15TH EDITION

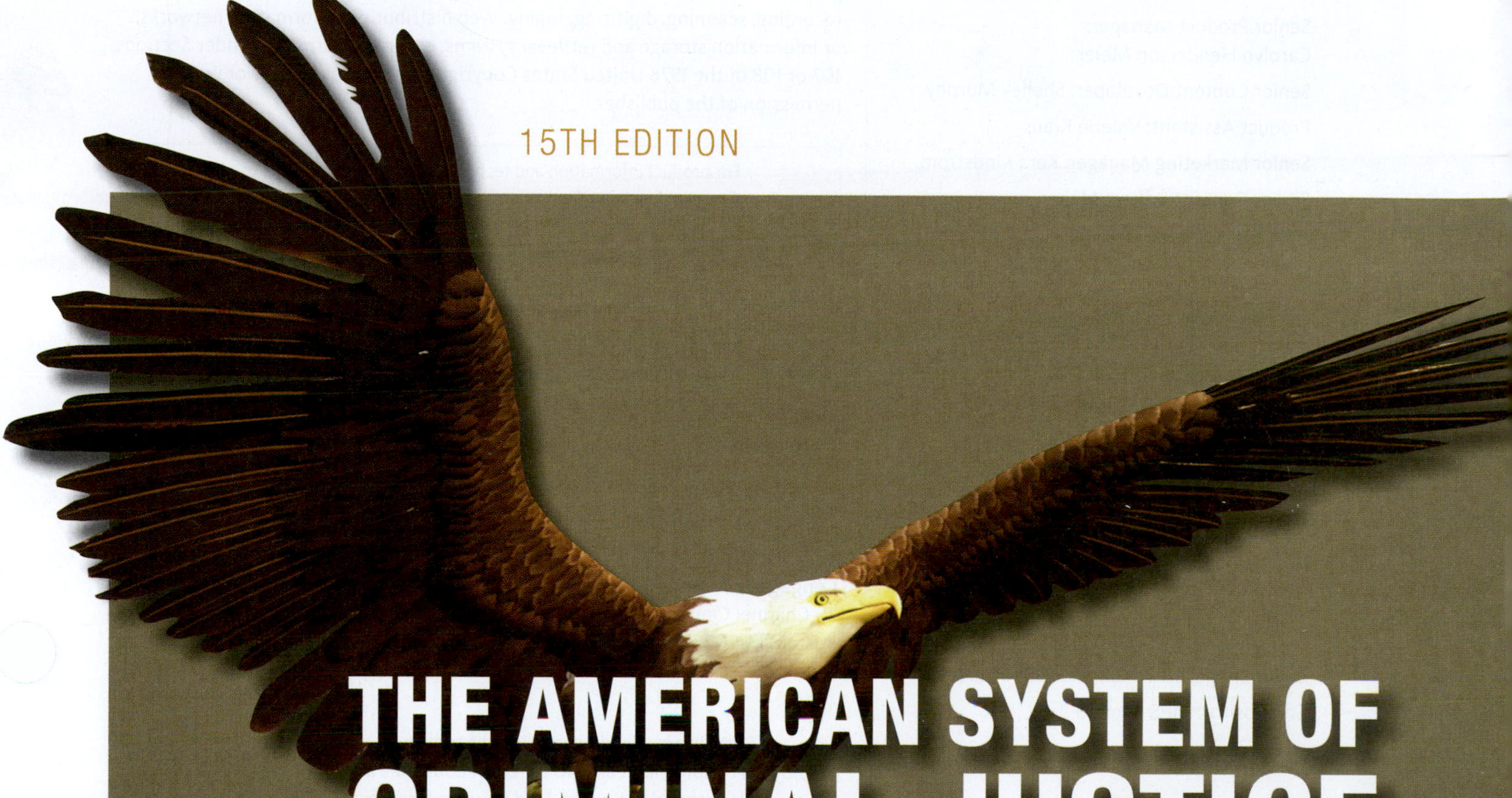

THE AMERICAN SYSTEM OF CRIMINAL JUSTICE

GEORGE F. COLE
University of Connecticut

CHRISTOPHER E. SMITH
Michigan State University

CHRISTINA DEJONG
Michigan State University

CENGAGE Learning

Australia • Brazil • Mexico • Singapore • United Kingdom • United States

CENGAGE Learning

The American System of Criminal Justice,
Fifteenth Edition
George F. Cole, Christopher E. Smith, and Christina DeJong

Product Director: Marta Lee-Perriard

Senior Product Manager: Carolyn Henderson Meier

Senior Content Developer: Shelley Murphy

Product Assistant: Valerie Kraus

Senior Marketing Manager: Kara Kindstrom

Senior Content Project Manager: Christy Frame

Managing Art Director: Andrei Pasternak

Senior Manufacturing Planner: Judy Inouye

Production Service: Greg Hubit Bookworks

Photo Development: Sarah Evertson
Photo Researcher: Jananie Kulasekaran, Lumina Datamatics

Text Researcher: Ranipadma Thamodaran, Lumina Datamatics

Copy Editor: Marne Evans

Proofreader: Carrie Crompton

Illustrator: Lotus Art

Text and Cover Designer: Jennifer Wahi

Cover Image: Steve Collender/Shutterstock

Compositor: MPS Limited

Library of Congress Control Number: 2015946268

Student Edition:
ISBN: 978-1-305-63374-2

Looseleaf Edition:
ISBN: 978-1-305-66446-3

Cengage Learning
20 Channel Center Street
Boston, MA 02210
USA

Cengage Learning is a leading provider of customized learning solutions with employees residing in nearly 40 different countries and sales in more than 125 countries around the world. Find your local representative at **www.cengage.com**

Cengage Learning products are represented in Canada by Nelson Education, Ltd.

To learn more about Cengage Learning Solutions, visit **www.cengage.com**

Purchase any of our products at your local college store or at our preferred online store **www.cengagebrain.com**

Printed in China
Print Number: 02 Print Year: 2016

ABOUT THE AUTHORS

George F. Cole, Ph.D., is Professor Emeritus of Political Science at the University of Connecticut. A specialist in the administration of criminal justice, he has published extensively on such topics as prosecution, courts, and corrections. George Cole is also coauthor with Christopher Smith and Christina DeJong of *Criminal Justice in America,* coauthor with Todd Clear, Michael Reisig, and Carolyn Petrosino of *American Corrections,* and coauthor with Marc Gertz and Amy Bunger of *The Criminal Justice System: Politics and Policies.* He developed and directed the graduate corrections program at the University of Connecticut and was a Fellow at the National Institute of Justice (1988). Among his other accomplishments, he has been granted two awards under the Fulbright-Hays Program to conduct criminal justice research in England and the former Yugoslavia. In 1995 he was named a Fellow of the Academy of Criminal Justice Sciences for distinguished teaching and research.

Trained as a lawyer and social scientist, **Christopher E. Smith**, J.D., Ph.D., is Professor of Criminal Justice at Michigan State University, where he teaches courses on criminal justice policy, courts, corrections, and law. He holds degrees from several universities, including Harvard University and the University of Connecticut. In addition to writing more than 110 scholarly articles, he is the author of 25 books, including several other titles with Cengage Learning: *Criminal Procedure; Law and Contemporary Corrections; Courts, Politics, and the Judicial Process; The Changing Supreme Court: Constitutional Rights and Liberties* with Thomas R. Hensley and Joyce A. Baugh; *Courts and Public Policy; Politics in Constitutional Law; and Courts and the Poor.*

Christina Dejong, Ph.D., is Associate Professor of Criminal Justice at Michigan State University. She earned her degrees at the University of Texas and the University of Maryland. At Michigan State, she is a noted researcher and award-winning teacher for a variety of criminology topics, including recidivism, violence against women, police–community relations, and genocide. She is the coauthor of *The Supreme Court, Crime, and the Ideal of Equal Justice* and numerous articles in such journals as *Justice Quarterly, Criminology, Women and Criminal Justice,* and *Violence and Victims.*

BRIEF CONTENTS

CONTENTS

PART 1 CRIME AND THE CRIMINAL JUSTICE SYSTEM 1

3 THE CRIMINAL JUSTICE SYSTEM 90

4 CRIMINAL JUSTICE AND THE RULE OF LAW 138

PART 2 POLICE 185

5 POLICE 186

PREFACE

Most students come to the introductory course in criminal justice intrigued by the prospect of learning about crime and the operation of the criminal justice system. Many of them look forward to the roles they may one day fill in allocating justice, either as citizens or in careers with the police, courts, or corrections. All have been exposed to a great deal of information—and misinformation—about criminal justice through the news and entertainment media. Whatever their views, few are indifferent to the subject they are about to explore.

Like all newcomers to a field, however, introductory students in criminal justice need, first, *content mastery*—a solid foundation of valid information about the subject—and second, *critical understanding*—a way to think about this information. They need conceptual tools that enable them not only to absorb a large body of factual content but also to process that information critically, reflect on it, and extend their learning beyond the classroom. This text aims at providing both the essential content and the critical tools involved in understanding criminal justice.

This edition continues the book's recent unifying emphasis on citizens' varied and important roles in influencing criminal justice policies and processes. Social commentators and political scientists have long noted that young Americans seem insufficiently interested and engaged in public affairs. Participation rates for youthful voters lag behind those of older demographic groups. Surveys indicate that many young people lack knowledge about both current events and the operation of their country's governing system. Such trends raise questions about the vibrancy of the American democracy and the range of values and opinions that inform decisions about public policies.

Young Americans are certainly entitled to make their own choices about whether and how they become involved in public affairs. If, however, their lack of participation is due to insufficient knowledge about their important potential roles in democratic processes, then the study of criminal justice—a high-interest subject for college students—presents an opportunity to make clearer to them all citizens' inevitable and unavoidable roles in affecting criminal justice.

The American public is accustomed to seeing officials in the criminal justice system—legislators, prosecutors, judges, defense attorneys, and corrections officials—as constituting the decision makers who shape criminal justice policies and processes. Students who aspire to careers in these positions undoubtedly recognize their potential importance to the system. Less well recognized, however, are the influence and importance of all citizens in their roles as voters, members of neighborhood associations and community organizations, and even as renters and homeowners. In these roles, all Americans influence criminal justice through a variety of activities, ranging from formal decisions about voting or buying security systems for businesses and churches to less formal actions in personal crime-prevention decisions (e.g., locking cars, reporting suspicious activity) that guide the nature and extent of crime problems as well as the allocation of law enforcement resources. The influence of all Americans on criminal justice will be highlighted throughout the book, especially in the feature Civic Engagement: Your Role in the System, which gives students concrete opportunities to analyze and make decisions about real-life examples. Three other features in the book reinforce this theme. The Doing Your Part boxes highlight regular citizens' contributions to the justice system and to the prevention of crime problems, even though they are not criminal justice professionals. In addition, a critical-thinking element, Stop and Analyze, which follows each subsection within every chapter, poses questions to students about issues concerning the material that they have just read. Many of these Stop and Analyze questions challenge students to develop arguments and conclusions about their own positions on contemporary controversies. A similar feature, Debate the Issue, included in the Close Up boxes within each chapter, also leads students to engage in analytical thinking about concrete problems and issues in criminal justice. These exercises help students to become intellectually engaged in relevant issues and problems as a means to move away from citizens' passive acceptance of other people's exclusive control over decision making and policy formulation.

This unifying emphasis on civic engagement draws from all three of the book's major themes because active and informed citizens must use knowledge of the *system's characteristics* and *American values* in order to understand and improve their own actions that influence *public policy*.

The Approach of This Text: Three Key Themes

Criminal justice is a complex subject encompassing an array of topics that cannot be evaluated through a limited or narrow focus. To understand what happens to people who are drawn into the American system of criminal justice, one must analyze such varied subjects as societal problems, determinants of individuals' behavior, government processes, and conceptions of morality and justice. This text tackles the challenge of this complexity by drawing from an interdisciplinary foundation of research, with contributions from criminology, law, history, sociology, psychology, and political science. The interdisciplinary approach supplies the analytical tools and information needed to evaluate the varied institutions, processes, and social phenomena of criminal justice. Although breadth of perspective is necessary for understanding criminal justice, it does not automatically provide an appropriate basis for explaining the American system of justice to students. Information and analysis must be organized and presented in ways that highlight the key elements that shape and drive criminal justice in the United States. We use three organizing themes to bring the complexity of criminal justice into focus and to highlight continuing issues and controversies that affect this dynamic subject:

1. *Criminal justice involves public policies* that are developed within the political framework of the democratic process.
2. *The concept of social system is an essential tool* for explaining and analyzing the way criminal justice is administered and practiced.
3. *American values provide the foundation on which criminal justice is based.* With concerns about terrorism and civil liberties at the forefront of the national agenda, an awareness of basic American values—individual liberty, equality, fairness, and the rule of law—is as vital today as it has ever been in our history.

Over the years the approach of *The American System of Criminal Justice* has enjoyed broad acceptance as it addresses new challenges. Instructors at hundreds of colleges and universities throughout the nation have chosen this book, and during its more than 30 years of use in their classrooms, more than a half million of their students have used it. Yet, textbook authors cannot afford to rest on their laurels, particularly in a field as dynamic as criminal justice. The social scene changes, research multiplies, theories are modified, and new policies are proposed and implemented while old ones become unpopular and fade away. Students and their needs change as well. Accordingly, we have made this Fifteenth Edition even more current, vital, cohesive, and appealing to students and instructors alike.

Highlights of the Fifteenth Edition

This edition encompasses important revisions in content and presentation. Users of the Fourteenth Edition will find many significant additions and changes. We have also strengthened focus on the various important roles of citizens in affecting criminal justice in their states, communities, and neighborhoods. This focus draws together the book's themes concerning American values, public policy, and system conception of criminal justice. The remainder of this section considers the major content changes and expanded discussions in the book and then examines the new elements in each chapter.

Highly Publicized, Contemporary Controversies

Among the most significant developments affecting the justice system are contemporary controversies that have captured the public's attention through heavy news media coverage. In particular, key events in 2014 and 2015 included videotaped incidents of police officers' use of force, especially white officers' actions leading to the deaths of African American suspects. Incidents such as those in Ferguson, Missouri; New York City; Cleveland, Ohio; North Charleston, South Carolina; and Baltimore led to large-scale public protests, including civil disorder in Ferguson and Baltimore that produced extensive property damage and arrests. These incidents brought into sharp focus debates about use of force, police–community relations, and discrimination in the justice system. In order to highlight and examine these and other issues, we introduce a new box, Inside Today's Controversies. Two of these new features appear in each of the first four parts of the book, and an additional one is in the final chapter on Juvenile Justice. The focus on current controversies is used to illuminate aspects of each segment of the system, from policing to courts to corrections to juvenile justice.

Several of these features concern police use of force and police–community relations. For example, one Inside Today's Controversies box examines the human consequences of aggressive, racially skewed stop-and-frisk practices. Others focus on issues elsewhere in the justice system, such as questions about the fairness of grand jury proceedings and the introduction of less-lethal weapons, such as chemical sprays and Tasers, into the hands of traditionally unarmed corrections officers inside the walls of prisons.

Proposals for Reform of the Justice System

In recent decades, the primary focus of the justice system has been on crime control and punishment. The past few years, however, have seen a shift toward concerns about the effectiveness and costs of policies and practices in criminal justice. There is greater recognition among policy makers about the high financial costs of incarceration and the significant societal costs of failing to prepare offenders for reintegration into society. In addition, social media and the proliferation of shared photos and videos have highlighted questions about police practices and fairness in the justice system in ways that have heightened public awareness and concern. Throughout the Fifteenth Edition, there are examples of reform initiatives and proposals intended to increase fairness, enhance effectiveness, and limit budgetary expenditures in criminal justice. Among the new Inside Today's Controversies topics, for example, are President Obama's task force on police reform, proposals for police officers to wear body cameras, and the U.S. Department of Justice's report on the City of Ferguson using its justice system for the purpose of raising revenue for the city budget. Other contemporary reform issues include federal proposals to ease civil disabilities experienced by ex-offenders in the community and the debates over the use of solitary confinement. In addition, the Fifteenth Edition continues the prior edition's attention to the trend toward evidence-based policies and practices that are supported by research results. Thus the New Directions in Criminal Justice boxes emphasize evidence-based practices in policing, courts, and corrections.

Real Ethical Problems and Dilemmas Facing Officials in Each Segment of the Criminal Justice System

As in previous editions, each chapter ends with A Question of Ethics, but each of these features has new, updated content. These contemplative exercises provide real situations drawn from recent news reports. Students are asked to consider genuine cases concerning police honesty in reporting crime statistics, sentencing disparities, departmental quotas imposed on officers for writing tickets or frisking pedestrians, corrections officers' use of violence to punish prisoners, and problems with privatization of prison services. Students are then challenged to place themselves in the position of administrators who must think about how to organize or reform training, supervision, and other elements that are essential for addressing ethical lapses by justice system officials.

Expanded Focus on Technology and Criminal Justice

The rapid pace of technological development and change has profound effects on criminal justice. Technology creates new opportunities for lawbreakers to steal money, corporate assets, and trade secrets. The public is familiar with some aspects of these problems through publicity about identity theft and hackers' success in stealing credit card numbers. Technology poses other problems for criminal justice, such as the sophisticated weapons that police officers encounter in the hands of organized crime groups, gangs, and individual criminals. Technology also presents opportunities for criminal justice officials to prevent crime, investigate crime, maintain order, and control incarcerated populations. In addition, technology can raise questions about collisions between citizens' constitutional rights and officials' efforts to catch criminal offenders. New aspects of technology develop each year that impact criminal justice. Thus the Technology and Criminal Justice features throughout the book now focus on current issues of critical importance to students, including transnational cybercrime; controversies concerning the use of drones; military equipment used by local police agencies; surveillance technology; and electronic monitoring of probationers, parolees, and defendants released on bail.

Expanded Coverage of Prison Population Reduction, Parole, and Reentry

Reconsideration of sentencing practices as well as financial pressures have led to state and federal efforts to reduce prison populations. The reasons and ramifications of these policy decisions are addressed in several chapters. New material on such topics as conditional release, reentry institutions, and reentry programs help to illuminate recent developments. This subject is one of the most important issues facing legislatures around the country and is essential knowledge for contemporary students of criminal justice.

Key Chapter-by-Chapter Changes

Chapter 1, Crime and Justice in America

A new chapter opener focuses on the 2014 shooting in downtown Austin, Texas, when a gunman fired hundreds of rounds at the police department headquarters, the federal courthouse, and the Mexican consulate. The opening illuminates questions about criminal behavior, policy debates, and systemic responses. A new Close Up feature examines state legislatures' responses to the Newtown, Connecticut, Sandy Hook Elementary School shootings. This chapter introduces the new feature box, Inside Today's Controversies, by focusing on whether and why people should criticize criminal justice system officials, including police officers who put their lives on the line every day for their fellow citizens. A new Civic Engagement feature looks at a cyberbullying law in New Jersey. There is also new material on such topics as transnational crime, motorcycle gangs, and former congresswoman Gabrielle Giffords's efforts to advance new gun control policies. In addition, the new Question of Ethics box focuses on a 2014 investigation revealing that Los Angeles police misclassified crimes and effectively reduced the reported violent-crime rate for the city.

Chapter 2, Victimization and Criminal Behavior

The new chapter opener on the 2014 shooting at Seattle Pacific University, as well as the embezzlement of over $3 million from a charitable organization in Maine, provide the context for comparison and lead students to think about crime causation. There is new material in the Technology and Criminal Justice feature on data breaches suffered by major retailers and the ensuing costs and consequences. A new Close Up examines victimization of the elderly. The Doing Your Part feature includes new information on programs for crime victims. The New Directions in Criminal Justice Policy feature now focuses on evidence-based practices and victims' services. There is a new figure illustrating the relationship between poverty and the risk of victimization. In addition, the Question of Ethics feature examines domestic violence perpetrated by police officers.

Chapter 3, The Criminal Justice System

A new chapter opener examines the Jacksonville, Florida, trial and conviction of Michael Dunn, who shot and killed an African American teenager in a convenience store parking lot after an argument about loud music. A new Civic Engagement feature presents a November 2014 report on a Seattle neighborhood group's effort to organize and communicate to city officials their concerns about the increase in area property crimes at the same time that police staffing and police presence was reduced in their precinct. In New Directions in Criminal Justice Policy, there is a focus on the U.S. Justice Department's "smart on crime" report from August 2013 that outlined goals and principles for making the justice system fairer and more efficient. The new Civic Engagement feature concerns the 2014 arrest of a Pittsburgh high school teacher outside a community meeting and the resulting financial settlement of the related lawsuit and the resultant changes in police procedures intended to reduce disparate racial treatment. Within the chapter, there is new material on the impact of budget cuts on the criminal justice system; controversy over the Ferguson, Missouri, grand jury proceedings; police discretion to stop enforcing certain laws; reemergence of heroin problems as an example of whites' involvement in crime; research documenting unconscious bias in decision making. The latter issue is further illustrated by the example of North Miami Beach police using mugshots of African American men—but not whites or Hispanics—as targets at the shooting range. The new Inside Today's Controversies feature examines stop-and-frisk practices in New York City from the perspective of a white father looking at the experiences of his biracial son who is treated in society as an African American. The Question of Ethics compares sentences in two 2014 domestic violence cases: sentence of counseling and record expungement for a federal judge and a 17-month prison sentence for another man.

Chapter 4, Criminal Justice and the Rule of Law

The new chapter opener highlights three different insanity-defense murder cases in Iowa in 2013 and 2014. Two of the individuals were found not guilty by reason of insanity and sent to mental institutions, with attendant uncertainty about the likelihood of their eventual release. However, the teenager who was convicted of second-degree murder when his insanity defense failed, will, by contrast, eventually be released from custody. A new Civic Engagement focuses on a 2014 ballot issue to legalize the possession and personal use of marijuana by adults. The new Technology and Criminal Justice feature focuses on the Supreme Court's 2015 case of *Elonis v. United States* concerning whether certain statements posted on social media should be regarded as criminal threats rather than free expression. There is new material on a variety of topics: *Hall v. Florida* (2014), the Supreme Court decision that invalidated a state law narrowly defining whose developmental disabilities made them ineligible for the death penalty; "stand your ground" laws concerning lethal self-defense in interpersonal conflicts; police forfeiture practices of seizing millions of dollars in cash and property during traffic stops without any search warrants or charges pursued against the drivers; and the *Rodriguez v. United States* (2015) Supreme Court ruling against holding drivers beyond the completion of the traffic matter that caused a traffic stop. The new Question of Ethics concerns police officers' use of false statements while questioning suspects in order to elicit incriminating statements.

Chapter 5, Police

The new chapter opener focuses on the November 2014 public demonstrations, property damage, and confrontations between protesters and police in Ferguson, Missouri, in the aftermath of the grand jury's decision in the Michael Brown shooting case. A new Technology and Criminal Justice feature concerns the widespread acquisition of surplus military equipment by local police departments and the risks that the use of military-style clothing and equipment will change the public's view of police as well as the police officers' attitudes and behavior toward the public. The New Directions in Criminal Justice Policy feature examines evidence-based policing practices in dealing with people suffering from mental illness. New 2014 public opinion data illustrates attitudes toward police by race and urban/nonurban place of residence. A new Doing Your Part focuses on 2014 national Crime Stoppers award won by students at Ball State University for their role in investigating and publicizing unsolved murder cases. The new Civic Engagement feature uses the example of Dalton, Georgia, police reorganizing their Neighborhood Policing Plan in 2014. The new Question of Ethics feature presents testimony by a police officer in the 2013 federal trial in New York City about the racially biased stop-and-frisk practices of the police department and the retaliation he claimed to have experienced when he refused to follow those practices.

Chapter 6, Police Officers and Law Enforcement Operations

The new chapter opener highlights the shooting in 2014 of two Pennsylvania State Police troopers and the 48-day manhunt that followed to catch the survivalist hidden in the woods who was responsible for the shooting. New examples of police shootings in Cleveland and Albuquerque raise questions about the extent to which police departments may fail to completely follow selection procedures when hiring new officers. New material discusses the lack of demographic representativeness among police forces in Ferguson, Missouri, and North Charleston, South Carolina. Another new example examines a volunteer police officer in Tulsa, Oklahoma, charged with manslaughter for shooting a suspect during arrest when—he claimed—he mistakenly grabbed his gun instead of his Taser. There is new detailed information on federal law enforcement salaries and on state legislature bans on police departments basing officer productivity on quotas for traffic tickets. An Inside Today's Controversies feature concerns President Obama's response to the demonstrations after the grand jury decisions in Ferguson, Missouri, and Staten Island, New York, concerning the deaths, at police hands, of unarmed African American men. In December 2014, President Obama appointed the Task Force on 21st Century Policing, which held hearings in early 2015 on ways to improve community policing and police–community relations. This new topic includes examples of the group's recommendations from the preliminary report in March 2015. This task force's approach highlighted questions about whether and how the president and the federal government can influence policing practices in the country's decentralized law enforcement system. New material in the Technology and Criminal Justice feature about crime prediction software affects many departments' evidence-based strategy of using "hot spot" policing. The new Question of Ethics feature examines specific ticket-writing and arrest expectations for officers that are characterized by police administrators as "performance standards" rather than as "quotas."

Chapter 7, Policing: Contemporary Issues and Challenges

Consistent with the chapter opening's presentation on the use of technology in catching the Boston Marathon bomber, new material in the chapter strengthens coverage of technology relevant to policing. For example, material on the use of drones includes new information from 2015 on the drone crashing on the White House lawn, a drug-carrying drone crashing near the U.S.-Mexican border, and the Michigan State Police request to the FAA for permission to fly drones statewide to photograph traffic collisions and public emergencies. New security management material focuses on cloud-computing hacking and the cyber attack on Sony Entertainment. The new Inside Today's Controversies feature considers the debates, costs, and consequences over requiring police officers to wear body cameras in order to deter police misconduct and reduce false claims about police misconduct. With respect to other topics, a new What Americans Think illuminates differences in whites' and African Americans' views on the existence of police brutality, and a new Close Up focuses on 2014 consent decree between the U.S. Justice Department and the Albuquerque police department to change hiring, training, and supervision after a relatively high number of police shootings and unnecessary uses of force. There are also new examples of police corruption from news reports in 2014 and 2015. The new Question of Ethics concerns a Florida sheriff's captain in 2015 who ordered an investigation of individuals seeking to set up a firearms business that would compete with the company that had retained the captain in a part-time, second job. The case raises issues about what constitutes an actual conflict of interest and what can be considered simply the appearance of a conflict.

Chapter 8, Police and Constitutional Law

The new chapter opener discusses the Supreme Court decision in *Riley v. California* (2014) clarifying that police officers do not have the authority to conduct warrantless examinations of the contents of cell phones as part of searches incident to a lawful arrest. There is also a new comparison of the use of drug-sniffing dogs around vehicles in public places (*Illinois v. Cabelles,* 2005) and at the front door of residences (*Florida v. Jardines,* 2013) to illustrate how reasonable expectations of privacy help to define situations that are "searches" requiring warrants. Other new Supreme Court decisions include *Navarette v. California* (2014), concerning an anonymous tip serving as the basis for a traffic stop, and *Missouri v. McNeely* (2013), which rejected an automatic exigent circumstances claim for drawing blood from a suspected drunk driver. There is a new discussion of *Heien v. North Carolina* (2014) regarding an officer's traffic stop based on the mistaken belief that his state's law required both taillights on a vehicle to be working. The Supreme Court did not find any rights violation or require any exclusion of evidence. The new Technology and Criminal Justice feature concerns the public backlash against two police surveillance technologies: red-light cameras and automatic license plate readers. There is also new material on U.S. Department of Justice policy announcement in 2014 requiring videotaping of most interrogations of suspects, a rule that applies to FBI, DEA, BATF, and U.S. Marshals. A new exclusionary rule example is based on drug-selling charges being dropped against the man suspected of selling heroin to Philip Seymour Hoffman, the Oscar-winning actor who died of a drug overdose in 2014. The prosecutor dropped the charges because police officers failed to inform the man of his *Miranda* rights when they initially questioned him after his arrest. A new Question of Ethics asks what a police chief can do to strengthen the ethical climate in a department so that officers would actually feel less free to engage in misconduct without fear of being reported by any colleagues. The example is based on a 2014 report of California officers sharing motorists' personal photos with each other after seizing drivers' cell phones during traffic incidents.

Chapter 9, Courts and Pretrial Processes

The new chapter opener discusses Curtis Reeves, former police officer who shot another patron in a Florida movie theater after arguments over the use of a cell phone during film previews. The Reeves case illustrates the steps in the court process. He was held in a jail for a month after arrest in January 2014; still detained after his bail hearing in February 2014; in July 2014 the court of appeals told the judge that Reeves qualified for bail, so he was released on bail in July 2014. He went through a pretrial hearing in November 2014 and then again in January 2015 with a trial date set for August 24, 2015. He also faced several preliminary hearings scheduled between January and August 2015. There are new examples of increased spending by out-of-state groups to influence judicial elections. There is new information on a 2014 lawsuit against a Mississippi county where poor defendants languish for months in jail, unable to make bail but also not provided with the services of a defense attorney. New attention is given to states that no longer rely on private bail agents as a means for arrestees to gain pretrial release. A new Technology and Criminal Justice feature examines the use of electronic monitoring to relieve the burdens of pretrial detention and thereby reduce jail costs, transfer costs to defendants, and permit additional people to have pretrial release. This feature includes information on GPS monitors as well as SCRAM ankle monitors that use skin detection to identify any alcohol use. The new Question of Ethics concerns a state judge in Florida who was removed by the state supreme court because of activities related to the ministry that she founded, including trying to sell religious materials to lawyers and others at court as well as using a photo of herself in her judicial robe to promote the sale of products on her ministry website.

Chapter 10, Prosecution and Defense

The new chapter opener examines the 2015 murder trial of former NFL football star Aaron Hernandez, highlighting the strategies of both the prosecutor and the defense attorney. For example, the prosecutor granted immunity to the defendant's fiancée so that she would testify, and the defense attorney raised issues about potentially sloppy police work in gathering evidence. The chapter includes the recent example in 2015 of Loretta Lynch's strong record as a federal prosecutor helping her to overcome partisan divide in Congress and gain votes from key Republican senators in nomination process to be U.S. attorney general. A new Technology and Criminal Justice feature discusses state laws that mandate taking DNA samples from unconvicted arrestees, a practice approved by the Supreme Court in *Maryland v. King* (2013). The new Inside Today's Controversies feature concerns the Ferguson grand jury, the unusual procedures used in that case, and the risk that prosecutors will appear to protect police officers from being charged with crimes. The new Question of Ethics examines recent examples in which prosecutors opposed DNA testing of evidence in old cases. In one case, a Michigan man was freed after many years in prison. In another case, a New Jersey man who claimed to be innocent was seeking to have residency and employment restrictions removed. The restrictions had been imposed after a long-ago rape conviction.

Chapter 11, Determination of Guilt: Plea Bargaining and Trials

The new chapter opener describes the "American Sniper trial" and conviction of Eddie Ray Routh, a former Marine with PTSD who used an unsuccessful insanity defense after killing Chris Kyle, a former Navy SEAL and best-selling author, and Kyle's friend Chad Littlefield. A new Close Up concerns the risks of relying on elections as the basis to choose local prosecutors and hold them accountable for their decisions. The new Technology and Criminal Justice feature examines potential issues with the presentation of DNA evidence to jurors, including scandals about improper procedures and falsified results in several government crime labs as well as the risks that trace DNA can be transferred from innocent people and inadvertently end up at crime scenes. There is new material on jury reform, including issues with clarifying jurors' understanding of judges' jury instructions. A new Question of Ethics illustrates defense attorneys' obligations to inform defendants of plea offers from the prosecutor and accurately educate the defendant about potential consequences from declining offers in the plea bargaining process.

Chapter 12, Punishment and Sentencing

The new chapter opener compares recent sentences from various states imposed on teachers convicted of having sexual relationships with underage students. The sentences range from ten days in jail to 20 years in prison. They illustrate differences in state laws, discretionary decisions, and local legal culture and courtroom workgroups. To illustrate how sentences may be tailored to advance particular purposes, new hypothetical statements from a sentencing judge illustrate how a prison sentence for a statutory rape conviction can be explained under several different justifications. There is new material on a number of topics, including Florida's post-adjudicatory expansion drug courts as a tool to implement intermediate sanctions, the concept of justice reinvestment, and the division between Democrats and Republicans on capital punishment. The New Directions in Criminal Justice Policy feature illuminates evidence-based sentencing. Inside Today's Controversies focuses on the role of the municipal court in Ferguson, Missouri, in perpetuating unfair treatment of people for minor municipal citations, as illustrated by the U.S. Department of Justice's scathing investigative report on Ferguson. The new Question of Ethics concerns the 2014 case of a wealthy white youth sentenced to ten years of probation for killing four people and seriously injuring others while driving drunk. This sentence was imposed by the same judge who levied a ten-year incarceration sentence on an African American youth who threw one punch that resulted in the victim dying after falling and hitting his head on the floor.

Chapter 13, Corrections

The new chapter opener describes shocking news reports in 2015 about corrections officers' abuse of detainees and prisoners at New York City's Rikers Island jail, as well as the criminal charges against officers for viciously beating a prisoner at New York's Attica prison. There is new material on Douglas Blackmon's Pulitzer Prize–winning book *Slavery by Another Name*, about the use of the southern corrections system to perpetuate forms of slavery on many African Americans into the mid-twentieth century to better serve the interests of business owners in the lease system for convict labor. There is also expanded coverage of different types and security levels for prisons using the examples of the Oklahoma and Minnesota corrections systems. The New Directions in Criminal Justice feature discusses evidence-based practices for addressing the needs of individuals with mental illness who enter jails. A new Close Up on freedom of religion in prison focuses on the successful lawsuit by John Walker Lindh, known to the public as the "American Taliban," to gain the right to participate in group prayer with other Muslims in federal prison. There is related coverage of a new Supreme Court decision, *Holt v. Hobbs* (2015), which permitted a Muslim prisoner to grow a beard for religious reasons. The new Question of Ethics examines problems in 2014 with Michigan's privatization of food service inside its prison system, including misbehavior by dozens of company employees and potential health problems for prisoners associated with the lack of cleanliness in food service areas.

Chapter 14, Community Corrections: Probation and Intermediate Sanctions

The new chapter opener highlights the 2014 arrests of singer Justin Bieber by discussing the punishments levied by the courts and whether his fame and fortune resulted in more-lenient treatment as compared to that given to other offenders. There is new material explaining risk assessment instruments for probationers as a way to assess their risk of committing new crimes and their specific needs for supervision and services. There is also new material on the potential effectiveness of boot camps with post-release treatment, including potential cost savings. The Technology and Criminal Justice feature updates probation monitoring technology, including facial recognition software and smartphone apps. A new Close Up examines the controversy over civil forfeiture for individuals suspected of committing crimes and the recent changes to federal policy to diminish the risk that innocent people will lose cash and property. The New Directions in Criminal Justice feature highlights the EPICS program (Effective Practices in Community Supervision), which utilizes cognitive-behavioral strategies to reduce the risk of future crime. A new Question of Ethics raises issues about criminal activity by probation and parole officers.

Chapter 15, Incarceration and Prison Society

The new chapter opener shows the continuity of daily schedules in secure prisons, comparing 1950s Alcatraz in California with contemporary North Carolina prisons, even as many factors inside prisons have changed as society changed. There is new material on a variety of topics: a corrections officer sentenced to prison for trying to smuggle cell phones and tobacco to prisoners; the variation in corrections officers' salaries across several states as part of a discussion of recruitment; New York Governor Cuomo's effort to reactivate the use of public funds for college education courses inside prisons; prison health care costs and the risks of privatizing medical services for prisoners; and mental illness in prison as well as the associated risks of violent victimization for prisoners with psychological problems. The Inside Today's Controversies feature focuses on the new introduction of chemical sprays and conducted energy devices inside the walls of prisons. This development represents a move away from the tradition of having outnumbered officers remain unarmed inside the walls. The new Question of Ethics concerns 15 corrections officers in Maryland facing prison sentences in 2014 for severely beating a prisoner as revenge for his having punched an officer.

Chapter 16, Reentry into the Community

The new chapter opener describes education and training programs in New Orleans, Louisiana, and Anchorage, Alaska, to help integrate parolees back into society. The New Directions in Criminal Justice Policy feature provides several examples of evidence-based reentry programs focused on enhancing employment opportunities for offenders and working to reduce substance abuse problems. There is new material on several topics, including state budget cuts affecting corrections programs, innovative reentry facilities created in repurposed factories and prisons, and the impact of reentry programming. The Technology and Criminal Justice feature updates the use of GPS technology to track parolees. The Inside Today's Controversies feature examines the REDEEM Act, introduced to Congress in 2014 as a way to ease civil disabilities on ex-inmates returning to the community. The new Question of Ethics explores neighborhood resistance to the placement of community corrections centers.

Chapter 17, Juvenile Justice

The new chapter opener discusses the "Slender Man case" concerning two 12-year-old juvenile offenders in Wisconsin who stabbed a classmate 19 times in order to please a fictional character. The juveniles were charged as adults with attempted homicide. A new What Americans Think feature examines the practice of charging juvenile offenders as adults. The new Close Up describes youth violence reduction programs in Philadelphia and Stockton, California. The New Directions in Criminal Justice Policy feature provides several examples of evidence-based juvenile diversion programs in New York, Michigan, and Texas. These programs focus on keeping juvenile offenders out of formal processing in the court system. The Technology and Criminal Justice feature updates material on cases of sexting and cyberbullying. The Inside Today's Controversies feature examines the use of solitary confinement for juveniles and related court cases that have attempted to block this practice. There is new information on the Baltimore Juvenile Detention Facility and ongoing investigations into the mistreatment of residents. The new Question of Ethics examines the use of less-lethal weapons, such as pepper spray, on juveniles in detention facilities.

To help students identify and master core concepts, the text provides several study and review aids.

Study Aids

- **Chapter outlines** preview the structure of each chapter.
- **Chapter-opening vignettes** introduce the chapter topic with a high-interest, real-life episode. These vignettes include such recent examples as the random shootings in downtown Austin, Texas, and Seattle Pacific University; prominent murder trials of NFL star Aaron Hernandez and of the man who killed the best-selling author of *American Sniper*; public protests in Ferguson, Missouri, after a police officer shot teenager Michael Brown; as well as sentencing examples involving singer Justin Bieber for various misdemeanor arrests; and for teachers from across the country who received widely varying sentences for sexual contact with students.
- **Chapter Learning Objectives** highlight the chapter's key topics and themes. The numbered learning objectives have been carefully matched to individual bullet points in the end-of-chapter Summary for maximum learning reinforcement.
- **Checkpoints** throughout each chapter allow students to test themselves on content as they proceed through the chapter.
- **Chapter Summaries and Questions for Review** reinforce key concepts and provide further checks on learning.
- **Key Terms and Cases** are defined throughout the text in the margins of each chapter and can also be located in the Glossary.

Promoting Critical Understanding

Aided by the features just described, diligent students can master the essential content of the introductory course. Although such mastery is no small achievement, most instructors aim higher. They want students to complete this course with the ability to take a more thoughtful and critical approach to issues of crime and justice. *The American System of Criminal Justice*, Fifteenth Edition, provides several features that help students learn how to think about the field.

- **Inside Today's Controversies** This new feature examines contemporary controversies as a means to gain new insights and challenge assumptions about criminal justice. This feature also highlights a variety of proposals to reform the criminal justice system. These new boxes give attention to specific highly-publicized examples that illuminate police use of force, police–community relations, President Obama's commission to develop reform proposals, the use of police body cameras, the application of solitary confinement to juvenile offenders, and other current issues. Each of these features includes questions for students to consider under the Critical Thinking and Analysis segments that conclude each presentation.
- **Civic Engagement: Your Role in the System** In order to gain a clear understanding of the inevitable, important, and varied ways that citizens influence criminal justice policy and process, two Civic Engagement features in each chapter pose scenarios and questions drawn from real-life examples. Students are asked to place themselves in roles as voters, members of neighborhood organizations, jurors, members of citizen advisory committees, and a host of other real-life contexts where Americans make decisions that impact criminal justice. For each situation they are asked to use their analytical skills to present reasons for a decision or other suggestions related to policy problems. At the conclusion of each feature, students are guided to a website that describes what actually happened in a particular city or state when Americans were confronted with this specific problem or issue.
- **Stop and Analyze** features after each Checkpoint pose critical-thinking questions and ask students to concretely articulate arguments and analytical conclusions about issues.
- **Close Ups** Understanding criminal justice in a purely theoretical way does not give students a balanced understanding of the field. The wealth of examples in this book shows how theory plays out in practice and what the human implications of policies and procedures are. In addition to the many illustrations in the text, the Close Up features in each chapter draw on newspapers, court decisions, first-person accounts, and other current sources.
- **New Directions in Criminal Justice Policy** To illustrate criminal justice policies that have been proposed or are being tested, we include a box called New Directions in Criminal Justice Policy in many of our chapters. Most of these discuss evidence-based practices, such as those concerning patrol strategies, identification procedures, and jury reform, so that students will be prepared to face the new realities of criminal justice.
- **Debate the Issue** Within the Close Up, New Directions in Criminal Justice, and Technology and Criminal Justice features, the book poses questions to students and asks them to articulate arguments and analytical conclusions about controversies concerning criminal justice policies.
- **Doing Your Part** Many Americans have contributed to criminal justice through voluntary activities or by promoting reforms. In selected chapters the roles played by individuals who are assisting the police, crime victims, courts, and prisoners are described in each Doing Your Part feature. Consistent with the theme of civic engagement, we hope that these illustrations will encourage students to consider how they might contribute to a just society.
- **A Question of Ethics** Criminal justice requires that decisions be made within the framework of law but also be consistent with the ethical norms of American society. At the end of each chapter the A Question of Ethics activity places students in the role of decision makers for actual situations presented in newspaper reports. These examples promote critical thinking and analysis and offer students a more well-rounded view of what is asked of criminal justice professionals every day.
- **What Americans Think** Public opinion plays an important role in the policy-making process in a democracy. As such, we present the opinions of Americans on controversial criminal justice issues as collected through surveys. Students are encouraged to compare their own opinions with the national perspective.

Supplements

To access additional course materials, please visit **www.cengagebrain.com**. At the CengageBrain.com home page, search for the ISBN of your title (from the back cover of your book) using the search box at the top of the page. This will take you to the product page where these resources can be found.

For the Instructor

MindTap for Criminal Justice

MindTap Criminal Justice from Cengage Learning represents a new approach to a highly personalized, online learning platform. A fully online learning solution, MindTap combines all of a student's learning tools—readings, multimedia, activities, and assessments into a singular Learning Path that guides the student through the curriculum. Instructors personalize the experience by customizing the presentation of these learning tools for their students, allowing instructors to seamlessly introduce their own content into the Learning Path via "apps" that integrate into the MindTap platform. Additionally, MindTap provides interoperability with major Learning Management Systems (LMS) via support for industry standards and fosters partnerships with third-party educational application providers to provide a highly collaborative, engaging, and personalized learning experience.

Online Instructor's Resource Manual

Includes learning objectives, key terms, a detailed chapter outline, a chapter summary, lesson plans, discussion topics, student activities, "what if" scenarios, media tools, a sample syllabus, and an expanded test bank with 30 percent more questions than the prior edition. The learning objectives are correlated with the discussion topics, student activities, and media tools.

Online Test Bank

Each chapter of the test bank contains questions in multiple-choice, true/false, completion, essay, and new critical-thinking formats, with a full answer key. The test bank is coded to the learning objectives that appear in the main text, and includes the section in the main text where the answers can be found. Finally, each question in the test bank has been carefully reviewed by experienced criminal justice instructors for quality, accuracy, and content coverage, so instructors can be sure they are working with an assessment and grading resource of the highest caliber.

Cengage Learning Testing Powered by Cognero

This assessment software is a flexible, online system that allows instructors to import, edit, and manipulate test bank content from *The American System of Criminal Justice* test bank or elsewhere, including their own favorite test questions; create multiple test versions in an instant; and deliver tests from their LMS, classroom, or wherever they want.

Online PowerPoint® Lectures

Helping instructors make their lectures more engaging while effectively reaching visually oriented students, these handy Microsoft PowerPoint slides outline the chapters of the main text in a classroom-ready presentation. The PowerPoint slides are updated to reflect the content and organization of the new edition of the text, are tagged by chapter learning objective, and feature some additional examples and real-world cases for application and discussion.

For the Student

MindTap for Criminal Justice

MindTap Criminal Justice from Cengage Learning represents a new approach to a highly personalized, online learning platform. A fully online learning solution, MindTap combines all of your learning tools—readings, multimedia, activities, and assessments into a singular Learning Path that guides you through the course.

A Group Effort

No one can be an expert on every aspect of the criminal justice system. Authors need help in covering new developments and ensuring that research findings are correctly interpreted. This revision has greatly benefited from the advice of two groups of criminal justice scholars (see the inside front cover for a complete list). The first group of reviewers teach at a wide range of colleges and universities throughout the country and have used previous editions of the text in the classroom, so their comments concerning presentation, levels of student abilities, and the requirements of introductory courses at their institutions were especially useful. Reviewers in the second group we consulted are nationally recognized experts in the field; they focused their attention on the areas in which they specialize. Their many comments helped us avoid errors and drew our attention to points in the literature that had been neglected.

The many criminal justice students and instructors who used the Fourteenth Edition also contributed abundantly to this edition. Their comments provided crucial practical feedback. Many of them gave us their comments personally when we lectured in criminal justice classes around the country.

Others have helped us as well. Chief among them was Senior Product Manager Carolyn Henderson Meier, who has supported our efforts. Our Senior Content Developer, Shelley Murphy, provided invaluable comments as we revised the book.

The project has benefited much from the attention of Senior Content Project Manager Christy Frame, and Product Assistant Valerie Kraus was invaluable in helping us develop the supplements. Marne Evans used her effort and skill to contribute to the copyediting process. As always, Greg Hubit used his managerial skills to oversee the project from manuscript submission to bound books. Jennifer Wahi designed the interior and cover of the book. Carrie Crompton made valuable suggestions in her role as proofreader.

We acknowledge the reviewers for this Fifteenth Edition, along with all who reviewed our previous fourteen editions, listed on the front pages inside the cover of our text. We are grateful for their contributions, and their valuable comments and suggestions for our revisions. Ultimately, however, the full responsibility for the book is ours alone. We hope you will benefit from it, and we welcome your comments.

George F. Cole (georgefrasercole@gmail.com)
Christopher E. Smith (smithc28@msu.edu)
Christina DeJong (dejongc@msu.edu)

PART 1

Laura Skelding/TNS/Landov

CRIME AND THE CRIMINAL JUSTICE SYSTEM

The American system of criminal justice is a response to crime—a problem that has demanded the attention of all societies throughout history. To understand how the system works and why crime persists in spite of our efforts to control it, we need to examine both the nature of criminal behavior and the functioning of the justice system itself. As we shall see, the reality of crime and justice involves much more than "cops and robbers," the details of legal codes, and the penalties for breaking laws. From defining which behavior counts as criminal to deciding the fate of offenders who are caught, the process of criminal justice is a social process subject to many influences other than written law.

By introducing the study of this process, Part 1 provides a broad framework for analyzing how our society—through its police, courts, and corrections—tries to deal with the age-old problem of crime.

CHAPTER FEATURES

- **New Directions in Criminal Justice Policy** Drug Policy: Questioning the Necessity and Desirability of Imprisonment
- **Close Up** The Politics of Gun Control Law and Policy
- **Inside Today's Controversies** Criticism of Justice System Officials: Improper or Useful?
- **Technology and Criminal Justice** Transnational Cybercrime
- **Doing Your Part** The Fight against Cybercrime

CHAPTER 1 CRIME AND JUSTICE IN AMERICA

CHAPTER LEARNING OBJECTIVES

1 Discuss how public policies on crime are formed

2 Recognize how the crime control and due process models of criminal justice help us understand the system

3 Be able to explain: "What is a crime?"

4 Describe the major types of crime in the United States

5 Analyze how much crime there is and understand how it is measured

CHAPTER OUTLINE

Laura Skelding/TNS/Landov

The sound of gunfire shattered the relative calm in downtown Austin, Texas, in the early morning hours of November 28, 2014. Larry McQuilliams, age 49, stepped out of his minivan and began to shoot. Shortly before 2:30 A.M., callers to 911 operators reported automatic weapons fire. McQuilliams fired more than 100 rounds at the federal courthouse and the Austin Police Department headquarters. He also attempted to set fire to the Mexican consulate using small propane tanks that are normally intended for camping stoves ("Police: Man Fired 100-Plus Rounds," 2014). Within minutes, a police officer from Austin's mounted patrol encountered McQuilliams outside of police headquarters and fired his weapon at McQuilliams. McQuilliams was fatally wounded at the scene and died as police tried to determine if he was wearing a bomb vest or if his minivan was rigged with bombs. Despite significant damage to several buildings, police officials felt very relieved that no one other than the shooter was killed in the dangerous incident.

This frightening event was not a typical crime. Thefts and burglaries occur every day. Computer hackers steal financial information on a daily basis. Yet the Austin shooting was the kind of incident that can influence people's perceptions about crime. When significant news media coverage reports unexpected, seemingly random violence in which people are put at risk of death by a complete stranger, people's fears may affect their assumptions and behavior. They may become suspicious of certain people or avoid being in public at certain times and places. Such incidents also raise questions about how American society should respond in order to protect against dangerous events. Think about the possible questions that are raised by the Austin shooting:

- Does the incident show that high-powered firearms are too easily available to people who cannot be trusted? Alternatively, does this actually show that rapid-fire weapons should be more easily available to all citizens so that people can defend themselves?

- McQuilliams had spent time in prison. Does this incident show that we should keep people in prison longer or supervise them in the community more closely when they are released from prison?
- McQulliams was reportedly motivated by his opposition to government immigration policies that he viewed as too weak to prevent people from improperly entering and remaining in the United States. Should the incident be viewed as an act of politically motivated "terrorism" instead of a regular "crime"? If so, how does that affect efforts to prevent such incidents in the future? (Barragan and Toohey, 2014)

Debating and addressing these questions intelligently requires information and understanding about complex issues. To what extent are Americans knowledgeable about the realities of crime? This is an important question because our understanding of crime—or our lack of understanding—can affect how we influence public policy when we act as voters, as members of community organizations, or for some college students, as future justice system officials.

All Americans influence criminal justice policy. We make judgments about political candidates, in part, based on their stance on gun control, capital punishment, and other criminal justice issues. We express our views and fears to city councils, school boards, state legislatures, and other policy-making bodies that decide whether and how to spend money on safety and security in our communities. We make choices about the neighborhoods where we will reside, the schools where we will send our children, and the stores where we will shop based, in part, upon our perceptions about risk and crime. Even these decisions can have important impacts on economic development and neighborhood stability within communities. Moreover, many college students who study criminal justice will eventually become professionals in the justice system and thereby have even more influence over how policies develop and how policies are applied to the lives of others within American society. In light of the importance of criminal justice to all Americans—and, conversely, the important contributions that all Americans play in shaping criminal justice policy—it is essential that Americans develop realistic understandings of the nature of crime and justice in their society.

A Gallup Poll taken in October 2014 revealed that 37 percent of Americans fear walking alone at night within a mile of their home (A. Dugan, 2014). That same Gallup Poll found that nearly two-thirds of Americans believe that crime rates increased in 2014 (J. McCarthy, 2014). Given Americans' concerns about criminal justice issues, politicians attempt to gain favor with voters by proposing policies to address crime. These proposals do not always reflect careful analysis of the costs and benefits of different policy choices. In fact, politicians often try to outdo one another in being "tough on crime" without fully understanding the costs and consequences of such policies. This toughness has led to many shifts in public policies: adding 100,000 police officers nationwide, building more prisons, extending the death penalty to cover 60 federal offenses, mandating longer sentences, and requiring certain parolees to register with the police. The public's perception of crime tends to encourage the government to spend millions of dollars in ways that affect individuals drawn into the criminal justice system for punishment.

In the face of politicians' desire to appear tough on crime, an important question arises: Are concerns about crime justified? Polls indicate that many Americans do not realize that serious crime declined steadily from the record-setting years of the early 1980s through 2000. Additional drops occurred for various crimes during the early years of the twenty-first century. Despite widespread beliefs in constantly rising crime rates (J. McCarthy, 2014), there is no national crime wave. Violent crime rates decreased from 758 per 100,000 people in 1991 to 387 per 100,000 in 2012 (BJS, 2015a). The homicide rate was nearly 10 per 100,000 people in 1991. By 2012, the homicide rate was less than 5 per 100,000 people, just half of what it had been 20 years earlier (BJS, 2015a). Because beliefs and fears about crime seem to ignore the actual drops in crime rates (A. Dugan, 2014), many critics believe that people in the United States are unduly preoccupied with and insufficiently informed about crime as a policy issue.

The Main Themes of This Book

The study of criminal justice offers a fascinating view of a crucial social problem. Drawing from the perspectives of such academic disciplines as economics, history, law, political science, psychology, and sociology, the field of criminal justice aims at supplying knowledge and developing policies to deal with criminality. This aim, however, poses a fundamental challenge in a democratic society: how to develop policies that deal with crime while still preserving individual rights, the rule of law, and justice.

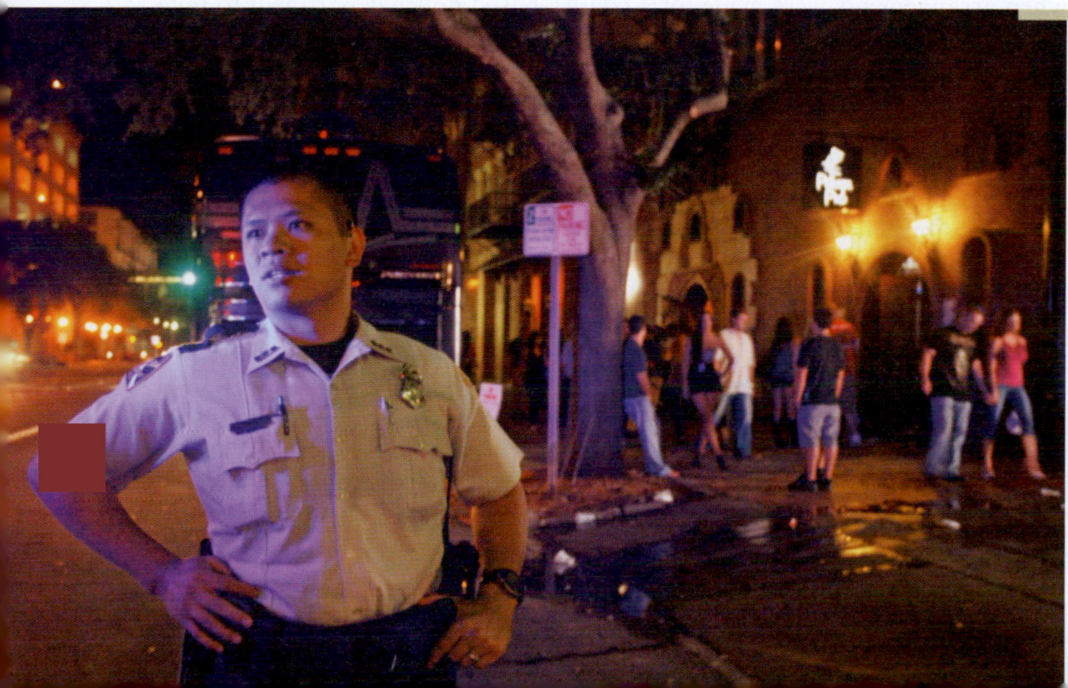

Chris Zuppa/St. Petersburg Times/The Image Works

Many Americans are fearful of walking at night near their own homes. Other Americans have inaccurate beliefs about crime steadily increasing. If government budget cuts lead to a reduction in police services, how will that affect Americans' fears and beliefs about crime?

Democracy in the United States is defined and guided by historic American values, including individual liberty, the preservation of constitutional rights, an expectation of personal privacy, and the protection of private property and free enterprise. These American values guide the development of public policy in all areas of government, including criminal justice. The application of American values, however, creates special tensions and problems in criminal justice. For example, people's sense of liberty may depend on how freely they can walk the streets without fearing crime; therefore, they want tough crime-control policies. On the other hand, other aspects of American values emphasize the protection of the criminal defendant's rights in order to ensure that no one is improperly denied his or her liberty. Finding the proper balance between conflicting values may pose an even greater challenge during the current era, in which fears about terrorism have enhanced citizens' concerns about crime and public safety. In the aftermath of the September 11, 2001, terrorist attacks on the World Trade Center in New York and the Pentagon in Washington, D.C., more than half of Americans believed it would be necessary to sacrifice some civil liberties in order to gain greater security. A survey in 2011 revealed that 40 percent of Americans still expressed that view ten years after the attacks of 9-11 (BJS, 2015a). If there were to be another large-scale terrorist attack on the United States or elsewhere, new laws and policies produced in response to such an event may strike a new balance that diminishes individuals' rights in favor of enhancing order and security.

To facilitate the exploration of these issues and others, this book presents three major themes: (1) crime and justice are public policy issues; (2) criminal justice can best be seen as a social system; and (3) the criminal justice system embodies society's effort to fulfill American values, such as liberty, privacy, and individuals' rights.

An additional minor theme will be highlighted in each chapter. This fourth theme is a reflection of the times in which we live: the impact of widespread federal, state, and local budget cuts on crime and criminal justice. Many states are seeking to save money by reducing their prison populations. As a result, governments must simultaneously develop and expand mechanisms for punishing offenders in the community and for reintegrating former prisoners into society. In addition, many cities and counties are laying off police officers. For example, there were 16 percent fewer police officers statewide in Michigan in 2013 as compared to a decade earlier (S. Miller, 2013). Camden, New Jersey, a poor community with significant crime problems, laid off more than one-third of its police force in 2011 and eliminated the department completely in 2013 when arrangements were made for a county-based police department to take over (Wood, 2014). These changes in priorities—and the subsequent impact on communities—were a direct result of budget reductions stemming from a loss of tax revenue as the national economy struggled to regain its footing from the economic recession of 2008. The problems and choices involved in cutting budgets while still seeking to protect the public are components of the first major theme of this book: crime and justice as public policy issues. However, these decisions and their results have assumed such importance for contemporary criminal justice agencies at all levels of government that we will highlight these problems throughout the book.

As we shall see, values can come into conflict as choices are made about how to operate the system and define public policies. These themes are important for all Americans because of people's involvement in shaping criminal justice policy through their roles as voters, members of community organizations, and, for many students of criminal justice, as future criminal justice professionals. All Americans are affected by criminal justice issues through perceptions that guide their choices about how to behave, where to live, and how to protect themselves and their families from victimization. All Americans also influence criminal justice when they vote on statewide ballot issues, vote for specific political candidates, make suggestions to their neighborhood associations, and express their views to elected officials. A knowledge of criminal justice from a public policy perspective and an understanding of the operation of the criminal justice system are essential tools for Americans. Individuals can use this knowledge to make decisions about their own behavior and to inform their voting decisions and other involvement in shaping public policy. In asserting their influence over criminal justice, Americans also need to bear in mind the third theme: the need to uphold and strike an appropriate balance between our nation's values, including personal privacy and due process, and the necessary government authority for maintaining safety and security in society.

This chapter focuses on the first theme, concerning crime and justice as public policy issues. The third theme, American values, is also presented in this chapter and will appear in each chapter throughout the book. Chapter 1 also examines the nature and definition of **crime**. Crime is those behaviors defined by law as so harmful or undesirable that individuals proven to have undertaken them should be punished by the government. As you learn about crime and the criminal justice system, take note of the many different academic disciplines that contribute to our knowledge in these areas. For example, the study of criminal justice requires psychologists to analyze the thinking and behavior of individuals. Criminologists develop and test theories about the causes of criminal behavior. Sociologists and economists examine the impact of society on crime as well as crime's impact on society. Political scientists explore the development of public policy and the operations of criminal justice agencies. Increasingly, chemists, biologists, and engineers play important roles in criminal justice because of the development of new scientific methods for investigating crimes and new technologies for weapons, surveillance, databases, and other essential aspects of law enforcement administration. Clearly, criminal justice provides a multidisciplinary area of study that appeals to people with varied interests and expertise.

crime
A specific act of commission or omission in violation of the law, for which a punishment is prescribed.

An understanding of the crime problem and U.S. society's definition of this problem as a public policy issue will give you the groundwork for later discussions about criminal justice as a social system in which actors and agencies interact and make decisions. To guide your study, we address the following themes.

Crime and Justice as Public Policy Issues

Who bears responsibility for addressing issues of crime and justice? The answer to this question depends on the organization of a society and the nature of its governing system. Looking back at human history, one can see many approaches to crime and punishment. For example, in a sparsely populated rural society that lacked effective control by government, crime and justice were often viewed as private matters. When one individual harmed another through violence or theft, a measure of justice could be obtained through vengeful acts by the victim's family or through the payment of compensation by the perpetrator. Such approaches were common in the centuries before central governments became dominating forces in modern nations. Alternatively, local leaders could rely on cultural traditions to impose punishments upon wrongdoers.

In the United States, by contrast, crime and justice are public policy issues, because the government addresses them. Institutions and processes of government produce laws to define crimes; create and operate agencies to investigate, prosecute, and punish criminals; and allocate resources to address the problems of crime and justice. Moreover, these institutions and processes are influenced by the actions of American citizens, as they cast their votes for specific candidates; bring issues and problems to the attention of elected officials; and publicly protest against those policies that they see as unfair, inappropriate, or ineffective.

public policy
Priorities and actions developed by government to use public resources as a means to deal with issues affecting society.

Crime and justice are important and difficult **public policy** issues in the United States. In a democracy, we struggle to strike a balance between maintaining public order and protecting individual freedom. Both sides of this equation represent American values. To enjoy the liberty that we value so highly, we want to feel safe to move freely in society. On the other hand, if we push too strongly to ensure safety, we could limit individual rights and liberty by unnecessarily restricting, detaining, or punishing too many individuals. For example, we could impose policies that make us feel safe from crime, such as placing a police officer on every street corner or by executing suspected criminals. Such severe practices have been used elsewhere in the world. Although they may reduce crime, they also fly in the face of democratic values. If we gave law enforcement officers a free hand to work their will on the public, we would be giving up individual freedom, due process, and the American conception of justice. Liberty and legal rights are so important that they are enshrined in the nation's founding document, the U.S. Constitution. However, the protection of these democratic values can impede the ability of criminal justice officials to catch and punish offenders. Thus we continually struggle to find the proper balance between stopping crime and preventing government officials from violating individuals' rights.

Some critics of criminal justice, such as Jeffrey Reiman, argue that our system is designed not to reduce crime or to achieve justice but to project to the American people a visible image of the threat of crime (Reiman, 1996: 1). This is done by maintaining a sizable population of criminals while at the same time failing to reduce crime. Reiman argues that we need to move away from a system of *criminal* justice to one of criminal *justice*. He urges policies that

- End crime-producing poverty.
- Criminalize the harmful acts of affluent and white-collar offenders.
- Create a corrections system that promotes human dignity.
- Make the exercise of police, prosecution, and judicial power more just.
- Establish economic and social justice.

If adopted, Reiman's thought-provoking critical perspective would produce significant changes in priorities in the criminal justice system and effect changes in programs, policies, and the distribution of government resources affecting the rest of society.

Evidence-Based Practices

Dealing with the crime problem concerns not only the arrest, conviction, and punishment of offenders; it also requires the development of policies to deal with a host of issues such as gun control, stalking, hate crimes, computer crime, drugs, child abuse, and global criminal organizations. Many of these issues are controversial; policies must be hammered out in the political arenas of state legislatures and Congress. Any policy choice carries with it costs and consequences as well as potential benefits. Predicting consequences can be difficult. In addition, legislators often enact laws based on their *beliefs* about the nature of a problem and the responses that will be effective in addressing the problem. These beliefs are not necessarily based on a thorough understanding of available research on the nature of problems in criminal justice. Similarly, police chiefs, prison wardens, and others who carry out laws and policies may rely heavily on practices they are accustomed to using, rather than exploring the full range of possible effective alternatives. Decision makers' reliance on unsupported beliefs or customary practices may result in missed opportunities to develop policies and practices that might more effectively advance desired goals.

One emerging trend in creating policies within criminal justice is the use of **evidence-based practices**. These are practices that have proven to be effective in research studies. Social scientists examine many aspects of criminal justice, including the causes of crime, the effectiveness of crime control strategies, and efficiency in police procedures. These studies can demonstrate that some approaches are more useful and cost effective than others in addressing problems. Research also shows that some approaches are unproven or ineffective. As described by Faye Taxman and Steven Belenko, evidence-based practices are "practices that *should* be widely used because research indicates that they positively alter human behavior" (Taxman and Belenko, 2013: 3). Thus legislators, police chiefs, prison wardens, and other decision makers are increasingly looking to scholars' research for guidance about which laws and policies to develop. Ideally, working partnerships can be formed between researchers and justice system officials in order to increase the effectiveness of communication, understanding, and application of reforms (E. Davis and Robinson, 2014). However, even when research-supported approaches are available, evidence-based practices are not always followed. Sometimes decision makers are not aware of relevant research about a problem that they are addressing. Legislators and other policy makers also may resist adopting evidence-based practices when the research findings underlying those practices conflict with their own strongly held beliefs or their commitment to familiar, customary approaches. Read the New Directions in Criminal Justice Policy feature in this chapter to see a contemporary debate about drug policy that is influenced by research studies and evidence-based practices.

evidence-based practices
Policies developed through guidance from research studies that demonstrate which approaches are most useful and cost-effective for advancing desired goals.

The Role of Public Opinion

In a democracy, public opinion greatly influences political leaders. They know that if they develop policies contrary to public views, they may lose the next election and diminish the legitimacy of those policies. As a result, these leaders often enact policies that are thought by researchers to have little potential impact on crime but that nonetheless allay the general public's anxiety about crime and safety.

Throughout this book, you will find marginal items labeled "What Americans Think." These features present the results of public opinion surveys on issues concerning crime and the administration of justice. As you read each chapter, consider these expressions of public opinion. Do you agree with the majority of Americans on each issue? Or does your understanding of criminal justice give you a different perspective on the policies that might better address these problems? See, for example, "What Americans Think" about the criminal justice system.

WHAT AMERICANS THINK

QUESTION: "I am going to read you a list of institutions in American society. Please tell me how much confidence you, yourself, have in each one—a great deal, quite a lot, some, or very little: the criminal justice system?"

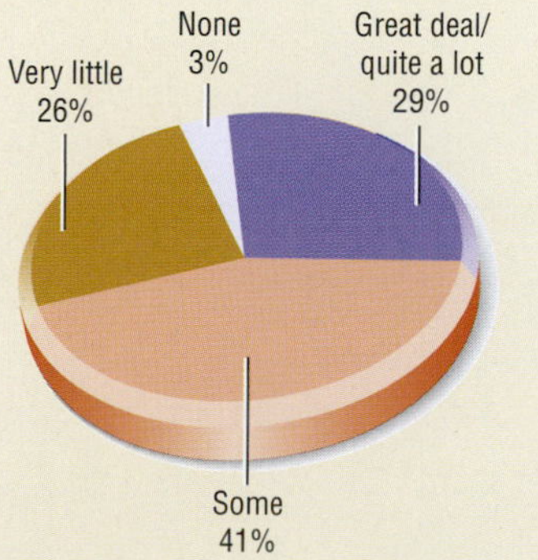

Source: Bureau of Justice Statistics, *Sourcebook of Criminal Justice Statistics* (2015), Table 2.11.2012.

Contemporary Policies

Over the past several decades, both conservatives and liberals have promoted policies for dealing with crime. Each group has its own perspective on what works best to advance justice. Conservatives believe that solutions will come

NEW DIRECTIONS IN CRIMINAL JUSTICE POLICY

DRUG POLICY: QUESTIONING THE NECESSITY AND DESIRABILITY OF IMPRISONMENT

Many Americans have asked the question: Why is it legal to consume alcoholic beverages but the use of marijuana and other intoxicants labeled as "drugs" leads to criminal convictions and punishments? It would be possible to treat the use of addictive and intoxicating substances as a public-health problem rather than as a crime problem. Why not apply the education and treatment approaches, often used for nicotine addiction and alcoholism, to marijuana and perhaps to the addictive substances cocaine, methamphetamine, heroin, and prescription painkillers as well?

One answer to these questions is that it can be difficult to shift viewpoints about behavior that has been perpetually and loudly condemned as "illegal" and "wrong" for many years. It is all the more difficult to change approaches when millions and millions of dollars have been spent on law enforcement efforts and correctional institutions that treat marijuana and other drugs as a crime problem.

In recent years, however, two factors have pushed legislators and other decision makers to reconsider American drug policy. First, the public's attitude toward marijuana is changing. In several states, voters have approved ballot issues that legalize the use of marijuana for medical purposes by people who have the approval of a doctor. In 2012, the voters in Colorado and Washington went a step further and approved ballot issues that legalized the possession and use of marijuana by individuals. Voters in Oregon, Alaska, and Washington, D.C., followed suit by approving their own legalization ballot issues in November 2014. These decisions caused new problems as officials encountered matters such as driving under the influence of marijuana, children's access to marijuana-infused snacks, and a potential increase in young people's possession of marijuana at schools. Despite these issues, the slow spread of decriminalization efforts through ballot issues approved by voters clearly indicates that the public is less supportive of treating marijuana use as a crime issue.

Second, government budget cuts throughout the country have led officials to look for ways to send fewer people to prison and to reduce the sentence lengths that dramatically expanded the country's prison population over the last three decades. In 1980, there were 320,000 offenders serving sentences in American prisons. By 2013, that number had risen to more than 1.5 million, despite the fact that crime rates generally fell steadily after 1992. A tough-on-crime approach to sentencing led hundreds of thousands of additional offenders to be imprisoned. Many of these offenders were imprisoned on drug charges or for crimes, such as thefts and robberies, that were committed to support a drug habit. Imprisonment has been enormously expensive with respect to building and staffing new prisons and supplying food, shelter, medical care, and supervision for the swelling prison population. This increase has also created huge monetary and emotional costs for the spouses and children of prisoners, because a parent and breadwinner can be sent away for years for committing the relatively minor crime of illegal drug possession.

These two influences will not necessarily lead to the legalization of drugs, because the U.S. Department of Justice maintains that marijuana and other drugs, remain illegal under federal law no matter what voters in any state decide. However, these factors have pushed officials to look at research studies in considering how to cut costs by using more-effective, evidence-based practices.

Research indicates that it is cheaper to provide drug-addicted offenders with treatment than it is to send them to prison. Although many people with substance abuse problems

from stricter enforcement of the law through the expansion of police forces and the enactment of laws that require swift and certain punishment of criminals (Pickett, Tope and Bellandi, 2014; Logan and DiIulio, 1993). Advocates of such policies have dominated since the early 1980s. They argue that we must strengthen crime control, which they claim has been hindered by certain decisions of the U.S. Supreme Court and by programs that substitute government assistance for individual responsibility (Rushford, 2009).

In contrast, liberals argue that stronger crime-control measures endanger the values of due process and justice (A. Schwartz, 2013; S. Walker, 1993). They claim that strict measures are ineffective because progress will come from reshaping the lives of offenders and changing the social and economic conditions from which criminal behavior springs. Thus they advocate programs to reduce poverty, increase educational opportunities for poor youths, and provide counseling and drug rehabilitation (Edelman, 2010).

will eventually fall back into their old ways, research shows that those who have undergone treatment are more likely to stay away from drugs and avoid committing new crimes than are those who are sent to prison and receive no treatment. In one New York program, it cost only $32,000 to send drug-addicted offenders to a two-year residential treatment program that included job training, whereas it would have cost taxpayers twice that amount to send them to prison for the same time period. It is even less expensive for those offenders who pose no danger to society to attend outpatient treatment programs while living at home. Treatment programs inside prisons can also improve offenders' likelihood of avoiding drugs upon release, an important consideration as states speed up early releases in order to reduce the costs of imprisonment.

Research studies also provide guidance for dealing with risks that emerge as a result of easier access to decriminalized marijuana and other substance abuse issues. For example, studies indicate that specific family counseling programs and school-based intervention programs can reduce teenage alcohol and drug abuse. Such early intervention programs may save society from long-term problems if these youths are guided away from a path that might otherwise have led them to engage in criminal acts, and consequently, expensive periods of imprisonment.

Budgetary pressures and changes in public attitudes have combined to produce reconsideration of several aspects of drug policy. Looking at these issues in a new light creates the opportunity to seek guidance from evidence-based practices. However, it remains to be seen whether states will devote significant resources to prevention and treatment. Governments could save resources by merely reducing enforcement of marijuana laws, shortening prison sentences, and moving prisoners out through early release. But in the long run, more money might be saved through investments in research-based treatment programs that reduce the problem of drug abuse.

Sources: G. H. Brody et al., "Family Centered Program Deters Substance Use, Conduct Problems, and Depressive Symptoms in Black Adolescents," *Pediatrics* 129 (2012): 108–15; E. A. Carson, "Prisoners in 2013," Bureau of Justice Statistics *Bulletin*, September 2014, NCJ 247282; J. Healy, "After 5 Months of Sales, Colorado Sees the Down Side of a Legal High," *New York Times*, May 31, 2014 (www.nytimes.com); D. McVay et al., *Treatment or Incarceration? National and State Findings on the Efficacy and Cost Savings of Drug Treatment versus Imprisonment* (Washington, DC: Justice Policy Center, 2004); D. Merica, "Oregon, Alaska, and Washington, D.C. Legalize Marijuana," CNN.com, November 5, 2014 (www.cnn.com); F. S. Taxman and S. Belenko, *Implementing Evidence-Based Practices in Community Corrections and Addiction Treatment* (New York: Springer, 2013); N. D. Volkow, R. D. Baler, W. M. Compton, and S. R. B. Weiss, "Adverse Health Effects of Marijuana Use," *New England Journal of Medicine*, 370 (2014): 2219–27; K. C. Winters et al., "Brief Intervention for Drug-Abusing Adolescents in a School Setting: Outcomes and Mediating Factors," *Journal of Substance Abuse Treatment* 42 (2012): 279–88.

DEBATE THE ISSUE

Should the United States legalize the consumption of marijuana and treat it in the same manner as alcoholic beverages? What problems and issues may emerge from that policy choice? Should addictive drugs, such as heroin, methamphetamines, cocaine, and prescription painkillers, be regarded as public-health problems instead of crime problems? Should resources be focused on education and treatment for drug abuse, as is done with nicotine addiction and alcoholism? What problems might emerge from using the public-health approach? Give two arguments that present your position on whether the United States should treat substance abuse as a public-health problem instead of a crime problem.

As you consider these arguments, think about how they relate to crime trends. In the 1960s, when we were trying the liberal approach of rehabilitating offenders, crime increased. Does this mean that the approach does not work? Perhaps these programs were merely overwhelmed by the sheer number of people who were in their crime-prone years (between the ages of 16 and 24). Perhaps there would have been even more crime if not for the efforts to rehabilitate people. On the other hand, crime rates decreased when tough policies were implemented in the 1980s and thereafter. But was that because of the conservative policies in effect, or because there were fewer people in the crime-prone age group? If conservative policies are effective, then why did violent-crime rates rise in the early 1990s, when tough policies were still in force? Clearly, there are no easy answers. Nonetheless, we cannot avoid making choices about how to use the police, courts, and corrections system most effectively.

Crime and Justice in a Democracy

Americans agree that criminal justice policies should control crime by enforcing the law and should protect the rights of individuals. But achieving both objectives is difficult. They involve questions such as the amount of power police should have to search people without a warrant, the rules judges must follow in deciding if certain types of evidence may be used, and the extent to which prison wardens may punish inmates. These questions are answered differently in a democracy than they would be in an authoritarian state.

The administration of justice in a democracy also differs from that in an authoritarian state in the nature and extent of the protections provided for an accused person while guilt is determined and punishment imposed. The police, prosecutors, judges, and correctional officials are expected to act according to democratic values—especially respect for the rule of law and the maintenance of civil rights and liberties. Further, citizens must view the criminal justice system as legitimate and have confidence in its actions.

Laws in the United States begin with the premise that all people—the guilty as well as the innocent—have rights. Moreover, unlike laws in some other countries, U.S. laws reflect the desire to avoid unnecessarily depriving people of liberty, either by permitting the police to arrest people at will or by punishing a person for a crime that he or she did not commit.

Although all Americans prize freedom and individual rights, they often disagree about the policies that deal with crime. Our greatest challenge as we move through the twenty-first century may be to find ways to remain true to the principles of fairness and justice while operating a system that can effectively protect, investigate, and punish.

✔POINT
1. What are evidence-based practices?
2. What criminal justice policies are advocated by conservatives?
3. What are liberals' criticisms of contemporary policies?

STOP AND ANALYZE: Do you see yourself as more inclined to take the conservative or the liberal position with respect to criminal justice policy? If the approach that you chose was implemented as the dominant guide to policy, what forms of injustice might occur? List two situations in which something you regard as an injustice might arise under your approach.

(Answers are at the end of the chapter.)

AP Images/Alex Menendez

In a democracy, citizens must take an interest in the criminal justice system, as they are doing here in this 2014 demonstration after publicized incidents of police using lethal force on unarmed people. Here, demonstrators seek to raise awareness about aspects of officials' performance that need to improve and change. As a citizen, how can you become involved in criminal justice issues?

Crime Control versus Due Process

In one of the most important contributions to systematic thought about criminal justice, Herbert Packer (1968) describes two competing models of criminal justice administration: the **crime control model** and the **due process model**. These are contrasting ways of looking at the goals and procedures of the criminal justice system. The crime control model is much like an assembly line, whereas the due process model is like an obstacle course.

In reality, of course, no criminal justice official or agency functions according to one model or the other. Elements of both models appear throughout the system. However, the two models reveal key tensions within the criminal justice process, as well as the gap between how we describe the system and the way most cases are actually processed. Table 1.1 presents the main elements of each model.

crime control model
A model of the criminal justice system that assumes freedom is so important that every effort must be made to repress crime; it emphasizes efficiency, speed, finality, and the capacity to apprehend, try, convict, and dispose of a high proportion of offenders.

due process model
A model of the criminal justice system that assumes freedom is so important that every effort must be made to ensure that criminal justice decisions are based on reliable information; it emphasizes the adversarial process, the rights of defendants, and formal decision-making procedures.

Crime Control: Order as a Value

The crime control model assumes that every effort must be made to repress crime. It emphasizes efficiency and the capacity to catch, try, convict, and punish a high proportion of offenders; it also stresses speed and finality. This model places the goal of controlling crime uppermost, putting less emphasis on protecting individuals' rights. As Packer points out, the crime control model calls for efficiency in screening suspects, determining guilt, and applying sanctions to the convicted; this will achieve liberty for all citizens. High rates of crime and the limited resources of law enforcement make speed and finality necessary. All of these elements depend on informality, uniformity, and few challenges by defense attorneys or defendants.

In this model, police and prosecutors decide early on how likely the suspect is to be found guilty. If a case is unlikely to end in conviction, the prosecutor may drop the charges. At each stage—from arrest to preliminary hearing, arraignment, and trial—established procedures are used to determine whether the accused should be passed on to the next stage. Rather than stressing the combative aspects of the courtroom, this model promotes bargaining between the state and the accused. Nearly all cases are processed through such bargaining, and they typically end with the defendant pleading guilty. Packer's description of this model as an assembly-line process conveys the idea of quick, efficient decisions by actors at fixed stations that turn out the intended product—guilty pleas and closed cases.

Due Process: Law as a Value

If the crime control model looks like an assembly line, the due process model looks more like an obstacle course. This model assumes that freedom is so important that every effort must be made to ensure that criminal justice decisions

TABLE 1.1 DUE PROCESS MODEL AND CRIME CONTROL MODEL COMPARED

What other comparisons can be made between the two models?

	GOAL	VALUE	PROCESS	MAJOR DECISION POINT	BASIS OF DECISION MAKING
Due Process Model	Preserve individual liberties	Reliability	Adversarial	Courtroom	Law
Crime Control Model	Repress crime	Efficiency	Administrative	Police, pretrial processes	Discretion

stem from reliable information. It stresses the adversarial process, the rights of defendants, and formal decision-making procedures. For example, because people are poor observers of disturbing events, police and prosecutors may well be wrong in presuming a defendant to be guilty. Thus, people should be labeled as criminals only on the basis of conclusive evidence. To reduce error, the government must prove beyond a reasonable doubt that the defendant is guilty of the crime. Therefore, the process must give the defense every opportunity to show that the evidence is not conclusive, and an impartial judge and jury must decide the outcome. According to Packer, the assumption that the defendant is innocent until proved guilty has a far-reaching impact on the criminal justice system.

In the due process model, the state must prove that the person is guilty of the crime as charged. Prosecutors must prove their cases while obeying rules dealing with such matters as the admissibility of evidence and respect for defendants' constitutional rights. Forcing the state to prove its case in a trial protects citizens from wrongful convictions. Thus the due process model emphasizes justice as protecting the rights of individuals and reserving punishment for those who unquestionably deserve it. These values are stressed even though some guilty defendants may go free because the evidence against them is not conclusive enough. By contrast, the crime control model values efficient case processing and punishment over the possibility that innocent people might get swept up in the process.

✔POINT

4. What are the main features of the crime control model?

5. What are the main features of the due process model?

STOP AND ANALYZE: The due process model is most frequently portrayed in television dramas and movies that show criminal cases argued in trials before juries. List two reasons why this model represents only a small fraction of criminal cases.

The Politics of Crime and Justice

Criminal justice policies are developed in national, state, and local political arenas. There is always a risk that politicians will simply do what they believe voters want, rather than seriously weighing whether the policies will achieve their intended goals. For example, the crime bill passed by Congress in 1994 expanded the death penalty to cover 60 additional offenses, including the murder of members of Congress, the Supreme Court, and the president's staff. These are tough provisions, but did they actually accomplish anything? When highly publicized actions are narrowly directed at rarely committed crimes or undertaken without careful study of underlying problems, the appearance of strong action does not translate into actual impacts on crime rates.

Frequently, "knee-jerk" reactions inform the political process. A problem occurs and captures significant public attention. Calls to do something arise. Politicians respond with (1) outrage, (2) a limited examination of the problem, and (3) a law—often poorly thought out and with little regard for unintended consequences. Politicians often propose laws without carefully studying the nature and extent of the problem they claim to address (Socia, 2014; Gest, 2001).

If not written carefully, laws may affect more people than the original targets of the law. In one example, a 12-year-old Boy Scout and honors student in Texas forgot to remove a small pocketknife from his jacket pocket after a weekend camping trip. When he found the knife in his pocket at school, he placed it in his locker. Another student reported him to school officials. Because the state's Safe Schools Act of 1995 imposed a "zero tolerance" policy for weapons in schools, the boy was arrested and taken to a juvenile-detention facility without officials informing his parents. After being expelled from school and spending weeks in a school for juvenile offenders, he began contemplating suicide (Axtman, 2005).

Other examples of laws with unanticipated consequences might include residence restrictions on sex offenders who are often forbidden from living near schools and playgrounds after their release from prison. Because of the geographic distribution of schools in cities and towns, this can make it difficult for these offenders to find anywhere to live and thereby hinder their ability to reenter society as productive citizens (Socia, 2014; Schwirtz, 2013). In Miami, for example, dozens of sex offenders ended up sleeping every night in tents under a bridge. Evidence-based practice indicates that a stable home is a key element for the rehabilitation of ex-offenders. Thus the policy choice of residence restrictions was counterproductive. A more workable and effective approach would be to enforce anti-loitering laws to prevent these offenders from being in specific locations during the day (Skipp, 2010).

The clearest link between politics and criminal justice shows up in the statements of Republicans and Democrats who try to outdo each other in exhibiting how tough they can be on crime. Just as important are the more "routine" links between politics and the justice system. Legislators, who are motivated by their desire for reelection, respond to voters' expectations by enacting laws to define crimes, adjust mandated punishments, and decide how much money will go to the annual budgets of criminal justice agencies. Unfortunately, the effort to satisfy voters and project an image of "doing something about crime" may lead to policy choices that are based on beliefs and perceptions about crime rather than on research and evidence-based practices. Read the Close Up about gun control laws and consider the challenges of making effective policies when reactions to criminal justice problems are often guided by politics and personal beliefs.

Many other types of political decisions affect criminal justice, some of which create undesirable consequences. For example, Congress appropriates millions of dollars to help states and cities wage the "war on drugs," funding that leads to the arrest of more people but fails to allocate additional funds to provide attorneys for poor defendants. A legislature may create a budget crisis for local police agencies by requiring the collection of DNA samples from everyone in local jails when it does not provide additional funds for technicians

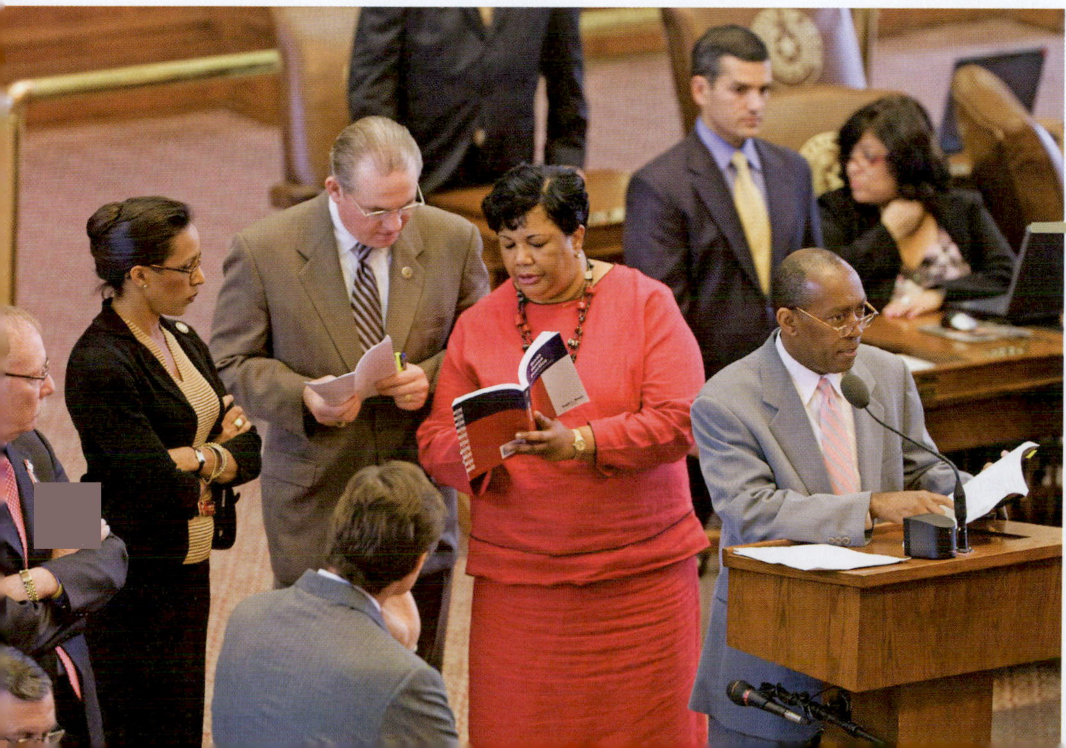

Bob Daemmrich/The Image Works

Criminal justice policies are decided by legislators who respond to voters' concerns and perceptions about crime. Legislators also determine priorities for government spending on various policy issues. Do you think your state and local government spends too little, too much, or just enough on criminal justice as compared to issues such as education and transportation?

and labs to gather, store, and test samples. At the state and local levels, many criminal justice authorities—including sheriffs, prosecutors, and judges—are also elected officials. There are no elected justice officials in the federal system except the president of the United States, who appoints federal prosecutors throughout the country. The decisions of state and local elected officials will be influenced by the concerns and values of their communities, because these officials must please a majority of voters in order to be reelected. Because the decisions of prosecutors, sheriffs, and judges are affected by their efforts to please voters, there are concerns that these officials will lose sight of other important values, such as equal treatment for all defendants.

As you learn about each part of the criminal justice system, keep in mind the ways that decision makers and institutions are connected to politics and government. Criminal justice is closely linked to society and its institutions, and to understand it fully we must be aware of those links.

CLOSE UP

THE POLITICS OF GUN-CONTROL LAW AND POLICY

The entire nation was shocked in December 2012 when a mentally troubled young man, Adam Lanza, entered an elementary school in Newtown, Connecticut, and opened fire on students and staff. The dead included 20 six- and seven-year-old first graders. In the aftermath of the shooting, President Obama spoke to the nation about the need to enact laws aimed at reducing gun violence. He proposed new federal laws, yet none were ever passed by Congress.

The subject of gun control is highly emotional for many Americans, as there is a divide between those who see firearms as an essential element of personal liberty and those who believe that many deaths needlessly occur because guns are too freely available. Many opponents of restrictive gun laws point to the Constitution's Second Amendment, which contains the phrase " . . . the right of the people to keep and bear arms shall not be infringed," as a basis for arguing for greater access to firearms. However, the U.S. Supreme Court, which is the ultimate authority over the meaning of the Second Amendment, has declared that the right to "keep and bear arms" is guaranteed only with respect to law-abiding citizens' entitlement to keep handguns in their homes for self-protection (*District of Columbia v. Heller*, 2008; *McDonald v. City of Chicago*, 2010). Thus Congress, state legislatures, and city councils have the authority to impose gun regulations as long as those regulations do not violate the right to keep a handgun in the home. Whether or not regulations are actually created depends on political values, lobbying, and beliefs about gun policies in each city and state.

After the Newtown shooting, state legislatures in Connecticut and New York, as well as a few other states, enacted laws to create new limitations. The laws were intended to do such things as limit the number of bullets that can be loaded into a weapon, keep certain mentally ill people from acquiring guns, require registration of weapons and background checks for gun purchasers, and ban certain rapid-fire weapons. Critics argued that such restrictions violated their own visions of the Second Amendment's meaning and claimed that people with mental issues will stop their contacts with medical professionals in order to avoid being placed on lists of people forbidden to buy guns. They also argued that the laws would be ineffective because troubled people who want to cause harm would find other ways to acquire the weapons that they want.

Other states followed the views of these critics and these state legislatures enacted new laws to make firearms more readily available and to permit people to carry concealed weapons in a wider variety of locations. These decision makers typically held quite different views about the Second Amendment's meaning than those maintained by Supreme Court justices, President Obama, and legislators in New York and Connecticut. In addition, legislators in these states with more lenient gun laws often expressed the view that an increase in the availability of firearms makes society safer because people are better prepared to defend themselves against criminals. Opponents to that view countered that laws providing easier access to guns are associated with an increased number of suicides and accidental shootings. These critics also argued that such laws make it easier for people who want to cause harm to bring weapons to highly populated locations without any impediments or suspicion. They pointed to Georgia's expansion of opportunities to carry weapons into bars, churches and schools, and Idaho's removal of universities' authority to ban guns on their own campuses, as examples of laws that would increase danger.

Specific news stories highlight incidents of "road-rage" shootings and instances of drunk people waving firearms in bars and restaurants. Other stories point to children finding their parents' guns and shooting siblings or friends accidently. Indeed, a professor at Idaho State University accidently shot himself in the

✔POINT 6. At what level of government are many justice officials elected to office?
7. How do politics influence criminal justice policies?

STOP AND ANALYZE: If a legislator asked you to provide two suggestions for improving policy making in criminal justice by decreasing the influence of politics, what would you say?

Citizens and Criminal Justice Policy

Americans should not view themselves as passive observers of criminal justice policy. In fact, they are intimately involved in the processes that produce public policy. Most obviously, citizens vote for the elected officials who create criminal laws, run the criminal justice system, and implement criminal justice policies. Often, votes are based on concerns about issues, such as economic

foot during class with his concealed weapon just weeks after the state legislature broadened opportunities to carry weapons on campus. These individual incidents illustrate risks that exist, but they do not clearly inform legislators about the best course of action. Moreover, legislators, like other people, tend to filter out information and accept selected evidence in ways that reinforce their existing beliefs.

What laws and policies might be produced if legislators could step back from their beliefs and ignore the financial contributions and lobbying directed at them from gun-rights interest groups? What would happen if a legislature sought to take an evidence-based approach to gun policy? In January 2013, Johns Hopkins University in Baltimore hosted a conference at which leading researchers shared the findings of their studies in an effort to develop a set of evidence-based proposals for gun regulation. For example, studies showed a reduction in intimate partner homicides (i.e., murders of spouses, girlfriends, etc.) in those jurisdictions that both regulated gun ownership and investigated the backgrounds of individuals subject to restraining orders from domestic violence incidents. In the aftermath of a 1996 mass shooting, Australia banned various weapons and instituted government buyback programs in 1996 and 2003. Comparative studies following the enactment of that legislation showed a significant reduction in firearms suicides and coincided with a trend toward fewer gun homicides.

One of the impediments for developing evidence-based regulation in the United States stems from political pressure that led Congress to restrict the ability of federal government research agencies to conduct or fund studies of gun violence. Other aspects of criminal justice are studied by researchers with assistance from government funding, but firearms issues are singled out for restrictions on funding and data sharing. In effect, a law is in place that makes it difficult to examine an important policy issue and blocks the government's ability to consider whether there would be benefits from recommending changes based on evidence-based research findings. Thus, gun policy, in particular, is likely to continue to be guided by beliefs, political values, and lobbying without a concerted effort to use research as a means to produce evidence about the effects of different policy choices.

Sources: Drawn from M. Cruz, "Georgia's 'Guns Everywhere' Law Stirs Controversy among Students, Teachers," *USA Today*, July 14, 2014 (www.usatoday.com); M. Eversley, "Ionia Police: Tailgating Led to Deadly Road Rage Shooting," *Detroit Free* Press, September 20, 2013 (www.freep.com); Christine Jamieson, "Gun Violence Research: History of the Federal Funding Freeze," *Psychological Science Agenda*, February 2013 (http://www.apa.org/science/about/psa/2013/02/gun-violence.aspx); T. Kaplan, "Cuomo's Gun Law Plays Well Downstate but Alienates Upstate," *New York Times*, October 24, 2014 (www.nytimes.com); L. Mungin and B. Brady, "Connecticut Governor Signs Sweeping Gun Measure," CNN.com, April 4, 2013 (www.cnn.com); H. Schwartz, "Idaho Professor Shoots Himself in Foot Two Months after State Legalizes Guns on Campuses," *Washington Post*, September 5, 2014 (www.washingtonpost.com); D. W. Webster and J. S. Vernick, eds., *Reducing Gun Violence in America: Informing Policy with Evidence and Analysis* (Baltimore: Johns Hopkins University Press, 2013, including specific articles such as A. M. Zeoli and S. Frattaroli, "Evidence for Optimism: Policies to Limit Batterers' Access to Guns," 53–63 and P. Alpers, "The Big Melt: How One Democracy Changed after Scrapping a Third of Its Firearms," 205–11.

DEBATE THE ISSUE

Many Americans enter the gun-control debate with firmly fixed views and an unwillingness to listen to opposing evidence and arguments. Are there any views about gun-control policy that you hold which you would be willing to consider changing if research evidence could demonstrate that you have relied on faulty assumptions? Are you willing to consider evidence that contradicts your current views? Challenge yourself to step back from your current views by writing down the five strongest arguments and evidence that contradict your current viewpoint.

problems or wars, which are regarded as more pressing than criminal justice issues at a given moment in time. At other times, citizens may vote based on loyalty to a political party or perceptions about a candidate's leadership abilities. Americans who move beyond simple beliefs and assumptions about criminals by gaining knowledge about crime trends and the criminal justice system can

INSIDE TODAY'S CONTROVERSIES

CRITICISM OF JUSTICE SYSTEM OFFICIALS: IMPROPER OR USEFUL?

The year 2014 brought forth visible public controversies concerning the unequal treatment of African Americans and whites by certain police officers. Complaints about excessive use of force by police against unarmed African Americans and the failure of police officers to be punished for such actions were brought to the forefront. Public protest marches took place around the country in the aftermath of grand juries declining to criminally charge the police officer who fatally shot unarmed teenager Michael Brown after an altercation in Ferguson, Missouri, or to send to trial the officer who used a neckhold that contributed to the death of Eric Garner, a man accused of illegally selling individual cigarettes on a New York street. In late December 2014, two NYC police officers were gunned down as they sat in their patrol vehicle. Prior to the attack, the killer had shot a girlfriend in Baltimore. He then traveled to New York during which time he indicated on social media posts, which also referenced Brown and Garner, his intention to kill police officers. After ambushing the officers, the killer subsequently committed suicide before he could be apprehended.

In the aftermath of the police officers' murders, New York City police union officials and Republican politicians claimed that Democratic New York City Mayor Bill de Blasio had "blood on his hands" and bore responsibility for the killings because he had previously expressed an understanding of the protesters' concerns relating to improper police actions. In fact, de Blasio generated anger from police a year earlier, during his successful election campaign, by opposing their stop-and-frisk practices targeting young minority men (an issue that will be discussed in Chapter 3). At the same time, former NYC mayor and Republican political candidate Rudolph Giuliani publicly claimed that President Barack Obama bore responsibility for the police officers' murders because, according to Giuliani, the president had spent months since the Brown and Garner deaths saying "that everybody should hate the police." It is notable that the *Washington Post* newspaper carefully examined all of Obama's public statements in the preceding months, found nothing to support Giulani's claim, and awarded Giuliani's statement a "Four Pinocchios" rating as being a complete falsehood.

The newspaper investigation and the New York police officers' previously established opposition to the mayor's criticisms of stop-and-frisk tactics, which a federal judge found to be unconstitutional, serve as reminders that criticisms are often politically motivated. Republican politicians consistently look for ways to criticize Democratic President Obama during his time in office, and the New York police union was posturing to place the mayor at a disadvantage in ongoing negotiations over a new labor contract. However, these stark—albeit not entirely genuine—condemnations of political leaders for purportedly improperly criticizing criminal justice officials raise a question that often causes discomfort in individual citizens: To what extent should citizens strongly support, rather than criticize, public employees who work to improve public safety—especially when the employees in question are police officers who put their lives at risk on a daily basis?

Professors who teach criminal justice courses will sometimes be asked by a student: "Why do you hate the police?" This formulation of the question makes clear that some people improperly equate the act of criticism—a practice that professors often undertake—with hatred—a feeling that is highly unlikely to be held by criminal justice professors who typically have strong, continuing relationships with former students who enter careers in law enforcement.

How might one consider the question of whether it is proper to criticize the police or other criminal justice officials? The first step might be to pose the question: Do all of these officials act properly in all circumstances? Clearly not. It is easy to find news stories about officers who engaged in improper conduct. In November and December 2014, for example, the following stories appeared in the news:

- A Buffalo, New York, police officer was convicted of beating a handcuffed suspect after the man fled on foot during a traffic stop;
- A Detroit police officer was convicted of sexually assaulting a woman when he came to her home in response to her 911 call about being a domestic violence victim at the hands of her boyfriend;
- A Tulsa, Oklahoma, police officer was convicted of bribery after accepting money in exchange for information he obtained from police databases and supplied to criminals for their use in planning burglaries and drug transactions;
- A New York City police officer was convicted of involvement in drug trafficking.

While it would be wrong to criticize *all* police based on the actions of a few officers, clearly there is good reason to criticize officers who do behave improperly.

position themselves to incorporate consideration of these issues into their decisions about whom to support on Election Day.

Because the United States is a democracy, there are opportunities for citizens to go beyond merely voting and act to directly affect policy decisions. For example, a specific, tragic criminal event can lead individual Americans to devote time and

At times there are also good reasons to criticize police operations and procedures. In November 2014, a caller to 911 in Cleveland reported watching someone at a park who had a gun and he was pointing it at various people. The caller told the 911 operator that the gun could likely be a toy. As later seen nationwide on a security video, when the Cleveland police patrol vehicle arrived at the scene, within seconds an officer had fatally shot the young man, Tahir Rice, who turned out to be a 12-year-old holding a realistic-looking toy gun. It was soon revealed that the 911 operator neglected to tell the officers that the caller had said the gun might be a toy. In addition, the officers used poor approach tactics by driving the car right up to the boy on the playground rather than arriving at some distance to give themselves time to assess the situation. Moreover, the officer who fired the fatal shot had been found unfit for duty in his previous employment at a suburban police department because of dismal performance in shooting handguns, inability to follow orders, and inability to remain unemotional and think clearly. Yet, the Cleveland Police Department never reviewed the personnel file from his previous job before hiring him. At the scene, the police officers did not render any first aid to the bleeding boy. Four minutes passed after the shooting before an FBI agent arrived and began to attempt to save the boy with emergency first aid. No one knows if he might have survived if given immediate first aid for his wounds.

Might this tragedy have been averted with better hiring procedures and training for officers and 911 operators? Perhaps so. Thus, the Cleveland tragedy highlights the fact that *critical analysis* and criticism are necessary. You cannot fix anything unless you see and understand its flaws. One can only identify necessary and realistic plans for improving criminal justice agencies by honestly and critically identifying flaws. Thus criticism is a necessary element toward improving the justice system for the benefit of society. If justice system officials or politicians simply try to portray criticism as "tearing down" agencies that automatically deserve to be praised, then they are likely hindering opportunities to identify problems or to subsequently seek improvements.

In a democratic society it is necessary to criticize public officials, in criminal justice and elsewhere in government; such scrutiny makes those officials more responsive to the citizens and raises awareness of the need to make improvements in personnel or procedure. Sometimes criticisms will be misguided or unfair, but because we live in a democracy, there will also opportunities for other voices to provide information that will inform those critics (as well as citizens wanting to examine the arguments for themselves) about why certain criticisms are not accurate or useful. Often, such disagreements become the basis for policy debates, a hallmark of a democratic society in which citizens have a role in contributing to either preservation or reform of policies and practices. Of course, all forms of criticism are not equally useful: Acts of violence and vandalism, for example, create problems rather than effectively clarifying or communicating ideas. Yet, fundamentally, criticism of public agencies and officials is a key element in the exchange of ideas that can help improve government and society. In short, criticism of police practices should not automatically be equated with "hating" the police. In fact, such criticism can actually reflect a high regard for the police and a strong belief in the possibility that police and other criminal justice actors can move ever closer to the ideal of consistently and ethically enforcing laws with effectiveness and fairness while respecting citizens' constitutional rights.

Sources: B. Blackwell, "Tamir Rice Killing Caused by Catastrophic Chain of Events: Analysis," Cleveland.com, December 10, 2014 (www.cleveland.com); A. Bland, "Former Tulsa Police Officer Sentenced in Bribery Case," *Tulsa World*, December 18, 2014 (www.tulsaworld.com); G. Damron and E. Anderson, "Ex-Detroit Cop Gets up to 15 Years in Sex Assault Case," *Detroit Free Press*, November 18, 2014 (www.freep.com); FBI, "Buffalo Police Officer Involved in Videotaped Beating Sentenced on Civil Rights Charges," FBI Press Release, December 1, 2014 (www.fbi.gov); M. Lee, "Guilani's Claim That Obama Launched Anti-Police 'Propaganda'," *Washington Post*, December 23, 2014 (www.washingtonpost.com); C. Mai-Duc, "Cleveland Cop Who Killed Boy, 12, Was Deemed Unfit for Duty," *Los Angeles Times*, December 4, 2014 (www.latimes); D. Meminger, "Ex-Police Officer Sentenced to over 12 Years in Drug Case," New York One News, December 10, 2014 (www.ny1.com); "Police Unions, Others Blast de Blasio after Shooting Deaths of Two NYPD Cops," CBS New York online, December 20, 2014 (newyork.cbslocal.com).

CRITICAL THINKING AND ANALYSIS

In light of the nation's need for and gratitude to police officers for their essential service to society, are there any criticisms that should never be directed at police, either because the assessments are inherently unfair or because citizens are not positioned to really know the reality of policing? How should police officials react and respond when they hear criticisms from politicians, community activists, and ordinary citizens? Write a memo in which you make at least two points about each of the foregoing questions.

WHAT AMERICANS THINK

QUESTION: "Do you think the use of marijuana should be made legal or not?" (2014)

QUESTION: "When a person has a disease that cannot be cured, should doctors be allowed by law to assist the patient to commit suicide if the patient requests it?" (2014)

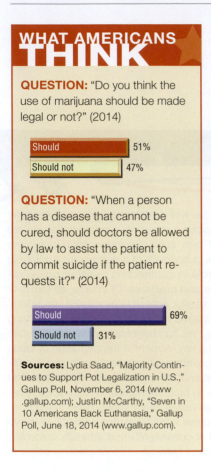

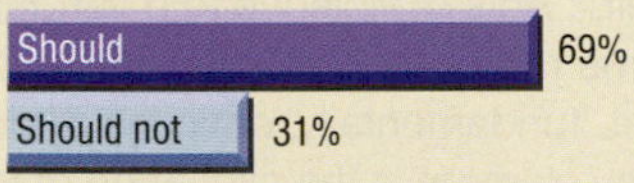

Sources: Lydia Saad, "Majority Continues to Support Pot Legalization in U.S.," Gallup Poll, November 6, 2014 (www.gallup.com); Justin McCarthy, "Seven in 10 Americans Back Euthanasia," Gallup Poll, June 18, 2014 (www.gallup.com).

energy toward shaping justice policy. Candy Lightner, whose teenage daughter was killed by a hit-and-run drunk driver, founded Mothers Against Drunk Driving (MADD), an organization that became very influential throughout the United States in shaping the development and enforcement of criminal laws concerning drunken driving. Similarly, Sarah Brady, whose husband James was seriously injured in the 1981 assassination attempt on President Ronald Reagan, founded the Brady Center to Prevent Gun Violence, an organization that pursues her vision of sensible gun-control laws. In another example, Carolyn McCarthy became dedicated to influencing criminal justice policy after a random shooting by a mentally ill man killed her husband and seriously injured her son. She successfully ran for a seat in Congress and represents a New York district. A similar example is Gabrielle Giffords who, as a member of Congress, was severely injured when shot in the head in an assassination attempt outside a supermarket in Tucson, Arizona, in 2011. Giffords and her husband, NASA astronaut Mark Kelly, founded an organization called Americans for Responsible Solutions to advocate for specific gun regulations. Other individuals have used their personal motivation to educate and mobilize their fellow citizens and thereby influence capital punishment, sex offender registration laws, and other aspects of criminal justice policy.

Individual Americans also influence criminal justice policy through their involvement in community organizations, such as neighborhood associations, parent–teacher organizations, and church groups. They frequently must make decisions about how to keep their homes, schools, and churches safe and secure. This often requires communication and cooperation with police agencies as well as decisions about policies regarding lighting, alarms, public education, and other matters that affect people's vulnerability to criminal victimization.

It is important for Americans to become knowledgeable about criminal justice issues. In our daily lives, we cannot escape making decisions that impact the risk of victimization for ourselves and others. Do we click a link in an unsolicited email message and risk becoming a victim of cybercrime? Do we approach an ATM machine in a dark, isolated corner at night? What do we teach our children about how to handle situations when they are approached by strangers? We also face other questions about how we will influence public policy. How will we vote on ballot issues that will change laws concerning criminal sentences, drug rehabilitation, gambling, and other policy issues? Do we remain silent and passive if our elected officials in local, state, or national government pursue criminal justice policies with which we disagree? Because criminal justice issues affect the lives of all Americans, there are important reasons for educated citizens to recognize their role and impact. Think about these questions as you read Inside Today's Controversies.

✔POINT **8.** Who are some individual Americans who have influenced criminal justice policy?

9. How do average citizens affect criminal justice?

STOP AND ANALYZE: List three things that you are conscious of doing to reduce the risk of crime for yourself and others.

Defining Crime

Why does the law label some types of behavior as "criminal" but not others? In the preceding section's feature on New Directions in Criminal Justice Policy, we saw that consumption of intoxicating alcoholic beverages is generally legal nationwide, whereas the consumption of intoxicating marijuana is still a crime in most American jurisdictions. Criminal laws are not necessarily developed through consistent logical reasoning. Instead, these statutes reflect societal values—some of which may be inconsistent—and reveal the preferences of politicians.

Criminal law is defined by elected representatives in state legislatures and Congress who make choices about the behaviors that government will punish. Some of those choices reflect a broad consensus in society that certain actions, such as rape, assault, and murder, are so harmful that they must be punished. Such crimes have traditionally been called **mala in se**—wrong in themselves. However, legislatures also create criminal laws concerning certain acts whose harm the public is still debating. These crimes are referred to as **mala prohibita**—they are crimes because they are prohibited by the government and not because they are wrong in themselves. Everyone does not agree, for example, that gambling, prostitution, drug use, and assisted suicide should be punished. Today, some people view these behaviors as free choices that adults should be able to make themselves (see "What Americans Think"). Indeed, these behaviors have not been illegal at all times and in all places. Gambling, for example, is illegal in Utah and Hawaii, but it represents an important legitimate business in Nevada, New Jersey, Michigan, on Native American reservations, and in other locations in the United States. Regulated prostitution is legal in Nevada and in many countries of the world, but not in most U.S. states. Although the federal government has blocked the implementation of state laws that relax drug regulations, voters in several U.S. states have expressed their views on the subject by voting to permit people to smoke marijuana (Bruni, 2013). Thus the designation of such activities as crimes does not reflect values that are universally shared throughout the United States.

mala in se
Offenses that are wrong by their very nature.

mala prohibita
Offenses prohibited by law but not wrong in themselves.

Evidence from a national survey helps show the extent to which Americans agree about the behaviors that should be defined as crimes (BJS, 1988). In this classic study, respondents were asked to rank the seriousness of 204 illegal events. The results (Table 1.2) showed wide agreement on the severity

TABLE 1.2 HOW DO PEOPLE RANK THE SEVERITY OF A CRIME?

Respondents to a survey were asked to rank 204 illegal events ranging from school truancy to planting a deadly bomb. A severity score of 40 indicates that people believe the crime is twice as bad as a crime receiving a severity score of 20.

SEVERITY SCORE	TEN MOST SERIOUS OFFENSES	SEVERITY SCORE	TEN LEAST SERIOUS OFFENSES
72.1	Planting a bomb in a public building. The bomb explodes and 20 people are killed.	1.3	Two persons willingly engage in a homosexual act.*
52.8	A man forcibly rapes a woman. As a result of physical injuries, she dies.	1.1	Disturbing the neighborhood with loud, noisy behavior.
43.2	Robbing a victim at gunpoint. The victim struggles and is shot to death.	1.1	Taking bets on the numbers.
39.2	A man stabs his wife. As a result, she dies.	1.1	A group continues to hang around a corner after being told by a police officer to break up.
35.7	Stabbing a victim to death.	0.9	A youngster under 16 runs away from home.
35.6	Intentionally injuring a victim. As a result, the victim dies.	0.8	Being drunk in public.
33.8	Running a narcotics ring.	0.7	A youngster under 16 breaks a curfew law by being on the street after the hour permitted by law.
27.9	A woman stabs her husband. As a result, he dies.	0.6	Trespassing in the backyard of a private home.
26.3	An armed person skyjacks an airplane and demands to be flown to another country.	0.3	A person is vagrant. That is, he has no home and no visible means of support.
25.8	A man forcibly rapes a woman. No other physical injury occurs.	0.2	A youngster under 16 is truant from school.

*No longer illegal after the U.S. Supreme Court decision in *Lawrence v. Texas*, 2003.

Source: Bureau of Justice Statistics, *Report to the Nation on Crime and Justice*, 2nd ed. (Washington, DC: U.S. Government Printing Office, 1988), 16.

of certain crimes. However, crime victims scored those acts higher than did nonvictims. The ratings assigned by minority group members tended to be lower than those assigned by whites. Thus there is disagreement about which behaviors to punish as crimes. Examine your own views by considering the proposed cyberbullying legislation in "Civic Engagement: Your Role in the System."

✔POINT
10. Who defines certain behaviors as criminal?
11. What is meant by *mala in se* and by *mala prohibita*?

STOP AND ANALYZE: Think of an act that is currently a crime and give two arguments for why it should not be a crime. Then think of an act that is currently not a crime and make two arguments for why it should be a crime.

Types of Crime

Crimes can be classified in various ways. As we have seen, scholars often use the distinction between *mala in se* and *mala prohibita*. Crimes can also be classified as either felonies or misdemeanors. **Felonies** are serious crimes punishable by incarceration for more than one year in prison or the death penalty. **Misdemeanors** are less serious offenses that are punishable by jail sentences of less than one year, probation, fines, or other intermediate sanctions. A third scheme classifies crimes by the nature of the act. This approach produces seven types of crime: visible crime, victimless crime, political crime, occupational crime, organized crime, transnational crime, and cybercrime. Each type has its own level of risk and reward, each arouses varying degrees of public disapproval, and each is committed by a certain kind of offender. New types of crime emerge as society changes. Cybercrimes committed via the Internet with computers are becoming a major global problem.

felonies
Serious crimes usually carrying a penalty of incarceration for more than one year or the death penalty.

misdemeanors
Offenses less serious than felonies and usually punishable by incarceration of no more than one year, probation, or intermediate sanctions.

visible crime
An offense against persons or property that is committed primarily by members of the lower social classes. Often referred to as "street crime" or "ordinary crime," this type of offense is the one most upsetting to the public.

Visible Crime

Visible crime, often called "street crime" or "ordinary crime," ranges from shoplifting to homicide. For offenders, such crimes are the least profitable and, because they are visible, the least protected. These are the acts that the public regards as "criminal," and they receive the majority of law enforcement resources. We can divide visible crimes into three categories: violent crimes, property crimes, and public order crimes.

Violent Crimes

Acts against people in which death or physical injury results are **violent crimes**. These include criminal homicide, assault, rape, and robbery. The criminal justice system treats these as the most serious offenses and punishes them accordingly. Although the public is most fearful of violence by strangers, many of these offenses are committed by people who know their victim.

Property Crimes

Property crimes are acts that threaten property held by individuals or by the state. Many types of crimes fall under this category, including theft, larceny, shoplifting, embezzlement, and burglary. Some property offenders are amateurs who occasionally commit these crimes because of situational factors such as financial need or peer pressure. In contrast, professional criminals make a significant portion of their livelihood from committing property offenses.

CIVIC ENGAGEMENT

YOUR ROLE IN THE SYSTEM

A state enacts a cyberbully statute making it a crime "if any juvenile makes 'a communication in an online capacity via any electronic device or through a social networking site . . . with the purpose to harass another" ("New Cyberbully Law," 2014). How do you evaluate this new law? *Make a list of three arguments that are important for your evaluation of the issue.* Would you have voted for this as a legislator? Read more about the about the law online and about the first juvenile prosecution of a 15-year-old under this law in New Jersey.

Public Order Crimes

Acts that threaten the general well-being of society and challenge accepted moral principles are defined as **public order crimes**. They include public drunkenness, aggressive panhandling, vandalism, and disorderly conduct. Although the police tend to treat these behaviors as minor offenses, there is concern that this type of disorderly behavior instills fear in citizens, leads to more-serious crimes, and hastens urban decay (Gau, Corsaro, and Brunson, 2014; Kelling and Coles, 1996). The definition and enforcement of such behaviors as crimes highlights the tensions between different interpretations of American values. Many people see such behavior as simply representing the liberty that adults enjoy in a free society to engage in offensive and self-destructive behavior that causes no concrete harm to other people. By contrast, other people see their own liberty limited by the need to be wary and fearful of actions by people who are intoxicated or out of control.

Those charged with visible crimes are often young, male, and poor. In many cities, members of minority groups are overrepresented among arrestees. Some argue that this is due to the class bias of a society that has singled out visible crimes for priority enforcement. They note that law enforcement officials do not focus as much attention on other kinds of crimes.

violent crimes
Crimes against people in which force is employed to rob, produce physical injury, or cause death.

property crimes
Crimes in which property is damaged or stolen.

public order crimes
Acts, such as public drunkenness and disorderly conduct, that threaten society's well-being and make citizens fearful.

Victimless Crimes

Crimes that involve a willing and private exchange of goods or services that are in strong demand but illegal are called **victimless crimes**. These are offenses against morality in which the participants do not see themselves as victims. Examples include gambling and illegal drug sales and use. Prostitution may be included in this category except for situations when sex workers are physically abused and are unwillingly held captive by pimps. Similarly, when gamblers are cheated and exploited by those who run gambling venues, this situation cannot be regarded as victimless. These activities can be closely connected with organized crime and other harmful influences on society; on the other hand, when there is willing participation, then these activities are sometimes labeled as "victimless crimes" because those involved do not feel that they are being harmed. This is a controversial concept because inevitably even voluntary participants are exploited and suffer harm even if they do not recognize or acknowledge that fact.

victimless crimes
Offenses involving a willing and private exchange of illegal goods or services that are in strong demand. Participants do not feel they are being harmed, but these crimes are prosecuted on the ground that society as a whole is being harmed.

Prosecution for these offenses is justified on the grounds that society as a whole is harmed because the moral fabric of the community is threatened. Moreover, there are social costs for the entire country as the nation's medical systems must cope with the spread of sexually transmitted diseases and drug overdoses for people who often do not have adequate health insurance or money to pay for their own medical care.

In the eyes of critics who characterize these activities as matters of individual choice and personal liberty, using the law to enforce moral standards is costly. The system is swamped by these cases, which often require the use of police informers and thus open the door for payoffs and other kinds of corruption.

The "war on drugs" is the most obvious example of policies against one type of victimless crime. Possession and sale of drugs—marijuana, heroin, cocaine, opium, amphetamines—have been illegal in the United States for over 100 years. Especially during the past 40 years, extensive government resources have been used to enforce these laws and punish offenders.

Political Crime

Political crime refers to criminal acts either by the government or against the government that are carried out for ideological purposes (Hagan, 1997). Political criminals believe they are following a morality that is above the

political crime
An act, usually done for ideological purposes, that constitutes a threat against the state (such as treason, sedition, or espionage) or a criminal act by a state.

law. For example, the shooting incident in downtown Austin, Texas, in the chapter opener may have been carried out for ideological purposes by an individual who opposed national immigration policies (Jonsson, 2014). In 2010 Scott Roeder was convicted of first-degree murder for walking into a church in Wichita, Kansas, at the start of a church service and shooting Dr. George Tiller point-blank in the head because he objected to the fact that Dr. Tiller performed abortions. During the trial, Roeder testified in his own defense and openly admitted that he had planned for years to kill Dr. Tiller and finally carried out the act because he viewed Tiller as a murderer for performing abortions (M. Davey, 2010). Similarly, shocking acts of violence that are labeled as terrorism, including the 1995 bombing of the federal building in Oklahoma City by Timothy McVeigh, and the 2001 attacks on the World Trade Center and Pentagon, spring from political motivations.

In some authoritarian states, merely criticizing the government is a crime that can lead to prosecution and imprisonment. In Western democracies today, there are few political crimes other than treason, which is rare. Although many illegal acts, such as the World Trade Center attack and the Oklahoma City bombings, can be traced to political motives, they are prosecuted as visible crimes under laws against bombing, arson, and murder, rather than as political crimes per se.

Political crimes against the government include activities such as treason, sedition (rebellion), and espionage. Since the nation's founding, many laws have been passed in response to perceived threats to the established order. The Sedition Act of 1789 made it a crime to utter or publish statements against the government. The Smith Act of 1940 made it a crime to call for the overthrow of the government by force or violence. During the Vietnam War, the federal government used charges of criminal conspiracy to deter those who opposed its military policies. The foregoing examples became obsolete as federal judges' interpretations of the Constitution expanded the definition of free speech, thereby limiting the government's authority to pursue prosecutions based on an individual's expression of political beliefs and policy preferences. However, in the aftermath of September 11, the U.S. government entered a new era in which people were investigated and prosecuted based on their alleged connections to organizations employing terror tactics.

Occupational Crime

occupational crime
A criminal offense committed through opportunities created in a legal business or occupation.

Occupational crimes are committed in the context of a legal business or profession. Often viewed as shrewd business practices rather than as illegal acts, they are crimes that, if done right, are never discovered. An important American value is economic liberty. Each person is presumed to have the opportunity to make his or her own fortune through hard work and innovative ideas. The success of the American economic system is built, in part, on the creativity of people who invent new products, develop new technologies, or discover new ways to market goods. Although we admire entrepreneurial activities, some individuals go too far in using their creativity within our free enterprise system. The freedom to make financial transactions and other decisions in fast-moving private businesses also creates opportunities to steal from employers or defraud customers and investors. These crimes cost society billions of dollars each year. Many estimates indicate that the money stolen through occupational crime far exceeds the total amounts stolen through visible crimes such as robbery and larceny. Some estimates indicate for every $1 lost in street crime, about $60 is lost as a result of occupational crime (Friedrichs, 2010).

Crimes committed in the course of business were first described by criminologist Edwin Sutherland in 1939, when he developed the concept of white-collar crime. He noted that such crimes are committed by respectable offenders taking advantage of opportunities arising from their business dealings. He forced criminologists to recognize that criminal behavior was not confined to lower-class people (so-called blue-collar crime) but reached into the upper levels of society (Shover, 1998: 133; Sutherland, 1949).

The white-collar/blue-collar distinction has lost much of its meaning in modern society. Since the 1970s, much of the research on white-collar crime has shifted from the individual to the organization (Simpson, 2013; van de Brunt and Huisman, 2007). Gary Green has described four types of occupational crimes (Green, 1997: 17–19):

1. *Occupational crimes for the benefit of the employing organizations.* Employers rather than offenders benefit directly from these crimes. They include price fixing, theft of trade secrets, and falsification of product tests. In these cases an employee may commit the offense but will not benefit personally, except perhaps through a bonus or promotion. It is the company that benefits. These crimes are "committed in the suites rather than in the streets."

   In 2011, after government investigations of the mortgage crisis that significantly harmed the American economy beginning in 2008, seven officials from Taylor, Bean & Whitaker Mortgage Company and the Colonial Bank of Alabama were convicted of fraud crimes that cost banks around the world $2.9 billion (Norris, 2011). Additional investigations and prosecutions were aimed at other mortgage companies and banks.
2. *Occupational crimes through the exercise of government authority.* In these crimes the offender has the legal power to enforce laws or command others to do so (C. Matthews, 2014). Examples include removal of drugs from the evidence room by a police officer, acceptance of a bribe by a public official, and falsification of a document by a notary public. For example, in March 2011 a former U.S. Army officer, Eddie Pressley, and his wife were convicted of bribery and money laundering for accepting more than $2 million in bribes for steering military contracts in Kuwait to specific companies that provided bottled water, fences, and other goods and services for American military forces. His wife's conviction was based on her activities in setting up overseas bank accounts to hide the bribe money (Lawson, 2011).
3. *Occupational crimes committed by professionals in their capacity as professionals.* Doctors, lawyers, and stockbrokers may take advantage of clients by, for instance, illegally dispensing drugs, using funds placed in escrow, or using "insider" stock-trading information for personal profit or, if their offices are not prospering, to keep their businesses going (Cliff and Desilets, 2014). In 2014, for example, a prominent cancer physician in Michigan pleaded guilty to running a $35 million Medicare fraud scheme in which he diagnosed healthy people as having cancer in order to charge for their treatment and giving unnecessary drug treatments to people dying of cancer (Baldas, 2014). Many commentators believe that the American value of economic liberty led the government to reduce the regulation of businesses. Thus some individuals exploited the lack of government control to manipulate corporate stock values in ways that gave them great profits but ultimately harmed millions of investors. As a result of the scandals involving mortgage companies, investment banks, and other corporations, Congress has examined new public policy choices that will reduce corporate executives' freedom to make decisions without supervision and accountability (Konczal, 2013).

4. *Occupational crimes committed by individuals as individuals, where opportunities are not based on government power or professional position.* Examples of this type of crime include thefts by employees from employers, filing of false expense claims, and embezzlement (Shigihara, 2013; Kidder, 2005). Employee crime is believed to account for about 1 percent of the gross national product and causes consumer prices to be 10 to 15 percent higher than they would be otherwise. Employee theft is involved in about a third of business failures. The total loss due to employee theft, therefore, is greater than all business losses from shoplifting, burglary, or robbery (Friedrichs, 2010).

Although they are highly profitable, most types of occupational crime do not come to public attention. Regulatory agencies, such as the Federal Trade Commission and the Securities and Exchange Commission, often do not enforce the law effectively. Many business and professional organizations "police" themselves, dropping employees or members who commit offenses.

Organized Crime

organized crime
A framework for the perpetration of criminal acts—usually in fields, such as gambling, drugs, and prostitution—providing illegal services that are in great demand.

money laundering
Moving the proceeds of criminal activities through a maze of businesses, banks, and brokerage accounts in order to disguise their origin.

The term **organized crime** refers to a framework within which criminal acts are committed, rather than referring to the acts themselves. A crime syndicate has an organizational structure, rules, a division of labor, and the capacity for ruthless violence and corrupting law enforcement, labor and business leaders, and politicians (Levin, 2013; J. B. Jacobs and Panarella, 1998). Members of organized crime groups provide goods and services to millions of people. These criminals will engage in any activity that provides minimum risk and maximum profit. Thus organized crime involves a network of activities, usually cutting across state and national borders, that range from legitimate businesses to shady deals with labor unions to providing "goods"—such as drugs, sex, and pornography—that cannot be obtained legally. In recent years organized crime has been involved in new services such as commercial arson, illegal disposal of toxic wastes, and **money laundering**. Some crime syndicates have also acquired significant funds through illegal recycling operations (Coleman, 2011). Few individuals involved in organized crime are arrested and prosecuted.

Although the public often associates organized crime with Italian Americans—indeed, the federal government indicted 73 members of the Genovese New York crime family in 2001 (R. F. Worth, 2001)—other ethnic groups have dominated at various times. Thirty-five years ago, one scholar noted the strangeness of America's "ladder of social mobility," in which each new immigrant group uses organized crime as one of the first rungs of the climb (Bell, 1967: 150). However, debate about this notion continues, because not all immigrant groups have engaged in organized crime (Kenney and Finckenauer, 1995). In addition, nonimmigrants have also become involved in these crime syndicates (Mallory, 2012).

Over the last few decades, law enforcement efforts have greatly weakened the long-standing organized crime groups. Beginning in 1978 the federal government mounted extraordinary efforts to eradicate the well-established groups. Using electronic surveillance, undercover agents, and mob turncoats, as well as the FBI, the federal Organized Crime Task Forces, and the U.S. attorneys' offices, law enforcement launched investigations and prosecutions. As James Jacobs notes, "The magnitude of the government's attack on Cosa Nostra is nothing short of incredible." By 1992, convictions were successfully brought against 23 bosses, and the leadership and soldiers of five New York City families (Bonanno, Colombo, Gambino, Genovese, and Lucchese) were decimated (J. B. Jacobs, Panarella, and Worthington, 1994).

Today African Americans, Hispanics, Russians, and Asians have formed organized crime groups in some cities. Drug dealing has brought Colombian and Mexican crime groups to U.S. cities, and Vietnamese-, Chinese-, and Japanese-led groups have formed in California. In recent years, there has been increased concern about criminal gangs from eastern Europe and Central America. Specific gangs from El Salvador, which have thousands of members there and in the United States, have gained reputations for horrific violence. As a result, the U.S. government has sought to establish formal links with police in El Salvador and elsewhere in order to make a coordinated international effort against criminal organizations (Archibold, 2007).

Criminal organizations are not exclusively based on ethnic groups. For example, the U.S. Department of Justice regularly investigates and prosecutes members of motorcycle gangs who are involved in selling drugs and weapons (U.S. Department of Justice, 2014). For example, in August 2014, federal prosecutors in western New York state announced that a motorcycle gang member entered a guilty plea and faced a possible sentence of 20 years in prison for conspiracy to distribute methamphetamine. He had been charged along with eight other members of the same gang in New York and California.

Transnational Crime

National borders define the boundaries of law enforcement agencies' authority and the definitions of particular crimes. Each country has its own police agencies that enforce its own laws. Borders do not, however, define or limit the nature of criminal activity (Bersin, 2012). The growth of global transportation systems, international trade, computerized financial transactions, and worldwide availability of information through the Internet have facilitated the expansion of the international economy. Simultaneously, these factors provided the basis for **transnational crime**. These are crimes with planning, execution, or victimization that crosses the borders of countries. Jay Albanese distinguishes profit-seeking transnational crimes from "international crimes," which are acts

transnational crime
Profit-seeking criminal activities that involve planning, execution, or victimization that crosses national borders.

AP Images/Steven K. Doi

Organized crime has changed significantly from the stereotyped images of Italian American mobsters portrayed in the movies. These motorcycle gang members charged with crimes also show that organized crime groups need not be based strictly on ethnicity. How would you explain why people become involved in organized crime groups? What, if anything, can society do to persuade young people to pursue careers other than those involving illegal activities?

of terrorism, genocide, human rights abuses, or other crimes against humanity that violate international law (Albanese, 2011). Transnational crimes, by contrast, involve theft, fraud, counterfeiting, smuggling, and other violations of individual countries' criminal laws that involve transborder activities.

Transnational crimes can be grouped into three categories (Albanese, 2011: 3). The first category, *provision of illicit goods,* includes such transnational crimes as drug trafficking and moving stolen property, such as automobiles and artwork, from one country to another for sales that are difficult to trace back to the original theft (Alderman, 2012). It also includes the transportation and sale of counterfeit goods, such as prescription medications and designer clothing. The second category, *provision of illegal services,* includes human trafficking, such as transporting sex workers or undocumented immigrants illegally into a country (Shamir, 2012). This category also includes various cybercrimes that often involve fraudulent financial investments as well as child pornography. Bribery, extortion, and money laundering activities define the third category, called *infiltration of business or government* (Albanese, 2011).

TECHNOLOGY & CRIMINAL JUSTICE

TRANSNATIONAL CYBERCRIME

Virtually every American with an email address has likely been touched by transnational cybercrime. It seems as if everyone has received an unsolicited email requesting they transfer a modest sum of money—to unfreeze a foreign bank account—and stating that they will be sent a large sum money as the return on that small investment. This particular scam is associated with independent operators in Nigeria, although it is also used by would-be thieves located in other countries. Unfortunately, it is just the tip of the iceberg when considering the kinds of technology-enabled criminal acts that can be directed at Americans and remotely carried out from international locations.

The FBI's website posts multiple press releases every week about indictments, arrests, and convictions for cybercrimes, including transnational scams. These crimes can be directed at individuals in order to steal money; directed at corporations to steal financial information and trade secrets; or directed at corporations and government agencies whose computers contain secret information related to national security, military affairs, and related matters. A few examples from 2014 illustrate the breathtaking frequency, scope, and harm of transnational cybercrime:

- In December 2014, a Romanian man worked with others to fraudulently post on eBay and other online selling sites fictional advertisements for vehicles. People wishing to purchase the vehicles were directed to wire money to specific bank accounts. The conspirators stole nearly $700,000 from gullible buyers. The man was arrested in the United States using a false passport and was sentenced to serve five years in prison and ordered to pay back the money to victims.
- Nigerian cybercriminals organized a scheme in which they created fake websites and domain names that appeared quite similar to those of universities and schools. They ordered millions of dollars' worth of computer equipment from office supply stores that erroneously believed that the orders were coming from their established customers among educational institutions. The purchased equipment was delivered to unsuspecting individuals who had been recruited as employees in a "work-from-home" business that paid them to receive packages at their residences; the "employees" would then ship those packages to Nigeria. Because the office supply stores thought they were dealing with established institutional customers, the items were shipped first and billed later with 30 days to pay. When universities and schools received the bills for items they had never ordered, the effective scam was uncovered—but the criminals were overseas, beyond the reach of American law enforcement. In October 2014, the FBI sought to publicize the scam in order to warn businesses and schools to be on the lookout for such activities.
- In May 2014, federal prosecutors filed criminal charges against five Chinese military officers accused of hacking into the computer systems of numerous American corporations, including Westinghouse, U.S. Steel, and Alcoa, to steal information about nuclear power plants, solar energy technology, and metals processing. The thefts of information were allegedly undertaken on behalf of the Chinese government. The officers involved in the alleged computer hacking crimes were in China and beyond the reach of American law enforcement officials.

Organized crime groups are involved in all of the foregoing transnational crimes. Individual lawbreakers can victimize people in other countries through Internet scams or the cybertheft of financial information. However, most of the harms from transnational crimes come from the activities of formal criminal organizations or, alternatively, criminal networks that connect individuals and organizations who undertake specific criminal acts together. According to the United Nations, annual proceeds from transnational organized crime activities amount to more than $870 billion annually, with drug trafficking producing the largest individual segment of that total amount (United Nations, 2011).

In addition to drug trafficking, governments and international organizations are especially concerned about the human harms from sexual slavery. This occurs when women and children are lured or transported across international borders and held as prisoners while being forced to sell their bodies in the sex trade for the benefit of their captors (Lehti and Aromaa, 2006). Human trafficking also occurs to obtain inexpensive laborers, who are held prisoner and forced to work under deplorable conditions (Feingold, 2005).

- In September 2014, four young men, ages 18 to 28, from the United States and Canada, as well as an additional associate in Australia, were charged with hacking into corporate and government computers in the United States to steal millions of dollars' worth of trade secrets and valuable data. They allegedly stole such things as software and data from Microsoft related to Xbox gaming systems and the U.S. Army's Apache helicopter training software. They were charged with planning to sell or share the valuable data. Law enforcement officials seized from them more $600,000 that was allegedly the proceeds from their crimes.

In the final example, the arrests and criminal charges resulted from the coordinated efforts of the FBI, the U.S. Department of Homeland Security, the Regional Police of Ontario, Canada, and the Western Australia Police. This example helps to show the necessity of international cooperation and coordination in attacking criminal activities that can be undertaken remotely via the Internet. Such multi-country cooperation is necessary because international lawbreakers many never even set foot in the country where the victimization is taking place. As a related matter, the Nigerian and Chinese examples illustrate the limitations of effective law enforcement involving transnational cybercrime since the perpetrators of these crimes cannot be arrested and punished—unless their home countries decide to join with other countries in attacking this significant international problem. In the case of China, of course, if the prosecutors are accurate in their allegations that the Chinese government sponsored and gained benefits from the cyberhacking, then there is little hope for organizing the necessary cooperation to put an end to such activities or to punish the individuals involved.

Agencies in various countries are seeking to improve their ability to cooperate and share information. Law enforcement officials throughout the world are not equally committed to or capable of catching cyberthieves and hackers. In some countries, criminals may have better computer equipment and expertise than do the officials trying to catch them. The FBI provides assistance to many countries to help identify and catch cybercriminals within their own borders, especially those who are operating schemes that harm Americans and American interests.

Sources: J. Albanese, *Transnational Crime and the 21st Century* (New York: Oxford University Press, 2011); FBI, "FBI Cyber Action Teams: Traveling the World to Catch Cyber Criminals," March 6, 2006 (www.fbi.gov); U.S. Department of Justice, "Department of Justice Disrupts International Cyber Crime Rings Distributing Scareware," *FBI National Press Releases*, June 22, 2011 (www.fbi.gov); FBI, "Five Chinese Military Hackers Charged with Cyber Espionage against U.S.," *FBI National Press Releases*, May 19, 2014 (www.fbi.gov); FBI, "Four Members of International Computer Hacking Ring Indicted for Stealing Gaming Technology, Apache Helicopter Training Software," *FBI National Press Releases*, September 30, 2014 (www.fbi.gov); FBI, "Cyber Crime: Purchase Order Scam Leaves a Trail of Victims," *FBI National Press Releases*, October 17, 2014 (www.fbi.gov); FBI, "Romanian Man Sentenced to Prison for Role in International Fraud Scheme Involving Online Marketplace Websites," *FBI National Press Releases*, December 11, 2014 (www.fbi.gov).

DEBATE THE ISSUE

What should the United States do to reduce the extent and impact of transnational cybercrime? Should cybercrime be considered the price of "open" Internet access? Is it reasonable to argue that Americans must simply become more educated to better protect themselves from scams? Alternatively, should the United States create tougher criminal penalties for cybercrime and more-aggressively seek to apprehend cybercriminals operating from other countries? Are there other policy choices available? Make two arguments for the approaches that you would recommend.

Law enforcement officials face huge challenges in attempting to combat transnational crime. Because American police agencies cannot operate in other countries without permission, they must depend on assistance from officials abroad. It can be difficult to coordinate efforts with agencies in other countries that operate under different laws and have different priorities. There can also be problems if bribery and other forms of corruption encourage officials in some countries to tolerate or protect transnational criminal organizations. The United Nations Office on Drugs and Crime (UNODC) seeks to gather and disseminate information about transnational crime. The UNODC and other organizations seek to facilitate communication and cooperation between countries so that there is an ongoing framework for international coordination rather than repeated requests for assistance from one country to another in response to specific criminal acts.

In the aftermath of September 11, American law enforcement and intelligence officials increased their efforts to monitor and thwart criminal organizations that help those who seek to attack the United States and its citizens. Transnational criminal organizations can be the source of weapons and explosives that terrorists seek to obtain. In addition, organizations that seek to advance terrorism goals may themselves use criminal transactions, such as drug smuggling and stolen credit card numbers, to fund their efforts. Because the flow of money and weapons to organizations that employ terrorist tactics for political purposes is so closely connected to international crime networks, the United States will continue to devote personnel and resources to this issue.

Research has identified several factors that can increase effectiveness in combating transnational crimes. Laws need consistent definitions of illegal activities in order for different countries to cooperate effectively and work toward the same goals. Courts and law enforcement agencies need to emphasize international cooperation as a central component of their operations against transnational criminal groups and activities. In addition, law enforcement agencies need appropriate powers that will permit them to conduct searches, surveillance, and computer activities in order to discover and gain evidence concerning criminal activities. Above all, justice system officials in different countries must improve their capacity for sharing information (Le, Bell, and Lauchs, 2013).

As we will see in the next section, one of the most difficult forms of transnational crime to combat is cybercrime. Sophisticated criminals using technology that equals or exceeds that available to law enforcement officials can steal large sums of money or business trade secrets with the touch of a button as they hack into American computer systems from thousands of miles away. Read the Technology and Criminal Justice feature to learn about the transnational nature of many cybercrime offenses.

Cybercrime

As new technologies emerge, so do people who take advantage of them for their own gain. One has only to think of the impact of the invention of the automobile to realize the extent to which the computer age will lead to new kinds of criminality. News reports in recent years have been filled with shocking reports of very damaging cybercrimes, such as hackers' thefts of unreleased motion pictures, emails, and employees' social security numbers at Sony Pictures in 2014 (C. Kang, Timberg, and Nakashima, 2014). Even more significant for individual Americans, major computer thefts regularly compromise the credit card numbers for tens of millions of customers at such major retailers as Home Depot and Target (Sidel, 2014). Today, the justice system is facing the ramifications of cybercrimes (T. Holt and Bossler, 2014).

Cybercrimes involve the use of computers and the Internet to commit acts against people, property, public order, or morality (de Villiers, 2011). Some use computers to steal information, resources, or funds. These thefts can be aimed at simply stealing money or they can involve the theft of company trade secrets, chemical formulas, and other information that could be quite valuable to competing businesses. Others use computers for malicious, destructive acts, such as releasing Internet viruses and "worms" to harm computer systems. In addition, there are widespread problems with people illegally downloading software, music, videos, and other copyrighted materials (Hinduja, 2007). Although such acts, which are done by millions of Americans every day, are actually federal crimes, they are seldom prosecuted unless the government ties individuals or organizations to substantial involvement in such activities. In addition, new issues continually arise that produce suggestions about criminalizing new forms of cyber behavior, such as cyberbullying between teens that leads to psychological harm and behavioral problems (Hinduja and Patchin, 2013).

cybercrimes
Offenses that involve the use of one or more computers.

Identity theft has become a huge problem affecting many middle-class and affluent Americans who would otherwise seldom find themselves victimized by criminals (Edwards, 2014; Daleiden, 2012). Perpetrators of identity theft use other people's credit card numbers and social security numbers to secure fraudulent loans and steal money and merchandise (Segal, Ngugi, and Mana, 2011). Sometimes they accomplish their thefts through "phishing" schemes in which they set up phony websites for banks and other fake organizations, thereby tricking people into supplying personal information. A government study found that 16.6 million Americans, or 7 percent of the population age 16 and older, were victims of identity theft in 2012, mostly through fraudulent use of bank account or credit card information (Harrell and Langton, 2013). Read the Doing Your Part feature, "The Fight against Cybercrime," to see how some college students help combat this modern crime.

identity theft
The theft of social security numbers, credit card numbers, and other information in order to secure loans, withdraw bank funds, and purchase merchandise while posing as someone else. The unsuspecting victim will eventually lose money in these transactions.

Other offenders use the Internet to disseminate child pornography, to advertise sexual services, or to stalk the unsuspecting. Police departments have given special emphasis to stopping computer predators who establish online relationships with juveniles in an effort to manipulate those children into sexual victimization (E. T. Jacobs, 2012). Toward this end, officers often pretend to

DOING YOUR PART

THE FIGHT AGAINST CYBERCRIME

Joseph Weber, a computer science student, spends hours in front of a computer at the University of Alabama at Birmingham (UAB) going through spam email messages in an effort to identify phony bank websites. He and other UAB students are part of an effort to find counterfeit websites that trick people into providing information, such as bank account numbers and social security numbers, which they are misled to believe is needed by their bank. With the expansion of online banking, many criminals have discovered lucrative opportunities to trick unsophisticated consumers into opening their bank accounts and lines of credit. The work of Weber and the other students is used to remove these websites from the Internet and to provide evidence that can be used against these cybercriminals when they are prosecuted. The UAB program is not alone in this effort. In November 2014, the Department of Homeland Security advertised its "Secretary's Honors Program Cyber Student Volunteer" opportunities for college students to engage in similar work throughout the country as part of an increasing national effort to combat cyberthreats.

Sources: Drawn from Agency Job Announcement for "Secretary's Honors Program Cyber Student Volunteer," November 24, 2014 (www.usajobs.gov); Honora Gathings, "Scholarship to Help Students Fight Crime Online," WBMA News, January 27, 2011 (www.abc3340.com).

AP Images/Manuel Balce Ceneta

Cybercrime is a growing problem that costs American businesses and individuals millions of dollars each year. Law enforcement officials work diligently to keep up with criminals' computer expertise, technology, and methods of deception. How can American police effectively combat the evolving and spreading threat of cybercrime, especially when so many cybercriminals are located in other countries?

be juveniles in online conversations in "chat rooms" in order to see if sexual predators will attempt to cultivate a relationship and set up a personal meeting (Eichenwald, 2006).

In attacking these problems, the FBI's National Computer Crime Squad lists its responsibilities as covering the following:

- Intrusions of the Public Switched Network (the telephone company)
- Major computer network intrusions
- Network integrity violations
- Privacy violations
- Industrial espionage
- Pirated computer software
- Other crimes where the computer is a major factor in committing the criminal offense

In advancing these priorities, the FBI seeks to develop cooperative partnerships, both domestically and internationally, to help fight cybercrime. In Pittsburgh, for example, the FBI has joined with computer scientists at Carnegie Mellon University and the National Cyber Forensic Training Alliance to crack the cases of several especially destructive cybercriminals (R. Lord and Anderson, 2014).

It is extremely difficult to know how many cybercrimes occur and how much money is lost through identity theft, auction fraud, investment fraud, and other forms of financial computer crime. The federal government's Internet Crime Complaint Center (IC3) publishes reports that provide perspective on the question by compiling information on complaints filed each year. In 2010, the IC3 received 303,890 complaints about cybercrime financial losses. The largest number of complaints in 2010 concerned nondelivery of payment or merchandise from Internet transactions, scams impersonating the FBI, and identity theft. These cybercrimes primarily were committed by perpetrators in the United States (66 percent), but people in other countries also victimized Americans regularly. The other leading countries of origin for cybercriminal enterprises were Great Britain (10 percent), Nigeria (6 percent), China (3 percent) and Canada (2 percent) (Internet Crime Complaint Center, 2011). According to a report by the Center for Strategic and International Studies in

2014, cybercrime and economic espionage cost the world economy more than $445 billion each year (Nakashima and Peterson, 2014). As discussed previously with respect to transnational crime, efforts to create and enforce effective laws that will address such activities have been hampered by the international nature of cybercrime.

Since the events of September 11, many countries' law enforcement agencies have increased their international communication and cooperation in order to thwart terrorist activities. As these countries cooperate in investigating and monitoring the financial transactions of groups that employ terror tactics, it seems likely that they will also improve their capacity to discover and pursue cybercriminals (Cade, 2012). For example, the FBI has also joined forces with the national police agencies of Australia, Canada, New Zealand, and the United Kingdom to form the Strategic Alliance Cyber Crime Working Group, an international organization for sharing information and cooperating in cybercrime investigations (FBI, 2008).

How significant is the problem of cybercrime? The following is an excerpt from a U.S. Department of Justice press release about the conviction of one computer hacker in 2011 and the extent of the harm he caused:

> Rogelio Hackett, Jr., 26, of Lithonia, Ga., pleaded guilty today . . . to trafficking in credit cards and aggravated identity theft, . . . U.S. Secret Service special agents executing a search warrant in 2009 at Hackett's home found more than 675,000 stolen credit card numbers and related information in his computers and email accounts. Hackett admitted . . . he has been trafficking in credit card information he obtained either by hacking into business computer networks and downloading credit card databases, or purchasing the information from others using the Internet. . . . He also admitted that he sold credit card information, manufactured and sold counterfeit plastic cards, and used the credit card information to acquire gift cards and merchandise. According to court documents, credit card companies have identified tens of thousands of fraudulent transactions using the card numbers found in Hackett's possession, totaling more than $36 million. . . . Hackett will face maximum penalties of 10 years in prison and a $250,000 fine . . . (U.S. Department of Justice, 2011: 1).

Law enforcement agencies cannot prevent cybercrimes from occurring. Typically, they react to such harmful activities in order to limit theft and damage. People cannot rely on law enforcement efforts to protect them from harm. The first defense against some forms of cybercrime is citizen awareness and caution (Pinguelo, Lee, and Muller, 2012). How much do you know about cybercrime? Consider how you would address the problem presented in "Civic Engagement: Your Role in the System."

Of these seven main types of crime that we've just discussed, which is of greatest concern to you? If you are like most people, you are troubled most by visible crime. Thus, as a nation, we devote most of our criminal justice resources to dealing with such crimes. To develop policies to address these crimes, however, we need to know more about the amount of crime and all the types of crimes that occur in the United States. Within the various categories of crime, new types of offenses can emerge as society evolves and changes. Further, new types of offenses can arise within a given category of crime. As we have seen, creative thieves continually find new ways to exploit technology for profit in various forms of cybercrime. For example, criminals have become increasingly skilled at creating phony websites that look identical to websites of legitimate businesses and at stealing information from laptop computers that are connected to wireless networks. Because of the dynamic and innovative nature of contemporary criminal activities, law enforcement officials must attempt to match the creativity and resources of lawbreakers in order to protect society.

CIVIC ENGAGEMENT

YOUR ROLE IN THE SYSTEM

Your elderly grandparents have finally decided to buy a computer, sign up with an Internet service provider, and begin participating in the cyber universe through email, online banking, and all of the computer activities that they have seen described in newspapers and television. They ask you, "How do we protect ourselves from this identity theft stuff that we've heard about?" *Make a list of suggestions to help these newcomers avoid becoming victims of cybercrime.* How do your suggestions compare to the advice provided for the public by the federal government?

CHECKPOINT

12. What are the seven main types of crime?

13. What groups are overrepresented among those arrested for visible or street crimes?

14. What is meant by the term *victimless crimes*?

15. What are political crimes?

16. Why is the term *occupational crime* more useful today than the term *white-collar crime*?

17. What is transnational crime?

18. What types of criminal activities are labeled as cybercrime?

STOP AND ANALYZE: What do you think of the concept of "victimless crimes"? Aren't participants harmed by participation in pornography, gambling, and drug use? Aren't there also harms to society when people spread disease, lose their family's money, or need medical treatment as a result of participating in these illegal activities? List the three strongest reasons for decriminalizing these activities and the three strongest reasons for maintaining their status as illegal.

The Crime Problem Today

Although the crime rate generally declined from the 1990s through the initial years of the twenty-first century, 68 percent of respondents to a national survey in December 2012 expressed the belief that crime would increase in 2013 (Newport, 2013). The gaps between the public's perceptions and available information highlight several important questions for students of criminal justice. How much crime actually exists in the United States? Is the United States the most crime-ridden nation of the world's industrial democracies? How do we measure the amount of crime? What are the current and future trends? By trying to answer these questions, we can gain a better understanding of the crime problem and the public's beliefs about it.

The Worst of Times?

There has always been too much crime. Ever since the nation's founding, people have felt threatened by it. Outbreaks of violence erupted after the Civil War, after World War I, during Prohibition, and during the Great Depression (Friedman, 1993). But the nation has also seen extended periods, such as the 1950s, marked by comparatively little crime. Thus, ours is neither the best nor the worst of times.

Although crime is an old problem, the amount and types of crime do not remain consistent. During both the 1880s and the 1930s, pitched battles took place between strikers and company police. Race riots causing deaths and property destruction occurred in Chicago, Omaha, Tulsa, and other cities between 1919 and 1921. These riots typically occurred when white mobs attacked African Americans because of a rumored crime, such as the Omaha riot that erupted after a black man was accused of assaulting a white woman. Organized crime was rampant during the 1930s. The murder rate, which reached a high in 1933 and a low during the 1950s, rose to a new high of 10.2 per 100,000 people in 1980. The rate declined initially to 7.9 in 1984, then had an uptick in the early 1990s, with a high point of 9.8 in 1991, before subsequently showing a decline to a new low of 4.7 per 100,000 in 2012. The most recent rates match the low rates at the start of the 1960s (BJS, 2015a: Table 3.106.2012). As illustrated in Figure 1.1, the trends show a steady decline since 1993.

What if we examine crimes other than murder? Overall rates for violent crimes and property crimes have dropped since 1991, but the rates for 2012 remained well above the crime rates experienced by Americans at the close

FIGURE 1.1 **A CENTURY OF MURDER**

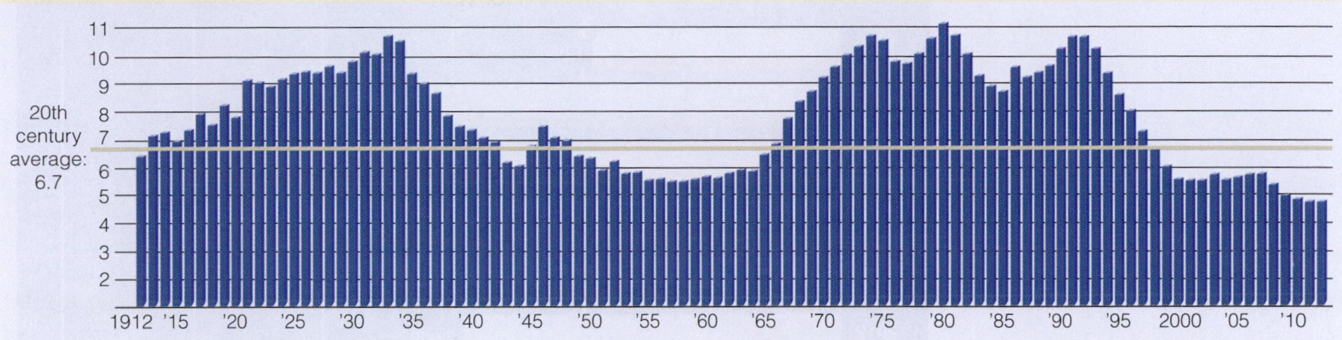

Sources: *Sourcebook of Criminal Justice Statistics, 1999* (Washington, DC: U.S. Government Printing Office, 2000), Table 3.146; *Sourcebook of Criminal Justice Statistics* (2015), Table 3.106.2012.

of the relatively peaceful 1950s. The rate of violent crime was 158 offenses per 100,000 people in 1961. That rate rose over the next three decades until it peaked in 1991 and 1992 at 758 violent offenses per 100,000 (Figure 1.2). However, from 1992 to 2004, the violent crime rate dropped steadily to 463 offenses per 100,000, a rate lower than any year since 1977, followed by a slight uptick to 469 in 2005 and 480 in 2006 and then another downward move to 387 per 100,000 in 2012 (BJS, 2015a: Table 3.106.2012).

Rates of property crimes show a similar pattern, rising dramatically from 1960 through 1991 before falling each year through 2011 (see Figure 1.3 for an overview). Property crimes rates went from 1,748 per 100,000 people in 1961 to more than 5,000 per 100,000 in the first years of the 1980s. Although there was a small drop during the mid-1980s, with a low point of 4,498 per 100,000 in 1984, the rate pushed back up toward 5,000 in the first years of the 1990s. After falling steadily through the rest of the 1990s, the property crime rate was only 2,859 in 2012. Although this figure was nearly double the rate of 1961, it returned property crime rates to a level not seen since 1968 (BJS, 2015a: Table 3.106.2011). Americans may not accurately recognize that crime rates have fallen for more than a decade, yet they may be justified in labeling

FIGURE 1.2 **VIOLENT CRIME RATES PER 100,000 PEOPLE**

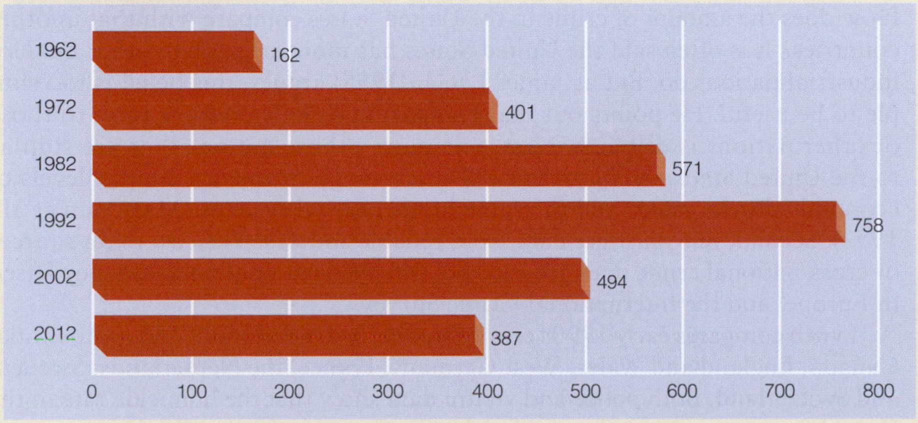

Source: *Sourcebook of Criminal Justice Statistics* (2015), Table 3.106.2012.

FIGURE 1.3 PROPERTY CRIME RATES PER 100,000 PEOPLE

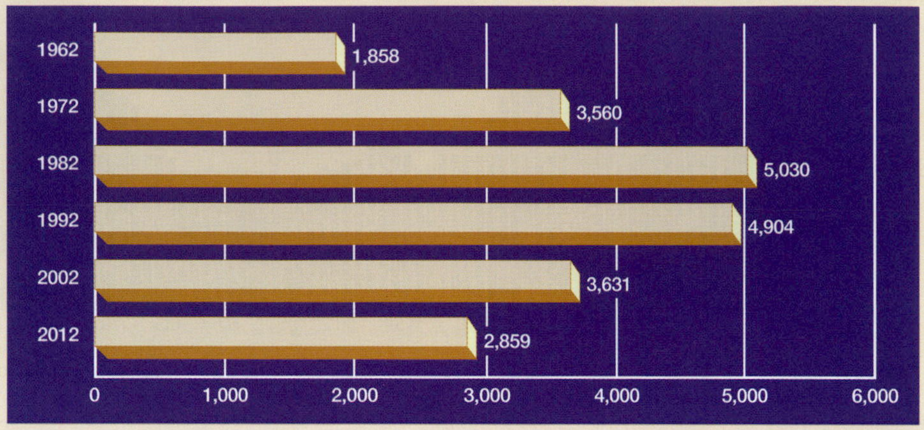

Source: *Sourcebook of Criminal Justice Statistics* (2015), Table 3.106.2012.

crime as a serious national problem, especially if they are comparing today's crime rates with those of the early 1960s.

The drop in crime rates raises interesting questions about why crime has declined in the United States. Some observers argue that reductions in crime since the 1980s occurred as a result of the policy of increasing the number of offenders held in prison and holding them for longer sentences. As you read subsequent chapters in the book, you will encounter other possible explanations for changes in crime rates. For example, demographic changes over time affect the number of young men who are in their crime-prone years (ages 16–24) at any given moment in history. Economic changes affect the number of people who are unemployed and living in poverty from year to year. In addition, police officials constantly experiment with new law enforcement strategies, some of which may have affected crime rates in the past decade. For example, New York City officials claim that their police department's policy of aggressively stopping and frisking young men has led to a decrease in crime, despite controversies about the policy being overwhelmingly applied to young African American and Latino men and not to other New Yorkers (C. Smith, 2014). As you consider subsequent chapters concerning theories of crime and law enforcement policies, think about how various factors can affect trends in crime rates.

The Most Crime-Ridden Nation?

How does the amount of crime in the United States compare with that in other countries? It is often said the United States has more crime than other modern industrial nations do. But as James Lynch (1995) argues, this belief is too simple to be useful. He points out that comparing American crime rates to those of other nations is difficult. First, one must choose nations that are similar to the United States—nations with democratic governments, similar levels of economic development, and the same kinds of legal systems (MacCoun et al., 1993). Second, one must get data from reliable sources. The two main sources of cross-national crime data are Interpol (the international police agency based in Europe) and the International Crime Survey.

Lynch compares early 1990s crime rates in the United States and in Australia, Canada, England and Wales, West Germany, France, the Netherlands, Sweden, and Switzerland. Both police and victim data show that the homicide rate in the United States was more than twice that in Canada, the next highest country,

TABLE 1.3 COMPARATIVE INTENTIONAL HOMICIDE RATES PER 100,000 PEOPLE, 2011

Homicide rates in the United States exceed those of industrialized democracies, but some developing democracies have higher rates.

NATION	HOMICIDE RATE
United States	4.7
Spain	0.8
England and Wales	1.0
France	1.5
Canada	1.7
Finland	2.5
Estonia	6.2
Lithuania	6.2

Sources: Bureau of Justice Statistics, *Sourcebook of Criminal Justice Statistics* (2015), Table 3.106.2012; Shannon Brennan, "Police-Reported Crime Statistics in Canada, 2011," Statistics Canada website (www.statcan.gc.ca); *European Sourcebook of Crime and Criminal Justice Statistics: 2014*, Table 1.2.1.5.

and many times that in the other countries. The same was generally true at that time for robbery, but American robbery rates subsequently declined in the later 1990s to levels comparable to that of several other countries.

Other studies examine the data concerning property crimes, with surprising results. Police statistics do not show all property crime rates in the United States to be higher than those in several other countries. In 2011, for example, the motor vehicle theft rate in the United States was 230 per 100,000 population. By contrast, equal or higher vehicle theft rates were experienced in Canada (239 per 100,000), France (294 per 100,000 population) and Sweden (366 per 100,000 population) (BJS, 2015a; European Institute, 2014). As in Lynch's study, other data indicate that the main difference between the countries lies in homicide rates, which were nearly 4 times higher in the United States than in England in 2011 (see Tables 1.3 and 1.4). Firearms play a much greater role in violent crimes in the United States, where they are used in two-thirds of murders compared with their use in fewer than 10 percent of intentional homicides in England.

TABLE 1.4 COMPARATIVE CRIME RATES, RATES OF REPORTED CRIME PER 100,000 POPULATION, 2011

These data from the Government of Canada and the *European Sourcebook of Crime and Criminal Justice Statistics* indicate that the United States does not lead the world in all rates of non-homicide offenses.

NATION	AUTO THEFT	BURGLARY	ROBBERY
United States	230	701	114
Canada	239	526	86
England and Wales	164	892	133
France	294	544	193
Netherlands	126	Not available	92
Sweden	366	1002	103

Sources: U.S. Bureau of Justice Statistics, *Sourcebook of Criminal Justice Statistics* (2015), Table 3.106.2012; Shannon Brennan, "Police-Reported Crime Statistics in Canada, 2011," Statistics Canada website (www.statcan.ga.ca); *European Sourcebook of Crime and Criminal Justice Statistics: 2014*, Tables 1.2.1.16, 1.2.1 17, 1.2.1.13.

In sum, the risk of lethal violence is much higher in the United States than in other well-established industrial democracies. However, the homicide rate in the United States is lower than in industrialized countries, such as Lithuania, Russia, and South Africa, which have sought to move from authoritarian governments to democracy in the past two decades (Harrendorf, Heiskanen, and Malby, 2010).

Interestingly, crime rates in Western countries besides the United States may have begun to decline (Tonry, 1998). Crime rates in Canada fell for a decade before rising 6 percent in 2003 as a result of increases in counterfeiting and property crime. The rates subsequently declined again in 2004 and 2005. Canada experienced continued declines for most violent crimes (Gannon, 2006; Brennan, 2012). According to the British Crime Survey, crime in England and Wales fell 42 percent from 1995 to 2007, with burglaries reduced by nearly 60 percent and violent crimes dropping by 40 percent (Nicholas, Kershaw, and Walker, 2007). Significant declines in crime appeared in crime data from many of the 11 industrial countries in the International Crime Victimization Surveys during the 1990s (Mayhew and van Dijk, 1997). We can gain more insight into the nature and extent of crime in the United States by looking at countries, such as Iceland, where there is little crime. Some might say that because Iceland is small, homogeneous, and somewhat isolated, we cannot compare the two countries. But as you will see in the Comparative Perspective, "Iceland: A Country with Little Crime," on the companion website, other factors help explain differences in the amount and types of crime in different countries.

The preceding discussions indicate that, contrary to public perceptions, crime rates in the United States have declined since the early 1990s and that the United States does not lead the world in crime. This information warns us to avoid accepting an image of the contemporary United States as an especially crime-ridden nation. According to the data, we must recognize that the level and nature of crime in the United States can change over time and that other countries have crime problems of their own. Bear in mind, however, that all the conclusions rest on one factor: our reliance on data about crime and crime rates. What if our data are not accurate? Can we really know for sure that crime declined or that our country compares favorably with other countries in the world? Further, the development of public policies in criminal justice often rests on crime statistics. Thus we work hard to identify ways to improve our knowledge about, and measurement of, crime. We know, however, that crime data can be flawed. Let's look closely at the sources of crime data and ask ourselves if they give us a true picture of crime in the United States.

Keeping Track of Crime

One of the frustrations in studying criminal justice is the lack of accurate means of knowing the amount of crime that takes place. Surveys reveal that much more crime occurs than is reported to the police. This is referred to as the **dark figure of crime**.

dark figure of crime
A metaphor referring to the significant yet undefined extent of crime that is never reported to the police.

Most homicides and auto thefts are reported to the police. In the case of a homicide, a body must be accounted for, and insurance companies require a police report before they will pay for a stolen car. However, according to surveys of victims, a majority of rape or sexual assault victims do not report the attack; almost one-half of robbery victims and nearly 60 percent of victims of simple assault do not do so. Figure 1.4 shows the percentage of victimizations not reported to the police.

Crimes go unreported for many reasons. Some victims of rape and assault do not wish to be embarrassed by public disclosure and police questioning; the most common reason for not reporting a violent crime is that it was viewed

FIGURE 1.4 PERCENTAGE OF VICTIMIZATIONS NOT REPORTED TO THE POLICE

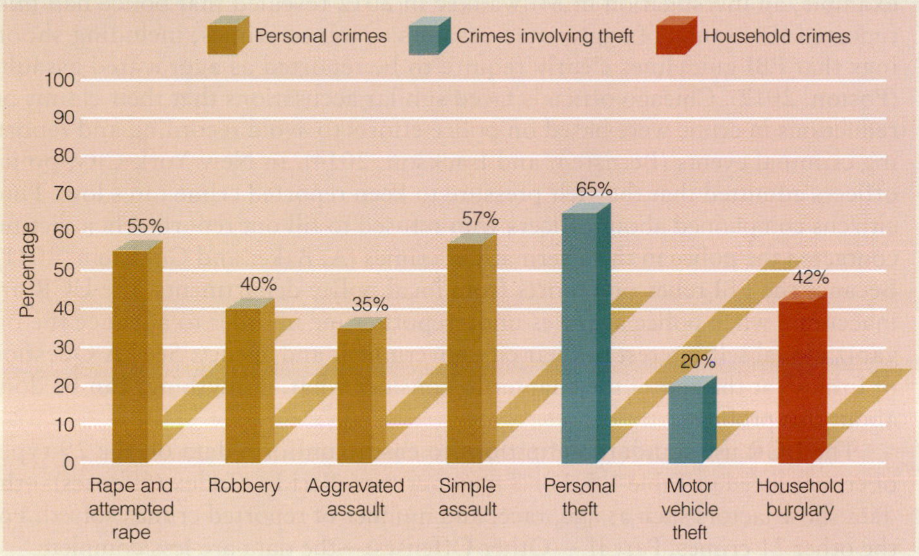

Source: Bureau of Justice Statistics, *Criminal Victimization in the United States, 2008*, May 2011, Table 91.

by the victims as a personal, private matter. In the case of larceny, robbery, or burglary, the value of the property lost may not be worth the effort of calling the police. Many people refrain from reporting crimes because they do not want to become involved, fill out papers at the station house, perhaps go to court, or appear at a police lineup. They may not want police to come to their homes to ask questions if they have stolen property, drugs, unregistered guns, or other evidence of their own illegal activities there. In some neighborhoods, people may fear retaliation from gangs or individual criminals if they go to the police. As these examples suggest, many people feel the costs and risks of reporting crimes outweigh the gains.

Until 1972, the only crimes counted by government were those that were known to the police and that the police reported to the Federal Bureau of Investigation for the FBI's Uniform Crime Reports (UCR). Since then, the Department of Justice has sponsored the National Crime Victimization Surveys (NCVS), which pose questions to a sample of the public to find out how much victimization has occurred. One might hope that the data from these two sources would give us a clear picture of the amount of crime, crime trends, and the characteristics of offenders. However, the picture remains blurred and imperfect because of differences in the way crime is measured by the UCR and the NCVS, and because of flaws contained in the data reported by each of these sources.

The Uniform Crime Reports

Issued each year by the FBI, the **Uniform Crime Reports (UCR)** are a statistical summary of crimes reported to the police. At the urging of the International Association of Chiefs of Police, Congress in 1930 authorized this system for compiling crime data (Rosen, 1995). The UCR come from a voluntary national network of some 16,000 local, state, and federal law enforcement agencies, policing 93 percent of the U.S. population. The main publication of the UCR is an annual volume, *Crime in the United States*.

Uniform Crime Reports (UCR)
Annually published statistical summary of crimes reported to the police, based on voluntary reports to the FBI by local, state, and federal law enforcement agencies.

With the drop in crime in recent years, police executives have faced new pressures to show that their cities are following the national trend. Some officials have even falsified their crime statistics as promotions, pay raises, and department budgets have become increasingly dependent on positive data. For example, an investigation in Milwaukee in 2012 revealed that police had misreported thousands of aggravated assaults as minor crimes, including shootings that FBI guidelines clearly require to be reported as aggravated assaults (Poston, 2012). Chicago officials faced similar accusations that their claims on reductions in crime were based on police efforts to avoid recording and reporting criminal events (Bernstein and Isackson, 2014). In New York City, police officers admitted that they felt pressure to keep reported crime rates low. Thus citizens complained about officers who refused to fill out reports when victims contacted the police in the aftermath of crimes (A. Baker and Goldstein, 2011). Because the FBI relies on reports from local police departments, the UCR are inaccurate when police agencies underreport crime in order to advance the organizational self-interest of their city government and agency. See "A Question of Ethics" at the end of the chapter to consider what, if anything, can be done about this problem.

The UCR use standard definitions to ensure uniform data on the 29 types of crimes listed in Table 1.5. For 8 major crimes, Part I—(Index Offenses)—the data show factors such as age, race, and number of reported crimes solved. For the other 21 crimes, Part II—(Other Offenses)—the data are less complete.

TABLE 1.5 UNIFORM CRIME REPORTS OFFENSES

The UCR present data on 8 index offenses and 21 other crimes for which there is less information. Data are collected on Part II offenses based solely on arrests and not for all incidents reported to police.

PART I (INDEX OFFENSES)	PART II (OTHER OFFENSES)
1. Criminal homicide	9. Simple assaults
2. Forcible rape	10. Forgery and counterfeiting
3. Robbery	11. Fraud
4. Aggravated assault	12. Embezzlement
5. Burglary	13. Buying, receiving, or possessing stolen property
6. Larceny/theft	14. Vandalism
7. Auto theft	15. Weapons (carrying, possession, etc.)
8. Arson	16. Prostitution and commercialized vice
	17. Sex offenses
	18. Violation of narcotic drug laws
	19. Gambling
	20. Offenses against the family and children
	21. Driving under the influence
	22. Violation of liquor laws
	23. Drunkenness
	24. Disorderly conduct
	25. Vagrancy
	26. All other offenses (excluding traffic)
	27. Suspicion
	28. Curfew and loitering (juvenile)
	29. Juvenile runaways

Source: Federal Bureau of Investigation, *Crime in the United States, 2013* (2014) (www.fbi.gov).

The UCR present crime data in three ways: (1) as *aggregates* (a total of 345,031 robberies were reported to the police in 2013), (2) as *percentage changes* over different periods (there was a 3.5 percent decrease in robberies from 2012 to 2013), and (3) as a *rate per 100,000 people* (the robbery rate in 2013 was 109) (FBI, 2014a).

The UCR provide a useful but incomplete picture of crime levels. These reports fail to provide an accurate picture of crime in the United States for many reasons, including the following:

- They count only crimes reported to the police.
- They count and classify crimes but do not provide complete details about offenses.
- They rely on voluntary reports from local police departments.
- Local police may adjust the classification of crimes in order to protect the image of a police department or community.
- The definitions of specific crime categories can be interpreted inconsistently.
- They count only a specific set of crimes and do not focus on corporate, occupational, and computer crime.
- Seven percent of Americans live in jurisdictions where police agencies do not make reports to the UCR.

In response to criticisms of the UCR, the FBI has made some changes in the program that are now being implemented nationwide. Some offenses have been redefined, and police agencies are being asked to report more details about crime events. Using the **National Incident-Based Reporting System (NIBRS)**, police agencies are to report all crimes committed during an incident, not just the most serious one, as well as data on offenders, victims, and the places where they interact. For example, the NIBRS seeks to gather detailed information on such matters as the race, sex, and age of the victim and offender; types of weapons used; value of property stolen; victim injuries; and relationship, if any, between the victim and offender. While the UCR now count incidents and arrests for the 8 index offenses and count arrests for other crimes, the NIBRS provides detailed incident data on 46 offenses in 22 crime categories. The NIBRS distinguishes between attempted and completed crimes as well.

National Incident-Based Reporting System (NIBRS)
A reporting system in which the police describe each offense in a crime incident, together with data describing the offender, victim, and property.

The National Crime Victimization Surveys

A second source of crime data is the **National Crime Victimization Surveys (NCVS)**. Since 1972, the Census Bureau has done surveys to find out the extent and nature of crime victimization. Thus data have been gathered on unreported as well as reported crimes. Interviews are conducted twice each year with a national probability sample of approximately 76,000 people in 43,000 households. The same people are interviewed twice a year for three years and asked if they have been victimized in the last six months.

National Crime Victimization Surveys (NCVS)
Interviews of samples of the U.S. population conducted by the Bureau of Justice Statistics to determine the number and types of criminal victimization, and thus, the extent of unreported as well as reported crime.

Each person is asked a set of screening questions (for example, did anyone beat you up, attack you, or hit you with something such as a rock or a bottle?) to determine whether he or she has been victimized. The person is then asked questions designed to elicit specific facts about the event, the offender, and any financial losses or physical disabilities caused by the crime.

Besides the household interviews, separate studies are also done to find out about the victimization of businesses. These data allow us to estimate how many crimes have occurred, learn more about the offenders, and note demographic patterns. The results show that for the crimes measured (rape, robbery, assault, burglary, theft), there were fewer than 21 million victimizations in 2008 (down from 43 million in 1973). This level is much higher than the number of crimes actually reported to the police suggests.

In reporting data from the NCVS, the Bureau of Justice Statistics often emphasizes households as the unit of analysis in order to present a more accurate picture of the dispersion of crime. All households do not experience the same risks of victimization. Most households are not victimized at all during a given year, whereas others experience multiple victimizations. In 2005, for example, only 14 percent of American households reported experiencing criminal victimization (Klaus, 2007).

Although the NCVS provide a more complete picture of the nature and extent of crime than do the UCR, they too have flaws. Because government employees administer the surveys, the people interviewed tend not to report crimes in which they or members of their family took part. They also may not want to admit that a family member engages in crime, or they may be too embarrassed to admit that they have allowed themselves to be victimized more than once.

The NCVS are also imperfect because they depend on the victim's *perception* of an event. The theft of a child's lunch money by a bully may be reported by one person but not by another. People may say that their property was stolen when in fact they lost it. Moreover, people's memories of dates may fade, and they may misreport the year in which a crime occurred even though they remember the event itself clearly. In addition to the problem of victims' perceptions, Clayton Mosher, Terance Miethe, and Dretha Phillips (2002: 168), have identified other problems in relying on victim surveys:

- Surveys only cover a limited range of crimes.
- Surveys are based on a relatively small sample of people; there are risks that they will not be representative of the national population or that errors in data analysis will lead to erroneous conclusions about the nation as a whole.
- The identification of victimization can depend on how the survey questions are phrased.

The FBI describes the UCR and NCVS as complementary. Each is intended to supply information that is missing through the other's approach to measuring crime. Table 1.6 compares the Uniform Crime Reports and the National Crime Victimization Surveys.

In describing the two approaches, the FBI acknowledges that these reports do not provide a complete picture of crime in the United States. For example, the NCVS do not interview children under the age of 12 and do not include questions about certain crimes, such as arson and crimes against businesses. If such crimes are not reported to the police, and therefore not recorded in the UCR, they are therefore not included in the two main sources of crime data used by government policy makers.

Because there is no perfect way to measure crime, government agencies work to keep improving the available methods for counting, classifying, and analyzing the occurrence of crime each year. Students of criminal justice must recognize the limitations of crime data, so that they can discuss crime with the awareness that a complete and accurate picture of criminal offenses and victimization does not exist.

Trends in Crime

Experts agree that, contrary to public opinion and the claims of politicians, crime rates have not been steadily rising. The NCVS show that the victimization rate peaked in 1981 and has declined since then. The greatest declines are in property crimes, but crimes of violence have also dropped, especially since

TABLE 1.6 THE UCR AND THE NCVS

Compare the data sources. Remember that the UCR tabulate only crimes reported to the police, whereas the NCVS are based on interviews with victims.

	UNIFORM CRIME REPORTS	NATIONAL CRIME VICTIMIZATION SURVEYS
Offenses Measured		
	Homicide Rape Robbery (personal and commercial) Assault (aggravated) Burglary (commercial and household) Larceny (commercial and household) Motor vehicle theft Arson	Rape Robbery (personal) Assault (aggravated and simple) Burglary (household) Larceny (personal and household) Motor vehicle theft
Scope		
	Crimes reported to the police in most jurisdictions; considerable flexibility in developing small-area data	Crimes both reported and not reported to police; all data are for the nation as a whole; some data are available for a few large geographic areas
Collection Method		
	Police department reports to Federal Bureau of Investigation	Survey interviews: periodically measures the total number of crimes committed by asking a national sample of 43,000 households representing 76,000 people over the age of 12 about their experiences as victims of crime during a specific period
Kinds of Information		
	In addition to offense counts, provides information on crime clearances, persons arrested, persons charged, law enforcement officers killed and assaulted, and characteristics of homicide victims	Provides details about victims (such as age, race, sex, education, income, and whether the victim and offender were related) and about crimes (such as time and place of occurrence, whether or not reported to police, use of weapons, occurrence of injury, and economic consequences)
Sponsor		
	Department of Justice's Federal Bureau of Investigation	Department of Justice's Bureau of Justice Statistics

1993. From 2003 to 2012, rates of violent crime fell overall by 19 percent, although there was a rise in reported violent victimizations for simple assaults that raised the violent crime rate between the years 2011 to 2012. Rates for property crime decreased by 10 percent from 2003–2012 but there was also an increase in reported in thefts from 2011–2012 (Truman, Langton, and Planty, 2013).

The UCR show similar results, revealing a rapid rise in crime rates beginning in 1964 and continuing until 1980, when the rates began to level off or decline before rising again until 1992 when the significant, steady decline began to occur. In fact, according to the UCR, property crimes have gone from a peak rate of 5,353 per 100,000 people in 1980 to a rate of 2,859 in 2012. Reported violent crime fell steadily from its peak of 758 per 100,000 in 1991 and 1992 to 387 in 2011 and 2012 (BJS, 2015a). Interestingly, people surveyed for the NCVS indicated that there was an upswing in crime from 2010 to 2012, although the UCR presents a decline in crimes reported by local police to the FBI during that two-year period (Truman, Langton, and Planty, 2013).

Table 1.7 displays three measures of violent crime. One measure is based on the victimization survey, whereas crimes recorded by the police and arrests are from the UCR. Remember that the differences in the trends indicated by the NCVS and the UCR are explained in part by the different data sources and different populations on which their tabulations are based. The UCR are based on crimes reported to the police, while the NCVS record crimes experienced by victims. Apparent inconsistencies in the two sources of data are likely to stem from a combination of problems with victims' memories, inaccuracies in crime records in individual police agencies, and inconsistencies in the data projections used to produce the NCVS and UCR. Notice that the crime rates decline, even if the actual numbers of crimes do not decline, because steady increases in the nation's population have meant fewer crimes recorded per 100,000 population.

Earlier in the chapter, we saw that the reasons for the decline in crime in the United States produce much debate. Among the reasons given by analysts are the aging of the baby boom population, the increased use of security systems, the aggressive police efforts to keep handguns off the streets, and the dramatic decline in the use of crack cocaine. Other factors may include the booming economy of the 1990s and the quadrupling of the number of people incarcerated since 1970. There are concerns about the final two factors, in that economic downturns could fuel an increase in crime, as could the release from prison of hundreds of thousands of parolees and offenders who complete their sentences each year. Yet, despite the economic problems affecting the nation from the mortgage crisis of 2007–2008 and the large numbers of offenders leaving prison each year in the same time period, crime rates generally continued to decline from 2007 through 2012. Other factors that may be associated with crime rates, such as the decline of urban neighborhoods, gang activity, the availability of drugs, and an increase in poverty, still exist and may affect crime in specific areas. However, the national crime rates have shown an overall decline in the past two decades. For now, though, let's look more closely at one other factor—age—as a means of assessing future crime levels.

TABLE 1.7 THREE MEASURES OF VIOLENT CRIME

The difficulty in accurately counting crimes and calculating crime rates stems from different sources of information, none of which capture the complete picture of crime. Because the population of the United States has steadily increased, the crime rate can fall even without a drop in reported victimizations and recorded crimes. The crime rate is calculated as the number of recorded crimes per 100,000 population.

YEAR	VIOLENT VICTIMIZATIONS (NATIONAL SURVEY)	VIOLENT CRIMES RECORDED BY POLICE (REPORTED TO FBI)	ARRESTS FOR VIOLENT CRIMES	CRIME RATE—VIOLENT CRIMES
1984	5,954,000	1,273,282	493,960	540
1995	9,604,570	1,798,792	796,230	685
2004	5,182,670	1,360,088	586,558	463
2012	6,842,590	1,214,462	521,196	387

Sources: Bureau of Justice Statistics, *Sourcebook of Criminal Justice Statistics*, 2015; Howard N. Snyder and Joseph Mulako-Wangota, online "Arrest Data Analysis Tool," Bureau of Justice Statistics website, 2014 (www.bjs.gov); Jennifer Truman, Lynn Langton, and Michael Planty, "Criminal Victimization, 2012"; *Bureau of Justice Statistics Bulletin*, October 2013, NCJ 243389; Patsy Kaus and Cathy Maston, *Criminal Victimization in the United States, 1995*, Bureau of Justice Statistics, May 2000, NCJ 171129; Anita Timrots and Marshall DeBerry, "Criminal Victimization 1984," *Bureau of Justice Statistics Bulletin*, October 1985, NCJ 98904.

AP Images/Mel Evans

In light of the association between certain kinds of crimes and males in a certain age group, should police officers be especially suspicious of young men? Would such an approach to crime control create risks that innocent young men will be needlessly followed and stopped? Alternatively, if we see associations between age and crime, should that be a reason to emphasize social and educational programs that provide support to young men to steer them away from crime?

Age

Changes in the age makeup of the population are central to the analysis of crime trends. It has long been known that men aged 16 to 24 are the most crime-prone group. The rise in crime in the 1970s has been blamed on the post–World War II baby boom. By the 1970s the boomers had entered the high-risk crime group of 16- to 24-year-olds. They made up a much larger portion of the U.S. population than ever before. Between 40 and 50 percent of the total arrests during that decade resulted from the growth in the total population and in the size of the crime-prone age group. Likewise, the decline in most crime rates that began during the 1980s has been attributed to the maturing of the post–World War II generation.

During the 1990s the 16- to 24-year age cohort was smaller than it had been at any time since the early 1960s, and many people believe that this contributed to the decline in crime. One controversial study argues that contributing to the small age cohort and the decline in crime in the 1990s was the Supreme Court's 1973 decision legalizing abortions (Samuelson, 1999). Abortions reduced the size of the 1973–1989 age cohort by about 40 percent. The study, by Steven Levitt and John Donahue, suggests that those who would have been at greatest risk for criminal activity during their crime-prone years—"the unwanted offspring of teenage, poor and minority women—were aborted at disproportionately high rates" (Brandon, 1999). In 1994, a small but influential group of criminologists predicted that by the year 2000 the number of young men in the 14- to 24-year-old cohort would greatly increase. They argued that the decline in crime experienced in the 1990s was merely the "lull before the storm" (J. Steinberg, 1999: 4-WK). In the words of James Fox, "To prevent a blood bath in 2005, when we will have a flood of 15-year-olds, we have to do something today with the 5-year-olds" (Krauss, 1994: 4). However, this link between increases in the juvenile population and a rise in violent crime has not occurred. For most years since the prediction was made, the homicide rate among teenage offenders has been falling, although individual cities have experienced increases in homicides during specific years.

Crime Trends: What Do We Really Know?

Pointing to specific factors that cause an increase or decrease in crime rates is difficult. Once, people thought that with the proper tools they could analyze and solve the crime problem. However, crime is complex. Key questions remain: Do changes in crime rates occur because of demography, unemployment rates, housing conditions, and changes in family structure? Or do crime rates result from interactions among these and other factors? How do the policies of law enforcement, sentencing, and corrections affect criminality? Until we know more about the causes of criminal behavior, we can neither blame nor praise government policies for shifts in crime rates.

CHECKPOINT

19. Has crime in the United States reached record levels?

20. For which crimes does the crime rate in the United States exceed that of most industrialized democracies?

21. What are the two main sources of crime data?

22. What factors may affect crime trends?

STOP AND ANALYZE: Why do so many Americans believe that crime in the United States is increasing when, in fact, it has been decreasing for years? List three factors that may contribute to this erroneous belief.

A QUESTION OF ETHICS

In 2014, an investigation by journalists at the *Los Angeles Times* found that in the preceding year the Los Angeles Police Department had misclassified nearly 1,200 violent crimes as minor offenses when reporting crime data to the FBI. In one example, a man choked his wife, stabbed her in the face with a screwdriver, and threw her down a flight of stairs. The man was sent to prison for six years, yet the police reported it as a "simple assault," even though his use of a weapon should have made it automatically a more serious "aggravated assault." Although some misclassifications can be based on errors in recordkeeping, several police officers said that they were under relentless pressure from top officials to demonstrate that crime rates were down. Those pressures, they said, made some officers knowingly misclassify crimes. The investigation found that aggravated assaults would have been 14 percent higher if the crimes had been properly classified, thus increasing the city's actual overall violent crime rate by 7 percent for the preceding year.

Source: Ben Poston and Joel Rubin, "LAPD Misclassified Nearly 1,200 Violent Crimes as Minor Offenses." *Los Angeles Times*, August 9, 2014 (www.latimes.com).

CRITICAL THINKING AND ANALYSIS

If you were a police officer, is there anything that you could do to resist the pressure to misclassify or otherwise underreport crimes? How would you view this situation if you were the mayor? Aside from the fact that you would benefit politically from a perception of low crime rates during your time in office, as mayor, you would also recognize that the public is not fully informed. Write a memo describing what, if anything, could be done about this issue. Moreover, clearly identify who should take action and what, realistically, could be accomplished.

Summary

1 Discuss how public policies on crime are formed

- Crime and justice are high on the agenda of national priorities.
- Crime and justice are public policy issues.
- Public opinion and citizen involvement affect criminal justice.
- Criminal justice can best be seen as a social system.
- As a democracy, the United States faces a struggle to strike a balance between maintaining public order and protecting individual freedom, especially because of the tensions between conflicting American values.

2 Recognize how the crime control and due process models of criminal justice help us understand the system

- The crime control model and the due process model are two ways of looking at the goals and procedures of the criminal justice system.
- The crime control model focuses on efficiency in an administrative process that relies on discretionary decisions.
- The due process model focuses on reliable decisions in an adversarial process that relies on law.

3 Be able to explain: "What is a crime?"

- Crimes are those behaviors defined by law as so harmful or undesirable that individuals proven to have undertaken them should be punished by the government.
- Politicians define crimes through laws that they enact, and they do not always anticipate the consequences of laws. Politics affect the development of laws concerning criminal justice at the national, state, and local levels.
- Criminal laws may reflect a consensus in society or may reflect conflicts about values and morality in contexts in which the preferences of the majority of legislators will prevail.

4 Describe the major types of crime in the United States

- There are seven broad categories of crime: visible crime, victimless crimes, political crime, occupational crime, organized crime, transnational crime, and cybercrime.
- Each type of crime has its own level of risk and profitability, each arouses varying degrees of public disapproval, and each has its own group of offenders with their own characteristics.

5 Analyze how much crime there is and understand how it is measured

- Today's crime problem is not unique. Throughout the history of the United States, crime has reached high levels at various times.
- Homicide is the primary type of crime that occurs at higher rates in the United States than in other industrialized democracies.
- The amount of crime is difficult to measure. The Uniform Crime Reports and the National Crime Victimization Surveys are the best sources of crime data.
- The complexity of crime statistics makes monitoring trends in crime a challenge.
- Crime rates are affected by changes in social factors, such as the size of the cohort of young males in their crime-prone years (ages 16–24) and the introduction of new drugs or other criminal activities that affect social contexts in certain communities.

Questions for Review

1 What are the goals of criminal justice in a democracy?

2 What are the major elements of Packer's due process model and crime control model?

3 What are the seven types of crime?

4 What are the positive and negative attributes of the two major sources of crime data?

Key Terms

crime (p. 7)
crime control model (p. 13)
cybercrimes (p. 31)
dark figure of crime (p. 38)
due process model (p. 13)
evidence-based practices (p. 9)
felonies (p. 22)
identity theft (p. 31)
mala in se (p. 21)
mala prohibita (p. 21)
misdemeanors (p. 22)
money laundering (p. 26)
National Crime Victimization Surveys (NCVS) (p. 41)
National Incident-Based Reporting System (NIBRS) (p. 41)
occupational crime (p. 24)
organized crime (p. 26)
political crime (p. 23)
property crimes (p. 23)
public order crimes (p. 23)
public policy (p. 8)
transnational crime (p. 27)
Uniform Crime Reports (UCR) (p. 39)
victimless crimes (p. 23)
violent crimes (p. 23)
visible crime (p. 22)

Checkpoint Answers

1 What are evidence-based practices?

✓ Policies developed through guidance from research studies that demonstrate which approaches are most useful and cost-effective for advancing desired goals.

2 What criminal justice policies are advocated by conservatives?

✓ Stricter enforcement of the law through the expansion of police forces and the enactment of laws that require swift and certain punishment of offenders.

3 What are liberals' criticisms of contemporary policies?

✓ Stronger crime measures endanger the values of due process and justice.

4 What are the main features of the crime control model?

✓ Every effort must be made to repress crime through efficiency, speed, and finality.

5 What are the main features of the due process model?

✓ Every effort must be made to ensure that criminal justice decisions are based on reliable information. The model stresses the adversarial process, the rights of defendants, and formal decision-making procedures.

6 At what level of government are many justice officials elected to office?

✓ State and local levels of government.

7 How do politics influence criminal justice policies?

✓ Penal codes and budgets are passed by legislatures, many criminal justice officials are elected, and criminal justice policies are developed in political arenas.

8 Who are some individual Americans who have influenced criminal justice policy?

✓ Candy Lightner, founder of MADD; Sarah Brady, founder of Brady Center to Prevent Gun Violence; Congresswomen Carolyn McCarthy and Gabrielle Giffords.

9 How do average citizens affect criminal justice?

✓ Voting, participating in community organizations, taking steps to impact their own potential vulnerability to victimization.

10 Who defines certain behaviors as criminal?

✓ Elected representatives in state legislatures and Congress.

11 What is meant by *mala in se* and by *mala prohibita*?

✓ *Mala in se:* offenses that are wrong in themselves (murder, rape, assault). *Mala prohibita:* acts that are crimes because they are prohibited (vagrancy, gambling, drug use).

12 What are the seven main types of crime?

✓ Visible crime, victimless crime, political crime, occupational crime, organized crime, transnational crime, cybercrime.

13 What groups are overrepresented among those arrested for visible or street crimes?

✓ Young, male, poor.

14 What is meant by the term *victimless crimes?*

✓ These are crimes against morality in which the people involved do not believe they have been victimized.

15 What are political crimes?

✓ Crimes such as treason committed for a political purpose.

16 **Why is the term *occupational crime* more useful today than the term *white-collar crime*?**

✓ Workplace-related crimes are committed by all occupational groups.

17 **What is transnational crime?**

✓ Crime that crosses national borders in its planning, execution, or victimization.

18 **What types of criminal activities are labeled as cybercrime?**

✓ Using computers to steal valuable information and assets, identity theft, illegal downloading, malicious viruses.

19 **Has crime in the United States reached record levels?**

✓ No, there have been other eras when crime was higher.

20 **For which crimes does the crime rate in the United States exceed that of most industrialized democracies?**

✓ Violent crimes such as murder.

21 **What are the two main sources of crime data?**

✓ Uniform Crime Reports, National Crime Victimization Surveys.

22 **What factors may affect crime trends?**

✓ Demography (e.g., age cohorts); changing social contexts that may impact jobs, neighborhoods, and families, such as the spread of new drugs or other criminal activities (e.g., crack, gangs, business closures). Anticrime strategies of law enforcement agencies may also play a role.

CHAPTER FEATURES

- **Technology and Criminal Justice** Hacking of Customer Data
- **Close Up** Victimization of the Elderly
- **Doing Your Part** Crime Victims' Assistance Volunteer
- **New Directions in Criminal Justice Policy** Evidence-Based Practices and Victim Services

CHAPTER 2

VICTIMIZATION AND CRIMINAL BEHAVIOR

CHAPTER LEARNING OBJECTIVES

1. Describe who is likely to be victimized by crime
2. Discuss the impacts of crime on society
3. Identify the justice system's responses to the needs of crime victims
4. Describe the theories put forward to explain criminal behavior
5. Analyze crime-causation theories and apply them to different groups of offenders

CHAPTER OUTLINE

Crime Victimization
- Who Is Victimized?
- Acquaintances and Strangers
- Recurring Victimization
- The Impact of Crime
- The Experience of Victims within the Criminal Justice System
- The Role of Victims in Crime

Causes of Crime
- Classical and Positivist Theories
- Biological Explanations
- Psychological Explanations
- Sociological Explanations
- Life Course Explanations
- Women and Crime
- Assessing Theories of Criminality

AP Images/Elaine Thompson

AP Images/Elaine Thompson

On the afternoon of June 5, 2014, Aaron Ybarra entered Otto Miller Hall on the campus of Seattle Pacific University and began shooting. He killed one student and injured three others before being subdued by students at SPU and held while awaiting the arrival of police (M. Kang and Stokes, 2014; McLaughlin, 2014). In his personal journal, Ybarra explained that he was seeking revenge on people who had humiliated him, and wanted to kill everyone in the world, except his family and friends. He also indicated that he chose Seattle Pacific University because he was unfamiliar with the campus, and thought that the University of Washington and Seattle University "represent Seattle more. I didn't want to have to attack my own city." (Cruz, 2014).

According to his attorney, Ybarra had been diagnosed with a mental illness, yet he had not been taking his prescription medication for some time prior to the shootings (Cruz, 2014). Psychological illness seems to be one possible explanation for his behavior, but are there others? At home, he lived with an alcoholic father and was himself treated for alcohol addiction, and his home life was described as "tumultuous" by reporters investigating his background (Cruz & Baker, 2014). How might these factors help explain his crimes? Could they also help explain other shootings, such as those that occurred at Columbine High School in 1999, or the Aurora, Colorado, movie shootings in 2012?

In September 2014, Russell "Rusty" Brace, an attorney in Maine, was accused of stealing $3.8 million from Midcoast Charities, an organization for which he served as president from 2001 through August 2014 (Betts, 2014). The funds raised by Midcoast were meant to help the needy in two counties on the coast of Maine—for example, one recipient of Midcoast funds ran a soup kitchen for residents facing hard times (Ramos, 2014).

Brace was born into a wealthy family and graduated from an Ivy League university. He ran large corporations, ran for state Senate in 1984 (and lost), and accrued significant wealth, including three separate homes—his main residence has been valued at $774,800 (Ramos, 2014). Brace's assets have been frozen during the court process, and they may be awarded to Midcoast Charities to offset the funds he has stolen, but clearly, many people have been harmed by his actions.

It is obvious that Brace was not lacking for money—so, what was his motivation for stealing from a charity that helps those in need? Does greed sufficiently explain his motivations? Did he feel any guilt about defrauding the people he was tasked with helping? Many victims are stunned and left seeking answers to these questions because, while he awaits the filing of criminal charges, Brace has not spoken about his motivations for his actions. The victims in this crime include people (and organizations) that made sizable donations to Midcoast, as well as those who might have received important assistance from the organization. In what ways does a crime involving misappropriation of money meant for the needy differ from a violent shooting that left one victim dead and two others injured? Are there "ripple effects" that continue to affect victims and their families after both kinds of crimes?

The Seattle Pacific University shooting was highly publicized because it occurred on a peaceful college campus. It was the type of crime that raises the public's worst fears about becoming victims of random violence. The incident also brought forth significant questions about why anyone would commit such a terrible act. Yet as we consider the possible causes that led to this crime, it is important to recognize that this shooting is not the typical crime. It is no surprise that crime statistics indicate that thefts, minor assaults, and credit card fraud are much more common than murders are. Do the underlying motivations for all crimes have a common core? Or are there distinctly different causes of crime, depending on which crimes are examined? These and other questions serve to illuminate the issues of victimization and crime causation, the topics of this chapter.

The Seattle Pacific University shooting provides a context we can use to examine a number of important questions related to crime. For example, who are the crime victims in this case? Clearly, the SPU students who were killed and wounded are victims. But what about their families? Are they also victims because they suffered psychological and emotional harm? Paul Lee, the only fatality in the shooting, used to help his father by working in the family restaurant (Brink, 2014). His death was not only a devastating loss to his family and friends, but also those who worked at the restaurant, as well as other members of the surrounding community. What about the city of Seattle? Has its reputation as a safe place to live been tarnished? Will fewer people decide to move to Seattle, or will potential students decide not to attend SPU? What financial losses might the university experience if it is known as the location of a terrible crime? And how does a shooting on a university campus affect college students, faculty, and staff in general? Would it be proper to say that *all* people in society could be viewed as victims of the crime?

Brace's actions cost Midcoast donors and charitable groups millions of dollars. The community of Camden, Maine, feels betrayed by one of their own, and people in need have not had access to services that were funded through the organization. Do incidents such as this cause people to rethink their decision to donate (or not) to charity if they cannot be sure how the funds are used? How will this hurt people who benefit from charities such as Midcoast, which provides much-needed services to the community?

These are important questions to contemplate, because how society answers them will define the scope of the subject of criminal victimization. In other words, when we talk about the victimizing consequences of crime, should we only consider the individuals most directly harmed by a crime, or should we also include those who have suffered less direct, but equally real, experiences? These discussions actually have practical consequences because we must define what we mean by “victim” before we can implement any policy that recognizes victims’ rights or victim compensation.

A further question arises when we ask whether people bear any responsibility for their own victimization. If young women sit in parked cars in dark, out-of-the-way places, do they place themselves in danger? What about young men who walk alone late at night down empty, unfamiliar streets while wearing eye-catching expensive watches and rings? Is such a line of inquiry unfair and inhumane? Yet, as we study criminal events, we cannot help but notice that some crimes occur when victims make themselves more vulnerable or when they take actions that appear to trigger a violent response from the wrongdoer. Do such questions imply that victims are at *fault* for the crime directed at them? No. Clearly, people who commit criminal acts must be punished as the ones responsible for those acts. However, an understanding of criminal events and victim behavior may help us discover how to teach people to reduce their risk of criminal victimization.

An additional important question looms when considering the SPU shooting and the Midcoast embezzlement, and every other criminal case: Why did the perpetrators do what they did? Criminal behavior is the main cause of criminal victimization. Research scholars, policy makers, and the public have long pondered questions such as “What causes crime?” and “Why do criminal offenders cause harm to other human beings?” These questions have significant implications for the subject of criminal victimization. Theories about crime causation often influence government policies for controlling and punishing violators of criminal laws.

In this chapter, we examine the many facets of crime victimization, including aspects that the general public does not usually recognize. In addition, we discuss the causes of crime. Many complex and controversial theories center on why people commit crimes. In considering this subject, we realize that no single theory can be expected to explain all crimes. Remember that “crimes” are whatever actions a legislature defines as deserving punishment at a particular moment in history. Thus, we should not assume that a man who steals money from a charitable organization has the same motives as the man who opens fire on a college campus in Seattle, Washington. The fact that crime has many causes, however, does not mean that all proposed theories about crime causation are equally useful or valid. We need to look closely at these theories and determine whether evidence supports them.

Crime Victimization

victimology
A field of criminology that examines the role the victim plays in precipitating a criminal incident and the impact of crimes on victims.

Until the past few decades, researchers paid little attention to crime victims. The field of **victimology**, which emerged in the 1950s, focused attention on four questions: (1) Who is victimized? (2) What is the impact of crime? (3) What happens to victims in the criminal justice system? (4) What role do victims play in causing the crimes they suffer? We discuss these questions in the following sections.

Who Is Victimized?

Not everyone has an equal chance of becoming a crime victim. Research shows that people who are victimized by crime in one year are also more likely to be victimized by crime in a subsequent year (Daigle and Fisher, 2013). Moreover, members of certain demographic groups are more likely to be victimized than others. As Andrew Karmen notes, "Victimization definitely does not appear to be a random process, striking people just by chance" (Karmen, 2001: 87). Victimologists have puzzled over this fact and come up with several answers for it. One explanation is that demographic factors (age, gender, income) affect lifestyle—people's routine activities such as work, home life, and recreation. Even cybercrime can be explained by the behavior of computer users, with those involved in computer crime being more likely to be victimized themselves (T. J. Holt and Bossler, 2009).

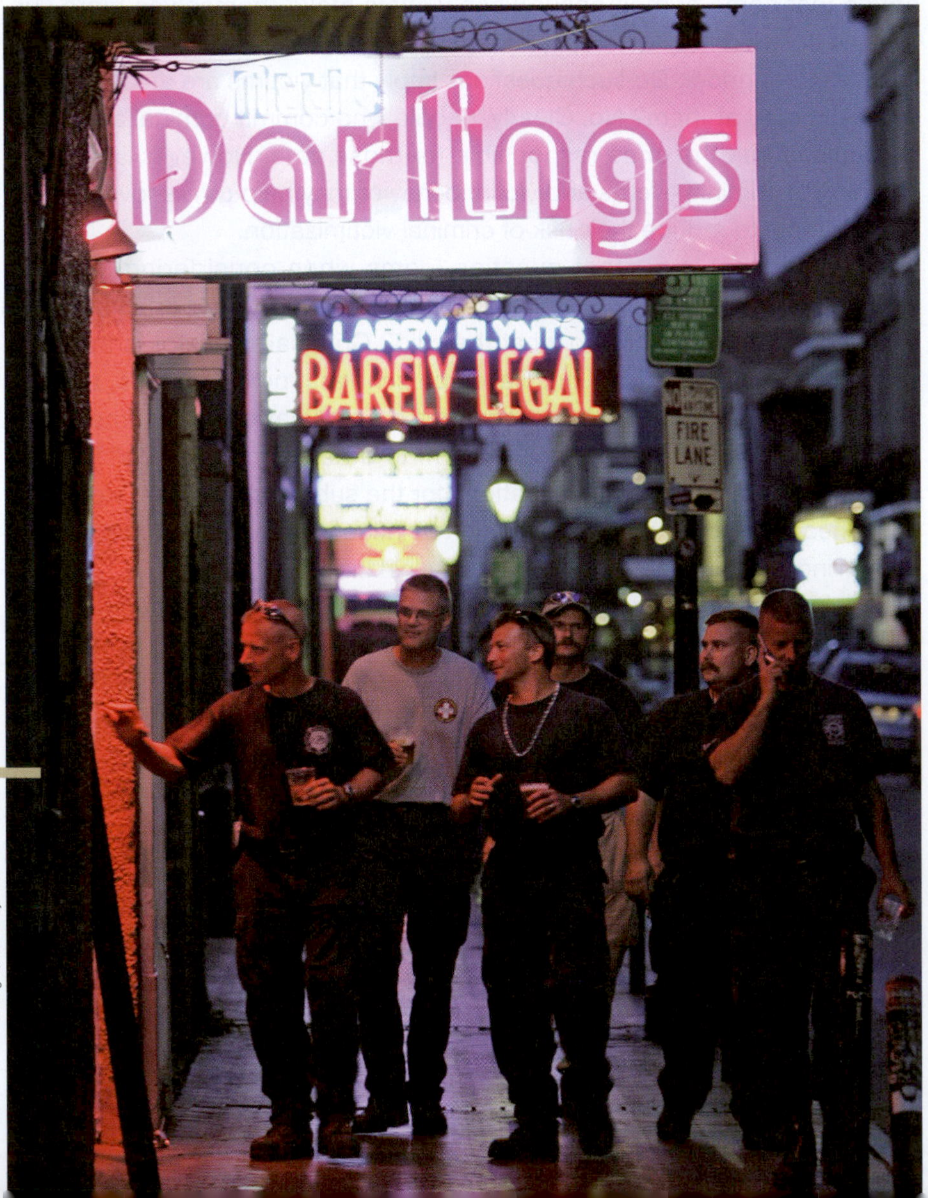

According to lifestyle-exposure theory, demographic factors (age, gender, income) and exposure to dangerous places, times, and people influence the probability of being victimized. Based on this theory, how would you assess your own risk of victimization?

AP Images/Kevork Djansezian

Lifestyles and routine activities, in turn, affect people's exposure to victimization risks in encounters with specific places and people (Xie, Heimer, and Lauritsen, 2012; Varano et al., 2004). Thus, differences in lifestyles and routine activities lead to varying degrees of exposure to risks (Meier and Miethe, 1993).

As indicated in the foregoing description, the **lifestyle-exposure theory** focuses on the unequal distribution of crime within society by identifying demographic groups, such as young people and the poor, who often face greater exposure to certain kinds of crime, especially violent crimes like robbery (Bunch, Clay-Warner, and Lei, 2012). A related focus of research by scholars who study crime causation and victimization is **routine activities theory**. This variation of the lifestyle approach examines the contexts of crime and sees crime arise in times and places where there is a convergence of specific elements: motivated offenders; suitable victims or buildings to target; and a lack of capable guardians or security technology that can prevent or deter the criminal acts in that time and place (Bunch et al., 2012; M. Felson and Boba, 2010). Lifestyle elements may place motivated offenders and vulnerable people together in specific places at specific times as part of their overlapping routine activities—such as hanging out at bars or pool halls.

lifestyle-exposure theory
Approach to understanding the unequal distribution of crime and victimization that examines the differential exposure to crime of demographic groups, such as the young or the poor, based on where they live and work and engage in leisure activities.

routine activities theory
A variation of the lifestyle approach that sees crime arise in times and places where there is a convergence of specific elements: motivated offenders, suitable victims, and a lack of capable guardians to prevent or deter criminal acts.

Figure 2.1 shows the links among the factors used in the lifestyle-exposure model of personal victimization. Using this model, think of a person whose lifestyle includes going to nightclubs in a "shady" part of town. Such a person runs the risk of being robbed if she walks alone through a dark, high-crime area at two o'clock in the morning to reach her luxury car. By contrast, an older person who watches television at night in her small-town home has a very low chance of being robbed. But these cases do not tell the entire story. What other factors make victims more vulnerable than nonvictims?

Women, Youths, Nonwhites

The lifestyle-exposure model and survey data shed light on the links between personal characteristics and the chance that one will become a victim. Figure 2.2 shows the influence of gender, age, and race on the risk of being victimized by a violent crime such as rape, robbery, or assault. If we apply these findings to the lifestyle-exposure model, we might suggest that African American teenagers and young adults are most likely to be victimized because of where they may live (urban, high-crime areas), how they may spend their leisure time (outside, late at night), and the people with whom they may associate (violence-prone youths). Lifestyle factors may also explain why elderly white men and women are least likely to be victimized by a violent crime. Perhaps it is because they do not go out at night, do not associate with people who are prone to crime, carry

FIGURE 2.1 LIFESTYLE-EXPOSURE MODEL OF VICTIMIZATION

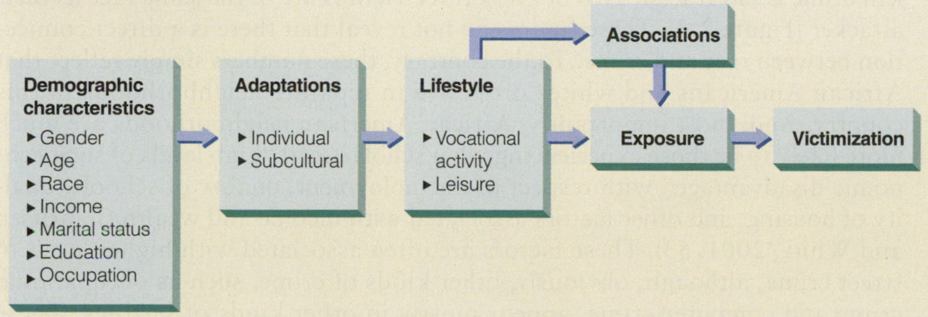

Adapted with permission from Robert F. Meier and Terance D. Miethe, "Understanding Theories of Criminal Victimization" in *Crime and Justice: A Review of Research.* Edited by Michael Tonry (Chicago: University of Chicago Press, 1973), 467.

FIGURE 2.2 VICTIMIZATION RATES FOR VIOLENT CRIMES

African American male youths generally have the highest victimization rates. Why are these young people more likely than other age, gender, and racial groups to be robbed or assaulted?

Note: Figures reflect average victimization rates for each demographic group for the time period 2003–2008. For specific demographic groups, data for an individual year would be excluded from the calculation of the average if there were fewer than ten sample cases in the category.

Sources: Bureau of Justice Statistics, *Criminal Victimization in the United States, 2003: Statistical Tables* (July 2005), Table 10; Bureau of Justice Statistics, *Criminal Victimization in the United States, 2004: Statistical Tables* (June 2006), Table 10; Bureau of Justice Statistics, *Criminal Victimization in the United States, 2005: Statistical Tables* (December 2006), Table 10; Bureau of Justice Statistics, *Criminal Victimization in the United States, 2006: Statistical Tables* (August 2008), Table 10; Bureau of Justice Statistics, *Criminal Victimization in the United States, 2007: Statistical Tables* (February 2010), Table 10; M. R. Rand and J. E. Robinson, *Criminal Victimization in the United States 2008: Statistical Tables* (May 2011), Table 10.

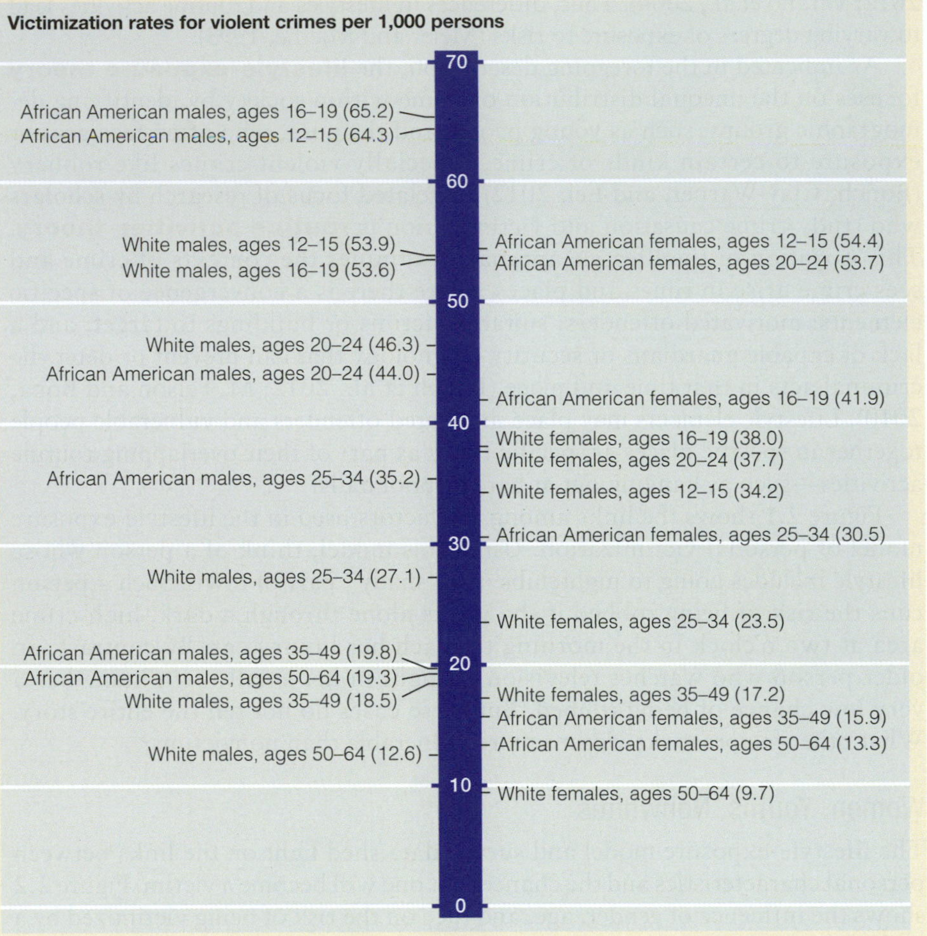

few valuables, and take precautions such as locking their doors. Thus, lifestyle opportunities and choices directly affect the chance of victimization.

Race is a key factor in exposure to crime. African Americans and other minorities are more likely than whites to be raped, robbed, and assaulted. The rate of violent crime victimization for whites is 22 per 1,000 people, compared to 25 per 1,000 for African Americans. Hispanics have a rate of violent victimization similar to African Americans, at 25 per 1,000 (Truman and Rand, 2014). Many white Americans are fearful of being victimized by African Americans (Skogan, 1995; Pickett, Chiricos, et al., 2012). However, most violent crime is intraracial: Two of every three victims are of the same race as their attacker (Figure 2.3). These figures do not reveal that there is a direct connection between race and crime. To the contrary, these numbers simply reflect that African Americans and whites often live in separate neighborhoods in this country. And, most importantly, African American neighborhoods are much more likely to be those experiencing what scholars call "high levels of socioeconomic disadvantage" with respect to unemployment, quality of schools, quality of housing, and other factors associated with income and wealth (Lauritsen and White, 2001: 53). These factors are often associated with higher levels of street crime, although, obviously, other kinds of crime, such as occupational crime and computer crime, appear mostly in other kinds of settings. These

FIGURE 2.3 VICTIMS AND OFFENDERS ARE OF THE SAME RACE IN 2 OUT OF 3 VIOLENT CRIMES

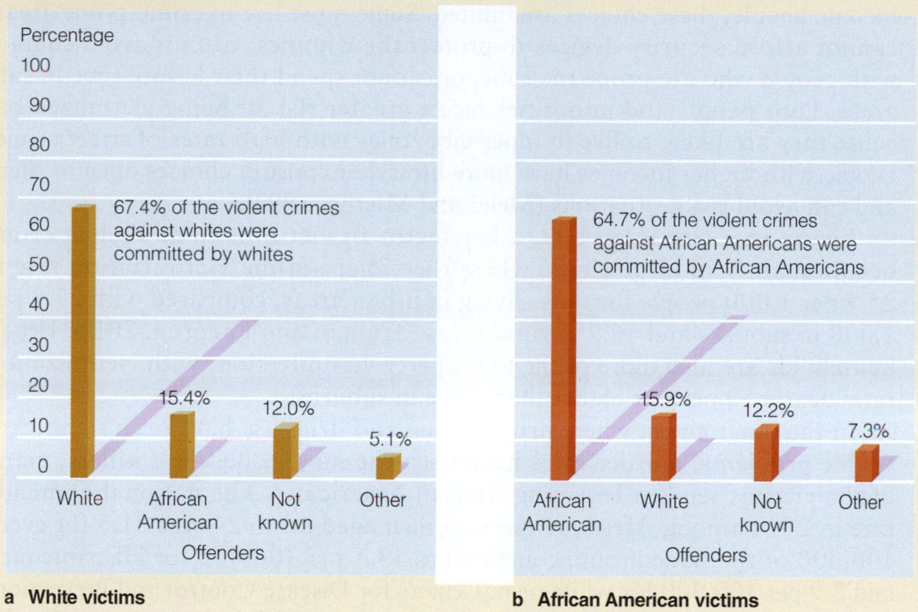

Although whites seem most fearful of being victimized by African Americans, most violent crime is intraracial. Why do people have such misperceptions?

Source: M. R. Rand and J. E. Robinson, *Criminal Victimization in the United States, 2008: Statistical Tables,* "Personal Crimes of Violence," Table 42 (Washington, DC: U.S. Department of Justice) May 2011.

same factors of race are also associated with property crimes: Most victims and offenders are of the same race and social class. The street crimes that people fear most occur among people who are in proximity to each other. Again, in modern America, many people come into contact mainly with others of the same race, especially in the neighborhoods in which they live.

Low-Income City Dwellers

Income is closely linked to exposure to violent crime. As Figure 2.4 shows, the lower the income, the more likely people are to be victims of crime, across

FIGURE 2.4 POVERTY AND RISK OF VICTIMIZATION

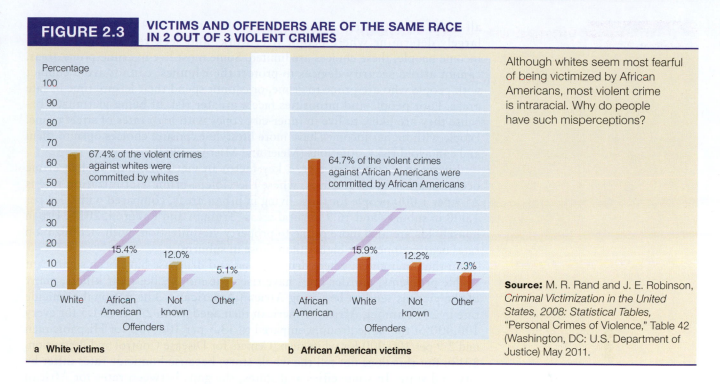

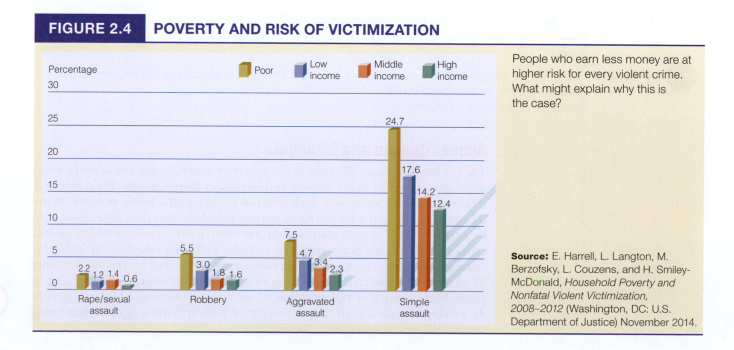

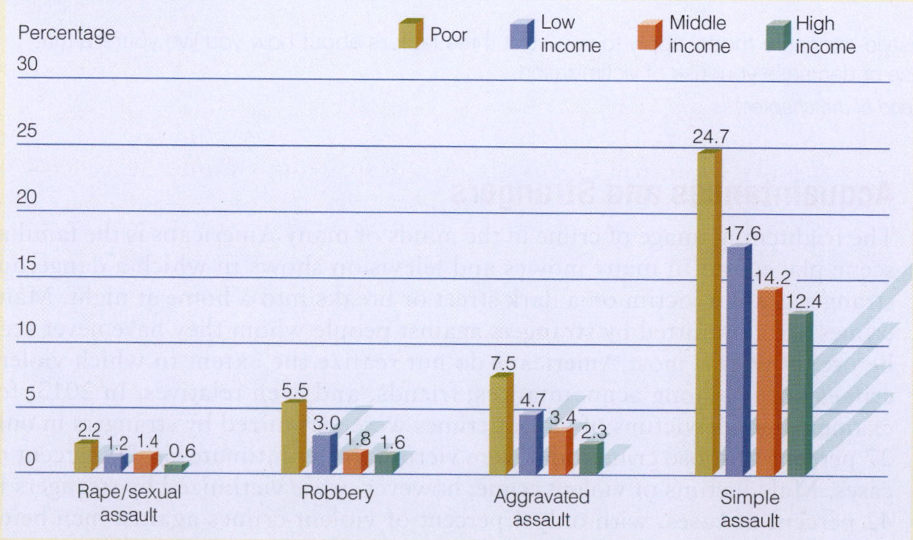

People who earn less money are at higher risk for every violent crime. What might explain why this is the case?

Source: E. Harrell, L. Langton, M. Berzofsky, L. Couzens, and H. Smiley-McDonald, *Household Poverty and Nonfatal Violent Victimization, 2008–2012* (Washington, DC: U.S. Department of Justice) November 2014.

all crime types (Harrell, Langton, Berzofsky, et al., 2014). Economic factors largely determine where people live, work, and seek recreation. For low-income people, these choices are limited. Some must live in crime-prone areas, cannot afford security devices to protect their homes, cannot avoid contact with people who are prone to crime, or cannot spend their leisure time in safe areas. Poor people and minorities face a greater risk of being victimized because they are likely to live in inner-city zones with high rates of street crime. People with higher incomes have more lifestyle-exposure choices open to them and can avoid risky situations (Meier and Miethe, 1993).

Living in a city is, in fact, a key factor in victimization. Violent crime occurs mainly in large cities, where the violent-crime victimization rate is 25.9 per 1,000 people for those living in urban areas, compared with 23.3 per 1,000 in suburbs and 16.9 in rural areas (Truman and Langton, 2014). Urban households are also more prone to property victimization, with victimization rates nearly 50 percent higher than those in suburbs.

In the inner cities, where drug dealing and drug use have been significant visible problems, murder rates have risen the most. Like their killers, many of the victims tend to be young African Americans. The national homicide rate in 2010 among African American men aged 10 to 24 was 51.5 for every 100,000 of the same group, compared to 13.5 per 100,000 for Hispanic men and 2.9 per 100,000 for white men (Centers for Disease Control and Prevention, 2013). But this does not tell the whole story, because homicide rates differ by city and state. In some cities and states, the gaps between rates for African Americans and whites are even greater.

Furthermore, we cannot conclude that crime rates will be equally high in all poor urban areas or that increases in poverty will necessarily result in increases in crime (Hipp and Yates, 2011). There is more crime in some poor areas than in others. Many factors besides poverty—such as home ownership rates, the physical condition of the neighborhood, the residents' attitudes toward society and the law, the extent of opportunities for crime, and social control by families and government—may affect the crime rate of a given area (Slocum, Rengifo, et al., 2013; Velez, Lyons, and Boursaw, 2012).

✔POINT

1. What are the main elements of the lifestyle-exposure model?
2. What are the characteristics of the group that is most victimized by violent crime? Of the least-victimized group?

STOP AND ANALYZE: How might the lifestyle-exposure model apply to you? List three factors about how you live your life that might either increase or decrease your risk of victimization.

(Answers are at the end of the chapter.)

Acquaintances and Strangers

The frightening image of crime in the minds of many Americans is the familiar scene played out in many movies and television shows in which a dangerous stranger grabs a victim on a dark street or breaks into a home at night. Many crimes are committed by strangers against people whom they have never seen before; however, most Americans do not realize the extent to which violent crimes occur among acquaintances, friends, and even relatives. In 2013, for example, female victims of violent crimes were victimized by strangers in only 27 percent of those crimes and were victimized by intimates in 20 percent of cases. Male victims of violent crime, however, were victimized by strangers in 42 percent of cases, with only 4 percent of violent crimes against men being committed by intimates (BJS, 2015b).

As we have seen, people's odds of being victimized depend in part on the people with whom they associate. An element of the lifestyle-exposure model includes consideration of the places that people frequent and the people with whom they interact. Some people increase their vulnerability to victimization by spending time with people who steal property and commit acts of violence. In the case of female victims, who suffer over 20 percent of their violent victimizations from intimate partners, this may mean that they misjudged their partners or that they could not anticipate how marital conflicts and other interpersonal stress would affect interactions and behavior. This does not mean, however, that these victims have necessarily chosen to place themselves at risk. Our legal system, at least theoretically, does not blame victims for the harms they suffer. Individuals who commit crimes, including domestic violence, are responsible for their own behavior.

There are other contexts in which people's risk of victimization is high because of the people with whom they associate, yet they cannot readily prevent such situations from arising. For example, people who live in neighborhoods with active drug trafficking may be acquainted with neighbors, former schoolmates, and even relatives who rob and steal because they have become dependent on illegal drugs and they need money to support their drug habits. When these acquaintances commit crimes, people who live nearby may find it difficult to avoid victimization. They cannot stop walking down the streets or avoid leaving their homes unoccupied and vulnerable to burglary when they go to work or school. Moreover, they may be reluctant to report

AP Images/Rod Aydelotte, Pool

Although Americans often fear violent victimization at the hands of strangers, most violence against women is perpetrated by those with whom they are intimate—husbands, boyfriends, and former lovers. What policies could address this problem?

some crimes because they fear that the offenders will take revenge. People may also be reluctant to report theft committed by a relative with a drug habit. They may be upset about losing their valuables, but they do not want to see their son, daughter, or cousin arrested and sent to prison. If the perpetrators of such crimes know that their relatives will not report them, they may feel encouraged to victimize these people further in order to support a drug habit. Prior relationships among people may facilitate some crimes and keep victims from seeking police assistance. In effect, life circumstances that are separate from lifestyle choices can greatly increase an individual's risk of victimization (G. S. Armstrong and Griffin, 2007).

Recurring Victimization

The understanding of crime victimization is complicated by the fact that victims do not experience crime in the same way. Obviously, victims are affected differently depending on the particular crime for which they were targeted. Someone shot in a robbery does not have the same experience as someone whose purse was stolen. More importantly, many people are victimized repeatedly whereas some people seldom or perhaps never experience crime victimization. In effect, a small portion of the population experiences a disproportionate share of crime through repeat victimization. Thus researchers are interested in this subject with the idea that the prevention of repeat victimization on these targeted individuals and locations may have significant benefits for overall crime prevention (G. Farrell, 1995).

repetitive victimization
The victimization of an individual or household by more than one crime during a relatively short period of time.

Scholars distinguish between **repetitive victimization** and revictimization (Daigle and Fisher, 2013). Repetitive victimization or repeat victimization refers to individuals who are victimized by crime more than once during a relatively brief period of time, such as within a year or less. An individual may be assaulted more than once or may experience property thefts within a short time after experiencing an assault or other crime. Some houses are burglarized repeatedly after burglars conclude that these properties are vulnerable targets. Repetitive victimization has implications for understanding the extent of harm suffered by some victims as well as raising questions about how individuals or locations come to be targeted. The neighborhood of residence and lifestyle factors can be associated with repetitive victimization (Daigle and Fisher, 2013).

revictimization
The victimization of an individual more than once over a long period of time, such as repeated incidents of domestic violence spread out over several years.

Revictimization refers to repeat offenses directed at an individual over a long period of time, such as domestic violence incidents directed at a spouse repeatedly but spread over a number of years (Daigle and Fisher, 2013). As in the foregoing domestic violence example, some instances of revictimization are attributable to violent crimes committed by family, friends, and acquaintances of the victim. Such situations create risks that observers will blame the victims for maintaining relationships or contact with those who have victimized them previously. Yet there are many complex reasons that victims may be unable to avoid family members, especially if the victims are young or financially dependent on others. So, too, adults may maintain personal relationships due to fear of increased abuse if they attempt to leave, or they may stay in an optimistic effort to improve the situation.

victim precipitation
The role of victims in fostering the context or triggering the action that led to their victimization in a crime.

One area of research for scholars has been **victim precipitation** or the role of victims in fostering the context or triggering the action that led to their victimization in a crime. What began with research on homicide and assault victims who may have thrown the first punch or hurled the first insult in an incident led to studies exploring other kinds of crimes, such as occur when people leave their houses unlocked or their keys in their cars (Muftic and Hunt, 2012). With respect to domestic violence and sexual assault, however, there are grave concerns that a victim-precipitation approach to analysis can reinforce stereotypes that blame women for their own victimization (Miethe, 1985; Grubb and Turner, 2012). Thus scholars who study revictimization must be aware of stereotypes about traditional gender roles as well as the complex circumstances of individual contexts and relationships. Although there may be situations in which observers can identify actions that a victim could have taken to reduce risk, the justice system is based on the principle that the offender, not victim, is responsible for criminal acts.

✔POINT

3. Which type of violent crime is most likely to be committed by nonstrangers?
4. Which type of crime is most likely to be committed by strangers?
5. Why is recurring victimization a significant concern to research scholars and policy makers?

STOP AND ANALYZE: After examining the issue of crimes committed by strangers and nonstrangers, do you have a different perception of the risks and causes of crime? Imagine you had to explain to a group the risks and frequency of certain crimes. List three points you would want to make about the matter of crimes by strangers and nonstrangers.

The Impact of Crime

Crime affects not only the victim but all members of society. We all pay for crime through higher taxes, higher prices, and fear. These factors impinge on key American values such as individual liberty and protection of private property and personal wealth. Thus, many people advocate crime-control policies as a means to restore American values.

As we have seen, crime can diminish our sense of liberty by making us fearful about going certain places, being out after dark, and trusting strangers. In addition, the money that we work so hard to earn is reduced by the costs of increased insurance premiums to cover thefts throughout society and increased taxes to pay for police and other government services. There may be other costs, too. For example, research shows an increased probability of people deciding to move to a new home after being victimized by a crime in their neighborhood (Dugan, 1999). Moving produces financial costs, personal costs in the loss of friendships and the social isolation of arriving in a new location, and the hassles of becoming settled in a new neighborhood, especially for a family with children. Estimating the precise impact of crime is difficult; however, it is clear that we all share the burdens of crime, and these burdens clash with long-held American values.

Costs of Crime

Crime has many kinds of costs. First, there are the economic costs—lost property, lower productivity, and the cost of medical care. Second, there are psychological and emotional costs—pain, trauma, and lost quality of life. Third, there are the costs of operating the criminal justice system.

It is extremely difficult to get a firm estimate of the costs of crime. Periodic studies by the government, industry, or university researchers tend to focus on only certain aspects of costs or certain kinds of crime. When one looks at the various surveys, however, it is clear that the costs of crime to society are staggering. The economic costs from crime in 2008 were estimated at $17.4 billion (Rand and Robinson, 2011: Table 82). However, this value only includes the property lost through events such as theft and vandalism. Costs associated with lost work time and medical expenses increase that value

TECHNOLOGY & CRIMINAL JUSTICE

HACKING OF CUSTOMER DATA

Several major retail chains have been the victims of major data breaches in recent years. In 2014, Home Depot reported a hacking event that resulted in the loss of 56 million customers' credit card numbers and 53 million email addresses. In the same year, Target Corporation revealed that a major data breach had allowed 100 million customer credit card numbers to be stolen along with the personal information associated with each account. Online auction house eBay lost the personal information of over 100 million members; but in this case, the company claims no financial information was compromised.

The increasingly widespread use of technology to make purchases leaves consumers and retailers vulnerable to hackers, who steal personal information and then sell it to others for illegal use. Theft of credit card numbers and other information can be especially prevalent during the winter holiday season, when retailers may sacrifice security in order to process large numbers of transactions during their busiest time of the year. Security experts warn that it only takes one knowledgeable hacker with a single computer to steal data from a major corporation.

The theft of this information results in huge profit losses for companies. Target is expected to have lost a total of $1 billion, after compensating victims, increasing security and insurance, and through the loss of customers who no longer trust the company to keep their data safe. The data breach experienced by eBay resulted in the loss of value in their stock in the weeks following the hack. eBay also experienced a hack on its site "Stubhub.com," which resulted in over $1 million of fraudulent sales. Retail outlets that have been victimized may mitigate their losses by increasing prices in their stores. Thus, consumers end up paying more for products as a result of stolen data.

Corporations can mount preventive measures by increasing security and keeping up with the latest technological advances, but this can be costly. Experts advise that companies collect the least amount of information from their customers, which can make

significantly. One study found that the resultant costs to government from shooting deaths and injuries exceeded $3.2 billion in 2010, because many victims' medical expenses are covered by government programs. In addition, there was $5.4 billion in lost tax revenue for governments because shooting victims were unable to work, and $4.7 billion in court costs for the criminal prosecutions after shooting incidents (Kennedy, 2013). Operating the overall criminal justice system costs taxpayers more than $210 billion a year to pay for police, courts, and corrections (Kyckelhahn, 2014). Further, in the aftermath of the September 11 tragedy, government costs increased as more money was spent on airport security, border patrols, and counterterrorism activities. These figures do not include the costs of occupational, organized, or cybercrime. For example, in 2013 cybercrime victims who contacted the Internet Crime Complaint Center reported losses in excess of $781 million (Internet Crime Complaint Center, 2014).

The surge in the use of technology by most Americans has increased the risk of personal financial loss if that technology were stolen. While technology can help the criminal justice system identify and prosecute offenders, it can also make individuals more prone to victimization. Read the Technology and Criminal Justice feature, "Hacking of Customer Data," to consider how our reliance on technology has increased the likelihood of victimization but also how it has enhanced society's ability to react to crime.

WHAT AMERICANS THINK

QUESTION: Is there any area right around here—that is, within a mile—where you would be afraid to walk alone at night?" (Responses from 2011 survey.)

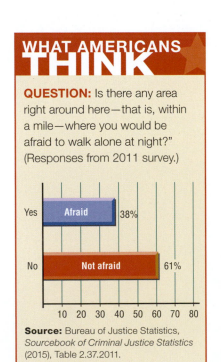

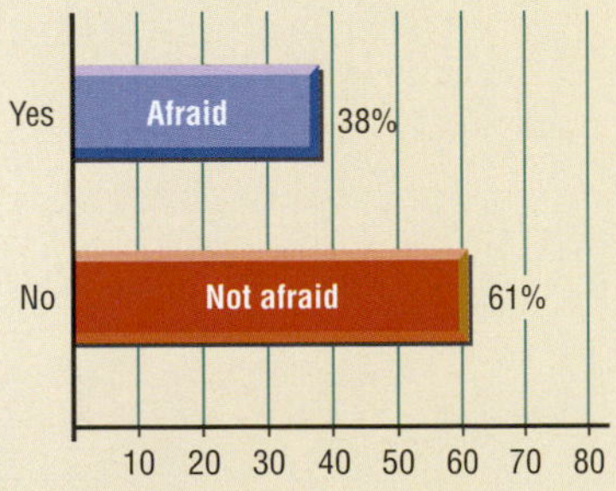

Source: Bureau of Justice Statistics, *Sourcebook of Criminal Justice Statistics* (2015), Table 2.37.2011.

Fear of Crime

One impact of crime is fear. Fear limits freedom. Because they are fearful, many people limit their activities to "safe" areas at "safe" times. Fear also creates anxieties that affect physiological and psychological well-being. What are the costs to people's quality of life if they spend time worrying about victimization every day? Given that the location of one's home has a significant effect on fear of crime (Scarborough et al., 2010), what is the cost of human suffering their databases less attractive targets for thieves. Consumers can protect themselves by regularly checking credit, debit, and bank statements for fraudulent charges; it is also prudent to avoid making purchases over Wi-Fi networks because they can be easily hacked. However, critics claim that the security used by credit card companies in the United States has lagged far behind that of European companies, which use an EMV chip to encrypt data. These recent breaches, however, have encouraged some banks to start issuing cards with data encryption chips.

Sources: "Arrests Made after eBay's Stubhub Suffers Cyber-Thefts," BBC.COM, July 23, 2014 (www.bbc.com); Rachel Abrams, "Target Puts Data Breach Costs at $148 Million, and Forecasts Profit Drop," *New York Times*, August 5, 2014 (www.nytimes.com); Kroll Inc., "Data Breach Prevention Tips," (www.kroll.com); Don Reisinger, "eBay Hacked, Requests All Users Change Passwords," *CNET Magazine*, May 21, 2014 (www.cnet.com); Anisha Sekar, "How to Protect Your Credit Card from a Data Breach," *U.S. News & World Report*, January 6, 2014 (www.usnews.com); Heather Somerville, "Retailers' Data Breaches Could Get 'Ugly' During Holiday Season," *San Jose Mercury News*, November 27, 2014 (www.mercurynews.com); Tom Groenfeldt, "American Credit Cards Improving Security with EMV, At Last," Forbes, January 28, 2014 (www.forbes.com); Veronica Waters, "Hearings Begins in Home Deport Data Breach," WSB Radio, January 16, 2015 (www.wsbradio.com).

DEBATE THE ISSUE

Data breaches of personal information target two victims—the corporation holding the data and the individual who owns the data. How much responsibility should retail companies take when data breaches occur? Corporations are victims in these types of crimes—should they be recognized as victims in the same way as individuals are? Should corporations be forced to repay fraudulent charges to consumers as a result of data theft? As you read the section "Causes of Crime" in this chapter, think about which of those theories would best explain this type of crime.

if people cannot get a good night's sleep because they awaken at every sound, fearing that an intruder is breaking in? The very people who face the least chance of being victimized by violent crime, such as women and the elderly, are often the most fearful (Miethe, 1995). All Americans do not experience the same fears, but many do adjust their daily activities to avoid being victimized. Elderly people, though, are at risk of being victimized by scam artists. Read the Close Up about victimization of the elderly and think about which explanations may best explain their victimization.

Since 1965, public opinion polls have asked Americans whether they "feel more uneasy" or "fear to walk the streets at night" (see "What Americans Think"). From 1972 to 1993, more than 40 percent of respondents indicated that fear of crime limited their freedom. Coinciding with the declining crime rates during the 1990s, the percentage of respondents who were fearful of walking near their homes dropped to 30 percent in 2001. Despite the improvement in quality of life indicated by the lower figure, this number still represents a significant segment of the American public. Further, the figure had risen to 38 percent by 2011.

A 2011 survey indicated nearly identical levels of fear among whites and African Americans concerning their risk of victimization for burglary and vehicle theft (BJS, 2015a). For some crimes, however, higher levels of fear are found among nonwhites and people with low incomes, the groups that are most likely to be victimized. In the 2011 survey, for example, 38 percent of African Americans feared that their children could be physically harmed at school, but only 30 percent of whites expressed the same fear. Thirty percent of African Americans frequently or occasionally feared being murdered, while the same was true for only 17 percent of whites. The most significant gap was evident for the 29 percent of African Americans who feared being victimized by a hate crime, when only 11 percent of whites had similar fears (BJS, 2015a: Table 2.39.2011). In 2002, the most recent year with race-specific data

CLOSE UP

VICTIMIZATION OF THE ELDERLY

Senior citizens have become attractive targets for scam artists looking to earn easy money; the elderly can also be subject to physical victimization by caretakers. As the baby boomer generation ages, the number of potential victims for scammers and abusers subsequently increases.

Many of these financial scams take advantage of older retirees, who may be living on a fixed budget and seeking to increase their income through reverse mortgages and the like. In general, senior citizens tend to be at home more often than other sectors of the population and are therefore more likely to be targeted in daytime telemarketing scams and door-to-door sales. In addition, health-care scams (those selling "cure-alls" or anti-aging drugs) prey on elderly people in poor health who may not be able to afford private health care. Scammers may pose as Medicare representatives to obtain private information from seniors or provide unauthorized services and keep funds paid to them by victims.

In one type of scam, con artists target those people who have already been victims of a scam. The offender approaches the victim, pretending to be a police officer investigating the crime. The "detective" tells the victim that the police department needs money from them to travel out of town to arrest a suspect; seniors are vulnerable to this kind of scam if they are not aware that police departments would never make such a request.

The elderly are also frequently victims of physical abuse, typically perpetrated against them by caretakers—mainly, family members or nursing-home staff. In Long Island, nine people were arrested for failing to respond to a medical alert alarm for two hours, which was signaling that a temporary resident's ventilator had become disconnected. The deceased's family was told she had died of a heart attack. The postmortem proved otherwise. Severe crimes lead to questions concerning the level of attention generally given by staff to patients in residential care settings and about how many uninvestigated incidents there are in which elderly residents may have been neglected at nursing homes. The owner of this particular nursing home is also accused of stealing money from Medicaid. He is suspected of pocketing government payments intended to help run the facility for his personal use. At other care facilities, elderly victims have been physically assaulted, and even raped. Abuse is more likely to occur against people who have physical or mental disabilities, who may be less likely to report such crimes to the police.

available on this question, 41 percent of African Americans but only 30 percent of whites expressed fears about walking at night in their own neighborhoods. In another study, 50 percent of those with incomes below $20,000 expressed these fears, while only 28 percent of those with incomes over $50,000 made such statements. These differences may reflect what people actually observe in their own neighborhoods. In addition, researchers suggest that the degree to which certain crimes are feared depends on two factors: the seriousness of the offense and the chances that it will occur. However, not all fears are based on realistic assessments of risk. For example, women and the elderly are more fearful than the average citizen, despite these groups' lower-than-average rates of victimization (BJS, 2015a: Table 2.38; Warr, 1993: 25). As you examine Table 2.1, consider how Americans' overall levels of fear for specific crimes compare to your own concerns.

Although crime rates are down, Americans' fears seem to exceed the actual victimization risks. People do not have a clear picture of the true risk of crime in their lives. They gain perceptions about crime from talk at their workplace and from politicians' statements and campaign promises. Their views about crime also seem to be shaped more by what they see on television than by reality (Chiricos, Padgett, and Gertz, 2000). Although fewer than 8 percent of victimizations are due to violent crime, such crimes are the ones most frequently reported by the media.

Most people do not experience crime directly but instead learn about it indirectly (Skogan and Maxfield, 1981). Local television news has a major impact on attitudes about crime (H. Kurtz, 1997). Fictional television dramas, such as the various *Law and Order* and *CSI* programs, may enhance the effect. In addition, television news magazine shows such as *Dateline* and *60 Minutes*

Some criminal justice agencies have created special task forces to investigate and prosecute crimes against the elderly. In California, the Los Angeles County District Attorney's Office provides special information to seniors to help them recognize legitimate businesses from those peddling scams. State legislatures have also been identifying gaps in their current laws that may allow abusers to escape punishment. For example, seniors can give a relative a "Power of Attorney" (POA), which allows that person to make legal decisions on their behalf in case they fall ill or become incapacitated. However, POAs are easily abused—lawmakers in Iowa have created laws specifically designed to prosecute individuals who have POA for elderly family members and misuse that power to steal funds from them. In Pennsylvania, laws are being passed that make it easier for elderly victims to sue those who have stolen from them in order to recoup some of their financial losses.

Thieves and abusers prey on the elderly due to the group's general vulnerability and dependence on others. The criminal justice system and state legislatures recognize that the elderly population is increasingly at risk of falling victim to financial scams and caretaker abuse. Current trends in public policy and increased attention to these issues may help reduce rates of financial theft and physical abuse of senior citizens in the United States.

Sources: Associated Press, "9 Arrested in L.I. Nursing Home Probe Following Patient's Death," CBS News, February 11, 2014 (http://newyork.cbslocal.com); CBS NewYork, "Aide Accused in Rape of Woman, 64, at Bronx Nursing Home," CBS News, February 18, 2014 (http://newyork.cbslocal.com); K. Brugger, "Better Protections for Vulnerable Victims," *Santa Barbara Independent*, February 27, 2014 (http://www.independent.com); Clay County (Florida) Sheriff's Office (http://www.claysheriff.com/CrimesAgainstElderly.asp); S. Tisinger, "Elder Abuse Bills 'Moving in the Right Direction,'" *Muscatine Journal*, March 4, 2014 (http://muscatinejournal.com); Los Angeles County (California) District Attorney's Office (http://da.co.la.us/seniors); National Center on Elder Abuse, U.S. Department of Health and Human Services (http://www.ncea.aoa.gov/); National Council on Aging, "Top 10 Scams Targeting Seniors" (http://ncoa.org); F. Sacco, "Proposed Bill Would Allow Elderly Victims of Fraud to Pursue Civil Action," *Observer-Reporter*, February 28, 2014 (http://www.observer-reporter.com).

DEBATE THE ISSUE

Should special punishments be leveled against offenders who target vulnerable groups such as the elderly? How can we better inform potential victims of the threats against them, particularly if this group is less likely to be engaged in technology and surfing the net than younger people?

TABLE 2.1 PERCENTAGE OF AMERICANS WHO FEAR DIFFERENT TYPES OF CRIME

How often do you, yourself, worry about the following things—frequently, occasionally, rarely, or never?

CRIMES	PERCENT RESPONDING "FREQUENTLY" OR "OCCASIONALLY"
Being the victim of identity theft	67%
Your home being burglarized when you are not there	47
Having your car stolen or broken into	44
Getting mugged	34
Having a school-aged child of yours physically harmed while attending school	32
Your home being burglarized when you are there	30
Being a victim of terrorism	30
Being sexually assaulted	22
Getting murdered	20
Being attacked while driving your car	19
Being the victim of a hate crime	17
Being assaulted or killed by a coworker or other employee while you are at work	6

Source: Bureau of Justice Statistics, *Sourcebook of Criminal Justice Statistics* (2015), Table 2.39.2011.

frequently have stories about crimes. Researchers believe that conversations with friends also tend to magnify the perception of local violence. Such conversations often focus on crimes against women, the elderly, and children. Stories about defenseless victims create a feeling that violent crime lurks everywhere.

Fear of crime is also linked to disorderly conditions in neighborhoods and communities (Skogan, 1990; Snedker, 2010; J. Q. Wilson and Kelling, 1982). As discussed by George Kelling and Catherine Coles, in urban areas, disorderly behavior—public drunkenness, public urination, aggressive panhandling, and menacing behavior—offends citizens and instills fear. Unregulated disorderly behavior may signal to citizens that an area is unsafe. Because of this fear, they "will stay off the streets, avoid certain areas, and curtail their normal activities and associations" (Kelling and Coles, 1996: 20). Avoidance of "unsafe" business areas may lead to store closings, decline in real estate values, and flight to more orderly neighborhoods. However, avoidance due to fear can help to reduce the likelihood an individual will be victimized or commit a crime in the future, thereby reducing violence overall (Melde, Berg and Esbensen, 2014).

Actions that might reduce the fear of crime are costly, and those who can best afford to protect themselves are those who are least threatened by crime. Some responses to the perceived risk of crime, such as staying at home after dark, may not seem costly; yet even such a simple measure is often far easier for the rich than for the poor. The rich tend to work during the day, with some control over their hours of work. Poorer people are more likely to work evenings and nights as waiters, security guards, or convenience store clerks. Other measures, such as moving to the suburbs, installing home security systems, and hiring private security companies, are also most available to those who possess financial resources.

✓POINT

6. What are some of the impacts of crime?

7. How is fear of crime shaped, and how does it relate to actual crime rates?

8. Why are poor people often less likely than others to take actions to reduce the risk of crime?

STOP AND ANALYZE: What is your perception of the level of crime in your neighborhood? How would you describe the risk of crime to someone who was interested in moving to your neighborhood? List three things that you would say to this person. What is the basis for your list? Perceptions? Personal experiences? Actual government statistics on crime?

The Experience of Victims within the Criminal Justice System

After a crime has occurred, the victim is often forgotten. Although victims may have suffered physical, psychological, and economic losses, the criminal justice system focuses on finding and prosecuting the offender.

Too often the system is not sensitive to the needs of victims. For example, defense attorneys may ask crime victims hostile questions and attempt to paint them, rather than the defendant, as causing the offense to occur. Likewise, although victims provide key evidence, the police may question them closely—and in a hostile fashion—to find out if they are telling the truth. Often a victim never hears the outcome of the case. Sometimes a victim comes face-to-face with the assailant, who is out on bail or on probation. This can be quite a shock, especially if the victim assumed that the offender was in prison.

Victims may be forced to miss work and lose pay in order to appear at judicial proceedings. They may be summoned to court again and again, only to

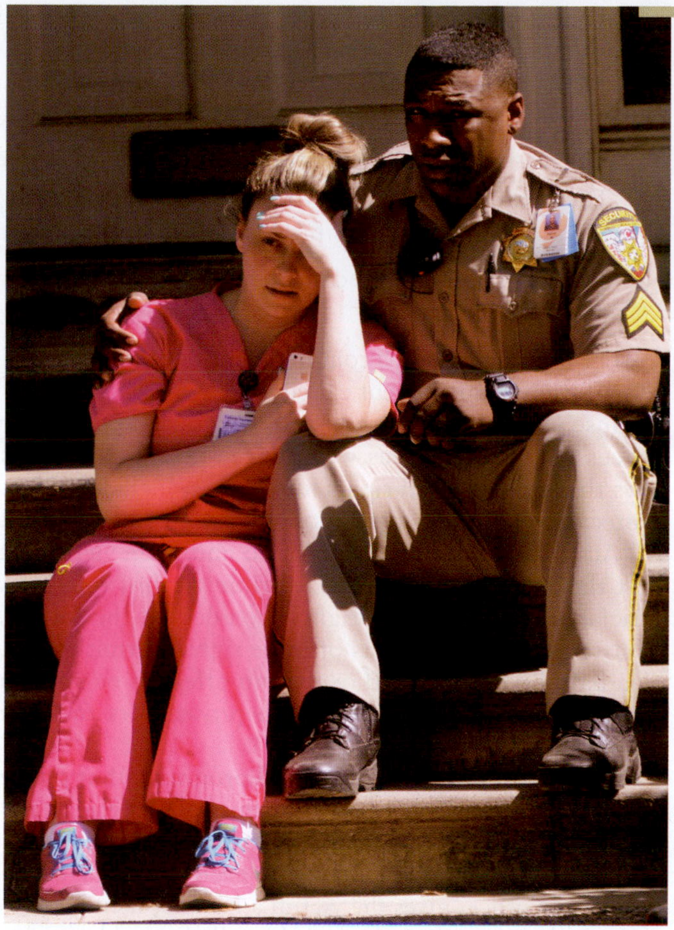

AP Images/John Walker

Officials in the criminal justice system must learn to use understanding and sensitivity when dealing with victims of crime. Police officers are often the first officials to encounter victims and it can be challenging to keep the victims' needs in mind as officers are also gathering evidence and pursuing criminal offenders. What kind of training do officers need in order to treat victims appropriately?

learn that the arraignment or trial has been postponed. Any recovered property may be held by the court for months as the case winds its way through the system. In short, after cases have been completed, victims may feel that they have been victimized twice, once by the offender and once by the criminal justice system.

During the past two decades, justice agencies have become more sensitive to the interests of crime victims. This has happened partly because victims often are the only witnesses to the crime and their help is needed. Many victims are not willing to provide such help if it involves economic and emotional costs. Some research indicates that victims are more likely to cooperate with the prosecutor if victims' assistance workers meet with them to provide comfort as well as information about how the court system operates (Erez and Roberts, 2013). Many victims' assistance workers are volunteers from the community. As you think about the issue presented in "Civic Engagement: Your Role in the System," consider what assistance you think should be provided to someone who has been traumatized by a criminal event.

In October 2004, President George W. Bush signed into law the Justice for All Act. The statute contains provisions concerning a variety of matters, such as DNA testing of offenders and compensation for people wrongly convicted of federal crimes. The statute also includes rights for crime victims in federal criminal cases. These rights include the following:

1. The right to be reasonably protected from the accused
2. The right to reasonable notice of any court proceeding, parole proceeding, release, or escape of the accused

CIVIC ENGAGEMENT

YOUR ROLE IN THE SYSTEM

Your roommate is having nightmares after witnessing a shooting in an unfamiliar part of town. Your friend rushed to aid the fallen victim and came home with his shirt soaked with the victim's blood. *Make a list of symptoms that you might look for as indicators of serious problems affecting someone who has witnessed or been victimized by a crime. Then note some things that might help such people recover from the event.* Go to the Special Victims' Recovery Project to see how victims' assistance volunteers in Sacramento deal with such situations.

3. The right not to be excluded from any court proceeding unless attendance might affect the victim's testimony
4. The right to be reasonably heard at any public proceeding regarding release, plea, sentencing, or parole
5. The reasonable right to confer with the federal prosecutor
6. The right to full and timely restitution as provided by law
7. The right to proceedings free of unreasonable delay
8. The right to be treated with fairness and with respect for the victim's dignity and privacy

The rights for victims contained in the statute resemble those in a proposed constitutional amendment called the Crime Victims' Bill of Rights. However, because Congress never took action to initiate the constitutional amendment process, these provisions were placed into a statute instead. All states have laws that provide legal rights for victims, including 32 states that have placed protections in their constitutions (Howley and Dorris, 2013). The Justice for All Act enhances communication to and from victims. It is notable, however, that the act does not authorize crime victims to file lawsuits if government officials fail to fulfill the rights provided by the statute. Only in limited circumstances will violations of these rights permit the victim to request that a plea bargain be rescinded or that an offender be resentenced. In effect, crime victims might have no way to make prosecutors and other court officials obey the statute.

Many states have implemented programs that give information, support, and compensation to victims. Information programs are designed (1) to sensitize justice officials to the need to treat crime victims courteously and (2) to let victims know what is happening at each stage of a case. In some states the investigating officer gives the victim a booklet listing the steps that will be taken and telephone numbers that can be called should questions arise.

Support matters most when the victim faces medical, emotional, or financial problems as a result of a crime. Such support comes from rape crisis centers, victims' assistance programs, and family shelters (Zweig and Yahner, 2013). These programs may be administered by courts, prosecutors' offices, or private agencies. These programs can face challenges in attempting to identify and provide services to victims from special populations, such as the homeless, rural residents, and victims with disabilities (J. A. Walsh and Muscat, 2013). Often these programs rely heavily on volunteers, who may not know enough to recognize the full range of victims' needs, especially the need for psychological assistance to deal with lingering emotional harm. In most states, compensation programs help victims of violent crime by paying the medical expenses of those who cannot afford them. When property has been stolen or destroyed, compensation programs encourage judges to order restitution by the offender as part of the sentencing. Some states also have victim–offender mediation programs to permit victims to express themselves and help offenders learn about the harmful consequences of their behavior (Lightfoot and Umbreit, 2004).

Crime victims can also file civil lawsuits against the offenders who injured them. Such lawsuits are not difficult to win, especially after an offender's guilt has been proven in a criminal case. However, most offenders cannot afford to pay restitution, especially if they are sitting in prison. Thus, victims typically do not receive full compensation for their losses and the continuing emotional harms that they suffer. See the Doing Your Part feature, "Crime Victims' Assistance Volunteer," for more on victims' rights; see also "A Question of Ethics," at the end of this chapter.

In response to the nation's economic downturn that began in 2007–2008, resulting budget reductions in state and local government posed particularly dire threats to many victims' assistance programs. When pushed to choose between cutting police and fire protection or cutting victims' services, it is no surprise that victims' services ended up on the chopping block. Officials in Texas used their state's crime victims' compensation fund to provide grants to victim-services agencies (previously funded by other state monies), and nearly depleted the monies available to crime victims (Mashhood and O'Rourke, 2013). Iowa's attorney general considered proposals to reorganize victims' services in the wake of reductions of more than $1.7 million in federal and state funding ("Attorney General," 2012). In King County, Washington, the largest share of proposed budget cuts in human services was directed at assistance for domestic violence survivors and sexual assault victims (Radford, 2010). In Los Angeles, budget cuts for victims' services led to greater reliance on volunteers, who may lack the expertise and training to be as effective as full-time professionals (Hunnicutt, 2010). These examples are repeated throughout the country, and current cuts may increase in the near future. These budget reductions illustrate the policy priorities of state and local government. When pressed to make choices, officials need to make sure that emergency-response and crime-prevention services are maintained. As a result, crime victims may bear even greater burdens as government is less willing or able to provide services.

DOING YOUR PART

CRIME VICTIMS' ASSISTANCE VOLUNTEER

When the prosecutor's office in Washington County, Oregon, sought to initiate a crime victims' assistance program in 2002, Rita and Vern Strobel became the first volunteers. The Strobels assist victims by accompanying them to court hearings, keeping them informed of the schedule for hearings and trials, explaining how the court system operates, and assisting with the paperwork necessary to get victims' compensation and other benefits.

In St. Louis, Missouri, the Bridgeway Sexual Assault Center provides emergency services to victims 24 hours per day, 7 days per week. Because police typically need to keep victims' clothing as evidence, Bridgeway volunteers provide victims with a change of clothes as well as emotional support. Local victims' assistance programs throughout the country rely on volunteers to provide comfort, support, and assistance to victims of crime. Some of these programs are administered by local prosecutors' offices, whereas others develop in neighborhood centers or faith centers. In 2003, a group of volunteers in Freehold, New Jersey, started a program to provide the homeless with a warm place to sleep in the winter. Today, six different houses of worship collaborate to provide food and shelter to those in need. In Jacksonville, Florida, 72-year-old Peg Chassman has helped her community in a number of ways, including speaking out for victimized children. In Lansing, Michigan, local volunteers assist at the Refugee Development Center to help individuals fleeing conflict in their home countries. Volunteers help children with homework, lead classes on English, and generally help refugees—many of whom have experienced victimization by conflict—adjust to American culture.

Agencies that administer victims' assistance programs are constantly searching for dedicated volunteers interested in serving their communities by helping their fellow citizens who are experiencing the trauma and crisis that accompanies crime victimization. The program in Travis County, Texas, for example, provides three evenings of training to prepare volunteers who commit to be on call for four-hour shifts four times per month.

Sources: J. Brown, "Any Time of the Night: Aerin Kaiser, GRCQB Award Winner," *Stlouisrams.com*, January 16, 2015 (http://stlouisrams.com); S. Cervenka, "Clergy Save Homeless from the Cold," *Asbury Park Press*, January 2, 2015 (http://app.com); S. Hillman, "Making a New Life in Lansing as a Refugee," *Capital Gains*, February 5, 2014; "Meet Your Neighbor: Shepherding Crime Victims," *Portland Oregonian*, April 4, 2002, p. 12; M. Ward, "Peg Chassman: Helping Those in Need with Access to Medicine," *Florida Times-Union*, April 21, 2011 (www.jacksonville.com); "Victim Services Unit Seeks Volunteers," KXAN-TV, July 17, 2012 (www.kxan.com).

✔POINT **9.** Why do some crime victims feel mistreated by the justice system?

10. What rights have been provided in federal criminal cases by the Justice for All Act?

STOP AND ANALYZE: If a "victim's right" is violated, as when the system fails to fulfill one of the promises in a victim's rights statute, who should be held responsible? How should those at fault be held responsible? List two things that should happen to police, prosecutors, or others if a victim's right is neglected or omitted as a criminal case is processed.

The Role of Victims in Crime

Victimologists study the role victims play in some crimes. Researchers have found that many victims behave in ways that invite the acts committed against them. Remember that routine activities theory, which was discussed earlier in this chapter, included a suitable target as a key element for creating a context in which crimes occur (Bunch et al., 2012). Victims' actions or inaction may contribute to making them targets of motivated offenders. This does not mean that it was the victim's fault that the crime occurred. It means instead that the victim's behavior may have increased the risk of the crime.

What do studies tell us about these situations? First, some people do not take proper precautions to protect themselves. For example, they leave keys in their cars or enter unsafe areas. Using common sense may be a requirement of living in modern society. Second, some victims provoke or entice another person to commit a crime. Third, some victims of nonstrangers are not willing to help with the investigation and prosecution. Although these behaviors do not excuse criminal acts, they do force us to think about other aspects of the crime situation.

Andrew Karmen points out that some victims are partly to blame for motor vehicle theft (2001). In some cases the victims are legally blameless, yet in others they have posed as victims to commit insurance fraud. Victim contributions to motor vehicle theft can include *negligence* (leaving the keys in the vehicle), *precipitation* (leaving the car in a vulnerable location so it can be stolen), and *provocation* (arranging to have a vehicle damaged or destroyed). According to Karmen, survey research indicates that 75 percent of vehicle owners have not installed alarms, 30 percent do not always lock their car doors, and 10 percent admit that they sometimes leave their keys in parked cars (2001).

Victimologists now recognize that victims play a key role—positive or negative—in many crimes. Research shows that their behavior may facilitate crimes (J. Kenny, 2012). On the other hand, resistance by some victims may prevent offenders from completing robberies and other crimes (Tark and Kleck, 2004).

Clearly, victims affect and are affected by crime in many ways. But victims represent only one of the many factors that help explain crime. We now turn to the major theories of the causes of crime.

✔POINT **11.** What victim behaviors can invite crime?

STOP AND ANALYZE: Do you observe your friends, roommates, or family members engaging in any behaviors that may provoke or precipitate crimes? List two such behaviors that you have personally observed.

Causes of Crime

Whenever news of a crime hits the headlines, whether the crime is a grisly murder or complex bank fraud, the first question is "Why did he (or she) do it?" Do people commit crimes because they are poor, greedy, mentally ill, or just plain stupid? If you look at any newspaper on a single day, you can see reports on a variety of crimes. For example, newspaper stories on March 21, 2013, reported on the targeted killing of the director of the Colorado Department of Corrections, who was shot when he opened the front door of his home; two high school seniors in Connecticut accused of sexually assaulting 13-year-old girls; and the imprisonment of a political consultant convicted of stealing $750,000 in campaign funds from New York City Mayor Michael Bloomberg (Healy, 2013; A. Baker, 2013; Buettner, 2013). Can we link all of these crimes to a single cause? Are there differences between the motivations for these crimes and the causes of other offenses, such as a young man who sells illegal drugs or a repeat sex offender who kidnaps and murders a young child? These and similar difficult questions serve as the focus of the field of academic study known as *criminology.*

Criminology centers on learning about criminal behavior, the nature of offenders, and how crime can be prevented. Research focuses mainly on the offender. Fewer questions are asked about how factors such as the economy, government policy, family, and education affect crime (Messner and Rosenfeld, 2006). In this section we look at the two major schools of criminological thought—classical and positivist. We then examine biological, psychological, sociological, and life course theories of the causes of criminal behavior. Finally, we explore the relationship between gender and crime and assess the various theories that help understand gender differences in criminality.

Classical and Positivist Theories

Two major schools of criminological thought are the classical and positivist schools. Each was pioneered by scholars influenced by the dominant intellectual ideas of their times.

The Classical School

Until the eighteenth century, most Europeans explained criminal behavior in supernatural terms—as the work of the devil. Those who did wrong were "possessed" by the devil. Some Christians believed that all humanity had fallen with Adam and had remained in a state of total depravity ever since. Indictments often began, "[John Doe], not having the fear of God before his eyes but being moved and seduced by the instigation of the devil, did commit [a certain crime]." Such approaches to crime stemmed from a clear differentiation between good people and evil people. In addition, by attributing crime to the devil, this viewpoint did not allow for the possibility that lawbreakers could control their own behavior.

Before the eighteenth century, defendants had few rights. The accused had little chance to put forth a defense, confessions were obtained through torture, and the penalty for most offenses was physical punishment or death.

In 1764 Cesare Beccaria published his *Essays on Crime and Punishments;* this was the first attempt to explain crime in secular, or worldly, terms instead of religious terms. The book also pointed to injustices in the administration of criminal laws. Beccaria's ideas prompted reformers to try to make criminal law and procedures more rational and consistent. From this movement came **classical criminology**, whose main principles are as follows:

classical criminology
A school of criminology that views behavior as stemming from free will, that demands responsibility and accountability of all perpetrators, and that stresses the need for punishments severe enough to deter others.

1. Criminal behavior is rational, and most people have the potential to engage in such behavior.
2. People may choose to commit a crime after weighing the costs and benefits of their actions.

3. Fear of punishment is what keeps most people in check. Therefore, the severity, certainty, and speed of punishment affect the level of crime.
4. The punishment should fit the crime, not the person who committed it.
5. The criminal justice system must be predictable, with laws and punishments known to the public.

Classical ideas declined in the nineteenth century, partly because of the rise of science and partly because its principles did not take into account differences between individuals or the way the crime was committed.

Neoclassical Criminology

After remaining dormant for almost a hundred years, classical ideas took on new life in the 1980s, when America became more conservative. Some scholars argue that crimes may result from the *rational choice* of people who have weighed the benefits to be gained from the crime against the costs of being caught and punished. But they also recognize that the criminal law must take account of differences among individuals. To a large extent, sentencing reform, criticisms of rehabilitation, and greater use of incarceration stem from this renewed interest in classical ideas, or *neoclassicism*. However, the positivist school of thought has dominated American criminology since the start of the twentieth century.

Positivist Criminology

positivist criminology
A school of criminology that views behavior as stemming from social, biological, and psychological factors. It argues that punishment should be tailored to the individual needs of the offender.

By the middle of the nineteenth century, as the scientific method began to take hold, the ideas of the classical school seemed old-fashioned. Instead, **positivist criminology** used science to study the body, mind, and environment of the offender. Science could help reveal why offenders committed crimes and how they could be rehabilitated. Here are the key features of this approach:

1. Human behavior is controlled by physical, mental, and social factors, not by free will.
2. Criminals are different from noncriminals.
3. Science can be used to discover the causes of crime and to treat deviants.

Positivism has served as the foundation for many types of theories, which we explore in the following sections. Understanding the main theories of crime causation is important because they affect how laws are enforced, guilt is determined, and crimes are punished. As we describe each of the theories, consider its implications for crime policies. For example, if biological theories are considered sound, then the authorities might try to identify potential offenders through genetic analysis and then segregate or supervise them. On the other hand, the acceptance of sociological theories might lead to efforts to end poverty, improve education, and provide job training.

✔POINT **12.** What were the main assumptions of the classical school?
13. What are the main assumptions of the positivist school?

STOP AND ANALYZE: As you think about crime, do you see criminals as rational—namely, do they weigh the costs and benefits of their actions before deciding to commit a crime? Alternatively, do you believe other reasons likely lead to most crimes? Give two examples to support your view.

Biological Explanations

The medical training of Cesare Lombroso (1836–1909) led him to suppose that physical traits distinguish criminals from law-abiding citizens. He believed that some people are at a more primitive state of evolution and hence are born criminal. These "throwbacks" have trouble adjusting to modern society. Lombroso's ideas can be summarized as follows (Lombroso, 1968 [1912]):

1. Certain people are born criminals with **criminogenic traits**.
2. They have primitive physical traits such as strong canine teeth, huge jaws, and high cheekbones.
3. These traits are acquired through heredity or through alcoholism, epilepsy, or syphilis.

criminogenic traits
Factors thought to bring about criminal behavior in an individual.

Around the turn of the twentieth century, researchers studying crime turned their attention from physical traits to inherited traits that affect intelligence. Some scholars believed that criminals commit crimes to alleviate pathological urges inherited from mentally defective ancestors. They studied genealogies to find the links between these traits and the criminal records of family members.

Two studies, first published in 1875 and 1902, of families with the fictitious names of Jukes and Kallikak, presented evidence that genetic defects passed on to offspring could condemn them to lives of crime. Richard Dugdale studied more than 1,000 descendants of the woman he called Ada Jukes, whom he dubbed the "mother of criminals." Among them were 280 paupers, 60 thieves, 7 murderers, 140 criminals, 40 people with venereal diseases, and 50 prostitutes (Dugdale, 1910). Similar data collected by Henry H. Goddard (1902) supported the belief that the Kallikak family, whose members were all related to the illegitimate son of Martin Kallikak, contained more criminals than did the descendants of Martin's later marriage into a "good" family.

These early studies may no longer seem credible to us, but they were taken seriously in their time and affected criminal justice for decades. For example, many states passed laws that required repeat offenders to be sterilized. It was assumed that crime could be controlled if criminal traits were not passed from parents to children. Not until 1942 did the U.S. Supreme Court declare required sterilization unconstitutional (*Skinner v. Oklahoma*).

Renewed Interest in Biological Explanations

Although **biological explanations** of crime were ignored or condemned as racist after World War II, they have attracted renewed interest. *Crime and Human Nature,* by James Q. Wilson and Richard Herrnstein, reviews the research on this subject (J. Q. Wilson and Herrnstein, 1985). Unlike the early positivists, the authors do not claim that any one factor explains criminality. Instead, they argue that biological factors predispose some people to a crime. Genetic makeup, body type, and IQ may outweigh social factors as predictors of criminality (Beaver et al., 2008). The findings of research on nutrition, neurology, genetics, and endocrinology give some support to the view that these factors may contribute to violent behavior in some people (P. A. Brennan, Mednick, and Volavka, 1995: 65). Other researchers have identified physiological factors associated with antisocial behavior, which they see as a step toward considering a possible link between biology and offending (Cauffman, Steinberg, and Piquero, 2005).

biological explanations
Explanations of crime that emphasize physiological and neurological factors that may predispose a person to commit crimes.

These new findings have given biological explanations a renewed influence and reduced the dominance of sociological and psychological explanations. Scientists are doing further research to see if they can find biological factors that make some people prone to violence and criminality (J. C. Barnes, Beaver, and Boutwell, 2011; Fishbein, 1990). For example, a study published in 2002 found that a single gene can help predict which abused children will become violent or antisocial adults. Although most abused children do not commit crimes, studies indicate that abused children are twice as likely as other children to commit crimes later in life. Maltreated children with a specific gene identified in the study were less likely to be violent as adults compared to other abused children (Caspi et al., 2002). This study provides evidence that genetic makeup may "protect" some individuals from engaging in violent behavior, even if they have experienced events that increase criminality; and it provides an interesting indication of how genetic factors (such as a specific gene) may interact with life experiences (such as victimization by child abuse) to trigger or facilitate later criminal behavior.

Contemporary research does not merely look at genes as providing a biological basis for behavior that can lead to crime. Researchers also examine specific physical and environmental conditions that affect the human body and thereby potentially influence behavior. In one obvious example, individuals who receive certain kinds of head injuries or suffer from tumors in particular locations of the brain can experience impairments affecting their knowledge, perception, and behavior. Other people may have abnormal levels of certain chemicals in their brains that affect hyperactivity, irritability, and risk-taking behavior. If such conditions are diagnosed and people have access to treatment, doctors may prescribe certain drugs to counteract the chemical imbalance. People who suffer from specific medical conditions, such as attention-deficit hyperactivity disorder (ADHD), may be prone to aggressiveness and impulsive behavior that can lead to the violation of criminal laws, such as fighting, substance abuse, and improper operation of motor vehicles (Vogel and Messner, 2012). Their problems may be compounded if they come from poor families in which they lacked opportunities for diagnosis, treatment, and supervision.

Other studies examine links between nutrition and behavior. Many studies explore possible connections between sugar consumption or vitamin deficiencies and aggressiveness, intelligence, or specific psychological problems. For example, one study found that consumption of fish rich in omega-3, such as salmon, is associated with lower levels of hostility in young adults (Iribarren et al., 2004). A study of young offenders in a British prison found a decrease in antisocial behavior among those who received vitamins and nutritional supplements (Gesch et al., 2002). Such studies raise interesting possibilities for affecting some potential offenders through greater understanding of the links between diet and behavior.

Studies also examine environmental influences on brain development and behavior. Herbert Needleman, a medical researcher who has studied the effects of lead on children for 30 years, stated in a 2005 report to the American Association for the Advancement of Sciences that "when environmental lead finds its way into the developing brain, it disturbs neural mechanisms responsible for regulation of impulse. That can lead to antisocial and criminal behavior" (University of Pittsburgh Medical Center, 2005). Medical researchers have long known that children's exposure to lead paint affects brain development, but Needleman's research has found a link between lead exposure and juvenile delinquency. Because people in modern society are exposed to lead and other chemicals through polluted air and water, factory operations, and other sources, additional research on exposure to environmental contaminants may steer researchers to greater understanding of the connections between chemical effects on the human body and antisocial behavior.

Policy Implications of Biological Explanations

A policy based on biological theories of crime would attempt to identify people who have traits that make them prone to crime and then treat or control those people. This might lead to selective incarceration, intensive supervision, or drug therapies. Special education might be required for those with learning disabilities. In addition, research concerning environmental influences on the human body, such as excessive exposure to lead or the need for better nutrition, could produce policies that attempt to limit environmental harms and provide better nutrition and medical care for targeted populations. Because modern research has never established a simple connection between biology and criminality, however, these policy approaches are highly problematic. As indicated by the Caspi et al. study, there are genetic markers that appear to indicate *lower* levels of violent behavior—how could policy be created that is relevant to those kinds of genetic factors? Moreover, there appears to be an interaction between life experiences and genetic indicators of criminality—in some cases, negative life experiences can "turn on" a genetic predisposition to crime. Thus, basing policies merely on the gene or some other biological connection would lead to the treatment or punishment of too many people.

POINT 14. What were the main elements of Lombroso's theory?

STOP AND ANALYZE: The recent attention to biological and genetic factors demonstrates a broad use of science in examining possible causes for crime. If we accept these recent research studies, do they seem to relate to all kinds of crime or only to specific kinds of criminal behavior? List two kinds of crime that might flow from the findings about brains, nutrition, and other biological factors. List two kinds of crime that seem more likely to flow from other underlying causes.

Psychological Explanations

People have often viewed criminal behavior as being caused by a mental condition, a personality disturbance, or limited intellect. **Psychological explanations** of crime center on these ideas.

psychological explanations Explanations of crime that emphasize mental processes and behavior.

AP Images/Steve Helber

George Huguely, a former University of Virginia lacrosse player, was convicted of second-degree murder and sentenced to 23 years in prison in 2012 for the beating death of his ex-girlfriend, Yeardley Love, also a University of Virginia varsity athlete. Does criminological theory help us to understand what motivated a privileged, prominent student-athlete to commit this act?

Before the eighteenth century, as we have seen, those who engaged in such behavior were thought to be possessed by demons. However, some scholars suggested that defects in the body and mind caused people to act "abnormally." One early advocate of this idea was Henry Maudsley (1835–1918), an English psychologist who believed that criminals were "morally insane." Moral insanity, he argued, is an innate characteristic, and crime is a way of expressing it. Without crime as an outlet, criminals would become insane (Maudsley, 1974).

Sigmund Freud (1856–1939), now seen as one of the foremost thinkers of the twentieth century, proposed a *psychoanalytic theory* that crime is caused by unconscious forces and drives. Freud also claimed that early childhood experiences greatly affected personality development. He theorized that the personality is made up of three parts: the id, ego, and superego (Freud, 1923). The id controls drives that are primarily sexual, the ego relates desires to behavior, and the superego (often referred to as the conscience) judges actions as either right or wrong. Psychoanalytic theory explains criminal behavior as resulting from either an undeveloped or an overdeveloped superego. For example, a person who commits a violent sex crime is thought to have an undeveloped superego, because the urges cannot be controlled. Alternatively, a person with an overdeveloped superego may suffer from guilt and anxiety. To reduce the guilt, the person may commit a crime, knowing that punishment will follow. To ensure punishment, the offender will unconsciously leave clues at the crime scene. Psychoanalysts say this occurred in the famous Loeb–Leopold murder of Bobby Franks in 1924 (Regoli and Hewitt, 1994).

Psychiatrists have linked criminal behavior to such concepts as innate impulses, psychic conflict, and the repression of personality. Such explanations propose that crime is a behavior that takes the place of abnormal urges and desires. Although the psychological approach takes many different forms, all are based on the idea that early personality development influences later behavior.

NEW DIRECTIONS IN CRIMINAL JUSTICE POLICY

EVIDENCE-BASED PRACTICES AND VICTIM SERVICES

Many treatment and counseling program options are available to people who have been victims of crime. While most programs designed to help victims are well intended, it is not always clear whether they actually achieve the goals they are designed to meet. The only way to be certain that programs are effective is to collect data that measure program results and then make evidence-based decisions related to those findings. Increasingly, victim services agencies are incorporating evidence from academic research to help select and develop their programs. For example, the Domestic Violence Evidence Project (http://www.dvevidenceproject.org) uses science-based evaluations to identify promising programs that reduce domestic violence. One such program, Caminar Latino, is aimed specifically at Latino women, men, and children living in Georgia. Evaluations of this program indicate that individuals who complete its training have an increased awareness of personal safety and are more aware of domestic violence and strategies they can use to increase their safety (National Resource Center on Domestic Violence, 2012).

One important finding from academic research is that there are several different types of domestic violence, and each one requires a different response by criminal justice and advocacy agencies. According to researcher Michael P. Johnson (2008), there are four categories of domestic violence: intimate terrorism, violent resistance, situational couple violence, and mutual violent control. *Intimate terrorism* is likely what comes to mind when people think about domestic violence—a male abuser holding emotional and physical control over a female victim. It is this model on which most domestic violence programs are based. Programs to provide emergency shelter to female victims assume they require shelter. However, in the case of *situational couple violence*—in which both parties are mutually combative with low levels of violence—each person may be considered both "offender" and "victim," and the usual services provided may not be appropriate. In cases such as these, research suggests that couples counseling may be a suitable option, although it would not be the correct service for a couple

Psychopathology

The terms *psychopath, sociopath,* and *antisocial personality* refer to a person who is unable to control impulses, cannot learn from experience, and does not feel emotions, such as love. This kind of person is viewed as psychologically abnormal, as a crazed killer or sex fiend.

During the 1940s, after several widely publicized sex crimes, many state legislatures passed "sexual psychopath laws" designed to place "homicidal sex fiends" in treatment institutions. Such laws were later shown to be based on false assumptions. They reveal the political context within which the criminal law is fashioned (Sutherland, 1950).

Psychological theories have been widely criticized. Some critics point to the fact that measuring emotional factors is difficult, as is identifying people thought to be prone to crime. Others note the wide range of theories—some contradicting one another—that take a psychological approach to crime.

Policy Implications of Psychological Explanations

Despite the criticisms, psychological explanations have played a major role in criminal justice policy during the twentieth century and beyond. The major implication of these theories is that people with personality disorders should receive treatment, while those whose illegal behaviors stem from learning should be punished so that they will learn that crime is not rewarded.

Policies that stress rehabilitation attempt to change the offender's personality and, hence, behavior. From the 1940s to the mid-1970s, psychotherapy, counseling, group therapy, behavior modification, and moral development programs were used in efforts to rehabilitate criminals. However, the past three decades have seen less reliance on these policies, except as a justification to confine repeat sex offenders even after they have served their full criminal

engaged in a relationship characterized by intimate terrorism. The evidence indicating that there are different types of domestic violence can help determine the most appropriate service for each victim's situation.

Services personnel also rely heavily on program evaluations and feedback provided by victims. This type of evidence can help improve the services received by victims at each stage of the process. The Sexual Assault Response Team in San Diego, California, asks victims to rate the service they received from police, trauma personnel, and crisis counselors. The feedback from clients is used in conjunction with other data sources collected from police, health-care systems, and advocacy organizations to ensure that the services provided to victims are effective (San Diego County, 2012).

While there are many good notions about what services are most effective and most useful to victims, it is vital that evidence from research be used to develop services appropriate to all victims, and to recognize that different victims have different needs. Only through careful analysis of "what works," can governments and community groups develop services that can truly help victims of crime recover.

Sources: M. P. Johnson. *Typologies of Domestic Violence* (Boston: Northeastern University Press, 2008); National Resource Center on Domestic Violence, *Program and Practice Profiles: Caminar Latino.* (Harrisburg, PA: National Resource Center on Domestic Violence, 2012). Retrieved January 14, 2015 (www.dvevidenceproject.org); San Diego County (2012, November). Sexual Assault Response Team Systems Review Committee Report, 2008–2011 (http://www.sandiegocounty.gov/hhsa/programs/phs/emergency_medical_services/sexual_assault_response_team.html).

DEBATE THE ISSUE

Social science research is vitally important for determining whether specific programs are working as intended; however, some victim advocates have expressed concern that surveying and studying victims can be harmful, particularly if individuals are asked to recall details of their victimization. Should researchers be interviewing victims to determine if individual needs were served by victim service agencies? How can researchers demonstrate sensitivity to victims when doing this kind of research?

sentences. The reentry of sex offenders into the community poses difficult challenges as legislators react to highly publicized crimes by troubled individuals without necessarily looking closely at evidence-based practices. As you read the New Directions in Criminal Justice Policy feature, "Evidence-Based Practices in Victim Services," consider what you regard as appropriate policies for helping victims deal with the aftermath of crime.

CHECKPOINT **15.** What is meant by the term *psychopath*?

STOP AND ANALYZE: Think of the example of Aaron Ybarra and the shooting at Seattle Pacific University that opened this chapter. Ybarra had been under the care of a psychiatrist—should that fact affect how he is punished? Should he receive psychological treatment or otherwise be treated differently than other murderers? List two reasons for your answers to these questions.

Sociological Explanations

sociological explanations
Explanations of crime that emphasize the social conditions that bear on the individual as causes of criminal behavior.

In contrast to psychological approaches, **sociological explanations** focus on the way that belonging to social groups shapes people's behavior. Sociologists believe that criminality results from external factors rather than from inborn influences. Thus, sociological theories of crime assume that contact with the social world, as well as such factors as race, age, gender, and income, molds the offender's personality and actions.

Social theorist Emile Durkheim (1858–1917) argued that when a simple rural society develops into a complex urbanized one, traditional standards decline. Some people cannot adjust to the new rules and will engage in criminal acts.

In the 1920s a group of researchers at the University of Chicago looked closely at aspects of urban life that seemed linked to crime: poverty, bad housing, broken families, and the problems faced by new immigrants. They found high levels of crime in those neighborhoods that had many opportunities for delinquent behavior and few legitimate means of earning a living.

From a sociological perspective, criminals are made, not born. Among the many theories stressing the influence of societal forces on criminal behavior, three types deserve special mention: social structure theories, social process theories, and social conflict theories.

Social Structure Theories

social structure theories
Theories that attribute crime to the existence of a powerless lower class that lives with poverty and deprivation and often turns to crime in response.

Social structure theories suggest that criminal behavior is related to social class. People in various social classes have quite different amounts of wealth, status, and power. Those in the lower class suffer from poverty, poor education, bad housing, and lack of political power. Therefore, members of the lower class, especially the younger members, are the most likely to engage in crime. Crime thus is created by the structure of society.

anomie
A breakdown in and disappearance of the rules of social behavior.

Sociologist Robert Merton extended Durkheim's ideas about the role of social change and urbanization on crime. He stressed that social change often leads to a state of **anomie**, in which the rules or norms that guide behavior have weakened or disappeared. People may become anomic when the rules are unclear or they are unable to achieve their goals. Under such conditions, antisocial or deviant behavior may result.

It is said, for example, that American society highly values success but makes it impossible for some of its members to succeed. It follows that those who are caught in this trap may use crime as a way out. Theorists believe that this type of situation has led some ethnic groups into organized crime. Others argue that social disorganization brings about conditions in which, among other things, family structure breaks down, alcohol or drug abuse becomes more common, and criminal behavior increases. They assert that poverty must be ended and the social structure reformed if crime is to be reduced.

Contemporary Theories Contemporary theorists have drawn from social structure concepts and Merton's anomie theory to develop certain theories of crime causation. Prominent among modern approaches is the general theory of strain (S. K. Matthews, 2011). According to this approach, negative relationships can lead to negative emotions. These emotions, particularly anger, are expressed through crime and delinquency. *Strain* results from the failure to achieve valued goals, which may particularly affect poor people in a society that values financial success. Strain is also produced by negative experiences, including unemployment, child abuse, criminal victimization, and family problems, which also may prevail in poor communities. Under the theory, those who cannot cope with negative experiences may be predisposed to criminal behavior (Listwan et al., 2013; Liska and Messner, 1999).

As these ideas have become more refined, they have been applied to white-collar crime. Although one may assume that the affluent would benefit most from American social structure, theorists have raised this question: Do business people measure their success against the wealth and power of those that they see above them in their corporate settings and affluent communities? To achieve even higher levels of success in a structure that values ever-increasing wealth, individuals may break rules and violate laws in order to enhance their personal success. Thus, structure theories have been used to explain the behavior of corporate leaders who manipulate stock prices and take other actions to add to their wealth, despite already being millionaires (Liska and Messner, 1999).

Policy Implications of Social Structure Theories If crime is caused by social conditions, then actions should be taken to reform the conditions that breed crime. Such actions include policies to combat the effects of poverty, including education and job training, urban redevelopment, better health care, and economic development. Theorists who apply structural theories to white-collar crime are likely to see such criminality as an inevitable component of a society with a free-market economy that equates wealth with success.

Social Process Theories

Many criminologists believe that the social structure approach does not adequately explain criminality by middle-class and affluent people. They fear that a focus on social structure erroneously presents crime as a problem mainly of the poor. **Social process theories**, which date from the 1930s but did not gain recognition until the 1960s and 1970s, assume that any person, regardless of education, class, or upbringing, has the potential to become a criminal. However, some people are more likely to commit criminal acts because of the circumstances of their lives. Thus, these theories try to explain the processes by which certain people become criminals.

social process theories
Theories that see criminality as normal behavior. Everyone has the potential to become a criminal, depending on (1) the influences that impel one toward or away from crime and (2) how one is regarded by others.

Three Social Process Theories There are three main types of social process theories: learning theories, control theories, and labeling theories.

Learning theories hold that criminal activity is learned behavior. Through social relations, some people learn how to be a criminal and acquire the values associated with that way of life. This view assumes that people imitate and learn from one another. Thus, family members and peers are viewed as major influences on a person's development.

learning theories
Theories that see criminal behavior as learned, just as legal behavior is learned.

theory of differential association
The theory that people become criminals because they encounter more influences that view criminal behavior as normal and acceptable than influences that are hostile to criminal behavior.

control theories
Theories holding that criminal behavior occurs when the bonds that tie an individual to society are broken or weakened.

labeling theories
Theories emphasizing that the causes of criminal behavior are found not in the individual but in the social process that labels certain acts as deviant or criminal.

social conflict theories
Theories that assume criminal law and the criminal justice system are primarily a means of controlling the poor and the have-nots.

CIVIC ENGAGEMENT

YOUR ROLE IN THE SYSTEM

Imagine that your state's governor has identified you as a local community leader and asked you to serve on your county's juvenile crime prevention council. Your team is tasked with suggesting and planning programs to prevent youth crime. *Which theories of crime causation would provide the basis for your suggestions? Make a list of three suggestions to prevent youth crime, and identify which theory or theories of crime causation relate to each suggestion.* Then examine the website of the North Carolina Juvenile Crime Prevention Councils to see what programs are actually being advanced in that state.

In 1939 Edwin Sutherland proposed a type of learning theory called the **theory of differential association**, which states that people learn behavior through interactions with others, especially family members (Sutherland, 1947). Criminal behavior occurs when a person encounters others who are more favorable to crime than opposed to it. If a boy grows up in a family where, say, an older brother is involved in crime, he will tend to learn criminal behavior. If people in the family, neighborhood, and gang believe that illegal activity is not shameful, this belief increases the chance that the young person will engage in crime.

Control theories hold that social links keep people in line with accepted norms (M. Gottfredson and Hirschi, 1990; Hirschi, 1969). In other words, all members of society have the potential to commit crime, but most are restrained by their ties to family, church, school, and peer groups. Thus, sensitivity to the opinion of others, commitment to a conventional lifestyle, and belief in the standards or values shared by friends all influence a person to abide by the law. A person who lacks one or more of these influences may engage in crime (Vogel and Messner, 2012).

Finally, **labeling theories** stress the social process through which certain acts and people are labeled as deviant. As Howard Becker notes, society creates deviance—and, hence, criminality—"by making the rules whose infraction constitutes deviance, and by applying those rules to particular people and labeling them outsiders" (Becker, 1963: 9).

Becker studied the process through which people become deviant. Social control agencies, such as the police, courts, and corrections, are created to label certain people as outside the normal, law-abiding community. When they have been labeled, those people come to believe that the label is true. They take on a deviant identity and start acting in deviant ways. Once labeled, the person is presumed by others to be deviant, and they react accordingly. This reinforces the deviant identity.

Labeling theory has generated criticism and debate. Many scholars question whether evidence exists to support the theory, especially when one looks broadly at the various kinds of activities and types of people involved in acts that constitute crimes.

Policy Implications of Social Process Theories If crime is a learned behavior, it follows that people need to be treated in ways that build conventional bonds, develop positive role models, and avoid labeling. Policies to promote stable families and develop community agencies to help those in need are based on this view. Examine the issue in "Civic Engagement: Your Role in the System" and consider whether social process theories—or other theories about the causes of criminal behavior—would provide the basis for suggestions that you make about how to reduce crimes committed by juveniles.

Social Conflict Theories

In the mid-1960s, the then-current biological, psychological, and sociological explanations of criminal behavior were challenged by **social conflict theories**. These theories assume that criminal law and the justice system are designed mainly to control the poor. The rich commit as many crimes as do the poor, it is argued, but the poor are more likely to be caught and punished. Those in power use the law to impose their version of morality on society in order to protect their property and safety. They use their power to change the definitions of crime to target acts they view as threatening.

Types of Social Conflict Theories There are different types of social conflict theories. One type, proposed by critical, radical, or Marxist criminologists, holds that the class structure causes certain groups to be labeled as deviant. In this view, "deviance is a status imputed to groups who share certain structural characteristics (e.g., powerlessness)" (Spitzer, 1975: 639). Thus, the criminal law is aimed at the behavior of specific groups or classes. One result is that the poor are deeply hostile toward the social order, and this hostility is one factor in criminal behavior. Moreover, when the status quo is threatened, legal definitions of crime are changed in order to trap those who challenge the system. For example, vagrancy laws have been used to arrest labor union organizers, civil rights workers, and peace activists when those in power believed that these groups threatened their interests.

Policy Implications of Social Conflict Theories Conflict theories require policies that would reduce class-based conflict and injustice. Policies to help women, the poor, and minorities deal with government agencies would follow. Criminal justice resources would focus on crimes committed by upper-class as well as lower-class offenders.

Like other theories about the causes of criminal behavior, sociological theories have met with criticism. Their critics argue that these theories are imprecise, unsupported by evidence, and based on ideology. Even so, sociological theories have served as the basis for many attempts to prevent crime and rehabilitate offenders.

✔POINT

16. What is the main assumption of social structure theories?
17. What is the main assumption of social process theories?
18. What is the main assumption of social conflict theories?

STOP AND ANALYZE: If it turns out sociological theories provide the most comprehensive or widely applicable explanations for crime causation, what, if anything, should government do to address the problem of crime? Give two examples or reasons for your answer.

Life Course Explanations

Life course theories seek to identify factors that shape criminal careers; these theories attempt to explain when and why offenders begin to commit crimes and to determine which factors lead individuals to stop their participation in crimes.

life course theories
Theories that identify factors affecting the start, duration, nature, and end of criminal behavior over the life of an offender.

Studies in this area often try to follow individuals from childhood through adulthood in order to identify the factors associated with beginning, avoiding, continuing, or ceasing criminal behavior (Loeffler, 2013). Criminal careers often begin at an early age; people who eventually become involved with crime often exhibit disruptive behavior, lack family support, and experiment with drinking and drugs as youths. Recent research explores associations between delinquent behavior by juveniles and the experience of having a father who has been imprisoned (Roettger and Swisher, 2011). Some theorists discuss *pathways* into crime, which may begin with minor habits of lying and stealing that lead to serious misbehavior. However, pathways into crime are not identical for all kinds of offenders (S. R. Maxwell and Maxwell, 2000). For example, those youths who engage in bullying and fighting may begin a pathway toward different kinds of crimes and criminal careers than do those who start out using and selling drugs.

The factors identified by life course theorists that can impact criminal careers can overlap with factors discussed in psychological, social structure, and social process theories, such as unemployment, failure in school, impulsiveness, and unstable families. In other words, life course theorists' ideas about factors associated with criminal behavior are consistent with factors identified in other theories. However, these theorists study criminal behavior from a broader perspective as something that develops, evolves, changes, and sometimes ends over the course of a person's life.

The research of Robert Sampson and John Laub is among the most influential in examining the life course and criminal careers (Sampson and Laub, 1993; Laub and Sampson, 2003). They reanalyzed and built on the famous studies of Sheldon and Eleanor Glueck that had followed the lives of 1,000 Boston-area boys from 1940 through the 1960s (Glueck and Glueck, 1950). The Gluecks' studies had matched and compared the lives of 500 delinquent boys with those of 500 nondelinquent boys from the same neighborhoods who possessed similar backgrounds and characteristics. Sampson and Laub gathered data on the same men in the 1990s, by which time the surviving "boys" from the original study were becoming senior citizens.

Based on their research, Sampson and Laub discuss informal and formal social controls over the life course. Unlike some researchers, who see youthful criminality as setting into place behavior patterns that continue into adulthood, Sampson and Laub emphasize *turning points* in life that move individuals away from criminal careers. For example, their study showed that military service, employment, and marriage served as particularly important factors leading away from criminal careers, while incarceration and alcohol abuse were associated with continued lawbreaking. Other researchers have tested the theory by, for example, examining how the experience of incarceration may diminish an offender's prospects for positive life course developments, such as marriage and employment (Huebner, 2005). In another example, researchers examined whether the development of religiosity may be another turning-point factor, but the evidence in that regard is weak and requires further long-term studies (Giordano et al., 2008). Moving to a new location after release from incarceration can also be a turning point away from crime (Kirk, 2012). As indicated by this summary, life course explanations do not seek to identify a single or primary factor as the cause of criminal behavior. Instead, they try to identify and evaluate the timing, interaction, and results of complex factors that affect people's lives.

What factors might shape the future behavior of these children? How do life course explanations contribute to our understanding of why some people commit crimes?

David Grossman/Alamy

Another influential life course theorist is Terrie Moffitt, who hypothesized that there are two main types of juvenile offending: life-course-persistent and adolescence-limited (Moffitt, 1993). After more than ten years of research, Moffitt revised her theory to include several new categories to account for other types of juvenile offending (Farrington, 2010). Generally, her research has focused on the psychological and social factors related to delinquent behavior.

Policy Implications of Life Course Theories

Although life course theories highlight the complex factors and situations that can affect individuals differently throughout their lives, several elements emerge for policy makers. They might, for instance, try to diminish the use of incarceration for young offenders, because such experiences are associated with criminal careers that continue into adulthood. Policies might also be developed to encourage and support key turning points, such as marriage, military service, and stable employment, that are associated with individuals' moves away from criminal activities.

CHECKPOINT 19. What are potential turning points for criminal careers according to life course theories?

STOP AND ANALYZE: If life course theories turn out to provide the best explanations for criminal careers, what, if anything, do you believe the government should do to address the problem of crime? List two examples or reasons for your answer.

Women and Crime

Theories about causes of crime were historically developed based on observations of male behavior. The fact that women commit crime less often than men (and the fact that most criminologists have historically been male) has helped to explain this fact (D. Klein, 1973). Many people assumed that most women, because of their nurturing and dependent nature, could not commit serious crimes. Those who did commit crimes were labeled as "bad" or "fallen" women. Unlike male criminals, then, female criminals were viewed as "immoral."

Most traditional theories of crime cannot explain two important facts about gender and offending. First, a theory that purports to explain crime causation must explain why women are less likely to commit crime than men are (the "gender gap"). Women accounted for approximately 26 percent of all arrests in 2013, with men responsible for the remaining 74 percent (FBI, 2014a). This represents an increase over arrest rates in prior decades. During the past 15 years, as overall crime rates have declined, there have been increases in women's share of arrests for violent crime and some other categories of offenses—although women's rates of offending are still well behind those of men. Second, an effective theory must explain why women commit different kinds of crime than men do—women are less likely to be arrested for violent crimes than are men, and they are more likely to be arrested for crimes such as prostitution (FBI, 2014a). Although it is a challenge to explain some gender differences in criminal behavior, criminologists must also remind themselves to avoid overgeneralizing about the behavior of men versus the behavior of women. Individual offenders who are male or female may have similar motivations or personal circumstances that shape their criminal behavior (Kruttschnitt and Carbone-Lopez, 2006).

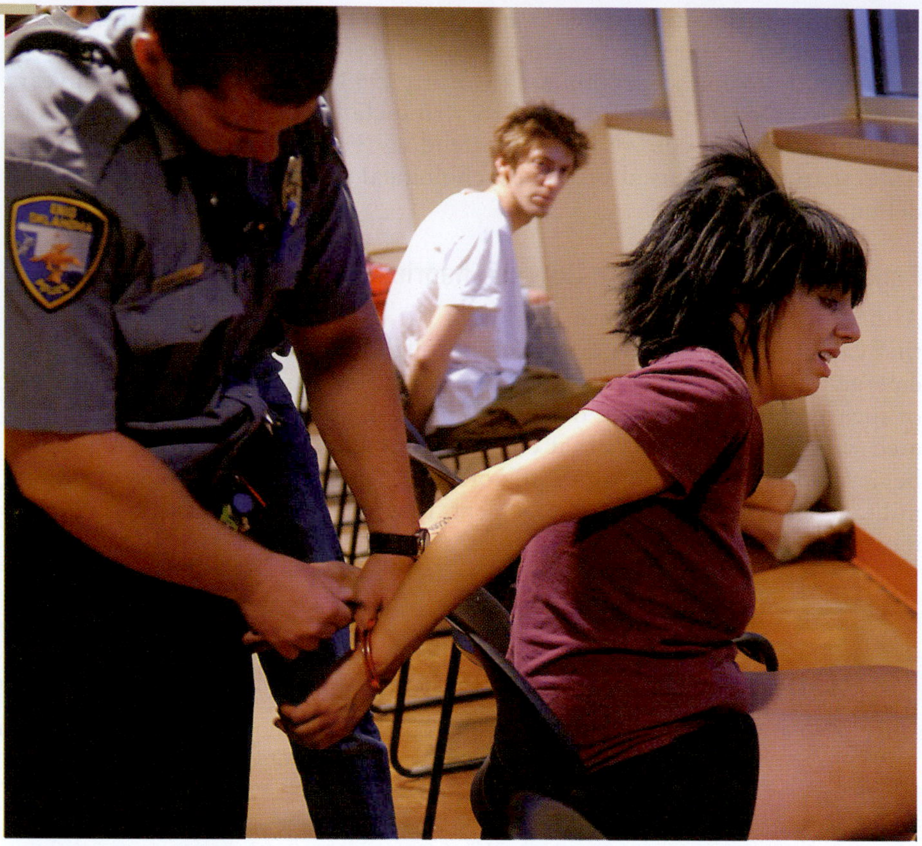

AP Images/Bonnie Vculek/Enid News & Eagle

Women's share of serious offenses and arrests has increased even as overall crime rates have decreased. Although men commit offenses and go to prison at much higher rates, there are concerns about increases in women's involvement in serious crimes. Should the government develop specific policies to attempt to steer young women away from crime and to provide special attention to women who are convicted of criminal offenses?

Figure 2.5 shows that most serious crimes are committed by men. Female offenders are less likely than male offenders to be arrested for any type of offense. In addition, women are more likely to be arrested for larceny/theft than for any other offense (approximately 44 percent of all arrests for theft were women), but men are still more likely than women to be arrested for larceny/theft.

FIGURE 2.5 HOW DO THE TYPES OF CRIME COMMITTED BY MEN AND WOMEN DIFFER?

Although most arrests are of men, women make up a relatively high percentage of arrests for larceny/theft.

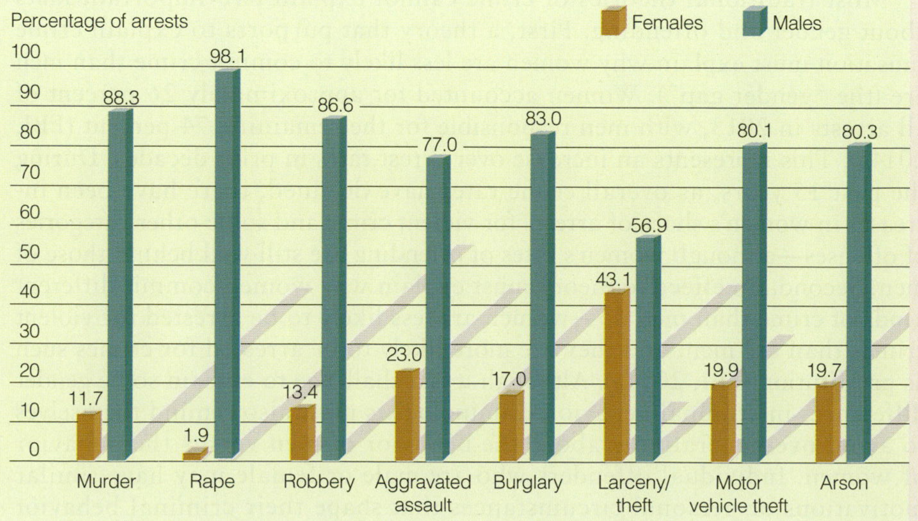

Source: Federal Bureau of Investigation, *Crime in the United States, 2013* (2014), Table 42 (www.fbi.gov).

Two books published in 1975 attempted to explain these facts about female offending. Rita Simon's *Women and Crime* and Freda Adler's *Sisters in Crime* both hypothesized that the movement for women's equality would result in increases in female offending. Although Adler and Simon disagreed about how the *types* of crime committed by women would be affected by women's liberation, both agreed the gender gap would be reduced significantly. It can be a challenge, however, to test predictions with complete accuracy. For example, an apparent increase in violence by women as measured by arrests might also be affected by changing police policies, such as the adoption of "zero tolerance" for any domestic violence situation, rather than an actual widespread change in offending by women (Steffensmeier, Schwartz, et al., 2005).

Beginning in the 1990s, theorists recognized the importance of *social structure* in explaining female criminality. These theorists posit that our society is structured in such a way as to create different opportunities for men and women in the workforce, that power differentials exist between men and women, and that important differences in sexuality shape the behavior of men and women (Messerschmidt, 1993). Behavioral differences between male and female offenders can have adverse consequences for women. For example, corrections officials may apply predictive tools for the risk of re-offending that do not accurately account for differences in offending patterns by some women and thereby disadvantage women in classification processes and in the allocation of resources in corrections programs (Reisig, Holtfreter, and Morash, 2006).

In recent decades, scholars have increased their attention to testing various crime-causation theories using data about women suspects and offenders. For example, the impact of "strain" from sociological theory has been found to affect changes in offending and drug-use patterns among a sample of female subjects (Slocum, Simpson, and Smith, 2005). Recent developments related to women and crime include life course theories, which focus on the paths taken by individuals through life and identify important turning points in people's lives. These "transitions" can affect individual behavior and lead people either toward or away from criminal activity (Sampson and Laub, 1993). To better explain gender and crime, feminist pathways researchers focus on the impact of critical life events, such as victimization, to determine why some women engage in criminal behavior. It is well documented, for example, that many women working as prostitutes were sexually abused as children (Widom, 1995).

As the status of women changes and as more women pursue careers in business and industry, some scholars believe that women will commit more economic and occupational crimes, such as embezzlement and fraud. However, research continues to show that female offenders, like their male counterparts, tend to come from poor families in which physical and substance abuse are present (Rosenbaum, 1989). Other researchers believe that the rising crime rates among women are due in part to a greater willingness of police and prosecutors to treat them like men. More research is needed to reach comprehensive conclusions about gender differences and crime.

✔POINT
20. What have feminist researchers contributed to theories of female criminality?
21. How do the number and trends in arrests compare for male and female arrestees?

STOP AND ANALYZE: Why is it useful to examine gender differences in criminal behavior and the treatment of arrestees and offenders in the criminal justice system? Give three reasons why it may be useful to study and monitor statistics for men and women rather than just looking at "criminals" as a single category covering all offenders.

Assessing Theories of Criminality

Undoubtedly, many of the theories of crime described here contain at least an element of truth (see Table 2.2). However, none is powerful enough to predict criminality or establish a specific cause for an offender's behavior. The theories are limited in other ways as well. They tend to focus on visible crimes and the poor. They have less to say about upper-class or organized crime. Most of the theories also focus on male behavior. What is missing, and truly needed, is a verifiable theory that merges these disparate ideas about the causes of crime. Once we have a complete and testable account of what causes crime, we can develop better policies to deal with it.

TABLE 2.2 MAJOR THEORIES OF CRIMINALITY AND THEIR POLICY IMPLICATIONS

Scholars and the public support various types of policies. We know little about the real causes of crime, but note how many people think they have the answers!

THEORY	MAJOR PREMISE	POLICY IMPLICATIONS	POLICY IMPLEMENTATION
Biological	Genetic, biochemical, or neurological defects cause some people to commit crime.	Identification and treatment or control of persons with crime-producing biological factors. Selective incapacitation, intensive supervision.	1. Use of drugs to inhibit biological urges of sex offenders. 2. Use of controlled diet to reduce levels of antisocial behavior caused by biochemical imbalances. 3. Identification of neurological defects through CAT scans. Use of drugs to suppress violent impulses. 4. Special education for those with learning disabilities.
Psychological	Personality and learning factors cause some people to commit crime.	Treatment of those with personality disorders to achieve mental health. Those whose illegal behavior stems from learning should have their behavior punished so they will realize that crime is not rewarded.	1. Psychotherapy and counseling to treat personality disorders. 2. Behavior modification strategies, such as electric shock and other negative impulses, to change learned behavior. 3. Counseling to enhance moral development. 4. Intensive individual and group therapies.
Social Structure	Crime is the result of underlying social conditions such as poverty, inequality, and unemployment.	Actions taken to reform social conditions that breed crime.	1. Education and job-training programs. 2. Urban redevelopment to improve housing, education, and health care. 3. Community development to provide economic opportunities.
Social Process	Crime is normal, learned behavior and is subject to either social control or labeling effects.	Individuals to be treated in groups, with emphasis on building conventional bonds and avoiding stigmatization.	1. Youth programs that emphasize positive role models. 2. Community organizing to establish neighborhood institutions and bonds that emphasize following society's norms. 3. Programs designed to promote family stability.
Social Conflict	Criminal definitions and punishments are used by some groups to control other groups.	Fundamental changes in the political and social systems to reduce class conflict.	1. Development of programs to remove injustice in society. 2. Provision of resources to assist women, minorities, and the poor in dealing with the criminal justice system and other government agencies. 3. Modification of criminal justice to deal similarly with crimes committed by upper-class members and crimes committed by lower-class members.
Life Course	Offenders have criminal careers that often begin with pathways into youth crime but can change and end through turning points in life.	Fostering positive turning points such as marriage and stable employment.	1. Policies to reduce entry pathways associated with youth incarceration and substance abuse. 2. Policies to promote educational success, full employment, successful marriages, and stable families.

A QUESTION OF ETHICS

In September 2014, the police chief of Weare, New Hampshire, was put on administrative leave and placed under a restraining order after being accused of domestic violence. Incidents such as this, in which individuals who are authorized to carry firearms engage in threatening or violent acts, raise grave concerns. A worst-case scenario from this kind of risk played out in 2003 when Tacoma (Washington) Police Chief David Brame fatally shot his estranged wife, and then killed himself. This event occurred after repeated domestic violence incidents involving Brame, none of which had been pursued or investigated by the Tacoma city manager—the only local government employee with authority over the police chief.

Police officers are given the authority to enforce law, but these same officials also have the capability to break the law. Because they are part of the law enforcement hierarchy, they may be able to avoid serious punishment if caught. In 1997, a legal assistant working on a case against the Los Angeles Police Department uncovered evidence showing that 79 officers had been charged with domestic violence, yet none had been prosecuted. While civilian offenders were facing serious punishment for similar instances of domestic violence, the LAPD officers were not charged with crimes against their significant others—in fact, all the officers accused of intimate partner violence (some repeat offenders) were allowed to remain on the force, and some were even promoted.

A victim who experiences domestic violence at the hands of a police officer is in an extremely difficult position. As members of law enforcement, these abusers own guns and know how to manipulate the system to their own benefit; they often also know the locations of most women's shelters (which are typically kept secret to keep victims safe). Victims may be reluctant to call the police if they've been abused, for fear that the responding officers will be friends with their abuser, that they won't be believed, and that the crime may not be sufficiently investigated or that it will be covered up—as occurred in the LAPD cases.

Sources: Jeremy Blackman, "Details of Domestic Violence Claim against Weare, Police Chief Emerge," *Concord Monitor,* September 16, 2014 (www.concordmonitor.com); Jim Crogan, "Life of a Whistleblower." *LA Weekly,* June 5, 2003 (http://laweekly.com); Conor Friedersdorf, "Police Have a Much Bigger Doemstic-Abuse Problem Than the NFL Does," *The Atlantic*, September 19, 2014 (http://theatlantic.com); Donald W. Meyers, "Activist: Men Need to Help End Domestic Violence," *Yakima Herald*, October 7, 2014 (http://yakimaherald.com); National Center for Women and Policing, *Police Family Violence Fact Sheet* (http://womenandpolicing.com); Sean Robinson, "10 Years Later: Looking Back at Former Tacoma Police Chief David Brame," *News Tribune*, April 21, 2013 (http://thenewstribune.com); United States Department of Justice, *The United States Attorney's Manual* (http://justice.gov).

CRITICAL THINKING AND ANALYSIS

Is it ethical for a police department to investigate a crime committed by one of its own officers? Where should victims of domestic violence turn for help with the offender is a police officer? The Lautenberg Amendment was passed in 1996 as an attempt to restrict the possession of firearms by domestic violence abusers; however, some believe this is a violation of the right to bear arms as specified in the U.S. Constitution. Should officers accused of domestic violence be allowed to retain possession of their guns, or does this place their families at undue risk?

Summary

1 Describe who is likely to be victimized by crime

- Young residents of lower-income communities are among those most likely to be victimized by crime.
- Because of the connection between race and social status in the United States, African Americans are more frequently victimized by crime than are whites.
- A significant percentage of crimes, especially those against women, are committed by acquaintances and relatives of victims.
- Recurring victimization is a serious problem that imposes a disproportionate share of crime's harm on a small portion of the population.

2 Discuss the impacts of crime on society

- Because of the financial and other costs it produces, crime significantly affects all of society.
- Financial costs from white-collar crime, employee theft, and fraud lead to huge financial losses for businesses.
- Medical costs and lingering psychological effects impose heavy burdens on victims.
- Fear of crime may make everyone in society feel less free to go to certain places or to live their daily lives without being nervous and fearful.

3 Identify the justice system's responses to the needs of crime victims

- Government agencies have begun to be more sensitive to the needs of crime victims. Thus, many states support programs to provide services and compensation.

- State and federal legislation has provided new rights for crime victims, including compensation, forms of assistance, and current information about the offender who victimized them.
- Scholars have begun to study the role that victims may play in facilitating crimes.

4 Describe the theories put forward to explain criminal behavior

- The classical school of criminology emphasized reform of criminal law, procedures, and punishments.
- The rise of science led to the positivist school, which viewed behavior as stemming from social, biological, and psychological factors.
- Positivist criminology has dominated the study of criminal behavior since the beginning of the twentieth century.
- Biological theories of crime claim that physiological and neurological factors may predispose a person to commit crimes. Some of these factors may be associated with genes, but others may be affected by nutrition, environmental pollution, medical conditions, or brain injuries.
- Psychological theories of crime propose that mental processes and behavior hold the key to understanding the causes of crime.
- Sociological theories of crime emphasize the social conditions that bear on the individual as causes of criminal behavior. Three types of sociological theory are social structure theories, social process theories, and social conflict theories.
- Life course theories are based on long-term studies and identify factors associated with pathways into criminal careers and turning points away from criminal activity.

5 Analyze crime-causation theories and apply them to different groups of offenders

- All criminal theories have implications for policy decisions.
- The criminality of women has been studied for the past 30 years. Some argue that as women become more equal with men in society, the number of crimes committed by women will increase.
- Theories of criminality are criticized for focusing too exclusively on lower-class and male perpetrators.

Questions for Review

1. Who is most likely to be victimized by crime?
2. What are the costs of crime?
3. How does the criminal justice system treat victims?
4. What are the major theories of criminality?
5. What have researchers learned about criminal behavior by women?

Key Terms

anomie (p. 78)
biological explanations (p. 73)
classical criminology (p. 71)
control theories (p. 80)
criminogenic traits (p. 73)
labeling theories (p. 80)
learning theories (p. 79)
life course theories (p. 81)
lifestyle-exposure theory (p. 55)
positivist criminology (p. 72)
psychological explanations (p. 75)
repetitive victimization (p. 60)
revictimization (p. 60)
routine activities theory (p. 55)
social conflict theories (p. 80)
social process theories (p. 79)
social structure theories (p. 78)
sociological explanations (p. 78)
theory of differential association (p. 80)
victim precipitation (p. 60)
victimology (p. 54)

Checkpoint Answers

1 What are the main elements of the lifestyle-exposure model?

✓ Demographic characteristics, adaptations, lifestyle, associations, exposure.

2 What are the characteristics of the group that is most victimized by violent crime? Of the least-victimized group?

✓ Most victimized: teenage African Americans, male or female, varies by year. Least victimized: elderly white females.

3 Which type of violent crime is most likely to be committed by nonstrangers?

✓ Rape/sexual assault.

4 Which type of crime is most likely to be committed by strangers?

✓ Robbery.

5 Why is recurring victimization a significant concern to research scholars and policy makers?

✓ A small portion of individuals bear a disproportionate share of harm through recurring criminal victimization.

6 What are some of the impacts of crime?

✓ Fear, financial costs, emotional costs, lifestyle restrictions.

7 How is fear of crime shaped, and how does it relate to actual crime rates?

✓ People gain perceptions about crime through the news media, movies, and television shows; thus, perceptions and fears about crime often exceed the actual risks of victimization.

8 Why are poor people often less likely than others to take actions to reduce the risk of crime?

✓ Poor people often reside in higher-crime areas without being able to afford home security systems. They are also more likely to travel to and from work in the evening if they work third shifts or have service occupations.

9 Why do some crime victims feel mistreated by the justice system?

✓ The system focuses on finding and punishing the offender; police and lawyers often question victims closely, in an unsympathetic manner; victims do not always receive assistance that covers their medical expenses and other losses.

10 What rights have been provided in federal criminal cases by the Justice for All Act?

✓ Receive notice about hearings, attend hearings, consult with the federal prosecutor, gain restitution, and avoid unnecessary delays.

11 What victim behaviors can invite crime?

✓ Failing to take precautions, taking actions that may provoke or entice, refusing to assist police with investigations.

12 What were the main assumptions of the classical school?

✓ Criminal behavior is rational, and the fear of punishment keeps people from committing crimes.

13 What are the main assumptions of the positivist school?

✓ Criminal behavior is the product of social, biological, and psychological factors.

14 What were the main elements of Lombroso's theory?

✓ Offenders are born criminals and have traits that mark them.

15 What is meant by the term *psychopath?*

✓ A person who is unable to control impulses, cannot learn from experience, and does not have normal human emotions.

16 What is the main assumption of social structure theories?

✓ Crime is caused by people's negative reactions to social inequality, lack of opportunity, and the success of others that does not seem to be attainable in a society that values wealth and status.

17 What is the main assumption of social process theories?

✓ Everyone has the potential of becoming a criminal, depending on influences such as learning or labeling, which can move one toward or away from crime and on how one is regarded by others.

18 What is the main assumption of social conflict theories?

✓ Criminal law and the criminal justice system are primarily a means of controlling the poor and the have-nots.

19 What are potential turning points for criminal careers in life course theories?

✓ Marriage, military service, and stable employment are associated with moving away from criminal careers.

20 What have feminist researchers contributed to theories of female criminality?

✓ The idea that women and men commit crimes for different reasons, and that these reasons must be taken into account when studying gender differences.

21 How do the number and trends in arrests compare for male and female arrestees?

✓ Women constitute a small percentage of arrestees for all crimes except larceny/theft, although arrests of women for violent crimes rose recently even as arrests of men declined.

CHAPTER FEATURES

- **Technology and Criminal Justice** Evidence-Based Practice and Public Surveillance
- **New Directions in Criminal Justice Policy** Contemporary Criminal Justice Reform
- **The Criminal Justice Process** The State of Michigan versus Christopher Jones
- **Inside Today's Controversies** "What I Learned about Stop-and-Frisk from Watching My Black Son"
- **Close Up** Racial Profiling

CHAPTER 3 THE CRIMINAL JUSTICE SYSTEM

CHAPTER LEARNING OBJECTIVES

1 Describe the goals of the criminal justice system

2 Discuss the different responsibilities of federal and state criminal justice operations

3 Analyze criminal justice from a system perspective

4 Identify the authority and relationships of the main criminal justice agencies, and understand the steps in the decision-making process for criminal cases

5 Describe the criminal justice "wedding cake" concept

6 Discuss the possible causes of racial disparities in criminal justice

CHAPTER OUTLINE

AP Images/Will Dickey

Standing in the courtroom between two defense attorneys and dressed in an orange jail-inmate shirt and pants, 47-year-old Michael Dunn listened as Jacksonville, Florida, Circuit Court Judge Russell Healey announced his sentence. The October 17, 2014, sentencing hearing concerned the events that had occurred in November 2012, nearly two years earlier. At that time, a confrontation took place when Dunn, a white man, argued with several African American teenagers in a convenience-store parking lot about how loudly they were playing their music. The process from incident to sentencing for Dunn illustrates the length and nature of the steps that affect criminal suspects from the initial investigation of a crime through the ultimate determination of guilt and punishment.

According to witnesses' testimony at the trial, when Dunn argued with the teens on Friday, November 23, 2012, he pulled out a handgun that he kept in his car and began shooting at the teens' vehicle. Dunn fired ten bullets, including shots as the teens were driving away. Three bullets struck 17-year-old Jordan Davis, a passenger in the vehicle, causing fatal wounds. Dunn left the scene and returned to his hotel without calling police. The next day he drove to his home 170 miles south of Jacksonville, where he was arrested later in the day. On Monday, November 26, Dunn appeared in court, where he was denied pretrial release on bail and informed that he faced homicide charges. Thus he faced the prospect of remaining in jail until his case was processed and decided (Maddox, 2012).

Dunn's attorney told the news media that the shooting was based on self-defense because Dunn claimed that he had seen the barrel of a gun sticking out of a window of the teens' vehicle. However, police did not find any weapons in the vehicle or in the area of the convenience-store parking lot where the vehicle was driven during the shooting. The Florida prosecutor (called a state attorney), later decided to seek first-degree murder charges against Dunn. This is the most serious homicide charge under criminal law, requiring proof that the killing was done deliberately without any justification. Under Florida law for first-degree murder charges, the prosecutor must present evidence to a grand jury, and that body of citizens must decide if there is appropriate evidence to pursue this most serious of all charges. In this case, the grand jury issued an indictment—the formal approval of the charge—and Dunn returned to court in mid-December 2012 for another arraignment hearing, where he was informed of the new charge (Eastman, 2012; Maddox, 2012). Dunn was also charged with three counts of attempted murder because some of his bullets had been directed at the other three teenagers in the vehicle.

By entering and maintaining a plea of "not guilty," unlike the majority of people facing serious charges, Dunn was unwilling to accept a plea bargain that would have reduced his potential punishment. Dunn claimed he was not guilty of a crime because he had acted in self-defense; he feared for his life in the confrontation. Since he was not released on bail, Dunn remained in county jail for many months awaiting his trial. In February 2014, after more than a year of preparation by the prosecutors and the defense attorney, Dunn's trial moved forward in Duval County Circuit Court before Judge Healey. The twelve-member jury heard testimony from police officers and the three surviving teenagers. Dunn testified in person that he saw a gun pointed at him. This in itself was unusual, because many defendants prefer not to testify, to avoid subjecting themselves to harsh questioning from prosecutors in the open courtroom. Most defendants hope that their attorneys can poke holes in the testimony of the prosecution's witnesses. However, a self-defense claim fundamentally rests on the defendant personally convincing the jury or judge that he reasonably feared for his life (Alvarez, 2014).

The prosecutor's questions to Dunn pointed out inconsistencies between his courtroom testimony and statements that he had made to police officers and the three surviving teenagers. Dunn testified and claimed that he saw a gun pointed at him. Moreover, Dunn's fiancée, who had been present at the shooting, damaged his credibility by testifying that, contrary to his statements in court, he never told her in the hours after the shooting that he saw the teens with a gun (Alvarez, 2014). At the conclusion of the trial, the jury spent more than 30 hours deliberating over the charges. They decided that Dunn was guilty of the three counts of attempted murder concerning the three teens in the vehicle, but they were deadlocked on whether he was guilty of first-degree murder or of some lesser charge in the killing of Jordan Davis. Thus the state attorney announced that she would seek a new trial focused solely on the undecided issue of Dunn's guilt in the death of Davis (Quesada, 2014).

For the second trial, the judge rejected the defense attorney's request for a change of venue. Dunn's lawyer had asked that the next trial be moved to a different city because of concerns that publicity from the event and the first trial would make it difficult to find twelve unbiased jurors who did not already have opinions about the case. A new jury at the second trial in September 2014 heard from many of the same witnesses and ultimately found Dunn guilty of first-degree murder in the death of Davis. Judge Healey gave Dunn a mandatory life sentence for the first-degree-murder conviction plus an additional 90 years—30 years for each conviction—for the attempted murder of the other teens in the car (Associated Press, 2014; Richinick, 2014; Long, 2014).

The criminal case against Michael Dunn illustrates many elements of the criminal justice system that will be discussed in this chapter. The case was processed through a series of steps in which justice system officials made decisions about whether the case would move forward or leave the system. The police provided the prosecutor with crime scene evidence and witness descriptions from the event. The prosecutor concluded that this evidence, when examined in light of Dunn's statements and behavior after the shooting, justified serious criminal charges.

A judge made decisions about whether Dunn could be released on bail while awaiting the start of his trial. Many of these court decisions depended on the arguments formulated and presented by the prosecutors and defense attorneys. Later, the judge determined the length of Dunn's prison sentence based on Florida laws concerning which offenses draw mandatory sentences and which permit judges to use discretion in determining the length of the prison term.

Think about the key factors in the Dunn case: discretionary decisions by justice system officials; a series of steps in sequence; interactions between attorneys, prosecutors, judges, grand jurors, and trial jurors; several months of delay for defendants who plead not guilty and wait for the attorneys to prepare evidence and arguments for trial; the expense and stress of living under conditions of bail or in jail while worrying about the possibility of prison. These are all elements that affect criminal cases throughout the United States, and they reflect many essential characteristics of the justice system.

In this chapter, we examine the goals of the criminal justice system and how American criminal justice operates as a system. Moreover, we shall see how that system's processes are shaped by scarce resources, individual decision makers, and other factors that can lead to divergent treatment for similar criminal cases. In the United States, our history has taught us the importance of knowing that differences in the treatment of suspects, defendants, and offenders may be related to issues of race, ethnicity, and social class—and the interaction of these demographic factors with the criminal justice system's processes. Anyone in the United States, including law-abiding college students, can be drawn into the criminal justice system in a variety of roles: victim, witness, juror, defendant. Thus, all Americans need to gain an understanding of the system, how it operates, and how it affects people's lives.

The Goals of Criminal Justice

To begin our study of the criminal justice system, we must ask, What goals does the system serve? Although these goals may seem straightforward in theory, saying exactly what they mean in practice can be difficult.

In 1967 the President's Commission on Law Enforcement and Administration of Justice described the criminal justice system as an apparatus that society uses to "enforce the standards of conduct necessary to protect individuals and the community" (U.S. President's Commission, 1967: 7). This statement will form the basis for our discussion of the goals of the system. Although there is much debate about the purposes of criminal justice, most people agree that the system has three goals: (1) doing justice, (2) controlling crime, and (3) preventing crime.

Doing Justice

"Doing justice" is the foundation of the rules, procedures, and institutions that make up the American criminal justice system. Without the principle of justice, there would be little difference between criminal justice in the United States and that in authoritarian countries. Fairness is essential: We want to have fair laws. We want to investigate, judge, and punish fairly. Doing justice also requires upholding the rights of individuals and punishing those who violate the law. All of these elements reflect American values and appear in the U.S. Constitution. Thus, the goal of doing justice embodies three principles: (1) offenders will be held fully accountable for their actions, (2) the rights of persons who have contact with the system will be protected, and (3) like offenses will be treated alike and officials will take into account relevant differences among offenders and offenses (DiIulio, 1993).

TECHNOLOGY & CRIMINAL JUSTICE

EVIDENCE-BASED PRACTICE AND PUBLIC SURVEILLANCE

Cities and private businesses invest in CCTV (closed-circuit television) systems as means to provide crime-prevention surveillance. The use of such security cameras is familiar to Americans because they are frequently installed in convenience stores and gas stations, locations often targeted by armed robbers. From their early use by businesses, security cameras have become increasingly visible in housing projects, apartment buildings, airports, malls, bus stations, and other locations where their presence is intended to deter crime and provide visual evidence that can be used to solve crimes that do occur. Following the examples of London and other overseas cities, Chicago and other U.S. municipalities have placed cameras along streets and parks as a means of preventing crime in public spaces.

There is no question that these CCTV systems have helped to solve highly publicized criminal events. When a Wesleyan University student was murdered in a bookstore, images from the store's security camera enabled police to quickly disseminate photos of the gunman through news outlets. In Florida, the security camera at a carwash recorded a man with a long criminal record abducting a young girl whose dead body was later found nearby. Most famously, store security cameras helped to identify the men who detonated bombs amidst the crowds of spectators at the Boston Marathon in 2013. However, the examples of cases in which security cameras help to solve crimes do not answer the question of whether electronic video surveillance prevents crime or if it is a cost-effective way to do so.

Brandon Welsh and David Farrington systematically examined studies of CCTV surveillance in public places in an effort to produce evidence-based conclusions about best practices for public surveillance. They found that research indicated positive effects on crime prevention in some contexts, especially parking lots. Some studies indicated greater crime-prevention impacts in Great Britain than in other countries, and researchers speculated that this may be the result of the British practice of linking CCTV use with other interventions, such as increased lighting in public areas.

Significant questions remain about exactly how and where to use technology for surveillance in public spaces. These issues

John Moore/Staff/Getty Images

Periodically people undertake public protests to call attention to social problems and crime in their communities. How can the interest and energy generated by such public events be translated into concrete action to prevent crime?

Doing justice successfully is a tall order, and we can easily identify situations in which criminal justice agencies and processes fall short of this ideal. In authoritarian political systems, criminal justice clearly serves the interests of those in power, but in a democracy, people can try to improve the capacity of their institutions to do justice. Thus, however imperfect they may be, criminal justice institutions and processes can maintain public support. In a democracy, a system that makes doing justice a key goal is viewed as

include how many cameras are necessary for effectiveness and whether video should be continuously monitored by officials or examined periodically. The latter issue highlights concerns about cost. There are also questions about whether criminals will simply move their activities to locations that are not under surveillance. Certainly, society could make a heavy investment in security cameras and the personnel to continuously monitor them. However, any government agency must be concerned about the effective use of resources, especially in an era of budget cuts. Thus officials must weigh whether it would be more cost-effective to simply increase the number of police officers patrolling specific areas where crimes are regularly reported.

Technology can increase society's capacity for crime prevention, yet its use should be supported by evidence-based research concerning its effectiveness. Otherwise, officials may use limited law enforcement funds in ways that do not maximize the effectiveness of society's investments for purposes of crime prevention.

Sources: R. Eckert, "Florida Girl Abducted on Video Is Found Dead: Mechanic with Criminal Record Is Charged," *New York Times,* February 7, 2004; H. Kelly, "After Boston: The Pros and Cons of Surveillance Cameras," CNN.com, April 26, 2013 (www.cnn.com); R. Shah and J. Braithwaite, "Spread Too Thin: Analyzing the Effectiveness of the Chicago Camera Network on Crime," *Police Practice and Research: An International Journal,* April 4, 2012 (www.tandfonline.com); L. Sievert, "Wesleyan Murder Trial, Day 2: Suspect Walked around Scene after Killing Wesleyan Senior," *Middletown (CT) Press,* December 1, 2011 (www.middletownpress.com); B. C. Welsh and D. P. Farrington, *Making Public Places Safer: Surveillance and Crime Prevention* (New York: Oxford University Press, 2009).

DEBATE THE ISSUE

Would you be willing to pay more taxes to enable your city or town to install CCTV surveillance systems along roadways and parks? Do you have any concerns that CCTV violates individuals' privacy and leads to "Big Brother" watching too many aspects of people's everyday activities? Provide two arguments for either increasing the use of CCTV or investing in alternative crime-prevention approaches.

legitimate and can therefore pursue the secondary goals of controlling and preventing crime.

Controlling Crime

The criminal justice system is designed to control crime by arresting, prosecuting, convicting, and punishing those who disobey the law. A major constraint on the system, however, is that efforts to control crime must be carried out within the framework of law. This reflects a central tension within American values, in that we do not fully enjoy our liberty if we live in fear of crime, yet the value that we place on rights may inhibit our effectiveness in controlling crime. The criminal law not only defines what is illegal but also outlines the rights of citizens and the procedures officials must use to achieve the system's goals.

In any city or town, we can see the goal of crime control being actively pursued: police officers walking a beat, patrol cars racing down dark streets, lawyers speaking before a judge, probation officers visiting clients, or the wire fences of a prison stretching along a highway. Taking action against wrongdoers helps to control crime, but the system must also attempt to keep crimes from happening.

Preventing Crime

Crime can be prevented in various ways. Perhaps most important is the deterrent effect of the actions of police, courts, and corrections. These entities not only punish those who violate the law but also provide examples that will likely keep others from committing wrongful acts. For instance, a racing patrol car responding to a crime also serves as a warning that law enforcement is at hand.

Crime prevention depends on the actions of criminal justice officials and citizens. Increasingly, technology is used for crime prevention purposes. For individuals, such approaches as car alarms and "find me" GPS (global positioning system) applications for missing laptops and smartphones are used by many people to prevent property crimes. Read the Technology and Criminal Justice feature about evidence-based practices related to public surveillance and consider whether government investment in such technologies as a means of crime prevention is a worthwhile endeavor.

Citizens do not have the authority to enforce the law. Society has assigned that responsibility to the criminal justice system. Thus, citizens must rely on the police to stop criminals; they cannot take the law into their own hands. Still, they can and must be actively engaged in preventing crime. Examine "Civic Engagement: Your Role in the System" to consider what concrete steps people can take to address a specific crime problem within a neighborhood. Also read "A Question of Ethics" at the end of this chapter as you consider how far citizens should be permitted to go in trying to prevent crime.

Any decision made in the justice system—whether in doing justice, controlling crime, or preventing crime—will reflect particular legal, political, social, and moral values. As we study the system, we must be aware of the possible conflicts among these values and the implications of choosing one value over another. The tasks assigned to the criminal justice system are most easily performed when they are clearly defined, so that citizens and officials can act with precise knowledge of their duties.

CIVIC ENGAGEMENT

YOUR ROLE IN THE SYSTEM

You live in a neighborhood experiencing an increase in burglaries and property crimes. A television news report based on an internal police memo reveals that the number of detectives in your precinct has been reduced from 14 to 2 and thus the police have less ability to investigate all burglaries and other crimes. You are asked to lead a neighborhood effort to reduce crime and disorder on your block. *Make a list of suggestions of what you could do.* Then read about what happened when such a situation arose in a Seattle neighborhood, especially how they organized and who they sought to bring into their discussions.

✔POINT 1. What are the three goals of the criminal justice system?
2. What is meant by "doing justice"?

STOP AND ANALYZE: What is the role of the individual citizen in crime prevention? List two things that you do right now that contribute to crime prevention. What are two additional things that you could easily incorporate into your daily life that would also contribute to crime prevention?

(Answers are at the end of the chapter.)

Criminal Justice in a Federal System

Like other aspects of American government, criminal justice is based on **federalism**, in which power is divided between a central (national) government and regional (state) governments. States have a great deal of authority over their own affairs, but the federal government handles matters of national concern. Because of federalism, no single level of government is solely responsible for the administration of criminal justice.

federalism
A system of government in which power is divided between a central (national) government and regional (state) governments.

The structure of the U.S. government was created in 1789 with the ratification of the U.S. Constitution. The Constitution gave the national government certain powers—to raise an army, to coin money, to make treaties with foreign countries—but all other powers, including police power, were retained by the states. No national police force with broad powers may be established in the United States.

The Constitution does not include criminal justice among the federal government's powers. However, the government participates in criminal justice in many ways. For example, the Federal Bureau of Investigation (FBI) is a national law enforcement agency. In addition, certain criminal cases are tried in U.S. district courts, which are federal courts, and there are federal prisons throughout the nation. Most criminal justice activity, however, occurs at the state rather than the national level.

Two Justice Systems

Both the national and state systems of criminal justice enforce laws, try criminal cases, and punish offenders, but their activities differ in scope and purpose. The vast majority of criminal laws are written by state legislatures and enforced by state agencies. However, Congress has enacted a variety of national criminal laws, which the FBI, the Drug Enforcement Administration, the Secret Service, and other federal agencies enforce.

Except in the case of federal drug offenses, relatively few offenders break federal criminal laws, compared with the large numbers who break state criminal laws. For example, only small numbers of people violate the federal law against counterfeiting and espionage, while large numbers violate state laws against assault, larceny, and drunken driving. Some criminal activities violate both state and federal laws. When football star Michael Vick was investigated and prosecuted for running a dog-fighting operation in 2007, his actions violated laws in both systems. His conviction on federal charges led him to serve 19 months in federal prison and two additional months of home confinement (Maske, 2009). While serving his federal prison sentence, he also entered a guilty plea to state charges in Virginia after his attorneys negotiated a suspended state sentence that would not require him to spend any additional time in prison (Zinser, 2008).

Expansion of Federal Involvement

Since the 1960s the federal government has expanded its role in dealing with crime, a policy area that has traditionally fallen to state and local governments. As Willard Oliver notes, the federal role has become much more active in "legislating criminal activity, expanding [the] federal law enforcement bureaucracy, widening the reach and scope of the federal courts, and building more federal prisons" (2002: 1).

The report of the U.S. President's Commission on Law Enforcement and Administration of Justice (1967: 613) emphasized the need for greater federal involvement in local crime control and urged that federal grants be directed to the states to support criminal justice initiatives. Since then, Congress has allocated billions of dollars for crime control efforts and passed legislation, national in scope, to deal with street crime, the "war on drugs," violent crime, terrorism, and juvenile delinquency. Although most criminal justice expenditures and personnel remain at the local level, over the past 40 years the federal government has increased its role in fighting street crime (Oliver, 2002; Gest, 2001).

Because many crimes span state borders, we no longer think of some crimes as being committed at a single location within a single state. For example, crime syndicates and gangs deal with drugs, pornography, and gambling on a national level. In addition, technology-based crimes, such as computer-fraud schemes and Internet-sourced child pornography have spurred new national laws from Congress and enforcement actions by federal agencies because these illegal activities can cross both state and international borders (Hermann, 2014). Thus, Congress has expanded the powers of the FBI and other federal agencies to pursue criminal activities that formerly were the responsibility of the states.

Congress enacts laws designed to allow the FBI to investigate situations in which local police forces will likely be less effective. Under the National Stolen Property Act, for example, the FBI may investigate thefts worth over $5,000 when the offenders have probably transported the stolen property across state lines. As a national agency, the FBI is better able than any state agency to pursue criminal investigations across state borders.

In addition, technology-based crimes, such as computer fraud schemes, have also spurred new laws from Congress because these illegal activities can cross both state and international borders. Federal officials have become

Federal law enforcement agencies bear special responsibility for certain crimes. In addition, they can provide special expertise to assist state and local police in matters involving forensic science, drug analysis, and intelligence about organized crime. If shrinking police budgets in state and local government lead to more requests for assistance, will federal agencies be expected to assume increased responsibilities for crimes, such as drug and gun offenses, that can be covered under both federal and state laws?

AP Images/Laura Skelding/Austin American-Statesman

increasingly active in pursuing arms dealers, narcotics traffickers, and terrorists who operate in other countries but whose harmful activities violate the laws of the United States. For example, Russian arms dealer Viktor Bout was arrested in Thailand and brought to the United States, as was reputed Jamaican drug kingpin Christopher Coke, who was brought from Jamaica to New York to face trial in 2010 (Weiser, 2011).

Disputes over jurisdiction may occur when an offense violates both state and federal laws. If the FBI and local agencies do not cooperate, they may each seek to catch the same criminals. This can have major implications if the agency that makes the arrest determines which court tries the case. Usually, however, law enforcement officials at all levels of government seek to cooperate and to coordinate their efforts.

After the September 11 attacks on the World Trade Center and the Pentagon, the FBI and other federal law enforcement agencies focused their resources and efforts on investigating and preventing terrorist threats against the United States, including tightening security at airports and national borders. As a result, the role of the FBI as a law enforcement agency may be changing. One month after the attacks, 4,000 of the agency's 11,500 agents were dedicating their efforts to the aftermath of September 11. So many FBI agents were reassigned from their traditional law enforcement activities to anti-terror initiatives that some observers claimed that other federal crimes, such as bank robberies, were no longer being vigorously investigated (Kampeas, 2001). In a 2013 speech, FBI Director James Comey emphasized that "counterterrorism remains our top priority" while also focusing attention on the FBI's increasing attention to cyber crimes (Comey, 2013). The federal government's response to potential threats to national security and other priorities may ultimately diminish the federal role in traditional law enforcement and thereby effectively transfer responsibility for many criminal investigations to state and local officials.

The reorientation of the FBI's priorities is just one aspect of changes in federal criminal justice agencies that have been made to address the threat of terrorism. The Transportation Security Administration (TSA), was established as a new agency within the Department of Transportation in November 2001. The TSA assumed responsibility for protecting travelers and interstate commerce. Most visibly, federal employees of the TSA took over the screening of passengers and their luggage at airports throughout the country. In light of the ease with which the September 11 hijackers brought box cutters onboard commercial airliners, there were grave concerns that employees of private security agencies were neither adequately trained nor sufficiently vigilant to protect the traveling public.

The biggest change in federal criminal justice occurred in November 2002, when Congress enacted legislation to create a new Department of Homeland Security (DHS). This department was charged with centralizing the administration and coordinating many existing federal agencies that were previously scattered throughout various departments. The Secretary of Homeland Security oversees the Coast Guard, the Immigration and Naturalization Service, the Border Patrol, the Secret Service, the Federal Emergency Management Agency, the TSA, and other agencies concerned with protecting our food supply, nuclear power facilities, and other potential terrorism targets. The Secretary of Homeland Security faces a continuing challenge in seeking to integrate departments that previously operated separately, as well as coordinating efforts with other government agencies (J. G. Carter and Rip, 2013). The DHS trains emergency first responders, coordinates federal agencies' actions with those of state and local agencies, and analyzes domestic intelligence information obtained by the CIA, FBI, and other sources (Table 3.1).

TABLE 3.1 **DEPARTMENT OF HOMELAND SECURITY**

Congress approved legislation to create a federal agency dedicated to protecting the United States from terrorism. The legislation merged 22 agencies and nearly 170,000 government workers.

	AGENCIES MOVED TO THE DEPARTMENT OF HOMELAND SECURITY	PREVIOUS DEPARTMENT OR AGENCY
Border and Transportation Security	Immigration and Naturalization Service enforcement functions	Justice Department
	Transportation Security Administration	Transportation Department
	Customs Service	Treasury Department
	Federal Protective Services	General Services Administration
	Animal and Plant Health Inspection Service (parts)	Agriculture Department
Emergency Preparedness and Response	Federal Emergency Management Agency	(*Independent agency*)
	Chemical, biological, radiological, and nuclear response units	Health and Human Services Department
	Nuclear Incident response teams	Energy Department
	National Domestic Preparedness Office	FBI
	Office of Domestic Preparedness	Justice Department
	Domestic Emergency Support Teams	(*From various departments and agencies*)
Science and Technology	Civilian biodefense research program	Health and Human Services Department
	Plum Island Animal Disease Center	Agriculture Department
	Lawrence Livermore National Laboratory (parts)	Energy Department
Information Analysis and Infrastructure Protection	National Communications System	Defense Department
	National Infrastructure Protection Center	FBI
	Critical Infrastructure Assurance Office	Commerce Department
	National Infrastructure Simulation and Analysis Center	Energy Department
	Federal Computer Incident Response Center	General Services Administration
Secret Service	Secret Service including presidential protection units	Treasury Department
Coast Guard	Coast Guard	Transportation Department

Source: *New York Times,* November 20, 2002, p. A12.

Because both state and federal systems operate in the United States, criminal justice here is highly decentralized. As Figure 3.1 shows, almost two-thirds of all criminal justice employees work for local governments. The majority of workers in all of the subunits of the system—except corrections—are tied to local government. Likewise, the costs of criminal justice are distributed among federal, state, and local governments.

Laws are enforced and offenders are brought to justice mainly in the states, counties, and cities. As a result, local traditions, values, and practices shape the way criminal justice agencies operate. Local leaders, whether members of the city council or influential citizens, can help set law enforcement priorities by putting pressure on the police. Will the city's police officers crack down on illegal gambling? Will juvenile offenders be turned over to their parents with stern warnings, or will they be sent to state institutions? The answers to these and other important questions vary from city to city.

The nation's economic problems since 2007 have reduced government budgets for criminal justice in many cities, counties, and states. Federal agencies have been affected, too. When budget disagreements created a deadlock between Republicans and Democrats in Congress during 2013, automatic budget

FIGURE 3.1 PERCENTAGE (ROUNDED) OF CRIMINAL JUSTICE EMPLOYEES AT EACH LEVEL OF GOVERNMENT

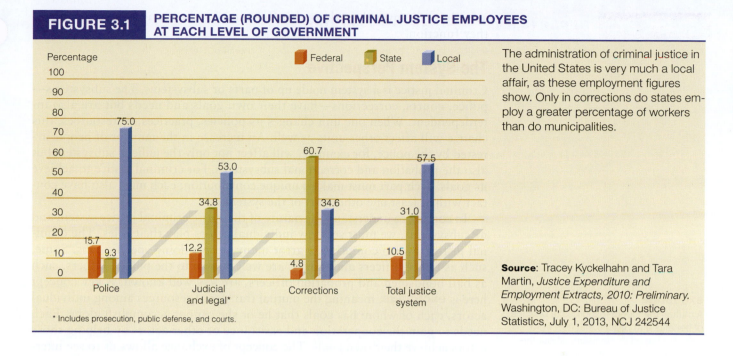

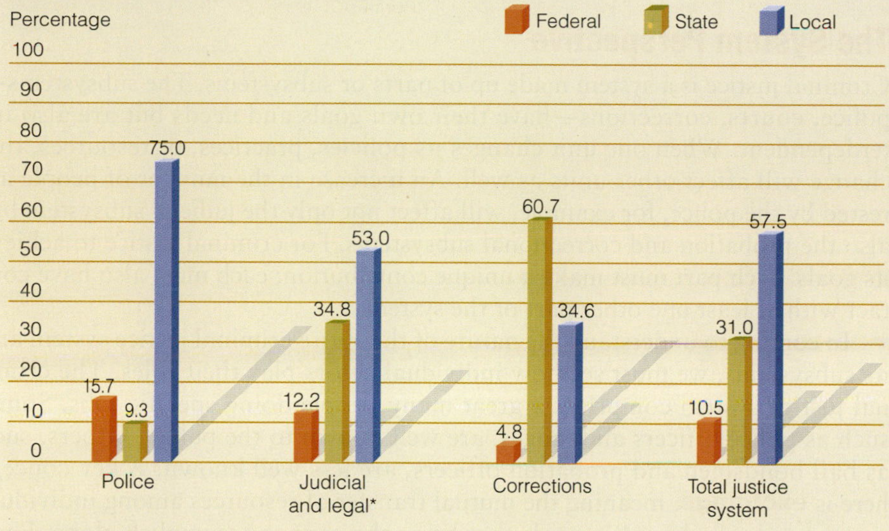

* Includes prosecution, public defense, and courts.

The administration of criminal justice in the United States is very much a local affair, as these employment figures show. Only in corrections do states employ a greater percentage of workers than do municipalities.

Source: Tracey Kyckelhahn and Tara Martin, *Justice Expenditure and Employment Extracts, 2010: Preliminary.* Washington, DC: Bureau of Justice Statistics, July 1, 2013, NCJ 242544

cuts were imposed by the federal government ("sequestration"), resulting in a law enforcement hiring freeze, reduced training, and an inability to open new investigations by the FBI and other agencies (Horwitz, 2013). Indeed, as we shall see throughout this book, budget problems during the last several years have led criminal justice agencies at all levels of government to reduce aspects of their law enforcement activities, release offenders early from prison, and take other measures to cope with limited resources (Bluestein, 2011). These issues can have their greatest impact at the local level, especially when there are no longer enough police officers on duty to respond quickly to citizens' calls for assistance (LeDuff, 2011).

✔POINT

3. What are the key features of federalism?
4. What power does the national government have in the area of crime and justice?
5. What main factor has caused federal involvement in criminal justice to expand?

STOP AND ANALYZE: Is there a risk that the American system of criminal justice is too fragmented because authority is divided between federal, state, and local government? List three problems that can arise because the United States lacks a single, specific authority to be in charge of running criminal justice agencies throughout the nation.

Criminal Justice as a System

To achieve the goals of criminal justice, many kinds of organizations—police, prosecution, courts, corrections—have been formed. Each has its own functions and personnel. We might assume that criminal justice is an orderly process in which a variety of professionals act on each case on behalf of society. To know how the system really works, however, we must look beyond its formal organizational chart. In doing so, we can use the concept of a **system**: a complex whole made up of interdependent parts whose actions

system
A complex whole consisting of interdependent parts whose operations are directed toward goals and are influenced by the environment within which they function.

are directed toward goals and influenced by the environment in which they function.

The System Perspective

Criminal justice is a system made up of parts or subsystems. The subsystems—police, courts, corrections—have their own goals and needs but are also interdependent. When one unit changes its policies, practices, or resources, this change will affect other units as well. An increase in the number of people arrested by the police, for example, will affect not only the judicial subsystem but also the probation and correctional subsystems. For criminal justice to achieve its goals, each part must make a unique contribution; each must also have contact with at least one other part of the system.

In coming to understand the nature of the entire criminal justice system and its subsystems, we must see how individual actors play their roles. The criminal justice system comprises a great many people doing specific jobs. Some, such as police officers and judges, are well known to the public. Others, such as bail bondsmen and probation officers, are less well known. A key concept here is **exchange**, meaning the mutual transfer of resources among individual actors, each of whom has goals that he or she cannot accomplish alone. Each needs to gain the cooperation and assistance of other actors by helping those actors achieve their own goals. The concept of exchange allows us to see interpersonal behavior as the result of individual decisions about the benefits and costs of different courses of action.

exchange
A mutual transfer of resources; a balance of benefits and deficits that flow from behavior based on decisions about the values and costs of alternatives.

There are many kinds of exchange relationships in the criminal justice system, some more visible than others. Probably the most obvious example is the **plea bargain**, in which the defense attorney and the prosecutor reach an agreement: The defendant agrees to plead guilty in exchange for a reduction of charges or a lighter sentence. As a result of this exchange, the prosecutor gains a quick, sure conviction; the offender receives a shorter sentence; and the defense attorney can move on to the next case. Thus, the cooperation underlying the exchange promotes the goals of each participant.

plea bargain
A defendant's plea of guilty to a criminal charge with the reasonable expectation of receiving some consideration from the state for doing so, usually a reduction of the charge. The defendant's ultimate goal is a penalty lighter than the maximum punishment formally warranted by the original charge.

The concept of exchange reminds us that decisions are the products of interactions among individuals and that the subsystems of the criminal justice system are tied together by the actions of individual decision makers. Figure 3.2 presents selected exchange relationships between a prosecutor and other individuals and agencies involved in the criminal justice process.

AP Images/Pool, Chuck Liddy

The system perspective emphasizes that criminal justice is made up of parts or subsystems, including police, courts, and corrections. Here, Judge Orlando Hudson confers with prosecutors and defense attorneys during the Durham, North Carolina, trial of Michael Peterson, who was convicted of murdering his wife, Kathleen. How do decisions by actors in each subsystem affect the ultimate fate of a defendant, such as Peterson, who is convicted of a crime?

FIGURE 3.2 EXCHANGE RELATIONSHIPS BETWEEN PROSECUTORS AND OTHERS

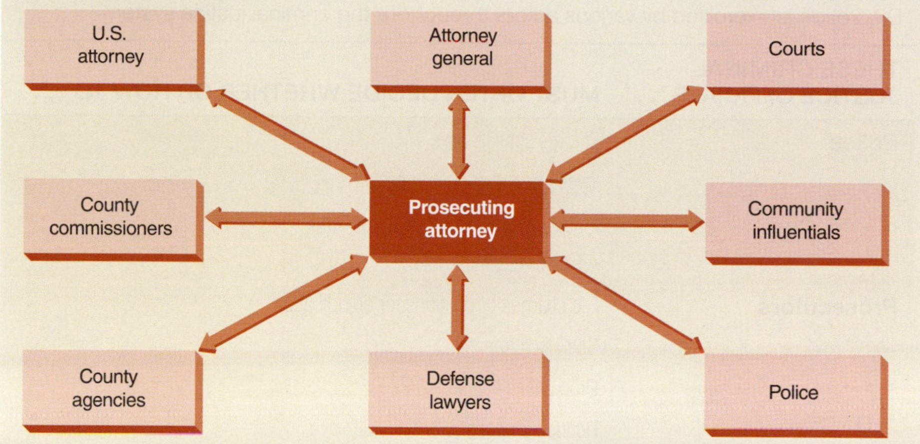

The prosecutor's decisions are influenced by relationships with other agencies and members of the community.

The concepts of system and exchange are closely linked. In this book, these concepts serve as an organizing framework to describe individual subsystems and actors and help us see how the justice process really works. Let's turn now to the main characteristics of the system, all of which shape the decisions that determine the fates of defendants.

Characteristics of the Criminal Justice System

The workings of the criminal justice system have four major characteristics: (1) discretion, (2) resource dependence, (3) sequential tasks, and (4) filtering.

Discretion

All levels of the justice process reveal a high degree of **discretion**. This term refers to officials' freedom to act according to their own judgment and conscience (see Table 3.2). For example, police officers decide how to handle a crime situation, prosecutors decide which charges to file, judges decide how long a sentence will be, and parole boards decide when an offender will be released from prison.

discretion
The authority to make decisions without reference to specific rules or facts, using instead one's own judgment; allows for individualization and informality in the administration of justice.

The extent of such discretion may seem odd, given that the United States is ruled by law and has created procedures to ensure that decisions are made in accordance with law. However, instead of being a mechanical system in which the law dominates decisions, criminal justice is a system in which actors may take various factors into account and exercise many options as they dispose of a case. The role of discretion opens the door for individual police officers, prosecutors, defense attorneys, and judges to make decisions based, at least in part, on their own self-interest. They may want to save time, save resources, or move a case to completion. Whenever people base criminal justice decisions on self-interest, however, they run the risk that American values, such as individual liberty and constitutional rights, will receive inadequate consideration and protection. For example, in December 2014, when New York City police officers, amid negotiations over a new contract, expressed their strong disapproval of what they labeled the mayor's lack of support for their department, there was a sharp drop in traffic citations, parking violations, and drug arrests. The drops—including a 94 percent decline in traffic citations over a one-year period—were so dramatic that critics interpreted them as a\ protest against

TABLE 3.2 WHO EXERCISES DISCRETION?

Discretion is exercised by various actors throughout the criminal justice system.

THESE CRIMINAL JUSTICE OFFICIALS . . .	MUST OFTEN DECIDE WHETHER OR HOW TO . . .
Police	Enforce specific laws Investigate specific crimes Search people, vicinities, buildings Arrest or detain people
Prosecutors	File charges or petitions for adjudication Seek indictments Drop cases Reduce charges
Judges or Magistrates	Set bail or conditions for release Accept pleas Determine delinquency Dismiss charges Impose sentences Revoke probation
Correctional Officials	Assign to type of correctional facility Award privileges Punish for infractions of rules Determine date and conditions of parole Revoke parole

Source: Bureau of Justice Statistics, *Report to the Nation on Crime and Justice,* 2nd ed. (Washington, DC: U.S. Government Printing Office, 1988), 59.

the mayor—a protest that many feared could endanger public safety (Editorial Board, 2014).

Two arguments are often used to justify discretion in the criminal justice system. First, discretion is needed because the system lacks the resources to treat every case the same way. If every violation of the law were pursued through trial, for example, the costs would be immense. Second, many officials believe that discretion permits them to achieve greater justice than rigid rules would produce. However, the second justification can only be true when officials emphasize justice in their decisions. If they emphasize other considerations, such as efficiency or cost, their use of discretion may clash with justice and other important American values that supposedly form the foundation of the criminal justice system. As you read New Directions in Criminal Justice Policy, consider how reform proposals may seek to affect the exercise of discretion by criminal justice officials.

Resource Dependence

Criminal justice agencies do not generate their own resources; rather, they depend on other agencies for funding. Therefore, actors in the system must cultivate and maintain good relations with those who allocate resources—that

NEW DIRECTIONS IN CRIMINAL JUSTICE POLICY

CONTEMPORARY CRIMINAL JUSTICE REFORM

In 2013, U.S. Attorney General Eric Holder ordered a comprehensive review of the criminal justice system in an effort to identify possible reforms that would help the system operate more efficiently, and at the same time enforce federal laws more fairly. The project focused on five goals:

1. To ensure that finite resources are devoted to the most important law enforcement priorities;
2. To promote fairer enforcement of the laws and alleviate disparate impacts of the criminal justice system;
3. To ensure just punishments for low-level, nonviolent convictions;
4. To bolster prevention and prisoner reentry efforts to deter crime and reduce recidivism;
5. To strengthen protections for vulnerable populations.

In seeking to advance these goals, the Justice Department put forward five principles for being "smart on crime" in using the limited resources of the criminal justice system.

The first principle was "prioritize prosecutions to focus on the most serious cases." This was in recognition that different parts of the country face different crime problems, with cybercrime, drugs, smuggling, human trafficking, and other federal crimes varying in significance and frequency in each of the nation's 94 federal district court jurisdictions. To advance this principle, the Justice Department called for the creation of new guidelines for federal prosecutors to use in deciding which cases to prosecute in their own districts. In effect, the attorney general wanted U.S. attorneys in each district to carefully construct directives to guide their own discretion as prosecutors. The guidelines would then be followed to better prioritize criminal problems and to allocate resources more effectively.

The second principle was "reform sentencing to eliminate unfair disparities and reduce overburdened prisons." Attorney General Holder announced that he would work with Congress to reform laws that impose mandatory sentences. He also used his authority to create greater flexibility for the federal Bureau of Prisons to expand compassionate releases for elderly or chronically ill prisoners who pose no threat to public safety. In addition, Attorney General Holder announced a change in federal prosecution policies "so that certain people who have committed low-level, nonviolent drug offenses, who have no ties to large-scale organizations, gangs, or cartels will no longer be charged with offenses that impose draconian mandatory minimum sentences." In effect, these changes limited discretionary decisions that might seek the harsh penalties for relatively minor offenders and also created criteria that push for compassionate releases from prison that otherwise might have been prohibited or left to the discretion of prison authorities.

The third principle was "pursue alternatives to incarceration for low-level, non-violent crimes." The Justice Department encouraged the expanded use of diversion programs and specialty courts, such as drug courts and veterans courts, that would enable prosecutors to pursue treatment and community supervision for low-level drug and theft offenders who otherwise might have been subjected to imprisonment at great expense to society.

The fourth principle was "improve reentry to curb repeat offenses and revictimization." Offenders who are released from prison often have great difficulty reentering society successfully. They may lack education and job skills and find themselves unable to compete for jobs in communities facing difficult economic circumstances. When obstacles to reentry are severe, there are grave concerns that these ex-offenders will commit new offenses and return to the justice system when, with additional assistance and resources, they might otherwise have succeeded in becoming productive members of society. Attorney General Holder directed the U.S. attorneys in each federal district to designate a reentry coordinator who would monitor progress on these issues. The Justice Department also called on federal prosecutors to give attention to the issue and consider it a component of their jobs in the federal criminal justice system.

The fifth principle was "'surge' resources to violence protection and protecting most vulnerable populations." For this principle, the Justice Department required federal prosecutors, FBI agents, and U.S. marshals to work with local law enforcement officials in developing strategies and sharing information to address problems of violent crime. The Justice Department also increased resources for programs to combat the victimization of women and children, including more money for School Resource Officers (SROs), police officers who are assigned to work with students in schools.

Source: U.S. Department of Justice, *Smart on Crime: Reforming the Criminal Justice System for the 21st Century.* August 2013 (http://www.justice.gov/sites/default/files/ag/legacy/2013/08/12/smart-on-crime.pdf).

DEBATE THE ISSUE

Are these appropriate goals and strategies for the federal government to pursue? Are there any goals and strategies that are undervalued or missing? Do these approaches appear to be those that will increase fairness and efficiency in the criminal justice system? Provide three additional suggestions for actions by the federal government as well as three criticisms or questions about the prospects for success of the current plans.

is, political decision makers, such as legislators, mayors, and city council members. Some police departments gain revenue through traffic fines and property forfeitures, but these sources generate too little to sustain their budgets.

Because budget decisions are made by elected officials who seek to please the public, criminal justice officials must also maintain a positive image and good relations with voters. If the police have strong public support, for example, the mayor will be reluctant to reduce the law enforcement budget. Criminal justice officials also seek positive coverage from the news media. Because the media often provide a crucial link between government agencies and the public, criminal justice officials may announce notable achievements but try to limit publicity about controversial cases and decisions.

Sequential Tasks

Decisions in the criminal justice system follow a specific sequence. The police must make an arrest before a defendant is passed along to the prosecutor; the prosecutor's decisions determine the nature of the court's workload; and so forth. If officials act out of sequence, they cannot achieve their goals. For example, prosecutors and judges cannot bypass the police by making arrests, and correctional officials cannot punish anyone who has not passed through the earlier stages of the process.

The sequential nature of the system is a key element in the exchange relationships among decision makers who depend on one another to achieve their goals. It thus contributes to the strong interdependence within the system.

Filtering

filtering process
A process by which criminal justice officials screen out some cases while advancing others to the next level of decision making.

The criminal justice system also serves as a **filtering process**. At each level, some defendants are sent on to the next stage, while others are either released or processed under changed conditions. As shown in Figure 3.3, people who have been arrested may be filtered out of the system at various points. Note that few suspects who are arrested are then prosecuted, tried, and convicted. Some go free because the police decide that a crime has not been committed or that the evidence is not sound. The prosecutor may decide that justice would be better served by sending the suspect to a substance abuse clinic. Although many defendants will plead guilty, the judge may dismiss charges against others, and the jury may acquit a few defendants. Most of the offenders who are actually tried, however, will be convicted. Thus, the criminal justice system is often described as a funnel—many cases enter it, but only a few result in conviction and punishment.

To summarize, the criminal justice system is composed of a set of interdependent parts (subsystems). This system has four key attributes: (1) discretion, (2) resource dependence, (3) sequential tasks, and (4) filtering. Within this framework, we look next at the operations of criminal justice agencies and then examine the flow of cases through the system.

✔POINT
6. What is a system?
7. What is one example of an exchange relationship?
8. What are the major characteristics of the criminal justice system?

STOP AND ANALYZE: What is the most surprising aspect of Figure 3.3? Describe two aspects of the information presented in the figure that differ from your assumptions about the criminal justice system.

FIGURE 3.3 CRIMINAL JUSTICE AS A FILTERING PROCESS

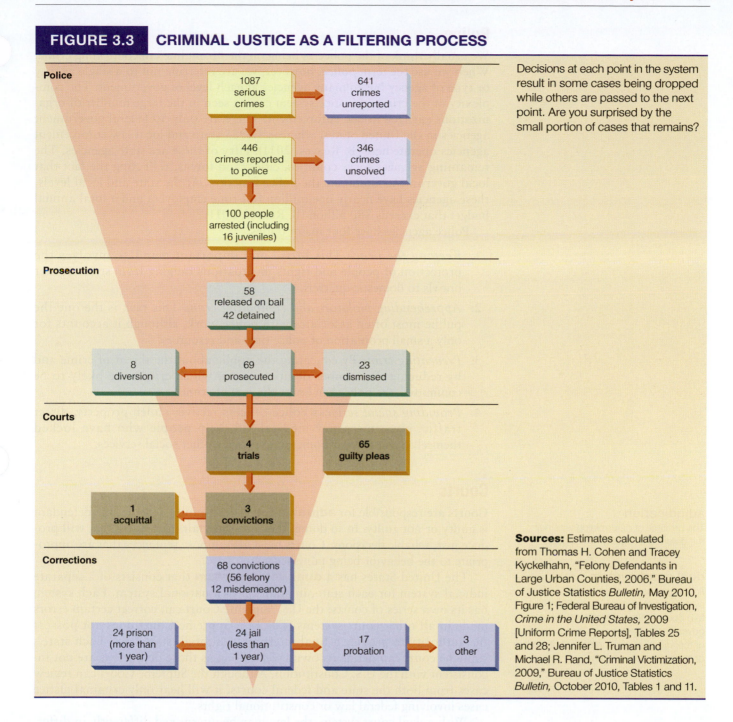

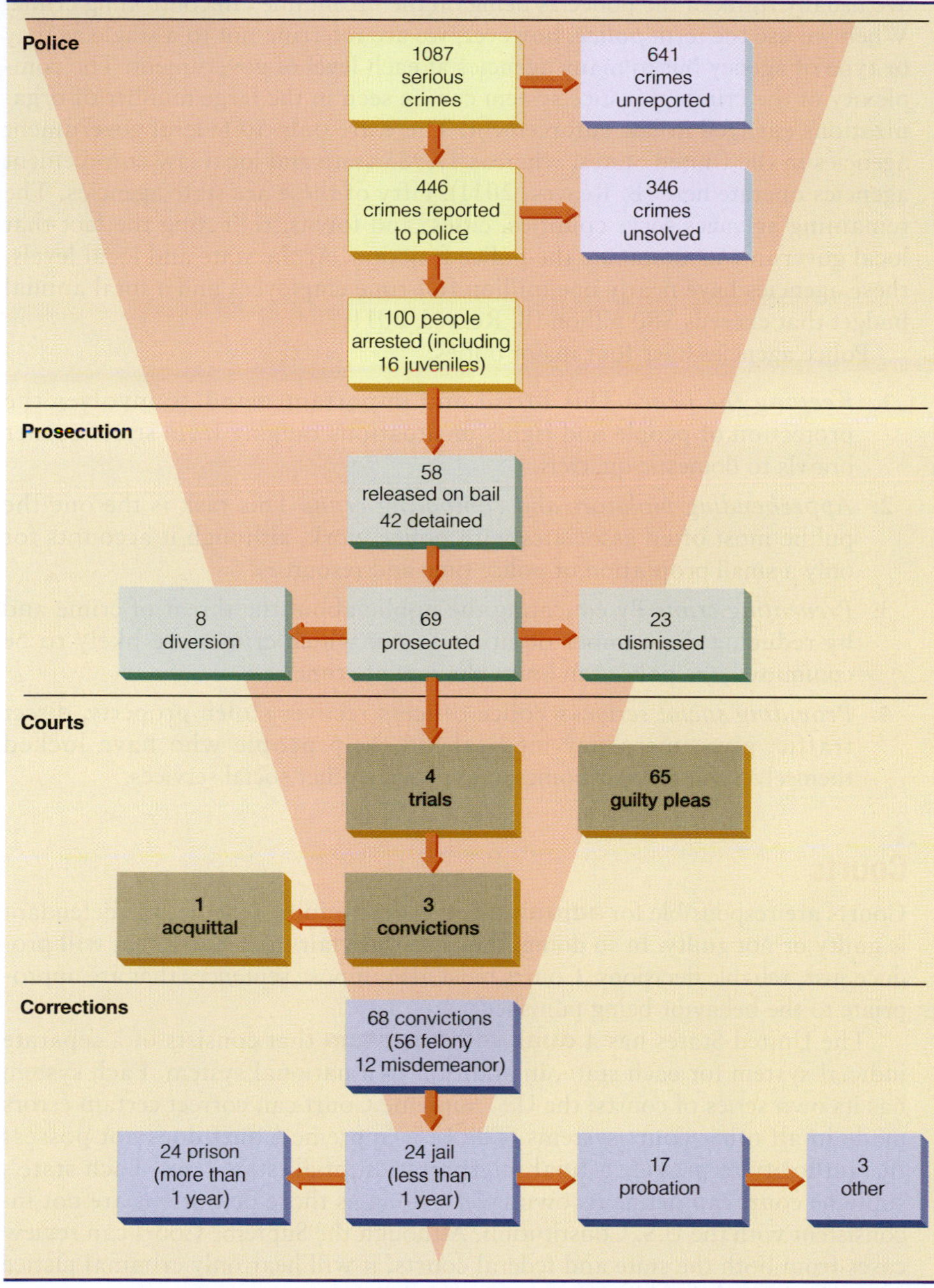

Decisions at each point in the system result in some cases being dropped while others are passed to the next point. Are you surprised by the small portion of cases that remains?

Sources: Estimates calculated from Thomas H. Cohen and Tracey Kyckelhahn, "Felony Defendants in Large Urban Counties, 2006," Bureau of Justice Statistics *Bulletin,* May 2010, Figure 1; Federal Bureau of Investigation, *Crime in the United States,* 2009 [Uniform Crime Reports], Tables 25 and 28; Jennifer L. Truman and Michael R. Rand, "Criminal Victimization, 2009," Bureau of Justice Statistics *Bulletin,* October 2010, Tables 1 and 11.

Operations of Criminal Justice Agencies

The criminal justice system has been formed to deal with people accused of violating the criminal law. Its subsystems consist of more than 60,000 public and private agencies with an annual budget of more than $250 billion and more than 2.5 million employees (Kyckelhahn and Martin, 2013). Here we review the main parts of the criminal justice system and their functions.

Police

We usually think of the police as being on the "front line" in controlling crime. When we use the term *police,* however, we are referring not to a single agency or type of agency but to many agencies at each level of government. The complexity of the criminal justice system can be seen in the large number of organizations engaged in law enforcement. There are only 50 federal government agencies in the United States, whereas 17,985 state and local law enforcement agencies operate here (B. Reaves, 2011). Fifty of these are state agencies. The remaining agencies serve counties, cities, and towns, reflecting the fact that local governments dominate the police function. At the state and local levels, these agencies have nearly one million full-time employees and a total annual budget that exceeds $80 billion (B. Reaves, 2011).

Police agencies have four major duties:

1. *Keeping the peace* This broad and important mandate involves the protection of people and rights in situations ranging from street-corner brawls to domestic quarrels.
2. *Apprehending violators and combating crime* This task is the one the public most often associates with police work, although it accounts for only a small proportion of police time and resources.
3. *Preventing crime* By educating the public about the threat of crime and by reducing the number of situations in which crimes are likely to be committed, the police can lower the rate of crime.
4. *Providing social services* Police officers recover stolen property, direct traffic, give emergency medical aid, help people who have locked themselves out of their homes, and provide other social services.

Courts

adjudication
The process of determining whether the defendant is guilty or not guilty.

dual court system
A system based on a separate judicial system for each state, in addition to a court system under the national government. Each case is tried in a court of the same jurisdiction as that of the law or laws allegedly broken.

Courts are responsible for **adjudication**—determining whether the defendant is guilty or not guilty. In so doing, they must use fair procedures that will produce just, reliable decisions. Courts must also impose sentences that are appropriate to the behavior being punished.

The United States has a **dual court system** that consists of a separate judicial system for each state, in addition to a national system. Each system has its own series of courts; the U.S. Supreme Court can correct certain errors made in all other court systems. The U.S. Supreme Court does not possess the authority to provide a final interpretation of all state laws. Each state's supreme court can define its own laws as long as those definitions are not inconsistent with the U.S. Constitution. Although the Supreme Court can review cases from both the state and federal courts, it will hear only criminal justice cases involving federal law or constitutional rights.

With a dual court system, the law may be interpreted differently in different states. Although the wording of laws may be similar, state courts have the power to interpret and define their own laws for application within their own states. To some extent, these variations reflect regional differences in social and political conditions; that is, although a common set of American values concerning liberty and rights exists throughout the country, the interpretation and weight of those values may vary in the minds of citizens and judges in various regions. Thus, the nature of expectations about personal privacy, equal treatment, and the role of private gun ownership as elements of liberty is viewed differently in the northeastern and Great Lakes states than in the southern and mountain states. For example, the Washington State courts' interpretations of their state constitution "resulted in outcomes that reflect greater protection for the right to privacy than is enforced under the federal constitution. For example, [Washington] courts have found that [the state constitution] protects against unwarranted searches of a person's garbage cans, government invasion of bank and telephone records, and unwarranted searches of vehicles, even those driven by a felon on work release" (Bindas et al., 2010: 49). Other states' courts would not necessarily make the same decisions.

Corrections

On any given day, nearly seven million (1 of every 35) American adults fall under the supervision of local, state, and federal correctional systems (L. E. Glaze and Kaeble, 2014). There is no typical correctional agency or official. Instead, a variety of agencies and programs are provided by private and public organizations—including federal, state, and local governments—and carried out in many different community and closed settings.

While the average citizen may equate corrections with prisons, less than 23 percent of convicted offenders are in prisons and jails; the rest are being supervised in the community. Probation and parole have long been important aspects of corrections, as have community-based halfway houses, work release programs, and supervised activities.

The federal government, all the states, most counties, and all but the smallest cities engage in corrections. Nonprofit private organizations such as the YMCA have also contracted with governments to perform correctional services. In recent years, for-profit businesses have also entered into contracts with governments to build and operate correctional institutions.

The police, courts, and corrections are the main agencies of criminal justice. Each is a part, or subsystem, of the criminal justice system. Each is linked to the other two subsystems, and the actions of each affect the others. These effects can be seen as we examine the flow of decision making within the criminal justice system.

✔POINT

9. What are the four main duties of police?
10. What is a dual court system?
11. What are the major types of state and local correctional agencies?

STOP AND ANALYZE: What kinds of problems can arise from having state and federal law enforcement agencies and courts operating in the same city? Briefly describe two problems that may face citizens living under the authority of two separate justice systems that handle their own sets of laws simultaneously in every American city and state. Now describe two problems that may face either police or prosecutors.

The Flow of Decision Making in the Criminal Justice System

The processing of cases in the criminal justice system involves a series of decisions by police officers, prosecutors, judges, probation officers, wardens, and parole board members. At each stage in the process, they decide whether a case will move on to the next stage or be dropped from the system. Although the flowchart shown in Figure 3.4 appears streamlined, with cases entering at the top and moving swiftly toward the bottom, the actual route may be quite long, with many detours. At each step, officials have the discretion to decide what happens next. Many cases are filtered out of the system, others are sent to the next decision maker, and still others are dealt with by informal means.

FIGURE 3.4 THE FLOW OF DECISION MAKING IN THE CRIMINAL JUSTICE SYSTEM

Each agency is responsible for a part of the decision-making process. Thus police, prosecution, courts, and corrections are bound together through a series of exchange relationships.

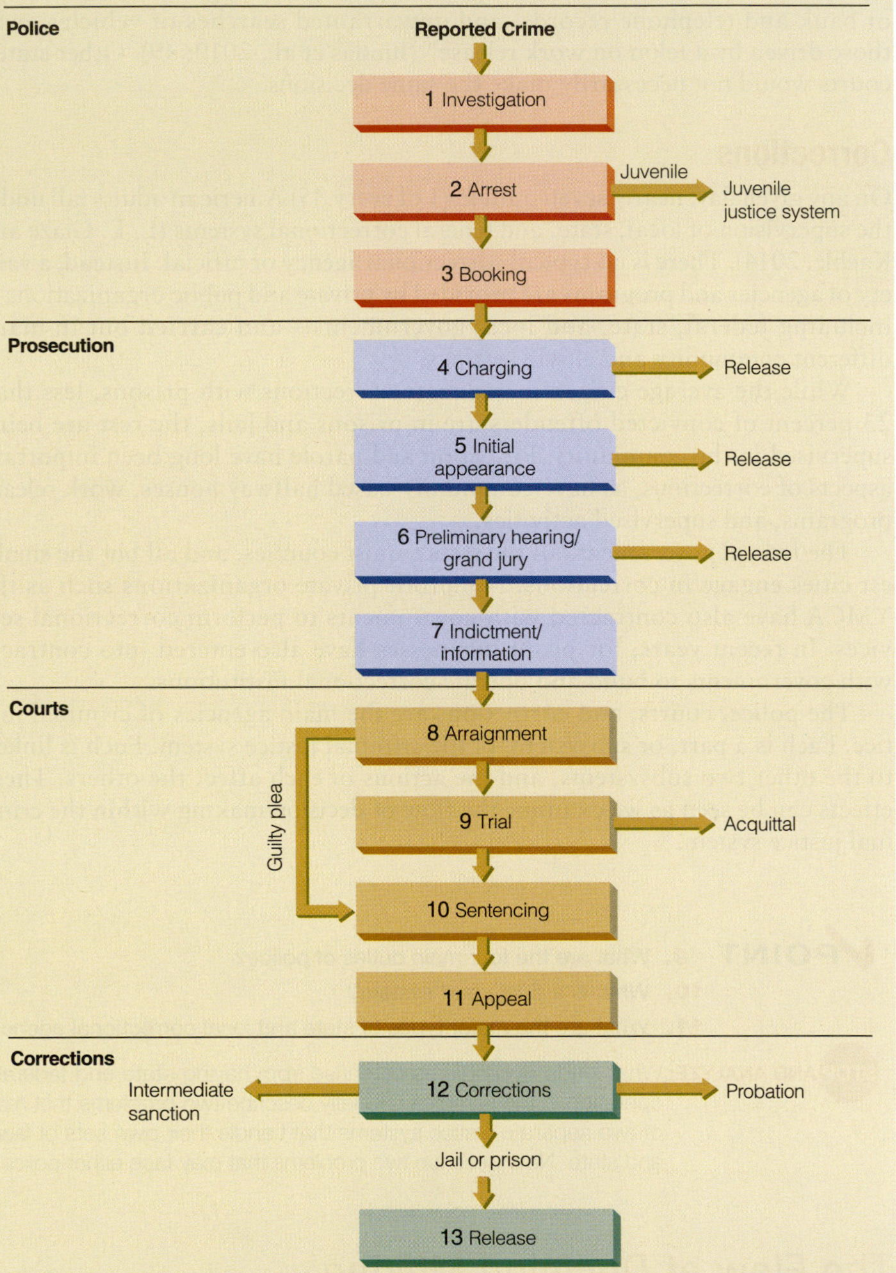

Moreover, the flowchart does not show the influences of social relations or the political environment. For example, in 2006 a retired FBI agent was charged with providing inside information to organized-crime figures so that informants could be murdered. It was then discovered that 30 years earlier this agent had been caught illegally selling unlicensed handguns to undercover agents of the U.S. Bureau of Alcohol, Tobacco, and Firearms. If this FBI agent had been prosecuted for the handgun sales, his career in the FBI would have been over and he would never have achieved the high-level position that later allegedly allowed him to assist mobsters. However, according to one former federal prosecutor involved in the handgun case in 1976, a high official in the

U.S. Justice Department used his discretion to drop the gun charges. According to the former prosecutor, the high official "expressed no other reason not to prosecute the guy except the guy was a cop—and he didn't want to embarrass the [FBI]" (Feuer, 2006). The flowchart does not take into account that someone in authority might exercise discretion unfairly in favor of certain people, such as those with wealth, important positions, or political connections.

Many factors can influence prosecutors' decisions to use their full powers or, alternatively, to decline to prosecute even when evidence of wrongdoing exists. Thus, as we describe the 13 steps in the criminal justice process, we must bear in mind that other factors affecting decisions by police, prosecutors, and judges may not be fully evident in these descriptions. Discretion, political pressure, and other factors can alter the outcomes for different defendants.

Steps in the Decision-Making Process

The criminal justice system consists of 13 steps that cover the stages of law enforcement, adjudication, and corrections. The system looks like an assembly line where decisions are made about defendants—the raw material of the process. As these steps are described, recall the concepts discussed earlier: system, exchange, discretion, sequential tasks, and filtering. Be aware that the terms used for different stages in the process may differ from state to state, and the sequence of the steps differs in some parts of the country, but the flow of decision making generally follows this pattern.

1. *Investigation.* The process begins when the police believe that a crime has been committed. At this point, an investigation is begun. The police normally depend on a member of the community to report the offense. Except for traffic and public order offenses, the police rarely observe illegal behavior themselves. Because most crimes have already been committed and offenders have left the scene before the police arrive, the police are at a disadvantage in quickly finding and arresting the offenders.
2. *Arrest.* If the police find enough evidence showing that a particular person has committed a crime, they can make an arrest. An **arrest** involves physically taking a person into custody pending a court proceeding. This action not only restricts the suspect's freedom, but it is also the first step toward prosecution.

   Under some conditions, arrests may be made on the basis of a **warrant**—a court order issued by a judge authorizing police officers to take certain actions, such as arresting suspects or searching premises. In practice, most arrests are made without warrants. In some states, police officers may issue a summons or citation that orders a person to appear in court on a certain date. This avoids the need to hold the suspect physically while waiting for decisions to be made about the case.
3. *Booking.* After an arrest, the suspect is usually transported to a police station for booking, in which a record is made of the arrest. When booked, the suspect may be fingerprinted, photographed, interrogated, and placed in a lineup to be identified by the victim or witnesses. All suspects must also be warned that they have the right to counsel, that they may remain silent, and that any statement they make may be used against them later. Bail may be set so that the suspect learns what amount of money must be paid or what other conditions must be met to gain release from custody until the case is processed.
4. *Charging.* Prosecuting attorneys are the key link between the police and the courts. They must consider the facts of the case and decide whether there is reasonable cause to believe that an offense was committed and

arrest
The physical taking of a person into custody on the grounds that probable cause exists to believe that he or she has committed a criminal offense. Police may use only reasonable physical force in making an arrest. The purpose of the arrest is to hold the accused for a court proceeding.

warrant
A court order authorizing police officials to take certain actions; for example, to arrest suspects or to search premises.

that the suspect committed the offense. The decision to charge is crucial, because it sets in motion the adjudication of the case.

5. *Initial appearance.* Within a reasonable time after arrest, the suspect must be brought before a judge. At this point, suspects are given formal notice of the charge(s) for which they are being held, advised of their rights, and, if approved by the judge, given a chance to post bail. At this stage, the judge decides whether there is enough evidence to hold the suspect for further criminal processing. If enough evidence has not been produced, the judge will dismiss the case.

   The purpose of bail is to permit the accused to be released while awaiting trial and to ensure that he or she will show up in court at the appointed time. The concept of bail is connected to the important American value of liberty. Bail represents an effort to avoid depriving presumptively innocent people of liberty before their guilt has been proven in court. Bail requires the accused to provide or arrange a surety (or pledge), usually in the form of money or a bond. The amount of bail is based mainly on the judge's view of the seriousness of the crime and the defendant's prior criminal record. Suspects may also be released *on their own recognizance*—a promise to appear in court at a later date. In a few cases bail may be denied and the accused held because he or she is viewed as a threat to the community or there is a high risk that the individual will flee.

6. *Preliminary hearing/grand jury.* After suspects have been arrested, booked, and brought to court to be informed of the charge and advised of their rights, a decision must be made as to whether there is enough evidence to proceed. The preliminary hearing, used in about half the states, allows a judge to decide whether there is probable cause to believe that a crime has been committed and that the accused person committed it. If the judge does not find probable cause, the case is dismissed. If there is enough evidence, the accused is bound over for arraignment on an **information**—a document charging a person with a specific crime. In the federal system and in some states, the prosecutor appears before a grand jury, which decides whether there is enough evidence to file an **indictment** or *true bill* charging the suspect with a specific crime. The preliminary hearing and grand jury are designed to prevent hasty and malicious prosecutions, to protect people from mistakenly being humiliated in public, and to decide whether there are grounds for prosecution. The use of the grand jury reinforces the American value of limited government. By giving citizens the authority to overrule the police and prosecutor in determining whether criminal charges should be pursued, the grand jury represents an effort to reduce the risk that government officials will use their power to deprive people of liberty in unjustified circumstances.

   In 2014, controversies arose concerning whether the grand jury process could be used by prosecutors seeking to avoid filing criminal charges themselves. These officials could thereby claim that citizens, rather than the prosecutor, had decided against prosecution. One particular example of this occurred with the grand jury proceedings to examine the evidence relating to the shooting of unarmed teenager Michael Brown by Ferguson, Missouri, police officer Darren Wilson. Specific concerns were raised about the proceedings of this grand jury, namely, that the prosecutor intentionally overwhelmed and confused the jury with contradictory evidence, including evidence that he knew to be untrue; and that he gave the jury improper instructions on the law concerning police shootings (M. M. Davey, Wines, et al., 2014; Walton, 2014).

7. *Indictment/information.* If the preliminary hearing leads to an information or the grand jury vote leads to an indictment, the prosecutor prepares the formal charging document and presents it to the court.

information
A document charging an individual with a specific crime. It is prepared by a prosecuting attorney and presented to a court at a preliminary hearing.

indictment
A document returned by a grand jury as a true bill charging an individual with a specific crime on the basis of a determination of probable cause from evidence presented by a prosecuting attorney.

8. *Arraignment.* The accused person appears in court to hear the indictment or information read by a judge and to enter a plea. Accused persons may plead guilty or not guilty or, in some states, stand mute. If the accused pleads guilty, the judge must decide whether the plea is made voluntarily and whether the person has full knowledge of the consequences. When a guilty plea is accepted as knowing and voluntary, there is no need for a trial, and the judge imposes a sentence. Plea bargaining can take place at any time in the criminal justice process, but it tends to be completed shortly before or soon after arraignment. Very few criminal cases proceed to trial. Most move from the entry of the guilty plea to the sentencing phase.
9. *Trial.* For the small percentage of defendants who plead not guilty, the Sixth Amendment guarantees the right to a trial by an impartial jury if the charges are serious enough to warrant a prison sentence of more than six months. In many jurisdictions, lesser charges do not entail a right to a jury trial. Most trials are summary or bench trials—that is, they are conducted without a jury. Because the defendant pleads guilty in most criminal cases, fewer than 10 percent of cases go to trial, and only a portion of those are heard by juries. Whether a criminal trial is held before a judge alone or before a judge and jury, the procedures are similar and are set out by state law and Supreme Court rulings. A defendant may be found guilty only if the evidence proves beyond a reasonable doubt that he or she committed the offense.
10. *Sentencing.* Judges are responsible for imposing sentences. The intent is to make the sentence suitable to the offender and the offense within the limits set by the law. Although criminal codes define the boundaries of sentences, the judge often still has leeway. Among the judge's options are a suspended sentence, probation, imprisonment, or other sanctions such as fines and community service.
11. *Appeal.* Defendants who are found guilty may appeal convictions to a higher court. An appeal can be based on the claim that the trial court failed to follow the proper procedures or that the defendant's constitutional rights were violated by the actions of police, prosecutors, defense attorneys, or judges. The number of appeals is small compared with the total number of convictions, and in about 80 percent of appeals, trial judges and other officials are ruled to have acted properly. Even defendants who win appeals do not necessarily go free. Normally the defendant is given a second trial, which may result in an acquittal, a second conviction, or a plea bargain to lesser charges.
12. *Corrections.* The court's sentence is carried out by the correctional subsystem. Probation, intermediate sanctions such as fines and community service, and incarceration are the sanctions most often imposed. Probation allows offenders to serve their sentences in the community under supervision. Youthful offenders, first offenders, and those convicted of minor violations are most likely to be sentenced to probation rather than incarceration. The conditions of probation may require offenders to observe certain rules—to be employed, maintain an orderly life, or attend school—and to report to their supervising officer from time to time. If these requirements are not met, the judge may revoke the probation and impose a prison sentence. Many new types of sanctions have been used in recent years. These intermediate sanctions are more restrictive than probation but less restrictive than incarceration. They include fines, intensive supervision probation, boot camp, home confinement, and community service. Whatever the reasons used to justify them, prisons exist mainly to separate criminals from the rest of society. Those convicted of misdemeanors usually serve their time in city or county jails, while felons serve time in state

prisons. Isolation from the community is one of the most painful aspects of incarceration. Visits are restricted and supervision is ever present. To maintain security, prison officials make unannounced searches of inmates and subject them to strict rules.

13. *Release.* Release may occur when the offender has served the full sentence imposed by the court, but most offenders are returned to the community under the supervision of a parole officer. Parole continues for the duration of the sentence or for a period specified by law. Parole may be revoked and the offender returned to prison if the conditions of parole are not met or if the parolee commits another crime.

The case of Christopher Jones is described in The Criminal Justice Process feature. Jones, a then 31-year-old man from Battle Creek, Michigan, was arrested, charged, and convicted of serious crimes arising from the police investigation of a series of robberies. His case illustrates how the steps just discussed can play out in the real world.

✔POINT 12. What are the steps of the criminal justice process?

STOP AND ANALYZE: How powerful is discretionary decision making in the criminal justice process? Make a list of all of the actors who make such decisions and all of the steps in the process where discretionary decisions occur.

The Criminal Justice Wedding Cake

Although the flowchart shown in Figure 3.4 is helpful, we must note that not all cases are treated equally. The process applied to a given case, as well as its outcome, is shaped by the importance of the case to decision makers, the seriousness of the charge, and the defendant's resources.

Some cases are highly visible either because of the notoriety of the defendant or victim or because of the shocking nature of the crime. At the other extreme are "run-of-the-mill cases" involving unknowns charged with minor crimes.

As shown in Figure 3.5, the criminal justice process can be compared to a wedding cake. This model shows clearly how different cases receive different kinds of treatment in the justice process.

FIGURE 3.5 THE CRIMINAL JUSTICE WEDDING CAKE

This figure shows that different cases are treated in different ways. Only a very few cases are played out as "high drama"; most are handled through plea bargaining and dismissals.

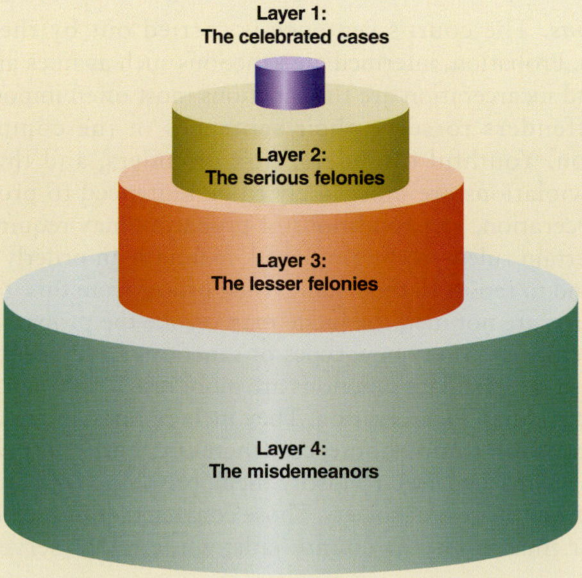

Drawn from Samuel Walker, *Sense and Nonsense about Crime and Drugs,* 4th ed. (Belmont, CA: Wadsworth, 1998), 20–37.

THE CRIMINAL JUSTICE PROCESS

The State of Michigan versus Christopher Jones

INVESTIGATION

In October 1998, police in Battle Creek, Michigan, investigated a string of six robberies that occurred in a ten-day period. Assaults occurred during some of the robberies. One victim was beaten so badly with a power tool that he required extensive reconstructive surgery for his face and skull. The police received an anonymous tip on their Silent Observer hotline, which led them to put together a *photo lineup*—an array of photographs of local men who had criminal records. Based on the anonymous tip and photographs identified by the victims, the police began to search for two men who were well known to them, Christopher Jones and his cousin Fred Brown.

ARREST

Christopher Jones had shut himself into a bedroom at his parents' house. He was a 31-year-old African American man whose life was in shambles. A dozen years of struggles with cocaine addiction had cost him his marriage and several jobs in local factories. In addition, he had a criminal record, stretching back several years, from pleading guilty to charges of attempted larceny and attempted breaking and entering in separate incidents. Thus he had a record of stealing to support his drug habit, and he had previously spent time on probation and done a short stretch in a minimum-security prison and a boot camp. But he had never been caught with drugs, and he had never been accused of committing an act of violence.

Because his family feared that he would be injured or killed by the police if he tried to run or resist arrest, his parents called the police and told them where he was. At approximately 10:00 P.M. on October 28, as officers surrounded the house, the family opened the door and showed the officers the way to the bedroom. When Jones heard the knock on the door, he knew he had to face the inevitable. He surrendered peacefully and was led to the waiting police car in handcuffs.

The officers took him to the police station. A detective with whom Jones was acquainted offered him a cup of coffee and then read him his *Miranda* rights, including his right to remain silent and his right to an attorney. The detective then informed Jones that he was looking at the possibility of a life sentence in prison unless he helped the police by providing information about Fred Brown. Jones said that he did not want to talk to the police yet, and he asked for an attorney. Because arrested suspects are entitled to have an attorney present during questioning if they ask for one, the police ceased questioning Jones. He was taken next door to the jail.

BOOKING

At the jail, Jones was strip-searched. After removing all of his clothes so that officers could make sure he had not hidden weapons or drugs in his clothing or on his body, he was given a bright-orange jumpsuit to wear. He was photographed and fingerprinted. He was told that he would be arraigned the next morning. The police handed him a blanket and locked him in the *holding cell*—a large cell where people are placed immediately upon arrest. The holding cell was big enough to hold approximately ten people and it had four cement benches to serve as beds. As Jones looked for a space to lie down on the floor with his blanket, he estimated that 16 men were sleeping in the crowded cell that night.

ARRAIGNMENT

The next morning, the men in the holding cell were taken to a neighboring room for video arraignment. A two-way camera system permitted Jones to see the district courtroom in the neighboring courthouse at the same time that the judge and others in the courtroom could view him on a television screen. The judge informed Jones that he was being charged with breaking and entering, armed robbery, and assault with intent to commit murder. The final charge alone could draw a life sentence. Under Michigan law, these charges can be filed directly by the prosecutor without being presented to a grand jury for indictment as required in federal courts and some other states. The judge set bond (bail) at $200,000, an amount that an unemployed, penniless person like Jones would have no hope of obtaining.

At a second video arraignment several days later, Jones was informed that he faced seven additional counts of assault with intent to commit murder, armed robbery, unarmed robbery, and home invasion for four additional robberies. Bond was set at $200,000 for each alleged robbery. Thus he faced ten felony charges for the five robberies, and his total bail was $1 million.

STOP AND ANALYZE: At this point, Jones was considered "presumptively innocent" as he had not been convicted for the crimes of which he was accused. Was the bail too high? Write down two purposes that the judge may have been advancing by setting such a high bail.

JAIL

After arraignment, jail officers examined Jones's current charges and past record in order to determine the level of security and supervision he would need in the jail. Prisoners charged with violent offenses or who have substantial criminal records are kept in areas separate from people charged with property crimes. Jones was placed in a medium-security area with 55 others who were charged with serious felonies. Jones would eventually spend nine months at the jail before his case concluded.

DEFENSE ATTORNEY

Under state court procedures, Jones was supposed to have a preliminary hearing within two weeks after his arraignment. At the preliminary hearing, the prosecution would be required to present enough evidence to justify the charges. If the evidence was inadequate, the district judge could dismiss the charges. If there was enough evidence to raise the possibility of guilt, the district judge would send the case up to the Calhoun County Circuit Court, the court that handled felony trials.

Jones received a letter informing him of the name of the private attorney appointed by the court to represent him, but he did not get to meet the attorney until he was taken to court for his first preliminary hearing. Minutes before the hearing, the attorney, David Gilbert, introduced himself to Jones. Jones wanted to delay any preliminary hearing until a lineup could be held to test the victims' identification of him as a robber. According to Jones, Gilbert said they must proceed with the preliminary hearing for one of the charges, because the victim had traveled from another state in order to testify. The preliminary hearing covering the rest of the charges was postponed, but the out-of-town witness's testimony led the district judge to conclude that sufficient evidence existed to move one of Jones's cases to the circuit court on an armed robbery charge.

LINEUP

Jones waited for weeks for the lineup to be scheduled. When he was taken to his rescheduled preliminary hearing, his attorney complained to the judge that the lineup had never been conducted. The judge ordered that the lineup be held as soon as possible.

Jones and the other men were told to stand and turn around in front of a one-way mirror. One by one, the victims of each robbery looked at the men in the room and attempted to determine if any of them were the robbers. At the end of each identification, one of the men in the lineup was asked to step forward, and Jones presumed this meant that the victim had identified that man as one of the robbers. Jones was only asked to step forward twice, and other men were asked to step forward at other times. Jones guessed that he was picked out by two of the victims, but that the other three victims either picked other men or were unable to identify anyone.

Jones's defense attorney was unable to attend the lineup. Another attorney arrived and informed Jones that he would take Mr. Gilbert's place. Although Jones protested that the other men in the lineup were much shorter and older, he was disappointed that the substitute attorney was not more active in objecting that the men looked too different from Jones to adequately test the victims' ability to make an identification. He later claimed that he learned that his substitute attorney had just entered private practice after serving as an assistant prosecutor at Jones's first preliminary hearing.

STOP AND ANALYZE: Was there anything wrong with the identification procedure? Describe two aspects of lineup procedures that may create risks of inaccurate identification of suspects.

PRELIMINARY HEARING

At the next preliminary hearing, the victims in each case provided testimony about what happened. Because the testimony generally focused on Brown as the perpetrator of the assaults and robberies, the defense attorney argued that many of the charges against Jones should be dropped. The judge determined that the victims' testimony provided enough evidence to send most of the charges against Jones to the circuit court.

PLEA BARGAINING

Jones waited for weeks in jail without hearing much from his attorney. Although he did not know it, the prosecutor was formulating a plea agreement and communicating to the defense attorney the terms under which charges would be dropped in exchange for a guilty plea from Jones. Outside the courtroom a few minutes before a hearing on the proposed plea agreement, Gilbert told Jones that the prosecutor had offered to drop all of the other charges if Jones would plead guilty to one count of unarmed robbery for the incident in which the victim was seriously injured by Brown and one count of home invasion for another robbery. Jones did not want to accept the deal, because he claimed that he was not even present at the robbery for which he was being asked to plead guilty for home invasion. According to Jones, the attorney insisted that this was an excellent deal compared with all of the other charges that the prosecutor could pursue. Jones still resisted. In the courtroom, Judge James Kingsley read the offer to Jones, but Jones refused to enter a guilty plea. Like the defense attorney, the judge told Jones that this was a favorable offer compared with the other serious charges that the prosecutor could still pursue against him. Again, Jones declined.

Jones was worried that he was making a mistake by turning down the plea offer. He wondered if he could end up with a life sentence, even for a crime he did not commit, if one of the victims identified him by mistake as having done a crime that was actually committed by Brown. Outside the courtroom, he told his attorney that he had changed his mind. They went right back into the courtroom and told the judge that he was ready to enter a guilty plea. As they prepared to enter the plea, the prosecutor said that they also expected Jones to provide information about the five robberies and testify against Brown as part of the plea agreement. The defense attorney protested that this condition had not been part of the plea agreement offered by the prosecutor. Jones told the judge that he could not provide any information about the home invasion to which he was about to plead guilty because he was not present at that robbery and had no knowledge of what occurred. Judge Kingsley declared that he would not accept a guilty plea when the defendant claimed to have no knowledge of the crime.

After the hearing, the prosecutor and defense attorney renewed their discussions about a plea agreement. Jones agreed to take a polygraph (lie detector) test so that the prosecutor could try to confirm which robberies he actually knew about. Although Jones waited for weeks for the polygraph test in hopes that it would show prosecutors that his criminal involvement with Brown was limited, no test was ever administered.

SCHEDULED TRIAL AND PLEA AGREEMENT

Jones waited for several more weeks in jail. According to Jones, when Gilbert came to visit, he informed Jones that the armed robbery trial was scheduled for the following day. In addition, the prosecutor's plea offer had changed. Fred Brown pleaded guilty to armed robbery and assault with intent less than murder, and he was facing a sentence of 25 to 50 years in prison. Because Brown pleaded guilty, the prosecutor no longer needed Jones as a potential witness in any trial against Brown. Thus the prosecutor no longer offered the unarmed robbery and home invasion pleas. He now wanted Jones to plead to the same charges as Brown in exchange for dropping the other pending charges. According to Jones, Gilbert claimed the prosecutor would be very angry if he did not take the plea, and the attorney encouraged Jones to accept the plea by arguing that the prosecutor would otherwise pursue all of the other charges, which could bring a life sentence. Jones refused to plead guilty.

The next day, Jones was given his personal clothes to wear instead of the orange jail jumpsuit, because he was going to court for trial instead of for a hearing. Gilbert again encouraged him to consider the plea agreement. He raised the possibility of a life sentence if the prosecutor pursued all of the pending charges and, according to Jones, he said that the guilty plea could be withdrawn if the sentencing recommendation made by the probation office was too high. Because he did not want to risk getting a life sentence and he believed he could later withdraw the plea if he wanted, Jones decided to accept the offer.

With his attorney's advice, he entered a plea of no contest to the two charges. A no contest plea is treated the same as a guilty plea for punishment purposes. However, the plea means that crime victims must prove their case in any subsequent civil lawsuit against the defendant for injuries suffered in the alleged crime, rather than automatically winning the lawsuit because the offender admitted guilt.

Before taking the plea, Judge Kingsley informed Jones that by entering the plea he would be waiving his right to a trial, including his right to question witnesses and to have the prosecutor prove his guilt beyond a reasonable doubt. After Judge Kingsley read the charges of armed robbery and assault with intent to do great bodily harm and asked,"What do you plead?" Jones replied, "No contest." Then the judge asked Jones a series of questions.

> Judge Kingsley: Mr. Jones, has anyone promised you anything other than the plea bargain to get you to enter this plea?
>
> Jones: No.
>
> Judge Kingsley: Has anyone threatened you or forced you or compelled you to enter the plea?
>
> Jones: No.
>
> Judge Kingsley: . . . Are you [entering this plea] of your own free will?
>
> Jones: Yes.

The judge reminded Jones that there had been no final agreement on what the ultimate sentence would be and gave Jones one last opportunity to change his mind about pleading no contest. Jones repeated his desire to enter the plea, so the plea was accepted.

Immediately after the hearing, Jones had second thoughts about pleading no contest. According to Jones, "I was feeling uneasy about being pressured [by my attorney] to take the plea offer . . . [so I decided] to write to the Judge and tell him about the pressures my attorney put upon me as well as [the attorney] telling me I had a right to withdraw my plea. So I wrote the Judge that night." Jones knew he was guilty of stealing things at one robbery, but he had been unarmed. He felt as if he had been pressured into pleading guilty to an armed robbery and assault that he did not commit because the prosecutor threatened him with so many other charges and his own attorney seemed so eager for him to accept the plea agreement. He subsequently learned that the law did not permit him to withdraw the plea.

STOP AND ANALYZE: Does the threat of multiple serious charges create improper pressure on defendants to plead guilty? Did any of the aspects of the plea bargaining process strike you as undesirable or improper? List two suggestions you might make for improving the process of plea bargaining in order to make sure that pleas are genuinely voluntary and defendants are fully aware of their rights.

PRESENTENCE INVESTIGATION

Probation officers are responsible for conducting presentence investigations in which they review offenders' records and interview the offenders about their education, work history, drug use, and family background before making recommendations to the judge about an appropriate punishment. Jones felt that his interview with the probation officer went well, but he was dismayed to discover that his file erroneously stated that he had three prior criminal convictions instead of two. The extra conviction would mean additional years tacked on to his sentence unless he could get his file corrected. When the errors were eventually corrected, the presentence report prepared by the probation office ultimately recommended 5 to 25 years for armed robbery and 4 to 7 years for assault.

When Gilbert learned that Jones had written the letter to Judge Kingsley that was critical of Gilbert's performance in the case, he asked the judge to permit him to withdraw as Jones's attorney. Judge Kingsley initially refused to permit him to withdraw. However, when Jones spoke in open court at the first scheduled sentencing hearing about his criticisms of Gilbert as well as his complaints about the prosecution's handling of the lineup and the failure to administer the polygraph test, the judge decided to appoint a new defense attorney to handle sentencing at a rescheduled hearing. It was apparently clear that the relationship between Gilbert and Jones had deteriorated to the point that it would be difficult for them to cooperate in preparing for the sentencing hearing.

SENTENCING PREPARATION

The new defense attorney, Virginia Cairns, encouraged Jones's parents, siblings, ex-wife, and minister to write letters to the judge describing Jones's positive qualities and his prospects for successful rehabilitation after prison. Jones was pleased with his attorney. According to Jones, "She came to visit me within a week or so. . . . She said she would fight for me to get a lesser sentence than what was recommended."

SENTENCING

Although he was arrested in October 1998, Jones's case did not complete its processing until the sentencing hearing in July 1999. When his case was called, Jones was led into the courtroom wearing an orange jail jumpsuit and escorted by a deputy sheriff. Judge Kingsley called on Jones to make his statement first. Jones faced the judge as he spoke, glancing occasionally at his family and at the victim when he referred to them in his remarks.

> First and foremost, I would like to say what happened to the victim was a tragedy. I showed great remorse for that. He is in my prayers along with his family. Even though, your Honor, I'm not making any excuses for what I'm saying here today, the injuries the victim sustained were not at the hands of myself and nor did I actually rob this victim. I was present, your Honor, as I told you once before, yes, I was. And it's a wrong. Again I'm not making any kind of excuse whatsoever . . . .
>
> Your Honor, I would just like to say that drugs has clouded my memory, and my choices in the past. I really made some wrong decisions. Only times I've gotten into trouble were because of my drug use. . . . One of the worst decisions I really made was my involvement of being around the co-defendant Fred Brown. That bothers me to this day because actually we didn't even get along. Because of my drug use again I chose to be around him.

Jones also used his statement to talk about his positive record as a high school student and athlete, his work with the jail minister, and his desire to talk to young people about his experiences in order to steer them away from drugs.

Cairns spoke next. She emphasized the letters of support from Jones's family and argued that this support system would help him to become rehabilitated after serving his prison term. She argued that Jones should receive a less severe sentence than the long prison term imposed on the co-defendant, Brown.

The courtroom was completely silent as the victim spoke about his severe injuries and how his $40,000 worth of medical bills had driven him to bankruptcy.

> I went from having perfect vision to not being able to read out of my left eye any more. I got steel plates in my head. . . . They left me to die that morning. He took the keys to my car. . . . So today it's true, I don't think Mr. Jones should be sentenced same as Brown. That's who I want—I want to see him sentenced to the maximum. He's the one that crushed my skull with a drill. But Jones did hit me several times while Mr. Brown held me there to begin with. It's true that I did hit him with a hammer to get them off me. But he still was there. He still had the chance of not leaving me without keys to my car so I could get to a hospital. He still had the choice to stop at least and phone on the way and say there's someone that could possibly be dead, but he didn't. . . . You don't treat a human being like that. And if you do, you serve time and pretty much to the maximum. I don't ask the Court for 25 years. That's a pretty long time to serve. And I do ask the Court to look at 15 to 20. I'd be happy. Thank you.

Gary Brand, the assistant prosecutor, recommended a 20-year sentence and noted that Jones should be responsible for $35,000 in restitution to the victim and to the state for medical expenses and lost income.

After listening to the presentations, Judge Kingsley spoke sternly to Jones. He agreed that Jones's drug problem had led to his involvement in this crime and the crimes that led to Jones's prior convictions. He also noted that Jones's family support was much stronger than that of most defendants appearing in circuit court. He chastised Jones for falling into drugs when life got tougher after enjoying a successful career in high school. Judge Kingsley then proceeded to announce his sentencing decision.

> You are not in my view as culpable as Mr. Brown. I agree with [the victim] that you were there. When I read your handwritten letter, Mr. Jones, I was a bit disturbed by your unwillingness to confront the reality of where you found yourself with Mr. Brown. You were not a passive observer to everything that went on in my view. You were not as active a participant as Mr. Brown, but you were not an innocent victim in the sense that "I simply walked into the store. I had no idea what was going on. I just stood there in amazement as my acquaintance brutalized this man." I don't think that's the case. But what I'm going to do, Mr. Jones, is as follows: Taking everything into consideration as it relates to the armed robbery count, it is the sentence of the Court that you spend a term of not less than 12 years nor more than 25 years with the Michigan Department of Corrections. I will give you credit for the [261 days] that you have already served.

The judge also ordered the payment of $35,000 in restitution as a condition of parole. He also noted that the sentence was within the state's new sentencing guidelines and remarked that the cost to the taxpayers would be approximately $500,000 to hold Jones in prison during the sentence. He concluded the hearing by informing Jones of his right to file an application for a leave to appeal.

STOP AND ANALYZE: Was the sentence fair and appropriate? Should it matter whether Jones was sufficiently apologetic or whether his family wrote letters of support? Taking into consideration the statement by the victim and the statement by Jones, what sentence would you have imposed? Write a brief statement explaining your sentence and the reasons for it.

PRISON

After spending a few more weeks in jail awaiting transfer to the state prison system, Jones was sent to the state correctional department's classification center at a state prison in Jackson. At the center, newly incarcerated prisoners are evaluated. Based on their criminal history, presentence report, psychological and medical problems, and age, they are assigned to one of nearly 40 correctional facilities in the state. Jones spent one month in the center, confined to a cell with one other prisoner. Because there was no mirror in the cell, he shaved by looking at his reflection in the pipes on back of the toilet. Each day the prisoners were released from their cells for ten minutes at each meal and one hour in the recreation yard.

He was eventually assigned to a Level IV prison, where he lived with a cellmate in a space designed to house one prisoner. Prisons' security classifications range from Level I for minimum security to Level VI for "super maximum," high security. At prison, conditions were better than at the classification center. Inmates were given more time at each meal and more choices of foods. There were longer periods in the morning and the afternoon for recreation, prison jobs, and school. Because Jones was a high school graduate who had previously attended a community college—and therefore was one of the most highly educated prisoners in his institution—he became head clerk in the prison library. Over the years, he was transferred to seven different prisons, both for medical reasons and to move him into lower-security facilities as he proved himself to be well behaved.

REENTRY

Ten years and three months after his arrest, Jones was released on parole with the requirements that he live at his parents' house, take regular drug tests, and report to his parole officer. At one point during his two-year parole period, he was placed in the county jail for several weeks for missing meetings and drug tests. However, his parole was not revoked, so he was released again under his parole conditions rather than sent back to prison. The brief taste of jail renewed his determination to obey the rules and do something productive. He volunteered at a program to help troubled youths and he gave speeches to church youth groups in an effort to steer teens away from drugs and crime. By the end of his two-year parole period, he had been hired for a full-time job as a youth counselor with an agency that provided job training and counseling for high school dropouts. However, after several months, the program lost its funding. Jones attended community college while looking for another job, but his criminal record, in addition to his lack of work experience and skills, made it difficult to find a job. Eventually, he was hired by a different program that provided substance abuse counseling and other services for people on probation and parole. Like other ex-offenders, he continues to experience significant challenges in attempting to reenter society as a productive citizen.

STOP AND ANALYZE: Did the outcome of the case achieve "justice"? List three possible issues concerning the processing of the case or the length and nature of the punishment. If you were the victim of the crime for which Jones was imprisoned, would you feel that justice had been achieved?

Sources: T. Christenson, "Two Charged in Violent Robberies," *Battle Creek Inquirer,* October 30, 1998, p. 1A; Interview with Christopher Jones, St. Louis Correctional Facility, St. Louis, Michigan, October 19, 1999; Letters to author from Christopher Jones, October and November 1999; Calhoun County Circuit Court transcripts for plea hearing, May 20, 1999, and sentencing hearing, July 16, 1999.

Layer 1 of the "cake" consists of celebrated cases that are highly unusual, receive much public attention, result in a jury trial, and often drag on through many appeals. These cases embody the ideal of an adversary system of justice in which each side actively fights against the other, either because the defendant faces a stiff sentence or because the defendant has the wealth to pay for a strong defense. Further, Layer 1 cases in a sense serve as morality plays. People see the carefully crafted arguments of the prosecution and defense as expressing key issues in society or tragic flaws in individuals. The trials of Michael Dunn, described in the opening of this chapter, represent the top of the wedding cake. So, too, do the 2012 trial of former presidential candidate John Edwards for improper use of campaign funds and the 2011 trial of Dr. Conrad Murray. Murray was convicted of causing singer Michael Jackson's death by improperly prescribing medication. Cases may go to trial because of the long prison sentences at stake for the defendants if they are convicted, as was true in the homicide cases of Dunn and Murray, or because the defendants are very wealthy and can afford to fight the charges in expensive trials, as was true of Edwards.

The Layer 1 cases fit the ideals of American values concerning liberty, due process, and constitutional rights. In such cases, attorneys work vigorously to make sure that the defendant's rights are protected and that the trial process produces a careful, fair decision about the defendant's guilt and punishment. The drawn-out, dramatic procedures of such trials fulfill the picture of the American justice process that is taught to schoolchildren and reinforced in movies and television shows. When people in other countries ask Americans to describe the U.S. legal system, they are most likely to draw from their idealized image of American values and describe the Layer 1 process. Too often, however, the public's belief in the prevalence of idealistic American values leads to the erroneous conclusion that most criminal cases follow this model.

In 2014, Dinesh D'Souza, a best-selling author, former college president, and conservative political activist, pleaded guilty to a federal felony charge of making illegal political campaign contributions. He benefited from hiring an experienced private attorney who could help negotiate a plea deal that permitted him to avoid any jail time. Federal sentencing guidelines recommended a sentence of 10–16 months in prison. Instead, he received five years' probation including spending eight months sleeping at a community confinement center while he was free in the community during the day. Does the United States achieve its motto of "equal justice under law" if not all defendants have the resources to gain the services of experienced, effective defense attorneys?

AP Images/Richard Drew

Layer 2 consists of serious *felonies:* violent crimes committed by people with long criminal records, against victims unknown to them. Police and the prosecutors speak of these as "heavy" cases that should result in "tough" sentences. In such instances the defendant has little reason to plead guilty and the defense attorney must prepare for trial.

Layer 3 also consists of felonies, but the crimes and the offenders are seen as less important than those in Layer 2. The offenses may be the same as in Layer 2, but the offender may have no record, and the victim may have had a prior relationship with the accused. The main goal of criminal justice officials is to dispose of such cases quickly. For this reason, many are filtered out of the system prior to trial, usually through plea bargaining.

Layer 4 is made up of *misdemeanors*. About 90 percent of all cases fall into this category. They concern such offenses as public drunkenness, shoplifting, prostitution, disturbing the peace, and traffic violations. Looked on as the "garbage" of the system, these cases are handled by the lower courts, where speed is essential. Prosecutors use their discretion to reduce charges or recommend probation as a way to encourage defendants to plead guilty quickly. Trials are rare; processes are informal; and fines, probation, or short jail sentences result.

The wedding cake model provides a useful way of viewing the criminal justice system. Cases are not treated equally: Some are seen as quite important, others as merely part of a large number that must be processed. When one knows the nature of a case, one can predict fairly well how it will be handled and what its outcome will be.

✔POINT **13.** What is the purpose of the wedding cake model?

14. What types of cases are found in each layer?

STOP AND ANALYZE: Where in the wedding cake model is there a risk of incorrect or unjust outcomes? At the top—if effective defense lawyers persuade a judge or jury to acquit a guilty person? At the bottom—where quick, administrative processing lacks the opportunity for defense attorneys to challenge the nature and quality of evidence? Make an argument about which part of the wedding cake and its related processes carries the greatest risk of error.

Crime and Justice in a Multicultural Society

One important aspect of American values is the principle of equal treatment. The overarching value of equality is prominently announced and displayed in our national documents. The Declaration of Independence speaks of every American being "created equal," and the Fourteenth Amendment to the Constitution guarantees the right to "equal protection." Critics of the criminal justice system argue that discretionary decisions and other factors produce racial discrimination. Discrimination calls into question the country's success in fulfilling the values that it claims to regard as supremely important. Therefore, we should look closely at whether or not discrimination exists in various criminal justice settings.

Disparity and Discrimination

African Americans, Hispanics, and other minorities are subjected to the criminal justice system at much higher rates than are the white majority (A. Baker, 2010; T. H. Cohen and Kyckelhahn, 2010; Epp, Maynard-Moody, and Haider-Markel, 2014; L. Glaze, 2011; J. McKinley, 2014; "New NYCLU Report,"

2012; Poston, 2011; Rainville and Smith, 2003; B. Reaves, 2006; Spohn, 2011; Ulmer, Light, and Kramer, 2011). For example:

- African American men are sent to jails and prisons at a rate 6 times that of whites. The incarceration rate for Hispanic men is nearly 3 times that for whites. For women, the rates are 2.5 times greater (African American) and 1.5 times greater (Hispanics).
- In sentencing for federal crimes, African American male offenders, on average, received sentences more than 20 percent longer than those imposed on comparable white offenders, and sentences for Hispanic men were nearly 7 percent longer.
- A 2014 study in New York City found that African American and Hispanic defendants are more likely to be held in jail before trial and more likely to be offered plea bargains that include a prison sentence than are whites and Asians charged with the same crimes.
- Studies of traffic stops regularly find that police stop and search African American and Hispanic drivers more frequently than white drivers, even though they are no more likely than whites to be found with weapons or drugs. In 2011 in Milwaukee, for example, African American drivers were 7 times more likely to be stopped and Hispanic drivers were 5 times more likely to be stopped. African American drivers were twice as likely to be searched.
- A 2014 study of traffic stops in Kansas City found that African American and white drivers were equally likely to be stopped when there was a clear traffic violation and officers quickly issued tickets focused on that stop. However, African American drivers were three times more likely to be subjected to investigatory stops involving prolonged questioning and vehicle searches.
- Forty-five percent of felony defendants in the 75 largest, most populous counties were African American, although African Americans comprised only 14 percent of the population of those counties. Hispanics constituted 24 percent of felony defendants while only comprising 19 percent of the population.
- In the country's 40 most populous counties, more than 60 percent of juvenile felony defendants were African Americans.
- A 2010 study in New York City concluded that African American and Hispanic pedestrians were nine times more likely than whites to be stopped and searched by the police, although they were less frequently found to be carrying illegal weapons and were no more likely than whites to be arrested.
- A 2012 study found that of the 685,724 people stopped and questioned by New York City police in the preceding year, 87 percent were African American or Hispanic. Among those stopped, 90 percent were innocent and were neither ticketed nor arrested. Fifty-seven percent of these innocent people were also searched by police. Although young African American and Hispanic men in the 14 to 24 age group account for only 4.7 percent of the city's population, they were subjected to nearly 42 percent of police stops; 90 percent of those stopped were innocent people about whom there was no evidence of wrongdoing.

The experiences of minority group members with the criminal justice system may contribute to differences in their expressions of confidence about actors and institutions in the criminal justice system (Epp et al., 2014; Lundman and Kaufman, 2003). Many young men, in particular, can describe multiple incidents when they were followed by officers, temporarily taken into custody,

WHAT AMERICANS THINK

QUESTION: "I am going to read you a list of institutions in American society. Please tell me how much confidence you, yourself, have in each one."

Confidence in the police*

Whites

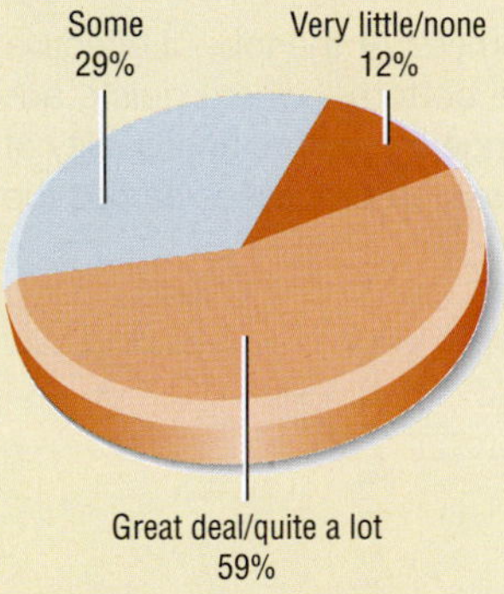

African Americans

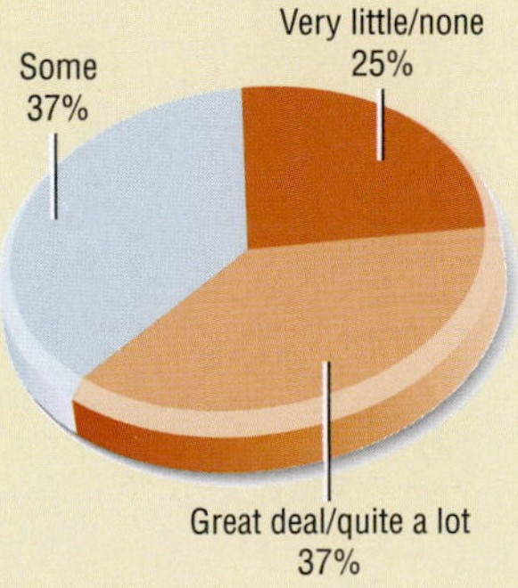

*Gallup Poll aggregate surveys conducted 2011–2014.

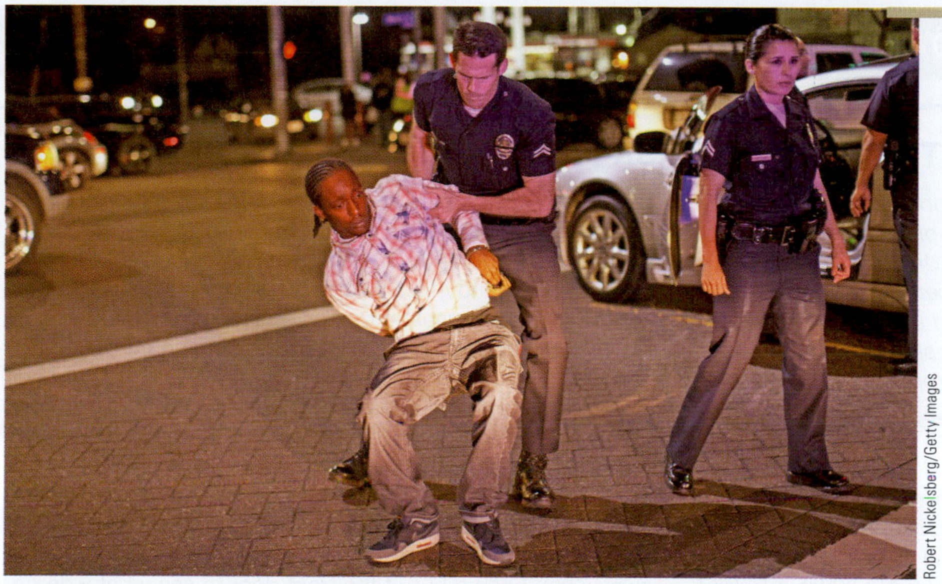

Young African American and Hispanic men often complain that police follow, stop, and search them without proper justification. In light of your own experiences, do you see evidence that a person's race may play a role in arousing the suspicions of some police officers? What about other factors that may enhance police suspicions? Gender? Social status? Residence in a specific neighborhood? Driving a certain kind of car or wearing certain clothes?

(Continued)

WHAT AMERICANS THINK

Confidence in the criminal justice system*

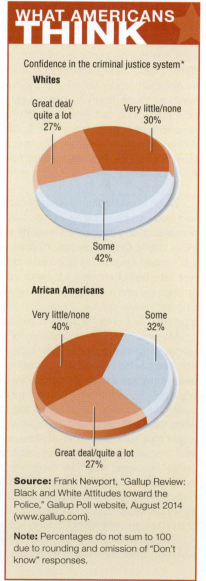

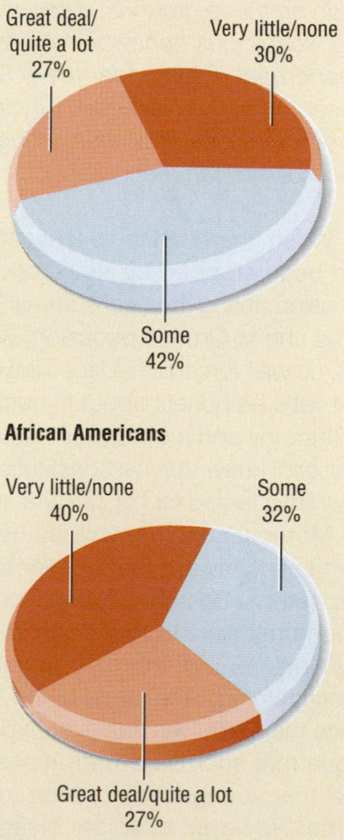

Source: Frank Newport, "Gallup Review: Black and White Attitudes toward the Police," Gallup Poll website, August 2014 (www.gallup.com).

Note: Percentages do not sum to 100 due to rounding and omission of "Don't know" responses.

forced by police to hand over money or property, or subjected to physical force for no reason other than walking down the sidewalk (Peart, 2011; Brunson, 2007). A lawsuit in New York City revealed that its police department had a policy of pressuring officers to make frequent stops and searches of pedestrians, and testimony from officers showed that they were specifically expected to stop young minority men. As mentioned earlier, this led to hundreds of thousands of stops that primarily targeted African American and Hispanic men, 90 percent of whom had done nothing wrong. As an African American college student in New York City wrote after the fifth time he was searched for no reason and, in the last search, actually handcuffed while the officers took his keys and illegally entered his apartment, "The police should consider the consequences for a generation of young people who want nothing to do with them—distrust, alienation, and more crime" (Peart, 2011). See "What Americans Think" for more on this topic.

In 2014, significant debates emerged about the role of race in the criminal justice system, especially with respect to claims that police officers in some communities treat whites and African Americans unequally. The conflict was highlighted by public reactions against grand juries in New York City and St. Louis that declined to approve criminal charges against police officers for the deaths of unarmed African Americans who were placed in a chokehold by an officer (Eric Garner in New York City) and shot after an altercation with a police officer (Michael Brown in Ferguson, Missouri). These events led to large public protest demonstrations in many cities, including some protesters blocking highways and, in Missouri and California, causing property damage and fires (Almasy and Yan, 2014). People on both sides of debates about race and criminal justice can feel challenged to understand the experiences and perspectives of those voicing an opinion different from their own. Defenders of police argue that the public cannot understand the extent to which officers need to make split-second decisions and take strong steps to preserve public safety. By contrast, minority group members claim that others in society do not really see and understand the degree to which they are unfairly regarded as criminal suspects without justification and that they are treated unfairly by the criminal justice system. It is impossible to stand in the shoes of other people, but sometimes interaction and communication with others of different backgrounds and

INSIDE TODAY'S CONTROVERSIES

WHAT I LEARNED ABOUT STOP-AND-FRISK FROM WATCHING MY BLACK SON

Note: One of the authors of this textbook, Dr. Christopher E. Smith, wrote this essay in 2014 as part of a series of perspectives on the New York City Police Department's stop-and-frisk practices. He wrote it based on his experiences as a white father of biracial children who are treated as African Americans by others in U.S. society based on their skin color and physical appearance. As previously noted, New York City adopted a policy of stopping and frisking (i.e., a search of the outer clothing) hundreds of thousands of people, nearly 90 percent of whom were African American and Hispanic—although 90 percent of those stopped were innocent of any offense. Among these stops, 42 percent were directed at young minority men, although that cohort made up less than 5 percent of the city's population. This routine procedure was the subject of lawsuit in which a federal judge condemned the practice because, under U.S. law, such stops are only permissible when an individual has engaged in suspicious behavior that reasonably leads the officer to believe that the person is armed and involved in criminal activity (Terry v. Ohio, 1968). Members of the public are not supposed to be detained simply because of their age, race, or gender. Stops made on those grounds, without any justification based on specific, suspicious behaviors, would violate the individual's Fourth Amendment rights under the U.S. Constitution. In the evidence presented in the New York City lawsuit, a patrol officer secretly taped his supervisor instructing him to stop and frisk young African American men.

When I heard that my 21-year-old son, a student at Harvard, had been stopped by New York City police on more than one occasion during the brief summer he spent as a Wall Street intern, I was angry. On one occasion, while wearing his best business suit, he was forced to lie face-down on a filthy sidewalk because—well, let's be honest about it, because of the color of his skin. As an attorney and a college professor who teaches criminal justice classes, I knew that his constitutional rights had been violated. As a parent, I feared for his safety at the hands of the police.

Moreover, as the white father of an African American son, I am keenly aware that I never face the suspicion and indignities that my son continuously confronts. In fact, all of the men among my African American in-laws—and I literally mean every single one of them—can tell multiple stories of unjustified investigatory police stops of the sort that not a single one of my white male relatives has ever experienced. Some commentators argue that such stop-and-frisk searches are merely a "special tax" that young minority men must endure in order to reduce crime. However, scholars disagree about whether crime rate data really substantiate the claim that such tactics make society safer. New York City saw crime rates decline while using its widespread stop-and-frisk tactics, but other cities also saw crime rate declines without using such tactics.

Proponents of stop-and-frisk often suggest that the imposition on their liberty and their equal right to walk unimpeded down city sidewalks would be tolerable for minority group members if officers were trained to be polite rather than aggressive and authoritarian. We need to remember, however, that with respect to African American men, we are talking about imposing an additional burden on a demographic that *already* experiences a set of alienating "taxes" not shared by the rest of society.

I can tell myriad stories about the ways my son is treated with suspicion and negative presumptions in nearly every arena of his life. I can describe the terrorized look on his face when, as a 7-year-old trying to learn how to ride a bicycle on the sidewalk in front of our suburban house, he was followed at 2-miles-per-hour from a few feet away by a police patrol car—a car that sped away when I came out of the front door to see what was going on. I can tell stories of teachers, coaches, and employers who have forced my son to overcome a presumption that he will cause behavior problems or that he lacks intellectual capacity. I can tell you about a U.S. Customs official inexplicably ordering both of us to exit our vehicle and enter a building at the Canadian border crossing so that a team of officers could search our car without our watching—an event that never occurs when I am driving back from Canada by myself.

If I had not witnessed all this so closely, I never would have fully recognized the extent of the indignities African American boys and men face. Moreover, as indicated by research recently published in the *American Journal of Preventive Medicine,* the cumulative physical toll this treatment takes on African American men can accelerate the aging process and cause early death. Thus, no "special tax" on this population can be understood without recognizing that it does not exist as a small, isolated element in people's lives.

It is equally important to recognize the more acute dangers posed by these encounters. When my son was walking home one night during his summer in New York City, two men jumped out of the shadows and grabbed him. Any reasonable person would instantly have been jolted into wondering, "Am I being robbed?" That question demands quick decision-making: "Do I defend myself? Do I break free and try to run away?"

However, because cautious African Americans learn that they are frequent targets of sudden and unexplained police stops, they must suppress their rational defensive reactions with self-imposed docility. What if these were plainclothes police officers? Any resistance could have led to my son's being tasered or even shot. And if the police were to shoot him in this context—all alone in the shadows on an empty street late at night—that act would likely have been judged as a justifiable homicide. In my son's case, it turned out that they *were* plainclothes police officers who failed to identify themselves until the encounter was well underway.

This example is by no means unique. My African American brother-in-law, a white-collar professional who works for a major corporation, was driving to my house on Thanksgiving Day with his 20-something son when their car was stopped and surrounded by multiple police vehicles. The police officers immediately pointed guns at my relatives' heads. If my brother-in-law or nephew—or one of the officers—had sneezed, there could have been a terrible tragic police shooting. After the officers looked them over and told them that they could go, my relatives asked why they had been stopped. The officers hemmed and hawed before saying, "You fit the description of some robbery suspects—one was wearing a Houston Astros jersey just like the one your son is wearing."

In reality, if my in-laws had fit the description of the robbery suspect so well, there is no way the police could have ruled them out as the robbers without searching their car. Sadly, it seems likely that the police were stopping—and presumably pointing guns at—every African American male driver who happened by. I have heard similar stories from other African American friends—and never from any white friend or relative.

Many have noted that stop-and-frisk practices hinder important constitutional values: the liberty to walk freely down the sidewalk; the reasonable expectation of privacy against unjustified invasion of one's person by government officials; and the equal protection of the laws. But even the best-intentioned white writers often gloss over the actual human impacts of these encounters. Now and again, an individual white elite will have an experience that personalizes this principle of individualized suspicion.

For example, Linda Greenhouse, the Yale Law School Research Scholar and *New York Times* columnist, once wrote about the "unnerving" experience of being "unaccountably pulled over by a police officer" in a quiet, residential neighborhood in Washington, DC, at night. As Greenhouse wrote, "My blood pressure goes up as I recall it years later." Michael Powell, another *New York Times* columnist, learned from his two 20-something sons that they had never been stopped by police despite traveling regularly all over New York City. By contrast, when he interviewed eight male African American students at a New York City college, they told him they had cumulatively been stopped a total of 92 times—in encounters that included rough physical treatment. Neither of these writers lacked knowledge about these issues, but their experiences obviously humanized and heightened their awareness.

My son's experiences aside, I can only call on one personal reference when the issue of stop-and-frisk is raised. As a graduate student in April 1981, I spent spring break traveling around Europe. When I visited Germany at this historical moment when the Berlin Wall was still in place and the Communist Party still ruled East Germany, I decided to spend one afternoon walking around Communist East Berlin. I quickly found myself being stopped at every single street corner by police officers whose suspicions were undoubtedly raised by my American clothing. Because of my limited knowledge of German, every encounter involved emphatic demands and raised voices, accompanied by threatening hand-slapping gestures. While Linda Greenhouse described her one-time experience with a police officer as "unnerving," my encounter with a Communist police state would be better described as "suffocating." I had the sense of being helplessly trapped, aware that no matter which direction I chose to walk, I would find more police waiting for me on the next block. I often wonder whether suspicionless stop-and-frisk searches regularly force African American males into an East Berlin-like sense of oppression—while the rest of us go our merry way without noticing.

I understand the necessity and inevitability of police discretion. I also understand the pressures we place on law enforcement agencies to prevent and control crime. However, stop-and-frisk practices frequently disregard the basic requirements laid out in the seminal 1968 Supreme Court case *Terry v. Ohio*. The Court ruled that an officer preforming a stop should note "unusual conduct which leads him reasonably to conclude in light of his experience that criminal activity may be afoot and that the persons with whom he is dealing may be armed and presently dangerous." By contrast, in their reports on stop-and-frisk encounters, contemporary New York City police officers can merely check a box that says "furtive movements" or one that implausibly just says "other."

If we truly believe that we must impose the "special tax" of setting aside Fourth Amendment constitutional rights against "unreasonable searches and seizures" by using suspicionless searches to control crime, then shouldn't we all share the burden of that "special tax"? Is it fair to impose that burden on an already overburdened demographic group (young African American males) because of their age, gender, and skin color? If we believe in this approach to crime control and think it is more important than constitutional rights, then wouldn't we control even more crime by also searching white men and women, the wealthy as well as the poor? Some might say, "Wait, it's a waste of the officers' time to impose these searches on innocent people instead of searching people who might actually be criminals." But the evidence shows that New York City police were already imposing stop-and-frisk searches on innocent people nearly 90 percent of the time—it is just that the burden of those stops and searches was overwhelmingly imposed on young minority men. If police start stopping and frisking hundreds of thousands of white women and men in the manner they have been searching young minority men, they will undoubtedly issue some citations and make some arrests. There are middle-class white people in possession of illegal guns—not to mention heroin, illegal prescription painkillers, and marijuana. The success rates of these searches may not be high. But low success rates have not stopped them from searching young minority men for contraband and weapons.

If police were actually to apply this idea, even for a short while, it would test society's disregard for individualized suspicion and force us to think more deeply about what it means to impose stop-and-frisk on large numbers of innocent people. It is easy enough to accept and rationalize away a "special tax" when we apply it to "them." But how will we feel about that burden once it's shared by all of us?

(*Continued*)

INSIDE TODAY'S CONTROVERSIES (CONT.)

Source: Adapted from Christopher E. Smith, "What I Learned about Stop-and-Frisk from Watching My Black Son," *The Atlantic* online, April 1, 2014 (http://www.theatlantic.com/national/archive/2014/04/what-i-learned-about-stop-and-frisk-from-watching-my-black-son/359962/). Copyright 2014 by Christopher E. Smith. Used by permission. **Other sources cited:** D. H. Chae, A. M. Nuru-Jeter, N. E. Adler, G. H. Brody, J. Lin, E. H. Blackburn, and E. S. Epel, "Discrimination, Racial Bias, and Telomere Length among African American Men, *American Journal of Preventive Medicine* 46: 103–11; Joseph Goldstein, "Judge Rejects New York's Stop-and-Frisk Policy," *New York Times,* August 12, 2013 (www.nytimes.com); Linda Greenhouse, "Justice in Dreamland," *New York Times,* May 18, 2011 (www.nytimes.com); Michael Powell, "Former Skeptic Now Embraces Divisive Tactic," *New York Times*, April 9, 2012 (www.nytimes.com).

CRITICAL THINKING AND ANALYSIS

If you were the mayor of New York City, what would you do? Is there additional research about stop-and-frisk that you would seek to conduct in order to understand the consequences more fully? Would you feel obligated to defend the practice for fear that crime rates might increase if the practice were stopped? Are there specific changes to the practice—or to training for police officers—that would help the situation? Write a memo describing four things that you would say or do in addressing the controversial use of widespread stop-and-frisk searches.

races can provide information and insights that are not generally available to everyone in society. Read the Inside Today's Controversies box for an unusual perspective on the impact of race on lives of African American men and boys.

A central question is whether racial and ethnic disparities like those listed at the beginning of this section result from discrimination or from some other cause (C. R. Mann, 1993: vii–xiv; Wilbanks, 1987). A **disparity** is a difference between groups that legitimate factors can explain. For example, the fact that 18- to 24-year-old men are arrested out of proportion to their numbers in the general population is a disparity explained by the fact that they commit more crime. It is not thought to be the result of a public policy that singles out young men for arrest. **Discrimination** occurs when groups are differentially treated without regard to their behavior or qualifications. Discrimination can include overt, intentional acts, such as police officers targeting people for stop-and-frisk searches because of their skin color. It can also include less-obvious acts that may reflect subconscious biases, such as judges routinely sentencing people of color to prison regardless of their criminal history.

disparity
The unequal treatment of members of one demographic group by the criminal justice system, compared with treatment accorded members of other groups.

discrimination
Differential treatment of individuals or groups based on race, ethnicity, sexual orientation, or economic status, instead of treatment based on the actual behavior or qualifications of each individual.

Explanations for Disparities

Three differing theories can be examined as possible explanations for the existence of racial disparities in criminal justice:

1. people of color commit more crimes,
2. the criminal justice system is racist, with the result that people of color are treated more harshly, or
3. the criminal justice system expresses the racism found in society as a whole.

We consider each of these views in turn.

Explanation 1: People of Color Commit More Crimes

Nobody denies that the proportion of minorities arrested and placed under correctional supervision (probation, jail, prison, parole) exceeds the proportion of minorities in the general population. However, people disagree over whether bias accounts for the disparity.

In theory, disparities in arrests and sentences may be due to legitimate factors. For example, prosecutors and judges are supposed to take into account differences between serious and petty offenses, and those between repeat and first-time offenders. It follows that more people of color will end up in the courts and prisons if they are more likely than whites to commit more-serious crimes and have more-serious prior records (S. Walker, Spohn, and DeLeone, 2012).

But why would minorities commit more crimes? The most extreme argument is that they are more predisposed to criminality. This assumes that people of color make up a "criminal class." The available evidence does not support this view. Behavior that violates criminal laws is prevalent throughout all segments of society. For example, police made 6.2 million arrests of *whites* in 2013, including 183,000 arrests for aggravated assault, 33,000 arrests for robbery, and 3,800 arrests for murder and manslaughter (FBI, 2014a). There are similar rates of illegal drug and marijuana use for whites, African Americans, and Hispanics, with whites much more likely than African Americans to illegally abuse prescription drugs (U.S. Department of Health and Human Services, 2007). Furthermore, self-report studies, in which people are asked to report on their own criminal behavior, have shown that nearly everyone has committed a crime, although most are never caught. Other offenses committed by large segments of affluent people, whites, and other population groups include drunken driving, misreporting income for taxation purposes, and falsifying reimbursement forms for business expenses. Former President George W. Bush and Vice President Dick Cheney both had drunken driving convictions; further, in secretly taped conversations released in 2005, President Bush indicated that he had used marijuana and said, "I haven't denied anything," with respect to questions about whether he had used cocaine (Kirkpatrick, 2005b).

Many of these kinds of crimes are difficult to detect or are low priorities for law enforcement agencies. In other instances, affluent perpetrators are better positioned to gain dismissals or light sentences because of their status within the community, social networks, or access to high-quality legal representation.

In evaluating theories about possible links between race and crime, we must be aware that many commentators may be focusing on only specific kinds of crimes, such as burglaries, robberies, and murders. In addition, analysts may focus only on crimes that resulted in prosecutions. Such limitations may distort an accurate understanding of this important issue. Race itself is not linked to crime as a cause of criminal behavior. Instead, any apparent associations between crime and race relate to subcategories of people within racial and ethnic groups, such as poor, young men, as well as certain categories of crimes that are commonly investigated and prosecuted. Research links crime to social contexts, not to race (Bruce, 2003).

Crime problems evolve and change over time. An examination of new problems and trends helps demonstrate that criminal behavior is not linked to race. Identity theft and computer crime, for example, cause economic harms and losses in the billions of dollars, yet no one has claimed a link between these crimes and race. Even if we look at developments affecting "street crimes," we can see that factors other than race appear to create the contexts for criminal behavior. For example, one of the most significant crime problems to hit the United States at the dawn of the twenty-first century is the "meth crisis": the spread of highly addictive methamphetamine that can be "cooked" in homemade labs using over-the-counter medicines and readily available chemicals. Americans use this inexpensive, dangerous drug more often than crack cocaine or heroin. Yet, this drug's use has been most prevalent among poor whites in rural areas and has contributed to burglaries and robberies by white addicts seeking to support their drug habits. Similarly, in 2014, the death of actor Phillip Seymour Hoffman generated news media attention to the soaring rates of addiction and overdose deaths from heroin among white people in suburbs and small towns (Chen and Wilbur, 2014; Riddell, 2014). As with meth addiction, heroin use can lead to theft crimes and burglaries as addicts seek money to support their drug habits. Indeed, even the son of a U.S. senator was arrested for several thefts and car break-ins as he struggled with his heroin problem (Heil, 2014). Many parts of the country have also seen soaring rates of addiction, mostly among white people, to prescription painkillers such as Vicodin and OxyContin, leading to burglaries and robberies (Goodnough, 2011; Tavernise, 2011).

The link between crime and economic disadvantage is significant (R. Peterson, 2012; Steffensmeier, Feldmeyer, et al., 2011; McNulty and Bellair, 2003). As mentioned earlier, the "meth crisis" has spread among poor whites in rural areas and small towns. Other kinds of crimes prevail among the poor in urban areas. Further, minority groups suffer greatly from poverty. Less than 10 percent of whites live in poverty, compared with more 27 percent of African Americans and 25 percent of Hispanics (U.S. Department of Health and Human Services, 2012). Unemployment rates are highest among people of color, and family income is lowest. In November 2014, white males over age 20 were unemployed at a rate of 4.6 percent, while the unemployment rate for African American men was 11.2 percent (Bureau of Labor Statistics, 2014b). The gap may actually be even larger if minorities are overrepresented among the half-million people classified as "discouraged workers" who are not counted in government unemployment statistics because they have given up trying to find a job.

Poor people do not have the same opportunities that affluent Americans do to acquire money unlawfully through tax cheating, employee theft, and illegal stock transactions. If poor people seek to steal, they tend to do so through means available to them, whether that be burglaries at farmhouses by white meth addicts in rural areas or such crimes as shoplifting, street-corner drug sales, and robbery by minority offenders in urban areas. Further, police and prosecutors can more easily detect such crimes and emphasize them as enforcement priorities than they can white-collar crimes, identity theft, or computer offenses. In light of the association between race and poverty as well as the criminal opportunities associated with economic status, it would not be surprising to find Native Americans, Hispanics, and African Americans to be overrepresented among perpetrators of certain categories of crimes.

Explanation 2: The Criminal Justice System Is Racist

Other explanations focus on the possible existence of racism in the criminal justice system. Many writers have discussed and analyzed evidence concerning biased attitudes among criminal justice officials, the system's perpetuation of inequalities created by discrimination throughout American history, and other facets of racism. These explanations are particularly disturbing because they violate important American values about equality and fairness. These values are embodied in the Fourteenth Amendment, which purports to guarantee equal protection for people of different races when they are subjected to government laws, policies, and procedures. The contemporary Supreme Court has not been active in evaluating and supporting claims concerning alleged violations of equal protection in the criminal justice system. Its inaction has left open more opportunities for discrimination to be a source of racial disparities (Starkey, 2012; C. E. Smith, DeJong, and Burrow, 2002).

Racial disparities may result if people who commit similar offenses are treated differently by the criminal justice system because of their race or ethnicity. From this perspective, the fact that people of color are arrested more often than whites does not mean that they are more crime prone. Critics point to *racial profiling* as evidence of unequal treatment (K. Johnson, 2010a). For example, if law enforcement officials single out drivers for traffic stops because of their race, then African Americans, Hispanics, Arabs, and others are subjected to discriminatory treatment that critics regard as evidence of racism. Evidence of racial profiling by officers in many law enforcement agencies has led to new laws and policies that require police to keep records about their traffic law enforcement patterns (Diedrich and Barton, 2013; Engel, Calnon, and Bernard, 2002).

Despite efforts to monitor and prevent such activities, evidence that some police officers use race as the basis for stopping, searching, and arresting individuals persists (Epp et al., 2014; Diedrich and Barton, 2013; Rojek, Rosenfeld, and Decker, 2012). Obviously, racial profiling activities—or the lack thereof—can vary from officer to officer and police department to police department (P. Warren et al., 2006). A 2005 study of Texas law enforcement agencies reported, for example, that the Houston Police Department searched 12 percent of African American drivers and 9 percent of Hispanic drivers stopped by its officers but searched only 3.7 percent of the white drivers who were pulled over (Steward and Totman, 2005). A national study of traffic stops found that the odds of being searched were 50 percent higher for African American drivers and 42 percent higher for Hispanic drivers than for white drivers (M. R. Durose, Schmitt, and Langan, 2005; Engel and Calnon, 2004). These searches took place despite a finding that white drivers were more likely than minority drivers to be carrying contraband. Figure 3.6 shows the results of a government study that found more frequent searches and police use of force against Hispanic and African American motorists (M. R. Durose et al., 2005).

If minority group members are stopped, searched, and arrested at higher rates than whites, even if they do not have higher rates of committing offenses, then they will be overrepresented among those drawn into the criminal justice system. Read the Close Up feature, "Racial Profiling," to examine additional aspects of this problem.

The disparities among crime rates, arrest rates, and rates of incarceration are central to the claim by some that the criminal justice system is biased against minority groups. The arrest rate of minority citizens is indeed greater than their offense rates justify. According to data from the Bureau of Justice Statistics, victims of aggravated assault identified their assailants as African Americans in 24 percent of cases, yet African Americans comprised 34 percent of suspects arrested for aggravated assault. African Americans constituted

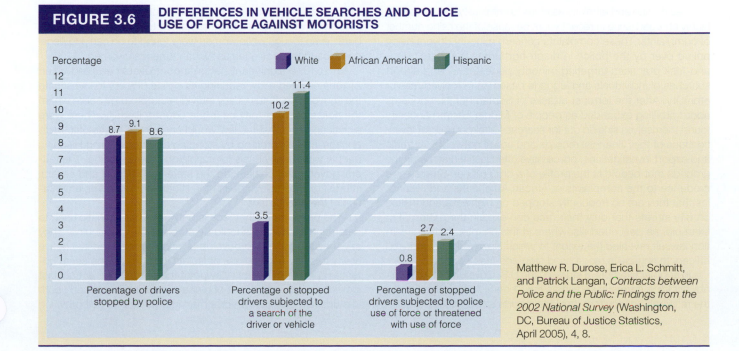

FIGURE 3.6 DIFFERENCES IN VEHICLE SEARCHES AND POLICE USE OF FORCE AGAINST MOTORISTS

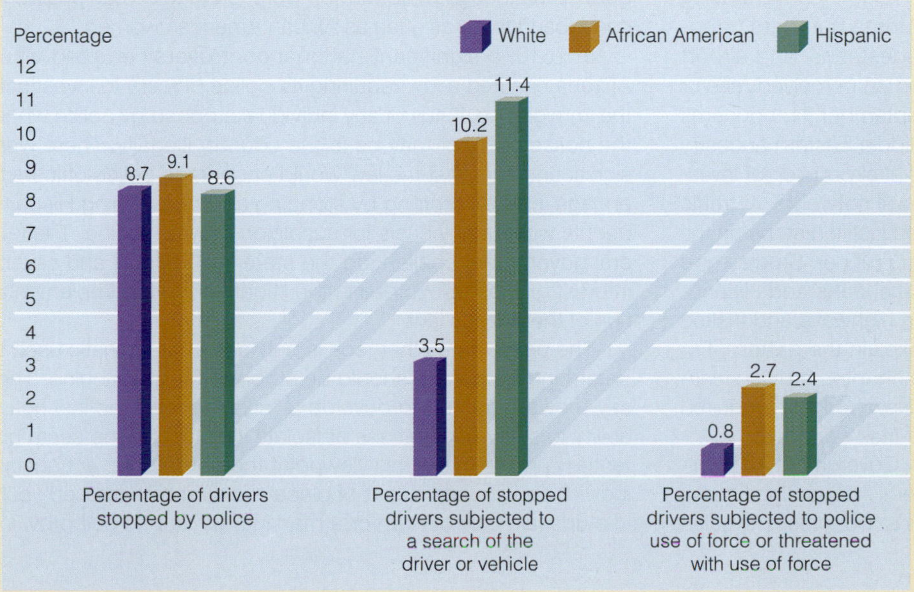

Matthew R. Durose, Erica L. Schmitt, and Patrick Langan, *Contracts between Police and the Public: Findings from the 2002 National Survey* (Washington, DC, Bureau of Justice Statistics, April 2005), 4, 8.

57 percent of suspects arrested for robbery although robbery victims reported that the robbers were African Americans in only 42 percent of cases (Rand and Robinson, 2011). In sum, the odds of arrest are higher for African American suspects than for white suspects.

In comparison with other demographic groups, African American men are treated less favorably in decisions about pretrial release on bail, an important decision that can affect the likelihood of being convicted and imprisoned, in addition to the disruption of employment and family situations for those individuals who are denied bail (J. Wooldredge, 2012). With respect to sentencing, research indicates that African American and Hispanic men are less likely to receive the benefit of prosecutors' discretionary recommendations for charge reductions for federal weapons crimes and lesser sentences in cocaine prosecutions (Shermer and Johnson, 2010; R. Hartley, Madden, and Spohn, 2007). A similar finding of racial disparities emerged in a study of who benefits from Florida judges' discretionary authority to "withhold adjudication" for people sentenced to probation so that they can avoid having a felony record if they successfully complete the terms of their probation (Bontrager, Bales, and Chiricos, 2005). African Americans and Hispanics, especially young men, were less likely than whites to benefit from these discretionary decisions and other faqctors. Thus, in the findings of recent study, "young black and Hispanic males bear the disproportionate brunt of sentencing in the federal courts" (Doerner and Demuth, 2010: 23).

Logic alone suggests that higher arrest rates and prosecutions will lead minority group members to be overrepresented among those receiving criminal punishment, including prison sentences. Further, research has found that judges' discretion in sentencing produces longer sentences for African

CLOSE UP

RACIAL PROFILING

The use of race and ethnicity as clues to criminality has become a highly charged issue in recent years because of the rising number of complaints. These complaints concern minority drivers being pulled over by the police in disproportionate numbers, stop-and-frisk practices targeting minority pedestrians, and airport searches of individuals and luggage based on perceived race or ethnicity. After the terrorist attacks of September 11, concerns about profiling expanded as people of Middle Eastern ancestry found themselves singled out for searches at airports or for investigations of their financial records and social networks. In traffic and airport investigations, police have often justified stops on the grounds that people fit the profile of a drug runner. Studies give credence to the complaints of African Americans and Hispanics that they are so frequently stopped on highways and frisked on city streets that only their race can explain the pattern. For example, as described elsewhere in this chapter, a discrimination lawsuit revealed the extent to which New York City required officers to engage in race-based stop-and-frisk searches.

In another example, a study by the U.S. Government Accountability Office (formerly known as the General Accounting Office), the research agency that provides reports to Congress, revealed that African American women returning from abroad were 9 times as likely as white women to be subjected to X-ray searches at airports, even though white women were found to be carrying illegal contraband twice as often as African American women.

In 2010, a significant national controversy erupted when Arizona enacted a law requiring its police officers to investigate the immigration status of any individual stopped by police whom the police suspect may be in the country illegally. There were significant fears that the law would encourage police officers to engage in racial profiling by stopping and questioning Hispanic people without any basis for suspicion of wrongdoing. The federal government challenged the state law in court and several interest groups also joined in the litigation to stop implementation of the Arizona law.

The police argue that race is only one characteristic used to determine if a person should be stopped for questioning. They say they are trained to develop a "sixth sense," the instinctive ability to sniff out situations or isolate individuals who seem potentially unsafe. From this viewpoint the police often act against individuals who seem "out of place"—a shabbily dressed youth in a upscale part of town or a man in a pinstriped suit prowling

Americans in some jurisdictions, even when studies control for other factors (Bales and Piquero, 2012; S. D. Bushway and Piehl, 2001).

Criminal justice officials need not act in racist ways to cause disparities in arrest and incarceration rates. At each stage of the process, the system itself operates in ways that may put minority group members at a disadvantage. The number of minority arrests may be greater because police patrols are more heavily concentrated in areas where nonwhites live, where drug use is more open, and where users are more likely to be observed by police. Most pretrial release practices take into account factors such as employment status, living arrangements, and prior criminal record. Prosecutors may be less likely to dismiss charges against poor, unemployed defendants, among whom African Americans and Hispanics are overrepresented. These offender characteristics may further skew sentencing as well.

For example, a study of sentencing of women convicted of misdemeanors found that race and ethnicity did not directly affect sentencing. African American and Hispanic women were more likely than their white counterparts to receive jail sentences because of other factors, including socioeconomic status, prior criminal record, and the severity of the charges pursued against them (P. K. Brennan, 2006). These factors create racial and ethnic disparities, but we cannot attribute them to a single decision maker.

Is the criminal justice system racist? The result of the system's decisions cannot be disputed—African American and Hispanic men end up in prison and jails in higher proportions than their crime and arrest rates can explain. These results do not mean that every minority defendant is treated disadvantageously compared with whites. Instead, the existence, nature, and extent of

a gritty ghetto. Often, however, a person's furtive look or uneasy gait may give officers a vague sense that something is not right.

Determining when and how the police should use race to assess suspects and situations involves a complicated balancing of public safety and civil liberties. Law enforcement experts insist that effective police work depends on quick analysis and that skin color is one factor among many—like dress or demeanor—that officers must consider. But minority leaders say that racial profiling is based on the presumption that African Americans and Hispanics are linked to crime or that Arab Americans might be linked to terrorism. This has led to the humiliation and physical abuse of innocent citizens. As a result, some police agencies have attempted to develop specific policies to steer their officers away from improper use of race and ethnicity as factors in their decisions to make stops and conduct searches.

Sources: Drawn from American-Arab Anti-Discrimination Committee, "ADC Reiterates Objection to Government Investigations Based on Racial Profiles," Press release, March 20, 2002 (www.adc.org); American Civil Liberties Union, "Driving While Black: Racial Profiling on Our Nation's Highways," June 1999 (www.aclu.org); Al Baker, "New York Police Release Data Showing Rise in Number of Stops on Streets," *New York Times*, May 12, 2012 (www.nytimes.com); Ralph Blumenthal, "Study in Texas Sees Race Bias in Searches," *New York Times*, February 25, 2005 (www.nytimes.com); Joseph Goldstein, "Recording Points to Race Factor in Stops by New York Police," *New York Times*, March 21, 2013 (www.nytimes.com); Jennifer Medina, "Federal Appeals Court Weighs Arizona Law on Immigration," *New York Times*, November 1, 2010 (www.nytimes.com); U.S. General Accounting Office, *U.S. Customs Service: Better Targeting of Airline Passengers for Personal Searches Could Produce Better Results* (Washington, DC: U.S. Government Printing Office, 2000); Kate Taylor, "Stop-and-Frisk Policy 'Saves Lives,' Mayor Tells Black Congregation," *New York* Times, June 10, 2012 (www.nytimes.com).

DEBATE THE ISSUE

Is there any way to stop police from engaging in racial profiling? Police have broad discretion to make stops. They can create after-the-fact justifications for the stops by later claiming that they saw evidence of criminal activity even if they did not actually view anything suspicious. Some observers believe that increased training on ethics, law, and sensitivity to race will reduce profiling. Others believe that there must be an increase in record keeping and supervision, including the use of body cameras by officers to record their interactions and statements. Although a department could follow both approaches, give two arguments for why one approach might be more effective than the other.

discrimination can vary by community (Britt, 2000). Thus, racial discrimination may be limited to certain types of cases, circumstances, and defendants (S. Walker, Spohn, and DeLeone, 2012).

Explanation 3: America Is a Racist Society

Some people claim that the criminal justice system is racist because it is embedded in a racist society. In fact, some accuse the system of being a tool of a racist society.

Evidence of racism appears in the way society asks the criminal justice system to operate. For example, even after Congress reduced the amount of crack cocaine needed for a specific mandatory sentence in 2010, federal sentencing guidelines still punish users of crack cocaine more harshly than users of powder cocaine, even though the drugs are virtually identical in their chemical composition and effect on users (Eckholm, 2010). A primary difference is that whites tend to use cocaine in its powder form, while people of color in the inner cities tend to use crack cocaine. Thus, the imposition of significantly harsher punishments for one form of the drug produces racial disparities in imprisonment rates. These critics argue that these effects are enhanced by police officers' emphasis on arresting visible crack dealers on the streets in poor neighborhoods rather than pursuing as vigorously the more-difficult-to-find powder cocaine traffickers who set up shop in suburban motels or who rely on suburban social networks.

By contrast, government responses to the meth crisis of the early twenty-first century placed greater emphasis on prevention, such as limiting sales of over-the-counter medications used to manufacture meth, as well as treatment. For example, the state of Iowa's 2006 annual report entitled *Iowa's Drug Control Strategy* said, "More treatment and related resources need to be targeted to meth-addicted offenders. . . . It is only by reducing the demand for meth and other drugs that we can to break the cycle of addiction" (Governor's Office on Drug Control Policy, 2006: 8). Some observers suspect that the less punitive orientation toward meth offenders, as well as drunk drivers, who are predominantly white, may reflect race-based attitudes that perceive crack cocaine offenders, many of whom have been African American, as more dangerous and less worthy of rehabilitation (M. Alexander, 2012).

In one example related to this risk about negative assumptions concerning African American men, a controversy emerged in 2015 concerning the use by police in North Miami Beach, Florida, of old mug shots of African American men—but not whites or Hispanics—as targets for firearms shooting practice (M. Winter, 2015). Instead of using the generic human form targets typically used at shooting ranges, these officers practiced by firing bullets into the photo image faces of actual African American men who had been arrested, some of whom had been arrested many years earlier. Did the choice of using only African American faces for target practice reflect thoughtless, negative stereotypes about the dangerousness and criminality of men from a specific demographic group? Did the use of such targets reinforce or harden stereotypes in the minds of officers? The police department's practice came to light when a National Guard sergeant went to the shooting range and was shocked to see a bullet-riddled photo of her brother, who had been arrested ten years earlier for participating in a road-racing incident that led to a serious collision.

In addition, the country's history of racial discrimination that produced high minority populations in impoverished neighborhoods that lack economic development may contribute to increased reimprisonment of minority ex-offenders who face more-difficult challenges in succeeding within these communities (Reisig, Bales, et al., 2007).

Society's economic impacts on racial groups also affect other decisions in the justice system. These can flow from the role of racial disparities in educational resources and racial discrimination in employment opportunities. The greater rates of unemployment for African Americans and Hispanics can contribute to differential treatment in the bail process. Moreover, poor defendants are less likely to be able to make bail and hire their own lawyer.

Other evidence of racism in American society shows up in the stereotyping of offenders and evidence that, under some circumstances, perceptions of certain minority groups as threatening may increase the extent to which they are subject to arrest (Eitle and Monahan, 2009). Thus, for example, the fact that Asian American defendants in federal court receive sentences similar to those of whites and less severe than those imposed on African Americans and Hispanics may show that courtroom decision makers reflect society's negative stereotypes about defendants from the latter two groups (B. Johnson and Betsinger, 2009). Recent psychology research has shown the role of unconscious, ingrained racial bias against African Americans in the decision making by police, prosecutors, judges, and jurors in the criminal justice system (T. Jacobs, 2015; Sommers and Marotta, 2014).

That racist stereotyping affects police actions can be seen in cases of African American and Hispanic professionals who have been falsely arrested when the police were looking for persons of color and these individuals were viewed as out of place. Judge Claude Coleman was handcuffed and dragged through crowds of shoppers in Short Hills, New Jersey, while protesting his innocence; Princeton University Professor Cornel West was stopped on false cocaine charges while traveling to Williams College; and law student Brian Roberts was pulled over by the police as he drove through an affluent St. Louis neighborhood on his way to interview a judge for a class project (Tonry, 1995).

In June 2009, nationally prominent Harvard University Professor Henry Louis Gates, an African American man, was arrested for arguing with a police officer on the front porch of his home after a passerby, who saw Gates

Frederick M. Brown/Getty Images

Harvard professor Henry Louis Gates, a famous scholar in the field of African American Studies, was arrested on the front porch of his home after a passerby called police upon seeing him struggle to push open the front door. Gates reacted angrily to being asked to identify himself inside his own home. Whether or not race actually affected the officer's perception of events, do you understand why the professor's knowledge of history and his own personal experiences led him to suspect race was a factor?

A QUESTION OF ETHICS

Fairness requires that similarly situated people receive equivalent treatment by the justice system, yet factors such as discretionary decisions and resources can create situations that raise concern about favoritism and disadvantage. In 2014, U.S. District Judge Mark Fuller from Birmingham, Alabama, was arrested for domestic violence when his wife called the 911 operator from an Atlanta hotel room and pleaded for help. Mrs. Fuller said her husband dragged her around the room by her hair and hit her in the face when she accused him of having an affair. The 911 operator could hear the Fullers yelling at each other, and police officers found Mrs. Fuller to have cuts to her mouth and forehead. It appeared that Judge Fuller had been drinking. News reports indicated that in a previous divorce proceeding, the judge's first wife asserted claims about domestic violence, drug abuse, and infidelity, but the records of the first divorce were sealed, so the precise details of that case were unavailable.

The prosecutor charged Judge Fuller with misdemeanor battery. He was released after 35 hours in jail by promising to pay $5,000 if he did not appear for scheduled court dates in the case. Eventually, the Georgia judge presiding over the case approved a plea agreement reached between the prosecutor and Fuller's attorney that required him to undergo weekly counseling on domestic violence and be monitored for alcohol and drug use for 24 weeks. During that entire time, he would still be paid his $199,000 salary as a federal judge, even though the federal courts temporarily removed him from overseeing any legal matters. In addition, upon successful completion of the counseling and drug testing, his record would be expunged—meaning he would not have any criminal record.

By contrast, also in 2014, Joseph Mayle in Marietta, Ohio, was intoxicated and got into an argument with his aunt about a bag of potato chips. He hit his aunt and then choked his mother when she intervened in the altercation. Mayle was charged with two felony counts of domestic violence, jailed for 125 days because he did not have enough money to pay bail, and then was sentenced to 17 months in prison after pleading guilty.

Although the two cases are not identical, do the dramatically different consequences raise concerns about unfairness in the system? Prosecutors' discretionary decisions about whether to pursue serious felony charges instead of lesser misdemeanor charges can have big impact on case outcomes. Is there a risk that favoritism will be shown to a federal judge who is accused of a crime? Access to expensive representation by the best, most-experienced defense attorneys that only people with financial means can afford can also be a factor in individual cases.

Sources: R. Cook, "Federal Judge's Cases Reassigned Due to Pending Domestic Violence Case," *Atlanta Journal Constitution*, August 13, 2014 (www.ajc.com); "Editorial: Public Needs to Know What's in Judge Mark Fuller's Sealed Divorce File: Opinion," AL.Com (Alabama News), October 13, 2014 (www.al.com); "Man Sentenced for Domestic Violence," *Marietta* (Ohio) *Times*, October 8, 2014 (www.mariettatimes.com); D. Reese, "From Ray Rice to a Federal Judge, Is the System Too Lenient in Domestic Violence Cases?," *Washington Post*, September 10, 2014 (www.washingtonpost.com); S. Visser, "GOP Senator Urges Alabama Judge Accused of Wife Assault to Resign," *Atlanta Journal Constitution*, September 17, 2014 (www.ajc.com).

CRITICAL THINKING AND ANALYSIS

Do these cases create the appearance of unfairness? If so, are there ways to adjust how the system operates in order to equalize treatment of similarly situated offenders? Write a memo describing three ideas for reforming the criminal justice system in order to counteract the potentially unfair effects of discretionary decisions and inequality in resources available to defendants.

struggling with a broken lock on his front door, called the police to investigate whether a break-in might be occurring. Gates perceived that race played a role in the officer's motives for asking for his identification and actually entering the house without justification. An element of race appeared in the officer's written report on the incident when the officer claimed that the witness had said that two black men were attempting to enter the home, even though 911 tapes and the witness herself refuted the claim that there had been any report that the men involved were black (Drash, 2009). Other observers discussed whether the officer arrested Professor Gates primarily for showing disrespect to the officer notwithstanding the accusations of racism in the case (Cooper, 2010).

The highly publicized case generated national debates about the continuing existence of racism in society and the criminal justice system. Ultimately, the disorderly conduct charges were dropped and President Obama hosted both men for beer and conversation at the White House in an effort to defuse the controversy that temporarily dominated the national news. In the aftermath of the event, an unanswerable question remained: Would a 58-year-old white Harvard professor have been subjected to the same suspicion and arrest (Lopez, 2010)?

If people of color are overrepresented in the justice system because the larger society is racist, the solution may seem daunting. Nobody knows how to quickly rid a society of racist policies, practices, and attitudes.

As you consider these three potential sources of racial disparities, consider whether citizens can play a role in diminishing any of these causes. Individuals can try to be educated about issues of race and be self-conscious about their own attitudes and behavior. However, controlling one's self is not going to change how justice system officials act or reshape the nature of society. Does that mean the problem of racial disparities is beyond the reach of citizen action? Consider the problem of racial profiling presented in "Civic Engagement: Your Role in the System." After reading it, contemplate how citizens can help to educate, monitor, or change law enforcement officials.

CIVIC ENGAGEMENT

YOUR ROLE IN THE SYSTEM

Imagine that an African American high school teacher is arrested while being interviewed by a news reporter outside of a community meeting about police–community relations. The teacher claims that the arrest is based on racially discriminatory treatment and asks you what can be done to counteract the arrest and push the police to change how they treat people. *Make a list of suggestions that you would give both for the teacher's next step and for the police, so that they could demonstrate to the community their commitment to prevent racial profiling and disparate treatment.* Then read about what happened in Pittsburgh in 2014 when this situation occurred.

✔POINT

15. What is meant by racial or ethnic disparities in criminal justice?

16. What three alternative explanations are used to account for such disparities?

STOP AND ANALYZE: If race is influential in the justice system, what are three steps that might be taken to attempt to reduce the negative impact of this factor?

Summary

1 Describe the goals of the criminal justice system

- The three goals of criminal justice are doing justice, controlling crime, and preventing crime.
- Doing justice concerns the foundation of rules, procedures, and institutions of the system.
- Controlling crime involves arresting, prosecuting, and punishing those who commit offenses.
- Preventing crime requires the efforts of citizens as well as justice system officials.

2 Discuss the different responsibilities of federal and state criminal justice operations

- Both the national and state systems of criminal justice enforce laws, try cases, and punish offenders.
- Federal officials enforce crimes defined by Congress.
- Federal involvement in criminal justice has expanded in recent decades.
- Federal justice agencies shifted their priorities in the aftermath of 9/11.
- Most criminal laws and criminal cases are under the authority of state criminal justice systems.

3 Analyze criminal justice from a system perspective

- Criminal justice is composed of many organizations that are interdependent and interact as they seek to achieve their goals.
- The primary subsystems of criminal justice are police, courts, and corrections.
- Key characteristics of the criminal justice system influence activities within the system.
- The key characteristics of the criminal justice system are discretion, resource dependence, sequential tasks, and filtering.

- Discretion occurs at all levels of the system and gives freedom to justice system officials in some aspects of their decision making.
- Resource dependence requires justice system agencies to maintain good relationships with government officials.
- Decisions and tasks in the criminal justice system occur in a sequential manner.
- Discretionary decisions in the criminal justice system create a filtering process that moves suspects and convicted offenders out of the system at different points.

4 Identify the authority and relationships of the main criminal justice agencies, and understand the steps in the decision-making process for criminal cases

- Police possess authority over the investigation, arrest, and booking steps in the criminal justice process.
- Prosecutors possess authority over charging, initial appearances and arraignments, plea bargaining, and trials.
- Judges are involved in preliminary hearings, bail, plea agreements, and sentencing.
- Corrections officials administer punishments and release decisions.
- Criminal justice officials must interact and cooperate in the sequential process in order to achieve the system's goals.

5 Describe the criminal justice "wedding cake" concept

- The criminal justice "wedding cake" concept provides a way to describe the frequency through which certain processes and outcomes occur in the criminal justice system.
- The small top of the wedding cake represents the relatively small number of very serious cases that are processed through trials.
- The lower, larger portions of the wedding cake represent the increasing frequency of plea bargaining for larger numbers of cases as one moves downward toward less serious offenses.

6 Discuss the possible causes of racial disparities in criminal justice

- Research does not support any theories about race causing criminal behavior.
- Race in the United States can be associated with poverty, and evidence exists that some kinds of crimes can be associated with poverty and neighborhood contexts.
- Evidence exists concerning differential treatment of members of various racial groups by criminal justice officials in some contexts.
- More frequent stops, searches, and arrests of minority group members can explain disparities in outcomes, even without a greater frequency of criminal behavior by members of minority groups.
- Evidence of differential treatment exists in some studies of judges' sentencing decisions.
- The existence of racial attitudes in American society can affect how laws are written and enforced, such as the imposition of more severe sentences for crack cocaine offenses, which are frequently committed by members of minority groups.

Questions for Review

1. What are the goals of the criminal justice system?
2. What is a system? How is the administration of criminal justice a system?
3. What are the 13 steps in the criminal justice decision-making process?
4. Why is the criminal justice wedding cake a better depiction of reality than the 13-step model of the system?
5. What is the challenge of criminal justice in a multicultural society?

Key Terms

adjudication (p. 108)
arrest (p. 111)
discretion (p. 103)
discrimination (p. 126)
disparity (p. 126)
dual court system (p. 108)
exchange (p. 102)
federalism (p. 97)
filtering process (p. 106)
indictment (p. 112)
information (p. 112)
plea bargain (p. 102)
system (p. 101)
warrant (p. 111)

Checkpoint Answers

1 What are the three goals of the criminal justice system?

✓ Doing justice, controlling crime, preventing crime.

2 What is meant by "doing justice"?

✓ Offenders are held fully accountable for their actions, the rights of people who have contact with the system will be protected, and like offenses will be treated alike and officials will take into account relevant differences among offenders and offenses.

3 What are the key features of federalism?

✓ A division of power between a central (national) government and regional (state) governments.

4 What power does the national government have in the area of crime and justice?

✓ Enforcement of federal criminal laws.

5 What main factor has caused federal involvement in criminal justice to expand?

✓ The expansion of criminal activities across state and national borders.

6 What is a system?

✓ A complex whole made up of interdependent parts whose actions are directed toward goals and influenced by the environment within which it functions.

7 What is one example of an exchange relationship?

✓ Plea bargaining.

8 What are the major characteristics of the criminal justice system?

✓ Discretion, resource dependence, sequential tasks, filtering.

9 What are the four main duties of police?

✓ Keeping the peace, apprehending violators and combating crime, preventing crime, providing social services.

10 What is a dual court system?

✓ A separate judicial system for each state in addition to a national system.

11 What are the major types of state and local correctional agencies?

✓ Prisons, jails, probation, parole, community programs. Public, nonprofit, and for-profit agencies carry out correctional programs on behalf of state and local governments.

12 What are the steps of the criminal justice process?

✓ (1) investigation, (2) arrest, (3) booking, (4) charging, (5) initial appearance, (6) preliminary hearing/grand jury, (7) indictment/information, (8) arraignment, (9) trial, (10) sentencing, (11) appeal, (12) corrections, (13) release.

13 What is the purpose of the wedding cake model?

✓ To show that all cases are not treated alike.

14 What types of cases are found in each layer?

✓ Layer 1: celebrated cases in which the adversarial system is played out in full; Layer 2: serious felonies committed by people with long criminal records against victims unknown to them; Layer 3: felonies in which the crimes and the offenders are viewed as less serious than in Layer 2; Layer 4: misdemeanors.

15 What is meant by racial or ethnic disparities in criminal justice?

✓ That racial and ethnic minorities are subjected to the criminal justice system at much higher rates than are the white majority.

16 What three alternative explanations are used to account for such disparities?

✓ Minorities commit more crime; the criminal justice system is racist; U.S. society is racist.

CHAPTER FEATURES

- **Technology and Criminal Justice** Posting on Social Media: Distinguishing Threats from Free Expression
- **Close Up** The Insanity Defense and Its Aftermath
- **Doing Your Part** Criminal Defense Internship

CRIMINAL JUSTICE AND THE RULE OF LAW

CHAPTER LEARNING OBJECTIVES

1. Describe the bases and sources of American criminal law
2. Discuss how substantive criminal law defines a crime and the legal responsibility of the accused
3. Describe how procedural criminal law defines the rights of the accused and the process for dealing with a case
4. Analyze the United States Supreme Court's role in interpreting the criminal justice amendments to the Constitution

CHAPTER OUTLINE

Foundations of Criminal Law
- Substantive Law and Procedural Law
- Sources of Criminal Law
- Felony and Misdemeanor
- Criminal versus Civil Law

Substantive Criminal Law
- Seven Principles of Criminal Law
- Elements of a Crime
- Statutory Definitions of Crimes
- Responsibility for Criminal Acts
- Justification Defenses
- Excuse Defenses

Procedural Criminal Law
- The Bill of Rights
- The Fourteenth Amendment and Due Process
- The Due Process Revolution
- The Fourth Amendment: Protection Against Unreasonable Searches and Seizures
- The Fifth Amendment: Protection Against Self-Incrimination and Double Jeopardy
- The Sixth Amendment: The Right to Counsel and a Fair Trial
- The Eighth Amendment: Protection Against Excessive Bail, Excessive Fines, and Cruel and Unusual Punishments

The Supreme Court Today

AP Images/Arian Schuessler

In July 2013, a woman returned home one evening to find her 43-year-old son in the garage covered with blood, claiming that he just killed Satan. Inside the house, she found her 73-year-old husband, a prominent restaurant owner in Mason City, Iowa, dead from stab wounds. The son, Thomas Barlas Jr., was charged with murder for killing his father ("Man Found," 2014).

As the defense attorney and the prosecutor began to prepare their cases for trial, Aaron Hamrock, the attorney for Barlas, announced that he would present an insanity defense. Under American law, if someone is judged to be insane at the time they commit a crime, then they can be found not guilty of the crime. As we will see later in this chapter, the standard to evaluate whether or not someone should be declared not guilty by reason of insanity is determined by each state. Under Iowa law, it must be shown that the individual (in this case, Barlas) either did not know right from wrong or did not understand the nature of his actions at the time the murder was committed. Defendants are evaluated by psychiatrists, who then provide testimony in the trial. This expert testimony will typically have significant impact on the decision. The ultimate finding of insane or not insane is often difficult because the defense and prosecution typically hire their own psychiatrists to bolster their side's argument—and it is not unusual for there to be conflicting psychiatric diagnoses between these experts (Senzarino, 2013a).

After the long trial preparation process, in August 2014 Judge Gregg Rosenbladt ruled that Barlas was not guilty by reason of insanity. Judge Rosenbladt concluded that Barlas had suffered a psychotic episode on the night of the killing and that he could not comprehend right from wrong or understand the nature and consequences of his actions (Senzarino, 2014). Even though Barlas clearly had committed the crime, he avoided being sent to prison and instead went to a mental health institution where he would be periodically reevaluated to

legal responsibility
The accountability of an individual for a crime because of the perpetrator's characteristics and the circumstances of the illegal act.

determine whether, if ever, he could be released into the community because he no longer posed a threat to himself or others.

A criminal defendant's claim of insanity raises difficult questions for the justice system. Critics question whether such a defense should be available to permit people to avoid **legal responsibility** and punishment for their criminal acts. Should an individual avoid imprisonment after committing as horrible a deed as the one Barlas was responsible for? In the Barlas case, the psychiatrists for the defense and the prosecution both agreed that he was insane at the time of the killing. But in other cases, the psychiatrists who testify will disagree in their diagnoses. In one 2013 case in Iowa, a 13-year-old boy was charged with attempting to sexually assault his mother and of shooting her 22 times; in another case the same year, a 17-year-old was charged with beating his 5-year-old foster brother in the head with a brick and drowning the youngster in a pond (Senzarino, 2013a; Nelson, 2014). Both cases presented insanity defenses with disputed testimony about the young killers' mental capacity. Without having any training in psychology or medicine, are judges, or in other cases, a jury, the most appropriate decision makers to determine whether a defendant is legally insane? Although this is a difficult challenge for these individuals, our justice system places this important responsibility in the hands of the community's representatives in the courtroom rather than deferring only to experts' conclusions.

Because of the insanity-based "not guilty" verdict, Barlas could not be punished for the crime. A verdict of not guilty by reason of insanity does not, however, mean that a criminal defendant will be released from custody. Barlas could be released in the future if psychiatrists judge him fit for release, but there is no guarantee that he will ever be released. Noah Crooks, the 13-year-old who killed his mother, was found guilty of second-degree murder; however, the prosecution did not successfully convince the jury that the boy had committed the sexual assault. Under Iowa law concerning juvenile offenders, he was to be held in a juvenile detention facility until his 18th birthday and then reevaluated by the court to determine if he should serve a longer period of time in prison. In any event, he is likely to be released eventually (Senzarino, 2013b).

By contrast, Cody Metzker-Madsen, the older teen who killed his young foster brother, was found not guilty by reason of insanity. He was sent to a secure mental institution where he will be periodically evaluated. Commentators noted, though, that the nature of his mental problems could mean that the insanity verdict might keep him confined forever, whereas a murder conviction would have created a likelihood of eventual release (Wheater, 2014). A term of confinement to the psychiatric hospital is not considered *punishment* in the criminal justice system. Instead, it is mandatory *treatment* in a secure facility within the mental health system. Thus there is a loss of liberty as a result of the killing, despite the lack of legal *responsibility* for the killing.

In this chapter, we shall examine the primary components of criminal law. Substantive criminal law is developed through statutes enacted by the American people's elected representatives in state legislatures and

Congress. It addresses the specific acts for which people will be punished as well as the circumstances in which people may not be held fully responsible for their actions. We shall also introduce procedural criminal law, which defines the procedures used in legal processes and the rights possessed by criminal suspects and defendants. Even though Barlas, Crooks, and Metzker-Madsen all acknowledged that they committed the killings for which they were charged, they were still entitled to a trial and representation by an attorney as they attempted to show why they should not be held fully responsible for their actions. The right to counsel and the right to a fair trial are two of the elements provided by procedural criminal law. The precise nature of individuals' rights under procedural criminal law is determined by judges' interpretations of the U.S. Constitution, state constitutions, and relevant statutes enacted by Congress and state legislatures.

Foundations of Criminal Law

Like most Americans, you probably realize that law and legal procedures are key elements of the criminal justice system. Americans are fond of saying that "we have a government of laws, not of men (and women)." According to our American values, we do not have a system based on the decisions of a king or dictator. Our judges and elected representatives in legislatures create laws that shape the rules for society, and those rules are supposed to apply to everyone. Does that mean that every citizen, police officer, and member of Congress obeys those rules? No. But the rules of law set the standards for their behavior, and they can face consequences for their failure to comply.

Historically, presidents, governors, and mayors have not had the power to legally punish people they dislike. Even our most powerful leaders have had to make decisions within limits imposed by law. The government could seek to punish people only if they had violated defined laws, and their guilt had to be determined through procedures established by law. After the attacks on the World Trade Center and the Pentagon on September 11, 2001, however, some commentators expressed fears that the federal government moved away from traditional constitutional values by jailing suspected terrorists without charging them with any crimes or presenting any evidence in court to prove their involvement in wrongdoing (C. E. Smith, 2004a). Thus we find ourselves in a new era that raises challenges to the traditional operation of American criminal law.

Laws tell citizens what they can and cannot do. Laws also tell government officials when they can seek to punish citizens for violations and how they must go about it. Government officials who take actions according to their own preferences run the risk that judges will order them to take different actions that comply with the law. The president of the United States is no exception. In 2004, for example, the U.S. Supreme Court ordered President George W. Bush's administration to permit a U.S. citizen being held as a suspected terrorist to meet with an attorney and have opportunities to make arguments in court (*Hamdi v. Rumsfeld*). Government officials are expected to follow and enforce the law. Thus, in a democracy, laws provide a major tool to prevent government officials from seizing too much power or using power improperly.

Substantive Law and Procedural Law

civil law
Law regulating the relationships between or among individuals, usually involving property, contract, or business disputes.

substantive criminal law
Law defining acts that are subject to punishment and specifying the punishments for such offenses.

procedural criminal law
Law defining the procedures that criminal justice officials must follow in enforcement, adjudication, and corrections.

Criminal law is only one category of law. Peoples' lives and actions are also affected by **civil law**, which governs business deals, contracts, real estate, and the like. For example, if you harm other people in an automobile collision or damage their property, they may sue you to pay for the harm or damage. By contrast, the key feature of criminal law is the government's power to punish people for damage they have done to society.

Of the two categories of criminal law, **substantive criminal law** defines actions that the government can punish. It also defines the punishments for such offenses. Often called the *penal code,* substantive law answers the question "*What* is illegal?" Elected officials in Congress, state legislatures, and city councils write the substantive criminal laws. These legislators decide which kinds of behaviors are so harmful that they deserve to be punished. They also decide whether each violation should be punished by imprisonment, a fine, probation, or another kind of punishment. When questions about the meaning of substantive criminal laws arise, judges interpret the laws by seeking to fulfill the legislators' intentions.

Criminal laws can also be created and changed through ballot issues in those states that permit statewide voting as a means to create law. Here citizens are directly involved in shaping their own criminal laws, although this process typically affects only a small number of laws. Usually a petition drive is required to obtain the required number of signatures to place a specific proposal on the ballot. Criminal law ballot issues often concern the issues of gambling and drug use. Ballot issues may also be aimed at sentencing and other aspects of criminal justice. Think about whether the general population of voters is sufficiently knowledgeable to create criminal laws as you consider the issue in "Civic Engagement: Your Role in the System."

By contrast, **procedural criminal law** defines the rules that answer the question, "*How* shall the law be enforced?" It protects the constitutional rights of defendants and provides the rules that officials must follow in all areas of the criminal justice system. It embodies the American values of liberty and individual rights by seeking to ensure that no one will be incarcerated or otherwise punished unless the government proves criminal guilt through proper procedures that respect constitutional rights. Legislatures define many aspects of procedural criminal law, such as how bail will be set and which kind of preliminary hearing will take place before a trial. However, the U.S. Supreme Court and state supreme courts also play a key role in defining procedural criminal law. These courts define the meaning of rights in the U.S. Constitution and in state constitutions. Their interpretations of constitutional provisions create rules on such issues as when and how police officers can question suspects and when defendants can receive advice from their attorneys.

CIVIC ENGAGEMENT

YOUR ROLE IN THE SYSTEM

In several states, voters made decisions about ballot proposals to remove criminal penalties for the personal possession and use of marijuana by adults. *Make a list of contrasting arguments for and against the legalization of marijuana for personal use (not for selling). How would you vote on the issue?* Then look at the proposal and the competing arguments for such a ballot issue presented to voters in Oregon in 2014.

✔POINT
1. What is contained in a state's penal code?
2. What is the purpose of procedural criminal law?

STOP AND ANALYZE: In 2011, the mayor of Baltimore proposed that the Maryland legislature enact a new law requiring a minimum 18-month prison sentence for anyone caught with an illegal, loaded firearm. Are legislators capable of predicting all of the consequences of such a law? List three of your own predictions about the consequences of such a law. In light of your predictions, is the law a good idea?

(Answers are at the end of the chapter.)

Sources of Criminal Law

The earliest known codes of law appeared in the Sumerian law of Mesopotamia (3100 B.C.E.) and the Code of Hammurabi (1750 B.C.E.). These written codes were divided into sections to cover different types of offenses. Other important ancestors of Western law are the Draconian Code, produced in the seventh century B.C.E. in Greece, and the Law of the Twelve Tables created by the Romans (450 B.C.E.). However, the main source of American law is the common law of England.

Common Law

Common law was based on custom and tradition as interpreted by judges. In continental Europe, a system of *civil law* developed in which the rules were set down in detailed codes produced by legislatures or other governing authorities. By contrast, the common law of England was not written down as a list of rules. Rather, it took its form from the collected opinions of the judges, who looked to custom in making their decisions. The judges created law when they ruled on specific cases. These rulings, also known as *precedents,* established legal principles to be used in making decisions on similar cases. When such cases arose, judges looked to earlier rulings to find principles that applied to the type of case they were deciding. Over time, as new kinds of situations emerged, judges had to create new legal principles to address them. As more rulings on various kinds of legal issues were written down, they grew into a body of law—composed of principles and reasoning—that other judges could use in deciding their own cases. The use of a common set of precedents made the application of law more stable and consistent. Moreover, the judges' ability to adjust legal principles when new kinds of situations arose made the common law flexible enough to respond to changes in society.

common law
The Anglo-American system of uncodified law, in which judges follow precedents set by earlier decisions when they decide new but similar cases. The substantive and procedural criminal law was originally developed in this manner but was later codified—set down in codes—by state legislatures.

The American colonies maintained the English precedents and procedures, but after independence the states began to make some changes in the law. For example, state legislatures often formalized the definitions of crimes and punishments in the English common law by enacting statutes that placed these definitions into the penal code. These statutes then became subject to interpretation by judges. American judges still create precedents when they interpret statutes, state constitutions, the U.S. Constitution, and prior judicial opinions. These judicial rulings guide the decisions of other courts on issues concerning both substantive and procedural criminal law.

Written Law

Most people would agree that having a document that clearly states the criminal law, both substantive and procedural, would be helpful. It would allow citizens to know definitively when they might be in danger of committing an illegal act and to be aware of their rights if official action is taken against them. If such a document could be written in simple language, society would probably need fewer lawyers. However, writing such a document is impossible. Our criminal laws and procedures are too complex to be reduced to simple terms. In part, the complexity stems from the unpredictable array of individual circumstances that can arise in criminal cases. If you pick up someone's wallet in the fitness center locker room because you mistakenly thought it was yours, should we treat that act the same as when a person intentionally runs away with someone else's wallet? Further, we are constantly expanding the scope and complexity of criminal law. When we try to define new illegal acts, such as secretly photographing people with camera-equipped cell phones or intercepting information from wireless Internet connections, we see how the law must constantly respond to new, unforeseen problems. Moreover, any effort to reduce rules to words on a page creates opportunities for those words to be interpreted in different ways. If we have a crime called negligent homicide, for example, how will we define *negligence?* The need for interpretation means that lawyers and judges will always have a role in shaping and changing the meaning of both substantive and procedural law.

Because we cannot compile a single, complete document that provides all the details of criminal law, we continue to rely on four sources of law: constitutions, statutes, court decisions (also known as case law), and administrative regulations.

constitution
The basic laws of a country or state defining the structure of government and the relationship of citizens to that government.

Constitutions contain basic principles and procedural safeguards. The Constitution of the United States was written in Philadelphia in 1787 and went into effect in 1789 after the required number of states ratified it. This document sets forth the country's governing system and describes the institutions (legislature, courts, and president) that will make its laws. The first ten amendments to the Constitution, known together as the Bill of Rights, were added in 1791. Most of these amendments provide protections against government actions that would violate basic rights and liberties. Several of the amendments affect criminal law, because they guarantee the rights of due process, jury trial, and representation by counsel, as well as protection against unreasonable searches and cruel and unusual punishments. Most state constitutions also contain protections against actions by state and local governments. During the 1960s the U.S. Supreme Court decided to require state and local governments to respect most of the rights listed in the Bill of Rights. (Before that time most criminal justice provisions of the Bill of Rights protected citizens only against actions by the federal government.) As a result of court decisions, the power of police officers, prosecutors, and judges is limited by the U.S. Constitution as well as the constitution of the state in which they work.

statutes
Laws passed by legislatures. Statutory definitions of criminal offenses are found in penal codes.

Statutes are laws passed by legislative bodies; the substantive and procedural rules of most states are found in their statutes. Although state legislatures write the bulk of criminal law, Congress and local governments play a role in shaping it. Federal criminal laws passed by Congress deal mainly with violations that occur on property of the U.S. government (such as national parks, military bases) or with actions that involve the national interest (such as terrorism, counterfeiting) or more than one state (such as taking a kidnap victim across state lines). State constitutions and legislatures give cities and towns limited authority to create laws dealing with local problems, including minor offenses. National, state, and local rules governing certain kinds of criminal conduct do overlap. Possession or sale of drugs, for example, may violate criminal laws at all three levels of government. In such situations, law enforcement agencies must decide which one will prosecute the offender.

If we want to know the definition of a crime covered by a statute, we consult a state's penal code. This code clearly specifies the acts that constitute a crime and the penalty to be imposed. Although the laws of most states are similar, differences inevitably arise in the lawmaking process. To make state laws more uniform, the American Law Institute has developed the *Model Penal Code,* which it urges legislatures to follow when creating state criminal laws.

case law
Court decisions that have the status of law and serve as precedents for later decisions.

Court decisions, often called **case law**, provide a third source of criminal law. As noted earlier, the main characteristic of the common-law system is that judges look to earlier decisions to guide their rulings. Although statutes have replaced much of the common law of crime, precedent remains an important aid to lawyers and judges in interpreting penal codes.

Administrative regulations are laws and rules made by federal, state, and local agencies. The legislature, president, or governor has given those agencies the power to make rules governing specific policy areas such as health, safety, and the environment. Most regulations produced since the mid-twentieth century deal with modern concerns, such as wages and work hours, pollution, traffic, workplace safety, and pure food and drugs. Many of the rules are part of the criminal law, and violations are processed through the criminal justice system.

As you can see, the criminal law is more than just a penal code written by a state legislature or Congress. Figure 4.1 summarizes the sources of criminal law.

administrative regulations
Rules made by government agencies to implement specific public policies in areas such as public health, environmental protection, and workplace safety.

FIGURE 4.1 SOURCES OF CRIMINAL LAW

Although codes of law existed in ancient times, American criminal law is derived mainly from the common law of England. The common law distinguishes English-speaking systems from civil-law systems of the rest of the world.

CONSTITUTIONAL LAW
The Constitution of the United States and the state constitutions define the structure of government and the rights of citizens.

STATUTORY LAW
The substantive and procedural criminal laws are found in laws passed by legislative bodies such as the U.S. Congress and state legislatures.

CASE LAW
Consistent with the common-law heritage, legal opinions by judges in individual cases have the status of law.

ADMINISTRATIVE LAW
Also having the status of law are some decisions of federal and state governmental agencies that have been given the power to regulate such areas as health, safety, and the environment in the public interest.

✔POINT
3. How does the common law shape criminal law?
4. What are the forms of written law?

STOP AND ANALYZE: Consider this portion of the Minnesota statute defining the crime of "disorderly conduct." Is it obvious how it would apply to every possible situation? List three issues of interpretation or uncertain application that might arise.

> Whoever does any of the following in a public or private place, including on a school bus, knowing, or having reasonable grounds to know that it will, or will tend to, alarm, anger or disturb others or provoke an assault or breach of the peace, is guilty of disorderly conduct, which is a misdemeanor: . . . (3) Engages in offensive, obscene, abusive, boisterous, or noisy conduct or in offensive, obscene, or abusive language tending reasonably to arouse alarm, anger, or resentment in others.

Felony and Misdemeanor

Crimes are classified by how serious they are. The distinction between a felony and a misdemeanor is one of the oldest in criminal law. Most laws define felonies and misdemeanors in terms of punishment. Conviction on a felony charge usually means that the offender may be given a prison sentence of more than a year of imprisonment. The most serious felonies, such as planned murders, may draw the death penalty. Those who commit misdemeanors are dealt with more leniently; the sentence might be a fine, probation, or a jail sentence of less than a year. Some states define the seriousness of the offense according to the place of punishment: prison for felonies, jail for misdemeanors. Be aware, however, that if someone is convicted of multiple misdemeanors, he can receive a sentence of one year for each crime and thereby serve a longer sentence. For example, movie star Wesley Snipes was convicted of three misdemeanors for willfully failing to file tax returns, and a federal judge sentenced him to three years in prison, one year for each misdemeanor, with the requirement that the three years be served consecutively (Itzkoff, 2010).

Whether a defendant is charged with a felony or a misdemeanor determines not only how the person is punished, but also how the criminal justice system will process the defendant. Certain rights and penalties follow from this distinction. The seriousness of the charge determines, in part, the conditions under which the police may make an arrest and the court level where the charges

AP Images/Jacquelyn Martin

In 2011, a Virginia judge dismissed misdemeanor assault charges against former professional football player Albert Haynesworth after he agreed to a settlement providing financial compensation to the victim of an alleged road-rage incident. Does this example show that wealthy defendants may be able to "buy" their way out of criminal charges by anticipating the possibility of civil lawsuits and paying money to victims in advance of such lawsuits? Should the settlement of potential civil lawsuits by victims affect judges' and prosecutors' decisions about whether or not to drop criminal charges?

will be heard. For example, although the Sixth Amendment to the U.S. Constitution says criminal defendants are entitled to a right to trial by jury, in 1996 the U.S. Supreme Court declared that this provision applies only to people accused of serious offenses. People who face less than six months in jail for a charge are not entitled to a jury trial—although their own state's laws may grant them one under those circumstances. However, the U.S. Constitution requires only that they be tried in front of a judge when facing petty charges *(Lewis v. United States)*.

The distinction between types of crimes also can affect a person's future. People with felony convictions may be barred from certain professions, such as law and medicine, and in many states they are also barred from certain other occupations, such as bartender, police officer, and barber. Depending on a state's laws, felony convictions may also keep people from ever voting, serving on juries, or running for election to public office (Grovum, 2014; Olivares, Burton, and Cullen, 1996).

Criminal versus Civil Law

As mentioned earlier, the legal system makes basic distinctions between criminal and civil law. A violation of criminal law is an offense against society as a whole, while civil law regulates relations between individuals. Criminal law focuses on the intent of the wrongdoer. We view intentional acts as most deserving of punishment, but we may decide to press criminal charges even when a harmful event was an "accident." By contrast, civil law centers on fixing the blame for the damage or harm.

In some cases, both criminal and civil proceedings arise from the same event. When hunting, if you carelessly fire a shot that crashes through the window of a home and wounds the homeowner, the homeowner may bring a civil lawsuit against you to recover the cost of the damage you caused. The cost might include medical bills and the price of fixing the window. This legal action falls within the area of civil law known as *torts,* which deals with compensation for damage to property or for people's injuries. In a separate action, the state may charge you with a violation of the criminal law, because your actions broke society's rules for the lawful use of firearms. Although criminal and civil law are distinct, both attempt to control human behavior by steering people to act in a desired manner and by imposing costs on those who violate social rules.

Increasingly, civil lawsuits are being brought against offenders who previously were subject only to criminal charges. For example, some department stores now sue shoplifters for large amounts, and some rape victims bring civil lawsuits against their attackers. Other rape victims successfully sue apartment complexes for failing to maintain secure conditions that would prevent criminal attacks. Victims can win civil lawsuits even against defendants who have been acquitted of criminal charges. In December 2012, a jury found a bus driver not guilty of manslaughter after his bus struck a guardrail and flipped over in New York City, resulting in the deaths of 15 passengers and serious injuries to many others. Even though the jury acquitted him of criminal charges, he still faced civil lawsuits for negligence that could result in substantial financial awards for the survivors and the families of the deceased passengers (Hu and Schweber, 2012).

Civil law is also important for the criminal justice system because citizens can file lawsuits against police officers, correctional officers, and other government actors if they believe those individuals have violated their constitutional rights (Rembert and Henderson, 2014). Such lawsuits can result in multimillion dollar verdicts, especially when innocent citizens are seriously injured or killed through improper high-speed driving or the use of weapons by the police. These civil lawsuits help shape police training and departmental policies, because government agencies want to avoid the high costs of defending and losing civil rights litigation (Epp, 2009).

Civil lawsuits also provide the vehicle for citizen involvement in shaping criminal law by challenging whether a law enacted by a legislature is proper. If a citizen believes that a criminal law clashes with a legal right that is guaranteed by the U.S. Constitution or a state constitution, the individual can use court processes to challenge that law by filing a lawsuit against the government. For example, residents of Washington, D.C., filed a lawsuit and took their case all the way to the U.S. Supreme Court in 2008 to challenge whether the city's laws regulating private gun ownership violate individuals' constitutional rights (D. G. Savage, 2008). Such laws can also be challenged through the criminal process if someone is charged with a crime and challenges the legality of the criminal law. In 2014, for example, the postconviction review of a murder case led the U.S. Supreme Court to declare that a Florida law violated the Eighth Amendment right against "cruel and unusual punishments" by rigidly defining the IQ test score level that made defendants eligible for the death penalty (*Hall v. Florida,* 2014). The Court required that states take a flexible approach that would consider various kinds of evaluations to determine if an individual's intellectual disability was significant enough to eliminate consideration of execution as the punishment for a murder conviction. As you read "Civic Engagement: Your Role in the System," consider what you would do if you thought one of your state's statutes or one of your city's ordinances was unconstitutional.

CIVIC ENGAGEMENT

YOUR ROLE IN THE SYSTEM

Imagine that you live in a state with criminal libel laws that permit prosecutions for making false statements about other individuals. If someone reported to the police that you were posting criticisms of a professor on your personal website, what would you do? *Make a brief list of your options for protecting yourself and resolving the controversy.* Then read about what happened to a high school student who posted threatening comments about a school principal on a website.

Another example of a link between criminal and civil law is **civil forfeiture** (Schaldenbrand, 2010). This concept, derived from English common law, allows for government to take privately owned property, and it has frequently been applied in drug law enforcement (M. B. Stahl, 1992). Forfeiture can even affect property owners who are not guilty of any crime. In 1996 the U.S. Supreme Court decided that, despite her innocence, a wife lost her ownership rights to a car when her husband used the vehicle to pick up a prostitute *(Bennis v. Michigan).* Forfeiture laws frequently permit law enforcement agencies to sell seized property and use the money to buy equipment for themselves and otherwise enhance their annual budgets.

civil forfeiture
Confiscation by the state of property used in or acquired through a crime. In recent years the police have used civil forfeiture to seize property that they believe was purchased with drug profits.

The use of forfeiture by law enforcement agencies has generated controversy, especially when applied against people who have never been convicted of any crime and when used by police departments to enhance their own budgets. Over the course of a decade, state and local police officers made nearly 62,000 cash seizures in traffic stops, totaling more than $2.5 billion, without obtaining any search warrants or charging the drivers with any crimes (O'Harrow and Rich, 2014).

In 2015, in response to a newspaper investigation of the cash-seizure practices of police, U.S. Attorney General Eric Holder announced new restrictions on a federally-sponsored program that had authorized state and local law enforcement officials to seize cash and property from drivers in highway traffic stops. These stops and seizures had often taken place without the individual being charged with any crime, or having been convicted of engaging in wrongdoing. The seized money and property was divided among the federal government and the state and local agencies that had made the traffic stops. State and local departments kept more than $1.7 billion under the program since 2011. With the new rules, seizures under the program can occur only with a search warrant or if the stop and seizure result in criminal charges (O'Harrow, Horwitz, and Rich, 2015).

In summary, the bascs of American criminal law are complex. English common law and the laws found in such written sources as constitutions, statutes, case law, and administrative regulations all contribute to what most people call "criminal law." Within this body of law, there is a major division between substantive criminal law and procedural criminal law.

✔POINT
5. What is the difference between a felony and a misdemeanor?
6. What types of legal issues arise in civil-law cases?

STOP AND ANALYZE: Could we save a significant amount of money in federal, state, and local budgets by ending criminal prosecutions in many kinds of non-homicide cases and instead punish criminals solely through civil lawsuits? List two reasons why you agree or disagree with this approach.

Substantive Criminal Law

As we have seen, substantive criminal law defines acts that are subject to punishment and specifies the punishments. It is based on the doctrine that no one may be convicted of or punished for an offense unless the offense has been defined by the law. In short, people must know in advance what is required of them. Thus, no act can be regarded as illegal until it has been defined as punishable under the criminal law. While this sounds like a simple notion, the language of law is often confusing and ambiguous. As a result, judges must interpret the law so that the meaning intended by the legislature can be understood.

Seven Principles of Criminal Law

The major principles of Western criminal law were summarized in a single statement by legal scholar Jerome Hall (1947). To convict a defendant of a crime, prosecutors must prove that all seven principles have been fulfilled (Figure 4.2).

1. **Legality.** There must be a law that defines the specific action as a crime. Offensive and harmful behavior is not illegal unless it was already prohibited by law before it was committed. The U.S. Constitution forbids ex post facto laws, or laws written and applied after the fact. Thus, when the legislature defines a new crime, people can be prosecuted only for violations that occur after the new law has been passed.

FIGURE 4.2 THE SEVEN PRINCIPLES OF CRIMINAL LAW

A crime is	
1 legally proscribed	(legality)
2 human conduct	(*actus reus*)
3 causative	(causation)
4 of a given harm	(harm)
5 which conduct coincides	(concurrence)
6 with a blameworthy frame of mind	(*mens rea*)
7 and is subject to punishment	(punishment)

These principles of Western law are the basis for defining acts as criminal and defining the conditions required for successful prosecution.

2. ***Actus reus.*** Criminal laws are aimed at human acts, including acts that a person failed to undertake. The U.S. Supreme Court has ruled that people may not be convicted of a crime simply because of their status. Under this *actus reus* requirement, for a crime to occur a person must perform an act of either commission or omission. In *Robinson v. California* (1962), for example, the Supreme Court struck down a California law that made being addicted to drugs a crime. States can prosecute people for using, possessing, selling, or transporting drugs when they catch them performing these acts, but states cannot prosecute them merely for the status of addiction.
3. **Causation.** For a crime to have been committed, there must be a causal relationship between an act and the harm suffered. In Ohio, for example, a prosecutor tried to convict a burglary suspect on a manslaughter charge when a victim, asleep in his house, was killed by a stray bullet as officers fired at the unarmed, fleeing suspect. The burglar was acquitted on the homicide charge because his actions in committing the burglary and running away from the police were not the direct cause of the victim's death (Bandy, 1991). However, states can write their criminal statutes to account for specific situations by attributing causation to lawbreakers. For example, Alabama state law permits murder convictions for those involved in a crime that results in a collaborator being killed. A homeowner shot and killed a Faulkner University student in Montgomery, Alabama, when he and three of his football teammates allegedly attempted to commit a robbery. In 2015, the three surviving students faced murder charges for the death of their teammate because of their alleged participation in the crime that resulted in his death, despite the fact that none of them pulled the trigger and directly caused the death (Associated Press, 2015).
4. **Harm.** To be a crime, an act must cause harm to some legally protected value. The harm can be to a person, property, or some other object that a legislature deems valuable enough to deserve protection through the government's power to punish. This principle is often questioned by those who feel that in causing harm only to themselves they are not committing a crime. Laws that require motorcyclists to wear helmets have been challenged on this ground. Such laws, however, have been written because legislatures see enough forms of harm to require protective laws. These forms of harm include injuries to helmetless riders, tragedy and loss for families of injured cyclists, and the medical costs imposed on society for head injuries that could have been prevented.

   An act can be deemed criminal if it might lead to harm that the law seeks to prevent; this is called an **inchoate offense**. Thus, criminal law includes conspiracies and attempts, even when the lawbreaker does not complete the intended crime. For example, people can be prosecuted for planning to murder someone or hiring a hit man to kill someone. The potential for grave harm from such acts justifies the application of the government's power to punish.

inchoate offense
Conduct that is criminal even though the harm that the law seeks to prevent has been merely planned or attempted but not done.

5. **Concurrence.** For an act to be considered a crime, the intent and the act must be present at the same time (J. Hall, 1947). Let's imagine that Joe is planning to murder his archenemy, Bill. He spends days planning how he will abduct Bill and carry out the murder. While driving home from work one day, Joe accidentally hits and kills a jogger who suddenly—and foolishly—has run across the busy street without looking. The jogger turns out to be Bill. Although Joe had planned to kill Bill, he is not guilty of

murder, because the accidental killing was not connected to Joe's intent to carry out a killing.

6. ***Mens rea.*** The commission of an act is not a crime unless it is accompanied by a guilty state of mind. This concept is related to intent (Ginther, Shen, et al., 2014). It seeks to distinguish between harm-causing accidents, which generally are not subject to criminal punishment, and harm-causing crimes, which involve some level of intent. Certain crimes require a specific level of intent; examples include first-degree murder, which is normally a planned, intentional killing, and larceny, which involves the intent to permanently and unlawfully deprive an owner of his or her property. Later in this chapter we examine several defenses, such as necessity and insanity, that can be used to assert that a person did not have **mens rea**—"guilty mind" or blameworthy state of mind—and hence should not be held responsible for a criminal offense. The element of *mens rea* becomes problematic when there are questions about an offender's capability of understanding or planning harmful activities, as when the perpetrator is mentally ill or is a child (D. W. Klein, 2010). The defense attorneys in the murder cases of Thomas Barlas, Noah Crooks, and Cody Metzker-Madsen, described at the beginning of the chapter, sought to attack the *mens rea* element by claiming these defendants were legally insane at the time that the crimes were committed.

   Exceptions to the concept of *mens rea* are strict liability offenses involving health and safety, in which showing intent is not necessary (J. Greenberg and Brotman, 2014). Legislatures have criminalized certain kinds of offenses in order to protect the public. For example, a business owner may be held responsible for violations of a toxic waste law whether or not the owner actually knew that his employees were dumping polluting substances into a river. Other laws may apply strict liability to the sale of alcoholic beverages to minors. The purpose of such laws is to put pressure on business owners to make sure that their employees obey regulations designed to protect the health and safety of the public. Courts often limit the application of such laws to cases that involve recklessness or indifference.

7. **Punishment.** There must be a provision in the law calling for punishment of those found guilty of violating the law. The punishment is enforced by the government and may carry with it loss of freedom, social stigma, a criminal record, and loss of rights.

mens rea
"Guilty mind" or blameworthy state of mind, necessary for legal responsibility for a criminal offense; criminal intent, as distinguished from innocent intent.

The seven principles of substantive criminal law allow authorities to define certain acts as being against the law and provide the accused with a basis for mounting a defense against the charges. During a criminal trial, defense attorneys often try to show that one of the seven elements either is unproven or can be explained in a way that is acceptable under the law. In contemporary forms of computer-related crimes, there can be challenges for both the prosecutor and the defense in accurately establishing the existence, or lack thereof, of necessary actions and intent. Read the Technology and Criminal Justice feature to consider these potential challenges in evaluating material posted on social media.

These seven principles are by no means adopted throughout the world; other countries base their laws on different principles (Souryal, Potts, and Alobied, 1994). Laws typically reflect the values and traditions of a society. Criminal law may stem from religious tenets, for example, rather than laws enacted by legislatures. The values protected by the law may also differ. In the United States, *defamation*—slander or libel by making false statements that

TECHNOLOGY & CRIMINAL JUSTICE

POSTING ON SOCIAL MEDIA: DISTINGUISHING THREATS FROM FREE EXPRESSION

Clearly, the proliferation of technology in the form of smartphones, digital tablets, and personal computers has created new opportunities for communication. Every day, hundreds of thousands of statements and photos are posted through such social-media outlets as Facebook and Twitter. Interactions can range from person-to-person chats via social messaging to uploads on YouTube that go viral nation- or even worldwide. The sheer quantity of information being communicated daily via social media has made these outlets useful to both criminals and law enforcement officers. For example, there have been burglaries traced to Facebook, Twitter, and other postings in which people announce to the world that they are away on vacation. On the other hand, such postings have also led to arrests and convictions when criminal offenders announce their locations or share with friends information about crimes that they have committed. More difficult problems arise when the social-media postings themselves are potentially the basis for a prosecution and conviction for a crime.

In December 2014, the U.S. Supreme Court heard oral arguments in the case of *Elonis v. United States.* Anthony Elonis posted statements on Facebook that appeared to be angry reactions to being left by his wife and losing his employment for on-the-job sexual harassment of coworkers. Regarding his coworkers, he said "I have sinister plans for all of my friends. . . . " With respect to his wife, he said such things as "I'm not going to rest until your body is a mess, soaked in blood and dying from all the little cuts." He also posted statements alluding to the possibility he might engage in a shooting at a school and kill law enforcement officers.

These statements resulted in federal charges, a conviction for transmitting interstate threats to injure another person, and a sentence of several years in federal prison. In challenging

harm someone else's reputation—is addressed by civil tort law. A person can sue to gain compensation from someone who harms his or her reputation. By contrast, under Islamic law, society may punish certain kinds of defamation as criminal offenses. As they do between countries, differences in traditions, values, and social structures also create variations among the state laws within the United States. For example, although many states sponsor lotteries as a means to raise money for public education, Utah's state constitution says that the "legislature shall not authorize any game of chance, lottery or gift enterprise." Utah's laws officially make gambling a crime, whereas other states have casinos and other forms of legalized gambling. As you read the next section, think about differences in the definitions of crimes and punishments—in the United States and throughout the world—which also reflect the way law is shaped by values and traditions.

✔POINT 7. What are the seven principles of criminal law?

STOP AND ANALYZE: Which of the seven elements is likely to be most difficult to prove? Why? Give two reasons for your answer.

Elements of A Crime

Legislatures define certain acts as crimes when they fulfill the seven principles under certain attendant circumstances while the offender is in a certain state of mind. These three factors—the act *(actus reus),* the attendant circumstances, and the state of mind *(mens rea)*—are together called the elements of a crime. They can be seen in the following section from a state penal code:

> Section 3502. Burglary Offense defined: A person is guilty of burglary if he enters a building or occupied structure, or separately secured or occupied portion thereof,

the conviction, Elonis claimed that he was not making threats. He said his statements were therapeutic in helping him to cope with his divorce and job loss. He said that the statements were much like rap music lyrics—stark expressions, but not actual threats.

The Supreme Court confronted the question of how criminal law should regard expressions posted on social media, especially because social-media sites are recognized outlets for creativity and personal expression. Prior to the advances in technology, a criminal threat would have been easier to identify as such, because it would have been said directly to someone or written in a letter. Yet some of the Supreme Court's justices expressed reluctance to permit stark threats to be freely made because they are like song lyrics or labeled by the author as merely expressing emotions. In 2015, Elonis won. The Supreme Court demanded clearer proof of intent in such cases.

Sources: D. Citron, "*United States v. Elonis* and the Rarity of Threat Prosecutions," *Forbes,* December 3, 2014 (www.forbes.com); G. Epps, "When Does the First Amendment Protect Threats?," *The Atlantic* online, November 29, 2014 (www.theatlantic.com); M. K. Mallonee and P. Brown, "Facebook Threats Case Heard at Supreme Court," CNN.com, December 1, 2014 (www.cnn.com).

DEBATE THE ISSUE

Is there a straightforward test that could be developed to distinguish criminal threats from creative expression? Is there a risk that the Supreme Court's decision could limit the ability of rappers, songwriters, and poets to express themselves in stark terms? Is the risk of harm different, either greater or reduced, because any threat-like statements are announced to a broader audience than traditional criminal threats sent to an individual? Create two examples of expressions that you believe show sufficient intent to justify a criminal conviction for making threats.

> with intent to commit a crime therein, unless the premises are at the time open to the public or the actor is licensed or privileged to enter.

The elements of burglary are, therefore, entering a building or occupied structure (*actus reus*) with the intent to commit a crime therein (*mens rea*) at a time when the premises are not open to the public and the actor is not invited or otherwise entitled to enter (attendant circumstances). For an act to be a burglary, all three elements must be present.

The elements of crimes and required proof before punishment in the American system differ from those in other systems. The definitions of crimes and punishments reflect the values of a particular system of justice. An act committed in one country may not be a crime, yet if that same act were committed elsewhere, it might be punished harshly. For example, journalists in Iran have been imprisoned for writing articles critical of the government, while journalists in the United States can write such articles under the protection of freedom of the press in the U.S. Constitution's First Amendment.

Statutory Definitions of Crimes

Federal and state penal codes often define criminal acts somewhat differently. To find out how a state defines an offense, one must read its penal code; this will give a general idea of which acts are illegal. To understand the judge's interpretations of the code, one must analyze the judicial opinions that have sought to clarify the law.

In the following discussion we focus on two of the eight index crimes of the Uniform Crime Reports (UCR), homicide and rape. The elements of these crimes are interpreted differently in different states.

Murder and Nonnegligent Manslaughter

The common-law definition of criminal homicide has been subdivided into degrees of murder and voluntary and involuntary manslaughter. In addition, some states have created new categories, such as reckless homicide, negligent homicide, and vehicular homicide. Each of these definitions involves slight variations in the *actus reus* and the *mens rea*. Table 4.1 provides examples of differences in states' definitions of crimes by comparing the Ohio and Wyoming statutes on murder and rape. Each state has additional crime definitions for other homicide offenses, such as manslaughter, that result from nonpremediated angry actions or negligence. For an additional comparison that illuminates the differences between law in the United States and that applied elsewhere in the world, see the feature on Islamic law on the book's website.

In legal language, the phrase *malice aforethought* is used to distinguish murder from manslaughter. This phrase indicates that murder is a deliberate, premeditated, and willful killing of another human being. Most states extend the definition of murder to these two circumstances: (1) defendants knew their behavior had a strong chance of causing death, showed indifference to life, and thus recklessly engaged in conduct that caused death; or (2) defendants caused death while committing a felony. Mitigating circumstances, such as the heat of passion or extreme provocation, would reduce the offense to manslaughter, because the requirement of malice aforethought would be absent or reduced. Likewise, manslaughter would include a death resulting from an attempt to defend oneself that was not fully excused as self-defense. It might also include a death resulting from recklessness or negligence.

Rape

In recent decades, pressure mounted, especially from women's groups, for stricter enforcement of laws against rape and for greater sensitivity toward victims (Shen, 2011). Successful prosecution of suspected rapists is difficult because proving *actus reus* and *mens rea* may not be possible (Hickey, 1993).

Scott Olson/Getty Images

Police gather evidence at the scene of a 2013 murder in Chicago. When suspects are arrested for the crime, what will the prosecutor need to prove in order to gain a murder conviction?

TABLE 4.1 DEFINITIONS OF OFFENSES IN THE CRIMINAL CODES OF OHIO AND WYOMING

Each state defines its own crimes. Their definitions are usually quite similar but not identical. Examine the definition of crimes for these two states and identify any differences that you see.

Ohio Aggravated Murder

(A) No person shall purposely, and with prior calculation and design, cause the death of another or the unlawful termination of another's pregnancy.

(B) No person shall purposely cause the death of another or the unlawful termination of another's pregnancy while committing or attempting to commit, or while fleeing immediately after committing or attempting to commit, kidnapping, rape, aggravated arson, arson, aggravated robbery, robbery, aggravated burglary, burglary, trespass in a habitation when a person is present or likely to be present, terrorism, or escape.

(C) No person shall purposely cause the death of another who is under thirteen years of age at the time of the commission of the offense.

(D) No person who is under detention as a result of having been found guilty of or having pleaded guilty to a felony or who breaks that detention shall purposely cause the death of another.

(E) No person shall purposely cause the death of a law enforcement officer whom the offender knows or has reasonable cause to know is a law enforcement officer. . . .

Wyoming Murder

6-2-101. Murder in the first degree . . .

Whoever purposely and with premeditated malice, or in the perpetration of, or attempt to perpetrate, any sexual assault, sexual abuse of a minor, arson, robbery, burglary, escape, resisting arrest, kidnapping or abuse of a child under the age of sixteen (16) years, kills any human being is guilty of murder in the first degree.

6-2-104. Murder in the second degree . . .

[W]hoever purposely and maliciously, but without premeditation, kills any human being is guilty of murder in the second degree, and shall be imprisoned in the penitentiary for any term not less than twenty (20) years, or during life.

Ohio Rape

(1) No person shall engage in sexual conduct with another who is not the spouse of the offender or who is the spouse of the offender but is living separate and apart from the offender, when any of the following applies:

(a) For the purpose of preventing resistance, the offender substantially impairs the other person's judgment or control by administering any drug, intoxicant, or controlled substance to the other person surreptitiously or by force, threat of force, or deception.

(b) The other person is less than thirteen years of age, whether or not the offender knows the age of the other person.

(c) The other person's ability to resist or consent is substantially impaired because of a mental or physical condition or because of advanced age, and the offender knows or has reasonable cause to believe that the other person's ability to resist or consent is substantially impaired because of a mental or physical condition or because of advanced age.

(2) No person shall engage in sexual conduct with another when the offender purposely compels the other person to submit by force or threat of force.

Wyoming: Sexual Assault in the First Degree

6-2-302. Sexual assault in the first degree.

(a) Any actor who inflicts sexual intrusion on a victim commits a sexual assault in the first degree if:

(i) The actor causes submission of the victim through the actual application, reasonably calculated to cause submission of the victim, of physical force or forcible confinement;

(ii) The actor causes submission of the victim by threat of death, serious bodily injury, extreme physical pain or kidnapping to be inflicted on anyone and the victim reasonably believes that the actor has the present ability to execute these threats;

(iii) The victim is physically helpless, and the actor knows or reasonably should know that the victim is physically helpless and that the victim has not consented; or

(iv) The actor knows or reasonably should know that the victim through a mental illness, mental deficiency or developmental disability is incapable of appraising the nature of the victim's conduct.

Source: Ohio Revised Code, Title 29, Chapters 2903 and 2907; Wyoming Statutes, Title 6, Chapter 2.

Because the act usually takes place in private, prosecutors may have difficulty showing that sexual intercourse took place without the victim's consent (Decker and Baroni, 2011). These issues are compounded by the desire of many victims to avoid reliving the trauma of the event by talking about it in court and facing tough questioning from defense attorneys.

One potential problem in prosecuting rape is that rape victims often feel humiliated when their identities are revealed and they are questioned in court about actions that could indicate consent to engage in sex. Many victims therefore are reluctant to press charges (Gruber, 2012; Bast, 1995). In 2004, for example, Colorado prosecutors dropped rape charges against NBA basketball star Kobe Bryant after the alleged victim decided that she did not want to endure the experience of a trial. Thus, jurors never faced the difficult matter of determining whether to believe Bryant's claim that the woman consented to the sexual encounter. Some victims are unwilling to report rape because of the insensitive way victims have been treated. In recent decades many states have enacted laws that limit the kinds of questions that can be asked of rape victims in courts, especially questions concerning the victim's reputation or past sexual history.

If a state's laws divide sex offenses by degrees, as is typically done with murder and manslaughter, rape is the most serious or first-degree offense. Lesser sex offenses typically lack all of the elements of rape. Michigan's criminal code, for example, uses the phrase *sexual penetration* for first-degree criminal sexual conduct and *sexual contact* for the second-degree offense. States that do not divide their sex offenses by degrees may use other terms, such as *sexual assault,* to designate lesser crimes.

From this review of the crimes of murder and rape, we can see that substantive criminal law defines the conditions that must be met before a person can be convicted of an offense. The seven principles of Western law categorize these doctrines, and the penal code of each of the states and the laws of the United States define offenses in specific terms. However, the crafting of precise definitions for criminal offenses does not necessarily enable us to determine when a crime has been committed. Often, difficult issues arise concerning evidence and the reliability of witnesses that will ultimately determine whether an individual is punished for a specific act. With respect to sex crimes, for example, many questions can arise no matter how carefully legislators write their states' statutes. How can the court system determine if rape occurred when the defendant claims that the victim consented to have sex? Does the task of reaching judgment become even more difficult when the victim and alleged assailant are dating and have previously engaged in consensual sex? It is difficult for the criminal justice process to reach accurate conclusions in every case.

✔POINT 8. What is the difference between murder and manslaughter?

STOP AND ANALYZE: Imagine that you are a state legislator proposing a law to make it a crime to neglect a pet (let's call the crime "criminal neglect of an animal"). Write the precise wording of your proposed statute to protect these animals against neglect. Could your law be used to punish anyone in any circumstances that you do not intend?

Responsibility for Criminal Acts

Thus far we have described the elements of crime and the legal definition of offenses; we now need to look at the question of responsibility. Of the seven principles of criminal law, *mens rea* is crucial in establishing responsibility for the act. To obtain a conviction, the prosecution must show that the offender not only committed the illegal act but also did so in a state of mind that makes it appropriate to hold him or her responsible for the act. In October 2011, for example, two 12-year-olds pushed a shopping cart off the fourth floor of a parking garage in New York City. It struck a pedestrian on the sidewalk below, leaving her unconscious and suffering with a life-threatening head injury

(L. Robbins, 2011). Were these children capable of anticipating the risks and potential consequences of their actions? This case raises the question of whether a child can form the same intent as an adult. The analysis of *mens rea* is difficult, because the court must inquire into the defendant's mental state at the time the offense was committed. In other words, it must determine what someone was thinking when he or she performed an act.

Many defendants who admit they committed a harmful act still plead not guilty. They do so not only because they know that the state must prove them guilty but also because they—or their attorneys—believe that *mens rea* was not present. Accidents provide the clearest examples of such situations: The defendant argues that it was an accident that the gun went off and the neighbor was killed, or that the pedestrian suddenly crossed into the path of the car. As U.S. Supreme Court Justice Oliver Wendell Holmes (1841–1935) once said, "Even a dog distinguishes between being stumbled over and being kicked" (O. W. Holmes, 1881: 3).

The courts say that events are "accidents" when responsibility is not fixed; *mens rea* is not present, because the event was not intentional. But a court may not accept the claim that an event was an accident. In some cases the offender is so negligent or reckless that the court holds him or her responsible for some degree of the resulting harm. If a passing pedestrian was killed as the result of a game of throwing a loaded gun into the air and watching it fire when it hit the ground, the reckless gun-tossers could be held responsible. If a pedestrian was killed by a car in which the driver was preoccupied with speaking on a cellular phone, the reckless driver could be charged with a crime. The court holds people accountable for irresponsible actions that cause serious harms; such actions are not easily justified as being "mere accidents" for which no one should be punished.

Note that *mens rea,* or criminal responsibility, may occur even when the defendant had no motive or specific intention to cause harm. In other words, motives do not establish *mens rea;* rather, the nature and level of one's intent do. The *Model Penal Code* lists four mental states that can be used to meet the requirement of *mens rea:* The act must have been performed intentionally, knowingly, recklessly, or negligently. Some offenses require a high degree of intent. For example, larceny requires a finding that the defendant intentionally took property to which she knew she was not entitled, intending to deprive the rightful owner of it permanently.

As we have seen, a major exception to the *mens rea* principle has to do with public welfare offenses or **strict liability** offenses—criminal acts that require no showing of intent. Most of these offenses are defined in a type of law first enacted in England and the United States in the late 1800s. This sort of law dealt with issues arising from urban industrialization, such as sanitation, pure food, decent housing, and public safety. Often the language of the law did not refer to *mens rea*. Some courts ruled that employers were not responsible for the carelessness of their workers, because they had no knowledge of the criminal offenses being committed by them. An employer who did not know that the food being canned by his employees was contaminated, for example, was not held responsible for a violation of pure food laws, even if people who ate the food died. Other courts, however, ruled that such owners were responsible to the public to ensure the quality of their products, and therefore they could be found criminally liable if they failed to meet the standards set forth in the law. Some experts believe that the principle should be applied only to violations of health and safety regulations that carry no prison sentence or stigma. In practice, the penalty in such cases is usually imposed on business owners only after many failed attempts to persuade them to obey the law.

strict liability
An obligation or duty that when broken is an offense that can be judged criminal without a showing of *mens rea,* or criminal intent; usually applied to regulatory offenses involving health and safety.

The absence of *mens rea,* then, does not guarantee a verdict of not guilty in every case. In most cases, however, it relieves defendants of responsibility for acts that would be labeled criminal if they had been intentional. Besides the defense of accidents, there are eight defenses based on lack of criminal intent: self-defense, necessity, duress (coercion), entrapment, infancy, mistake of fact, intoxication, and insanity. These defenses are often divided into two categories: justifications and excuses.

Justification Defenses

Justification defenses focus on whether the individual's action was socially acceptable under the circumstances despite causing a harm that the criminal law would otherwise seek to prevent.

Self-Defense

A person who has a reasonable fear that he or she is in immediate danger of being harmed by another person may ward off the attack in self-defense. The laws of most states also recognize the right to defend others from attack, to protect property, and to prevent a crime. For example, in August 2002, T. J. Duckett, an African American football player for the NFL's Seattle Seahawks at the time of the incident, was attacked by three white men who yelled racial slurs at him as he walked toward his car after a concert. Duckett lost a tooth and suffered a cut, which required four stitches, when he was struck with a bottle in the surprise attack. The 250-pound running back then defended himself, knocking one attacker unconscious and causing a second attacker to be hospitalized with injuries. The third attacker ran away. Although the attackers received the most serious injuries, they faced criminal charges because Duckett was entitled to defend himself with reasonable force against an unprovoked criminal assault (Winkeljohn, 2002).

The level of force used in self-defense cannot exceed the person's reasonable perception of the threat. Thus, a person may be justified in shooting a robber who is holding a gun to her head and threatening to kill her, but not justified in doing so if the robber is clearly unarmed. A Kentucky woman who was nine months pregnant killed another woman in 2005 when the woman lured her into an apartment and attacked her with a knife in an apparent effort to cut her open and steal her baby. She struck her attacker with an ashtray, wrestled the knife away, and stabbed the assailant (CNN, 2005). Because the pregnant woman was attacked with a lethal weapon, she was justified in killing her attacker. By contrast, homeowners generally are not justified in shooting an unarmed burglar who has left the house and is running across the lawn.

Is it possible that self-defense claims will increase as a result of budget cuts affecting law enforcement agencies? In Ashtabula County, Ohio, a judge advised citizens to arm themselves and form neighborhood watch groups after budget cuts reduced by half the number of sheriff's deputies serving the county (Sheeran, 2010). If people who live in areas that experience reductions in police services decide to buy and carry more guns, there is a risk that weapons will be brandished in situations, such as encounters with trespassers on rural land, that would previously have been handled by calling the police. If shots are fired by a homeowner and the local prosecutor questions the justification for the discharge of the weapon, juries may be asked to consider self-defense claims more frequently. Such legal proceedings pose risks for people who believe that they are acting in self-defense but who find themselves being second-guessed by jurors who believe the degree of force was unreasonable or the use of firearms was not justified in the situation.

State legislatures have the authority to enact laws that refine or change the definitions of self-defense and other justifications and excuses recognized in criminal proceedings. A controversial recent development involves the expansion of so-called "stand your ground" laws, through which legislatures in various states have changed or eliminated the traditional requirement of retreating and using deadly force only when necessary as a means of self-defense. In Florida, for example, the expanded concept of self-defense has been used successfully by people using guns to kill others who were threatening them only with fists (Coker, 2014). Critics claim that such laws unnecessarily lead to avoidable deaths by encouraging people to be aggressive rather than make an effort to avoid escalating conflicts (Hundley, Martin, and Humburg, 2012).

Necessity

Unlike self-defense, in which a defendant feels that he or she must harm an aggressor to ward off an attack, the necessity defense is used when people break the law in order to save themselves or prevent some greater harm. A person who speeds through a red light to transport an injured child to the hospital or breaks into a building to seek refuge from a hurricane could claim to be violating the law out of necessity.

The English case *The Queen v. Dudley and Stephens* (1884) offers a famous example of necessity. After their ship sank, four sailors found themselves adrift in the ocean without food or water. Twenty days later, two of the sailors, Thomas Dudley and Edwin Stephens, killed the youngest sailor, the cabin boy, and ate his flesh. Four days later, a passing ship rescued them. When they returned to England, they were tried for murder. The court found that

> if the men had not fed upon the body of the boy they would . . . within the four days have died of famine. That the boy, being in a much weaker condition, was likely to have died before them. That at the time of the act there was no sail in sight, nor any reasonable prospect of relief. That under these circumstances there appeared to the prisoners that unless they then fed or very soon fed upon the boy or one of themselves they would die of starvation. That there was no appreciable chance of saving life except by killing some one for the others to eat.

Despite these findings, the court did not accept their defense of necessity. Lord Coleridge, the chief justice, argued that regardless of the degree of need, standards had to be maintained and the law not weakened. Dudley and Stephens were convicted and sentenced to death, but the Crown later reduced the sentence to six months in prison.

Excuse Defenses

Excuse defenses focus on the actor and whether he or she possessed the knowledge or intent needed for a criminal conviction.

Duress (Coercion)

The defense of duress arises when someone commits a crime because another person coerces him or her. During a bank robbery, for instance, if an armed robber forces one of the bank's customers at gunpoint to drive the getaway car, the customer would be able to claim duress. However, courts generally do not accept this defense if people do not try to escape from the situation. After heiress Patty Hearst was kidnapped by a radical political group and held for many months in the 1970s, she took part in some of the group's armed robberies. She could not use the defense of duress because, in the court's view, she took part in the crimes without being directly coerced by her captors. Despite claiming that she had been psychologically coerced and physically abused while in captivity, she was convicted and ultimately served 21 months in prison before her sentence was commuted by President Jimmy Carter.

Entrapment

entrapment
The defense that the police induced the individual to commit the criminal act.

Entrapment is a defense that can be used to show lack of intent. The law excuses a defendant when it is shown that government agents have induced the person to commit the offense (D. A. Carter, 2009). That does not mean the police may not use undercover agents to set a trap for criminals, nor does it mean the police may not provide ordinary opportunities for the commission of a crime. But the entrapment defense may be used when the police have actually encouraged the criminal act.

During the twentieth century, the defense of entrapment evolved through a series of court decisions (Costinett, 2011). In earlier times, judges were less concerned with whether the police had baited a citizen into committing an illegal act and were more concerned with whether or not the citizen had taken the bait. Today when the police implant the idea for a crime in the mind of a person who then commits the offense, judges are more likely to consider entrapment. This issue raises tough questions for judges, who must decide whether the police went too far toward making a crime occur that otherwise would not have happened (J. Roth, 2014). In addition, it raises difficult problems for defendants who may be reluctant to assert entrapment or other defenses for fear that such efforts will be held against them if, after conviction, the court's sentencing guidelines lead to harsher punishments for defendants who did not admit their guilt (Bridges, 2004).

The key question is the predisposition of the defendant. In 1992 the Supreme Court stressed that the prosecutor must show beyond a reasonable doubt that a defendant was predisposed to break the law before he or she was approached by government agents. The Court's decision invalidated the conviction of a Nebraska farmer who purchased child pornography after receiving multiple solicitation letters from law enforcement officials pretending to be pen pals and bookstore operators. In the majority opinion, Justice Byron White wrote that government officials may not "originate a criminal design, implant in an innocent person's mind the disposition to commit a criminal act, and then induce commission of the crime so that the government may prosecute" (*Jacobson v. United States).*

Infancy

Anglo-American law excuses criminal acts by children younger than age seven on the grounds of their immaturity and lack of responsibility for their actions—*mens rea* is not present. Although common law has presumed that children aged 7 to 14 are not liable for their criminal acts, prosecutors have been able to present evidence of a child's mental capacity to form *mens rea*. Juries can assume the presence of a guilty mind if it can be shown, for example, that the child hid evidence or tried to bribe a witness. As a child grows older, the assumption of immaturity weakens. Since the development of juvenile courts in the 1890s, children above age seven generally have not been tried by the same rules as adults. In some situations, however, children can be tried as adults if, for example, they are repeat offenders or are charged with a particularly heinous crime. Indeed, fear about perceived increases in violent crimes by youths led many states to rewrite their laws in order to give prosecutors or judges greater authority to prosecute youths as adults (Henning, 2013). In 2008, the U.S. Supreme Court declined to hear an appeal from Christopher Pittman, who as a 12-year-old killed his grandparents, was tried as an adult, and sentenced to 30 years in prison, despite debates about whether his antidepressant medication may have contributed to his violent behavior (Greenhouse, 2008).

Mistake of Fact

The courts have generally upheld the view that ignorance of the law is no excuse for committing an illegal act. But if an accused person has made a mistake of fact in some crucial way, that may serve as a defense (Meese and Larkin, 2012). For example, suppose some teenagers ask your permission to grow sunflowers in a vacant lot behind your home. You help them weed the garden and water the plants. Then it turns out that they are growing marijuana. You were not aware of this because you have no idea what a marijuana plant looks like. Should you be convicted for growing an illegal drug on your property? The answer depends on the specific degree of knowledge and intent that the prosecution must prove for that offense. The success of such a defense may also depend on the extent to which jurors understand and sympathize with your mistake.

For example, in 2008 a college professor attending a professional baseball game bought his seven-year-old son a bottle of "lemonade." Because he and his family seldom watch television, however, he had no idea that "hard lemonade" even existed. Thus he made a mistake of fact by purchasing an alcoholic beverage for his very underage son. When police officers spotted the child with the beverage, the boy was taken from the custody of his parents for a few days until officials decided that it was an unintentional mistake. If prosecutors had pursued criminal charges against the professor, his fate would have depended on whether the jury believed his claim of making an ignorant mistake of fact in purchasing the alcoholic "lemonade" for a child (Dickerson, 2008).

Intoxication

The law does not relieve an individual of responsibility for acts performed while voluntarily intoxicated. There are, however, cases in which intoxication can be used as a defense, as when a person has been tricked into consuming a substance without knowing that it may cause intoxication. People may try to argue, for example, that an expected side effect of prescription medication caused violent behavior. Other complex cases arise when the defendant must be shown to have had a specific, rather than a general, intent to commit a crime. For example, someone may claim that they were too drunk to realize that they had left a restaurant without paying the bill. If permitted under state law, drunkenness can also be used as a mitigating factor to reduce the seriousness of a charge.

Insanity

As illustrated by the cases that opened this chapter, the defense of insanity provides an opportunity to avoid responsibility for a crime (A. Griffin, 2012). Debates about insanity have become more complicated as we gain increased medical knowledge about such conditions as postpartum depression (A. Cohen, 2012). The public believes that many criminals "escape" punishment through the skillful use of psychiatric testimony. Yet only about 1 percent of incarcerated offenders are held in mental hospitals because they were found "not guilty by reason of insanity." The insanity defense is rare, generally used only in serious cases or where there is no other valid defense. In four states (Idaho, Montana, Kansas, Utah), defendants cannot use the insanity defense to gain acquittal (Bennion, 2011). Instead, juries may find defendants to be "guilty but insane" or "guilty but mentally ill." In other American jurisdictions, defendants found to be "not guilty by reason of insanity" are not automatically released. They are typically confined to a mental institution until doctors determine that they have recovered enough to be released (Laski, 2012). Some people acquitted of crimes may be confined to such institutions for a longer time than if they had been convicted and sent to prison.

TABLE 4.2 INSANITY DEFENSE STANDARDS

The standards for the insanity defense have evolved over time.

TEST	LEGAL STANDARD BECAUSE OF MENTAL ILLNESS
M'Naghten (1843)	"Didn't know what he was doing or didn't know it was wrong."
Irresistible Impulse (1897)	"Could not control his conduct."
Durham (1954)	"His criminal act was caused by his mental illness."
Model Penal Code (1972)	"Lacks substantial capacity to appreciate the wrongfulness of his conduct or to control it."
Comprehensive Crime Control Act (1984)	"Lacks capacity to appreciate the wrongfulness of his conduct."

Source: National Institute of Justice, Crime File, *Insanity Defense,* a film prepared by Norval Morris (Washington, DC: U.S. Government Printing Office, n.d.).

Over time, American courts have used five tests of criminal responsibility involving insanity: the *M'Naghten* Rule, the Irresistible Impulse Test, the *Durham* Rule, the *Model Penal Code*'s Substantial Capacity Test, and the test defined in the federal Comprehensive Crime Control Act of 1984 (Hollander-Blumoff, 2012). These tests are summarized in Table 4.2, and the tests used in the various states are shown in Figure 4.3, later in the chapter.

AP Images/Mark Garfinkel, Pool

Christian Karl Gerhartsreiter, a German immigrant who lived in the United States as "Clark Rockefeller," purporting to be a member of the famous family, sought unsuccessfully to use the insanity defense in his 2009 trial for kidnapping his daughter in a custody dispute. In 2013, while in prison serving his five-year kidnapping sentence, Gerhartsreiter was convicted of having killed a California man in 1985, when he lived in the man's home while pretending to be a member of a wealthy British family. He was given a prison sentence of 27 years to life. Even if he had to convince a court that he was insane at the time of the murder, should he have avoided a criminal conviction if he did, in fact, commit the crime?

FIGURE 4.3 STANDARDS FOR INSANITY USED BY THE STATES

State laws differ in the standards used to determine insanity.

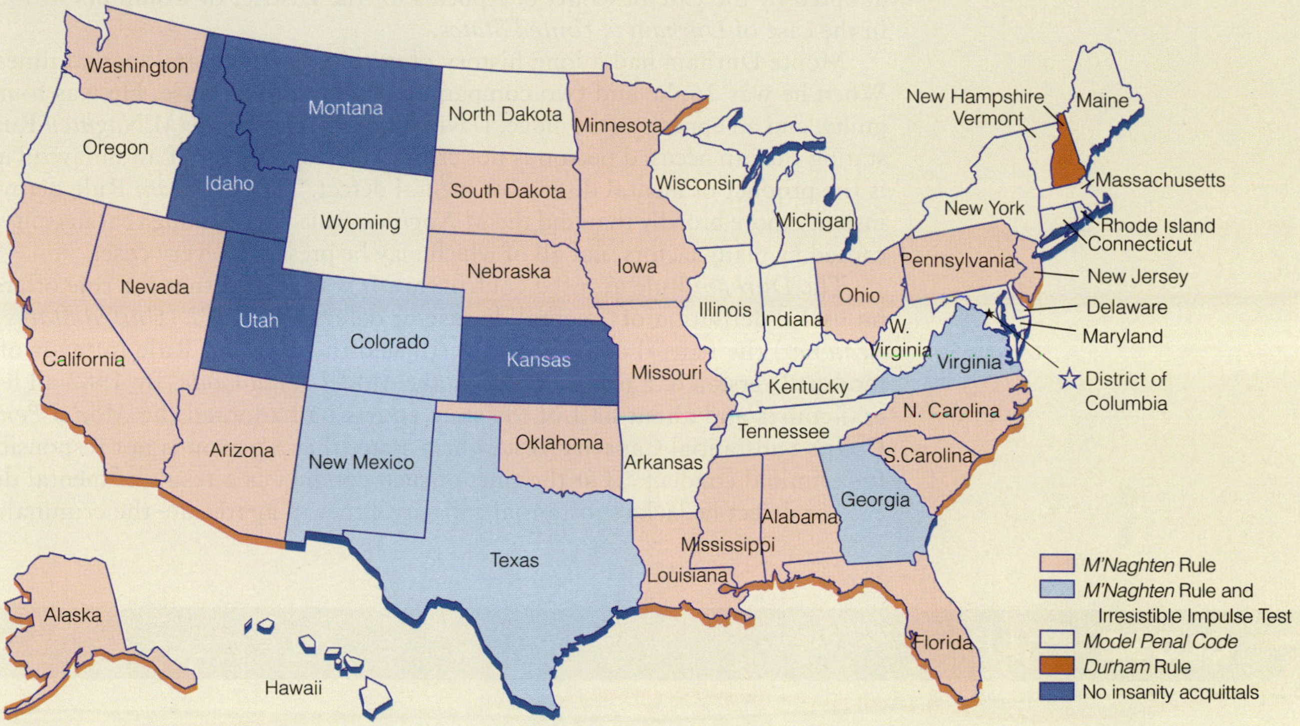

Source: "The Insanity Defense among the States," FindLaw.com (criminal.findlaw.com/criminal-procedure/the-insanity-defense-among-the-states.html).

Before 1843 the insanity defense could be used only by those who were so lacking in understanding that they could not know what they were doing. In that year Daniel M'Naghten was acquitted of killing Edward Drummond, a man he had thought was Sir Robert Peel, the prime minister of Great Britain. M'Naghten claimed that he had been delusional at the time of the killing, but the public outcry against his acquittal caused the House of Lords to ask the court to define the law with regard to delusional persons. The judges of the Queen's Bench answered by saying that a finding of guilt cannot be made if,

> at the time of the committing of the act, the party accused was laboring under such a defect of reason, from disease of the mind, as not to know the nature and quality of the act he was doing, or if he did know it, that he did not know he was doing what was wrong.

This test, often referred to as the "right-from-wrong test," is accepted by many states today.

Over the years many have criticized the *M'Naghten* Rule as not in keeping with modern concepts of mental disorder. Some have argued that people may be able to distinguish right from wrong and still be insane in the psychiatric sense, and that terms such as *disease of the mind, know,* and *nature and quality of the act* have not been defined adequately. Some states allow defendants to plead that, while they knew what they were doing was wrong, they could not control an urge to commit the crime. The Irresistible Impulse Test excuses defendants when a mental disease was controlling their behavior even though they knew that what they were doing was wrong. Five states use this test along with the *M'Naghten* Rule.

The *Durham* Rule, originally developed in New Hampshire in 1871, was adopted by the Circuit Court of Appeals for the District of Columbia in 1954 in the case of *Durham v. United States*.

Monte Durham had a long history of criminal activity and mental illness. When he was 26, he and two companions broke into a house. He was found guilty, and an appeals court judge, David Bazelon, rejected the *M'Naghten* Rule, stating that an accused person is not criminally responsible "if an unlawful act is the product of mental disease or mental defect." The *Durham* Rule defined insanity more broadly than did the *M'Naghten* Rule by assuming that insanity is caused by many factors, not all of which may be present in every case.

The *Durham* Rule aroused controversy. It was argued that the rule offered no useful definition of "mental disease or defect." By 1972 (*United States v. Brawner*) the federal courts had overturned the *Durham* Rule in favor of a modified version of a test proposed in the *Model Penal Code*. By 1982 all federal courts and about half of the state courts had adopted the *Model Penal Code*'s Substantial Capacity Test, which states that a person is not responsible for criminal conduct "if at the time of such conduct as a result of mental disease or defect he lacks substantial capacity either to appreciate the criminality

CLOSE UP

THE INSANITY DEFENSE AND ITS AFTERMATH

Defendants who are judged "not guilty by reason of insanity" are typically committed to mental hospitals. If medical experts subsequently determine that they are not a danger to themselves or the community, they may be released. With regard to the recent Iowa cases described in the chapter opener, in which the insanity defense was used successfully, the court has ordered periodic examinations of Thomas Barlas and Cody Metzker-Madsen to determine when, if ever, either of them will be released. New York law provides the opportunity for a jury trial if a person acquitted through the insanity defense wants to challenge a judge's decision to extend the length of confinement in a mental hospital. In April 1999 Albert Fentress, a former schoolteacher, sought such a jury trial. Twenty years earlier, he had tortured, killed, and cannibalized a teenager, but he had been found not guilty by reason of insanity. The jury listened to four expert witnesses, presented by the prosecution, who asserted that Mr. Fentress had not changed during two decades in the hospital. They also listened to four expert witnesses, including doctors from the state's psychiatric facility, who said that Mr. Fentress no longer posed a danger to society. How could the average juror know which set of experts presented the most accurate diagnosis? In the end, the jury voted 5 to 1 that although Fentress was still mentally ill, he no longer needed to be confined to the hospital.

Undoubtedly, many members of the public would be shocked to think that someone who has committed an outrageous, gruesome murder could be released to walk freely in society. Many members of the public were probably equally shocked in 2003 when John Hinckley Jr., the man who shot President Ronald Reagan in 1981, was allowed to take unsupervised outings, away from the mental hospital where he had been confined, after successfully presenting an insanity defense. Some states have sought to prevent the release of mentally ill, violent offenders by enacting statutes that permit the state to hold such people in mental hospitals after they have finished serving prison sentences. In 1997 the U.S. Supreme Court approved the use of such laws for people diagnosed as "sexually violent predators" (*Kansas v. Hendricks*). However, such laws apply only to people who are convicted of crimes, not to those found not guilty by reason of insanity.

The jury's decision in the Fentress case led the then governor of New York to complain that "individuals like Albert Fentress can hide behind an insanity plea to avoid the prison time they deserve" (LeDuff, 1999: B1). However, an insanity acquittal does not always lead to more-lenient treatment for people committed to mental hospitals. In Virginia, for example, one-quarter of the 239 people confined to mental hospitals after asserting the insanity defense were accused only of misdemeanors. If they had been convicted, they would have served a jail sentence of a year or less. Instead, some of them may serve much longer commitments in the hospital. A man named Leroy Turner has spent more than 13 years in Virginia's Central State Hospital after having been found not guilty, by reason of insanity, of breaking a window. His doctors say that his substance abuse problems are in remission and he is not psychotic. Even though some mental health experts estimate that as many as 40 percent of Virginia's insanity acquittees no longer need to be hospitalized, the state's Forensic Review Panel approves relatively few petitions for [wrongfulness] of his conduct or to conform his conduct to the requirements of law." The Substantial Capacity Test broadens and modifies the *M'Naghten* and Irresistible Impulse rules. Key terms have been changed to conform better with modern psychological concepts, and the standards lacking in *Durham* have been supplied. By stressing substantial capacity, the test does not require that a defendant be unable to distinguish right from wrong.

All of the insanity tests are difficult to apply. Moreover, as you will see in the Close Up feature, "The Insanity Defense and Its Aftermath," significant difficulties arise in deciding what to do with someone who has been found not guilty by reason of insanity. Jurors' fears about seeing the offender turned loose might even affect their decisions about whether the person was legally insane at the time of the crime.

John Hinckley's attempt to assassinate President Ronald Reagan in 1981 reopened the debate on the insanity defense. Television news footage showed that Hinckley had shot the president. Yet, with the help of psychiatrists, Hinckley's lawyers counteracted the prosecution's efforts to persuade the jury that Hinckley was sane. When Hinckley was acquitted, the public was outraged, and several states acted to limit or abolish the insanity defense. Twelve states introduced the defense of "guilty but mentally ill." This defense allows a jury to find the accused guilty but requires that he or she be given psychiatric

release. Is it fair for people to lose their liberty for long periods when they have been acquitted of minor crimes?

In the case of Albert Fentress, a judge blocked the jury's release decision. Fentress later withdrew his petition for release when new victims came forward to contradict his claim that the murder was a one-time psychotic event and he had never before victimized anyone with sex abuse or violence.

As the foregoing examples show, the insanity defense presents significant problems. How can we follow our tradition of reserving criminal convictions for people with sufficient mental capacity yet also protect society from dangerous people and avoid unduly long hospital commitments for insanity acquittees charged with minor offenses?

These problems may be especially difficult when decision-making responsibilities land in the hands of jurors who lack knowledge about psychiatry and mental illness. In 2002, a jury in Houston, Texas, convicted Andrea Yates of murdering her five young children by drowning them in the bathtub. The prosecution and the defense agreed that she was mentally ill, but the prosecutors claimed that she understood right from wrong. By contrast, a jury in Tyler, Texas, in 2004 acquitted Deanna Laney, whom they found to be insane when she claimed to follow God's orders by beating her sons to death with rocks in her front yard. In Laney's case, all five mental health experts for the prosecution and defense testified that she suffered from psychotic delusions. In the case of Yates, one expert claimed she knew what she was doing. A portion of that expert's testimony was later found to be erroneous because he said Yates might have copied the plot of a specific episode from a television show—but that episode never existed. Thus a court of appeals overturned Yates's conviction and she was found not guilty by reason of insanity at her second trial, leading to confinement in a state mental hospital. Can jurors accurately determine if someone was insane when a crime was committed? Are decisions by different juries consistent? When experts contradict each other in their assessments, will jurors tend to play it safe by convicting the defendant? If there are so many problems, then why do we keep the insanity defense? What would you do about this issue?

Sources: Drawn from CNN, "Yates Attorneys Won't Seek Release," January 6, 2005 (www.cnn.com); Russell D. Covey, "Temporary Insanity: The Strange Life and Times of the Perfect Defense," *Boston University Law Review* 91 (2011): 1597–1668; Fox News, "Laney Acquitted of All Charges," April 3, 2004 (www.foxnews.com); David M. Halbfinger, "Verdict in Cannibalism Case Is Set Aside," *New York Times,* June 11, 1999, p. B4; "In Virginia, Insanity Plea Can Bring Long Incarceration," *Washington Post,* June 21, 1999, p. B3; Charlie LeDuff, "Jury Decides Hospitalized Killer in Cannibalism Case Can Go Free," *New York Times,* April 22, 1999, p. B1; Man Gets Life Sentence in Killing, *Lansing State Journal,* August 4, 1999, p. 3B; Bill Miller, "Judges Let Stand Hinckley Ruling; St. Elizabeths Officials Have Right to Decide on Day Trips," *Washington Post,* April 28, 1999, p. A7; Press release of NY Attorney General Eliot Spitzer, December 11, 2001 (www.oag.state.ny.us).

DEBATE THE ISSUE

Should the insanity defense exist at all? Should everyone receive punishment through imprisonment for serious crimes, even if they have serious mental problems? Doesn't society need to demonstrate that everyone will be punished for wrongdoing? State your position on whether the insanity defense should exist. Give three reasons for your position. What is the strongest argument against your position?

In the adversary process, attorneys for each side are obligated to provide zealous advocacy and attempt to refute the evidence presented by the opposing side. Do the formal proceedings of a criminal trial truly protect the rights of defendants or do they just create opportunities for attorneys to obscure the truth by manipulating the presentation of evidence?

AP Images/Dominick Reuter/Pool

treatment while in prison (L. A. Callahan et al., 1992). Hinckley gained permission to take supervised day trips away from the hospital in 1999. In 2003 a judge granted Hinckley permission to make six *unsupervised* day trips within Washington, D.C., with his parents as well as two overnight stays at a local hotel with his family (CBS News, 2004). The fact that the man who shot the president of the United States could walk among other members of the public aroused new debates about the insanity defense. By 2013, Hinckley was permitted to make monitored overnight stays at his mother's house in Virginia that lasted for ten days. The mental hospital and his attorneys argued to a judge that these overnight stays should be lengthened in preparation for his eventual release to live with his mother. However, federal prosecutors vigorously opposed any expansion of Hinckley's time spent away from the secure setting of the hospital (Marimow, 2013; Muskal, 2013).

The Comprehensive Crime Control Act of 1984 changed the federal rules on the insanity defense by limiting it to those who cannot, because of severe mental disease or defect, understand the nature or the wrongfulness of their acts. This change means that the Irresistible Impulse Test cannot be used in the federal courts. It also shifts the burden of proof from the prosecutor, who in some federal courts had to prove beyond a reasonable doubt that the defendant was not insane, to the defendant, who has to prove his or her insanity. The act also creates a new procedure whereby a person who is found not guilty only by reason of insanity must be committed to a mental hospital until he or she no longer poses a danger to society. Although these rules originally applied only to federal courts, they are spreading to several states.

The movement away from the insanity defense reduces the importance of *mens rea*. Many reform efforts have aimed at punishing crimes without regard for the knowledge and intentions of the offender (March, 2010).

The U.S. Supreme Court has reminded states that they cannot do away with all considerations of mental competence, because it affects many phases of the criminal justice process. The insanity defense focuses on the mental state of people at the moment when they commit crimes. A second issue arises concerning their mental state at the time of trial. In the past, people who lacked the mental competence to understand the charges against them and to assist in their own defense were committed to mental hospitals until they were able to stand trial (Ho, 1998; Winick, 1995). In 1996 the justices unanimously declared that states cannot require defendants to meet an excessively high standard in proving incompetence to stand trial. Such standards would result in too many trials of people who lack the necessary mental competence to face charges (*Cooper v. Oklahoma*).

In practice, the outcomes of the various insanity tests frequently depend on jurors' reactions to the opinions of psychiatrists presented as expert witnesses by the prosecution and defense. For example, the prosecution's psychiatrist will testify that the defendant does not meet the standard for insanity, while the defendant's psychiatrist will testify that the defendant does meet that standard. The psychiatrists themselves do not decide whether the defendant is responsible for the crime. Instead, the jurors decide, based on the psychiatrists' testimony and other factors. They may take into account the seriousness of the crime and their own beliefs about the insanity defense. The rules for proving insanity thus clearly favor wealthy defendants who can afford to hire psychiatrists as expert witnesses.

There is nothing automatic about the insanity defense, even for defendants who engage in highly abnormal behavior. In fact, it is rare for anyone to present a successful insanity defense. In 1991, for example, Jeffrey Dahmer was arrested for drugging and killing more than a dozen men and boys whom he had lured to his Milwaukee apartment. He had sex with the corpses, cut up and ate the bodies, and saved body parts in his refrigerator. Despite his shocking behavior, a Wisconsin jury rejected his insanity defense, perhaps because they feared that he might be released some day if he were not held fully responsible for the crimes.

The few defendants acquitted by reason of insanity are nearly always committed to a mental hospital (Laski, 2012). Although the criminal justice system does not consider hospitalization to be "punishment," commitment to a psychiatric ward results in loss of liberty and often a longer period of confinement than if the person had been sentenced to prison (L. Cunningham, 2010). A robber may have faced only ten years in prison, yet an acquittal by reason of insanity may lead to a lifetime of hospital confinement if the psychiatrists never find that the accused has recovered enough to be released. Thus the notion that those acquitted by reason of insanity have somehow "beaten the rap" may not reflect reality.

✔POINT

9. What kind of offense has no *mens rea* requirement?

10. What are the defenses in substantive criminal law?

11. What are the tests of criminal responsibility used for the insanity defense?

STOP AND ANALYZE: Look through the list of defenses and choose one that you think is the least important or necessary. (Pick one other than the insanity defense that was discussed in the Close Up feature.) Make three arguments for abolishing that defense. What would be the consequences if that defense were to be abolished? What is the strongest argument in favor of keeping that defense in the law?

Procedural Criminal Law

Procedural law defines how the state must process cases. According to **procedural due process**, accused people must be tried in accordance with legal procedures. The procedures include providing the rights granted by the Constitution to criminal defendants. As we saw in Chapter 1, the due process model is based on the premise that freedom is so valuable that efforts must be made to prevent erroneous decisions that would deprive an innocent person

procedural due process
The constitutional requirement that all people be treated fairly and justly by government officials. An accused person can be arrested, prosecuted, tried, and punished only in accordance with procedures prescribed by law.

WHAT AMERICANS THINK

Percentage of first-year college students who agree with the statement, "There is too much concern in the courts for the rights of criminals."

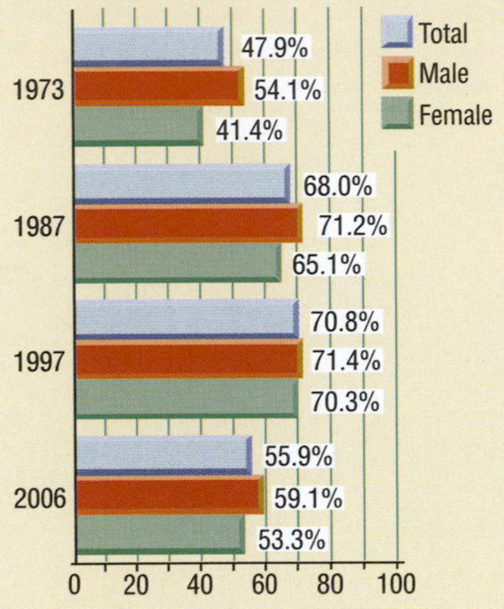

Source: Bureau of Justice Statistics, *Sourcebook of Criminal Justice Statistics* (2015), Table 2.92.2006.

of his or her freedom. Rights are not only intended to prevent the innocent from being wrongly convicted; they also seek to prevent unfair police and prosecution practices aimed at guilty people, such as conducting improper searches, using violence to pressure people to confess, and denying defendants a fair trial.

The concept of due process dates from the thirteenth century, when King John of England issued the Magna Carta, promising that "no free man shall be arrested, or imprisoned, or disseized, or outlawed, or exiled, or in any way molested; nor will we proceed against him unless by the lawful judgment of his peers or by the law of the land." This rule, that people must be tried not by arbitrary procedures but according to the process outlined in the law, became a basic principle of procedural law.

The importance of procedural law has been evident for centuries. American history contains many examples of police officers and prosecutors harassing and victimizing those who lack political power, including poor people, racial and ethnic minorities, and unpopular religious groups. The development of procedural safeguards through the decisions of the U.S. Supreme Court has helped protect citizens from such actions. Because of the weight it places on protecting procedural rights and preventing police misconduct, the Supreme Court may favor guilty people by ordering new trials or may even release them from custody.

Individuals' rights and the protection against improper deprivations of liberty represent central American values. However, the protection of rights for the criminally accused can clash with competing American values that emphasize the control of crime as an important component of protecting all citizens' freedom of movement and sense of security. Because the rules of procedural criminal law can sometimes lead to the release of guilty people, some observers believe that it is weighted too heavily in favor of American values emphasizing individuals' rights rather than equally valid American values that emphasize the protection of the community.

Public opinion does not always support the decisions by the Supreme Court and other courts that uphold the rights of criminal defendants and convicted offenders. Many Americans would prefer that other priorities for society, such as stopping drugs and ensuring that guilty people are punished, would come before the protection of rights. Such opinions raise questions about Americans' commitment to the Bill of Rights. According to public opinion data, most first-year college students believe that courts have placed too much emphasis on the rights of criminal defendants. Moreover, this sentiment has grown over the past 30 years. In addition, although male and female students' support for rights differed in 1973, the two groups show less difference today. Do you agree that there are too many rights? Can you identify specific rights that give too much protection to criminal defendants? Would reducing the rights available in the criminal justice process create any risks? See "What Americans Think."

Unlike substantive criminal law, which is defined by legislatures through statutes, procedural criminal law is defined by courts through judicial rulings. Judges interpret the provisions of the U.S. Constitution and state constitutions, and these interpretations establish the procedures that government officials must follow. Because it has the authority to review cases from state supreme courts as well as from federal courts, the U.S. Supreme Court has played a major role in defining procedural criminal law. The Supreme Court's influence stems from its power to define the meaning of the U.S. Constitution, especially the Bill of Rights. Although public opinion may clash with Supreme Court rulings, the Supreme Court can make independent decisions because the voters cannot remove its members from office.

The Bill of Rights

When it was ratified in 1789, the U.S. Constitution contained few references to criminal justice. Because many people were concerned that the document did not set forth the rights of individuals in enough detail, in 1791 ten amendments were added that list legal protections against actions of the government. These are the Bill of Rights. Four of these amendments concern criminal justice issues. The Fourth Amendment bars unreasonable searches and seizures. The Fifth Amendment outlines basic due process rights in criminal cases. For example, consistent with the assumption that the state must prove the defendant's guilt, protection against **self-incrimination** means that people cannot be forced to respond to questions whose answers may reveal that they have committed a crime. The protection against **double jeopardy** means that a person may be subjected to only one prosecution or punishment for a single offense within the same jurisdiction. The Sixth Amendment provides for the right to a speedy, fair, and public trial by an impartial jury, as well as the right to counsel. The Eighth Amendment bars excessive bail, excessive fines, and cruel and unusual punishments.

For most of U.S. history, the Bill of Rights did not apply to most criminal cases, because it was designed to protect people from abusive actions by the federal government. Specifically, it did not seek to protect people from state and local officials, who handled nearly all criminal cases. This view was upheld by the U.S. Supreme Court in the 1833 case of ***Barron v. Baltimore.*** However, as we shall see shortly, this view gradually changed in the middle of the twentieth century.

self-incrimination
The act of exposing oneself to prosecution by being forced to respond to questions whose answers may reveal that one has committed a crime. The Fifth Amendment protects defendants against compelled self-incrimination. In any criminal proceeding, the prosecution must prove the charges by means of evidence other than the involuntary testimony of the accused.

double jeopardy
The subjecting of a person to prosecution more than once in the same jurisdiction for the same offense; prohibited by the Fifth Amendment.

***Barron v. Baltimore* (1833)**
The protections of the Bill of Rights apply only to actions of the federal government.

The Fourteenth Amendment and Due Process

After the Civil War, three amendments were added to the Constitution. These amendments were designed to protect individuals' rights against infringement by state and local government officials. Two of the amendments had little impact on criminal justice: The Thirteenth Amendment abolished slavery, and the Fifteenth Amendment attempted to prohibit racial discrimination in voting. The other amendment, however, profoundly affected criminal justice.

The Fourteenth Amendment, ratified in 1868, barred states from violating people's right to due process of law. It states that "no State shall . . . deprive any person of life, liberty, or property without due process of law; nor deny to any person within its jurisdiction the equal protection of the laws." These rights to due process and equal protection served as a basis for protecting individuals from abusive actions by local criminal justice officials. However, the terms *due process* and *equal protection* are so vague that it was left to the U.S. Supreme Court to decide if and how these new rights applied to the criminal justice process.

For example, in ***Powell v. Alabama* (1932)**, the Supreme Court ruled that the due process clause required states to provide attorneys for poor defendants facing the death penalty. This decision stemmed from a notorious case in Alabama in which nine African American men, known as the "Scottsboro boys," were quickly convicted and condemned to death for allegedly raping two white women, even though one of the alleged victims later admitted that she had lied about the rape (J. Goodman, 1994).

***Powell v. Alabama* (1932)**
An attorney must be provided to a poor defendant facing the death penalty.

In these early cases, the justices had not developed clear rules for deciding which specific rights applied against state and local officials as components of the due process clause of the Fourteenth Amendment. They implied that procedures must meet a basic standard of **fundamental fairness**. In essence, the justices simply reacted against brutal situations that shocked their consciences. In doing so, they showed the importance of procedural criminal law in protecting individuals from abusive and unjust actions by government officials.

fundamental fairness
A legal doctrine supporting the idea that so long as a state's conduct maintains basic standards of fairness, the Constitution has not been violated.

The Due Process Revolution

From the 1930s to the 1960s, a majority of the Supreme Court justices supported the fundamental fairness doctrine. Even so, they applied it on a case-by-case basis, not always in a consistent way. After Earl Warren became chief justice in 1953, he led the Supreme Court in a revolution that changed the meaning and scope of constitutional rights for criminal justice. Instead of requiring state and local officials merely to uphold fundamental fairness, the Court began to require them to abide by the specific provisions of the Bill of Rights. Through the process of **incorporation**, the Supreme Court during the Warren Court era declared that elements of the Fourth, Fifth, Sixth, Eighth, and other amendments were part of the due process clause of the Fourteenth Amendment. Up to this point, states could design their own criminal justice procedures, so long as those procedures passed the fairness test. Under Warren's leadership, however, the Supreme Court's new approach imposed detailed procedural standards on the police and courts. As it applied more and more constitutional rights against the states, the Court made decisions that favored the interests of many criminal defendants. These defendants had their convictions overturned and received new trials, because the Court believed that it was more important to protect the values underlying criminal procedure than to single-mindedly seek convictions of criminal offenders.

incorporation
The extension of the due process clause of the Fourteenth Amendment to make binding on state governments the rights guaranteed in the first ten amendments to the U.S. Constitution (the Bill of Rights).

In the eyes of many legal scholars, the Warren Court's decisions made criminal justice processes consistent with the American values of liberty, rights, and limited government authority. To critics, however, these decisions made the community more vulnerable to crime and thereby harmed American values by diminishing the overall sense of liberty and security in society (Nowlin, 2012). Politicians, police chiefs, and members of the public strongly criticized Warren

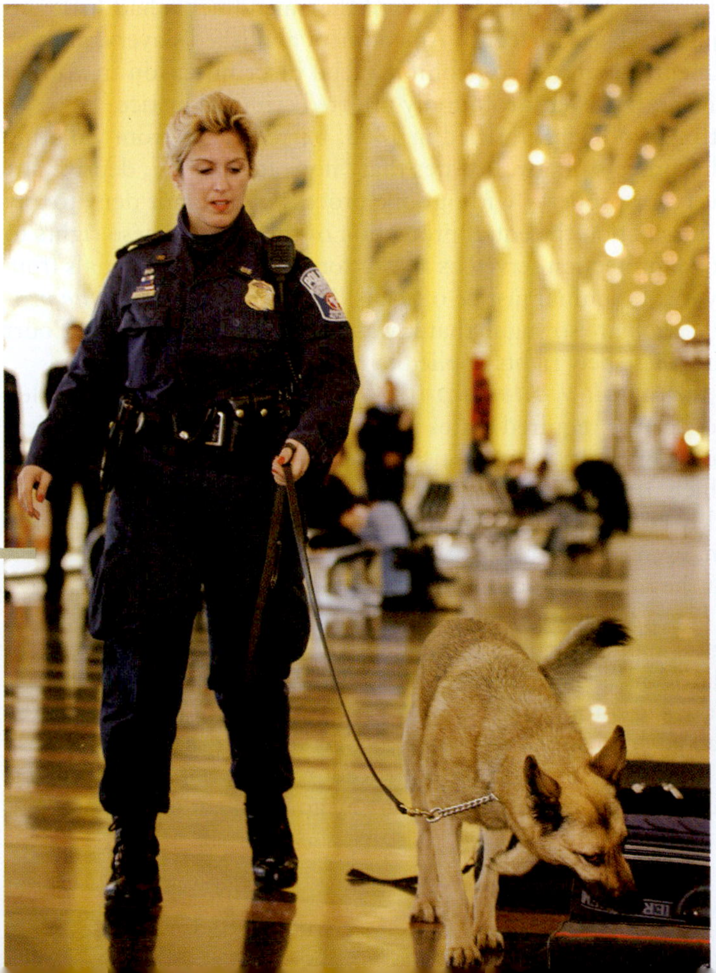

AP Images/Evan Vucci

Security officials at airports, as well as police patrol units, use dogs that sniff for bombs, drugs, or large amounts of cash. Should such dogs be used to investigate anyone selected by police officers or should they only be used when people engage in suspicious behavior?

and the other justices. These critics believed that the Warren Court was re-writing constitutional law in a manner that gave too many legal protections to criminals who harm society (J. M. Burns, 2009). In addition, Warren and his colleagues were criticized for ignoring established precedents that defined rights in a limited fashion. Some people alleged that the justices were advancing their own political views rather than following the true meaning of the Constitution.

From 1962 to 1972 the Supreme Court, led by Chief Justices Earl Warren (1953–1969) and Warren Burger (1969–1986), applied most criminal justice rights in the U.S. Constitution against the states. By the end of this period, the process of incorporation was nearly complete. Criminal justice officials at all levels—federal, state, and local—were obligated to respect the constitutional rights of suspects and defendants.

✓POINT

12. What is incorporation?

13. Prior to incorporation, what test was used by the Supreme Court to decide which rights applied to the states?

14. Which Supreme Court era (named for the chief justice) most significantly expanded the definitions of constitutional rights for criminal defendants?

STOP AND ANALYZE: How might the criminal justice system be different today if the Supreme Court had never initiated the incorporation process? List three ways that the justice system might be different as a result.

The Fourth Amendment: Protection Against Unreasonable Searches and Seizures

> The right of the people to be secure in their persons, houses, papers, and effects, against unreasonable searches and seizures, shall not be violated, and no Warrants shall issue, but upon probable cause, supported by Oath or affirmation, and particularly describing the place to be searched, and the persons or things to be seized.

The Fourth Amendment limits the ability of law enforcement officers to search a person or property in order to obtain evidence of criminal activity. It also limits the ability of the police to detain a person without justification (Taslitz, 2010). When police take an individual into custody or prevent an individual from leaving a location, such detentions are considered to be seizures under the Fourth Amendment. As we shall examine in greater detail in Chapter 8, the Fourth Amendment does not prevent the police from conducting searches or making arrests; it merely protects people's privacy by barring unreasonable searches and arrests. It is up to the Supreme Court to define the situations in which a search or seizure is "reasonable" or "unreasonable."

The justices also face challenges in defining such words as *searches* and *seizures*. For example, in 2005 the Supreme Court ruled that no issues concerning Fourth Amendment rights arose when a K-9 officer had a trained police dog sniff the exterior of a vehicle that was stopped for a traffic violation in a public place (Lunney, 2009). The dog indicated to the officer that the car's trunk contained marijuana, and that discovery led to a criminal conviction. However, unlike a *search,* for which officers must have proper justifications, the use of the dog in this situation did not require any justification, because the dog's scent-based examination of the vehicle's exterior did not invade the driver's right to privacy (*Illinois v. Caballes*).

By contrast, in 2013, the Supreme Court said a search occurred and violated the rights of a homeowner when an unverified informant's tip led an officer to take a drug-sniffing dog to the front door of a house. The dog detected marijuana in the house and the police obtained a warrant to do a search based on the dog's indication. However, because the officer lacked sufficient justification to bring the dog to the front door of a house, the homeowner's rights were violated by the improper search (*Florida v. Jardines*). In essence, as compared to the limited privacy protections for cars in public places, the Supreme Court applies much greater Fourth Amendment protection to examinations of houses.

The justices decided *Florida v. Jardines* (2013) by a 5-to-4 vote. Clearly the justices disagreed about whether the use of the drug-sniffing dog at a house constituted a "search" under the Fourth Amendment. Because Supreme Court justices do not always agree on the Constitution's meaning, the definitions of these words and the rules for police searches can change as the makeup of the Court changes (Soree, 2013).

In 2015, the Supreme Court further clarified the use of drug-sniffing dogs when it prohibited police officers from prolonging traffic stops in order to wait for a trained dog to be brought to the scene (*Rodriguez v. United States*). In this case, the driver was only delayed for eight minutes after being given a written warning from the officer. However, a majority of justices said that drivers must be free to go when the officer has completed the traffic matter that led to the stop, unless the officer has a specific basis for reasonable suspicion that the driver's vehicle carries drugs or other illegal items. This case did not focus on whether the use of the dog constituted a search. Instead, it concluded that holding a driver beyond the time necessary to complete the traffic stop constitutes an "unreasonable seizure" under the Fourth Amendment.

The wording of the Fourth Amendment makes clear that the authors of the Bill of Rights did not believe that law enforcement officials should have the power to pursue criminals at all costs. The Fourth Amendment's protections apply to suspects as well as law-abiding citizens. Police officers are supposed to follow the rules for obtaining search warrants, and they are not permitted to conduct unreasonable searches even when trying to catch dangerous criminals. As we shall see in Chapter 8, improper searches that lead to the discovery of criminal evidence can lead judges to bar police and prosecutors from using that evidence to prove the suspect's guilt. Thus, police officers need to be knowledgeable about the rules for searches and seizures and to follow those rules carefully in conducting criminal investigations. Defense attorneys will look closely at police actions in order to attempt to protect the rights of their clients by challenging the use of evidence obtained through improper searches. Read the Doing Your Part feature, "Criminal Defense Internship," to learn how students may find opportunities to simultaneously learn about and assist with the protection of these rights in the criminal justice process.

Police face challenges in attempting to respect Fourth Amendment rights while also actively seeking to prevent crimes and catch offenders. There are risks that officers may be tempted to go too far in investigating crimes without an adequate basis for suspicion and thereby violate Fourth Amendment rights. The discussion of racial profiling in Chapter 3 illustrates one aspect of the risk that officers will use their authority in ways that collide with the Fourth Amendment, by conducting stops and searches without an appropriate basis. Read "A Question of Ethics" at the end of the chapter to consider police officers' use of new technology that tests the boundaries of the Fourth Amendment.

The Fifth Amendment: Protection Against Self-Incrimination and Double Jeopardy

> No person shall be held to answer for a capital, or otherwise infamous crime, unless on a presentment or indictment of a Grand Jury, except in cases arising in the land or naval forces, or in the Militia, when in actual service in time of war or public danger;

DOING YOUR PART

CRIMINAL DEFENSE INTERNSHIP

Many college students studying criminal justice are interested in learning about careers in law enforcement. Many can find opportunities as police cadets with local police departments or as summer interns with law enforcement agencies at all levels of government. Few people realize that there are also opportunities to learn about and contribute to cases through the perspective of protecting the rights of people drawn into the criminal justice system. For example, the Public Defender Service of Washington, DC, has a long-established program called the Criminal Law Internship Program (CLIP) that permits college students to become actively involved in investigating and preparing cases on behalf of poor criminal defendants. Although many defendants will be found guilty of the crimes for which they are accused, the American system still emphasizes that even guilty defendants are entitled to have the police and prosecutor respect their constitutional rights under the Fourth, Fifth, and Sixth Amendments. While learning about the justice system, these students are able to contribute to the protection of rights and, in some cases, potentially help innocent people avoid being erroneously convicted of crimes that they did not commit.

> nor shall any person be subject for the same offense to be twice put in jeopardy of life or limb; nor shall be compelled in any criminal case to be a witness against himself, nor be deprived of life, liberty, or property, without due process of law; nor shall private property be taken for public use, without just compensation.

The Fifth Amendment clearly states some key rights related to the investigation and prosecution of criminal suspects. For example, the protection against compelled self-incrimination seeks to prevent authorities from pressuring people into acting as witnesses against themselves (C. E. Smith, 2010b). Presumably, this right also helps to protect against torture or other rough treatment when police officers question criminal suspects (Kamisar, 2012). In Chapter 8, we shall discuss the Fifth Amendment rules that guide officers in questioning criminal suspects. The right against double jeopardy seeks to keep prosecutors from putting defendants on trial over and over again in repeated efforts to convict them of the same offense. One of the rights in the Fifth Amendment, the entitlement to indictment by a grand jury before being prosecuted for a serious crime, applies only in federal courts. This is one of the few rights in the Bill of Rights that the Supreme Court never applied to the states. A **grand jury** is a body of citizens drawn from the community to hear evidence from the prosecutor in order to determine whether there is a sufficient basis to move forward with a criminal prosecution. Some states use grand juries by their own choice; they are not required to do so by the Fifth Amendment. Other states simply permit prosecutors to file charges directly against criminal suspects.

grand jury
A body of citizens that determines whether the prosecutor possesses sufficient evidence to justify the prosecution of a suspect for a serious crime.

Because of the limit imposed by the Fifth Amendment, a person charged with a criminal act may be subjected to only one prosecution or punishment for that offense in the same jurisdiction. As interpreted by the Supreme Court, however, the right against double jeopardy does not prevent a person from facing two trials or receiving two sanctions from the government for the same criminal acts (J. M. Barry, 2012). Because a single criminal act may violate both state and federal laws, for example, a person may be tried in both courts. Thus, when Los Angeles police officers were acquitted of assault charges in a state court after they had been videotaped beating motorist Rodney King in 1992, they were later convicted in a federal court for violating King's civil rights. The Supreme Court further refined the meaning of double jeopardy in 1996 by ruling that prosecutors could employ both property forfeiture and criminal charges against someone who grew marijuana at his home. The Court did not apply the double jeopardy right in the case, because the property forfeiture was not a "punishment" (*United States v. Ursery*). In yet another case, the Supreme Court permitted Alabama to pursue kidnapping and murder charges against a man who had already been convicted for the same murder in Georgia when the victim was kidnapped in one state and killed in the other (*Heath v. Alabama*, 1985). Thus, the protection against double jeopardy does not prevent two different trials based on the same criminal acts as long as the trials are in different jurisdictions and based on different charges.

✔POINT **15.** What rights are protected by the Fourth Amendment?

16. What rights are protected by the Fifth Amendment?

STOP AND ANALYZE: What is the underlying purpose of the Fifth Amendment right against double jeopardy? Is that purpose nullified when defendants, who are acquitted on state charges, are later convicted on separate federal charges arising out of the same incident? List two arguments against permitting such consecutive prosecutions. List two arguments supporting such prosecutions.

The Sixth Amendment: The Right to Counsel and a Fair Trial

> In all criminal prosecutions, the accused shall enjoy the right to a speedy and public trial, by an impartial jury of the State and district wherein the crime shall have been committed, which district shall have been previously ascertained by law, and to be informed of the nature and cause of the accusation; to be confronted with the witnesses against him; to have compulsory process for obtaining witnesses in his favor, and to have the assistance of counsel for his defense.

The Sixth Amendment includes several provisions dealing with fairness in a criminal prosecution. These include the right to counsel, to a speedy and public trial, and to an impartial jury.

The Right to Counsel

Gideon v. Wainwright (1963)
Indigent defendants have a right to counsel when charged with serious crimes for which they could face six months or more incarceration.

indigent defendants
People facing prosecution who do not have enough money to pay for their own attorneys and court expenses.

Although the right to counsel in a criminal case had prevailed in federal courts since 1938, not until the Supreme Court's landmark decision in ***Gideon v. Wainwright* (1963)** was this requirement made binding on the states when indigent defendants faced serious criminal charges. **Indigent defendants** are those who cannot afford to hire their own attorney. Many states already provided attorneys for indigents, but the Court forced all of the states to meet Sixth Amendment standards. In previous cases the Court, applying the doctrine of fundamental fairness, had ruled that states must provide poor people with counsel only when this was required by the special circumstances of the case. A defense attorney had to be provided when conviction could lead to the death penalty, when the issues were complex, or when a poor defendant was either very young or mentally handicapped. After the *Gideon* decision and the later case of *Argersinger v. Hamlin* (1972), all indigent defendants facing the possibility of a jail or prison sentence were entitled to be provided with attorneys. Defendants who have enough money to hire their own defense attorneys must do so without any assistance from the government.

Although the *Gideon* ruling directly affected only states that did not provide poor defendants with attorneys, it set in motion a series of cases that affected all the states by deciding how the right to counsel would be applied in various situations. Beginning in 1963, the Court extended the right to counsel to preliminary hearings, initial appeals, postindictment identification lineups, and children in juvenile court proceedings. Later, however, the Burger Court declared that attorneys need not be provided for discretionary appeals or for trials in which the only possible punishment is a small fine (*Ross v. Moffitt,* 1974; *Scott v. Illinois,* 1979).

The Right to a Speedy and Public Trial

The nation's founders were aware that in other countries accused people often languished in jail awaiting trial and faced conviction in secret proceedings. At the time of the American Revolution, the right to a speedy and public trial was recognized in the common law and included in the constitutions of six of the original states. But the word *speedy* is vague, and the Supreme Court has recognized that the desire for quick processes may conflict with other interests of society (such as the need to collect evidence) as well as with interests of the defendant (such as the need for time to prepare a defense).

The right to a public trial is intended to protect the accused against arbitrary conviction. The Constitution assumes that judges and juries will act in accordance with the law if they must listen to evidence and announce their decisions in public. Again, the Supreme Court has recognized that there may be cases in which the need for a public trial must be balanced against other interests. For example, the right to a public trial does not mean that all members of the public have the right to attend. The courtroom's seating capacity and the interests of a fair trial, free of outbursts from the audience, may be considered. In hearings on sex crimes when the victim or witness is a minor, courts have barred the public in order to spare the child embarrassment. Alternatively, in some states trials have become even more public than the authors of the Sixth Amendment ever imagined, because court proceedings are televised, with some carried on the Internet and national cable systems through cnn.com/Justice and truTV (formerly known as Court-TV).

These Sixth Amendment rights obviously represent important American values related to liberty and fair judicial proceedings. In the aftermath of the September 11 attacks, however, the federal government's antiterrorism efforts have challenged these values (C. E. Smith, 2004a). The Bush administration sought to limit the rights available for American citizens suspected of involvement in terrorism. Foreign citizens taken into custody by U.S. military forces in Afghanistan and elsewhere who are labeled as "unlawful combatants" are being held at the U.S. Navy base in Cuba and other American military installations around the world. In the case of one jailed American, the U.S. Supreme Court said that he was entitled to meet with an attorney and file court actions to challenge the basis for his detention (*Hamdi v. Rumsfeld,* 2004). The Supreme Court also said that the foreign citizens being held in Cuba may file legal actions in U.S. courts to challenge their continued confinement (*Rasul v. Bush,* 2004). Later, the federal government tried and convicted a terrorism suspect as well as Somali pirates who had attacked American ships off the east coast of Africa by providing regular criminal trials with full constitutional rights (Mackey, 2010; Weiser and Savage, 2010). However, the government later decided to try the alleged 9-11 masterminds in military trials with limited rights at Guantánamo Bay rather than bring them to the United States for

WHAT AMERICANS THINK

QUESTION: "What concerns you more about the government's antiterrorism policies: that they have gone too far in restricting the average person's civil liberties or that they have not gone far enough to adequately protect the country?"

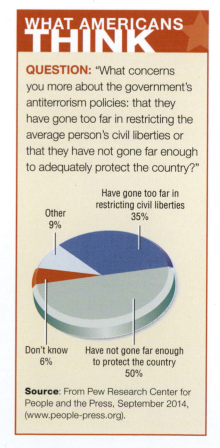

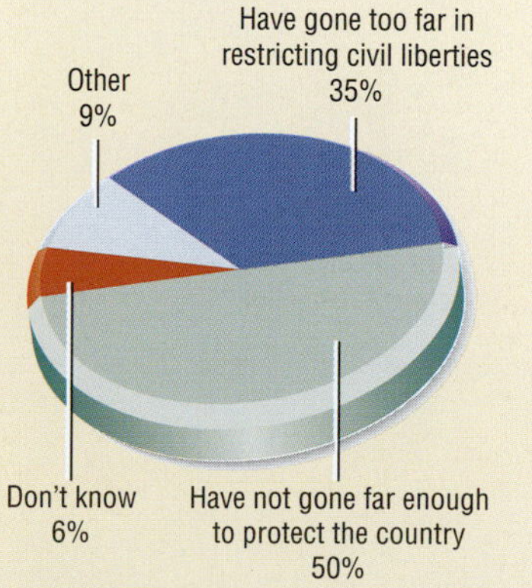

Source: From Pew Research Center for People and the Press, September 2014, (www.people-press.org).

regular criminal trials (C. Savage, 2011b). As the presidential administrations of both George W. Bush and Barack Obama have struggled with making decisions about the best course of action for these trials, Americans are divided on whether the nation is appropriately committed to protecting people's rights and liberties in a time of terrorism fears. See "What Americans Think" and consider how you would answer the question.

The Right to an Impartial Jury

The right to a jury trial was well established in the American colonies at the time of the Revolution (Gertner, 2010). In their charters, most of the colonies guaranteed trial by jury, and it was referred to in the First Continental Congress's debates in 1774, the Declaration of Independence, the constitutions of the 13 original states, and the Sixth Amendment to the U.S. Constitution. Juries allow citizens to play a role in courts' decision making and to prevent punishments in cases that do not have enough evidence for a proper conviction.

Several Supreme Court decisions have dealt with the composition of juries. The Magna Carta required that juries be drawn from "peers" of the accused person who live in the area where the crime was committed. However, the Sixth Amendment does not refer to a jury of one's peers. Instead, the Supreme Court has held that the amendment requires selection procedures that create a jury pool made up of a cross section of the community (T. White and Baik, 2010). Most scholars believe that an impartial jury can best be achieved by drawing jurors at random from the broadest possible base (Levine, 1992). The jury is expected to represent the community, and the extent to which it does is a central concern of jury administration (M. Rose and Abramson, 2011). Prospective jurors are usually summoned randomly from voter registration lists or drivers' license records. After the jury pool has been formed, attorneys for each side may ask potential jurors questions and seek to exclude specific jurors (Burke, 2012). Thus, the final group of jurors may not, in fact, reflect the diversity of a particular city's or county's residents (Preller, 2012). In addition, a specific jury may be even less representative of the community because of the ability of lawyers to influence its composition in the selection process, such as prosecutors' ability to exclude capital punishment opponents from juries in death penalty cases (*Uttecht v. Brown*, 2007).

The Eighth Amendment: Protection Against Excessive Bail, Excessive Fines, and Cruel and Unusual Punishments

> Excessive bail shall not be required, nor excessive fines imposed, nor cruel and unusual punishments inflicted.

The briefest of the amendments, the Eighth Amendment, deals with the rights of defendants during the pretrial (bail) and correctional (fines, punishment) phases of the criminal justice system.

Release on Bail

The purpose of bail is to allow for the release of the accused while he or she is awaiting trial (Gerstein, 2013). The Eighth Amendment does not require that all defendants be released on bail, only that the amount of bail not be excessive. Despite these provisions, many states do not allow bail for those charged with particular offenses, such as murder, and there seem to be few limits on the amounts that can be required. In 1987 the Supreme Court, in *United States v. Salerno and Cafero,* upheld provisions of the Bail Reform Act of 1984 that allow federal judges to detain without bail suspects who are considered dangerous to the public.

Excessive Fines

The Supreme Court ruled in 1993 that the forfeiture of property related to a criminal case can be analyzed for possible violation of the excessive fines clause (*Austin v. United States*). In 1998 the Court declared for the first time that a forfeiture constituted an impermissible excessive fine. In that case, a man failed to comply with the federal law requiring that travelers report if they are taking $10,000 or more in cash outside the country (C. E. Smith, 1999a). There is no law against transporting any amount of cash. The law only concerns filing a report to the government concerning the transport of money. When one traveler at the Los Angeles airport failed to report the money, which was detected in his suitcase by a cash-sniffing dog trained to identify people who might be transporting money for drug dealers, he was forced to forfeit all of the $357,000 that he carried in his luggage. Because there was no evidence that the money was obtained illegally and because the usual punishment for the offense would only be a fine of $5,000, a slim, five-member majority on the Supreme Court ruled that the forfeiture of all the traveler's money constituted an excessive fine (*United States v. Bajakajian*). It is unclear whether the Court's decisions have had any significant impact on law enforcement agencies' practices in forcing criminal defendants to forfeit cash and property.

Cruel and Unusual Punishments

Because the nation's founders were concerned about the barbaric punishments that had been inflicted in seventeenth- and eighteenth-century Europe, where offenders were sometimes burned alive or stoned to death, they banned "cruel and unusual punishments." The Warren Court set the standard for judging issues of cruel and unusual punishment in a case dealing with a former soldier who was deprived of U.S. citizenship for deserting his post during World War II (*Trop v. Dulles,* 1958). Chief Justice Earl Warren declared that judges must use the values of contemporary society to determine whether a specific punishment is cruel and unusual. This test has been used in death penalty cases; however, the justices have strongly disagreed over the values of American society concerning the death penalty. For example, only a few justices concluded that society's contemporary values have developed to the point that the death penalty violates the Eighth Amendment's ban on cruel and unusual punishments in all circumstances. Justices William Brennan and Thurgood Marshall advanced that viewpoint from the 1970s through their retirements at the beginning of the 1990s. Justice Harry Blackmun reached the same conclusion just prior to his retirement in the early 1990s. Most recently, Justice John Paul Stevens announced in 2008 that he had reached the same conclusion *(Baze v. Rees,* 2008), but he was the only recent member of the Court to express that viewpoint (C. E. Smith, 2010a). However, Stevens retired in 2010 after serving on the Court for 35 years, and none of the current justices have expressed similar support for banning capital punishment.

The use of the contemporary standards test caused controversy when a slim majority of justices applied it to declare that states violate the cruel and unusual punishments clause when they apply the death penalty for murders committed by youths under the age of 18 (*Roper v. Simmons,* 2005) and for murders committed by developmentally disabled offenders (*Atkins v. Virginia,* 2002). They declined, however, to reach the same conclusion about the use of lethal injection as a method of execution (*Baze v. Rees,* 2008). We shall examine these and other death penalty issues in greater detail in Chapter 12.

The test from *Trop v. Dulles* is also used to evaluate whether the conditions of confinement in prisons constitute cruel and unusual punishment. If, for example, prison officials were to deprive incarcerated offenders of medical care, food, or shelter, such actions could violate the Eighth Amendment (C. E. Smith, 2007).

Since the 1950s the rights of defendants in state criminal trials have greatly expanded. The Supreme Court has incorporated most of the Fourth, Fifth, Sixth, and Eighth Amendments, as shown in Figure 4.4. Figure 4.5 shows the amendments that protect defendants at various stages of the criminal justice process.

FIGURE 4.4 **RELATIONSHIP OF THE BILL OF RIGHTS AND THE FOURTEENTH AMENDMENT TO THE RIGHTS OF THE ACCUSED**

For most of U.S. history, the Bill of Rights protected citizens only against violations by officials of the federal government. The Warren Court used the process of incorporation to interpret the Fourteenth Amendment as applying portions of the Bill of Rights against actions by state officials.

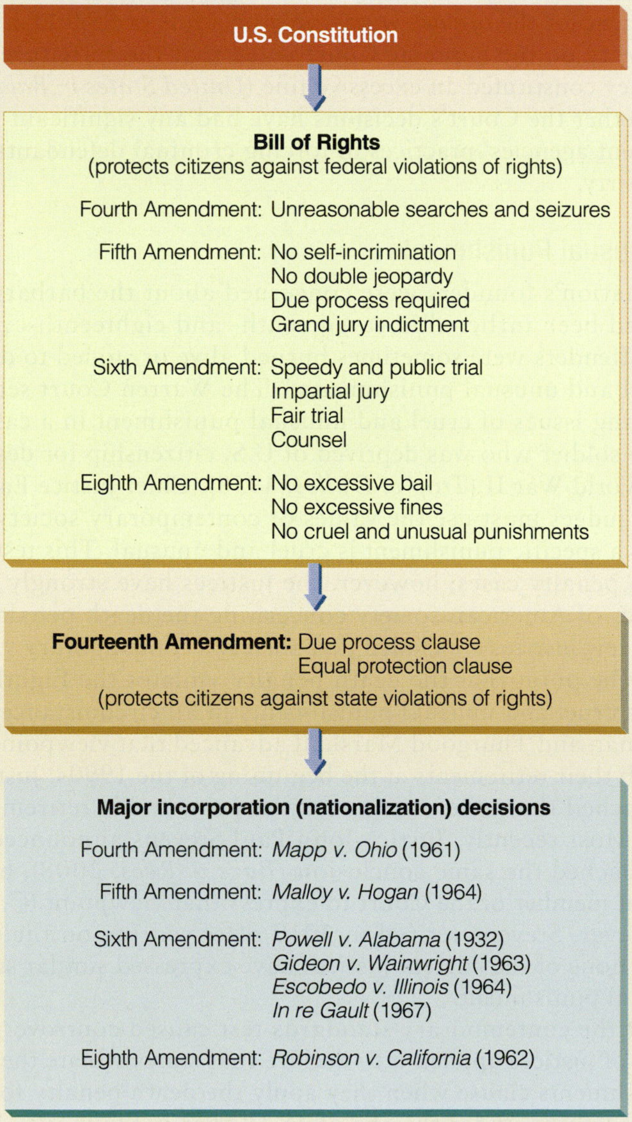

FIGURE 4.5 PROTECTIONS OF THE BILL OF RIGHTS

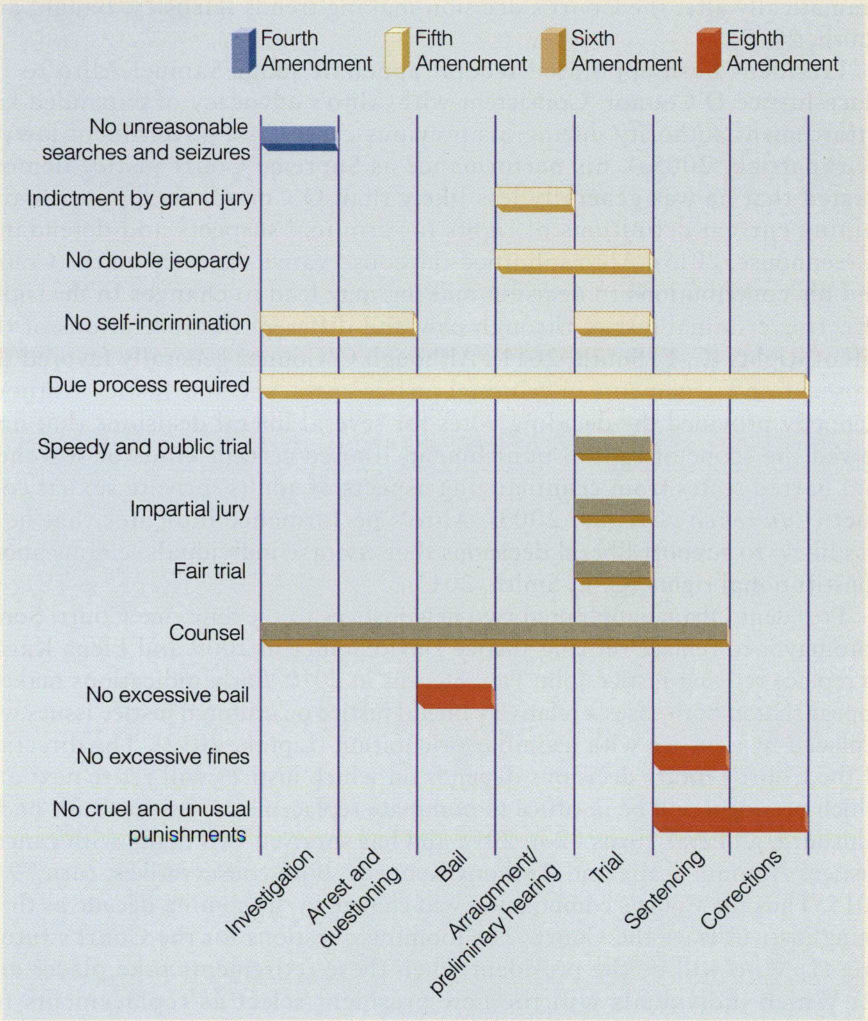

The Bill of Rights protects defendants during various phases of the criminal justice process.

✔POINT

17. What are the main criminal justice rights set forth in the Sixth Amendment?

18. What are the main criminal justice rights set forth in the Eighth Amendment?

STOP AND ANALYZE: If the phrase "cruel and unusual punishments" is to be interpreted according to contemporary values, what exactly does it mean? Consider the sentence of life in prison without possibility of parole for someone who drove the getaway car in a robbery in which a store owner was shot and killed by someone else involved in the robbery. Does that sentence violate the Eighth Amendment by being "cruel and unusual"? Make two arguments about whether that sentence violates contemporary values by being too severe and disproportionate to the driver's involvement in the crime.

The Supreme Court Today

After a remarkable 12-year period (1994–2005) in which the same nine men and women served on the Supreme Court together, in 2005 Justice Sandra Day O'Connor announced her retirement and Chief Justice William Rehnquist died. John Roberts, a federal judge, was appointed to serve as the new chief justice. Because Roberts, a former Rehnquist law clerk, shared similar views as the late chief justice, his initial performance did not dramatically alter the Court's decision-making trends (Hensley, Baugh, and Smith, 2007).

President Bush appointed federal appellate judge Samuel Alito to replace Justice O'Connor. Consistent with Alito's advocacy of expanded law enforcement authority during his previous career as a government lawyer (Kirkpatrick, 2005a), his performance as Supreme Court justice demonstrated that he was generally less likely than O'Connor to support maintaining current definitions of rights for criminal suspects and defendants (Greenhouse, 2015). Alito solidified the conservative majority on the Court, and his contributions to decision making may lead to changes in decisions affecting criminal justice through new and different interpretations of the Bill of Rights (C. E. Smith, 2011). Although O'Connor generally favored the prosecution's arguments in criminal justice cases, she and Justice Anthony Kennedy provided the deciding votes for several liberal decisions that narrowed the scope of capital punishment, limited certain kinds of searches, and barred states from criminalizing aspects of adults' private sexual conduct (*Lawrence v. Texas,* 2003). Alito's performance indicates that he is less likely to support liberal decisions that endorse individuals' claims about constitutional rights (C. E. Smith, 2013).

President Obama appointed two new justices to the Supreme Court: Sonia Sotomayor to replace retiring Justice David Souter in 2009 and Elena Kagan to replace retiring Justice John Paul Stevens in 2010. Early indications make it appear that in both cases a relatively liberal justice on criminal justice issues was replaced by a justice with a similar orientation (Liptak, 2012). The direction of the Court's future decisions depends on which justices will retire next and which president will be in office to nominate replacements. Justice Ruth Bader Ginsburg, a liberal, turns 82 in 2015 and has survived two bouts with cancer. Justices Antonin Scalia and Anthony Kennedy, both conservatives, turn 79 in 2015. Thus the Court's composition will change in the coming decade as these aging justices leave the Court. The looming questions for the Court's future are: (1) Who will be the president when these retirements take place? and (2) Which individuals will the new president select as replacements for retiring justices? President Obama's reelection in 2012 may prove to be a pivotal moment for determining the future makeup of the Supreme Court if any conservative justices leave the Court during his final four-year term. Alternatively, if these justice remain on the Court when a new president takes the oath of office in 2017, then the next president is likely to shape the Court's composition. Future changes in the Court's composition are likely to be quite different depending on whether President Obama is followed by a Republican president or a Democratic president.

Although changes in the Court's composition may make its decisions tend to be more liberal or more conservative, this will not necessarily produce dramatic changes in the rules and rights affecting criminal justice. Most of the fundamental principles concerning Fourth Amendment searches and seizures, Fifth Amendment self-incrimination, and Sixth Amendment right to counsel have remained remarkably stable since the 1960s. Thus the Court's liberal and conservative justices have all conveyed the message that police officers and other criminal justice officials must be aware of the Bill of Rights in carrying out their responsibilities.

A QUESTION OF ETHICS

Police officers in New Rochelle, New York, questioned the boyfriend of a woman who had taken a drug overdose. Instead of informing the man that the woman had died from the overdose, the police told him that in order to try to save her life at the hospital they needed to know what drugs she had taken. The man admitted that he had injected her with heroin and given her a Xanax. The police tactic raised the question of when, if ever, it is proper for police to lie to a suspect during questioning in order to obtain incriminating information. An intermediate appellate court ruled that the police improperly pressured the suspect to incriminate himself by leading him to believe that his silence could lead to the woman's death and result in him being charged with a homicide. However, in other cases, appellate courts have approved police officers' use of deception and false statements in order to obtain confessions.

Source: James McKinley, "Court Weighs Police Role in Coercing Confessions," *New York Times*, January 14, 2014 (www.nytimes.com).

CRITICAL THINKING AND ANALYSIS

Are there reasons to require police officers to be truthful in their statements to criminal suspects? If not, are there any deceptive or untrue statements that a police officer might make to a suspect that are improper or unacceptable? If we adopt a blanket endorsement of the use of lying by police in order to obtain confessions, does that raise any troubling risks?

Summary

1 Describe the bases and sources of American criminal law

- Criminal law focuses on state prosecution and punishment of people who violate specific laws enacted by legislatures, whereas civil law concerns disputes between private citizens or businesses.
- Criminal law is divided into two parts: substantive law, which defines offenses and penalties; and procedural law, which defines individuals' rights and the processes that criminal justice officials must follow in handling cases.
- The common-law tradition, which was inherited from England, involves judges shaping law through their decisions.
- Criminal law is found in written constitutions, statutes, judicial decisions, and administrative regulations.

2 Discuss how substantive criminal law defines a crime and the legal responsibility of the accused

- Substantive criminal law involves seven important elements that must exist and be demonstrated by the prosecution in order to obtain a conviction: legality, *actus reus,* causation, harm, concurrence, *mens rea,* and punishment.
- The *mens rea* element, concerning intent or state of mind, can vary with different offenses, such as various degrees of murder or sexual assault. The element may also be disregarded for strict liability offenses that punish actions without considering intent.
- Criminal law provides opportunities to present several defenses, divided between justifications and excuses, based on lack of criminal intent: self-defense, necessity, duress (coercion), entrapment, immaturity, mistake of fact, intoxication, and insanity.
- Standards for the insanity defense vary by jurisdiction, with various state and federal courts using several different tests: the *M'Naghten* Rule, the Irresistible Impulse Test, the *Durham* Rule, the Substantial Capacity Test (from the *Model Penal Code*), and the federal Comprehensive Crime Control Act.

3 Describe how procedural criminal law defines the rights of the accused and the process for dealing with a case

- The U.S. Supreme Court did not apply the provisions of the Bill of Rights to state and local officials until the mid-twentieth century, when the Court incorporated most of the specific provisions in the Bill of Rights into the due process clause of the Fourteenth Amendment.
- The Fourth Amendment prohibition on unreasonable searches and seizures provides guidance to

police about what actions they may take in looking for evidence of a crime or carrying out an arrest.

- The Fifth Amendment provides protections against compelled self-incrimination and double jeopardy. The protection against double jeopardy does not always prevent a person from being tried twice for the same criminal act.
- The Sixth Amendment includes the right to counsel, the right to a speedy and public trial, and the right to an impartial jury.
- The Eighth Amendment includes protections against excessive bail, excessive fines, and cruel and unusual punishments. Decisions concerning cruel and unusual punishments affect the death penalty as well as conditions in prisons.

4 Analyze the United States Supreme Court's role in interpreting the criminal justice amendments to the Constitution

- Changes in the Supreme Court's composition will affect decisions concerning specific legal issues, as a new president will replace retiring justices with appointees who may interpret rights in new ways.
- Both liberal and conservative justices convey the message that criminal justice officials must be aware of the Bill of Rights in carrying out their responsibilities, so future decisions affecting criminal justice will not necessarily produce many dramatic changes.

Questions for Review

1. What two functions does law perform? What are the two major divisions of the law?
2. What are the sources of criminal law? Where would you find it?
3. What are the seven principles of criminal law?
4. What is meant by *mens rea?* Give examples of defenses that defendants can use to deny that *mens rea* existed when the crime was committed.
5. What is meant by the incorporation of the Bill of Rights into the Fourteenth Amendment?
6. Which amendments in the Bill of Rights protect people in the criminal justice system?

Key Terms and Cases

administrative regulations (p. 145)
case law (p. 144)
civil forfeiture (p. 148)
civil law (p. 142)
common law (p. 143)
constitution (p. 144)
double jeopardy (p. 169)
entrapment (p. 160)
fundamental fairness (p. 169)
grand jury (p. 173)
inchoate offense (p. 150)
incorporation (p. 170)
indigent defendants (p.174)
legal responsibility (p. 140)
mens rea (p. 151)
procedural criminal law (p. 142)
procedural due process (p. 167)
self-incrimination (p. 169)
statutes (p. 144)
strict liability (p. 157)
substantive criminal law (p. 142)
Barron v. Baltimore (1833) (p. 169)
Gideon v. Wainwright (1963) (p. 174)
Powell v. Alabama (1932) (p. 169)

Checkpoint Answers

1 What is contained in a state's penal code?

✓ Penal codes contain substantive criminal law that defines crimes and also punishments for those crimes.

2 What is the purpose of procedural criminal law?

✓ Procedural criminal law specifies the defendant's rights and tells justice system officials how they can investigate and process cases.

3 How does the common law shape criminal law?

✓ Based on English tradition, judges make decisions relying on the precedents of earlier cases.

4 **What are the forms of written law?**

✓ Constitutions, statutes, judicial decisions, and administrative regulations.

5 **What is the difference between a felony and a misdemeanor?**

✓ A felony usually involves a potential punishment of a year or more in prison; a misdemeanor carries a shorter term of incarceration, probation, fines, or community service.

6 **What types of legal issues arise in civil-law cases?**

✓ Civil law includes tort lawsuits (for example, personal-injury cases), property law, contracts, and other disputes between two private parties.

7 **What are the seven principles of criminal law?**

✓ Legality, *actus reus,* causation, harm, concurrence, *mens rea,* punishment.

8 **What is the difference between murder and manslaughter?**

✓ Murder requires malice aforethought whereas manslaughter involves homicides that are not planned or that result from recklessness.

9 **What kind of offense has no *mens rea* requirement?**

✓ Strict liability offense.

10 **What are the defenses in substantive criminal law?**

✓ Self-defense, necessity, duress (coercion), entrapment, infancy, mistake of fact, intoxication, insanity.

11 **What are the tests of criminal responsibility used for the insanity defense?**

✓ *M'Naghten* Rule (right-from-wrong test), Irresistible Impulse Test, *Durham* Rule, *Model Penal Code,* the test defined in the federal Comprehensive Crime Control Act.

12 **What is incorporation?**

✓ Taking a right from the Bill of Rights and applying it against state and local officials by making it a component of the due process clause of the Fourteenth Amendment.

13 **Prior to incorporation, what test was used by the Supreme Court to decide which rights applied to the states?**

✓ Fundamental fairness.

14 **Which Supreme Court era (named for the chief justice) most significantly expanded the definitions of constitutional rights for criminal defendants?**

✓ Warren Court.

15 **What rights are protected by the Fourth Amendment?**

✓ Protection against unreasonable searches and seizures.

16 **What rights are protected by the Fifth Amendment?**

✓ The right against compelled self-incrimination and against double jeopardy; the right to due process.

17 **What are the main criminal justice rights set forth in the Sixth Amendment?**

✓ The right to counsel, to a speedy and fair trial, to a jury trial, and to confrontation and compulsory process.

18 **What are the main criminal justice rights set forth in the Eighth Amendment?**

✓ The right to protection against excessive bail, excessive fines, and cruel and unusual punishments.

PART 2

istockphoto.com/thall

POLICE

Although the police are the most visible agents of the criminal justice system, our images of them come mainly from fiction, especially movies and television. The reality of police experiences, however, differs greatly from the dramatic exploits of the cops in *Law and Order* and other television shows.

In Part 2 we examine the police as the key unit of the criminal justice system: the one that confronts crime in the community. Chapter 5 traces the history of policing and looks at its function and organization. Chapter 6 explores the recruitment of officers and the daily operations of the police. Chapter 7 analyzes current issues and trends in policing. Chapter 8 examines the relationship between the police and constitutional law. As we shall see, police work is often done in a hostile environment in which life and death, honor and dishonor are at stake. Police officers have discretion to deal with many situations; how they use it greatly affects the way society views policing.

CHAPTER FEATURES

- **Technology and Criminal Justice** Military Equipment and Local Police
- **New Directions in Criminal Justice Policy** Evidence-Based Practices and Issues with Mental Illness
- **Close Up** Living under Suspicion
- **Doing Your Part** Students Examine Unsolved Cases

CHAPTER 5 POLICE

CHAPTER LEARNING OBJECTIVES

1. Describe how policing evolved in the United States
2. Discuss the main types of police agencies
3. Analyze the functions of the police
4. Describe how the police are organized
5. Analyze influences on police policy and styles of policing
6. Discuss how police officers balance actions, decision making, and discretion
7. Describe the importance of connections between the police and the community

CHAPTER OUTLINE

The Development of Police in the United States
- The English Roots of the American Police
- Policing in the United States

Law Enforcement Agencies
- Federal Agencies
- State Agencies
- County Agencies
- Native American Tribal Police
- Municipal Agencies
- Special Jurisdiction Agencies

Police Functions
- Order Maintenance
- Law Enforcement
- Service
- Implementing the Mandate

Organization of the Police
- Bureaucratic Elements
- Operational Units
- The Police Bureaucracy and the Criminal Justice System

Police Policy

Everyday Action of Police
- Encounters Between Police and Citizens
- Police Discretion
- Domestic Violence

Police and the Community
- Special Populations
- Policing in a Multicultural Society
- Community Crime Prevention

AP Images/Jeff Roberson

In the third week of November 2014, crowds of angry people gathered on consecutive nights in Ferguson, Missouri, and expressed their outrage about a local prosecutor's failure to convince a grand jury to issue criminal charges against a white police officer who shot and killed an unarmed African American teenager. There were reports of gunfire, arson, and property damage as businesses in the vicinity of the shooting site were burned to the ground, a police car was overturned, and protesters threw rocks and bricks that struck police officers' helmets and riot shields (Fernandez, 2014). Protesters and news reporters had traveled from across the nation to gather in Ferguson to await the announcement of the grand jury's decision. Thus television reports and newspapers carried troubling images of burning buildings and angry crowds confronted by heavily armed police with military-style weapons and equipment (M. Davey and Bosman, 2014).

The public disorder in Ferguson serves as a stark reminder of the expectations the public holds about police behavior in a democratic society as well as the challenges facing police in fulfilling their role for society. The turmoil in Ferguson, Missouri, began in late summer with the police shooting of unarmed teenager Michael Brown. Darren Wilson, the policeman who shot and killed the teen, claimed that Brown had tried to grab his gun after the officer spoke to the young man about walking in middle of the street. From witness accounts, it is not clear whether Brown was raising his hands in surrender as Wilson fired a dozen shots or if he was moving toward the officer in a threatening manner. Because Wilson, a white officer, was not charged with a crime for shooting Brown, an African American teenager, in the minds of many observers, the shooting incident and the grand jury's decision declining to charge Wilson with a crime reinforced concerns about unequal treatment of minorities by criminal justice officials. Moreover, it raised echoes of

America's long history of police violence directed against the poor, minorities, and political protesters.

Abusive behavior by police was common throughout American history. However, many people assumed that controversial incidents of police violence rarely occur today, because police became highly trained and professionalized during the second half of the twentieth century. Yet the widespread availability of cell-phone cameras, building security cameras, and cameras in police patrol cars led to publicly available video and news media reports throughout 2014 and 2015 of police officers injuring and killing people in circumstances that seemed clearly improper and illegal. The jarring images of police violence, especially the frequency with which controversial applications of force are directed at young minority men, clash with Americans' expectations about how police are supposed to serve the public.

In a democracy, the public expects police to follow the law and to exercise equal treatment and fairness in their interactions with the public. By contrast, police in authoritarian governing systems are often permitted to use any means at their disposal to suppress dissent. In these systems, police are tasked with preserving the power of dictatorial leaders, and equal treatment at the hands of officers is replaced with favoritism toward certain groups in society. Yet, as discussed with respect to racial disparities and disparate treatment in Chapter 3, there is evidence that some police officers, as well as other criminal justice officials, engage in behaviors that produce unequal treatment and, at times, violate the laws and policies they have sworn to uphold.

The uniformed men and women who patrol American streets are the most visible presence of government in the United States. They are joined by thousands of plainclothes officers who share various law enforcement responsibilities. Whether they are members of the local or state police, sheriff's departments, or federal agencies, the more than 700,000 sworn officers in the country play key roles in U.S. society. Citizens look to them to perform a wide range of functions: crime prevention, law enforcement, order maintenance, and community services. In performing their functions, police officers are given a great deal of authority. Using their powers to arrest, search, detain, and use force, they can interfere with the freedom of any citizen. If they abuse such powers, they can threaten the basic values of a stable, democratic society.

Police officers have challenging jobs. They must respond to emergency calls, which can range from rendering first aid to injured motorists to rescuing elderly people from rising flood waters to rushing into the potential dangers of a robbery in progress. They must make quick decisions about what actions they will take to restore order, protect citizens, or confront lawbreakers. There are risks that the police will face situations for which they are not fully trained or for which they lack needed resources to be completely effective. In their difficult jobs, they typically receive strong support from the general public. However, specific officers and police departments may, as in Ferguson, face strong criticism and opposition for decisions and actions that clash with high expectations about their performance and adherence to the rules of law. Moreover, because all members of the public do not share either identical expectations about the police or common experiences in their interactions with the them, officers experience mixed reactions and differing levels of support from people they encounter in their work.

In this chapter we examine several aspects of policing. A brief history of the police precedes discussions of the types of law enforcement agencies: their functions, organization, and policies; and their actions and interactions with citizens and the community as a whole.

As you read about the police in this and subsequent chapters, bear in mind that contemporary law enforcement agencies are feeling significant effects from budget cuts at all levels of government. By 2013, the federal program that provides hundreds of millions of dollars in funding to state and local law enforcement agencies had been cut by 40 percent from 2009 levels, and faced the prospect of additional cuts. Most state and local governments have budget issues of their own and cannot readily make up that reduction in federal funding (M. Clark, 2013). Over a three-year period, for example, the number of police officers in California shrank by 4,000, and there were 3,000 fewer civilian support personnel in California police departments over the same time period (KGO-TV, 2013). San Diego alone lost 300 police officer positions (Eigeman, 2013). In 2014, cities such as Mobile, Alabama; York, Pennsylvania; and Troy, New York, discussed plans to cut their police forces in response to budget problems (Crowe, 2014; C. Murphy, 2014; Robinson, 2014). Such cuts inevitably affect the police services provided for the community. Budget problems also reduce training and prevent the acquisition of needed equipment. Such choices about the use of resources are inevitable, but these decisions can have important potential consequences for society.

The Development of Police in the United States

Law and order is not a new concept; it has been a subject of debate since the first police force was formed in London in 1829. Even further back, the Magna Carta of 1215 placed limits on constables and bailiffs. Reading between the lines of that historic document reveals that the modern problems of police abuse, maintenance of order, and the rule of law also existed in thirteenth-century England. Further, current remedies—recruiting better-qualified people to serve as police, stiffening the penalties for official misconduct, creating a civilian board of control—were suggested even then to ensure that order was kept in accordance with the rule of law.

The English Roots of the American Police

The roots of American policing lie in the English legal tradition. Three major aspects of American policing evolved from that tradition: (1) limited authority, (2) local control, and (3) fragmented organization. Like the British police, but unlike police in continental Europe, the police in the United States have limited authority; their powers and duties are specifically defined by law. England, like the United States, has no national police force; instead, 43 regional authorities are headed by elected commissioners who appoint the chief constable. Above these local authorities is the home secretary of the national government, which provides funding and can intervene in cases of police corruption, mismanagement, and discipline. In the United States, policing is fragmented: There are many types of agencies—constable, county sheriff, city police, FBI—each with its own special jurisdiction and responsibilities.

frankpledge
A system in old English law in which members of a tithing, a group of ten families, pledged to be responsible for keeping order and bringing violators of the law to court.

Systems for protecting citizens and property existed before the thirteenth century. The **frankpledge** system required that groups of ten families, called *tithings,* agree to uphold the law, keep order, and bring violators to a court. By custom, every male person above the age of 12 was part of the system. When a man became aware that a crime had occurred, he was obliged to raise a hue and cry and to join others in his tithing to track down the offender. The tithing was fined if members did not perform their duties.

Over time, England developed a system in which individuals within each community were chosen to take charge of catching criminals. The Statute of Winchester, enacted in 1285, set up a parish constable-watch system. Members of the community were still required to pursue criminals, just as they had been under the frankpledge system, but now a constable supervised those efforts. The constable was a man chosen from the parish to serve without pay as its law enforcement officer for one year. The constable had the power to call the entire community into action if a serious disturbance arose. Watchmen, who were appointed to help the constable, spent most of their time patrolling the town at night to ensure that "all's well" and to enforce the criminal law. They were also responsible for lighting street lamps and putting out fires.

Not until the eighteenth century did an organized police force evolve in England. With the growth of commerce and industry, cities expanded and farming declined as the main source of employment and the focus of community life. In the larger cities these changes produced social disorder.

In the mid-eighteenth century, the novelist Henry Fielding and his brother, Sir John Fielding, led efforts to improve law enforcement in London. They wrote newspaper articles to inform the public about crime, and they published flyers describing known offenders. After Henry Fielding became a magistrate in 1748, he organized a small group of "thief-takers" to pursue and arrest lawbreakers. The government was so impressed with Fielding's Bow Street Amateur Volunteer Force (known as the Bow Street Runners) that it paid the participants and attempted to form similar groups in other parts of London.

After Henry Fielding's death in 1754, these efforts declined. As time went by, however, many saw that the government needed to assert itself in enforcing laws and maintaining order. London, with its unruly mobs, had become an especially dangerous place.

In the early 1800s, several attempts were made to create a centralized police force for London. Although people saw the need for social order, some feared that a police force would threaten the freedom of citizens and lead to tyranny. Finally, in 1829 Sir Robert Peel, home secretary in the British Cabinet, pushed Parliament to pass the Metropolitan Police Act, which created the London police force. This agency was organized like a military unit, with a 1,000-man force commanded by two magistrates, later called "commissioners." The officers were called "bobbies" after Sir Robert Peel. In the British system, cabinet members who oversee government departments are chosen from the elected members of Parliament. Thus, because it was supervised by Peel, the first police force was under the control of democratically elected officials.

Under Peel's direction, the police had a four-part mandate:

1. To prevent crime without using repressive force and to avoid having to call on the military to control riots and other disturbances
2. To maintain public order by nonviolent means, using force to obtain compliance only as a last resort
3. To reduce conflict between the police and the public, and
4. To show efficiency through the absence of crime and disorder rather than through visible police actions (P. K. Manning, 1977: 82).

In effect, this meant keeping a low profile while maintaining order. Because of fears that a national force would threaten civil liberties, political leaders made every effort to focus police activities at the local level. These same concerns soon came to the United States.

✔POINT

1. What three main features of American policing were inherited from England?
2. What was the frankpledge and how did it work?
3. What did the Statute of Winchester (1285) establish?
4. What did the Metropolitan Police Act (1829) establish?
5. What were the four mandates of the English police in the nineteenth century?

STOP AND ANALYZE: To what extent do you see American police carry out the four early mandates of English police? Based on your experience, list two examples that fall within the four mandates and two examples that do not seem consistent with the mandates.

(Answers are at the end of the chapter.)

Policing in the United States

As with other institutions and areas of public policy, the development of formal police organizations reflected the social conditions, politics, and problems of different eras in American history. The United States drew from England's experience but implemented policing in its own way.

The Colonial Era and the Early Republic

From the earliest colonies through the westward expansion of the nineteenth century, those Americans who pushed the boundaries of the expanding frontier inevitably needed to take care of themselves. As settlers moved westward from the East Coast, they relied on each other for assistance and protection in all matters, from weather disasters to conflicts with Native Americans. They also needed to protect themselves and their neighbors from those who might cause harm through theft or other crimes. Although we are accustomed to seeing police officers in every contemporary American community, early settlements needed every able-bodied person to devote themselves to clearing land, farming, and contributing to survival. Governing institutions and occupational specialization developed more fully after communities—and the economic basis for their survival—became more firmly established.

Along the East Coast, the colonists drew from their experiences in England in adopting the English offices of constable, sheriff, and night watchman as the first positions with law enforcement responsibilities. Before the Revolution, American colonists shared the English belief that members of a community had a duty to help maintain order. The **watch system** served as the primary means of keeping order, warning of danger, and responding to reports of crime. Boston's watch system began before 1640. Each citizen was required to

watch system
Practice of assigning individuals to night observation duty to warn the public of fires and crime that was first introduced to the American colonies in Boston and that later evolved into a system of paid, uniformed police.

be a member of the watch, but paid watchmen could be hired as replacements. Although the watch system originally operated at night, cities eventually began to have daytime watchmen, too. Over time, cities began to hire paid, uniformed watchmen to deal with public danger and crime (S. Walker, 1999).

After the formation of the federal government in 1789, police power remained with the states, in response to fear of centralized law enforcement. However, the American police developed under conditions that differed from those in England. Unlike the British, police in the United States had to deal with ethnic diversity, local political control, regional differences, the exploration and settling of the West, and a generally more violent society.

slave patrols
Distinctively American form of law enforcement in southern states that sought to catch and control slaves through patrol groups that stopped and questioned African Americans on the roads and elsewhere in public places.

For example, in the South, **slave patrols** developed as organized forces to prevent slave revolts and to catch runaway slaves. These patrols had full power to break into the homes of slaves who were suspected of keeping arms, to physically punish those who did not obey their orders, and to arrest runaways and return them to their masters. Under the watch system in northern cities, watchmen reacted to calls for help. By contrast, the mobility of slave patrols positioned them to operate in a proactive manner by looking for African Americans whom whites feared would disrupt society, especially the economic system of slavery. Samuel Walker (1999) describes the slave patrols as a distinctly American form of law enforcement and the first modern police forces in the United States.

Beginning in the 1830s and continuing periodically for several decades, many American cities experienced violent riots. Ethnic conflict, election controversies, hostility toward nonslave blacks and abolitionists, mob actions against banks during economic declines, and violence in settling questions of morality—such as the use of alcohol—all these factors contributed to fears that a stable democracy would not survive. The militia was called in to quell large-scale conflicts, because constables and watchmen proved ineffective in restoring order (Uchida, 2005). These disorders, along with perceptions of increased problems with serious crime, helped push city governments to consider the creation of professional police forces.

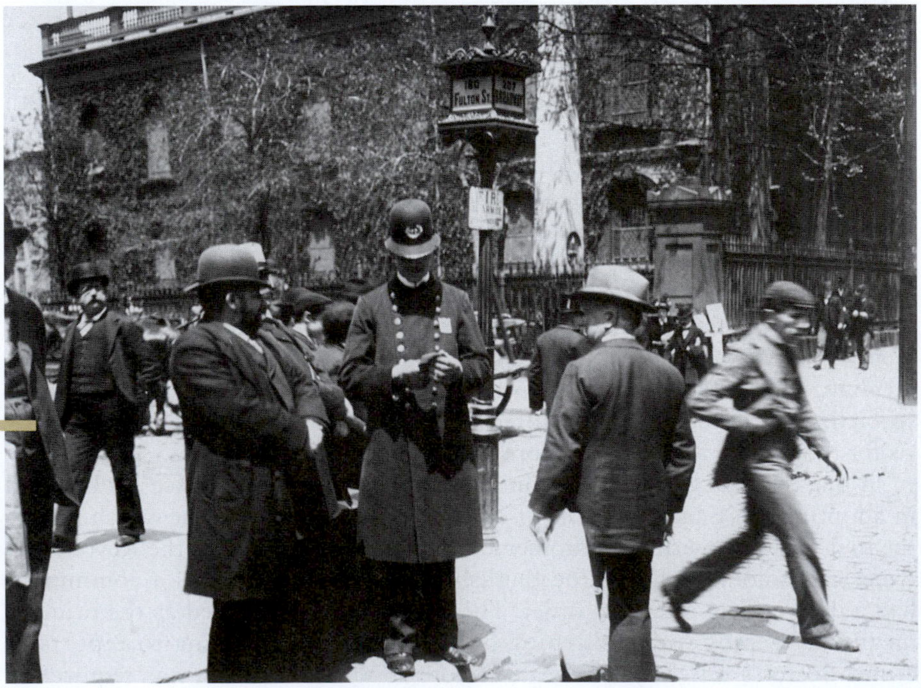

During the political era, the officer on a neighborhood beat dealt with crime and disorder as it arose. Police also performed various social services, such as providing beds and food for the homeless. Should today's police officers devote more time to providing social services for the public?

Museum of the City of New York/Byron Collection/Getty Images

American policing after this early period is often described in terms of three subsequent historical periods: the political era (1840–1920), the professional model era (1920–1970), and the community policing era (1970–present) (Kelling and Moore, 1988). This description has been criticized because it applies only to the urban areas of the Northeast while largely ignoring the very different development of the police in rural areas of the South and West. Still, it remains a useful framework for exploring the organization of the police, the focus of police work, and the strategies employed by police (H. Williams and Murphy, 1990).

The Political Era: 1840–1920

The period from 1840 to 1920 is called the political era because of the close ties between the police and local political leaders at that time. In many cities the police seemed to work for the mayor's political party rather than for the citizens. This relationship served both groups in that the political "machines" recruited and maintained the police, while the police helped the machine leaders get out the vote for favored candidates. Ranks in the police force often went for sale to the highest bidder, and many officers took payoffs for not enforcing laws on drinking, gambling, and prostitution (S. Walker, 1999: 26).

In the United States, as in England, the growth of cities led to pressures to modernize law enforcement. Social relations in cities differed from those in towns and the countryside.

In 1845, New York City established the first full-time, paid police force. Boston and Philadelphia were the first to add a daytime police force to supplement the night watchmen; other cities—Chicago, Cincinnati, New Orleans—quickly followed. By 1850 most major U.S. cities had created police departments organized on the English model. A chief, appointed by the mayor and city council, headed each department. The city was divided into precincts, with full-time, paid patrolmen assigned to each. Early police forces sought to prevent crimes and keep order through the use of foot patrols. The officer on the beat dealt with crime, disorder, and other problems as they arose.

In addition to foot patrols, the police performed service functions, such as caring for derelicts, operating soup kitchens, regulating public health, and handling medical and social emergencies. In cities across the country, the police provided beds and food for homeless people. In station houses, overnight "lodgers" slept on the floor or in clean bunkrooms (Monkkonen, 1981: 127). Because they were the only government agency that had close contact with life on the streets of the city, the police became general public servants as well as crime control officers. Because of these close links with the community and service to it, they had the citizens' support (Monkkonen, 1992: 554).

Police developed differently in the South because of the existence of slavery and the agrarian nature of that region. As noted previously, the first organized police agencies with full-time officers developed in cities with large numbers of slaves (Charleston, New Orleans, Richmond, and Savannah), where white owners feared slave uprisings (Rousey, 1984: 41).

Westward expansion in the United States produced conditions quite different from those in either the urban East or the agricultural South. The frontier became settled before order could be established. Thus, those who wanted to maintain law and order often had to take matters into their own hands by forming vigilante groups.

One of the first official positions created in rural areas was that of **sheriff**. Although the sheriff had duties similar to those of the "shire reeves" of seventeenth-century England and the sheriffs appointed by British governors in the early New England colonies, American sheriffs took on a different role: They were elected and had broad powers to enforce the law. As elected officers,

sheriff
Top law enforcement official in county government. The sheriff was an exceptionally important police official during the country's westward expansion and continues to bear primary responsibility for many local jails.

sheriffs had close ties to local politics. They also depended on the men of the community for assistance. This is how the *posse comitatus* (Latin for "power of the county"), borrowed from fifteenth-century Europe, came into being. Local men above the age of 15 were required to respond to the sheriff's call for assistance, forming a body known as a *posse*.

U.S. marshals
Federal law enforcement officials appointed to handle duties in western territories and today bear responsibility for federal court security and apprehending fugitives.

After the Civil War, the federal government appointed **U.S. marshals** to help enforce the law in the western territories. Some of the best-known folk heroes of American policing were U.S. Marshals Wyatt Earp, Bat Masterson, and Wild Bill Hickok, who tried to bring law and order to the "Wild West" (Calhoun, 1990). Although some marshals did extensive law enforcement work, most had mainly judicial duties, such as keeping order in the courtroom and holding prisoners for trial.

During the twentieth century, urban centers developed throughout the country. This change blurred some of the regional differences that had helped define policing in the past. In addition, growing criticism of the influence of politics on the police led to efforts to reform the nature and organization of the police. Specifically, reformers sought to make police more professional and to reduce their ties to local politics.

The Professional Model Era: 1920–1970

American policing was greatly influenced by the Progressive movement. The Progressives were mainly upper-middle-class, educated Americans with two goals: more-efficient government and more government services to assist the less fortunate. A related goal was a reduction of the influence of party politics and patronage (favoritism in handing out jobs) on government. The Progressives saw a need for professional law enforcement officials who would use modern technology to benefit society as a whole, not just local politicians.

The key to the Progressives' concept of professional law enforcement is found in their slogan, "The police have to get out of politics, and politics has to get out of the police." August Vollmer, chief of police of Berkeley, California, from 1909 to 1932, stood as one of the leading advocates of professional policing. He initiated the use of motorcycle units, handwriting analysis, and fingerprinting. With other police reformers, such as Leonhard Fuld, Raymond Fosdick, Bruce Smith, and O. W. Wilson, he urged that the police be made into a professional force, a nonpartisan agency of government committed to public service. This model of professional policing has six elements:

1. The force should stay out of politics.
2. Members should be well trained, well disciplined, and tightly organized.
3. Laws should be enforced equally.
4. The force should use new technology.
5. Personnel procedures should be based on merit.
6. The main task of the police should be fighting crime.

Refocusing attention on crime control and away from maintaining order probably did more than anything else to change the nature of American policing. The narrow focus on crime fighting broke many of the ties that the police had formed with the communities they served. By the end of World War I, police departments had greatly reduced their involvement in social services. Instead, for the most part, police became crime fighters.

O. W. Wilson, a student of Vollmer, was a leading advocate of professionalism. He earned a degree in criminology at the University of California in 1924 and became chief of police in Wichita, Kansas, in 1928. He came to national attention by reorganizing the department and fighting police corruption.

During the professional era, the police saw themselves as crime fighters. Yet many inner-city residents saw them as a well-armed, occupying force that did not support efforts to advance civil rights and racial equality. If the police see themselves as crime fighters, how might that orientation interfere with efforts to gain citizens' cooperation and improve police–community relationships?

He promoted the use of motorized patrols, efficient radio communication, and rapid response. He believed that one-officer patrols were the best way to use personnel and that the two-way radio, which allowed for supervision by commanders, made officers more efficient (Reiss, 1992: 51). He rotated assignments so that officers on patrol would not become too familiar with people in the community (and thus prone to corruption). In 1960, Wilson became superintendent of the Chicago Police Department with a mandate to end corruption there.

The new emphasis on professionalism spurred the formation of the International Association of Chiefs of Police (IACP) in 1902 and the Fraternal Order of Police (FOP) in 1915. Both organizations promoted the use of new technologies, training standards, and a code of ethics.

Advocates of professionalism urged that the police be made aware of the need to act lawfully and to protect the rights of all citizens, including those suspected of crimes. They sought to instill a strong—some would even say rigid ("Just the facts, ma'am")—commitment to the law and to equal treatment (H. Goldstein, 1990).

By the 1930s the police were using new technologies and methods to combat serious crimes. They became more effective against crimes such as murder, rape, and robbery—an important factor in gaining citizen support. By contrast, efforts to control victimless offenses and to maintain order often aroused citizen opposition. As Mark Moore and George Kelling have noted, "The clean, bureaucratic model of policing put forth by the reformers could be sustained only if the scope of police responsibility was narrowed to 'crime fighting'" (1983: 55).

In the 1960s the civil rights and antiwar movements, urban riots, and rising crime rates challenged many of the assumptions of the professional model. In their attempts to maintain order during public demonstrations, the police in many cities seemed to be concerned mainly with maintaining the status quo. Thus, police officers found themselves enforcing laws that tended to discriminate against African Americans and the poor. The number of low-income racial minorities living in the inner cities was growing, and the professional style kept the police isolated from the communities they served. In the eyes of many inner-city residents, the police were an occupying army keeping them at the bottom of society, not public servants helping all citizens.

Although the police continued to portray themselves as crime fighters, citizens became aware that the police often were not effective in this role. Crime rates rose for many offenses, and the police could not change the perception that the quality of urban life was declining.

The Community Policing Era: 1970–Present

Beginning in the 1970s, calls were heard for a move away from the crime-fighting focus and toward greater emphasis on keeping order and providing services to the community. Research studies revealed the complex nature of police work and the extent to which day-to-day practices deviated from the professional ideal. The research also questioned the effectiveness of the police in catching and deterring criminals.

Three findings of this research are especially noteworthy:

1. Increasing the number of patrol officers in a neighborhood had little effect on the crime rate.
2. Rapid response to calls for service did not greatly increase the arrest rate.
3. Improving the percentage of solved crimes is difficult.

Such findings undermined acceptance of the professional crime-fighter model (M. Moore, 1992). Critics argued that the professional style isolated the police from the community and reduced their knowledge about the neighborhoods they served, especially when police patrolled in cars. Use of the patrol car prevented personal contacts with citizens. Instead, it was argued, police

TECHNOLOGY & CRIMINAL JUSTICE

MILITARY EQUIPMENT AND LOCAL POLICE

Television news crews and newspaper photographers from around the nation gathered in Ferguson, Missouri, in November 2014 to cover the anticipated protests—or potential public celebrations—that would follow from the grand jury's decision on whether or not to bring criminal charges against Officer Darren Wilson for the shooting death of unarmed teenager Michael Brown. Upon the prosecutor's announcement that no indictment would be issued, protests ignited that led to acts of arson and property damage. During the height of the protests, some of the most striking news footage to come from Ferguson was that of unarmed protesters, in hands-up "surrender" mode, standing face-to-face with helmeted police officers wearing military-style gear and carrying high-powered military-style weapons. In the days following the grand jury decision, that gesture, as well as the chant of "Hands up, don't shoot"—to emulate witnesses' statements that Michael Brown was surrendering to police when he was shot—became a common element of nationwide protests. These images from Ferguson contributed to new national debates about the so-called militarization of American police and, especially, the transfer of millions of dollars' worth of military weapons and vehicles surplused from the U.S. Department of Defense to local police departments.

As described by one news report, "Since President Obama took office, the Pentagon has transferred to police departments tens of thousands of machine guns; nearly 200,000 ammunition magazines; thousands of pieces of camouflage and night-vision equipment; and hundreds of silencers, armored cars, and aircraft" (Apuzzo, 2014). The drawing-down of American military forces from the wars in Iraq and Afghanistan left the federal government with surplus equipment that local police departments eagerly requested. Law enforcement agencies in Florida alone received $266 million worth of equipment, including 45 Mine-Resistant Ambush Protected (MRAP) armored vehicles designed to withstand blasts from roadside bombs.

Many police officials see military equipment as useful for several reasons. There may be hostage situations and armed standoffs for which the police need vehicles and equipment that can take officers close to the buildings while providing protection from gunshots. Police officers may need to be able to have firepower equal to that of lawbreakers who are using high-powered semiautomatic weapons. In addition, one component of homeland security planning since 2001 has been the idea that police officers need to be ready to respond to any kind of terrorism attack in their local communities, including coordinated efforts by multiple attackers who might plant bombs and use military-style weapons against the police.

There are grave concerns, however, that the use of military equipment and tactics will alter the attitudes and behavior of police and that it will have detrimental consequences for citizens' perception of and cooperation with the police. In countries should get out of their cars and spend more time meeting and helping residents. This would permit the police to help people with a range of problems and in some cases to prevent problems from arising or growing worse. For example, if the police know about conflicts between people in a neighborhood, they can try to mediate and perhaps prevent a conflict from growing into a criminal assault or other serious problem. Reformers hoped that closer contact with citizens would not only permit the police to help them in new ways but would also make them feel safer, knowing that the police were available and interested in their problems.

In a provocative article titled "Broken Windows: The Police and Neighborhood Safety," James Q. Wilson and George L. Kelling argued that policing should work more on little problems such as maintaining order, providing services to those in need, and adopting strategies to reduce the fear of crime (1982). They based their approach on three assumptions:

1. Neighborhood disorder creates fear. Areas with street people, youth gangs, prostitution, and public drunkenness are high-crime areas.
2. Just as broken windows are a signal that nobody cares and can lead to worse vandalism, untended disorderly behavior is a signal that the community does not care. This also leads to worse disorder and crime.
3. If the police are to deal with disorder and thus reduce fear and crime, they must rely on citizens for assistance.

governed by dictators, military forces are mobilized to suppress freedom and control people. By contrast, policing in the American democracy is based on ensuring that police officers work as public servants who are members of the community. Citizens retain control over their community's police force, because law enforcement policies and practices are directed by mayors and other officials who are elected by the voters. The birth of community policing in the 1970s was driven, in part, by heavy-handed police tactics. These police actions often occurred during civil rights protests, both peaceful and those that involved civil disorder. It was common for people in poor neighborhoods to view the police as an occupying force acting in opposition to their desires for racial equality and the freedom to go about their daily affairs without surveillance and suspicion. Because police who are clad and equipped as soldiers renewed concerns about police roles and relationships in the community, President Obama and members of Congress acted after the events in Ferguson to consider whether to tighten the rules and conditions for the transfer of military equipment to local police.

Does the use of military-style uniforms and equipment make citizens see the police as more impersonal, distant, and hostile? Do people feel less free to approach and interact in a friendly manner with officers in military-style dress and military vehicles as compared to the officers in traditional uniforms on foot, riding bicycles, and driving squad cars? If so, are there also risks that a militarized self-image will affect how police officers treat people? Tom Nolan, a criminal justice scholar and former lieutenant in the Boston Police Department says, "When you equip domestic police officers in civilian law enforcement with military uniforms, military equipment, and military weapons—they'll conduct themselves as if they're waging war in our communities" (Ledbetter, 2014). Many police officials disagree with this viewpoint, but clearly there are widespread concerns about the impact of the militarization of American police.

Sources: Matt Apuzzo, "What Military Gear Your Local Police Department Bought," *New York Times,* August 20, 2014 (www.nytimes.com); Radley Balko, *Rise of the Warrior Cop,* New York: Public Affairs, 2013; Mark Landler, "Obama Offers New Standards on Police Gear in Wake of Ferguson Protests," *New York Times*, December 1, 2014 (www.nytimes.com); Stewart Ledbetter, "Surplus Military Hardware Finds Way into Area Police Agencies," WPTZ-News Channel 5, November 11, 2014 (www.wptz.com); Paul Shinkman, "Ferguson and the Militarization of Police," *U.S. News and World Report*, August 14, 2014 (www.usnews.com).

DEBATE THE ISSUE

Do military-style uniforms and equipment create risks that the public's view of and voluntary cooperation with police officers will change? What hazards, if any, exist concerning potential changes in police officers' attitudes and actions? If you were a police chief, what three arguments would you give concerning your view of the risks—or benefits—of acquiring surplus military equipment?

Advocates of the community policing approach urge greater use of foot patrols so that officers will become known to citizens, who in turn will cooperate with the police. They believe that through attention to little problems, the police may not only reduce disorder and fear but also improve public attitudes toward policing. When citizens respond positively to police efforts, the police will have "improved bases of community and political support, which in turn can be exploited to gain further cooperation from citizens in a wide variety of activities" (Kelling, 1985: 299). There are recent developments, however, as illustrated by the police response to the civil disorder and protests in Ferguson, Missouri, that raise concerns about the risk of deterioration in police–community relations. Read Technology and Criminal Justice to consider debates about the impact of local police departments' acquisition and use of military equipment and technology.

Closely related to the community policing concept is problem-oriented policing (see Chapter 6). Herman Goldstein, the originator of this approach, argued that instead of focusing on crime and disorder, the police should identify the underlying causes of such problems as noisy teenagers, battered spouses, and abandoned buildings used as drug houses. In doing so they could reduce disorder and fear of crime (H. Goldstein, 1979). Closer contacts between the police and the community can then reduce the hostility that has developed between officers and residents in many urban neighborhoods (Sparrow, Moore, and Kennedy, 1990). Research indicates that problem-oriented policy can have positive effects on the problems of crime and disorder (D. Weisburd, Telep, et al., 2010).

In *Fixing Broken Windows,* a book written in response to the Wilson and Kelling article, George L. Kelling and Catherine Coles (1996) call for strategies to restore order and reduce crime in public spaces in U.S. communities. In Baltimore, New York, San Francisco, and Seattle, police are paying greater attention to "quality-of-life crimes"—by arresting subway fare-beaters, rousting loiterers and panhandlers from parks, and aggressively dealing with those who are obstructing sidewalks, harassing others, and soliciting. By handling these "little crimes," the police not only help restore order but also often prevent worse crimes. In New York, for example, searching fare-beaters often yielded

Community policing encourages personal contact between officers and citizens, especially interactions that facilitate citizens' cooperation with and support for the police. Is your own involvement in criminal justice affected by your view of police officers and interactions with them?

Bob Daemmrich/The Image Works

weapons, questioning a street vendor selling hot merchandise led to a fence specializing in stolen weapons, and arresting a person for urinating in a park resulted in discovery of a cache of weapons.

Although reformers argue for a greater focus on order maintenance and service, they do not call for an end to the crime-fighting role. Instead, they want a shift of emphasis. The police should pay more attention to community needs and seek to understand the problems underlying crime, disorder, and incivility (Reisig, 2010). These proposals have been adopted by police executives in many cities and by influential organizations such as the Police Foundation and the Police Executive Research Forum.

The high point for community policing came in the 1990s. The federal government created the Office of Community Oriented Policing Services, more commonly known as the "COPS Office," which provided grants to local police agencies for hiring new officers and developing community policing programs. Between 1995 and 2003, the COPS Office supplied nearly $7 billion to 13,000 state and local agencies to hire 118,000 new officers and implement training and programs for community policing (Uchida 2005: 37).

The new focus for the police did not go unchallenged (Reichers and Roberg, 1990). Critics question whether the professional model really isolated police from community residents (S. Walker, 1984). Taking another view, Carl Klockars doubted whether the police would give higher priority to maintaining order and wondered whether Americans want their police to be something other than crime fighters (1985). Others wonder whether the opportunity to receive federal money and hire new officers led departments to use the language of community policing in portraying their activities, even though they never fully adopted the new methods.

The Next Era: Homeland Security? Evidence-Based Policing?

The hijackers' attacks on the World Trade Center and the Pentagon on September 11, 2001, made homeland security and antiterrorism efforts among the highest priorities for the U.S. government. As we shall see in Chapter 7, this

AP Images/Charles Eckert/Newsday

The FBI bears special responsibility for investigating federal crimes. The agency also provides assistance to state and local police. In the past decade, it has shifted its focus and resources to give greater emphasis to homeland security and counterterrorism efforts. Could the agency focus solely on these two important issues and leave other crimes entirely to state and local agencies? Why?

event shifted the federal government's funding priorities for law enforcement and led to a reorganization of federal agencies. According to Craig Uchida, "Priorities for training equipment, strategies, and funding have transformed policing once again—this time focusing on homeland security" (2005: 38). Instead of focusing funds on community policing, federal money shifted toward supplying emergency-response training, hazardous materials gear, and equipment for detecting bombs and other weapons of mass destruction, and collection of intelligence data. In public comments, a few police officials have made reference to "terrorist-oriented policing," but it is not clear how such a concept or emphasis would be defined at the local level (Kerlikowske, 2004). Some observers believe that a shift toward homeland security may appeal to traditionalists in law enforcement who prefer to see themselves as heroically catching "bad guys" rather than solving problems within neighborhoods. Yet a by-product of the increased emphasis on homeland security may be better-coordinated services for society in non-crime-fighting situations, such as public emergencies. For example, in 2007, Minneapolis police officials credited their training in a course on Integrated Emergency Management, conducted by the federal government, as one of the reasons that they could respond so quickly and effectively when the I-35W bridge collapsed, killing 13 people, injuring 145 others, and forcing quick rescues of drivers in sinking vehicles that fell from the bridge and into the river below (Karnowski, 2008).

intelligence-led policing
An approach to policing, in conjunction with concerns about homeland security, that emphasizes gathering and analyzing information to be shared among agencies in order to develop cooperative efforts to identify, prevent, and solve problems.

In considering whether we have reached a new era in policing, the emphasis on homeland security has grown in conjunction with the development of **intelligence-led policing** (J. G. Carter, Phillips and Gayadeen, 2014). For policing, the concept of intelligence means an emphasis on gathering, analyzing, and sharing information while incorporating these elements into community policing (M. Peterson, 2005). Intelligence-led policing is based on cooperation and coordination among law enforcement agencies as well as between law enforcement officials and those in other sectors of government and business. Even though many police departments may not be directly affected by homeland security considerations in all of their daily operations, departments throughout the country have been affected by the spread of data analysis techniques. Departments analyze crime trends, locations of events, informants' tips, surveillance observations and tapes, and other sources of information in order to distribute personnel and take action to prevent crimes from occurring (Kirby, Quinn, and Keay, 2010). The gathering and analysis of intelligence data are now central features of policing, as these techniques spread both from federal homeland security activities and from the example of cities that used crime analysis techniques to address street crime (M. Peterson, 2005).

As discussed in previous chapters, when data on problems in local communities are combined with social science research on "what works" in crime prevention and crime control, then departments are attempting to incorporate the principles of evidence-based practices into policing. An awareness of evidence-based practices has become a major emphasis in policing and could develop in ways to define the next era of policing. However, the dedicated use of evidence-based practices varies from department to department. Departments' ability to use evidence-based policing depends on their resources and effectiveness in gathering and analyzing data about their communities and on their openness and effectiveness in utilizing the results of scholars' research studies. Unfortunately, the contemporary era of budget cuts affecting personnel resources, training, and technology acquisition poses a significant barrier to the prospects of carrying out evidence-based policies and practices (Bueermann, 2012). It remains to be seen whether the establishment of priorities, the allocation of resources, and the implementation of practices will define a new era in policing.

Community policing will not disappear. Many police executives remain committed to its purposes and principles. However, federal agencies have clearly made homeland security their top priority, and federal funding for local police departments has shifted as well. Further development of a homeland security focus throughout policing may depend on whether American cities suffer additional terror attacks. Thus, whether the early years of the twenty-first century will be regarded as the dawn of a new era for all levels of policing remains to be seen.

Whichever approach the police take—professional, crime fighting, or community policing—it must be carried out through a bureaucratic structure. We therefore turn to a discussion of police structure, function, and organization in the United States.

✔POINT

6. What are the major historical periods of American policing?
7. What was the main feature of the political era?
8. What were the major recommendations of the Progressive reformers?
9. What are the main criticisms of the professional model era?
10. What is community policing?

STOP AND ANALYZE: List the key historical circumstances or developments that led to the definition of each era of policing. Project into the future: What are some developments that could very well change policing and define one or more new eras in your lifetime?

Law Enforcement Agencies

As discussed in Chapter 3, the United States has a federal system of government with separate national and state structures, each with authority over certain functions. Police agencies at the national, state, county, and municipal levels are responsible for carrying out three functions: (1) maintaining order, (2) enforcing the law, and (3) providing services to the community. Each of these functions contributes to the prevention of crime. They together employ more than 1 million people, both sworn and unsworn personnel. Nearly 765,000 full-time sworn officers serve in state and local agencies, and an additional 120,000 sworn officers operate in federal agencies. Police agencies include the following (B. Reaves, 2012; B. Reaves, 2011):

- 12,501 local police departments
- 3,063 sheriff's departments
- 50 state police departments
- 135 Native American tribal police agencies
- 24 federal agencies that employ 250 or more full-time officers authorized to carry firearms and make arrests

In addition, there are 1,733 special police agencies (jurisdictions limited to transit systems, parks, schools, and so on) as well as additional federal agencies each with fewer than 250 sworn officers.

This list shows both the fragmentation and the local orientation of American police. Seventy percent of expenditures for policing are spent at the local level. Each level of the system has different responsibilities, either for different kinds of crimes, such as the federal authority over counterfeiting, or for different geographic areas, such as state police authority over major highways. The broadest authority tends to lie with local units. Table 5.1 shows

TABLE 5.1 PERSONNEL IN FEDERAL, STATE, COUNTY, AND LOCAL LAW ENFORCEMENT AGENCIES

The decentralized nature of U.S. law enforcement is shown by the fact that 52 percent of all full-time sworn officers are in local departments.

TYPE OF AGENCY	NUMBER OF FULL-TIME SWORN OFFICERS	PERCENTAGE OF TOTAL
Local Police	463,063	52%
County Police	182,979	21%
State Police	60,772	7%
Special Police*	56,968	6%
Federal	120,348	14%

*Officers in state and local parks, transportation, animal control, housing, and so forth.

Sources: Brian A. Reaves, *Federal Law Enforcement Officers, 2008* (Washington, DC: Bureau of Justice Statistics, 2012); Brian A. Reaves, *Census of State and Local Law Enforcement Agencies, 2008* (Washington, DC: U.S. Bureau of Justice Statistics, 2011).

the number of full-time sworn officers in federal, state, county, and local law enforcement agencies.

As we examine the differing law enforcement agencies, we should recognize that the events of 9-11 have triggered an expansion and reorganization, especially among federal law enforcement agencies. The creation of the Department of Homeland Security, the reordering of crime control policies away from street crime and drugs to international and domestic terrorism, and the great increase in federal money to pursue the war against terrorism are greatly affecting law enforcement at all levels of government.

Federal Agencies

Federal law enforcement agencies are part of the executive branch of the national government. They investigate a specific set of crimes defined by Congress. Recent federal efforts against drug trafficking, organized crime, insider stock trading, and terrorism have attracted attention to these agencies, even though they handle relatively few crimes and employ only 120,348 full-time officers authorized to make arrests.

The FBI

The Federal Bureau of Investigation (FBI) is an investigative agency within the U.S. Department of Justice with the power to investigate all federal crimes not placed under the jurisdiction of other agencies. Established as the Bureau of Investigation in 1908, it came to national prominence under J. Edgar Hoover, its director from 1924 until his death in 1972. Hoover made major changes in the bureau (renamed the Federal Bureau of Investigation in 1935) to increase its professionalism. He sought to remove political factors from the selection of agents, established the national fingerprint filing system, and oversaw the development of the Uniform Crime Reporting System. Although Hoover has been criticized for many things, such as FBI spying on civil rights and antiwar activists during the 1960s, his role in improving police work and the FBI's effectiveness is widely recognized.

As of September 2012, there were 13,907 FBI special agents and 22,141 support professionals (intelligence analysts, language translators, scientists, and computer experts) working out of 56 field offices and 400 additional satellite offices known as "resident agencies" (FBI, 2014b). After the attacks of 9-11, the FBI announced a new list of priorities that describes its work:

1. Protect the United States from terrorist attack.
2. Protect the United States against foreign intelligence operations and espionage.
3. Protect the United States against cyberbased attacks and high-technology crimes.
4. Combat public corruption at all levels.
5. Protect civil rights.
6. Combat transnational and national criminal organizations and enterprises.
7. Combat major white-collar crime.
8. Combat significant violent crime.
9. Support federal, state, county, municipal, and international partners.
10. Upgrade technology to successfully perform the FBI's mission.

The advancement of the FBI's mission requires skilled professionals in addition to the traditional law enforcement-trained special agents. The emphasis on counterterrorism led to tripling the number of intelligence analysts within the agency, from 1,023 in September 2001 to nearly 3,000 in 2011, as well as doubling the number of foreign-language specialists (Mueller, 2011; Mueller, 2008).

As indicated by its priority list, the FBI has significant responsibilities for fighting terrorism and espionage against the United States. In addition, it continues its traditional mission of enforcing federal laws, such as those aimed at organized crime, corporate crime, corrupt government officials, and violators of civil rights laws. The bureau also provides valuable assistance to state and local law enforcement through its crime laboratory, training programs, and databases of fingerprints, stolen vehicles, and missing persons. With the growth of cybercrime, the FBI has become a leader in using technology to counteract crime as well as to prevent terrorism and espionage.

Specialization in Federal Law Enforcement

The FBI is the federal government's general law enforcement agency. Other federal agencies, however, enforce specific laws. Elsewhere in the Department of Justice, for example, the Drug Enforcement Administration (DEA) investigates illegal importation and sale of controlled drugs. The activities of the DEA's nearly 5,000 agents range from investigations of individual drug traffickers to monitoring of organized crime's involvement in the drug trade to coordinating drug enforcement efforts with state and local police as well as foreign governments. The Internal Revenue Service (IRS) pursues violations of tax laws, and the Bureau of Alcohol, Tobacco, Firearms, and Explosives (ATF) deals with crimes connected to the words in its name.

The Department of Justice also contains the U.S. Marshals Service. Federal marshals provide security at courthouses, transport federal prisoners, protect witnesses, and pursue fugitives within the United States who are wanted for domestic criminal charges or who are sought by police officials in other countries. Because of the FBI's increased emphasis on terrorism, its agents are now less involved in the pursuit of fugitives. This development increased the marshals' responsibilities for this duty. In 2013, U.S. marshals apprehended more than 36,000 fugitives on federal warrants and assisted in the capture of 74,000 individuals wanted by local police departments (U.S. Marshals Service, 2014).

As described in Chapter 3, several federal law enforcement agencies were reorganized and relocated in conjunction with the creation of the Department of Homeland Security. These agencies include those responsible for Customs and Border Protection (formerly known as the Customs Service and the Border Patrol), the Secret Service, and the Transportation Security Administration. The Secret Service was created in 1865 to combat counterfeit currency. After the assassination of President William McKinley in 1901, it received the additional duty of providing security for the president of the United States, as well as for other high officials and their families. The Secret Service has 2,100 special agents in Washington, D.C., and field offices throughout the United States. It also has 1,200 uniformed police officers who provide security at the White House, the vice president's residence, and foreign embassies in Washington.

Many other federal agencies include law enforcement personnel. Some of these agencies are well recognized, but others are not. Within the Department of the Interior, for example, officers responsible for law enforcement serve as part of the National Park Service. Other officers in the Fish and Wildlife Service protect wildlife habitats, prevent illegal hunting, and investigate illegal trafficking of wildlife. Many people know about conservation officers and other law enforcement officials, such as postal inspectors in the Office of Inspector General of the U.S. Postal Service. By contrast, few people realize that special agents in the U.S. Department of Education investigate student loan fraud, and similar officers in the U.S. Department of Health and Human Services investigate fraud in Medicare and Medicaid programs. Law enforcement functions exist in many federal agencies, including those whose overall mission has little to do with the criminal justice system.

Internationalization of U.S. Law Enforcement

Law enforcement agencies of the U.S. government have increasingly stationed officers overseas, a fact little known by the general public. In a shrinking world with a global economy, terrorism, electronic communications, and jet aircraft, much crime is transnational, giving rise to a host of international criminal law enforcement tasks. American law enforcement is being "exported" in response to increased international terrorism, drug trafficking, smuggling of illegal immigrants, violations of U.S. securities laws, and money laundering, as well as the potential theft of nuclear materials (Albanese, 2011).

To meet these challenges, U.S. agencies have dramatically increased the number of officers stationed in foreign countries. The FBI has 63 overseas offices known as Legal Attachés or legats (FBI, 2013b). These offices focus on coordination with law enforcement personnel in other countries. Their activities are limited by the formal agreements negotiated between the United States and each host country. In many other countries, American agents are authorized only to gather information and facilitate communications between countries. American agencies are especially active in working with other countries on counterterrorism, drug trafficking, and cybercrime. These international partnerships help the United States find people who finance terrorism, help prevent terrorists from getting access to nuclear materials, and contribute to investigations of child pornography and human trafficking (Mueller, 2008).

According to the FBI (2013b: 14):

> Each legat works with law enforcement and security agencies in their host country to coordinate investigations of interest to both countries. . . . In addition to the work of legats, the Bureau often deploys agents and crime scene experts to assist in the investigation of attacks in other countries as requested and stations personnel overseas in such global partnerships as Interpol and Europol.

The United States contributes to the activities of **Interpol**, the International Criminal Police Organization. Interpol was created in 1946 to foster cooperation among the world's police forces. Based today in Lyon, France, Interpol maintains an intelligence data bank and serves as a clearinghouse for information gathered by agencies of its 186 member nations. Interpol officially describes its four core functions as providing:

1. Secure global police communications
2. Data services and databases for police
3. Support to police services
4. Police training and development

Interpol's six priority crime areas are: (1) drugs and criminal organizations, (2) public safety and terrorism, (3) financial and high-tech crime, (4) trafficking in human beings, (5) fugitive apprehension, and (6) corruption (www.interpol.int). Many criminal suspects and prison escapees have been caught after fleeing to a different country because Interpol is able to disseminate information about fugitives. Despite the benefits of international cooperation, Interpol's secretary general has complained that individual countries have not shared enough information with Interpol in a timely manner (Noble, 2006). It appears that countries may be wary of sharing information about terrorism and other investigations. It may be that they are inclined to assess specific events as "local," and thus not consider it worthwhile to explore the possibility that there are international connections behind a specific incident of criminal or terrorist activity.

The U.S. Interpol unit, the U.S. National Central Bureau, is a division of the Department of Justice. Based in Washington, DC, this bureau facilitates communication with foreign police agencies. It has a permanent staff plus officers assigned by 13 federal agencies including the FBI, the Secret Service, and the DEA. Interpol has also formed links with state and local police forces in the United States.

International involvement by American law enforcement officials extends beyond the activities of federal agencies. Since the end of the Cold War, American police organizations have assisted United Nations peacekeeping operations in Bosnia, Cyprus, Haiti, Kosovo, Panama, and Somalia. In these countries more than 3,000 police officers from around the world "have engaged in monitoring, mentoring, training, and generally assisting their local counterparts." Effective policing and following the rule of law are considered essential elements for achieving peace, safety, and security within a society. In countries that are developing democratic systems of government, trainers emphasize that policing is to be conducted by civilian police forces whose officers are trained in basic law enforcement skills and who display respect for the law and for human rights. The U.S. government relied on private companies to supply police trainers and training facilities in Iraq and Afghanistan. Evaluation reports have questioned whether these private companies have been effective in providing the needed training for countries that desperately need professional police in order to achieve stability and order (Glanz and Rohde, 2006; E. Schmitt and Rohde, 2007).

Interpol
The International Criminal Police Organization, through which countries cooperate in investigating crimes, especially situations in which lawbreakers have crossed international borders or participated in multicountry criminal activities.

State Agencies

Every state has its own law enforcement agency with statewide jurisdiction. In about half of the states, state police agencies carry out a wide range of law enforcement tasks. The others have state highway patrols with limited authority, primarily the task of enforcing traffic laws. In Hawaii, the agency conducts statewide drug investigations and provides police services at state facilities and courts (Hawaii Department of Public Safety, 2013). The American reluctance to centralize police power has generally kept state police forces from replacing local ones.

Before 1900 only Texas had a state police force. The Texas Rangers, a quasi-military force, protected white settlers from bandits and Native American raids. It had already been established by 1836, when Texas declared its independence from Mexico. Modern state police forces were organized after the turn of the century, mainly as a wing of the executive branch that would enforce the law when local officials did not. The Pennsylvania State Constabulary, formed in 1905, was the first such force. By 1925 almost all of the states had police forces.

All state forces regulate traffic on main highways, and two-thirds of the states have also given them general police powers. In only about a dozen populous states such as Massachusetts, Michigan, New Jersey, New York, and Pennsylvania can these forces perform law enforcement tasks across the state. For the most part, they operate only in areas where no other form of police protection exists or where local officers ask for their help. In many states, for example, the crime lab is run by the state police as a means of assisting local law enforcement agencies.

County Agencies

Sheriffs are found in almost all of the counties in the United States (except those in Alaska). The 3,063 sheriff's departments nationwide employ 182,979 full-time sworn officers (B. Reaves, 2011). Sheriff's departments are responsible for policing rural areas, but over time, especially in the Northeast, the state or local police have assumed many of these criminal justice functions. In parts of the South and West, however, the sheriff's department is a well-organized force. In 33 states, sheriffs are elected and hold the position of chief law enforcement officer in the county. Even when the sheriff's office is well organized, however, it may lack jurisdiction over cities and towns. In these situations, the sheriff and his or her deputies patrol unincorporated parts of the county or small towns that do not have police forces of their own. In addition to performing law enforcement tasks, the sheriff often serves as an officer of the court; sheriffs may operate jails, serve court orders, and provide bailiffs, who maintain order in courtrooms.

Native American Tribal Police

Through treaties with the United States, Native American tribes are separate, sovereign nations that maintain a significant degree of legal autonomy. They have the power to enforce tribal criminal laws against everyone on their lands, including non–Native Americans (Mentzer, 1996). More than 2.4 million Native Americans and Alaska Natives belong to approximately five hundred tribes (Humes, Jones, and Ramirez, 2011). However, many tribes are not recognized by the federal government, and many Native Americans do not live on reservations. Traditionally, Native American reservations have been policed either by federal officers of the Bureau of Indian Affairs (BIA) or by their own tribal police. The Bureau of Justice Statistics identified 178 tribal law enforcement agencies with nearly 3,000 full-time sworn officers (BJS, 2013b). Police on some reservations face especially daunting problems due to high rates of unemployment, poverty, and crime (T. Williams, 2012).

Municipal Agencies

The police departments of cities and towns have general law enforcement authority. City police forces range in size from 36,023 full-time sworn officers in the New York City Police Department to only one sworn officer in more than 500 small towns. There are 461,063 full-time sworn local police officers in the United States. Sworn personnel are officers with the power to make arrests.

Nearly three-quarters of municipal police departments employ fewer than 25 sworn officers. Nearly 90 percent of local police agencies serve populations of 25,000 or less, but half of all sworn officers work in cities of at least 100,000. The five largest police departments—New York, Chicago, Los Angeles, Philadelphia, and Houston—together employ more than 15 percent of all local police officers (B. Reaves, 2011).

In a metropolitan area composed of a central city and many suburbs, policing is usually divided among agencies at all levels of government, giving rise to conflicts between jurisdictions that may interfere with efficient use of police resources. The city and individual suburbs buy their own equipment and often deploy their officers without coordinating with those of nearby jurisdictions. In some areas with large populations, agreements have been made to enhance cooperation between jurisdictions.

Special Jurisdiction Agencies

Nearly 1,700 law enforcement agencies serve a special geographic jurisdiction. Among them are 508 college and university police forces, along with 253 additional two-year college police departments with sworn officers who can make arrests. These agencies employ approximately 57,000 sworn officers. More than 10,000 of these officers serve on college campuses (B. Reaves, 2011). Another large group of special jurisdiction agencies enforce laws as conservation officers and police in parks and recreation settings. For example, they may be responsible for law enforcement and safety in county parks, including the enforcement of laws for safe boating on lakes. These settings account for 14,571 sworn officers working for 246 agencies. In addition, there are 167 special jurisdiction agencies that enforce law and protect safety at specific mass transit systems, airports, bridges, tunnels, and ports. These agencies employ 11,508 sworn officers (B. Reaves, 2011). These agencies must coordinate and communicate with state and local officials and agencies that have general law enforcement responsibilities in the immediate vicinity. For example, if there is a major criminal event or large public disturbance on a college campus, state and local police are often called to provide assistance or special technical expertise for the campus police department.

In essence, the United States is a nation of small police forces, each of which is authorized, funded, and operated within the limits of its own jurisdiction. This is in direct contrast to the centralized police forces found in many other countries. For example, in France the police are a national force divided between the Ministry of Interior and the Ministry of Defense. All French police officers report to these national departments.

Despite this fragmentation among federal, state, and local agencies, law enforcement officials often seek to coordinate their efforts. Most recently, issues of homeland security and emergency preparedness have drawn agencies together to plan their coordinated responses to large-scale emergencies. Agencies also work together through such initiatives as "Amber Alerts," the plan used in increasing numbers of metropolitan areas to notify all police agencies and media outlets immediately if a child has been abducted.

✔POINT

11. What is the jurisdiction of federal law enforcement agencies?

12. Why are some law enforcement agencies of the U.S. government located overseas?

13. What are the functions of most state police agencies?

14. Besides law enforcement, what functions do sheriffs perform?

15. What are the main characteristics of the organization of the police in the United States?

STOP AND ANALYZE: What are the advantages and disadvantages of having a fragmented system of separate police agencies? List two advantages and two disadvantages.

Police Functions

The police are expected to maintain order, enforce the law, and provide services as they seek to prevent crime. However, they perform other tasks as well, many of them having little to do with crime and justice and more to do with community service. They direct traffic, handle accidents and illnesses, stop noisy parties, find missing persons, enforce licensing regulations, provide ambulance services, take disturbed people into protective custody, and so on. The list is long and varies from place to place. Some researchers have suggested that the police have more in common with social service agencies than with the criminal justice system.

The American Bar Association has published a list of police goals and functions that includes the following (H. Goldstein, 1977: 5):

1. Prevent and control conduct considered threatening to life and property (serious crime).
2. Aid people who are in danger of harm, such as the victim of a criminal attack.
3. Protect constitutional rights, such as the rights of free speech and assembly.
4. Facilitate the movement of people and vehicles.
5. Aid those who cannot care for themselves: the drunk or the addicted, the mentally ill, the disabled, the old, and the young.
6. Resolve conflict, whether between individuals, groups of individuals, or individuals and government.
7. Identify problems that could become more serious for the citizen, for the police, or for government.
8. Create a feeling of security in the community.

How did the police gain such broad responsibilities? In many places the police are the only public agency that is available 7 days a week, 24 hours a day to respond to calls for help. They are usually best able to investigate many kinds of problems. Moreover, the power to use force when necessary allows them to intervene in problematic situations.

We can classify the functions of the police into three groups, each of which can contribute to crime prevention: (1) order maintenance, (2) law enforcement, and (3) service. Police agencies divide their resources among these functions on the basis of community need, citizen requests, and departmental policy.

Order Maintenance

order maintenance
The police function of preventing behavior that disturbs or threatens to disturb the public peace or that involves face-to-face conflict among two or more people. In such situations, the police exercise discretion in deciding whether a law has been broken.

The **order maintenance** function is a broad mandate to prevent behavior that either disturbs or threatens to disturb the peace or involves face-to-face conflict among two or more people. A domestic quarrel, a noisy intoxicated person, loud music in the night, a panhandler on the street, a tavern brawl—all are forms of disorder that may require action by the police.

Unlike most laws that define specific acts as illegal, laws regulating disorderly conduct deal with ambiguous situations that different police officers could view in different ways. For many crimes, determining when the law has been broken is easy. However, order maintenance requires officers to decide not only whether a law has been broken but also whether any action should be taken and, if so, who should be blamed. In a bar fight, for example, the officer must decide who started the fight, whether an arrest should be made for assault, and whether to arrest people other than those who started the conflict.

Patrol officers deal mainly with behavior that either disturbs or threatens to disturb the peace. They confront the public in ambiguous situations and have wide discretion in matters that affect people's lives. If an officer decides to arrest someone for disorderly conduct, that person could spend time in jail and lose his or her job even without being convicted of the crime.

Officers often must make judgments in order maintenance situations. They may be required to help people in trouble, manage crowds, supervise various kinds of services, and help people who are not fully accountable for what they do. The officers have a high degree of discretion and control over how such situations will develop. Patrol officers are not subject to direct control. They have the power to arrest, but they may also decide not to make an arrest. The order maintenance function is made more complex by the fact that the patrol officer is normally expected to "handle" a situation rather than to enforce the law, usually in an emotionally charged atmosphere. In controlling a crowd outside a rock concert, for example, the arrest of an unruly person may restore order by removing a troublemaker and also serving as a warning to others that they could be arrested if they do not cooperate. However, an arrest may cause the crowd to become hostile toward the officers, making the situation worse. Officers cannot always predict precisely how their discretionary decisions will promote or hinder order maintenance.

To uphold important American values of equal treatment and respect for constitutional rights, police officers must make decisions fairly and within the boundaries of their authority. Officers may face a difficult, immediate situation that leads them to use force or target specific individuals for restraint. The volatile context of order maintenance situations, where emotions are running high and some people may be out of control, can produce anger and hostility toward officers. If officers must stop a disturbance in a bar, for example, they will inevitably seek to restrain individuals who are contributing to the disturbance. However, if they cannot restrain everyone, they may choose specific individuals or focus their attention on the people standing close at hand. As a result, some citizens may believe that officers are applying unequal treatment or targeting individuals because of their race or ethnicity. Thus the immediacy of order maintenance problems and the need to make quick decisions can create risks that officers will be viewed as acting in a manner contrary to American values.

AP Images/The (Athens) Post, Greg Roberts

Police in Athens, Ohio, forcibly cleared the area during an annual street party adjacent to Ohio University that turned into a near riot. In such situations, police officers must control their own emotions and avoid escalating the conflict even as they risk injury from thrown objects. Given that each situation can take on a life of its own, is it possible to train officers to make appropriate decisions in all situations?

Law Enforcement

law enforcement
The police function of controlling crime by intervening in situations in which the law has clearly been violated and the police need to identify and apprehend the guilty person.

The **law enforcement** function applies to situations in which the law has been violated and the offender needs to be identified or located and then apprehended. Police officers who focus on law enforcement serve in specialized branches such as the vice squad and the burglary detail. Although the patrol officer may be the first officer at the scene of a crime, in serious cases a detective usually prepares the case for prosecution by bringing together all the evidence for the prosecuting attorney. When the offender is identified but not located, the detective conducts the search. If the offender is not identified, the detective must analyze clues to find out who committed the crime.

The police often portray themselves as enforcers of the law, but many factors interfere with how effectively they can do so. For example, when a property crime is committed, the perpetrator usually has some time to get away. This limits the ability of the police to identify, locate, and arrest the suspect. Burglaries, for instance, usually occur when people are away from home. The crime may not be discovered until hours or days have passed. The effectiveness of the police also decreases when assault or robbery victims cannot identify the offender. Victims often delay in calling the police, reducing the chances that a suspect will be apprehended.

As in the case of order maintenance, the important American values of equal treatment and respect for rights can be threatened if officers do not make their law enforcement decisions professionally and objectively. If people believe that such decisions target specific neighborhoods or particular ethnic groups, police actions might generate suspicion and hostility. People in some communities have complained that police enforce narcotics laws primarily in poor neighborhoods populated by members of minority groups. Such perceptions of the police clash with the American values of equal treatment and respect for rights.

Service

service
The police function of providing assistance to the public, usually in matters unrelated to crime.

Police perform a broad range of services, especially for lower-income citizens, that are not related to crime. This **service** function—providing first aid, rescuing animals, helping the disoriented, and so on—has become a major police function. Crime prevention has also become a major component of police service to the community. Through education and community organizing, the police can help the public take steps to prevent crime.

Research has shown how important the service function is to the community. Studies have shown that most calls to the police do not involve reports of crimes. Instead, they are requests for service or information. Because the police are available 24 hours a day, people turn to them in times of trouble. For example, if someone has a bat flying around inside the house at night, it will likely lead to a call to the police for advice or assistance. People also call the police for medical emergencies or assistance with gaining entry into a car or home in which the owners have left the keys inside. Many departments provide information, operate ambulance services, locate missing persons, check locks on vacationers' homes, and intervene in suicide attempts. Categories of frequent calls can include such service matters as automobile collisions, requests to check on the welfare of someone, and complaints about someone parking illegally.

Critics claim that valuable resources are being inappropriately diverted from law enforcement to services. However, performing service functions can help police control crime. Through the service function, officers gain knowledge about the community, and citizens come to trust the police. Checking the security of buildings clearly helps prevent crime, but other activities—dealing with runaways, intoxicated people, and public quarrels—may help solve problems before they lead to criminal behavior.

Implementing the Mandate

Although people may depend most heavily on the order maintenance and service functions of the police, police chiefs act as if law enforcement—the catching of lawbreakers—is the most important function. According to public opinion polls, the crime-fighter image of the police remains firmly rooted in citizens' minds and is the main reason given by recruits for joining the force.

Public support for budgets is greatest when the crime-fighting function is stressed. This emphasis appears in the organization of big-city departments. The officers who perform this function, such as detectives, have high status. The focus on crime leads to the creation of special units to deal with homicide, burglary, and auto theft. All other tasks fall to the patrol division. In some departments, this pattern creates morale problems, because extra resources are allocated and prestige devoted to a function that is concerned with a small percentage of the problems brought to the police. In essence, police are public servants who keep the peace, but their organization reinforces their own law enforcement image and the public's focus on crime fighting.

But do the police prevent crime? David Bayley claims that they do not. He points to the fact that no link has been found between the number of police officers and crime rates. For example, Philadelphia is major city with a relatively high number of police officers for its population. Philadelphia has 44 officers per 10,000 residents. Yet, in 2013, Philadelphia reported a relatively high rate of violent crime: 114 violent crimes per 10,000 people. Miami had a similarly high reported rate of violent crime (118 violent crimes per 10,000 residents) with the same number of police officers per population (28 per 10,000 residents) as Seattle, which only had a crime rate of 58 violent crimes per 10,000 residents. By contrast, Los Angeles (25 officers per 10,000) had fewer police officers for its population, yet also had a lower reported rate of violent crime: 42 violent crimes per 10,000 residents. (FBI, 2014a; individual city websites).

In addition, the strategies traditionally used by modern police have little or no effect on crime. Those strategies are street patrolling by uniformed officers, rapid response to emergency calls, and expert investigation of crime by detectives. Bayley says that the police have seen these strategies as essential to protect public safety, but little evidence exists that they achieve this goal (Bayley, 1994). Yet the inability of police to affect the major crime trends over the course of American history has not made law enforcement leaders and researchers resigned to the inevitability of limited impact. As evidence-based policing continues its development in the twenty-first century, there are indications that police may draw from research to implement strategies that can affect certain types of crimes in specific locations.

✔POINT

16. What is the order maintenance function? What are officers expected to do in situations where they must maintain order?

17. How do law enforcement situations compare with order maintenance situations?

STOP AND ANALYZE: Which of the police functions do you see as most difficult to carry out? Give three reasons for your answer.

Organization of the Police

Most police agencies are organized in a military manner with a structure of ranks and responsibilities. But police departments are also bureaucracies designed to achieve objectives efficiently. Bureaucracies are characterized by a division of labor, a chain of command with clear lines of authority, and rules to guide the activities of staff. Police organization differs somewhat from place to place, depending on the size of the jurisdiction, the characteristics of the population, and the nature of the local crime problems. However, the basic characteristics of a bureaucracy appear in all sizable departments.

Bureaucratic Elements

The police department in Odessa, Texas, reveals the elements of bureaucracy in a typical urban police force. Figure 5.1 shows the Odessa Police Department's 2012 organizational chart, which we refer to in the following discussion.

Division of Labor

As indicated in Figure 5.1, the Odessa Police Department is divided into three divisions and bureaus—the Administrative Division, the Operations Bureau, and

FIGURE 5.1 ORGANIZATION OF ODESSA, TEXAS, POLICE DEPARTMENT

This is a typical structure. Note the divisions between administrative services, operations, and special operations.

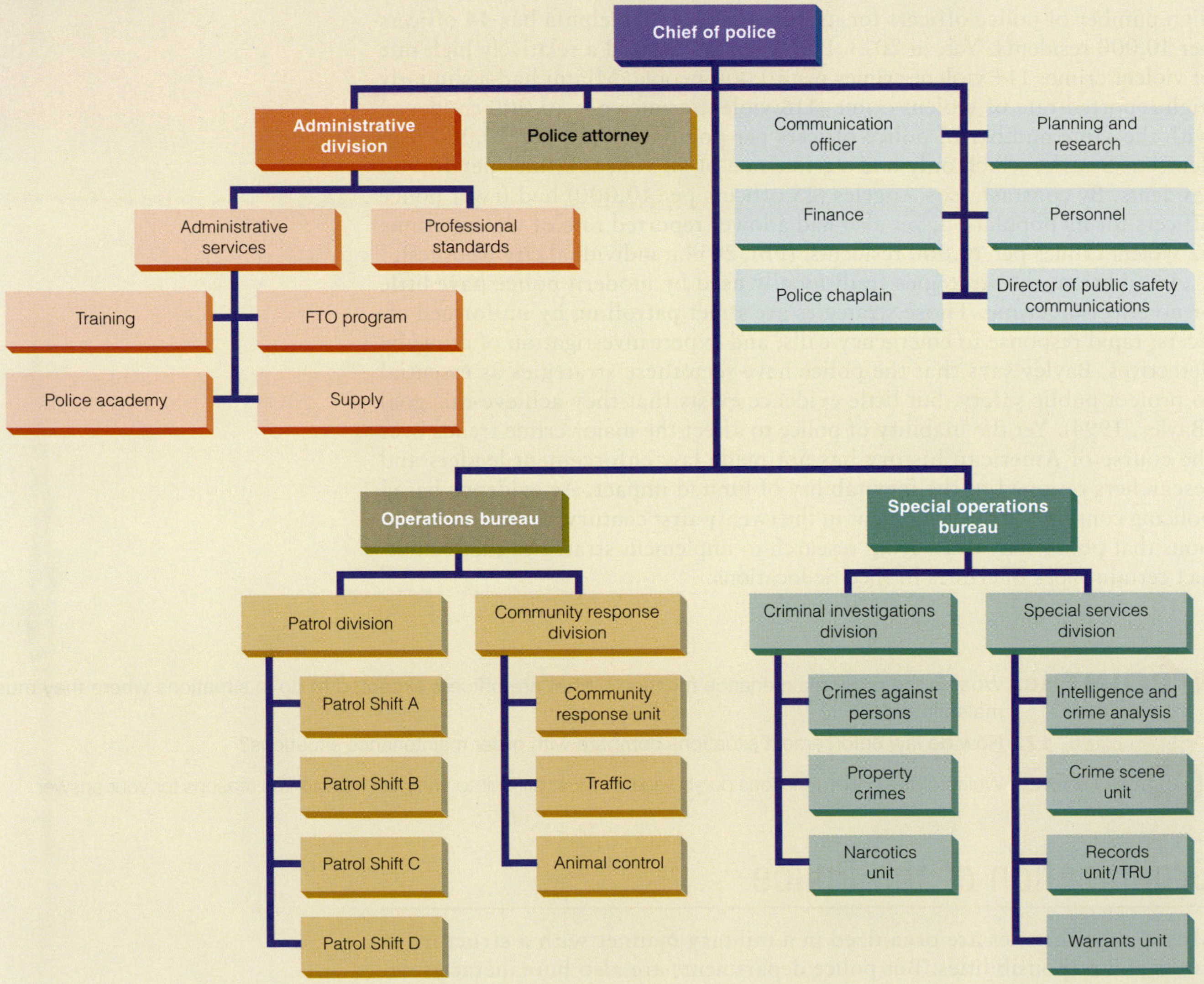

Odessa, Texas, Police Department website 2013 (www.odessapd.com).

the Special Operations Bureau—and specific offices under the Chief of Police. In each of these divisions and bureaus, authority is further delegated to offices and units that have special functions for such matters as training, finance, and communications. The Operations Bureau is divided into specific **patrol units**, designated by shift and function. The Special Operations Bureau may give an officer higher status and greater freedom than that enjoyed by patrol officers.

patrol units
The core operational units of local police departments that deploy uniformed officers to handle the full array of police functions for service, order maintenance, and law enforcement.

The bureaucratic organization of a city police department such as Odessa allows the allocation of resources and the supervision of personnel, taking into account the needs and problems of each district.

Chain and Unity of Command

The military character of police departments is illustrated by the **chain of command** according to ranks—officer, commander, sergeant, lieutenant, captain, major, and chief. These make clear the powers and duties of officers at each level. Relationships between superiors and subordinates emphasize discipline, control, and accountability. Each officer has an immediate supervisor who has authority and responsibility for the actions of those below. Such priorities help officers mobilize resources. They also ensure that civil liberties are protected; if police officers are accountable to their superiors, they are less likely to abuse their authority by needlessly interfering with the freedom and rights of citizens.

chain of command
Organizational structure based on a military model with clear definition of ranks to indicate authority over subordinates and obligations to obey orders from superiors.

Rules and Procedures

Complex bureaucracies such as police departments depend on clearly stated rules and procedures to guide officers. These rules are usually found in operations manuals so that officers will know the procedures they should take when confronted by particular types of incidents. In some departments the rules are so detailed that they tell officers when they may unholster their gun, what precautions to take when stopping a vehicle, arrest procedures, and actions to take in domestic squabbles. Obviously, rules cannot define all police actions, and the specificity of some rules may detract from law enforcement effectiveness. Critics say that the rules of too many departments are inflexible and cannot possibly cover all circumstances. They argue that officers must be encouraged to use discretion without fear of sanctions for not strictly following the rules.

Operational Units

All but the smallest police departments assign officers to operational units that focus on specific functions: patrol, investigation, traffic, vice, and juvenile. These units perform the basic tasks of crime prevention and control. The patrol and investigation (detective) units form the core of the modern department. The patrol unit handles a wide range of functions, including preventing crime, catching suspects, mediating quarrels, helping the ill, and giving aid at accidents. The investigation unit identifies, apprehends, and collects evidence against lawbreakers who commit serious crimes. Because of their overlapping duties, the separation of patrol and investigation can cause problems. Although the investigation unit usually focuses on murder, rape, and major robberies, the patrol unit has joint responsibility for investigating those crimes but is also solely responsible for investigating the more numerous lesser crimes.

The extent to which departments create specialized units may depend on the size of the city and its police force. Many departments have traffic units, but only those in midsized to large cities also have vice and juvenile units. Large departments usually have an internal affairs section to investigate charges of officer corruption, as well as other problems associated with the staff and officers. The juvenile unit works with young people, focusing mainly on crime prevention. All special units depend on the patrol officers for information and assistance.

The traditional top-down military structure of the police, with designated ranks and superior officers who have command authority over subordinates, and the development of specific law enforcement specializations, may lead citizens to feel they have little influence over the organization of the police in their communities. It is possible that they can lobby the city council to create a new, specialized division to deal with a specific problem, such as juvenile delinquency, traffic, or vice, but it is generally difficult to think about a drastic restructuring of police organization and functions. Consider the issue in "Civic Engagement: Your Role in the System," and think about whether you have any ideas to improve police organization.

CIVIC ENGAGEMENT

YOUR ROLE IN THE SYSTEM

A new mayor has proposed that the police department be reorganized by merging it with the fire department and the emergency medical response department. The proposal would require that every frontline officer be trained to work as a police officer, firefighter, and emergency medical technician. Thus each officer could perform any safety service needed by the public. *Make a list of the arguments supporting and opposing this proposal. Do you support the proposal?* Then look at the description of the combined police–fire department in Amberley Village, Ohio.

The Police Bureaucracy and the Criminal Justice System

The police play an important role as a bureaucracy within the broader criminal justice system. Three issues arise in the organizational context within which the police operate.

First, the police are the gateway through which information and individuals enter the justice system. Police have the discretion to determine which suspects will be arrested. Cases that are sent to the prosecutor for charging and then to the courts for adjudication begin with an officer's decision that there is probable cause for an arrest. The care taken by the officer in making the arrest and collecting evidence greatly affects the ultimate success of the prosecution. The outcome of the case, whether through plea bargaining by lawyers or through a trial with a judge and jury, hinges on the officer's judgment and evidence-gathering activities.

Second, police administration is influenced by the fact that the outcome of a case is largely in the hands of others. The police bring suspects into the criminal justice process, but they cannot control the decisions of prosecutors and judges. In some cases, the police officers feel that their efforts have been wasted. For example, the prosecutor sometimes agrees to a plea bargain that does not, in the eyes of the officer, adequately punish the offender.

Third, as part of a bureaucracy, police officers are expected to observe rules and follow the orders of superiors while at the same time making independent, discretionary judgments. They must stay within the chain of command, yet also make choices in response to events on the streets. The tension between these two tasks affects many aspects of their daily work, which we shall explore further in this chapter and in Chapter 6.

CHECKPOINT

18. What are three characteristics of a bureaucracy?

19. What are the five operational units of police departments with sufficient size for specialization?

STOP AND ANALYZE: In light of the budget cuts affecting contemporary police departments throughout the country, if you were a police chief, what would you cut and why? Describe and explain two possible budget cuts.

Police Policy

The police cannot enforce every law and catch every lawbreaker. Legal rules limit the ways officers can investigate and pursue offenders. For example, the constitutional ban on unreasonable searches and seizures prevents police from investigating most crimes without a search warrant.

Because the police have limited resources, they cannot have officers on every street at all times of the day and night. This means that police executives must develop policies regarding how the members of their department will implement their mandate. These policies guide officers in deciding which offenses to address and which tactics to use. They develop policies, for example, on whether to have officers patrol neighborhoods in cars or on foot. Changes in policy—such as increasing the size of the night patrol or tolerating prostitution and other public order offenses—affect the amount of crime that gets official attention and the system's ability to deal with offenders.

Police frequently emphasize their role as crime fighters. As a result, police in most communities focus on the crimes covered by the FBI's Uniform Crime Reports. These crimes make headlines, and politicians point to them when they call for increases in the police budget. They are also the crimes that poor people tend to commit. Voters pressure politicians and the police to enforce laws that help them feel safe in their daily lives. They see occupational crimes, such as forgery, embezzlement, or tax fraud, as less threatening. Because these crimes are less visible and more difficult to solve, they receive less attention from the police.

Decisions about how police resources will be used affect the types of people who are arrested and passed through the criminal justice system. Think of the hard choices you would have to make if you were a police chief. Should more officers be sent into high-crime areas? Should more officers be assigned to the central business district during shopping hours? What should the mix of traffic control and crime fighting be? These questions have no easy answers. Police officials must answer them according to their goals and values.

American cities differ in racial, ethnic, economic, and government characteristics as well as in their degree of urbanization. These factors can affect the style of policing expected by the community. In a classic study, James Q. Wilson found that citizen expectations regarding police behavior affect the political process in the choice of the top police executive. Chiefs who run their departments in ways that antagonize the community tend not to stay in office very long. Wilson's key finding was that a city's political culture, which reflects its socioeconomic characteristics and its government organization, had a major impact on the style of policing found there. Wilson described three different styles of policing—the *watchman, legalistic,* and *service* styles (J. Q. Wilson, 1968). Table 5.2 documents these styles of policing and the types of communities in which they appear.

Departments with a **watchman style** stress order maintenance. Patrol officers may ignore minor violations of the law, especially those involving traffic and juveniles, as long as there is order. The police exercise discretion and deal with many infractions in an informal way. Officers make arrests only for flagrant violations and when order cannot be maintained. The broad discretion

watchman style
Style of policing that emphasizes order maintenance and tolerates minor violations of law as officers use discretion to handle small infractions informally but make arrests for major violations.

TABLE 5.2 STYLES OF POLICING

James Q. Wilson found three distinct styles of policing in the communities he studied. Each style emphasizes different police functions, and each is linked with the specific characteristics of the community.

STYLE	DEFINING CHARACTERISICS	COMMUNITY TYPE
Watchman	Emphasis on maintaining order	Declining industrial city, mixed racial/ethnic composition, blue-collar
Legalistic	Emphasis on law enforcement	Reform-minded city government, mixed socioeconomic composition
Service	Emphasis on service with balance between law enforcement and order maintenance	Middle-class suburban community

Source: Drawn from James Q. Wilson, *Varieties of Police Behavior* (Cambridge, MA: Harvard University Press, 1968).

exercised by officers can produce discrimination when officers do not treat members of different racial and ethnic groups in the same way.

legalistic style
Style of policing that emphasizes strict enforcement of laws and reduces officers' authority to handle matters informally.

In departments with a **legalistic style**, police work is marked by professionalism and an emphasis on law enforcement. Officers are expected to detain a high proportion of juvenile offenders, act vigorously against illicit enterprises, issue traffic tickets, and make a large number of misdemeanor arrests. They act as if a single standard of community conduct exists (as prescribed by the law) rather than different standards for juveniles, minorities, substance abusers, homeless people, and other groups. Thus, although officers do not discriminate in making arrests and issuing citations, the strict enforcement of laws, including traffic laws, can seem overly harsh to some groups in the community.

service style
Style of policing in which officers cater to citizens' desire for favorable treatment and sensitivity to individual situations by using discretion to handle minor matters in ways that seek to avoid embarrassment or punishment.

Suburban middle-class communities often experience a **service style** of policing. Residents feel that they deserve individual treatment and expect the police to provide service. Burglaries and assaults are taken seriously, while minor infractions tend to be dealt with by informal means such as stern warnings. The police are expected to deal with the misdeeds of local residents in a personal, nonpublic way so as to avoid embarrassment.

In all cases, before officers investigate crimes or make arrests, each police chief decides on policies that will govern the level and type of enforcement in the community. Given that the police are the entry point to the criminal justice system, the decisions made by police officials affect all segments of the system. Just as community expectations shape decisions about enforcement goals and the allocation of police resources, they also shape the cases that prosecutors and correctional officials will handle.

✔POINT

20. What are the characteristics of the watchman style of policing?

21. What is the key feature of the legalistic style of policing?

22. Where are you likely to find the service style of policing?

STOP AND ANALYZE: If you were a police chief, which style of policing would you seek to have your officers carry out? Would it depend on the type of city for which you have responsibility, or is there one style that is actually the ideal approach? Give three reasons for your choice of style.

Everyday Action of Police

We have seen how the police are organized and which three functions of policing—law enforcement, order maintenance, and service—define police duties. We have also recognized that police officers must be guided by policies developed by their superiors as to how policing is to be implemented. Now let us look at the everyday actions of the police as they deal with citizens in often highly discretionary ways. We shall then discuss domestic violence to show how the police respond to serious problems.

Encounters Between Police and Citizens

To carry out their mission, the police must have the public's confidence, because officers depend on the public to help them identify crime and carry out investigations. Each year approximately 1 in 5 Americans age 16 and older has face-to-face contact with law enforcement officers. One-fifth of the contacts occur when police respond to a call for assistance or come to the scene of an automobile collision. Another fifth involve people reporting a crime. Another fifth involve police investigating crimes or providing service and assistance. The remaining 40 percent of these contacts involve drivers and passengers stopped by a patrol officer. Overall, 90 percent of people who had contact with the police believed that the police acted properly. However, among drivers stopped by the police, African Americans were less likely than whites or Hispanics to believe that the police had stopped them for a legitimate reason (Eith and Durose, 2011). People's contacts with the police may shape their perceptions of the police and affect their willingness to cooperate.

Although most people are willing to help the police, fear, self-interest, and other factors keep some from cooperating. Many people avoid calling the police, because they think it is not worth the effort and cost. They do not want to spend time filling out forms at the station, appearing as a witness, or confronting a neighbor or relative in court. In some low-income neighborhoods, citizens are reluctant to assist the police because their past experience has shown that contact with law enforcement "only brings trouble." Without information about a crime, the police may decide not to pursue an investigation. Clearly, then, citizens have some control over the work of the police through their decisions to call or not to call them.

Citizens expect the police to act both effectively and fairly—in ways consistent with American values. Departmental policy often affects fairness in encounters between citizens and police. When should the patrol officer frisk a pedestrian or the driver of a stopped vehicle? When should a deal be made with the addict-informer? Which disputes should be mediated on the spot and which left to more-formal procedures? Surprisingly, conflicts between fairness and policy are seldom decided by heads of departments, but fall largely to the officer on the scene. In many areas the department has little control over the actions of individual officers.

Police Discretion

Police officers have the power to deprive people of their liberty—to arrest them, take them into custody, and use force to control them. In carrying out their professional responsibilities, officers are expected to exercise discretion—to make choices in often ambiguous situations as to how and when to apply the law. Discretion can involve ignoring minor violations of the law or holding some violators to rule-book standards. It can mean arresting a disorderly person or taking that person home.

In the final analysis, the officer on the scene must define the situation, decide how to handle it, and determine whether and how the law should be applied. Five factors are especially important:

1. *The nature of the crime.* The less serious a crime is to the public, the more freedom officers have to ignore it.
2. *The relationship between the alleged criminal and the victim.* The closer the personal relationship, the more variable the use of discretion. Family squabbles may not be as grave as they appear, and a spouse may later decide not to press charges, so police are wary of making arrests.
3. *The relationship between the police and the criminal or victim.* A polite complainant will be taken more seriously than a hostile one. Likewise, a suspect who shows respect to an officer is less likely to be arrested than one who does not.
4. *Race/ethnicity, age, gender, class.* Although subject to debate, research shows that officers are more likely to strictly enforce the law against young, minority, and poor men while being more lenient to the elderly, whites, and affluent women.
5. *Departmental policy.* The policies of the police chief and city officials promote more or less discretion.

Patrol officers—who are the most numerous, the lowest-ranking, and the newest to police work—have the most discretion. For example, if they chase a young thief into an alley, they can decide, outside of the view of the public, whether to make an arrest or just recover the stolen goods and give the offender a stern warning.

As we have seen, patrol officers' primary task is to maintain order and enforce ambiguous laws such as those dealing with disorderly conduct, public drunkenness, breach of the peace, and other situations in which it is unclear if a law has been broken, who committed the offense, and whether an arrest should be made. James Q. Wilson describes a patrol officer's role as "unlike that of any other occupation . . . one in which subprofessionals, working alone, exercise wide discretion in matters of utmost importance (life and death, honor and dishonor) in an environment that is apprehensive and perhaps hostile" (J. Q. Wilson, 1968: 30).

Although some people call for detailed guidelines for police officers, such guidelines would probably be useless. No matter how detailed they were, the officer would still have to make judgments about how to apply them in each situation. At best, police administrators can develop guidelines and training that, one hopes, will give officers shared values and make their judgments more consistent.

Domestic Violence

domestic violence
The term commonly used to refer to intimate partner violence or violent victimization between spouses, boyfriends and girlfriends, or those formerly in intimate relationships. Such actions account for a significant percentage of the violent victimizations experienced by women.

How the police deal with **domestic violence** can show the links between police–citizen encounters, the exercise of discretion, and actions taken (or not taken) by officers. Domestic violence, also called "battering," "spouse abuse," and "intimate partner violence," is assaultive behavior involving adults who are married or who have a prior or an ongoing intimate relationship.

Violence by an intimate (husband, ex-husband, boyfriend, or ex-boyfriend) accounted for about 26 percent of all violence experienced by female victims in 2009, compared with 5 percent for male victims. In that year, more than 500,000 incidents of intimate partner violence were reported with women as victims (Truman and Rand, 2010; Truman and Planty, 2012). In 2013, intimate partner violence remained a significant problem; more than 700,000 incidents were reported in the National Crime Victimization Survey, combining totals for both female and male victims (Truman and Langton, 2014). The highest rates of victimization from nonlethal violence by an intimate occur among African American women, women aged 20 to 24, and women in households in the lowest income categories. In addition, from 2001 through 2005, a reported 30 percent of female homicide victims were killed by intimate partners, whereas the comparable figure for men was only 5 percent (Catalano, 2007).

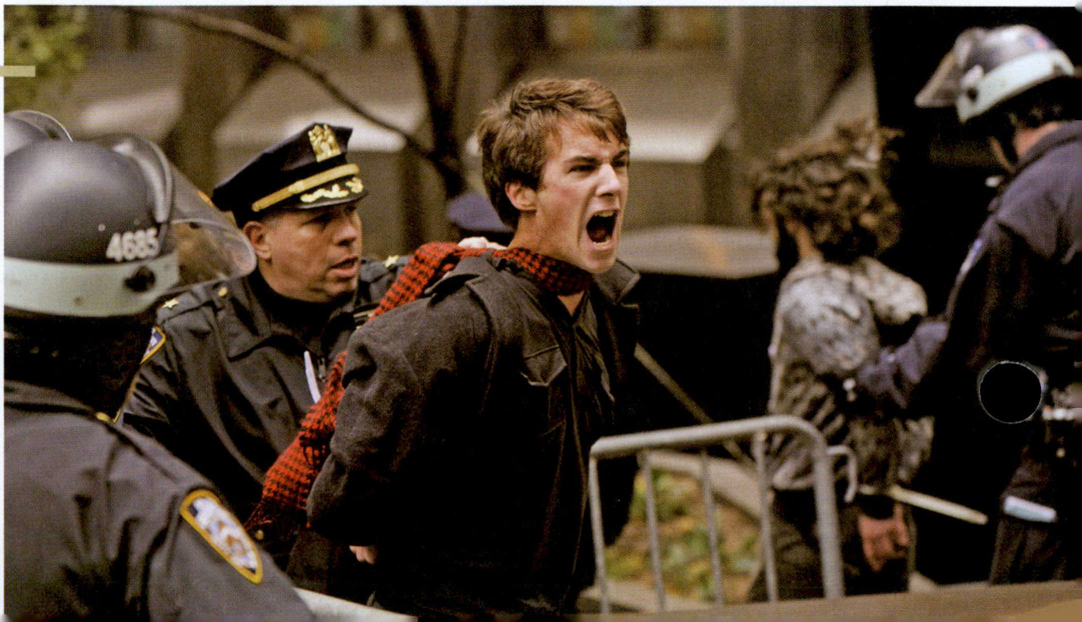

Justin Lane/EPA/Newscom

Police officers often encounter citizens in moments of fear, anger, and trauma. As a result, people can lash out at an officer or otherwise become emotionally out of control. Can officers be effectively trained to keep their own emotions in check when verbally abused by an upset citizen? How can we be sure officers will not resort too quickly to their discretionary authority to arrest or use force?

Before 1970, most citizens and criminal justice agencies viewed domestic violence as a "private" affair best settled within the family. It was thought that police involvement might make the situation worse for the victim because it raised the possibility of reprisal. Even today, though a large number of calls to the police involve family disturbances, about half go unreported.

From the viewpoint of most police departments, domestic violence was a "no-win" situation in which one or both disputants often challenged or attacked the officers responding to calls for help. If an arrest was made, the police found that the victim often refused to cooperate with a prosecution. In addition, entering a home to deal with an emotion-laden incident was thought to be more dangerous than investigating "real" crimes. Many officers believed that trying to deal with family disputes was a leading cause of officer deaths and injury. However, this belief has been challenged by researchers who have found that domestic violence cases are no more dangerous to officers than are other incidents.

Prodded by the women's movement and research on the usefulness of making arrests in domestic violence situations (Dixon, 2008), police departments began to rethink this policy of leniency. In many states, policies also changed as a result of lawsuits by injured women who claimed that the police ignored evidence of assaults and in effect allowed the spouses to inflict serious injuries (Jain, 2011). The increased awareness of domestic violence appears in other aspects of criminal justice law and policy, too. For example, in 2015, the governor of Michigan blocked a bill passed by the state legislature that would have made it easier for citizens to obtain permits to carry concealed firearms. He said he vetoed the measure because he feared it might increase the danger faced by some domestic violence victims (M. Davey, 2015).

There is a growing sense that domestic violence can no longer be left to the discretion of individual patrol officers. Today, most large departments and police academies have programs to educate officers about domestic violence (Luthern, 2014). In addition, two dozen states require the arrest without a warrant of suspects in violent incidents within the past 24 hours, even if the officer did not witness the crime but has probable cause to believe that the suspect committed it. It is not clear, however, that mandatory arrest policies advance effectiveness as a form of evidence-based policing. Recent research indicates rates of victimization are lower in those cities with more police officers and social service workers per capita than in those with mandatory arrest policies (Xie, Lauritsen, and Heimer, 2012).

Even though we can point to policy changes imposed to deal with domestic violence, the officer in the field remains the one who must handle these situations. Laws, guidelines, and training can help; however, as is often true in police work, the discretion of the officer inevitably determines what actions will be taken.

It should also be noted that although police decisions determine whether there is an official law enforcement intervention into a situation of domestic violence, the ultimate outcomes are also affected by prosecutors' decisions about whether or not to press charges. Just as budget cuts that reduce police resources may lead to diminished enforcement of domestic violence laws and other crimes, budget reductions may also reduce prosecutors' attention to domestic violence. For example, in 2011 when the Wisconsin state government ordered additional unpaid furlough days for prosecutors throughout the state, one county's district attorney wrote a letter to the state's secretary of administration warning that domestic violence and other cases might no longer be pursued. District Attorney Allen Brey wrote that the "only classes of cases available to cut and meet our projected [reduction] are criminal traffic . . . and misdemeanors (wife beaters, drug users, [etc.]. . . .) [Y]our decision requires a choice to not prosecute one group or the other" (Srubas, 2011).

POINT **23.** Why do patrol officers have so much discretion?

24. Why have police in the past failed to arrest in domestic violence situations?

STOP AND ANALYZE: Discretion is a necessary element of police officers' tools to handle situations that they encounter. Yet discretion may be used inappropriately. List two approaches you would use, if you were a police chief, to improve the discretionary decision making of your officers.

Police and the Community

The work of a police officer in an American city can be very difficult, involving hours of boring, routine work interrupted by short spurts of dangerous crime fighting. Although police work has always been frustrating and dangerous, officers today must deal with situations ranging from helping the homeless to dealing with domestic violence to confronting shoot-outs at drug deals gone sour. Yet police actions are sometimes mishandled by officers or misinterpreted by the public, making some people critical of the police.

Special Populations

Urban police forces must deal with a complex population. City streets contain growing numbers of people suffering from mental illness, homelessness, alcoholism, drug addiction, or serious medical conditions such as acquired immunodeficiency syndrome (AIDS). In addition, they may find youthful runaways and children victimized by their parents' neglect. Several factors have contributed to increasing numbers of "problem" people on the streets. These factors include

NEW DIRECTIONS IN CRIMINAL JUSTICE POLICY

EVIDENCE-BASED PRACTICES AND ISSUES WITH MENTAL ILLNESS

Police departments are turning to evidence-based practices to inform policies and procedures for dealing with special populations, including individuals with mental illness, addiction, or serious problems. Statistics have shown that in large cities, at least 10 percent of police calls are thought to involve persons with mental illness. For example, in some communities, a portion of the homeless population includes those suffering from mental health problems, and these individuals' problems may be quite visible and problematic with respect to issues of behavioral self-control, property damage, and public intoxication.

Too often, police officers lack sufficient knowledge about mental illness. In fact, officers' inability to recognize and properly respond to behavior caused by mental illness may escalate problems during encounters with this population. For example, police officers may use force inappropriately and cause injuries when other strategies may have been safer and more effective. Highly publicized incidents have occurred when police officers have used deadly force in dealing with someone's unpredictable and apparently threatening behavior. These situations might have ended peacefully with better training and understanding of mental illness by officers. Research has shown that training that focuses on effective communication skills and knowledge-based methods can help officers de-escalate situations involving persons with mental health issues.

For police, developing relationships and coordinating with mental health services providers in the local community are key to successfully implementing evidence-based practices. Officers need to be aware of the available resources for treatment, housing, and medical services when they encounter mentally ill people who have no means to manage on their own. In addition, coordination is essential to police preparation for and participation in crisis intervention. Police training and planning toward these goals often emphasize Crisis Intervention Teams (CIT), which can be called to the scene of a problem. Members of the team are trained to defuse the situation in a manner that is safe for the individual, officers, and the community. They then quickly move the individual into appropriate treatment or identify which available health, housing, and other services are deemed to be most beneficial.

While police officers in CIT programs require extensive training to deal with the range of mental health incidents they may encounter, all police officers need training that will heighten their awareness and sensitivity to mental illness and help avoid regrettable outcomes during encounters with this population. Officers overcrowded jails, cutbacks in public assistance, and the closing of many psychiatric institutions, which must then release mental health patients. Although most of these "problem" people do not commit crimes, their presence disturbs many of their fellow citizens, and thus they may contribute to fear of crime and disorder.

Clearly, dealing with special populations poses a major challenge for police in most cities. Occasionally, major controversies erupt, especially when police officers are questioned in their use of deadly force against people who may not understand the officers' statements and commands, such as individuals who are mentally ill, developmentally disabled, or deaf (Romney, 2012; Hubert, 2010). Research indicates that officers who receive special training in crisis intervention are less likely to use force in dealing with mentally ill people (M. Rogers, 2010). However, the budget cuts that are currently causing police agencies to eliminate training programs may hamper progress in equipping officers to deal with special populations (K. Johnson, 2010b).

Patrol officers cooperate with social service agencies in helping individuals and responding to requests for order maintenance. The police must walk a fine line when requiring a person to enter a homeless shelter, obtain medical assistance, or be taken to a mental health unit. Police departments have developed various techniques for dealing with special populations (Morgan, 2013). Memphis, Houston, Atlanta, and Chicago use "crisis intervention teams" composed of selected officers who receive 40 hours of special training and who coordinate their efforts with social service agencies and families (Ellis, 2014; Twyman, 2005). Each community must develop policies so that officers will know when and how they are to intervene when a person has not broken the law but is upsetting residents. Read the New Directions in Criminal Justice Policy box for more information on evidence-based practices for dealing with people suffering from mental illnesses.

must be able to recognize problems and act appropriately without instantly assuming that force is required to control every individual who might appear to be out of control. Officers trained to approach with calmness and quiet speech an individual they suspect might be in a mental health crisis, can often address problems and avoid needlessly tragic outcomes.

Police can also become key actors in other evidence-based practices in the criminal justice system, especially the use of special mental health courts. These courts focus on the treatment and supervision needs of individuals, rather than applying punishments that offer no hope of helping the individual. Several communities have established such specialized courts as a means to avoid, if possible, jailing minor offenders who suffer from mental illness. Police officers can play a role in steering appropriate individuals into mental health courts and then monitoring and helping people who are released into the community under programs of treatment and supervision.

Sources: N. Bonfine, C. Ritter, and M. Munetz, "Police Officer Perceptions of the Impact of Crisis Intervention Team (CIT) Program," *International Journal of Law and Psychiatry* 37 (2014): 341–50; H. Ellis, "Effects of a Crisis Intervention Team (CIT) Training Program upon Police Officers before and after Crisis Intervention Team Training." *Archives of Psychiatric Nursing* 28 (February 2014): 10–16; F. Kara, "Police Interactions with the Mentally Ill: The Role of Procedural Justice," *Canadian Graduate Journal of Sociology and Criminology* 3 (2014): 79–94; V. Rose, "Police Procedures for Apprehending Mentally Ill Persons," Connecticut Government Report 2010-R-0310, July 21, 2010 (www.cga.ct.gov/2010/rpt/2010-R-0310.htm); M. Woody, "The Dutiful Mind: Police Training in Dealing with the Mentally Ill," Connecticut Alliance to Benefit Law Enforcement, 2015 (http://www.cableweb.org/resources/the-dutiful-mind-police-training-in-dealing-with-the-mentally-ill).

DEBATE THE ISSUE

Has society reduced budgets so much for mental health programs and treatment that there is inadequate attention to the needs of individuals, whose problems then confront police officers on patrol? Can police officers, in light of their varied responsibilities, ever have enough training and resources to deal with the problems of the mentally ill? If you were a big-city mayor, would you reduce the police budget (or the budget of another city agency) in order to provide more resources for mental health programs? Alternatively, would you increase the police training budget in order to give added attention to mental health issues in the community? Give two reasons for your choice. What impact could your choice have on the effectiveness of the police department?

Policing in a Multicultural Society

Carrying out the complex tasks of policing efficiently and according to the law is a tough assignment even when the police have the support and cooperation of the public. But policing in a multicultural society like the United States presents further challenges.

In the last half-century, the racial and ethnic composition of the United States has changed. During the mid-twentieth century, many African Americans moved from rural areas of the South to northern cities. In recent years, people from Puerto Rico, Cuba, Mexico, and South America have become the fastest-growing minority groups in many cities. Immigrants from eastern Europe, Russia, the Middle East, and Asia have entered the country in greater numbers than before. Since 1980 the United States has witnessed a huge increase in immigration, rivaling the stream of foreigners that arrived in the early 1900s.

Policing requires trust, understanding, and cooperation between officers and the public. People must be willing to call for help and provide information

CLOSE UP

LIVING UNDER SUSPICION

One of the most invasive discretionary decisions made by police officers is the determination of when to do a warrantless search. As we will see in Chapter 8. there are specific situations in which police officers are authorized to search people and places without seeking approval from a judge in the form of a search warrant. One key situation that interferes with people's privacy and liberty is a stop-and-frisk search. This does not mean that officers are supposed to have complete discretion to simply feel the outer clothing of anyone walking down the street to see if the individual is carrying a weapon, drugs, or evidence of criminal activity. Indeed, the original Supreme Court decision in *Terry v. Ohio* (1968) was quite specific about the circumstances in which such searches could be done on the spot, in order to avoid giving police officers complete freedom to do searches based on hunches or other unjustified grounds. According to the *Terry* decision, "where a police officer observes unusual conduct which leads him to reasonably conclude in light of his experience that criminal activity may be afoot and that the persons with whom he is dealing may be armed and presently dangerous," the officer may stop the individual and conduct a limited search of the outer clothing. Unfortunately, studies in a number of cities indicate that some officers may be more inclined to conclude that "criminal activity may be afoot" when they see African Americans or Latinos, while less likely to reach that conclusion when seeing whites engaging in the same behaviors.

A review of New York City police records showed that its officers conducted 575,000 stop-and-frisk searches in 2009. Whites constitute the largest racial group in the city, more than 40 percent of the city's population in the first decade of the twenty-first century, yet the number of African Americans and Latinos subjected to stop-and-frisk searches was many times more than the number of whites subjected to such searches. During 2009, there were nearly 490,000 stop-and-frisk searches of African Americans and Latinos and only 53,000 stop-and-frisk searches of whites. Yet 1.7 percent of whites were found illegally carrying weapons, versus only 1.1 percent of African Americans. Such findings raise concerns that officers are more likely to look for actual indications of potential criminal behavior before searching whites but more freely search African Americans and Latinos without the proper basis articulated in the *Terry v. Ohio* decision. A sophisticated statistical analysis of New York City stop-and-frisk searches from the late 1990s concluded that "police were more willing to stop minority group members with less reason" (Gelman, Fagan, and Kiss, 2007: 821).

Questions about racially motivated stop-and-frisk searches intensified as the number of stops in New York City increased to 685,724 in 2011 and 88 percent of those people were found to be completely innocent. A white *New York Times* reporter asked his college-age sons if they had ever been stopped by the police as they traveled all over New York City by subway and foot to visit their friends and attend social events. They both said "no." He posed the same question to eight African American students at the city's central community college and he learned that they had been stopped and frisked collectively a total of 92 times. These disparities led to a lawsuit against the city in 2013 in which a police officer testified that he was instructed to stop young black males.

Indicators of racial differences in the rate of discretionary stops and searches by police officers are not limited to large cities. For example, a 2011 study of the Lansing, Michigan, police department found that although Latinos make up only 10 percent of the city's population, they were subjected to 33 percent of the discretionary searches conducted by officers in conjunction with traffic stops.

What do these racial disparities mean for Americans who are members of racial and ethnic minority groups? Can minority citizens avoid feeling as if they are constantly under about wrongdoing. But in a multicultural society, relations between the police and minorities are complicated by stereotypes, cultural variations, and language differences. Most of the newer immigrants come from countries around the world with cultural traditions and laws that differ from those in the United States. American police officers may know little about these traditions, especially if the immigrants they serve cannot communicate easily in English. Moreover, after the September 11 attacks, law enforcement officials may have increased caution and suspicion when encountering people whom they believe, accurately or not, to be Middle Eastern or Muslim. Lack of familiarity, difficulties in communicating, and excessive suspicion can create risks that officers will violate the American value of equal treatment of all people.

Like other Americans who have limited personal experience and familiarity with people from different backgrounds, officers may attribute undesirable traits to members of minority groups (S. L. Miller, Zielaskowski, and Plant, 2012). Historically, many Americans have applied stereotypes to their fellow citizens. These

suspicion if they see, through their own experiences or the experiences of friends and relatives, that they are much more likely than white Americans to be stopped and searched by the police?

In 2007, New York City's number of stop-and-frisk searches of African Americans was equal to more than 21 percent of the African American population of the city. By contrast, the number of such searches directed at whites was equal to less than 3 percent of the white population. How might such figures—and the thousands of experiences that they represent—affect people's views about the police? Are there risks that discretionary decisions that lead to racial disparities will ultimately harm policing by making people distrustful and unwilling to help the police?

There are parallel concerns about the issue of whether some police officers act too quickly in using force against unarmed young men of color. Many critics argue that the Ferguson, Missouri, police shooting and subsequent protests and civil disorder in 2014 demonstrate that if community residents perceive police actions as being overly aggressive and racially motivated, serious harm will be dealt to police–community cooperation. The nation witnessed the same issue arise in April 2015 when mass street protests led to arson and property damage in Baltimore after a young African American man mysteriously died from a broken spine while in police custody.

Although these disparities in the application of police discretion are cause for concern, there is also visible progress toward fair and appropriate treatment. Like many other departments, the Lansing police department pays outside researchers to study their traffic stops and searches each year because the department wants to be educated about its officers' actions in order to conduct additional training and improve supervision, if necessary. In 2010, the Arizona state legislature sought to require officers to ask people about their immigration status. The law raised fears that it would push officers to engage in racial profiling, especially with respect to Latinos. Although the law was put on hold by a court order, police departments moved forward with additional training for their officers about the proper bases for searches and about avoiding accusations of racial profiling. Some observers believe that the additional training is helping to reduce bias and errors in officers' decisions about when a stop is legally justified.

Sources: Al Baker, "Minorities Frisked More but Arrested at Same Rate," *New York Times,* May 12, 2010 (www.nytimes.com); Andrew Gelman, Jeffrey Fagan, and Alex Kiss, "An Analysis of the New York City Police Department's 'Stop-and-Frisk' Policy in the Context of Claims of Racial Bias," *Journal of the American Statistical Association,* 102: 813–23 (2007); Joseph Goldstein, "Stop-and-Frisk Trial Turns to Claim of Arrest Quotas," *New York Times,* March 20, 2013 (www.nytimes.com); Kevin Grasha, "Report Finds LPD Searched Minorities' Cars More Than Whites," *Lansing State Journal,* May 5, 2011 (www.lsj.com); J. J. Hensley, "Arizona Immigration Law: Police Profiling Training Paid Off, Some Say," *Arizona Republic,* April 23, 2011 (www.azcentral.com); Michael Powell, "Former Skeptic Now Embraces Divisive Tactic," *New York Times,* April 9, 2012 (www.nytimes.com).

DEBATE THE ISSUE

Are racial and ethnic disparities in the number of stop-and-frisk searches a cause for concern, or is there no real reason to be bothered, because the rate of arrests for whites from such searches is actually higher than that for African Americans and Latinos—at least in New York City? Should we worry about a brief frisk of the external clothing when such actions may help to reduce crime by deterring criminals from carrying guns and give us greater ability to catch terrorists and other dangerous individuals? List two arguments supporting the position that this is a small intrusion that helps to make society safer. List two opposing arguments that portray these disparities as a matter of serious concern. Where do you stand?

stereotypes may include assumptions that certain people are prone to involvement with drugs or other criminal activities. Treating people according to stereotypes, rather than as individuals, creates tensions that harden negative attitudes.

In the "Inside Today's Controversies" feature in Chapter 3, you saw a white father's perspective on race-based suspicions generating stop-and-frisk searches by the police. As you read the Close Up feature, "Living under Suspicion," consider how this impacts the lives of people who are subjected to searches. Moreover, think about the policy of aggressive stop-and-frisk searches that overwhelmingly affect the liberty of innocent young men of color in apparent violation of the constitutional rights of many of them. What are the benefits and harms of such police practices? Also read A Question of Ethics at the end of the chapter and consider whether there are any options for an officer who objects to a department's stop-and-frisk practices.

Very few officers can speak a language other than English. Often, only large urban departments have officers who speak any of the many languages used by new immigrants. People who speak little English and who report crimes, are arrested, or are victimized may not be understood. Language can be a barrier for the police in responding to calls for help and dealing with organized crime. Languages and cultural diversity make it harder for the FBI or local police to infiltrate the Russian, Vietnamese, and Chinese organized-crime groups now found in East and West Coast cities.

Public opinion surveys have shown that race and ethnicity are key factors shaping attitudes toward the police. As seen in "What Americans Think," questions of confidence in the police differ among racial groups as well as according to whether they live in urban areas. Young, low-income racial-minority men have the most negative attitudes toward the police (S. Walker, Spohn, and DeLeone, 2011). These attitudes may stem from their experiences in encounters with police officers.

Residents of inner-city neighborhoods—the areas that need and want effective policing—often significantly distrust the police; citizens may therefore fail to report crimes and refuse to cooperate with the police. Encounters between officers and members of these communities can be hostile and sometimes lead to public protests or large-scale disorders, as was seen in the events of 2014 in Ferguson, Missouri, an urban area adjacent to St. Louis.

Why do some residents in predominantly minority neighborhoods resent the police? One likely factor is the differential treatment of Americans by police officers that lead Hispanics and African Americans to be disproportionately chosen for searches and other unwanted encounters with police (Rojek, Rosenfeld, and Decker, 2012). Many African Americans perceive themselves as targeted for suspicion when they are engaging in routine activities such as driving their cars or shopping. If both police and citizens view each other with suspicion or hostility, then their encounters will be strained and the potential for conflict will increase.

In addition, according to John DiIulio (1993), the police are also accused of failure to give protection and services to minority neighborhoods and of abusing residents physically or verbally. The police are seen as permissive when an officer treats an offense against a person of the same ethnic group as the offender more lightly than a similar offense in which the offender and victim are members of different groups. The police say that such differences occur because they are working in a hostile environment. The white patrol officer may fear that breaking up a street fight among members of a minority group will provoke the wrath of onlookers, but community residents may in fact view inaction as a sign that the police do not care about their neighborhood. It is said that the police do not work effectively on crimes such as drug sales, gambling, petty theft, and in-group assault, although these are the crimes that are most common in urban neighborhoods and are the ones that create the

WHAT AMERICANS THINK

QUESTION: "Please tell me how much confidence you, yourself, have in the police?" Confidence in Police, by Race and Place of Residence. Figures are percentages saying they have a great deal or quite a lot of confidence in the police.

Confidence in police, by race and place of residence

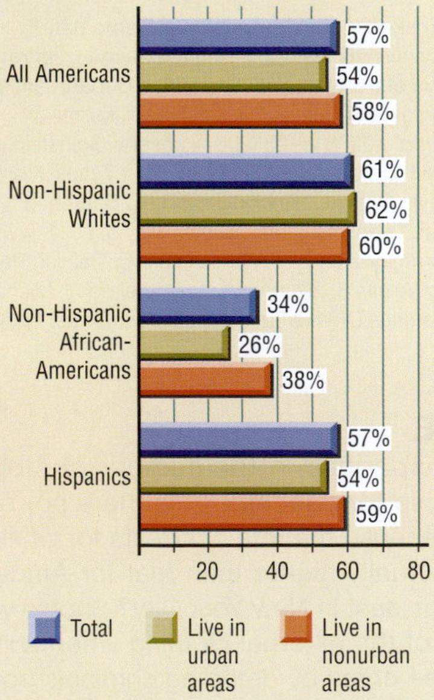

Source: Gallup Poll, 2006–2014 aggregated data. Jeffrey M. Jones, "Urban Blacks in U.S. Have Little Confidence in Police," Gallup Poll, December 8, 2014 (www.gallup.com) Reprinted by permission.

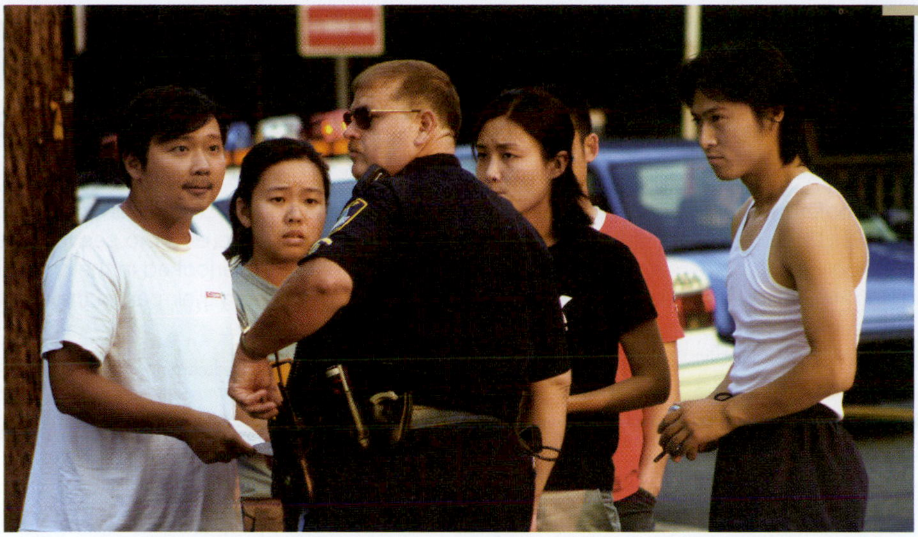

Tom carter/Alamy

In multicultural America, police officers must be sensitive to the perspectives and customs of many groups. They must uphold civil liberties and treat people equally while upholding the law. These responsibilities can be difficult in highly emotional situations in which people are uncooperative. How can police be trained to overcome suspicion and gain cooperation? What do police need to understand in order to accomplish that goal?

greatest insecurity and fear among residents. If both police and citizens view each other with suspicion or hostility, then their encounters will be strained and the potential for conflict will increase. All aspects of officers' responsibilities, including service, order maintenance, and crime control, can suffer when police officers and the communities they serve lack cooperation and trust.

Community Crime Prevention

There is a growing awareness that the police cannot control crime and disorder on their own. Social control requires involvement by all members of the community. When government agencies and neighborhood organizations cooperate, community crime prevention can improve. As one expert says, "Voluntary local efforts must support official action if order is to be preserved within realistic budgetary limits and without sacrificing our civil liberties" (Skogan, 1990: 125). Across the country, community programs to help the police have proliferated. We now look at several such approaches.

Citizen crime-watch groups have been formed in many communities. More than 6 million Americans belong to such groups, which often have direct ties to police departments. One of the challenges for community prevention programs is to include young people as participants rather than treat youths as targets of surveillance and suspicion (J. Forman, 2004).

One of the most well-known programs is Neighborhood Watch, a program that developed in the 1960s and that the National Sheriffs' Association (NSA) adopted as a nationwide initiative in 1972. The NSA provides information and technical assistance for groups that want to start Neighborhood Watch programs in their communities. Reflecting the changing themes of contemporary policing, the NSA's website touts Neighborhood Watch as important for homeland security as well as for crime prevention.

The Crime Stoppers Program is designed to enlist public help in solving crimes. Founded in Albuquerque, New Mexico, in 1975, it has spread across the country. Television and radio stations present the "unsolved crime of the week," and cash rewards are given for information that leads to the conviction of offenders. Although these programs help solve some crimes, the numbers of solved crimes remain small compared with the total number of crimes committed. Read the Doing Your Part feature on the students at Ball State University in Indiana who were recipients of a national award from the Crime Stoppers program in 2014 for their work in investigating unsolved criminal cases.

DOING YOUR PART

STUDENTS EXAMINE UNSOLVED CASES

The Crime Stoppers USA National Training Conference presented its "2014 Best Community Initiative Award" to criminal justice students at Ball State University and the police and community agencies with which they worked. Eighteen students worked individually on unsolved murder cases in order to update reports on these "cold" cases and produce video Public Service Announcements (PSA) for the Indiana Crime Stoppers website. Their objective was to bring these cases back into the public eye with the hope of generating tips or new information that might lead to solving these crimes. Their work included interviewing the families of victims in the effort to see if some aspect of the case might have been overlooked in the original investigation. These students were doing their part in the effort to address problems of crime and justice.

Sources: Kara Berg, "Unsolved Deaths Immersive Learning Project Wins National Award," *Ball State Daily,* September 28, 2014 (www.ballstatedaily.com); "Crime Stoppers of Central Indiana Wins '2014 Best Community Initiative' Award," WISH-TV website, September 17, 2014 (wishtv.com).

In 1991 the federal government initiated the Operation Weed and Seed program as a means to coordinate citizens' and agencies' efforts in community crime prevention and to encourage neighborhood revitalization. The program is administered by the Community Capacity Development Office of the U.S. Department of Justice. The government awards grants to local programs designed to address problems in targeted neighborhoods. Under the "Weed" segment of the program, the local U.S. Attorney's Office works with law enforcement agencies and state prosecutors to crack down on violence, drugs, and gang activity. At the same time, human services agencies work with neighborhood associations in the "Seed" activities designed to clean up neighborhoods, repair homes, encourage small businesses to develop, and institute delinquency-prevention programs for youths. By 2005, Weed and Seed programs existed at 300 sites around the nation. In the Providence, Rhode Island, program, for example, residents of the targeted neighborhood are directly involved in Neighborhood Watch, mentoring programs for youths, and community cleanup and home repair projects.

Successful community-based crime prevention programs typically work with the police and other government agencies to restore order and control crime. Many police chiefs and community leaders work continuously to develop new ways to involve citizens in crime prevention and to increase participation in existing programs (Christensen, 2008). Scholars say that the citizens of a community must take responsibility for maintaining civil and safe social conditions. Experience has shown that "while police might be able to retake a neighborhood from aggressive drug dealers, police could not hold a neighborhood without significant commitment and actual assistance from private citizens" (Kelling and Coles, 1996: 248). Think about what strategies you would suggest for preventing and reducing crime in your home neighborhood as you read "Civic Engagement: Your Role in the System."

CIVIC ENGAGEMENT

YOUR ROLE IN THE SYSTEM

Your local police chief has asked you to lead a citizens' committee to develop effective ways for citizens to communicate with police as part of a "neighborhood policing plan." *Make a list of recommendations for designing such a plan and for facilitating communication.* Then look at the reorganization undertaken by the Dalton, Georgia, Police Department to enhance communication in its Neighborhood Policing Plans.

As the federal budget deficit grows and the federal government shifts funding toward homeland security, state and local governments may face decisions about whether to continue community initiatives such as Operation Weed and Seed. The Pennsylvania Commission on Crime and Delinquency (PCCD), for example, has taken a leading role in facilitating the development and continuation of community-based programs. The PCCD has expanded the Weed and Seed concept to smaller Pennsylvania communities that were not targeted for federal grants. The PCCD also provides funding and technical assistance for other community prevention programs that seek to build coalitions of citizens who will work to improve the quality of life within their neighborhoods (Feinberg, Greenwood, and Osgood, 2004).

A QUESTION OF ETHICS

When testifying in the 2013 federal trial challenging the racial targeting of young men for stops and frisks by the New York City police, one officer presented taped conversations with superior officers in which he was ordered to make more stop-and-frisk stops. His superior specifically said, "The problem was what? Black males. And I told you that at roll call, and I have no problem telling you this: male blacks 14 to 20 [in age]." The officer in question was deeply troubled by these orders, especially because he was Hispanic and had been stopped many times himself when he was off duty. He testified that he was the subject of retaliation when he refused to meet mandated quotas for stops and frisks, and he faced further harassment when he sought to report the situation to the police department's internal affairs investigative office.

Source: Marina Carver, "NYPD Officers Say They Had Stop and Frisk Quotas," CNN.com, March 26, 2013 (www.cnn.com).

CRITICAL THINKING AND ANALYSIS

What, if anything, can an officer do when he or she believes that the police department's policies and practices are improper or, as in this case, impose violations of citizens' constitutional rights? Are there any realistic options for police officers who are supposed to obey orders from superiors? Imagine that you are a fellow police officer and friend of the officer in question, and he seeks advice from you. What advice would you give? Write a memo detailing the actions you would propose and predict the possible consequences of those actions.

✔POINT

25. What "special populations" pose challenges for policing?

26. What factors make policing in a multicultural society difficult?

27. What are the two basic reasons that urban residents sometimes resent the police?

28. How are citizen watch groups and similar programs helpful to the police?

STOP AND ANALYZE: Imagine that you are a police chief who is concerned about police–community relations as well as your officers' approach to dealing with special populations. List three ideas you have for improving your department's performance with respect to these issues.

Summary

1 Describe how policing evolved in the United States

- The police in the United States owe their roots to early nineteenth-century developments in policing in England.
- Like their English counterparts, the American police have limited authority, are under local control, and are organizationally fragmented.
- The three eras of American policing are the political era (1840–1920), the professional model era (1920–1970), and the community policing era (1970–present).

2 Discuss the main types of police agencies

- In the U.S. federal system of government, police agencies are found at the national, state, county, and municipal levels.
- Federal agencies include the FBI, DEA, Secret Service, and sworn officers in dozens of other agencies.
- Most states have a state police force, and sheriff's departments are the primary county-level policing agencies.

3 Analyze the functions of the police

- The functions of the police are order maintenance, law enforcement, and service.
- Police have cultivated an image as crime fighters preoccupied with the law enforcement function.
- The service function is actually the basis for most calls to police departments.

4 Describe how the police are organized

- The police are organized along military lines so that authority and responsibility can be located at appropriate levels.
- Larger police departments have specialized units.

5 Analyze influences on police policy and styles of policing

- Police executives develop policies on how they will allocate their resources according to one of three styles: the watchman, legalistic, or service styles.
- The development of differing styles can be affected by the nature of the community and the political context.
- Suburban middle-class communities often have a service style; the legalistic style emphasizes law enforcement; the watchman style emphasizes order maintenance.

6 Discuss how police officers balance actions, decision making, and discretion

- Discretion is a major factor in police actions and decisions. Patrol officers exercise the greatest amount of discretion.
- The problem of domestic violence illustrates the links between encounters with citizens by police, their exercise of discretion, and the actions they take.

7 Describe the importance of connections between the police and the community

- Police face challenges in dealing with special populations, such as the mentally ill and homeless, who need social services yet often disturb or offend other citizens as they walk the streets.
- Policing in a multicultural society requires an appreciation of the attitudes, customs, and languages of minority group members.
- To be effective, the police must maintain their connection with the community.

Questions for Review

1. What principles borrowed from England still underlie policing in the United States?
2. What are the eras of policing in the United States and what are the characteristics of each?
3. What are the functions of the police?
4. How do communities influence police policy and police styles?
5. How does the problem of domestic violence illustrate basic elements of police action?
6. What problems do officers face in policing a multicultural society?

Key Terms

chain of command (p. 213)
domestic violence (p. 218)
frankpledge (p. 190)
intelligence-led policing (p. 200)
Interpol (p. 205)
law enforcement (p. 210)
legalistic style (p. 216)
order maintenance (p. 208)
patrol units (p. 213)
service (p. 210)
service style (p. 216)
sheriff (p. 193)
slave patrols (p. 192)
U.S. marshals (p. 194)
watch system (p. 191)
watchman style (p. 215)

Checkpoint Answers

1 What three main features of American policing were inherited from England?

✓ Limited authority, local control, organizational fragmentation.

2 What was the frankpledge and how did it work?

✓ A rule requiring groups of ten families to uphold the law and maintain order.

3 What did the Statute of Winchester (1285) establish?

✓ Established a parish constable-watch system. Citizens were required to pursue criminals.

4 What did the Metropolitan Police Act (1829) establish?

✓ Established the first organized police force in London.

5 What were the four mandates of the English police in the nineteenth century?

✓ To prevent crime without the use of repressive force, to manage public order nonviolently, to minimize and reduce conflict between citizens and the police, and to demonstrate efficiency by the absence of crime.

6 What are the major historical periods of American policing?

✓ Political era, professional model era, community policing era.

7 What was the main feature of the political era?

✓ Close ties between the police and local politicians, leading to corruption.

8 **What were the major recommendations of the Progressive reformers?**

✓ The police should be removed from politics; police should be well trained; the law should be enforced equally; technology should be used; merit should be the basis of personnel procedures; the crime-fighting role should be prominent.

9 **What are the main criticisms of the professional model era?**

✓ The professional, crime-fighting role isolated the police from the community. The police should try to solve the problems underlying crime.

10 **What is community policing?**

✓ The police should be close to the community, provide services, and deal with the little problems.

11 **What is the jurisdiction of federal law enforcement agencies?**

✓ Enforce the laws of the federal government.

12 **Why are some law enforcement agencies of the U.S. government located overseas?**

✓ Because of the increase in international criminality in a shrinking world.

13 **What are the functions of most state police agencies?**

✓ All state police agencies have traffic law enforcement responsibilities, and in two-thirds of the states they have general police powers.

14 **Besides law enforcement, what functions do sheriffs perform?**

✓ Operate jails, move prisoners, and provide court bailiffs.

15 **What are the main characteristics of the organization of the police in the United States?**

✓ Local control, fragmentation.

16 **What is the order maintenance function? What are officers expected to do in situations where they must maintain order?**

✓ Police have a broad mandate to prevent behavior that either disturbs or threatens to disturb the peace or involves face-to-face conflict among two or more people. Officers are expected to handle the situation.

17 **How do law enforcement situations compare with order maintenance situations?**

✓ The police in order maintenance situations must first determine if a law has been broken. In law enforcement situations, that fact is already known; thus, officers must only find and apprehend the offender.

18 **What are three characteristics of a bureaucracy?**

✓ A bureaucracy has (1) division of labor, (2) chain of command, and (3) rules and procedures.

19 **What are the five operational units of police departments with sufficient size for specialization?**

✓ Patrol, investigation, traffic, vice, and juvenile.

20 **What are the characteristics of the watchman style of policing?**

✓ Emphasis on order maintenance, extensive use of discretion, and differential treatment of racial and ethnic groups.

21 **What is the key feature of the legalistic style of policing?**

✓ Professionalism and using a single standard of law enforcement throughout the community.

22 **Where are you likely to find the service style of policing?**

✓ Suburban middle-class communities.

23 **Why do patrol officers have so much discretion?**

✓ They deal with citizens, often in private, and are responsible for maintaining order and enforcing laws. Many of these laws are ambiguous and deal with situations in which the participants' conduct is in dispute.

24 **Why have police in the past failed to arrest in domestic violence situations?**

✓ These situations were often viewed as family problems rather than criminal events; police also feared making the situation worse.

25 **What "special populations" pose challenges for policing?**

✓ Runaways and neglected children; people who suffer from homelessness, drug addiction, mental illness, or alcoholism.

26 **What factors make policing in a multicultural society difficult?**

✓ Stereotyping, cultural differences, and language differences.

27 **What are the two basic reasons that urban residents sometimes resent the police?**

✓ Permissive law enforcement and police abuse of power.

28 **How are citizen watch groups and similar programs helpful to the police?**

✓ They assist the police by reporting incidents and providing information.

CHAPTER FEATURES

- **Inside Today's Controversies** The President's Task Force on 21st Century Policing
- **Close Up** The Use of Volunteers in Law Enforcement
- **New Directions in Criminal Justice Policy** Evidence-Based Policing and Patrol
- **Technology and Criminal Justice** Specialized Software, Information Analysis, and Crime Control

CHAPTER 6 POLICE OFFICERS AND LAW ENFORCEMENT OPERATIONS

CHAPTER LEARNING OBJECTIVES

1. Discuss why people become police officers and how they learn to do their jobs
2. Describe the elements of the police officer's "working personality"
3. Analyze factors that affect police response
4. Describe the main functions of police patrol, investigation, and special operations units
5. Analyze patrol strategies that police departments employ

CHAPTER OUTLINE

Emily Paine/Allentown Morning Call/MCT /Landov

On Friday, September 12, 2014, Corporal Byron Dickson, a 38-year-old trooper in the Pennsylvania State Police, was leaving the Blooming Grove state trooper barracks at the end of his workday. Suddenly, shots rang out and he fell with mortal wounds. Trooper Alex Douglass, who was just arriving to begin his shift, came to the fallen officer's aid; he, too, was shot but survived his wounds. Unbeknownst to the troopers, Eric Frein, a survivalist who liked to dress up and pretend that he was a Communist soldier from Cold War–era Eastern Europe, had hidden himself in the woods across from the entrance to the barracks. With the shooting, Frein had carried out his plan to kill a law enforcement officer; he then fled into the woods (D. Barry, 2014).

With the help of other law enforcement agencies, the Pennsylvania State Police organized a manhunt that involved searching many miles of thick woods. Within days, officers working the case had identified Frein as the suspect when they found his vehicle abandoned in a pond two miles away from the site of the shooting. Because of his advance planning and skills as a woodsman, the fugitive eluded capture for many weeks (Southall, 2014). The hundreds of law enforcement officers who participated in the search knew that Frein continued to be armed and dangerous. Moreover, they knew that his goal was to kill police officers. Each police officer was aware that the gunman might be set up as an elusive sniper, hiding out somewhere in the dark woods without any of the officers knowing his exact vantage point. In sum, they all knew they were risking their lives in searching for him, yet they pressed ahead, determined to capture him. After a 48-day search, Frein was arrested by U.S. marshals who spotted him at a small abandoned airport in the Poconos Mountains. Fortunately, no additional law enforcement officers were injured in the long manhunt that resulted in Frein's capture (McGraw and Gabriel, 2014).

What motivates a person to choose a career in policing—an occupation that carries with it the risk of being killed or injured in the course of serving the public? Sadly, police officers' deaths in the line of duty occur with troubling regularity. During 2013, there were 27 law enforcement officers killed in the United States through the felonious actions of lawbreakers, and another 49 died as a result of accidents while on duty (FBI, 2014b). Obviously, police officers face significant potential risks in their jobs, and they never know when they may be called upon to courageously save a life—or put their own lives on the line while protecting society.

In this chapter, we focus on the actual work of the police as they pursue suspects, prevent crimes, and otherwise serve the public. The police must be organized so that patrol efforts can be coordinated, investigations carried out, arrests made, evidence gathered, crimes solved, and violators prosecuted. At the same time, patrol officers must be prepared to maintain order and provide needed services for the citizens in a community. Much of the time, police work may seem quite boring, as officers drive for hours along quiet streets, direct traffic, and respond to complaints about noisy teenagers or illegally parked cars. At any moment, however, grave dangers may arise and officers may be called upon to make quick decisions that will profoundly affect the lives of others as well as their own. Because American society depends so much on police officers for service, order maintenance, and crime control, it is important to understand who these public servants are, and what they do in their jobs every day.

Who Are the Police?

Police officers never know what they might encounter around the next corner as they walk or drive on patrol. What if an armed fugitive surprises officers by opening fire? What if they come upon a ticking bomb? What if they are surrounded and outnumbered by 20 angry gang members? The possibility of such dangerous situations arising leads to questions about the motives for those who choose policing as a career. These questions are important because they help to determine which people will be granted the authority to carry firearms and make discretionary decisions about arrests, searches, and even ending the lives of other human beings by pulling the trigger during stressful, fast-moving, and dangerous scenarios.

Because policing is such an important occupation, society would obviously benefit from recruiting its most thoughtful, athletic, and dedicated citizens as police officers. Happily, many such individuals are attracted to this field. Yet, many other people who would make fine law enforcement officers turn to other occupations, because policing is such a difficult job. The modest salaries, significant job stress, and moments of danger involved in police work can deter individuals from choosing this public service occupation.

If you or someone you know plans a career in law enforcement, ask yourself what aspects of the job make it more appealing than other kinds of work. Some people might want the adventure and excitement of investigating crimes and catching suspects. Others might be drawn to the satisfactions that come from being a public servant. Still others may be attracted to a civil service job with good benefits.

Table 6.1 presents the reasons people give for choosing police work as a career. As you look at the ranking of reasons given by police recruits detailed in Table 6.1, consider that a later survey of the same officers found slightly different results. After they had been on the job for several years, the officers indicated that "job security" had risen to be the top-ranked motivation and "opportunity to help people" dropped below job-related aspects such as benefits, early retirement, and career advancement (M. D. White, Cooper, et al., 2010). How might the officers' motivations at different stages of their careers affect how they interact with citizens and how they do their jobs?

TABLE 6.1 RANKING OF REASONS FOR CHOOSING POLICE WORK AS A CAREER

To what extent do the reasons for choosing police work differ from those that might be given for choosing other careers? What explains the different responses given by men and women? What about differences among racial and ethnic groups?

RANKING OF REASONS	MEN	WOMEN
Opportunity to help people	1	1
Job security	1	3
Job benefits	2	3
Career advancement opportunities	3	2
Early retirement opportunity	3	4
Excitement of the work	4	6
To fight crime	5	5
Good companionship among co-workers	6	9
Profession carries prestige	7	9
Job as stepping stone to better career	9	8
To enforce the laws of society	10	7
To fulfill lifelong dream or aspiration	8	10

RANKING OF REASONS	WHITE	HISPANIC	BLACK
Opportunity to help people	1	1	1
Job security	1	2	2
Job benefits	2	3	3
Career advancement opportunities	4	4	4
Early retirement opportunity	3	6	5
Excitement of the work	5	6	7
To fight crime	6	5	6
Good companionship among co-workers	7	9	13
Profession carries prestige	8	7	10
Job as stepping stone to better career	10	10	8
To enforce the laws of society	11	8	9
To fulfill lifelong dream or aspiration	9	11	12
Ability to work on your own a lot	12	12	11

Source: Anthony J. Raganella and Michael D. White, "Race, Gender, and Motivation for Becoming a Police Officer: Implications for Building a Representative Police Department," *Journal of Criminal Justice* 32(2004): 506, 507.

Recruitment

How can departments recruit well-rounded, dedicated public servants who will represent the diversity of contemporary America? All agencies require recruits to pass physical fitness tests, and they check to see if applicants have criminal records. Agencies increasingly require recruits to undergo psychological evaluations, because each officer will ultimately make important discretionary decisions, including those that may determine life and death in stressful situations (Dantzker, 2011). When agencies cut corners or make mistakes in their evaluation processes, there are concerns that they will hire people who are unsuited to make the life-and-death decisions that sometimes confront police officers. For example, the Cleveland, Ohio, police officer who shot a 12-year-old boy holding a toy gun in 2014 had been discharged earlier, from a suburban police agency, for emotional reactions that cast doubt on his decision-making abilities. Although this information was in his record, the Cleveland police hired him without looking at his complete personnel file from the prior agency (Ferrise, 2014). Similarly, there were criticisms that the Albuquerque, New Mexico, police department let applicants bypass the full range of testing during a period in which administrators were eager to quickly expand the size of the force. However, reports in 2015 indicated that a surprising number of these quickly hired officers were involved in controversial police shootings (Aviv, 2015).

Besides these requirements, what other factors determine who is hired by specific law enforcement agencies? Compensation is one factor that influences which people apply for law enforcement jobs. Some people who might have been outstanding local police officers decline to apply because they seek jobs that have higher salaries. According to the most recent federal government study, the average starting salary was $39,263 for local departments with collective bargaining (i.e., officers represented by unions or police officers' associations) but only $28,376 for departments without collective bargaining (B. A. Reaves, 2010). The foregoing figures are national averages, but salaries in different regions vary significantly. For example, starting salaries for new police officers in Seattle were more than $69,000 in 2015, with pay increases leading to salaries in excess of $90,000 after nine years of service (City of Seattle website, 2015). Obviously, such salaries are markedly higher than those departments that are below the national average. However, high salaries often exist in areas with a high cost of living, thus making the salaries less lucrative than they would appear to be in the eyes of people elsewhere in the country. Traditionally, officers have been able to earn additional money through overtime work, but budget cuts have reduced or eliminated these supplemental opportunities in many departments. Because of limited budgets, rural sheriff's departments, by contrast, may have a more difficult time recruiting a large applicant pool.

Federal agencies and others that provide good compensation and benefits tend to attract larger numbers of applicants. These positions typically require higher levels of education and experience than do many local law enforcement agencies. Starting salaries for U.S. border patrol agents are at least $38,619 per year, while FBI special agents begin at $43,441. As described by the FBI website (FBI, 2014c), agents may actually receive much higher pay if assigned to a city with a high cost of living.

For example, a new agent assigned to Washington, D.C., would make a base salary of $43,441 (GS-10, step 1 on the Law Enforcement Officers' salary table) + locality pay of $7,602 (based on the Washington, D.C., locality adjustment of 17.5 percent) + availability pay of $12,761 (25 percent of base + locality) for a total salary of $63,804 their first year. If the new special agent qualified for the relocation bonus (e.g., moving from Atlanta to Washington, D.C.), they would also receive a one-time payment of approximately $22,000.

Another factor is the educational level of potential recruits. Most local departments require only a high school diploma, but they actually may seek to recruit people with at least some college education. In the largest cities, with populations greater than 500,000, about one-third of departments require at least some college education and a small percentage require either a two-year or a four-year degree (B. A. Reaves, 2010). Some departments will accept years of military service as a replacement for an equal number of years of college education. The percentage of state and local law enforcement agencies that required education beyond high school tripled between 1990 and 2007 and likely will continue to increase over time (B. A. Reaves, 2010). The expansion of criminal justice programs at community colleges and universities throughout the United States has produced increasing numbers of law enforcement officers who have taken college courses in criminology, law, sociology, and psychology. Competitive entry-level positions in the most sought-after agencies, including federal law enforcement agencies, state police departments, and those in the cities and suburbs (which provide the most generous pay and benefits), now often effectively require a college education. Even if state and local departments formally require only a high school diploma, many of them attract enough applicants with college degrees to make it difficult for those with only a high school education to be hired. The expansion of college criminal justice programs has broadened opportunities to take college courses and increased the number of applicants with degrees in criminal justice and related fields. College-educated officers frequently seek advanced degrees by taking evening and Internet-based programs.

Debate continues about whether college-educated officers perform better than those who lack advanced education (Roberg and Bonn, 2004). The idea that college-educated officers would be better decision makers and make more-effective officers helped to spur the creation of the federal Police Corps program (Gest, 2001). Although some researchers found that a college education makes little difference for police performance, other scholars concluded that it is associated with fewer problems relating to the improper use of force and citizens' complaints, and that it improves report writing and other aspects of performance (Rydberg and Terrill, 2010; Paoline and Terrill, 2007; Lersch and Kunzman, 2001). Obviously, education alone does not determine performance; departmental training, supervision, and other factors also shape it.

In recent years, policing agencies seeking additional personnel have taken advantage of the budget cuts in other departments by hiring experienced officers who had lost their jobs. For example, in 2011 the Santa Cruz County sheriff's office hired four officers from the San Jose city police department, where 100 officers had been laid off in a budget cut (Baxter, 2011). Such lateral hiring reduces opportunities for inexperienced applicants to be hired as new recruits. Police departments throughout the country will be challenged to recruit and retain officers during the contemporary era of budget difficulties (J. M. Wilson, 2010).

The Changing Profile of the Police

For most of the nation's history, almost all police officers were white men. Today, women and minorities represent a growing percentage of officers within police departments in many areas (see Figure 6.1). There are several reasons for this. In 1968, the National Advisory Commission on Civil Disorders found that tense relationships between the police and minority group residents in inner-city neighborhoods contributed to the ghetto riots of the 1960s. Until the 1970s, many police departments rarely hired African Americans, Latinos, and other minority group members; women were also largely

FIGURE 6.1 **THE CHANGING PROFILE OF THE AMERICAN POLICE OFFICER**

Today about 1 in 10 local officers is female and 1 in 4 belongs to a racial or ethnic minority.

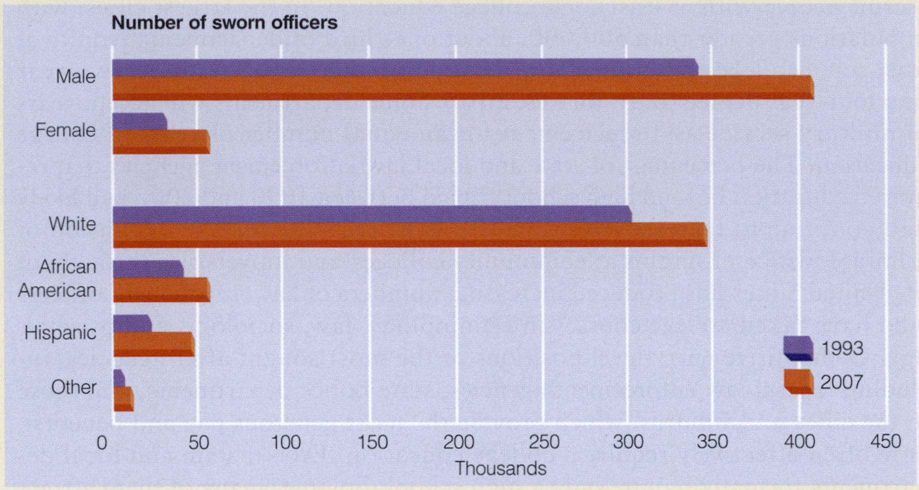

Sources: Brian A. Reaves, *Local Police Departments, 1993* (Washington, DC: Bureau of Justice Statistics, 1996); Brian A. Reaves, *Local Police Departments, 2007* (Washington, DC: Bureau of Justice Statistics, 2010).

excluded in the hiring process. Eventually, the Equal Employment Opportunity Act of 1972 barred state and local governments from discriminating in their hiring practices. Pressured by state and federal agencies as well as by lawsuits, most city police forces have mounted campaigns to recruit more minority and female officers (Lasley et al., 2011). Since the 1970s the percentage of minority group members and women has doubled. Approximately 25 percent of local police officers nationwide belong to minority groups. The percentage is even larger—40 percent—in police departments in cities with populations greater than 500,000 (B. A. Reaves, 2010).

Issues about the lack of diversity in police departments remain, especially in smaller cities. Stark examples arose in cities with two of the most controversial shootings of unarmed African Americans by white police officers in 2014 and 2015—Ferguson, Missouri, and North Charleston, South Carolina, cities in which African Americans represent the largest racial group among residents. In Ferguson, the city's population is only 29 percent white, but the police force is 94 percent white (Firozi, 2014a). Similarly, North Charleston's police department is 80 percent white in a city where only 37 percent of the residents are white (McCormack, 2015). Many critics believe that police departments will be more responsive to community needs and less likely to regularly engage in biased actions when the officer corps reflects the diversity of the community.

In those cities where recruitment has changed the composition of police forces, the advancement of diversity reflects the American value of equal opportunity. Although the United States has a long history of racial and gender discrimination, such actions clash with the Constitution's equal protection clause. In addition to promoting equality, the expansion of employment opportunities to additional groups may provide significant benefits for law enforcement officials. If people in neighborhoods composed largely of members from a specific ethnic or racial group view the police as "outsiders" who are different and hostile, developing the community cooperation needed to prevent and investigate crimes can be difficult. When a force employs police officers from all demographic groups, the police gain legitimacy because they are seen as reflecting the interests of all people and there may be reductions in race-based disparities affecting who is stopped, searched, or arrested (Cochran and Warren, 2012; R. A. Brown and Frank, 2006). Further, the officers may gain concrete benefits in communication and cooperation.

CHIP EAST/Reuters/Landov

The police are no longer exclusively made up of white males. Women and minorities now represent an increasing portion of the force, especially in urban areas. Are women and minority group members visible among the police officers that you see where you live?

Unfortunately, many of the minority and female officers who served as trailblazers to desegregate departments faced hostility and harassment from their colleagues as they attempted to prove themselves. Many of these courageous men and women also faced disrespect and hostility from citizens who did not believe that these nontraditional officers could perform effectively. Although the employment discrimination lawsuits that arise periodically indicate that some officers believe racial and gender discrimination still exists, especially with respect to promotions, female and minority officers have become well accepted as capable and valuable law enforcement professionals throughout the country.

Minority Police Officers

Before the 1970s, many police departments did not hire nonwhites. As this practice declined, the makeup of police departments changed, especially in large cities. The fact that minority officers now constitute 40 percent of the officers in the nation's largest cities represents a dramatic change in staff composition over the past two decades. In the most recent federal study, African Americans composed 12 percent of officers in local police departments. Latino officers constituted more than 10 percent of officers and Asian, Pacific Islander, Native American, and multiracial officers were an additional 3 percent of local police forces nationally. For cities with populations in excess of 1 million residents, 23 percent of officers were Latino and nearly 18 percent were African American (B. A. Reaves, 2010). In light of the growing population of Latinos in many regions, some police departments are showing greater interest in recruiting bilingual Latino officers. For example, in 2011 the Charlotte, North Carolina, police department sent a team of recruiters to Puerto Rico in an attempt to recruit bilingual officers (Ordonez, 2011). Such efforts can be a source of controversy, especially in areas burdened by unemployment, as local people complain that the police should recruit bilingual people locally as well as train officers to speak Spanish or other needed languages to provide service to the newcomers within the Latino community and other ethnic-group members who may not be fluent in English (Ordonez, 2011).

As the population and political power shift toward minorities in some American cities, the composition of their police forces reflects this change.

Three-quarters of Detroit's population is now African American, as is about 63 percent of the city's police officers. In El Paso and San Antonio, Texas, which have large Hispanic populations, 72 percent and 42 percent of those police departments are Hispanic, respectively. The extent to which the police reflect the racial composition of a city is believed to affect police–community relations and thus the quality of law enforcement. For example, the presence of an African American police chief can reduce the rise in distrust of police that can follow a controversial police shooting (E. Sharp and Johnson, 2009).

Women on the Force

Women have been police officers since 1905, when Lola Baldwin became an officer in Portland, Oregon. Prior to that time, many cities had "police matrons" to assist in handling women and children in jails, but they did not have the power to arrest or engage in investigative and patrol activities (Horne, 2006). After Baldwin became the trailblazing first officer, the number of women officers remained small for most of the twentieth century because of the belief that policing was "men's work." This attitude changed as the result of federal and state laws against employment discrimination as well as court decisions enforcing those laws. Court decisions opened up police work for women by prohibiting job assignments by gender; changing minimum height, weight, and physical fitness requirements; and insisting that departments develop job classification and promotion criteria that were nondiscriminatory (*Blake v. Los Angeles,* 1979; *Griggs v. Duke Power Company,* 1971).

The percentage of female officers rose from 1.5 percent of local police officers in 1970 to nearly 12 percent (Hickman and Reaves, 2006; B. A. Reaves, 2010). Interestingly, the larger the department, the higher the proportion of women who are sworn officers. In cities of more than 1 million inhabitants, women make up nearly 18 percent of officers, but women make up less than 8 percent of officers, on average, in cities with fewer than 10,000 residents (B. A. Reaves, 2010). In large police agencies, women hold less than 10 percent of the supervisory positions and only 7 percent of the top command spots (ranks of captain and higher) are held by women (Horne, 2006).

Although some male police officers still question whether women can handle dangerous situations and physical confrontations, most policewomen have easily met the expectations of their superiors. Studies done by the Police Foundation and other researchers have found that, in general, male and female officers perform in similar ways. Alissa Worden's research (1993) found few differences in the ways male and female officers viewed "their role, their clientele, or their departments." Research has also found that most citizens have positive things to say about the work of policewomen. Some researchers believe that women have generally superior performance in avoiding excessive use of force and when interviewing crime victims, especially in cases of sexual assault and domestic violence (Prussel and Lonsway, 2001). Rape victims may also specifically request to be interviewed by a female officer, so gender diversity on a police force may be valuable for investigating specific types of crimes or dealing with specific victims and witnesses (Riccucci, Van Ryzin, and Lavena, 2014; Jordan, 2002).

Despite these findings, women can still have trouble breaking into police work and being recognized equally for promotion (C. Barrett, Bergman, and Thompson, 2014; Crooke, 2013). Cultural expectations of women often conflict with ideas about the proper behavior of officers (Morash and Haarr, 2012). Many people do not think women are tough enough to confront dangerous suspects. Especially with regard to patrol duty, questions like the following often come up:

- Can women handle situations that involve force and violence?
- What changes must be made in training and equipment in order to accommodate women?
- Should women and men have equal opportunities for promotion?
- Does assigning men and women as patrol partners tend to create tension with their spouses?

As these questions reveal, women must work hard to overcome resistance from their fellow officers and citizens in the community. In particular, policewomen encounter resistance when they assert their authority; they must often endure sexist remarks and more-troubling forms of sexual harassment. Initially, many male officers were upset by the entry of women into what they viewed as a male world. They complained that if their patrol partner was a woman, they could not be sure of her ability to provide necessary physical help in times of danger. The challenges for female officers from ethnic minority groups may be even more difficult if they perceive others as doubting their qualifications and ability based on their race as well as their gender (Dodge and Pogrebin, 2001).

According to Susan Martin, the statistics on women in policing provide both "good news and bad news . . . because the steady numerical and proportional gains [are counterbalanced] by the concentrat[ion] of women at the bottom of the police hierarchy" (S. E. Martin, 2005: 352). In a few cities, such as Atlanta, Boston, Detroit, and Portland, Oregon, a small number of women have risen to the top ranks of police departments. Elsewhere, employment discrimination lawsuits have helped open promotion opportunities for women. In many other departments, however, few women have been promoted to supervisory jobs. Identifying and combating remaining barriers to the recruitment, retention, and promotion of female officers can be challenging, especially if the responsibility falls solely to male administrators (D. Kurtz, 2012; S. Walker and Turner, 1992).

The role of women in police work will undoubtedly evolve along with changes in the nature of policing, in cultural values, and in the organization of law enforcement. As communities become accustomed to women on patrol, female officers will find it increasingly easier to gain citizen cooperation.

Training

The performance of the police is not based solely on the types of people recruited; it is also shaped by their training (Conti, 2011). There are several models for preservice training. Depending on the agency in which they will serve, new federal law enforcement officers attend training at one of the Federal Law Enforcement Training Centers (FLETC), with the primary facility located in Glynco, Georgia. The FBI and DEA train their new agents at their training academies on a Marine Corps base in Quantico, Virginia. In this model, college graduates are hired based on characteristics and qualifications and enrolled in a training program run by their employing agency. Police departments in large cities often use a similar approach in running their own police academies to train newly hired officers.

An alternative approach requires candidates for law enforcement positions to pay their own way through a police academy program, often held at a community college or university. After passing the police academy program, these individuals can then seek employment as police officers. The state of New York uses a variation of this approach, in which people can enroll at their own expense in the Pre-Employment Police Basic Training Course offered at specific community colleges that work closely with nearby police agencies. Unlike police academy programs in some other states, the New York approach grants academic college credit for those who successfully complete the program. This preliminary education is referred to as providing "pre-credentialing" for potential law enforcement officers and thereby eases the recruitment and training burdens on individual police agencies. Program graduates can seek employment with New York law enforcement agencies. If hired, they must complete the second segment of basic training that is run by their employing agency (New York Division of Criminal Justice Services, 2013).

Police training programs range from two-week sessions that stress the handling of weapons, to academic four-month programs followed by fieldwork. Recruits hear lectures on social relations, learn foreign-language phrases, and study emergency medical treatment. Recruits need formal training in order to gain an understanding of legal rules, weapons use, and other aspects of the job. However, the police officer's job also demands social skills that cannot be learned from a lecture or a book. Training programs begin the process of giving recruits the outlook, values, and orientation of police officers (Chappell and Lanza-Kaduce, 2010). However, much of the most important training of police officers takes place during a probationary period when new officers work with and learn from experienced officers. When new officers finish their classroom training and arrive for their first day of patrol duty, experienced officers may tell them, "Now, I want you to forget all that stuff you learned at the academy. You really learn your job on the streets."

socialization
The process by which the rules, symbols, and values of a group or subculture are learned by its members.

subculture
The symbols, beliefs, and values shared by members of a subgroup of the larger society.

The process of **socialization**—in which members learn the symbols, beliefs, and values of a group or **subculture**—includes learning the informal rather than the rule-book ways of law enforcement. New officers must learn how to look "productive," how to take shortcuts in filling out forms, how to keep themselves safe in dangerous situations, how to analyze conflicts so as to maintain order, as well as absorb a host of other bits of wisdom, norms, and folklore that define the subculture of a particular department. Recruits learn that loyalty to other officers, esprit de corps, and respect for police authority are highly valued.

In police work, the success of the group depends on the cooperation of its members. All patrol officers operate under direct supervision, and their performance is measured by their contribution to the group's work. Besides supervisors, the officers' colleagues also evaluate and influence them. Officers within a department may develop strong, shared views on the best way to "handle" various situations.

How officers use their personal skills and judgment can mean the difference between defusing a conflict or making it worse so that it endangers citizens and other officers. Thus new recruits must learn the ways of the world from the other officers.

✔POINT
1. What are the main requirements for becoming a police officer?
2. How has the profile of American police officers changed?
3. What type of training do police recruits need?
4. Where does socialization to police work take place?

STOP AND ANALYZE: Why might it be important for police department personnel to reflect the racial and ethnic composition of the community that they serve? List three potential benefits of a diverse police force.

(Answers are at the end of the chapter.)

The Star-Ledger/John Munson/The Image Works

Police officers receive formal training in classroom settings but much of their most important training occurs during the first months of patrol. The "rookies" work with senior officers and are socialized into the police subculture. Are there any risks created by this method of training that may undercut a police chief's expectations about how police officers should perform?

The Police Subculture

A subculture is made up of the symbols, beliefs, values, and attitudes shared by members of a subgroup within the larger society. The subculture of the police helps define the "cop's world" and each officer's role in it. Like the subculture of any occupational group that sees itself as distinctive, police develop shared values that affect their view of human behavior and their role in society. For example, research indicates that officers' use of coercive methods, such as physical force, is associated with alignment between those officers' attitudes and the elements of the police subculture (Terrill, Paoline, and Manning, 2003).

The recruit learns the norms and values of the police subculture through a process of socialization (Oberfield, 2012). This begins at the training academy but really takes hold on the job through the new recruit's interactions with experienced officers. The characteristics of a subculture are not static: They change as new members join the group and as the surrounding environment changes. For example, the composition of the police has changed dramatically during the past 30 years in terms of race, gender, and education. We should thus expect that these "new" officers will bring different attitudes and cultural values to the police subculture (S. Walker, 1999).

Four issues are key to understanding the police subculture: the concept of the "working personality," the role of police morality, the isolation of the police, and the stressful nature of much police work.

The Working Personality

Social scientists have demonstrated that there is a relationship between one's occupational environment and the way one interprets events. The police subculture produces a **working personality**—that is, a set of emotional and behavioral characteristics developed by members of an occupational group in response to the work situation and environmental influences. The working personality of the police thus influences the way officers view and interpret their occupational world. Two elements of police work define this working personality: (1) the threat of danger and (2) the need to establish and maintain one's authority (Skolnick, 1966: 44).

working personality
A set of emotional and behavioral characteristics developed by a member of an occupational group in response to the work situation and environmental influences.

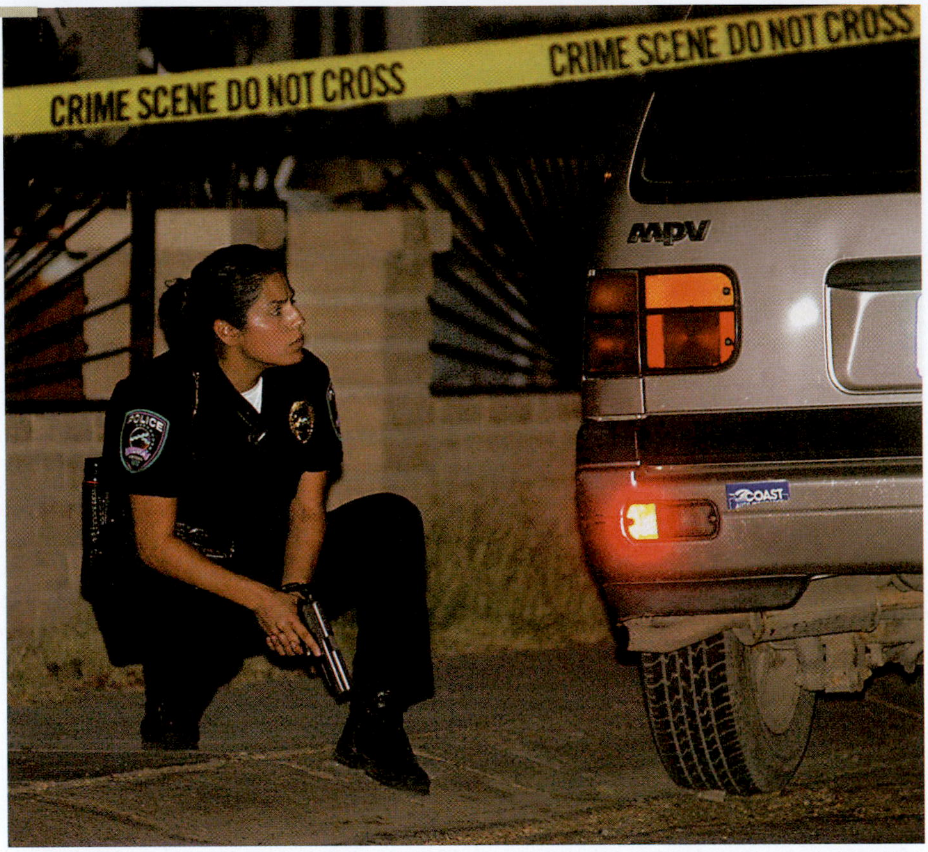

AP Images/Yuma Sun, Alfred Hernandex

Although many officers never fire their guns throughout their entire careers, every day on the job brings the potential for sudden danger. Do the danger and stress police officers face create a risk that they will overreact when citizens fail to cooperate with their requests and instructions?

Danger

Because they often face dangerous situations, officers are keenly aware of clues in people's behavior or in specific situations that indicate that violence and lawbreaking are imminent. As they drive the streets, they notice things that seem amiss—a broken window, a person hiding something under a coat—anything that looks suspicious. As sworn officers, they are never off duty. People who know that they are officers will call on them for help at any time, day or night.

Throughout the socialization process, experienced officers warn recruits to be suspicious and cautious. Rookies are told about officers who were killed while trying to settle a family squabble or writing a traffic ticket. The message is clear: Even minor offenses can escalate into extreme danger. Constantly pressured to recognize signs of crime and be alert to potential violence, officers may become suspicious of everyone, everywhere. Thus, police officers maintain a constant state of "high alert," always on the lookout and never letting down their guard.

Being surrounded by risks creates tension in officers' lives. They may feel constantly on edge and worried about possible attack. This concern with danger can also affect their interactions with citizens and suspects. Citizens who come into contact with them may perceive their caution and suspicion as hostility, and officers' evident suspicion may generate angry or uncooperative reactions from suspects. As a result, on-the-street interrogations and arrests may lead to confrontations.

Authority

The second aspect of the working personality is the need to exert authority. Unlike many professionals, such as doctors, psychiatrists, and lawyers—whose clients recognize and defer to their authority—police officers must establish authority through their actions. Although the police uniform, badge, gun, and nightstick are symbols of position and power, the officer's demeanor and behavior are what determine whether people will defer to him or her.

Victims are glad to see the police when they are performing their law enforcement function, but the order maintenance function puts pressure on officers' authority. If they try too hard to exert authority in the face of hostile reactions, officers may cross the line and use excessive force. For example, when sent to investigate a report of a fight, drunken neighbor, or domestic quarrel, they usually do not find a cooperative complainant. Instead, they must contend not only with the perpetrators but also with onlookers who might escalate the conflict. In such circumstances the officers must "handle the situation" by asserting authority without getting emotionally involved. Even when citizens challenge the conduct of police and their right to enforce the law, they expect the police to react in a detached or neutral manner. For officers who feel burdened with the twin pressures of danger and authority, this may not be easy. Thus, in the daily work of policing, the rules and procedures taught at the academy may affect officers' actions less than does the need to preserve and exert authority in the face of potential danger.

At times, officers must give orders to people with higher status. Professionals, businesspeople, and others sometimes respond to the officer not as a person working for the benefit of the community but as a public servant whom they do not respect. Poor people may also challenge officers' authority when, for example, they are angry about a situation or believe officers are targeting them unfairly. Police officers present themselves in the best light to the public when they perform their jobs in ways that demonstrate a commitment to fair treatment for everyone (Tyler and Wakslak, 2004). In stressful, conflict-laden situations, this may be difficult to do.

Researchers have studied expressions of disrespect by officers toward members of the public and vice versa (Reisig, McCluskey, et al., 2004). One finding indicates that police officers' own expressions of disrespect in encounters with citizens, such as name-calling and other kinds of derogatory statements, occur most often when those citizens had already shown disrespect to the officers (Mastrofski, Reisig, and McCluskey, 2002). Thus, police officers can help to influence the nature of their interactions with citizens through their own professional behavior (Braga, Winship, et al., 2014).

In sum, working personality and occupational environment are closely linked and constantly affect the daily work of the police. Procedural rules and the structure of policing come second to the need to exert authority in the face of potential danger in many contexts in which citizens are angry, disrespectful, or uncooperative.

Police Morality

In his field observations of Los Angeles patrol officers, Steve Herbert found a high sense of morality in the law enforcement subculture. He believes that three aspects of modern policing create dilemmas that their morality helps officers overcome. These dilemmas include (1) the contradiction between the goal of preventing crime and the officers' inability to do so, (2) the fact that officers must use their discretion to "handle" situations in ways that do not strictly follow procedures, and (3) "the fact that they invariably act against at least one citizen's interest, often with recourse to coercive force that can maim or kill" (Herbert, 1996: 799).

Herbert believes that justifying their actions in moral terms, such as upholding the law, protecting society, and chasing "bad guys," helps officers lessen the dilemmas of their work. Thus use of force may be condoned as necessary

WHAT AMERICANS THINK

QUESTION: "Please tell me how you would rate the honesty and ethical standards of people in these different fields—very high, high, average, low, or very low. Policemen?"

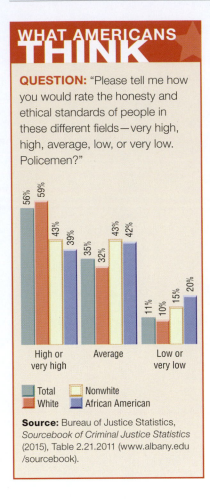

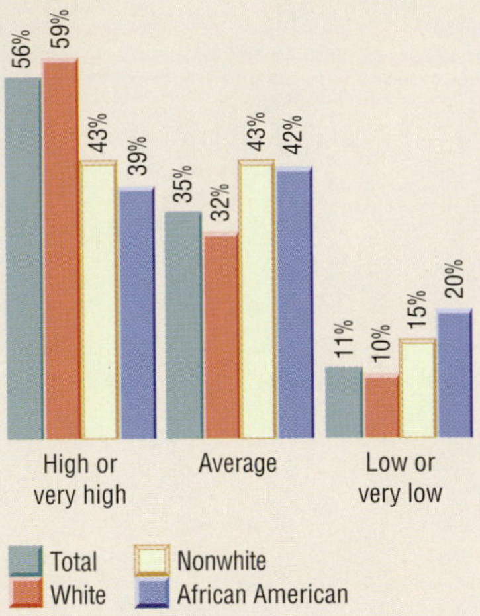

Source: Bureau of Justice Statistics, *Sourcebook of Criminal Justice Statistics* (2015), Table 2.21.2011 (www.albany.edu/sourcebook).

for "ridding evil from otherwise peaceable streets." It is the price we pay to cleanse society of the "punks," "crazies," and "terrorists." But police morality can also be applauded: Officers work long hours and are genuinely motivated to help people and to improve their lives, often placing themselves at risk. Nonetheless, to the extent that police morality crudely categorizes individuals and justifies insensitive treatment of some community members, it contributes to police–citizen tensions.

Police Isolation

Police officers' suspicion of and isolation from the public may increase when they believe that the public is hostile to them. Many officers feel that people regard them with suspicion, in part because they have the authority to use force to gain compliance. Some research scholars argue that this attitude increases officers' desire to use force on citizens (Regoli, Crank, and Culbertson, 1987). Public opinion polls have found that a majority of people have a high opinion of the police; however, as shown in "What Americans Think," various groups of people have different opinions regarding police officers' ethical standards (Y. Wu, 2014). Research shows that young people in high-crime neighborhoods may develop negative attitudes based on their own experiences in being watched and questioned by the police (P. J. Carr, Napolitano, and Keating, 2007). In the most recent version of the poll, for which complete results were not available, the percentage of nonwhites who rated police officers' honesty and ethical standards as "high" or "very high" dropped 20 points to 23 percent in 2014 (Jones, 2014). Many observers fear that several highly publicized deaths of unarmed African American men at the hands of police officers in 2014 contributed to this sudden drop in confidence in the police. The deaths, including that of Michael Brown in Ferguson, Missouri, described in the beginning of Chapter 5, contributed to President Obama's decision to form a national task force to make recommendations on how to strengthen trust between police and communities. As you read about the task force in the Inside Today's Controversies feature, bear in mind that these issues remain deeply troubling and inflamed people in various cities as incidents continued in 2015 in Baltimore and North Charleston, South Carolina.

Police officers' isolation from the public is made worse by the fact that many officers interact with the public mainly in moments of conflict, emotion, and crisis. Victims of crimes and accidents are often too hurt or distraught to thank the police. Citizens who are told to stop some activity when the police are trying to keep order may become angry at the officers. Even something as minor as telling someone to turn down the volume on a stereo can turn the police into the "bad guys" in the eyes of people who believe that the officers' authority limits citizens' entitlement to personal freedom. Ironically, these problems may be at their worst in poor neighborhoods where effective policing is needed most. There, pervasive mistrust of the police may keep citizens from reporting crimes and cooperating with investigations.

Because they believe that the public is hostile to them and that the nature of their work makes the situation worse, the police tend to separate themselves from the public and to form strong in-group ties. The police culture also encourages the bonding that often occurs among people who deal with violence.

One result of the demands placed on the police is that officers often cannot separate their job from other aspects of their lives. From the time they obtain badges and guns, they must always carry these symbols of the position—the tools of the trade—and be prepared to use them. Their obligation to remain vigilant, even when off duty, and to work at odd hours, reinforces the values shared with other officers. Strengthening this bond is officers' tendency to socialize mainly with their families and other officers; indeed, they may have little social contact with people other than police officers. Further, their contacts with citizens can reinforce their perceptions that members of the public view them narrowly as police officers and not as neighbors, friends, and fellow community members. Wherever they go, the police are recognized by people who want to "talk shop"; others harangue them about what is wrong with police service. These incidents can also contribute to isolation.

Job Stress

In addition to isolation, stress often results from the work environment and subculture of the police (Dabney, Copes, Tewksbury, et al., 2013; Schaible and Gecas, 2010; Noblet, Rodwell, and Allisey, 2009). Stemming from the elements of danger and authority, this stress can affect not only the way officers treat the citizens they encounter but also the officer's own health (G. Anderson, Litzenberger, and Plecas, 2002). Stress can also affect how officers interact with one another (Haarr and Morash, 1999). Researchers have found that work environment, work–family conflict, and individual coping mechanisms are the most significant predictors of stress for individual officers (Zhao, He, Loverich, et al., 2003).

Always on alert, police sometimes face grave danger and yet feel unappreciated by a public they perceive to be hostile. Thus, that their physical and mental health suffers at times comes as no surprise. In fact, police officers, like military personnel and firefighters, are regularly listed as having one of the most stressful occupations (McKendrick, 2013). The effects of stress are compounded by the long hours many officers work, including double shifts that deprive them of sleep and make them work under conditions of severe fatigue (Vila and Kenney, 2002). The stress of police work may help explain why officer suicide poses a problem for some law enforcement agencies (Hackett and Violanti, 2003). However, there are debates among researchers about whether police officers' suicide rates are actually higher than those of other individuals who are similarly affected by factors such as marital problems and alcohol abuse, which can be associated with higher rates of suicide (Goode, 2002).

Psychologists have identified four kinds of stress to which officers are subjected, and the factors that cause each (Cullen et al., 1985):

1. *External stress.* This is produced by real threats and dangers, such as the need to enter a dark and unfamiliar building, to respond to "man with a gun" alarms, and to chase lawbreakers at high speeds.
2. *Organizational stress.* This is produced by the nature of work in a paramilitary structure: constant adjustment to changing schedules, irregular work hours, and detailed rules and procedures.
3. *Personal stress.* This can be caused by an officer's racial or gender status among peers, which can create problems in getting along with other officers and adjusting to group values that differ from one's own. Social isolation and perceptions of bias also contribute to personal stress.
4. *Operational stress.* This reflects the total effect of dealing with thieves, derelicts, and the mentally ill; being lied to so often that all citizens become suspect; being required to face danger to protect a public that seems hostile; and always knowing that one may be held legally liable for one's actions.

Some departments now have stress-prevention, group-counseling, liability insurance, and family-involvement programs.

As we have seen, police officers face special pressures that can affect their interactions with the public and even harm their physical and mental health.

INSIDE TODAY'S CONTROVERSIES

THE PRESIDENT'S TASK FORCE ON 21ST-CENTURY POLICING

During 2014, Americans witnessed widespread public protests, including civil disorder, after grand juries declined to bring criminal charges against police officers in Missouri and New York whose actions caused the deaths of unarmed African American men. President Obama appealed for calm and consulted with advisers about what, if anything, could be done to address the controversies. In December 2014, the president announced the creation of the "Task Force on 21st Century Policing." The members of the task force were asked to gather information and ideas in order to "strengthen community policing and strengthen the trust among law enforcement officers and the communities they serve." The task force would study problems and provide a report with recommendations for improvement.

The task force had eleven appointed members, including co-chairs Charles Ramsey, the Commissioner of the Philadelphia Police Department, and Laurie Robinson, a criminal justice professor and former U.S. Assistant Attorney General responsible for providing federal advice and assistance to police departments. The other commission members included police chiefs, the leader of a police officers' association, executives from non-profit organizations, and civil rights attorneys.

The group was instructed to hold "listening sessions" in various cities in order to "hear testimony, including proposed recommendations for consideration, from invited witnesses and also receive comments and questions from the public." The process was intended to occur at a rapid pace so that the task force would produce a report less than three months after its formation.

At a two-day session in Cincinnati in January 2015, the task force members heard from researchers, police union leaders, prosecutors, police chiefs, and activist citizens. Testimony from police emphasized how infrequently police officers use force with fatal results. Community activists stressed how issues of police–community relations represented long-standing problems and were not a new development. Researchers underlined the need for greater training for police on how to de-escalate situations to avoid the use of violence. There was also discussion of using body cameras and other means to oversee police actions. A prosecutor advocated greater oversight by the U.S. Department of Justice, such as independent audits of police departments rather than waiting to investigate *after* there was a complaint about a troubling series of incidents. One police official raised the important question of who would provide the

How would you react to the prospect of facing danger and being on the lookout for crime at every moment, even when you were not actually working? It seems understandable that police officers become a close-knit group, yet their isolation from society may decrease their understanding of other people. It may also strengthen their belief that the public is ungrateful and hostile. Are there risks that this belief will increase the probability that officers' actions toward members of the public may be unnecessarily hostile, gruff, or forceful?

In sum, the effects of the police subculture on the behavior of officers are stronger in situations that produce conflict between the police and society. To endure their work, the police find they must relate to the public in ways that protect their own self-esteem. If the police view the public as hostile and see police work as adding to that hostility, they will isolate themselves by developing strong values and norms to which all officers conform. In the rest of this chapter, we examine the contexts in which police officers work. Bear in mind how the elements of the police subculture could impact officers' behavior in these contexts.

✔POINT

5. What are the two key elements of police work that define the officer's working personality?

6. What are the four types of stress felt by the police?

STOP AND ANALYZE: As you have read, several factors may contribute to police officers' feelings that they are separate from the other citizens in the community. If you were a police chief, what three steps would you take to encourage your officers to become acquainted with and feel connected to other residents of their community?

funds for additional training and equipment, such as body cameras, in an era in which many police departments were facing budget cuts.

The group's preliminary report was issued in March 2015. The report made 63 recommendations including independent investigations of cases in which people died as the result of a police officer's use of force. The report also suggested increased efforts to diversify police forces so that they reflect the demographic makeup of the communities that they serve. In addition, the report called for the elimination of department policies that require officers to conduct a specific number of stops or write a certain number tickets on each shift. Moreover, the group recommended that, in the absence of specific grounds for suspicion, officers seek individuals' consent before conducting searches and inform people that they have a right to refuse to be searched when there is no search warrant or probable cause to believe that a crime has been committed. It remains to be seen whether these recommendations will move forward as actual policies and practices adopted by local police departments.

Sources: Lisa Cornwell, "President's Task Force on Policing Looks at Use of Force," *Springfield* (OH) *News-Sun*, January 30, 2015 (www.springfieldnewssun.com); Julie Hirschfeld Davis, "Obama Calls for Changes in Policing After Task Force Report," *New York Times*, March 2, 2015 (www.nytimes.com); Chelsey Levingston, "Cincinnati's Community Policing Efforts Attract President's Task Force," *Springfield* (OH) *News-Sun*, January 31, 2015; (www.springfieldnewssun.com); Office of the Press Secretary, The White House, "Press Release: Fact Sheet: Task Force on 21st Century Policing," White House website, December 18, 2014 (www.whitehouse.gov).

CRITICAL THINKING AND ANALYSIS

Police agencies and actions are primarily local matters. The decentralized nature of American policing means that the culture, organization, training, and practices of police vary from city to city and town to town. Can the president of the United States and a national task force influence policing throughout the country? Will the task force's recommendations merely serve to call attention to issues and ideas? Does the federal government need to offer money to local police departments—with strings attached—in order to induce them to adopt certain practices, training programs, and methods of supervision? Write a memo making two arguments about potential beneficial impacts from the task force recommendations and two arguments with reasons that the recommendations may have little or no impact.

Police Response and Action

In a free society, people do not want police on every street corner asking them what they are doing. Thus, the police are mainly **reactive** (responding to citizen calls for service). Studies of police work show that 81 percent of actions result from citizen telephone calls, 5 percent from citizens who approach an officer, and only 14 percent from officers in the field. These facts affect the way departments are organized and the way the police respond to cases.

reactive
Acting in response, such as police activity in response to notification that a crime has been committed.

However, there can be benefits for society when police are **proactive** (initiating actions in the absence of citizen requests). Research indicates that a proactive approach can have positive impacts on crime and disorder (Lum, Koper, and Telep, 2011). Thus there are strong reasons to consider whether and how police can be proactive without intruding too much into the privacy and liberty of innocent people who are going about their daily activities.

proactive
Acting in anticipation, such as an active search for potential offenders that is initiated by the police without waiting for a crime to be reported. Arrests for victimless crimes are usually proactive.

Because they are mainly reactive, the police usually arrive at the scene only after the crime has been committed and the perpetrator has fled. This means that the police are hampered by the time lapse and sometimes by inaccurate information given by witnesses. For example, a mugging may happen so quickly that victims and witnesses cannot accurately describe what happened. In about a third of cases in which police are called, no one is present when the police arrive on the scene.

Citizens have come to expect that the police will respond quickly to every call, whether it requires immediate attention or can be handled in a more routine manner. This expectation has produced **incident-driven policing**. Members of the public call the police department to request assistance, and officers are dispatched to respond to the reported incident. Studies have shown,

incident-driven policing
A reactive approach to policing emphasizing a quick response to calls for service.

though, that less than 30 percent of calls to the police involve criminal law enforcement—most calls concern order maintenance and service (S. Walker, 1999). To a large extent, then, reports by victims and observers define the boundaries of policing.

The police do use proactive strategies such as surveillance and undercover work to combat some crimes. When investigating victimless crimes, for example, they must rely on informers, stakeouts, wiretapping, stings, and raids. Police resources in many cities have been assigned to proactive efforts to apprehend people who use or sell illegal drugs. Because calls from victims reporting these crimes are few, crime rates for such offenses are nearly always reported as rates of arrest rather than rates of known criminal acts. Police efforts with respect to terrorism and homeland security also have a proactive emphasis. Law enforcement personnel attempt to intercept communications, monitor financial transactions and travel patterns, keep suspects under surveillance, and cultivate relationships with potential informers.

Increasingly, police administrators look to evidence-based policing as a tool for making decisions about deployment of personnel and officers' duties on patrol (Gross-Shader, 2011). As described in prior chapters, evidence-based policing involves the examination of social science research on crime and policing, and the translation of that research into practical strategies for police departments to employ when addressing crime and other problems. With respect to crime prevention, for example, evidence-based policing draws from research studies that guide police to proactively employ specific strategies aimed at targeted locations within a city or town (Lum, Koper, et al., 2011). Otherwise, officers deployed on general patrols throughout an entire city would be less effective in preventing crime than when they are engaged in specific activities at targeted trouble spots. The effective use of evidence-based policing can be enhanced through cooperation and communication between law enforcement officials and criminal justice researchers.

Organizational Response

The organization of the police bureaucracy influences how the police respond to citizens' calls. Factors that affect the response process include the separation of police into various functional groups (patrol, vice, investigation, and so on), the quasi-military command system, and the techniques used to induce patrol officers to respond in desired ways.

Police departments are being reshaped by new communications technology, which tends to centralize decision making. The core of the department is the communications center, where commands are given to send officers into action. Patrol officers are expected to remain in constant touch with headquarters and must report each of their actions. Two-way radios, cell phones, and computers are the primary means by which administrators monitor the decisions of officers in the field. In the past, patrol officers might have administered on-the-spot justice to a mischievous juvenile, but now they must file a report, take the youth into custody, and start formal proceedings. Because officers must contact headquarters by radio or computer with reports about each incident, headquarters is better able to guide officers' discretion and ensure that they comply with departmental policies.

By 2007, more than 90 percent of departments in cities with 25,000 or more inhabitants used onboard computers (B. A. Reaves, 2010). In cities with populations between 2,500 and 10,000, however, only 59 percent of departments used in-car computers. Only 43 percent of departments in towns smaller than 2,500 had such equipment (B. A. Reaves, 2010). From these figures we can see that the availability of communications and information technology

John Klicker/The New York Times/Redux Pictures

New high-tech tools, connected to high-speed wireless communications, have become widely available to officers in the field. Here, Officer Mike Frome of Portland, Oregon, uses a mobile device that can scan a person's fingerprints and compare them with others in a database.

varies, depending on departmental resources. In light of contemporary budget cuts and reduced availability of federal grants for equipment, it may be difficult for many departments to catch up with their larger-city colleagues' acquisition of new technology. In New York City, for example, the police department began a pilot project in 2012 to enable 400 foot patrol officers to use smartphones that have access to computerized arrest records, mugshots, and Department of Motor Vehicles databases. Thus the officers have ultraportable devices that permit them to check identities, records of crimes at specific locations, and other important matters as they walk through a housing project or make a stop-and-frisk search of a pedestrian (Ruderman, 2013). It remains to be seen whether or how soon smaller police departments will be able to acquire such useful technology for their officers.

Nearly all Americans can call 911 to report a crime or to obtain help or information, as even 86 percent of towns with populations less than 2,500 have 911 systems (B. A. Reaves, 2010). The 911 system has brought a flood of calls to police departments—many not directly related to police responsibilities. In many places, the number of calls increased significantly as the spread of cell phones made it easier for people to make reports as incidents arose. In 1997, the Federal Communications Commission (FCC) set aside the 311 number for cities to use, if they choose, as a nonemergency number. Baltimore was the first city to implement the new number, and it soon experienced a 42 percent reduction in 911 calls, as many nonemergency calls were placed to 311 instead. Other cities, such as Detroit and New York, followed in Baltimore's footsteps, but not all cities have implemented a 311 call system. The FCC later set aside the 211 number for social services information and the 511 number for traffic information, but relatively few cities have yet implemented call centers to make use of those other numbers (McMahon, 2002).

Although 911 systems can automatically trace the location of calls made from landlines, many cities are struggling to upgrade their 911 systems so that they can trace wireless calls to the vicinity of the nearest cell-phone tower (Dewan, 2007). Such efforts to upgrade equipment, procedures, and training become more visible in the aftermath of tragedies. One such example was the murder of a University of Wisconsin student in 2008 who dialed 911 from her cell phone, apparently when confronted by an intruder in her apartment,

differential response
A patrol strategy that assigns priorities to calls for service and then determines the appropriate response depending on the importance or urgency of the call.

yet the operator did not know her precise location or the nature of the emergency (Arnold, 2008). The 911 system remains the primary means for callers to reach their local government, but there are always concerns that those lines may become too tied up with emergency calls and thereby disrupt the ability of police and other emergency responders to receive quick reports about urgent situations.

To improve efficiency, police departments use a **differential response** system that assigns priorities to calls for service. This system assumes that it is not always necessary to rush a patrol car to the scene when a call is received. The appropriate response depends on several factors—such as whether the incident is in progress, has just occurred, or occurred some time ago, as well as whether anyone is or could be hurt. A dispatcher receives the calls and asks for certain facts. The dispatcher may (1) send a sworn officer to the scene right away, (2) give the call a lower rank so that the response by an officer is delayed, (3) send someone other than a sworn officer, or (4) refer the caller to another agency. Evaluations of differential response policies have found that they contribute to effective use of police resources and satisfying public expectations about an agency's responsiveness.

The policy of differential response clearly saves police resources. It provides other benefits as well. For example, with trained officers answering 911 lines, (1) more-detailed information is gathered from callers, (2) callers have a better sense of when to expect a response, and (3) patrol officers have more information about the case when they respond.

Some experts criticize centralized communications and decision making. Many advocates of community policing believe that certain technologies tend to isolate the police from citizens. By contrast, community-policing strategies ideally attempt to enhance interaction and cooperation between officers and citizens (Morash and Ford, 2002). Widespread use of motorized patrols has meant that residents may get only a glimpse of the officers cruising through their neighborhoods. Community-oriented policing attempts to overcome some of the negative aspects of centralized response, often by placing officers on foot or on bicycles or by dedicating specific officers' time to particular neighborhoods.

Productivity

Following the lead of New York's CompStat program, police departments in Baltimore, New Orleans, Indianapolis, and even smaller cities emphasized precinct-level accountability for crime reduction (F. Santos, 2008b). Through twice-weekly briefings before their peers and senior executives, precinct commanders must explain the results of their efforts to reduce crime. In the CompStat approach, they are held responsible for the success of crime control efforts in their precincts as indicated by crime statistics (D. Weisburd, Mastrofski, et al., 2003). Essential to this management strategy is timely, accurate information. Computer systems have been developed to put up-to-date crime data into the hands of managers at all levels (Willis, Mastrofski, and Weisburd, 2004). This allows discussion of department-wide strategies and puts pressure on low producers. Cities with populations as small as 50,000, such as Albany, Oregon, have pointed to how the data-driven policing underlying CompStat has led to major reductions in a wide range of crimes (Odegard, 2015). This innovation brought major changes to police operations and raised questions as to how police work should be measured. It has also raised questions about whether measures of performance based on data tend to move departments away from community policing by emphasizing a centralized hierarchy focused on accountability and control (W. F. Walsh and Vito, 2004).

In addition, critics raise issues about whether it creates incentives for precinct-level police to avoid reporting crime data accurately and whether the nation's two-decade-long drop in crime rates is attributable to these new techniques or to larger social forces.

Quantifying police work is difficult in part because of the wide range of duties and day-to-day tasks of officers (Coutts and Schneider, 2004). In the past, the crime rate and the clearance rate have been used as measures of "good" policing. A lower crime rate might be cited as evidence of an effective department, but critics note that other factors besides policing affect this measure.

The **clearance rate**—the percentage of crimes known to police that they believe they have solved through an arrest—is a basic measure of police performance. The clearance rate varies by type of offense. In reactive situations, this rate can be low. For example, the police may first learn of a burglary hours or even days later; the clearance rate for such crimes is only about 13 percent. Police find more success in handling violent crimes, especially if victims can identify their assailants; the clearance rate for violent offenses is 47 percent (BJS, 2015a).

clearance rate
The percentage rate of crimes known to the police that they believe they have solved through an arrest; a statistic used to measure a police department's productivity.

In proactive situations, the police are not responding to the call of a crime victim; rather, they seek out crimes. Hence, at least in theory, arrests for prostitution, gambling, and drug selling have a clearance rate of 100 percent, because every crime known to the police is matched with an arrest.

The arrest of a person often results in the clearance of other reported offenses, because the police can link some arrested persons with similar, unsolved crimes. Interrogation and lineups are standard procedures, as is the lesser-known practice of simply assigning unsolved crimes to the suspect. When an offender enters a guilty plea, the bargain may include an admission that he or she committed prior crimes. Professional thieves know that they can gain favors from the police in exchange for "confessing" to unsolved crimes that they may not have committed.

These measures of police productivity are sometimes supplemented by other data, such as the number of traffic citations issued, illegally parked cars ticketed, and suspects stopped for questioning, as well as the value of stolen goods recovered by officers. These additional ways of counting work done reflect the fact that an officer may work hard for many hours yet have no arrests to show for his or her efforts (Kelling, 1992). Some of these measures, however, may have adverse consequences for police–community relations. Citizens are usually not happy with the perception that officers may be expected to issue a specific number of traffic citations each day, because it leads residents to believe that officers make unjustified traffic stops simply to impress superiors. The Illinois legislature enacted a law in 2014 to ban the use of traffic ticket quotas by police departments to require officers to engage in a measurable activity. A similar ban was proposed in New Jersey (Firozi, 2014b). In New York City, during a 2013 lawsuit about racial profiling in stop-and-frisk searches of pedestrians that predominantly affected young African American and Hispanic men, a police chief testified about criticizing officers for not making enough frisks. His description about the pressure applied by supervisory officers raised questions about whether this productivity measure contributed to discriminatory treatment of citizens (J. Goldstein, 2013). How do we weigh the costs and benefits of using traffic and frisk stops as productivity measures that may effectively encourage officers to employ this strategy too frequently? Read A Question of Ethics at the end of the chapter to consider the use of ticket and arrest quotas as a means to evaluate police performance.

Society may benefit even more when officers spend their time in activities that are hard to measure, such as calming disputes, becoming acquainted with people in the neighborhood, and providing services to those in need. Some research indicates that officers who engage in activities that produce higher levels of measurable productivity, such as issuing citations or making arrests, also receive higher numbers of citizen complaints about alleged misconduct (Lersch, 2002). Would officers better serve the community by spending time in difficult-to-measure activities? Only further research can provide an answer.

✔POINT

7. What is incident-driven policing?
8. What is differential response?
9. What are the basic measures of police productivity?

STOP AND ANALYZE: If you were a police chief, how would you measure your officers' productivity? Suggest two possible measures, and list the advantages and disadvantages of each.

Delivery of Police Services

line functions
Police components that directly perform field operations and carry out the basic functions of patrol, investigation, traffic, vice, juvenile, and so on.

In service bureaucracies like the police, a distinction is often made between line and staff functions. **Line functions** are those that directly involve field operations such as patrol, investigation, traffic control, vice, juvenile crimes, and so on. By contrast, *staff functions* supplement or support the line functions. Staff functions are based in the chief's office and the support or services bureau, as well as in the staff inspection bureau. An efficient department maintains an appropriate balance between line and staff duties.

Patrol Functions

Patrol is often called the backbone of police operations. The word *patrol* is derived from a French word, *patrouiller,* which once meant "to tramp about in the mud." This is an apt description of a function that one expert describes as "arduous, tiring, difficult, and performed in conditions other than ideal" (Chapman, 1970: ix). For most Americans the familiar sight of a uniformed and armed patrol officer, on call 24 hours a day, is what they would call "policing."

sworn officers
Police employees who have taken an oath and been given powers by the state to make arrests and use necessary force, in accordance with their duties.

Every local police department has a patrol unit. Even in large departments, patrol officers account for up to two-thirds of all **sworn officers**—those who have taken an oath and been given the powers to make arrests and use necessary force in accordance with their duties. In small communities, police operations are not specialized, and the patrol force is the entire department. The patrol officer must be prepared for any imaginable situation and must perform many duties.

Television portrays patrol officers as always on the go—rushing from one incident to another and making several arrests in a single shift. A patrol officer may indeed be called to deal with a robbery in progress or to help rescue people from a burning building. However, the patrol officer's life is not always so exciting, often involving routine and even boring tasks such as directing traffic at minor accident scenes and road construction sites.

Most officers, on most shifts, do not make even one arrest. To better understand patrol work, note in Figure 6.2 how the police of Wilmington, Delaware, allocate time to various activities. The information from this classic study of time allocation shows that crime-related activities account for a smaller portion of police officers' time than many people realize.

preventive patrol
Making the police presence known, in order to deter crime and to make officers available to respond quickly to calls.

The patrol function has three parts: answering calls for help, maintaining a police presence, and probing suspicious circumstances. Patrol officers are well suited to answering calls, because they usually are near the scene and can move quickly to provide help or catch a suspect. At other times, they engage in **preventive patrol**—that is, making the police presence known in an effort to

FIGURE 6.2 TIME ALLOCATED TO PATROL ACTIVITIES BY THE POLICE OF WILMINGTON, DELAWARE

The time spent on each activity was calculated from records for each police car unit. Note the range of activities and the time spent on each.

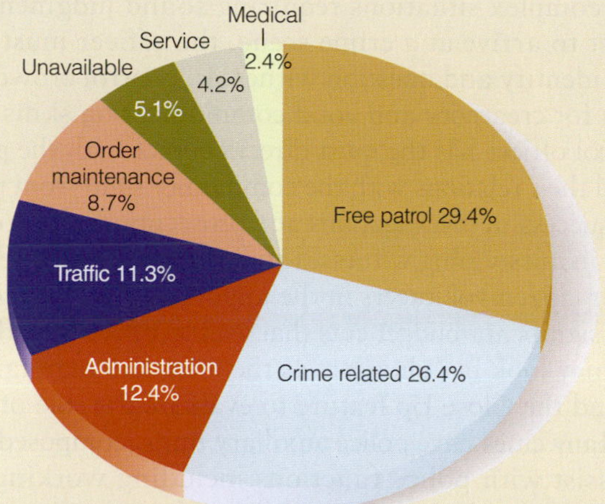

Free patrol: park and walk

Crime related: officer in trouble, suspicious person/vehicle, crime in progress, alarm, investigate crime not in progress, service warrant/subpoena, assist other police

Administration: meal break, report writing, firearms training, police vehicle maintenance, at headquarters, court related

Traffic: accident investigation, parking problems, motor vehicle driving problems, traffic control, fire emergency

Order maintenance: order maintenance in progress, animal complaint, noise complaint

Service: service related

Medical: medical emergency, at local hospital

Source: Jack R. Greene and Carl B. Klockars, "What Police Do," in *Thinking about Police*, 2nd ed. Edited by Carl B. Klockars and Stephen D. Mastrofski (New York: McGraw-Hill, 1991), 279.

deter crime and to make officers available to respond quickly to calls. Whether walking the streets or cruising in a car, the patrol officer is on the lookout for suspicious people and behavior. With experience, officers come to trust in their own ability to spot signs of suspicious activity that merit stopping people on the street for questioning.

Patrol officers also help maintain smooth relations between the police and the community. As the most visible members of the criminal justice system, they can profoundly affect the willingness of citizens to cooperate. When officers earn the trust and respect of the residents of the neighborhoods they

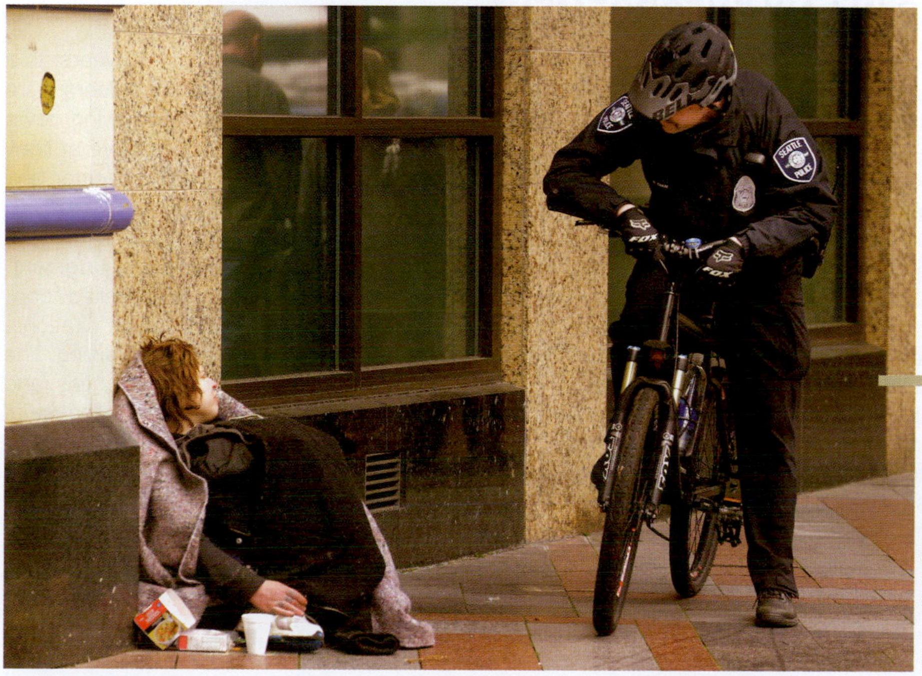

AP Images/Ted S. Warren

Patrol officers must be skilled at interacting with all kinds of people in order to do their jobs effectively. They must also make quick decisions in dangerous situations. Which job requires a wider array of skills—a patrol officer dealing with a variety of daily situations or a detective investigating a crime?

CIVIC ENGAGEMENT

YOUR ROLE IN THE SYSTEM

Your town's mayor has asked you to lead a community committee to study whether a volunteer auxiliary police unit should be established to assist the regular police. *Make a list of the benefits and risks of using citizen-volunteers. Would you support or oppose the creation of the unit?* Then look at the description of the police auxiliary unit in Baltimore County, Maryland.

patrol, people become much more willing to provide information about crimes and suspicious activities. Effective work by patrol officers can also help reduce citizens' fear of crime and foster a sense of security.

Patrol officers' duties sound fairly straightforward, yet these officers often find themselves in complex situations requiring sound judgment and careful actions. As the first to arrive at a crime scene, the officer must comfort and give aid to victims, identify and question witnesses, control crowds, and gather evidence. This calls for creativity and good communication skills.

Because the patrol officer has the most direct contact with the public, the image of the police and their relations with the community stem from patrol officers' actions. Moreover, successful investigations and prosecutions often depend on patrol officers' actions in questioning witnesses and gathering evidence after a crime.

Is there a role for citizen-volunteers in the important patrol function of policing? In the midst of significant budget cuts that lead to officer layoffs, local police chiefs and sheriffs may look to volunteers as the means to maintain services for the community. Read the Close Up feature to evaluate the role of volunteers in law enforcement. Many cities have police auxiliary units, composed of uniformed volunteers, who assist with police functions including working as unarmed officers on patrol. Consider the benefits and risks of using citizen-volunteers on police patrols as you examine "Civic Engagement: Your Role in the System."

Because the patrol officer's job involves the most contact with the public, the best-qualified officers should be chosen to perform it. However, because of the low status of patrol assignments, many officers seek higher-status positions such as that of detective. A key challenge facing policing is to grant to patrol officers a status that reflects their importance to society and the criminal justice system.

CLOSE UP

THE USE OF VOLUNTEERS IN LAW ENFORCEMENT

Budget reductions since 2008 have caused many police departments to experience significant cuts in patrol personnel. In order to minimize the impact of these cuts on the fulfillment of police functions, some departments utilize citizen-volunteers as auxiliary police officers. Many cities have police auxiliary units composed of uniformed volunteers who assist with police functions. In 2011, the Los Angeles Police Department had 700 unpaid citizens in its Reserve Corps. When these volunteers go through police academy training, they can be deployed on the streets as armed, uniformed officers who assist regular officers in order maintenance, crime investigation, and other police functions. The services provided by these volunteer officers save the city $5 million each year.

In New York City, 4,500 volunteer auxiliary officers serve as unarmed, uniformed officers who are extra "eyes and ears" for the police department as they patrol the streets on foot, observe subway platforms, and call regular officers via police radio when their suspicions are aroused. Eight auxiliary officers in New York have been killed in the line of duty in the past 50 years. In a highly publicized tragedy in 2007, two auxiliary officers were killed by a shooting suspect whom they were following down the street. One victim was a 19-year-old sophomore at New York University who was intent on a career as a prosecutor, and the other was a 27-year-old aspiring novelist.

The usefulness of such officers has been questioned, especially with respect to issues about training and judgment. In Tennessee, there is a traditional elective office called "constable," through which unpaid citizens patrol, issue citations, and make arrests after receiving only 40 hours of training. The constables' powers have been eliminated in four counties, and critics seek to abolish the office statewide, in part because of the misbehavior of several constables for wrongful arrests and sexual assaults.

Other problems can also emerge. A Florida volunteer officer used his position to obtain a woman's address and stalk her in

✔POINT **10.** What is the difference between line and staff functions?

11. What are the three parts of the patrol function?

STOP AND ANALYZE: How important is preventive patrol—the visible, mobile presence of police? If budget cuts reduce the size of police departments, should police adopt different strategies, such as solely responding to calls or patrolling in high-crime areas only? If you were a police chief in such circumstances, what choice would you make? List three reasons for either continuing or ending preventive patrol during a budget crisis.

Investigation

All cities with a population of more than 250,000, and 90 percent of smaller cities, have officers called *detectives* assigned to investigative duties. Detectives make up 15 percent of police personnel. Compared with patrol officers, they have a higher status in the department. Their pay is higher, their hours are more flexible, and they are supervised less closely. Detectives do not wear uniforms, and their work is considered more interesting than that of patrol officers. In addition, they engage solely in law enforcement rather than in order maintenance or service work; hence, their activities conform more closely to the image of the police as crime fighters.

Within federal law enforcement agencies, the work of special agents is similar to that of detectives. Several federal agencies, such as Customs and Border Protection and the Fish and Wildlife Service, have uniformed officers. However, the work in many other agencies, such as the FBI, DEA, and Secret Service, is primarily carried out by plainclothes officers who focus on investigations. One key difference between federal special agents and detectives in local departments is that federal agents are more likely to be proactive in initiating

2012. In 2011, the Illinois attorney general raised questions about the legality of using volunteer officers in her state, because some departments used such officers in ways that collided with state laws on carrying handguns and impersonating a police officer.

Issues concerning the use of volunteer officers captured national attention in 2015 when a 73-year-old volunteer officer in Tulsa, Oklahoma, shot and killed an unarmed suspect who was on the ground and apparently struggling to resist the handcuffing process during an arrest. The volunteer officer claimed that he mistakenly grabbed and fired his gun instead of his Taser when trying to assist with the arrest. The incident was captured on video through the body camera of one of the arresting officers. The volunteer officer was charged with manslaughter amid investigations about whether such officers receive adequate training and whether they are given opportunities to work with police through friendships with senior officers or financial contributions to a police department.

Sources: Natalie Neysa Alund, "Value of Tennessee Constables Debated," *Knoxville News Sentinel*, December 11, 2011 (www.knoxnews.com); "Cops: Volunteer Law Enforcement Officer Used Position to Stalk Woman," WFTV .com, July 25. 2012 (www.wftv.com); Alan Feuer and Al Baker, "Greenwich Village Gunfight Leaves Four Dead," *New York Times*, March 15, 2007 (www .nytimes.com); Gloria Hillard, "In Tight Times, L.A. Relies on Volunteer Police," National Public Radio, May 19, 2011 (www.npr.org); Richard Perez-Pena, "Tulsa Sheriff Defends Volunteer Deputy in Shooting," *New York Times*, April 20, 2015 (www.nytimes.com); Larry Yellen, "Illinois Attorney General: Auxiliary Police Are Breaking Law," Fox Chicago News, March 1, 2011 (www.myfoxchicago.com).

DEBATE THE ISSUE

Should police departments rely on volunteer officers? Should there be specific requirements for their training and specific limits on their authority and tasks? Does a police department have enough control over volunteer officers who, if fired, are not actually losing their paying jobs? If you were a police chief, would you use volunteer officers? Give three reasons for your answer.

investigations to prevent terrorism, drug trafficking, and other crimes. Local police detectives are typically reactive, responding to crimes that have been discovered or reported.

Detectives in small departments are generalists who investigate whatever crimes occur, but in large departments they are assigned to special units such as homicide, robbery, auto theft, forgery, and burglary. In recent decades, because of public pressures, some departments have set up new special units to deal with bias crimes, child abuse, sexual assault, computer crime, and crimes targeting tourists (Mawby, Boakye, and Jones, 2014; Bayley, 1994).

Most investigative units are separated from the patrol chain of command. Many argue that this results in duplication of effort and lack of continuity in handling cases. It often means that vital information known by one branch is not known by the other.

Like patrol, criminal investigation is largely reactive. Detectives become involved after a crime has been reported and a patrol officer has done a preliminary investigation. The job of detectives is mainly to talk to people—victims, suspects, witnesses—in order to find out what happened (Patterson, 2011). On the basis of this information, detectives develop theories about who committed the crime and then set out to gather the evidence that will lead to arrest and prosecution.

Herman Goldstein (1977: 55) outlines the process of investigation as follows:

- When a serious crime occurs and the suspect is identified and caught right away, the detective prepares the case to be presented to the prosecuting attorney.
- When the suspect is identified but not caught, the detective tries to locate him or her.
- When the offender is not identified but there is more than one suspect, the detective conducts investigations to determine which one committed the crime.
- When there is no suspect, the detective starts from scratch to find out who committed the crime.

In performing an investigation, detectives depend not only on their own experience but also on technical experts. Much of the information they need comes from criminal files, lab technicians, and forensic scientists. Many small departments turn to the state crime laboratory or the FBI for such information. Detectives are often pictured as working alone, but in fact they are part of a team.

Although detectives focus on serious crimes, they are not the only ones who investigate crimes. Patrol, traffic, vice, and juvenile units may also do so. In small towns and rural areas, patrol officers must conduct investigations because police departments are too small to have separate detective bureaus. In urban areas, because they tend to be the first police to arrive at the scene of a crime, patrol officers must do much of the initial investigative work. As we have seen, the patrol unit's investigation can be crucial. Successful prosecution of many kinds of cases, including robbery, larceny, and burglary, is closely linked to the speed with which a suspect is arrested. If patrol officers cannot obtain information from victims and witnesses right away, the chance of arresting and prosecuting the suspect greatly decreases.

Apprehension

The discovery that a crime has been committed sets off a chain of events leading to the capture of a suspect and the gathering of the evidence needed to convict that person. It may also lead to several dead ends, such as a lack

FIGURE 6.3 THE APPREHENSION PROCESS

Apprehension of a felony suspect results from a sequence of actions by patrol officers and detectives. Coordination of these efforts is key to solving major crimes.

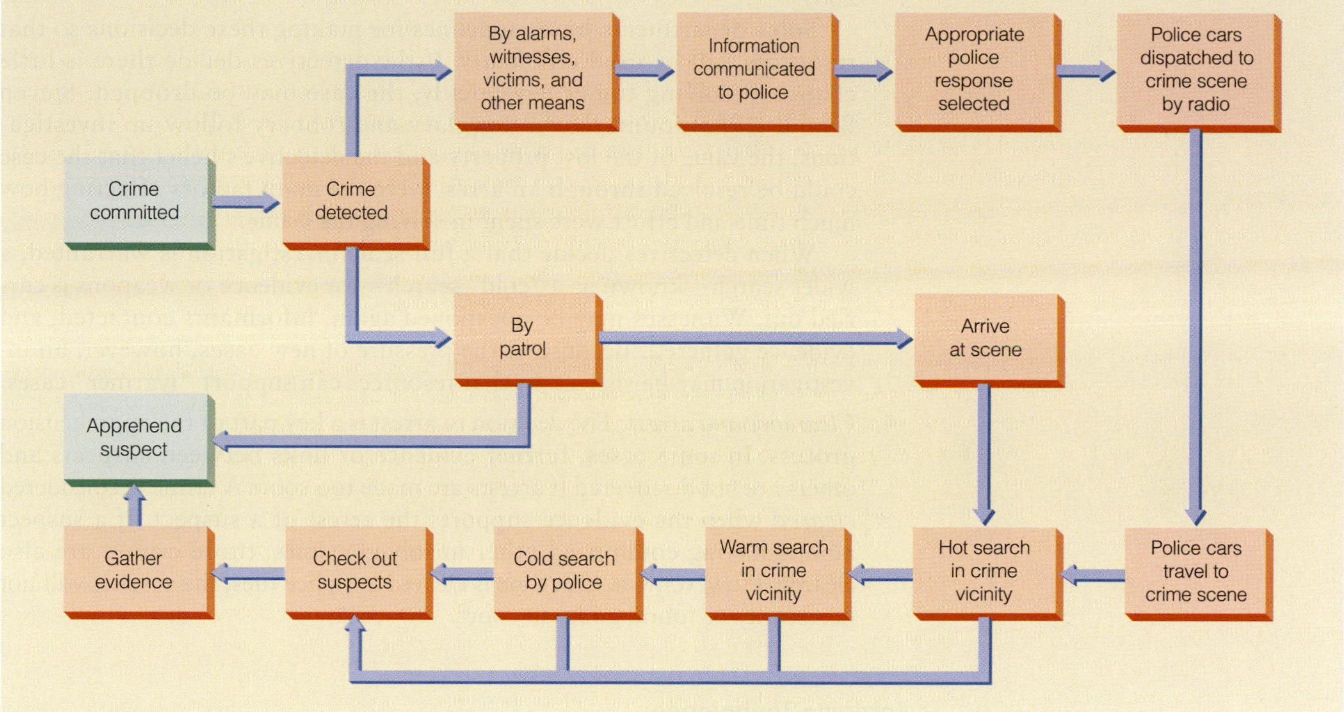

of clues pointing to a suspect or a lack of evidence to link the suspect to the crime.

The process of catching a suspect has three stages: detection of a crime, preliminary investigation, and follow-up investigation. Depending on the outcome of the investigation, a fourth step may follow: clearance and arrest. As shown in Figure 6.3, these actions are designed to use criminal justice resources to arrest a suspect and assemble enough evidence to support a charge. Here is a fuller description of each step.

1. *Detection of a crime.* Although patrol officers sometimes discover crimes, information that a crime has been committed usually comes in a call to the police. For example, automatic alarms linked to police headquarters could alert the police to a crime on business premises. Such direct communications help shorten response time and increase the chances of catching the suspect.
2. *Preliminary investigation.* The first law enforcement official on the scene is usually a patrol officer who has been dispatched by radio. The officer helps the victim, secures the crime scene for investigation, and documents the facts of the crime. If a suspect is present or nearby, the officer conducts a "hot" search and may apprehend the suspect. This initial work is crucial. The officer must gather the basic facts, including the name of the victim, a description of the suspect, and the names of witnesses. After the information is collected, it is sent to the investigation unit.
3. *Follow-up investigation.* After a crime has been brought to the attention of the police and a preliminary investigation has been made, the detective

decides what course of action to pursue. In big-city departments, incident reports from each day are analyzed the next morning. Investigators receive assignments based on their specialties. They study the information, weigh each factor, and decide whether the crime can likely be solved (D. Carson, 2009).

Some departments have guidelines for making these decisions so that resources will be used efficiently. If the detectives decide there is little chance of solving the crime quickly, the case may be dropped. Steven Brandl (1993) found that in burglary and robbery follow-up investigations, the value of the lost property and the detective's belief that the case could be resolved through an arrest were the main factors affecting how much time and effort were spent in solving the crime.

When detectives decide that a full-scale investigation is warranted, a wider search—known as a "cold" search—for evidence or weapons is carried out. Witnesses may be questioned again, informants contacted, and evidence gathered. Because of the pressure of new cases, however, an investigation may be shelved so that resources can support "warmer" cases.

4. *Clearance and arrest.* The decision to arrest is a key part of the apprehension process. In some cases, further evidence or links between suspects and others are not discovered if arrests are made too soon. A crime is considered *cleared* when the evidence supports the arrest of a suspect. If a suspect admits having committed other unsolved crimes, those crimes are also cleared. However, when a crime is cleared in police files, the suspect will not necessarily be found guilty in court.

Forensic Techniques

American police have long relied on science in gathering, identifying, and analyzing evidence. Through the *CSI: Crime Scene Investigation* television drama and its spin-offs, the public has become increasingly aware of the wide range of scientific testing techniques used for law enforcement purposes. Scientific analysis of fingerprints, blood, semen, hair, textiles, soil, weapons, and other materials has helped the police identify criminals. It has also helped prosecutors convince jurors of the guilt of defendants. Beginning in the 1990s, these techniques have also increasingly helped defense attorneys establish the innocence of people who are in prison for such crimes as rape and murder (C. E. Smith and Sanford, 2013). Although all states and many large cities have forensic labs, this does not guarantee that the latest tests can be used in all cases. Not all labs have the same technical equipment and personnel. In addition, some police departments, especially those in small towns and rural areas, have little access to crime labs and other technology. For example, although more than 90 percent or more of agencies in cities with populations greater than 25,000 have access to Automated Fingerprint Identification Systems (AFIS)—computerized systems to match fingerprints—only 64 percent of agencies in towns with 2,500 to 10,000 residents have such access. Only 47 percent of agencies with fewer than 2,500 inhabitants have access to such systems (Hickman and Reaves, 2006). We shall examine issues concerning forensic techniques in greater detail in Chapter 7.

Research on Investigation

The results of several studies raise questions about the value of investigations and the role detectives play in apprehension. This research suggests that the police have attached too much importance to investigation as a means of solving crimes and shows that most crimes are cleared because of arrests made by the patrol force at or near the scene. Response time is key to apprehension, as is the information given by the victim or witnesses.

A classic study of 153 large police departments found that a key factor in solving crimes was identification of the perpetrator by the victim or witnesses. Of those cases that were not solved right away but were cleared later, most were cleared by routine procedures such as fingerprint searches, tips from informants, and mug-shot "show-ups." The report found that actions by the investigative staff mattered in very few cases. In sum, about 30 percent of the crimes were cleared by on-scene arrest and another 50 percent through identification by victims or witnesses when the police arrived. Thus, only about 20 percent could have been solved by detective work. Even among this group, however, the study found that most crimes "were also solved by patrol officers, members of the public who spontaneously provide further information, or routine investigative practices" (P. Greenwood, Chaiken, and Petersilia, 1977: 227).

In many cities, the amount of serious crime has gone down during the past decade, but the percentage of unsolved cases has remained relatively stable. In part this may be due to the lack of resources allocated to pursuing "cold cases." Detectives emphasize that although forensic tools are important, solving crimes "the old fashioned way" through much street work is still effective.

Does this research show that detectives are not important? No. Some cases are weak with little evidence, some are strong with a lot of evidence. Police need not devote a great deal of effort in these polar cases. However, in between lie cases with moderate evidence. These do require additional effort by detectives, and, as one researcher found, this "is extremely important with respect to subsequent making of follow-up arrests" (Bayley, 1998: 149). A study of a midwestern department's follow-up investigations of burglary and robbery backs up this finding (Brandl and Frank, 1994: 163).

The detective's role is important in at least two ways besides solving crimes. First, the status of detective provides a goal to which patrol officers can aspire and thereby gives them an incentive to excel in their work. Second, the public expects the police to conduct investigations. Citizens may have more trust in the police or feel more willing to cooperate with them when they see investigations being conducted, even if those investigations do not always lead to arrests.

✔POINT **12.** What is the job of the detective?

13. What are the four steps of the apprehension process?

STOP AND ANALYZE: Could a police department function effectively without detectives? Give three reasons to support your answer to this question.

Special Operations

Patrol and investigation are the two largest and most important units in a police department. In metropolitan areas, however, special units are set up to deal with specific types of problems. The most common such units concern traffic, vice, and juveniles. Some cities also have units to deal with organized crime and drugs. As discussed with respect to specialized drug units, it is increasingly common for police agencies to cooperate with each other in multiagency task forces to better address specialized problems that are not confined to a specific spot in one city. Such task-force participation is especially prevalent for the largest cities. For example, more than 80 percent of cities larger than 250,000 participate in antiterrorism task forces, and more than a third of such cities participate in human-trafficking task forces (B. A. Reaves, 2010). Even with special units in place, however, patrol officers and investigators continue to deal with the same problems.

school resource officers (SROs)
Police officers assigned for duty in schools to assist in order maintenance while also developing positive relationships with students that may assist in delinquency prevention.

As we examine the special units used by many departments, bear in mind that individual officers may receive special assignments, too. A good example is the development of **school resource officers (SROs)**, police officers assigned to high schools under contractual arrangements between public schools and local police departments. More than 85 percent of police departments in cities ranging in size from 25,000 to 500,000 have officers assigned to SRO duty. Percentages are slightly lower for larger cities and significantly lower for the smallest towns. In the aftermath of the school shooting in Newtown, Connecticut, there were many proposals in 2013 to increase the number of SROs in schools around the country.

School resource officers provide a visible presence that may deter student misconduct; they have full authority to enforce laws as well as school rules. Furthermore, SROs are expected to develop relationships with students that will permit them to provide advice and guidance. They are positioned to help develop positive relationships between young people and police. In addition, SROs frequently give formal talks in classrooms to educate students about law and the criminal justice system (B. Finn et al., 2005). However, there are concerns that teenage students may be unnecessarily routed into the criminal justice system as a result of SRO-issued misdemeanor citations for minor behavioral violations—incidents that would traditionally be handled by the high school principal's office (Na and Gottfredson, 2013; Eckholm, 2013). Overall, the use of SROs represents a particularly important form of individualized special assignment because it shows how, in one specific setting, police officers' functions and duties extend well beyond the crime-fighting image that is commonly associated with law enforcement.

Traffic

Traffic regulation is a major job of the police. The police regulate the flow of vehicles, investigate accidents, and enforce traffic laws. This work may not seem to have much to do with crime fighting or order maintenance, but in fact it does. Besides helping maintain order, enforcement of traffic laws educates the public by promoting safe driving habits and provides a visible service to the community.

Traffic duty can also help the police catch criminals. In enforcing traffic laws, patrol officers can stop cars and question drivers. Stolen property and suspects linked to other criminal acts are often found this way. Most departments can now automatically check license numbers against lists of wanted vehicles and suspects.

Enforcement of traffic laws offers a good example of police discretion. When officers stop drivers for traffic violations, they choose from among various options that include issuing a citation, giving a warning, making an arrest for drunk driving or other offense, or letting the driver go. An officer's specific decision in any situation may depend on a number of factors including department policies, the attitude of the driver, and the amount of time involved in processing paperwork for a citation or arrest.

Traffic work is mostly proactive, and the level of enforcement depends in part on departmental policies. Guided by these policies, officers target certain kinds of violations or certain highways. Some departments expect officers to issue a prescribed number of citations during each shift. Although these norms may be informal, they offer a way of gauging the productivity of traffic officers. For the most part, selective enforcement is the general policy, because the police have neither the desire nor the resources to enforce all traffic laws.

Vice

Enforcement of vice laws depends on proactive police work, which often involves the use of undercover agents and informers. Most big-city police departments have a vice unit. Vice officers often must engage in degrading activities, such as posing as prostitutes or drug dealers, in order to catch lawbreakers. The special nature of vice work requires members of the unit to be well trained in the legal procedures that must be followed if arrests are to lead to convictions.

The potential for corruption in this type of police work presents administrative problems. Undercover officers are in a position to blackmail gamblers and drug dealers and may also be offered bribes. In addition, officers must be transferred when their identities become known.

The growth of undercover work and electronic surveillance, common in vice patrols, troubles critics who favor more open policing. They fear that the use of these tactics violates civil liberties and increases government intrusion into the private lives of citizens, whether or not those citizens commit crimes.

Drug Law Enforcement

Many large cities have a bureau to enforce drug laws. More than 80 percent of cities with populations larger than 100,000 have such units, but these are less common in smaller cities (Hickman and Reaves, 2006). Many city police departments also participate in multiagency task forces focused on drugs. Only 35 percent of all police departments participate in multiagency drug task forces, but this includes more than 80 percent of all agencies in cities with populations over 50,000. Thus such task forces are primarily tools used by larger cities, especially the nation's largest cities, as more than 94 percent of cities with populations greater than 250,000 participate (B. A. Reaves, 2010). These agencies may also be linked to task forces that deal with organized crime or with gangs involved in drug dealing. More than two-thirds of departments in cities with populations greater than 250,000 participate in gang task forces (B. A. Reaves, 2010). They may use sting operations to arrest drug sellers on the street or to provide drug education in the community.

Drug enforcement sometimes reflects the goal of *aggressive patrol,* or assigning resources so as to get the largest number of arrests and stop street dealing. Police executives believe that they must show dealers and the community that drug laws are enforced.

The police use various strategies to attack drug dealing. One of these involves inspections of houses and buildings used by drug dealers. Those that do not meet city standards can be boarded up in order to rid the neighborhood of

AP Images/Karie Hamilton

Special drug units are common within police departments, especially in large cities. Through specialization and concentrated attention, police departments hope to impact continuous problems such as drug sales and prostitution. Special units are proactive and therefore provide officers with opportunities to plan strategies for catching lawbreakers. If you were a police officer, would you rather deal with a wide array of different problems each day as a patrol officer or focus your attention on a particular crime problem day after day?

dealers. Streets where drugs are dealt openly can be flooded with officers who engage in proactive stops and questioning.

Another strategy is to disrupt the drug market. By flooding an area with officers and closing off abandoned buildings, the police can shut down drug sales in a specific location. This approach has been used in New York City, Los Angeles, and other cities. But how effective is it? Do these efforts simply shift the drug market to another area, or do they actually reduce the availability of drugs?

Although arrests for drug sale or possession have increased dramatically, some observers believe that this is not the best way to deal with the problem. Many public officials argue that drugs should be viewed as a public-health problem rather than as a crime problem. Critics of current policies believe that society would benefit if more resources went to drug treatment programs than to police actions that fill prisons and jails without doing much to reduce drug use.

✓POINT 14. What kinds of special operations units do police departments often employ?

STOP AND ANALYZE: Think about the city or town where you live. Is there a need for a special operations unit in your police department? Why or why not? Give two reasons for your answer.

Issues in Patrolling

Patrol officers are the frontline personnel who bear the primary responsibility for all of the major functions of policing, including law enforcement, order maintenance, and service. The effectiveness of patrol officers relies in part on the strategies that police administrators use to distribute personnel throughout a city or county and to instruct officers about practices and priorities. For each specific problem that arises, police agencies instruct their officers to perform in ways tailored to each problem; different problems require different modes of operation.

NEW DIRECTIONS IN CRIMINAL JUSTICE POLICY

EVIDENCE-BASED POLICING AND PATROL

Police administrators make decisions about how to deploy their personnel. They must determine where their officers will patrol, when and how often officers will move down specific streets and sidewalks, and what officers will do at particular locations. Early research findings called into question the usefulness of having officers randomly patrol a city and wait for calls from citizens about crimes or other problems. Instead, studies point to the benefits of officers devoting their attention to specific locations, typically referred to as "hot spots," where crimes or related issues of disorder repeatedly occur. Because crime and disorder are not randomly or evenly distributed around a city or town, there are benefits gained from targeting attention and resources to those places where trouble is known to occur. Evidence indicates that reductions in crime can take place when patrols focus their attention on known hot spots within a community.

Research also indicates that there are benefits from officers spending time at hot spots rather than just passing through the area. By spending 15 minutes at a hot spot, patrol officers may create deterrent effects that lead potential lawbreakers to avoid the area or to be careful about their unlawful behavior. Moreover, there may be benefits from officers actively seeking to solve problems that they see in the vicinity of hot spots. This proactive approach presents officers with the opportunity to merge problem-oriented policing (POP) with a patrol emphasis on hot spots. In addition, spending a longer time in hot spots may enable officers to identify and plan remediation for certain vulnerabilities to crime that exist for businesses and residences in such areas. Extended presence in the vicinity of hot spots also gives officers the opportunity to interact with residents to learn their concerns about crime and safety, and to speak to individuals whose behavior troubles other residents in the neighborhood.

Another form of police intervention that shows promising results in research involves direct interactions between potential offenders and officers to provide clear communications about the consequences of criminal activity. For example, this may involve direct contact with gang members to let them know that

For example, certain New York City precincts sought to reduce crime by sending "waves of rookies, teamed with seasoned officers, into high-crime areas" (Hauser, 2008). By contrast, departments that can focus on long-term trends in crime control or service instead of an immediate crisis may be able to establish specific patterns of patrol that emphasize having officers walk within neighborhoods and build personal relationships with individual citizens.

In the last 30 years, many studies have been done on police methods of assigning tasks to patrol officers, mobilizing them, and communicating with them. Much of this evidence points toward the importance of place-based policing, such as focusing officers' attention on crime "hot spots" in a community where crimes are repeatedly committed (Telep and Weisburd, 2012). These studies have caused experts to rethink some aspects of patrolling. However, even when researchers agree on which patrol practices are the most effective and provide a basis for evidence-based policing, those practices often run counter to the desires of departmental personnel (Lum, Telep, et al., 2012). For example, foot patrol may be important for some community-policing strategies, but many officers would prefer to remain in squad cars rather than pound the pavement. Police administrators therefore must deal with many issues in order to develop and implement effective patrol strategies. Read the New Directions in Criminal Justice Policy feature to see the role of research in developing evidence-based policing strategies for patrol.

Assignment of Patrol Personnel

In the past it has been assumed that patrol officers should be assigned where and when they will be most effective in preventing crime, keeping order, and serving the public. For the police administrator, the question has been "Where should the officers be sent, when, and in what numbers?" There are no guidelines to answer this question, and most assignments seem to be based on the

they are being watched and that any use of guns or other illegal activities will be dealt with harshly in the criminal justice system.

These evidence-based patrol strategies are proactive in that they lead police officers to plan and carry out a set of activities at particular locations. As such, they differ from the traditional reactive approach to policing that long characterized standard procedures—waiting for and responding to calls from the public. In addition, the evidence-based approach can lead to the removal of regular patrols from neighborhoods that seldom experience problems. However, this may cause unhappiness among citizens who had previously felt reassured by the regular presence of police patrols in their neighborhoods. Because of these and other changes that occur when moving toward a focus on evidence-based policing, there can be reluctance among officers and members of the public to embrace new police patrol practices that are guided by research findings.

Sources: Anthony A. Braga, Andrew V. Papachristos, and David M. Hureau, "The Effects of Hot Spots Policing on Crime: An Updated Systematic Review and Meta-Analysis," *Justice Quarterly*. 31 (2014): 633–63; Cynthia Lum, Christopher S. Koper, and Cody W. Telep, "The Evidence-Based Policing Matrix," *Journal of Experimental Criminology* 7 (2011): 3–26; Cynthia Lum, Cody W. Telep, Christopher S. Koper, and Julie Grieco, "Receptivity to Research in Policing," *Justice Research and Policy* 14 (2012): 61–95; Bruce Taylor, Christopher S. Koper, and Daniel J. Woods, "A Randomized Controlled Trial of Different Policing Strategies at Hot Spots of Violent Crime," *Journal of Experimental Criminology* 7 (2011): 149–81; Cody W. Telep and David Weisburd, "What Is Known about the Effectiveness of Police Practices in Reducing Crime and Disorder?" *Police Quarterly* 15 (2012): 331–57.

DEBATE THE ISSUE

If you were a police chief, how would you incorporate newer research into your plans for patrolling neighborhoods? How will you persuade your officers to adopt new approaches with enthusiasm? How will you reassure citizens who experience a reduction of patrols in their neighborhoods? Give three reasons for your position on these questions.

notion that patrols should be concentrated in "problem" neighborhoods or in areas where crime rates and calls for service are high. Thus, the assignment of officers to particular patrol areas is based on factors such as crime statistics, 911 calls, degree of urbanization, pressure from business and community groups, and socioeconomic conditions.

Patrol officers are assigned to shifts and to geographic areas. Demands on the police differ according to the time of day, day of the week, and even season of the year. Most serious crimes occur during the evening hours, and the fewest occur in the early morning. Police executives try to allocate their patrol resources according to these variables to achieve what they believe to be the most productive use of officers. Departments monitor patterns in reported crimes and calls for service in order to adjust their plans for deploying patrol officers.

The assignment of officers to specific locations is only one aspect of patrol strategies. Law enforcement officials must also decide how police will travel on patrol and what activities the officers will emphasize. Experimentation with different strategies in various cities has led to numerous choices for police leaders. In addition, research on these strategies sheds light on the strengths and weaknesses of various options. We shall examine several options in greater detail: (1) preventive patrol, (2) hot spots, (3) rapid response time, (4) foot versus motorized patrol, (5) one-person versus two-person patrol units, and (6) aggressive patrol.

Preventive Patrol

Preventive patrol has long been thought to help deter crime. Since the days of Sir Robert Peel, experts have argued that a patrol officer's moving through an area will keep criminals from carrying out illegal acts. In 1974 this assumption was tested in Kansas City, Missouri. The surprising results shook the theoretical foundations of American policing (Sherman and Weisburd, 1995).

In the Kansas City Preventive Patrol Experiment, a 15-beat area was divided into three sections, each with similar crime rates, population characteristics, income levels, and numbers of calls to the police. In one area, labeled "reactive," all preventive patrol was withdrawn, and the police entered only in response to citizens' calls for service. In another section, labeled "proactive," preventive patrol was raised to as much as four times the normal level; all other services were provided at the same levels as before. The third section was used as a control, with the usual level of services, including preventive patrol, maintained. After observing events in the three sections for a year, the researchers concluded that the changes in patrol strategies had had *no* major effects on (1) the amount of crime reported, (2) the amount of crime as measured by citizen surveys, or (3) citizens' fear of crime (Kelling, Pate, et al., 1974). Neither a decrease nor an increase in patrol activity had any apparent effect on crime.

Despite contradictory findings of other studies using similar research methods, the Kansas City experiment "remains the most influential test of the general deterrent effects of patrol on crime" (Sherman and Weisburd, 1995: 626). Because of this study, many departments increased their emphasis on maintaining order and serving the public rather than thinking of themselves as primarily engaged in crime control. The Kansas City study called into question the inflexible aspects of preventive patrol. By contrast, as discussed in the New Directions in Criminal Justice Policy feature, contemporary police departments can use evidence-based practices to focus their crime control activities on hot spots and problem-oriented policing as a means of using patrol officers to impact crime.

Hot Spots

In the past, patrols were organized by "beats." It was assumed that crime can happen anywhere, and the entire beat must be patrolled at all times. Research shows, however, that crime is not spread evenly over all times and places (Braga, Papachristos, and Hureau, 2010). Instead, direct-contact predatory crimes, such as muggings and robberies, occur when three elements converge: motivated offenders, suitable targets, and the absence of anyone who could prevent the violation. This means that resources should center on "hot spots," places where crimes are likely to occur (Telep, Mitchell, and Weisburd, 2014).

Advocates of evidence-based policing argue that "place-based policing," such as focusing on hot spots, can prevent crime and also reduce arrests and costs of processing cases (Telep and Weisburd, 2012; Aden and Koper, 2011). According to David Weisburd (2011: 16), "If place-based policing were to become the central focus of police crime prevention, rather than arrest and apprehension of offenders, we would likely see at the same time a reduction in prison populations and an increase in crime prevention effectiveness of the police."

In a classic study of crime in Minneapolis, researchers found that a small number of hot spots—3 percent of streets and intersections—produced 50 percent of calls to the police. By analyzing the places from which calls were made, administrators could identify those areas that produced the most crime (Sherman, Gartin, and Buerger, 1989). Because research casts doubt on the ability of officers to identify hot spots for themselves, departments need to gather data about crimes and order maintenance problems (Bichler and Gaines, 2005).

With this knowledge, officers can be assigned to **directed patrol**—a proactive strategy designed to direct resources to known high-crime areas. Research indicates that directed patrol activities focused on suspicious activities and locations can reduce violent gun crime (C. S. Koper and Mayo-Wilson, 2006; McGarrell et al., 2001). There is a risk, however, that the extra police pressure may simply cause lawbreakers to move to another neighborhood. On the other hand, one study that found increased activity in areas adjacent to the hot spots targeted by police was likely attributable to citizens in those areas increasing their willingness to call the police when they knew that police were nearby and eager to address community problems. Thus there may have been an increase in reported crimes but perhaps no actual increase in crime (B. Taylor, Koper, and Woods, 2010).

directed patrol
A proactive form of patrolling that directs resources to known high-crime areas.

Police administrators know that the amount of crime varies by season and time. Rates of predatory crimes such as robbery and rape increase in the summer months, when people are outdoors. By contrast, domestic violence occurs more frequently in winter, when intimates spend more time indoors in close proximity to one another.

There are also "hot times," generally between 7:00 P.M. and 3:00 A.M. The Minneapolis study found that 51.9 percent of crime calls to the police came during this period, whereas the fewest calls were made between 3:00 A.M. and 11:00 A.M. With this knowledge, the department increased patrol presence in hot spots and at hot times (C. Koper, 1995). Although this strategy resulted in less crime, many officers disliked the new tactics. Being a "presence" in a hot spot might deter criminals, but the officers grew bored. Preventing crime is not as glamorous as catching criminals (Sherman and Weisburd, 1995).

A new technical development that can assist police departments in utilizing a strategy of policing hot spots is the existence of data-analysis software that helps to make predictions about the timing and locations of certain kinds of criminal activity. Read the Technology and Criminal Justice feature to examine this new tool for law enforcement.

Rapid Response Time

Most departments are organized so that calls for help come to a central section that dispatches the nearest officers by radio to the site of the incident. Because most citizens have access to phones, most cities have 911 systems, and because

TECHNOLOGY & CRIMINAL JUSTICE

SPECIALIZED SOFTWARE, INFORMATION ANALYSIS, AND CRIME CONTROL

In 2013, police officials in Tempe, Arizona, credited information analysis and data sharing for significant decreases in crime. New software helps officers to analyze crime trends and to immediately update records databases. Thus information on reported crimes, suspects, and other aspects of investigations can be accessed immediately by officers in the field. In addition, information is instantly added to national databases so that departments can share information about suspects and crime trends. Information sharing has led to greater cooperation with neighboring police departments as well as with state and federal officials, and contributed to solving a number of crimes.

Police officials in Santa Cruz, California, contacted researchers who had developed software to predict earthquakes and asked them to develop prediction software to anticipate when and where crimes such as burglary, bicycle thefts, and assaults were likely to take place. Based on existing crime data, officers were given reports at the start of each shift about the likeliest times and locations for specific crimes to occur. The city saw nearly a 20 percent reduction in burglaries over the course of a year even as a decrease in police personnel occurred due to budget cuts. Based on the example of California cities following the lead of Santa Cruz, the Seattle police department began to use prediction software to address its own crime problems.

Microsoft Corporation worked with New York City to develop software called the Domain Awareness System. The system incorporates information from public surveillance cameras, license-plate readers at the city's entry bridges and tunnels, radiation detection devices around the city, and other information, such as emergency calls within New York City. The system proved very useful in solving several highly publicized crimes. Other cities began inquiring about purchasing the system and now employ it to address their own issues.

most officers patrol in squad cars linked to headquarters by two-way radios, cell phones, and computers, police can respond quickly to calls. But are response times short enough to catch offenders?

Several studies have measured the impact of police response time on the ability of officers to intercept a crime in progress and arrest the criminal. In a classic study, William Spelman and Dale Brown (1984) found that the police succeeded in only 29 of 1,000 cases. It made little difference whether they arrived 2 minutes or 20 minutes after the call. What did matter, however, was how soon the police were called.

Although delayed arrival of the police is often due to slowness in calling, it seems unlikely that one could improve arrest rates merely by educating the public about their key role in stopping crime. As Spelman and Brown (1984) point out, three decision-making delays slow the process of calling the police:

1. *Ambiguity delays*. Some people are not sure whether the police should be called, because the situation seems ambiguous. They might see an event but not know whether it is a robbery or two young men "horsing around."
2. *Coping delays*. Other people are so busy coping—taking care of the victim or directing traffic—that they cannot leave the scene to call the police.
3. *Conflict delays*. Still other people must first resolve conflicts before they call the police. For example, they may call someone else for advice about whether to call the police.

Although delay is a major problem, reducing delay would only slightly increase arrest rates. In about three-quarters of crime calls, the police are reactive, in that the crimes (burglary, larceny, and the like) are discovered long after they have occurred. A much smaller portion are "involvement" crimes (robbery, rape, assault) that victims know about right away and for which they can call the police promptly (Spelman and Brown, 1984). Rapid response time

Although these advances in the analysis of data place cities in the position to employ evidence-based practices, certain risks arise from the acquisition of new technology. An audit of the Oakland, California, police department in 2012 found that the department purchased several expensive anticrime technology systems yet did not end up using them. With one system, it did not work as expected and then the company that sold it went out of business so no refund or repair was possible. The use of other systems can be affected by the need to periodically upgrade software or upgrade equipment at moments when budget cuts limit resources available for new technology purchases.

Sources: Jackee Coe, "Police: Technology Helped with Drop in Tempe Crime," *Arizona Republic*, March 13, 2013 (www.azcentral.com); John deLeon, "Seattle Police Turn to Computer Software to Predict, Fight Crime," *Seattle Times*, February 27, 2013 (www.seattletimes.com); Chris Kanaracus, "Audit: Police Wasted Millions on Software, Crime-Fighting Tech They Never Used," *Computer World*, August 1, 2012 (www.computerworld.com); Heather Kelly, "Police Embracing Tech That Predicts Crime," CNN.com, July 9, 2012 (www.cnn.com); Sam Roberts, "Police Surveillance May Earn Money for City," *New York Times*, April 3, 2013 (www.nytimes.com).

DEBATE THE ISSUE

Is there a risk of excessive reliance on technology? Could unanticipated flaws or unexpected failures cause problems that would have been avoided by relying on old-fashioned human observation and record keeping? Is there a risk that police officers will no longer develop the same useful knowledge and skills for investigating and preventing crimes when they rely on computers for so many tasks? Should police departments exercise caution in relying on new software and related computer technology? Give three reasons for your answer to this last question.

helps in only a small fraction of all calls. In sum, the costs of police resources and the danger created by high-speed response may outweigh any increase in effectiveness due to faster response times (Sherman, 1995).

✔POINT

15. What factors affect patrol assignments?:
16. What did the Kansas City study show about preventive patrol?
17. What is a hot spot?
18. What is directed patrol?
19. What types of delays reduce response time?

STOP AND ANALYZE: Do you find the results of the Kansas City Preventive Patrol Experiment surprising? Why or why not? Give two reasons for your answer.

Foot versus Motorized Patrol

One of the most frequent citizen requests is for officers to be put back on the beat. This was the main form of police patrol until the 1930s, when motorized patrol came to be viewed as more effective. Foot patrol and bicycle patrol are used in the majority of cities larger than 10,000 residents, including approximately 90 percent or more of cities with 50,000 or more inhabitants (Hickman and Reaves, 2006). However, departments typically use these patrol strategies in selected neighborhoods or districts with a high business or population density. Most patrolling is still conducted in cars. Squad cars increase the amount of territory that officers can patrol. With advances in communication technologies and onboard computers, patrol officers have direct links to headquarters and to criminal information databases. Now they can be quickly sent where needed, with crucial information in their possession.

However, as we have seen, many citizens and some researchers claim that patrol officers in squad cars have become isolated from the people they protect and less aware of their needs and problems. Because officers rarely leave the patrol car, they cannot easily anticipate and mediate disputes, investigate suspected criminal activities, and make residents feel that the police care about their well-being. When officers are distant from the people they serve, citizens may be less inclined to call for help or provide information. Indeed, some departments are keenly aware of the risks of too much distance from the public and the benefits of cultivating communications and relationships. Thus, for example, the Community Affairs division of the New York City Police Department makes a special effort to include meetings with neighborhood religious leaders, and arranges visits to meet residents in housing projects as part of officers' training (Hauser, 2008).

Because of citizens' demands for a familiar figure walking through the neighborhood, the past three decades have seen a revived interest in foot patrol (J. Ratcliffe, Taniguchi, Groff, et al., 2011). Studies have shown that although foot patrols are costly and do not necessarily reduce crime, they reduce people's fear of crime. In addition, citizen satisfaction with the police increases, and the officers gain a greater appreciation of neighborhood values. In terms of the cost and benefit, foot patrols are effective in high-density urban neighborhoods and business districts.

One-Person versus Two-Person Patrol Units

The debate over one-person versus two-person patrol units has raged in police circles for years. Patrolling is costly, and two one-officer units can cover twice as much territory and respond to twice as many calls as can a single two-officer unit. Officers and their union leaders support the two-person squad car. They claim that police are safer and more effective when two officers work together in dangerous or difficult situations. However, police administrators contend that the one-person squad car is much more cost-effective and permits them to deploy more cars on each shift. With more cars to deploy, each can be assigned to a smaller area and response time can be decreased. They also contend that an officer working alone is more alert and attentive because he or she cannot be distracted by idle conversation with a colleague. In light of contemporary financial pressures felt by police departments in an era of budget cuts, it may be difficult to maintain the expense of two-person patrol cars.

Aggressive Patrol

aggressive patrol
A patrol strategy designed to maximize the number of police interventions and observations in the community.

Aggressive patrol is a proactive strategy designed to maximize police activity in the community. It takes many forms, such as "sting" operations, firearms confiscation, raids on crack houses, programs that encourage citizens to list their valuables, and the tracking of high-risk parolees. In their classic study, James Q. Wilson and Barbara Boland (1979) have shown the link between lower crime rates and patrol tactics that increase the risk of arrest. They argue that the effect of the police on crime depends less on how many officers are deployed in an area than on what they do while they are there.

This classic study showed that officers in an "anticrime patrol" in New York worked the streets of high-crime areas in civilian clothes. Although they accounted for only 5 percent of the officers assigned to each precinct, during one year they made more than 18 percent of the felony arrests, including more than half of the arrests for robbery and about 40 percent of the arrests for burglary and auto theft (J. Q. Wilson and Boland, 1979). Research provides some evidence for the role of such proactive measures in reducing rates of robbery (Kubrin et al., 2010).

"broken windows" theory
Influential theory about increases in fear and crime within neighborhoods when there is insufficient police attention to seemingly minor public order offenses such as vandalism, loitering, aggressive panhandling, and prostitution.

The zero-tolerance policing in New York City is an example of aggressive patrol linked to the **"broken windows" theory** posited by James Q. Wilson and George Kelling (1982). This theory asserts "that if not firmly suppressed, disorderly behavior in public will frighten citizens and attract predatory criminals, thus leading to more serious crime problems" (Greene, 1999: 172). Thus, the police should focus on minor, public order crimes such as aggressive panhandling, graffiti, prostitution, and urinating in public. By putting more police on the streets, decentralizing authority to the precinct level, and instituting officer accountability, the zero-tolerance policy was assumed to be a major factor in reducing New York City's crime rate (Silverman, 1999). However, New York City also saw increasing cries of outrage from citizens, especially those living in low-income, minority neighborhoods, that the police were being too aggressive. Thus the surge in police stop-and-frisks on New York City's streets in the early twenty-first century led to widespread complaints and a major lawsuit alleging that the police had expanded tactics in a manner that was overly intrusive and discriminatory (J. Goldstein, 2013; A. Baker, 2008).

Aggressive, zero-tolerance police practices reduced gang-related crime in targeted precincts in Detroit (Bynum and Varano, 2002). Police departments also use aggressive patrol strategies to track high-risk parolees and apprehend them if they commit new offenses. However, other studies raise questions about whether aggressive patrol actually contributed to the New York City's crime rate over the past few decades (Rosenfeld and Fornango, 2014; Harcourt and Ludwig, 2006).

Although aggressive patrol strategies reduce crime, they may also lead to citizen hostility. In New York, Pittsburgh, Charlotte, and other cities, polls show support for the strategy. However, some neighborhoods complain that aggressive patrol has gone too far and is straining police relations with young African Americans and Hispanics. This issue pits the need to respect the rights of individuals against the community's interest in order.

Community Policing

As we saw in Chapter 5, the concept of community policing has taken hold in many cities. As characterized by Stephen Mastrofski and James Willis, "community and problem-oriented policing have probably had the greatest impact in challenging American departments' commitment to the standard approach to police patrol" (2010: 82). To a great extent, community policing has been seen as the solution to problems with the crime-fighter stance that prevailed during the professional era (P. V. Murphy, 1992). In addition, many cities have turned to community policing because the federal government has provided funding for the development of community-policing strategies and programs.

Joe Raedle/Staff/Getty Images

Police chiefs credit aggressive take-back-the-streets tactics with reducing urban crime rates in the past two decades. In some cities, however, there are questions about whether such tactics have harmed police–community relations through searches and arrests that neighborhood residents view as unjustified. If you were a police chief, what patrol strategy would you choose and what specific goals would you seek to advance?

CIVIC ENGAGEMENT

YOUR ROLE IN THE SYSTEM

You attend a neighborhood meeting in which police officers ask community residents for help in implementing and improving community policing. *Make a list of specific things that neighborhood residents can do to assist in the effectiveness of community policing.* Then look online at a report on public involvement in community policing in Chicago.

Community policing consists of attempts by the police to involve residents in making their own neighborhoods safer. Based on the belief that citizens may be concerned about local disorder as well as crime in general, this strategy emphasizes cooperation between the police and citizens in identifying community needs and determining the best ways to meet them (M. Moore, 1992).

Community policing has four components (Skolnick and Bayley, 1986):

1. Community-based crime prevention
2. Changing the focus of patrol activities to nonemergency services
3. Making the police more accountable to the public
4. Including residents in decision making

As indicated by these four components, community policing requires a major shift in the philosophy of policing. In particular, police officials must view citizens as customers to be served and as partners in the pursuit of social goals, rather than as a population to be watched, controlled, and served reactively (Morash, Ford, White, et al., 2002). Although crime control may still be a priority in community policing, the change in emphasis can strengthen police effectiveness for order maintenance and service (Zhao, He, and Loverich, 2003).

Departments that view themselves as emphasizing community policing do not necessarily implement identical patrol strategies and initiatives (Thurman, Zhao, and Giacomazzi, 2001). Some departments emphasize identifying and solving problems related to disorder and crime. Other departments work mainly on strengthening local neighborhoods. A department's emphasis can affect which activities become the focus of officers' working hours.

Organizational factors can also affect the implementation of community policing. For example, community policing may be carried out by patrol officers assigned to walk neighborhood beats so that they can get to know residents better. It may entail creating police mini-stations in the community and police-sponsored programs for youth and the elderly. Police departments may also survey citizens to find out about their problems and needs (Reisig, 2002). The common element in community policing programs is a high level of interaction between officers and citizens, and the involvement of citizens in identifying problems and assisting the development of solutions. As such, departments need to provide training in problem identification and give officers greater authority to make decisions (Giacomazzi, Riley, and Merz, 2004). As you read "Civic Engagement: Your Role in the System," consider the problem of encouraging public involvement in community policing.

problem-oriented policing
An approach to policing in which officers routinely seek to identify, analyze, and respond to the circumstances underlying the incidents that prompt citizens to call the police.

A central feature of community policing for many departments is **problem-oriented policing**, a strategy that seeks to find out what is causing citizen calls for help (H. Goldstein, 1990). The police seek to identify, analyze, and respond to the conditions underlying the events that prompt people to call the police (DeJong, Mastrofski, and Parks, 2001). Knowing those conditions, officers can enlist community agencies and residents to help resolve them (Braga, 1999). Research indicates that problem-solving approaches can impact homicide rates (S. Chermak and McGarrell, 2004). A scholarly analysis of multiple research studies focused on problem-oriented policing found positive impacts on problems of crime and disorder from this policing approach (D. Weisburd, Telep, et al., 2010). By contrast, an Oakland, California, study, which invested heavily in adding dozens of problem-solving officers, found no statistical evidence that the program was associated with reductions in crime and violence (J. M. Wilson, 2008). However, there may have been an impact on crime that was not detected in the study. There may also have been other positive effects that were not the focus of the study because police using this approach do not just fight crime; they address a broad array of problems that affect the quality of life in the community.

Many departments train their officers to use the **SARA** strategy for problem solving (Thurman et al., 2001: 206). SARA stands for a four-step process:

1. Scanning the social environment to identify problems
2. Analysis of the problem by collecting information
3. Response to the problem by developing and employing remedies
4. Assessment of the remedies to evaluate the extent to which the problem has been solved

Regardless of whether the police focus their resources on order maintenance, law enforcement, or service, they tend to respond to specific incidents. In most cases, a citizen's call or an officer's field observation triggers a police response. The police are often asked to respond to a rash of incidents in the same location. Because the police traditionally focus on incidents, they do not try to identify the roots of these incidents. By contrast, those engaged in problem-oriented policing seek to address the underlying causes.

Although community policing has won support from police executives, the Police Foundation, the Police Executive Research Forum, and police researchers, it may be difficult to put into effect. As with any reform, change might not come easily (Schafer, 2002). Police chiefs and midlevel managers, who usually deal with problems according to established procedures, may feel that their authority is decreased when responsibility goes instead to precinct commanders and officers on the streets (Alley, Bonello, and Schafer, 2002). Another problem with implementing community policing is that it does not reduce costs; it requires either additional funds or redistribution within existing budgets. Measuring the success of this approach in reducing fear of crime, solving underlying problems, maintaining order, and serving the community is also difficult. In addition, debate centers on how far the police should extend their role beyond crime fighting to remedying other social problems. Police officers may resist committing themselves to daily activities that emphasize goals other than the crime-fighting role that may have attracted them to a career in law enforcement (Mastrofski, Willis, and Snipes, 2002).

Crime and the Impact of Patrol

As previously discussed, the famous Kansas City experiment raised questions about whether and how police patrol impacts crime and crime rates. Thus police departments have tried various means to use patrol in order to provide service, order maintenance, and to achieve improvements in crime prevention and crime control. Research has begun to provide direction for police administrators by finding crime reductions through a focus on hot spots and problem-oriented policing (Telep and Weisburd, 2012). As indicated by the discussion of the various approaches to police patrol, experimentation with patrol will continue, especially as technological advances may increase the resources and efficiency of patrol officers as they walk a beat or drive through a neighborhood.

In recent decades, as discussed in Chapter 1, crime rates have generally declined in the United States. Many observers have attributed the decrease in crime, at least in part, to aggressive patrol strategies that flow from the "broken windows" thesis. According to these observers, police officers' attention to small matters and more-frequent questioning of citizens helped to catch wanted suspects, discover criminal activity, deter potential criminal activity, and reduce the fear of crime within communities. However, even research that finds a crime-reduction impact from these patrol strategies concedes that they explain only a portion of the reduction in crime (Rosenfeld, Fornango, and Rengifo, 2007; Messner, Galea, et al., 2007).

Other observers see the development and spread of community policing as an important element in crime reduction as officers become more closely connected to neighborhoods and receive greater cooperation from residents. Indeed, beginning in the 1990s the federal government actively encouraged the spread of community policing principles and even provided substantial funding for local communities to hire nearly 100,000 new police officers and carry out community policing programs. Yet, recent research analyses of crime trends have questioned whether community policing and the introduction of additional police officers across the nation actually had any effect on crime rates (Worrall and Kovandzic, 2007).

If we cannot demonstrate that crime rates declined because of new policing strategies, then what explains the reduction in crime? This is a complex question that is subject to debate. We might like to believe that we can address crime problems by simply adjusting the resources devoted to policing and the methods of deploying the police, but we lack strong evidence to support such a belief. Crime rates may have complex connections to the state of the American economy, employment opportunities, family stability, neighborhood cohesion, and other factors. Recently new debates have emerged about how changing social conditions in the United States may affect crime rates. For example, although some political commentators claim that the infusion of illegal immigrants into the United States contributes to increases in street crime, several prominent scholars have reached the opposite conclusion (R. J. Sampson, Morenoff, and Raudenbush, 2005). Despite highly publicized criminal activities by Central American-based gangs, these scholars argue that illegal immigrants typically add to stability in poor neighborhoods by gaining employment, promoting marriage and family stability, and avoiding behaviors that will draw the attention of police (Press, 2006; Bermudez, 2008). This is a subject that will undoubtedly be studied by scholars and debated by social commentators.

Other debates surround the impact of stiff sentences, high incarceration rates, and the subsequent reentry each year of nearly 700,000 ex-prisoners into American communities. Will the steady return of offenders to communities have an impact on crime rates? Research and debates about these issues will also become part of the complex picture of crime and the limited ability of criminal justice agencies to know precisely how to deal with it (Zernike, 2007; Fields, 2008; Solomon et al., 2008). There is certainly an important role for police patrol in providing service and order maintenance. And patrol officers also are essential in responding to and investigating criminal events. It is less clear, however, how much effect patrol can have on crime rates.

The Future of Patrol

Preventive patrol and rapid response to calls for help have been the hallmarks of policing in the United States for the past half-century. However, research has raised many questions about which patrol strategies police should employ. The rise of community policing has shifted law enforcement toward problems that affect the quality of life of residents. Police forces need to use patrol tactics that fit the needs of the neighborhood. Neighborhoods with crime hot spots may require different strategies than do neighborhoods where residents are concerned mainly with order maintenance.

The current era of budget cuts and reductions in police-force personnel may constrict police chiefs' flexibility in their use of officers. In Flint, Michigan, for example, a high-crime city that was economically devastated by the decline of the auto industry, there were so few officers after two-thirds of the force was laid off by early 2011 that it could take hours for the few officers on each shift to respond to calls concerning serious crimes such as kidnapping and armed robbery (LeDuff, 2011). Undoubtedly, other cities will look to Flint as an example of what they hope to avoid as the future of their own police patrols. In the case of Flint, the state of Michigan provided assistance by sending Michigan State Police troopers to help patrol the city (Goheen, 2013).

One promising development in recent years is the emphasis on evidence-based policing. Researchers and police executives have become much more conscious of the need to work together in planning rigorous studies that will provide useful guidance about how best to deploy officers and plan police patrols. As discussed in this chapter, research indicates that there are beneficial effects from directed patrol, an emphasis on hot spots, and problem-oriented policing. Because of the new emphasis on evidence-based policing, scholars are increasingly aware of their responsibility for designing studies and translating research results in ways that are usable by police departments. There are questions about whether and how well police agencies are using research results (Rojek, Alpert, and Smith, 2012). Yet, many police executives are clearly working to identify impediments to adoption of research-based practices and seeking to persuade their officers about the value of switching from traditional policing approaches, such as preventive patrol, to new emphases that have demonstrated benefits, such as hot-spot policing.

✔POINT

20. What are the advantages of foot patrol? Of motorized patrol?

21. How do one-person and two-person patrol units compare?

22. What is aggressive patrol?

23. What are the major elements of community policing?

STOP AND ANALYZE: If you were a police chief, what approach to patrol would you choose to implement? Give three reasons for your answer.

A QUESTION OF ETHICS

In 2014, a police officer in Chesterfield, Virginia, resigned his position when he was denied a raise for failing to write enough traffic tickets and make enough arrests to meet his department's standards. He showed a news reporter his performance evaluation, which said his work goals should be two or three traffic stops per day and one arrest per day. The evaluation also said, "Failure to meet expectations during this work performance plan will result in further disciplinary action." State legislators expressed concern about the department requiring officers to produce a certain number of tickets and arrests each day. However, the police administrator said the plan set out "performance standards" and did not constitute a "quota." The administrator said the performance standard simply reflected the average number of tickets and arrests per day that officers in the department had produced in the prior year. The prior year's average was simply used to mandate expectations to ensure that officers are productive.

Source: Melissa Hipolit, "Former Police Officer Exposes Chesterfield's Ticket Quota Goals," CBS6 News, July 14, 2014 (http://wtvr.com).

CRITICAL THINKING AND ANALYSIS

When police administrators state specific expectations about numbers of tickets and arrests to be produced by officers each day and promise to discipline officers who do not achieve those numbers, do ethical issues arise? Might an officer make unjustified traffic stops or arrests just to meet or exceed the mandated numbers? Is there a difference between a "performance standard" and a "quota" in this context? If you were asked to advise a police department about this issue, what ethical issues, if any, would you identify? Would you have advice about how to resolve discomfort with quotas and the desire to measure police productivity?

Summary

1 Discuss why people become police officers and how they learn to do their jobs

- To meet current and future challenges, the police must recruit and train individuals who will uphold the law and receive citizen support.
- Improvements have been made during the past quarter century in recruiting more women, racial and ethnic minorities, and well-educated people as police officers.

2 Describe the elements of the police officer's "working personality"

- The police work in an environment greatly influenced by their subculture.
- The concept of the working personality helps us understand the influence of the police subculture on how individual officers see their world.
- The isolation of the police strengthens bonds among officers but can also add to job stress.

3 Analyze the factors that affect police response

- The police are mainly reactive rather than proactive, which often leads to incident-driven policing.
- The organization of the police bureaucracy influences how the police respond to citizens' calls.
- The productivity of a force can be measured in various ways, including the clearance rate; however, measuring proactive approaches is more difficult.

4 Describe the main functions of police patrol, investigation, and special operations units

- Police services are delivered through the work of the patrol, investigation, and specialized operations units.
- The patrol function has three components: answering calls for assistance, maintaining a police presence, and probing suspicious circumstances.
- The investigative function is the responsibility of detectives in close coordination with patrol officers.
- The felony apprehension process is a sequence of actions that includes crime detection, preliminary investigation, follow-up investigation, clearance, and arrest.
- Large departments usually have specialized units dealing with traffic, drugs, vice, and juveniles.

5 Analyze patrol strategies that police departments employ

- Police administrators must make choices about possible patrol strategies, which include directed patrol, foot patrol, and aggressive patrol.
- Community policing seeks to involve citizens in identifying problems and working with police officers to prevent disorder and crime.
- Research has raised questions about the effectiveness of police patrol techniques and community policing for reducing crime.

Questions for Review

1. How do recruitment and training practices affect policing?
2. What is meant by the *police subculture*, and how does it influence an officer's work?
3. What factors in the police officer's "working personality" influence an officer's work?
4. What issues influence police administrators in their allocation of resources?
5. What is the purpose of patrol? How is it carried out?
6. Why do detectives have so much prestige on the force?
7. What has research shown about the effectiveness of patrol?

Key Terms

aggressive patrol (p. 268)
"broken windows" theory (p. 268)
clearance rate (p. 251)
differential response (p. 250)
directed patrol (p. 265)
incident-driven policing (p. 247)
line functions (p. 252)
preventive patrol (p. 253)
proactive (p. 247)
problem-oriented policing (p. 270)
reactive (p. 247)
school resource officers (SROs) (p. 260)
socialization (p. 240)
subculture (p. 240)
sworn officers (p. 252)
working personality (p. 241)

Checkpoint Answers

1 **What are the main requirements for becoming a police officer?**
✓ High school diploma, good physical condition, absence of a criminal record.

2 **How has the profile of American police officers changed?**
✓ Better educated, more female and minority officers.

3 **What type of training do police recruits need?**
✓ Preservice training, usually in a police academy.

4 **Where does socialization to police work take place?**
✓ On the job.

5 **What are the two key elements of police work that define the officer's working personality?**
✓ Danger, authority.

6 **What are the four types of stress felt by the police?**
✓ External stress, organizational stress, personal stress, operational stress.

7 **What is incident-driven policing?**
✓ Citizen expectation that the police will respond quickly to every call.

8 **What is differential response?**
✓ Policy that prioritizes calls according to whether an immediate or delayed response is warranted.

9 **What are the basic measures of police productivity?**
✓ Clearance rate—the percentage of crimes known to the police that they believe they have solved through an arrest—is the traditional productivity measure, now supplemented by such measurable activities as traffic tickets and stop-and-frisk searches.

10 **What is the difference between line and staff functions?**
✓ Personnel assigned to line functions are directly involved in field operations; those assigned to staff functions supplement and support the line function.

11 **What are the three parts of the patrol function?**
✓ Answering calls for assistance, (2) maintaining a police presence, and (3) probing suspicious circumstances.

12 **What is the job of the detective?**
✓ Detectives examine the crime scene, question witnesses and victims, and focus on gathering evidence to solve crimes.

13 **What are the four steps of the apprehension process?**
✓ (1) Detection of crime, (2) preliminary investigation, (3) follow-up investigation, and (4) clearance and arrest.

14 **What kinds of special operations units do police departments often employ?**
✓ Traffic, vice, narcotics, juvenile

15 **What factors affect patrol assignments?**
✓ Crime rates, "problem neighborhoods," degree of urbanization, pressures from business people and community groups, and socioeconomic conditions.

16 **What did the Kansas City study show about preventive patrol?**
✓ Crime rates do not seem to be affected by changes in patrolling strategies, such as assigning more officers.

17 **What is a hot spot?**
✓ A location that generates a high number of calls for police response.

18 **What is directed patrol?**
✓ A proactive patrol strategy designed to direct resources to known high-crime areas.

19 **What types of delays reduce response time?**
✓ Decision-making delays caused by ambiguity, coping activities, and conflicts.

20 **What are the advantages of foot patrol? Of motorized patrol?**
✓ Officers on foot patrol have greater contact with residents of a neighborhood, thus gaining their confidence and assistance. Officers on motorized patrol have a greater range of activity and can respond speedily to calls.

21 **How do one-person and two-person patrol units compare?**
✓ One-person patrols are more cost-efficient; two-person patrols are thought to be safer.

22 **What is aggressive patrol?**
✓ A proactive strategy designed to maximize the number of police interventions and observations in a community.

23 **What are the major elements of community policing?**
✓ Community policing emphasizes order maintenance and service. It attempts to involve members of the community in making their neighborhoods safe. Foot patrol and decentralization of command are usually part of community-policing efforts.

CHAPTER FEATURES

- **Technology and Criminal Justice** Gunshot Detection Technology
- **Doing Your Part** Homeland Security
- **New Directions in Criminal Justice Policy** The Use of Drones by Law Enforcement Agencies
- **Inside Today's Controversies** Should Police Officers Wear Individual Body Cameras?
- **Close Up** Federal Consent Decrees and Oversight over Local Police

CHAPTER 7

POLICING: CONTEMPORARY ISSUES AND CHALLENGES

CHAPTER LEARNING OBJECTIVES

1 Describe the new technologies that facilitate crime, assist police investigations, and affect citizens' rights

2 Discuss the issues and problems that emerge from law enforcement agencies' increased attention to homeland security

3 Analyze the policing and related activities undertaken by private-sector security management

4 Discuss the ways police can abuse their power and the challenges of controlling this abuse

5 Identify the methods that can be used to make police more accountable to citizens

CHAPTER OUTLINE

Policing and New Technology
- The Challenge of New Crimes
- Investigative Tools
- Weapons Technology

Homeland Security
- Preparing for Threats

Security Management and Private Policing
- Functions of Security Management and Private Policing
- Private Police and Homeland Security
- Private Employment of Public Police
- The Public–Private Interface
- Recruitment and Training

Police Abuse of Power
- Use of Force
- Corruption

Civic Accountability
- Internal Affairs Units
- Civilian Review Boards
- Standards and Accreditation
- Civil Liability Lawsuits

John Tlumacki/The Boston Globe/Getty Images

Dwindling crowds of people lined the sidewalks in downtown Boston on April 15, 2013. They cheered as the late-arriving finishers of the Boston Marathon came across the finish line. Suddenly, two loud explosions and clouds of smoke shattered the celebratory atmosphere. Amid screams and chaos, medical personnel on the scene as part of the marathon support crew found themselves suddenly providing first aid to spectators suffering catastrophic leg injuries from two crude bombs hidden in backpacks and left among the crowds on the sidewalk. Police officers and bystanders rushed to assist with moving the wounded to arriving ambulances. The unexpected and incomprehensible act of violence killed 3 people and wounded 170 others (Seelye, Rashbaum, and Cooper, 2013). In the immediate aftermath, the police did not have any specific suspects.

Reports on the bombing dominated news broadcasts throughout the day. For most Americans, the bombing at the Boston Marathon raised disturbing questions about the protection of homeland security. Government intelligence officials reported that there was no forewarning or specific threat about Boston being a target for suspected terrorist groups. As with the 2001 attacks on the World Trade Center and the Pentagon on 9-11, people were forced to wonder whether this was the act of a small group based in the United States or of an organized terrorist group directed and trained by enemies overseas. People could not avoid fearing that this might signal the beginning of new random attacks designed to kill Americans and instill fear throughout society.

Four days later, the entire nation sat transfixed watching live coverage of the substantial force of police from multiple local, state, and federal agencies moving door-to-door through Watertown, Massachusetts, to check each house for 19-year-old bombing suspect, Dzhokhar Tsarnaev. His brother

Tamarlan, the other bombing suspect, had been killed in a shoot-out with police the previous evening. Eventually, the police found the young bombing suspect, bleeding heavily from wounds, in his hiding place in a boat stored at the back of a driveway on a quiet street. He was arrested and taken to the hospital.

Modern technology served as the crucial element in solving this important criminal case affecting homeland security. Throughout much of history, it was nearly impossible to identify or apprehend criminals without eyewitnesses to the crime, the criminal being caught at the crime scene, or the criminal being found later in possession of stolen items or other incriminating evidence. In the case of a disguised assailant whose motive was murder rather than robbery, it could be exceptionally difficult to solve the case unless someone was caught with the murder weapon. This problem would be especially challenging in cases of individuals who leave bombs at a big public event and then disappear anonymously into the crowd. The development of technology, however, has altered the capabilities of law enforcement officers to identify and apprehend lawbreakers.

In little more than a day after the bombing, law enforcement authorities were able to isolate and enhance video from store security cameras at the bombing site in order to post photos of the two suspects carrying the bomb backpacks. Posting the photos nationwide via news media and social media led to the identification of the two brothers. Police also used cell-phone records to hunt for the bombers. In addition, forensic scientists analyzed bomb fragments to determine the contents of the explosive devices and whether they seemed to be built by professionals or amateurs. Further, during the hunt for Dzhokhar, the younger brother who escaped during a shoot-out with officers, helicopters with thermal-imaging devices and bomb-squad robots were brought to Watertown in anticipation of searching for the perpetrator and dismantling any bombs that he might be carrying.

Contemporary Americans take for granted the availability and usefulness of technology. American television viewers are fascinated by the *CSI: Crime Scene Investigation* television shows and other programs that depict the impressive ability of scientists to identify criminal suspects by examining microscopic bits of evidence. Because the United States is a relatively wealthy and technologically sophisticated country, it can fund and benefit from the development of new technologies that provide crucial assistance in various operations of the criminal justice system. As we learn about the role and impact of technology in criminal justice, we must also remember that existing technological resources are not necessarily available for use in all state and county criminal justice systems.

In this chapter we discuss several new developments as well as continuing issues relating to the police and their role in society. The issues include new technology, homeland security, the growing private sector of policing, and continuing concerns about police misbehavior and accountability. For each topic, questions emerge about the role of police in a democratic society, including the risk that police actions will threaten citizens' constitutional rights. For example, technological developments and the shifting emphasis toward homeland security raise concerns about the surveillance and searches of citizens who have done nothing wrong. Similarly, any shooting or other use of force by police that injures a citizen raises concerns that officers may have disregarded the constitutional rights guaranteed to people under the U.S. Constitution. In a democratic society, police must act within legal guidelines, remain under the control of elected officials, and be accountable for their actions. These principles can be violated when law enforcement personnel exhibit unethical and illegal behavior. Problems also arise if legislators permit police powers to expand too far because of public fear, a situation that some critics believe is developing with respect to certain aspects of homeland security policies.

We first look at how technological changes have both opened the door to new crime problems and given police innovative abilities to investigate criminal activity and monitor people's behavior. We also examine how these cutting-edge technologies raise new questions about the role of police and the preservation of citizens' rights. Second, we discuss the expansion of police activities related to homeland security, especially with respect to federal agencies. Third, we look at private-sector policing, which falls under the title of "security management," a growing industry that is increasingly affecting police operations and requiring unprecedented cooperation between public and private agencies. Finally, we explore troubling issues that arise when police abuse their power, and also examine what is being done to make police more accountable.

Policing and New Technology

Policing has long made use of technological developments. As discussed in Chapter 5, police departments adopted the use of automobiles and radios in order to increase the effectiveness of their patrols, including better response time to criminal events and emergencies. Technology has affected the investigation of crime as well. As early as 1911, fingerprint evidence was used to convict an offender. Police officers seek to collect fingerprints, blood, fibers, and other crime-scene materials to be analyzed through scientific methods in order to identify and convict criminal offenders.

Police officers also use polygraphs, the technical name for "lie detectors," that measure people's heart rates and other physical responses as they answer questions. Although polygraph results are typically not admissible as evidence in court, police officers have often used these examinations on willing suspects and witnesses as a basis for excluding some suspects or for pressuring others to confess. These traditional uses of technology still exist, but the resources and attention of law enforcement officials must now focus significantly on new technology-based crimes that increasingly confront society. Officers must now concentrate on the development of sophisticated technologies to combat such crimes and to aid in investigating other crimes.

The Challenge of New Crimes

Although technological developments have long provided benefits for police officers in fulfilling their duties, those developments also create opportunities for new kinds of crimes. In addition, the spread of technology can provide people with tools that permit them to evade responsibility for violating the law. In 2011, for example, controversy arose from the availability of a cell-phone "app"—software that provides an application for a specific purpose—that enabled drivers to pinpoint and avoid traffic cameras that identify red-light and speeding violations, radar speed traps, and drunk-driving checkpoints. Congress launched an investigation and asked cell-phone makers to stop offering this software for sale to consumers (Copeland, 2011). The use of new technology to break laws presents difficult and fast-changing challenges for law enforcement officials who seek to understand lawbreakers' techniques and keep pace with their technology. In Chapter 1, we discussed the worldwide problem of cybercrime, a form of crime that costs businesses, individuals, and government billions of dollars each year. There are also other technology-based crimes that present serious challenges for law enforcement officials.

Counterfeiting

Traditional counterfeiting involves the creation of fake currency that can be deposited into banks, used to purchase items, and otherwise enables criminals to achieve financial gains by passing worthless paper into the economic system. Counterfeiting not only constitutes theft by permitting criminals to exchange fake bills for actual products and services, it also harms the economy by placing into circulation bills that have no monetary value. Subsequent additional victims may receive the worthless paper as change in a purchase transaction or in payment for products and services. Historically, currency counterfeiters in the United States had difficulty matching the paper, ink, and intricate designs of real currency. Although they may be able to produce counterfeit bills that would fool individual clerks in stores, restaurants, and banks, it was difficult to avoid the eventual discovery that the bills were fakes. As image-reproduction technology developed, especially in the form of photocopiers and scanners, criminals found new ways to seek financial gain from counterfeiting. Among the reasons that it is a crime to make reproductions of U.S. currency is that counterfeiters initially found ways to copy currency images and feed those images into change machines. In went the fake paper currency and out came an equal amount of coins with real monetary value that the counterfeiters could then take to a bank and exchange for real paper money.

Continued improvements in computer and printing technology permitted counterfeiters to produce fake currency of increasingly better quality. Thus, in 1996, the United States began to redesign American currency and to employ new technological techniques that make it more difficult for counterfeiters to produce authentic-looking imitations due to the paper, intricate designs, and mix of colors (Mihm, 2006). The advancement and availability of copying and printing technologies create risks when in the hands of terrorist organizations and traditional organized crime groups. This threat leads American officials to constantly seek to improve U.S. capability to identify fake currency. In addition to improvements in the federal government's capacity to create difficult-to-copy bills, the countermeasures range from the use of special felt-tipped markers by retail store cashiers to detect fake bills to the establishment of scientific laboratories for the detection of forgeries by the U.S. Treasury (Mihm, 2006).

Currency is not the only product susceptible to counterfeiting through the use of available production technologies. In 2015, it was revealed that college students in the United States were ordering online Chinese-made counterfeit drivers' licenses for various American states in order to engage in underage drinking (Fliegelman, 2015). Such counterfeiting is not limited to college students seeking to avoid specific laws. These licenses can also be used by identity thieves and people plotting threats to American homeland security who wish to disguise their identities for far more damaging purposes.

In another example, legitimate businesses lose billions of dollars in potential sales each year when consumers purchase illegally copied, or "pirated,"

Hollywood movie DVDs and counterfeit luxury products purported to be name brands, such as Gucci, Chanel, Louis Vuitton, and Prada. It is estimated by the International Chamber of Commerce that counterfeit goods worth more than $650 billion were sold worldwide in 2008 at the cost of 2.5 million jobs for people who might otherwise have been employed by legitimate manufacturers. There are estimates that counterfeit products globally will exceed $1.7 trillion in value in 2015 (Hargreaves, 2012). More importantly, some of these counterfeit products, such as counterfeit insecticides, can be deadly to people who are exposed to them. Although American law enforcement agencies can attempt—with limited success—to prevent the importation of such counterfeit and pirated products, they can do little to prevent the manufacture of such products without the cooperation of authorities in countries where the counterfeiters are located.

Although counterfeit consumer products impose significant costs on American businesses, far more serious human costs are imposed by the counterfeiting of another product: prescription drugs. During the first decades of the twenty-first century, technological advancements produced a sharp increase in the problematic effects of counterfeit medications (Orlov, 2014; "Man Gets 1 Year," 2014). The discovery of counterfeit versions of specific medications increased from five different prescription and over-the-counter drugs per year in the late 1990s to more than 20 different kinds of new counterfeit drugs per year beginning in 2000 (Grady, 2003). The dangers of counterfeit drugs are obvious: Their use can cause the deaths of patients who believe that they are taking genuine drugs, or prevent patients from recovering appropriately from nonfatal illnesses. In 2008, a counterfeit version of the blood-thinning drug heparin came to the United States from China and led to the deaths of 19 Americans as well as triggering hundreds of serious allergic reactions (Bogdanich, 2008). There are estimates that as much as 50 percent of antimalarial medication worldwide may be counterfeit. Thus a curable disease that kills more than 500,000 people each year causes needless tragedy in Africa and South Asia due to the greed and heartlessness of counterfeiters (Hargreaves, 2012). New efforts to combat counterfeit prescriptions include the development of microscopic additives to medications that are detectable by a smartphone app to reassure consumers, doctors, and pharmacists that medications are genuine (Graber, 2013; C. Winter, 2013).

Crime-Enabling Technology

In addition to cybercrime and counterfeiting, other forms of crime are made possible by the development of technology. For example, the widespread use of credit cards, debit cards, and ATM cards provides an attractive target for thieves who, with the proper codes from those cards, instantly steal large sums of money by using the credit cards or emptying a consumer's bank account. A particularly damaging criminal device is the ATM skimmer, used by thieves to capture bank account information and PIN numbers. Thieves install their own card reader over the actual card reader of an ATM machine and mount a tiny hidden camera in a strategic position as a PIN-capturing device. When unwary bank customers place their debit or ATM cards into the reader, the thieves are able to gain bank account information, and the tiny camera records the users punching their PIN code into the numeric keyboard. Although the frustrated consumers will walk away thinking that the ATM is broken—as it will not dispense any money based on the fake card reader—the thieves will quickly be able to access the individuals' bank accounts using the card information and their PINs (Schultz, 2011).

Law enforcement officials work with bank representatives to devise new technological approaches to prevent such victimizations. They also create public education campaigns to show customers how to scrutinize an ATM before using it. An alert consumer can often notice glue or something else that looks unusual about an ATM and thus avoid using that particular machine. As with many other aspects of crime, defeating criminals' use of technology relies heavily on members of the public taking proactive measures to avoid victimization.

A parallel criminal scheme involves handheld credit card skimmers that a restaurant server or retail cashier can use to steal credit card numbers. As these thieves prepare to run a customer's credit card to pay for a purchase, they run the card first through their own small skimmer to steal the credit card number, which they then sell to criminals who use the numbers to purchase merchandise. In 2009, eight people in Washington, D.C., including five servers at three expensive restaurants, pleaded guilty to stealing credit numbers through this scheme after they were tracked down by the U.S. Secret Service. People who had eaten at the restaurants noticed unfamiliar charges for merchandise showing up on their credit card bills. The thieves in this scheme stole a total of $736,000 before they were caught (Markon, 2009). The use of such skimmers continues to be a problem. For example, transportation officials in Denver discovered credit card skimming devices attached to ticket-purchasing machines at suburban commuter rail stations in November 2014 ("RTD Finds," 2014).

One aspect of the availability of technology that presents grave concerns for police officials is the proliferation of high-powered weapons and body armor. Federal law forbids convicted felons from owning body armor—also known as bulletproof vests. However, because such items are legally available in most states, people intent on committing robberies and other criminal acts can obtain them and wear them in order to blunt the threat from police officers' firearms (McLamb, 2011). If police officers are fired upon by a criminal wearing body armor, it can be very difficult for them to prevent danger to themselves and the public with return fire intended to stop the assailant (Saletan, 2012). These challenges are enhanced by the spread of high-powered weapons that may leave police officers outgunned by criminals. In August 2010, Oklahoma City police officer Katie Lawson was ambushed from 20 feet away by a teenager shooting an AR-15 rifle—the civilian version of the M-16 military assault rifle. The assailant fired 26 rounds, striking her six times. Body armor will not normally stop the high-powered AR-15 ammunition, but Officer Lawson's life was saved because the bullets passed through her patrol car window before striking her bulletproof vest. The glass presumably slowed their velocity enough to prevent penetration of the vest (Dean, 2011). These aspects of technology affect the training and practices of police officers as well as the desire of departments to purchase weapons that will permit them to match the criminals' firepower (Harrington, 2010).

One response to the issue of criminals' high-powered firearms has been the federal government's effort to test and improve bulletproof vests through the U.S. Department of Justice's Body Armor Safety Initiative. In addition, the federal government assists local police departments in obtaining body armor. Since 1999, under the Bulletproof Vest Partnership, over 13,000 agencies have received a total of $277 million in federal funds to help with the purchase of 800,000 vests. Beginning in 2011, the federal government required local agencies to make it mandatory for officers to wear body armor in order to receive assistance from the program (www.ojp.usdoj.gov/bvpbasi/).

✔POINT

1. What actions have been taken to combat counterfeit currency in the United States?
2. What harms are caused by counterfeit products in the United States?
3. What aspects of weaponry increase the risks to police officers and the public?

STOP AND ANALYZE: In light of the fragmentation of policing in the United States—with so many different agencies at the federal, state, and local level, is it possible for all law enforcement officers to have access to the technology that they need to detect and combat contemporary crime? Give three suggestions for how the country might address this problem.

(Answers are at the end of the chapter.)

Investigative Tools

Throughout the chapters of the book, we are highlighting various aspects of technology, including investigative tools, in the Technology and Criminal Justice features. As these examples make clear, technological developments are key aspects of contemporary police departments' tools for investigating crimes and identifying offenders.

Computers

One of the most rapidly spreading technological tools for law enforcement officers is the computer, especially portable ones used in patrol cars. In addition, police departments increasingly equip officers with smartphones and tablets as devices with computer functions that are more portable than laptops installed inside vehicles. Among other benefits, computers enable instant electronic communication that permits the radio airwaves to be reserved for emergency calls rather than being used for requests to check license numbers or other routine matters.

Computers have become essential for investigating certain types of crimes, especially cybercrimes (E. Sullivan, 2013; Hinduja, 2004). Many police departments now train officers to investigate people who seek to meet children online and then lure them into exploitative relationships. Computer investigations also involve pursuing people who commit identity theft, steal credit card numbers, and engage in fraudulent financial transactions using computers (Collins, 2005). At the national level, federal officials must use computers to detect and prevent sophisticated efforts to hack into government and corporate computer systems in order to steal secrets or harm critical infrastructures, such as regional electrical systems and emergency warning systems (Markoff, 2009; Kilgannon and Cohen, 2009). Local police departments face greater challenges in training and equipping officers to investigate cybercrimes (Holt and Bossler, 2012).

Computers are also essential for crime analysis and "crime mapping," analytic methods used with increasing frequency by local police departments. Through the use of **geographic information system (GIS)** technology and software, police departments can analyze hot spots, crime trends, and other crime patterns with a level of previously unavailable sophistication and precision (Zhang, Hoover, and Zhao, 2014). By analyzing the locations and frequencies of specific crimes, such as burglary, or the nature of calls for service in various neighborhoods, police are better able to deploy their personnel effectively and plan targeted crime-prevention programs (Stroshine, 2005). Recall that the Technology and Criminal Justice feature in Chapter 6 discussed software programs that law enforcement officials increasingly use as part of predictive policing, an approach that utilizes the analysis of crime data concerning locations and times that specific categories of crimes occur (Kelly, 2012).

geographic information system (GIS)
Computer technology and software that enable law enforcement officials to map problem locations to better understand calls for service and the nature and frequency of crimes and other specific issues within specific neighborhoods.

The foregoing techniques are combined with weekly crime statistics for police departments that use CompStat-type approaches for allocating police resources to various neighborhoods and for holding police commanders responsible for crime control results in their precincts (Dabney, 2009). Under this approach, a police chief can press commanders to monitor information on crimes and crime locations in their districts and thereby respond proactively through decisions about how to allocate personnel on each shift and where to patrol. Commanders can be pressured to show results through their tailored responses to such measures, rather than by just following established routines that do not effectively address the problems revealed by the crime analysis data.

The crime analysis technology relies heavily on software that can analyze data. There is also hardware technology that can be useful to police officers seeking to solve crimes. The Technology and Criminal Justice feature discusses gunshot detection technology.

TECHNOLOGY & CRIMINAL JUSTICE

GUNSHOT DETECTION TECHNOLOGY

In January 2013, the U.S. Secret Service, the agency assigned to protect the president's safety, announced that it was interested in information about gunshot detection systems. Commentators presumed that the agency was interested in acquiring the technology for use in protecting the White House. The request called attention to a promising computerized tool that is able to analyze the location of a gunshot and instantly communicate the information to police without reliance on human witnesses to dial the phone and give what is, often, an uncertain estimate of where a shooting took place. These detection systems were originally developed for the military as a means to identify sniper locations. For police use, once the system is installed, it can electronically distinguish gunshots from other sounds and detect gunshot location through the interaction between a series of sound sensors placed in a specific neighborhood. As a result, the system can enable police officers to drive directly to the spot of the shooting and avoid driving around a neighborhood trying to find where a shooting occurred based on a 911 caller who heard the shot but didn't witness it. The precision in pinpointing the location of the shooting can help to save the lives of shooting victims who will receive first aid more quickly; it will also assist in catching whoever fired the shots.

The systems are expensive and thus difficult to acquire for many cities that are struggling with budget cuts. More than 70 cities, however, have decided that such systems are important enough for the expenditure of funds and the allocation of personnel to monitor the technology. Many cities have systems that rely on technicians at a remote corporate headquarters, who use satellite maps to quickly communicate the location of gunfire to the police department in the affected city. Obviously, it would be prohibitively expensive for most cities to install such systems broadly enough to provide coverage throughout an entire municipality. Typically, the systems are placed only in areas that have recurring crime problems involving gun violence.

As with any technology, there are questions about the accuracy of the system, particularly with respect to distinguishing

Databases

Police departments throughout the country can submit fingerprints from a crime scene in hope of finding the criminal's identity from among the more than 47 million sets of fingerprints stored in the FBI computers. Local and federal law enforcement officials routinely submit the fingerprints of everyone arrested for a serious charge so that the prints can be added to the database. If a suspect is found not guilty, the prints are supposed to be removed from the system (Engber, 2005). These databases may also be used for background checks on people who work in regulated industries such as casinos and banks (Engber, 2005).

A few years ago, matching fingerprints was time consuming because the impressions had to be sent to the FBI on cards. Since 1999, however, the Integrated Automated Fingerprint Identification System (IAFIS) has enabled police to send fingerprints electronically, and then have those prints matched against the millions of others in the database (Kaye, 2014). The FBI can also provide electronic images of individuals' fingerprints to local law enforcement agencies upon request. In addition, the FBI provides training for state and local police on taking fingerprints and transmitting those prints to the IAFIS for evaluation.

The Department of Homeland Security has developed its own fingerprint database from two primary sources. New rules established after the 9-11 terrorist attacks require the collection of fingerprints from every noncitizen entering the United States. This has created a database of more than 64 million fingerprints that can be linked to the FBI database containing an additional 40 million sets. Military and intelligence officials are also collecting unidentified **latent fingerprints** from cups, glasses, firearms, ammunition, doorknobs, and any other objects that they find overseas in

latent fingerprints
Impressions from the ridges on the fingertips that are left behind on objects due to natural secretions from the skin or contaminating materials, such as ink, blood, or dirt, which were present on the fingertips at the time of their contact with the objects.

gunshots from other sounds, such as firecrackers or car horns. In addition, there has been controversy when the systems pick up and record yelling or loud conversations, troubling many privacy experts about the prospect of this technology inadvertently becoming a government surveillance system that records the private verbal communications of citizens on the streets.

Police officials generally express enthusiasm about the usefulness of the gunshot detection technology. It can provide a huge advantage over the prior practice of waiting to respond to a 911 call about gunshots without always knowing the exact location of the shooting. In addition, there is often a delay of five minutes or longer as residents decide whether or not to call the police at the sound of a gunshot. Indeed, use of gunshot detection systems has demonstrated that in certain neighborhoods gunshots are so routine that residents do not even bother to call 911 when they hear shooting. The new technology can call police to the location even if no citizens are willing to report the gunfire. Enthusiasm for the systems is such that in Springfield, Massachusetts, a neighborhood group raised money to acquire a system for its residential area as a way to assist police at a moment of tight budgets (Tuthill, 2013).

Sources: Erica Goode, "Shots Fired, Pinpointed and Argued Over," *New York Times,* May 28 (www.nytimes.com); Michelle McGuinness, "Secret Service Seeks Gunshot Detection Technology," MSN.com, January 22, 2013 (news.msn.com/science-technology/secret-service-seeks-gunshot-detection-technology); Paul Tuthill, "Springfield Police Expand Use of Gunshot Detection Technology," WAMC.com, March 14, 2013 (www.wamc.org/post/springfield-police-expand-use-gunshot-detection-technology).

DEBATE THE ISSUE

If you were a mayor or police chief, how much would you be willing to spend to acquire a gunshot detection system? The systems can have annual costs of $40,000 to $60,000 per square mile of coverage. Would your answer depend on how many shootings your city typically experienced each year within a particular neighborhood? If you had to reduce any part of the police department's budget in order to acquire this technology, what cuts would you make? Describe how you would address these issues.

abandoned al-Qaida training camps, safe houses, and battle sites. The hope is that terrorists will be identified if their prints match those stored in the database (Richey, 2006).

As indicated elsewhere in the book, additional kinds of databases are used to check criminal records, DNA samples, tattoos, and other identifying information that is useful in investigating crimes.

Questions about the accuracy and effectiveness of technological developments persist, even though the developments were originally embraced with great confidence. For example, despite the long and confident use of fingerprint evidence by police and prosecutors, its accuracy has been questioned. In 2002 a federal judge ruled that expert witnesses could compare crime-scene fingerprints with those of a defendant, but they could not testify that the prints definitely matched. The judge pointed out that, unlike DNA evidence, fingerprint evidence processes have not been scientifically verified, the error rate for such identifications has never been measured, and there are no scientific standards for determining when fingerprint samples "match" (Loviglio, 2002). Prosecutors later persuaded the judge to reverse his original decision and admit the expert testimony about a fingerprint match, but the judge's first decision raises the possibility that other judges will scrutinize fingerprint and other forms of technical evidence more closely.

DNA Testing

In recent years, scientific advances have enabled police and prosecutors to place greater reliance on DNA "fingerprinting." This technique identifies people through their distinctive gene patterns (also called genotypic features). DNA, or deoxyribonucleic acid, is the basic component of all chromosomes; all the cells in an individual's body, including those in skin, blood, organs, and semen

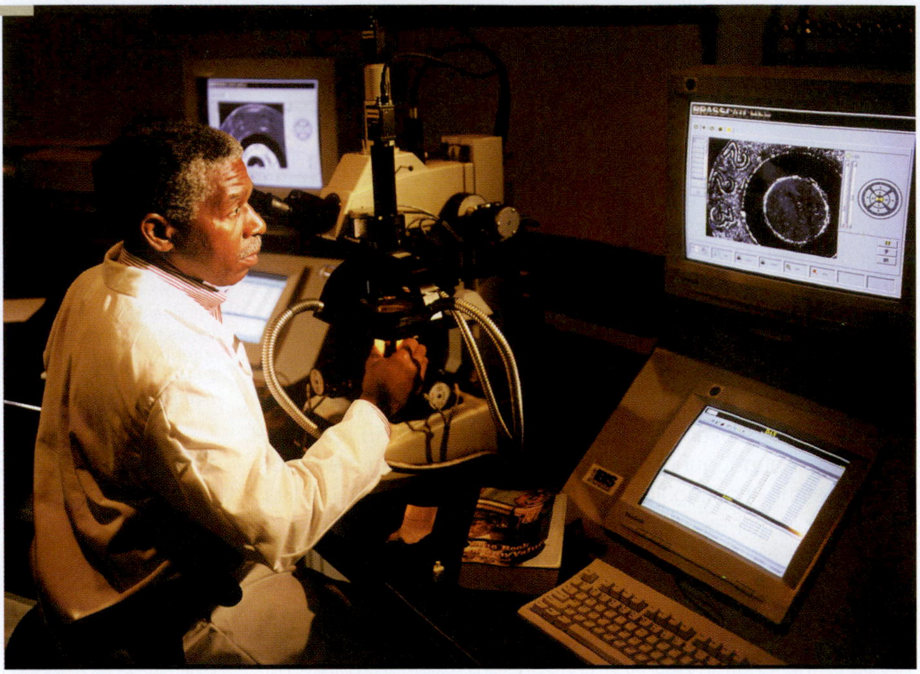

Brooks Kraft/Corbis

The development of databases and improvements in nationwide computer access to those databases helps investigators identify suspects through DNA samples, fingerprints, tattoos, and other markers. Here, the FBI's lead ballistics examiner, Walter Dandridge, studies the grooves of a .223 slug through a developing database of ballistics signatures from guns used in crimes. Is there any information about Americans that should *not* be centralized in these database collections?

contain the same unique DNA. The characteristics of certain segments of DNA vary from person to person and thus form a genetic "fingerprint." Forensic labs can analyze DNA from, for example, samples of hair and compare them with those of suspects. As described by several law enforcement officials, the increasing effectiveness of DNA testing as an investigative tool stems from "improved technology, better sharing of DNA databases among states and a drop in crime . . . that allowed detectives more time to work on unsolved cases" (Yardley, 2006). Table 7.1 shows the tests conducted by various government crime labs. Note that not all government forensic science labs conduct DNA tests. Indeed, some jurisdictions will hire private labs to handle certain tests, including DNA tests.

TABLE 7.1 PERCENTAGE OF LABS PERFORMING EACH FUNCTION, BY JURISDICTION TYPE

FORENSIC FUNCTION	TOTAL (%)	STATE (%)	COUNTY (%)	MUNICIPAL (%)	FEDERAL (%)
Controlled substances	82	86	85	75	59
Latent prints	60	54	63	78	65
Forensic biology (including DNA)	59	64	66	49	26
Firearms/toolmarks	55	55	63	62	21
Crime scene	52	44	62	71	44
Trace evidence	50	50	55	44	50
Impressions	44	44	53	43	24
Toxicology	42	50	43	35	9
Digital evidence	19	10	21	32	44
Questioned documents	16	13	13	24	29
Number of labs reporting	**397**	**211**	**88**	**63**	**35**

Source: Matthew R. Durose, Kelly A. Walsh, and Andrea M. Burch, "Census of Publicly Funded Forensic Crime Laboratories, 2009," Bureau of Justice Statistics *Bulletin,* August 2012, p. 2.

Critics worry that new technologies will create new collisions with citizens' constitutional rights. In several cities, police officers with DNA evidence from a rape have asked all of the men in a particular community to submit a DNA sample from a swab of saliva and cells inside the cheek in order to try to find a match with DNA of the perpetrator. Many critics believe that innocent citizens who have done nothing suspicious should not be pressured to provide the government with a sample of their DNA.

In spite of questions about which offenders should be required to submit DNA samples, many states and the federal government are building a national database of DNA records that is maintained by the FBI. Known as CODIS, which stands for Combined DNA Index System, the project began in 1990 as a pilot project serving a few state and local laboratories. CODIS has now grown to include 137 laboratories in 47 states and the District of Columbia.

The federal Justice for All Act, enacted in October 2004, greatly expanded the number of offenders in the federal justice system who must submit DNA samples. Previously, samples were taken only from those who had committed specific violent crimes. Now, samples are taken from offenders convicted of any felony, violent act, or conspiracy. In the federal correctional system, the Bureau of Prisons obtains DNA through blood samples from *all* incoming offenders. In addition, federal probation offices must now obtain samples under the new law. Federal probation offices are scrambling to find qualified phlebotomists (people trained to draw blood samples), and to acquire enough test kits for thousands of additional offenders. Moreover, Congress mandated that the samples be collected but did not provide any funds for the probation offices within federal courts to collect these samples (Administrative Office of the U.S. Courts, 2005). Thus, the new requirement is causing budget strains in the justice system.

States have their own laws governing DNA and which people are required to submit a sample. Efforts are underway to expand the collection of samples. In 2012, for example, New York officials began to collect samples from all convicted offenders; previously the state's law mandated collection only from those convicted of specific offenses (Eligon and Kaplan, 2012). In 2008, Maryland joined a dozen other states in collecting samples from people arrested, but not yet convicted, for murder, rape, and assault (Arena and Bohn, 2008). Georgia instituted a new law in 2008 to permit investigators to compare DNA evidence with samples collected from suspects when a search warrant is obtained in order to require those particular suspects to provide a sample. Thus the law required police to receive a judge's approval before using DNA from a suspect who was not yet convicted of a crime. Previously, DNA evidence in Georgia could only be compared to samples taken from convicted felons and not from unconvicted suspects ("Perdue OKs Bill," 2008). In 2013, the legal controversy over collecting DNA samples from arrestees who were not yet convicted of crimes was settled when the U.S. Supreme Court approved the practice in its decision in ***Maryland v. King* (2013)** (Kaye, 2014).

***Maryland v. King* (2013)**
U.S. Supreme Court decision that endorsed the legality of collecting DNA samples from individuals arrested but not yet convicted of serious offenses.

Another proposal to expand the use of DNA testing and evidence concerns searches that look for relatives rather than the exact person whose DNA was left at the crime scene. Although only exact matches of crime-scene evidence and an individual's DNA are supposed to be used in court, it is possible to identify other suspects through wider comparisons. For example, DNA comparisons may indicate that a convicted felon whose sample is in the database is not the perpetrator of a rape, but that he is a relative of the rapist. Thus police would have reason to undertake further investigations of the convicted felon's close male relatives. So-called "kinship-based DNA searching" is already used in Great Britain but is not used as widely in the United States (Wade, 2006).

As one critic noted about this approach, "it subjects family members to police scrutiny based solely on the misdeeds of their relatives" (A. Roth, 2010).

By taking samples from people convicted of specific crimes in the state and federal systems, officials hope that CODIS will enable them to close unsolved crimes that involve DNA evidence. Unfortunately, problems and delays in collecting and processing the samples persist. Nonetheless, the use of DNA testing and databases has led to arrests in a growing number of unsolved cases.

Many examples illustrate the use of DNA identification in cold cases. In March 2011, DNA tests on a discarded cigarette butt led to the arrest of a Connecticut man who was tied through DNA testing to 17 rapes in various eastern states from 1997 to 2009 (T. Moore, 2011). In April 2005, DNA tests linked a man in Georgia with 25 unsolved rapes in three states, including a rape committed in New York in 1973. The man had fled New York nearly 20 years earlier when facing different rape charges. He was eventually located when Georgia conducted a routine background check when the man attempted to purchase a gun. At the time, officials did not know he was linked to the other unsolved rapes, but the matches emerged when his sample was run through the national database (Preston, 2005). The successful use of the DNA database to close an old case raised officials' optimism about solving other cold cases by testing evidence that had been saved from many years ago. Such was the case, for example, of an imprisoned man in Georgia whose DNA analysis in 2006 indicated that he was responsible for four unsolved murders in Connecticut in the late 1980s and early 1990s (Yardley, 2006) and a serial murderer-rapist in Buffalo, New York, whose unsolved crimes spanned two decades (Staba, 2007).

Problems exist when officers do not submit crime-scene DNA for testing. Officers are accustomed to submitting DNA samples taken from suspects but not samples taken from crime scenes. When they fail to submit such samples, it is impossible to match crime-scene evidence with individuals who are already in the database (K. J. Strom and Hickman, 2010). Another problem is the delay resulting from a scarcity of laboratories and inadequate staff and equipment, which plague many states and the federal government (Ritter, 2010). It only took police five days to learn that a man's DNA sample in Vermont identified him as a murder suspect. Unfortunately, however, five years had already passed from the time that the man provided the DNA sample to the time when Vermont crime lab officials could put the sample in the state's database (Ring, 2005). Thus, the long delay prevented quick identification and arrest after he provided the sample.

Another potential problem with DNA testing, and with other aspects of forensic science, concerns the ethics and competence of scientists and technicians. Such problems have emerged in the FBI crime lab as well as in various states. For example, crime laboratories in Houston and Fort Worth, Texas, were investigated and shut down after improper handling and analyzing of DNA evidence led to the convictions of people who were actually innocent. For instance, a man sent to prison because of the Houston lab's DNA analysis was exonerated when a private lab retested the sample. Scandals involving improper lab procedures and erroneous testimony by forensic scientists have led states such as Oklahoma and Texas to enact laws requiring crime labs to meet national accreditation standards (Kimberly, 2003). The federal government now requires crime labs to meet accreditation standards in order to receive federal funds, but many labs have not yet gone through the accreditation process. Moreover, critics contend that accreditation will not prevent mistakes and erroneous testimony by scientists and technicians with questionable ethics, skills, or knowledge. This is especially true in the worst cases, such as that of a West Virginia forensic scientist who falsified test results and provided false testimony in order to help prosecutors gain convictions (Roane and Morrison, 2005). Scientists have an obligation to present truthful analyses, and they must avoid seeing themselves as part of the law enforcement team that seeks to convict people of crimes.

DNA is an investigative tool for police, but it can also be used to prevent and correct grave errors by exonerating wrongly convicted people. However, it can only serve this aspect of justice when evidence is properly preserved and available for later testing as DNA technology steadily improves. Fewer than half of the states require that evidence be preserved, and errors by court clerks and lab technicians have led to the disposal of relevant evidence, even in states with laws that require preservation. A more uniform and structured system of evidence preservation is necessary in order for DNA to provide its full potential benefits for the justice system.

Surveillance and Identification

Many cities use surveillance cameras in public spaces, including traffic cameras to identify cars that run red lights or exceed speed limits (B. C. Welsh and Farrington, 2009; J. H. Ratcliffe, Taniguchi, and Taylor, 2009). In addition, American law enforcement officials have experimented with other surveillance and detection technologies. The National Institute of Justice provides funding to help scientists develop devices that will assist the police. For example, scanners have been developed that will permit officers to detect whether individuals are carrying weapons, bombs, or drugs. Some of these devices detect foreign masses hidden on the human body, whereas others detect trace particles and vapors that are differentiated from those associated with human bodies and clothing (Oxley, 2014). For example, there are mobile scanners that can be installed in vans and trucks. These models were originally designed for use by the military to detect car bombs, but they are available for broader use in border security to detect contraband in vehicles (A. Greenberg, 2010). As technology advances, police officers on the streets might eventually use smaller, more-mobile versions, especially if they could point a handheld device at an individual passerby to detect whether the person is carrying weapons or contraband.

The most controversial application of new scanners thus far concerns those used by the Transportation Safety Administration (TSA) in checking passengers at airports. TSA began to use full-body, backscatter X-ray scanners that provide a view of passengers as if they were virtually naked, because it allows the operator to see through clothes to detect if any weapons or contraband are carried on the body. The use of the scanners led to a backlash of complaints by many travelers who felt as if such devices unnecessarily invaded their privacy, especially after the federal government revealed that, contrary to earlier promises, it had recorded and stored thousands of images of people (McCullagh, 2010). Such controversies illustrate the potential for clashes to arise between government's claimed need to take specific action to protect the public and citizens' sense of entitlement to personal privacy and legal rights.

The use of surveillance technology is likely to expand as part of the government's efforts to identify suspected terrorists. The USA Patriot Act enhances federal law enforcement officials' authority to monitor electronic communications, including the use of "roving" surveillance aimed at particular individuals without identifying or limiting specific facilities and devices to be monitored (C. Savage, 2011a). In 2012, controversies emerged about cell-phone companies providing information to local police agencies that sought to monitor individuals without obtaining a court order (Lichtblau, 2012). President Obama gave a speech in 2014 that acknowledged risks to citizens' privacy and constitutional rights from improper practices by government agencies intercepting private communications, but he also defended the necessity of certain kinds of electronic monitoring to protect national security ("Obama's Speech," 2014).

Scientists are working to develop technology to detect deceptions that suspects may use when questioned by police. Polygraph tests are considered unreliable as evidence, because some liars are very calm when they lie, and thereby avoid detection, whereas some truthful people are quite nervous when asked questions. Thus truthful people may look like liars on a polygraph test if their palms sweat and their heart rates increase as they answer. One approach under investigation is the use of a thermal-imaging camera that can detect faint blushing in the faces of people who answer questions in an untruthful manner (Ioannou, Gallese, and Merla, 2014). Critics warn, however, that this technology may simply reproduce the problems with polygraphs by looking only at physical responses that vary by individual (R. Callahan, 2002). Some people will have physical reactions from nervousness in unfamiliar situations even when they are being truthful.

United States v. Jones (2012)
Law enforcement officials cannot place a GPS device on a vehicle to monitor its movements based on their own discretion without obtaining a warrant or having another proper justification.

Kyllo v. United States (2001)
Law enforcement officials cannot examine a home with a thermal-imaging device unless they obtain a warrant.

The U.S. Supreme Court has already given a sign that it will look critically at some new police technologies. In **_United States v. Jones_ (2012)**, the justices decided that placing a global positioning system (GPS) device on a car to follow a suspected drug traffickers' movement constituted a "search." Thus the action required that police obtain a warrant from a judge or provide a justification for an approved warrantless search under the categories to be discussed in Chapter 8. Officers cannot freely place electronic monitoring devices on vehicles.

In **_Kyllo v. United States_ (2001)**, law enforcement officials pointed a thermal-imaging device at a house to detect unusual heat sources that might indicate marijuana being cultivated under grow lights. Their efforts led to a search of the home and the discovery of 100 marijuana plants. In the majority opinion, Justice Antonin Scalia declared the use of the device in this manner to be an illegal search. According to Scalia, "Obtaining by sense-enhancing technology any information regarding the interior of the home that could not otherwise have been obtained without physical intrusion into a constitutionally protected area constitutes a search" and is therefore covered by the limitations of the Fourth Amendment, especially the warrant requirement (*Kyllo v. United States,* 2001: 2043). In light of these decisions, it is not clear how judges may evaluate the permissibility of new technologies as specific uses of each device are tested in court cases.

✔POINT

4. What kinds of new technologies are assisting police with their investigative functions?
5. What problems are associated with the use of new technologies?

STOP AND ANALYZE: Among the investigative technologies described in this section, which ones raise concerns for you about adverse effects on people's privacy and rights? Give three reasons for your answer.

Weapons Technology

less-lethal weapons
Weapons such as pepper spray and air-fired beanbags or nets that intend to incapacitate a suspect without inflicting serious injuries.

Police officers have been sued in many cases when they injured or killed people without proper justification. Some of these lawsuits have resulted in cities and counties paying millions of dollars to people who were injured when police used guns or nightsticks improperly or in an inappropriate situation. To avoid future lawsuits, departments have given greater attention to the training of officers. They have also sought nonlethal weapons that could be used to incapacitate or control people without causing serious injuries or deaths. Traditional **less-lethal weapons**, such as nightsticks and pepper spray, can be used only when officers are in close contact with suspects, and they are not suitable for all situations that officers face.

The police need to have the ability to incapacitate agitated people who are threatening to harm themselves or others. This need arises when officers confront someone suspected of committing a serious crime as well as when they are attempting to control a crowd causing civil disorder. They also seek to enhance their ability to stop criminal suspects from fleeing. A variety of less-lethal weapons have been developed to accomplish these goals. Police use some of these weapons widely, whereas others are still undergoing testing and refinement.

Projectile weapons shoot objects at people whom the police wish to subdue. Some projectiles, such as rubber bullets, can travel a long distance. Others are employed only when suspects are within a few yards of the officers. Rubber bullets have been used for many years. Although they are generally nonlethal, they can cause serious injuries or death if they hit someone in the eye or elsewhere in the head. Many departments have turned to the use of beanbags, small canvas bags containing tiny lead beads, fired from a shotgun (Spencer, 2000). These are intended to stun people on impact without causing lasting injury. Several police departments in the Los Angeles area, however, abandoned the use of beanbags because of concerns about injuries and a few deaths caused by these projectiles as well as dissatisfaction with their accuracy when fired at a target (J. Leonard, 2002). In 2015, a suburban Chicago police officer was tried and acquitted on criminal charges after a 95-year-old nursing home resident, who was in an agitated state and holding a knife, died as a result of being shot by the officer with a beanbag projectile weapon ("Police Officer Acquitted," 2015).

Other departments have begun to use airguns that shoot "pepperballs," small plastic pellets filled with a peppery powder that causes coughing and sneezing on release after the suspect is stunned by the impact of the pellet. This weapon drew increased scrutiny after an Emerson College student died when she was hit in the eye by a projectile that disperses pepper spray as police officers attempted to control a crowd of revelers who were celebrating a Boston Red Sox victory (CNN, 2004a). Officers can also fill the pellets with green dye in order to mark and later arrest individuals in an out-of-control crowd (Randolph, 2001). Other weapons under development include one that shoots nets that wrap around individual suspects and another that sprays a fountain of foam that envelops the suspect in layers of paralyzing ooze.

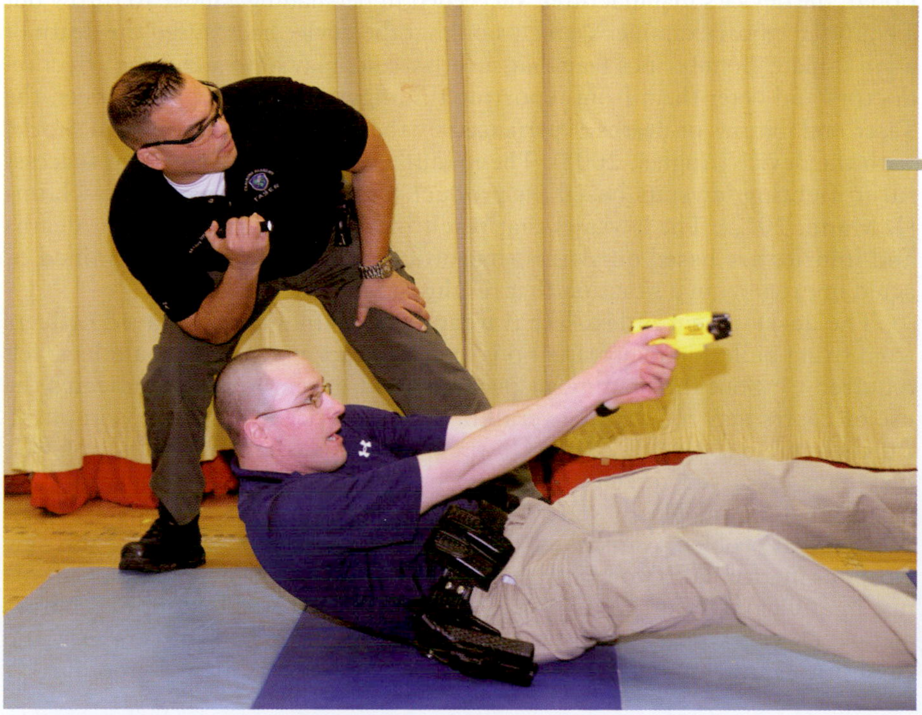

AP Images/The News-Item, Mike Staugaitis

Tasers and similar conducted energy devices give police officers the opportunity to incapacitate threatening people with less-than-lethal force when in prior years they might have used firearms. Because some people have died after being subjected to these weapons, controversies exist about whether their use should be strictly limited to truly dangerous situations. Are there risks that new weapons technology will be used in the field without a full understanding of how they may cause serious harm to people with specific medical conditions or other special vulnerabilities?

Law enforcement agencies may also eventually have versions of new weapons being developed for the military, such as devices that send out incapacitating blasts of heat or blinding flash explosions (Hambling, 2005). For example, a new military weapon called Silent Guardian shoots a focused beam of radiation that is tuned precisely to stimulate human pain nerves. It inflicts unbearable, incapacitating pain, but, according to the inventors, does not cause injuries (Hanlon, 2007). A law enforcement version, if it worked as intended, could be an alternative to using lethal firearms in some situations.

For suspects who are close at hand, many police departments use CEDs—conducted energy devices—the most well-known of which is the Taser, a weapon with prongs that sends an incapacitating electric jolt of 50,000 volts into people on contact (A. O'Brien and Thom, 2014; Ith, 2001). More than 12,000 law enforcement agencies in the United States use these devices. However, the human rights organization Amnesty International has documented more than 150 cases since 2001 in which people died after police used a Taser on them. The manufacturer of Tasers, as well as some researchers, dispute whether the device actually caused the deaths. Researchers are identifying factors that may be associated with higher risk from death after Taser use, including the subject's mental illness or drug use and multiple administrations of shocks (M. D. White and Ready, 2009). Issues have also arisen about whether officers are too quick to use Tasers when they could use persuasion or other means to calm agitated or uncooperative people. The controversy reached an initial high point when Miami police officers used a Taser on a six-year-old child who was threatening to harm himself (CNN, 2004b). In late 2012 and early 2013, there were news reports of cities in Utah, Ohio, North Carolina, and elsewhere paying large sums to settle significant lawsuits based on deaths and permanent injuries that occurred after police officers' use of CED weapons (D. G. Callahan, 2013; B. Adams, 2012; T. Reaves, 2012). One man's death in Utah led that state's legislature to enact a resolution encouraging police departments to participate in specific training on how to handle uncooperative mentally ill people without resorting quickly to the use of force (M. Rogers, 2011).

A related controversy expanded in 2008 when lawsuits by Taser International, the device's manufacturer, succeeded in persuading a judge to throw out a county medical examiner's conclusion that the device had caused the death of a jail inmate. Some critics fear that such lawsuits may have a chilling effect on doctors and deter them from reporting findings about any links between the Taser and injuries or deaths experienced by those who receive electrical shocks with the device (Anglen, 2008). The manufacturer of Taser has been successful in fighting lawsuits based on product liability or warning label claims (J. Mann, 2012). The lawsuits that result in financial settlements for deaths and injuries are based on claims that officers were insufficiently trained or acted improperly in a situation that resulted in the use of a CED.

The development of less-lethal weapons has undoubtedly saved officers from firing bullets in many situations in which they previously would have felt required to shoot threatening suspects. Indeed, recent research indicates the use of Tasers may reduce the overall injuries to officers and citizens in physical encounters (Bulman, 2010). On the other hand, the availability of CEDs may have increased citizen injuries in encounters with police. Clearly, these weapons do not magically solve the problem of incapacitating suspects safely. Mechanical problems, mistakes, or misuse by the officer may make the new weapons ineffectual. Two highly publicized incidents, one in Oakland, California, in 2009 and the other in Tulsa, Oklahoma, in 2015 led to criminal charges against officers who killed suspects when the officers mistakenly grabbed and fired pistols instead of CED devices. In addition, officers may act too quickly in firing a less-lethal weapon during inappropriate situations. In such circumstances, needless minor injuries may be inflicted, or the targeted person may become more enraged and thus more threatening to the officers who later must transport the person to jail. Moreover, an officer can carry only so many weapons in his or her arms. The officer whose shooting of Michael Brown in Ferguson, Missouri, in 2014 led to civil disorder and protests claimed that on the day of the shooting he had too much to carry and was unable to take a CED with him. The existence of less-lethal weapons will not ensure that such weapons are actually handy when officers must make difficult, on-the-spot decisions about how to handle a threatening situation.

No matter what new technologies are developed by scientists for identification, investigation, and weaponry, there is no guarantee that new devices and techniques will be widely available. New technology brings with it additional expenses for equipment, training, and maintenance. In an era of budget cutting at all levels of government, police agencies are likely to forgo opportunities to acquire new technology in favor of retaining personnel to undertake the essential tasks of policing.

✔POINT 6. What kinds of new weaponry have police employed?

STOP AND ANALYZE: Critics fear that officers will be too quick to use less-lethal weapons when they should first try to talk an agitated person into cooperating, or wait to see if the person in question will stop arguing. What guidelines would you give to officers concerning when they should use a less-lethal weapon, such as a Taser? Write a description of your preferred rules for using such weapons.

Homeland Security

We have seen how the contemporary emphasis on homeland security has changed policing. In the months following the September 11 attacks, the federal government reorganized various agencies, including law enforcement agencies, in creating the Department of Homeland Security (DHS). Shifts in the FBI's priorities and in the availability of federal funds created new burdens, opportunities, and objectives for local law enforcement agencies. Even traditional programs, such as Neighborhood Watch, now include discussions of moving beyond crime prevention toward contributing more to homeland security. Note, however, that both the FBI and the DHS have been criticized for failing to do enough to make the country fully prepared. For example, in 2008 the U.S. Senate Intelligence Committee issued a report criticizing the FBI's failure to fill key supervisory positions responsible for al-Qaida-related cases, inadequate training of newly hired intelligence analysts, and delays in the development of a program to collect intelligence on foreign powers operating in the United States (R. B. Schmitt, 2008). The FBI has also been criticized for its arguments with ATF (Bureau of Alcohol, Tobacco, Firearms, and Explosives) over which agency will take charge of specific cases (Esposito, 2010).

Although the emphasis on homeland security accelerated and generated a sense of urgency after the hijackers' attacks on September 11, 2001, many police departments gained awareness about their role in homeland security prior to that date. For example, Timothy McVeigh, an antigovernment radical, detonated a truck bomb in front of the Oklahoma City Federal Building on April 19, 1995. The bomb killed 168 people and injured hundreds more. In both of these examples, local police officers, as well as firefighters, were first responders who rescued survivors, rendered first aid, and began to collect criminal evidence that would be used to identify and punish the perpetrators.

DOING YOUR PART

HOMELAND SECURITY

In a single-engine plane flying along the northern coast of California, three retirees use binoculars to look for suspicious activities on ships and docks. They are volunteers in the Coast Guard Auxiliary. They underwent background investigations and received training, but their only direct compensation is partial reimbursement for the fuel and maintenance of the privately owned aircraft. In other parts of the country, truck drivers receive instruction on how to spot suspicious activities, such as people photographing bridges, nuclear power plants, or other important elements of the country's infrastructure. In some cities, volunteers patrol airports, gas pipelines, and municipal water facilities. Although some critics worry that overzealous civilians may harass innocent people, the government sees citizen involvement as an essential component of homeland security. The Department of Homeland Security has discouraged the thought of using citizen-volunteers to patrol the border with Mexico to detect and apprehend undocumented immigrants. Privately organized groups have sought to participate in border patrol work, but the government is concerned that overzealous, under-trained volunteers may use force inappropriately, thus leading to injuries to themselves and others.

The Department of Homeland Security sponsors the Citizen Corps, a network of volunteer organizations. As stated on its website,

> Citizen Corps asks you to embrace the personal responsibility to be prepared; to get training in first aid and emergency skills; and to volunteer to support local emergency responders, disaster relief, and community safety.

The Citizens Corps volunteers provide training in emergency preparedness through Community Emergency Response Team (CERT) academies, two-week programs on various topics including disaster preparedness, first aid, fire safety, and search and rescue. What contribution could you make to the homeland security effort?

Sources: Based on Dean E. Murphy, "Retirees Answer the Call to Hunt for Terrorists," *New York Times,* May 4, 2005, p. A12; "Sheriff's Citizen Corps Offer Free Emergency Preparation and Response Training," This Is Reno website, February 14, 2013 (thisisreno.com/2013/02/sheriffs-citizen-corps-offers-free-emergency-preparation-and-response-training/).

The events of September 11 served to teach Americans that terrorist attacks could not be treated as isolated incidents or rare events. Instead, government officials and citizens alike were forced to recognize that specific groups around the world were making plans to inflict large-scale damage on the United States and harm Americans on U.S. soil. These lessons altered the priorities of government agencies and pushed law enforcement at federal, state, and local levels to devise contingency plans for potential threats in the future. Such plans have been helpful in mobilizing and coordinating agencies for such events as the Boston Marathon bombing in 2013, as described in the chapter opener, and the attempted car bombing in New York City's busy Times Square in 2010 (P. Baker and Shane, 2010).

Although this section focuses on law enforcement agencies' efforts to combat terrorism, bear in mind that the government needs assistance from citizens in order to identify suspicious activities and respond to emergencies. As you read about the contributions of regular citizens to homeland security in the Doing Your Part feature, think about whether there may be a role for you.

Preparing for Threats

As discussed in prior chapters, the FBI and DHS make concerted efforts to identify and combat risks to reduce the threat of additional attacks. The FBI shifted a significant portion of its personnel away from traditional crime-control activities in order to gather intelligence on people within the United States who may pose a threat to the nation. The FBI also received budget allocations to enable it to expand the number of special agents and intelligence analysts working on counterterrorism issues. The agency seeks to coordinate its efforts with state and local officials. Federal officials also seek cooperation and coordination with their counterparts in many countries around the world.

Kevin Steele/Aurora/Getty Images

Police officers through the nation have increased their training in emergency-response procedures in light of threats concerning terrorism and homeland security. In an environment of shrinking budgets, do local police have the time and resources to effectively add homeland security responsibilities to their traditional duties of law enforcement, service, and order maintenance?

At the same time, the creation of DHS reflected a desire to have better coordination among agencies that were previously scattered throughout the federal government. The DHS also instituted new security procedures at airports and borders as a means of seeking to identify individuals and contraband that pose threats. Many critics believe that the federal government has not done enough to protect ports and critical infrastructure, including nuclear power plants, information systems, subway systems, and other elements essential for the functioning of American society. Attacks with devastating consequences could range from computer hackers disabling key military information systems or computerized controls at energy companies to a suicide airline hijacker hitting a nuclear power plant or chemical manufacturing site. If an attack should target and disable any of these entities, it would fall to local police to maintain order and to rescue victims.

Police agencies have traditionally gathered **law enforcement intelligence** information about criminal activities and organizations, especially in their efforts to monitor motorcycle gangs, hate groups, drug traffickers, and organized crime. The new emphasis on homeland security broadens the scope of information that agencies need to gather. According to Jonathan White (2004: 73), police must be trained to look for and collect information about such things as

law enforcement intelligence Information, collected and analyzed by law enforcement officials, concerning criminal activities and organizations such as gangs, drug traffickers, and organized crime.

- Emergence of radical groups, including religious groups
- Suspicious subjects observing infrastructure facilities
- Growth of phony charities that may steer money to terrorists
- Groups with links to foreign countries
- Unexpected terrorist information found during criminal searches
- Discovery of bomb-making operations

Local police agencies need training about what to look for and who to contact if any suspicious activities or materials are discovered (Meyer, 2008).

One of the disconcerting aspects of the September 11 tragedy was that specific agencies and officers possessed suspicions about unusual students at flight schools and individuals who had entered the country. If the agencies had shared information more effectively, some people believe that at least some of the September 11 hijackers would have been apprehended and questioned. In light of this lesson, law enforcement agencies at all levels are working harder to coordinate their efforts and share information. However, even more than a decade after 9-11, local police officials still complain that the FBI and other federal agencies do not share enough information with them about potential threats within their communities.

fusion centers
Centers run by states and large cities that analyze and facilitate sharing of information to assist law enforcement and homeland security agencies in preventing and responding to crime and terrorism threats.

Efforts to share information emerged in the form of **fusion centers** (Perrine, Speirs, and Horwitz, 2010). These are state and local intelligence operations that "use law enforcement analysts and sophisticated computer systems to compile, or fuse, disparate tips and clues and pass along the refined information to other agencies" (O'Harrow, 2008). The federal government has provided nearly $250 million for the development and operation of these centers. It is hoped that the gathering, processing, and sharing of information can help prevent plots from being executed. In retrospect, many wonder if 9-11 might have been preventable if the FBI had access to the CIA's reports on suspicions about the presence in the United States of two of the hijackers. Would the attack have been thwarted if officials in different states had been able to share their suspicions about the behavior of foreigners taking flying lessons in different parts of the country? If information can be passed down to local law enforcement officers, they may be able to discover suspected terrorists in their everyday activities of making traffic stops or encountering unusual behavior of people in the act of photographing bridges and government buildings (Sheridan and Hsu, 2006). The preparedness of police agencies, swift action, dissemination of information to the public, and cooperation between agencies appeared to contribute significantly to the capture of the second Boston Marathon bombing suspect in April 2013. Perhaps the training, equipment acquisition, and emphasis on coordination and sharing information has become a fixture in the operation of many law enforcement agencies after a decade of drawing lessons from the experience of September 11.

The emphasis on information analysis and coordination among agencies at all levels of the U.S. government, as well as coordination with foreign governments, also impacts law enforcement operations concerning other major problems. Information and coordination are essential to address drug trafficking, money laundering, gun smuggling, and border security. For example, homeland security efforts overlap with initiatives to combat transnational street gangs. For instance, the MS-13 gang from Central America has spread from Los Angeles to such places as Washington, D.C., and Charlotte, North Carolina, bringing with it various criminal activities, including a series of gang-related homicides (Lineberger, 2011).

There are lingering public suspicions about fusion centers and other law enforcement intelligence operations (Regan and Monahan, 2014). These concerns stem from revelations about government agents spying on American citizens during the 1960s and 1970s for merely expressing their views about civil rights and the Vietnam War. For example, as fusion centers in various states create massive databases that include such information as citizens' credit reports, car-rental records, unlisted cell-phone numbers, drivers' license photographs, and identity-theft reports, there are concerns that the government is unnecessarily intruding too broadly into the lives of all Americans, including those who are not suspected of any wrongdoing (O'Harrow,

2008; German and Stanley, 2007). In addition, the accumulation of so much information into databases and connected networks raises concerns about the risk of a security breach, either through the work of an ingenious hacker or through a government employee losing a laptop computer on a business trip, which will create massive problems with identity theft and computer crime. As law enforcement agencies in the United States continue to develop methods to combat terrorism and protect homeland security, many people will reexamine the balance between providing the government with appropriate tools and safeguarding the rights of Americans against government intrusions (K. Martin, 2008).

Within local police departments, the emphasis on homeland security has led to changes in training, equipment, and operations to prepare first responders to deal with the possibility of weapons of mass destruction and terrorist attacks. The police must also develop regional coordination with neighboring communities and state governments, because large-scale emergencies require the resources and assistance of multiple agencies. Communities need plans for conducting evacuations of buildings and neighborhoods. Police officials must work more closely with firefighters, public-health officials, and emergency medical services to prepare for anything from a bomb to a bioterror attack using anthrax, smallpox, or other harmful agents. Some of these threats require the acquisition of new equipment, such as protective suits to guard against suspected biological or chemical hazards, or communications equipment that can be used to contact multiple agencies. Many police departments are giving renewed attention to training specialized teams, such as bomb squads and SWAT teams, that will intervene in emergency situations. In addition, they must give all officers additional training on hazardous materials; on coordination with outside agencies; and on evacuation procedures for malls, central business districts, and hospitals.

For example, in the aftermath of the killing of Osama bin Laden by U.S. military forces in Pakistan in May 2011, the FBI and Department of Homeland Security issued warnings to police departments in cities throughout the country. The federal intelligence experts feared that retaliation could come in the form of "lone wolf" terrorists—angry bin Laden sympathizers who were not guided by any formal terrorist organization but who simply would decide on their own to build a bomb or fire a gun in an attempt to cause fear and harm (Bennett, 2011). Such an event could happen in any city in the country; thus all local police departments need to be vigilant and prepared for an event in their communities. There is an awareness that organized terrorist groups would most like to inflict maximum casualties in very visible attacks on big cities such as New York, Washington, or Los Angeles. However, this awareness should not make local officials throughout the country forget that any community could face danger. These dangers may be enhanced if the community is home to a chemical plant, nuclear power facility, or other component of the nation's critical infrastructure that might be a tempting target.

Just as the development of better communication and coordination among agencies can help combat drug trafficking, gun smuggling, and other crimes unrelated to terrorism, so too can training and equipment serve dual purposes. For example, new equipment for detecting and defusing bombs obtained under homeland security grants can be used for pipe bombs and other explosive devices created by people unconnected to terrorism. Similarly, training in the detection and dismantling of chemical weapons threats has applications in police efforts to find and destroy meth labs and thereby address one of the nation's growing problems with illegal drugs.

CIVIC ENGAGEMENT

YOUR ROLE IN THE SYSTEM

What could you see that would arouse your suspicions enough to lead you to call law enforcement officials with information about a potential threat to homeland security? *Make a list of things that you might observe that should be reported to authorities.* Then look at the things that Nevada's homeland security officials recommend that citizens report.

A key element of homeland security planning is the development of the Incident Command System (ICS). The principles of ICS were first developed to help multiple agencies coordinate their efforts in addressing large wildfires in western states. ICS strategies include planning to determine what individual will take charge of managing resources and operations in response to a critical incident. They also include the development of an Incident Action Plan that coordinates the resources, activities, and responsibilities of various agencies and individuals involved in responding to an emergency. By using ICS, agencies are not taken by surprise when emergencies arise and they can spring into action with well-coordinated efforts to maintain order, address primary threats such as fires or bombings, evacuate endangered people, and provide medical aid. The awareness of homeland security needs after September 11 has encouraged police departments to work closely with state officials, firefighters, public-health officials, hospitals, and others to develop local and regional ICS plans. Also consider the role of citizens in homeland security as you read "Civic Engagement: Your Role in the System."

POINT 7. What have law enforcement officials done to enhance homeland security?

STOP AND ANALYZE: In light of the budget cuts affecting state and local government, imagine that you are a governor who must recommend choices about how to allocate shrinking resources. If faced with the following choices—reduce money for homeland security and law enforcement intelligence, reduce money for state police patrols and criminal investigations, or raise taxes—which would you choose and why? Give three reasons for your answer.

New Laws and Controversies

Controversies arose concerning new state and federal statutes created after September 11. Both Congress and state legislatures enacted new laws aimed at addressing various aspects of homeland security. More than 30 states added new terrorism-related laws. These laws ranged from narrow to broad—from statutes addressing a specific problem to broad authorizations of new powers for law enforcement officials and the definition of new crimes. At the narrow end of the spectrum, for example, after it was discovered that several of the September 11 hijackers had Virginia driver's licenses, Virginia passed a new law to make it more difficult for foreign nationals to obtain a driver's license without possession of specific legal documents.

An example of a broader law is Arizona's statute concerning money laundering, weapons of mass destruction, terrorism and terrorism hoaxes, eavesdropping on communications, and a prohibition of bail for people accused of violent terrorist acts. Some of the purposes and uses of these laws raise questions about whether government powers will grow beyond appropriate boundaries in a democracy that is supposed to place a high value on the protection of individuals' rights.

In 2011, the National Defense Authorization Act, which provides annual funding for the military, included provisions permitting terrorism suspects to be arrested and detained indefinitely and permitting the military to detain and question terrorism suspects on American soil. These provisions generated harsh criticism from civil libertarians who feared the expansion of governmental powers and the potential for Americans to be denied their rights (Jenks, 2015). However, members of Congress claimed that the wording was carefully designed to balance individuals' rights with national security. President Obama expressed misgivings about the language but signed the bill into law in December 2011 (Klain, 2012; Nakamura, 2011).

Because new laws provide tools for justice system officials, controversies can arise when those officials apparently stretch their authority beyond the intentions of the relevant statutes. For example, prosecutors in several cases have used new terrorism laws as a means to prosecute people for criminal acts that are not commonly understood to be related to terrorism. In New York, for example, one of the first prosecutions under the state's antiterrorism laws enacted after September 11 arose when the Bronx district attorney charged street gang members for various crimes. There was no allegation that the gang members had connections to any foreign terrorist networks. Instead, the prosecutor used the state's antiterrorism law to charge gang members with shootings "committed with the intent to intimidate or coerce a civilian population" (Garcia, 2005). Virginia used nearly identical language under its post-September 11 statute as one basis for applying the death penalty to John Muhammad, one of the infamous D.C. snipers who frightened the nation's capital in October 2002, even though there was no proof that he pulled the trigger in any of the shootings (Hegsted, 2005). In other examples, a North Carolina prosecutor charged the operator of a small meth lab under a terrorism statute for "manufacturing a nuclear or chemical weapon," and a Michigan prosecutor used the state's antiterrorism law to charge a high school student for writing up a "hit list" of classmates and school officials ("Charging Common Criminals under Terrorism Laws Doesn't Fit in America's Justice Values," 2003; "Concern Mounts over Anti-Terrorism Law," 2005). These cases generated criticism in newspaper editorials and raised concerns that government officials would exploit terrorism laws for improper purposes. The language of many terrorism laws is sufficiently vague to give prosecutors greater flexibility in seeking convictions. The severe penalties for terrorism-related acts can also give prosecutors more leverage to pressure defendants to plead guilty to lesser charges (Hirten, 2014).

Read the New Directions in Criminal Justice Policy feature to consider how the spread of unmanned "drone" aircraft from the military to domestic law enforcement has become a source of controversy and has resulted in new laws from state legislatures (Salter, 2014; M. Smith, 2015).

USA Patriot Act

The most controversial anti-terrorism legislation came from Congress in the form of the "Uniting and Strengthening America by Providing Appropriate Tools Required to Intercept and Obstruct Terrorism Act." It became best known by its shorthand name, the **USA Patriot Act**. The Patriot Act moved quickly through Congress after the September 11 attacks and covered a wide range of topics including the expansion of government authority for searches and surveillance and the expansion of definitions and penalties for crimes related to terrorism. Critics raised concerns about many provisions because of fears that the government's assertions of excessive power would infringe on individuals' rights (Ahmadi, 2011; Dority, 2005). The Patriot Act made it easier for law enforcement officials to monitor email and obtain "sneak-and-peek" warrants in which they secretly conduct searches without informing a home or business owner until much later that the premises had been searched (K. M. Sullivan, 2003). The Patriot Act also authorizes warrantless searches of third-party records, such as those at libraries, financial institutions, phone companies, and medical facilities. This provision sparked an outcry from librarians and booksellers who argued that government monitoring of the reading habits of citizens without sufficient evidence to obtain a warrant violates their rights of privacy and free expression. This provision, in particular,

USA Patriot Act
A federal statute passed in the aftermath of the terrorist attacks of September 11, 2001, which broadens government authority to conduct searches and wiretaps and that expands the definitions of crimes involving terrorism.

NEW DIRECTIONS IN CRIMINAL JUSTICE POLICY

THE USE OF DRONES BY LAW ENFORCEMENT AGENCIES

Unmanned aircraft called "drones" were developed for use by the military. They can carry cameras to follow and record the movement of enemy forces or to spy on areas that are too dangerous to view from helicopters or planes. In addition, drones can carry missiles and be used to kill enemies by remote command. The Obama administration has drawn sharp criticism for using drones overseas to kill suspected terrorists, including Americans. Drone strikes in such places as Pakistan and Yemen are alleged to have killed people other than the intended targets. Moreover, there are questions about the proof that should be required before someone is assassinated by a drone.

In 2011, the first use of a drone by local American law enforcement officials occurred in North Dakota. Drones had already been used for specific investigations by federal agencies such as the FBI and the Drug Enforcement Administration. A North Dakota county sheriff who was chased off a ranch by armed men asked for assistance from drones stationed at a nearby Air Force Base. U.S. Customs and Border Protection had begun using drones in 2005 to monitor the North Dakota-Canada border to prevent illegal immigrants and smuggling. An unarmed drone flew over the ranch and helped local officials determine when the men had set down their guns so that they could be arrested by sheriff's deputies. These and other limited missions in support of local law enforcement were done without detailed consideration of important legal and ethical questions. For example, does the use of drones piloted by military officers violate the legal and traditional limitations on activity within the United States by American armed forces? Does the use of drones threaten the privacy of individuals because a drone can fly over a house or business for many hours while transmitting high-quality photos and video to those monitoring the activity on computer screens?

By 2013, two developments contributed to major debates about the use of drones. First, the price of drones decreased and their availability from manufacturers increased so that it became possible for police departments to acquire these devices. A small drone can cost as little as $3,000. Thus businesses and non–law enforcement government agencies also sought to use drones to inspect pipelines and monitor highway traffic. The risk that small, private drones could threaten public safety was illustrated in 2015 when an off-duty government employee accidently crashed a hobby drone on the White House lawn. In another example from 2015, a drone being used to smuggle small quantities of drugs crashed while flying from Mexico to the United States ("Police: Drug-Laden Drone," 2015).

Second, there were intensified debates about the use of drones to kill suspected terrorists and the fear that the federal government might claim the authority to make such assassination strikes within the United States. Eventually, the Obama administration provided reassurances about not using drones for lethal domestic missions, yet controversy remained about the legality, ethics, and effects of raining death from the sky.

was cited by many of the 150 communities across the country that passed resolutions protesting the excessive authority granted to government by the Patriot Act (J. Gordon, 2005).

Some of the concerns about the Patriot Act arose because it sailed through Congress in the aftermath of September 11 with very little close examination or debate. Because the law is several hundred pages long, members of Congress had not likely studied the entire law before voting on it. Some of the provisions in the Patriot Act, such as those expanding powers for searches and wiretaps, had been sought by some federal law enforcement officials prior to September 11. Critics claim that the terrorist attacks provided the momentum for powers that these officials had sought to use for crime control purposes unrelated to homeland security. Moreover, some people fear that the Patriot Act authorizes law enforcement officials to undertake investigatory activities that cannot be readily supervised or monitored by judges and legislators (Banks and Tauber, 2014). In light of their new powers, will law enforcement officials act too swiftly in investigating and even arresting people without an adequate basis for suspicion?

The Patriot Act received criticism from both liberals and conservatives. Politicians expressed concern that law enforcement officials could too easily search people's homes, obtain their personal records, and intercept their communications without a firm basis for suspicion of wrongdoing. Further, the

In response to the growing debates, states and cities began to take action to define and limit the possibilities for the use of drones within the United States. No one denied the usefulness of drones for tracking suspects, port security, search and rescue, and finding missing persons. However, there were grave concerns about privacy and other aspects of overhead surveillance. For example, Virginia initially enacted legislation to ban unmanned aircraft in the state for two years but later sought to change the law to permit specific uses by law enforcement agencies. Idaho's law required police to obtain warrants for most uses of drones. Proposals in North Carolina followed Idaho's approach. The Seattle City Council required that any use of drones have prior approval by the council, but created a controversial exception for police investigations and circumstances approved by a search warrant. By contrast, in 2015, the Michigan State Police sought permission from the Federal Aviation Agency to become the first law enforcement agency with statewide authority to use drones. They wanted to use drones for aerial photographs for traffic collisions and public emergencies, a need that seemed compelling after a deadly 193-vehicle pileup amid a blinding snowstorm on a Michigan highway.

Clearly, inexpensive unmanned aircraft carrying cameras can have useful purposes for law enforcement agencies. However, the publicity and debates surrounding the military uses of drones overseas heightened sensitivity to the risks that might be posed if use of such aircraft in the United States is not carefully defined and controlled. It remains to be seen how law enforcement agencies will, under the watchful eye of state legislatures, develop proposals for clearly defining the uses of this new technology.

Sources: Jim Acosta and Jeremy Diamond, "U.S. Intel Worker Blamed for White House Drone Crash," CNN.com, January 27, 2015 (www.cnn.com); Brian Bennett, "Police Employ Predator Drone Spy Planes on Home Front," *Los Angeles Times,* December 10, 2011 (www.latimes.com); John Hinton, "Legislation Would Restrict Use of Drones by Police and Deputies," *Winston-Salem Journal,* March 24, 2013 (www.journalnow.com); Jason Koebler, "Virginia Governor on Drone Ban: Police Use OK," *U.S. News and World Report,* March 26, 2013 (www.usnews.com); Chad Livengood, "State Police Float Michigan-Wide Drone Use," *Detroit News,* January 26, 2015 (www.detroitnews.com); Lynn Thompson, "Except for Police, Use of Drones Would Need City's OK," *Seattle Times,* March 18, 2013 (www.seattletimes.com); Laura Zuckerman, "Idaho Restricts Drone Use by Police Agencies amid Privacy Concerns," Reuters, April 11, 2013 (www.reuters.com).

DEBATE THE ISSUE

Should local law enforcement agencies be able to use drones? For what purposes? Should prior approval by a judge or city council be required for each use? Are there any situations in which police could use an armed drone capable of firing at targets on the ground? Give three reasons for either endorsing the use of drones by police or imposing strict limitations on such use.

Patriot Act defined "domestic terrorism" as criminal acts dangerous to human life that appear intended to intimidate civilians or influence public policy by intimidation. Conservatives feared the law could be used against antiabortion protesters who block entrances at abortion clinics, whereas liberals feared that it could be used against environmental activists who take direct actions to prevent the destruction of forests and wildlife. Other critics of the Patriot Act pointed to provisions making it a crime to provide material support for terrorism; they raised concerns that people who donate money to the antiabortion movement or environmental causes could unwittingly find themselves prosecuted for serious terrorism offenses (Lithwick and Turner, 2003). The law requires periodic reexamination and approval by Congress. Despite the controversies, Congress approved an extension of the Patriot Act's key provisions in 2011 (Mascaro, 2011).

The debates about new laws enacted as part of homeland security and counterterrorism efforts illustrate the struggle to maintain American values of personal liberty, privacy, and individual rights while simultaneously ensuring that law enforcement personnel have sufficient power to protect the nation from catastrophic harm. There are no easy answers for the questions raised about whether the government has too much power and whether Americans' rights have been violated.

Now that we have considered the government's role in homeland security, we turn our attention to the private sector. Corporations and other entities must safeguard their assets, personnel, and facilities. They, too, have heightened concerns about terrorism and other homeland security issues. For example, nuclear power plants, chemical factories, energy companies, and other private facilities make up part of the nation's critical infrastructure. Because terrorists might target such facilities, private-sector officials must address these concerns, just as they have long needed to address other security issues such as employee theft, fires, and trade secrets.

CHECKPOINT 8. What are the criticisms directed at the USA Patriot Act?

STOP AND ANALYZE: Are you willing to give up any of your rights and liberties in order to grant the government more power to take actions to strengthen homeland security? If so, which rights and liberties? If not, why not?

Security Management and Private Policing

Only a few years ago, the term *private security* called to mind the image of security guards, people with marginal qualifications for other occupations who ended up accepting minimal wages to stand guard outside factories and businesses. This image reflected a long history of private employment of individuals who served limited police patrol functions. Private policing existed in Europe and the United States before the formation of public police forces. Examples include Fielding's Bow Street Runners in England and the bounty hunters of the American West. In the late nineteenth century, the Pinkerton's National Detective Agency provided industrial spies and strikebreakers to thwart labor union activities, and Wells Fargo and Company was formed to provide security for banks and other businesses.

In recent years, by contrast, private-sector activities related to policing functions have become more complex and important. Today, if one speaks of people employed in "private security," it would be more accurate to envision a variety of occupations ranging from traditional security guards to computer security experts to high-ranking corporate vice presidents responsible for planning and overseeing safety and security at a company's industrial plants and office complexes around the world. The aftermath of September 11 has brought a heightened awareness of the importance of security management and private-sector employees in handling police functions.

Retail and industrial firms spend nearly as much for private protection as all localities spend for police protection. Many government entities hire private companies to provide security at specific office buildings or other facilities. In addition, private groups, such as residents of wealthy suburbs, have hired private police to patrol their neighborhoods. Each year businesses, organizations, and individuals together spend about $100 billion on private security. There are now more officers hired by private security companies than there are public police (K. Strom et al., 2010).

Private agencies have gained success for several reasons. Private companies recognize the need to be conscientious about protecting their assets, including buildings, financial resources, and personnel. They must be prepared for fires and other emergencies as well as for criminal activity. Next, many threats have spurred an expansion in security management and private policing; these include (1) an increase in crime in the workplace; (2) an increase in fear (real or perceived) of crime; (3) the fiscal crises of the states, which have limited public police protection; and (4) increased public and business awareness and use of more cost-effective private security services (W. C. Cunningham, Strauchs, and Van Meter, 1990).

Functions of Security Management and Private Policing

Top-level security managers have a range of responsibilities that require them to fulfill multiple roles that separate individuals would typically handle in the public sector. For their corporations, they simultaneously function as police chiefs, fire chiefs, emergency-management administrators, and computer-security experts. They hire, train, and supervise expert personnel to protect corporate computer systems that may contain credit card numbers, trade secrets, confidential corporate financial information, and other data sought by hackers intent on causing destruction or stealing money. These challenges become even more difficult as the technology and environment of computing change, such as the increased reliance on "cloud" storage for computer data (Tse, Chen, et al., 2014). In 2014, hackers reportedly compromised Apple Computer's iCloud storage and released many private photos of celebrities who had relied on the security of Apple's system (Peterson, Yahr, and Warrick, 2014). Although Apple denied that its system had been hacked and pointed to other photo storage systems, the incident raised concerns about consumer confidence in cloud-storage systems and potential harm to Apple's reputation. Even more threatening risks occur when hackers gain access to files at companies that store customers' personal financial and identity information, such as social security numbers. In 2015, for example, one of the nation's largest health insurance companies reported that hackers had gained access to information that could put the company's 80 million customers at risk of identity theft (Weise, 2015).

Frequently they combat cybercriminals who are attacking company computer resources from overseas and are therefore beyond the reach of U.S. law enforcement officials. Most notably, in 2014 hackers gained access to a wealth of private information in the computer systems of Sony Entertainment leading to the early release of movies, executives' emails, and personal information about employees. The U.S. government blamed the North Korean government for the hacking scheme. The incident illustrated the extent to which private companies must have security systems in place to counteract the potential of concerted hacker attacks, not just from individual criminal groups, but from specific foreign countries (K. Johnson, Dorrell, and Weise, 2014).

Security managers also plan asset security systems in addition to fire and other disaster-response plans for buildings and other property owned by companies. Such plans include provisions for evacuating large buildings and coordinating their efforts with local police and fire departments in a variety of locales. In addition, they develop security systems to prevent employee theft that may involve sophisticated schemes to use company computer systems to transfer financial assets in improper ways. Because so many American companies own manufacturing plants and office buildings overseas, security companies must often implement their services in diverse countries around the globe.

Security managers are responsible for risk management in their facilities. They need a clear understanding of the assets that must be protected in their corporations, hospitals, and other institutional settings. They must also identify the potential vulnerabilities their organizations face. Effective risk management depends on identifying specific threats ahead of time and considering how those threats can be minimized or avoided. Some security managers conduct their own risk assessments by inspecting facilities and developing a checklist that includes assets to be protected; vulnerabilities; and resources for surveillance, asset protection, and emergency response. Outside consultants are sometimes hired to undertake such security studies, especially because

Contemporary security managers are well-educated professionals with administrative experience and backgrounds in management and law. They bear responsibility for such matters as computer security, corporate asset protection, and physical security and fire protection at industrial plants. Can you think of any business enterprises or industries that do not need professional security managers in today's ever-changing world of computer technology and international criminal organizations?

Juice Images/Alamy

many professionals believe that an "outsider" may spot vulnerabilities that people who work in a facility every day minimize, take for granted, or ignore (Gill and Howell, 2014; Garvey, 2002).

At lower levels, specific occupations in private security compare more closely to those of police officers. Many security personnel are the equivalent of private-sector detectives. They must investigate "attacks" on company computer systems or activities that threaten company assets. Thus, for example, credit card companies have large security departments that use computers to monitor unusual activity on individual customers' credit cards, which may signal that a thief is using the card. Private-sector detectives must also investigate employee theft. Because this criminal activity extends beyond simple crimes such as stealing money from a store's cash register, investigations might examine whether people are making false reports on expense accounts, using company computers to run private businesses, or misspending company money.

Other activities are more directly comparable to those of police patrol officers, especially those of security officers who must guard specific buildings, apartments, or stores. The activities of these private security personnel vary greatly: Some act merely as guards and call the police at the first sign of trouble, others have the power to carry out patrol and investigative duties similar to those of police officers, and still others rely on their own presence and the ability to make a "citizen's arrest" to deter lawbreakers. In most cases, citizens are authorized by law to make an arrest only when a felony has been committed in their presence. Thus, private security companies risk being held liable for false arrest and violation of civil rights.

Some states have passed laws that give civil immunity to store personnel who reasonably but mistakenly detain people suspected of shoplifting. More ambiguous is the search of a suspect's person or property by a private guard. The suspect may resist the search and file a civil suit against the guard. If such a search yields evidence of a crime, the evidence might not be admitted in court. Yet, the Supreme Court has not applied the *Miranda* ruling to private police. In any case, federal law bars private individuals from engaging in wiretapping, and information gathered by such methods cannot be entered as evidence at trial.

Security managers are often willing to accept responsibility for dealing with minor criminal incidents that occur on their employer's premises. They might perform such tasks as responding to burglar alarms, investigating misdemeanors, and carrying out preliminary investigations of other crimes. Some law enforcement administrators have indicated that they might be willing to transfer some of these tasks to private security firms. They cite several police tasks—such as providing security in public buildings and enforcing parking regulations—that private security might perform more efficiently than the police. In some parts of the country, personnel from private firms already perform some of these tasks. Using a little-known law, 16 of the nation's 450 airports have opted out of using TSA screeners for passenger safety checks prior to boarding. Instead they use private security officers, with the idea that private officers are less expensive but just as effective as TSA officers. Two dozen additional airports have applied for permission to switch to private screeners (R. Nixon, 2012).

Private Police and Homeland Security

Private-sector corporations control security for vital facilities in the United States, including nuclear power plants, oil refineries, military manufacturing facilities, and other important sites (Nalla, 2002). Fires, tornadoes, or earthquakes at such sites could release toxic materials into the air and water. Thus, emergency planning is essential for public safety. Moreover, because these sites are now recognized as potential targets of terrorist attacks, the role and effectiveness of security managers matter more than ever to society (Faddis, 2010). They must work closely with law enforcement executives and other government officials to institute procedures that reduce known risks and to participate in emergency preparedness planning. The potential importance of private security's role was illustrated by the Boston Marathon bombing described at the opening of the chapter. Ultimately, it was security cameras from private businesses that provided the basis for identifying the bombers when the images were broadcast around the nation.

Unfortunately, significant problems have emerged in delegating essential homeland security responsibilities to private companies. For example, private security personnel guard the headquarters of the U.S. Department of Homeland Security. Yet security guards assigned to the building claim that they do not have proper training or equipment to handle the job. In 2005, guards at the building opened an envelope containing a mysterious white powder. A well-trained security force would have known to don hazardous materials clothing and carefully seek to dispose of a potentially dangerous chemical or biological hazard. Instead, the private security personnel "carried [the envelope] by the office [of then Homeland Security] Secretary Michael Chertoff, took it outside and then shook it outside Chertoff's window without evacuating people nearby" (Margasak, 2006). Because of the improper handling of the situation, if it had been a deadly chemical or biological agent, it might have been inhaled by and consequently killed a number of important officials, including the secretary of Homeland Security. Fortunately, it turned out to be harmless. Other guards at the same building failed tests conducted by the Secret Service, which sent personnel into the building with fake identification cards. Other guards could not tell what to do when a fire alarm sounded; without radios they could not learn if it was real or a test. And yet another guard said, "I didn't have a clue what to do" when a suspicious bag was reported to have been abandoned in the parking lot (Margasak, 2006).

As indicated by the foregoing examples, the federal government has become increasingly dependent on private contractors for a variety of functions, including safety and security (Shane and Nixon, 2007). Private security firms handle a variety of tasks for government, from guarding military bases, nuclear power plants, and government buildings to providing personal security for diplomats traveling in Iraq and other dangerous locations. In guarding buildings and other sites within the United States, the private guards are often paid less than half of what a police officer would be paid. Moreover, they often do not have the same training, equipment, or qualifications as police or military personnel. There have been a number of scandals when private guards were caught intoxicated or sleeping on duty, which is especially troubling when it occurs at essential security locations such as nuclear power plants, or when companies hire guards with criminal records who then commit crimes (J. Newman, 2012). Because of the problems and the risk of even greater disasters, a number of large private security companies actually lobby the government to seek more rules and regulations for their industry (Margasak, 2007).

Private Employment of Public Police

The officials responsible for asset protection, safety, and security at the top levels of major corporations are often retired police administrators or former military personnel. For example, former New York Police Commissioner Raymond Kelly served as senior managing director of Global Corporate Security for a Wall Street financial firm after he left his position as director of the U.S. Customs Service and before he was appointed to serve as police commissioner. The reliance on people with public-sector experience for important positions in private security management reflects the fact that asset protection and security management have only recently become emphasized as topics in college and university programs. Thus, relatively few professionals have yet gained specific educational credentials in this important area. As a result, the placement of retired law enforcement officials in high-level positions has often created opportunities for strategic communication and coordination between top-level security managers and public-sector police administrators. Both entities have reason to seek cooperation throughout the hierarchy of their respective organizations. Unfortunately, however, they cannot always ensure that individual police officers and lower-level security personnel will sufficiently communicate and coordinate with each other when incidents arise.

At operational levels of security management, private security and local police often make frequent contact. Private firms are usually eager to hire public police officers on a part-time basis. About 20 percent of departments forbid their officers from "moonlighting" for private employers. By contrast, some departments simultaneously facilitate and control the hiring of their officers by creating specific rules and procedures for off-duty employment. For example, the New York City police department coordinates a program called the Paid Detail Unit. Event planners, corporations, and organizations can hire uniformed, off-duty officers for $37 per hour. The police department must approve all events at which the officers will work, and the department imposes an additional 10 percent administrative fee for the hiring of its officers. Thus the department can safeguard against officers working for organizations and events that will cause legal, public relations, or other problems for the police department. The department can also monitor and control how many hours its officers work so that private, part-time employment does not lead them to be exhausted and ineffective during their regular shifts.

These officers retain their full powers and status as police personnel even when they work for a private firm while off duty. New York and other cities have specific regulations requiring an on-duty officer to be called when a situation arises in which an arrest will be made. Although the use of off-duty officers expands the number and visibility of law enforcement officers, it also raises questions, two of which are discussed next.

Conflict of Interest

Police officers must avoid any appearance of conflict of interest when they accept private employment. They are barred from jobs that conflict with their public duties. For example, they may not work as process servers, bill collectors, repossessors, or preemployment investigators for private firms. They also may not work as investigators for criminal defense attorneys or as bail bondsmen. They may not work in places that profit from gambling, and many departments do not allow officers to work in bars or other places where regulated goods, such as alcohol, are sold. No department can know the full range of situations in which private employment of an officer might harm the image of the police or create a conflict with police responsibilities. Thus, departments need to keep tabs on new situations that might require them to refine their regulations for private employment of off-duty officers.

Management Prerogatives

Another issue concerns the impact of private employment on the capabilities of the local police department. Private employment cannot be allowed to tire officers and impair their ability to protect the public when they are on duty. Late-night duties as a private security officer, for example, can reduce an officer's ability to police effectively the next morning.

Departments require that officers request permission for outside work. Such permission can be denied for several reasons. Work that lowers the dignity of the police, is too risky or dangerous, is not in the home jurisdiction, requires more than eight hours of off-duty service, or interferes with department schedules is usually denied.

Several models have been designed to manage off-duty employment of officers. Some approaches can lead to controversy, as in New Orleans in 2011 when several high-ranking police officials were revealed to be earning six-figure incomes beyond their police salaries by imposing "coordination fees" as part of their authority over choosing which officers would perform security work at movie sets, football games, and other private settings (B. McCarthy, 2011). Read the Question of Ethics feature at the end of the chapter to consider how actual conflicts of interest or the appearance of such conflicts may affect the image of police when officers engage in outside employment.

The *department contract model* permits close control of off-duty work, because firms must apply to the department to have officers assigned to them. New York City's system fits this model. Officers chosen for off-duty work are paid by the police department, which is reimbursed by the private firm, along with an overhead fee. Departments usually screen employers to make sure that the proposed use of officers will not conflict with the department's needs. When the private demand for police services exceeds the supply, the department contract model provides a way of assigning staff so as to ensure that public needs are met.

The *officer contract model* allows each officer to find off-duty employment and to enter into a direct relationship with the private firm. Officers must apply to the department for permission, which is granted if the employment standards listed earlier are met. Problems can arise when an officer acts as an employment "agent" for other officers. This can lead to charges of favoritism and nepotism, with serious effects on discipline and morale.

In the *union brokerage model,* the police union or association finds off-duty employment for its members. The union sets the standards for the work and bargains with the department over the pay, status, and conditions of the off-duty employment.

Each of these models has its backers. Albert Reiss notes another complication: The more closely a department controls off-duty employment, the more liability it assumes for officers' actions when they work for private firms (Reiss, 1988).

What remains unknown is how uniformed off-duty patrol affects crime prevention and the public's perception of safety. Public fears may decrease because of the greater visibility of officers whom citizens believe to be acting in their official capacity.

The Public–Private Interface

The relationship between public and private law enforcement is a concern for police officials. Because private agents work for the people who employ them, their goals might not always serve the public interest. Questions have arisen about the power of private security agents to make arrests, conduct searches, and take part in undercover investigations. A key issue is the boundary between the work of the police and that of private agencies. Lack of coordination and communication between public and private agencies has led to botched investigations, destruction of evidence, and overzealousness.

Growing awareness of this problem has led to efforts to have private security agents work more closely with the police. Current efforts to enhance coordination involve emergency planning, building security, and general crime prevention. In other areas, private security managers still tend to act on their own without consulting the police.

One such area is criminal activity within a company. Many security managers in private firms tend to treat crimes by employees as internal matters that do not concern the police. They report UCR index crimes to the police, but employee theft, insurance fraud, industrial espionage, commercial bribery, and computer crime tend not to be reported to public authorities. In such cases the chief concern of private firms is to prevent losses and protect assets. Most of these incidents are resolved through internal procedures (private justice). When such crimes are discovered, the offender may be convicted and punished within the firm by forced restitution, loss of the job, and the spreading of information about the incident throughout the industry. Private firms often bypass the criminal justice system so they do not have to deal with prosecution policies, administrative delays, rules that would open the firms' internal affairs to public scrutiny, and bad publicity.

Recruitment and Training

Higher-level security managers are increasingly drawn from college graduates with degrees in criminal justice who have taken additional coursework in such subjects as business management and computer science to supplement their knowledge of policing and law. These graduates are attracted to the growing private-sector employment market for security-related occupations because the jobs often involve varied, complex tasks in a white-collar work environment. In addition, they often gain corporate benefits such as quick promotion, stock options, and other perks unavailable in public-sector policing.

By contrast, the recruitment and training of lower-level private security personnel present a major concern to law enforcement officials and civil libertarians (Enion, 2009; Strickland, 2011). These personnel handle the important responsibility of guarding factories, stores, apartments, and other buildings. Often on the scene when criminal activity occurs, they are the private security personnel most likely to interact with the public in emergency situations. Moreover, any failure to perform their duties could lead to a significant and damaging event, such as a robbery or a fire. In spite of these important responsibilities, which parallel those of police patrol officers, studies have shown that such personnel often have little education and training. A national study found that 46 percent of private security officers had a high school diploma or even less education and only 12 percent had bachelor's degrees. In addition, the median annual pay for private security officers is less than half that of police officers. Many private security officers are paid only minimum wage (K. Strom, Berzofsky, et al., 2010). Because the pay is low, the work often attracts people who cannot find other jobs or who seek temporary work. Private security firms in San Francisco reported annual staff turnover rates as high as 300 percent because their low pay and benefits led employees continually to seek higher-paying jobs, especially when better-paid public security jobs opened up, such as security work at state office buildings (Lynem, 2002). City police departments and other public law enforcement agencies do not experience these kinds of staffing problems, because they have better pay and benefits.

The growth of private policing has brought calls for the screening and licensing of its personnel. However, there has been no systematic national effort to standardize training and licensing for private security personnel. As indicated in Figure 7.1, only 8 states require all private security officers to be licensed. Other states require licensing only for contractual security officers or those carrying firearms. Remarkably, 16 states require no licensing at all (K. Strom, Berzofsky, et al., 2010).

FIGURE 7.1 LICENSING REQUIREMENTS FOR SECURITY OFFICERS BY STATE, 2009

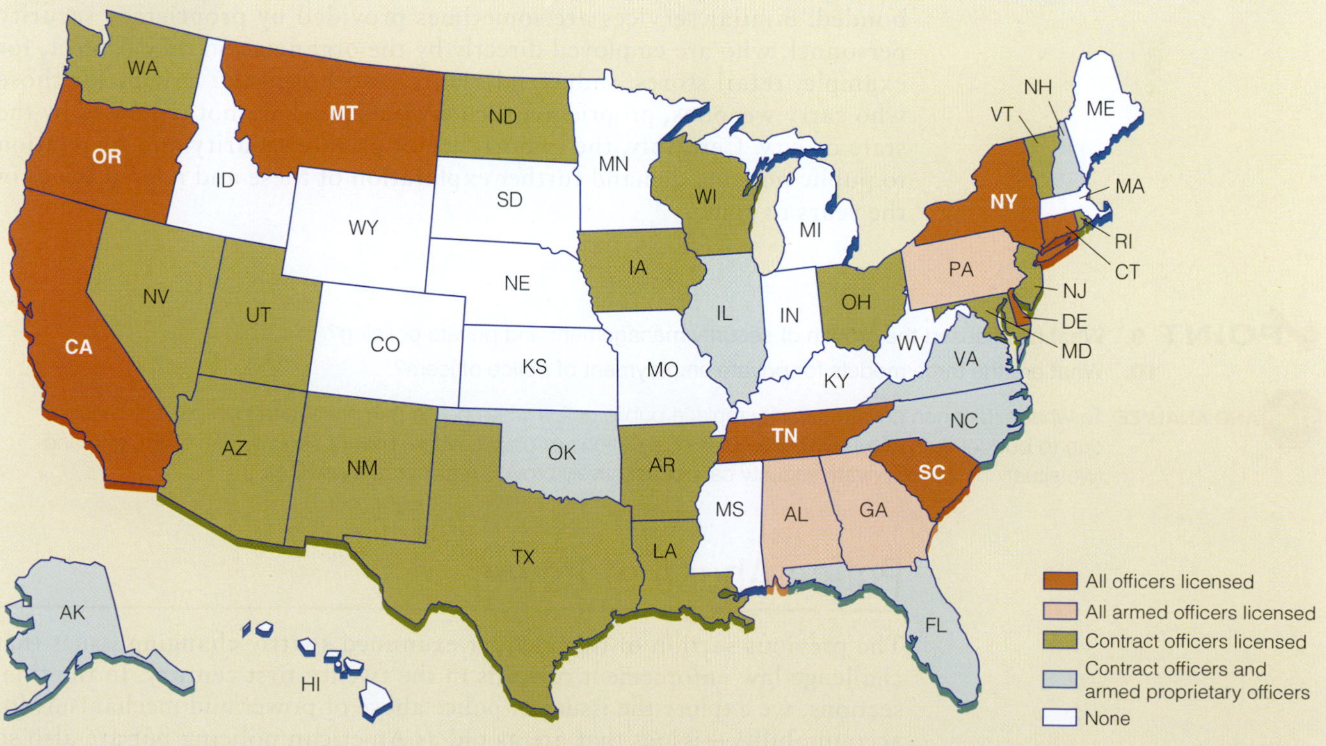

Source: K. Strom, M. Berzofsky, B. Shook-Sa, K. Barrick, C. Daye, N. Horstmann, and S. Kinsey. *The Private Security industry: A Review of the Definitions, Available Data Sources, and Paths Moving Forward.* Report prepared for Bureau of Justice Statistics, December 2010 (www.ncjrs.gov/pdffiles1/bjs/grants/232781.pdf).

Today's security personnel must be aware of numerous potential threats and have the necessary training and equipment to communicate with law enforcement officials. If security guards are merely hourly minimum-wage employees, are they likely to have the qualifications and commitment to provide adequate security at important private enterprises such as chemical factories and nuclear power plants?

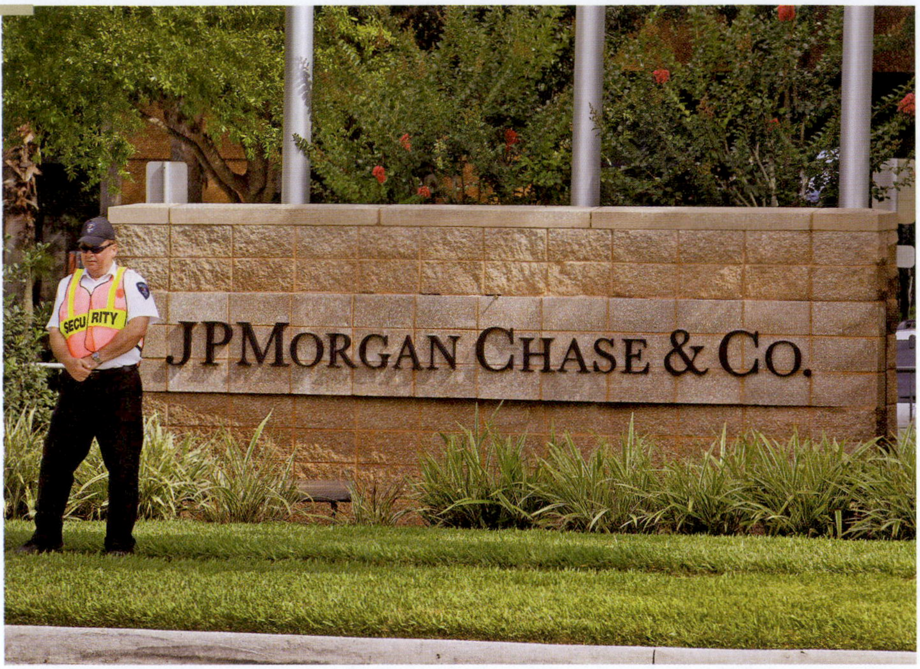

Joe Raedle/Staff/Getty Images

The regulations that do exist tend to focus on contractual, as opposed to proprietary, private policing. Contractual security services are provided for a fee by locksmiths, alarm specialists, polygraph examiners, and firms such as Brink's, Burns, and Wackenhut, which provide guards and detectives. States and cities often require contract personnel to be licensed and bonded. Similar services are sometimes provided by proprietary security personnel, who are employed directly by the organization they protect, for example, retail stores, industrial plants, and hospitals. Except for those who carry weapons, proprietary security personnel are not regulated by the state or city. Certainly, the importance of private security and its relation to public policing demand further exploration of these and related issues in the years to come.

✓POINT
9. What has caused the growth of security management and private policing?
10. What are the three models for private employment of police officers?

STOP AND ANALYZE: To what extent can private security replace public police when police personnel and services are reduced due to budget cuts? Give two examples of situations or places where private security can fill the gap and two situations where private security cannot effectively provide replacement services.

Police Abuse of Power

The previous section of this chapter examined swiftly changing issues that challenge law enforcement officials in the twenty-first century. In the final sections, we explore the issues of police abuse of power and mechanisms for accountability—issues that are as old as American policing but are also so persistent that they effectively remain challenges in the new century. For example, in May 2008, fifteen Philadelphia police officers were suspended from duty after a television news helicopter videotaped them repeatedly kicking and beating three suspects as they lay on the ground being handcuffed (Slobodzian, 2008). In 2011, five Chicago police officers pleaded guilty to various charges related to the theft of $600,000 from drug dealers who were kidnapped and robbed by the officers (Main and Korecki, 2011). In 2014, a man in Portland, Oregon, was awarded $562,000 by a trial jury after a security camera recorded three police officers striking him and injuring his face and shoulder when he was pinned to the ground after being uncooperative ("Mayor Disagrees with Verdict," 2014). These examples represent deviations from the professionalism that we see in most police officers, yet such incidents arise regularly year after year. Although such scandals have occurred throughout U.S. history, only in the past few decades has the general public become keenly aware of the problems of police misconduct, especially the illegal use of violence by law enforcement officers and the criminal activities associated with police corruption. These issues raise questions about whether there are individual officers who are prone to break rules or whether the supervision, practices, and cultures of specific departments encourage or permit improper activities to occur (Kane and White, 2009; Kutnjak Ivkovic, 2009).

As indicated in the "What Americans Think" feature, there have been stark differences in the views of and experience with the police among different members of various racial groups in American society. In light of the highly publicized deaths of African American men and boys in Ohio, Missouri, New York, and elsewhere in 2014, it is possible that a more recent poll might show either starker divisions or, possibly, larger numbers of white Americans expressing concern about the issue ("Police Silence, 2015). Read the Inside Today's Controversies feature to examine the growing belief that the use of body cameras by police can diminish the risks that police officers will use excessive force.

WHAT AMERICANS THINK

QUESTION: "In some places in the nation there have been charges of police brutality. Do you think there is any police brutality in your area, or not?"

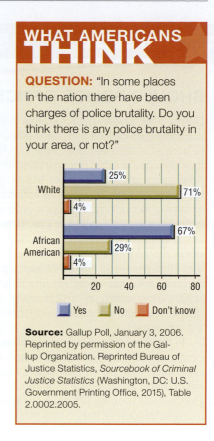

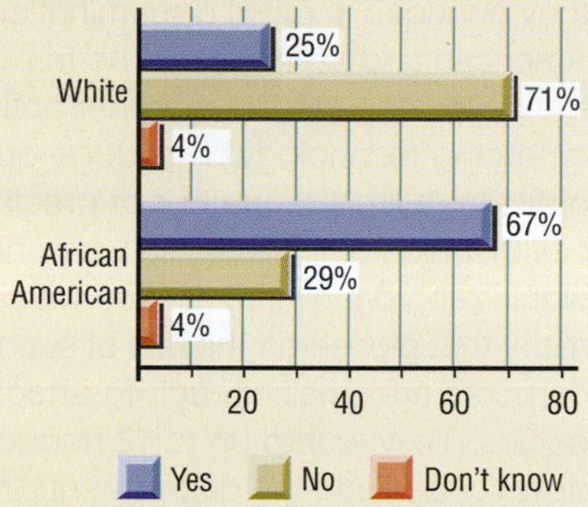

Source: Gallup Poll, January 3, 2006. Reprinted by permission of the Gallup Organization. Reprinted Bureau of Justice Statistics, *Sourcebook of Criminal Justice Statistics* (Washington, DC: U.S. Government Printing Office, 2015), Table 2.0002.2005.

Use of Force

Most people cooperate with the police, yet officers must at times use force to arrest, control disturbances, and deal with the intoxicated or mentally ill (Thompson, 2001). As noted by Jerome Skolnick and James Fyfe (1993: 37),

> As long as some members of society do not comply with the law and resist the police, force will remain an inevitable part of policing. Cops, especially, understand that. Indeed, anybody who fails to understand the centrality of force in police work has no business in a police uniform.

Thus police may use legitimate force to do their job. It is when they use excessive force that they violate the law. But which situations and actions constitute **excessive use of force**? Both officers and experts debate this question.

excessive use of force Applications of force against individuals by police officers that violate either departmental policies or constitutional rights by exceeding the level of force permissible and necessary in a given situation.

In cities where racial tensions are high, conflicts between police and residents often result when officers are accused of acting in unprofessional ways. Citizens use the term *police brutality* to describe a wide range of practices, from the use of profane or abusive language to physical force and violence.

Stories of police brutality are not new. However, unlike the untrained officers of the early 1900s, today's officers are supposed to be professionals who know the rules and understand the need for proper conduct. Thus, reports of unjustified police shootings and beatings are particularly disturbing (Ogletree et al., 1995). Moreover, when abusive behavior by police comes to light, the public cannot know how often police engage in such actions, because most violence is hidden from public view (Weitzer, 2002). If the TV-news helicopter had not been flying above the scene, would we know that the Philadelphia police officers were kicking and beating suspects who were not resisting arrest in 2008? How can we prevent such incidents, especially when they occur without witnesses?

INSIDE TODAY'S CONTROVERSIES

SHOULD POLICE OFFICERS WEAR INDIVIDUAL BODY CAMERAS?

During 2013, a highly publicized trial took place in New York City concerning allegations that police officers improperly performed hundreds of thousands of stop-and-frisk searches and that they engaged in racial discrimination in targeting young African American and Latino men. The trial judge's decision finding that the police engaged in improper actions brought attention to an emerging technology. The judge ordered a one-year pilot program for a limited number of precincts spread throughout the city in which officers would wear individual body cameras that would record their interactions with citizens. In Rialto, California, a city that pioneered the use of such cameras in 2012, the $900 cameras are small enough to attach to officers' sunglasses or collars. They record up to 12 hours of color video and are then downloaded into the department's central computer storage at the end of each shift.

In the aftermath of protest marches in 2014 concerning the controversial deaths of young, unarmed African Americans in encounters with police in Missouri, New York, and Ohio, interest in body cameras grew even more. President Obama asked Congress to allocate $75 million in federal funds to help communities throughout the country obtain 50,000 more body cameras for police.

Many observers see this technology as beneficial to both police officers and citizens. The cameras can help police refute false claims that they used excessive force or engaged in improper searches. At the same time, the cameras can provide evidence if police officers violate citizens' rights. However, other observers fear that the cameras may fail to fulfill expectations and create risks of new problems. In the cities that have begun using the cameras, many police officers initially resist the requirement of using the cameras because, in effect, the devices put them under constant surveillance when the recording device in operating.

In the discussions about the use of body cameras, lists of benefits and drawbacks are regularly presented. Among the benefits are:

- Cameras can provide evidence of police errors and wrongdoing in conducting searches and using force on people.
- The presence of the camera will force officers to be very conscious of following proper rules of police procedure and thereby reduce the risks of mistakes and misbehavior by police. Visible cameras may also make some citizens more self-conscious and careful about their own behavior and statements in interacting with officers.
- The cameras can help protect police officers against false claims of improper searches and excessive use of force.
- The cameras will provide a basis for supervisors to review officers' actions in order to identify errors, hold officers accountable, and identify needs for additional policies and training.
- The city of Rialto, California, experienced an 89 percent drop in complaints against officers during the first year of using the cameras.

The cameras, however, do not present a cure for the risk of improper police actions. The drawbacks often discussed include:

- Equipping entire police departments with individual cameras is expensive and not necessarily the best use of scarce resources during a time of budget shortfalls.
- The limited field in the camera's view may not record a complete and accurate picture of the circumstances facing an officer at the moment when decisions are made to use force or conduct searches. Something that an officer sees but is not in the direct line of vision of the camera may be the basis for a statement or action, yet the video does not adequately portray

The concept "use of force" takes many forms in practice. We can arrange the various types of force on a continuum ranging from most severe (civilians shot and killed) to least severe ("come-alongs," or being grasped by an officer). Table 7.2 lists many of these forms of force according to their frequency of use in a representative study. The frequency of use will vary by individual officer and the particular policies and training of each department. How often must police use force? Most research has shown that in contacts with suspects, police use force infrequently and the type of force used is usually at the low end of the continuum—toward the less severe. Resistance by a suspect can contribute to the officers' decision to use force (R. Johnson, 2011; Garner, Maxwell, and Heraux, 2002). However, research also documents use of force by police against people who show no resistance. A report by the National Institute of Justice (K. Adams, 1999) summarized knowledge about use of force:

1. Police use force infrequently.
2. Police use of force typically occurs in the lower end of the force spectrum, involving grabbing, pushing, or shoving.

everything that the officer observed. In addition, even events clearly recorded by the camera may be subject to interpretation in second-guessing officers' decisions and actions.

- Camera breakdowns or limited camera views may lead to assumptions that police have intentionally failed to use the equipment properly, and then any dispute about events will weigh against the officer, even when the officer is telling the truth about what happened.
- A significant increase in the number of cameras used by a police department, in addition to the already-in-use patrol car cameras, will lead to enormous expenditures of time and money when reviewing footage in order to respond to requests for evidence or public information. Many cities are finding that they face costs of hundreds of thousands of dollars in computer storage costs and the paid time of technicians and officers in downloading and reviewing video footage.
- The costs of such programs are affected by whether departments require officers to run the cameras continuously while on duty or turn on the cameras during encounters with citizens. The latter policy may save video storage costs, but also creates risks that officers will neglect to turn on the cameras, either intentionally or unintentionally.
- There are risks to officers' privacy if they forget to turn the cameras off, as the device will be running when they are on bathroom breaks and when they engage in private phone conversations with their own family members.

By 2014, roughly 3,000 law enforcement agencies had begun using the cameras with at least some of their officers. In some departments, the use of the technology has gone smoothly, and officers have come to view the device as protecting them against false allegations. In other departments, concerns have arisen about the development of appropriate policies and practices. If there is an allegation against the officer, should the officer be able to view the footage before answering questions about the incident? If the officer is not allowed to view the footage, will inconsistencies between the footage from the camera and the officer's statement be viewed with sensitivity to the fact that officers' honest perceptions and memories of the entire context are not fully captured in the recording? In the New York City case, the judge's order was presented in order to consider how to address a specific problem. In such situations, the cameras have a very specific purpose: ensure that officers properly follow the law in a city where evidence has shown that improper behavior occurred. In places that have not been proven to have problems with police behavior, is there enough reason to undertake the expense and risks of using the cameras?

Sources: Associated Press, "For Police Body Cameras, Big Costs Loom in Storing Footage," *New York Times,* February 6, 2015 (www.nytimes.com); Harry Bruinius, "Body Cams for NYC Police as a Check on 'Stop and Frisk': A Good Idea?" *Christian Science Monitor,* August 14, 2013 (www.csmonitor.com); Harry Bruinius, "New York Police Test Body Cameras: Effective Deterrent or Privacy Violation?" *Christian Science Monitor,* September 5, 2014 (www.csmonitor.com); Rory Carroll, "California Police Use of Body Cameras Cuts Violence and Complaints," *Guardian,* November 4, 2013 (www.theguardian.com); Justin T. Ready and Jacob T.N. Young, "Three Myths about Police Body Cams," Slate.com, September 1, 2014 (www.slate.com); Derek Thompson, "Forcing America's Weaponized Police to Wear Cameras," *Atlantic,* August 14, 2014 (www.theatlantic.com).

CRITICAL THINKING AND ANALYSIS

Imagine that you are an advisor to a city's mayor and police chief. Consider the competing arguments and issues surrounding the use of body cameras by police. Prepare a recommendation that includes the three most significant issues for them to address in implementing your recommendation.

3. Use of force typically occurs when police are trying to make an arrest and the suspect is resisting.

Although more studies are needed, research indicates that use of force is not linked to an officer's personal characteristics such as age, gender, and ethnicity (Klahm and Tillyer, 2010). However, a small percentage of officers may be disproportionately involved in use-of-force situations. In addition, use of force occurs more frequently when police are dealing with people affected by drugs, alcohol, or mental illness (V. B. Lord and Sloop, 2010). By law, the police have the authority to use force if necessary to make an arrest, keep the peace, or maintain public order. But the questions of just how much force is necessary and under what conditions force may be used are complex and open to debate.

When the police kill a suspect or bystander while trying to make an arrest, their actions may produce public outrage and hostility. Fears about the possibility of public disorders arose in 2005 when a Los Angeles police officer fired ten shots that killed a 13-year-old boy who was driving a stolen car. The officer

TABLE 7.2 REPORTED USES OF FORCE BY BIG-CITY POLICE

Police have the legal right to use force to make an arrest, keep the peace, and maintain order. Of the many types of force available to police, the less severe types are used most often.

TYPE OF FORCE	RATE PER THOUSAND SWORN OFFICERS
Handcuff/leg restraint	490.4
Bodily force (arm, foot, or leg)	272.2
Come-alongs	226.8
Unholstering weapon	129.9
Swarm	126.7
Twist locks/wrist locks	80.9
Firm grip	57.7
Chemical agents (Mace or Cap-Stun)	36.2
Batons	36.0
Flashlights	21.7
Dog attacks or bites	6.5
Electrical devices (Taser)	5.4
Civilians shot at but not hit	3.0
Other impact devices	2.4
Neck restraints/unconsciousness-rendering holds	1.4
Vehicle ramming	1.0
Civilians shot and killed	0.9
Civilians shot and wounded but not killed	0.2

Source: Drawn from Bureau of Justice Statistics, *National Data Collection on Police Use of Force* (Washington, DC: U.S. Government Printing Office, 1996), 43.

fired in the aftermath of a chase, when the boy skidded across a sidewalk and then struck a police car while backing up (Chavez, 2005). The incident led Los Angeles police officials to revise their policies for firing at moving vehicles.

There are no accurate data on the number of people shot by the police. The numbers vary by police department, presumably affected by both the specific situations that arise in a given year and also the training and culture of a particular department with respect to using firearms. The FBI reports annually on the number of fatal shootings by police, but their figures are widely acknowledged to underreport actual incidents. One study found that the number of fatal police shootings reported by the FBI was only half of the number that police departments nationwide had in their own reports (Wines, 2015; Klinger, 2012a). Obviously, fatal shootings are only a portion of the total police shootings. There are larger numbers of shootings in which officers miss the person targeted or wound the person. In some shootings, police bullets wound bystanders as well.

The most troubling aspect of police shootings in recent decades has been the fact that many of those shot are young African American men. The U.S. Department of Justice launched an investigation of the Miami police in 2011 after seven African American men were shot and killed by police during an eight-month period. In each case, the fatal shots were fired by Latino officers. The final event that triggered the investigation was the shooting of Travis McNeil, who was unarmed and never left the driver's seat of his rental car when he was shot in the chest by Officer Reinaldo Goyo. One of the concerns about the Miami Police Department was that it had undertaken an aggressive strategy for proactively seeking out suspected gang members and others believed to be responsible for violent crimes at the time that the rash of shootings occurred (Van Natta, 2011). Because of America's long history of racial discrimination by law enforcement officials, any racial disparities in the treatment of citizens raise questions about whether race was a contributing factor to the amount of force used in particular instances. In particular, it raises fears that police officers are quicker to use lethal force against minority group members.

Many police departments have increased their focus on training and the development of very specific policies to guide officers' decisions about when and how firearms may be used (Klinger, 2012b). In 2010, Houston police officers fired their weapons in 46 incidents, resulting in the deaths of 13 people. This was a reduction from the prior year's 60 shooting incidents that killed 27 people. The reduction was attributed, in part, to new policies and training, as well as to the increased use of Tasers (Pinkerton, 2011). In Seattle in 2011, controversy surrounding police officers' actions in several videotaped use-of-force incidents led police officials to initiate new training. According to Sue Rahr, the King County Sheriff in Seattle:

> What we've done very well over the last decade is we have taught very strong rules about physical tactics to use different ways to approach problems. What we haven't been clear and concrete on is the communication skills that we expect our officers to use ("Big Changes," 2011).

Until the 1980s the police had broad authority to use deadly force in pursuing suspected felons. Police in about half the states were guided by the common-law principle that allowed the use of whatever force was necessary to arrest a fleeing felon. In 1985 the Supreme Court set a new standard in ***Tennessee v. Garner* (1985)**, ruling that the police may not use deadly force in apprehending fleeing felons "unless it is necessary to prevent the escape and the officer has probable cause to believe that the suspect poses a significant threat of death or serious physical injury to the officer or others."

***Tennessee v. Garner* (1985)**
Deadly force may not be used against an unarmed and fleeing suspect unless necessary to prevent the escape and unless the officer has probable cause to believe that the suspect poses a significant threat of death or serious injury to the officers and others.

The case dealt with the killing of Edward Garner, a 15-year-old eighth grader who was shot by a member of the Memphis Police Department. Officers Elton Hymon and Leslie Wright were sent to answer a "prowler-inside" call. When they arrived at the scene, they saw a woman standing on her porch and gesturing toward the adjacent house. She told them she had heard glass breaking and someone was inside. While Wright radioed for help, Hymon went to the back of the house, heard a door slam, and saw someone run across the backyard toward a 6-foot chain-link fence. With his flashlight, Hymon could see that Garner was unarmed. He called out, "Police! Halt!" but Garner began to climb the fence.

Convinced that Garner would escape if he made it over the fence, Hymon fired, hitting him in the back of the head. Garner died in the operating room, the $10 he had stolen still in his pocket. Hymon had acted under Tennessee law and Memphis Police Department policy.

The standard set by *Tennessee v. Garner* presents problems because judging a suspect's dangerousness can be difficult. Because officers must make quick decisions in stressful situations, creating rules that will guide them in every case is impossible. The Court tried to clarify its ruling in the case of *Graham v. Connor* (1989). Here, the justices established the standard of "objective reasonableness," saying that the officer's use of deadly force should be judged in terms of the "reasonableness at the moment." This means that the use of the deadly force should be judged from the point of view of the officer on the scene. The Court's decision says that it must be recognized that

CLOSE UP

FEDERAL CONSENT DECREES AND OVERSIGHT OVER LOCAL POLICE

An Albuquerque, New Mexico, police officer's helmet camera filmed the group of heavily armed officers approaching James Boyd, a homeless man with a history of mental illness, as he stood on a hillside where he was camping at the edge of the city. The March 2014 incident later generated protest marches and national attention to the police department's record when, upon being released to the public, the video showed officers shooting Boyd as he waved two knives and made threats. Critics claimed that the heavily armed police, who outnumbered Boyd, could have avoided shooting him as it did not appear that he was positioned to actually inflict any harm on officers if they had stood back and attempted to de-escalate the situation and seek advice from mental health professionals.

At the time of Boyd's death, the Albuquerque Police Department was already under investigation by the U.S. Department of Justice for excessive use-of-force practices that potentially violated people's rights and caused needless deaths. The investigation, which began in November 2012, found that even prior to the shooting of James Boyd, in the preceding four years Albuquerque officers had shot 37 people, killing 23 and wounding 14 others. The federal investigation also raised issues concerning improper use of force involving conducted energy weapons, citing the use of stun guns "at a 75-year-old homeless man for refusing to leave a bus stop, at a 16-year-old boy for refusing to lie on a floor covered in broken glass, and at a young man so drunk he could not get up from a couch" (Santos, 2014).

A consent decree is a mechanism through which a government agency can avoid a lawsuit by agreeing to requirements that will serve as needed remedies to solve problems. The consent decree required changes in the hiring and training of Albuquerque police officers. There were reports of the police department failing to follow its own usual hiring standards because they were eager to fill a large number of vacant positions. The training was to include attention to strategies to

"officers are often forced to make split-second judgments—in circumstances that are tense, uncertain, and rapidly evolving—about the amount of force that is necessary in a particular situation."

The risk of lawsuits by victims of improper police shootings looms over police departments and creates a further incentive for administrators to set and enforce standards for the use of force. In 2011, the city of Philadelphia agreed to pay $1.2 million to the family of an unarmed man who was shot in the head by a police officer on New Year's Eve. The officer claimed that he thought he saw the man pointing a gun at him but the federal judge presiding over the lawsuit rejected that claim in light of the testimony of other witnesses (Gorenstein, 2011). Litigation over improper use of force and other police misconduct can be very expensive. In 2009, Philadelphia paid amounts ranging from $690 to $750,000 to resolve 220 lawsuits and complaints against the police (Gorenstein, 2011). The threat of lawsuits cannot, however, prevent improper use of force from happening. As long as officers carry weapons, some improper shootings will occur. Training, internal review of incidents, and disciplining or firing of quick-trigger officers may help reduce the use of unnecessary force. Read the Close Up feature on the Albuquerque, New Mexico, police department to see the federal government's role in pressuring police agencies to engage in careful use-of-force practices.

The risk of deaths, injuries, and subsequent lawsuits does not stem from police shootings alone. Police officers have also caused deaths by improperly conducting high-speed pursuit driving, using chokeholds, and striking people in the head with batons. Injuries also result from other forms of physical force, including such seemingly routine procedures as placing a suspect in handcuffs, if the handcuffs are too tight.

As a result of lawsuits by people injured at the hands of the police, departments have sought new means of applying force in ways that will not produce injuries. Some of the new methods are taught through training about specific de-escalate situations, avoid the use of force, and to be especially aware of how to handle mentally ill people without resorting to violence. The decree also required Albuquerque to disband specific police units that had developed reputations for using especially aggressive tactics. The Department of Justice appointed a well-known expert on police reform as the outside monitor to keep track of Albuquerque's progress and make sure that Albuquerque followed the commitments that it made in the consent decree.

Sources: Cindy Carcamo, "Justice Department Orders Reforms, Monitor for Albuquerque Police," *Los Angeles Times,* October 31, 2014 (www.latimes.com); Russell Contraras, "U.S. Justice Department, Albuquerque Announce Police Monitor to Oversee Troubled Police Force," *U.S. News and World Report*, January 20, 2015 (www.usenews.com); Trip Jennings, "Protesters Cite New Details of Albuquerque Police Shooting as Reason for Rally," *New York Times*, June 3, 2014 (www.nytimes.com); Ian Lovett, "Albuquerque Agrees to Changes on Use of Force," October 31, 2014 (www.nytimes.com); Fernanda Santos, "Justice Dept. Accuses Albuquerque Police of Excessive Force," *New York Times*, April 10, 2014 (www.nytimes.com)

DEBATE THE ISSUE

Albuquerque is not the only city to agree to have its police department placed under supervision after being pressured by the threat of a U.S. Department of Justice lawsuit. Other cities under consent decrees include New Orleans and Seattle. Can the federal Department of Justice effectively change practices at local police departments? Are these merely issues of hiring and training, or are there also issues concerning changing the attitudes and culture within a department? Will a city's police department necessarily change by following the requirements of a consent decree? What factors might limit the potential for change? If you were a police chief or a mayor, would you agree to a consent decree? Would you find ways to change your police department yourself without having requirements placed upon you through federal government pressure? What would you do?

holds and pressure points that officers can use to incapacitate people temporarily without causing permanent harm. In addition, as previously discussed in the section on weapons technology, police departments seek new weapons that use less-than-lethal force.

Although progress has been made in reducing improper and excessive use of force by police, corruption remains a major problem. We turn to this issue next.

Corruption

Police corruption has a long history in America. Early in the twentieth century, city officials organized liquor and gambling businesses for their personal gain. In many cities, ties between politicians and police officials assured that favored clients would be protected and competitors harassed. Much of the Progressive movement to reform the police aimed at combating such corrupt arrangements.

Although these political ties have diminished in most cities, corruption still exists. A Georgia police chief was sentenced to prison in February 2015 for accepting money to protect an illegal gambling operation (Skutch, 2015). In December 2014, two San Francisco police officers were convicted of stealing property and cash from drug suspects, with evidence of their misdeeds caught on motel security cameras (Egelko, 2014). Earlier in 2014, a Kansas City police officer was convicted of corruption for accepting sexual favors from prostitutes in exchange for agreeing not to arrest them ("Kansas City Police Officer," 2014). Sadly, a number of such cases appear in the news each year.

Sometimes "corruption" is defined so broadly that it ranges from accepting a free cup of coffee to robbing businesses or beating suspects. Obviously, corruption is not easily defined, and people disagree about what it includes. As a useful starting point, we can focus on the distinction between corrupt officers who are "grass eaters" and those who are "meat eaters."

Officers are placed in situations where they can be tempted to enrich themselves by stealing money, property, or drugs, or by accepting favors, gifts, and bribes. If you were a police chief, how would you reduce the risks of police corruption?

AP Images/Paul Sancya

Grass Eaters and Meat Eaters

Grass eaters are officers who accept payoffs that the routines of police work bring their way. *Meat eaters* are officers who actively use their power for personal gain. Although meat eaters are few, their actions make headlines when discovered. By contrast, because grass eaters are numerous, they make corruption seem acceptable and promote a code of secrecy that brands as a traitor any officer who exposes corruption. Grass eaters make up the heart of the problem and are often harder to detect than meat eaters.

In the past, low salaries, politics, and poor hiring practices have been cited as factors contributing to corruption. However, these arguments fall short of explaining today's corruption. Whereas some claim that a few rotten apples should not taint an entire police force, corruption in some departments has been so rampant that the rotten-apple theory does not fully explain the situation. Some explanations center on the structure and organization of police work. Much police work involves enforcement of laws in situations in which there is no complainant or it is unclear whether a law has been broken. Moreover, most police work takes place under the officer's own discretion, without direct supervision. Thus, police officers may have many opportunities to gain benefits by using their discretion to protect people who engage in illegal conduct.

If police administrators judge success merely by the maintenance of order on the streets and a steady flow of arrests and traffic citations, they may not have any idea what their officers actually do while on patrol. Officers therefore may learn that they can engage in improper conduct without worrying about supervisors' investigations as long as they maintain order on the streets and keep their activities out of the public spotlight. In some cities the profits for drug dealers and organizers of prostitution rings are so high that they can easily afford to make large payments to unethical officers for protection against prosecution.

Over time, illegal activity may become accepted as normal. Ellwyn Stoddard, who conducted the classic study "blue-coat crime," says that it can become part of an "identifiable informal 'code.'" He suggests that officers are socialized to the code early in their careers. Those who "snitch" on other officers may be ostracized (Stoddard, 1968: 205). Recent research shows that officers risk retaliation from peers if they break the code (Cancino and Enriquez, 2004).

When corruption comes to official attention, officers protect the code by distancing themselves from the known offender rather than stopping their own improper conduct. Activities under this blue-coat code may include the following (Stoddard, 1968: 205):

- *Mooching:* Accepting free coffee, cigarettes, meals, liquor, groceries, or other items, which are thought of as compensation either for being underpaid or for future favoritism to the donor.
- *Bribery:* Receiving cash or a "gift" in exchange for past or future help in avoiding prosecution. The officer may claim to be unable to identify a criminal, may take care to be in the wrong place when a crime is to occur, or may take some other action that can be viewed as mere carelessness.
- *Chiseling:* Demanding discounts or free admission to places of entertainment, whether on duty or not.
- *Extortion:* Demanding payment for an ad in a police magazine or purchase of tickets to a police function; holding a "street court" in which minor traffic tickets can be avoided by the payment of cash "bail" to the arresting officer, with no receipt given.
- *Shopping:* Picking up small items such as candy bars, gum, and cigarettes at a store where the door has been left unlocked at the close of business hours.
- *Shakedown:* Taking expensive items for personal use during an investigation of a break-in or burglary. Shakedown is distinguished from shopping by the value of the items taken and the ease with which former ownership of items can be determined if the officer is caught.
- *Premeditated theft:* Using tools, keys, or other devices to force entry and steal property. Premeditated theft is distinguished from shakedown by the fact that it is planned, not by the value of the items taken.
- *Favoritism:* Issuing license tabs, window stickers, or courtesy cards that exempt users from arrest or citation for traffic offenses (sometimes extended to family members and friends of recipients).
- *Perjury:* Lying to provide an alibi for fellow officers engaged in unlawful activity or otherwise failing to tell the truth so as to avoid sanctions.
- *Prejudice:* Treating members of minority groups in a biased fashion, especially members of groups that lack the political influence in City Hall to cause the arresting officer trouble.

Police corruption has three major effects on law enforcement: (1) suspects are left free to engage in further crime, (2) morale is damaged and supervision becomes lax, and (3) the image of the police suffers. The image of the police agency is very important in light of the need for citizen cooperation. When people see the police as not much different from the "crooks," effective crime control falls even further out of reach. Indeed, recent research has identified connections between violent crime and compromised police legitimacy in disadvantaged communities (Kane, 2005).

Surprisingly, many people do not equate police corruption with other forms of crime. Some believe that police corruption is tolerable as long as the streets remain safe. This attitude ignores the fact that corrupt officers are serving only themselves and are not committed to serving the public.

Controlling Corruption

The public has a role to play in stopping police corruption. Scandals attract the attention of politicians and the news media, but it is up to citizens to file complaints about improper actions. Once a citizen files a complaint, however, questions remain about how best to respond. All departments have policies about proper police behavior and ways of dealing with complaints, but some departments tend to sweep corruption complaints under the rug. The most effective departments often have strong leaders who clearly demonstrate to the public and to officers that corruption will not be tolerated and that complaints will be investigated and pursued seriously. Specific innovations are possible. Because of its highly publicized scandals, for example, the city of New York in 1995 created the Commission to Combat Police Corruption, a permanent agency with a full-time staff that is completely separate from the New York City Police Department that it monitors.

✔POINT

11. What kinds of practices may be viewed as police abuse?
12. When may the police use force?
13. How did the Supreme Court rule in *Tennessee v. Garner*?
14. What is the difference between grass eaters and meat eaters?
15. What are five of the ten practices cited by Stoddard as blue-coat crime?

STOP AND ANALYZE: Is it ever appropriate for police officers to receive gifts or monetary "tips" from the public? Create arguments in favor of two circumstances that could be acceptable. Then point out two risks or two arguments against permitting any such practices.

Civic Accountability

Relations between citizens and the police depend greatly on citizen confidence that officers will behave in accordance with the law and departmental guidelines. Rapport with the community is enhanced when citizens feel sure that the police will protect their persons and property and the rights guaranteed by the Constitution. Making the police responsive to citizen complaints without burdening them with a flood of such complaints is difficult. The main challenge in making the police more accountable is to use citizen input to force police to follow the law and departmental guidelines without placing too many limits on their ability to carry out their primary functions. At present, four less-than-perfect techniques are used in efforts to control the police: (1) internal affairs units, (2) civilian review boards, (3) standards and accreditation, and (4) civil liability lawsuits. We now look at each of these in some detail.

Internal Affairs Units

Controlling the police is mainly an internal matter that administrators must give top priority. The community must be confident that the department has procedures to ensure that officers will protect the rights of citizens. Many police departments' formal complaint procedures almost seem designed to discourage citizen input.

Depending on the size of the department, a single officer or an entire section can serve as an **internal affairs unit** that receives and investigates complaints against officers. An officer charged with misconduct can face criminal prosecution or disciplinary action leading to resignation, dismissal, or suspension. Officers assigned to the internal affairs unit have duties similar to those of the inspector general's staff in the military. They must investigate complaints against other officers. Hollywood films and television dramas depict dramatic

internal affairs unit
A branch of a police department that receives and investigates complaints alleging violations of rules and policies on the part of officers.

investigations of drug dealing and murder, but investigations of sexual harassment, alcohol or drug problems, misuse of force, and violations of departmental policies are more common.

The internal affairs unit must be given enough resources to carry out its mission, as well as direct access to the chief. Internal investigators who assume that a citizen complaint is an attack on the police as a whole will shield officers against such complaints. When this happens, administrators do not get the information they need to correct a problem. The public, in turn, may come to believe that the department condones the practices they complain of and that filing a complaint is pointless. Moreover, even when the top administrator seeks to attack misconduct, he or she may find it hard to persuade police to testify against other officers.

Internal affairs investigators find the work stressful, because their status prevents them from maintaining close relationships with other officers. A wall of silence rises around them. Such problems can be especially severe in smaller departments where all the officers know each other well and regularly socialize together.

Civilian Review Boards

If a police department cannot show that it effectively combats corruption among officers, the public will likely demand that a **civilian review board** investigate the department. The Bay Area Regional Transit (BART) system in California created such a citizens' board in the aftermath of a BART police officer's fatal shooting of an unarmed African American man under controversial circumstances (Melendez, 2011). Atlanta created such a board amid public controversy after drug task force officers shot and killed a 92-year-old woman in her home (Jonsson, 2015). These boards allow complaints to be channeled through a committee of people who are not sworn police officers. The organization and powers of civilian review boards vary, but all oversee and review how police departments handle citizen complaints. The boards may also recommend remedial action. They do not have the power to investigate or discipline individual officers, however (S. Walker and Wright, 1995).

civilian review board
Citizens' committee formed to investigate complaints against the police.

The main argument made by the police against civilian review boards is that people outside law enforcement do not understand the problems of policing. The police contend that civilian oversight lowers morale and hinders performance, and that officers will be less effective if they are worried about possible disciplinary actions. In reality, however, the boards have not been harsh. Indeed, research on the public's views on appropriate punishment for police misconduct reveals that "the public brings a temperate lens, or one that does not demonstrate a propensity toward harsh punishments" when examining police behavior and the circumstances in which that behavior occurred (Seron, Pereira, and Kovath, 2006: 955).

Review of police actions occurs some time after the incident has taken place and usually comes down to the officer's word against that of the complainant. Given the low visibility of the incidents that lead to complaints, a great many complaints are not substantiated (Skolnick and Fyfe, 1993). The effectiveness of civilian review boards has not been tested; their presence may or may not improve police–citizen relations. Even so, filing a complaint against the police can be quite frustrating. As you read "Civic Engagement: Your Role in the System," consider the best way for a civilian review board to approach complaints against the police.

CIVIC ENGAGEMENT

YOUR ROLE IN THE SYSTEM

Imagine that the mayor of your city asks you to design a civilian review board to handle complaints against police officers. *Present the design of your proposed board and the complaint process, including number of members and their selection process, procedural steps to which the citizen is entitled, and the specific people responsible for investigating complaints. What potential impediments may hinder the effective creation and operation of your board and process?* Then compare your process with that of Seattle's Office of Professional Accountability review board.

Standards and Accreditation

Commission on Accreditation for Law Enforcement Agencies (CALEA)
Nonprofit organization formed by major law enforcement executives' associations to develop standards for police practices and policies; on request, will review police agencies and award accreditation upon meeting those standards.

One way to increase police accountability is to require that police actions meet nationally recognized standards. The movement to accredit departments that meet these standards has gained momentum during the past decade. It has the support of the **Commission on Accreditation for Law Enforcement Agencies (CALEA)**, a private nonprofit corporation formed by four professional associations: the International Association of Chiefs of Police (IACP), the National Organization of Black Law Enforcement Executives (NOBLE), the National Sheriffs' Association (NSA), and the Police Executive Research Forum (PERF).

The CALEA *Standards,* first published in 1983, have been updated from time to time. The latest edition, published in 2006, has 188 specific standards for first-tier accreditation and 482 standards for departments seeking advanced accreditation. Each standard is a statement, with a brief explanation, that sets forth clear requirements. For example, under Limits of Authority, Standard 1.2.7 requires that "a written directive [govern] the use of discretion by sworn officers" (Commission on Accreditation for Law Enforcement Agencies, 2006). Because police departments traditionally have said almost nothing about their use of discretion, this statement represents a major shift. However, the standard still is not specific enough to necessarily cover all situations in which officers use discretion. Police accreditation is voluntary. Departments contact CALEA, which helps them in their efforts to meet the standards. This process involves self-evaluation by departmental executives, the development of policies that meet the standards, and the training of officers. The CALEA representative acts like a military inspector general, visiting the department, examining its policies, and seeing if the standards are met in its daily operations. Departments that meet the standards receive certification. Administrators can use the standards as a management tool, training officers to know the standards and to be accountable for their actions.

Obviously, the standards do not guarantee that police officers in an accredited department will not engage in misconduct. However, the standards are a major step toward providing clear guidelines to officers about proper behavior. Accreditation can also show the public that the department is committed to making sure officers carry out their duties in an ethical, professional manner.

Civil Liability Lawsuits

Section 1983 lawsuits
Civil lawsuits authorized by a federal statute against state and local officials and local agencies when citizens have evidence that their federal constitutional rights have been violated by these authorities.

Civil lawsuits against departments for police misconduct can increase civic accountability. In 1961 the U.S. Supreme Court ruled that Section 1983 of the Civil Rights Act of 1871 allows citizens to sue state and local officials for violations of their civil rights. The high court extended this opportunity to file **Section 1983 lawsuits** in 1978 when it ruled that individual officials and local agencies may be sued when a person's civil rights are violated by an agency's "customs and usages." If an individual can show that a rights violation was caused by employees whose wrongful acts were the result of these "customs, practices, and policies, including poor training and supervision," then he or she can win the lawsuit (*Monell v. Department of Social Services of the City of New York,* 1978).

Lawsuits charging brutality, false arrest, and negligence are being brought in both state and federal courts. In several states people have received damage awards in the millions of dollars, and police departments have settled some suits out of court. In 2013, for example, Chicago paid $4.1 million to the family of an unarmed man who was shot in the back multiple times by a police officer as he lay on the ground (St. Clair and Gorner, 2013). In the same year, five Connecticut towns agreed to pay $3.5 million to the family of an apparently innocent man who was killed by a combined SWAT team made up of officers from several towns (Tepfer, 2013).

Civil liability rulings by the courts tend to be simple and severe: Officials and municipalities are ordered to pay a sum of money, and the courts can enforce that judgment. Most departments have liability insurance, and many officers have their own insurance policies. The potential for costly judgments gives police departments an incentive to improve the training and supervision of officers (Vaughn, 2001). One study asked a sample of police executives to rank the policy issues most likely to be affected by civil liability decisions. The top-ranked issues were use of force, pursuit driving, and improper arrests (C. E. Smith and Hurst, 1996). The fear of lawsuits and adverse jury verdicts on these issues pushes police departments to create and refine their policies to guide officers' decision making.

✔**POINT**

16. What are the four methods used to increase the civic accountability of the police?

17. What is an internal affairs unit?

18. Why are civilian review boards relatively uncommon?

19. What is the importance of the decision in *Monell v. Department of Social Services of the City of New York?*

STOP AND ANALYZE: Police officers often voice concerns about being judged after the fact by citizens who do not understand the dangers and need for quick decisions in daily police work. Thus they criticize the role of citizens on review boards and juries. What are two arguments in favor of using only professionals in investigating and deciding whether police acted inappropriately? What are two arguments in favor of treating citizens as essential participants in these processes? Which set of arguments is more persuasive?

A QUESTION OF ETHICS

In Volusia, Florida, a captain in the county sheriff's department ordered a subordinate officer to investigate the possible theft of trade secrets at a firearms company. The alleged theft was undertaken by two former employees who were trying to set up a competing firearms business. The two former employees were charged with crimes, but a judge dismissed several charges at a pretrial hearing, including clearing one defendant of all charges. At the hearing in 2015, it was revealed that the captain worked part-time for the firearms company and was reportedly planning to continue his work for the company when he retired from the sheriff's department. When the captain testified at the hearing, the defense attorney used a question to make a pointed accusation about a conflict of interest: "What better way to please your future co-owner than to eliminate your competition?" The defense attorney later remarked to a news reporter, "That just to me is the appearance of impropriety. . . . I don't know if anything improper happened. It just looks bad."

Source: Frank Fernandez, "Volusia Officer Ordered Investigation on Behalf of His Part-Time Employer," *Daytona Beach News-Journal,* February 7, 2015 (www.news-journalonline.com).

CRITICAL THINKING AND ANALYSIS

Imagine that you are the sheriff in the department where these actions related to the officer's second job have been revealed. Do you see any appearance of a conflict of interest? Let us presume that you would want to diminish any risk that improper actions would occur or those that the public may view as improper. Would you seek to ban outside employment? Would you seek full, public disclosure of outside employment commitments? Would you limit any contact between officers' official decisions and their outside employers? Write a memo describing the rules concerning outside employment that you would seek to impose on your officers.

Summary

1 Describe the new technologies that facilitate crime, assist police investigations, and affect citizens' rights

- The development of new technologies has assisted police investigations through the use of computers, databases, surveillance devices, DNA testing and other identity tests, and methods to detect deception.
- Questions arise concerning the reliability of technology, the adequacy of resources for using technology, and the ethics and competence of personnel using new technology.
- Police departments are seeking to identify less-lethal weapons that can incapacitate suspects and control unruly crowds without causing serious injuries and deaths.

2 Discuss the issues and problems that emerge from law enforcement agencies' increased attention to homeland security

- Homeland security has become an important priority for law enforcement agencies at all levels of government since September 11, 2001.
- Agencies need planning and coordination in order to gather intelligence and prepare for possible threats and public emergencies.
- The federal government provides funding for state and local fusion centers and emergency preparedness equipment.
- New laws, such as the USA Patriot Act, have caused controversy about the proper balance between government authority and citizens' rights.

3 Analyze the policing and related activities undertaken by private-sector security management

- The expansion of security management and private policing reflects greater recognition of the need to protect private assets and to plan for emergencies.
- Security management produces new issues and problems, including concerns about the recruitment, training, and activities of lower-level private security personnel.
- Public–private interaction affects security through such means as joint planning for emergencies, hiring private firms to guard government facilities, and hiring police officers for off-duty private security work.

4 Discuss the ways police can abuse their power and the challenges of controlling this abuse

- Police corruption and misuse of force erode community support.
- Police use of deadly force occurs infrequently and can no longer be applied to unarmed fleeing felons.
- Police corruption includes "meat eaters" who actively seek corrupt activities and "grass eaters" who accept favors and payoffs that come their way.

5 Identify the methods that can be used to make police more accountable to citizens

- Internal affairs units, civilian review boards, standards and accreditation, and civil liability lawsuits increase police accountability to citizens.

Questions for Review

1 What controversies exist concerning new technologies employed by the police?

2 What have law enforcement agencies done to enhance homeland security?

3 What problems are associated with private policing?

4 What are the major forms of police abuse of power?

5 What has the Supreme Court ruled regarding police use of deadly force?

6 What are the pros and cons of the major approaches to making the police accountable to citizens?

Key Terms and Cases

civilian review board (p. 321)
Commission on Accreditation for Law Enforcement Agencies (CALEA) (p. 322)
excessive use of force (p. 311)
fusion centers (p. 296)
geographic information system (GIS) (p. 283)
internal affairs unit (p. 320)
latent fingerprints (p. 284)
law enforcement intelligence (p. 295)
less-lethal weapons (p. 290)
Section 1983 lawsuits (p. 322)
USA Patriot Act (p. 299)
Kyllo v. United States (2001) (p. 290)
Maryland v. King (2013) (p. 287)
Tennessee v. Garner (1985) (p. 315)
United States v. Jones (2012) (p. 290)

Checkpoint Answers

1 What actions have been taken to combat counterfeit currency in the United States?

✓ Redesign of U.S. currency; efforts to detect counterfeit currency from the level of individual cashiers at stores to international investigations leading to the seizure of large quantities of fake currency.

2 What harms are caused by counterfeit products in the United States?

✓ Billions of dollars in losses for American businesses due to counterfeit and pirated products; deaths and other harmful health consequences from counterfeit medications.

3 What aspects of weaponry increase the risks to police officers and the public?

✓ The availability of high-powered weapons and body armor permit some criminals to outgun the police and avoid being easily stopped by police weapons.

4 What kinds of new technologies are assisting police with their investigative functions?

✓ Smartphones, tablets, and laptop computers in patrol cars connect to various databases, geographic information systems (GIS), and DNA testing.

5 What problems are associated with the use of new technologies?

✓ Questions about the accuracy and reliability of the technology, inadequate resources to utilize technology fully, and ethics and competence of personnel.

6 What kinds of new weaponry have police employed?

✓ Less-lethal weapons, including beanbag projectiles, Tasers, and pepperball projectiles.

7 What have law enforcement officials done to enhance homeland security?

✓ Planning and coordinating with other agencies, new equipment and training, and Incident Command System.

8 What are the criticisms directed at the USA Patriot Act?

✓ Permits too much government authority for searches and wiretaps; defines domestic terrorism in ways that might include legitimate protest groups.

9 What has caused the growth of security management and private policing?

✓ Companies' recognition of the need to protect assets and plan for emergencies, problems with employee theft, computer crime, and other issues that require active prevention and investigation.

10 What are the three models for private employment of police officers?

✓ Department contract model, officer contract model, and union brokerage model.

11 What kinds of practices may be viewed as police abuse?

✓ Profanity, abusive language, physical force, and violence.

12 When may the police use force?

✓ The police may use force if necessary to make an arrest, to keep the peace, or to maintain public order.

13 How did the Supreme Court rule in *Tennessee v. Garner*?

✓ Deadly force may not be used in apprehending a fleeing felon unless it is necessary to prevent the escape and unless the officer has probable cause to believe that the suspect poses a significant threat of death or serious physical injury to the officer or others.

14 What is the difference between grass eaters and meat eaters?

✓ Grass eaters are officers who accept payoffs that police work brings their way. Meat eaters are officers who aggressively misuse their power for personal gain.

15 What are five of the ten practices cited by Stoddard as blue-coat crime?

✓ Mooching, bribery, chiseling, extortion, shopping, shakedown, premeditated theft, favoritism, perjury, and prejudice.

16 What are the four methods used to increase the civic accountability of the police?

✓ Internal affairs units, civilian review boards, standards and accreditation, and civil liability suits.

17 What is an internal affairs unit?

✓ A unit within the police department designated to receive and investigate complaints alleging violation of rules and policies on the part of officers.

18 Why are civilian review boards relatively uncommon?

✓ Opposition by the police.

19 What is the importance of the decision in *Monell v. Department of Social Services of the City of New York?*

✓ Allows citizens to sue individual officers and the agency when an individual's civil rights are violated by the agency's customs and usages.

CHAPTER 8 POLICE AND CONSTITUTIONAL LAW

CHAPTER FEATURES

- **Doing Your Part** American Civil Liberties Union
- **Technology and Criminal Justice** The Public Backlash Against Police Surveillance Technology
- **Close Up** Determining Justification for Police Searches
- **New Directions in Criminal Justice Policy** Evidence-Based Practices in Identification Procedures

CHAPTER LEARNING OBJECTIVES

1 Know the extent of police officers' authority to stop and search people and their vehicles

2 Understand when and how police officers seek warrants in order to conduct searches and make arrests

3 Know whether police officers can look in people's windows or their backyards to see if evidence of a crime exists there

4 Analyze the situations in which police officers can conduct searches without obtaining a warrant

5 Understand the purpose of the privilege against compelled self-incrimination

6 Understand the exclusionary rule and the situations in which it applies

CHAPTER OUTLINE

Legal Limitations on Police Investigations
- Search and Seizure
- Arrest
- Warrants and Probable Cause

Plain View Doctrine
- Open Fields Doctrine
- Plain Feel and Other Senses

Warrantless Searches
- Special Needs beyond the Normal Purposes of Law Enforcement
- Stop and Frisk on the Streets
- Search Incident to a Lawful Arrest
- Exigent Circumstances
- Consent
- Automobile Searches

Questioning Suspects
- *Miranda* Rules
- The Consequences of *Miranda*

The Exclusionary Rule
- Application of the Exclusionary Rule to the States
- Exceptions to the Exclusionary Rule

AP Images/Reed Saxon

Police officers stopped David Riley's vehicle in August 2009 when they noticed that his license tags had expired. When they checked his driver's license, they discovered that it, too, had expired. Following departmental procedure in situations of drivers without valid licenses, they impounded his vehicle, namely, seizing it so that it would be in police possession. Impounded vehicles are typically released after the owner has complied with registration requirements and has paid any fines for traffic violations, such as lapsed registrations. Such vehicles are subject to a warrantless inventory search so that officers can make a list of what is inside the vehicle and thereby avoid later claims that they lost or destroyed an individual's property after impounding and taking possession of the vehicle. Inventory searches also serve as a permissible way to look for criminal evidence when there is a basis for impounding a vehicle. In this case, they found two handguns, so they arrested Riley for illegal possession of concealed weapons.

Upon arrest, individuals are subject—at the scene of arrest—to a pat-down search of their clothing so officers can make sure that they are not concealing any weapons or evidence. The search revealed that Riley had a cell phone in his pants pocket as well as items associated with membership in a street gang. About two hours after the arrest, a detective specializing in gangs accessed photographs and information from Riley's cell phone. Among the photos on the phone was one of Riley standing in front of a vehicle that police believed was involved in a shooting a few weeks earlier.

Riley was ultimately charged with several offenses related to the shooting, including attempted murder. Under a state statute he also faced enhanced sentencing for being convicted of a felony that was committed to advance the interests of a street gang. Riley's defense attorney asked the judge to exclude from consideration all evidence obtained from the cell phone by claiming that the examination of its contents was an improper police search in violation of Riley's Fourth Amendment rights against "unreasonable searches." The judge rejected that argument, photos from the cell phone were introduced into evidence against Riley, and officers testified about photos and videos that they viewed on the phone. Riley was convicted and given a sentence of 15 years to life in prison.

Riley's attorney appealed, based on the Fourth Amendment claim originally rejected by the trial judge. The California Court of Appeals endorsed the trial judge's decision, based on an earlier California Supreme Court case, that police officers can make warrantless examinations of the contents of cell phones seized upon the arrest of criminal suspects. The California Supreme Court declined to hear the case, so the attorney took the case to the U.S. Supreme Court in 2013. Cases typically move slowly through the various stages of the court system, so the Supreme Court did not actually hear arguments in the case until nearly five years after the original arrest.

After hearing oral arguments from attorneys for both sides in the case on April 29, 2014, the Supreme Court issued a unanimous majority opinion written by Chief Justice John Roberts on June 25, 2014. The Court declared that Riley's attorney was correct. The warrantless search of Riley's cell phone to obtain information for use against him in a criminal trial violated his Fourth Amendment rights. Such successful claims in the appellate courts do not automatically declare that an individual is innocent and must be set free. Instead, they typically mean that an individual is entitled to a new trial in which the improperly obtained evidence is excluded from consideration. However, there is often other evidence, such as witness testimony, fingerprints on guns, and crime scene evidence, that can be used to convict the individual again at a second trial.

The Supreme Court noted that police officers are entitled to search the clothing and immediate area around anyone that they arrest, to make sure that there are no weapons that could harm the officers or others and that no nearby evidence can be destroyed by the arrestee. Thus the Court approved examining a cell phone found in such a search to make sure that no razor blades or other weapons are physically concealed in the phone. However, in order to examine the data contained within a cell phone, officers must obtain a warrant from a judicial officer. In order to obtain a warrant, police would need to persuade the judicial officer that there is a basis to conclude that the cell phone contains criminal evidence. The Supreme Court opinion provided a clear acknowledgement that for people in contemporary society, cell phones can contain an extensive array of deeply personal information that government officials should not automatically be able to access and examine simply by making an arrest.

As you will see in A Question of Ethics at the end of this chapter, news reports have periodically surfaced indicating that some male officers in California, Texas, and presumably other places had been seizing cell phones from people at traffic stops and automobile collisions solely to look for nude or bathing-suit photos of female drivers in order to share those photos with other male officers for their personal entertainment (Friedersdorf, 2014). In one particularly outrageous case, an officer was caught not only stealing nude photos from a woman's phone after a traffic stop, but actually calling the woman later to invite her out to dinner (McVicker, 2005). The Supreme Court's opinion did not discuss this example of privacy invasions that can occur when police feel free to examine the contents of cell phones at their own discretion. Obviously, most Americans are likely to view such actions by police as serious and unjustified invasions of personal privacy. By clarifying the law concerning warrantless cell phone searches, the Supreme Court's opinion provided a very clear basis for citizens to sue police officers for constitutional rights violations when such searches occur.

In *Riley v. California* (2014), the U.S. Supreme Court justices and lower court judges in California were interpreting the ambiguous words "unreasonable searches" from the Fourth Amendment. As we examine other Supreme Court decisions, think about the challenge presented by the necessity of applying brief phrases from the Bill of Rights to actual situations, thereby determining which people can be searched and questioned and, more importantly, whether certain individuals will spend many years in prison.

In this chapter we examine individual rights and how those legal protections define the limits of police officers' powers of investigation and arrest. In particular, we look closely at two rights that were introduced in Chapter 4: the Fourth Amendment protection against unreasonable searches and seizures, and the Fifth Amendment privilege against compelled self-incrimination (see Appendix A for the complete text).

Legal Limitations on Police Investigations

In our democracy, the rights of individuals contained in the Bill of Rights embody important American values (see Chapter 4). They reflect the historic belief that we do not want to give government officials absolute power to pursue criminal investigations and prosecutions, because that approach to crime control would impose excessive costs on the values of individual liberty, privacy, and due process. If police could do whatever they wanted to do, then people would lack protections against arbitrary searches and arrests. On the other hand, crime control is an important policy goal. We do not want individuals' expectations about legal protections to block the ability of law enforcement officers to protect citizens from crime and punish wrongdoers. Judges must therefore interpret the Constitution in ways that seek to achieve a proper balance between crime control and the protection of individual rights.

Many police actions fall under the Fourth Amendment because they involve searches, seizures, and warrants. If officers exceed their authority by conducting an improper search of a person or a home, judges may release the arrestees or forbid certain evidence from being used. Officers might also be disciplined by their superiors or even sued by people whose rights were violated if investigatory activities violate the rules of law. Clearly, police officers need to know the legal rules that apply to their investigative activities, such as searches, arrests, and the questioning of suspects.

How can an officer know when his or her actions might violate the Fourth Amendment? The officer must depend on information and training provided at the police academy and subsequent updates from city and state attorneys who monitor court decisions. Individual police officers do not have time to follow the details of the latest court decisions. That responsibility rests with those who train and supervise law enforcement officers. Thus, police officers' compliance with the law depends on their own knowledge and decisions as well as the supervision and training provided by their departments. As described in the Doing Your Part feature, college students can play a role in ensuring police officers' compliance with the law.

Search and Seizure

search
Officials' examination of and hunt for evidence in or on a person or place in a manner that intrudes on reasonable expectations of privacy.

reasonable expectations of privacy
Standard developed for determining whether a government intrusion of a person or property constitutes a search because it interferes with individual interests that are normally protected from government intrusion.

The Fourth Amendment prohibits police officers from undertaking "unreasonable searches and seizures." The Supreme Court defines **searches** as actions by law enforcement officials that intrude on people's **reasonable expectations of privacy**. For example, someone who places a personal diary in a locked drawer within a bedroom of his or her home has demonstrated a reasonable expectation. Police officers cannot simply decide to enter the home and bedroom in order to open the locked door and read the diary.

Many situations raise questions about people's reasonable expectations. For example, should people reasonably expect that a police officer will not reach into their pockets in order to see if they have guns? Should people reasonably expect a police officer not to walk up to their houses and peer into the windows? Should people reasonably expect that government officials will not intercept and read their email messages? (Bagley, 2011).

Although judges do not always answer these questions in clear, consistent ways, people's reasonable expectations about their privacy are important elements in judges' determinations about legal guidelines for police investigations. For example, the Supreme Court has said that no warrant is required and no search has occurred if police bring a drug-sniffing dog to walk around your vehicle when an officer has stopped you for a traffic violation (*Illinois v. Cabelles*, 2005). On the other hand, the Court has also said that a search has occurred and a warrant is required if police officers bring a drug-sniffing dog to your front door in an attempt to determine whether there may be marijuana in your house (*Florida v. Jardines*, 2013). The difference between the two situations hinges on the greater reasonable expectation of privacy to which people are entitled with respect to their homes as opposed to their vehicles on a public roadway.

seizure
Situations in which police officers use their authority to deprive people of their liberty and property.

In defining **seizure**, the Supreme Court focuses on the nature and extent of officers' interference with people's liberty and freedom of movement. If an officer who is leaning against the wall of a building says to a passing pedestrian, "Where are you going?" and the person replies, "To the sandwich shop down the street" as she continues to walk without interference by the officer, there is virtually no intrusion on her liberty and freedom of movement. Thus, officers are free to speak to people on the street. If people voluntarily stop in order to speak with the officer, they have not been "seized," because they are free to move along whenever they choose. However, if people are not free to leave when officers assert their authority to halt someone's movement, then a seizure has occurred, and the Fourth Amendment requires that the seizure be reasonable. One form of seizure is an arrest, which involves taking a suspect into custody. In 2005, the Supreme Court endorsed another form of seizure: holding an individual in handcuffs for three hours while officers conduct a search of a home (*Muehler v. Mena*). The detention was reasonable because the individual was present on the property where officers searched for weapons and drugs. Property can also be subject to seizure, especially if it is evidence in a criminal case.

DOING YOUR PART

AMERICAN CIVIL LIBERTIES UNION

The American Civil Liberties Union (ACLU) is an organization dedicated to protecting constitutional rights. There is a national ACLU organization as well as individual chapters in states throughout the country. These chapters lobby for laws that respect rights and they also handle legal cases concerning rights issues. For example, the Arizona chapter was responsible for winning the famous Supreme Court case that established the obligation for police officers to inform arrested suspects of their rights (*Miranda v. Arizona,* 1966).

ACLU chapters regularly use college students as volunteers and interns to educate the public about constitutional rights. These students also interview people who claim that their rights were violated by police officers and other government officials. The website of the ACLU of Northern California provides a description of an internship opportunity for college students:

> You can play a crucial role in our mission by interning as a civil liberties counselor. The ACLU gets a large number of its cases, some of which lead to landmark decisions, from individuals who call our intake line. The civil liberties counselor then assesses each call and either provides referrals or meets with staff attorneys to present unique cases.

The enforcement of proper legal limitations on police officers' authority requires that citizens be knowledgeable about their rights and have access to lawyers who will challenge police misbehavior and mistakes. Some people may believe that the ACLU's activities interfere with police officers' efforts to stop crime. However, research by Charles Epp showed that police officers' professionalism and training improved through pressure from outside lawyers combined with police executives' new ideas for creating clear departmental policies and practices that protect rights (Epp, 2009).

Do you agree that working to protect constitutional rights makes a contribution to the professionalism of police? Would you feel as if you were improving the justice system if you volunteered to educate people about their rights?

Sources: Website of the American Civil Liberties Union of Northern California (www.aclunc.org); Charles R. Epp, *Making Rights Real: Activists, Bureaucrats, and the Creation of the Legalistic State* (Chicago: University of Chicago Press, 2009).

When a seizure is very brief, it is called a **stop**, defined as a brief interference with a person's freedom of movement with a duration that can be measured in minutes, albeit a total of minutes that might add up to a half-hour or more under some circumstances. When police require a driver to pull over in order to receive a traffic citation, that is a stop. To be permissible under the Fourth Amendment, stops must be justified by **reasonable suspicion**—a situation in which specific aspects of the person's appearance, behavior, and circumstances lead the officer to conclude that the person should be stopped in order to investigate the occurrence of a crime. Officers cannot legally make stops based solely on hunches.

stop
Government officials' interference with an individual's freedom of movement for a duration that typically lasts for a limited number of minutes and only rarely exceeds one hour.

reasonable suspicion
A police officer's belief, based on articulable facts, that criminal activity is taking place, so that intruding on an individual's reasonable expectation of privacy is necessary.

As we shall see, courts permit police officers to make stops without reasonable suspicion in many kinds of situations. For example, these stops can occur in locations where preventing illegal activities is especially important, such as border-crossing points where smuggling and drug trafficking often occur. Thus, everyone can be stopped in these special situations even if there is no specific basis to suspect them of wrongdoing.

✔POINT
1. What is a search?
2. What justification do police officers need to make a stop?

STOP AND ANALYZE: What are two examples of situations that you believe should be considered "unreasonable searches" in violation of the Fourth Amendment? What is it about those searches that makes them "unreasonable"?

(Answers are at the end of the chapter.)

Arrest

An *arrest* is a significant deprivation of liberty, because a person is taken into police custody, transported to the police station or jail, and processed into the criminal justice system. A seizure need not be lengthy to be an arrest. Indeed, some "stops" may be longer than "arrests" if, for example, a person taken to the police station is released on bail within an hour but a person stopped along a roadside must wait a longer period for the officer to write out a slew of traffic citations. Typically, however, arrests last much longer than stops.

Because arrests involve a more significant intrusion on liberty, they necessitate a higher level of justification. Unlike stops, which require only reasonable suspicion, all arrests must be supported by probable cause. **Probable cause** requires that sufficient evidence exists to support the reasonable conclusion that a person has committed a crime. In order to obtain an arrest warrant, police officers must provide a judicial officer with sufficient evidence to support a finding of probable cause. Alternatively, police officers' determinations of probable cause can produce discretionary warrantless arrests in public places (Dow, 2010). A judge subsequently examines such arrests for the existence of probable cause, in a hearing that must occur shortly after the arrest, typically within 48 hours. If the judge determines that the police officer was wrong in concluding that probable cause existed to justify the arrest, then the suspect is released from custody.

probable cause
Reliable information indicating that evidence will likely be found in a specific location or that a specific person is likely to be guilty of a crime.

Officers may make arrests when they see people commit criminal acts or when witnesses provide them with sufficient information so that they believe probable cause exists to arrest an individual. Arrest authority is not limited to felonies and misdemeanors, however. The Supreme Court has expanded the discretionary authority of police officers to make arrests. In 2001, the justices decided that police officers can make a warrantless arrest for a traffic offense, such as a failure to wear a seat belt, that would draw only a fine upon conviction (*Atwater v. City of Lago Vista*, 2001). In *Hiibel v. Sixth Judicial District Court of Nevada* (2004), the Court declared that officers can arrest an individual for refusing to give his name to the police when the state has a statute that requires such self-identification during police stops.

Warrants and Probable Cause

Imagine that you are a judge. Two police officers come to your chambers to ask you to authorize a search warrant. They swear that they observed frequent foot traffic of suspicious people going in and out of a house. Moreover, they swear that a reliable informant told them that he was inside the house two days earlier and saw crack cocaine being sold. Does this information rise to the level of "probable cause," justifying issuance of a search warrant? Can you grant a warrant based purely on the word of police officers, or do you need other concrete evidence?

Bill Pugliano/Getty Images

Arrest is the physical taking of a person into custody. What legal requirements must be met to make this a valid arrest? What, if anything, prevents officers from making an improper arrest that is not supported by sufficient evidence of wrongdoing?

Search Warrant Requirements

The Fourth Amendment requires that "no Warrants shall issue, but upon probable cause, supported by Oath or affirmation, and particularly describing the place to be searched, and the persons or things to be seized." These particular elements of the Amendment must be fulfilled in order to issue a warrant. If they are not fulfilled, then a defendant can later challenge the validity of the warrant. The important elements are, first, the existence of probable cause. Second, the evidence that police officers present to the judicial officer must be supported by "oath or affirmation," which typically means that police officers say "yes" when the judicial officer asks them if they swear or affirm that all the information presented is true to the best of their knowledge. Officers can also fulfill this requirement by presenting an **affidavit**, which is a written statement confirmed by oath or affirmation. Third, the warrant must describe the specific place to be searched; a "general warrant" to search many locations cannot be issued. Fourth, the warrant must describe the person or items to be seized. Thus, if the warrant authorizes a search for a person suspected of robbery, the officers should not open small dresser drawers or other places where they know a person could not be hiding.

affidavit
Written statement of fact, supported by oath or affirmation, submitted to judicial officers to fulfill the requirements of probable cause for obtaining a warrant.

The U.S. Supreme Court has attempted to guide judicial officers in identifying the existence of probable cause. Mere suspicion cannot constitute probable cause, yet the level of evidence to establish it need not fulfill the high level of proof needed to justify a criminal conviction. In essence, probable cause is a level of evidence sufficient to provide a reasonable conclusion that the proposed objects of a search will be found in a location that law enforcement officers request to search. For an arrest warrant, the essential issue is whether sufficient evidence is presented to lead reasonably to the conclusion that a specific person should be prosecuted for an arrestable criminal offense. There is no hard-and-fast definition of *probable cause* that judicial officers can apply to every situation; rather, it serves as a flexible concept that judicial officers can apply in different ways.

In *Illinois v. Gates* (1983), the Supreme Court endorsed a flexible **totality of circumstances test**. Under this test, judges make a generalized determination about whether the evidence is both sufficient and reliable enough to justify a warrant. They are not required to prove the specific reliability of the source of the evidence.

totality of circumstances test
Flexible test established by the Supreme Court for identifying whether probable cause exists to justify the issuance of a warrant.

As illustrated by the example of cell phones and the Supreme Court's decision in *Riley v. California* (2014), the use of new technologies for following or examining people, cars, buildings, and other property raises challenging questions about which decisions by police lead to "unreasonable" searches and when they must seek a warrant (R. Simmons, 2012). As Amy Vorenberg says, "New technologies challenge us to adapt legal principles to new circumstances and social norms" (Vorenberg, 2012). In *Kyllo v. United States* (2001), for example, the Supreme Court said police violated the Fourth Amendment through the warrantless use of a heat-detection device pointed at the outside of a home to identify "hot spots" that might indicate the existence of grow lights for marijuana cultivation. Similarly, in *United States v. Jones* (2012), the Court said that police officers exceeded their authority in attaching a GPS device to a drug suspect's car after the expiration date for the search warrant authorizing use of the device. Read the Technology and Criminal Justice feature to consider recent issues that create collisions between the public's expectations about the use of technological devices and police officers' goal of obtaining evidence of criminal wrongdoing.

TECHNOLOGY & CRIMINAL JUSTICE

THE PUBLIC BACKLASH AGAINST POLICE SURVEILLANCE TECHNOLOGY

Although the American public is concerned about the need to protect society and catch lawbreakers, there are recent examples of public backlash against the expanded use of certain kinds of technology for these purposes. Some commentators believe that news stories about the National Security Agency gathering information about phone calls and emails sent and received by millions of Americans, including those who are not suspected of committing any crimes or engaging in any conspiracies, has made the public less willing to automatically accept the government's use of certain technologies.

Red-light cameras are used in a number of states to identify drivers who violate traffic laws by disobeying traffic signals at intersections. These cameras typically take photos of vehicles that run red lights, which generates a ticket that is then mailed to the vehicle owner and requires the payment of a fine. Research shows that these cameras can reduce fatal accidents at intersections. However, other research shows that they may *increase* the number of rear-end collisions as drivers slam on their brakes in the presence of a yellow light out of fear of being issued a ticket if the camera detects a violation.

In a number of cities, voters have either cast ballots directly or pressured their local officials to limit or ban the use of such cameras. Certain cities have experienced mechanical failures with their cameras that led to tickets being issued erroneously to innocent drivers. In addition, the cameras strike a nerve with people who do not like to feel as if their everyday activities are being monitored and photographed by the government. The devices also generate opposition because of the significant income that local governments earn from using the cameras. For example, red-light cameras reportedly produced $69 million in proceeds for Chicago in 2010, so the city decided to expand the use of such cameras as well as add devices that could detect speeding violations. Thus many citizens question whether the cameras are actually being used for public safety purposes.

✔POINT **3.** What is the difference between an arrest and a stop?
4. What do police officers need to demonstrate in order to obtain a warrant?

STOP AND ANALYZE: In the warrant process, describe the responsibilities of police officers. Also describe the responsibilities of judges. Which of these actors has the more difficult job in the process of determining whether probable cause exists? Why?

Plain View Doctrine

Although the warrant requirement is a central feature of the Fourth Amendment, the Supreme Court has identified situations in which warrants are not required. What if a police officer is walking down the street and sees a marijuana plant growing in the front window of a home? Has the officer conducted a search by looking into the window? If so, is the search legal even though it took place by chance but was not supported by reasonable suspicion or probable cause? In *Coolidge v. New Hampshire* (1971), the Court discussed the **plain view doctrine**, which permits officers to notice and use as evidence items that are visible to them when the officers are where they are permitted to be. Officers may not break into a home and then claim that the drugs found inside were in plain view on a table. However, if a homeowner invited officers into his home in order to file a report about a burglary, the officers do not need to obtain a warrant in order to seize drugs that they see lying on the kitchen table. Because the drugs were in plain view and the officers had a legal basis for their presence in the house, the owner lost any reasonable expectation of privacy that would otherwise require officers to demonstrate probable cause for a search.

plain view doctrine
Officers may examine and use as evidence, without a warrant, contraband or evidence that is in open view at a location where they are legally permitted to be.

Open Fields Doctrine

open fields doctrine
Officers are permitted to search and to seize evidence, without a warrant, on private property beyond the area immediately surrounding the house.

Related to the plain view doctrine is the **open fields doctrine**. Under this doctrine, first announced by the Supreme Court in *Hester v. United States* (1924),

A similar public backlash has emerged against automatic license plate readers, devices attached to police cars that automatically snap photos of thousands of license plates each day. These photos have provided the basis for recovering many stolen vehicles and identifying the locations of suspected criminals who are wanted by the police. For example, license plate readers helped police to reconstruct and trace the location of the Boston Marathon bombing suspects in 2013. On the other hand, many privacy advocates worry that police officials are storing records concerning the whereabouts of thousands of law-abiding citizens. Thus there has been a push for laws that limit how long police officials can store data on license plates. In some places, such as New Hampshire, there have been successful efforts to prevent the use of license plate readers by police.

Sources: Taylor W. Anderson, "Lawmakers Still Hot on License Plate Camera Restrictions," *Bend* (OR) *Bulletin*, September 2, 2014 (www.bendbulletin.com); Maggie Clark, "License Plate Readers Spark Privacy, Public Safety Debate," *Stateline* (Pew Charitable Trust online publication), November 20, 2013 (www.pewtrusts.org); Rhonda Cook, "Are Automatic License Plate Readers a Violation of Privacy?," November 30, 2012 (www.ajc.com); Corey Dade, "What's Driving the Backlash against Traffic Cameras," National Public Radio, February 22, 2012 (www.npr.org); Daniel C. Vock, "Backlash for Red-Light Cameras Hasn't Slowed Spread," *Stateline* (Pew Charitable Trust online publication), February 26, 2013 (www.pewtrusts.org).

DEBATE THE ISSUE

In your view, is there a basis for citizens' opposition to the use of red-light cameras and automatic license plate readers? Does the potential threat to citizens' interests, including privacy interests, outweigh the benefits to society from catching and deterring lawbreakers? If you were a mayor, what would be your position on the use of these devices? Describe whether and how you would use these devices in your city, including any limitations on their use.

property owners have no reasonable expectation of privacy in open fields on and around their property. Thus, if criminal evidence is visible, then probable cause has been established for its seizure. The Court has approved cases in which police officers, acting without a warrant, walked past "no trespassing" signs and found marijuana plants in fields on private property (*Oliver v. United States,* 1984). The Court limited this doctrine by refusing to apply it to the *curtilage,* or the yard area immediately surrounding the home. Although protected against physical intrusion by officers, that area remains subject to the plain view doctrine if evidence of criminal activity is clearly visible from the vantage point of a location where officers can lawfully stand. For example, the plain view doctrine includes any areas visible from the air when police officers hover above property in a helicopter. Thus the frequency of the application of this doctrine is likely to increase as more police departments seek to use drones for aerial photography or surveillance of land.

Plain Feel and Other Senses

If law enforcement officers may conduct a warrantless search under the plain view doctrine, what about using other senses to detect criminal evidence? If officers smell the distinctive odor of an illegal substance, such as marijuana, they are justified in investigating further. Bear in mind that the sense of smell may be employed by a trained police dog, too. Court decisions have established that police dogs who sniff luggage in public places are not conducting searches and therefore are not subject to the requirements of the Fourth Amendment.

Does an officer's sense of "feel" apply to searches of property? As we shall see in the discussion of stop-and-frisk searches, a police officer with reasonable suspicion may conduct a pat-down search of a person's outer clothing. If the officer feels something that is immediately recognizable as a weapon, crack pipe, or other contraband, the item may be seized (*Minnesota v. Dickerson,* 1993). However, police officers cannot aggressively feel and

TABLE 8.1 SEARCHES BY SIGHT AND FEEL

The Fourth Amendment's protection for reasonable expectations of privacy does not cover criminal evidence that can be seen or felt by officers in specific situations.

CASE	DECISION
Plain View	
Coolidge v. New Hampshire (1971)	Officers are permitted to notice and use as evidence items in plain view when the officers are where they are legally permitted to be.
Open Fields	
Oliver v. United States (1984)	Officers are permitted to intrude on private lands that are open areas, such as fields and pastures, but they may not search the yard area immediately surrounding a house (*curtilage*) without a warrant or a specific justification for a warrantless search.
Plain Feel	
Minnesota v. Dickerson (1993)	While conducting a pat-down search of a suspect's outer clothing, police may seize items in pockets or clothing as evidence if they are immediately identifiable by touch as weapons or contraband.

manipulate people's property, such as a duffel bag, in an attempt to detect criminal evidence, unless the luggage examination is part of a standard search in boarding a commercial airliner or crossing an international border into the United States (*Bond v. United States*, 2000).

Table 8.1 reviews selected cases concerning the Fourth Amendment's protection for reasonable expectations of privacy involving searches by sight and feel.

✓POINT

5. What is the plain view doctrine?

6. May officers use senses other than sight to find evidence of crime without a warrant?

STOP AND ANALYZE: If you saw a police officer at a train station poking and feeling another passenger's closed, soft-sided duffel bag, would you consider that action to be a violation of that passenger's reasonable expectation of privacy? Why or why not?

Warrantless Searches

The U.S. Supreme Court has identified specific categories of searches that do not require warrants. The Court has decided that society's law enforcement needs are so significant in these situations that police officers must have the authority to undertake searches without taking the time to seek a warrant. In the rest of this section, we examine six of these categories: (1) special needs beyond the normal purposes of law enforcement, (2) stop and frisk on the streets, (3) search incident to a lawful arrest, (4) exigent circumstances, (5) consent, and (6) automobile searches.

Special Needs Beyond the Normal Purposes of Law Enforcement

Law enforcement officials have a justified need to conduct warrantless searches of every individual in certain specific contexts (Reinert, 2012). The use of metal detectors to examine airline passengers, for example, is a specific context in which the need to prevent hijacking justifies a limited search of every passenger. Here the Court does not require officers to have any suspicions, reasonable or otherwise, about the illegal activities of any individual.

Permissible warrantless searches also take place at the entry points into the United States—border crossings, ports, and airports (Chacon, 2010). The government's interests in guarding against the entry of people and items (such as weapons, drugs, toxic chemicals) that are harmful to national interests outweigh the individuals' expectations of privacy. Typically, these border stops take only a few moments as customs officers check required documents, such as passports and visas, inquire about where the person traveled, and ask what the person is bringing into the United States. The customs officers may have a trained dog sniff around people and their luggage, checking for drugs or large amounts of cash. At the Mexican and Canadian borders and at international airports, people may be chosen at random to have their cars and luggage searched. They may also be chosen for such searches because their behavior or their answers to questions arouse the suspicions of U.S. Customs and Border Protection (CBP) officers.

The handbook for CBP officers permits an officer to base some types of searches on suspicion alone, even though mere suspicion does not meet the standard of "reasonable suspicion," which requires the support of articulable facts. The CBP instructs its personnel to consider six categories of factors in determining if suspicion exists to justify searching a traveler at a border crossing or an airport:

1. *Behavioral analysis*. Signs of nervousness, such as flushed face, avoidance of eye contact, excessive perspiration
2. *Observational techniques*. Unexplained bulges in clothing or awkwardness in walking
3. *Inconsistencies*. Discrepancies in answers to questions posed by customs officers

David McNew/Getty Images News/Getty Images

The special needs of law enforcement at borders and airports provide authority for warrantless searches based on decisions of the officers looking for suspicious behavior. The need to protect public safety and national security justifies these searches. When you go to an airport, do you feel as if your privacy and rights are being violated when you are subjected to searches?

4. *Intelligence.* Information provided to customs officers by informants or other law enforcement officials
5. *K-9.* Signals from law enforcement trained dogs who sniff around people and luggage
6. *Incident to a seizure or arrest.* The discovery of contraband in one suitcase, which can justify the search of the person and the rest of the person's property

As part of its intelligence-based searches, the CBP also relies on the Interagency Border Inspection System (IBIS), a database used by 20 federal agencies to track information on suspected individuals, businesses, vehicles, and vessels. Computer checks on individuals and vehicles at border points may provide the basis for searches. Table 8.2 contains the CBP's policies for personal searches, including the level of suspicion required for each search and whether supervisory approval is required. Do you believe these guidelines strike a proper balance between individuals' rights and societal interests in stopping the flow of contraband?

The Supreme Court has expanded the checkpoint concept by approving systematic stops along highways within the nation's interior in order to look for drunken drivers. Specifically, they approved a sobriety checkpoint program in Michigan. State police had set up a checkpoint at which they stopped every vehicle and briefly questioned each driver. The checkpoint program was challenged as a violation of the Fourth Amendment right to be free from unreasonable seizures, but the Court found no constitutional violation (*Michigan Department of State Police v. Sitz,* 1990). The Court approved checkpoints to ask drivers whether they had witnessed an accident (*Illinois v. Lidster,* 2004). A drunken driver caught at the checkpoint claimed that he was stopped improperly. However, the Court said that police can systematically stop drivers in order to seek information about a specific event.

TABLE 8.2 CUSTOMS AND BORDER PROTECTION POLICIES FOR PERSONAL SEARCHES

SEARCH TYPE	SUSPICION	LEVEL APPROVAL
1. Immediate pat-down (frisk): A search necessary to ensure that a person is not carrying a weapon	Suspicion that a weapon may be present	None required
2. Pat-down for merchandise: A search for merchandise, including contraband, hidden on a person's body	One articulable fact	
3. Partial body search: The removal of some clothing by a person to recover merchandise reasonably suspected to be concealed on the body	Reasonable suspicion, based on specific, articulable facts	On-duty supervisor
4. X-ray: Medical X-ray by medical personnel to determine the presence of merchandise within the body	Reasonable suspicion, based on specific, articulable facts	Port director and court order, unless person consents
5. Body-cavity search: Any visual or physical intrusion into the rectal or vaginal cavity	Reasonable suspicion, based on specific, articulable facts	Port director and court order, unless person consents
6. MBM (monitored bowel movement): Detention of a person for the purpose of determining whether contraband or merchandise is concealed in the alimentary canal	Reasonable suspicion, based on specific, articulable facts	Port director

Source: U.S. General Accounting Office, *U.S. Customs Service: Better Targeting of Airline Passengers for Personal Searches Could Produce Better Results* (Washington, DC: U.S. Government Printing Office, March 2000).

Although the U.S. Supreme Court has approved vehicle checkpoints that combat drunken driving and seek information as contexts for permissible warrantless stops and searches, this does not mean that these checkpoints are permissible for all law enforcement agencies. State supreme courts can interpret their own states' constitutions to provide greater limitations on state and local police than those imposed by the U.S. Supreme Court through the U.S. Constitution (S. Johnson, 2008). For example, the Michigan Supreme Court ruled that sobriety checkpoints used by the state police to identify drunken drivers violate the provisions of the Michigan Constitution concerning searches and seizures (*Sitz v. Department of State Police,* 1993). Decisions of the U.S. Supreme Court provide the baseline of rights for everyone in the country, and a state supreme court cannot give its citizens fewer or weaker rights. However, a state court can provide broader rights and stronger limitations on state and local police authority.

The U.S. Supreme Court has not given blanket approval for every kind of checkpoint or traffic stop that police might wish to use. The Court specifically forbids officers on patrol to conduct random stops of vehicles (*Delaware v. Prouse,* 1979). Officers must have a basis for a vehicle stop, such as an observed violation of traffic laws. The Court has also ruled that a city cannot set up a checkpoint in order to check drivers and passengers for possible involvement in drugs. In *City of Indianapolis v. Edmond* (2000), even though police officers stopped vehicles only briefly in order to ask a few questions and circle the car with a drug-sniffing dog, the Court declared that checkpoints cannot be justified by a general search for criminal evidence. Such stops must focus narrowly on a specific objective, such as checking for drivers under the influence of alcohol.

✔POINT 7. In what situations do law enforcement's special needs justify stopping an automobile without reasonable suspicion?

STOP AND ANALYZE: If you were a Supreme Court justice, would you approve checkpoints to stop all drivers after the reported kidnapping of a child? What about after the reported theft of a laptop computer? Explain your decisions. Is the reasonable expectation of privacy for drivers different in either of these situations? Are society's interests different in either of these situations? If so, why?

Stop and Frisk on the Streets

Police officers possess the authority to make stops and limited searches of individuals on the streets when specific circumstances justify such actions. The U.S. Supreme Court endorsed this authority in the landmark case of ***Terry v. Ohio* (1968)**. The Court's decision recognized that seizures short of arrest could be "reasonable" under the Fourth Amendment. In this case, the suspects were not free to leave, yet the officer would presumably have released them if he had not found the weapons. Thus the stop and search occurred as part of the investigation process before any arrest occurred. The justices were clearly concerned about striking an appropriate balance between Fourth Amendment rights and necessary police authority to investigate and prevent crimes.

Although the justices in *Terry* supported law enforcement authority, they struck the balance by carefully specifying the circumstances in which this sort of pat-down search—more commonly known as a **stop-and-frisk search**—can occur. The Court appeared to demand that several specific facts exist in each situation in which a permissible stop and frisk can occur. If we break

***Terry v. Ohio* (1968)**
Supreme Court decision endorsing police officers' authority to stop and frisk suspects on the street when there is reasonable suspicion that they are armed and involved in criminal activity.

stop-and-frisk search
Limited search approved by the Supreme Court in *Terry v. Ohio* that permits officers to pat down clothing of people on the streets if there is reasonable suspicion of dangerous criminal activity.

apart the Court's own words, we can see that the justices explicitly say "We merely hold today that

1. where a police officer observes unusual conduct
2. which leads him reasonably to conclude in light of his experience
3. that criminal activity may be afoot and
4. that the persons with whom he is dealing may be armed and presently dangerous,
5. where in the course of investigating this behavior
6. he identifies himself as a policeman and makes reasonable inquiries,
7. and where nothing in the initial stages of the encounter serves to dispel his reasonable fear for his own or others' safety,
8. he is entitled for the protection of himself and others in the area to conduct a carefully limited search of the outer clothing of such persons in an attempt to discover weapons which might be used to assault him."

These specified factors imposed an obligation on police officers to make observations, draw reasonable conclusions, identify themselves, and make inquiries before conducting the stop-and-frisk search. In addition, the reasonableness of the search was justified by a reasonable conclusion that a person was armed and therefore the officer needed to act in order to protect him- or herself and the public.

Court decisions have given officers significant discretion to decide when these factors exist. For example, if officers see someone running at the sight of police in a high-crime neighborhood, their observation in that context can be a factor in their determination of sufficient suspicion to justify a stop and frisk (*Illinois v. Wardlow,* 2000). Thus, officers need not actually see evidence of a weapon or interact with the suspect prior to making the stop. In *Arizona v. Johnson* (2009), the Court approved an officer's authority to frisk a vehicle passenger during a traffic stop. The officer had concluded that the individual might be armed in light of his gang-associated clothing and admission that he had served time in prison. Critics claim that lower-court judges have been overly deferential to police officer's discretionary decisions. In the view of these critics, these judges fail to require the existence of the list of particularized facts described in the original *Terry* decision in

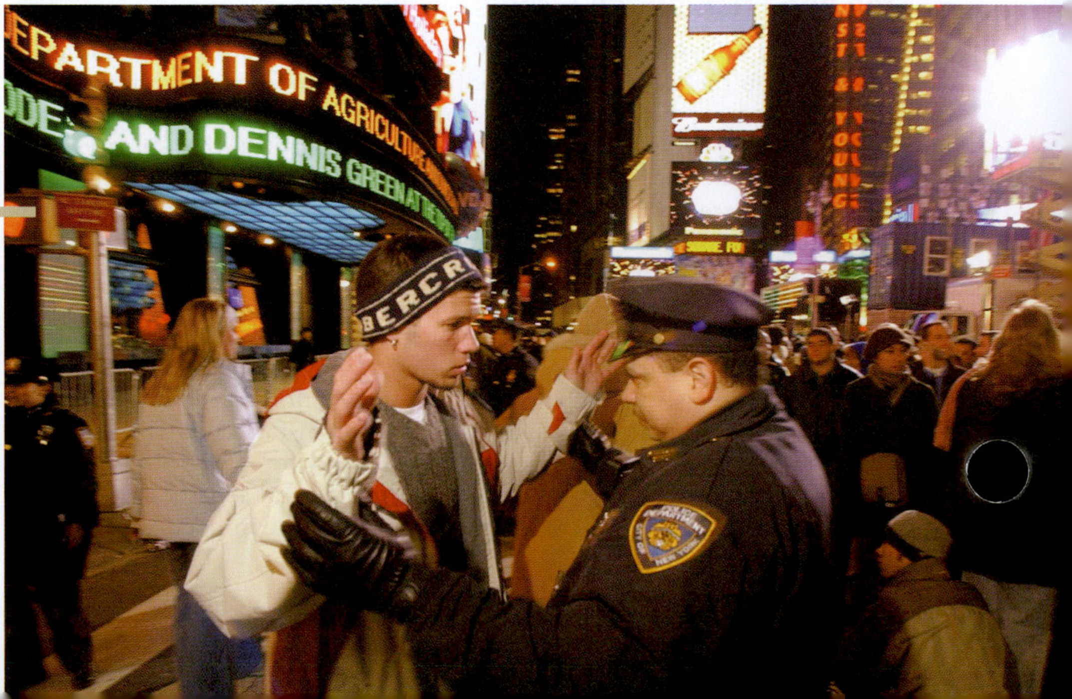

AP Images/Gregory Bull

The stopping and frisking of an individual on the streets must be carried out according to the standards first established by the U.S. Supreme Court in *Terry v. Ohio.* What are the standards? Are the standards clear enough to guide police officers and provide appropriate protection for citizens' liberty and privacy?

order to justify a frisk search. These lower-court judges allegedly endorse frisk searches that were based solely on the fact that an individual was present in a high-crime area or sought to avoid contact with the police (Withrow and Dailey, 2012).

The Supreme Court also expanded police authority by permitting officers to rely on reports from reliable witnesses as the basis for conducting the stop and frisk (*Adams v. Williams,* 1972). However, an unverified anonymous tip that an individual is carrying a handgun is not an adequate basis for a stop-and-frisk search **(*Florida v. J. L.,* 2000)**. The Court did not rule out the possibility that an anonymous tip alone might be sufficient in extraordinary circumstances in which a greater societal interest is at stake, such as a report that someone is carrying a bomb—a device with greater risk and likelihood of harm than a handgun. By contrast, the Supreme Court ruled in 2014 that an anonymous tip could provide the basis for a traffic stop (*Navarette v. California,* 2014). However, an officer's action in stopping a vehicle for a reported traffic violation in order to speak to the driver is a less intrusive action than when an officer places his or her hands on an individual in order to conduct a frisk search of clothing.

***Florida v. J. L.* (2000)**
Police officers may not conduct a stop-and-frisk search based solely on an anonymous tip.

Police officers possess the discretionary authority to make on-the-spot decisions to conduct searches. They provide justifications for those searches only when evidence of a crime is discovered and an arrested suspect uses a later court hearing to challenge the legality of the search. By that time, however, officers have had time to prepare an explanation for their actions. If officers are not completely honest and ethical, there are risks that they will manufacture justifications to fit the requirements of stop-and-frisk or other warrantless search categories. Because of the need to grant police the discretion to do certain kinds of searches without obtaining a judge's approval through the warrant process, we place great faith in the honesty and professionalism of police officers. Sometimes, however, officers do not fulfill their professional obligations because they are too intent on finding criminal evidence. It is very difficult for judges to know whether police officers are telling the truth about what happened before and during a search. Thus judges typically accept the police officer's version of events rather than that of the suspect who was arrested. This raises questions about whether we are able to adequately supervise police officers and hold them accountable for errors and rule violations (M. D. Wilson, 2010). As you read the Close Up feature about police officers failing to accurately describe the circumstances of their stops and searches, consider what might be done to reduce the risk of this problem.

Search Incident to a Lawful Arrest

The authority to undertake a warrantless search incident to a lawful arrest is not limited by the crime for which the arrestee has been taken into custody (Foley, 2013). Even someone arrested for a traffic offense can be searched. Although there is no reason to suspect the person has a weapon or to believe that evidence related to the offense will be found in the person's pockets, the arrestee is subject to the same arrest-scene search as someone taken into custody for murder (*United States v. Robinson,* 1973). As we saw in the discussion of *Riley v. California* (2014) that opened this chapter, officers are entitled to undertake a limited search whenever they make an arrest, but there are limits to the extent of such searches without a warrant.

The justification for searches of arrestees emerged in the Supreme Court's decision in **_Chimel v. California_ (1969)**. The officers must make sure that the arrestee does not have a weapon that could endanger the officers or others in the vicinity. The officers must also look for evidence on the person of the

***Chimel v. California* (1969)**
Supreme Court decision that endorsed warrantless searches for weapons and evidence in the immediate vicinity of people who are lawfully arrested.

CLOSE UP

DETERMINING JUSTIFICATION FOR POLICE SEARCHES

Imagine the courtroom scene after an individual has been stopped, searched, and found to be carrying drugs, stolen money, or exhibiting some other evidence of a crime. At the preliminary hearing, the accused's defense attorney argues that the search was illegal. The police officer swears under oath to tell the truth, and sits in the witness stand, prepared to answer questions from the defense attorney. What are the motives of the actors in this scene? The defense attorney is ethically obligated to argue zealously on behalf of the defendant's interests. Thus if there is a plausible basis to question the legality of the officer's actions, the adversarial system requires the attorney to vigorously challenge the police officer's version of events.

The judge is required to listen carefully to the police officer's testimony to determine if there was proper justification for the search. Even after hearing complete testimonies, evaluating the accuracy and strength of justifications can be a difficult task. How can a judge know if the officer is telling the truth about the reasons for the stop and search?

As a representative of community law enforcement, the police officer does not want someone guilty of a crime to go free without punishment. Presumably, the officer also wants to avoid criticisms from superiors for conducting an improper search. Are these motives enough to lead a member of law enforcement to testify untruthfully under oath? Unfortunately, in some courthouses veteran attorneys and judges feel so accustomed to seeing officers create untrue after-the-fact stories to justify their searches that such testimony is known by its own term: *testilying.*

How often is untruthful testimony presented by police officers? There is no way to know. Judges are placed in the difficult position of attempting to detect whether an officer is telling the truth. Yet, when a police officer's description of a search clashes with the defendant's version of events—and no other witnesses happened to be present at the scene—it is not surprising that judges typically side with the officers. Thus it is important for police officers to be committed to upholding the law and telling the truth. In many cases, they can get away with dishonesty,

arrestee that the arrestee might destroy or damage before or during transportation to jail.

Officers can search the arrestee and the immediate area around the arrestee. Officers can also make a protective sweep through other rooms where the suspect may recently have been. However, the arrest would not justify opening drawers and conducting a thorough search of an entire house. If, after the arrest, officers have probable cause to conduct a more thorough search, they must obtain a warrant that specifies the items they seek and the places they will search. However, in ***Arizona v. Gant* (2009)**, a majority of justices barred the search of an automobile after an arrest when the handcuffed driver posed no danger to the officers and could not reach into the car to destroy evidence. Thus officers cannot automatically conduct vehicle searches based on an arrest if the search will not fit the original *Chimel v. California* justifications of protecting officer safety or preventing the destruction of evidence.

***Arizona v. Gant* (2009)**
An arrest does not justify a vehicle search if the handcuffed driver has already been removed and poses no danger to officers or to the preservation of evidence.

Although a lawful arrest justifies a limited search and protective sweep, the Court has been unwilling to permit thorough warrantless searches at crime scenes, even when a murder victim is discovered. Officers should obtain a warrant to open luggage, packages, and filing cabinets at the murder scene (*Flippo v. West Virginia*, 1999).

✓POINT

8. What knowledge must an officer possess in order to conduct a stop-and-frisk search on the streets?

9. Where can officers search when conducting a warrantless search incident to a lawful arrest?

STOP AND ANALYZE: If officers believe that they can almost always justify a stop and frisk by describing circumstances that fit the *Terry v. Ohio* factors, what prevents them from justifying after the fact any stop and frisk that they want to do? List two factors that limit—at least for some officers—the exercise of authority for stop-and-frisk searches.

yet the proper operation of the criminal justice system and the protection of rights depend on their professionalism and integrity.

In 2013, a judge in Dallas concluded that two officers were untruthful in describing their observations and actions that led to the arrest of a man on drug charges. The Philadelphia District Attorney dropped 28 cases in January 2013 in addition to nearly 140 cases dropped a month earlier because of questions about the credibility of six narcotics officers. A court in Iowa overturned the conviction of a driver for operating a vehicle while intoxicated in 2012 because the video taken from the camera in the patrol car did not support the deputy's claim that he had stopped the man when the vehicle was observed weaving across the center line. When incidents such as these arise, there are risks that the public will lose confidence in law enforcement officers. If that happens, citizens may feel less willing to cooperate in reporting crimes and serving as witnesses for the prosecution.

Sources: Mark Fazlollah, "D.A. Pulls 28 More Prosecutions Linked to Six Officers," *Philadelphia Inquirer,* January 12, 2013 (www.philly.com); Rebecca Lopez, "Judge Questions Credibility of Dallas Police Officers," WFAA-TV, February 22, 2013 (www.wfaa.com); Christopher Slobogin, "Testilying: Police Perjury and What to Do about It," *University of Colorado Law Review,* 67 (1996): 1037–60; *State of Iowa v. Wilkerson,* No. 2-436/11-1522, Court of Appeals of Iowa, July 11, 2012; Melanie D. Wilson, "An Exclusionary Rule for Police Lies," *American Criminal Law Review* 47 (2010): 1–55.

DEBATE THE ISSUE

If judges conclude that police officers are not being truthful, then evidence is excluded and guilty offenders may go free. Should police officers face punishment if judges conclude that they are not honest and accurate in describing the justifications for searches? What punishment would be appropriate? Write an argument in favor of punishment for officers, as well as an opposing argument. If you were a police chief, what would you do? Why?

Exigent Circumstances

Officers can make an arrest without a warrant when there are **exigent circumstances**. This means that officers are in the middle of an urgent situation in which they must act swiftly and do not have time to go to court to seek a warrant. With respect to arrests, for example, when officers are in hot pursuit of a fleeing suspected felon, they need not stop to seek a warrant and thereby risk permitting the suspect to get away (*Warden v. Hayden,* 1967). Exigent circumstances can justify police entry into a home without a warrant (J. M. Huff, 2010). When police observed an altercation through a window and saw a teenager punch an adult in the face, the Supreme Court ruled that officers were justified in entering the home immediately and without a warrant in order to render emergency aid and prevent the escalation of violence and serious injuries (*Brigham City v. Stuart* 2006). The justices reiterated this conclusion in *Michigan v. Fisher* (2009) when officers entered a home upon observing through the window a man with a cut on his hand having a screaming fit in the living room. The warrantless entry under exigent circumstances was permissible despite the man yelling at officers that he did not need their aid and that they should "go get a warrant." Similarly, exigent circumstances can justify warrantless searches.

exigent circumstances
When there is a threat to public safety or the risk that evidence will be destroyed, officers may search, arrest, or question suspects without obtaining a warrant or following other usual rules of criminal procedure.

In *Cupp v. Murphy* (1973), a man voluntarily complied with police officers' request that he come to the police station to answer questions concerning his wife's murder. The couple resided in separate homes at the time. At the station, officers noticed a substance on the man's fingernails that they thought might be dried blood. Over his objections, they took a sample of scrapings under his fingernails and ultimately used that tissue as evidence against him when he was convicted of murdering his wife. The Supreme Court said the search was properly undertaken under exigent circumstances. If officers had taken the time to seek a warrant, the suspect might have gone to the bathroom to wash his hands and the evidence would have been lost.

***Kentucky v. King* (2011)**
Police officers can use the exigent circumstances justification to conduct a warrantless search even when their own actions, such as knocking loudly on the wrong door in an apartment building, lead to the sounds inside the dwelling that trigger the belief in the necessity of an immediate search.

The Supreme Court decided in ***Kentucky v. King* (2011)** that police can make a warrantless entry when they play a role in creating the exigent circumstances. Police pursuing a crack cocaine suspect knocked loudly on the door of an apartment from which the smell of marijuana emanated and, according to the defendants, demanded to be let in. When the police heard people moving around inside the apartment, the officers assumed evidence was being destroyed and they burst through the door based on exigent circumstances. They arrested the occupants that they discovered to be smoking marijuana, but it was the wrong apartment. The cocaine suspect had entered an apartment across the hall. When the unexpected banging and yelling by police caused people in the apartment to move around, did the police effectively create their own perception of evidence destruction that would not otherwise have existed? A majority of Supreme Court justices endorsed the search as permissible in spite of the debate about the officers' role in spurring people to move about inside the apartment. This case illustrates how new situations arise that lead the Supreme Court to reexamine, revise, and clarify their interpretations of constitutional rights and police authority.

Police officers can use the exigent circumstances justification for warrantless searches for the purpose of seeking evidence. To justify such searches, they do not need to show that there was a potential threat to public safety. As a practical matter, police officers make quick judgments about undertaking certain searches. If incriminating evidence is discovered, courts may be asked to make an after-the-fact determination of whether the urgency of the situation justified a warrantless search and whether the nature and purpose of the search were reasonable. Judges are often reluctant to second-guess a police officer's on-the-spot decision that the urgency of a situation required an immediate warrantless search.

In certain circumstances, however, the Supreme Court has barred automatic acceptance of claims concerning exigent circumstances. In *Missouri v. McNeely* (2013), for example, when a man arrested for drunk driving refused to consent to a blood alcohol test, officers ordered medical workers to draw a sample of the man's blood. Because alcohol will gradually dissipate in the body, the officers claimed the exigent circumstances required an immediate blood alcohol test in order to determine if the man's blood alcohol level exceeded legal limits for driving. However, the Supreme Court said that officers cannot automatically require such blood draws under the exigent circumstances rationale. Instead, they should normally seek a warrant for blood alcohol testing unless there are specific circumstances in a situation that would prevent them from obtaining a judge's approval in a timely manner.

Consent

If people consent to a search, officers do not need probable cause or even any level of suspicion to justify the search. The consent effectively absolves law enforcement officers of any risk that evidence will be excluded from use at trial or that they will be found liable in a civil lawsuit alleging a violation of Fourth Amendment rights. Individuals can waive their constitutional rights; a voluntary consent to search effectively waives the legal protections of the Fourth Amendment.

Consent searches provide a valuable investigatory tool for officers who wish to conduct warrantless searches. Officers in many police departments are trained to ask people if they will consent to a search. Thus, some officers ask every motorist during a traffic stop, "May I search your car?" Or, if called to the scene of a domestic dispute or a citizen complaint about noise, the officers may say, "Do you mind if I look around in the downstairs area of your house?" Criminal evidence is often uncovered in such consent searches, a fact which may indicate that many citizens do not know they have the option to say "no" when officers ask for permission to search. Moreover, some citizens may fear that they will look more suspicious to the officers if they say "no," so they agree to searches in order to act as if they have nothing to hide. In addition, in **United States v. Drayton (2002)**, the Supreme Court said very clearly that police officers do not have to inform people of their right to say "no" when asked if they wish to consent to a search. Read "Civic Engagement: Your Role in the System" to consider what you would do if an officer asked you to consent to a search.

One must address two key issues in deciding if a permissible consent search has occurred. First, the consent must be voluntary. Police officers could not have used coercion or threats in order to obtain consent. Even subtler tricks, such as dishonestly telling someone that there is a search warrant and thereby implying that the person has no choice but to consent, will result in the search being declared improper (*Bumper v. North Carolina,* 1968). Second, the consent must be given by someone who possesses authority to give consent and thereby waive the right. Someone cannot, for example, consent to have his or her neighbor's house searched. There is an exception to this second requirement, however. If police reasonably believe that an individual has the authority to consent, then the officers are permitted to rely on that belief in conducting the warrantless search. In ***Illinois v. Rodriguez* (1990)**, the suspect's girlfriend provided officers with a key to his apartment. The officers erroneously believed that she lived at the apartment and therefore had authority to consent to a search. Because their belief was reasonable under the circumstances, the officers were allowed to use the cocaine found during the warrantless search as evidence to convict the suspect.

CIVIC ENGAGEMENT

YOUR ROLE IN THE SYSTEM

Imagine that a friend says to you: "I was stopped for speeding and given a warning. The officer asked if she could search my car. I wanted to say 'no,' but I was afraid she would think I was guilty of something or that she would then write a speeding ticket. Can I really say 'no' to a police officer's request?" *Write a sentence to explain whether or not an individual can legally decline a request from an officer to conduct a "search." Write another sentence to explain what the individual could do if the officer conducted a search anyway after being told 'no' by a driver.* Then read *United States v. Cochrane* (2012) and consider how difficult it may be to persuade a judge that consent was not granted when a police officer says that voluntary consent to search was requested and given.

✔POINT **10.** What are exigent circumstances?

11. What two elements must be present for a valid consent to permit a warrantless search?

STOP AND ANALYZE: Imagine that a police officer knocked on the door of your apartment and asked, "Do you mind if I take a look around inside your bedroom?" Some people claim that only those who have something to hide would fail to cooperate with the police. Others believe that an individual's right to privacy is among the highest values to be protected by our society. What would you say to the officer? Why would you say that? What if the officer claimed that he had enough information to obtain a search warrant but that you could spare yourself time and hassle by simply consenting now?

Automobile Searches

Previous sections illustrated how automobiles can be searched under special needs and consent justifications. Vehicle searches may also occur in conjunction with arrests. Here we look at automobile searches in greater detail. In essence, because cars are mobile, they differ greatly from houses and other buildings. Automobiles can be driven away and can disappear in the time that it would take officers to ask a judicial officer for a search warrant. Thus officers have broad authority to search cars, depending on the circumstances.

During a traffic stop, for example, officers can order passengers as well as the driver to exit the vehicle, even if there is no basis for suspicion that the passengers engaged in any wrongdoing (*Maryland v. Wilson,* 1997). They can also charge everyone in a car with a crime when they find guns, drugs, or other criminal evidence and it is not clear which occupant of the vehicle is responsible (*Maryland v. Pringle,* 2003). As mentioned in the prior discussion

***United States v. Drayton* (2002)**
Police officers are not required to inform people of their right to decline when police ask for consent to search.

***Illinois v. Rodriguez* (1990)**
Officers may rely on reasonable beliefs that a person giving consent to a search has authority to do so even if the person actually lacks authority over the apartment, house, or vehicle.

of stop-and-frisk searches, drivers and passengers may also be subject to frisk searches if officers have sufficient justification (*Arizona v. Johnson,* 2009).

The two key questions that arise in automobile searches are (1) When can officers stop a car? and (2) How extensively can they search the vehicle? Many automobile searches arise as a result of traffic stops. A stop can occur when an officer observes a traffic violation, including defective safety equipment, or when there is a basis for reasonable suspicion concerning the involvement of the car, its driver, or its passengers in a crime. Police officers are free to make a visible inspection around a car's interior as they question a driver and ask for identification when preparing a citation for a traffic violation. All sworn officers can make traffic stops, even if they are in unmarked vehicles and serving in special vice or detective bureaus that do not normally handle traffic offenses (*Whren v. United States,* 1996). A traffic violation by itself, however, does not provide an officer with the authority to search an entire vehicle (*Knowles v. Iowa,* 1998). Specific factors must create reasonable suspicion or probable cause in order to authorize officers to do anything more than look inside the vehicle.

The arrest of a driver for possession of drugs justifies the search of a passenger's property, such as a purse, if that property could contain evidence of involvement in that crime (*Wyoming v. Houghton,* 1999). The search of a passenger's purse would not be justified, however, if the driver was arrested for illegal possession of a machine gun or another crime for which evidence could not be hidden in a purse. In addition, the Court has expanded officers' authority to search automobiles even when no formal arrest has yet occurred. In *Michigan v. Long* (1983), the Court approved a search of the car's interior around the driver's seat after officers found the car in a ditch and the driver standing outside the car appearing intoxicated. The Supreme Court justified the search as an expansion of the *Terry* doctrine. In effect, the officers were permitted to "frisk" the car in order to protect themselves and others by making sure no weapon was available to the not-yet-arrested driver. Such a search requires that the officers have reasonable suspicion that the person stopped may be armed and poses a potential danger to the officers.

Initially the Court treated containers and closed areas in automobiles differently from the passenger compartment. Even when officers had probable cause to search a car's trunk, they were expected to obtain a warrant for any containers found within the trunk. However, this rule changed with the Court's decision in *California v. Acevedo* (1991). Now police officers can search anywhere in the car for which they have probable cause to search. Further, unlike the situations with warrants, the officers themselves, rather than a judge, determine whether probable cause exists before conducting the warrantless search of the vehicle. If, however, a judge later disagrees with the officer's conclusion about the existence of probable cause, any evidence found in the search of the automobile will likely be excluded from use at trial.

Even if officers lack probable cause to believe that the vehicle has been stolen, an officer may enter the vehicle to see the vehicle identification number by the windshield when a car has been validly stopped pursuant to a traffic violation or other permissible justification (*New York v. Class,* 1986). In addition, the Court permits thorough searches of vehicles, without regard to probable cause, when police officers inventory the contents of impounded vehicles (*South Dakota v. Opperman,* 1976). Containers found within the course of the inventory search may also be opened and searched when the examination of such containers is consistent with a police department's inventory policies.

Table 8.3 reviews selected Supreme Court cases concerning those circumstances in which the police do not need a warrant to conduct a search or to seize evidence.

TABLE 8.3 WARRANTLESS SEARCHES

The Supreme Court has ruled that there are circumstances when a warrant is not required.

CASE	DECISION
Special Needs	
Michigan Department of State Police v. Sitz (1990)	Stopping motorists systematically at roadblocks designed for specific purposes, such as detecting drunken drivers, is permissible.
City of Indianapolis v. Edmond (2000)	Police traffic checkpoints cannot be justified as a generalized search for criminal evidence; they must be narrowly focused on a specific objective.
Stop and Frisk	
Terry v. Ohio (1968)	Officers may stop and frisk suspects on the street when there is reasonable suspicion that they are armed and involved in criminal activity.
Adams v. Williams (1972)	Officers may rely on reports from reliable witnesses as the basis for conducting a stop and frisk.
Illinois v. Wardlow (2000)	When a person runs at the sight of police in a high-crime area, officers are justified in using that person's flight as part of the basis for forming reasonable suspicion to justify a stop and frisk.
Incident to an Arrest	
Chimel v. California (1969)	To preserve evidence and protect the safety of the officer and the public after a lawful arrest, the arrestee and the immediate area around the arrestee may be searched for weapons and criminal evidence.
Arizona v. Gant (2009)	A warrantless search of an automobile incident to an arrest is not justified when the handcuffed arrestee has been moved to a location away from the vehicle that prevents any risk of danger to the officers or destruction of evidence.
Exigent Circumstances	
Warden v. Hayden (1967)	When officers are in hot pursuit of a fleeing suspect, they need not stop to seek a warrant and thereby risk permitting the suspect to get away.
Kentucky v. King (2011)	Officers may seize evidence to protect it if taking time to seek a warrant creates a risk of its destruction.
Consent	
Bumper v. North Carolina (1968)	Officers may not tell falsehoods as a means of getting a suspect to consent to a search.
United States v. Drayton (2002)	An officer does not have to inform people of their right to refuse when he or she asks if they wish to consent to a search.
Automobiles	
Carroll v. United States (1925)	Because by their nature automobiles can be easily moved, warrantless searches are permissible when reasonable suspicion of illegal activity exists.
New York v. Class (1986)	An officer may enter a vehicle to see the vehicle identification number when a car has been validly stopped pursuant to a traffic violation or other permissible justification.
California v. Acevedo (1991)	Officers may search throughout a vehicle when they conclude that they have probable cause to do so.
Maryland v. Wilson (1997)	During traffic stops, officers may order passengers as well as the driver to exit the vehicle, even if there is no basis for suspicion that the passengers engaged in any wrongdoing.
Knowles v. Iowa (1998)	A traffic violation by itself does not provide an officer with the authority to search an entire vehicle. There must be reasonable suspicion or probable cause before officers can extend their search beyond merely looking inside the vehicle's passenger compartment.

✔POINT 12. What defines the scope of officers' authority to search containers in automobiles?

STOP AND ANALYZE: Should the Supreme Court give officers even broader authority to search any vehicle that has been lawfully stopped? Why or why not? List two arguments supporting each side in this debate.

Questioning Suspects

As we saw in Chapter 4, the Fifth Amendment contains various rights, including the one most relevant to police officers' actions in questioning suspects. The relevant words of the Amendment are "No person shall . . . be compelled in any criminal case to be a witness against himself." The privilege against compelled self-incrimination should not be viewed as simply a legal protection that seeks to assist individuals who may be guilty of crimes. By protecting individuals in this way, the Fifth Amendment discourages police officers from using violent or otherwise coercive means to push suspects to confess.

In addition to discouraging the physical abuse of suspects, the privilege against compelled self-incrimination also diminishes the risk of erroneous convictions. When police officers use coercive pressure to seek confessions, some innocent people will succumb to the pressure by confessing to crimes that they did not commit. The worst-case scenario is illustrated by the film *In the Name of the Father* (1993), based on a true story in England in which police officers gain a confession from a bombing suspect, whom they know to be innocent, by placing a gun in the suspect's mouth and threatening to pull the trigger.

In the past, because of the Fifth Amendment protection against compelled self-incrimination, the validity of confessions hinged on their being voluntary. Under the doctrine of fundamental fairness, which was applied before the 1960s, the Supreme Court was unwilling to allow confessions that were beaten out of suspects, that emerged after extended questioning, or that resulted from the use of other physical tactics. Such tactics can impose inhumane treatment on suspects and create risks that innocent people will be wrongly convicted.

***Miranda v. Arizona* (1966)**
Before questioning a suspect held in custody, police officers must inform the individual of the right to remain silent and the right to have an attorney present during questioning.

In ***Miranda v. Arizona* (1966)**, the Warren Court outraged politicians, law enforcement officials, and members of the public by placing limits on the ability of police to question suspects without following specific procedures. The justices ruled that, prior to questioning, the police must inform detained suspects of their right to remain silent and their right to have an attorney present. In response, many police officers argued that they depended on interrogations and confessions as a major means of solving crimes (Cassell and Fowles, 1998). However, nearly four decades later, many suspects continue to confess for various reasons, such as feelings of guilt, inability to understand their rights, and the desire to gain a favorable plea bargain (Cleary, 2014; R. A. Leo, 1996a,

AP Images/Patrick Reddy/The Cincinnati Enquirer

When someone has been taken into custody by police, officers must provide *Miranda* warnings before asking questions. Are there risks that the fear that can accompany being handcuffed and detained will hinder people's ability to listen carefully and truly understand the nature of their rights before making statements without an attorney present?

1996b). Moreover, surveys indicate that many police officials accept the existence of the *Miranda* rules and do not want to see the Supreme Court reverse its original decision (Zalman and Smith, 2007).

Miranda Rules

Suspects in police custody must be told four things before they can be questioned:

1. They have the right to remain silent.
2. If they decide to make a statement, it can and will be used against them in court.
3. They have the right to have an attorney present during interrogation or to have an opportunity to consult with an attorney.
4. If they cannot afford an attorney, the state will provide one.

Prior to the *Miranda* decision, police officers in some places solved crimes by picking up poor people or African Americans and torturing them until a confession was produced. In *Brown v. Mississippi* (1936), the Supreme Court ruled that statements produced after police beat suspects were inadmissible, but it did not insist that counsel be available at the early stages of the criminal process. Moreover, there was no way for many suspects to prove that they had been abused by the police. It was just their word against that of the officers who tortured them.

Two rulings in 1964 laid the foundation for the *Miranda* decision. In *Massiah v. United States* (1964), the Supreme Court declared that an indicted defendant's rights were violated when he was questioned without his attorney present by someone secretly working for the police. In ***Escobedo v. Illinois* (1964)**, the Court made the link between the Fifth Amendment right against self-incrimination and the Sixth Amendment right to counsel. Danny Escobedo was questioned at the police station for 14 hours without counsel, even though he asked to see his attorney. He finally made incriminating statements that the police said were voluntary. The Court's ruling specified that defendants have a right to counsel when

> the investigation is no longer a general inquiry into an unsolved crime, but has begun to focus on a particular suspect, the suspect has been taken into police custody, [and] the police carry out a process of interrogations that lends itself to eliciting incriminating statements.

Escobedo v. Illinois (1964)
Police cannot refuse access to an attorney for arrested suspects who ask to see one.

The Court effectively expanded the right to counsel to apply at an early point in the criminal justice process as a means to guard against law enforcement officers' actions that might violate the Fifth Amendment privilege against compelled self-incrimination.

The *Miranda* warnings apply only to custodial interrogations. If police officers walk up to someone on the street and begin asking questions, they do not need to inform the person of his or her rights. The justices say that people know they can walk away when an officer asks them questions in a public place. When police have taken someone into custody, however, the Supreme Court sees it as an inherently coercive situation. The loss of liberty and isolation experienced by detained suspects can make them vulnerable to abusive interrogation techniques, especially when interrogations take place out of view of anyone other than police officers. When a suspect has been alone in a room with police officers, if the suspect claims to have been beaten, will anyone believe it, even if it is true? If the police say that the suspect confessed, will anyone believe the suspect who says that no confession was ever given? The *Miranda* warnings and the presence of counsel during questioning are meant to prevent such risks.

One circumstance in which the Court has permitted police officers to forgo *Miranda* warnings is when taking the time to provide the warnings would create a threat to public safety. This exception is similar to the exigent circumstance justification for warrantless searches. The underlying premise is that in some urgent situations, a larger social need outweighs individuals' rights. In the case that created the **public safety exception**, police officers chased an armed man into a supermarket after a reported assault. When they found him with an empty shoulder holster, they asked, "Where's the gun?" after he was handcuffed but before he had been informed of his *Miranda* rights (*New York v. Quarles*, 1984). His response to the question could be used against him in court because the public's safety might have been threatened if the police took the time to read him his rights before asking any questions.

public safety exception
When public safety is in jeopardy, police may question a suspect in custody without providing the *Miranda* warnings.

The Fifth Amendment protection against compelled self-incrimination applies only to testimonial evidence, which normally means incriminating statements made by suspects. The Fifth Amendment does *not* protect against the admission into evidence of nontestimonial evidence, such as objects or descriptions of behaviors manifested by the suspect. Thus, police could use evidence of a drunken driving suspect's slurred speech and inability to answer questions, because such evidence was nontestimonial. By contrast, the police could not use as evidence a statement made by the same arrested suspect in response to a question that was posed prior to the delivery of *Miranda* warnings (*Pennsylvania v. Muniz,* 1990).

Although some legal commentators and police officials have criticized *Miranda* warnings, the Supreme Court strongly repeated its endorsement of the *Miranda* requirement in 2000 (*Dickerson v. United States*). In 2010, however, the Supreme Court decided several cases that refined the *Miranda* requirements (L. A. Baker, 2010). Most importantly, in *Berghuis v. Thompson* (2010), the Court concluded that a suspect being questioned cannot assert his right to remain silent by remaining silent in the face of continued questioning by the officer. Instead, he must actually tell the officer that he is asserting his right to remain silent in order to seek an end to the officer's questioning. In *Florida v. Powell* (2010), the Court permitted police to vary the precise words used in providing the warnings. In the case, the officers informed the suspect that he had a right to consult with an attorney "before answering questions" and that he could invoke that right during questioning. Although three justices believed that this wording failed to make clear that the suspect has a right to consult with an attorney throughout the entire questioning process, the majority of justices concluded that this wording satisfied the requirements of *Miranda*.

The Court strengthened *Miranda*'s protections for juveniles in *J. D. B. v. North Carolina* (2011). In this case, police officers' questioning of a seventh grader at school led a majority of justices to declare that juveniles may be entitled to *Miranda* warnings in a wider array of situations than would apply to adults. In some circumstances in which an adult might feel free to walk away from the police and therefore not be considered as a detained suspect entitled to warnings, juveniles likely would not know that they could depart from a situation of a police officer asking questions (Cleary, 2014).

An additional controversy over *Miranda* and other suspects' rights concerns whether terrorism suspects should benefit from the same protections of the Bill of Rights that are granted to other criminal suspects (Guiora, 2012; D. Welsh, 2011). This debate about *Miranda* became most heated when federal law enforcement officials read the *Miranda* rights to a foreign citizen who was subsequently convicted of planning to blow up a commercial airliner (C. Savage, 2011a). Look at "What Americans Think" to see how the

WHAT AMERICANS THINK

QUESTION: "In order to curb terrorism in this country, do you think it will be necessary for the average person to give up some civil liberties, or not?"

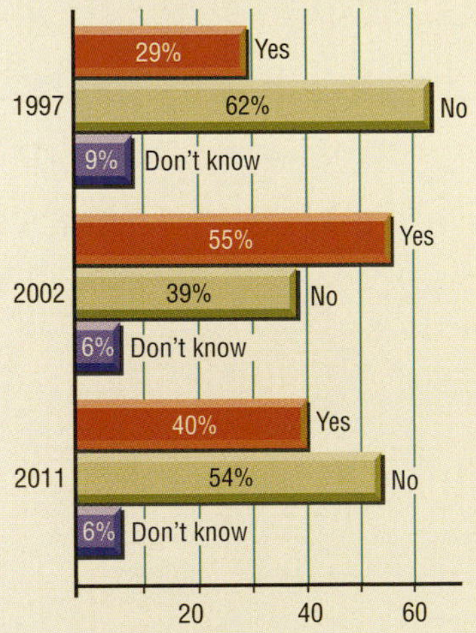

Source: Pew Research Center for the People and the Press, *United in Remembrance, Divided over Policies: Ten Years After 9/11* (September 1, 2011), p. 18. Reprinted in Bureau of Justice Statistics, *Sourcebook of Criminal Justice Statistics, 2015*, Table 2.31.2011.

public views the prospect of reducing the protections of constitutional rights for terrorism suspects and potentially everyone else, too, as part of the nation's antiterrorism efforts. The U.S. Supreme Court has granted the government a measure of flexibility with respect to certain antiterrorism policies that affect rights. For example, in *Clapper v. Amnesty International* (2013), by a 5-to-4 vote, the Court declined to examine or invalidate a law that permits intelligence officials to intercept Americans' international phone calls and emails (Liptak, 2013b).

CHECKPOINT **13.** What are *Miranda* rights?

14. What is the public safety exception?

STOP AND ANALYZE: If you were arrested and police officers informed you of your *Miranda* rights, what would you say or do? List three reasons why someone might talk to the police despite being informed of a right to remain silent.

The Consequences of *Miranda*

During oral arguments at the Supreme Court, the opponents of *Miranda* assumed that every subject would cease to talk upon being informed that there is a right to silence. However, in practice, this has not occurred. Police officers have adapted their techniques in order to question suspects without any impediment from the warnings.

Miranda rights must be provided before questions are asked during custodial interrogations. Many departments train their officers to read the *Miranda* warnings to suspects as soon as an arrest is made. This is done in order to make sure the warnings are not omitted as the suspect is processed in the system. The warnings may be read from a standard "*Miranda* card" to make sure that the rights are provided consistently and correctly. However, the courts do not require that police inform suspects of their rights immediately after arrest. The warnings do not have to be provided until the police begin to ask questions. Thus, after taking a suspect into custody, some officers may use their discretion to delay providing *Miranda* warnings in order to see if the suspect will talk on his or her own. The suspect may be kept in the backseat of a car as officers drive around town, or the suspect may be left alone in a room at the police station. Some suspects will take the initiative to talk to officers because of feelings of guilt. Other suspects may start conversations with officers because they are eager to convince the officers that they have an alibi or that they want to cooperate. The suspect might thus provide contradictory statements that will help build the case.

After suspects in custody have been informed of their *Miranda* rights, officers may attempt to defuse the potential impact of the rights by presenting them in a manner intended to encourage suspects to talk. For example, officers may inform suspects of their rights but then add, "But if you don't have anything to hide, why would you ask for an attorney or stay silent?"

Officers are also trained in interrogation techniques intended to encourage suspects to talk despite *Miranda* warnings. Officers may pretend to be sympathetic to the suspect (R. A. Leo, 1996b). They may say, for example, "We understand how bad stuff can happen that you never want to have happen. We know that you had a good reason to get mad and go after that guy with your knife. We probably would have done the same thing if we were in your situation. We know that you never really planned to stab him." Such statements are dishonest, but police officers are allowed to use deception to induce suspects to talk (R. Leo, 2008). It is not uncommon for officers to say, untruthfully, "We have five witnesses that saw you do it. If you tell us everything right now, we

WHAT AMERICANS THINK

QUESTION: "Do you agree with the following statement? The police should be able to search the houses of people who might be sympathetic to terrorists without a court order."

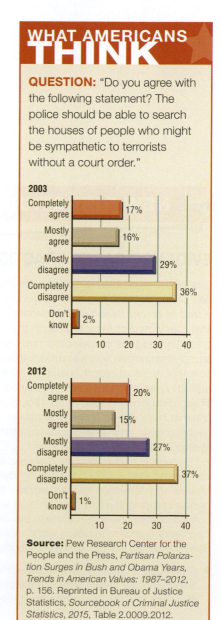

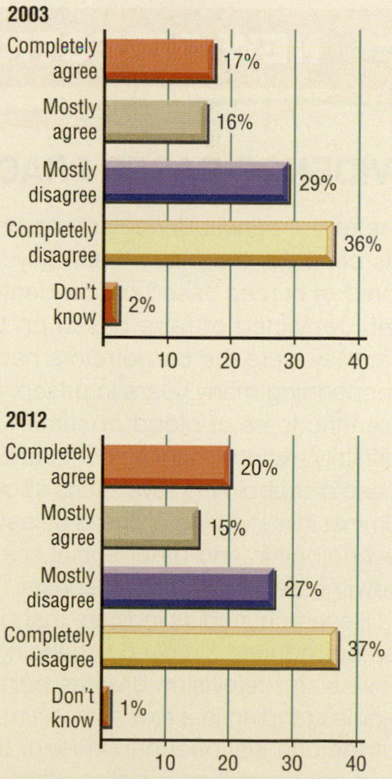

Source: Pew Research Center for the People and the Press, *Partisan Polarization Surges in Bush and Obama Years, Trends in American Values: 1987–2012*, p. 156. Reprinted in Bureau of Justice Statistics, *Sourcebook of Criminal Justice Statistics, 2015*, Table 2.0009.2012.

may be able to get you a good deal. If you don't help us, we don't know what we can do for you." Do such statements constitute coercion that would be regarded as improper pressure in violation of *Miranda?* Probably not—as long as the officers do not threaten suspects in ways that make them fear for their physical safety or the safety of their loved ones.

Jurors in criminal cases may increasingly have opportunities to see and evaluate the interrogation techniques used by law enforcement officers in their efforts to obtain confessions or incriminating statements. Police chiefs and prosecutors increasingly videotape interrogations so that jurors can see exactly what the suspect said to police officers. In 2006, the FBI formally prohibited its agents from videotaping most interrogations for fear that the presence of cameras would discourage suspects from talking and that jurors might react unfavorably to seeing some of the techniques used by law enforcement officers to elicit incriminating statements. However, in 2014 the U.S. Department of Justice reversed that policy and required the videotaping of most interrogations. The new policy applies to the FBI as well as the Drug Enforcement Administration (DEA), U.S. Marshals, and Bureau of Alcohol, Tobacco, Firearms, and Explosives. Officials decided that it was more important for jurors to see and hear the actual incriminating statements in order to obtain convictions than to worry about the reactions of certain suspects or jurors to the practice of videotaping in the interview rooms of federal law enforcement agencies (Schmidt, 2014).

Miranda rights have become very familiar to the American public through television shows and movies in which police officers inform arrested suspects

NEW DIRECTIONS IN CRIMINAL JUSTICE POLICY

EVIDENCE-BASED PRACTICES IN IDENTIFICATION PROCEDURES

One of the consequences of the development of DNA testing has been the discovery that many innocent people were convicted of crimes based on misidentifications by eyewitnesses. Men convicted of rape based on the victims' certain claims that they were the perpetrators have gained release, often after spending many years in prison, thanks to newly developed scientific tests of blood or semen from the crime scene that definitely exclude them as contributors of the biological material. These disappointing revelations about flaws and mistakes in the criminal investigation process helped to encourage research by psychologists and other social scientists about how and why eyewitnesses misidentify suspects.

Research studies indicate that risks of misidentification that can be reduced simply by changing identification procedures. Movies and television dramas portray the use of lineups with people standing in a row as a victim or witness attempts to pick out the criminal offender. Indeed, the use of such lineups has been very common in police work. However, research studies have identified a number of risks in lineups and other procedures.

- Show-ups, in which a single suspect is brought before a victim or witness, create risks that the police will be regarded as signaling that this is, indeed, the guilty individual. Moreover, the victim or witness will have no other individuals to consider or compare.
- In any procedure, victims or witnesses should be told that the guilty individual is not necessarily present in the lineup or array of photos. Otherwise there is a risk that an individual will be chosen, even if not well remembered, simply because of an assumption that one of these people must be the guilty individual.
- Some research indicates that fewer errors occur when victims or witnesses are shown individuals one at a time, either in person or in photos. In this way, they are pushed to compare each individual with their own memories. Otherwise they may believe that they are supposed to choose the individual who looks most like the perpetrator from among a lineup group or simultaneously viewed photos. Looking at individuals in sequences, rather than in a lineup, may increase the likelihood that victims and witnesses will honestly say "I don't see the individual here," rather than make an inaccurate selection from among the choices.
- Errors may be reduced if the identification procedure is supervised by a police official who has nothing to do with the case and has no idea which individual the police suspect of

of their rights. By the time television-watching Americans reach adulthood, they probably will have heard the *Miranda* warnings delivered hundreds of times on these shows. Many Americans can recite the warnings along with the television detectives. Ironically, this very familiarity with the warnings may impede the effective implementation of *Miranda,* because it interferes with suspects' ability to think about what the warnings actually mean (C. E. Smith, 2004b). Obviously, rights are most protective for people who have actually thought about the meaning of those rights. As you read "Civic Engagement: Your Role in the System," consider what you would do if stopped and questioned by the police.

Many suspects talk to the police despite being informed of their right to remain silent and their right to have an attorney present during questioning. Some suspects do not fully understand the rights. They may believe that they will look guilty by remaining silent or by asking for an attorney. Therefore they feel that they must talk to officers in order to have any hope of claiming innocence. Other suspects may be overly confident about their ability to fool the police and therefore talk to officers, despite the warnings, in an effort to act as if they have nothing to hide. More importantly, many suspects believe (often accurately) that they will gain a more favorable charge or plea bargain if they cooperate with officers as fully as possible and as early as possible. Thus, a trio of suspects arrested together after a robbery who are read their *Miranda* rights and who are placed in separate interrogation rooms may, in effect, race to be the first one to tell a version of events in order to pin greater responsibility on the other arrestees and to seek police assistance in gaining a favorable deal with the prosecutor.

CIVIC ENGAGEMENT

YOUR ROLE IN THE SYSTEM

Based on what you know about police authority to stop and question people, how would you advise your friends to behave during encounters with police officers? *Make a list of what to do and what not to do when stopped by the police.* Then look at the advice that the American Civil Liberties Union provides about how to handle encounters with police officers.

committing the crime. When active investigators run lineups or present photo arrays, there are risks that they will subtly or unconsciously signal through statements or body language that a specific individual is the actual person whom the police believe to be the perpetrator. Such actions, even if subtle, can influence the identifications made by victims and witnesses.

- Many reformers also argue that identification procedures must be videorecorded so that there are opportunities to see if the individuals supervising the procedures either intentionally or unintentionally provided cues about which individual to select. In addition, videorecording helps to show whether the victim or witness made a tentative, uncertain identification or if the identification was certain and confident.

In 2013, the Houston police department was criticized for continuing to use a photo-lineup procedure in which a victim or witness is shown photos of all possible suspects at one time. By contrast, many other Texas police departments, including Austin, Dallas, and San Antonio, had switched to showing photos one at a time in order to reduce the risks of misidentification discussed in the research studies. These examples show that many police departments have adjusted their practices in light of evidence produced by research studies. However, other departments have yet to adopt evidence-based practices to reduce the risk of misidentifications.

Sources: Beth Schuster, "Police Lineups: Making Eyewitness Identification More Reliable," *NIJ Journal* 258 (October 2007): 2–9; Gary L. Wells and Deah S. Quinlivan, "Suggestive Eyewitness Identification Procedures and the Supreme Court's Reliability Test in Light of Eyewitness Science: 30 Years Later," *Law and Human Behavior* 33 (2009): 1–24; Michael D. Cicchini and Joseph G. Easton, "Reforming the Law on Show-Up Identifications," *Journal of Criminal Law and Criminology* 100 (2010): 381–413; *United States v. Ford,* 11–2034, U.S. Court of Appeals, 7th Circuit, June 6, 2012; James Pinkerton, "HPD, Sheriff Using Questioned Photo Lineups," *Houston Chronicle,* January 14, 2013 (www.houstonchronicle.com).

DEBATE THE ISSUE

Should the courts order police departments to conduct identification procedures in one specific way? Alternatively, would such an approach create risks that police could not adapt as new research is produced that refines understandings about the risks and benefits of different approaches? List two reasons why you support either a specific, mandated set of procedures or opportunities for departments to develop their own methods? If you were a police chief, how would your officers conduct identification procedures? Describe your approach.

TABLE 8.4 QUESTIONING SUSPECTS

The Supreme Court has ruled that suspects' rights against self-incrimination are protected by the Fifth Amendment.

CASE	DECISION
Miranda Rules	
Miranda v. Arizona (1966)	Before suspects in police custody may be questioned, they must be told that they have the right to remain silent, that anything they say may be used against them, and that they have the right to counsel during questioning.
Public Safety Exception	
New York v. Quarles (1984)	Officers may direct questions to arrested suspects prior to reading the *Miranda* warnings if concerns about public safety require immediate questioning.

This incentive to cooperate can completely negate many of the fears about *Miranda*'s potentially detrimental effect on law enforcement's effectiveness. It can also create problems of its own, however. There are many cases in which the guiltiest suspect, for example, the one who pulled the trigger and killed a store owner during a robbery, is the most eager to cooperate with the police. If the police are not sufficiently skeptical and careful, the most serious offender may get the most favorable deal by having his or her version of events accepted by authorities, and the least culpable defendant, such as the driver of the getaway car, can sometimes end up with the severest punishment if he or she loses the "race" to confess.

Table 8.4 presents selected cases concerning Supreme Court decisions on how the Fifth Amendment protects suspects' rights against self-incrimination. The New Directions in Criminal Justice Policy feature examines another aspect of police investigations, lineups and other identification procedures, that may affect suspects during the same phase of the justice process where *Miranda* rights are so important. Efforts are underway to reform identification procedures so that they comply with evidence-based practices designed to reduce the risk that innocent people will be misidentified as guilty suspects by victims and witnesses. Misidentification by a victim or witness is a leading cause of innocent people being erroneously convicted of a crime (D. Walsh, 2013).

✔POINT 15. How have police officers changed their practices in light of *Miranda*?

STOP AND ANALYZE: Should police officers be permitted to lie to suspects during questioning, such as falsely claiming that they have eyewitnesses or other evidence of a suspect's guilt? Do such strategies create any risks, such as innocent people feeling hopelessly doomed and admitting guilt in order to seek a plea to a lesser charge? Write an argument in favor of giving police flexibility to use such strategies as well as an argument against permitting dishonest statements. Which argument do you support? Why?

The Exclusionary Rule

exclusionary rule
The principle that illegally obtained evidence must be excluded from a trial.

A primary remedy applied for rights violations by police officers is the exclusion of evidence from court. Thus, police may see evidence excluded when they conduct improper stops and searches as well as improper interrogations. Such exclusions of evidence are known as the **exclusionary rule**.

In *Weeks v. United States* (1914), the U.S. Supreme Court first endorsed the exclusion of evidence from trial as a remedy for improper searches conducted by federal law enforcement officials. The Court clearly declared that if prosecutors were permitted to use improperly obtained evidence, then the Fourth Amendment would lose all meaning, and people's rights under the Amendment would disappear. According to Justice William Day's opinion,

> If letters and private documents can thus be seized and held and used in evidence against a citizen accused of an offense, the protection of the 4th Amendment, declaring his right to be secure against such searches and seizures, is of no value, and, so far as those thus placed are concerned, might as well be stricken from the Constitution.

Newspaper stories periodically report on cases in which prosecutors decide or judges rule that evidence must be excluded due to police errors or intentional actions that violate individuals' rights. For example, when Oscar-winning film actor Philip Seymour Hoffman died of a heroin overdose in New York City in 2014, the police arrested Robert Aaron, a friend of Hoffman's from whom he had reportedly purchased heroin. The prosecutor ended up dropping the most serious drug-selling charges against Aaron because the police officers who first questioned him after his arrest had failed to inform him of his *Miranda* rights (Leland, 2014). Such decisions may come from prosecutors and judges at all levels of the state and federal court systems. One example is the U.S. Supreme Court's decision in *Arizona v. Gant* (2009) limiting police officers' ability to search vehicles based on the arrest of a driver who was handcuffed and moved away from the car. The Court's decision upheld the Arizona Supreme Court's 2007 decision that evidence from the search of the vehicle must be excluded from evidence in the prosecution of Gant due to the improper search. In another example, New York's highest court, called the state Court of Appeals, ordered the exclusion of evidence from a vehicle search in *People v. Garcia* (2012) when officers did not have a proper basis for questioning the vehicle's driver. In 2013, a judge on Michigan's lowest-level trial court ordered the exclusion of incriminating statements obtained from a homicide suspect when he had been held in custody too long without being formally charged with a crime (Misjak, 2013).

The exclusionary rule does not necessarily require that cases against defendants be dismissed when constitutional rights have been violated. The prosecution can continue, but it may not use improperly obtained evidence. In some cases, other valid evidence of guilt may exist in the form of witness testimony or confessions. Without such alternative evidence, however, the exclusionary rule can lead to charges being dropped. The rule clearly accepts the possibility that a guilty person may go free despite the fact that evidence, although illegally obtained, exists to demonstrate his or her guilt.

Application of the Exclusionary Rule to the States

In *Wolf v. Colorado* (1949), the Supreme Court incorporated the Fourth Amendment. However, the justices declined to apply the exclusionary rule to the states because they believed states could develop their own remedies to handle improper searches by police. The situation changed when the appointment of Earl Warren as Chief Justice in 1953 ushered in an era in which the Supreme Court expanded the definitions of constitutional rights affecting a variety of issues, including criminal justice. During the Warren era (1953–1969), the Court incorporated most of the criminal justice–related rights in a way that required state law enforcement officials to adhere to the same rules that federal law enforcement officials had to follow. Because the Warren Court justices decided to incorporate various Fifth, Sixth, and Eighth Amendment rights, they not surprisingly also applied the exclusionary rule to the actions of all law enforcement officials, including those in state and local agencies. The Supreme Court applied the exclusionary rule throughout the country in the famous case of ***Mapp v. Ohio* (1961)**.

***Mapp v. Ohio* (1961)**
Evidence obtained through illegal searches by state and local police must be excluded from use at trial.

Why did the Supreme Court see the exclusionary rule as necessary? Several reasons emerge in such cases as *Weeks* and *Mapp*. First, *Weeks* declared that the exclusionary rule is essential to making the Fourth Amendment meaningful. In essence, the justices believed that constitutional rights are nullified if government officials are permitted to benefit by violating those rights. Second, the *Mapp* decision indicates that the Constitution requires the exclusionary rule. Third, the majority opinion in *Mapp* concluded that alternatives to the exclusionary rule do not work. Justice Tom Clark's majority opinion noted that many states had found that nothing short of exclusion of evidence would work to correct constitutional rights violations and limit the number of violations that occur. Previously, some states had sought to prevent improper searches by permitting lawsuits against police officers rather than by excluding illegally obtained evidence. Fourth, the *Mapp* opinion argued that the use of improperly obtained evidence by officials who are responsible for upholding the law only serves to diminish respect for the law. In Clark's words, "Thus the State, by admitting evidence unlawfully seized, serves to encourage disobedience to the Federal Constitution which it is bound to uphold." Fifth, the *Mapp* decision indicates that the absence of an exclusionary rule diminishes the protection of all rights because it would permit all constitutional rights "to be revocable at the whim of any police officer who, in the name of law enforcement itself, chooses to suspend . . . [the] enjoyment [of rights]." Sixth, the exclusionary rule is justified as an effective means of deterring police and prosecutors from violating constitutional rights.

✔POINT 16. Why was the exclusionary rule created and eventually applied to the states?

STOP AND ANALYZE: Is the exclusion of valuable evidence too severe as a sanction for improper police actions? List two reasons why the exclusionary rule is necessary, or list two actions that could be used effectively in place of the exclusionary rule to deal with improper police investigation actions.

Exceptions to the Exclusionary Rule

The exclusionary rule has many critics, including justices on the Supreme Court. Earl Warren's successor, Chief Justice Warren Burger, who served from 1969 to 1986, criticized the rule as ineffective and misguided. He joined many law enforcement officials, commentators, and politicians in harshly criticizing the Court's decision in *Mapp*. Burger and his allies complained that the Court's decision would hamper police investigations and allow guilty criminals to go free. In Burger's view, there was no proof that the rule prevented officers from conducting improper searches. Moreover, he saw the rule as punishing prosecutors and society rather than the officers who violated people's rights.

Research has not clearly supported claims about the negative consequences of the exclusionary rule. Studies of the rule's impact have produced two consistent findings. First, only a small minority of defendants file a "motion to suppress," which is used to ask a judge to exclude evidence that has allegedly been obtained in violation of the defendant's rights. Second, only a small fraction of motions to suppress evidence are granted (Davies, 1983; Uchida and Bynum, 1991; S. Walker, 2001: 90–91). Amid continuing debates about the rule's impact and effectiveness, the Supreme Court began creating exceptions to the exclusionary rule after Burger became chief justice.

The Supreme Court created a **good faith exception** to the exclusionary rule when officers use search warrants (*United States v. Leon,* 1984). When officers have acted in good faith reliance on a warrant, the evidence will not be excluded even if the warrant was issued improperly. *Good faith* means that the officers acted with the honest belief that they were following the proper rules. In addition, the reliance and honest belief must be reasonable. If officers knew that a judge had issued a warrant based on no evidence whatsoever, officers could not claim that they reasonably and honestly relied on the warrant. However, if the officers had presented evidence of probable cause to the judge and the judge had made the error by issuing a warrant based on information that actually fell below the standard of probable cause, the officers could use evidence found in the resulting search.

good faith exception
When police act in honest reliance on a warrant, the evidence seized is admissible even if the warrant is later proved to be defective.

Importantly, the Supreme Court never created a general good faith exception to permit the admissibility of improperly obtained evidence when police officers make an honest mistake. In *Leon,* there was good faith reliance on a warrant, meaning that the fundamental error was made by the judge who issued the warrant. Evidence can still be excluded if officers undertook an improper warrantless search based on their own discretionary decision, even if they honestly (but wrongly) believed that a warrantless search was permitted.

Over the years the Supreme Court has recognized other circumstances where a good faith exception is applied to the exclusionary rule (Aviram, Seymour, and Leo, 2010). For example,

1. *Reliance on a warrant found to be incorrect* (*Maryland v. Garrison,* 1987). Police relied on a warrant that incorrectly designated the wrong apartment to search. They were able to use evidence found in the apartment, even though there had been no probable cause to search that apartment in the first place.
2. *Reliance on statutes later declared unconstitutional* (*Illinois v. Krull,* 1987). Officers conducted a search of a junkyard based on a state statute that authorized warrantless searches of such regulated locations. Although the statute was later declared unconstitutional, the evidence found during the improper search could be used against the defendant.
3. *Reliance on records maintained by justice system employees* (***Herring v. United States,* 2009**). Officers arrested a man based on an outstanding warrant for his arrest. They had searched him in conjunction with the arrest and found drugs and a pistol. Although it later turned out that there was no warrant and a court employee had failed to clear the warrant from his record, and therefore the arrest justifying the search was invalid, the evidence could be used against him because the officers took no deliberate improper actions.
4. *Reasonable reliance on a consent to search provided by someone who lacked the authority to grant such consent* (*Illinois v. Rodriguez,* 1990). A suspect's girlfriend provided the police with a key and granted permission to search an apartment even though she did not live in the apartment and she was not supposed to have a key. Evidence was admissible against the defendant because the officers reasonably believed that the girlfriend lived in the apartment.

***Herring v. United States* (2009)**
When officers act in good faith reliance on computerized records concerning outstanding warrants, evidence found in a search incident to arrest is admissible even if the arrest was based on an erroneous record that wrongly indicated the existence of a warrant.

One important exception to the exclusionary rule is the **inevitable discovery exception**. This rule arose from a case involving the tragic abduction and murder of a young girl. The police sought an escapee from a psychiatric hospital who was seen carrying a large bundle. The man being sought contacted an attorney and arranged to surrender to police in a town 160 miles away from the scene of the abduction. The Supreme Court subsequently found that the police improperly questioned the suspect outside of the presence of his attorney while driving him back to the city where the abduction occurred (*Brewer v. Williams,* 1977). The Supreme Court declared that the girl's body and the suspect's statements had to be excluded from evidence because they were obtained

inevitable discovery exception
Improperly obtained evidence can be used when it would later have inevitably been discovered without improper actions by the police.

Nix v. Williams (1984)
Decision in which the Supreme Court created the "inevitable discovery" exception to the exclusionary rule.

in violation of his rights. Thus, his murder conviction was overturned and he was given a new trial. At the second trial, at which he was convicted again, the prosecution used the body in evidence against him based on the claim that search parties would have found the body eventually even without his confession. There was a search team within two and one-half miles of the body at the time that it was found. In **Nix v. Williams (1984)**, the Supreme Court agreed that improperly obtained evidence can be used when it would later have been inevitably discovered without improper actions by the police.

Table 8.5 summarizes selected Supreme Court decisions regarding the exclusionary rule as it applies to the Fourth and Fifth Amendments.

The Supreme Court also created exceptions to the exclusionary rule by identifying stages in the criminal justice process in which the rule does not apply. Table 8.6 lists contexts outside of the standard criminal prosecution in which evidence is not excluded even if officials commit rights violations in the course of gathering evidence.

When the Supreme Court created the exclusionary rule in *Weeks v. United States* (1914) and later expanded its coverage to state and local criminal cases in *Mapp v. Ohio* (1961), it appeared to make strong statements against the use of improperly obtained evidence. As the Court refined the application of the rule from the 1970s onward, it became clear that the exclusion of evidence would arise only in specific situations. The justices have clarified their intention to apply the rule in criminal trials but not in other kinds of proceedings, such as grand jury proceedings and parole revocation hearings, that are not direct criminal prosecutions to determine guilt and punishment. In addition, the specific exceptions to the rule created by the Supreme Court show that the justices changed their approach to determining when evidence should be excluded.

When the Court issued its decisions in *Weeks* and *Mapp,* it appeared that the exclusion of evidence would be guided by a trial judge's answer to the question "Did police violate the suspect's rights?" By contrast, through the development of exceptions to the rule, the Court shifted its focus to the question "Did the police make an error that was so serious that the exclusion of evidence is

TABLE 8.5 EXCLUSIONARY RULE

The Supreme Court has ruled that improperly obtained evidence must be excluded from use by the prosecution, although the Court also created several exceptions to this general rule.

CASE	DECISION
Exclusionary Rule	
Mapp v. Ohio (1961)	Because the Fourth Amendment protects people from unreasonable searches and seizures by all law enforcement officials, evidence found through improper searches or seizures must be excluded from use at state and federal trials.
Good Faith Exception	
United States v. Leon (1984)	When officers act in good faith reliance on a warrant, the evidence will not be excluded even if the warrant was issued improperly.
Inevitable Discovery Exception	
Nix v. Williams (1984)	Improperly obtained evidence can be used when it would later have inevitably been discovered without improper actions by the police.
Erroneous Records Exception	
Herring v. United States (2009)	When officers act in good faith reliance on computerized records concerning outstanding warrants, evidence found in a search incident to arrest is admissible even if the arrest was based on an erroneous record that wrongly indicated the existence of a warrant.

TABLE 8.6 CONTEXTS OUTSIDE OF THE STANDARD CRIMINAL PROSECUTION IN WHICH THE EXCLUSIONARY RULE DOES NOT APPLY

CASE	DECISION
Grand Jury Proceedings	
United States v. Calandra (1974)	A witness summoned to appear before a grand jury cannot refuse to answer questions simply because the questions were based on evidence obtained from an improper search.
Parole Revocation Hearings	
Pennsylvania Board of Pardons and Parole v. Scott (1998)	Improperly obtained evidence can be used at parole revocation proceedings.
Immigration Deportation Hearings	
Immigration and Naturalization Service v. Lopez-Mendoza (1984)	Improperly obtained evidence can be used at deportation hearings.
Impeachment of Defendant	
Harris v. New York (1971)	Improperly obtained statements can be used to impeach the credibility of defendants who take the witness stand and testify in their own trials.

required?" For example, the good faith exception established in *United States v. Leon* (1984) emphasizes the fact that officers did what they thought they were supposed to do. The decision did not rest on the fact that the suspect's Fourth Amendment rights were violated by a search conducted with an improper warrant. Thus, the Supreme Court's creation of exceptions to the exclusionary rule has given police officers the flexibility to make specific kinds of errors without jeopardizing the admissibility of evidence that will help establish a defendant's guilt (Clancy, 2010; Cammack, 2010). Moreover, the Court reinforced its tolerance for police errors in 2014 when it decided that even though a police officer was wrong in believing that his state's law required both taillights on a vehicle to be working, no rights violation occurred and no

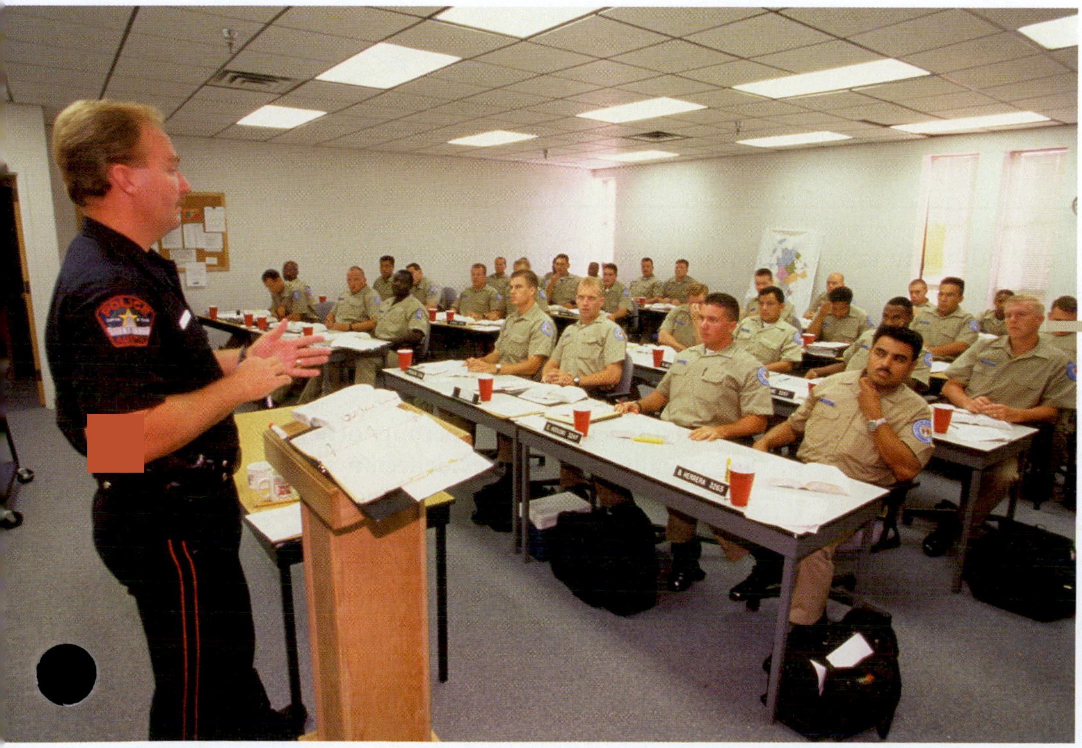

John Boykin/Stock Connection Distribution/Alamy

It is important for police to be educated, professional, and ethical. A properly educated officer must learn many rules, including the requirements for giving *Miranda* warnings and all of the exceptions to the exclusionary rule. Are the rules regarding proper police procedure and constitutional rights so numerous and complicated that it is difficult to imagine that an officer can truly remember and understand everything that he or she is supposed to do?

exclusion of evidence was required when a traffic stop based on this mistaken understanding of state law led to the discovery of criminal evidence in the vehicle (*Heien v. North Carolina*, 2014).

✔POINT **17.** What are some of the criticisms of the exclusionary rule?
18. What are the exceptions to the exclusionary rule?

STOP AND ANALYZE: Does the creation of multiple exceptions to the exclusionary rule significantly reduce the original purpose and effect of the rule? Describe a situation in which the exclusionary rule should apply. Then try to apply one of the exceptions to the rule to that situation, as if you were a prosecutor arguing against the exclusion of evidence. Are the exceptions sufficiently numerous and vague to give prosecutors broad opportunities to argue effectively against the exclusion of evidence?

A QUESTION OF ETHICS

Recall that the chapter's initial discussion of cell phone searches by police included the 2014 example of officers in California seizing motorists' cell phones in order to look for and steal revealing photos. In one case, an officer forwarded the image of a bikini-clad woman to a fellow officer as the woman whose cell phone contained the photo was being checked for injuries after an automobile collision. One writer described the incident by pointing sarcasm at the police: "The colleague upbraided him for violating a citizen's privacy, contacted the commanding officer, and arranged for [the fellow officer's] arrest on felony charges. I kid, of course. The colleague actually complained that the photo wasn't more explicit" (Friedersdorf, 2014). In actuality, the colleague complained that it was not a nude photo. Meanwhile, the officer who stole the photo requested that his colleague send him some photos from motorists' cell phones, too.

CRITICAL THINKING AND ANALYSIS

Clearly, these officers engaged in improper behavior. Moreover, the writer's comment pointed to a particular ethical problem even beyond the theft of the photo: Why didn't the officer who received the photo turn in his colleague for improper behavior that violated the rights of the motorist? Unfortunately, this behavior may indicate a police culture within the organization in which officers feel free to do what they want without fear that they will be caught and punished. As a result, there are grave risks that officers will freely violate the rights of the citizens they are paid to serve. Imagine that you are the police chief over these officers. What are two steps you would take to try to improve the ethical climate and sense of responsibility among your officers?

Summary

1 Know the extent of police officers' authority to stop and search people and their vehicles

- The Supreme Court has defined rules for the circumstances and justifications for stops, searches, and arrests in light of the Fourth Amendment's prohibition on "unreasonable searches and seizures."
- Most stops must be supported by reasonable suspicion; arrests, like search warrants, must be supported by enough information to constitute probable cause.

2 Understand when and how police officers seek warrants in order to conduct searches and make arrests

- In order to obtain a warrant, police officers present an affidavit (sworn statement) verifying the information presented to the judge that they believe constitutes probable cause to search or make an arrest.

3 Know whether police officers can look in people's windows or their backyards to see if evidence of a crime exists there

- The plain view doctrine permits officers to examine visually and use as evidence anything that is in open sight when they are in a place where they are legally permitted to be.

4 Analyze the situations in which police officers can conduct searches without obtaining a warrant

- Searches are considered "reasonable" and may be conducted without warrants in specific "special needs" circumstances that have purposes beyond those of normal law enforcement. For example, borders and airports often require searches without warrants.

- Limited searches may be conducted without warrants when officers have reasonable suspicions to justify a stop and frisk for weapons on the streets; when officers make a lawful arrest; under exigent circumstances; when people voluntarily consent to searches of their persons or property; and in certain situations involving automobiles.

5 Understand the purpose of the privilege against compelled self-incrimination

- The Fifth Amendment privilege against compelled self-incrimination helps protect citizens against violence and coercion by police as well as maintain the legitimacy and integrity of the legal system.
- The Supreme Court's decision in *Miranda v. Arizona* requires officers to inform suspects of specific rights before custodial questioning, although officers have adapted their practices to accommodate this rule, and several exceptions have been created.

6 Understand the exclusionary rule and the situations in which it applies

- In barring the use of illegally obtained evidence in court, the exclusionary rule is designed to deter police from violating citizens' rights during criminal investigations.
- The Supreme Court has created several exceptions to the exclusionary rule, including the "good faith" and "inevitable discovery" exceptions.

Questions for Review

1. What are the requirements for police officers with respect to stops, searches, arrests, and warrants?
2. What are the plain view doctrine and the open fields doctrine?
3. Under what circumstances are warrantless searches permissible?
4. How have police officers adapted to the requirements of *Miranda v. Arizona?*
5. What are the exceptions to the exclusionary rule?

Key Terms and Cases

affidavit (p. 333)
exclusionary rule (p. 354)
exigent circumstances (p. 343)
good faith exception (p. 357)
inevitable discovery exception (p. 357)
open fields doctrine (p. 334)
plain view doctrine (p. 334)
probable cause (p. 332)
public safety exception (p. 350)
reasonable expectations of privacy (p. 330)
reasonable suspicion (p. 331)
search (p. 330)
seizure (p. 330)
stop (p. 331)
stop-and-frisk search (p. 339)
totality of circumstances test (p. 333)
Arizona v. Gant (2009) (p. 342)
Chimel v. California (1969) (p. 341)
Escobedo v. Illinois (1964) (p. 349)
Florida v. J. L. (2000) (p. 341)
Herring v. United States (2009) (p. 357)
Illinois v. Rodriguez (1990) (p. 345)
Kentucky v. King (2011) (p. 344)
Mapp v. Ohio (1961) (p. 356)
Miranda v. Arizona (1966) (p. 348)
Nix v. Williams (1984) (p. 358)
Terry v. Ohio (1968) (p. 339)
United States v. Drayton (2002) (p. 345)

Checkpoint Answers

1 What is a search?

✓ A government intrusion into an individual's reasonable expectation of privacy.

2 What justification do police officers need to make a stop?

✓ Reasonable suspicion of wrongdoing based on articulable facts.

3 What is the difference between an arrest and a stop?

✓ An arrest requires probable cause and involves taking someone into custody for prosecution, whereas a stop is a brief deprivation of freedom of movement based on reasonable suspicion.

4 **What do police officers need to demonstrate in order to obtain a warrant?**

✓ The existence of probable cause by the totality of circumstances in the case.

5 **What is the plain view doctrine?**

✓ Officers can examine and use as evidence anything that is in open sight at a place where they are legally permitted to be.

6 **May officers use senses other than sight to find evidence of crime without a warrant?**

✓ Officers may use their sense of smell, especially for distinctive odors such as that of marijuana, but the Supreme Court has limited the authority to feel and manipulate luggage and other objects.

7 **In what situations do law enforcement's special needs justify stopping an automobile without reasonable suspicion?**

✓ Warrantless stops of automobiles are permitted at sobriety checkpoints (unless barred within a specific state by its own supreme court), and international borders, or when there is reasonable suspicion of a traffic violation or other wrongdoing.

8 **What knowledge must an officer possess in order to conduct a stop-and-frisk search on the streets?**

✓ A reasonable suspicion based on personal observation or information from a reliable informant that an individual is armed and involved in possible criminal activity.

9 **Where can officers search when conducting a warrantless search incident to a lawful arrest?**

✓ Officers can search in the immediate area of the arrestee and do a protective sweep of rooms where the arrestee may have recently been.

10 **What are exigent circumstances?**

✓ Urgent situations in which evidence may be destroyed, a suspect may escape, or the public would be endangered if officers took the time to seek a warrant for a search or arrest.

11 **What two elements must be present for a valid consent to permit a warrantless search?**

✓ The person must do it voluntarily and must have the proper authority to consent.

12 **What defines the scope of officers' authority to search containers in automobiles?**

✓ Officers can search any container or closed portion of an automobile for which probable cause exists to justify the search.

13 **What are *Miranda* rights?**

✓ Before custodial interrogation, officers must inform suspects of the right to remain silent, the prosecution's authority to use any of the suspect's statements, the right to the presence of an attorney during questioning, and the right to have an attorney appointed if the suspect cannot afford one.

14 **What is the public safety exception?**

✓ Officers can ask questions of suspects in custody without first providing *Miranda* warnings if public safety would be threatened by taking the time to supply the warnings.

15 **How have police officers changed their practices in light of *Miranda?***

✓ Officers ask questions before suspects are in custody, use techniques to pretend to befriend or empathize with suspects being questioned, and give suspects misinformation about the existence of evidence demonstrating guilt.

16 **Why was the exclusionary rule created and eventually applied to the states?**

✓ The exclusionary rule was created to deter officers from violating people's rights, and the Supreme Court considers it an essential component of the Fourth and Fifth Amendments.

17 **What are some of the criticisms of the exclusionary rule?**

✓ The rule is criticized as punishing the prosecutor and society rather than the police, imposing excessive costs on society, depriving the legal process of relevant evidence, and permitting some guilty people to go free.

18 **What are the exceptions to the exclusionary rule?**

✓ A good faith exception in warrant situations and in reliance on erroneous police or court records; an inevitable discovery exception when evidence would have been discovered by the police anyway; and no application of exclusion in grand jury proceedings and other contexts that do not involve the proof of guilt in a criminal prosecution.

PART 3

COURTS

In a democracy, the arrest of a person is but the first part of a complex process designed to separate the guilty from the innocent. Part 3 examines the process by which guilt is determined in accordance with the law's requirements, as well as the processes and underlying philosophies of the punishments that further separate the convicted from the acquitted. Here we look at the work of prosecutors, defense attorneys, bail agents, probation officers, and judges to understand the contribution each makes toward the ultimate decisions. In the adjudicatory stage, the goals of an administrative system blunt the force of the adversarial process prescribed by law. Although courtroom activities receive the most media attention, most decisions relating to the disposition of a case take place in less public surroundings. After the sentencing, the case recedes even further from the public eye. After studying these chapters, think about whether justice is served by processes that are more like bargaining than like adversarial combat between two lawyers. Also consider whether the punishments our courts hand out are doing the job they are supposed to be doing in punishing offenders.

CHAPTER FEATURES

- **Doing Your Part** Court-Appointed Special Advocates
- **New Directions in Criminal Justice Policy** Problem-Solving Courts
- **Close Up** The Image of Justice
- **Technology and Criminal Justice** Technology and Pretrial Release

CHAPTER 9

COURTS AND PRETRIAL PROCESSES

CHAPTER LEARNING OBJECTIVES

1. Describe the structure of the American court system
2. Analyze the qualities that we desire in a judge
3. Identify the ways that American judges are selected
4. Describe the pretrial process in criminal cases
5. Discuss how the bail system operates
6. Analyze the context of pretrial detention

CHAPTER OUTLINE

AP Images/Brendan Fitterer

In being arrested for a crime, suspects enter the judicial processes that will determine whether they are held in jail until their trials and, ultimately, whether they are guilty and must be punished. The initial processes of arrest and booking are typically the same for poor people accused of street crimes as for wealthy people accused of white-collar crimes. However, their ability to gain release from jail, as their cases are processed through the courts, often differs. These differences occur both because of the seriousness of the crime in different cases and because of the wealth of the defendants.

Curtis Reeves, a 71-year-old former police officer, faced second-degree murder charges for the shooting death of Chad Oulson, a 43-year-old former U.S. Navy petty officer. On January 13, 2014, according to police reports and witnesses at a movie theater, Reeves had told Oulson to put away his cell phone during previews prior to the scheduled movie. Oulson initially ignored Reeves, and Reeves went to the theater lobby to look unsuccessfully for a manager to complain about Oulson. When Reeves returned, the two men exchanged words. Oulson reportedly threw popcorn at Reeves, and Reeves shot Oulson with a .380-caliber semiautomatic handgun (Almasy and Payne, 2014).

Reeves was arrested at the scene. At his initial court appearance the following day, a judge rejected a defense attorney's claim that the preliminary evidence showed Reeves to be the victim in the incident. In effect, the judge refused to dismiss charges based on an initial claim of self-defense. The judge declined to release Reeves on bail after this probable cause hearing, so he remained locked up pending a formal bail hearing in which his defense attorney and the prosecutor would present their respective arguments about whether he should gain pretrial release and under what conditions that release should occur.

The two-day bail hearing was held during the first week of February 2014. At that time, prosecutors presented a grainy video of the shooting taken from a security camera inside the theater. The wives of both Reeves and Oulson had been eyewitnesses to the event. Their statements, taken in police interviews, were presented at the hearing, as well as statements that Reeves made to the police. Judge Pat Siracusa listened to additional hours of testimony from family, friends, and former colleagues of Reeves who claimed that he did not have an anger-management problem and that he would not present any risk of fleeing from Florida while awaiting his trial. Ultimately, Judge Siracusa concluded that the prosecutors had presented persuasive evidence about the need to deny bail ("Bail Denied," 2014), and he ordered Reeves to remain in jail until his trial.

Reeves's attorney appealed the bail decision to the state court of appeals. The appeals court ruled that the defense attorney had presented "exceptionally strong evidence in support for pretrial release" and sent the case back to Judge Siracusa. A new bail hearing was held in July 2014 and the judge set bail at $150,000—money that Reeves must hand over for court officials to hold and that would be permanently forfeited if he failed to appear at scheduled hearings. Judge Siracusa imposed additional bail conditions, too. Reeves was required to remain in his home, except when he went to church, doctors' appointments, or the grocery store. He was also required to wear an electronic ankle monitor, surrender his firearms, and avoid any contact with the victim's wife, who had testified against him at the bail hearings (Buie, 2014). Although the American justice system considered Reeves to be presumptively innocent because he had not yet been convicted of any crime, he spent more than six months in jail prior to his release on bail.

As attorneys for both sides prepared for trial by gathering evidence and interviewing dozens of witnesses, Reeves appeared in court again on November 19, 2014. Judge Siracusa had hoped to set a trial date at this hearing, but the attorney for Reeves asked for additional time so that more witnesses could be interviewed. The judge scheduled a new pretrial hearing for January 2015 (Osowski, 2014).

At the next pretrial hearing on January 29, 2015, more than one year after the shooting, Judge Siracusa, in consultation with the prosecutor and defense attorney, set the schedule for subsequent pretrial hearings leading up to the scheduled date to open the trial on August 24, 2015. The judge scheduled interim hearings to work through disputes about evidence and to hear motions from the defense on April 30, May 28, June 30, and August 3. Reeves would be required to appear at each of these hearings (WFTS Webteam, 2015).

As demonstrated by the lengthy pretrial process for Curtis Reeves, when people are arrested, they enter the court system where the decisions of judges, prosecutors, and defense attorneys largely determine their fate. Pretrial decisions can affect the ultimate outcome of a case. If defendants are not released on bail, they might have trouble helping their lawyers prepare arguments and evidence for the defense. In some cases, additional pretrial decisions must be made about the defendant's mental competence. Defendants found to lack the necessary mental competence to stand trial might never be convicted of a crime, even in homicide cases, yet they might still spend years confined in a state institution. Whether or not to perform a pretrial competency evaluation is just one key decision that can affect the defendant's ultimate fate. Important decisions take place in several other pretrial processes as well. These processes include formal events, such as preliminary hearings to determine if enough evidence exists to pursue criminal charges, and informal interactions, such as plea-bargaining discussions that might resolve the case prior to trial.

In this chapter we examine courts, the setting in which criminal defendants' cases are processed. We look at judges and their important role in criminal cases. In particular, we look at pretrial processes that help determine the fates of criminal defendants.

The Structure of American Courts

As we have seen, the United States has a dual court system, with separate federal and state court systems. Other countries have a single national court system, but American rules and traditions permit states to create their own court systems to handle most legal matters, including most crimes.

The federal courts oversee a limited range of criminal cases. For example, they deal with people accused of violating the criminal laws of the national government. Counterfeiting, kidnapping, smuggling, and drug trafficking are examples of federal crimes. But such cases account for only a small portion of the criminal cases that pass through American courts each year. For every offender sentenced to incarceration by federal courts, more than ten offenders are sent to prisons and jails by state courts, because most crimes are defined by state laws (BJS, 2015a). This disparity may grow wider as federal law enforcement agencies increasingly emphasize antiterrorism activities rather than traditional crime-control investigations. The gap is even greater for misdemeanors, because state courts bear primary responsibility for processing the lesser offenses, such as disorderly conduct, that arise on a daily basis.

State supreme courts each interpret their own state's constitution and statutes and ensure that lower courts within the state follow those interpretations. The U.S. Supreme Court oversees both federal and state court systems by interpreting the U.S. Constitution, which protects the rights of defendants in federal and state criminal cases.

The issues of complexity and coordination that the country's decentralized courts face are compounded by a third court system that operates in several states. Native Americans have tribal courts, whose authority is endorsed by congressional statutes and Supreme Court decisions. With **jurisdiction** over their own people on tribal land, these tribal courts permit Native American judges to apply their people's cultural values in

jurisdiction
The geographic territory or legal boundaries within which control may be exercised; the range of a court's authority.

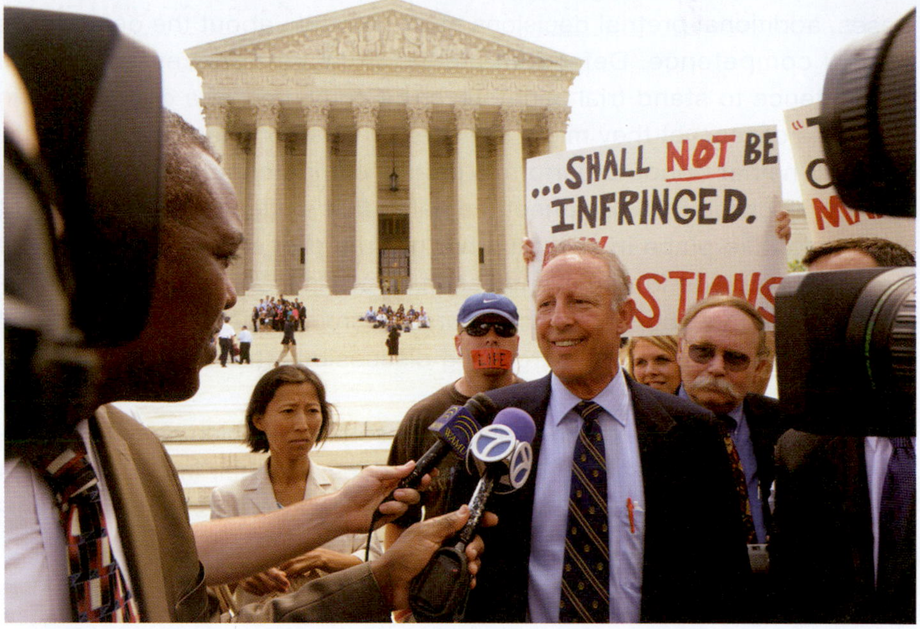

ROGER L. WOLLENBERG/UPI /Landov

Dick Anthony Heller speaks to reporters outside the U.S. Supreme Court prior to winning his case to strike down Washington, D.C.'s broad prohibition against handguns. Heller's case in 2008 established a limited Second Amendment right to keep handguns in private homes for self-protection. Does the Supreme Court possess too much power to strike down laws that are created by the people's elected representatives in city councils, state legislatures, and Congress?

resolving civil lawsuits and when processing certain criminal offenses (Goldberg, 2010).

Both the federal and state court systems have trial and appellate courts. There are three levels of courts: appellate courts, trial courts of general jurisdiction, and trial courts of limited jurisdiction.

Cases begin in a trial court, which handles determinations of guilt and sentencing. **Trial courts of limited jurisdiction** handle only misdemeanors and lawsuits involving small amounts of money. Felony cases and all other civil lawsuits are heard in **trial courts of general jurisdiction**. These are the courts in which jury trials take place and judges impose prison sentences. All federal cases begin in the general jurisdiction trial courts, the U.S. district courts.

trial courts of limited jurisdiction
Criminal courts with trial jurisdiction over misdemeanor cases and preliminary matters in felony cases. Sometimes these courts hold felony trials that may result in penalties below a specified limit.

trial courts of general jurisdiction
Criminal courts with jurisdiction over all offenses, including felonies. In some states, these courts also hear appeals.

appellate courts
Courts that do not try criminal cases but hear appeals of decisions of lower courts.

Cases move to intermediate **appellate courts** if defendants claim that errors by police or the trial court contributed to their convictions. Further appeals can be filed with a state supreme court or the U.S. Supreme Court, depending on which court system the case is in and what kind of legal argument is being made. All states have courts of last resort (usually called state supreme courts), and all but a few have an intermediate appellate court (usually called courts of appeals). In the federal system, the U.S. Supreme Court is the court of last resort, and the U.S. circuit courts of appeals are the intermediate appellate courts.

Although this basic three-tiered structure operates throughout the United States, the number of courts, their names, and their specific functions vary widely. For example, the federal system has no trial courts of limited jurisdiction. In state systems, 13,000 trial courts of limited jurisdiction handle traffic cases, small claims, misdemeanors, and other less serious matters. These courts handle 90 percent of all criminal cases. The federal system begins with the U.S. district courts, its trial courts of general jurisdiction. In the states, these courts have a variety of names (circuit, district, superior, and others) and are reserved for felony cases or substantial lawsuits. These are the courts in which trials take place, judges rule on evidence, and juries issue verdicts. Figure 9.1 shows the basic structure of the dual court system.

FIGURE 9.1 THE DUAL COURT SYSTEM OF THE UNITED STATES AND ROUTES OF APPEAL

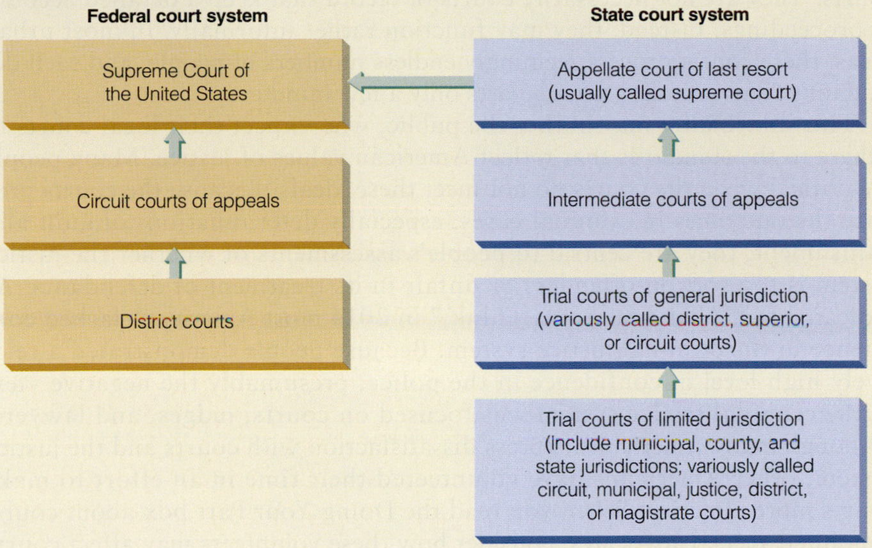

Whether a case enters through the federal or state court system depends on which law has been broken. The right of appeal to a higher court exists in either system.

Some states have reformed their court systems by simplifying the number and types of courts, whereas others still support a confusing assortment of lower courts. Figure 9.2 contrasts the reformed court structure of Alaska with Georgia's unreformed system. Both follow the three-tiered model, but Georgia has more courts and a more complex system for determining which court will handle which kind of case.

American trial courts are highly decentralized. Local political influences and community values affect the courts in many ways. Local officials determine their resources, residents make up the staff, and operations are managed so as to fit community needs. Only in a few small states is the court system organized on a statewide basis, with a central administration and state funding. In most of the country, the criminal courts operate under the state penal code but are staffed, managed, and financed by county or city government. The federal courts, by contrast, have centralized administration and funding, although judges in each district help shape their own courts' practices and procedures.

FIGURE 9.2 COURT STRUCTURES OF ALASKA (REFORMED) AND GEORGIA (UNREFORMED)

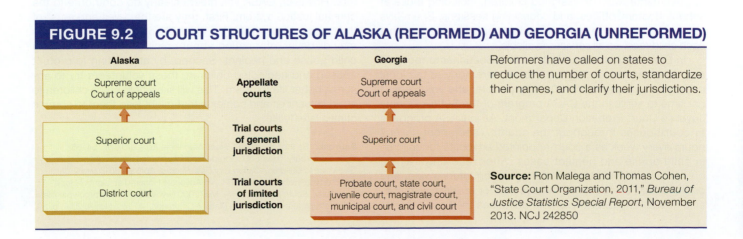

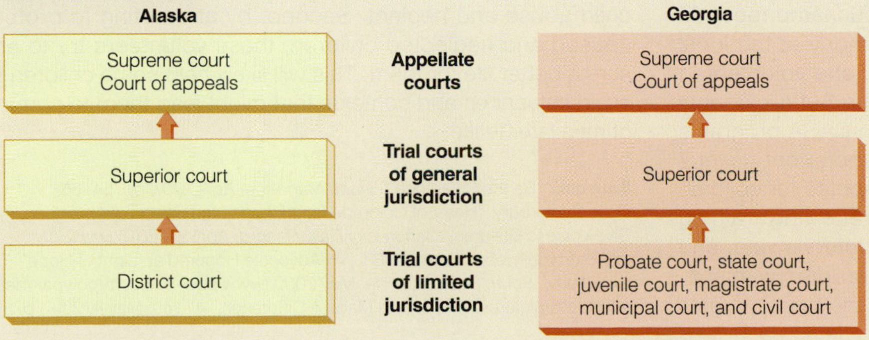

Reformers have called on states to reduce the number of courts, standardize their names, and clarify their jurisdictions.

Source: Ron Malega and Thomas Cohen, "State Court Organization, 2011," *Bureau of Justice Statistics Special Report*, November 2013. NCJ 242850

Lower courts, especially at the state level, do not always display the dignity and formal procedures of general jurisdiction trial courts and appellate courts. They are not necessarily courts of record that keep a detailed account of proceedings. Instead, they may function rather informally. In most urban areas, these courts process seemingly endless numbers of people, and each defendant's "day in court" usually lasts only a few minutes.

This informality may bother the public, who expect their local courts to adhere to the standards that reflect American values of justice. Many people are critical when the courts do not meet these ideals. Because the courts produce the outcomes in criminal cases, especially determinations of guilt and punishment, they are central to people's assessments of whether the justice system is too soft on offenders or unfair in its treatment of defendants. As indicated in "What Americans Think," in 2014 most Americans lacked confidence in the criminal justice system. Because people demonstrated a relatively high level of confidence in the police, presumably the negative view of the criminal justice system was focused on courts, judges, and lawyers. Although many Americans express dissatisfaction with courts and the justice system, other Americans have volunteered their time in an effort to make courts more effective. When you read the Doing Your Part box about court-appointed special advocates, consider how these volunteers may affect courts and criminal justice.

DOING YOUR PART

COURT-APPOINTED SPECIAL ADVOCATES

Because courts are institutions operated by trained professionals with special expertise in law, imagining how the average citizen can become involved and make a contribution is challenging. Some citizens are summoned to court to serve as jurors, but few others have contact with courts unless they are brought into a case as a defendant, witness, or victim. There is, however, a little-known but growing program that permits citizens to make a contribution: CASA, which stands for court-appointed special advocates.

In Colorado, Kathleen Sturgon, a retired educator, serves as an advocate for abused and neglected children. She attends appointments with her assigned children, including those at school, doctors' offices, and counseling sessions. She relays relevant information to the court and attempts to make sure that each child receives all services available.

In Boston, Massachusetts, Joanne Beauchamp received a special award in a "Light of Hope" ceremony at the local courthouse. Along with 100 other people, she volunteered her time to serve in the CASA program of the Suffolk County Juvenile Court Probation Department. As in CASA programs at courthouses throughout the country, she spent several hours every week as a court-appointed advocate for children in child abuse and neglect cases. After receiving training on the law of child abuse and neglect, on interviewing, and on advocacy, she became an advocate for children with specific needs. The CASA volunteer advances the best interests of each child by interviewing teachers, foster parents, and others; monitoring compliance with court orders; facilitating contacts with social services agencies; and reporting to the court on the status of the child. About 55,000 CASA volunteers in 948 communities serve more than 200,000 children throughout the nation.

Does CASA give volunteers the opportunity to affect the criminal justice system? This is a valid question, because CASA programs are typically connected not to criminal cases per se but to family courts or probate courts that have jurisdiction over child custody, parental rights, and related matters. However, CASA volunteers clearly do contribute to the criminal justice system. First, they are the "eyes and ears" of the court in supervising the child's best interests. Thus, they may discover information about criminal offenses involving child abuse and neglect. Second, by attempting to protect abused and neglected children, these volunteers try to ensure a better life for them. This will likely help some children to avoid influences and contexts that might lead them to commit crimes later in life.

Sources: "Be the Difference," *Grand Magazine,* April 2007, pp. 54–55; Carie Canterbury, "Heart of Colorado Court Appointed Special Advocates Give Voice to Children," *Cañon City Daily Record,* April 25, 2013 (www.canoncitydailyrecord.com); "SB Child Advocate Honored at 'Light of Hope' Ceremony," *South Boston Online,* May 2000 (www.pow-pak.com/powpak/data/etech266/pictures71.htm); "We Made A Difference," *All You,* May 4, 2007, p. 89.

Effective Management of the State Courts

Throughout the twentieth century and beyond, reformers have tried to change the structure, administration, and financing of the state courts so the courts can deal more effectively with their huge caseloads (Saufley, 2010). Problems with inadequate resources and the uneven quality of judges hurt the courts' effectiveness (Abrahamson, 2004). There is a need for professional court administrators with expertise and training (R. E. Hartley and Bates, 2006). However, people often see the fragmented structure of state courts as the biggest barrier to justice. Proposed solutions include the creation of a unified court system with four goals:

1. Eliminating overlapping and conflicting jurisdictional boundaries
2. Creating a hierarchical and centralized court structure with administrative responsibility held by a chief justice and a court of last resort
3. Having the courts funded by state government instead of local counties and cities
4. Creating a separate civil service personnel system run by a state court administrator

These goals stand at the forefront of the movement to promote the efficiency and fairness of state courts. However, local political interests often resist court reform. Local courts have long been used as a source of jobs to reward people loyal to the political party in power. Centralization of court administration and professionalization of court personnel would eliminate the opportunities to use court jobs in this manner.

Like other organizations within the justice system, courts face major problems in fulfilling their functions in an era of government budget crises and diminishing resources. Most of court budgets are allotted to pay judges and administrative staff, so options for implementing budget cuts are limited and tend to directly affect court personnel. In December 2013, Chief Justice John Roberts issued a report that warned Congress about the adverse consequences of budget cuts on the operations of the federal courts (Liptak, 2013a). Court systems in at least 15 states have put their staff on furloughs, whereas others have cut pay, imposed layoffs, and even closed courtrooms. California closed individual courthouses and eliminated staff, including a reduction in 800 positions in the Los Angeles Superior Court alone over a three-year period (Ofgang, 2013). Florida imposed both layoffs and pay cuts (W. M. Welch, 2010). Courts do not control their own workloads because they must process the criminal cases brought to them by prosecutors and police, and they must address civil lawsuits filed by individuals and businesses (Massey, 2011). Budget cuts that reduce staff and the availability of court time can delay the processing of civil cases and lead to pressures to find ways to conclude criminal cases more quickly, such as prosecutors' decisions to dismiss minor charges or offer more-attractive plea agreements.

WHAT AMERICANS THINK

QUESTION: "I am going to read you a list of institutions in American society. Please tell me how much confidence you have in each one—a great deal, quite a lot, some, or very little?" Responded "a great deal" or "quite a lot."

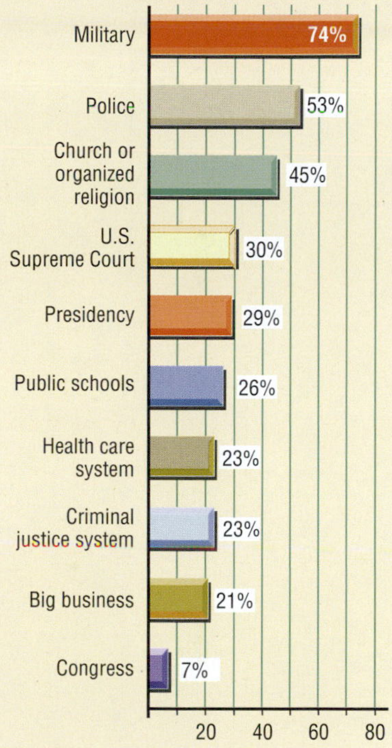

Source: Rebecca Riffkin, "Public Faith in Congress Falls Again, Hits Historic Low," Gallup Poll, June 19, 2014. www.gallup.com.

✓POINT

1. What is the dual court system?
2. What different categories of courts exist within each court system?
3. What does it mean for courts to be decentralized?
4. What are the main goals of advocates of judicial reform?

STOP AND ANALYZE: Will contemporary budget crises lead to greater centralization in state court systems? List three reasons that there may be resistance to centralization from officials who run city- and county-based systems.

(Answers are at the end of the chapter).

To Be a Judge

People tend to see judges as the most powerful actors in the criminal justice process. Their rulings and sentencing decisions influence the actions of police, defense attorneys, and prosecutors. If judges treat certain crimes lightly, for example, police and prosecutors may be less inclined to arrest and prosecute people who commit those offenses. Although judges are thought of primarily in connection with trials, they do some of their work—such as signing warrants, setting bail, arraigning defendants, accepting guilty pleas, and scheduling cases—outside the formal trial process.

More than any other person in the system, the judge is expected to embody justice, ensuring the defendant's right to due process and fair treatment. The prosecutor and the defense attorney each represent a "side" in a criminal case. By contrast, the judge's black robe and gavel are symbols of impartiality. Both inside and outside the courthouse, the judge is supposed to act according to a well-defined role. People expect judges to make careful, consistent decisions that uphold the ideal of equal justice for all citizens.

Who Becomes a Judge?

In U.S. society, the position of judge, even at the lowest level of the judicial hierarchy, carries a high status. Many lawyers take a significant cut in pay to assume a position on the bench. Public service, political power, and prestige in the community may matter more than wealth to those who aspire to the judiciary. The ability to control one's own work schedule is an additional attraction for lawyers interested in becoming judges. Unlike private practice attorneys, who often work over 50 hours per week preparing cases and counseling clients, judges can usually control their own working hours and schedules. Although judges face heavy caseloads, they frequently decide for themselves when to go home at the end of the workday.

Historically, the vast majority of judges have been white men with strong political connections. Women and members of minority groups had few opportunities to enter the legal profession prior to the 1960s and thus were seldom considered for judgeships. Although women judges have become more numerous, they still face challenges in running for election and being selected by a governor (M. S. Williams, 2006; Reid, 2004). In 2013, women comprised 29 percent of state judiciaries, including 34 percent of judges on state appellate courts, 27 percent on general jurisdiction trial courts, and 32 percent on limited jurisdiction courts (National Association of Women Judges, 2014).

In recent decades, political factors in many cities dictated that judges be drawn from specific racial, religious, and ethnic groups as political party leaders sought to gain the support of various segments of the voting public. Currently, 7 percent of state trial judges are African American, 4 percent are Latino, 2 percent are Asian or Pacific Islander in ancestry, and less than one-half of one percent are Native American (American Bar Association, 2010). This underrepresentation of ethnic diversity on the bench contrasts with the fact that the 2010 U.S. census showed the nation's population to be 12.6 percent African American, 16.3 percent Latino, 5.7 percent Asian or Pacific Islander, and 1 percent Native American plus an additional 3 percent of the population that labeled itself as belonging to two or more racial classifications (Humes, Jones, and Ramirez, 2011).

Comparing the racial and ethnic makeup of the judiciary with that of the defendants in urban courts raises many questions. Will people believe that decisions about guilt and punishment are being made in an unfair manner if

Like all judges, Judge Geraldine Hines of the Massachusetts Superior Court is expected to "embody justice," ensuring that the right to due process is respected and that defendants are treated fairly. What qualifications should someone possess in order to assume the important role and responsibilities of a judge?

middle-aged white men have nearly all the power to make judgments about people from other segments of society? Will people think that punishment is being imposed on behalf of a privileged segment of society rather than on behalf of the entire, diverse U.S. society?

Within these questions lurks an issue of American values. Americans often claim that equality, fairness, and equal opportunity are important values and, indeed, the equal protection clause in the Fourteenth Amendment of the Constitution demonstrates a formal commitment to use law to combat discrimination. However, the political connections and early career employment opportunities necessary to gain judgeships continue to disadvantage women and members of racial minority groups in many communities (Sen, 2014). Because judges symbolize the law as well as make important decisions about law, the lack of diversity in the judiciary provides a visible contrast with American values related to equal opportunity.

✓POINT

5. What is the image of the judge in the public's eye?
6. Why might it be important for judges to represent different segments of society?

STOP AND ANALYZE: If you were appointed to a special committee to create recommendations for ensuring that women and members of minority groups have equal opportunities to become judges—what would you propose? Present three recommendations.

Functions of the Judge

Although people usually think that the judge's job is to preside at trials, in reality, the work of most judges extends to all aspects of the judicial process. Defendants see a judge whenever decisions about their future are being made: when bail is set, pretrial motions are made, guilty pleas are accepted, a trial is conducted, a sentence is pronounced, and appeals are filed (see Figure 9.3). However, judges also perform administrative tasks outside the courtroom. Judges have three major roles: adjudicator, negotiator, and administrator.

FIGURE 9.3 ACTIONS OF A TRIAL COURT JUDGE IN PROCESSING A FELONY CASE

Throughout the process, the judge ensures that legal standards are upheld; he or she maintains courtroom decorum, protects the rights of the accused, meets the requirement of a speedy trial, and makes certain that case records are maintained properly.

Prearrest phase
Review requests for and issue or deny search and arrest warrants.

Initial appearance
Advise accused of constitutional rights; determine bail or pretrial release; decide if case should be dismissed.

Preliminary hearing
Evaluate prosecution and defense claims with regard to probable cause; decide whether evidence exists to hold accused for arraignment; rule on bail reduction request; continue to advise accused as to rights.

Arraignment
Evaluate indictment or information; advise defendant as to plea; ensure defendant understands impact of plea of guilty or *nolo contendere* ("no contest") with regard to waiver of some constitutional rights.

Pretrial
Rule on pretrial motions; answer requests for continuances.

Trial
Oversee jury selection; rule on evidence and other aspects of adversarial procedure; instruct jury as to legal rules affecting case; charge jury and receive report of deliberations; if nonjury trial, determine if guilty.

Sentence
Evaluate presentence report; hear opposing arguments of counsel with regard to sentence; impose sentence.

Adjudicator

Judges must assume a neutral stance in overseeing the contest between the prosecution and the defense. They must apply the law so that the rights of the accused are upheld in decisions about detention, plea, trial, and sentence. Judges have a certain amount of discretion in performing these tasks—for example, in setting bail—but they must do so according to the law. They must avoid any conduct that could appear biased.

Negotiator

Many decisions that determine the fates of defendants take place outside of public view in the judge's private chambers. These decisions are reached through negotiations between prosecutors and defense attorneys about plea bargains, sentencing, and bail conditions. Judges spend much of their time in their chambers talking with prosecutors and defense attorneys. They often encourage the parties to work out a guilty plea or agree to proceed in a certain way. The judge sometimes acts as a referee, keeping both sides on track in accordance with the law. Sometimes the judge takes a more active part in the negotiations, suggesting terms for an agreement or even pressuring one side to accept an agreement.

Administrator

A seldom-recognized function of most judges is managing the courthouse. In urban areas, professional court administrators rather than judges may actually direct the people who keep records, schedule cases, and do the many other jobs that keep a system functioning. But even then, judges remain in charge of their own courtroom and staff. In rural areas, where professional court administrators are not usually employed, the judge's administrative tasks may be more burdensome, and include responsibility for labor relations, budgeting, and maintenance of the courthouse building.

As administrators, all judges must deal with political actors such as county commissioners, legislators, and members of the state executive bureaucracy. For judges whose training as lawyers focused on courtroom advocacy skills, managing a complex organization with a sizable budget and many employees can pose a major challenge (C. E. Smith and Feldman, 2001).

Many observers argue that a fourth role of judges is emerging in some court systems. They see judges acting as "problem solvers" in newly developed courts that seek to address the problems of people arrested for drugs and other charges as an alternative to sending minor offenders to jail or prison. As discussed in the New Directions in Criminal Justice Policy feature, many states and cities have created specialized courts, such as **drug courts** to divert substance abusers away from incarceration. Drug users caught in possession of drugs or those charged with other lesser offenses may be required to appear in drug court regularly over the course of a year so that judges can monitor their progress with frequent drug tests, substance abuse counseling, and plans for education or employment (J. L. Nolan, 2010). If these individuals violate the conditions imposed by the judge for drug testing or counseling, then the judge can give them a regular criminal punishment, such as a jail sentence. Other jurisdictions have mental health courts to help mentally ill people who have been arrested for minor offenses (Cowell, Broner, and DuPont, 2004). Other kinds of specialized, problem-solving courts are also emerging, such as domestic violence courts, courts to handle homeless people's problems, and courts to help troubled veterans who commit minor offenses or have substance abuse issues (Melendez, 2014; Lee, 2013; J. L. Burns, 2010; Eaton and Kaufman, 2005).

drug courts
Specialized courts that impose drug testing and counseling requirements on substance abusers and monitor their progress instead of sending them immediately to jail or prison.

Because judges typically have no training in psychology or social work, critics worry that the development of a problem-solver role will lead judges to make decisions about matters for which they lack expertise. Moreover, some fear that this new role will cause judges to lose sight of their obligation to impose punishment on individuals who have violated criminal laws (J. Nolan, 2003).

How to Become a Judge

The quality of justice depends to a great extent on the quality of those who make decisions about guilt and punishment. Because judges have the power to deprive a citizen of his or her liberty through a prison sentence, judges should be thoughtful, fair, and impartial. The character, experience, and viewpoints of those selected for federal courts and state appellate courts are examined closely (Ringhand and Collins, 2011; S. Goldman and Slotnick, 1999). Trial judges in state criminal courts undergo less scrutiny. Ironically, these lower courts shape the public's image of a trial judge more than do other courts, because citizens have the most contact with judges there. When a judge is rude or hasty or allows the courtroom to become noisy and crowded, the public may lose confidence in the fairness and effectiveness of the criminal justice process. See the Close Up feature, "The Image of Justice," to consider the kinds of behavior by judges that can harm confidence in the courts. The "Question of Ethics" at the end of the chapter raises questions about the extent to which judges should be required to separate their outside activities from their role and identity as a judge.

NEW DIRECTIONS IN CRIMINAL JUSTICE POLICY

PROBLEM-SOLVING COURTS

In 1989, a judge in Miami began to emphasize treatment and intensive monitoring of low-level substance abusers as an alternative to incarceration. From these beginnings emerged drug courts and other specialized courts aimed at diverting troubled offenders from traditional criminal sanctions while also seeking to help them with their problems. As these courts spread to other jurisdictions, the federal government provided funding to encourage new developments and to evaluate the success of such programs. In addition, several other countries have begun to copy the problem-solving courts that originated in the United States and adapt them to their own issues and objectives.

Similar efforts began to surface in the first years of the twenty-first century as many cities also developed mental health courts (A. D. Redlich, Liu, et al., 2012). In these courts, judges placed mentally ill people arrested for minor offenses into treatment programs and employment training. Anchorage, Alaska, experimented with a court dedicated to the problems of veterans, some of whom were arrested regularly for drunkenness, substance abuse, and disorderly conduct. In addition to these courts that address minor criminal offenses, New York City developed a parallel court for civil matters that focuses on homelessness and attempts to prevent evictions, encourage employment opportunities, and solve disputes between tenants and landlords. As described by two observers, in these courts "judges are cheerleaders and social workers as much as jurists" (Eaton and Kaufman, 2005). Despite the positive intentions of such court programs, they raise questions about whether judges have sufficient training, knowledge, and resources to address individuals' significant personal problems.

Research shows that drug courts can have positive results in helping substance abusers and keeping them from going to jail. However, these programs do not always save money for the justice system, because they require funds to monitor, test, and provide services for troubled people. In addition, many people who could benefit from the programs do not gain access to the services and supervision that are available only to a limited number of offenders in certain communities due to the limited resources and availability of drug courts. Some other kinds of courts are too new to have been fully evaluated.

As discussed elsewhere in this chapter, critics wonder whether specialized courts place judges into a role of problem solver, a position for which they are not fully prepared. In addition, questions have arisen about whether these courts advance the interests of justice. Domestic violence courts, in particular, cause controversy. Some critics believe that they are too lenient on batterers by trying to solve their problems

CLOSE UP

THE IMAGE OF JUSTICE

The ethical rules for judges require them to speak and behave in ways that uphold the integrity, impartiality, and image of the courts. Unfortunately, these rules are broken with disappointing regularity in ways that attract public attention through newspaper articles about judges' improper statements and behavior. In the first few months of 2013 alone, a variety of examples emerged around the country in which judges were reprimanded for improper actions:

- Georgia: During a court proceeding, a judge told an attorney "Don't come back to this court" because the attorney had donated money to the election campaign of the judge's election opponent.
- Tennessee: A judge expressed the belief in court that one attorney was having a sexual relationship with another attorney.
- Minnesota: A judge joked about "women sleeping together" during jury selection after one juror noted that she had shared a hotel room with a defense attorney when they served as chaperones on a school trip for their children.
- Indiana: A judge said that it was inappropriate for taxpayers to pay for a sign language interpreter during a hearing concerning the custody of a deaf teenager, because one of the adults involved in the case had not paid taxes for several years.
- Oregon: A judge called a defendant a "piece of shit" who had no soul when sentencing the defendant for sexually abusing children.

rather than punishing them for committing acts of violence. Other critics contend that these courts favor alleged victims of domestic violence by pressuring the accused to accept anger-management treatment rather than letting the judicial processes take their course to determine whether the individual is actually guilty.

Veterans' courts, which first started in Buffalo, New York, in 2008 are subsequently spreading across the nation; they raise additional issues about how to handle issues of violence. These courts can help to facilitate the provision of mentors and treatment for those veterans who commit minor offenses while often struggling with issues of substance abuse, homelessness, unemployment, or psychological problems. There are debates, however, about whether such courts are appropriate settings to address issues of violence, such as intimate partner violence or other assaults that are regarded as connected to posttraumatic stress disorder or substance abuse. If such problems are related to reentering society after combat experience in a war zone, then many people are reluctant to see veterans incarcerated rather than helped with their problems. On the other hand, does diversion into treatment programs under veterans' court supervision leave family members and others in society inadequately protected against the risk of subsequent episodes of violence if treatment is not effective for a particular troubled veteran?

As these new courts develop, research is needed to determine precisely how they impact the roles of judges, the resources of the justice system, and the lives of both accused offenders and victims.

Sources: Bexar County Texas, Pretrial Services website, February 22, 2015 (http://gov.bexar.org); City of Denver, Pretrial Services website, February 22, 2015 (www.denver.org); John Gonzalez, "Bexar County to Crack Down on Second-Time DWI Offenders," *San Antonio Express-News* website, April 2, 2012 (www.mysanantonio.com); Paris Schutz, "Electronic Monitoring," WWTW-PBS news online, November 16, 2011 (http://chicagotonight.wttw.com); Kathleen Wilson, "Ventura County Expanding Electronic Monitoring of Jail Inmates," *Ventura County Star* online, November 1, 2011 (www.vcstar.com).

DEBATE THE ISSUE

Does electronic monitoring present an alternative to pretrial detention that can be used for poor people who are unable to make bail? If so, should this become a budget priority for local criminal justice systems? Is there a way to make this alternative available to homeless people and others who do not have stable family lives? Present three suggestions for how to use technology most effectively to avoid needless pretrial detention.

Do the statements reportedly made by these judges harm the image of the courts? If so, how? If these statements are improper, what should happen to judges who say such things? If the judges apologize, should they be forgiven and receive another opportunity to behave in a proper manner? Is there any way to make sure that judges always act according to the proper image of their judicial office?

Sources: Madeline Buckley, "Nemeth Reaches Pact," *South Bend Tribune,* January 8, 2013 (articles.southbendtribune.com); Lisa Coston, "Georgia State Judge Reprimanded and Suspended," *Courthouse News Service,* March 7, 2013 (www.courthousenews.com); Pat Pheifer, "Dakota County Judge Reprimanded for Inappropriate Jokes to Jurors," *Minneapolis Star Tribune,* March 29, 2013 (www.startribune.com); "Rhea County Judge Reprimanded for Comment, Language," *Times Free Press,* April 16, 2013 (www.timesfreepress.com); Sanne Specht, "Judge Sanctioned for Comments during Sentencing," *Ashland Daily Tidings,* February 9, 2013 (www.dailytidings.com).

DEBATE THE ISSUE

What is an appropriate sanction for a judge who speaks and acts inappropriately? Is it desirable to have such high standards that a judge would automatically be removed from office for improper conduct? List the punishments that you would impose on each of the five judges mentioned above. Assume that the misbehavior was by a judge who is selected through elections. Make an argument in favor of leaving it to the voters to pass judgment on the judge at the next election.

nonpartisan election
An election in which candidates' party affiliations are not listed on the ballot.

partisan election
An election in which candidates openly endorsed by political parties are presented to voters for selection.

adversarial system
Basis of the American legal system in which a passive judge and jury seek to find the truth by listening to opposing attorneys who vigorously advocate on behalf of their respective sides.

inquisitorial system
Basis of legal system in Europe in which the judge takes an active role in investigating the case and asking questions of witnesses in court.

Five methods are used to select state trial court judges: gubernatorial appointment, legislative selection, merit selection, **nonpartisan election**, and **partisan election**. Some states combine these methods; for example, in Pennsylvania a judge is initially elected by partisan election, but then at the end of the term there is a nonpartisan election (retention) for a second term. By contrast, federal judges are appointed by the president and confirmed by the U.S. Senate. Many of them are chosen as a result of their support for the president's political party and policy preferences (Epstein and Segal, 2007). Table 9.1 shows the method used in each of the states. All the methods bring up persistent concerns about the qualifications of those selected to serve as judges.

Selection by public voting occurs in more than half the states and has long been part of this nation's tradition. This method of judicial selection embodies the underlying American value of democracy, because it permits the citizens to control the choice of individuals who will be given the power to make decisions in civil and criminal cases. The fulfillment of this American value also helps to ensure that judges remain connected to the community and

TABLE 9.1 METHODS USED BY STATES TO SELECT JUDGES

States use different methods to select judges. Note that many judges are initially appointed to fill a vacancy, giving them an advantage if they must run for election at a later date.

PARTISAN ELECTION	NONPARTISAN ELECTION	GUBERNATORIAL APPOINTMENT	LEGISLATIVE SELECTION	MERIT SELECTION
Alabama	Arizona (some trial courts)	California (appellate)	South Carolina	Alaska
Illinois	Arkansas	Maine	Virginia	Arizona (appellate)
Indiana (trial)	California (trial)	Massachusetts (court of last resort)		Colorado
Louisiana	Florida (trial)	New Jersey		Connecticut
New Mexico	Georgia			Delaware
New York (trial)	Idaho			Florida (appellate)
Pennsylvania (initial)	Kentucky			Hawaii
Tennessee (trial)	Michigan			Indiana (appellate)
Texas	Minnesota			Iowa
West Virginia	Mississippi			Kansas
	Montana			Maryland
	Nevada			Massachusetts (trial, intermediate appellate)
	North Carolina			Missouri
	North Dakota			Nebraska
	Ohio			New Hampshire
	Oklahoma (trial)			New York (appellate)
	Oregon			Oklahoma (appellate)
	Pennsylvania (retention)			Rhode Island
	South Dakota (trial)			South Dakota (appellate)
	Washington			Tennessee (appellate)
	Wisconsin			Utah
				Vermont
				Wyoming

Source: American Judicature Society, *Judicial Selection in the States* (2012) (www.ajs.org).

demonstrate sensitivity to the community's priorities and concerns. The American value of democracy may, however, have detrimental consequences in the judiciary if it pressures judges to follow a community's prejudices rather than make independent decisions using their best judgment in each case (Canes-Wrone, Clark, and Park, 2012). Retired U.S. Supreme Court Justices Sandra Day O'Connor, David Souter, and John Paul Stevens have all criticized the use of elections to select judges because they believe it tarnishes both the image and the practice of judging to have judicial candidates solicit campaign contributions and make promises about their future decisions. In addition, voters are not well-positioned to evaluate the qualifications of judicial candidates. In O'Connor's view, judicial elections turn judges into "politicians in robes," when they should actually be neutral, knowledgeable, and committed to equal justice (J. Schwartz, 2009).

When lawyers are first elected to serve as judges, they obviously have no prior experience in deciding cases and supervising courthouse operations. Working as a lawyer differs a great deal from working as a judge, especially in the American **adversarial system**, in which lawyers serve as advocates for one party in each case. As a result, judges must "learn on the job." This method seems to counter the notion that judges are trained to "find the law" and apply neutral judgments (M. G. Hall, 1995). In Europe, by contrast, prospective judges receive special training in law school to become professional judges in what is called an **inquisitorial system**. These trained judges must serve as assistant judges and lower-court judges before they can become judges in general trial and appellate courts (Provine, 1996). Unlike American judges, these judges are expected to actively question witnesses during court proceedings.

Election campaigns for lower-court judgeships traditionally tended to be low-key contests marked by little controversy. Usually only a small portion of the voters participate, judgeships are not prominent on the ballot, and ethical considerations constrain candidates from discussing controversial issues. Research reveals, however, that even lower-level judicial races are becoming more competitive as candidates raise money and seek connections with interest groups (Brandenburg and Berg, 2012; Streb, Frederick, and LaFrance, 2007). In addition, a 2002 decision by the U.S. Supreme Court (*Republican Party of Minnesota v. White*) invalidated Minnesota's ethics rule that forbade judicial candidates from announcing their views on disputed legal or political issues (C. Gray, 2004). According to the Supreme Court, such rules violate candidates' First Amendment right to freedom of speech. The Court's decision also affects similar rules in other states. Thus, judicial elections might become as controversial and combative as elections for other public offices, as candidates attack each other and openly seek to attract voters to their announced positions on issues. Observers interested in preserving the integrity of courts worry that wide-open elections will ultimately diminish the image and effectiveness of judges, who may begin to look more and more like partisan politicians. On the other hand, if these electoral battles make voters more interested and involved in judicial elections, then perhaps there may be benefits for greater public attention and participation (M. Hall and Bonneau, 2013). Public opinion polls indicate that Americans are divided in their views about judges' honesty and ethics, and these divisions are based, in part, on race and income. It is unclear whether the perceived image of judges would improve if merit selection were more widespread (see "What Americans Think" for specific data).

Although the popular election of trial judges may be part of America's political heritage, until recently voters paid little attention to these elections. In many cities, judgeships are the fuel for the party machine. Because of the

WHAT AMERICANS THINK

QUESTION: "Please tell me how you would rate the honesty and ethical standards of people in these different fields—very high, high, average, low, or very low: Judges?"

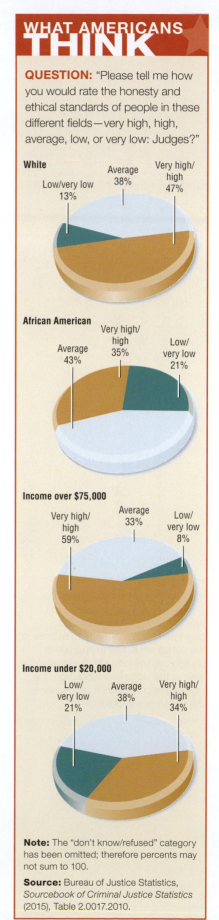

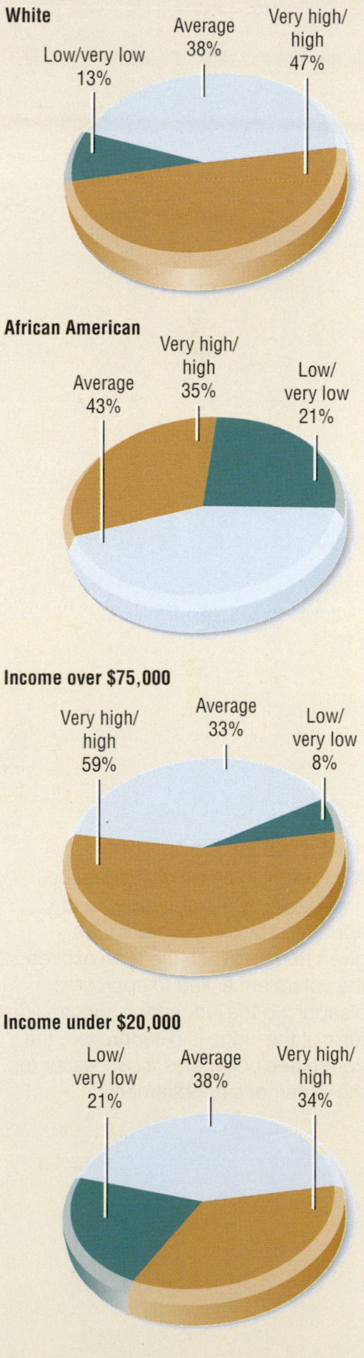

Note: The "don't know/refused" category has been omitted; therefore percents may not sum to 100.

Source: Bureau of Justice Statistics, *Sourcebook of Criminal Justice Statistics* (2015), Table 2.0017.2010.

honors and material rewards of a place on the bench, political parties get support—in the form of donated time and money—from attorneys seeking a judgeship. Parties also want judgeships to be elected posts, because they can then use courthouse staff positions to reward party loyalists. When a party member wins a judgeship, courthouse jobs may become available for campaign workers because the judge chooses clerks, bailiffs, and secretaries.

By contrast, elections for seats on state supreme courts frequently receive statewide media attention (M. Hall and Bonneau, 2013). Because of the importance of state supreme courts as policy-making institutions, political parties and interest groups often devote substantial resources to the election campaigns of their preferred candidates (Brandenburg and Berg, 2012; Bonneau, 2004). When organized interests contribute tens of thousands of dollars to judicial campaigns, questions sometimes arise about whether the successful candidates who received those contributions will favor the interests of their donors when they begin to decide court cases (Champagne and Cheek, 1996; Reid, 1996). There are also questions about the significance of out-of-state influence, such as when national interest groups contributed substantial amounts of money in 2010 to remove from office three justices on the Iowa Supreme Court who backed same-sex marriage (Mansker and Devins, 2011). As the U.S. Supreme Court has issued rulings that reduce restrictions on campaign spending by interest groups and political organizations, there has been an apparent increase in out-of-state groups spending money on advertising to influence judicial elections (Wolf, 2014).

Some states have tried to reduce the influence of political parties in the selection of judges while still allowing voters to select judges (Chertoff and Robinson, 2012). These states hold nonpartisan elections in which the ballot shows only the names of candidates, not their party affiliations. Nonetheless, political parties are often strongly involved in such elections. In Ohio, for example, the Republican and Democratic political parties hold their own primary elections to choose the judicial candidates whose names will go on the nonpartisan ballot for the general election (Felice and Kilwein, 1992). In other states, party organizations raise and spend money on behalf of candidates in nonpartisan elections. When candidates' party affiliations are not listed on the ballot, voters may not know which party is supporting which candidate. This occurs most often in low-visibility elections for local trial judgeships, which do not receive the same level of media attention as do elections for state supreme court seats.

merit selection
A reform plan by which judges are nominated by a commission and appointed by the governor for a given period. When the term expires, the voters are asked to approve or disapprove the judge for a succeeding term. If the judge is disapproved, the committee nominates a successor for the governor's appointment.

Merit selection, which combines appointment and election, was first used in Missouri in 1940 and has since spread to other states. When a judgeship becomes vacant, a nominating commission made up of citizens and attorneys evaluates potential appointees and sends the governor the names of three candidates, from which the replacement is chosen. After one year, a referendum is held to decide whether the judge will stay on the bench. The ballot asks, "Shall Judge X remain in office?" The judge who wins a majority vote serves out the term and can then be listed on the ballot at the next election.

Merit selection is designed to remove politics from the selection of judges and to allow the voters to unseat judges. However, studies have shown that voters in merit-selection states have removed relatively few judges (W. K. Hall and Aspin, 1987). Even so, interest groups sometimes seize the opportunity to mount publicity campaigns during retention elections in order to turn out judges with whom they disagree on a single issue or to open an important court seat so that a like-minded governor can appoint a sympathetic replacement. It may be difficult for judges to counteract a barrage of inflammatory television commercials focusing on a single issue such as capital punishment (Reid, 2000). If merit-selected judges feel intimidated by interest groups that might threaten their jobs at the next retention election, the independence of the judiciary will be diminished (Breslin, 2010).

Despite the support of bar associations, merit selection has not gone unchallenged. Although party politics may have been removed, some argue that it has been replaced by politics within the legal profession. Many lawyers see the system as favoring the selection of high-status attorneys with ties to corporations (Watson and Downing, 1969) or leading to the selection of judges whose values differ from the mainstream of society (Fitzpatrick, 2010).

In every selection system, critics contend that judges can accumulate too much power and remain beyond public accountability by being automatically reelected or reappointed when the public does not know enough about what judges have done in office. Read "Civic Engagement: Your Role in the System" to consider an approach to this issue. Remember that citizens can affect how the judicial branch is structured through their ability to vote on ballot issues or their ability to pressure their representatives in Congress and state legislatures to make new laws about how courts will operate.

CIVIC ENGAGEMENT

YOUR ROLE IN THE SYSTEM

Imagine that a ballot issue is placed before the voters that proposes limiting state appellate judges to no more than 10 years in office. *Make a list of arguments supporting and opposing this proposal.* How would you vote? Then see what Colorado voters did when faced with just such a proposal.

✓POINT

7. What are judges' main functions?
8. Why do political parties often prefer that judges be elected?
9. What are the steps in the merit-selection process?

STOP AND ANALYZE: What is the best way to select judges? List three arguments for the method that you favor. List three arguments against a method that you do not prefer.

From Arrest to Trial or Plea

At each stage of the pretrial process, key decisions are made that move some defendants to the next stage of the process and filter others out of the system. An innocent person could be arrested based on mistaken identification or misinterpreted evidence (Streib, 2010; C. R. Huff, 2002). However, pretrial processes are meant to force prosecutors and judges to review the available evidence and dismiss unnecessary or unjust charges. These processes are based on the American value of due process. Americans believe that people should be entitled to a series of hearings and other procedural steps in which their guilt is proven before they are subjected to punishments such as the loss of liberty through incarceration.

Although due process is an important value and is explicitly stated as a right in two different constitutional amendments, the Fifth and the Fourteenth, it can collide with Americans' interest in crime control if errors made by officials in carrying out these steps lead to the release of a guilty offender. For example, errors by judges in preliminary hearings or by police officers in lineups or other procedures can lead to the exclusion of evidence as a remedy for a rights violation. Thus, like other American values, due process can create results that undercut other priorities and objectives.

After arrest, the accused is booked at the police station. This process includes taking photographs and fingerprints, which form the basis of the case record. Usually the defendant must be taken to court for the initial appearance within 48 hours of a warrantless arrest. The purpose of this hearing is for the defendant to hear which charges are being pursued in light of the evidence gathered thus far, to be advised of his or her rights, and to be given the opportunity to post bail. Sometimes a separate bail hearing is scheduled shortly thereafter, especially when a case includes serious criminal charges. At the initial appearance, the judge also must make sure that probable cause exists to believe that a crime has been committed and that the accused should be

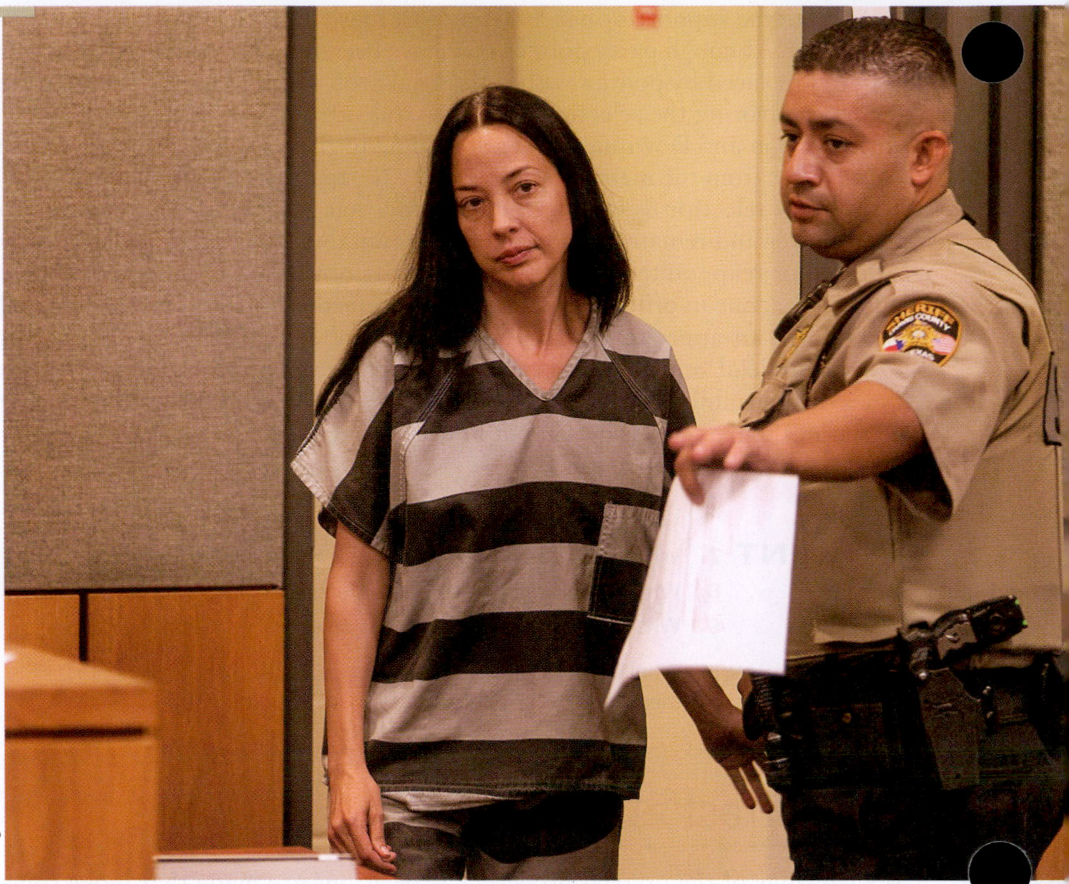

Criminal defendants typically make several court appearances as the judge makes decisions about evidence and the protection of each defendant's due process rights. Does the American system reduce the risk of error by using a multistep process to examine evidence, protect rights, and determine guilt?

AP Images/Rodolfo Gonzalez/Austin American-Statesman

prosecuted for the crime. Note that in the initial hearing for the Curtis Reeves case described in the chapter opener, the judge heard and rejected arguments from the defense attorney about dismissing charges.

If the police used an arrest warrant to take the suspect into custody, evidence has already been presented to a judge who believed that it was strong enough to support a finding of probable cause to proceed against the defendant. When an arrest is made without a warrant, the police must, at the initial appearance, present sufficient evidence to persuade the judge to continue the case against the defendant.

arraignment
The court appearance of an accused person in which the charges are read and the accused, advised by a lawyer, pleads guilty or not guilty.

Often, the first formal meeting between the prosecutor and the defendant's attorney is the **arraignment**: the formal court appearance in which the charges against the defendant are read and the defendant, advised by his or her lawyer, enters a plea of either guilty or not guilty. Most defendants will enter a plea of not guilty, even if they are likely to plead guilty at a later point. This is because, thus far, the prosecutor and defense attorney usually have had little chance to discuss a potential plea bargain. The more serious the charges, the more time the prosecutor and defense attorney will likely need to assess the strength of the other side's case. Only then can plea bargaining begin.

At the time of arraignment, prosecutors begin to evaluate the evidence. The lives of the defendants hinge on this screening process, because their fate depends largely on the prosecutor's discretion (K. Barnes, Sloss, and Thaman, 2009; C. W. Barnes and Kingsnorth, 1996). If the prosecutor believes the case against the defendant is weak, the charges may simply be dropped. Prosecutors do not wish to waste their limited time and resources on cases that will not stand up in court. A prosecutor may also drop charges if the alleged crime is minor, if the defendant is a first offender, or if the prosecutor believes that the few days spent in jail before arraignment are enough punishment for the alleged offense. Jail overcrowding or the need to work on more-serious cases can also influence the decision to drop charges. At times, the prosecutors making these decisions might discriminate against the accused because of race, wealth, or some other factor (Schlesinger, 2013); or they might discriminate against certain victims, such as women who are sexually assaulted by an intimate partner or other acquaintance as opposed to being victimized by a stranger (Spohn and Holleran, 2001). As cases move through the system, prosecutors' decisions to reduce charges for some defendants greatly affect the punishment eventually applied (Lippke, 2010; J. L. Miller and Sloan, 1994). Thus, individual prosecutors play a major role in deciding which defendants will receive criminal punishment (Covey, 2011).

As Figure 9.4 shows, prosecutors use their decision-making power to filter many cases out of the system. The 100 cases illustrated are typical felony cases. The percentage of cases varies from city to city, depending on such factors as the effectiveness of police investigations and prosecutors' policies about which cases to pursue. For example, nearly half of those arrested did not ultimately face felony prosecutions. A small number of defendants were steered toward diversion programs. A larger number had their cases dismissed for various reasons including lack of evidence, the minor nature of the charges, or first-time-offender status. Other cases were dismissed by the courts because the police and prosecutors did not present enough evidence to a grand jury or at a preliminary hearing to justify moving forward.

The proportion of cases dropped at the various stages of the pretrial process varies from city to city. In some cities, many cases are dropped before charges are filed. Prosecutors evaluate the facts and evidence and decide which cases are strong enough to carry forward. The others are quickly dismissed. In other cities, formal charges are filed almost automatically on the basis of police reports, but many cases are dismissed when the prosecutor takes the time to examine each defendant's situation closely.

During the pretrial process, defendants are exposed to the informal, assembly-line atmosphere of the lower criminal courts. Often, decisions are quickly made about bail, arraignment, pleas, and the disposition of cases. Moving

FIGURE 9.4 TYPICAL OUTCOMES OF 100 URBAN FELONY CASES

Prosecutors and judges make crucial decisions during the period before trial or plea. Once cases are bound over for disposition, guilty pleas are many, trials are few, and acquittals are rare.

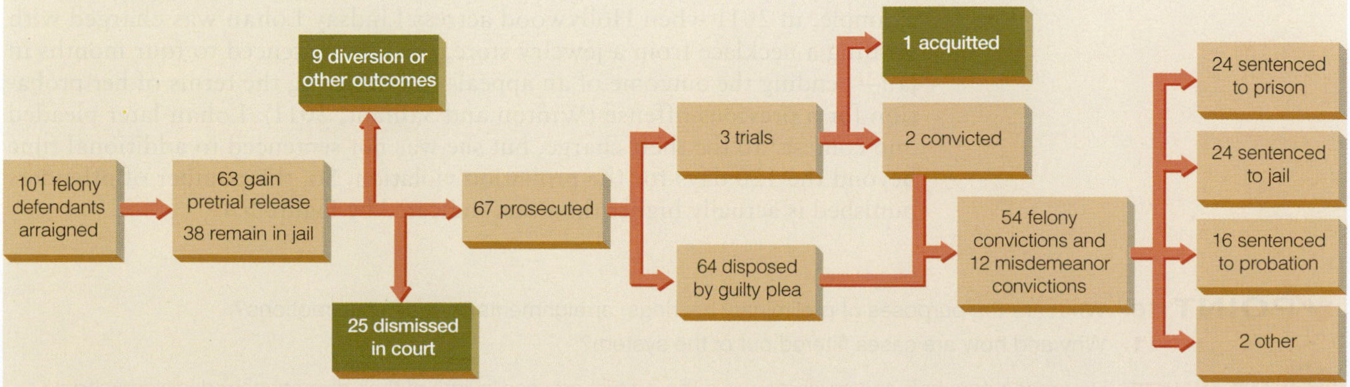

Source: Calculated from data in Brian A. Reeves, "Felony Defendants in Large Urban Counties, 2009—Statistical Tables," Bureau of Justice Statistics Statistical Tables, December 2013, NCJ 228944.

cases as quickly as possible seems to be the main goal of many judges and attorneys during the pretrial process. Courts throughout the nation face pressures to limit the number of cases going to trial. These pressures may affect the decisions of both judges and prosecutors as well as the defense attorneys who seek to maintain good relationships with them. American courts often have too little money, too few staff members, and not enough time to give detailed attention to each case, let alone a full trial.

motion
An application to a court requesting that an order be issued to bring about a specified action.

In American courts, the defense uses the pretrial period to its own advantage. Preliminary hearings provide an opportunity for defense attorneys to challenge the prosecution's evidence and make **motions** to the court requesting that an order be issued to bring about a specified action. Through pretrial motions, the defense may try to suppress evidence or learn about the prosecutor's case. The defense attorney making the motion must be able to support the claim being made about improper procedures used in the arrest, the insufficiency of the evidence, or the need for exclusion of evidence. Prosecutors also make motions, especially if they have disagreements with the defense about whether and how defense witnesses will be questioned. Judges may decide motions based on the written arguments submitted by each side, or they may schedule a motion hearing that will permit each attorney to present arguments about whether the motion should be granted. Decisions on motions can significantly affect the outcome of a case, especially if the motion hearing determines whether key pieces of evidence can be used in court against the defendant. In the Curtis Reeves case described in the chapter opener, the judge had been informed by the defense attorney that motions might be filed prior to trial, so the judge specifically scheduled pretrial hearings for motions when setting out the schedule of hearings prior to the planned trial date.

The large number of cases dismissed during pretrial proceedings need not be viewed as a sign of weakness in the system. Instead, one strength of the system is the power of prosecutors and judges to dismiss charges when a conviction would be either unfair or unlikely. A close look at Figure 9.4 shows that the offenses that a prosecutor decides to pursue have a high rate of conviction. Out of 67 typical cases carried forward, 64 will end with a guilty plea and two of the three defendants who had full trials will be convicted. These examples make it clear that the criminal justice system is effective in producing convictions when a prosecutor, with sufficient evidence, pursues a felony prosecution. In addition, recent research indicates that some of the people whose cases were dismissed will actually receive punishment. In the case of repeat offenders, prosecutors may dismiss criminal charges in favor of probation violation charges that lead the offender to serve time in jail or prison despite not being convicted of a new crime (Kingsnorth, MacIntosh, and Sutherland, 2002). For example, in 2011 when Hollywood actress Lindsay Lohan was charged with stealing a necklace from a jewelry store, she was sentenced to four months in jail—pending the outcome of an appeal—for violating the terms of her probation for a previous offense (Winton and Saillant, 2011). Lohan later pleaded "no contest" to the theft charge, but she was not sentenced to additional time beyond the 120 days for the probation violation. So, the number of offenders punished is actually higher than that indicated by Figure 9.4.

✔POINT

10. What are the purposes of preliminary hearings, arraignments, and defense motions?

11. Why and how are cases filtered out of the system?

STOP AND ANALYZE: Do prosecutors hold too much power in the pretrial process in light of their discretionary decisions about charging and plea bargaining? List two risks and two benefits from giving prosecutors significant authority over decisions in the pretrial process.

Bail: Pretrial Release

It is often stated that defendants are presumed innocent until proved guilty or until they enter a guilty plea. However, people who are arrested are taken to jail. They are deprived of their freedom and, in many cases, subjected to miserable living conditions while they await the processing of their cases. The idea that people who are presumed innocent can lose their freedom—sometimes for many months—as their cases work their way toward trial clashes with the American values of freedom and liberty. Moreover, research indicates that people unable to gain release on bail are at risk of ultimately receiving more severe sentences upon conviction (Oleson, Van Nostrand, et al., 2014). Such effects might be the result of several factors. For example, people held in jail are less able to help their attorneys prepare the case for plea bargaining or trial, or judges may unknowingly think about and treat differently defendants brought to hearings in jail jumpsuits as compared to those who arrive dressed up and in the company of friends and family.

On the other hand, government officials also feel an obligation to protect society from harm. A conflict is bound to occur between the American value of individual liberty and the need to keep some criminal suspects in jail in order to protect society from people who are violent or who may try to escape prosecution. Some suspects who are considered a threat to public safety could be held in pretrial detention without causing most Americans to believe that the values of freedom and liberty have been compromised. However, not every person who is charged with a criminal offense need be detained. Thus, bail and other methods of releasing defendants are used on the condition that the accused will appear in court as required.

Bail is a sum of money or property, specified by the judge, that the defendant must present to the court in order to gain pretrial release. The bail will be forfeited if the defendant does not appear in court as scheduled. Although people are generally entitled to a bail hearing as part of their right to due process, there is no constitutional right to release on bail, nor even a right to have the court set an amount as the condition of release. The Eighth Amendment to the U.S. Constitution forbids excessive bail, and state bail laws are usually designed to prevent discrimination in setting bail. They do not guarantee, however, that all defendants will have a realistic chance of being released before trial. A study in New York City found that among 19,137 cases for which bail was set at $1,000 or less, 87 percent of those defendants could not post bail and they remained in jail for an average of 16 days while their cases were processed (Secret, 2010). Such statistics about the risk of pretrial detention for large numbers of poor people raise the possibility that such defendants may feel pressured to plead guilty, whether or not they are in fact guilty, simply to obtain a sentence of probation for minor offenses and thereby more quickly regain their freedom.

bail
An amount of money specified by a judge to be paid as a condition of pretrial release to ensure that the accused will appear in court as required.

Because the accused is presumed to be innocent, bail should not be used as punishment. The amount of bail should therefore be high enough to ensure that the defendant appears in court for trial—but no higher. But this is not the only purpose of bail. The community must be protected from further crimes that some defendants might commit while out on bail. Except in the recent cases of suspected terrorists, criminal suspects are entitled to a hearing before they are denied bail or bail is set at such a high level that they are certain to be kept in jail despite the fact that they have not yet been convicted. Congress and some of the states have passed laws that permit preventive detention of defendants when the judge concludes that they pose a threat to others or to the community while awaiting trial.

The Reality of the Bail System

The reality of the bail system is far from the ideal. The question of bail may arise at the police station, at the initial court appearance in a misdemeanor case, or at the arraignment in most felony cases. For minor offenses, police officers may have a standard list of bail amounts. For serious offenses, a judge sets bail in court after hearing a recommendation from the prosecutor. In both cases, those setting bail may have discretion to set differing bail amounts for different suspects, depending on the circumstances of each case. The speed of decision making and lack of information available at the moment of setting bail can enhance differential treatment. As described by the prosecutor in Staten Island, one of the boroughs of New York City, "We have an assistant prosecutor who in about 30 seconds has to come up with a dollar figure that that young person believes is adequate [as an amount for bail]. . . . We don't get to interview the defendant; we have to make a determination without substantiating any of the information before us" (Secret, 2010).

In almost all courts, the amount of bail is based mainly on the judge's view of the seriousness of the crime and of the defendant's record. In part, this emphasis results from a lack of information about the accused. Because bail is typically determined 24 to 48 hours after an arrest, there is little time to conduct a more thorough assessment. As a result, judges in many communities have developed standard rates: so many dollars for such-and-such an offense. In some cases, a judge may set a high bail if the police or prosecutor want a certain person to be kept off the streets.

Critics of the bail system argue that it discriminates against poor people. Imagine that you have been arrested and have no money. Should you be denied a chance for freedom before trial just because you are poor? What if you have a little money, but if you use it to post bail you will not have any left to hire your own attorney? Professional criminals and the affluent have no trouble making bail; many drug dealers, for instance, can readily make bail and go on dealing while awaiting trial. In contrast, a poor person arrested for a minor violation may spend the pretrial period in jail. Should dangerous, wealthy offenders be allowed out on bail while nonviolent, poor suspects remain locked up?

The problems for poor defendants are compounded by the lack of a constitutional right to representation by an attorney at bail hearings (Gerstein, 2013). Defendants who cannot afford to hire an attorney may have no one to make arguments on their behalf at the bail hearing. Thus, the prosecutor's arguments in favor of a high bail or a denial of bail may be the only effective arguments presented to the judge. For many poor defendants, bail is set before an attorney has been appointed to represent them in the preparation of their defense. A lawsuit was filed against a county in Mississippi in 2014 because poor arrestees were spending months in jail, unable to make bail and never receiving the services of a defense attorney, and sometimes without ever being formally charged with a crime (Robertson, 2014).

According to a study of felony defendants in the nation's most populous counties, 62 percent were released before disposition of their cases, 34 percent could not make bail, and 4 percent were detained without bail (B. Reaves, 2013). Figure 9.5 shows the average amounts of bail set for various types of felony offenses. Those who cannot make bail must remain in jail awaiting trial, unless they can obtain enough money to pay a bail agent's fee. Given the length of time between arraignment and trial in most courts and the hardships of pretrial detention, defendants in many cities depend on bail agents. In 2009, there were 17,198 felony suspects in the 75 largest counties who could not make bail or use the services of a bail agent to gain release (B. Reaves, 2013). Far larger numbers of people lose their liberty when one adds the number of arrestees who cannot pay even small bail amounts when arrested for misdemeanor offenses.

FIGURE 9.5 MEDIAN BAIL AMOUNTS FOR FELONY DEFENDANTS BY OFFENSE TYPE

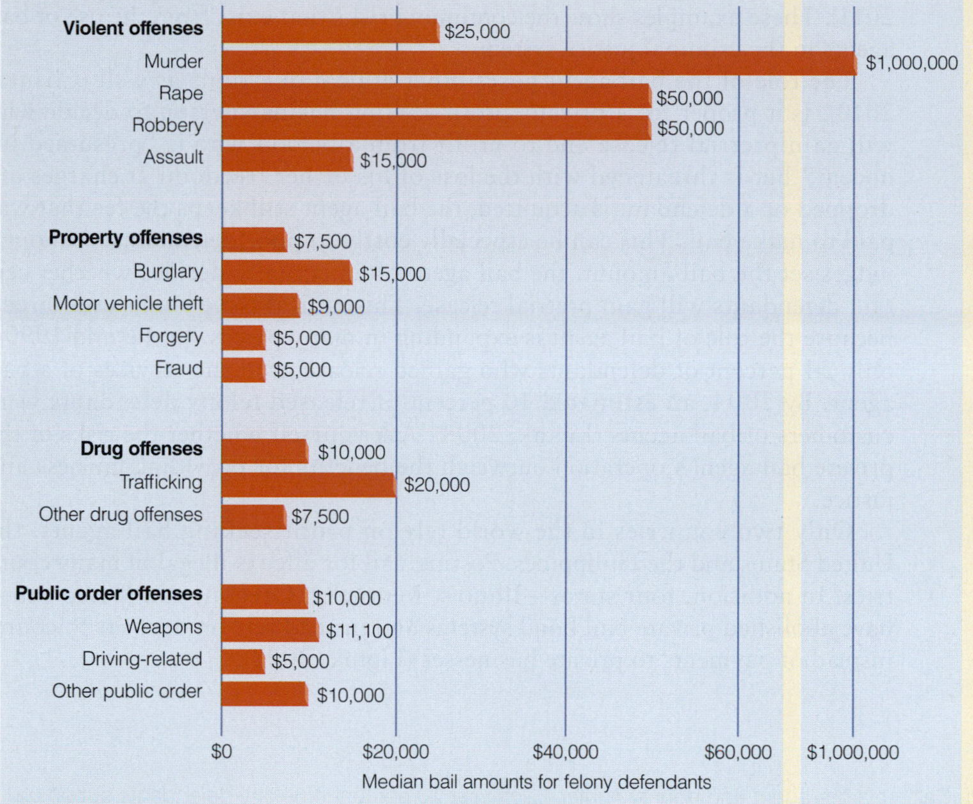

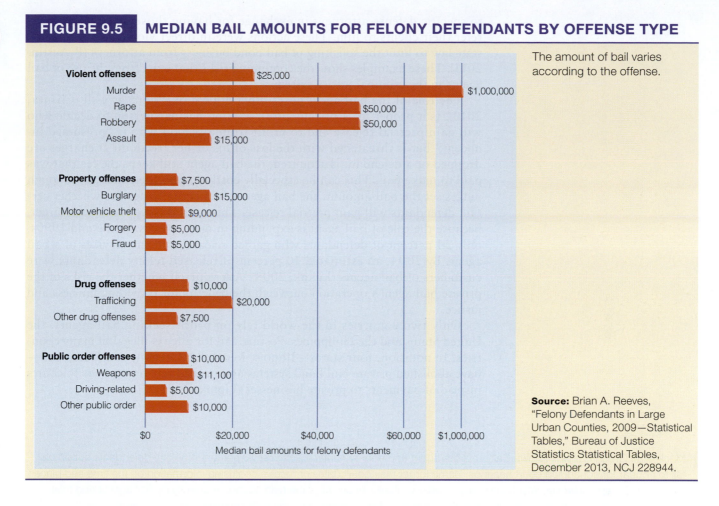

The amount of bail varies according to the offense.

Source: Brian A. Reeves, "Felony Defendants in Large Urban Counties, 2009—Statistical Tables," Bureau of Justice Statistics Statistical Tables, December 2013, NCJ 228944.

Bail Agents

The bail agent, also called a bail bondsman, is a key figure in the bail process. Bail agents are private businesspeople who loan money to defendants who lack the money to make bail. They are licensed by the state and choose their own clients. In exchange for a fee, which may be 5 to 10 percent of the bail amount, the bondsman will put up the money (or property) to gain the defendant's release. Again, bail agents are not obliged to provide bail money for every defendant who seeks to use their services. Instead, they decide which defendants are likely to return for court appearances. If the defendant skips town, the bail agent's money is forfeited.

Bail agents may build relationships with police officers and jailers to obtain referrals. Many defendants may not know whom to call for help in making bail, and officers can steer them to a particular bondsman. This can lead to corruption, if a bail agent pays a jailer or police officer to make such referrals. Moreover, these relationships can lead to improper cooperation, such as a bail agent refusing to help a particular defendant if the police would like to see that defendant remain in jail. A bail agent in Brownsville, Texas, for example, was sentenced to serve time in federal prison in 2012 after bribing a state judge to reduce an accused drug trafficker's bail (Brezosky, 2012). Similarly, a bail agent in Portsmouth, Virginia, went to prison in 2012 for paying bribes to a judge and an employee of the sheriff's department for referring defendants to him as bail bond clients (FBI Press Release, 2012). In 2011, a bail agent in California went to jail for one year after admitting that he referred clients to specific defense attorneys in exchange for having those defense attorneys refer their clients to him. These actions were in direct violation of a specific state law to limit the soliciting of bail bond business from attorneys (P. Austin, 2011). These examples show the continuing risks that exist from the use of bail agents in the criminal justice system.

The role of the bail agent poses other ethical questions as well (Clisura, 2010). Is it proper for a private, profit-seeking businessperson to decide who will gain pretrial release and to profit from a person who is "presumed innocent" but is threatened with the loss of his or her freedom? If charges are dropped or a defendant is acquitted, the bail agent still keeps the fee that was paid to make bail. This can be especially costly to poor defendants. Although judges set the bail amount, the bail agent often actually decides whether certain defendants will gain pretrial release. This ethical issue looms ever larger, because the role of bail agent is expanding in many places. In the mid-1990s, only 24 percent of defendants who gained release used the services of a bail agent. By 2004, an estimated 40 percent of released felony defendants were customers of bail agents (Liptak, 2008). Ask yourself whether the risks of the private bail agent's operation outweigh the benefits for providing fairness and justice.

Only two countries in the world rely on profit-seeking bail agents, the United States and the Philippines. Posting bail for a fee is illegal in many countries. In addition, four states—Illinois, Kentucky, Oregon, and Wisconsin—have abolished private bail bond systems and instead rely on deposits to courts instead of payments to private businesses (Liptak, 2008).

Mackenzie Green is a well-known California bail agent and bounty hunter. Each year 20 percent of felony defendants out on bail fail to appear for scheduled court hearings. Some forget their court dates or receive confusing information on the time and place to appear. Others, however, intentionally skip town. Eventually, nearly all of them are found, frequently by bail agents and their employees. Should such profit-seeking, private businesses be so deeply involved in the criminal justice process?

Left: Courtesy of Thane Plambeck; Right: Courtesy of Mackenzie Green

Despite the problems posed by their role, bail agents may benefit the criminal justice system. Although bail agents act in their own interest, they can contribute to the smooth processing of cases. For example, defendants who fail to appear for scheduled court appearances often do so because of forgetfulness and confusion about when and where they must appear. Courthouses in large cities are huge bureaucracies in which changes in the times and locations of hearings are not always communicated to defendants. Bail agents can help by reminding defendants about court dates, calling defendants' relatives to make sure that the defendant will arrive on time, and warning defendants about the penalties for failing to appear. Indeed, some officials in states that have done away with commercial bail bonds say that they have seen increases in failure-to-appear cases (Liptak, 2008).

Bounty hunters or bail-enforcement agents hired by bail agents find many of the defendants who have skipped out on bail. These independent operators have caused many problems. In highly publicized cases, bounty hunters have broken into the wrong homes, kidnapped innocent people mistaken for wanted criminals, and even shot and killed innocent bystanders (Drimmer, 1997; Liptak, 2008). Bounty hunters' disregard for people's rights and public safety has led to calls for new laws to regulate the activities of bail agents and the people they hire to hunt for fugitives. Consider the potential problems that can be caused by bounty hunters as you read "Civic Engagement: Your Role in the System."

The justice system may benefit in some ways from the activities of bail agents. However, court and law enforcement officials could provide the same benefits as well or better if they had the resources, time, and interest to make sure that released defendants return to court (VanNostrand, 2010). If all courts had pretrial services officers, such as those in the federal courts, defendants could be evaluated, monitored, and reminded to return to court without the risks of discrimination and corruption associated with the use of bail agents (Cooprider, 2014; J. G. Carr, 1993). Data collected by the U.S. Office of Probation and Pretrial Services, which handles the processing and monitoring of defendants released on bail by the federal courts, indicate that pretrial services activities produce low levels of failure-to-appear and rearrest while contributing to a significant decline in the use of bail agents in federal courts (Cadigan, 2007).

CIVIC ENGAGEMENT

YOUR ROLE IN THE SYSTEM

Imagine that a candidate for state legislature runs by claiming that she will propose a law to ban bounty hunters from taking people into custody, even when those people have skipped out on bail. *Make a list of the benefits and risks from such a proposed law.* Would you support the law? Then look at a news article that raises questions about how bounty hunters operate.

Setting Bail

When the police set bail at the station house for minor offenses, they usually use a standard amount for a particular charge. By contrast, when a judge sets bail, the amount of bail and conditions of release stem from interactions among the judge, prosecutor, and defense attorney, who discuss the defendant's personal qualities and prior record. The prosecutor may stress the seriousness of the crime, the defendant's record, and negative personal characteristics. The defense attorney, if one has been hired or appointed at this point, may stress the defendant's good job, family responsibilities, and status in the community. Like other aspects of bail, these factors may favor affluent defendants over the poor, the unemployed, or people with unstable families and thus be a basis for discrimination in the justice system (M. Johnson and Johnson, 2012). Yet many of these factors provide no clear information about how dangerous a defendant is or whether he or she is likely to appear in court. Moreover, judges may not have accurate information about these factors if pretrial services officers at the court do not carefully investigate the background and circumstances of each defendant (Marsh, 2001).

Research highlights the disadvantages of the poor in the bail process (Clisura, 2010). For example, a recent study in New Jersey found that the odds of having to produce money or property for bail, as opposed to being released on a promise to appear in court, were 63 percent higher for Hispanics and 65 percent higher for African American defendants than for white defendants. In addition, Hispanic and African American defendants were required to pay higher bail amounts than whites, even when charged with comparable offenses (Kazemian, McCoy, and Sacks, 2013). A study in Nebraska found an impact from gender as well as race and ethnicity. It found that "white females had a bail amount set that was substantially less than that of their white male counterparts," and "[n]on-white males, on the other hand, had a higher bail amount set than the white males" (K. B. Turner and Johnson, 2006: 61).

Some claim that bail setting should be guided by six principles:

1. The accused is entitled to release on his or her own recognizance.
2. Nonfinancial alternatives to bail will be used when possible.
3. The accused will receive a full and fair hearing.
4. Reasons will be stated for the decision.
5. Clear and convincing evidence will be offered to support a decision.
6. There will be a prompt and automatic review of all bail determinations.

Many people argue that these principles would hamper the ability of the justice system to deal with offenders and protect society. Others counter that personal freedom is so precious that failure to allow a person every opportunity to gain release creates an even greater injustice.

✔POINT

12. What factors affect whether bail is set and how much money or property a defendant must provide to gain pretrial release?

13. What positive and negative effects does the bail agent have on the justice system?

STOP AND ANALYZE: In light of the criticisms and problems with the bail system, how might it be improved? Give three suggestions for improving the system in ways that will both increase fairness and protect public safety.

Reforming the Bail System

Studies of pretrial detention in such cities as Philadelphia and New York have raised questions about the need to hold defendants in jail. Criticisms of the bail system focus on judges' discretion in setting bail amounts, the fact that the poor are deprived of their freedom whereas the affluent can afford bail, the negative aspects of bail agents, and jail conditions for those detained while awaiting trial. To address such criticisms, people have attempted for many years to reform the bail system. Such efforts have led to changes in the number of defendants held in jail. A recent survey found that 62 percent of felony suspects in the 75 most populous counties were released before disposition of their cases. Only 4 percent were denied bail (B. Reaves, 2013). The increase in defendants released on bail has occurred, in part, because of the use of certain pretrial release methods (see Table 9.2).

Citation

What people often call a ticket is more formally known as a **citation**. It is often issued to a person accused of committing a traffic offense or some other minor violation. Depending on the nature of the offense, the citation written out by the officer can also include a summons requiring an appearance in court.

citation
A written order or summons, issued by a law enforcement officer, often directing an alleged offender to appear in court at a specified time to answer a criminal charge.

TABLE 9.2 PRETRIAL RELEASE METHODS

FINANCIAL BOND	ALTERNATIVE RELEASE OPTIONS
Fully secured bail. The defendant posts the full amount of bail with the court.	*Release on recognizance (ROR).* The court releases the defendant on his or her promise to appear in court as required.
Privately secured bail. A bail agent signs a promissory note to the court for the bail amount and charges the defendant a fee for the service (usually 10 percent of the bail amount). If the defendant fails to appear, the bail agent must pay the court the full amount. The bail agent frequently requires the defendant to post collateral in addition to the fee.	*Conditional release.* The court releases the defendant subject to his or her following specific conditions set by the court, such as attendance at drug treatment therapy or staying away from the complaining witness.
Percentage bail. The courts allow the defendant to deposit a percentage (usually 10 percent) of the full bail with the court. The full amount of the bail is required if the defendant fails to appear. The percentage bail is returned after disposition of the case, although the court often retains 1 percent for administrative costs.	*Third-party custody.* The defendant is released into the custody of an individual or agency that promises to ensure his or her appearance in court. No monetary transactions are involved in this type of release.
Unsecured bail. The defendant pays no money to the court but is liable for the full amount of bail should she or he fail to appear.	

Source: Bureau of Justice Statistics, *Report to the Nation on Crime and Justice,* 2nd ed. (Washington, DC: U.S. Government Printing Office, 1988), 76.

By issuing the citation, the officer avoids taking the accused person to the station house for booking and to court for arraignment and setting of bail. Citations are now being used for more-serious offenses, in part because the police want to reduce the amount of time they spend booking minor offenders and waiting in arraignment court for their cases to come up.

Release on Recognizance

Pioneered in the 1960s by the Vera Institute of Justice in New York City, the **release on recognizance (ROR)** approach is based on the assumption that judges will grant releases if the defendant is reliable and has roots in the community. Soon after the arrest, court personnel talk to defendants about their job, family, prior record, and associations (K. Kim and Denver, 2011). They then decide whether to recommend release.

release on recognizance (ROR)
Pretrial release granted on the defendant's promise to appear in court, because the judge believes that the defendant's ties in the community guarantee that he or she will appear.

In the first three years of the Vera Institute of Justice's classic experiment, more than 10,000 defendants were interviewed and about 3,500 were released. Only 1.5 percent failed to appear in court at the scheduled time, a rate almost 3 times better than the rate for those released on bail (Goldfarb, 1965). Programs in other cities have had similar results, although Sheila Maxwell's research raises questions about whether women and property-crime defendants on ROR are less likely than other defendants to appear in court (S. R. Maxwell, 1999).

Ten Percent Cash Bail

Although ROR is a useful alternative to bail, not all defendants should be released on their own recognizance. Illinois, Kentucky, Nebraska, Oregon, and Pennsylvania have started bail programs in which the defendants deposit 10 percent of their bail in cash with the court. When they appear in court as required, 90 percent of this amount is returned to them. Begun in Illinois in 1964, this plan is designed to release as many eligible defendants as possible without using bail agents.

Bail Fund

An innovative program developed in New York City in 2009 is called the Bronx Freedom Fund. Poor defendants who are represented by the Bronx Defenders can receive loans from the fund in order to post bail and gain pretrial release (Clisura, 2010). The fund was created in order to prevent poor defendants from languishing in jail merely because they cannot pay a relatively small amount of money. Those freed on bail are monitored and assisted through the relationship between the fund and the defense attorneys. The organization's website claims that 93 percent of defendants assisted by the fund returned for their court appearances. In other locations, churches and other organizations have sometimes engaged in parallel activities by loaning money for bail. However, such programs are probably most effective when the loans are tied to contact, assistance, and supervision with people, such as counselors or defense attorneys, who remind defendants about court dates and otherwise help them to avoid violating conditions of bail.

Bail Guidelines

To deal with the problem of unequal treatment, reformers have written guidelines for setting bail. The guidelines specify the standards judges should use in setting bail and also list appropriate amounts. Judges are expected to follow the guidelines but deviate from them in special situations. The guidelines take into account the seriousness of the offense and the defendant's prior record, in order to protect the community and ensure that released offenders can be trusted to return for court appearances.

TECHNOLOGY & CRIMINAL JUSTICE

TECHNOLOGY AND PRETRIAL RELEASE

In 2011, the U.S. Supreme Court upheld a lower-court decision that ordered California to significantly reduce its prison population, largely because the state was unable to provide proper medical and mental health care for such a large number of prisoners (*Brown v. Plata*, 2011). The plan developed by California to reduce the population of its overcrowded prisons included an initiative to place nonviolent offenders in county jails to serve any sentences of three years or less. By increasing the number of convicted offenders slated to be housed in county jails, sheriffs found themselves considering how their facilities could be sure to have enough space for these offenders. Thus new efforts emerged for considering how counties might reduce the number of pretrial detainees. These efforts included a recognition that jails could use technology to monitor people awaiting trial without actually confining them inside jails.

Ventura County, California, for example, had previously only used electronic monitoring as a basis for releasing detainees with medical conditions that would pose challenges for jail officials. As a result, the sheriff's office developed criteria for identifying detainees who would be eligible for pretrial release with ankle monitors containing Global Positioning Systems that would show their locations at all times. Arrestees charged with using guns in their crimes and those facing the most serious charges were ineligible for the program. However, other places may include those charged with violent crimes within monitoring programs when technology is used in conjunction with other strict conditions, as was done with Curtis Reeves in the chapter opener's description of the Florida homicide case.

Prior to California counties focusing on electronic monitoring as an alternative to jail for pretrial detainees, Chicago had already proceeded with the use of such technology as a means to save money for the county and avoid jail overcrowding. It cost the county $143 per day to hold someone in jail but only $65 to use electronic monitoring as a form of home surveillance. The use of electronic monitoring also enabled nonviolent arrestees to maintain employment in order to support their families while they waited for their cases to be processed through the court system. Chicago's program primarily focused on nonviolent drug offenders, and initial evaluations found that only 3 percent of arrestees escaped from the ankle monitor or committed a new crime while on electronic monitoring.

In Denver and San Antonio, the forms of electronic monitoring of arrestees on pretrial release were not limited to GPS monitoring to ensure that they remained at home, traveled solely between work and home, and otherwise avoided "excluded areas" that can be programmed into GPS systems. These cities use Secure Continuous Remote Alcohol Monitoring (SCRAM), an ankle monitor for drunk-driving arrestees that

Read the Technology and Criminal Justice feature to consider how electronic monitoring can be used as an alternative to pretrial detention or in conjunction with other conditions of bail release.

Preventive Detention

Reforms have been suggested not only by those concerned with unfairness in the bail system but also by those concerned with stopping crime (J. S. Goldkamp, 1985). Critics of the bail system point to a link between release on bail and the commission of crimes, arguing that the accused may commit other crimes while awaiting trial. A study of the nation's most populous counties found that 16 percent of felony defendants released on bail were rearrested for another crime (B. Reaves, 2013). Sometimes these new arrests can arouse public concern by conveying the impression that the bail system is too lax, as when a man in Detroit was released on $10,000 bail in 2014 after being charged with attempted murder. When released from jail, the defendant went to original victim's house and shot him in the chest (Hunter, 2014). To address this problem, legislatures have passed laws permitting detention of defendants without bail.

For federal criminal cases, Congress enacted the Bail Reform Act of 1984, which authorizes **preventive detention**. Under the act, if prosecutors recommend that a defendant be kept in jail, a federal judge holds a hearing to

preventive detention
Holding a defendant for trial, based on a judge's finding that, if the defendant were released on bail, he or she would flee or would endanger another person or the community.

monitors the skin to detect any alcohol consumption. In these jurisdictions, as in many others, the arrestees are charged fees for electronic monitoring, thereby saving the cities even more money beyond avoiding the cost of feeding and guarding arrestees in jail. In San Antonio, monitored arrestees on release are charged $270 per month for a GPS ankle bracelet that monitors their location, $300 for an advanced GPS device that can be programmed for "excluded zones" and scheduled medical appointments, and $360 per month for SCRAM ankle monitors that analyze sweat on the skin for any presence of alcohol. In 2012, Denver saved nearly $1 million by using pretrial electronic monitoring while maintaining a 98 percent success rate for defendants appearing for scheduled court hearings.

If counties and cities have funds for electronic monitoring, this option can provide an additional alternative to traditional money bail. People who lack the funds to make bail could avoid being stuck in jail as they are monitored electronically while living at home. On the other hand, however, many local governments do not have the funds to pay for such programs themselves, so electronic monitoring may simply be an alternative form of pretrial release that is only available for people with enough money to pay monitoring fees. Moreover, such alternatives are less workable for homeless people and certain mentally ill people whose home lives and behavior will clash with a system based on residing in a specific location, especially for monitoring devices that must be keyed to landline home telephones.

Sources: "Jail Receives $50,000 in Technology Upgrades at No Cost to County," *Grayson Journal-Enquirer,* April 1, 2011 (journal-times.com); Drew Johnson, "Guardian RFID Brings Offender Management into the 21st Century," *CorrectionsOne News,* April 12, 2011 (www.correctionsone.com); Bob Link, "Telephone Revenues Help Pay for New Jail Technology," *Iowa Globe Gazette,* March 30, 2008 (www.globegazette.com); Quentin Misiag, "Johnson County Officials: Current Jail Technology 'on Its Last Leg,'" *Daily Iowan,* April 28, 2013 (www.dailyiowan.com); Scott Orr, "New Jail Technology at Camp Verde," *Tri-Valley Dispatch,* February 27, 2013 (www.trivalleycentral.com); Todd Razor, "Technology Boosts Efficiency at New Polk County Jail," *Business Record,* July 18, 2009 (www.businessrecord.com).

DEBATE THE ISSUE

Will the extensive use of technology reduce the person-to-person contact between detainees and jail officers, which previously was a potential source of counseling, information, and reassurance? Will the widespread surveillance aspects of technology harm morale in jails if officers feel as if they are being monitored as constantly and thoroughly as detainees and offenders? Provide what you think are the two strongest arguments in favor of new jail technology and the two strongest arguments in opposition.

determine (1) if there is a serious risk that the person will flee; (2) if the person will obstruct justice or threaten, injure, or intimidate a prospective witness or juror; or (3) if the offense is one of violence or one punishable by life imprisonment or death. On finding that one or more of these factors makes setting bail without endangering the community impossible, the judge can order the defendant held in jail until the case is completed (C. E. Smith, 1990).

Obviously, preventive detention provides a particularly powerful clash between important American values. The value placed on liberty for individuals seems to be denied when presumptively innocent individuals remain in jail. On the other hand, the value on all citizens' ability to enjoy the liberty of walking the streets without fear of crime may be advanced by detaining specific individuals who are found to threaten community safety.

Critics of preventive detention argue that it violates the Constitution's due process clause because the accused remains in custody until a verdict is rendered. However, the Supreme Court has ruled that it is constitutional. The preventive detention provisions of the Bail Reform Act of 1984 were upheld in ***United States v. Salerno and Cafero* (1987)**. The justices said that preventive detention was a legitimate use of government power, because it was not designed to punish the accused. Instead, it deals with the problem of people who commit crimes while on bail. By upholding the federal law, the Court also upheld state laws dealing with preventive detention (M. Miller and Guggenheim, 1990).

***United States v. Salerno and Cafero* (1987)**
The preventive detention provisions of the Bail Reform Act of 1984 are upheld as a legitimate use of government power designed to prevent people from committing crimes while on bail.

Supporters of preventive detention claim that it ensures that drug dealers, who often treat bail as a business expense, cannot flee before trial. Research has shown that the nature and seriousness of the charge, a history of prior arrests, and drug use all have a strong bearing on the likelihood that a defendant will commit a crime while on bail.

✔POINT

14. What methods are used to facilitate pretrial release for certain defendants?

15. How did the U.S. Supreme Court rule in cases involving preventive detention?

STOP AND ANALYZE: If you were the governor of a state that had never introduced reforms to reduce pretrial detention, which approach would you propose—10 percent cash bail, bail fund, release on own recognizance, bail guidelines, or citation? Make two arguments for regarding one of these options as being the best approach.

Pretrial Detention

People who are not released before trial must remain in jail. Often called "the ultimate ghetto," American jails hold more than 700,000 people on any one day (Minton and Golinelli, 2014). Most are poor, more than half are in pretrial detention, and the rest are serving sentences (normally of less than a year) or are waiting to be moved to state prison or to another jurisdiction (T. Clear, Cole, and Reisig, 2012).

Urban jails also contain troubled people, many with drug abuse and mental health problems, whom police have swept off the streets (Glasheen et al., 2012). Michael Welch calls this process, in which the police remove socially offensive people from certain areas, "social sanitation" (M. Welch, 1994: 262). The presence of troubled people poses challenges for jail staff as well as for the detainees sharing cells with people in need of counseling, psychiatric treatment, or medications (Desmarais et al., 2012).

Conditions in jails are often much harsher than those in prisons. People awaiting trial are often held in barracks-like cells with sentenced offenders. Thus, a "presumed innocent" pretrial detainee might spend weeks or months in the same confined space with troubled people or sentenced felons (A. J. Beck, Karberg, and Harrison, 2002).

The period just after arrest is the most frightening and difficult time for suspects. Imagine freely walking the streets one minute and being locked in a small space with a large number of troubled and potentially dangerous cell mates the next. Suddenly you have no privacy and must share an open toilet with hostile strangers. You have been fingerprinted, photographed, and questioned—treated like "the criminal" that the police and the criminal justice system consider you to be. You are alone with people whose behavior you cannot predict. You are left to worry and wonder about what might happen. If you are female, you may be placed in a cell by yourself if the jail is in a small community. Given the stressful nature of arrest and jailing, it is little wonder that many jail suicides and psychotic episodes occur during the first hours of detention. Fortunately, increased awareness about suicide risks in training programs and policies for jail staff have helped to reduce the frequency of this problem (Hayes, 2012).

The shock of arrest and detention can be made even worse by other factors. Many people are arrested for offenses they committed while under the influence of alcohol or some other substance and may therefore be that much less able to cope with their new situation. Young arrestees who face the risk of being victimized by older, stronger cell mates may sink into depression. Detainees also worry about losing their jobs while in jail, because they do not know if or when they will be released.

Pretrial detention can last a long time. Although most felony defendants have their cases adjudicated within six months, other felony defendants can wait more than a year. For example, in 15 percent of felony cases in one study the defendants waited for more than one year for their cases to be resolved (B. Reaves, 2013). If they are held in detention for that time period, they

Joe Amon/The Denver Post/Getty Images

Often jails holding pretrial detainees are crowded and have no education or work programs. Some detainees may sleep on the floor and spend their days in close quarters with many strangers as they wait days, weeks, or months for their trials or, if after trial, their transfer to a prison. What thoughts and feelings would you experience if you were arrested and detained in jail?

suffer from serious hardships, especially if the charges are eventually dropped or they are found to be not guilty. Thus, the psychological and economic hardships faced by pretrial detainees and their families can be major and prolonged.

Pretrial detention not only imposes stresses and hardships that can reach crisis levels, but it can also affect the outcomes of cases. People who are held in jail can give little help to their defense attorneys. They cannot help find witnesses and perform other useful tasks on their own behalf. In addition, they may feel pressured to plead guilty in order to end their indefinite stay in jail. Even if they believe that they should not be convicted of the crime charged, they may prefer to start serving a prison or jail sentence with a definite endpoint. Some may even gain quicker release on probation or in a community corrections program by pleading guilty, whereas they might stay in jail for a longer period by insisting on their innocence and awaiting a trial.

CHECKPOINT

16. People are detained in jail for many reasons. What categories of people are found in jails?

17. What sources of stress do people face while in jail awaiting trial?

STOP AND ANALYZE: Some people in jail have been convicted of crimes and are serving short sentences or awaiting transfer to prison. Others are presumptively innocent pretrial detainees awaiting the processing of their cases. Make two arguments in favor of treating pretrial detainees differently and better than convicted offenders inside jails. Now make two arguments about why such differential treatment is undesirable or too difficult to implement.

A QUESTION OF ETHICS

In October 2014, Judge Judith Hawkins was removed from office by the Florida Supreme Court primarily because of her activities in advancing a ministry that she founded and led on various mission trips. She was found to have sold and offered to sell her religious books and related items at the courthouse to lawyers and court employees. She also used a photo of herself in judicial robes to promote the sale of her religious items on her ministry's website. She also was found to have used her judicial assistant to promote the sale of her religious products. There were additional charges about misleading investigators and failing to fulfill her judicial obligations.

Sources: Karl Etters, "Court Orders Judge Judith Hawkins Be Removed from the Bench," *Tallahassee Democrat,* October 31, 2014 (www.tallahassee.com).

CRITICAL THINKING AND ANALYSIS

How did the actions of Judge Hawkins cause harm? Was she being required to surrender her right to religious liberty in order to work as a judge? Alternatively, is there a risk that lawyers and others might feel pressured to buy products sold by a judge in order avoid the fear that the judge might turn against them and their clients? Is removal from the bench too strong a punishment for these activities? Is there a more appropriate sanction, if a sanction is needed at all? Write a memo analyzing the nature and severity of the problem and recommending what actions, if any, should be taken with respect to the judge and her service on the county court.

Summary

1 Describe the structure of the American court system

- The United States has a dual court system consisting of state and federal courts that are organized into separate hierarchies.
- Trial courts and appellate courts have different jurisdictions and functions.
- Despite resistance from local judges and political interests, reformers have sought to improve state court systems through centralized administration, state funding, and a separate personnel system.

2 Analyze the qualities that we desire in a judge

- The judge is a key figure in the criminal justice process who assumes the roles of adjudicator, negotiator, and administrator.
- The recent development of specialized courts, such as drug courts, veterans courts, and mental health courts, places judges in the role of problem solver.

3 Identify the ways that American judges are selected

- State judges are selected through various methods, including partisan elections, nonpartisan elections, gubernatorial appointment, legislative appointment, and merit selection.
- Merit-selection methods for choosing judges have gradually spread to many states. Such methods normally use a screening committee to make recommendations of potential appointees who will, if placed on the bench by the governor, later go before the voters for approval or disapproval of their performance in office.

4 Describe the pretrial process in criminal cases

- Pretrial processes determine the fates of nearly all defendants through case dismissals, decisions defining the charges, and plea bargains, all of which affect more than 90 percent of cases.
- Defense attorneys use motions to their advantage to gain information and delay proceedings to benefit their clients.

5 Discuss how the bail system operates

- The bail process provides opportunities for many defendants to gain pretrial release, but poor defendants may be disadvantaged by their inability to come up with the money or property needed to secure release. Some preventive detention statutes permit judges to hold defendants considered dangerous or likely to flee.
- Bail agents, also known as bail bondsmen, are private businesspeople who charge a fee to provide money for defendants' pretrial release. Their activities create risks of corruption and discrimination in the bail process, but they may help the system by reminding defendants about court dates and by tracking down defendants who disappear.
- Although judges bear the primary responsibility for setting bail, prosecutors are especially influential in recommending amounts and conditions for pretrial release.
- Initiatives to reform the bail process include release on own recognizance (ROR), police-issued citations, and bail guidelines.

6 Analyze the context of pretrial detention

- Pretrial detainees, despite the presumption of innocence, are held in difficult conditions in jails containing mixed populations of convicted offenders, detainees, and troubled people. The shock of being jailed creates risks of suicide and depression.

Questions for Review

1 Discuss the effects that partisan election of judges may have on the administration of justice. Which system of judicial selection do you think is most appropriate? Why?

2 The judge plays several roles. What are they? In your opinion, do they conflict with one another?

3 What are the methods of securing pretrial release for the accused?

4 What are the criteria used to set bail?

Key Terms and Cases

adversarial system (p. 379)
appellate courts (p. 368)
arraignment (p. 382)
bail (p. 385)
citation (p. 390)
drug courts (p. 375)
inquisitorial system (p. 379)
jurisdiction (p. 367)
merit selection (p. 380)
motion (p. 384)
nonpartisan election (p. 378)
partisan election (p. 378)
preventive detention (p. 393)
release on recognizance (ROR) (p. 391)
trial courts of general jurisdiction (p. 368)
trial courts of limited jurisdiction (p. 368)
United States v. Salerno and Cafero (1987) (p. 394)

Checkpoint Answers

1 What is the dual court system?
✓ Separate federal and state court systems handling cases in the United States.

2 What different categories of courts exist within each court system?
✓ The federal system is made up of the Supreme Court of the United States, circuit courts of appeals, and district courts. State court systems are made up of an appellate court of last resort, intermediate courts of appeals, trial courts of general jurisdiction, and trial courts of limited jurisdiction.

3 What does it mean for courts to be decentralized?
✓ Operated and controlled by local communities, not a statewide administration. Most state and county courts are decentralized.

4 What are the main goals of advocates of judicial reform?
✓ To create a unified court system with consolidated and simplified structures, having centralized management, full funding by the state, and a central personnel system.

5 What is the image of the judge in the public's eye?
✓ That judges carefully and deliberately weigh the issues in a case before making a decision. Judges embody justice and dispense it impartially.

6 Why might it be important for judges to represent different segments of society?
✓ So that all segments of society will view the decisions as legitimate and fair.

7 What are judges' main functions?
✓ Adjudicator, negotiator, administrator.

8 Why do political parties often prefer that judges be elected?
✓ To secure the support of attorneys who aspire to become judges and to ensure that courthouse positions are allocated to party workers.

9 What are the steps in the merit-selection process?
✓ When a vacancy occurs, a nominating commission is appointed that sends the governor the names of approved candidates. The governor must fill the vacancy from this list. After a short term, a referendum is held to ask the voters whether the judge should be retained.

10 What are the purposes of preliminary hearings, arraignments, and defense motions?
✓ Preliminary hearings inform defendants of their rights and determine if there is probable cause. Arraignments involve the formal reading of charges and the entry of a plea. Motions seek information and the vindication of defendants' rights.

11 Why and how are cases filtered out of the system?
✓ Cases are filtered out through the discretionary decisions of prosecutors and judges when they believe that there is inadequate evidence to proceed, or when prosecutors believe that their scarce resources are best directed at other cases.

12 What factors affect whether bail is set and how much money or property a defendant must provide to gain pretrial release?
✓ Bail decisions are based primarily on the judge's evaluation of the seriousness of the offense and the defendant's prior record. The decisions are

influenced by the prosecutor's recommendations and the defense attorney's counterarguments about the defendant's personal qualities and ties to the community.

13 What positive and negative effects does the bail agent have on the justice system?

✓ Bail agents help the system by reminding defendants about their court dates and finding them if they fail to appear. However, bail agents also may contribute to corruption and discrimination.

14 What methods are used to facilitate pretrial release for certain defendants?

✓ Bail reform alternatives such as police citations, release on own recognizance (ROR), bail fund, and 10 percent cash bail.

15 How did the U.S. Supreme Court rule in cases involving preventive detention?

✓ Preventive detention does not violate the Constitution's ban on excessive bail because such detentions are not punishment and are merely a way to protect the public.

16 People are detained in jail for many reasons. What categories of people are found in jails?

✓ (1) Pretrial detainees for whom bail was not set or those who are too poor to pay the bail amount required, (2) people serving short sentences for misdemeanors, (3) people convicted of felonies awaiting transfer to prison, (4) people with psychological or substance abuse problems who have been swept off the streets.

17 What sources of stress do people face while in jail awaiting trial?

✓ The stress of living with difficult and potentially dangerous cell mates; uncertainty about what will happen to their case, their families, their jobs; and their ability to contribute to preparing a defense.

CHAPTER FEATURES

- **Technology and Criminal Justice** Mandatory DNA Samples
- **Inside Today's Controversies** Prosecutors, Police, and the Ferguson, Missouri, Grand Jury in 2014
- **Close Up** Pressure to Fulfill the Promise of Indigent Defense
- **New Directions in Criminal Justice** A Voucher System for Criminal Defense

CHAPTER 10 PROSECUTION AND DEFENSE

CHAPTER LEARNING OBJECTIVES

1. Describe the roles of the prosecuting attorney
2. Analyze the process by which criminal charges are filed, and what role the prosecutor's discretion plays in that process
3. Identify the other actors in the system with whom the prosecutor interacts during the decision-making process
4. Discuss the day-to-day reality of criminal defense work in the United States
5. Describe how counsel is provided for defendants who cannot afford a private attorney
6. Analyze the defense attorney's role in the system and the nature of the attorney–client relationship

CHAPTER OUTLINE

The Prosecutorial System
- Politics and Prosecution
- The Prosecutor's Influence
- The Prosecutor's Roles
- Discretion of the Prosecutor
- Key Relationships of the Prosecutor
- Decision-Making Policies

The Defense Attorney: Image and Reality
- The Role of the Defense Attorney
- Realities of the Defense Attorney's Job
- The Environment of Criminal Practice
- Counsel for Indigents
- Private versus Public Defense
- Attorney Competence

AP Images/Boston Herald, Ted Fitzgerald, Pool

Reporters for both news and sports publications gathered in the courthouse in Fall River, Massachusetts, in early 2015 to provide coverage of a highly publicized murder trial. Aaron Hernandez, a star player for the National Football League's New England Patriots, faced a trial on murder charges. He was accused of killing 27-year-old Odin Lloyd, the boyfriend of his fiancée's sister, in June 2013. A jogger found Lloyd's body in an industrial park less one mile from Hernandez's house in the town of North Attleborough. Lloyd had been shot with a .45-caliber handgun. Microscopic examinations of the five shell casings found near Lloyd's body by the Massachusetts State Police indicated they were likely fired by the same gun as the shell casing reportedly found in a car rented by Hernandez at the time of the shooting ("Shells Near Ex-NFL," 2015).

While Hernandez's fate would be determined by several factors, including the nature of the evidence against him and the jury's determinations about that evidence, the key actors who set the stage for that determination were the prosecutors and defense attorneys. In the adversarial setting of the trial, these attorneys bore responsibility for deciding which evidence to present and how to present it. For example, in order to gain additional evidence that might persuade the jury, prosecutor William McCauley strongly pressed Judge E. Susan Garsh to admit into evidence text messages sent from the victim to his sister shortly before he was murdered (K. Armstrong, 2015). The attorneys also challenged their opponents' evidence and formulated arguments that sought to persuade the jury to understand the case in a certain way. The strategies and effectiveness of prosecutors and defense attorneys significantly affect whether or not defendants are convicted and punished.

For example, one strategy used by William McCauley and Patrick Bomberg was to meet with Hernandez's fiancée, Shayanna Jenkins, presumably to talk about the potential for her to face criminal charges and imprisonment based on evidence she may have helped cover up the crime by destroying evidence. After the meeting, the judge announced that Jenkins had been granted immunity from prosecution, and her name was placed on the prosecution's list of witnesses. If she and Hernandez had been married, then she could not have been pressured to testify against him. Because they were merely engaged to be married, the prosecutors were positioned to raise the threat of potential prosecution and offer the incentive of immunity—namely, freedom from prosecution—in exchange for her testimony (Candiotti, 2015).

By contrast, defense attorney James Sultan pursued a strategy of challenging the procedures used for gathering evidence, thereby raising questions about whether there was sloppy police work. Sultan highlighted that the North Attleborough police department rarely handled murder investigations, only one every few years. He pressed Officer John Grim about why he failed to mention to the crime scene photographer the same information that he noted in his later statement when he said that he saw footprints at the scene. He also challenged Grim about changing his statement about how far a towel was found from the body. He later pressed Sergeant Paul Baker from the Massachusetts State Police about the failure to put certain items immediately in evidence bags to avoid contamination rather than just place them in the back of a truck. This approach seemed designed to cast doubts in the jurors' minds about whether they could trust the police officers' care in collecting evidence and the prosecutors' claims about the reliability of that evidence ("Aaron Hernandez Trial," 2015; "Hernandez Jurors," 2015). Ultimately, the defense attorney's efforts failed, and a jury found Hernandez guilty of first-degree murder. He was sentenced to life in prison without possibility of parole (Belson and Mather, 2015).

Prosecutors and defense attorneys are key decision makers in the criminal justice process, whether or not cases actually proceed all the way to a trial. In most cases, the prosecutors and defense attorneys negotiate a plea agreement. Yet in both plea bargaining and trials, the attorneys' decisions, strategies, interactions, and effectiveness determine the fates of individuals facing criminal prosecution. Prosecutors make decisions about whom to charge and the list of charges to pursue. In some cases, they worry that the evidence is not strong enough, so they offer a plea agreement to the defendant. In other cases, the evidence is so strong that the defendant is eager to accept a plea and a specified sentence rather than risk a longer sentence by going through a trial. By contrast, defense attorneys must advise their clients and make strategic decisions about whether to plead guilty and what tactics to use during trial. Unfortunately, the system does not ensure that all defendants receive equally effective representation. Defendants who can afford to hire their own attorneys and pay for the services of expert witnesses have advantages over poor defendants who must rely on defense attorneys provided for them.

As illustrated by the Hernandez case, the American system places great power and responsibility in the hands of attorneys for each side in a criminal case. The prosecutor and defense attorney are the most influential figures in determining the outcomes of criminal cases. Their discretionary decisions, strategies, negotiations, and effectiveness set the stage for the determination of people's fates. As we shall see in this chapter, the justice system's ability to handle cases and produce fair results depends on the dedication, skill, and enthusiasm of these lawyers.

The Prosecutorial System

Prosecuting attorneys make discretionary decisions about whether to pursue criminal charges, which charges to make, what sentence to recommend. They represent the government in pursuing criminal charges against the accused. Except in a few states, no higher authority second-guesses or changes these decisions. Thus, prosecutors are more independent than most other public officials. As with other aspects of American government, prosecution lies mainly in the hands of state and local governments. Because most crimes are violations of state laws, county prosecutors bring charges against suspects in court.

For cases involving violation of federal criminal laws, prosecutions are handled in federal courts by **United States attorneys**. These attorneys are responsible for a large number of drug-related and white-collar crime cases. Appointed by the president, they serve as part of the Department of Justice. One U.S. attorney and a staff of assistant U.S. attorneys prosecute cases in each of the 94 U.S. district courts. In 2015, President Obama nominated Loretta Lynch, a United States attorney from New York City, to be the next Attorney General of the United States, the official who heads the U.S. Department of Justice and oversees United States attorneys throughout the country. Lynch, the first African American woman to be nominated and confirmed by the Senate for the top Justice Department position, gained support from key Republican senators at a moment when Congress was deeply divided between the political parties. Her bipartisan support stemmed from her strong record as a federal prosecutor whose decisions were based on independent judgments and not politics (Huetteman, 2015).

United States attorneys
Officials responsible for the prosecution of crimes that violate the laws of the United States; appointed by the president and assigned to a U.S. district court jurisdiction.

Each state has an elected attorney general, who usually has the power to bring prosecutions in certain cases. A **state attorney general** may, for example, handle a statewide consumer fraud case if a chain of auto repair shops is suspected of overcharging customers. In Alaska, Delaware, and Rhode Island, the state attorney general also directs all local prosecutions.

state attorney general
A state's chief legal officer, usually responsible for both civil and criminal matters.

However, the vast majority of criminal cases are handled in the 2,341 county-level offices of the **prosecuting attorney**—known in various states as the district attorney, state's attorney, commonwealth attorney, or county attorney—who pursues cases that violate state law. In rural areas the prosecutor's office may consist of merely the prosecuting attorney and a part-time assistant. By contrast, some urban jurisdictions, such as Los Angeles, employ 500 assistant prosecutors and numerous legal assistants and investigators, and organize the office according to various types of crimes. Many assistant prosecutors seek to use the trial experience gained in the prosecutor's office as a means of moving on to a better-paying position in a private law firm.

prosecuting attorney
A legal representative of the state with sole responsibility for bringing criminal charges; in some states referred to as district attorney, state's attorney, or county attorney.

Prosecutors have the power to make independent decisions about which cases to pursue and what charges to file. They also have the power to drop charges and to negotiate arrangements for guilty pleas. Because of the local nature of most criminal prosecutions, prosecutors' offices are especially vulnerable to budget cuts as individual states and counties encounter financial shortfalls. As budget cuts continue to affect counties and cities in the years following the economic downturn of 2008, prosecutors' decisions in some places are affected by staff reductions. Thus prosecutors dismiss charges in certain cases solely because they do not have enough assistant prosecutors to handle all pending cases (Damron, Anderson, and Wisely, 2013). In the words of Gainesville, Florida, prosecutor Bill Cervone, "I have the discretion to prosecute or not prosecute anything that comes in. . . . If I have to concentrate on the violent crime as opposed to something petty, that's where my resources will go" (Swirko, 2012). Although many contemporary politicians typically vow that they will never raise taxes, it is possible that the reduction in resources to pursue criminal offenders may eventually make the public willing to pay more to keep the criminal justice system running at an acceptable pace.

Politics and Prosecution

Except in a few states, such as Alaska, Connecticut, and New Jersey, prosecutors are typically elected in county or municipal elections, usually for a four-year term; the office thus is heavily involved in local politics. By seeking to please voters, many prosecutors have tried to use their local office as a springboard to higher office—such as state legislator, governor, or member of Congress.

Although the power of prosecutors flows directly from their legal duties, politics strongly influence the process of prosecution. Prosecutors can often mesh their own ambitions with the needs of a political party. The appointment of assistant prosecutors offers a chance to recruit bright young lawyers to the party. Prosecutors may choose certain cases for prosecution in order to gain the favor of voters, or investigate charges against political opponents and public officials to get the attention of the public. Political factors can also cause prosecutors to apply their powers unevenly within a community. Prosecutors' discretionary power can create the impression that some groups or individuals receive harsher treatment, whereas others receive protection (Podgor, 2010).

The existence of discretionary decision making creates the risk that such decisions will produce discrimination. The limited research on prosecutorial decision making does not present consistent results. However, as summarized by scholars who looked at several studies, "a number of studies have found that African American and Hispanic suspects are more likely than white suspects to be charged with a crime and prosecuted fully" (S. Walker, Spohn, and DeLeone, 2012: 231). In addition, "[t]here also is evidence supporting charges of selective prosecution of racial minorities, especially for drug offenses" (S. Walker et al., 2012: 231). Several other studies raise questions about discrimination in specific situations, such as prosecutors' decisions to seek the death penalty (Unah, 2010). If prosecutors' discretionary decisions produce discriminatory results, these outcomes clearly clash with the American value of equal treatment and fairness (Butler, 2010). If the criminal justice system is going to fulfill American values concerning equality and fairness, then prosecutors must use their decision-making authority carefully to avoid inequality and injustice.

✔POINT **1.** What are the titles of the officials responsible for criminal prosecution at the federal, state, and local levels of government?

STOP AND ANALYZE: Would the justice system work better if all prosecutors were appointed and no local prosecutors were elected? List two reasons to favor appointed prosecutors and two reasons to favor elections. In your view, which approach is best for society?

(Answers are at the end of the chapter).

The Prosecutor's Influence

Prosecutors exert great influence because they are concerned with all aspects of the criminal justice process (Krischke, 2010; Jacoby, 1995). By contrast, other decision makers play a role in only part of the process. Throughout the entire process—from arrest to final disposition of a case—prosecutors can make decisions that will largely determine the defendant's fate. The prosecutor chooses the cases to be prosecuted, selects the charges to be brought, recommends the bail amount, approves agreements with the defendant, and urges the judge to impose a particular sentence (K. Kenny, 2009).

Throughout the justice process, prosecutors' links with the other actors in the system—police, defense attorneys, judges—shape the prosecutors' decisions. Prosecutors may, for example, recommend bail amounts and sentences that match the preferences of particular judges. They may make "tough" recommendations in front of "tough" judges, but tone down their arguments before judges who favor leniency or rehabilitation. Likewise, the other actors in the system may adjust their decisions and actions to match the preferences of the prosecutor. For example, police officers' investigation and arrest practices tend to reflect the prosecutor's priorities. Thus, prosecutors influence the decisions of others while also shaping their own actions in ways that reinforce their relationships with police, defense attorneys, and judges.

Prosecutors can gain additional power from the fact that their decisions and actions are hidden from public view. For example, a prosecutor and a defense attorney may strike a bargain whereby the prosecutor reduces a charge in exchange for a guilty plea or drops a charge if the defendant agrees to seek psychiatric help. In such instances, decisions are reached in a way that is nearly invisible to the public (J. Kim, 2009).

State laws do little to limit or guide prosecutors' decisions. Most laws describe the prosecutor's duties in such vague terms as "prosecuting all crimes and civil actions to which state or county may be party." Such laws do not tell the prosecutor which cases must be prosecuted and which ones dismissed. The prosecutor has significant discretion to make such decisions without direct interference from either the law or other actors in the justice system. When prosecutors' decisions are challenged, judges generally reject the claim. In addition, court decisions make it extremely difficult to affect prosecutors' decisions or hold them accountable through the threat of civil lawsuits, even when prosecutors intentionally hide evidence of innocence or engage in other forms of misconduct (Liptak, 2011a). Prosecutors' discretion is well protected by the law (Krischke, 2010).

Because most local prosecutors are elected, public opinion can influence their decisions. If they feel that the community no longer considers a particular act to be criminal, they may refuse to prosecute or they may try to convince the complainant not to press charges. Public influence over prosecutors can take two forms. First, because most prosecutors are elected, they must keep their decisions consistent with community values in order to increase their chances of gaining reelection. Second, because jurors are drawn from the local community, prosecutors do not want to waste their time and resources pursuing charges about which local jurors are unsympathetic or unconcerned. In some communities, for example, marijuana possession may be prosecuted actively, whereas in others this offense is ignored. About three-fourths of American prosecutors serve counties with populations of fewer than 100,000. There often is only one prosecutor in the community, and he or she may face strong local pressures, especially with regard to victimless crimes such as marijuana smoking, petty gambling, and prostitution. Prosecutors therefore develop policies that reflect community attitudes.

POINT **2.** What are the powers of the prosecuting attorney?

STOP AND ANALYZE: Are prosecutors too powerful? Should there be more mechanisms to control prosecutors' decision making? List two suggestions for making prosecutors less powerful. Now formulate the strongest argument you can against limiting prosecutors' discretion and power.

The Prosecutor's Roles

As "lawyers for the state," prosecutors face conflicting pressures to press charges vigorously against lawbreakers while also upholding justice and the rights of the accused (B. O'Brien, 2009). These pressures are often called "the prosecutor's dilemma." In the adversarial system, prosecutors must do everything they can to win a conviction; yet as members of the legal profession, they must see that justice is done even if it means that the accused is not convicted. This rule is enshrined in state statutes and lawyers' codes of ethics. For example, the Texas Code of Criminal Procedure states,

> It shall be the primary duty of all prosecuting attorneys, including any special prosecutors, not to convict, but to see that justice is done. They shall not suppress facts or secrete witnesses capable of establishing the innocence of the accused.

Even so, there is always a risk of prosecutor's bias, sometimes called a "prosecution complex." Although they are supposed to represent all the people, including the accused, prosecutors may view themselves as instruments of law enforcement. Thus, as advocates on behalf of the state, their strong desire to close each case with a conviction may keep them from recognizing unfair procedures or evidence of innocence (Weinberg, 2003). A comparison of prosecutors in the United States and Japan, for example, found that American prosecutors often proceed with the assumption that the facts weigh against the defendant, whereas Japanese prosecutors are more concerned with investigating the case to discover all available facts before making any decisions (D. T. Johnson, 1998). Read the Question of Ethics feature at the end of the chapter to consider prosecutors' roles and obligations when asked to support DNA testing of evidence from old cases.

What happens in the United States if prosecutors make a mistake and it appears that an innocent person may have been convicted? As Chapter 12 will discuss in greater detail, Americans have become much more aware about the existence of erroneous convictions as DNA testing on saved evidence has freed wrongly imprisoned people, sometimes after they have served for decades in prison. In reality, many wrongful convictions are based on mistaken identifications by witnesses or victims, false testimony by criminals seeking favors from police and prosecutors, and mistakes by incompetent defense attorneys. DNA evidence is not available to prove innocence in most cases. Unfortunately, wrongful convictions can also occur through unethical behavior by prosecutors and police, such as hiding evidence from the defense or making dishonest presentations in court in order to gain a conviction without regard for whether the defendant is actually guilty. Such circumstances raise serious issues about how the criminal justice system can ensure that its officials behave properly.

After a trial and the completion of the appellate process, sometimes a defendant has no realistic avenue to gain reconsideration of the conviction (Baude, 2010; Raeder, 2009). In 1999, a national commission appointed by then U.S. Attorney General Janet Reno recommended that prosecutors drop their adversarial posture and cooperate in permitting DNA testing of evidence saved from old cases that had produced convictions before sophisticated scientific tests were developed (N. Lewis, 1999). Despite the fact that dozens of convicted offenders have been proved innocent in rape and murder cases through after-the-fact DNA testing, some prosecutors have resisted the reexamination of old evidence (Moran, 2014; Dewan, 2009). Read the Technology and Criminal Justice feature to consider how the collection and potential use of DNA evidence has expanded beyond specifically selected criminal suspects and cases.

In contrast to prosecutors who resist DNA testing of evidence, when Craig Watkins became the new prosecutor of Dallas County, Texas, in 2007, he received national attention for seeking to reinvestigate cases of offenders convicted by previous prosecutors (Sylvester, 2011). Dallas County leads the nation in DNA exonerations. In April 2008, for example, James Woodard was the 17th person from Dallas County released from prison when DNA evidence demonstrated that he did not commit the rape and murder for which he had spent 27 years behind bars (Lavandera, 2008). Watkins sent shock waves through the legal community in Texas by proposing that the legislature create a new law that would make it a crime for prosecutors to knowingly hide or suppress evidence that could help a defendant. He made it clear that he thought some past prosecutors in Dallas County should be investigated for possible prosecution under such a law (Lavandera, 2008). Prosecutors are seldom punished for mistakes they have made in convicting innocent people, even when there is evidence of possible misconduct. They remain generally immune from civil lawsuits for their official actions (Liptak, 2011).

Although all prosecutors must uphold the law and pursue charges against lawbreakers, they can perform these tasks in different ways. Because of their personal values and professional goals, as well as the political climate of their city or county, they may define the prosecutor's role differently than do prosecutors in other places. For example, a prosecutor who believes that young offenders can be rehabilitated would likely define the role differently than one who believes that young offenders should receive the same punishments as adults. One might send juveniles to counseling programs, whereas the other may seek to process them though the adult system of courts and corrections (Sridharan, Greenfield, and Blakley, 2004). A prosecutor with no assistants and few resources for conducting full-blown jury trials may be forced to stress effective plea bargaining, whereas a prosecutor with a well-staffed office may have more options when deciding whether to take cases to trial.

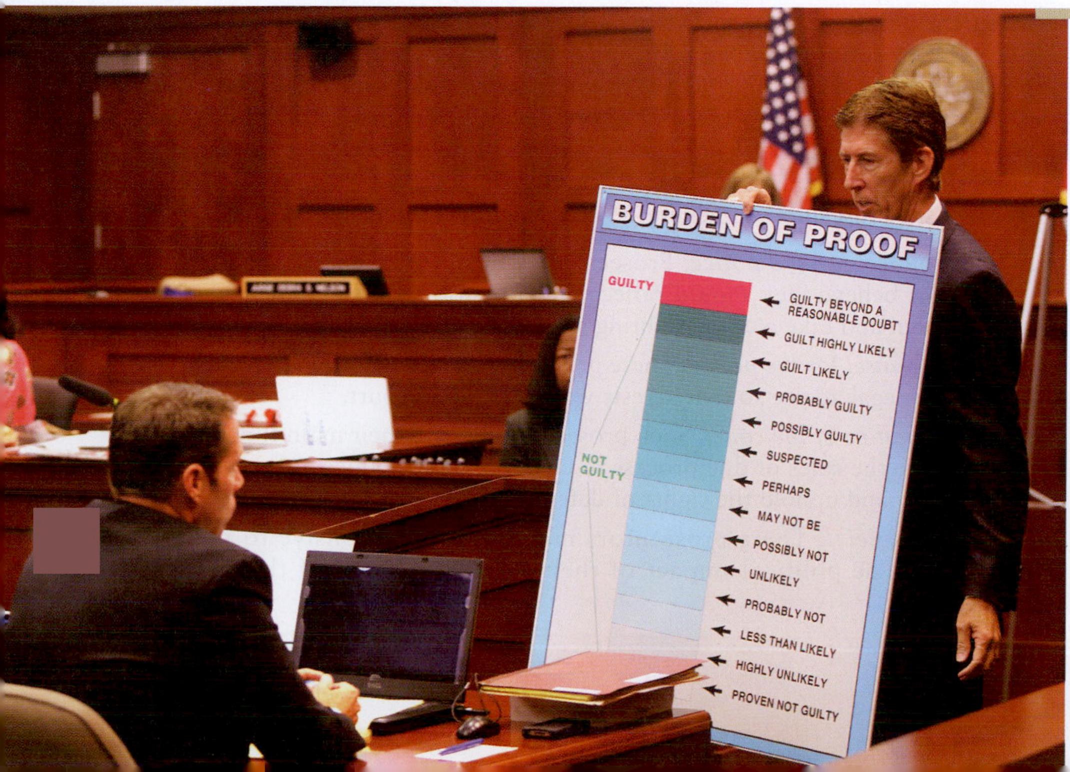

AP Images/Orlando Sentinel/Joe Burbank/Pool

What are the respective responsibilities of prosecutors and defense attorneys in conducting a criminal trial?

TECHNOLOGY & CRIMINAL JUSTICE

MANDATORY DNA SAMPLES

Maryland's DNA Collection Act requires that all people arrested for serious crimes must submit DNA samples through a quick swab of the inside of their cheek. Note that this sample is taken from people who have not yet been convicted of crimes and, indeed, inevitably includes people for whom charges will be dropped or who will avoid conviction by being acquitted at trial. A man named Alonzo King was arrested in 2009 for threatening a group of people with a shotgun. After arrest, a DNA sample was taken from him. When the sample was checked in the national computer database called the Combined DNA Index System (CODIS), his sample matched evidence taken from the victim's body after a brutal, unsolved rape in 2003. The DNA sample, test, and match led to his conviction for the rape.

King's attorneys argued that the taking of the DNA sample constituted a "search" under the Fourth Amendment that should only have been conducted after a judge issued a warrant for the specific search. Since King's 2009 arrest for threatening people with a shotgun did not in any way need to rely on DNA evidence, he could have been convicted of that crime solely based on the eyewitness testimony of the victims. Thus, they argued, there was no "probable cause" to justify this type of search, and the evidence obtained from this "unreasonable" search should be excluded from use against him in the rape case. King's case was decided by the U.S. Supreme Court in 2013.

In a narrow 5-to-4 vote, the Supreme Court approved the Maryland law. Although all of the justices saw the sampling as a "search" under the Fourth Amendment, a majority thought the search was justified. Justice Anthony Kennedy's majority opinion said that the mandatory DNA sampling of arrestees was justified by the need for law enforcement officials to be certain of the identities of the individuals that they had arrested. However, as Justice Antonin Scalia pointed out in his dissenting opinion, fingerprint matches can confirm arrestees' identities much more quickly than DNA tests, which can take several months to be returned from a laboratory in routine cases. Justice Kennedy also argued that the cheek swab was a very minor intrusion on an individual's privacy as it only takes a moment, causes no pain, and leaves no marks. He also noted that the DNA samples could

Role definition is further complicated by the prosecutor's need to maintain relationships with many other actors—police officers, judges, defense attorneys, political party leaders, and so forth—who may have conflicting ideas about what the prosecutor should do. The prosecutor's decisions affect the ability of the others to perform their duties and achieve their goals. If the prosecutor decides not to prosecute, the judge and jury will not get to decide the case, and police officers may feel that their efforts have been wasted. If the prosecutor decides to launch a campaign against drugs or pornography, this decision will impact both the political and criminal justice arenas. Police may feel that they must redirect their time and energy toward the crimes emphasized by the prosecutor. However, they may also pressure the prosecutor to set new priorities, by declining to devote their efforts to the kinds of crimes the prosecutor wants to concentrate on. Excessive attention to victimless crimes such as gambling and prostitution may produce a public backlash if citizens feel that the prosecutor should focus on more-serious crimes.

We can see prosecutors as generally following one of four distinct roles:

1. *Trial counsel for the police.* Prosecutors who see their main function in this light believe they should reflect the views of law enforcement in the courtroom and take a crime-fighting stance in public.
2. *House counsel for the police.* These prosecutors believe their main function is to give legal advice so that arrests will stand up in court.
3. *Representative of the court.* Such prosecutors believe their main function is to enforce the rules of due process to ensure that the police act according to the law and uphold the rights of defendants.
4. *Elected official.* These prosecutors may be most responsive to public opinion. The political impact of their decisions is one of their main concerns.

serve a positive purpose by freeing the wrongfully convicted if they happened to identify someone who was the perpetrator of a crime for which another person had been convicted.

By contrast, the four dissenters, led by Justice Scalia, saw the mandatory sampling as a violation of the fundamental ideas underlying the Fourth Amendment. In addition to criticizing in detail the weaknesses of the majority's justification based on identifying suspects, the dissenters argued that the real purpose of the law was to see if arrestees are responsible for unsolved crimes. The dissenting opinion noted that Maryland could have achieved its objective by waiting until King had been convicted on the shotgun charge and then taken the sample from him as a convicted felon, rather than as a presumptively innocent arrestee. In Justice Scalia's view, if it is supremely important to collect DNA from presumptively innocent arrestees, then the majority's preferred policy would actually justify taking DNA samples from everyone in the United States. Thus the government database would be complete enough to address any unsolved crime for which DNA evidence is available. However, according to Scalia, "Solving unsolved crimes is a noble objective, but it occupies a lower place in the American pantheon of noble objectives than the protection of our people from suspicionless law-enforcement searches. The Fourth Amendment must prevail."

Sources: *Maryland v. King*, 133 S.Ct. 1958 (2013); Richard Lempert, *Maryland v. King:* An Unfortunate Supreme Court Decision on the Collection of DNA Samples," *Up Front* (Brookings Institution blog), June 6, 2013 (www.brookings.edu).

DEBATE THE ISSUE

What, if anything, do we have to fear by permitting the taking of DNA samples from arrestees? Does this practice represent an abandonment of Bill of Rights principles that provide protections against unjustified searches? Given that samples will be taken from at least some people who are innocent, why should they be singled out for this treatment instead of simply testing the entire country, namely all of the innocent people in society? Make a list of the three issues that raise the most concern for you about the increased use of technology as it affects privacy related to DNA sampling and the retention of DNA records.

Each of these roles involves a different view of the prosecutor's "clients" as well as his or her own responsibilities. In the first two roles, prosecutors see the police as their primary clients. Take a moment to think about who might be the clients of prosecutors who view themselves as representatives of the court or as elected officials.

✔POINT 3. What are the roles of the prosecutor?

STOP AND ANALYZE: In your view, which of the four distinct roles should be the prosecutor's most important one? List two reasons for your conclusion. Now choose a different role and list two ways that a prosecutor might behave differently if she emphasized this second role rather than the role you preferred for the prosecutor.

Discretion of the Prosecutor

Because they have such broad discretion, prosecutors can shape their decisions to fit different interests (Ferguson, 2009). Their decisions might be based on a desire to impress voters through tough "throw-the-book-at-them" charges in a highly publicized case (Maschke, 1995). Their decisions might stem from their personal values and policy priorities, such as an emphasis on leniency and rehabilitation for young offenders or a desire to work with domestic violence victims to seek a desired result (M. Finn, 2013; Buzawa and Buzawa, 2013; Ferguson, 2009). Prosecutors might also shape their decisions to please local judges by, for example, accepting plea agreements that will keep the judges from being burdened by too many time-consuming trials. Such motives can shape prosecutors' decisions because there is usually no higher authority to tell prosecutors how they must do their jobs (MacLean and Wilks, 2012). From the time the police turn a case over to the prosecutor, he or she has almost complete control over decisions about charges and plea agreements (K. Griffin, 2009).

American prosecutors who have doubts about whether the available evidence actually proves the defendant's guilt may just shrug their shoulders and say, "I'll just let the jury decide," rather than face public criticism for dropping charges. In Japan, by contrast, prosecutors throughout the country work for a single nationwide agency and are not elected. As such, they must gain approval from superiors for many of their decisions rather than making independent decisions like those of local prosecutors in the United States (D. T. Johnson, 1998).

Although the rate of dismissals varies from place to place, in most cities up to half of all arrests do not lead to formal charges. In the nation's 75 largest counties, nearly a quarter of felony arrests result in charges being dismissed (Reaves, 2013). The percentage of dismissals is typically much larger in misdemeanor cases. Prosecutors may decide to drop charges because of factors related to a particular case or because they have a policy of not bringing charges for certain offenses. For example, the U.S. Department of Justice gives its prosecutors guidelines for deciding whether a case should be dismissed or pursued (U.S. Department of Justice, 1997). They include the following:

1. Federal law enforcement priorities
2. The nature and seriousness of the offense
3. The deterrent effect of prosecution
4. The person's culpability (blameworthiness) in connection with the offense
5. The person's history with respect to criminal activity
6. The person's willingness to cooperate in the investigation or prosecution of others
7. The probable sentence or other consequences if the person is convicted

In addition to these formal considerations, decisions to pursue felony charges may also be affected by the staffing levels of individual prosecutor's offices (P. Walker, 1998). If offices lack sufficient resources to pursue all possible cases, prosecutors may establish priorities and then reduce or dismiss charges in cases deemed less important. In light of the budget crises facing state and local government, prosecutors' offices increasingly confront these issues (Damron, Anderson, and Wisely, 2013; Swirko, 2012).

Jewel Samad/AFP/Getty Images

In June 2012, U.S. Secretary of Commerce John Bryson crashed his car into another vehicle and then drove away, only to smash into a second vehicle. He resigned his office shortly afterward. Despite the fact that tests indicated he was driving while having the sleep medication Ambien in his system, prosecutors decided not to file charges against him. Is there a risk that the public will view it as unfair when prominent or powerful people benefit from prosecutors' discretion to be lenient when other people are charged with crimes in similar situations?

Even after deciding that a case should be prosecuted, the prosecutor has great freedom in deciding what charges to file. In criminal incidents that involve several laws, the prosecutor can bring a single charge or more than one. Suppose that Smith, who is armed, breaks into a grocery store, assaults the proprietor, and robs the cash drawer. What charges can the prosecutor file? By virtue of having committed the robbery, the accused can be charged with at least four crimes: breaking and entering, assault, armed robbery, and carrying a dangerous weapon. Other charges or **counts** can be added, depending on the nature of the incident. A forger, for instance, can be charged with one count for each act of forgery committed. By filing as many charges as possible, the prosecutor strengthens his or her position in plea negotiations. In effect, the prosecutor can use discretion in deciding the number of charges and thus increase the prosecution's supply of "bargaining chips" (Simons, 2010).

counts
Each separate offense of which a person is accused in an indictment or an information.

The discretionary power to set charges does not give the prosecutor complete control over plea bargaining. Defense attorneys strengthen their position in the **discovery** process, in which the prosecutor discloses information from the case file to the defense. For example, the defense has the right to see any statements made by the accused during interrogation by the police, as well as the results of any physical or psychological tests. This information tells the defense attorney about the strengths and weaknesses of the prosecution's case. The defense attorney may use it to decide whether a case is hopeless or whether it is worthwhile to engage in tough negotiations.

discovery
A prosecutor's pretrial disclosure, to the defense, of facts and evidence to be introduced at trial.

The prosecutor's discretion does not end with the decision to file a certain charge. After the charge has been made, the prosecutor may reduce it in exchange for a guilty plea or enter a notation of ***nolle prosequi*** (*nol. pros.*). The latter is a freely made decision to drop the charge, either as a whole or as to one or more counts (J. Bowers, 2010). When a prosecutor decides to drop charges, no higher authorities can force him or her to reinstate them. When guilty pleas are entered, the prosecutor uses discretion in recommending a sentence.

nolle prosequi
An entry made by a prosecutor on the record of a case and announced in court to indicate that the charges specified will not be prosecuted. In effect, the charges are thereby dismissed.

✓POINT 4. How does a prosecutor use discretion to decide how to treat each defendant?

STOP AND ANALYZE: Why should prosecutors drop charges? List the four primary reasons that you believe should guide prosecutors' decisions about when to drop charges.

Key Relationships of the Prosecutor

Formal policies and role conceptions alone do not affect prosecutors' decisions (Fridell, 1990). Relationships with other actors in the justice system influence them as well. Despite their independent authority, prosecutors must consider how police, judges, and others will react. They depend on these officials in order to prosecute cases successfully. In turn, the success of police, judges, and correctional officials depends on prosecutors' effectiveness in identifying and convicting lawbreakers. Thus, these officials build exchange relationships in which they cooperate with one another.

Police

Prosecutors depend on the police to provide both the suspects and the evidence needed to convict lawbreakers. Most crimes occur before the police arrive at the scene; therefore, officers must reconstruct the crime on the basis of physical evidence and witnesses' reports. Police must use their training, experience,

AP Images/Paul Sancya

In order to be effective, elected county prosecutors must maintain cooperative relationships with a variety of others in their communities, including voters, crime victims, police, and judges. Does the need to maintain these relationships inevitably lead prosecutors to alter their decisions in order to accommodate the interests and feelings of others?

and work routines to decide whether arrest and prosecution would be worthwhile. Prosecutors cannot control the types of cases brought to them, because they cannot investigate crimes on their own. Thus, the police control the initiation of the criminal justice process through the ways they investigate crimes and arrest suspects. Various factors, such as pressure on police to establish an impressive crime-clearance record, can influence police actions. As a result, such actions can create problems for prosecutors if, for example, the police make many arrests without gathering enough evidence to ensure conviction.

Despite this dependence, prosecutors can influence the actions of the police. For example, prosecutors can return cases for further investigation and refuse to approve arrest warrants. Prosecutors and police have an exchange relationship in which the success of each depends on cooperation with the other.

Police requests for prosecution may be refused for reasons unrelated to the facts of the case. First, prosecutors regulate the workload of the justice system. They must make sure that a backlog of cases does not keep the court from meeting legal time limits for processing criminal cases. To keep cases from being dismissed by the judge for taking too long, prosecutors may themselves dismiss relatively weak or minor cases and focus on those with more-serious charges or clear proof of the defendant's guilt. Second, prosecutors may reject police requests for prosecution because they do not want to pursue poorly developed cases that would place them in an embarrassing position in the courtroom. Judges often scold prosecutors if weak cases are allowed to take up scarce courtroom time. Finally, prosecutors may return cases to make sure that police provide high-quality investigations and evidence.

In recent decades, criminal justice officials have expressed concern about coordination between police and prosecutors. Some claim that lack of coordination causes cases to be dismissed or lost. Part of the problem is that lawyers and police have different views of crime and work for different sponsoring organizations. The police often claim that they have made a valid arrest and that there is no reason an offender should not be indicted and tried, but prosecutors look at cases to see if the evidence will result in a conviction. These different perspectives often lead to conflicts.

In response to the need for greater coordination, many jurisdictions have formed police–prosecution teams to work together on cases. This approach is often used for drug or organized-crime investigations and cases in which conviction requires detailed information and evidence. Drug cases require cooperation between the police and prosecutors, because without a network of informers, the police cannot catch drug traffickers with evidence that can lead to convictions. Prosecutors can help the police gain cooperation from informants by approving agreements to reduce charges or even to *nolle prosequi* a case. The accused person may then return to the community to gather information for the police.

Relationships and cooperation with police provide advantages for prosecutors that are not enjoyed by defense attorneys. Prosecutors have, in effect, an entire agency of trained officers who conduct investigations for them without drawing from the budget and resources of the prosecutor's office. By contrast, defense attorneys typically have limited resources for gathering evidence and interviewing witnesses on behalf of their clients. Private practice defense attorneys and public defender offices may employ a few investigators, but their numbers and resources do not match those of the police. Read the Inside Today's Controversies feature to consider the risk that prosecutors' close relationships with and dependence on the police may impact decision making in ways that cause controversy.

Victims and Witnesses

Prosecutors depend on the cooperation of victims and witnesses (Rhodes et al., 2011). Although a case can be prosecuted whether or not a victim wishes to press charges, many prosecutors will not pursue cases in which the key testimony and other necessary evidence must be provided by a victim who is unwilling to cooperate. Prosecutors also need the cooperation of people who have witnessed crimes.

The decision to prosecute is often based on an assessment of the victim's role in his or her own victimization and the victim's credibility as a witness. If a victim has a criminal record, the prosecutor may choose not to pursue the case, in the belief that a jury would not consider the victim a credible witness—despite the fact that the jury will never learn that the victim has a criminal record. In fact, the decision not to prosecute may actually reflect the prosecutor's belief that someone with a criminal record is untrustworthy or does not deserve the protection of the law. In other words, the prosecutor's own biases in sizing up victims may affect which cases he or she pursues. If a victim is poorly dressed, uneducated, or inarticulate, the prosecutor may be inclined to dismiss charges out of fear that a jury would find the victim unpersuasive (Stanko, 1988).

Other characteristics of victims may play a similar role. For example, prosecutors might not pursue cases in which the victims are prostitutes who have been raped, drug abusers who have been assaulted by drug dealers, and children who cannot stand up to the pressure of testifying in court. Research indicates that victims' characteristics, such as moral character, behavior at time of incident, and age, influence decisions to prosecute sexual assault cases more than does the actual strength of the evidence against the suspect (J. W. Spears and Spohn, 1997). Prosecutors sometimes also base their decision on whether or not the victim and defendant had a prior relationship. Studies show that prosecutions succeed most when aimed at defendants accused of committing crimes against strangers (Boland et al., 1983). When the victim is an acquaintance, a friend, or even a relative of the defendant, he or she may refuse to act as a witness, and prosecutors and juries may view the offense as less serious

INSIDE TODAY'S CONTROVERSIES

PROSECUTORS, POLICE, AND THE FERGUSON, MISSOURI, GRAND JURY IN 2014

In prior chapters, we have seen examples of criminal justice issues that arose in 2014 related to public protests after grand juries declined to bring criminal charges against police officers whose actions caused the deaths of unarmed African American men. The Inside Today's Controversies feature in Chapter 6 highlighted how these events led President Obama to appoint the Task Force on 21st Century Policing. In light of the impact of these events, it is useful to take a closer look at the grand jury, and especially the role of the prosecutor in such proceedings. The grand jury proceedings that took place to examine the Ferguson, Missouri, shooting provide an especially thought-provoking and controversial example of the grand jury process. The prosecutors in the Ferguson grand jury hearing deviated from standard procedures, and their unusual actions raised questions about the fairness and legitimacy of the grand jury's decision not to indict the police officer who fired the fatal shot.

Grand jury proceedings are normally secret, so the public has no opportunity to know exactly what information is presented by prosecutors to the grand jurors who are responsible for deciding whether criminal charges are justified. In the Ferguson case, the county prosecutor appeared to be so concerned that news reporters and members of the public accept that the system was operating in a fair and objective manner that he released thousands of pages of documents about the testimony and other evidence presented to the grand jury. A close examination of this material revealed, however, that the county prosecutor and his assistant prosecutors made unusual and questionable choices about what to present to the grand jury.

In the typical grand jury proceeding, the jurors, who are citizens drawn from the community, meet in secret and hear only information presented to them by the prosecutor. During the hearing, the prosecutor identifies and explains the relevant charges being sought and presents enough evidence to justify those charges. No defense attorneys are present to argue for alternative versions of events or to present counterevidence. The grand jury is only asked to decide whether there is enough evidence to file criminal charges against an individual. The grand jurors do not need to be persuaded "beyond a reasonable doubt" that an individual committed a crime; they merely need to conclude that the evidence presented indicates that it seems more likely than not that the individual committed a crime. If the grand jury concludes that enough evidence exists, then it issues an indictment that serves to initiate charges against the targeted suspect.

Because the prosecutor controls the proceeding and determines what evidence is presented, a typical grand jury may hear evidence and issue indictments against dozens of suspects in a single day. Afterward, each case that ends in a grand jury indictment will then move to the plea bargaining and trial stages, where defense attorneys represent defendants and provide arguments and evidence on their behalf. For cases that eventually go to trial in front of a jury or judge, the prosecutor will face the full adversarial process, a much higher burden of proof, and an active battle with the accused's defense attorney in trying to prove the defendant's guilt beyond a reasonable doubt.

The Ferguson, Missouri, grand jury proceeding in the aftermath of Officer Darren Wilson's fatal shooting of unarmed teenager Michael Brown was different from the typical process in so many ways that it raised questions about the intentions of the prosecutor. This grand jury listened for more three weeks to the prosecution's presentation of information concerning the possibility of bringing criminal charges against Officer Wilson. The unusual length, structure, and content of the proceeding led critics to claim that it was conducted in a manner that was designed to help Officer Wilson avoid criminal charges. Critics pointed to various aspects of the Ferguson grand jury proceeding, including:

- Early in the proceeding, Officer Wilson testified at length about his version of events, and he did so without being closely questioned by the prosecutors, a sharp contrast to the prosecutors' questioning of several witnesses who were critical of Officer Wilson. Thus Wilson, who had been advised by an attorney and presumably knew from that advice how to present his version in the most favorable light, had the opportunity to provide the initial story that established the baseline of the grand jurors' understanding of events. Moreover, he was permitted to present this version without questioning that could have highlighted inconsistencies and weaknesses between his initial statements after the shooting and his later prepared testimony to the grand jury. This was especially unusual because defendants rarely testify at all in grand jury proceedings.

(Beichner and Spohn, 2012). Even if police make an arrest on the scene, a fight between spouses may strike a prosecutor as a weak case, especially if the complaining spouse has second thoughts about cooperating. A high percentage of victims of violent crimes are acquainted with their assailants. That some victims would rather endure victimization than see a friend or relative punished in the justice system creates problems for the prosecution's cases.

- Prosecutors prepared the grand jurors to hear and understand testimony by telling them about an inaccurate and outdated Missouri law that permitted officers to shoot people in order to prevent them from escaping. In reality, that law's legal principle had been declared unconstitutional by the U.S. Supreme Court in 1984 in a case that said the old "shoot-the-fleeing-felon" concept was invalid when officers did not see evidence that the individual was armed. Thus the grand jurors evaluated the testimony, including Wilson's, for several weeks through the lens of an erroneous understanding of permissible use of firearms by police officers. Prosecutors corrected their error near the end of the grand jury proceeding, but many observers concluded that the quick, vague way in which prosecutors presented the updated law to the grand jurors was likely to cause significant confusion.
- Prosecutors did not act in the usual manner to guide the grand jurors by specifying a charge and presenting evidence to provide a basis for issuing an indictment on that charge. Instead, they gave the grand jurors a list of charges to figure out for themselves and then presented a massive amount of evidence and testimony. Critics saw this approach as also likely to cause confusion by, in effect, overwhelming the grand jurors with excessive and contradictory evidence that would be difficult to sort and understand.
- Prosecutors permitted several witnesses to testify even though they knew these witnesses were not truthful, and their testimony had already been discredited by investigators. One of these witnesses had reportedly been caught lying in other cases, had posted racist comments online against the deceased, Michael Brown, and had her claims of being at the site of shooting already refuted by police investigators. Such discredited witnesses testified both for and against Office Wilson and, in the view of critics, enhanced the risk of confusion for the grand jurors who did not know which witnesses were already discredited.
- Prosecutors moved forward with the grand jury proceeding before local police and the FBI had completed their investigations. Thus, in claiming to present all evidence to the grand jury, the prosecutors actually acted prematurely without waiting to see complete law enforcement reports on the events and evidence.
- Critics claimed that the lengthy proceeding created the illusion in the minds of many members of the public that the grand jury had thoroughly investigated the case and produced a clear, evidence-supported determination that Wilson was "not guilty." In reality, however, the proceeding was not based on the adversarial process that would have occurred in a subsequent trial and therefore the evidence in the case was not rigorously questioned and challenged by attorneys, as would happen in a trial.

As indicated by these examples, public dissatisfaction with the Ferguson grand jury is not merely based on the disappointment of those who hoped to see Officer Wilson charged with a crime. The unusual manner in which the proceedings were conducted raised many questions for critics about whether prosecutors had decided in advance to keep Officer Wilson from facing criminal charges. Did the prosecutors design a confusing and arguably tilted proceeding to place responsibility for the failure to file charges on hopelessly confused grand jurors? Alternatively, did they feel pressured to have a lengthy proceeding that included as much information as possible in order to avoid possible accusations from critics that they were favoring Officer Wilson?

Sources: William Freivogel, "Grand Jury Wrangled with Confusing Instructions," St. Louis Public Radio online, November 26, 2014 (http://news.stlpublicradio.org); William Freivogel, "Was the Grand Jury Procedure in the Wilson Case Fair?," St. Louis Public Radio online, November 25, 2014 (http://news.stlpublicradio.org); Kimberly Kindy and Carol Leonnig, "In Atypical Approach, Grand Jury in Ferguson Shooting Receives Full Measure of Case," September 7, 2014 (www.washingtonpost.com); Lawrence O'Donnell, "Missouri Attorney General: Change Deadly Force Law," MSNBC.com, December 3, 2014 (www.msnbc.com); Colleen Shalby, "St. Louis DA Says He Knew of Lying Witnesses in Ferguson Grand Jury Trial," PBS New online, December 19, 2014 (www.pbs.org).

CRITICAL THINKING AND ANALYSIS

Prosecutors work closely with and depend on police in order to fulfill their responsibilities. Does this relationship create a risk that prosecutors will not treat police officers suspected of wrongdoing in the same manner as other citizen-suspects? Should a prosecutor from outside the county handle grand jury proceedings concerning police officers? If prosecutors were correct in their conduct of the grand jury proceeding for Officer Wilson, does that mean that other criminal suspects are being denied equal rights when their cases are handled in brief proceedings through prosecutors' presentation of evidence about a specific charge—and without any opportunity for the defendant to testify? Write a memo that describes how grand jury proceedings should operate when a police officer is suspected of committing a crime.

Prosecutors and police officers in several American cities express concern about the growth of a "stop snitching" movement that is essentially a means through which drug dealers and other criminals seek to intimidate witnesses into remaining silent. Beatings and murders of witnesses in Baltimore, Philadelphia, Newark, and other cities complicate prosecutors' efforts to gain convictions (Kocieniewski, 2007). Moreover, due to highly publicized "stop snitching" DVDs and T-shirts, the idea of refusing to cooperate with prosecutors and police seems to have become part of the code of behavior by which some young people apparently seek to live. Because prosecutors must rely on witnesses and victims to supply testimony and other evidence against offenders, officials have felt challenged to find ways to counteract the "stop snitching" message that is so widespread and powerful in some neighborhoods.

In recent years, many people have called for measures that would force prosecutors to make victims more central to the prosecution. Because the state pursues charges against the accused in criminal cases, the victim is often forgotten in the process. The victims' rights movement wants victims to receive a chance to comment on plea bargains, sentences, and parole decisions. In 2004, Congress enacted the Justice for All Act, which included entitlements for victims in federal criminal cases. Victims are entitled to the opportunity to be heard during court proceedings and to confer with the prosecutor. Some people would like to see such provisions added to the U.S. Constitution so that they would apply to all state courts as well as federal courts.

Judges and Courts

The sentencing history of each judge gives prosecutors an idea of how a case might be treated in the courtroom. Prosecutors may decide to drop a case if they believe that the judge assigned to it will not impose a serious punishment. Because prosecutors' offices have limited resources, they cannot afford to waste time pursuing charges in front of a judge who shows a pattern of dismissing those particular cases.

Prosecutors depend on plea bargaining to keep cases moving through the courts. If judges' sentencing patterns are not predictable, prosecutors find it hard to persuade defendants and their attorneys to accept plea agreements. If the defendants and their lawyers are to accept a lesser charge or a promise of a lighter sentence in exchange for a guilty plea, they need to see some basis for believing that the judge will support the agreement. Although some judges will informally approve plea agreements before the plea is entered, other judges believe early judicial action is improper. Because these judges refuse to state their agreement with the details of any bargain, the prosecutor and defense attorney must use the judges' past performance as a guide in arranging a plea that will be accepted in court.

In most jurisdictions, a person arrested on felony charges must receive a preliminary hearing within ten days. For prosecutors, this hearing is a chance to evaluate the testimony of witnesses, assess the strength of the evidence, and try to predict the outcome of the case, should it go to trial. After that, prosecutors have several options: recommend that the case be held for trial, seek to reduce the charge to a misdemeanor, or conclude that they have no case and drop the charges. The prosecutor's perception of both the court's caseload and the judge's attitudes greatly influences these decisions. If courts are overwhelmed with cases or if judges do not share the prosecutor's view about the seriousness of certain charges, the prosecutor may drop cases or reduce charges in order to keep the heavy flow of cases moving.

The Community

Studies have shown that the public usually pays little attention to the criminal justice system. Still, the community remains a potential source of pressure that leaders may activate against the prosecutor. The prosecutor's office generally keeps the public in mind when it makes its decisions. Public opinion and the media can play a crucial role in creating an environment that either supports or undermines the prosecutor. Like police chiefs and school superintendents, county prosecutors will likely not be retained if they are out of step with community values.

Public influence is especially important with respect to crimes that are not always fully enforced. Laws on the books may ban prostitution, gambling, and pornography, but a community may nonetheless tolerate them. In such a community the prosecutor will focus on other crimes rather than risk irritating citizens who believe that victimless crimes should not be strongly enforced. Other communities, however, may pressure the prosecutor to enforce morality laws and to prosecute those who do not comply with local ordinances and state statutes. As elected officials, prosecutors must remain sensitive to voters' attitudes.

Prosecutors' relationships and interactions with police, victims, defense attorneys, judges, and the community form the core of the exchange relations that shape decision making in criminal cases. Other relationships, such as those with news media, federal and state officials, legislators, and political party officials, also influence prosecutors' decisions. This long list of influences illustrates that these decisions are not based solely on whether a law was broken. The occurrence of a crime is only the first step in a decision-making process that may vary from one case to the next. Sometimes charges are dropped or reduced. Sometimes plea bargains are negotiated quickly. Sometimes cases move through the system to a complete jury trial. In every instance, relationships and interactions with a variety of actors both within and outside the justice system shape prosecutors' discretionary decisions.

One approach employed in some cities is **community prosecution**. Community prosecution represents an initiative to reduce crime and increase the effectiveness of the criminal justice system by bringing prosecutors into closer contact with citizens. This model program in Washington, D.C., gave individual assistant prosecutors responsibility for specific neighborhoods within the city. Some of the prosecutors were assigned exclusively to outreach functions that involved meeting with citizens and working with police to identify and remedy persistent crime problems. Other prosecutors took responsibility for prosecuting cases that arose in their assigned neighborhoods (J. Goldkamp, Irons-Guynn, and Weiland, 2002).

community prosecution
An approach to advance effective prosecution and crime prevention by placing prosecutors in close contact with citizens and neighborhood groups in an effort to identify and solve problems while enhancing cooperation between the community and the prosecutor's office.

By having responsibility for specific neighborhoods, the prosecutors could become well acquainted with the environment, social problems, crimes, and repeat offenders that burdened the residents of those neighborhoods. The residents could also gain personal familiarity with one or more specific prosecutors assigned to serve them. By contrast, prosecution in most cities is rather impersonal, because victims and witnesses must come to the courthouse to meet with prosecutors who may handle only specific aspects of one case or who have no reason to maintain continuing contacts with the citizens after the case is closed. Under the community prosecution model, individual prosecutors would become familiar to residents by working to resolve neighborhood problems and coordinate communications with police and other public service agencies.

The advocates of community prosecution argue that the initiative is not merely a public relations effort to gain favor with the public. Instead, it is a legitimate strategy for seeking to reduce crime, especially in neighborhoods burdened by the severest problems, and to increase cooperation between citizens and criminal justice officials. If you were a county prosecutor, would you want to experiment with community prosecution?

As you read "Civic Engagement: Your Role in the System," think about how cooperation and coordination among prosecutors, police, and the public can improve by connecting prosecutors more closely with the communities they serve.

CIVIC ENGAGEMENT

YOUR ROLE IN THE SYSTEM

Imagine that you are a neighborhood leader contacted by the local prosecutor. She wants to start a "community prosecution" program and she needs advice from citizens about which activities would be most useful. *Write a short memo that makes four suggestions to the prosecutor and explains how each one will both keep citizens involved and address neighborhood problems.* Then go to the website of the Center for Court Innovation to read about the programs at the Red Hook Community Justice Center in one New York neighborhood.

POINT **5.** What are the prosecutor's key exchange relationships?

STOP AND ANALYZE: Do the prosecutors' exchange relationships contribute to or distract from the goal of achieving justice in each case? List two arguments for recognizing benefits from exchange relationships and two arguments about negative consequences from such relationships.

Decision-Making Policies

Despite the many factors that can affect prosecutors' decisions, we can draw some general conclusions about how prosecutors approach their office. Prosecutors develop their own policies on how cases will be handled. These policies shape the decisions made by the assistant prosecutors and thus have a major impact on the administration of justice. In different counties, prosecutors may pursue different goals in forming policies on which cases to pursue, which ones to drop, and which ones to plea bargain. For example, prosecutors who wish to maintain a high conviction rate will drop cases with weak evidence. Others, concerned about using limited resources effectively, will focus most of their time and energy on the most serious crimes.

Some prosecutors' offices make extensive use of screening and are not inclined to press charges. Guilty pleas are the main method of processing cases in some offices, whereas pleas of not guilty strain the courts' trial resources in others. Some offices remove cases—by diverting or referring them to other agencies—soon after they are brought to the prosecutor's attention by the police; in others, disposition occurs as late as the first day of trial. The period from the receipt of the police report to the start of the trial is thus a time of review in which the prosecutor uses discretion to decide what actions should be taken.

Implementing Prosecution Policy

A classic study by Joan Jacoby analyzed policies that prosecutors use during the pretrial process and how they staff their offices to achieve their goals. On the basis of data from more than 3,000 prosecutors, she describes three policy models: legal sufficiency, system efficiency, and trial sufficiency. The choice of a policy model is shaped by personal aspects of the prosecutor (such as role conception), external factors such as crime levels, and the relationship of prosecution to the other parts of the criminal justice system (Jacoby, 1979).

The policy model adopted by a prosecutor's office affects the screening and disposing of cases. As shown in Figure 10.1, the policy models dictate that prosecutors select certain points in the process to dispose of most of the cases brought to them by the police. Each model identifies the point in the process at which cases are filtered out of the system. A particular model may be chosen to advance specific goals, such as saving the prosecutor's time and energy for the most clear-cut or serious cases. Each model also affects how and when prosecutors interact with defense attorneys in exchanging information or discussing options for a plea bargain.

legal sufficiency
The presence of the minimum legal elements necessary for prosecution of a case. When a prosecutor uses legal sufficiency as the customary criterion for prosecuting cases, a great many are accepted for prosecution, but the majority of them are disposed of by plea bargaining or dismissal.

In the **legal sufficiency** model, prosecutors merely ask whether there is enough evidence to serve as a basis for prosecution. Some prosecutors believe they should pursue any case that likely meets the minimum legal elements of the charge. Prosecutors who use this policy may decide to prosecute a great many cases. As a result, they must have strategies to avoid overloading the system and draining their own resources. Thus, assistant prosecutors, especially those assigned to misdemeanor courts, make extensive use of plea bargains to keep cases flowing through the courts. In this model, judges often dismiss

FIGURE 10.1 THREE POLICY MODELS OF PROSECUTORIAL CASE MANAGEMENT

Prosecutors develop policies to guide the way their offices will manage cases. These models all assume that a portion of arrests will be dropped at some point in the system so that few cases reach trial.

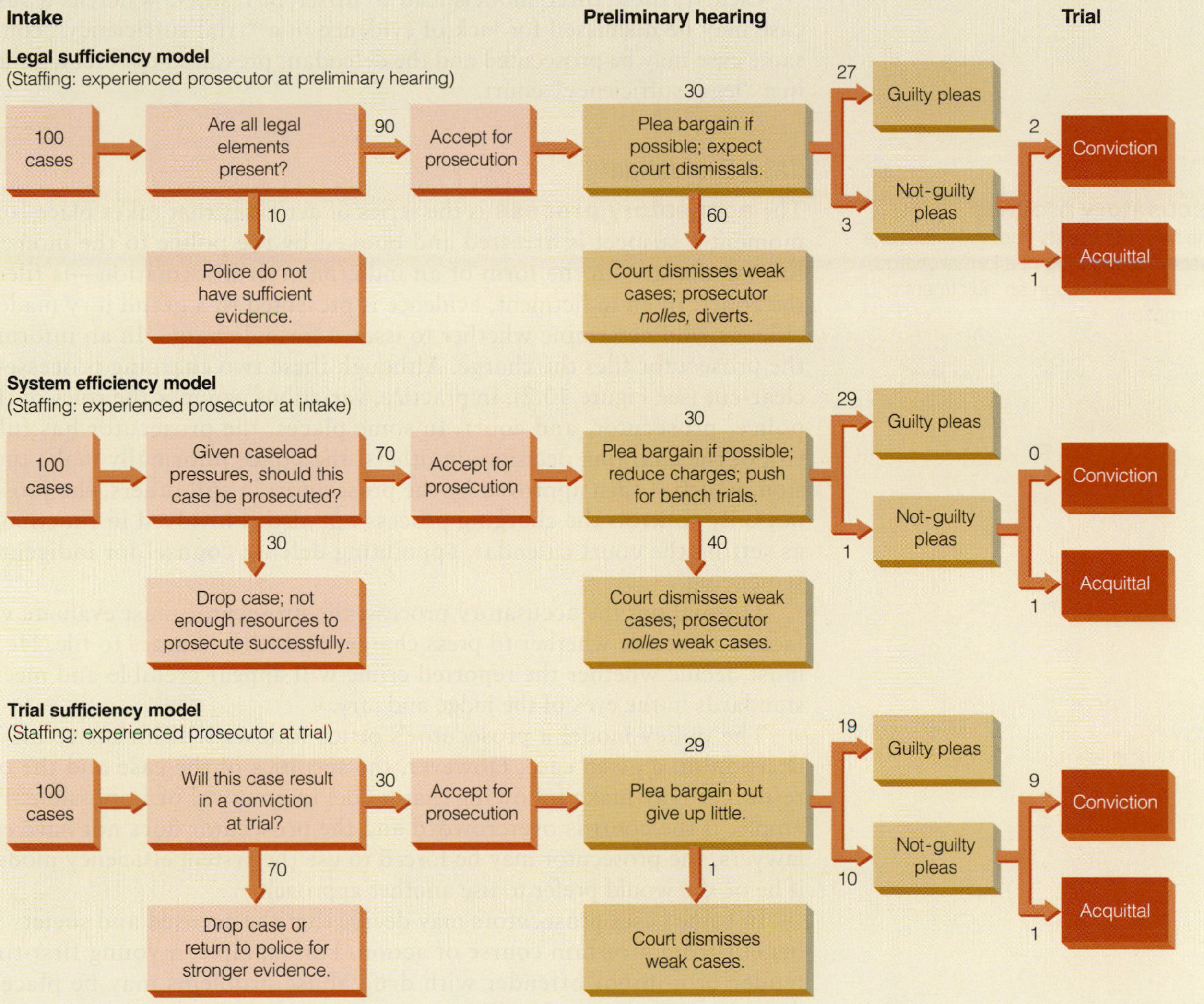

many cases after determining that there is not enough evidence for prosecution to continue.

The **system efficiency** model aims at speedy and early disposition of a case. Each case is evaluated in light of the current caseload pressures. To close cases quickly, the prosecutor might charge the defendant with a felony but agree to reduce the charge to a misdemeanor in exchange for a guilty plea. According to Jacoby's research, this model is usually followed when the trial court is backlogged and the prosecutor has limited resources.

In the **trial sufficiency** model, a case is accepted and charges are made only when there is enough evidence to ensure conviction. For each case the prosecutor asks, "Will this case result in a conviction?" The prosecutor might not correctly predict the likelihood of conviction in every case. However, the prosecutor will make every effort to win a conviction when he or she believes

system efficiency
Policy of the prosecutor's office that encourages speedy and early disposition of cases in response to caseload pressures. Weak cases are screened out at intake, and other nontrial alternatives are used as a primary means of disposition.

trial sufficiency
The presence of sufficient legal elements to ensure successful prosecution of a case. When a prosecutor uses trial sufficiency as the customary criterion for prosecuting cases, only cases that seem certain to result in conviction at trial are accepted for prosecution. Use of plea bargaining is minimal; good police work, and court capacity to go to trial are required.

there is evidence to prove that all necessary legal elements for a crime are present. This model requires good police work, a prosecution staff with trial experience, and—because there is less plea bargaining—courts that are not too crowded to handle many trials.

Clearly, these three models lead to different results. Whereas a suspect's case may be dismissed for lack of evidence in a "trial sufficiency" court, the same case may be prosecuted and the defendant pressured to enter a guilty plea in a "legal sufficiency" court.

Case Evaluation

accusatory process
The series of events from the arrest of a suspect to the filing of a formal charge with a court (through an indictment or information).

The **accusatory process** is the series of activities that takes place from the moment a suspect is arrested and booked by the police to the moment the formal charge—in the form of an indictment or information—is filed with the court. In an indictment, evidence is presented to a grand jury made up of citizens who determine whether to issue a formal charge. In an information, the prosecutor files the charge. Although these two charging processes seem clear-cut (see Figure 10.2), in practice, variations can mix the roles of the city police, prosecutor, and court. In some places, the prosecutor has full control of the charging decision; in others, the police informally make the decision, which is then approved by the prosecutor; in still others, the prosecutor not only controls the charging process but also is involved in functions such as setting the court calendar, appointing defense counsel for indigents, and sentencing.

Throughout the accusatory process, the prosecutor must evaluate various factors to decide whether to press charges and what charges to file. He or she must decide whether the reported crime will appear credible and meet legal standards in the eyes of the judge and jury.

The policy model a prosecutor's office follows will influence his or her decision on a given case. However, the specifics of the case and the office's resources may make following that model impractical or impossible. For example, if the court is overcrowded and the prosecutor does not have enough lawyers, the prosecutor may be forced to use the system efficiency model even if he or she would prefer to use another approach.

In some cases prosecutors may decide that the accused and society would benefit from a certain course of action. For example, a young first-time offender or a minor offender with drug abuse problems may be placed in a diversion program rather than prosecuted in the criminal justice system. In applying their own values in making such judgments, prosecutors may make decisions that run counter to the ideals of law. Prosecutors are, after all, human beings who must respond to some of the most troubling problems in American society. In evaluating cases, they may knowingly or unknowingly permit their personal biases to affect their decisions and thereby treat people differently according to their age, gender, race, or ethnicity. For example, recent research found no across-the-board discrimination by race in federal district courts nationwide for prosecutors' decisions about charge reductions. But apparent differences were identified in treatment by crime: "Male offenders were especially unlikely to be given charge reductions for drug and violent crimes and black and Hispanic offenders were disadvantaged in charging decisions for weapons offenses" (Shermer and Johnson, 2010: 421).

Clearly, the prosecutor's established policies and decisions play a key role in determining whether charges will be filed against a defendant. Keep in mind, however, that the prosecutor's decision-making power is not limited to

FIGURE 10.2 TWO MODELS OF THE ACCUSATORY PROCESS

Indictment and information are the two methods used in the United States to accuse a person of a crime. Note the role of the grand jury in an indictment and the preliminary hearing in an information. According to the ideal of due process, each method is designed to spare an innocent person the psychological, monetary, and other costs of prosecution.

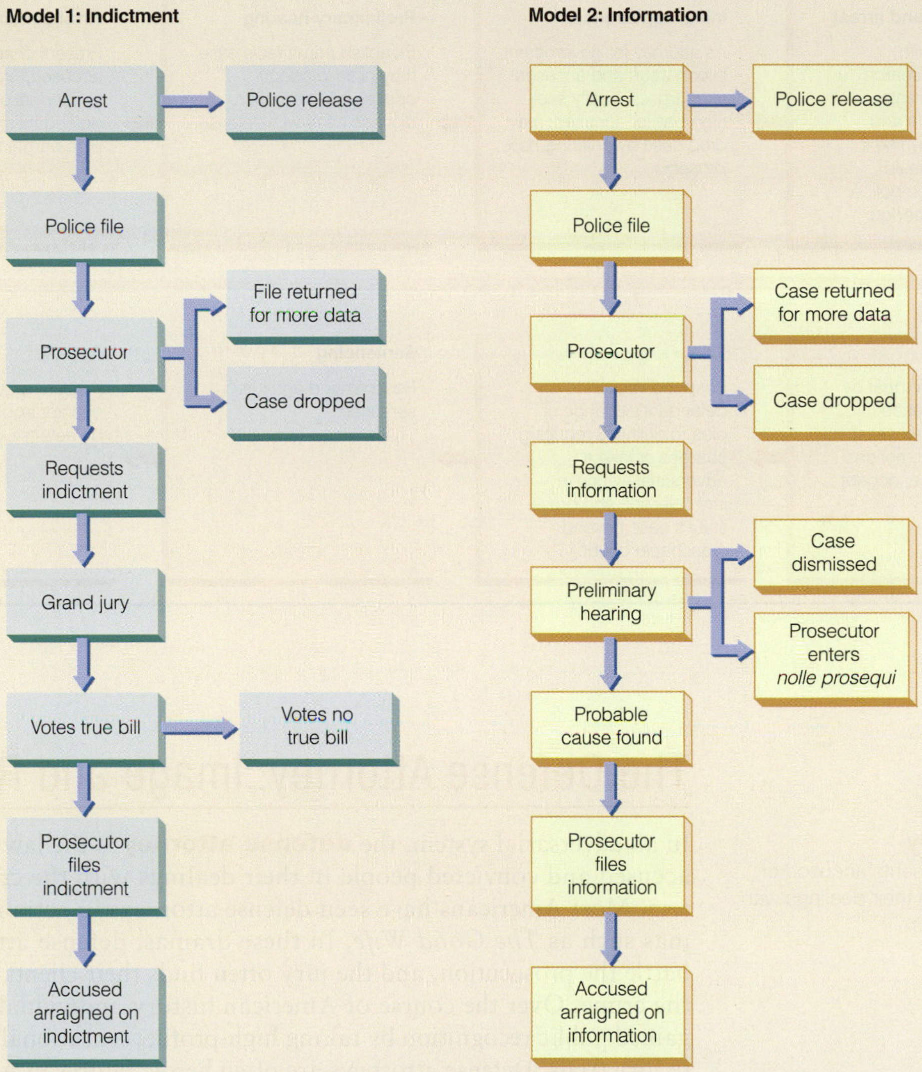

decisions about charges. As shown in Figure 10.3, the prosecutor makes important decisions at each stage, both before and after a defendant's guilt is determined. Because the prosecutor's involvement and influence span the justice process, from seeking search warrants during early investigations to arguing against postconviction appeals, the prosecutor is a highly influential actor in criminal cases. No other participant in the system is involved in so many different stages of the criminal process.

✔POINT 6. What are the three models of prosecution policy, and how do they differ?

STOP AND ANALYZE: If you were a prosecutor, which model of prosecution policy would you follow in your office? Give two reasons for your answer.

FIGURE 10.3 TYPICAL ACTIONS OF A PROSECUTING ATTORNEY IN PROCESSING A FELONY CASE

The prosecutor has certain responsibilities at various points in the process. At each point the prosecutor serves as an advocate for the state's case against the accused.

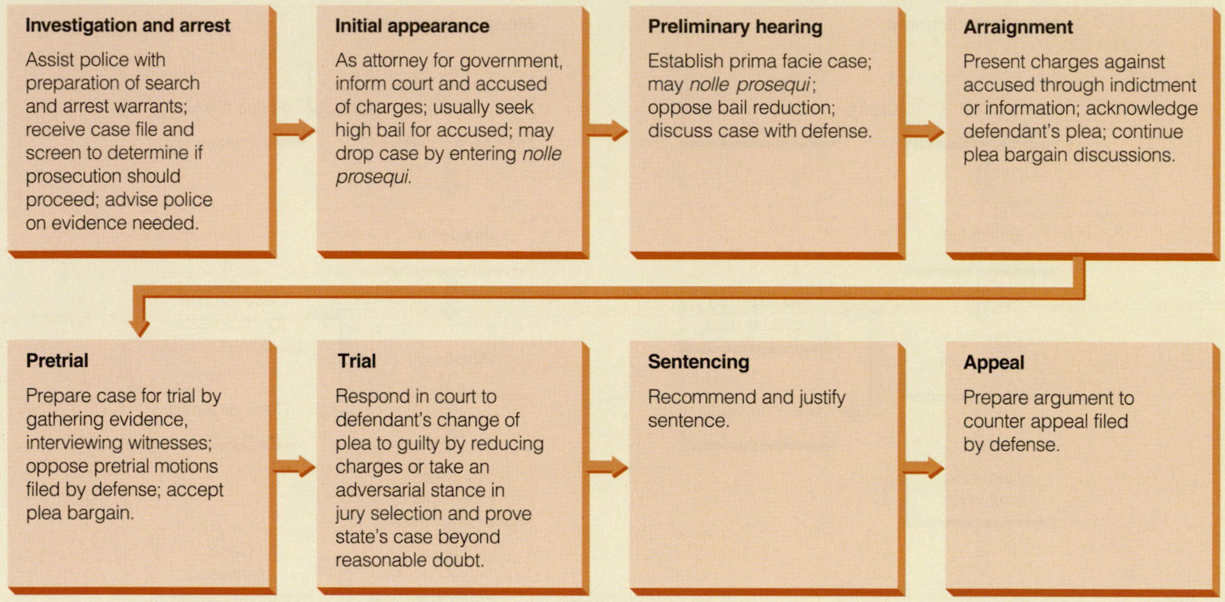
Investigation and arrest
Assist police with preparation of search and arrest warrants; receive case file and screen to determine if prosecution should proceed; advise police on evidence needed.
Initial appearance
As attorney for government, inform court and accused of charges; usually seek high bail for accused; may drop case by entering *nolle prosequi*.
Preliminary hearing
Establish prima facie case; may *nolle prosequi*; oppose bail reduction; discuss case with defense.
Arraignment
Present charges against accused through indictment or information; acknowledge defendant's plea; continue plea bargain discussions.
Pretrial
Prepare case for trial by gathering evidence, interviewing witnesses; oppose pretrial motions filed by defense; accept plea bargain.
Trial
Respond in court to defendant's change of plea to guilty by reducing charges or take an adversarial stance in jury selection and prove state's case beyond reasonable doubt.
Sentencing
Recommend and justify sentence.
Appeal
Prepare argument to counter appeal filed by defense.

The Defense Attorney: Image and Reality

defense attorney
The lawyer who represents accused or convicted offenders in their dealings with criminal justice officials.

In an adversarial system, the **defense attorney** is the lawyer who represents accused and convicted people in their dealings with the criminal justice system. Most Americans have seen defense attorneys in action on television dramas such as *The Good Wife*. In these dramas, defense attorneys vigorously battle the prosecution, and the jury often finds their clients to be not guilty of the crime. Over the course of American history, individual defense attorneys gained public recognition by taking high-profile, sensational cases that resulted in jury trials. Defense attorneys are often heroic figures in American literature. Think of attorney Atticus Finch defending the innocent African American rape suspect in *To Kill a Mockingbird* or various characters in the novels of John Grisham and Scott Turow.

In contrast, most cases are handled by criminal lawyers who must quickly process a large volume of cases for small fees. Rather than adversarial conflict in the courtroom, they process cases through plea bargaining, discretionary dismissals, and other means. In these cases the defense attorney may seem less like the prosecutor's adversary and more like a partner in the effort to dispose of cases as quickly and efficiently as possible through negotiation (Edkins, 2011).

The Role of the Defense Attorney

To be effective, defense attorneys must have knowledge of law and procedure, investigative skills, advocacy experience, and, in many cases, relationships with prosecutors and judges that will help a defendant obtain the best possible outcome. In the American legal system, the defense attorney performs the key function of making sure that the prosecution proves its case in court or has substantial evidence of guilt before a guilty plea is entered.

As shown in Figure 10.4, the defense attorney advises the defendant and protects his or her constitutional rights at each stage of the criminal justice process. The defense attorney advises the defendant during questioning by the police, represents him or her at each arraignment and hearing, and serves as advocate for the defendant during the appeals process if there is a conviction. Without a defense attorney, prosecutors and judges might not respect the rights of the accused. Without knowing the technical details of law and court procedures, defendants have little ability to represent themselves in court effectively.

While filling their roles in the criminal justice system, the defense attorneys also give psychological support to the defendant and his or her family. Relatives are often bewildered, frightened, and confused. The defense attorney is the only legal actor available to answer the question "What will happen next?" In short, the attorney's relationship with the client is crucial. An effective defense requires respect, openness, and trust between attorney and client. If the defendant refuses to follow the attorney's advice, the lawyer may feel obliged to withdraw from the case in order to protect his or her own professional reputation.

Realities of the Defense Attorney's Job

How well do defense attorneys represent their clients? The television image of defense attorneys is usually based on the due process model, in which attorneys are strong advocates for their clients. In reality, the enthusiasm and effectiveness of defense attorneys vary.

FIGURE 10.4 TYPICAL ACTIONS OF A DEFENSE ATTORNEY PROCESSING A FELONY CASE

Defense attorneys serve as advocates for the accused. They are obliged to challenge points made by the prosecution and to advise.

Police station
Provide advice during interrogation, ensure constitutional rights are not violated; counsel accused during booking; seek pretrial release; determine facts of case from police records.

Initial appearance
Appear with accused before judge; seek pretrial release (release on recognizance or bail); challenge basis for arrest.

Preliminary hearing
Challenge prosecutor's stand that probable cause exists; seek bail reduction if client not released; discover evidence held by prosecutor; counsel defendant as to nature of case; discuss case with prosecutor.

Arraignment
Learn charges listed in indictment or information; advise client as to plea; discuss plea bargain with prosecutor.

Pretrial
Continue plea negotiations; file pretrial motions challenging evidence and procedural errors.

Trial
Change plea from not guilty to guilty as result of bargain *or* assume adversarial stance in jury selection and presentation of defense.

Sentencing
Prepare client for expected outcome; urge lenient sentence.

Appeal
Develop appropriate basis for appeal; request that client be released pending appeal.

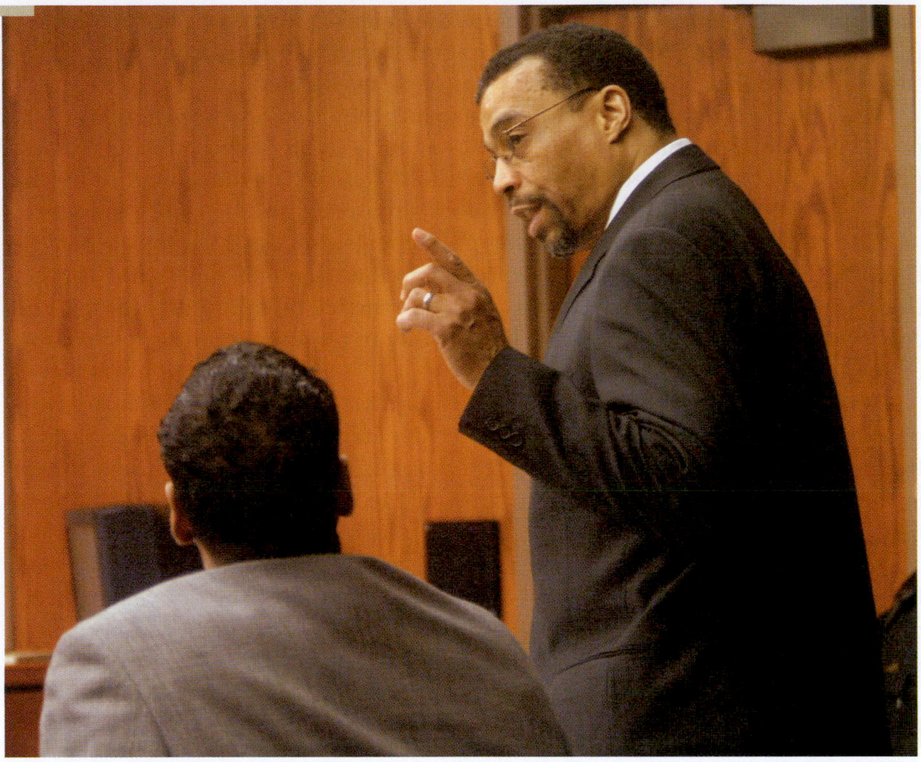

Billy Martin, a nationally known defense attorney, has represented such prominent clients as NFL quarterback Michael Vick and former NBA star Jayson Williams. The defense attorney must be persuasive and knowledgeable as well as creative in identifying useful arguments and flaws in the prosecutor's evidence. Could you use your creativity and skills to enthusiastically represent criminal defendants?

Attorneys who are inexperienced, uncaring, or overburdened have trouble representing their clients effectively. The attorney may quickly agree to a plea bargain and then work to persuade the defendant to accept the agreement. The attorney's self-interest in disposing of cases quickly, receiving payment, and moving on to other cases may cause the attorney to, in effect, work with the prosecutor to pressure the defendant to plead guilty.

Skilled defense attorneys, on the other hand, may also consider a plea bargain in the earliest stages of a case, but their role as an advocate for the defendant will guide them in their use of plea bargaining. An effective defense attorney does not try to take every case all the way to trial. In many cases, a negotiated plea with a predictable sentence will serve the defendant better than a trial spent fending off more-serious charges. Good defense attorneys seek to understand the facts of each case and to judge the nature of the evidence in order to reach the best possible outcome for their client. Even in the plea-bargaining process, this level of advocacy requires more time, effort, knowledge, and commitment than some attorneys are willing or able to provide.

The defense attorney's job is all the more difficult because neither the public nor defendants fully understand the attorney's duties and goals. The public often views defense attorneys as protectors of criminals. In fact, the attorney's basic duty is not to save criminals from punishment but to protect constitutional rights, keep the prosecution honest in preparing and presenting cases, and prevent innocent people from being convicted (Flowers, 2010). Surveys indicate that lawyers place much greater emphasis on the importance of right to counsel than does the public. Look at the questions presented in "What Americans Think." Do you think that the public underestimates the necessity of representation by an attorney? Do you agree with the majority of the defense attorneys in the survey? Are they too protective of rights or insufficiently concerned about threats to public safety? Could you work on behalf of people who might threaten American society?

In performing tasks that ultimately benefit both the defendant and society, the defense attorney must evaluate and challenge the prosecution's evidence. However, defense attorneys can rarely arrange for guilty defendants to go free. Keep in mind that when prosecutors decide to pursue serious charges, they have already filtered out weaker cases. The defense attorney often negotiates the most appropriate punishment in light of the resources of the court, the strength of the evidence, and the defendant's prior criminal record.

Defendants who, like the public, have watched hours of courtroom dramas on television, often expect their attorneys to fight vigorous battles against the prosecutor at every stage of the justice process. They do not realize that their best interest may require plea agreements negotiated in a friendly, cooperative way. Public defenders in particular are often criticized because the defendants tend to assume that if the state provided an attorney for them, the attorney must be working for the state rather than on their behalf.

✔POINT 7. How does the image of the defense attorney differ from the attorney's actual role?

STOP AND ANALYZE: Would you enjoy being a criminal defense attorney? List two reasons why you see the job as interesting or enjoyable. List two aspects of the job that you would find unpleasant or undesirable.

The Environment of Criminal Practice

Defense attorneys have a difficult job. Much of their work involves preparing clients and their relatives for the likelihood of conviction and punishment. Although they may know that their clients are guilty, they may become emotionally involved, because they are the only judicial actors who know the defendants as human beings and see them in the context of their family and social environment.

Most defense lawyers constantly interact with lower-class clients whose lives and problems are depressing. They sometimes must visit the local jail at all hours of the day and night—far removed from the fancy offices and expensive restaurants of the world of corporate attorneys. As described by one defense attorney, "The days are long and stressful. I spend a good deal of time in jail, which reeks of stale food and body odor. My clients often think that because I'm court-appointed, I must be incompetent" (Lave, 1998: 14).

Defense lawyers must also struggle with the fact that criminal practice does not pay well. Public defenders have relatively low salaries, and attorneys appointed to represent poor defendants are paid small sums. If private attorneys do not demand payment from their clients at the start of the case, they may find that they must persuade the defendants' relatives to pay—because many convicted offenders have no incentive to pay for legal services while sitting in a prison cell. To perform their jobs well and gain satisfaction from their careers, defense attorneys must focus on goals other than money, such as their key role in protecting people's constitutional rights. However, usually being on the losing side can make it hard for them to feel like professionals—with high self-esteem and satisfying work.

Defense attorneys face other pressures as well. If they mount a strong defense and gain an acquittal for their client, the public may blame them for using "technicalities" to keep a criminal on the streets. If they embarrass the prosecution in court, they may harm their prospects for reaching good plea agreements for future clients. Thus, criminal practice can bring major financial,

WHAT AMERICANS THINK

QUESTION: "The American Bar Association, the largest national association of lawyers, surveyed a small sample of defense attorneys about their views on issues related to the government's response to terrorism."*

The terrorism laws passed by Congress have made the U.S. safer.

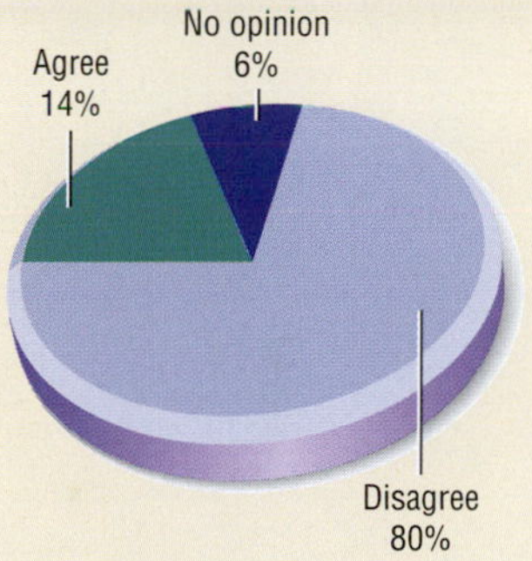

Privacy rights have been unduly compromised as a result of antiterror efforts.

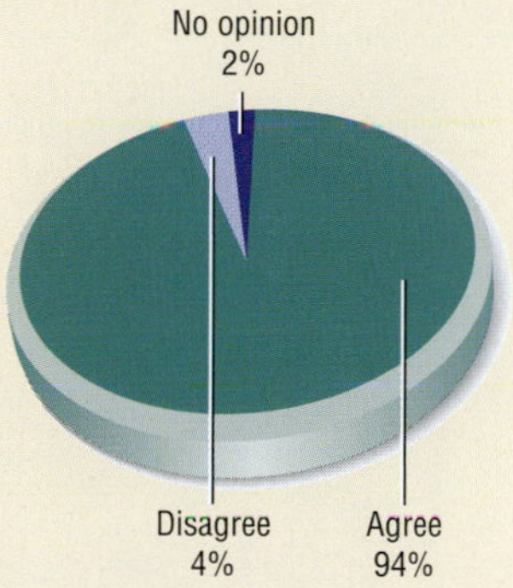

Would you be willing to represent Osama bin Laden in federal court?

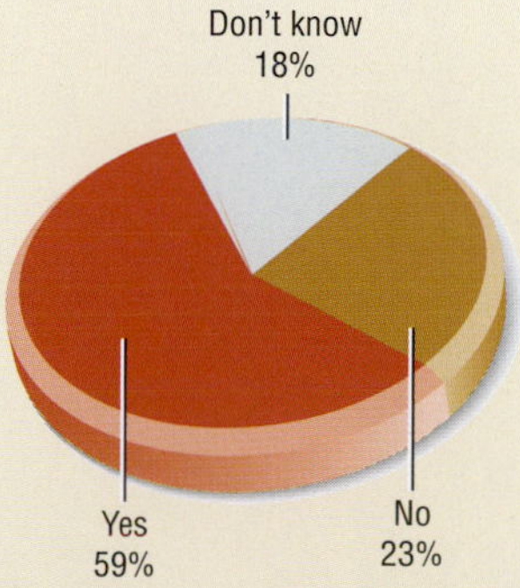

*Poll taken prior to the death of bin Laden in 2011.

Source: Mark Hansen and Stephanie Francis Ward, "The 50-Lawyer Poll," *ABA Journal*, September 2007 (www.abajournal.com).

social, and psychological burdens to attorneys. As a result, many criminal attorneys "burn out" after a few years and seek other career options.

Relationship to Court Officials

Because plea bargaining is the main method of deciding cases, defense attorneys believe they must maintain close personal ties with the police, prosecutor, judges, and other court officials. Critics point out that daily interaction with the same prosecutors and judges undermines the defenders' independence. When the supposed adversaries become close friends as a result of daily contact, the defense attorneys might no longer fight vigorously on behalf of their clients. Also, at every step of the justice process, from the first contact with the accused until final disposition of the case, defense attorneys depend on decisions made by other actors in the system. Even seemingly minor activities such as visiting the defendant in jail, learning about the case from the prosecutor, and setting bail can be difficult unless defense attorneys have the cooperation of others in the system. Thus defense attorneys may limit their activities in order to preserve their relationships with other courthouse actors.

For the criminal lawyer who depends on a large volume of petty cases from poor clients and assumes that they are probably guilty, the incentives to bargain are strong. If the attorney is to be assigned other cases, he or she must help make sure that cases flow smoothly through the courthouse. This requires a cooperative relationship with judges, prosecutors, and others in the justice system.

Despite their dependence on cooperation from other justice system officials to make their work go more smoothly, defense attorneys can sometimes use stubbornness as a tactic. They can, for example, threaten to take a case all the way through trial to test whether the prosecutor is really adamant about not offering a favorable plea agreement.

Some paying clients may expect their counsel to play the role of combatant in the belief that they are not getting their money's worth unless they hear verbal fireworks in the courtroom. Yet even when those fireworks do occur, one cannot be sure that the adversaries are engaged in a real contest. Studies have shown that attorneys whose clients expect a vigorous defense may engage in a courtroom drama commonly known as the "slow plea of guilty," in which the outcome of the case has already been determined, but the attorneys go through the motions of putting up a vigorous fight.

It is often difficult for defendants to understand the benefits of plea bargaining and friendly relationships between defense attorneys and prosecutors. Most cases that are pursued beyond the initial stages are not likely to result in acquittal, no matter how vigorously the attorney presents the defendant's case. In many cases, skilled lawyering simply cannot overcome the evidence of the defendant's guilt. Thus, good relationships can benefit the defendant by gaining a less-than-maximum sentence. At the same time, however, these relationships pose the risk that if the defense attorney and prosecutor are too friendly, the defendant's case will not be presented in the best possible way in plea bargaining or trial.

Relationship to Clients

Some scholars have called defense attorneys "agent-mediators" because they often work to prepare the defendant for the likely outcome of the case—usually conviction (A. Blumberg, 1967). Although such efforts may help the defendant gain a good plea bargain and become mentally prepared to accept the sentence, the attorney's efforts are geared to advancing the needs of the attorney and the legal system. By mediating between the defendant and the system—for example, by encouraging a guilty plea—the attorney helps save time for the prosecutor and judge in gaining a conviction and completing the case. In addition, appointed counsel and contract attorneys may have a financial interest in getting the defendant to plead guilty quickly, in that they can receive payment and move on to the next case (K. Armstrong, Davila, and Mayo, 2004).

A more sympathetic view of defense attorneys labels them "beleaguered dealers" who cut deals for defendants in a tough environment (Uphoff, 1992). Defense attorneys face tremendous pressure to manage large caseloads in a difficult court environment. From this perspective, their actions in encouraging clients to plead guilty result from the difficult aspects of their jobs rather than from self-interest.

✔POINT 8. What special pressures do defense attorneys face?

STOP AND ANALYZE: What knowledge, skills, and experiences are needed in order for a lawyer to be an effective criminal defense attorney? People's lives depend on the decisions and actions of defense attorneys. If you could require that defense attorneys have something more than a law degree in order to represent defendants, what other qualifications or experiences would you like to see? Make a list.

Counsel for Indigents

Since the 1960s, the Supreme Court has interpreted the "right to counsel" in the Sixth Amendment to the Constitution as requiring that the government provide attorneys for indigent defendants who face the possibility of going to prison or jail. Indigent defendants are those who are too poor to afford their own lawyers. The Court has also required that attorneys be provided early in the criminal justice process to protect suspects' rights during questioning and pretrial proceedings. See Table 10.1 for a summary of key rulings on the right to counsel.

Research on felony defendants indicates that 78 percent of those prosecuted in the 75 largest counties and 66 percent of those prosecuted in federal courts received publicly provided legal counsel (Harlow, 2000). The portion

TABLE 10.1 THE RIGHT TO COUNSEL: MAJOR SUPREME COURT RULINGS

CASE	YEAR	RULING
Powell v. Alabama	1932	Indigents facing the death penalty who are not capable of representing themselves must be given attorneys.
Johnson v. Zerbst	1938	Indigent defendants must be provided with attorneys when facing serious charges in federal court.
Gideon v. Wainwright	1963	Indigent defendants must be provided with attorneys when facing serious charges in state court.
Douglas v. California	1963	Indigent defendants must be provided with attorneys for their first appeal.
Miranda v. Arizona	1966	Criminal suspects must be informed about their right to counsel before being questioned in custody.
United States v. Wade	1967	Defendants are entitled to counsel at "critical stages" in the process, including postindictment lineups.
Argersinger v. Hamlin	1972	Indigent defendants must be provided with attorneys when facing misdemeanor and petty charges that may result in incarceration.
Ross v. Moffitt	1974	Indigent defendants are not entitled to attorneys for discretionary appeals after their first appeal is unsuccessful.
Strickland v. Washington	1984	To show that ineffective assistance of counsel violated the right to counsel, defendants must prove that the attorney committed specific errors that affected the outcome of the case.
Rothgery v. Gillespie County, Texas	2008	The right to counsel attaches at the initial hearing before a magistrate when the defendant is informed of the charges and restrictions on liberty are imposed.
Missouri v. Frye	2012	Defense attorneys are obligated to inform their clients about plea agreement offers made by the prosecutor.

of defendants who are provided with counsel because they are indigent has increased greatly in the past three decades. For example, in the 22 states with public defender offices funded by state government rather than county or city governments, criminal caseloads increased by 20 percent from 1999 to 2007 (Langton and Farole, 2010). Government-salaried public defenders alone received 5.5 million cases of indigent criminal defendants in 2007, a figure that does not include thousands of indigents represented by private attorneys who are paid by government on a case-by-case basis (Farole and Langton, 2010).

Many observers debate the quality of counsel given to indigent defendants. Ideally, experienced lawyers would be appointed soon after arrest to represent the defendant in each stage of the criminal justice process. However, inexperienced and uncaring attorneys are sometimes appointed. When the appointment occurs after initial court proceedings have already begun, the attorney has no time to prepare the case. Even conscientious attorneys may be unable to provide top-quality counsel if they have heavy caseloads or are not paid enough money to spend the time required to handle the case well. Excessive caseloads present a significant problem for defense attorneys for indigents, especially during a period of state and local government budget crises. For example, in 2007, in 15 of 22 states with state-funded public defender offices and three-quarters of the county-funded public defender offices in 27 other states, the defense attorneys had caseloads that exceeded the U.S. Department of Justice's recommended guidelines (Farole and Langton, 2010; Langton and Farole, 2010).

If they lack the time, resources, or desire to interview clients and prepare their cases carefully, government-paid attorneys may simply persuade defendants to plead guilty, right there in the courtroom during their first and only brief conversation. When the lawyers assigned to provide counsel to poor defendants cooperate with the prosecutor easily, without even asking the defendant about his or her version of events, it is little wonder that convicted offenders believe that their interests were not represented in the courtroom. Not all publicly financed lawyers who represent poor defendants ignore their clients' interests. However, the quality of counsel received by the poor may vary from courthouse to courthouse, depending on the quality of the attorneys, conditions of defense practice, and administrative pressure to reduce the caseload.

AP Photo/The Orange County Register/Kevin Sullivan

The quality of counsel received by the poor may vary from courthouse to courthouse, depending on the quality of attorneys, conditions of defense practice, and the administrative pressures to reduce caseloads. Should we spend more tax dollars on indigent criminal defense in order to increase resources and quality of representation?

Ways of Providing Indigents with Counsel

The three main ways of providing counsel to indigent defendants in the United States are (1) the **assigned counsel** system, in which a court appoints a private attorney to represent the accused; (2) the **contract counsel** system, in which an attorney, a nonprofit organization, or a private law firm contracts with a local government to provide legal services to indigent defendants for a specified dollar amount; and (3) **public defender** programs, which are public or private nonprofit organizations with full-time or part-time salaried staff. Figure 10.5 shows the states that have statewide, centrally administered public defender systems and the other states that have county-based systems for indigent defense that may include the use of appointed counsel, public defenders, or contract counsel. One study found that in the 100 most populous counties in the United States, 82 percent of indigent cases were handled by public defenders, 15 percent by assigned counsel, and 3 percent by contract attorneys ("Indigent Defense," 2011). Assigned counsel are likely to have a greater share of cases in less populous counties throughout the country.

The methods for providing defense attorneys and the quality of defense services may depend on the money available to pay attorneys. In the states where counties must fund their own defense services, resources—and the quality of indigent defense—may vary from county to county within a single state

assigned counsel
An attorney in private practice assigned by a court to represent an indigent. The attorney's fee is paid by the government with jurisdiction over the case.

contract counsel
An attorney in private practice who contracts with the government to represent all indigent defendants in a county during a set period of time and for a specified dollar amount.

public defender
An attorney employed on a full-time, salaried basis by the government to represent indigents.

FIGURE 10.5 STATE-RUN PUBLIC DEFENDER OFFICES AND COUNTY-RUN INDIGENT DEFENSE SYSTEMS

Note that county-run systems, in particular, may use different representation models (assigned, contract, or public defender) in counties within a given state or use more than one method within a county.

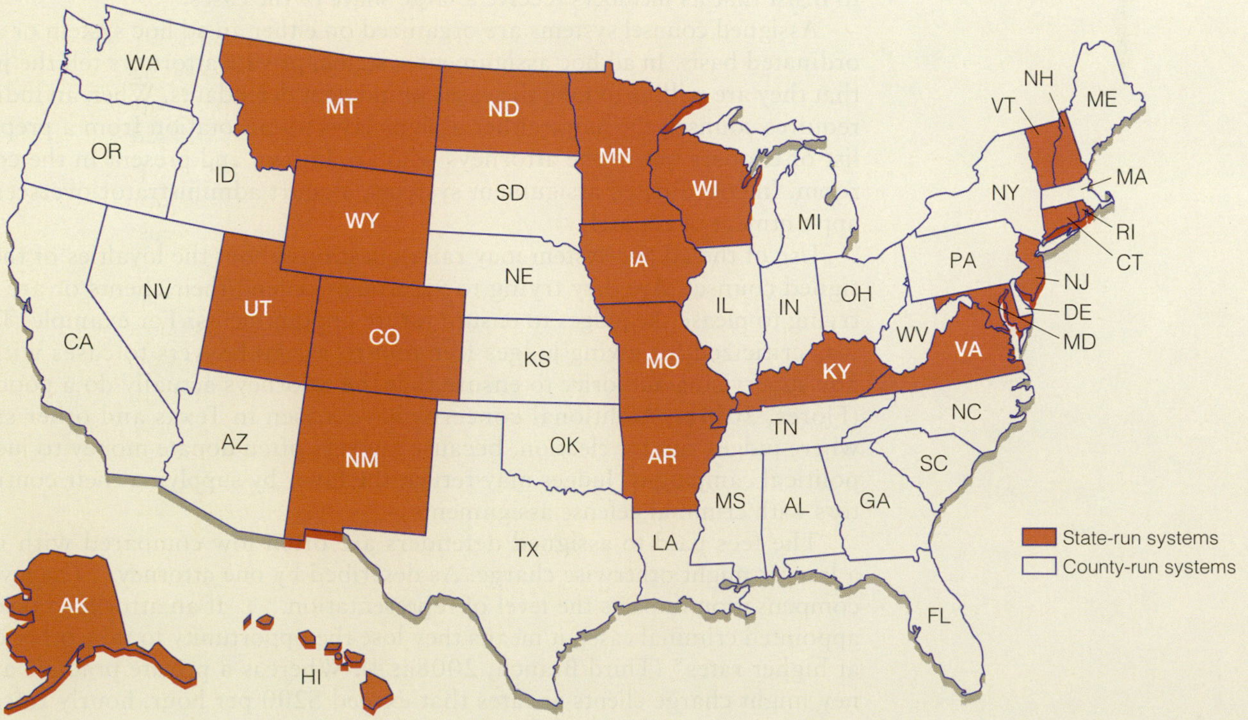

Source: Lynn Langton and Donald Farole Jr. "State Public Defender Programs, 2007." *Bureau of Justice Statistics Special Report*, September 2010. NCJ 228229.

(Flores, 2014b). As the chief state public defender in Ohio said with respect to the 88 counties in his state's county-run system, "When you have the state of Ohio law being enforced and defended in 88 different ways . . . you end up with huge disparities in cost, quality, and efficiency" (A. Manning, 2012).

Issues of resources and quality are complicated by budget cuts in the current era of economic recovery. In 2013, across-the-board cuts throughout the federal government forced public defenders who work in federal courts to take unpaid furloughs for several weeks. Such cuts affect the preparation of cases and timely representation of clients. They can also cause experienced public defenders to look for other jobs rather than fall into personal financial difficulties by being unable to pay rent or house payments because of uncertainties affecting their future working hours and paychecks (C. Johnson, 2013). Many states were affected by budget problems earlier than the federal government. For example, Gwinnett County, Georgia, cut the compensation for court-appointed defense attorneys from $75 to $65 per hour for serious felony cases, with even lower pay rates for misdemeanors and out-of-court activities (A. Simmons and Rankin, 2010). In Oklahoma, the indigent defense system suffered a $1.5 million budget cut resulting in its attorneys being assigned 400 to 500 cases per year (Bisbee, 2010). Some locations, however, are allocating more money for indigent defense, such as El Paso, Texas, which increased pay for appointed attorneys by $15 per hour in 2014 to $90 per hour for in-court work and $75 per hour for out-of-court work (Flores, 2014a).

Assigned Counsel In the assigned counsel system, the court appoints a lawyer in private practice to represent an indigent defendant. This system is widely used in small cities and in rural areas, but even some city public defender systems assign counsel in some cases, such as in a case with multiple defendants, where a conflict of interest might result if one of them were represented by a public lawyer. But in other cities, such as Detroit, the private bar has been able to insist that its members receive a large share of the cases.

Assigned counsel systems are organized on either an ad hoc system or a coordinated basis. In ad hoc assignment systems, private attorneys tell the judge that they are willing to take the cases of indigent defendants. When an indigent requires counsel, the judge either assigns lawyers in rotation from a prepared list or chooses one of the attorneys who are known and present in the courtroom. In coordinated assignment systems, a court administrator oversees the appointment of counsel.

Use of the ad hoc system may raise questions about the loyalties of the assigned counsel. Are they trying to vigorously defend their clients or are they trying to please the judges to ensure future appointments? For example, Texas was criticized for giving judges free rein to assign lawyers to cases without any supervising authority to ensure that the attorneys actually do a good job (Flores, 2014b). Additional concerns have arisen in Texas and other states where judges run for election, because lawyers often donate money to judges' political campaigns. Judges may return the favor by supplying their contributors with criminal defense assignments.

The fees paid to assigned defenders are often low compared with what a lawyer might otherwise charge. As described by one attorney, "The level of compensation impacts the level of representation. . . . If an attorney takes [an appointed criminal case], it means they lose the opportunity to take other cases at higher rates" (Third Branch, 2008a: 4). Whereas a private practice attorney might charge clients at rates that exceed $200 per hour, hourly rates for appointed counsel in Cook County (Chicago), Illinois, are merely $40 per hour for in-court tasks and $30 per hour for out-of-court tasks. These same rates have been in place for more than 30 years. Defense attorneys receive the low rate of $40 per hour for out-of-court work in Oklahoma, Oregon, Alabama,

South Carolina, and Tennessee. Many other states pay only $50 to $75 per hour (Spangenberg Group, 2007). The average hourly overhead cost for attorneys—the amount they must make just to pay their secretaries, office rent, and telephone bills—is $64 (Third Branch, 2008a). If their hourly fees fall short of their overhead costs, then attorneys actually lose money when spending their time on these cases. Look at Table 10.2 to see examples of fees paid to assigned defense counsel.

Low fees discourage skilled attorneys from taking criminal cases. Low fees may also induce a defense attorney to persuade clients to plead guilty to a lesser charge. Many assigned defenders find that they can make more money by collecting a preparation fee for a few hours work, payable when an indigent client pleads guilty, than by going to trial. Trials are very time-consuming, and appointed attorneys often feel that the fees paid by the state are too low to cover the amount of time required to prepare for trial, especially when the fee is a flat rate per case or trial rather than an hourly rate. It usually is more profitable to handle many quick plea bargains than to spend weeks preparing for a trial for which the total fee may be capped at $1,000 to $3,000.

Many organizations of judges and lawyers lobby Congress, state legislatures, and county councils to increase the amounts paid to assigned counsel. Courts may also pressure legislators to provide more money for indigent defense. In 2005, for example, the Louisiana Supreme Court ruled that trial judges can prevent prosecutors from proceeding against a defendant if there is not enough money available in the local government budget to pay the defense attorney (Maggi, 2005). Many members of Congress and state legislatures, however, do not wish to spend more money for the benefit of criminal defendants. In addition, even if legislators recognize that funding problems exist, state and local governments may have little ability to increase spending for indigent defense during periods when they face budget problems that affect their responsibilities for all issues, including schools, roads, and health care. This problem has become even worse in the second decade of the twenty-first century as states, counties, and cities cut services and lay off employees in every department.

Contract System The contract system is used in a few counties, mainly in western states. Most states using this method do not have large populations. The government contracts with an attorney, a nonprofit association, or a private law firm to handle all indigent cases (Gross, 2013). Some jurisdictions use

TABLE 10.2 FEES PAID TO ASSIGNED COUNSEL IN NONCAPITAL FELONY CASES

STATE	OUT-OF-COURT HOURLY RATE	IN-COURT HOURLY RATE	PER-CASE MAXIMUM
Alaska	$50	$60	$4,000 trial; $2,000 plea
Hawaii	$90	$90	$6,000
Illinois (Chicago)	$30	$40	$1,250
Maryland	$50	$50	$3,000
New York	$75	$75	$4,400
North Carolina	$65	$65	None
Ohio	$50	$60	$3,000
Wisconsin	$40	$40	None

Source: John P. Gross, "Rationing Justice: The Underfunding of Assigned Counsel Systems," *Part 1: Gideon at 50—A Three-Part Examination of Indigent Defense in America* (Washington, DC: National Association of Criminal Defense Lawyers), 2013, 20–32.

public defenders for most cases but contract for services in multiple-defendant cases that might present conflicts of interest, in extraordinarily complex cases, or in cases that require more time than the government's salaried lawyers can provide.

There are several kinds of contracts. The most common contract provides for a fixed yearly sum to be paid to the law firm that handles all cases. The laws in twenty states permit individual counties to enter into such contracts to handle indigent defense (Gross, 2013). Some people fear that this method encourages attorneys to cut corners in order to preserve their profits, especially if there are more cases than expected for the year. Other contracts follow a fixed price per case or per hour of work. Fixed price contracts, also known as flat fee contracts, can create perverse incentives if the amount varies depending on the specific tasks undertaken by the attorney. For example, in Detroit's system, defense attorneys are paid $200 more for a guilty plea than for a dismissal (Gross, 2013). How might that impact their motives and efforts? Still other jurisdictions use a cost-plus contract, in which a new contract is negotiated when the estimated cost of counsel is surpassed. According to Robert Spangenberg and Marea Beeman (1995: 49), "There are serious potential dangers with the contract model, such as expecting contract defenders to handle an unlimited caseload or awarding contracts on a low-bid basis only, with no regard to qualifications of contracting attorneys."

Public Defender The position of public defender developed as a response to the legal needs of indigent defendants. The concept started in Los Angeles County in 1914, when the government first hired attorneys to work full-time in criminal defense. The most recent national survey of the 100 most populous counties found that public defender systems handled 82 percent of the 6 million indigent criminal cases ("Indigent Defense," 2011). The public defender system,

CLOSE UP

PRESSURE TO FULFILL THE PROMISE OF INDIGENT DEFENSE

The structure of indigent defense systems and the allocation of money to pay for those systems rest in the hands of elected officials. In an era of budget difficulties and significant needs for expenditures on education, roads, and other priorities, why would elected officials steer funds to legal services for criminal defendants? There is no pressure from voters to devote more tax dollars to criminal defense, and wealthy interest groups focus on issues that advance their own policy priorities. Thus it is difficult to move state legislators and county commissioners to act on the issue of indigent defense, despite the obvious problems and shortcomings that exist in many jurisdictions. The problem is especially difficult because of the significant expenditures needed to truly fulfill the ideals of the Sixth Amendment right to counsel. For example, in 2010 the Missouri public defender's office said that it would need 125 more lawyers, 90 more secretaries, 109 more investigators, 130 more legal assistants, and more work space for these hoped-for new employees in order to fulfill their duties of timely and complete representation. In light of the state's budget woes, however, there was no possibility that the office would see its resources increase.

By 2013, efforts to call attention to the issue and push legislators to act had moved beyond civil rights interest groups and defense attorneys. Opinions by judges increasingly demonstrated concern about the need for legislative action to provide more funding for indigent defense systems. In *Boyer v. Louisiana* (2013), the U.S. Supreme Court dismissed a case that was to address whether a seven-year delay from arrest to trial violated the defendant's Sixth Amendment right to a speedy trial. A majority of justices concluded that the defense attorney had been primarily responsible for the defendant's seven-year pretrial detention in jail by requesting delays for various reasons. In dissent, however, Justice Sonia Sotomayor, supported by Justices Ruth Bader Ginsburg, Stephen Breyer, and Elena Kagan, argued that the Court should examine the failings of the Louisiana indigent defense system. According to Sotomayor, the Court originally accepted the case to determine "whether a delay caused by a State's failure to fund counsel for an indigent's defense should be weighed against the State in determining whether there was a deprivation" of the right to a speedy trial. The four dissenting justices showed their interest in examining and possibly issuing which is growing fast, is used in 43 of the 50 most populous counties and in most large cities. There are about 20 statewide, state-funded systems; in other states, the counties organize and pay for them. Only two states, North Dakota and Maine, do not have public defenders.

The public defender system is often viewed as better than the assigned counsel system because public defenders are specialists in criminal law. Because they are full-time government employees, public defenders do not sacrifice their clients' cases to protect their own financial interests. Public defenders do face certain special problems, however. Public defenders may have trouble gaining the trust and cooperation of their clients. Criminal defendants may assume that attorneys on the state payroll, even with the title "public defender," have no reason to protect the defendants' rights and interests. Lack of cooperation from the defendant may make it harder for the attorney to prepare the best possible arguments for use during hearings, plea bargaining, and trials.

Public defenders may also face heavy caseloads. Public defenders in Kentucky, for example, handled an average of 436 cases in 2007 (E. Lewis, 2007). Although the Washington State Bar Association recommends that defense attorneys handle no more than 300 cases per year, public defenders in Thurston County, Washington, each had as many as 900 misdemeanor cases per year in 2005 (Associated Press, 2005). Across New York State, the average was 680 cases in 2014 (Virtanen, 2014). Such heavy caseloads do not allow time for attorneys to become familiar with each case. Public defender programs are most effective when they have enough money to keep caseloads manageable. However, these programs do not control their own budgets and usually are not seen as high priorities by state and local governments (Jaksic, 2007). Thus, gaining the funds to give adequate attention to each defendant's case is difficult. As you read the Close Up feature, consider whether appellate courts should play a role in forcing states to provide adequate funding for indigent defense.

orders concerning the failings of Louisiana's underfunded indigent defense system.

At the state level, the Missouri Supreme Court supported the public defender's office request to decline additional cases because its caseload had exceeded capacity for several months (*State v. Waters and Orr,* 2012). Individual judges in Louisiana have issued orders blocking prosecutions from moving forward after a $2.5 million cut to the public defender budget in 2012 left 500 defendants with no attorneys appointed to represent them. At the same time, in places such as Michigan, civil rights groups continue to advocate for more funding, and even individual legislators who generally oppose government spending are starting to notice that increased financing can be less expensive than keeping people in jail awaiting delayed court proceedings or sending innocent people to prison because they did not receive proper representation.

With respect to other important issues of constitutional rights in the past, judges have ordered states to undertake expensive actions to uphold rights with respect to school desegregation and prison reform. Will judges eventually take the dramatic step of ordering states to spend more money on indigent defense?

Sources: Monica Davey, "Budget Woes Hit Defense Lawyers for the Indigent," *New York Times,* September 9, 2010 (www.nytimes.com); David Eggert, "Push to Fix Michigan Justice System Flaw Continues after Violations Uncovered," *Detroit Free Press,* May 5, 2013 (www.freep.com); Tom Gogola, "Slashed Budget Leaves Hundreds of Indigent Defendants Lawyerless," *The Lens,* March 6, 2013 (thelensnola.org); Vanita Gupta and Steve Hanlon, "Hitting Two Birds with One Stone: Strategies for Addressing the Indigent Defense Crisis and Overincarceration," *American Constitution Society* blog, September 4, 2012 (www.acslaw.org).

DEBATE THE ISSUE

Are there any ways to increase the effectiveness of indigent representation without additional budget expenditures during times of financial crisis? Should judges issue orders to increase funding in order to fulfill criminal defendants' constitutional rights? What impact might such orders have on taxpayers or on taking money away from other government programs? What would you do if you were a judge? Give two reasons for taking action or for declining to take action.

Some public defenders' offices try to make better use of limited resources by organizing assignments more efficiently. In some systems, every poor defendant has several public defenders, each handling a different stage or "zone" in the justice process. One attorney may handle all arraignments, another all preliminary hearings, and still another any trial work. No one attorney manages the entire case of any client. Although the zone system may increase efficiency, there is a risk that cases will be processed in a routine way, with no one taking into account special factors. With limited responsibility for a given case, the attorney is less able to advise the defendant about the case as a whole and is unlikely to develop the level of trust needed to gain the defendant's cooperation.

With or without zone systems, overburdened public defenders find it difficult to avoid making routine decisions. One case can come to be viewed as very much like the next, and the process can become routine and repetitive. Overworked attorneys cannot look closely at cases for any special circumstances that would justify a stronger defense.

Even when many governments are not experiencing budget crises, all three approaches to providing legal representation for indigent defendants face persistent challenges in gaining sufficient resources from local or state government. Defense offices frequently do not have staff investigators to help prepare cases in the manner that police departments help prosecutors to investigate and prepare their cases. In 2007, data showed that 40 percent of county-based public defender offices had no staff investigators at all, so that defense attorneys had to handle all aspects of their own cases (Farole and Langton, 2010). At times of financial difficulty, indigent defense will experience budget cuts just like most other government departments and programs. Because indigent defense provides services for many clients who have earned the fear and distrust of society, it is difficult to apply political influence to encourage legislators to meet the needs of these important programs.

As you ponder the challenges faced by states, counties, and cities throughout the country, read the New Directions in Criminal Justice Policy feature, "A Voucher System for Criminal Defense," to consider one suggestion for fixing the system.

POINT 9. What are the three main methods of providing attorneys for indigent defendants?

STOP AND ANALYZE: Which of the three methods of providing attorneys for indigent defendants works best? List the three strongest arguments in favor of each approach as well as two arguments against each approach. Which set of arguments is most persuasive?

Private versus Public Defense

Publicly funded defense attorneys now handle up to 85 percent of the cases in many places, and private defense attorneys have become more and more unusual in many courts. Retained counsel may serve only upper-income defendants charged with white-collar crimes or middle-class homeowners charged with various crimes who are able to obtain a second mortgage as means to borrow money that will be used to pay the attorney. In addition, they represent drug dealers and organized-crime figures who can pay the fees. This trend has made the issue of the quality of representation increasingly important.

Do defendants who can afford their own counsel receive better legal services than those who cannot? Many convicted offenders say "you get what you pay for," meaning that they would have received better counsel if they had been able to pay for their own attorneys. At one time, researchers thought public defenders entered more guilty pleas than did lawyers who had been either

NEW DIRECTIONS IN CRIMINAL JUSTICE POLICY

A VOUCHER SYSTEM FOR CRIMINAL DEFENSE

One suggestion for improving indigent defense systems relies on a different approach to attorney compensation. Under a voucher system, each defendant would be given a receipt, or "voucher," which would permit him to select his own attorney. The attorney would handle the case and then submit the voucher to the appropriate government agency in order to be paid, either for the number of hours worked or on a set fee per case. A fully implemented, universal voucher system might save money as the disbanding of public defender offices would eliminate the obligation of states, counties, and cities to provide medical benefits and retirement funds for the now-departed defense attorney employees.

The system would be similar to current medical reimbursement programs such as Medicare and Medicaid in which the client receives services from a private provider who is subsequently paid by the government agency. Vouchers are also used to help low-income people rent apartments.

One of the purported strengths of the proposal is that defendants would be able to choose their own attorneys. Thus they would presumably cooperate better and have less reason to complain about the case outcome, as compared to current systems in which an attorney is assigned to each defendant, even if the defendant does not like or have confidence in that particular attorney.

Many attorneys might decide that the voucher system does not pay sufficient compensation to induce them to take indigent criminal cases. This same issue exists in the medical realm as some doctors do not accept Medicaid or Medicare patients. On the other hand, other attorneys would seek to specialize in criminal defense, develop expertise, and implement efficient office procedures for a successful voucher-focused practice. Yet another group of attorneys would undoubtedly accept some voucher cases as part of a more general practice with paying clients for other kinds of cases.

Would states and counties be willing to pay enough through the voucher system to induce good attorneys to participate as indigent defense attorneys? Would criminal defendants have sufficient knowledge to choose good attorneys? These and other questions can only be addressed if a voucher system is implemented and evaluated.

Source: Stephen J. Schulhofer and David D. Friedman, "Reforming Indigent Defense: How Free Market Principles Can Help to Fix a Broken System," *Policy Analysis,* No. 666, September 1, 2010 (Washington, DC: Cato Institute).

DEBATE THE ISSUE

What are the three strongest arguments in favor of a voucher system? What are the three strongest arguments against a voucher system? What is your viewpoint? Why?

privately retained or assigned to cases. However, studies show little variation in case outcomes by various types of defense. For example, in a classic study of plea bargains in nine medium-sized counties in Illinois, Michigan, and Pennsylvania, the type of attorney representing the client appeared to make no difference in the nature of plea agreements (Nardulli, 1986). Other studies also find few differences among assigned counsel, contract counsel, public defenders, and privately retained counsel with respect to case outcomes and length of sentence (R. A. Hanson and Chapper, 1991).

CHECKPOINT 10. Are public defenders more effective than private defense attorneys?

STOP AND ANALYZE: If you were charged with a crime, would you prefer a private attorney that you selected and paid or a publicly financed defense attorney? Why? List three reasons for your preference.

Attorney Competence

The right to counsel is of little value when the counsel is neither competent nor effective. The adequacy of counsel provided to both private and public clients is a matter of concern to defense groups, bar associations, and the courts (Chiang, 2010). There are, of course, many examples of incompetent counsel (Gershman, 1993). Even in death penalty cases, attorneys have shown up for court so drunk that they could not stand up straight (Bright, 1994). In other

John Thompson spent 14 years on death row in Louisiana for a crime he did not commit. He was convicted because prosecutors illegally withheld evidence that would have shown that he was innocent. In 2011, the U.S. Supreme ruled that Thompson could not file a lawsuit against those prosecutors. If prosecutors cannot be sued for misconduct, how can we make sure that unethical prosecutors are held accountable for their misbehavior that harms people?

cases, attorneys with almost no knowledge of criminal law have made blunders that have needlessly sent their clients to death row (C. E. Smith, 1997). Lawyers have even fallen asleep during their clients' death penalty trials, yet one Texas judge found no problem with such behavior. He wrote that everyone has a constitutional right to have a lawyer, but "the Constitution does not say that the lawyer has to be awake" (Shapiro, 1997: 27). A divided appellate court later disagreed with this conclusion.

In other cases, the definition of "inadequate counsel" is less clear. What if a public defender's caseload is so large that he or she cannot spend more than a few minutes reviewing the files for most cases? What if, as a deliberate strategy to appear cooperative and thus stay in the judge's good graces, the defense attorney decides not to object to questionable statements and evidence presented by the prosecution? Because attorneys have discretion concerning how to prepare and present their cases, it is hard to define what constitutes a level of performance so inadequate that it violates the defendant's constitutional right to counsel.

The U.S. Supreme Court has examined the question of what requirements must be met if defendants are to receive effective counsel (Knake, 2010). In two 1984 cases, *United States v. Cronic* and *Strickland v. Washington,* the Court set standards for effective assistance of counsel. Cronic had been charged with a complex mail-fraud scheme, which the government had investigated for four and a half years. Just before trial, Cronic's retained lawyer withdrew and a young attorney—who had no trial experience and whose practice was mainly in real estate law—was appointed. The trial court gave the new attorney only 25 days to prepare for the trial, in which Cronic was convicted. The Supreme Court upheld Cronic's conviction on the grounds that, although the new trial counsel had made errors, there was no evidence that the trial had not been a "meaningful" test of the prosecution's case or that the conviction had not been justified.

In *Strickland v. Washington,* the Supreme Court rejected the defendant's claim that his attorney did not adequately prepare for the sentencing hearing in a death penalty case (the attorney sought neither character statements nor a psychiatric examination to present on the defendant's behalf). As it has done in later cases, the Court indicated its reluctance to second-guess a defense attorney's actions. By focusing on whether errors by an attorney were bad enough to make the trial result unreliable and to deny a fair trial, the Court has made it hard for defendants to prove that they were denied effective counsel, even when defense attorneys perform very poorly. As a result, innocent people who were poorly represented have been convicted, even of the most serious crimes (Radelet, Bedeau, and Putnam, 1992).

When imprisoned people are proved innocent and released—sometimes after losing their freedom for many years—we are reminded that the American justice system is imperfect. The development of DNA testing has produced regular reminders of the system's imperfections as new reports surface nearly every month of innocent people released from prison after evidence was reexamined. For example, in May 2008, Levon Jones was released from a North Carolina prison after serving 15 years on death row. At the time of Jones's release, a federal judge criticized his original defense attorneys for failing to investigate the credibility of the prosecution's star witness—someone who accepted reward money and was coached by police, but who later admitted to lying on the witness stand (Death Penalty Information Center, 2008). Such reminders highlight the importance of high-quality legal counsel for criminal defendants. However, because state and local governments have limited funds, concerns about the quality of defense attorneys' work will persist. Think about the importance of defense attorneys in the justice process as you consider "Civic Engagement: Your Role in the System."

CIVIC ENGAGEMENT

YOUR ROLE IN THE SYSTEM

Imagine that you must decide how to vote on a ballot issue that proposes denying access to a public defender or appointed counsel for appeals by indigent offenders whose convictions are based on guilty pleas. Should the public pay for an attorney to file an appeal for someone who admitted guilt in an open courtroom proceeding? *Make a list of three arguments favoring and three arguments opposing this ballot issue.* Then read the U.S. Supreme Court's decision concerning such a ballot issue that was passed by voters in Michigan (*Halbert v. Michigan,* 2005).

CHECKPOINT 11. How has the U.S. Supreme Court addressed the issue of attorney competence?

STOP AND ANALYZE: Are there mechanisms, such as aspects of attorney training or licensing, that could be employed to increase the competence and effectiveness of attorneys who handle criminal cases? List three suggestions for ways to improve attorney performance.

A QUESTION OF ETHICS

In 2015, a prosecutor in New Jersey opposed permitting DNA testing of preserved evidence from a rape case that occurred in 1988. According to the prosecutor, although DNA testing was not available at the time of the crime, the tests should not be conducted, because the man who was convicted of the crime had already served his prison sentence and been released many years earlier. Yet, as a result of the conviction, the man had difficulty finding employment or a place to live and had been arrested twice for failing to register properly with police as a convicted sex offender. In light of the severe continuing burdens affecting the man's life from the rape conviction, lawyers for the man argued that the interests of justice required going forward with the laboratory test to see if his claims of innocence could be verified.

In a Michigan case in 2014, defense attorneys alleged that prosecutors and a local judge spent 12 years blocking newly developed DNA tests of preserved evidence from a rape-murder. Meanwhile, a man with mental illness problems confessed to the crime. The man served a 15-year sentence and then was released from prison. When DNA testing finally took place after he had served his sentence, the test provided evidence that a different man, one of the original suspects under investigation in the case, was at the scene of the crime. No DNA evidence connected the imprisoned man to the crime.

Sources: Kathleen Hopkins, "Prosecutors Block DNA Test that Could Clear Man's Name," *USA Today*, January 9, 2015 (www.usatoday.com); David Moran, "On DNA, Prosecutors Can't Handle the Truth," *Detroit News*, October 13, 2014 (www.detroitnews.com); Jim Schaefer, "DNA Evidence Frees Northern Michigan Man in Prison for 15 Years," *Detroit Free Press*, September 6, 2014 (www.freep.com).

CRITICAL THINKING AND ANALYSIS

What is a prosecutor's highest obligation? To seek to convict people of crimes in the American adversary system? To make sure that justice is done? How do prosecutors' obligations translate into the decisions that they should make about supporting or opposing DNA testing? Write a memo describing the rules that you would create to guide prosecutors about what to do when asked to support or oppose DNA testing of evidence in old cases.

Summary

1 Describe the roles of the prosecuting attorney

- American prosecutors, both state and federal, have significant discretion to determine how to handle criminal cases.
- The prosecutor can play various roles, including trial counsel for the police, house counsel for the police, representative of the court, and elected official.

2 Analyze the process by which criminal charges are filed, and what role the prosecutor's discretion plays in that process

- There is no higher authority over most prosecutors that can overrule a decision to decline to prosecute (*nolle prosequi*) or to pursue multiple counts against a defendant.
- The three primary models of prosecutors' decision-making policies are legal sufficiency, system efficiency, and trial sufficiency.

3 Identify the other actors in the system with whom the prosecutor interacts during the decision-making process

- Prosecutors' decisions and actions are affected by their exchange relationships with many other important actors and groups, including police, judges, victims and witnesses, and the public.

4 Discuss the day-to-day reality of criminal defense work in the United States

- The image of defense attorneys as courtroom advocates often differs from the reality of pressured, busy negotiators constantly involved in bargaining with the prosecutor over guilty-plea agreements.
- Relatively few private defense attorneys make significant incomes from criminal work, but large numbers of private attorneys accept court appointments to handle indigent defendants' cases quickly for relatively low fees.
- Defense attorneys must often wrestle with difficult working conditions and uncooperative clients as they seek to provide representation, usually in the plea-negotiation process.

5 Describe how counsel is provided for defendants who cannot afford a private attorney

- Three primary methods for providing attorneys to represent indigent defendants are assigned counsel, contract counsel, and public defenders.
- Overall, private and public attorneys appear to provide similar quality of counsel with respect to case outcomes.

6 Analyze the defense attorney's role in the system and the nature of the attorney–client relationship

- The quality of representation provided to criminal defendants is a matter of significant concern, but U.S. Supreme Court rulings have made it difficult for convicted offenders to prove that their attorneys did not provide a competent defense.

Questions for Review

1. What are the formal powers of the prosecuting attorney?
2. How do politics affect prosecutors?
3. What considerations influence the prosecutor's decision about whether to bring charges and what to charge?
4. Why is the prosecuting attorney often cited as the most powerful office in the criminal justice system?
5. What problems do defense attorneys face?
6. How is the defense attorney an agent-mediator?
7. How are defense services provided to indigents?
8. Why might it be argued that publicly financed counsel serves defendants better than does privately retained counsel?

Key Terms and Cases

accusatory process (p. 420)
assigned counsel (p. 429)
community prosecution (p. 417)
contract counsel (p. 429)
counts (p. 411)
defense attorney (p. 422)
discovery (p. 411)
legal sufficiency (p. 418)
nolle prosequi (p. 411)
prosecuting attorney (p. 403)
public defender (p. 429)
state attorney general (p. 403)
system efficiency (p. 419)
trial sufficiency (p. 419)
United States attorneys (p. 403)

Checkpoint Answers

1 What are the titles of the officials responsible for criminal prosecution at the federal, state, and local levels of government?

✓ United States attorney, state attorney general, prosecuting attorney (the prosecuting attorney is also called district attorney, county prosecutor, state's attorney, county attorney).

2 What are the powers of the prosecuting attorney?

✓ Decides which charges to file, what bail amounts to recommend, whether to pursue a plea bargain, and what sentence to recommend to the judge.

3 What are the roles of the prosecutor?

✓ Trial counsel for the police, house counsel for the police, representative of the court, elected official.

4 How does a prosecutor use discretion to decide how to treat each defendant?

✓ The prosecutor can determine the type and number of charges, reduce the charges in exchange for a guilty plea, or enter a *nolle prosequi* (thereby dropping some or all of the charges).

5 What are the prosecutor's key exchange relationships?

✓ Police, victims and witnesses, defense attorneys, judges.

6 What are the three models of prosecution policy, and how do they differ?

✓ Legal sufficiency: Is there sufficient evidence to pursue a prosecution? System efficiency: What will be the impact of this case on the system with respect to caseload pressures and speedy disposition? Trial sufficiency: Does sufficient evidence exist to ensure successful prosecution of this case through a trial?

7 How does the image of the defense attorney differ from the attorney's actual role?

✓ The public often views defense attorneys as protectors of criminals. Defendants believe that defense attorneys will fight vigorous battles at every stage of the process. The defense attorney's actual role is to protect the defendant's rights and to make the prosecution prove its case.

8 What special pressures do defense attorneys face?

✓ Securing cases, collecting fees, persuading clients to accept pleas, having to lose most cases, maintaining working relationships with court officers, serving clients in unpleasant surroundings for little money, being viewed negatively by the public.

9 What are the three main methods of providing attorneys for indigent defendants?

✓ Assigned counsel, contract counsel system, public defender.

10 Are public defenders more effective than private defense attorneys?

✓ Research shows little difference in outcomes.

11 How has the U.S. Supreme Court addressed the issue of attorney competence?

✓ The Supreme Court has addressed the issue of "ineffective assistance of counsel" by requiring defendants to prove that the defense attorney made specific errors that affected the outcome of the case.

CHAPTER FEATURES

- **Close Up** Elected Prosecutors: Are There Risks and Benefits?
- **New Directions in Criminal Justice Policy** Jurors and Electronic Communications
- **Technology and Criminal Justice** DNA Evidence and the Risk of Error

CHAPTER 11

DETERMINATION OF GUILT: PLEA BARGAINING AND TRIALS

CHAPTER LEARNING OBJECTIVES

1. Describe the courtroom workgroup and how it functions
2. Discuss how and why plea bargaining occurs
3. Analyze why few cases go to trial and how jurors are chosen
4. Identify the stages of a criminal trial
5. Describe the basis for an appeal of a conviction

CHAPTER OUTLINE

AP Images/LM Otero, Pool

The nation's attention was drawn to a murder trial in Stephenville, Texas, in February 2015. Eddie Ray Routh, a former Marine who served in Iraq, stood trial for the murders of former Navy SEAL Chris Kyle and his friend Chad Littlefield. The case was known as the "American Sniper" trial, because Kyle was the author of the best-selling book by that name detailing his exploits as the U.S. military sniper credited with the most "kills" in the Iraq War. Moreover, an Academy Award–nominated Hollywood movie based on the book was released in the weeks prior to the trial and drew large audiences to movie theaters throughout the country (Jervis, 2015).

In February 2013, Kyle and Littlefield took Routh to a shooting range in an effort to help Routh with his struggles with posttraumatic stress disorder (PTSD). As Kyle and Littlefield shot at targets at the shooting range, Routh surprised them, putting six bullets into Kyle and seven into Littlefield. Routh then stole Kyle's truck and stopped at a Taco Bell for food before going to his sister's house and telling her what he had done. She called the police and Routh fled, eventually leading the police on a chase before surrendering (Fernandez and Jones, 2013).

Routh's attorney, Shay Isham, and his legal team presented an insanity defense based on the former soldier's PTSD symptoms, his hospitalization in mental institutions four times in the seven months prior to the shooting, and his ranting about voodoo and "pigs . . . taking over the earth" during his confession to the police. Indeed, while driving Routh to the shooting range, Kyle and Littlefield had exchanged text messages with each other referring to Routh as "straight-up nuts" (Jervis, 2015). By contrast, prosecutor Alan Nash pointed the jury to Routh's deliberate actions, including stealing Kyle's truck and fleeing from the police, as evidence that the defendant knew right from wrong and that he had killed the two men knowingly and intentionally.

The trial lasted nine days, with competing testimony from psychiatrists for each side providing opinions about the defendant's mental condition, numerous witnesses providing crime scene evidence, as well as the recounting of Routh's own words that had been given during his confession to the police (Lett and Ellis, 2015). There were concerns that jurors who had seen the movie *American Sniper* and its dramatization of Kyle as a war hero, husband, and father would be inclined to vote to convict Routh. However, Routh's attorneys believed the jurors would listen closely and determine the verdict based on the evidence (Effron and Keneally, 2015). Ultimately, the jury deliberated for only two hours before issuing a guilty verdict, deciding that Routh acted "intentionally and willingly" and that he knew right from wrong at the time of the shooting (Jervis, 2015). One juror later told a reporter that the jury saw a pattern of behavior by Routh that led them to conclude that he was not insane. According to the juror, "[The] pattern that we saw, he would get intoxicated, get in trouble, and then the police would show up and he would say, 'I'm a veteran, I have PTSD, I'm insane,' you know, and every time something bad happened he pulled that card" (Effron and Keneally, 2015). Not every jury would necessarily have interpreted Routh's behavior in this way, so there is a possibility that in a different court with different jurors the insanity defense may have been accepted. However, this was the conclusion of the ten women and two men who sat on the jury in this Texas county.

The prosecutor had declined to seek the death penalty for Routh so, in accordance with Texas law, upon conviction for these intentional murders, he was automatically sentenced to life in prison without possibility of parole. The prosecutor's choice could have been affected by his concern that jurors might hesitate to sentence a war veteran to death and that hesitation might have made them more inclined to consider accepting the insanity defense. It is also possible that the prosecutor's choice was made for financial reasons. Death penalty trials are much more expensive because of time-consuming jury selection processes and the inevitability of lengthy appeals. By contrast, for example, jury selection in the 2015 death penalty trial of Dzhokhar Tsarnaev, the defendant accused of the Boston Marathon bombing in 2013, took nearly two months and involved identifying 18 jurors and alternates from a pool of 1,373 potential jurors. Prosecutors in many small counties, like the one where Routh was tried, avoid seeking the death penalty because of the significant impact on their annual budgets (Izadi, 2015).

Can jurors drawn from the community accurately determine whether a defendant was insane at the time of a crime, especially when they hear contradictory opinions on the subject from psychiatrists for both sides in a trial? Can jurors set aside emotion when hearing evidence in a case involving the death of a well-known military hero? These are difficult challenges, yet the American system regards the trial as the best method for determining a defendant's guilt. This is especially true when the defendant can afford to pay for an attorney to mount a vigorous defense or when the potential punishment is so severe that appointed attorneys will fight all the way through trial rather than accept a plea agreement. The "American Sniper" case occupies the top layer of Samuel Walker's criminal justice wedding cake (see Chapter 3) as one of the relatively few cases that go to trial and command great public attention because a recognized public figure was the victim in the case. However, a trial is not a scientific process. Instead of calm, consistent evaluations of evidence, trials involve unpredictable human perceptions and reactions. Attorneys know that a mix of citizens drawn from society may react in different ways and reach different conclusions in response to the attorneys' presentations of evidence and the testimony of witnesses.

Because of the high stakes and uncertainty that surround criminal trials, most defendants plead guilty as they get closer to the prospect of being judged by a random group of citizens drawn from the community. Prosecutors also create incentives for guilty pleas by offering reductions in charges and sentences in exchange for admissions of guilt. Even if specific incentives are not offered, defendants may plead guilty in order to demonstrate to the judge that they are taking responsibility for their actions. They may hope that such honesty will lead the judge to soften the sentence.

Even the cases of prominent defendants who can afford to pay top-notch attorneys are often determined by plea bargaining. For example, multimillionaire movie star Mel Gibson entered a "no contest" plea in March 2011 to misdemeanor battery charges after he allegedly punched his girlfriend the year before (Cieply, 2011). A no contest plea means that the defendant is accepting a finding of criminal responsibility and is willing to take the punishment for the crime. Although such misdemeanor charges could carry a sentence of up to one year in jail, first offenders usually do not go to jail unless they have injured their victims.

As in other cases resolved through plea bargaining, Gibson's plea negotiations involved *exchange*, the system characteristic discussed in Chapter 3. The prosecutor agreed to recommend a specific sentence that did not involve jail time in exchange for Gibson's plea. In his plea deal, Gibson agreed to a sentence of 36 months of probation and 52 weeks of domestic violence counseling (McCartney, 2011). Gibson gained a definite sentence and spared his children from the embarrassment of a lengthy proceeding covered by newspapers and television. The prosecutor gained a quick conviction without expending time and other resources. Thus plea bargaining can advance the interests of both sides if they fear the cost and uncertainty of taking a case to trial.

In this chapter we discuss plea bargaining and trials as a way to examine the determination of guilt in criminal cases. We also explore the appeals process that occurs when a convicted offender challenges the validity of a criminal conviction. In all of these processes, defendants' fates depend on the interactions and decisions of many individuals in important roles: judges, prosecutors, defense attorneys, and jurors.

The Courtroom: How It Functions

Criminal cases follow similar rules and processes throughout the nation. However, courts differ in the precise ways they apply those rules and procedures. A study of criminal courts in nine communities in three states shows that similar laws and procedures can produce different results in the treatment of defendants (Eisenstein, Flemming, and Nardulli, 1988). Some courts sentence offenders to longer terms than do others (Wu and Spohn, 2010). In some places, court delays and tough bail policies keep many accused people in jail awaiting trial, whereas in other places defendants are more likely to be released before trial or have their cases resolved quickly. Guilty pleas may make up 90 percent of dispositions in some communities but only 60 percent in others. Such differences can appear even within different courthouses in the same city. How, then, can we explain such differences?

Social scientists are aware that the culture of a community greatly influences how its members behave. The definition of *culture* includes shared beliefs about proper behavior. These beliefs can span entire nations or pertain to smaller communities, including corporations, churches, or neighborhoods. In any community, large or small, the culture can exert a strong effect on people's decisions and behavior.

local legal culture
Norms, shared by members of a court community, which center on how cases should be handled and how a participant should behave in the judicial process.

Researchers have identified a **local legal culture**—values and norms shared by members of a particular court community (judges, attorneys, clerks, bailiffs, and others)—about how cases should be handled and the way court officials should behave (Church, 1985). The local legal culture influences court operations in three ways:

1. Norms (shared values and expectations) help participants distinguish between our court and other courts. Often a judge or prosecutor will proudly describe how we do the job differently and better than officials in a nearby county or city.
2. Norms tell members of a court community how they should treat one another. For example, one court may see mounting a strong adversarial defense as not in keeping with its norms, but another court may expect that sort of defense.
3. Norms describe how cases *should* be processed. The best example of such a norm is the **going rate**, the local view of the proper sentence based on the defendant's prior record and other factors. The local legal culture also includes attitudes on such issues as whether a judge should take part in plea negotiations, when **continuances**—lawyers' requests for delays in court proceedings—should be granted, and which defendants qualify for a public defender.

going rate
Local court officials' shared view of the appropriate sentence for the offense, based on the defendant's prior record and other case characteristics.

continuance
An adjournment of a scheduled case until a later date.

Differences among local legal cultures help explain why court decisions often differ even though the formal rules of criminal procedure are basically the same. For example, although judges play a key role in sentencing, the "going rate" concept shows us that sentences also result from shared understandings among the prosecutor, defense attorney, and judge. In one court, shared understandings may mean a court imposes probation on a first-time thief; in other courts, different shared values may send first offenders to jail or prison for the same offense.

✔POINT 1. How does the local legal culture affect criminal cases?

STOP AND ANALYZE: There are competing viewpoints about differences in case outcomes in different courts. On the one hand, different outcomes collide with notions of "equal justice." On the other hand, different outcomes may reflect the values of the individual communities in which they arise and therefore be, in some sense, democratic and embody the wishes of the local citizens. Which perspective seems most appropriate to you? List two reasons for your conclusion.

(Answers are at the end of the chapter.)

The Courtroom Workgroup

Television dramas such as *The Good Wife* present a particular image of the American courtroom. In these shows, prosecutors and defense attorneys lock horns in verbal combat, each side trying to persuade a judge or jury to either convict or acquit the defendant. However, this image of adversarial proceedings does not reflect the actual scene in most American courtrooms. A more realistic portrayal would stress the interactions among the actors, who are guided by the norms and expectations of the local legal culture. Many of these interactions take the form of calm cooperation among the prosecutor, defense attorney, and judge, rather than the battle of adversaries portrayed in fictional accounts (Haynes, Ruback, and Cusick, 2010).

Decisions in criminal cases rely on how the participants interact with each other. We can best understand how criminal justice officials and staff function when we view them as **workgroups**, or groups of people who interact with each other, share certain goals and values, and form relationships that facilitate cooperation. The better the judge, prosecutor, defense attorney, and courtroom staff can function as a workgroup, the more smoothly they can dispose of cases. The workgroup concept is especially important in analyzing urban courts, which have many courtrooms; large numbers of lawyers, judges, and other court personnel; and heavy caseloads.

workgroups
A collection of individuals who interact in the workplace on a continuing basis, share goals, develop norms regarding how activities should be carried out, and eventually establish a network of roles that differentiates the group from others and that facilitates cooperation.

In light of the factors that define the workgroup, we can expect differences among workgroups from courtroom to courtroom, depending on the strength of these factors in each setting. For example, a rotation system that moves judges between courtrooms in a large courthouse may limit the development of workgroup norms and roles. Although the same prosecutors and defense attorneys may be present every day, the arrival of a new judge every week or month will require them to learn and adapt to new ideas about how cases should be negotiated or tried. When shared norms cannot develop, cases tend to proceed in a relatively formal manner. The actors in such a courtroom have fewer chances to follow agreed-on routines than does a workgroup with a well-developed pattern of interactions.

By contrast, when there are shared expectations and consistent relationships, the business of the courtroom proceeds in a regular but informal manner, with many shared understandings among members easing much of the work (Worden, 1995). Through cooperation, each member can achieve his or her goals as well as those of the group. The prosecutor wants to gain quick convictions, the defense attorney wants fair and prompt resolution of the defendant's case, and the judge wants cooperative agreements on guilt and sentencing. All of these actors want efficient processing of the steady flow of cases that burden their working lives. Through cooperative decision making the courtroom workgroup can resist outside efforts to change case processing and sentencing through new laws and policies and thereby retain control of case outcomes (Gebo, Stracuzzi, and Hurst, 2006; Harris and Jesilow, 2000).

Each actor in the courtroom workgroup has a specific role with unique duties and responsibilities. If a lawyer moves from the public defender's office to the prosecutor's office and later to a judgeship, each new position calls for a different role in the workgroup because each represents a different sponsoring organization (Eisenstein and Jacob, 1977). One organization, loosely called the court, sends judges; the prosecuting attorney's office sends assistant prosecutors; the public defender's office sends counsel for indigents. In addition, other actors who work in the courtroom contribute to the workgroup's effectiveness. To determine an appropriate plea agreement and sentence, for example, members of the workgroup rely on the probation officer to provide accurate

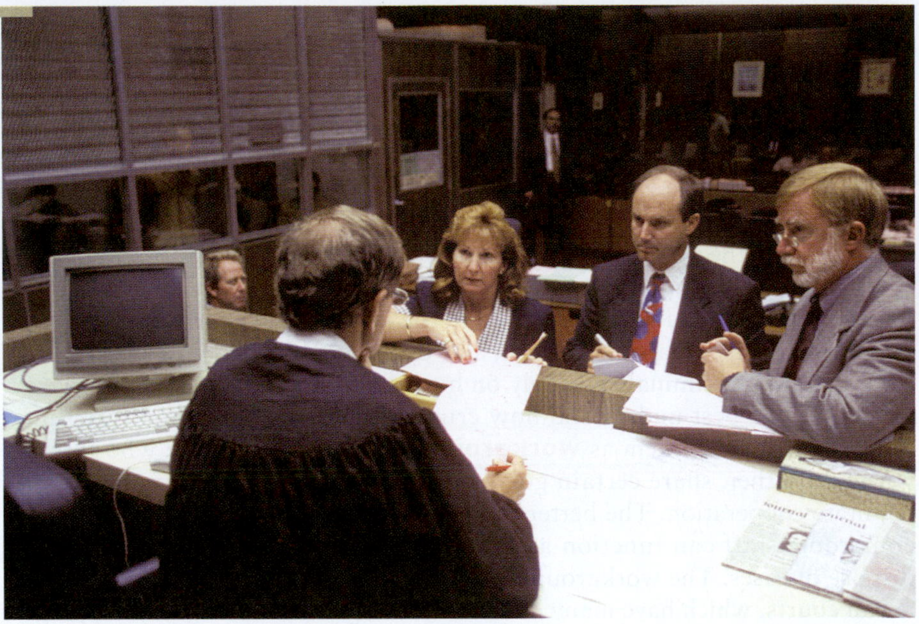

A. Ramey/PhotoEdit

Even in the most adversarial cases, courtroom participants form a workgroup that requires constant interaction, cooperation, and negotiation. Do workgroups help or hinder the attainment of justice?

information in the presentence report about the defendant's prior convictions and family history.

Figure 11.1 shows the elements of the courtroom workgroup and the influences that bear on decision making. Note that the workgroup operates in an environment in which decision making is influenced by the local legal culture; recruitment and selection processes; the nature of the cases; and the socioeconomic, political, and legal structures of the broader community.

The crime victim is the missing actor in the courtroom workgroup's processes that produce plea bargains. The workgroup members are interacting together on numerous cases, but each individual victim is only involved in one case. Many victims' rights advocates would like to see victims consulted by the prosecutor as the courtroom workgroup's interactions occur. Some observers believe that consulting with the victims would give the workgroup members more information and enhance the victims' satisfaction with the justice system (O'Hear, 2008). However, the interactions of the workgroup place an emphasis on shared understandings and efficiency—elements that could diminish through slowing their processes in order to consult with an outsider in each individual case.

Judges lead the courtroom team. They ensure that everyone follows procedures correctly. Even though prosecutors and defense attorneys make the key decisions, the judge must approve them. Judges are responsible for coordinating the processing of cases. Even so, each judge can perform this role somewhat differently. Judges who run a loose administrative ship see themselves as somewhat above the battle. They give other members of the team a great deal of freedom in carrying out their duties and will usually approve group decisions, especially when the members of the group have shared beliefs about the court's goals and the community's values. Judges who exert tighter control over the process play a more active role. They anticipate problems; provide cues for other actors; and threaten, cajole, and move the group toward efficient achievement of its goals. Such judges command respect and participate fully in the ongoing courtroom drama.

Because of their position in the justice system, judges can define the level of their involvement in the processing of criminal cases. How they define their

FIGURE 11.1 MODEL OF CRIMINAL COURT DECISION MAKING

This model ties together the elements of the courtroom workgroup, sponsoring organizations, and local legal culture. Note the effects on decision making. Should any other factors be taken into account?

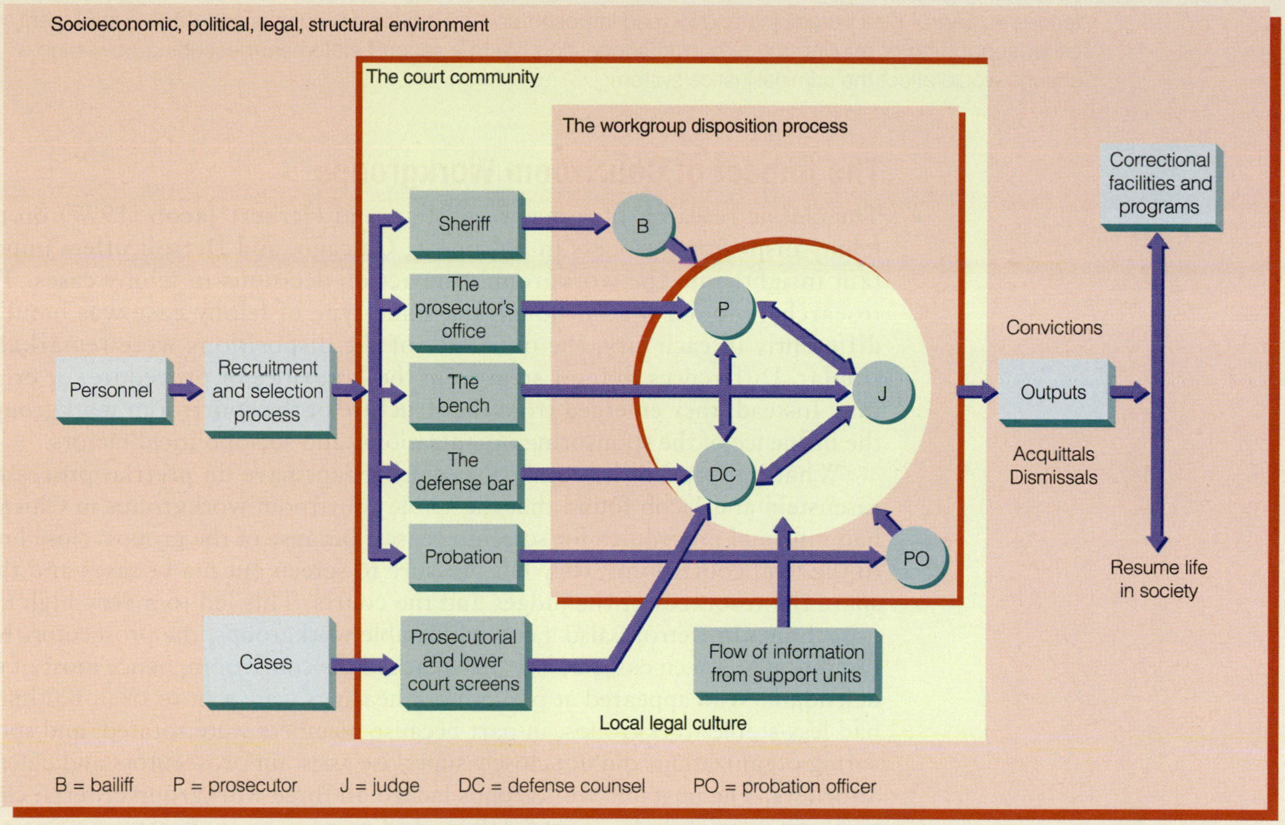

Source: Adapted from Peter Nardulli, James Eisenstein, and Roy Flemming, *Tenor of Justice: Criminal Courts and the Guilty Plea Process* (Urbana: University of Illinois Press, 1988). Copyright © 1988 by the Board of Trustees of the University of Illinois. Reprinted by permission of the authors.

role strongly affects interpersonal relations in the courtroom and the way the group performs its task, as measured by the way it disposes of cases. Judges' actions can, for example, pressure defense attorneys to encourage their clients to plead guilty instead of insisting on a trial (D. Lynch, 1999). Whether the judge actively participates in courtroom interactions or supervises from a distance will help define the speed, efficiency, and degree of cooperation involved in disposing cases.

The behavior of defendants greatly affects how they are treated. They are expected to act remorseful, repentant, silent, and submissive. When the defendant admits guilt in public and states that he or she is entering a guilty plea voluntarily, acceptance of the plea can be followed by a brief lecture from the judge about the seriousness of the crime or the harm the defendant has caused the victim as well as his or her own family. The judge can give a break to a defendant for having cooperated. A defendant who pleads not guilty or whose behavior is inappropriate in other ways may receive a more severe sentence (S. Bushway, Redlich, and Norris, 2014).

POINT 2. How does a courtroom workgroup form and operate?

STOP AND ANALYZE: Should the fates of defendants be shaped by the relationships between judges and attorneys and by the defendant's apologetic statements and appearance of remorse? Is there a way to enforce the same sentence for all offenders who committed the same crime? What if the courts abolished individualized sentences as part of plea bargaining and instead imposed uniform mandatory sentences? Write a statement either supporting or refuting the foregoing suggestion. Write a second statement describing how such a change would affect the criminal justice system.

The Impact of Courtroom Workgroups

The classic research of James Eisenstein and Herbert Jacob (1977) on the felony disposition process in Baltimore, Chicago, and Detroit offers important insights into the workgroup's impact on decisions in felony cases. The researchers found that although the same type of felony case was handled differently in each city, the outcomes of the dispositions were remarkably similar. Differences did not stem from the law, rules of procedure, or crime rate. Instead, they emerged from the structure of the courtroom workgroups, the influence of the sponsoring organizations, and sociopolitical factors.

What impact did the courtroom workgroups have on pretrial processes? Eisenstein and Jacob found that the stable courtroom workgroups in Chicago had informal procedures for screening cases. Because of the groups' close links to the trial courtrooms, they felt pressure to screen out many cases and thus spare the resources of the judges and the courts. This led to a very high dismissal rate. In Detroit, also a city with stable workgroups, the prosecutors had discretion to screen cases before they reached the courtroom; hence most of the defendants who appeared at preliminary hearings were sent to trial. Baltimore had less-stable workgroups, in part because members were rotated, and sponsoring organizations did not closely supervise assistant prosecutors and defense attorneys. The unstable workgroups lacked all three workgroup criteria: close working relationships, shared values, and reasons to cooperate. As a result, there were fewer guilty pleas, and most defendants were sent on to the grand jury and afterward to the trial courts.

The disposition of felony cases results from the interaction of members of the courtroom workgroup. The decisions made by each member are influenced by the policies of their sponsoring organizations. These interactions and policies may vary from courthouse to courthouse. The stability of workgroup interactions can be upset by changes such as a new docket system or adjustments in the policies and practices of sponsoring organizations.

POINT 3. Why are similar cases treated differently in different cities?

STOP AND ANALYZE: In your view, which actor appears to be most influential in the courtroom workgroup? Explain your conclusion in a brief statement.

Plea Bargaining

For the vast majority of cases, plea bargaining—also known as negotiating a settlement, copping a plea, or copping out—is the most important step in the criminal justice process. Few cases go to trial; instead, a negotiated guilty plea arrived at through the interactions of prosecutors, defense lawyers, and judges determines what will happen to most defendants.

TABLE 11.1 PLEA BARGAINING AND FELONY CASE DISPOSITIONS

	75 MOST POPULOUS COUNTIES NATIONWIDE (2006)	ALASKA STATEWIDE (2014)	BURLINGTON COUNTY, NEW JERSEY (2013)	OHIO STATEWIDE (2013)
Disposition by Plea	65%	72%	81%	79%
Disposition at Trial	3%	4%	1%	3%
Dismissal/Diversion/Other	32%	24%	18%	18%

Sources: "Alaska Court System: Annual Statistical Report 2014" (2015); "Burlington County (NJ) Prosecutor's Office 2013 Annual Report" (2014); Thomas H. Cohen and Tracy Kyckelhahn, *Felony Defendants in Large Urban Counties, 2006* (Washington, DC: Bureau of Justice Statistics, 2010); *Ohio Courts Statistical Report 2013* (2014).

Table 11.1 shows the role of plea bargaining in case dispositions in different jurisdictions. Although the percentage of dispositions based on pleas varies from place to place, it is clear that trials are relatively rare events. The differences in percentages also indicate that prosecutors' screening processes vary by jurisdiction. Some prosecutors screen out and dismiss all weak cases prior to charging defendants, whereas others wait until after charges have been filed to dismiss more cases or send defendants into diversion programs. The nature of the exchanges varies with each plea agreement, depending on the specific charges and whether the prosecutor expects a defendant to testify against other defendants.

Forty years ago, plea bargaining was not discussed or even acknowledged publicly; it was the criminal justice system's "little secret." Some observers felt that plea bargaining did not accord with American values of fairness. Doubts existed about whether it was constitutional, and it clashed with the image of the courtroom as a place where prosecutors and defense attorneys engage in legal battles as the jury watches "truth" emerge from the courtroom "combat." Yet a quick resolution of cases through negotiated guilty pleas has been a major means of disposing of criminal cases since at least the 1800s (Vogel, 1999). Researchers began to shed light on plea bargaining in the 1960s, and the U.S. Supreme Court endorsed the process in the 1970s and subsequently clarified certain aspects of attorneys' responsibilities in the process (Roberts, 2013). In ***Santobello v. New York* (1971)**, for example, Chief Justice Warren Burger ruled that prosecutors were obliged to fulfill promises made during plea negotiations. According to Burger, "'Plea bargaining' is an essential component of the administration of justice. Properly administered, it is to be encouraged." Burger also listed several reasons that plea bargaining was a "highly desirable" part of the criminal justice process:

***Santobello v. New York* (1971)**
When a guilty plea rests on a promise of a prosecutor, the promise must be fulfilled.

- If every case went to trial, federal and state governments would need many times more courts and judges than they now have.
- Plea bargaining leads to the prompt and largely final disposition of most criminal cases.
- Plea bargaining reduces the time that pretrial detainees must spend in jail.
- If defendants plead guilty to serious charges, they can be moved to prisons with recreational and educational programs instead of enduring the enforced idleness of jails.
- By disposing of cases more quickly than trials would, plea bargaining reduces the amount of time that released suspects spend free on bail. Therefore, the public is better protected from crimes that such suspects may commit while on pretrial release.
- Offenders who plead guilty to serious charges can move more quickly into prison counseling, training, and education programs designed to rehabilitate offenders.

In 1976, Justice Potter Stewart revealed the heart and soul of plea bargaining when he wrote in *Blackledge v. Allison* that plea bargaining "can benefit all concerned" in a criminal case. It offers advantages for defendants, prosecutors, defense attorneys, and judges. Defendants can have their cases completed more quickly and know what the punishment will be, instead of facing the uncertainty of a judge's sentencing decision. Moreover, the defendant is likely to receive less than the maximum punishment that might have been imposed after a trial. Prosecutors are not being "soft on crime" when they plea bargain. Instead, they gain an easy conviction, even in cases in which enough evidence may not have been gathered to convince a jury to convict the defendant. They also save time and resources by disposing of cases without having to prepare for a trial (Mongrain and Roberts, 2009). Private defense attorneys benefit by avoiding the expenditure of time and effort needed to prepare for a trial; they earn their fee quickly and can move on to the next case. Similarly, plea bargaining helps public defenders cope with large caseloads. Judges, too, avoid time-consuming trials and having to decide what sentence to impose on the defendant. Instead, they often adopt the sentence recommended by the prosecutor in consultation with the defense attorney, provided that it falls within the range of sentences that they deem appropriate for a given crime and offender.

The attraction of plea bargaining for prosecutors and defendants was evident in a notable plea-based conviction in 2011. Hall of Fame former football star Lawrence Taylor entered guilty pleas to two misdemeanor charges—sexual misconduct with an underage girl and patronizing a prostitute. When he was arrested in 2010, he was charged with third-degree rape and soliciting rape when a teenage girl had been brought to his room by a man who was subsequently charged with unlawful imprisonment, assault, and endangering the welfare of a child (Zinser and Schweber, 2010). Taylor's attorney admitted that the former football star intended to patronize a prostitute but that he had been deceived about the girl's age. Taylor, who had prior arrests on his record from earlier years when he had abused illegal drugs, faced the possibility of four years in prison. After the plea agreement, however, Taylor was sentenced to six years of probation, a $2,000 fine, and registration as a sex offender (Yaniv, 2011). For Taylor, the benefits of plea bargaining were clear: His charges were reduced, he avoided any time in jail or prison, and he gained certainty about what his sentence would be. The prosecutor gained a conviction without the time and expense of trial. It is possible that the prosecutor saw potential risk of acquittal in a trial if a jury accepted Taylor's claim that he honestly believed that the girl was 19 rather than 16. The victim expressed dissatisfaction with the plea agreement, but the prosecutor claimed that the victim had been consulted in advance and had expressed approval for the sentence (Yaniv, 2011). In some sex-crime cases, victims favor plea agreements because they do not wish to go through the process of being questioned intensively by the defense attorney about the details of the crime. In addition, some women's advocates fear that acquittals at trial send a message to victims that they should not bother enduring intensive questioning and verbal attacks in the courtroom if jurors will not believe their testimony (Loewen, 2013). In the case of Lawrence Taylor, did the plea agreement achieve justice? Such questions are difficult to answer, as conceptions of justice are in the eye of the beholder. However, these results spare the system and its decision makers from the risk of expending significant resources on uncertain outcomes.

Defenders of plea bargaining justify the practice by noting that it permits judges, prosecutors, and defense attorneys to individualize justice by agreeing to a plea and a punishment that fit the offender and offense. The process also helps to encourage the defendant to cooperate and accept the results (O'Hear, 2007). Some argue that plea bargaining is an administrative necessity because

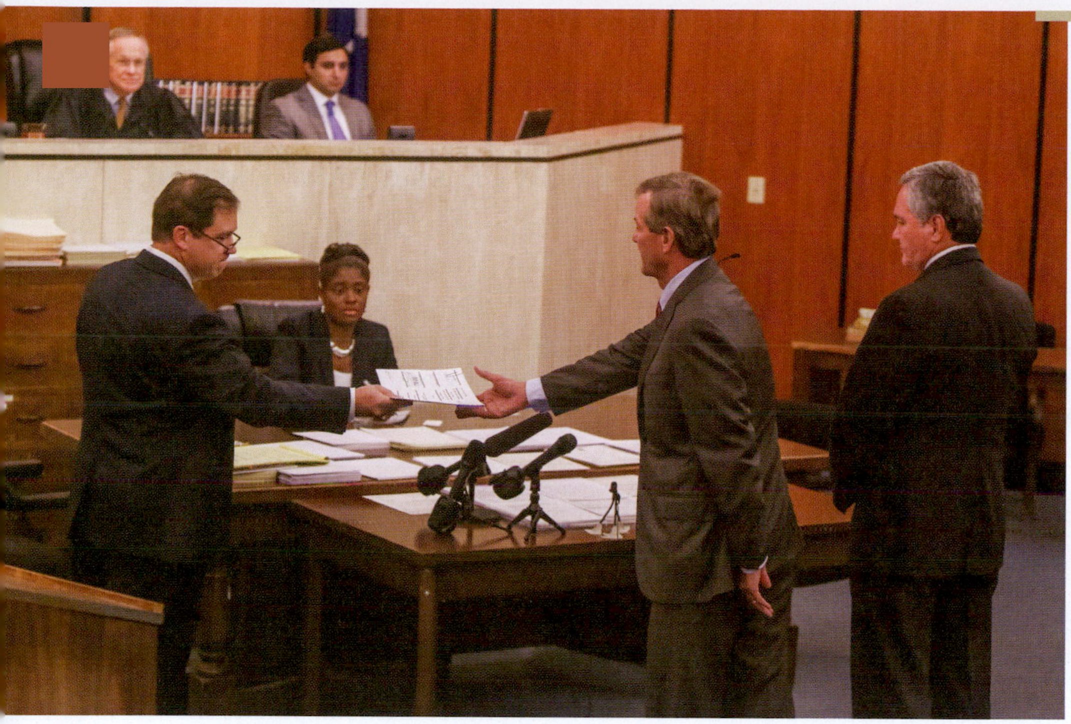

AP Images/Tim Dominick/The State

In 2014, South Carolina Speaker of the House Bobby Harrell pleaded guilty to criminal charges for taking political campaign funds for his own personal use. The judge suspended a six-year prison sentence and instead required him to serve three years of probation and pay more than $100,000 in fines and reimbursement. Should officials who violate the public's trust be permitted to gain reduced sentences through plea bargains?

courts lack the time and resources to conduct lengthy, expensive trials in all cases. Historical studies cast doubt on the latter justification, however, because during the nineteenth century, plea bargaining was a regular feature of case processing in courts with relatively few cases (Friedman, 1993; Heumann, 1978). Thus, instead of administrative need, the benefits of plea bargaining for the main participants appear to be the primary driving force behind the practice.

Because plea bargaining benefits all involved, it is little wonder that it existed long before the legal community publicly acknowledged it and that it still exists, even when prosecutors, legislators, or judges claim that they wish to abolish it. In California, for example, voters decided to ban plea bargaining for serious felony cases. Research showed, however, that when plea bargaining was barred in the felony trial courts, it did not disappear. It simply occurred earlier in the justice process, at the suspect's first appearance in the lower-level municipal court (McCoy, 1993). Efforts to abolish plea bargaining sometimes result in bargaining over the *charges* instead of over the *sentence* that will be recommended in exchange for a guilty plea. Moreover, if a prosecutor forbids his or her staff to plea bargain, judges may become more involved in negotiating and facilitating guilty pleas that result in predictable punishments for offenders.

Exchange Relationships in Plea Bargaining

Plea bargaining is a set of exchange relationships in which the prosecutor, the defense attorney, the defendant, and sometimes the judge participate. All have specific goals, all try to use the situation to their own advantage, and all tend to see the exchange as a success.

Plea bargaining does not always occur in a single meeting between prosecutor and defense attorney. One study showed that plea bargaining is a process in which prosecutors and defense attorneys interact again and again as they move along in the judicial process. As time passes, the prosecutor's hand may be strengthened by the discovery of more evidence or new information about the defendant's background (Caldwell, 2011; Emmelman, 1996). Often the prosecution rather than the defense is in the best position to obtain new evidence (Cooney, 1994). However, the defense attorney's position may gain strength if the prosecutor does not wish to spend time going further down the path toward a trial.

✔POINT 4. Why does plea bargaining occur?

STOP AND ANALYZE: Plea bargaining provides benefits for actors involved in individual cases. But does it provide benefits for society? Make a list of societal benefits of plea bargaining. Then make a list of the harms or costs. Is plea bargaining worth its price for society?

Tactics of Prosecutor and Defense

Plea bargaining between defense counsel and prosecutor is a serious game in which friendliness and joking may mask efforts to advance each side's cause. Each side tries to impress the other with its confidence in its own case while pointing out weaknesses in the other's. An unspoken rule of openness and candor helps keep the relationship on good terms. Little effort is made to conceal information that may later be useful to the other side in the courtroom. Studies show that the outcomes of plea bargaining may depend on the relationships between prosecutors and individual attorneys, as well as the defense counsel's willingness to fight for the client (Bowen, 2009; Champion, 1989).

A tactic that many prosecutors bring to plea bargaining sessions is the multiple-offense indictment. Multiple-offense charges are especially important to prosecuting attorneys in difficult cases in which, for instance, the victim is reluctant to provide information, the value of the stolen item is in question, and the evidence may not be reliable. The police often file charges of selling a drug when they know they can probably convict only for possession. Because the defendants know that the penalty for selling is much greater, they are tempted to plead guilty to the lesser charge rather than risk a severer punishment, even though conviction on the more serious charge is uncertain (Caldwell, 2011). Such tactics can be especially powerful when the potential punishment upon conviction at trial would be severe (Ehrhard, 2008).

In the view of many defense attorneys, prosecutors hold the upper hand through their ability to file and pursue multiple charges. Their position is further strengthened by the increasingly severe sentences that legislatures enacted in the 1990s (R. Oppel, 2011). Even without strong evidence, the defense attorney must be concerned that a jury might convict the defendant based on limited evidence, especially if the defendant already has a prior criminal record. As described by one public defender, "Plea bargaining is not give and take. The government has tremendous leverage over the defense. . . . It's more a take-it-or-leave-it situation" (Blankenship, 2013).

In some cases, defense attorneys may threaten to ask for a jury trial if concessions are not made (Bowen, 2009). Their hand is further strengthened if they have filed pretrial motions that require a formal response by the prosecutor. Another tactic is to seek to reschedule pretrial activities in the hope that, with delay, witnesses will become unavailable, media attention will die down, and memories of the crime will diminish by the time of the trial. Rather than resort to such legal tactics, however, some attorneys prefer to bargain on the basis of friendly interactions.

Neither the prosecutor nor the defense attorney is a free agent. Each needs the cooperation of defendants and judges. Attorneys often cite the difficulty of convincing defendants that they should accept the offered plea deal. Judges might not sentence the accused according to the prosecutor's recommendation. On the other hand, although their role requires that they uphold the public interest, judges may be reluctant to interfere with a plea agreement. Thus, both the prosecutor and the defense attorney often confer with the judge about the sentence to be imposed before agreeing on a plea. If a particular judge is unpredictable in supporting plea agreements, defense attorneys may be reluctant to reach agreements in that judge's court.

Pleas without Bargaining

Studies show that in many courts, give-and-take plea bargaining does not occur for certain types of cases, yet these cases have as many guilty pleas as they do in other courts (Bowen, 2009; Eisenstein, Flemming, and Nardulli, 1988). The term *bargaining* may be misleading in that it implies haggling. Many scholars argue that guilty pleas emerge after the prosecutor, the defense attorney, and sometimes the judge reach an agreement to settle the facts (Bowen, 2009; Utz, 1978). In this view, the parties first study the facts of a case. What were the circumstances of the event? Was it really an assault or was it more of a shoving match? Did the victim antagonize the accused? Each side may hope to persuade the other that provable facts back up its view of the defendant's actions. The prosecution wants the defense to believe that strong evidence proves its version of the event. The defense attorney wants to convince the prosecution that the evidence is not solid and a jury trial would likely result in acquittal.

In some cases, the evidence is strong and the defense attorney has little hope of persuading the prosecutor otherwise. Through their discussions, the prosecutor and defense attorney seek to reach a shared view of the provable facts in the case. Once they agree on the facts, they will both know the appropriate charge, and they can agree on the sentence according to the locally defined going rate. At that point a guilty plea can be entered without any formal bargaining, because both sides agree on what the case is worth in terms of the seriousness of the charge and the usual punishment. This process may be thought of as *implicit plea bargaining*, because shared understandings create the expectation that a guilty plea will lead to a less-than-maximum sentence, even without any exchange or bargaining.

The going rates for sentences for particular crimes and offenders depend on local values and sentencing patterns. Often both the prosecutor and the defense attorney belong to a particular local legal culture and thus share an understanding about how cases should be handled. On the basis of their experiences in interacting with other attorneys and judges, they become keenly aware of local practices in the treatment of cases and offenders (Worden, 1995). Thus they may both know right away what the sentence will be for a first-time burglar or second-time robber. The sentence may differ in another courthouse because the local legal culture and going rates can vary (S. Bushway et al., 2014).

These shared understandings are important for several reasons. First, they help make plea bargaining more effective, because both sides understand which sentences apply to which cases. Second, they help create a cooperative climate for plea bargaining, even if bad feelings exist between the prosecutor and the defense attorney. The local legal culture dictates how attorneys should treat each other and thereby reach agreements. Third, the shared understandings help maintain the relationship between the attorneys.

POINT 5. What is implicit plea bargaining?

STOP AND ANALYZE: Does plea bargaining place too much influence over people's fates into the discretionary decisions of prosecutors and defense attorneys? Should judges, as the officials most responsible for and committed to neutral decision making, have greater participation in and influence over plea agreements? List the pros and cons of having judges involved in all discussions through which plea agreements develop.

Legal Issues in Plea Bargaining

***Boykin v. Alabama* (1969)**
Defendants must state that they are voluntarily making a plea of guilty.

In ***Boykin v. Alabama* (1969)**, the Supreme Court ruled that defendants must state that they made their pleas voluntarily, before judges may accept those pleas. Judges have created standard forms that have questions for the defendant to affirm in open court before the plea is accepted. Trial judges also must learn whether the defendant understands the consequences of pleading guilty and confirm that the plea is not obtained through pressure or coercion. The judge's role ensuring that defendants know their rights is especially important because there is no constitutional right to withdraw a guilty plea after it has been entered. However, there may be a basis to do so in exceptional cases, depending on governing law. For example, in federal courts a plea may be withdrawn if the defendant shows "a just and fair reason" to do so (*United States v. Hyde,* 1997).

***North Carolina v. Alford* (1970)**
A plea of guilty may be accepted for the purpose of a lesser sentence from a defendant who maintains his or her innocence.

Can a trial court accept a guilty plea if the defendant claims to be innocent? In ***North Carolina v. Alford* (1970)**, the Court allowed a defendant to enter a guilty plea for the purpose of gaining a lesser sentence, even though he maintained that he was innocent (Gooch, 2010). However, the Supreme Court has stated that trial judges should not accept such a plea unless a factual

CLOSE UP

ELECTED PROSECUTORS: ARE THERE RISKS AND BENEFITS?

The United States is the only country in the world where local prosecutors are elected officials in most states. In other countries, prosecutors are appointed officials. In democracies elsewhere, prosecutors do not face the prospect of pressure from voters and the need for endorsements by police organizations during political campaigns. Questions inevitably arise concerning whether being elected may affect prosecutors' decisions about whom to charge, when to dismiss cases, and how they will conduct plea bargaining and trials.

In theory, elections are a mechanism to hold prosecutors accountable to local voters. If they do their jobs well, then the public will vote to keep them in office. If they make decisions with which the public disagrees, the voters will elect new prosecutors. In practice, however, there are concerns that the public does not fully understand criminal law and the obligations of prosecutors. Will voters punish a prosecutor for failing to prosecute a suspect who has received significant attention from the news media in a highly publicized crime even though the prosecutor believes that there is not enough evidence to establish the suspect's guilt? Will prosecutors feel pressure to avoid investigating allegations of police misconduct or decline to charge police officers with crimes because they know that endorsements from police officers' organizations may carry substantial weight with voters during the election? The controversy over how the St. Louis, Missouri, prosecutor conducted the grand jury inquiry in the Ferguson, Missouri, police shooting case, as described in Chapter 10, reinforced observers' concerns that prosecutors may be too influenced by external considerations. Would the justice system be more efficient and fair if prosecutors enjoyed greater independence from the voters, police, and political parties?

On the other hand, how will prosecutors be held accountable if they have greater independence? Prosecutors are almost completely immune from lawsuits if they make mistakes or violate people's rights. Thus they cannot be held responsible for improper actions in the same ways that other officials in the justice system (other than judges, who also enjoy immunity) face the threat of accountability through lawsuits.

The effectiveness of elections as an accountability mechanism is weakened by the fact that many members of the public have little knowledge about how particular prosecutors have handled individual cases. Instead, prosecutors may successfully gain reelection solely based on name recognition from their ability to basis exists for believing that the defendant is in fact guilty (Whitebread and Slobogin, 2000).

Another issue is whether the plea agreement has been fulfilled. If the prosecutor has promised to recommend a lenient sentence, he or she must keep that promise. The Supreme Court ruled that "when a [guilty] plea rests in any significant degree on a promise or agreement of the prosecutor, so that it can be said to be part of the inducement or consideration, such promise must be fulfilled" (*Santobello v. New York*, 1971). The Court also decided, in ***Ricketts v. Adamson* (1987)**, that defendants must also keep their side of the bargain, such as an agreement to testify against codefendants. However, defendants may forfeit their opportunity to challenge a prosecutor's failure to fulfill the agreement if the defense attorney does not raise an objection to the prosecutor's failure immediately when it occurs in the sentencing hearing (*Puckett v. United States*, 2009).

***Ricketts v. Adamson* (1987)**
Defendants must uphold the plea agreement or risk going to trial and receiving a harsher sentence.

May prosecutors threaten to penalize defendants who insist on their right to a jury trial? Yes, according to ***Bordenkircher v. Hayes* (1978)**. Prosecutors may, for example, threaten repeat offenders with life sentences under habitual offender statutes if they do not agree to plead guilty and accept specified terms of imprisonment. A threat of more-serious charges, as long as such charges are legitimate and supported by evidence, is not considered improper pressure that makes a guilty plea involuntary and hence invalid. Some scholars criticize this decision as imposing pressures on defendants that are not permitted elsewhere in the justice process (Dervan and Edkins, 2013; Caldwell, 2011; O'Hear, 2006). Read the Close Up to consider concerns about the motivations of elected prosecutors in the United States, including risks that improper motivations may influence their decisions about how to process cases (McCannon, 2013).

***Bordenkircher v. Hayes* (1978)**
A defendant's rights were not violated by a prosecutor who warned that failure to agree to a guilty plea would result in a harsher sentence.

get news media coverage for criminal cases as well as their ability to raise campaign funds and run commercials on television. Should attorneys gain and keep jobs as prosecutors primarily because of their ability to raise campaign funds from political parties and interest groups? Since money is a key element for success in elections, fundraising by prosecutors raises additional risks that favoritism will influence decision making when prosecutors' financial supporters may have broken criminal laws.

Because many members of the public may expect prosecutors to demonstrate a tough-on-crime attitude, there are risks that prosecutors will not be sufficiently careful to avoid using additional charges as threats to induce guilty pleas, even from people who may be innocent. Psychology research shows that innocent people may be susceptible to pleading guilty when faced with the possibility of severe punishments for extra charges if they assert their innocence and go to trial. Moreover, many people may not have confidence in the ability of juries to make correct decisions by identifying who is actually innocent. Thus they could plead guilty out of fear that a jury error will produce a much harsher sentence. Yet there is also a question about whether these risks would actually be reduced if prosecutors were appointed rather than elected.

Sources: Lucian Dervan and Vanessa Edkins, "The Innocent Defendant's Dilemma: An Innovative Empirical Study of Plea Bargaining's Innocence Problem." *Journal of Criminal Law and Criminology* 103 (2013): 1–48; Michael Ellis, "The Origins of Elected Prosecutors," *Yale Law Journal* 121 (2012): 1528–69; Letitia James, "Prosecutors and Police: The Inherent Conflict in Our Courts," MSNBC online, December 5, 2014 (www.msnbc.com); Daniel Knight, "We Elect Prosecutors for a Reason," *St. Louis Post-Dispatch*, October 31, 2014 (www.stltoday.com); Mara Leveritt, "Prosecutors Have All the Power," *Arkansas Times*, September 11, 2014 (www.arktimes.com); Ronald Wright, "Beyond Prosecutor Elections," *SMU Law Review* 67 (2014): 593–615.

DEBATE THE ISSUE

Should prosecutors be chosen by someone other than the voters? If so, how will they be held accountable for their actions? Do risks of favoritism, too-close relationships with police, and motivations to appear tough on crime exist for prosecutors no matter how they are chosen? Describe how prosecutors should ideally be chosen and held accountable. Give two reasons for the approach that you support.

In more-recent years, the Supreme Court has considered additional issues about plea bargaining. Although many of the Court's prior decisions focused on endorsing the legality of the practice, specifying the judge's responsibilities, and holding each side to its promises, a series of recent cases focused on protecting defendants against the consequences of mistakes by defense attorneys. Defendants do not possess enough knowledge and information to protect themselves in a negotiation process involving attorneys. Thus they are highly dependent on their attorneys' judgment and advice.

Despite its advantages for all parties involved, plea bargaining can present difficult decisions for defendants, especially if the prosecutor insists that a defendant accept a long prison sentence. Defendants may balk as they wonder if they might not do just as well by taking their chances in a trial. Defense attorneys are supposed to provide advice to defendants based on knowledgeable predictions about the possible results of going to trial. Trial outcomes are not, however, easily predictable. The sentences that judges may impose after trials might not be easy to predict either. Read the Question of Ethics feature at the end of the chapter to consider the difficulties faced by defense attorneys and their clients in deciding whether to accept a plea agreement offered by the prosecutor.

Criticisms of Plea Bargaining

Although plea bargaining is widely used, some critics deplore it. The criticisms are of two main types. The first stresses due process and argues that plea bargaining is unfair because defendants give up some of their constitutional rights, especially the right to trial by jury (O'Keefe, 2010). The second stresses sentencing policy and points out that plea bargaining reduces society's interest in appropriate punishments for crimes. In urban areas with high caseloads, harried prosecutors and judges are said to make concessions based on administrative needs, resulting in lighter sentences than those required by the penal code.

Plea bargaining also comes under fire because it is hidden from judicial scrutiny. Because the agreement is most often made at an early stage, the judge has little information about the crime and the defendant and thus cannot adequately evaluate the case. Nor can the judge review the terms of the bargain, that is, check on the amount of pressure put on the defendant to plead guilty. The result of bargain justice is that the judge, the public, and sometimes even the defendant cannot know for sure who got what from whom in exchange for what. In addition, plea bargaining does not happen in a uniform manner, so that decisions by different prosecutors about what deals to offer lead to unequal punishments for defendants originally charged with the same crimes (Devers, 2011).

Other critics believe that overuse of plea bargaining breeds disrespect and even contempt for the law. They say criminals look at the judicial process as a game or a sham, much like other "deals" made in life. Critics also contend that it is unjust to penalize people who assert their right to a trial by giving them stiffer sentences than they would have received if they had pleaded guilty. Indeed, the threat of severe sentences is so great in the federal court system that the number of trials in the federal system has dropped by two-thirds in the past 25 years even as the number of defendants has nearly tripled (Fields and Emshwiller, 2012; "Thumb on the Scale," 2013). Research provides evidence that an extra penalty is imposed on defendants who take up the court's time by asserting their right to a trial (Devers, 2011; Ulmer, Eisenstein, and Johnson, 2010). Critics note that federal sentencing guidelines also encourage avoidance of trial, because they include a two-point deduction from an offender's base score for a guilty plea—thus lowering the sentence—for "acceptance of responsibility" (McCoy, 1995).

Finally, another concern about plea bargaining is that innocent people will plead guilty to acts they did not commit. Although it is hard to know how often this happens, some defendants have entered guilty pleas when they have not committed the offense (McConville, 2000). Middle-class people might find it hard to understand how anyone could possibly plead guilty when innocent. However, people with little education, low social status, or mental problems may lack the confidence to say "no" to an attorney who pressures them to plead guilty (A. D. Redlich, Summers, and Hoover, 2010). Poor people may feel especially helpless in the stressful climate of the courthouse and jail. If they lack faith in the system's ability to protect their rights and to find them not guilty, they may accept a lighter punishment rather than risk conviction for a serious offense (Covey, 2009). The risk has been exacerbated by the severity of sentences, especially in the federal court system. News stories highlight examples of individuals who felt pressured to accept guilty pleas, despite believing in their own innocence, simply because they did not want to take the risk of being sent to prison for decades if a jury believed the prosecutor at trial (S. Bushway et al., 2014; Fields and Emshwiller, 2012; "Thumb on the Scale," 2013). Think about these criticisms as you examine "Civic Engagement: Your Role in the System."

CIVIC ENGAGEMENT

YOUR ROLE IN THE SYSTEM

Imagine that the voters of your state will consider a ballot issue to ban plea bargaining for serious crimes in the trial courts of general jurisdiction. *Make a list of the consequences that you predict if the ballot issue is approved by the voters. Would you vote in favor of the ban?* Then read a brief review that discusses what happened when California voters decided to approve such a ban.

✔POINT

6. What issues concerning plea bargaining has the Supreme Court examined?
7. What are the criticisms of plea bargaining?

STOP AND ANALYZE: The U.S. Supreme Court's decision in *North Carolina v. Alford* (1970) says that a judge can accept a guilty plea from someone who claims to be actually innocent. Does the acceptance of such pleas diminish the justice system's goal of punishing only those who are guilty of crimes? If you were a judge, would you accept such pleas? Write a brief statement explaining your position.

Trial: The Exceptional Case

Cases not dismissed or terminated through plea bargaining move forward for trial. The seriousness of the charge is probably the most important factor influencing the decision to go to trial. Defendants charged with property crimes rarely demand a trial. However, murder, felonious assault, or rape—all charges that bring long prison terms—are more likely to require judge and jury. In a study of the nation's 75 largest counties, 44 percent of murder cases went to trial, the largest percentage for any crime. For all other crimes, trials occurred in 6 percent of cases or less (T. H. Cohen and Kyckelhahn, 2010). When the penalty is harsh, many defendants seem willing to risk the possibility of conviction at trial.

Although such statistics suggest consistency in decisions about going to trial, the real practice varies considerably. Note in Table 11.2 the differences in the percentages of defendants going to trial for several offenses in various courts. What might explain the differences from one city to another and for one offense or another? Think about how prosecutors' policies or sentencing practices in different cities can increase or decrease the incentives for a defendant to plead guilty.

Most Americans are familiar with the image of the criminal trial. As portrayed in so many movies and television shows, the prosecutor and defense attorney face off in a tense confrontation in court. Each attorney attempts to use evidence, persuasion, and emotion to convince a jury of citizens to favor its arguments about the defendant's guilt or innocence.

TABLE 11.2 PERCENTAGE OF INDICTED CASES THAT WENT TO TRIAL, BY OFFENSE

The percentages of cases that went to trial differ both by offense and by jurisdiction. Typically, it seems that the stiffer the possible penalty, the greater the likelihood of a trial. However, a prosecutor may be able to gain guilty pleas even in the most serious cases.

JURISDICTION	HOMICIDE	RAPE/SEXUAL ASSAULT	ROBBERY	ASSAULT	DRUG OFFENSES
State courts, 75 largest counties	44%	7%	6%	6%	2%
Federal courts	15%	—	4%	8%	3%
Mercer County, NJ (Trenton)	12%	2%	3%	<1%	<1%

Sources: Adapted from Thomas H. Cohen and Tracy Kyckelhahn, *Felony Defendants in Large Urban Counties, 2006* (Washington, DC: Bureau of Justice Statistics, 2010); "Mercer County Prosecutor's Annual Report 2013" (2014); Bureau of Justice Statistics, *Sourcebook of Criminal Justice Statistics* (2015), Table 5.24.2010.

As we have seen in previous chapters, the trial process is based on the *adversary process*, an open battle between opposing lawyers that is assumed to be the best way to discover the truth. The authors of the Constitution apparently shared this assumption: The Sixth Amendment says the accused shall enjoy a speedy and public trial by an impartial jury in all criminal prosecutions. In theory, each side will present the best evidence and arguments it can muster, and the **jury** will make a decision based on thorough consideration of the available information about the case.

jury
A panel of citizens selected according to law and sworn to determine matters of fact in a criminal case and to deliver a verdict of guilty or not guilty.

However, because trials are human processes, many factors may keep a trial from achieving its goal of revealing the truth. The rules of evidence can prevent one side from presenting the most useful evidence. One side may have impressive expert witnesses that the other side cannot afford to counter with its own experts. One side's attorney may be more persuasive and likeable, thus swaying the jury in spite of the evidence. The jurors or judge may bring into the courtroom their own prejudices, which cause them to favor some defendants or automatically assume the worst about others (Ponulo et al., 2010). Fundamentally, we, as a society, place great faith in the trial process as the best means for giving complete consideration of a defendant's potential guilt, yet the process does not always work as it should. Thus there is inevitable uncertainty about how any given trial will turn out. As a result, most convictions are based on the plea bargaining process through which both sides can seek to gain a predictable outcome and defendants can reduce the risk of receiving the harshest possible sentence.

Trials determine the fates of very few defendants. Although the right to trial by jury is ingrained in American ideology—it is mentioned in the Declaration of Independence, three amendments to the Constitution, and countless opinions of the Supreme Court—trials produced only 3 percent of felony convictions in the nation's 75 most populous counties (T. H. Cohen and Kychkelhahn, 2010). Of these, most are typically jury trials; the rest are **bench trials** presided over by a judge without a jury. In federal trial courts, fewer than 1 percent of cases were decided by bench trials, while nearly 3 percent involved jury trials. Defendants may choose a bench trial if they believe a judge will be more capable of making an objective decision, especially if the charges or evidence are likely to arouse emotional reactions in jurors.

bench trial
Trial conducted by a judge who acts as fact finder and determines issues of law. No jury participates.

Trials take considerable time and resources. Attorneys frequently spend weeks or months preparing evidence, responding to their opponents' motions, planning trial strategy, and setting aside days or weeks to present the case in court. From the perspective of judges, prosecutors, and defense attorneys, plea bargaining is obviously an attractive alternative for purposes of completing cases quickly.

Going to Trial

Because the adversary process is designed to get to the truth, the rules of criminal law, procedure, and evidence govern the conduct of the trial. Trials are based on the idea that the prosecution and defense will compete before a judge and jury so that the truth will emerge. Above the battle, the judge sees to it that the rules are followed and that the jury impartially evaluates the evidence and reflects the community's interest (Walpin, 2003). The adversary process and the inclusion of citizen-jurors in decision making often make trial outcomes difficult to predict. The verdict hinges not only on the nature of the evidence but also on the effectiveness of the prosecution and defense and on the attitudes of the jurors. In a jury trial, the jury is the sole evaluator of the facts in a case. Does this adversarial, citizen-juried trial process provide the best mechanism for finding the truth and doing justice in our most serious criminal cases?

Most jury trials worldwide take place in the United States. Common-law countries, such as Australia, Canada, Great Britain, and the United States, are the places that historically have used a group of citizens drawn from the community to determine the guilt of criminal defendants. In civil-law countries, this function is usually performed by a judge or judges, often assisted by two or three nonlawyers serving as assessors. However, a few civil-law countries, including Russia and Spain, have incorporated juries into their legal processes (Thaman, 2000). Japan introduced criminal jury trials into their system in 2009 (Okada, 2006).

Juries perform six vital functions in the U.S. criminal justice system:

1. Prevent government oppression by safeguarding citizens against arbitrary law enforcement
2. Determine whether the accused is guilty on the basis of the evidence presented
3. Represent diverse community interests, so that no one set of values or biases dominates decision making
4. Serve as a buffer between the accused and the accuser

AP Images/Doug Finger/The Gainsville Sun

In 2014, a jury convicted 20-year-old Pedro Bravo of killing a University of Florida student and sentenced him to life without parole. Prosecutors alleged that Bravo was jealous of the victim for dating a woman for whom Bravo harbored obsessive feelings. What other kinds of cases are likely to lead to jury trials?

WHAT AMERICANS THINK

QUESTION: "How often do most people who are on trial have a jury that is fair and impartial?"

Perceptions of juries' fairness

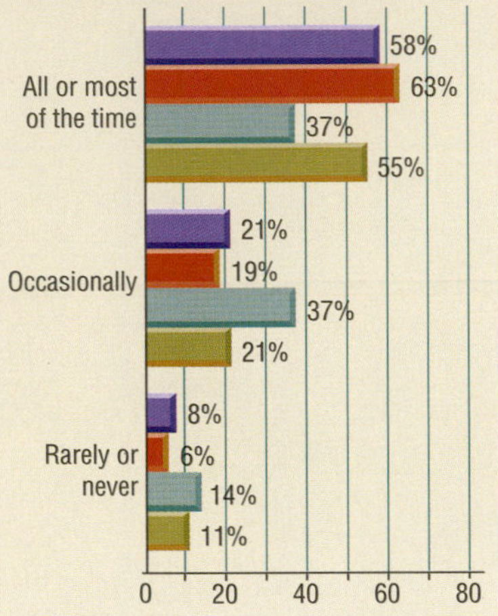

(Continues)

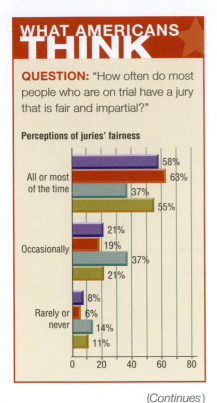

Williams v. Florida (1970)
Juries of fewer than 12 members are permitted by the U.S. Constitution.

5. Promote knowledge about the criminal justice system by learning about it through the jury-duty process
6. Symbolize the rule of law and the community foundation that supports the criminal justice system

As indicated by the responses in "What Americans Think," Americans have divided views on the fairness of the jury process.

As a symbol of law, juries demonstrate to the public—and to defendants—that decisions about depriving individuals of their liberty will be made carefully by a group of citizens who represent the community's values. In addition, juries provide the primary element of direct democracy in the judicial branch of government. Through participation on juries, citizens use their votes to determine the outcomes of cases (Heyman, 2014; C. E. Smith, 1994). This branch of government, which is dominated by judges and lawyers, offers few other opportunities for citizens to shape judicial decisions directly. Think about your own views of jury service as you read "Civic Engagement: Your Role in the System." In the United States, a criminal jury traditionally is composed of 12 citizens, but some states now allow as few as 6 citizens to make up a jury in noncapital cases. This reform was recommended to modernize court procedures and reduce expenses. It costs less for the court to contact, process, and pay a smaller number of jurors. The Supreme Court in **Williams v. Florida (1970)** upheld the use of small juries. In *Burch v. Louisiana* (1979), the Court ruled that six-member juries must vote unanimously to convict a defendant, but unanimity is not required for larger juries. Some states permit juries to convict defendants by votes of 10 to 2 or 9 to 3 (see Figure 11.2 for jury size requirements in each state). Critics of the change to six-person juries charge that the smaller group is less representative of the conflicting views in the community and too quick to bring in a verdict (Diamond et al., 2009; Amar, 1997).

FIGURE 11.2 JURY SIZE FOR FELONY AND MISDEMEANOR TRIALS

All states require 12-member juries in capital cases; six states permit juries of fewer than 12 members in felony cases. Does the smaller number of people on a jury create advantages or disadvantages? Would you rather have your case decided by a 12- or a 6-person jury?

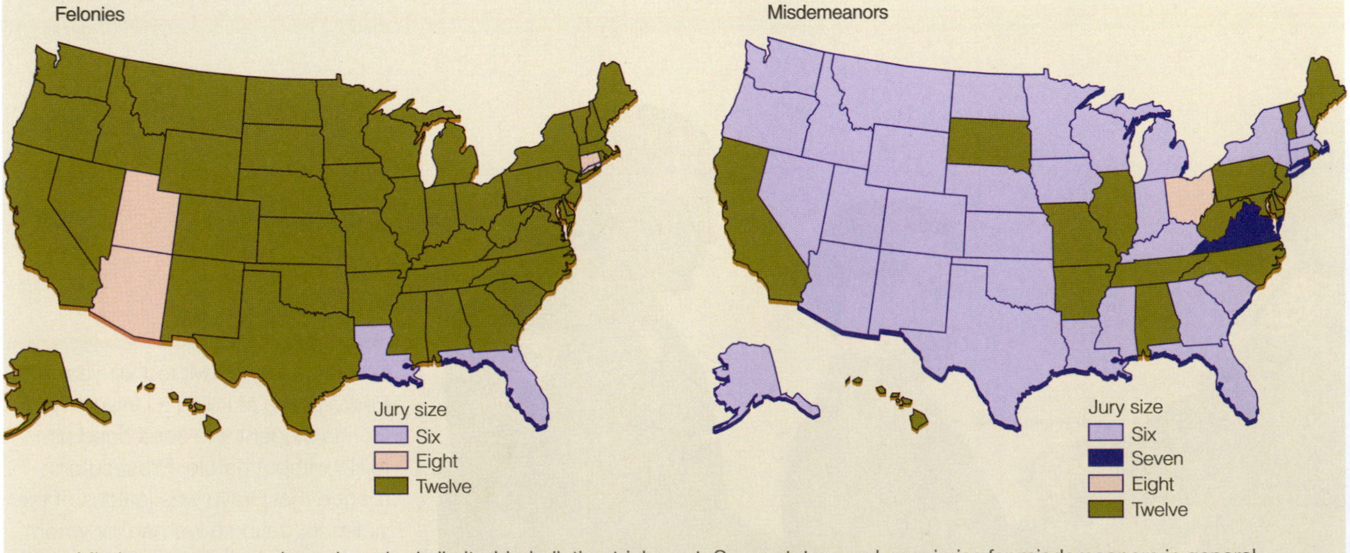

Note: Misdemeanors map shows jury size in limited-jurisdiction trial court. Some states use larger juries for misdemeanors in general jurisdiction trial court or for aggravated misdemeanors.

Source: Adapted from data by David B. Rottman and Shauna M. Strickland, *State Court Organization 2004* (Washington, DC: U.S. Government Printing Office, 2006), 233–37.

✔POINT

8. Approximately what percentage of felony cases reach conclusion through a trial?
9. What are three of the six functions that juries serve for the criminal justice system?
10. What has the Supreme Court decided concerning the size and unanimity requirements of juries?

STOP AND ANALYZE: Are citizens drawn from the community capable of setting aside their personal biases and able to understand complex or emotional testimony? Some other countries use "mixed tribunals" that include several judges and several citizens deciding cases together. List two reasons why you either favor or oppose the use of such mixed tribunals in the United States.

The Trial Process

The trial process generally follows eight steps:

1. Selection of the jury
2. Opening statements by prosecution and defense
3. Presentation of the prosecution's evidence and witnesses
4. Presentation of the defense's evidence and witnesses
5. Presentation of rebuttal witnesses
6. Closing arguments by each side
7. Instruction of the jury by the judge
8. Decision by the jury

The details of each step may vary according to each state's rules. Although only a small number of cases go to trial, understanding each step in the process and considering the broader impact of this institution are important.

Jury Selection

The selection of the jury, outlined in Figure 11.3, is a crucial first step in the trial process. Because people always incorporate their experiences, values, and biases in their decision making, prosecutors and defense attorneys actively seek to identify and select potential jurors who may be sympathetic to their side and to exclude potentially hostile jurors (Joy, 2015). Lawyers do not necessarily achieve these goals, because the selection of jurors involves the decisions and interactions of prosecutors, defense attorneys, and judges, each of whom has different objectives in the selection process.

Jurors are selected from among the citizens whose names have been placed in the jury pool. The composition of the jury pool tremendously impacts the ultimate composition of the trial jury. In most states, the jury pool is drawn from lists of registered voters and licensed drivers, but research has shown that nonwhites, the poor, and young people register to vote and maintain valid driver's licenses at lower rates than do the rest of the population. As a result, members of these groups are underrepresented on juries (Sommers, 2009).

In many cases, the presence or absence of these groups may make no difference in the ultimate verdict. In some situations, however, members of these groups will likely interpret evidence differently than will their older, white, middle-class counterparts who dominate the composition of juries (Cornwell and Hans, 2011). For example, poor people, nonwhites, and young people may be more likely to have had unpleasant experiences with police officers and therefore be less willing to believe that police officers always tell the truth (Forman, 2015). Today, courts may supplement the lists of registered voters

(Continued)

WHAT AMERICANS THINK

QUESTION: "Who would you trust more to give a fair verdict?"

Judge versus jury

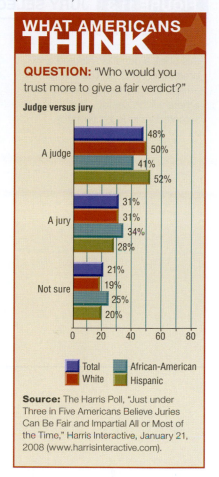

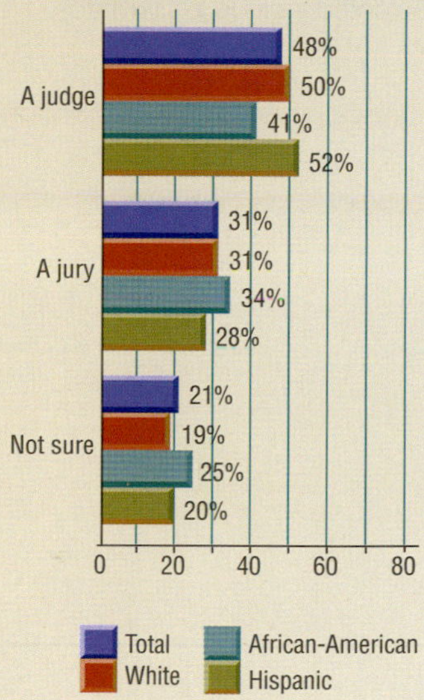

Source: The Harris Poll, "Just under Three in Five Americans Believe Juries Can Be Fair and Impartial All or Most of the Time," Harris Interactive, January 21, 2008 (www.harrisinteractive.com).

CIVIC ENGAGEMENT

YOUR ROLE IN THE SYSTEM

Imagine that you receive a notice to report to jury duty—but it is for the same day that you are supposed to drive four hours to an arena in order to attend a concert by your favorite musical group. A friend says to you, "Don't miss the concert. Just call in and say that you're sick." *Write down your responses to the following questions: is jury service an important civic duty? Should someone report for jury duty even when it is highly inconvenient? is jury service a burden to be avoided?* Then see how your responses compare to those of other Americans who were surveyed on a similar question.

FIGURE 11.3 JURY SELECTION PROCESS FOR A 12-MEMBER JURY

Potential jurors are drawn at random from a source list. From this pool, a panel is selected and presented for duty. The voir dire examination may remove some, while others will be seated. The 14 jurors selected include 2 alternates.

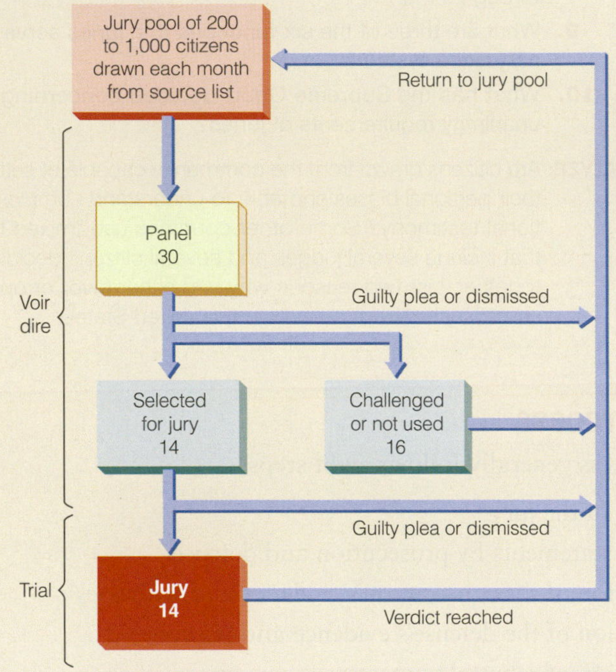

and driver's licenses with other lists, such as those for hunting licenses and utility bills, in order to diversify the jury pool (Hannaford-Agor, 2011).

Several states are considering increases in jurors' daily pay. In general, jurors receive minimal financial compensation for their service. Thus even increases tend to be small. Texas, for example, went from $6 per day to $40 per day in trials lasting more than one day. It is hoped that such efforts will make jury service more attractive for poor people who might otherwise avoid participating because they cannot afford to lose pay by missing work (Axtman, 2005).

Although some commentators believe that juror compensation must be increased in an effort to broaden participation, the budget crises affecting state and local governments have actually pushed compensation in the opposite direction. Many jurisdictions, including Cleveland, Ohio, and Topeka, Kansas, have reduced jurors' pay in order to save money (Dubail, 2009; KTKA News, 2011). Portage County, Ohio, actually suspended all pay for jurors because an unexpected increase in expensive murder trials drained the courts' budget during a period of financial cutbacks (Sever, 2010). In addition, lawyers and judges in many courts are concerned that potential jurors increasingly seek to be excused from service due to financial hardships. Small business owners feel that they cannot be away from their struggling businesses. Sole wage earners for a family cannot pay their bills with the minimal compensation provided to jurors (Weiss, 2009). Thus difficult economic times affect the composition of jury pools and potentially make them less representative of the entire community. Even worse, in some courthouses when judges refuse to excuse jurors for claims of financial hardship, those jurors may openly express their anger by asserting that they will not be objective in their decision making. Such expressions can lead attorneys on both sides to agree to have a bench trial in order to avoid problems in dealing with disgruntled jurors (C. J. Williams, 2010). Jury trials are also affected by other contemporary developments in society. Read

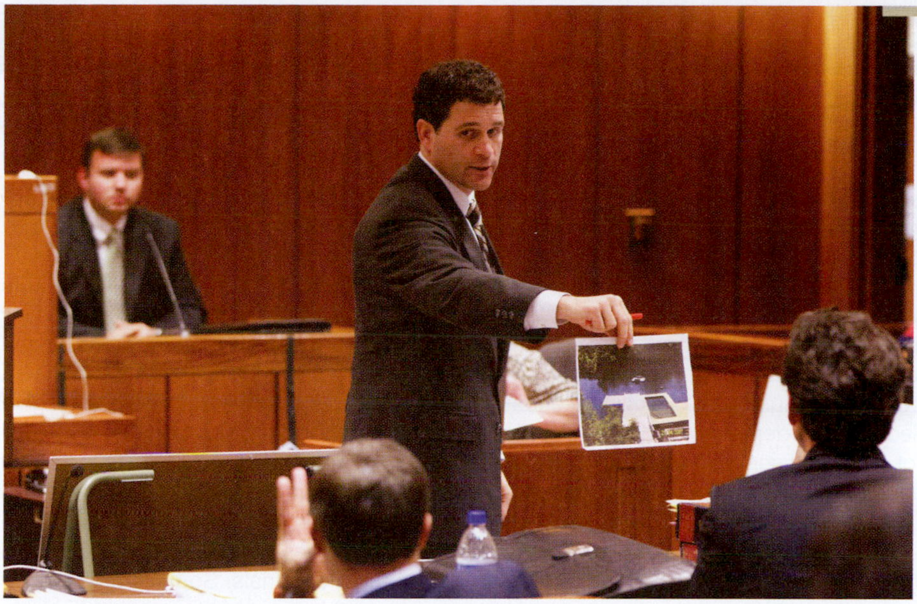

AP Images/Dave Martin

The prosecutor and defense attorney present evidence in their efforts to persuade the judge and jury. Their arguments and presentations are not neutral and objective, because they are professionally obligated to argue zealously for a particular perspective. In theory, this clash of advocates will make the truth emerge. Are there risks that the truth will actually be hidden? Are trials the most effective way to produce accurate determinations of guilt?

the New Directions in Criminal Justice Policy feature to consider the challenges judges and attorneys face in dealing with jurors who are accustomed to using the Internet and social media throughout the day.

Only about 15 percent of adult Americans have ever been called for jury duty. Retired people and homemakers with grown children tend to be overrepresented on juries because they are less inconvenienced by serving and are often less likely to ask to be excused because of job responsibilities or child-care problems. To make jury duty less onerous, many states have moved to a system called one-day, one-trial, in which jurors serve for either one day or the duration of one trial.

The courtroom process of **voir dire** (which means "to speak the truth") is used to question prospective jurors to screen out those who might be biased or incapable of making a fair decision (Harrison, 2011). Attorneys for each side, as well as the judge, may question jurors about their background, knowledge of the case, and their acquaintance with any participants in the case. Jurors will also be asked whether they or their immediate family members have been crime victims or otherwise involved in a criminal case in a manner that may prevent them from making open-minded decisions about the evidence and the defendant. If a juror's responses indicate that he or she will not be able to make fair decisions, an attorney may request a **challenge for cause**. The judge must rule on the challenge, but if the judge agrees with the attorney, then the juror is excused from that specific case. There is usually no limit on the number of jurors that the attorneys may challenge for cause. Nonetheless, identifying all of a juror's biases through brief questioning is not easy (Dillehay and Sandys, 1996).

voir dire
A questioning of prospective jurors in order to screen out people the judge or attorneys think might be biased or otherwise incapable of delivering a fair verdict.

challenge for cause
Removal of a prospective juror by showing that he or she has some bias or some other legal disability. The number of these challenges permitted to attorneys is potentially unlimited.

Although challenges for cause fall ultimately under the judge's control, the prosecution and defense can exert their own control over the jury's composition through the use of **peremptory challenges**. Using these challenges, the prosecution and defense can exclude prospective jurors without giving specific reasons. Attorneys use peremptory challenges to exclude jurors whom they think will be unsympathetic to their arguments (M. Hoffman, 1999). Attorneys usually use hunches about which jurors to challenge; there is little evidence that they can accurately identify which jurors will be sympathetic or

peremptory challenge
Removal of a prospective juror without giving any reason. Attorneys are allowed a limited number of such challenges.

NEW DIRECTIONS IN CRIMINAL JUSTICE POLICY

JURORS AND ELECTRONIC COMMUNICATIONS

In April 2013, a judge in Oregon noticed a strange glow in front of a juror just as the lights in the courtroom were being turned off in order to show video evidence. The judge cleared the courtroom of everyone except the juror in question and confronted the juror about the source of the glowing light: a smartphone being used for texting. The judge had specifically instructed the jurors prior to the trial that they were forbidden to use any technological devices in the courtroom. Suddenly, the 26-year-old juror found himself being led away by deputies. The judge ruled that he was in contempt of court and sent him to jail. After two days, the judge permitted the disobedient juror to be released.

The strong action taken by the Oregon judge appeared to reflect a key concern that he shared with other judges around the country: the need to keep jurors from using electronic devices, either as distractions or to communicate improperly during the course of a trial. A study published by the Federal Judicial Center in 2011 based on a survey of federal trial judges found that 30 judges had detected the use of social media by jurors during trials. It seems likely that jurors in other courthouses have engaged in the same behaviors, but perhaps were not caught by presiding judges.

The problem of improper use of technology affects state courts as much as federal courts. A Pennsylvania judge nearly declared a mistrial when a juror posted updates on Twitter and Facebook concerning developments and decisions in a trial. A mistrial ends a trial and forces the prosecutor to begin again after selecting a new jury. A Florida judge declared a mistrial when a witness sent a text message from the witness stand while the lawyers were engaged in a brief conference with the judge at the front of the courtroom. Jurors in other cases have been seen sending text messages or checking their email on smartphones during the middle of trials. Some jurors have attempted to do their own research on a case in progress by doing Internet searches for information while sitting in the jury box during a trial. Moreover, there have been problems in some cases with defendants' relatives contacting jurors during trials through Facebook, email, and text messages. Even worse, some jurors

unsympathetic to their side (M. S. White, 1995). Normally, the defense is allowed eight to ten peremptory challenges, and the prosecution six to eight.

The use of peremptory challenges has raised concerns that attorneys can use them to exclude, for example, African American jurors when an African American is on trial (Price, 2009). The same problem potentially exists with Latino jurors, members of the nation's largest minority group in the twenty-first century (Bagnato, 2010). In a series of decisions in the late 1980s and early 1990s, the Supreme Court prohibited using peremptory challenges to systematically exclude potential jurors because of their race or gender (e.g., *Batson v. Kentucky,* 1986). Jury-selection errors can provide the basis for appeals if a defendant is convicted at trial (Pizzi and Hoffman, 2001). In practice, however, the enforcement of this prohibition on race and gender discrimination falls to the trial judge (C. E. Smith and Ochoa, 1996). If a trial judge is willing to accept flimsy excuses for race-based and gender-based exclusions, then the attorneys can ignore the ban on discrimination (Bray, 1992). Ask yourself whether peremptory challenges have a positive or negative effect on jury selection. Do you think peremptory challenges should be abolished?

✔POINT
11. What is voir dire?
12. What is the difference between a peremptory challenge and a challenge for cause?

STOP AND ANALYZE: Should the voir dire process be standardized to be sure that all potential jurors for every case are asked the same questions? List two arguments favoring standardization and two in opposition. Which side is more persuasive?

Opening Statements

After the jury has been selected, the trial begins. The clerk reads the complaint (indictment or information) detailing the charges, and the prosecutor and the have been threatened by unknown individuals through text messages and cell phone calls. Because many older judges are not technologically savvy, there are fears that they do not even realize the risks posed by electronic communications. How should courts address these issues?

The Michigan Supreme Court imposed new rules in 2009 to bar all electronic communications by jurors during trials, including Twitter and Google searches. Judges all over the country now instruct jurors that they cannot use electronic devices during trials or during jury deliberations. It is very difficult, however, to make sure that jurors obey those instructions, especially during multiday trials when they can go home and send messages to their friends about the case or receive information and opinions from acquaintances and strangers. There are grave risks that jury deliberations will be distorted if one or more jurors have improperly obtained information from the Internet or outside sources that is either inaccurate or inadmissible under the rules of evidence for trials.

Sources: Associated Press, "Oregon Juror Jailed for Texting during Trial," *Seattle Times*, April 18, 2013 (www.seattletimes.com); Tresa Baldas, "For Jurors in Michigan, No Tweeting (or Texting or Googling) Allowed," *National Law Journal*, July 1, 2009 (www.law.com); Laura A. Bischoff, "Judges Combat Twitter, Facebook Use by Jurors during Trials," *Dayton Daily News*, February 12, 2010 (www.daytondailynews.com); Meghan Dunn, *Jurors' Use of Social Media During Trials and Deliberations* (Washington, DC: Federal Judicial Center, 2011); Nicola Haralambous, "Educating Jurors: Technology, the Internet and the Jury System," *Information and Communications Technology Law* 19 (2010): 255–66; Natasha Korecki, "Hale Juror: Neo-Nazi's Texts, Calls Terrifying," *Chicago Sun Times*, January 4, 2011 (www.suntimes.com); Amy St. Eve, Charles Burns, and Michael Zuckerman, "More from the #Jury Box: The Latest on Juries and Social Media," *Duke Law and Technology Review* 12 (2014): 64–91.

DEBATE THE ISSUE

How would you suggest that the justice system address the risks that social-media usage poses for jury trials? Can the problem be handled by educating jurors, or should there be sanctions, including possible criminal charges for violating a judge's instructions barring the use of electronic media? List two arguments in favor of the solution that you believe will be most appropriate and effective.

defense attorney may, if they desire, make opening statements to the jury to summarize the position that each side intends to take. The statements are not evidence. The jury is not supposed to regard the attorneys' statements as proving or disproving anything about the case.

Presentation of the Prosecution's Evidence

One of the basic protections of the American criminal justice system is the assumption that the defendant is innocent until proved guilty. The prosecution must prove beyond a reasonable doubt, within the demands of the court procedures and rules of evidence, that the individual named in the indictment committed the crime. This means that the evidence excludes all reasonable doubt; it does not have to determine absolute certainty.

By presenting evidence to the jury, the prosecution must establish a case showing that the defendant is guilty. Evidence is classified as real evidence, demonstrative evidence, testimony, direct evidence, and circumstantial evidence.

Real evidence might include such objects as a weapon, business records, fingerprints, or stolen property. These are real objects involved in the crime. **Demonstrative evidence** is any evidence presented for jurors to see and understand without testimony. Real evidence is one form of demonstrative evidence. Other forms of demonstrative evidence are items not involved in the crime but still used to make points to jurors. These include maps, X-rays, photographs, models, and diagrams.

Most evidence in a criminal trial, however, consists of the **testimony** of witnesses. Witnesses at a trial must be legally competent. Thus the judge may be required to determine whether the witness whose testimony is challenged has the intelligence to tell the truth and the ability to recall what was seen. Witnesses with inadequate intelligence or mental problems can be excluded as unqualified to present testimony. **Direct evidence** refers to eyewitness

real evidence
Physical evidence such as a weapon, records, fingerprints, stolen property—objects actually involved in the crime.

demonstrative evidence
Evidence that is not based on witness testimony but demonstrates information relevant to the crime, such as maps, X-rays, and photographs; includes real evidence involved in the crime.

testimony
Oral evidence provided by a legally competent witness.

direct evidence
Eyewitness accounts.

circumstantial evidence
Evidence, provided by a witness, from which a jury must infer a fact.

accounts for example, "I saw John Smith fire the gun." **Circumstantial evidence** requires that the jury infer a fact from what the witness observed: "I saw John Smith walk behind his house with a gun. A few minutes later I heard a gun go off, and then Mr. Smith walked toward me holding a gun." The witness's observation that Smith had a gun and that the witness then heard a gun go off does not provide the direct evidence that Smith fired his gun; yet the jury may link the described facts and infer that Smith fired his gun. After a witness has given testimony, he or she can be cross-examined by counsel for the other side.

Because many cases rely on scientific evidence, especially in the form of experts' testimony about DNA, blood spatters, bullet fragments and trajectories, and the nature of physical injuries, there are concerns that judges and jurors do not fully understand the information presented (Cheng, 2006). Determinations of guilt may hinge on the effectiveness of the presentation of such evidence rather than the accuracy and verifiability of the scientific conclusions (McAuliff and Duckworth, 2010). Judges' and jurors' lack of expertise about scientific matters means that there are risks that they cannot effectively question and analyze certain kinds of evidence, although recent research indicates most jurors are capable of comprehending scientific evidence (Hans, Kaye, et al., 2011).

The public's fascination with the forensic science portrayed in television shows, such as *CSI* [*Crime Scene Investigation*], has led some prosecutors to complain about an escalation in jurors' unrealistic expectations about the presentation of DNA analysis or other scientific evidence in order to establish guilt in each criminal trial. In reality, many criminal investigations and prosecutions are not based on DNA, fingerprints, or other scientific evidence. Instead,

TECHNOLOGY & CRIMINAL JUSTICE

DNA EVIDENCE AND THE RISK OF ERROR

The presumed reliability of DNA evidence for establishing the identity of someone who was at a crime scene has contributed to many criminal convictions. It has also contributed to several hundred exonerations when scientific evidence was used to free innocent people from prison. DNA evidence is widely regarded as providing definitive identifications and exclusions of suspects based on biological evidence at crime scenes and on the possessions of victims and suspects. However, there are risks that errors in the collection, testing, and use of DNA evidence may lead juries to erroneous conclusions when they hear testimony based on faulty evidence.

In a number of forensic science laboratories around the country, there have been scandals involving shoddy testing methods, unqualified lab technicians, and, worst of all, scientists who falsified test results in order to help prosecutors gain convictions. For example, an independent audit by retired FBI agents in 2010 found that the crime lab of the North Carolina State Bureau of Investigation had withheld or distorted evidence in more than 200 cases over a 16-year period. Previously, a key forensic scientist at the West Virginia state crime lab was found to have falsified test results in more than 100 cases. These are not the only examples of human problems that undercut the reliability of forensic science evidence presented to juries, including DNA test results. Fortunately, publicity about these scandals has led to increased efforts to provide oversight and standardization of procedures for crime labs. Hopefully, such efforts will reduce errors and misconduct.

Another significant challenge for the use of DNA evidence emerged in 2014 when a defense attorney successfully demonstrated her client's innocence, despite the fact that his DNA was found at the crime scene on the body of a murder victim. A Silicon Valley millionaire was murdered in his San Jose, California, home during a violent home invasion and robbery. Testing of DNA evidence demonstrated the presence of biological material from a homeless man on the victim's hand. Police assumed that such evidence would be present because the man was one of the robbers whom the victim tried to fend off with his hands. However, the defense attorney demonstrated that the homeless man was in the hospital at the time that the murder occurred. It turned out that Emergency Medical Technicians (EMTs) had placed an prosecutors more often present witness testimony and circumstantial evidence about a suspect's presence in a certain location and his or her relationship with the victim. However, some prosecutors have come to fear that jurors will not render a guilty verdict without the presentation of scientific evidence.

Research on the so-called CSI effect raises questions about whether jurors are actually less inclined to convict defendants in the absence of scientific evidence. Surveys indicate that jurors may expect to see specific kinds of scientific evidence, but this expectation may be related to a more general "tech effect" of Americans using technology in their daily lives rather than watching specific television shows. Moreover, the increased expectation for scientific evidence does not necessarily mean that jurors will not vote to convict a defendant without it (Huey, 2010; Shelton, 2008). Despite the reliance on scientific evidence, there are risks that errors in the investigation process will lead jurors, with their increasing faith in science and technology, to make errors. Read the Technology and Criminal Justice feature to consider the care that must be taken in order to use scientific evidence properly and avoid errors.

The attorney for each side can challenge the other side's presentation of evidence. If presented evidence violates the rules, reflects untrustworthy hearsay or opinions, or is not relevant to the issues in the case, an attorney will object to the presentation. In effect, the attorney is asking the judge to rule that the opponent's questionable evidence cannot be considered by the jury.

After the prosecution has presented all of the state's evidence against the defendant, he or she informs the court that the people's case rests. It is common for the defense then to ask the court to direct the jury to bring forth a verdict of not guilty. Such a motion is based on the defense argument that the state has not presented enough evidence to prove its case. If the motion is

oxygen-monitoring probe on the homeless man's hand when they found him unconscious in downtown San Jose and transported him to the hospital. Those same EMTs then went to the crime scene and placed the same oxygen-monitoring probe on the hand of the murder victim, thus transferring the homeless man's DNA that was present in cells on the probe to the hand of the victim.

The demonstration that a DNA transfer had occurred from an innocent man to the body of a murder victim has opened opportunities for defense attorneys to challenge the procedures of medical and law enforcement personnel. Moreover, it invites those attorneys to argue before juries that the example of the San Jose case should be regarded as raising the risk of DNA transfers happening in other cases. Will this example cause jurors to be more skeptical about the reliability of DNA evidence? No one knows. The incident should cause EMTs and others at crime scenes to be more careful. In addition, it should send a message to prosecutors that it may be more difficult now to rely on trace DNA evidence alone as the basis for gaining a criminal conviction. They must make extra efforts to find additional kinds of evidence that can link a defendant to a crime.

Sources: Mark Hansen, "Crime Labs under the Microscope after a String of Shoddy, Suspect and Fraudulent Results," *American Bar Association Journal,* September 1, 2013 (www.abajournal.com); Tracey Kaplan, "Monte Serro Murder Case Casts Doubts on DNA Evidence," *San Jose Mercury News,* June 28, 2014 (www.mercurynews.com); William Langley, "The Case against DNA," *The Telegraph,* March 6, 2012 (www.telegraph.com).

DEBATE THE ISSUE

Should the presence of skin cells at a crime scene or on a victim's body be a sufficient basis for DNA evidence alone to lead to a criminal conviction? What if someone has a skin condition involving shedding skin cells, such as psoriasis, and a crime victim picked up those cells unknowingly from riding in a taxicab where those skin cells were left behind by the previous passenger? Might the San Jose case make it significantly more difficult for prosecutors to persuade jurors to rely on DNA evidence? If you were a prosecutor, what specific things would you communicate to the police about their crime scene investigations? What specific things would you communicate to jurors about DNA evidence?

sustained by the judge (it rarely is), the trial ends; if it is overruled, the defense presents its evidence.

Presentation of the Defense's Evidence

The defense is not required to answer the case presented by the prosecution. As it is the state's responsibility to prove the case beyond a reasonable doubt, it is theoretically possible—and in fact sometimes happens—that the defense rests its case immediately. Usually, however, the accused's attorney employs one or more of the following strategies: (1) contrary evidence is introduced to rebut or cast doubt on the state's case, (2) an alibi is offered, or (3) an affirmative defense is presented. As discussed in Chapter 4, defenses include self-defense, insanity, duress, and necessity.

When singer R. Kelly was acquitted of child pornography charges by a Chicago jury in June 2008, the defense attorneys used every argument that they could, including arguments that were not consistent with each other, in order to cast doubt on the prosecution's case. The case hinged on whether a VHS tape showed Kelly having sex with a specific underage girl. The defense suggested that the tape showed another man who looked like Kelly, that computer manipulation had made the tape look like Kelly, or that the tape was made with models and prostitutes who looked like Kelly and the alleged victim (Streitfeld, 2008). The defense attorneys did not need to prove Kelly's innocence; they just needed to raise questions in the jurors' minds about the accuracy of the prosecution's claims.

A key issue for the defense is whether the accused will take the stand. The Fifth Amendment protection against self-incrimination means that the defendant is not required to testify. The Supreme Court has ruled that the prosecutor may not comment on, nor can the jury draw inferences from, the defendant's decision not to speak in his or her own defense. The decision is not made lightly, because if the defendant does testify, the prosecution may cross-examine him or her. *Cross-examination*, or questioning by the opposing attorney, creates risks for the defendant. The prosecutor may question the defendant not only about the crime but also about his or her past, including past criminal convictions. In R. Kelly's case, he never testified and thereby avoided cross-examination about his past sexual behavior and rumors about his attraction to teenage girls.

Presentation of Rebuttal Witnesses

When the defense's case is complete, the prosecution may present witnesses whose statements are designed to discredit or counteract testimony presented on behalf of the defendant. If the prosecution brings rebuttal witnesses, the defense can question them and present new witnesses in rebuttal.

Closing Arguments by Each Side

When each side has completed its presentation of the evidence, the prosecution and defense make closing arguments to the jury. The attorneys review the evidence of the case for the jury, presenting interpretations of the evidence that favor their own side. The prosecutor may use the summation to show how individual pieces of evidence connect to form a basis for concluding that the defendant is guilty. The defense may set forth the applicable law and try to show that (1) the prosecution has not proved its case beyond a reasonable doubt and (2) the testimony raised questions but did not provide answers. Each side may remind the jury of its duty to remain unswayed by emotion and to evaluate the evidence impartially. Some attorneys nonetheless hope that the jurors will react emotionally to benefit their side.

Judge's Instructions to the Jury

The jury decides the facts of the case, but the judge determines the law. Before the jurors depart for the jury room to decide the defendant's fate, the judge instructs them on how the law should guide their decision. The judge may discuss basic legal principles such as proof beyond a reasonable doubt, the legal requirements necessary to show that the prosecution has proved all the elements of the crime, or the rights of the defendant. Specific aspects of the law bearing on the decision, such as complicated court rulings on the nature of the insanity defense or the ways certain types of evidence have been gathered, may be included in the judge's instructions. In complicated trials, the judge may spend an entire day instructing the jury.

The concept of **reasonable doubt** lies at the heart of the jury system. The prosecution is not required to prove the guilt of the defendant beyond all doubt. Instead, if you as a juror are

> satisfied to a moral certainty that this defendant . . . is guilty of any one of the crimes charged here, you may safely say that you have been convinced beyond a reasonable doubt. If your mind is wavering, or if you are uncertain . . . you have not been convinced beyond a reasonable doubt and must render a verdict of not guilty. (Phillips, 1977: 214)

reasonable doubt
The standard used by a juror to decide if the prosecution has provided enough evidence for conviction.

The experience of listening to the judge may become an ordeal for the jurors, who must hear and understand perhaps two or three hours of instruction on the law and the evidence (C. Bradley, 1992). The length, complexity, and legalistic content of jury instructions make them difficult for many jurors to comprehend (Daftary-Kapur, Dumas, and Penrod, 2010). Scholars have concluded that there is "a serious problem [with] . . . the jury's documented difficulty in understanding legal instructions" (Hans and Vidmar, 2008: 228). There are also emerging concerns that jurors—as well as judges and other courtroom actors—can have their thinking and decision making affected by the high degree of stress they may feel about determining someone's fate (M. K. Miller, Flores, and Dolezilek, 2007). Not surprisingly, this stress may be particularly powerful in murder cases, especially those concerning the death penalty (Antonio, 2006).

Decision by the Jury

After they have heard the case and received instructions from the judge, the jurors retire to a room where they have complete privacy. They elect a foreperson to run the meeting, and deliberations begin. Until now, the jurors have been passive observers of the trial, unable to question witnesses or discuss the case among themselves; now they can discuss the facts that have been presented. Throughout their deliberations the jurors may be sequestered—kept together day and night, away from the influences of newspapers and conversations with family and friends. If jurors are allowed to spend nights at home, they are ordered not to discuss the case with anyone. The jury may request that the judge reread to them portions of the instructions, ask for additional instructions, or hear portions of the transcript detailing what specific witnesses said.

If the jury becomes deadlocked and cannot reach a verdict, the trial ends with a hung jury and the prosecutor must decide whether to retry the case in front of a new jury. When a verdict is reached, the judge, prosecution, and defense reassemble in the courtroom to hear it. The prosecution or the defense may request that the jury be polled: Each member individually tells his or her vote in open court. This procedure presumably ensures that no juror has felt pressured to agree with the other jurors.

✔POINT **13.** What are the stages in the trial process?

14. What are the kinds of evidence presented during a trial?

STOP AND ANALYZE: Because the trial process is expensive, current government budget problems make it likely that some prosecutors will offer increasing numbers of attractive plea agreements in order to save money on trials. Should Americans be willing to devote sufficient resources to prosecutors and courts so that there are no compromises with respect to ensuring appropriate punishments for serious criminal offenses? Are there certain crimes for which you, as a prosecutor, would always insist on a trial if the defendant refused to admit guilt for the actual offense committed? If so, make a list of the "priority crimes" that you consider are always worth incurring the expense of a trial.

Evaluating the Jury System

Individual jurors differ in their processing of information and interactions with others (Gunnell and Ceci, 2010). A classic study at the University of Chicago Law School found that, consistent with theories of group behavior, participation and influence in the jury process are related to social status. Men were found to be more active participants than were women, whites more active than minority members, and the better educated more active than those less educated (Strodtbeck, James, and Hawkins, 1957).

This research points to the potential influence of status and social context on jury deliberations. More-recent research has found that social status still affects participation rates as jurors with higher levels of education and income are more active in discussions. However, racial effects are less evident in contemporary juries, as African American jurors were as active—or moreso—than members of other groups. Additional differences were found that depended on the nature of the case. For example, there were higher rates of participation in murder cases. Geographic locations may also differ with respect to jury participation; for example, during trials in Los Angeles courts, Asian American women were less active in jury deliberations than were jurors from other demographic groups (Cornwell and Hans, 2011).

Jurors' deliberations are also affected by the procedures they follow in evaluating the case. Much of the discussion in the jury room is not necessarily directly concerned with the testimony, but rather with trial procedures, opinions about the witnesses, and personal reminiscences (Bornstein and Greene, 2011; Strodtbeck, James, and Hawkins, 1957). In 30 percent of the cases, a vote taken soon after entering the jury room was the only one necessary to reach a verdict; in the rest of the cases, the majority on the first ballot eventually prevailed in 90 percent of the cases (Broeder, 1959). More-recent research finds that the first ballot outcomes still ultimately prevail in nearly all cases, although immediate votes are generally not taken when considering the most serious criminal charges (Sundby, 2010). Because of group pressure, only rarely does a single juror produce a hung jury. Some jurors may doubt their own views or go along with the others if everyone else disagrees with them. Additional studies have upheld the importance of group pressure on decision making (Sundby, 2010; Hastie, Penrod, and Pennington, 1983).

Judges have more experience with the justice process. When they are the decision makers in bench trials, they are more likely than juries to convict defendants based on evidence that researchers characterize as moderately strong (T. Eisenberg et al., 2005). As explained by premier jury researchers Valerie P. Hans and Neil Vidmar (2008: 227):

> [T]he jury's distinctive approach of common sense justice, and the judges' greater willingness to convict based on the same evidence, best explain why juries and judges sometimes reach different conclusions. These juror values affect the verdicts primarily in trials in which the evidence is relatively evenly balanced and a verdict for either side could be justified.

By using research to gain an understanding of how jurors receive and understand information, it is hoped that court procedures could be adjusted in ways that will increase jurors' understanding of evidence and legal concepts. As a result, it is presumed that the quality of juries' decision making will improve, and thereby reduce the risk of error in jury verdicts.

Jurors face challenges in remembering and understanding information presented as evidence, especially when it is a long trial that lasts for many days. In addition, studies show that jurors have difficulty understanding the jury instructions read to them at the end of the trial by the judge (S. Gordon, 2013). As a result, many states have put effort into designing jury instructions that use plain language instead of confusing legal terms. Moreover, there is greater recognition that the length of jury instructions can exceed the attention span of jurors. Thus the extensive work on revising and delivering jury instructions seeks to address multiple concerns (Aaronson and Patterson, 2013).

Although there is not universal agreement on exactly what jury practices to implement based on research evidence, specific states have moved forward with reforms that seek to address the problems identified by research. Not all of the reforms have been verified by research and, indeed, some of the jury reform efforts are considered by the states to be experiments to see if they improve jury processes.

For example, in 2011 the Michigan Supreme Court issued an order concerning jury reforms for courts to try during a three-year evaluation period (Thomas, 2011). The reforms included:

- Providing pretrial jury instructions to jurors so that they could begin understanding their role and the relevant law before hearing evidence
- Providing a copy of the jury instructions for each juror rather than the traditional method of giving only one copy to the entire jury
- Permitting jurors to write down questions during the trial and then request that the judge consider posing these questions to specific witnesses, thus perhaps filling information gaps if the attorneys do not realize what else the jurors would like to know
- Permitting jurors to ask questions about the final jury instructions delivered by the judge at the end of the trial

Jury trials serve an important function for determining the fates of individuals, especially in serious cases, such as murder, that are likely to draw the most significant punishments. Thus any evidence-based practices produced through research studies have the potential to reduce errors and improve the quality of jury decisions.

✔POINT 15. What factors can make a jury's decision different from that of a judge?

STOP AND ANALYZE: If you were charged with tax evasion, would you prefer a trial in front of a judge or a jury? Why? Would you make a different choice if you were charged with injuring a small child when texting while driving?

Appeals

The imposition of a sentence does not mean that the defendant must serve it immediately. He or she typically has the right to appeal. Indigent offenders' right to counsel continues through the first appeal (Heise, 2009). Some states have limited the right to appeal when defendants plead guilty. For nonviolent crimes, judges sometimes permit newly convicted offenders to remain free as the appeal proceeds.

An **appeal** is based on a claim that one or more errors of law or procedure were made during the investigation, arrest, or trial process (Place, 2013). Such

appeal
A request to a higher court that it review actions taken in a completed lower-court case.

claims usually assert that the trial judge made errors in courtroom rulings or in improperly admitting evidence the police had gathered in violation of some constitutional right. A defendant might base an appeal, for example, on the claim that the judge did not instruct the jury correctly or that a guilty plea was not made voluntarily. Appeals are based on questions of procedure, not on issues of the defendant's guilt or innocence. The appellate court will not normally second-guess a jury. Instead it will check to make sure that the trial followed proper procedures (Shay, 2009). If the court finds significant errors in the trial, then the conviction is set aside. The defendant may be retried if the prosecutor decides to pursue the case again. Most criminal defendants must file an appeal shortly after trial to have an appellate court review the case; however, many states provide for an automatic appeal in death penalty cases. The quality of defense representation matters a great deal, because the appeal must usually meet short deadlines and carefully identify appropriate issues (Wasserman, 1990).

A case originating in a state court is usually appealed through that state's judicial system. When a state case involves a federal constitutional question, however, a subsequent review may be sought in the federal courts. Even so, state courts decide almost four-fifths of all appeals.

The number of appeals in both the state and federal courts has increased during recent decades. What is the nature of these cases? A classic five-state study by Joy Chapper and Roger Hanson (1989) shows that (1) although a majority of appeals occur after trial convictions, about a quarter result from nontrial proceedings, such as guilty pleas and probation revocations; (2) homicides and other serious crimes against people account for more than 50 percent of appeals; (3) most appeals arise from cases in which the sentence is five years or less; and (4) the issues raised at appeal tend to concern the introduction of evidence, the sufficiency of evidence, and jury instructions.

Most appeals do not succeed. In almost 80 percent of the cases Chapper and Hanson examined, the decision of the trial courts was affirmed. Most of the other decisions produced new trials or resentencing; only 9.4 percent of those whose convictions were overturned received acquittals on appeal. The appellate process rarely provides a ticket to freedom for someone convicted of a crime.

Habeas Corpus

After people use their avenues of appeal, they may pursue a writ of habeas corpus if they claim that their federal constitutional rights were violated during the lower-court processes (Primus, 2010). Known as "the great writ" from its traditional role in English law, a **habeas corpus** petition asks a judge to examine whether an individual is being properly detained in a jail, prison, or mental hospital (N. J. King and Hoffmann, 2010). If the detention is based on a rights violation or otherwise lacks a legal basis, then the judge will grant the writ of habeas corpus. A successful habeas corpus claim can lead to either an immediate release from government custody or an order for a new trial, which can require criminal defendants to remain in jail until the trial takes place. In the context of criminal justice, convicted offenders often claim that their imprisonment is improper because one of their constitutional rights was violated during the investigation or adjudication of their case. Statutes permit offenders convicted in both state and federal courts to pursue habeas corpus actions in the federal courts (N. J. King, Cheesman, and Ostrom, 2007). After first seeking favorable decisions by state appellate courts, convicted offenders can start their constitutional claims anew in the federal trial-level district courts and subsequently pursue their habeas cases in the federal circuit courts of appeal and the U.S. Supreme Court.

habeas corpus
A writ or judicial order requesting the release of a person being detained in a jail, prison, or mental hospital. If a judge finds the person is being held improperly, the writ may be granted and the person released or granted a new trial.

Only about 1 percent of habeas petitions succeed (Flango, 1994). In a recent study, less than one-half of one percent of noncapital habeas petitioners gained a favorable judicial decision, but more than 12 percent of habeas

Judges of the U.S. Court of Appeals for the Ninth Circuit hear arguments in San Francisco. The appeals process provides an opportunity to correct errors that occurred in trial court proceedings. What are the advantages or disadvantages of having a group of appeals court judges decide a case together?

petitioners in death penalty cases demonstrated a rights violation (N. J. King, Cheesman, and Ostrom, 2007). One reason may be that an individual has no right to be represented by an attorney when pursuing a habeas corpus petition. Few offenders have sufficient knowledge of law and legal procedures to identify and present constitutional claims effectively in the federal courts (R. A. Hanson and Daley, 1995). These challenges are especially difficult for offenders in noncapital cases. By contrast, legislatures have enacted statutes to provide extra resources for offenders on death row. Several statutes help to provide representation by lawyers in many capital cases, even though the U.S. Constitution does not give these offenders a constitutional right to counsel for their habeas petitions. In addition, judges may look more closely for rights violations in death penalty cases because the ultimate harm is so significant if an error goes undiscovered after review by the judges.

In the late 1980s and early 1990s, the U.S. Supreme Court issued many decisions that made it more difficult for convicted offenders to file habeas corpus petitions (H. L. Hoffmann, 2006; C. E. Smith, 1995a). The Court created tougher procedural rules that are more difficult for convicted offenders to follow. The rules also unintentionally created some new problems for state attorneys general and federal trial courts that must now examine the procedural rules affecting cases rather than simply addressing the constitutional violations that the offender claims occurred (C. E. Smith, 1995c). In 1996, Congress passed the Antiterrorism and Effective Death Penalty Act, which placed additional restrictions on habeas corpus petitions. The statute was quickly approved by the U.S. Supreme Court. These reforms were based, in part, on a belief that prisoners' cases were clogging the federal courts (C. E. Smith, 1995b). Ironically, habeas corpus petitions in the federal courts have increased by 50 percent since the passage of the restrictive legislation (Scalia, 2002). By imposing strict filing deadlines for petitions, the legislation may have inadvertently focused more prisoners' attention on the existence of habeas corpus and thereby encouraged them to move forward with petitions in order to meet the deadlines.

Evaluating the Appellate Process

The public seems to believe that many offenders are being let off through the appellate process. Frustrated by the problems of crime, some conservatives have argued that opportunities for appeal should be limited. They claim that too many offenders delay imposition of their sentences and that others seek to evade punishment by filing appeals endlessly. This practice not only increases the workload of the courts but also jeopardizes the concept of the finality of the justice process. However, because 90 percent of accused people plead guilty, the percentage of cases that might be appealed successfully is relatively small.

Consider what follows a defendant's successful appeal, which is by no means a total or final victory. An appeal that results in reversal of the conviction normally means that the case is remanded to the lower court for a new trial. At this point the state must consider whether the procedural errors in the original trial can be overcome and whether the costs of bringing the defendant into court again are justified. Frequently, the prosecutor pursues the case again and gains a new, proper conviction of the defendant. In some cases, however, the appeal process generates new plea negotiations that produce a second conviction with a lesser sentence that reflects the reduced strength of the prosecutor's case. Thus a successful appeal may place the defendant in a position to receive a more favorable offer from the prosecutor in exchange for a guilty plea.

The appeals process performs the important function of righting wrongs. It also helps to ensure consistency in the application of law by judges in different courts. Beyond that, its presence constantly influences the daily operations of the criminal justice system in that prosecutors and trial judges must consider how their decisions and actions might later be evaluated by a higher court.

✔POINT
16. How does the appellate court's job differ from that of the trial court?
17. What is a habeas corpus petition?

STOP AND ANALYZE: Do criminal offenders have too many opportunities to challenge convictions? List two pros and two cons of having an appeals process as well as a habeas corpus process.

A QUESTION OF ETHICS

Plea bargaining creates ethical challenges for defense attorneys. In a series of decisions, including *Padilla v. Kentucky* (2010) and *Missouri v. Frye* (2012), the U.S. Supreme Court made clear that defense attorneys are obligated to inform defendants of plea agreements offered by the prosecutor and to accurately inform defendants of the relevant law affecting those agreements, such as the prospect of deportation for noncitizens. In 2013, Tom Petters, a man serving a 50-year sentence in federal prison for a fraud scheme that bilked $3.6 billion from investors, claimed that his attorney had never informed him of a plea offer from prosecutors that would have given him a 30-year maximum sentence. His defense attorney, Jon Hopeman, responded by producing letters and notes to demonstrate that Petters knew about the offer and did not accept it. At the same time, Hopeman also acknowledged that he had not recommended Petters accept the offer because, as counsel, he believed that a 30-year sentence would be too severe. Arguably, Hopeman either underestimated what the ultimate sentence could be or overestimated his client's prospects for acquittal.

Source: Abby Simons, "Lawyer Says Petters Knew of Potential Plea Deal and Rejected It," *Minneapolis Star Tribune*, June 3, 2013 (www.startribune.com).

CRITICAL THINKING AND ANALYSIS

Defendants rely on their attorneys for expert advice. When the attorney advises against accepting a plea agreement and then the sentence turns out to be far more severe than what the defendant had expected, should the defendant be entitled to go back and accept the expired plea offer? How much good does it do for defendants to be informed of a plea offer if they lack personal knowledge and perspective on what the alternative sentence will be? Should the defense attorney, rather than the defendant, bear responsibility for inaccurate projections about the sentence that could be imposed after going to trial? Alternatively, if defendants maintain their innocence throughout the process, as Petters did, then isn't the defense attorney ethically obligated to advise against accepting a long sentence in a plea agreement? If you were a judge, would you rule that the defense attorney provided ineffective assistance of counsel and permit Petters to have the 30-year sentence from the plea offer? Give three reasons for your answer.

Summary

1 Describe the courtroom workgroup and how it functions

- A court's local legal culture, which defines the going rates of punishment for various offenses, significantly influences the outcomes in criminal cases.
- Courtroom workgroups made up of judges, prosecutors, and defense attorneys who work together can smoothly and efficiently handle cases through cooperative plea bargaining processes.

2 Discuss how and why plea bargaining occurs

- Most convictions are obtained through plea bargains, a process that exists because it fulfills the self-interest of prosecutors, judges, defense attorneys, and defendants.
- Plea bargaining is facilitated by exchange relations between prosecutors and defense attorneys. In many courthouses, there is little actual bargaining, as outcomes are determined through the implicit-bargaining process of settling the facts and assessing the going rate of punishment according to the standards of the local legal culture.
- The U.S. Supreme Court has endorsed plea bargaining and addressed legal issues concerning the voluntariness of pleas and the obligation of prosecutors and defendants to uphold agreements.
- Plea bargaining has been criticized for pressuring defendants to surrender their rights and for reducing the sentences imposed on offenders.

3 Analyze why few cases go to trial and how jurors are chosen

- Americans tend to presume that through the dramatic courtroom battle of prosecutors and defense attorneys, trials provide the best way to discover the truth about a criminal case.
- Less than 10 percent of cases go to trial, and half of those are typically bench trials in front of a judge, not jury trials.
- Cases typically go to trial because they involve defendants who are wealthy enough to pay attorneys to fight to the very end, or they involve serious disagreements between the prosecutor and defense attorney about the provable facts and the appropriate punishment.
- The U.S. Supreme Court has ruled that juries need not be made up of 12 members, and 12-member juries can, if permitted by state law, convict defendants by a supermajority vote instead of a unanimous vote. Juries serve vital functions for society by preventing arbitrary action by prosecutors and judges, educating citizens about the justice system, symbolizing the rule of law, and involving citizens from diverse segments of the community in judicial decision making.
- The jury-selection process, especially in the formation of the jury pool and the exercise of peremptory challenges, often creates juries that do not fully represent all segments of a community.

4 Identify the stages of a criminal trial

- The trial process consists of a series of steps: jury selection, opening statements, presentation of the prosecution's evidence, presentation of the defense's evidence, presentation of rebuttal witnesses, closing arguments, judge's jury instructions, and jury's decision.
- Rules of evidence dictate what kinds of information may be presented in court for consideration by the jury. The types of evidence are real evidence, demonstrative evidence, testimony, direct evidence, and circumstantial evidence.

5 Describe the basis for an appeal of a conviction

- Convicted offenders can appeal. However, defendants who plead guilty, unlike those convicted through a trial, often have few grounds for an appeal.
- Appeals focus on alleged errors of law or procedure in the investigation by police and prosecutors, or in the decisions by trial judges. Relatively few offenders win their appeals, and most of those simply gain an opportunity for a new trial, not release from jail or prison.
- After convicted offenders have used all their appeals, they may file a habeas corpus petition to seek federal judicial review of claimed constitutional rights violations in their cases. Very few petitions succeed.

Questions for Review

1. What is the courtroom workgroup and what does it do?
2. Why does plea bargaining exist?
3. Given that there are so few jury trials, what types of cases would you expect to find adjudicated in this manner? Why?
4. If so few cases ever reach a jury, why are juries such an important part of the criminal justice system?
5. What is the purpose of the appeals process?

Key Terms and Cases

appeal (p. 471)
bench trial (p. 458)
challenge for cause (p. 463)
circumstantial evidence (p. 466)
continuance (p. 444)
demonstrative evidence (p. 465)
direct evidence (p. 465)
going rate (p. 444)
habeas corpus (p. 472)
jury (p. 458)
local legal culture (p. 444)
peremptory challenge (p. 463)
real evidence (p. 465)
reasonable doubt (p. 469)
testimony (p. 465)
voir dire (p. 463)
workgroup (p. 445)
Bordenkircher v. Hayes (1978) (p. 455)
Boykin v. Alabama (1969) (p. 454)
North Carolina v. Alford (1970) (p. 454)
Ricketts v. Adamson (1987) (p. 455)
Santobello v. New York (1971) (p. 449)
Willams v. Florida (1970) (p. 460)

Checkpoint Answers

1 How does the local legal culture affect criminal cases?

✓ The local legal culture consists of norms that distinguish between one court and those in other jurisdictions. These norms dictate expectations about how members should treat one another and describe how cases should be processed.

2 How does a courtroom workgroup form and operate?

✓ The courtroom workgroup is made up of judge, prosecutor, defense counsel, and support staff assigned to a specific courtroom. Through the interaction of these members, goals and norms are shared, and a set of roles becomes stabilized.

3 Why are similar cases treated differently in different cities?

✓ Several factors can vary in different cities, including the structure of the courtroom workgroup and the influence of sponsoring organizations, which can affect such things as prosecution policies and public defender assignments.

4 Why does plea bargaining occur?

✓ It serves the self-interest of all relevant actors: defendants gain certain, less-than-maximum sentences; prosecutors gain swift, sure convictions; defense attorneys get prompt resolution of cases; judges do not have to preside over as many time-consuming trials.

5 What is implicit plea bargaining?

✓ Implicit plea bargaining occurs when prosecutors and defense attorneys use shared expectations and interactions to settle the facts of a case and reach a resolution based on the going rate for sentences in the local legal culture.

6 What issues concerning plea bargaining has the Supreme Court examined?

✓ The U.S. Supreme Court has examined whether the defendant pleads guilty in a knowing and voluntary way, guilty pleas from defendants who still claim to be innocent, and prosecutors' and defendants' obligations to fulfill their plea agreements.

7 What are the criticisms of plea bargaining?

✓ Concerns about pressures on defendants to surrender their rights and concerns that society's mandated criminal punishments are improperly reduced.

8 **Approximately what percentage of felony cases reach conclusion through a trial?**

✓ In most jurisdictions, only 3 to 4 percent of felony cases typically reach their conclusion through trials, although there may be slightly higher percentages in a specific year or at a specific courthouse.

9 **What are three of the six functions that juries serve for the criminal justice system?**

✓ (1) Safeguard citizens against arbitrary law enforcement, (2) determine the guilt of the accused, (3) represent diverse community interests and values, (4) serve as a buffer between accused and accuser, (5) become educated about the justice system, and (6) symbolize the law.

10 **What has the Supreme Court decided concerning the size and unanimity requirements of juries?**

✓ Juries can have as few as 6 jurors, except in death penalty cases, in which 12 are required, and convictions can occur through less-than-unanimous verdicts.

11 **What is voir dire?**

✓ The jury-selection process in which lawyers and/or judges ask questions of prospective jurors and make decisions about using peremptory challenges and challenges for cause to shape the jury's composition.

12 **What is the difference between a peremptory challenge and a challenge for cause?**

✓ A challenge for cause is based on an indication that a prospective juror cannot make a fair decision. Such challenges must be approved by the judge. A peremptory challenge can be made by the attorney without giving a reason, unless an allegation arises that the attorney is using such challenges systematically to exclude people because of their race or gender.

13 **What are the stages in the trial process?**

✓ Jury selection, attorneys' opening statements, presentation of prosecution's evidence, presentation of defense's evidence, presentation of rebuttal witnesses, closing arguments by each side, judge's instructions to the jury, and jury's decision.

14 **What are the kinds of evidence presented during a trial?**

✓ Real evidence, demonstrative evidence, testimony, direct evidence, and circumstantial evidence.

15 **What factors can make a jury's decision different from that of a judge?**

✓ Jurors may discount cases in which they dislike the victims. Jurors may also be more sympathetic to self-defense claims. Judges are more likely to convict defendants on evidence that is only moderately strong.

16 **How does the appellate court's job differ from that of the trial court?**

✓ Unlike trial courts, which have juries, hear evidence, and decide if the defendant is guilty or not guilty, appellate courts focus only on claimed errors of law or procedure in trial court proceedings. Victory in an appellate court may mean only a chance at a new trial—which often leads to a new conviction.

17 **What is a habeas corpus petition?**

✓ The habeas corpus process may be started after all appeals have been filed and lost. Convicted offenders ask a federal court to review whether any constitutional rights were violated during the course of a case's investigation and trial. If rights were violated, the person's continued detention in prison or jail may be improper.

CHAPTER FEATURES

- **Technology and Criminal Justice** Technological Innovation and Jail Administration
- **Close Up** The Death Penalty Debate
- **New Directions in Criminal Justice Policy** Evidence-Based Sentencing
- **Inside Today's Controversies** The U.S. Department of Justice's Investigation of the Ferguson, Missouri, Municipal Court

CHAPTER 12

PUNISHMENT AND SENTENCING

CHAPTER LEARNING OBJECTIVES

1. Describe the goals of punishment
2. Identify the types of sentences that judges can impose
3. Discuss what really happens in sentencing
4. Analyze whether the system treats wrongdoers equally

CHAPTER OUTLINE

The Goals of Punishment
- Retribution: Deserved Punishment
- Deterrence
- Incapacitation
- Rehabilitation
- New Approach to Punishment: Restorative Justice

Forms of the Criminal Sanction
- Incarceration
- Intermediate Sanctions
- Probation
- Death

The Sentencing Process
- The Administrative Context of the Courts
- Attitudes and Values of Judges
- Presentence Report
- Sentencing Guidelines
- Who Gets the Harshest Punishment?

AP Images/Houston Chronicle/Melissa Phillip

Among the many shocking crimes that occur with tragic regularity, one stands out as particularly distressing. Americans are rightly appalled at murders and other violent crimes. However, they cannot help but be both profoundly disappointed and alarmed when teachers exploit underage students and manipulate them into sexual relationships. These are adults who are trained for and entrusted with educational responsibilities for vulnerable young people. Sadly, these crimes reflect devastatingly harmful, self-interested behavior. Such crimes have the potential to psychologically damage young people for life.

What punishments do teachers deserve when they commit such harmful criminal acts against especially vulnerable victims? Does the American criminal justice system, with state-by-state differences in laws and legal culture, treat offenders in such cases fairly and equally? Are men and women teachers treated the same when they engage in such criminal acts? These are important questions that help illuminate the complexities of sentencing and punishment in a large country with a fragmented justice system. Given a structure governed by the varied laws of 50 different states as well as differences in courtroom workgroups within individual courthouses within each state, is it possible to treat all offenders equally?

In January 2015, Scott Tompkins, a 63-year-old high school teacher in rural northern Michigan, was accused of having a sexual relationship with a student. He entered a guilty plea to one criminal charge in exchange for the prosecutor dropping two additional charges. Tompkins was given an indeterminate sentence requiring him to spend from 18 months to 10 years in prison (Wolcott, 2015). The actual time he ultimately serves in prison will depend on when he becomes eligible for parole release based on his behavior and his completion of treatment programs. A few months earlier, in July 2014,

Torris Caston, a male ballet teacher in suburban St. Louis, Missouri, was sentenced to ten years in prison for his sexual relationship with a 15-year-old student, a girl who had taken his classes for several years. Caston had entered a "not guilty" plea and taken his case to trial. A jury convicted him of statutory rape and two other sexual offenses (Mann, 2014). Both Tompkins and Caston faced additional charges related to claims by other victims.

In evaluating these two cases, one must be begin with the difficult question of how much prison time is appropriate for this particular offense. Is a ten-year sentence too long, too short, or appropriate in severity? The two cases provide a clue to one important factor affecting punishment within the American justice system: defendants who admit guilt typically get lesser sentences than those who take their cases all the way through expensive and time-consuming trials. Should asserting one's Sixth Amendment right to trial by jury produce harsher sentences? Or does this just reflect the reality that going to trial typically means missing the opportunity to accept fewer or less serious charges?

An interesting contrast is presented by two other cases in 2014, both involving female teachers. Katie Fazekas, a high school teacher in Ohio, admitted she had a sexual relationship with a 17-year-old female student. After pleading guilty, she was sentenced to 17 months in prison (Feehan, 2014). In Houston, Texas, Kathryn Murray, a middle school teacher, pleaded guilty to having a sexual relationship with a 15-year-old male student. She was sentenced to two years in county jail. These sentences were significantly less harsh than those imposed in the Michigan and Missouri cases on male teachers. The victim's father in the Texas case complained that the sentence reflected a double standard favoring women as he told news reporters that a male teacher with a female student victim would have received a much longer sentence (B. Rogers, 2014). Was the father correct? Certainly, Texas has a reputation for handing out tough sentences for many offenses. In 2013, Brandon McDaniel, a male high school teacher in Texas was sentenced to 20 years in prison for sexual relationships with students. However, it is difficult to compare this precisely with Kathryn Murray's case because McDaniel had carried on relationships with several students over the course of a decade—and he took his case to trial (Crandall, 2013).

In considering the various factors that lead to significantly different sentences for the same type of shocking crime, consider one more case from 2014. In Annapolis, Maryland, Jason Webb, a 27-year-old martial arts teacher pleaded guilty to having a sexual relationship with one of his 14-year-old female students. His sentence: 10 *days* in jail ("Martial Arts Teacher," 2014). Was this sentence appropriate and fair? Can we explain why this sentence is so different from the others? It is not easy to know precisely why Webb received such a light sentence. As the foregoing examples illustrate, criminal behavior may produce a wide variety of punishments, which depend on the goals being pursued by officials who make laws and determine sentences. In essence, Webb's case highlights the fact that sentencing and punishment can vary drastically throughout the country as a result of different state laws, different local practices, and different discretionary decisions by judges and prosecutors.

The criminal justice system aims to solve three basic issues: (1) What conduct is criminal? (2) What determines guilt? (3) What should be done with the guilty? Earlier chapters emphasized the first two questions. The answers given by the legal system to the first question compose the basic rules of society: Do not murder, rob, sell drugs, commit treason, and so forth. The law also spells out the process for determining guilt or innocence; however, the administrative and interpersonal considerations of the actors in the criminal justice system greatly affect this process. In this chapter we begin to examine the third problem—sanction and punishment. First, we consider the four goals of punishment: retribution, deterrence, incapacitation, and rehabilitation. We then explore the forms punishment takes to achieve these goals. These are incarceration, intermediate sanctions, probation, and death. Finally, we look at the sentencing process and how it affects punishment.

The Goals of Punishment

Criminal sanctions in the United States have four main goals: retribution (deserved punishment), deterrence, incapacitation, and rehabilitation. Ultimately, all criminal punishment is aimed at maintaining the social order, but the justifications for sentencing speak of the American values of justice and fairness. However, the justice sought by crime victims often conflicts with fairness to offenders.

Punishments reflect the dominant values of a particular moment in history. By the end of the 1960s, for example, the number of Americans who were sentenced to imprisonment decreased because of a widespread commitment to rehabilitating offenders. By contrast, since the mid-1970s, record numbers of offenders have been sentenced to prison because of an emphasis on imposing strong punishments for the purposes of retribution, deterrence, and incapacitation. In the first decades of the twenty-first century, voices are calling for the addition of *restorative justice* as a fifth goal of the criminal sanction.

Retribution: Deserved Punishment

Retribution is punishment inflicted on a person who has infringed on the rights of others and so deserves to be penalized. The biblical expression "An eye for an eye, a tooth for a tooth" illustrates the philosophy underlying this kind of punishment. Retribution means that those who commit a particular crime should be punished alike, in proportion to the gravity of the offense or to the extent to which others have been made to suffer. Retribution is deserved punishment; offenders must "pay their debts."

retribution
Punishment inflicted on a person who has infringed on the rights of others and so deserves to be penalized. The severity of the sanction should fit the seriousness of the crime.

Some scholars claim that the desire for retribution is a basic human emotion. They maintain that if the state does not provide retributive sanctions to reflect community revulsion at offensive acts, citizens will take the law into their own hands to punish offenders. Under this view, the failure of government to satisfy the people's desire for retribution could produce social chaos.

This argument may not be valid for all crimes, however. If a rapist is inadequately punished, then the victim's friends, family, and other members of the community may be tempted to exact their own retribution. But what about a young adult smoking marijuana? If the government failed to impose retribution for this offense, would the community care? The same apathy may hold true for offenders who commit other nonviolent crimes that only modestly impact society. Even in these seemingly trivial situations, however, retribution may be useful and necessary to remind the public of the general rules of law and the important values they protect.

Since the late 1970s, retribution as a justification for the criminal sanction has aroused new interest, largely because of dissatisfaction with the philosophical basis and practical results of rehabilitation. Using the concept of "just deserts" or "deserved punishment" to define retribution, some theorists argue that one who infringes on the rights of others *deserves* to be punished. This approach rests on the philosophical view that punishment is a moral response to harms inflicted on society (Bronsteen, 2010). In effect, these theorists believe that basic morality demands that wrongdoers be punished (von Hirsch, 1976). According to this view, punishment should be applied only for the wrong that was inflicted and not primarily to achieve other goals such as deterrence, incapacitation, or rehabilitation.

Deterrence

Many people see criminal punishment as a basis for affecting the future choices and behavior of individuals. Politicians frequently talk about being "tough on crime" in order to send a message to would-be criminals. The roots of this approach, called deterrence, lie in eighteenth-century England among the followers of social philosopher Jeremy Bentham.

Bentham was struck by what seemed to be the pointlessness of retribution. His fellow reformers adopted Bentham's theory of utilitarianism, which holds that human behavior is governed by the individual's calculation of the benefits versus the costs of one's acts. Before stealing money or property, for example, potential offenders would consider the punishment that others have received for similar acts and would thereby be deterred.

general deterrence
Punishment of criminals that is intended to provide an example to the general public and to discourage the commission of offenses.

There are two types of deterrence. **General deterrence** presumes that members of the general public, on observing the punishments of others, will conclude that the costs of crime outweigh the benefits. For general deterrence to be effective, the public must be constantly reminded about the likelihood and severity of punishment for various acts. They must believe that they will be caught, prosecuted, and given a specific punishment if they commit a particular crime. Moreover, the punishment must be severe enough that the consequences of committing crimes will impress them. For example, public hanging was once considered to be an effective general deterrent. As a modern-day example, when movie star Wesley Snipes received three consecutive one-year prison sentences in 2008 for his three-year failure to file federal tax returns, many observers saw the maximum sentence on misdemeanor offenses as primarily focused on general deterrence to frighten other wealthy people from trying to evade their legal duty to pay taxes.

specific deterrence
Punishment inflicted on criminals to discourage them from committing future crimes.

By contrast, **specific deterrence** targets the decisions and behavior of offenders who have already been convicted. Under this approach, the amount and kind of punishment are calculated to discourage that criminal from repeating the offense. The punishment must be severe enough to cause the criminal to say, "The consequences of my crime were too painful. I will not commit another crime, because I do not want to risk being punished again." The three-month sentence of incarceration imposed on singer Lauryn Hill after pleading guilty in 2013 to charges of failing to file tax returns may have had an element of specific deterrence. The federal court demonstrated that it would send her behind bars for failing to file tax returns and pay taxes, thereby presumably reducing the likelihood that she would ever violate those laws again.

The concept of deterrence presents obvious difficulties (Stafford and Warr, 1993). Deterrence assumes that all people think before they act. It does not account for the many people who commit crimes while under the influence of drugs or alcohol, or those whose harmful behavior stems from psychological problems or mental illness. Deterrence also does not account for people who act impulsively in stealing or damaging property. In other cases, the low probability of getting caught defeats both general and special deterrence. To be generally deterrent, punishment must be perceived as relatively fast, certain, and severe (Mannheimer, 2011). But punishment does not always work this way.

Knowledge of the effectiveness of deterrence is limited (Kleck et al., 2005). For example, social science cannot measure the effects of general deterrence, because only those who are *not* deterred come to the attention of researchers. A study of the deterrent effects of punishment would have to examine the impact of different forms of the criminal sanction on various potential lawbreakers. How can we truly determine how many people (if any) stopped themselves from committing a crime because they were deterred by the prospect of prosecution and punishment? Therefore, although legislators often cite deterrence as a rationale for certain sanctions, no one really knows the extent to which sentencing policies based on deterrence achieve their objectives. Because contemporary U.S. society has shown little ability to reduce crime by imposing increasingly severe sanctions, the effectiveness of deterrence for many crimes and criminals should be questioned. Indeed, as indicated in "What Americans Think," the American public does not express confidence in the deterrent value of incarceration.

WHAT AMERICANS THINK

QUESTION: "Would you agree or disagree that serving time in prison or jail reduces the likelihood a person will commit more crime in the future?"

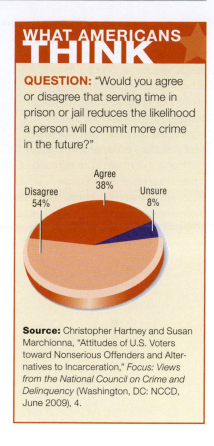

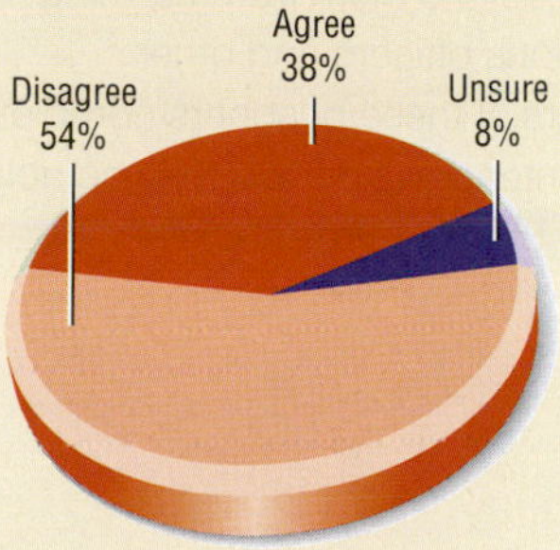

Source: Christopher Hartney and Susan Marchionna, "Attitudes of U.S. Voters toward Nonserious Offenders and Alternatives to Incarceration," *Focus: Views from the National Council on Crime and Delinquency* (Washington, DC: NCCD, June 2009), 4.

Incapacitation

Incapacitation assumes that society, by means of prison or execution, can keep an offender from committing further crimes. Many people express such sentiments, urging officials to "lock 'em up and throw away the key!" In primitive societies, banishment from the community was the usual method of incapacitation. In early America, offenders often agreed to move away or join the army as an alternative to some other form of punishment. In contemporary America, imprisonment is the usual method of incapacitation. Offenders can be confined within secure institutions and effectively be prevented from committing additional harm against society for the duration of their sentence. Long prison sentences impose sustained periods of incapacitation. Capital punishment is the ultimate method of incapacitation.

incapacitation
Depriving an offender of the ability to commit crimes against society, usually by detaining the offender in prison.

Any sentence that physically restricts an offender usually incapacitates the person, even when the underlying purpose of the sentence is retribution, deterrence, or rehabilitation. Sentences based on incapacitation are future oriented (Owens, 2009). Whereas retribution requires focusing on the harmful act of the offender, incapacitation looks at the offender's potential actions. If the offender is likely to commit future crimes, then a severe sentence may be imposed—even for a relatively minor crime.

For example, under the incapacitation theory, a woman who kills her abusive husband as an emotional reaction to his verbal insults and physical assaults could receive a light sentence. As a one-time impulse killer who felt driven to kill by unique circumstances, she will not likely commit additional crimes. By contrast, someone who shoplifts merchandise and has been convicted of the offense on ten previous occasions may receive a severe sentence. The criminal record and type of crime indicate that he or she will commit additional crimes if released. Thus, incapacitation focuses on characteristics of the offenders instead of characteristics of their offenses.

Does it offend your sense of justice that a person could receive a longer sentence for shoplifting than for manslaughter? This is one of the criticisms of

AP Images/Andy Manis

Prisoners who are considered to be exceptionally dangerous or who misbehave serve long sentences in high-security prisons. Long sentences incapacitate them from causing harm to society. In the highest security settings, they are kept in solitary confinement in order to incapacitate them from harming corrections officers and other prisoners. If these prisoners complete their sentences, how will they be able to adjust to life in free society?

incapacitation. Questions also arise about how to determine the length of sentence. Presumably, offenders will not be released until the state is reasonably sure that they will no longer commit crimes. However, can we accurately predict any person's behavior? Moreover, on what grounds can we punish people for anticipated future behavior that we cannot accurately predict? In addition, there are questions about whether incapacitative policies will lead to an overall reduction in crime rates if there are other social forces that continue to foster criminal behavior among people living in various contexts of American society (Stahlkopf, Males, and Macallair, 2010).

selective incapacitation
Making the best use of expensive and limited prison space by targeting for incarceration those individuals whose detention will do the most to reduce crime in society.

In recent years, greater attention has been paid to the concept of **selective incapacitation**, whereby offenders who repeat certain kinds of crimes receive long prison terms. Research has suggested that a relatively small number of offenders commit a large number of violent and property crimes (T. R. Clear, 1994). Burglars, for example, tend to commit many offenses before they are caught.

Thus, these "career criminals" should be locked up for long periods. Such policies could be costly, however. Not only would correctional facilities have to be expanded, but the number of expensive, time-consuming trials also might increase if longer sentences caused more repeat offenders to plead not guilty. Another difficulty with this policy is that we cannot accurately predict which offenders will commit additional crimes upon release.

Rehabilitation

rehabilitation
The goal of restoring a convicted offender to a constructive place in society through some form of vocational or educational training or therapy.

Rehabilitation refers to the goal of restoring a convicted offender to a constructive place in society through some form of training or therapy. Americans want to believe that offenders can be treated and resocialized in ways that allow them to lead a crime-free, productive life upon release. Over the last 100 years, rehabilitation advocates have argued for techniques that they claim identify and treat the causes of criminal behavior. If the offender's criminal behavior is assumed to result from some social, psychological, or biological imperfection, the treatment of the disorder becomes the primary goal of corrections.

Rehabilitation focuses on the offender. Its objective does not imply any consistent relationship between the severity of the punishment and the gravity of the crime. People who commit lesser offenses can receive long prison sentences if experts believe that rehabilitating them will take a long time. By contrast, a murderer might win early release by showing signs that the psychological or emotional problems that led to the killing have been corrected.

According to the concept of rehabilitation, offenders are treated, not punished, and they will return to society when they are "cured." Consequently, judges should not set fixed sentences but rather ones with maximum and minimum terms so that parole boards can release inmates when they have been rehabilitated. From the 1940s until the 1970s, the goal of rehabilitation was so widely accepted that people generally regarded the treatment and reform of the offender as the only issues worth serious attention. Most assumed that the problems affecting individuals caused crime, and that modern social sciences provided the tools to address those problems. During the past 30 years, however, researchers have questioned the assumptions of the rehabilitation model. Studies of the results of rehabilitation programs have challenged the idea that criminal offenders can be cured (Martinson, 1974). Moreover, scholars no longer take for granted that crime is caused by identifiable, curable problems such as poverty, lack of job skills, low self-esteem, and hostility toward authority. Instead, some argue that we cannot identify the cause of criminal behavior for individual offenders.

During the first decade of the twenty-first century, rehabilitation reemerged as a goal of corrections. As we shall see in Chapter 16, it came to be discussed and applied through the concept of "reentry" rather than through a declaration that rehabilitation is a primary goal of the justice system (Butterfield, 2004a). States and the federal government endured significant financial costs through the expansion of prison systems and the growth of prison populations, caused by the imposition of lengthy prison sentences during the preceding two decades. Eventually, they confronted the reality that hundreds of thousands of prisoners were returning to society each year after serving long sentences. In addition, as governments at all levels experienced budget crises, officials sought ways to reduce prison populations. Thus, policies and programs emerged that were intended to prepare offenders for successful integration into society (Eckholm, 2008b). These programs are rehabilitative in nature, by providing education, counseling, skill training, and other services to help change offenders' behavior and prospects for success in society. Public opinion generally supports efforts to reform offenders through such rehabilitative efforts (Pew Charitable Trusts, 2012).

New Approach to Punishment: Restorative Justice

In keeping with the focus on community justice—in policing, prosecution, courts, and corrections—many people are calling for **restoration** (through restorative justice) to be added to the goals of the criminal sanction (Abid, 2012; Braithwaite, 2007).

restoration
Punishment designed to repair the damage done to the victim and community by an offender's criminal act.

The restorative justice perspective views crime as more than a violation of penal law. The criminal act practically and symbolically denies community. It breaks trust among citizens and requires community members to determine how to counteract the moral message of the crime that the offender is above the law and the victim beneath its reach (T. Clear and Karp, 1999). Crime victims suffer losses involving damage to property and self. The primary aim of criminal justice should be to repair these losses. Crime also challenges the

CIVIC ENGAGEMENT

YOUR ROLE IN THE SYSTEM

The mayor of your city asks you to lead a committee to develop a proposal for the creation of restorative justice programs. *Make a list of activities in which citizens can assist in restorative justice processes.* Then look at the array of activities at the Montpelier Community Justice Center in Vermont.

very essence of community, to the extent that community life depends on a shared sense of trust, fairness, and interdependence. Shifting the focus to restorative justice requires a three-way approach that involves the offender, the victim, and the community (Rodriguez, 2005). This approach may include mediation in which the three actors devise ways that all agree are fair and just for the offender to repair the harm to the victim and community (L. Walker and Hayashi, 2007). Some initial research shows that juveniles in restorative justice programs may be less likely to reoffend (Rodriguez, 2007). Communities in Vermont have well-established restorative justice programs through which alternative punishments, public apologies, restitution, and interaction between offenders and victims seek to advance both accountability and restoration (Dzur, 2011). This new approach to criminal justice means that losses suffered by the crime victim are restored, the threat to local safety is removed, and the offender again becomes a fully participating member of the community. Think about the possible opportunities for citizen involvement in restorative justice programs as you read "Civic Engagement: Your Role in the System."

To see how these goals of punishment might be enacted in real life, consider again the sentencing of Torris Caston, the Missouri ballet teacher sentenced to ten years in prison for his sexual relationship with an underage student. What, if anything, could he be required to do in order to achieve restorative justice? Would an apology and payment of money to the victim ease the potential for lifelong psychological scars? Table 12.1 shows various hypothetical statements that the judge might have given during sentencing, depending on prevailing correctional goals.

As we next consider the ways that the goals are applied though the various forms of punishment, keep in mind the underlying goal—or mix of punishment goals—that justifies each form of sanction.

TABLE 12.1 THE GOALS OF PUNISHMENT

At sentencing, the judge usually gives reasons for the punishments imposed. Here are statements that Missouri Circuit Judge Jack Garvey might have given Torris Caston for the statutory rape of an underage girl, each statement promoting a different goal for the sanction.

GOAL	JUDGE'S POSSIBLE STATEMENT
Retribution	I am imposing this 10-year sentence because you deserve to be punished for the harms caused to this young woman and to society by exploiting and harming this young woman. *What you did to this woman has cut such a path of destruction, of humiliation and pain. I don't know if it can ever be fixed.* [Note: italicized words were actually said by Judge Garvey at sentencing (J. Mann, 2014)]. Your criminal behavior is the basis of the punishment. Justice requires that I impose a sanction at a level that illustrates the importance that the community places on respecting the law and contributing as a member of society.
Deterrence	I am imposing this 10-year sentence so that your punishment for statutory rape serves as an example and deters others who may contemplate similar actions. In addition, I hope that this sentence will deter you from ever again committing an illegal act, because the victim asked for strict punishment to make sure that others would not be victimized [Note: Judge Garvey actually made this last statement].
Incapacitation	I am imposing this 10-year sentence so that you will be incapacitated and hence unable to commit other sex offenses, in accordance with the victim's request for a sentence that would prevent you from victimizing other girls.
Rehabilitation	The trial testimony and information contained in the presentence report make me believe that there are aspects of your personality that contributed to your sex offenses. I am therefore imposing this 10-year sentence so that you will have time and opportunity to receive counseling treatment and correct your behavior in the future.

Source: Jeffrey Mann, "Webster Groves Ballet Teacher Sentenced to 10 Years for Sex with Student," St. Louis Post-Dispatch, July 7, 2014 (www.stltoday.com).

Restorative justice seeks to repair the damage that an offender's criminal act has done to the victim and the community. Victims and their families can convey to the offender the severity and enduring nature of the pain and harm caused by his or her actions. How do such meetings advance the idea of justice?

✓POINT
1. What are the four primary goals of the criminal sanction?
2. What are the difficulties in showing that a punishment acts as a deterrent?

STOP AND ANALYZE: What do you think should be the primary goal of the criminal sanction? List two problems or challenges to the achievement of that goal.

(Answers are at the end of the chapter.)

Forms of the Criminal Sanction

Incarceration, intermediate sanctions, probation, and death are the basic ways that the criminal sanction, or punishment, is applied. There is no overarching sentencing law for the United States. The criminal code of each state and of the federal government specify the punishments. Each code differs to some extent in the severity of the punishment for specific crimes and in the amount of discretion given judges to tailor the sanction to the individual offender.

Many judges and researchers believe that sentencing structures in the United States are both too severe and too lenient. That is, many offenders who do not warrant incarceration are sent to prison, and many who should receive more-restrictive punishment instead receive only minimal probation supervision.

Advocates for more-effective sentencing practices increasingly support a range of punishment options, with graduated levels of supervision and harshness. These advocates increasingly find support from public officials who are trying to cope with budget cuts in state and local government and therefore want to reduce the use of expensive incarceration. As Figure 12.1 shows, simple probation lies at one end of this range, and traditional incarceration lies at the other. It is argued that by using this type of sentencing scheme, authorities can reserve expensive prison cells for violent offenders. At the same time, they can use less restrictive community-based programs to punish nonviolent offenders.

As we examine the various forms of criminal sanctions, bear in mind that complex problems are associated with applying these legally authorized punishments. Judges are given wide discretion in determining the appropriate sentence within the parameters of the penal code.

Incarceration

Incarceration in jails and prisons is the most visible penalty imposed by U.S. courts. Although less than 30 percent of people under correctional supervision are in prisons and jails, incarceration remains the standard for punishing those who commit serious crimes. Imprisonment is thought to contribute significantly to deterring potential offenders. However, incarceration is expensive. It also creates the problem of reintegrating offenders into society upon release.

Sentences of one year or less are typically served in local jails while sentences in excess of one year are served in state or federal prisons. In California, as part of a court-ordered effort to reduce populations in overcrowded prisons, convicted felons serving sentences of up to three years now serve their time in jails. The presence of felons serving sentences longer than one year in jails changes the nature of populations inside places that generally had held only offenders with misdemeanor convictions in addition to pretrial detainees awaiting trials and plea negotiations. Read the Technology and Criminal Justice feature to see how computers, monitors, specialized software, and other innovations have increased efficiency in the administration of jails.

In penal codes, legislatures stipulate the type of sentences and the amount of prison time that may be imposed for each crime. Three basic sentencing structures are used: (1) indeterminate sentences, (2) determinate sentences, and (3) mandatory sentences. Each type of sentence makes certain assumptions

FIGURE 12.1 ESCALATING PUNISHMENTS TO FIT THE CRIME

This list includes generalized descriptions of many sentencing options used in jurisdictions across the country.

PROBATION
Offender reports to probation officer periodically, depending on the offense, sometimes as frequently as several times a month or as infrequently as once a year.

INTENSIVE SUPERVISION PROBATION*
Offender sees probation officer three to five times a week. Probation officer also makes unscheduled visits to offender's home or workplace.

RESTITUTION AND FINES
Used alone or in conjunction with probation or intensive supervision and requires regular payments to crime victims or to the courts.

COMMUNITY SERVICE
Used alone or in conjunction with probation or intensive supervision and requires completion of set number of hours of work in and for the community.

SUBSTANCE ABUSE TREATMENT
Evaluation and referral services provided by private outside agencies and used alone or in conjunction with either simple probation or intensive supervision.

*Some offenders consider intensive supervision probation to be so burdensome that they prefer to serve time in jail or prison rather than face such constant, close scrutiny in the community.

Source: W. M. DiMascio, Seeking Justice: Crime and Punishment in America (New York: Edna McConnell Clark Foundation, 1997), 32–33.

about the goals of the criminal sanction, and each provides judges with varying degrees of discretion (Bureau of Justice Assistance [BJA], 1998: 4; Wool, 2005; Zhang, Zhang, and Vaughn, 2011).

Indeterminate Sentences

During the period when the goal of rehabilitation dominated corrections, legislatures enacted **indeterminate sentences** (often called indefinite sentences). In keeping with the goal of treatment, indeterminate sentencing gives correctional officials and parole boards significant control over the amount of time a prisoner serves. Penal codes with indeterminate sentences stipulate a minimum and a maximum amount of time to be served in prison (for example, 1–5 years, 3–10 years, or 1 year to life). At the time of sentencing, the judge informs the offender about the range of the sentence. The offender also learns that he or she will probably be eligible for parole at some point after the minimum term has been served. The parole board determines the actual release date. Recall in the chapter opener about teachers' sex offenses against students that the Michigan teacher, Tompkins, was given a sentence from 18 months to 10 years, a good example of an indeterminate sentence (Wolcott, 2015).

indeterminate sentences
A period, set by a judge, that specifies a minimum and a maximum time to be served in prison. Sometime after the minimum, the offender may be eligible for parole. Because it is based on the idea that the time necessary for treatment cannot be set, the indeterminate sentence is closely associated with rehabilitation.

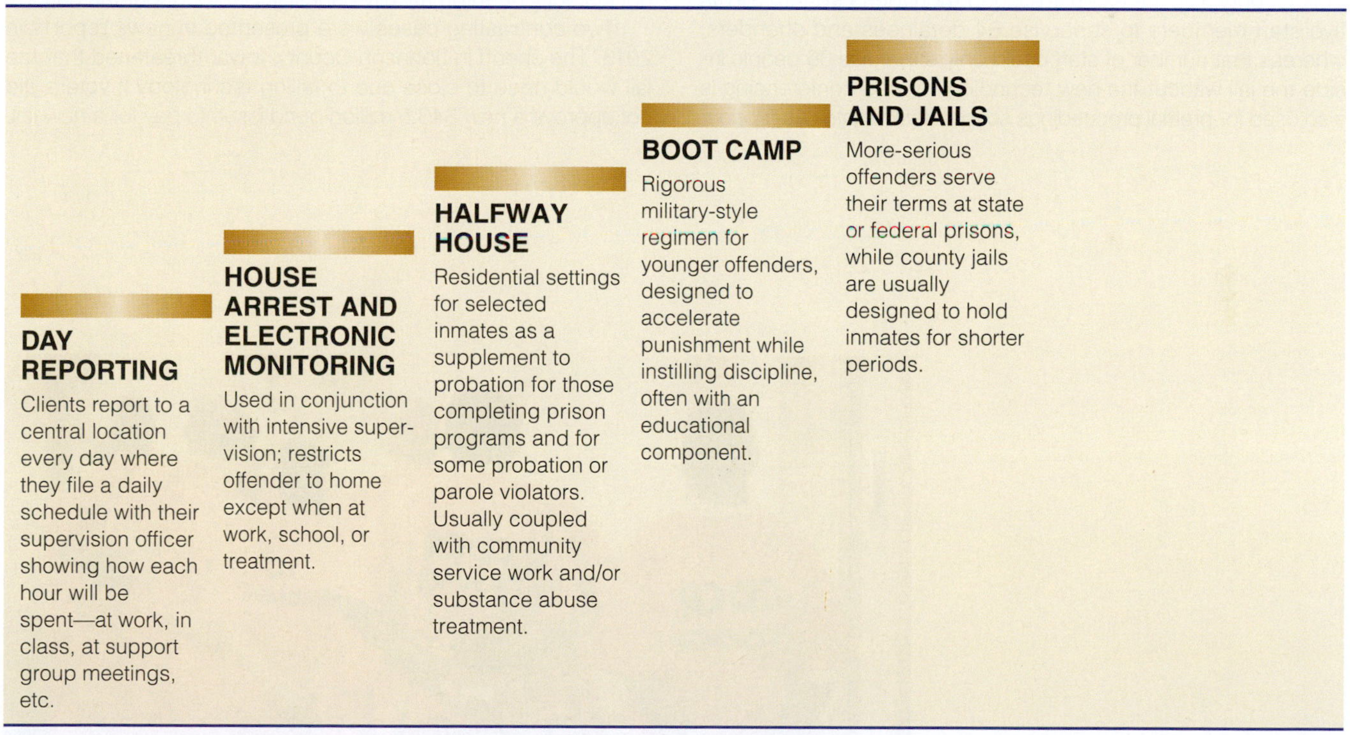

Determinate Sentences

Dissatisfaction with the rehabilitation goal and support for the concept of deserved punishment led many legislatures in the 1970s to shift to **determinate sentences** Dansky, 2008). With a determinate sentence, a convicted offender is imprisoned for a specific period of time (for example, 2 years, 5 years, 15 years). At the end of the term, minus credited good time (see later discussion), the prisoner is automatically freed. The time of release is tied

determinate sentences
A sentence that fixes the term of imprisonment at a specific period.

TECHNOLOGY & CRIMINAL JUSTICE

TECHNOLOGICAL INNOVATION IN JAIL ADMINISTRATION

When the new Polk County Jail opened outside Des Moines, Iowa, in November 2008, it boasted an array of technological innovations that enhanced the efficiency of jail administration and also reduced the number of staff members needed to supervise pretrial detainees and convicted offenders. In the lobby of the jail, a kiosk that looks like an ATM machine permits visitors to gain information about how to post bail for detainees and also permits them to deposit money into the accounts of people held in the jail. In addition, electronic visitation stations permit family members to converse with detainees and offenders through video conferencing, so that officers do not need to sign in visitors or escort detainees from housing units. These aspects of technology may help, in a small way, to ease a few of the burdens experienced by pretrial detainees.

Other aspects of technology in Polk County and elsewhere are designed to improve the efficiency of jail administration. At Polk County Jail, the extensive video monitoring system allows five staff members to supervise 64 detainees and offenders, whereas that number of staff could only supervise 36 people inside the jail without the new technology. Video conferencing is also used for pretrial proceedings so that defendants can "appear in court" without leaving the jail, thus reducing security risks and expenses for transporting defendants to a courthouse.

In the Sarasota, Florida, county jail and in other jails throughout the country, officers use handheld computers and sensors throughout a facility to count detainees and report on their status during rounds. The information from the handheld computers is instantly transferred to the main computer, avoiding the inaccuracy and delays that occurred through the traditional use of paper reports submitted throughout the day. An additional benefit for jail supervisors: They can track their own staff and make sure that officers are making their rounds through the jail completely and on schedule.

Technology is expensive. In times of budget cuts, those jails that had not previously obtained the new computers, software, and video systems are unlikely to be able to do so in the immediate future. Thus the existence of useful new technology will not instantly or automatically benefit jails throughout the nation.

Two contrasting cases were presented in news reports in 2013. The sheriff in Johnson County, Iowa, threatened that the jail would need to close due to failing technology if voters did not approve a new $43.5 million bond issue to pay for a new jail.

Tony Avelar/Christian Science Monitor/The Image Works

Of all correctional measures, incarceration represents the greatest restriction on freedom. Since 1980, the number of Americans held in prisons and jails has quadrupled. Beyond the significant financial costs, what are the other consequences for society from having such a large population of prisoners?

The voters had rejected the same proposal in November 2012, so it was uncertain if taxpayers would be willing to pay for the new jail. By contrast, the Yavapai County Jail in Arizona had the good fortune of acquiring some of its new technology free of charge by agreeing to help the manufacturer test the equipment at the jail. The manufacturer apparently hoped that it could use the Arizona jail's positive experience as a basis for persuading other jails around the country to buy its equipment. In addition to the sorts of technological equipment previously described in the Polk County, Iowa, jail, the Arizona jail also had two additional technological assets. Administrators there acquired a system to permit police officers to use their patrol car computers to provide most of the booking information on arrestees before the arrestees were brought to the jail. This innovation saved time when bringing arrestees into the jail and placing them into cells. In addition, the Arizona jail had iris-scanning technology to enable officials to scan the unique eyes of each detainee as a means of checking identities upon entry, during detention, and upon exit from the jail. Iris-scanning technology is faster and neater than traditional ink-based fingerprinting that is used at most jails to record the identity of detainees.

Sources: "Jail Receives $50,000 in Technology Upgrades at No Cost to County," *Grayson Journal-Enquirer,* April 1, 2011 (journal-times.com); Drew Johnson, "Guardian RFID Brings Offender Management into the 21st Century," *CorrectionsOne News,* April 12, 2011 (www.correctionsone.com); Bob Link, "Telephone Revenues Help Pay for New Jail Technology," *Iowa Globe Gazette,* March 30, 2008 (www.globegazette.com); Quentin Misiag, "Johnson County Officials: Current Jail Technology 'on Its Last Leg,'" *Daily Iowan,* April 28, 2013 (www.dailyiowan.com); Scott Orr, "New Jail Technology at Camp Verde," *Tri-Valley Dispatch,* February 27, 2013 (www.trivalleycentral.com); Todd Razor, "Technology Boosts Efficiency at New Polk County Jail," *Business Record,* July 18, 2009 (www.businessrecord.com).

DEBATE THE ISSUE

Will the extensive use of technology reduce jail officers' person-to-person contact with the offenders and detainees held in jail? Such contact has normally been viewed as a potential source of counseling, information, and reassurance. Will the widespread surveillance aspects of technology harm morale in jails if officers feel as if they are being monitored as constantly and thoroughly as detainees and offenders? Provide what you think are the two strongest arguments in favor of new jail technology and the two strongest arguments in opposition.

neither to participation in treatment programs nor to a parole board's judgment concerning the offender's likelihood of returning to criminal activities.

Some determinate-sentencing states have adopted penal codes that stipulate a specific term for each crime category. Others allow the judge to choose a range of time to be served. Some states emphasize a determinate **presumptive sentence**; the legislature or, often, a commission specifies a term based on a time range (for example, 14 to 20 months) into which most cases of a certain type should fall. Only in special circumstances should judges deviate from the presumptive sentence. Whichever variation is used, however, the offender theoretically knows at sentencing the amount of time to be served. One result of determinate sentencing is that by reducing the judge's discretion, legislatures have tended to limit sentencing disparities and to ensure that terms correspond to those the elected body thinks are appropriate (Griset, 1994).

presumptive sentence
A sentence for which the legislature or a commission sets a minimum and maximum range of months or years. Judges are to fix the length of the sentence within that range, allowing for special circumstances.

Mandatory Sentences

Politicians and the public have continued to complain that offenders gain release before serving sufficiently long terms, and legislatures have responded (Zimring, 2007). All states and the federal government created **mandatory sentences** (often called mandatory minimum sentences), stipulating some minimum period of incarceration that people convicted of selected crimes must serve. The judge may consider neither the circumstances of the offense nor the

mandatory sentences
A sentence determined by statutes and requiring that a certain penalty be imposed and carried out for convicted offenders who meet certain criteria.

Intermediate sanctions provide an array of choices for punishing offenders within the community. These sanction options include fines, community service, and home confinement—any of which may also be linked to a term of probation. Should judges have the power to individualize sentences depending on the prior record of each defendant and the circumstances of each crime?

background of the offender, and he or she may not impose nonincarcerative sentences. Mandatory prison terms are most often specified for violent crimes, drug violations, habitual offenders, or crimes in which a firearm was used. Mandatory sentences have contributed to expensive state corrections budgets and prison overcrowding. Thus some opinion polls indicate that the public has become less supportive of this approach to criminal punishment (Pew Charitable Trusts, 2012).

Use of mandatory minimum sentences expanded significantly during the 1980s as a weapon in the war on drugs. The result has been a significant increase in drug offenders, most for nonviolent offenses, spending very long terms in America's prisons (Gezari, 2008). Research has shown that these are low-level street dealers, mules (who deliver drugs), and addicts rather than the "kingpins" who import and distribute drugs to the market. Across the country, mandatory prison terms were applied more often to African American drug offenders than to their white counterparts (Crawford, 2000).

By 2009, years of lobbying by opponents of the harshness and disparities in mandatory sentencing converged with government officials' increasing concerns about the expense of incarceration. Many states looked for ways to reduce their prison populations, including changes in mandatory sentencing laws (Riccardi, 2009). New York revised its severe drug laws that had mandated a sentence of 15 years to life for many drug offenses. The New York reforms in 2009 returned sentencing discretion to judges for those possessing small quantities of drugs and immediately made 6,000 prisoners eligible to petition the courts for sentence reductions (Serwer, 2009). Voters in California approved a ballot issue in 2012 to reduce the applicability of that state's three-strikes law by no longer applying life sentences to offenders whose third offense was nonviolent (Staples, 2012). Similarly, in 2010, Congress reformed mandatory cocaine sentencing laws that had imposed mandatory five-year terms for the possession of 5 grams of crack cocaine, a sentence not mandated on powder-cocaine offenders unless they possessed 500 grams of the drug. After President

Obama signed the new law, it required 28 grams of crack cocaine to trigger the mandatory sentence, an amount that leads to a presumption that the drugs are for sale rather than for personal consumption (P. Baker, 2010).

The Sentence versus Actual Time Served

Regardless of how much discretion judges have to fine-tune the sentences they give, the prison sentences that are imposed may bear little resemblance to the amount of time served. In reality, parole boards in indeterminate-sentencing states have broad discretion in release decisions once the offender has served a minimum portion of the sentence. In addition, offenders can have their prison sentence reduced by earning **good time** for good behavior, at the discretion of the prison administrator.

good time
A reduction of an inmate's prison sentence, at the discretion of the prison administrator, for good behavior or participation in vocational, educational, or treatment programs.

Days are subtracted from prisoners' minimum or maximum term for good behavior or for participating in various types of vocational, educational, or treatment programs. Correctional officials consider these policies necessary for maintaining institutional order and reducing crowding (Demleitner, 2009). Good-time credit provides an incentive for prisoners to follow institutional rules. Prosecutors and defense attorneys also take good time into consideration during plea bargaining. In other words, they think about the actual amount of time a particular offender is likely to serve.

The amount of good time one can earn varies among the states, usually from five to ten days a month. In some states, once 90 days of good time are earned, they are vested; that is, the credits cannot be taken away as a punishment for misbehavior. Prisoners who then violate the rules risk losing only days not vested.

The budget crises of the early twenty-first century led officials in states that had abolished good-time credits to consider restoring the practice in order to reduce prison populations (Homan, 2010). Other states accelerated the awarding of good-time credits. Oregon increased good time from 20 percent reductions in time served to 30 percent reductions (Riccardi, 2009). In 2010, Louisiana allowed well-behaved prisoners eligible to receive a 35-day credit for every 30 days served. The change was expected to reduce the state's prison population by 2,386 prisoners in the first five years and save the state $7 million in the first year alone (KATC-TV, 2010).

More than 30 states also grant **earned time** that may be offered in addition to good time. Unlike good time, which is based on good behavior, earned time is awarded for participation in education, vocational, substance abuse, and other rehabilitation programs. Earned time may also be awarded for work assignments, such as when low-security prisoners work on disaster relief, conservation projects, or fighting wildfires (Lawrence, 2009). Several states have expanded the use of earned time as part of their budget-reduction strategies for shrinking expensive prison populations.

earned time
Reduction in a prisoner's sentence as a reward for participation in educational or other rehabilitation programs, and for work assignments, such as disaster relief and conservation projects.

Judges in the United States often prescribe long periods of incarceration for serious crimes, but good time, earned time, and parole reduce the amount of time spent in prison. Figure 12.2 shows the estimated time actually served by offenders sent to state prisons versus the average (mean) sentence according to the latest data published by the U.S. Bureau of Justice Statistics. The median prison sentence received for violent felony offenders decreased from ten years in 1994 to five years in 2006 (Rosenmerkel, Durose, and Farole, 2009). The portion of the sentence actually served increased for violent felonies in early twenty-first century from just under half to nearly two-thirds so that the average time served in prison for these offenders remained relatively stable from 1994 to 2004 (Durose and Langan, 2007).

FIGURE 12.2 **MEAN TIME SERVED IN STATE PRISON COMPARED WITH MEAN LENGTH OF SENTENCE (IN MONTHS)**

Many offenders serve a half or less of the mean sentences. Why is there such a difference between the sentence and the actual time served?

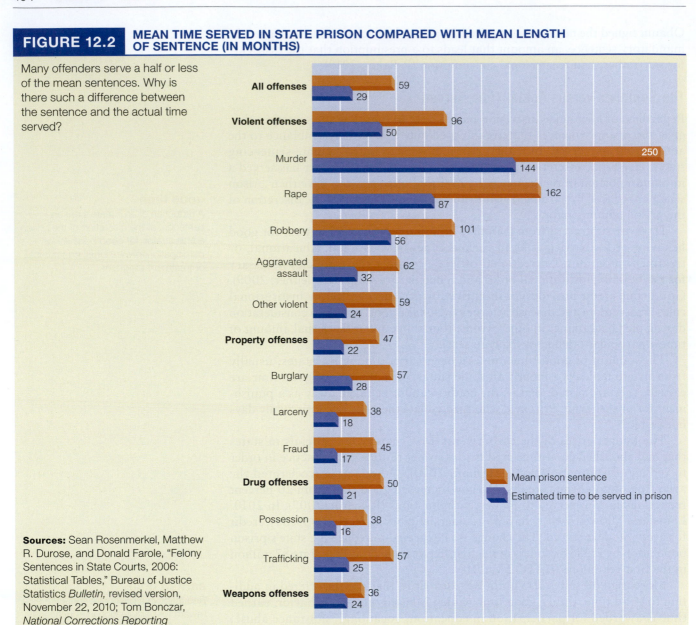

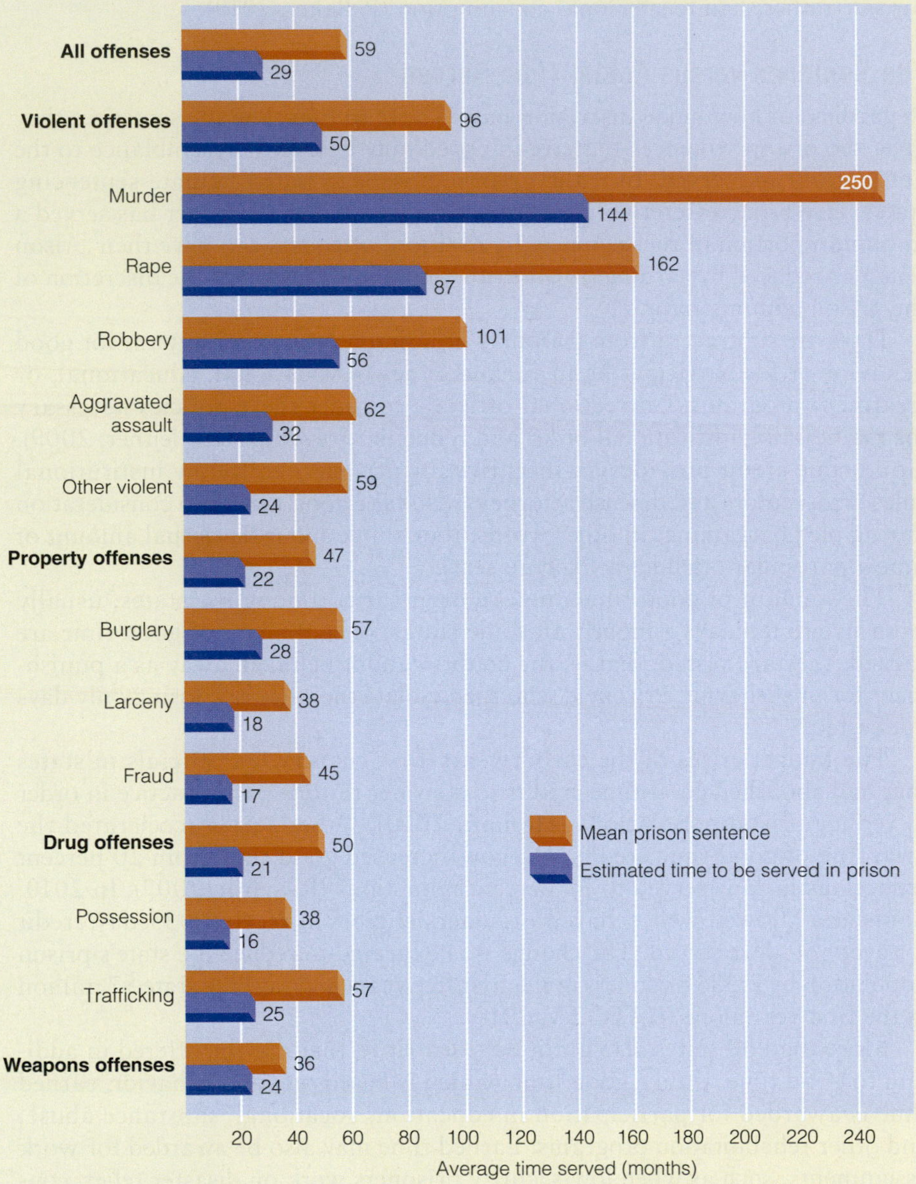

Sources: Sean Rosenmerkel, Matthew R. Durose, and Donald Farole, "Felony Sentences in State Courts, 2006: Statistical Tables," Bureau of Justice Statistics *Bulletin,* revised version, November 22, 2010; Tom Bonczar, *National Corrections Reporting Program, 2006,* U.S. Bureau of Justice Statistics, May 2010, Table 8;

This type of national data often hides the impact of variations in sentencing and releasing laws in individual states. In many states, because of prison crowding and release policies, offenders are serving less than 20 percent of their sentences. In other states, where three-strikes and truth-in-sentencing laws are employed, the average time served will be longer than the national average.

Truth in Sentencing

Truth in sentencing refers to laws that require offenders to serve a substantial proportion (usually 85 percent for violent crimes) of their prison sentence before being released on parole. These laws have three goals: (1) providing the public with more-accurate information about the actual length of sentences, (2) reducing crime by keeping offenders in prison for longer periods, and

(3) achieving a rational allocation of prison space by prioritizing the incarceration of particular classes of criminals (such as violent offenders). Most offenders serve two-thirds or less of their mean sentences. Why is there such a difference between the sentence and actual time served?

Truth in sentencing became such a politically attractive idea that the federal government allocated almost $10 billion for prison construction to those states adopting truth in sentencing in the 1990s (Donziger, 1996). Critics maintain, however, that truth in sentencing increased prison populations at a tremendous cost. The concept is less attractive today to many states beset by budget problems as they try to reduce their prison populations through greater flexibility in sentencing and early release (Riccardi, 2009).

Intermediate Sanctions

Prison crowding and low levels of probation supervision have spurred interest in the development of **intermediate sanctions**, punishments that are less severe and less costly than prison but more restrictive than traditional probation (R. Warren, 2007). Intermediate sanctions provide a variety of restrictions on freedom, such as fines, home confinement, intensive probation supervision, restitution to victims, community service, boot camp, and forfeiture of property. In 2010, Florida's Office of Program Policy Analysis and Government Accountability noted that more than 24,000 of the state's prison inmates were convicted of nonviolent offenses and had no prior convictions for violent offenses (Florida Office of Program Policy, 2010). As indicated in Table 12.2, the agency estimated that the state could enjoy substantial financial savings through the increased use of intermediate sanctions rather than imprisonment.

intermediate sanctions
A variety of punishments that are more restrictive than traditional probation but less severe and less costly than incarceration.

An example of contemporary innovation in intermediate sanctions is represented in Florida's expansion drug courts. Unlike most drug courts that employ *pretrial diversion* to provide treatment, conditions of release, and supervision to help drug arrestees avoid convictions and incarceration, Florida's program also involves *post-adjudicatory courts.* By focusing on offenders who have entered guilty pleas or been convicted at trial, as described by a state report, these courts "are funded to reduce state corrections costs by specifically targeting prison-bound, non-violent felony offenders who agree to participate in

TABLE 12.2 ESTIMATED COST SAVINGS FOR FLORIDA FROM INCREASED USE OF INTERMEDIATE SANCTIONS (BASED ON 2009 COSTS)

SANCTION	FIRST-YEAR COST PER OFFENDER	TOTAL FIRST-YEAR COST FOR 100 OFFENDERS[1]	POTENTIAL SAVINGS PER 100 OFFENDERS[2]
Prison	$20,272	$2,027,200	
Supervision with GPS monitoring	$5,121	$806,954	$1,220,246
Probation and restitution centers	$9,492	$1,639,211	$387,989
Day reporting	$4,191	$917,823	$1,109,377
Residential drug treatment	$10,539	$1,419,529	$607,671

[1]The first-year cost for 100 offenders is based on the actual program completion rates for 2008–2009. Offenders who do not complete the program are assumed to leave the program after 82 days and are sent to prison for the remaining 283 days of the year; the cost of prison for these offenders is included in the total first-year cost estimate.

[2]The savings for 100 offenders represents the difference between the cost of prison for one year based on $55.54 per day and the total first-year cost for intermediate sanctions.

Source: Florida Office of Program Policy Analysis and Government Accountability, *Intermediate Sanctions for Non-Violent Offenders Could Produce Savings,* Report No. 10-27, March 2010, 3.

drug court in lieu of incarceration" (Florida Office of Program Policy Analysis, 2014: 1). In these courts, judges, prosecutors, defense attorneys, probation officers, and treatment providers work as a team to facilitate and review offenders' participation and compliance with drug testing, treatment, counseling, and job training. Thus, intermediate sanctions as well postprison supervision in reentry programs and parole, as we will see in Chapter 16, are components of a major initiative in many states called **justice reinvestment**. States use evidence-based practices in an effort to reduce the number of offenders being sent into expensive confinement in prison or being returned to prison for parole violations. They use the money saved from reducing prison populations to fund alternative means to hold offenders accountable and protect public safety, such as rehabilitation-oriented intermediate sanctions and reentry programs that seek to help offenders avoid further criminal behavior (Lawrence and Lyons, 2013).

justice reinvestment
Evidence-based policies intended to reduce spending on imprisonment with the money saved being reinvested in alternative sanctions and programs that hold offenders accountable, protect public safety, and reduce the risk of reoffending.

Early advocates for intermediate punishments Norval Morris and Michael Tonry (1990) argued that these sanctions should not be used in isolation, but rather in combination to reflect the severity of the offense, the characteristics of the offender, and the needs of the community. In addition, intermediate punishments must be supported and enforced by mechanisms that take seriously any breach of the conditions of the sentence. Too often, criminal justice agencies have devoted few resources to enforcing sentences that do not involve incarceration. If the law does not fulfill its promises, offenders may feel that they have "beaten" the system, which makes the punishment meaningless. Citizens viewing the ineffectiveness of the system may develop the attitude that nothing but stiffer sentences will work.

Probation

The most frequently applied criminal sanction is **probation**, a sentence that an offender serves in the community under supervision. Nearly 60 percent of adults under correctional supervision are on probation. Ideally, under probation, offenders attempt to straighten out their lives. Probation is a judicial act, granted by the grace of the state, not extended as a right. The judge imposes conditions specifying how an offender will behave through the length of the sentence. Probationers may be ordered to undergo regular drug tests, abide by curfews, enroll in educational programs or remain employed, stay away from certain parts of town or certain people, and meet regularly with probation officers. If the conditions of probation are not met, the supervising officer recommends to the court that the probation be revoked and that the remainder of the sentence be served in prison. Probation may also be revoked for commission of a new crime.

probation
A sentence that the offender is allowed to serve under supervision in the community.

Although probationers serve their sentences in the community, the sanction is often tied to incarceration. In some jurisdictions, the court is authorized to modify an offender's prison sentence, after a portion is served, by changing it to probation. This is often referred to as **shock probation** (or split probation): An offender is released after a period of incarceration (the "shock") and resentenced to probation. An offender on probation may be required to spend intermittent periods, such as weekends or nights, in jail. Whatever its specific terms, a probationary sentence will emphasize guidance and supervision in the community.

shock probation
A sentence in which the offender is released after a short incarceration and resentenced to probation.

Probation is generally advocated as a way of rehabilitating offenders whose crimes are not serious or whose past records are clean. It is viewed as less expensive than imprisonment, and more effective. For example, imprisonment may embitter youthful or first-time offenders and mix them with hardened criminals so that they learn more-sophisticated criminal techniques. By contrast, the combination of regular supervision and threat of jail time for misbehavior while on probation imposes punishment while keeping these offenders connected to their families and, hopefully, motivated to change their behavior.

Death

Although other Western democracies abolished the death penalty years ago, the United States continues to use it (C. E. Smith, 2010a). Capital punishment was imposed and carried out regularly prior to the late 1960s. Amid debates about the constitutionality of the death penalty and with public opinion polls showing opposition to it, the U.S. Supreme Court suspended its use from 1968 to 1976. Eventually the Court decided that capital punishment does not violate the Eighth Amendment's prohibition of cruel and unusual punishments. Executions resumed in 1977 as a majority of states began, once again, to sentence murderers to death.

The numbers of people facing the death penalty increased dramatically from the late 1970s to the early 1990s and then stabilized. As you can see from Figure 12.3, there were 3,035 people awaiting execution in 2014 in the 32 death penalty states, and four states (Connecticut, Maryland, Nebraska, and New Mexico) that abolished capital punishment for future cases. Although California is the state with the most offenders sentenced to death, two-thirds of U.S. inmates on death row are in the South, with the greatest number of southern condemned prisoners in Florida, Texas, and Alabama (see Figure 12.4).

FIGURE 12.3 PEOPLE UNDER SENTENCE OF DEATH AND PEOPLE EXECUTED, 1955–2014

In the decade preceding 2013, an average of 118 new offenders were added to death row each year. Despite a total of more than 3,000 offenders on death row, an average of only 50 executions occurred each year during the same decade. What explains this fact?

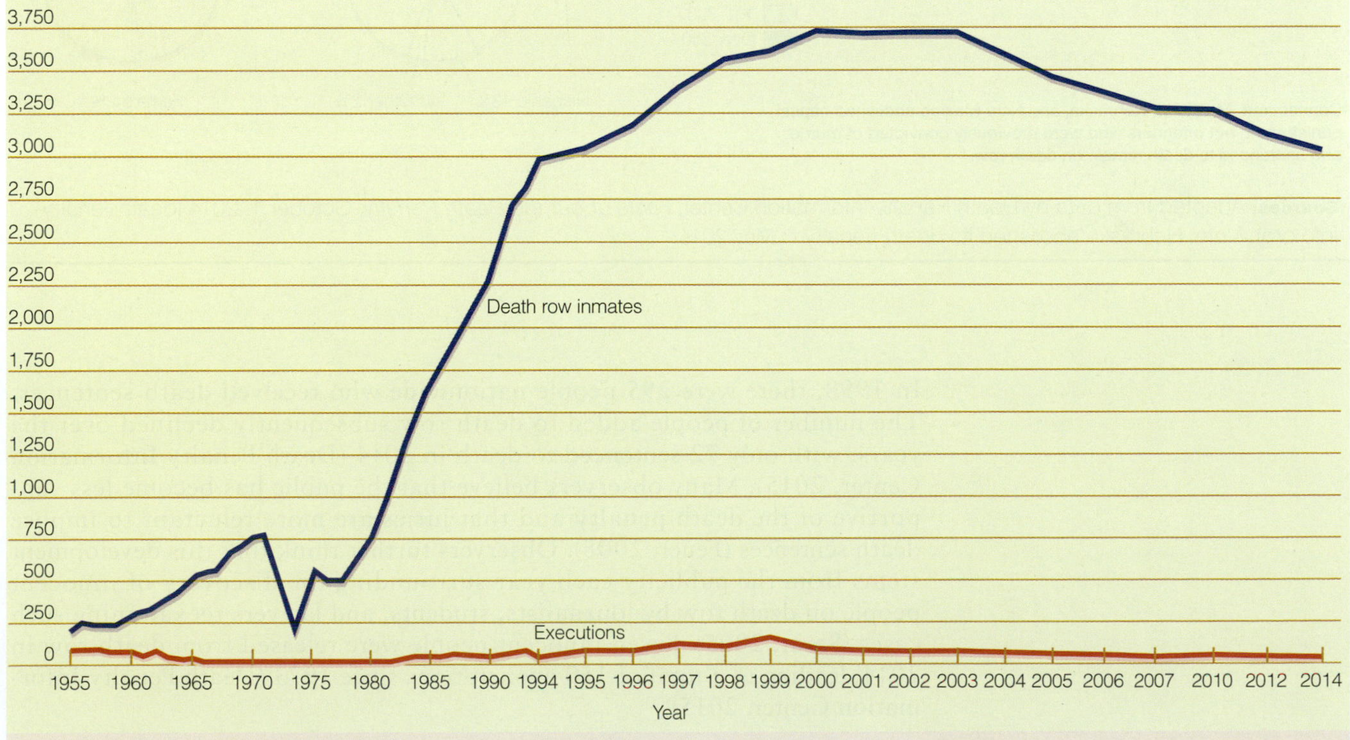

FIGURE 12.4 DEATH ROW CENSUS, 2014

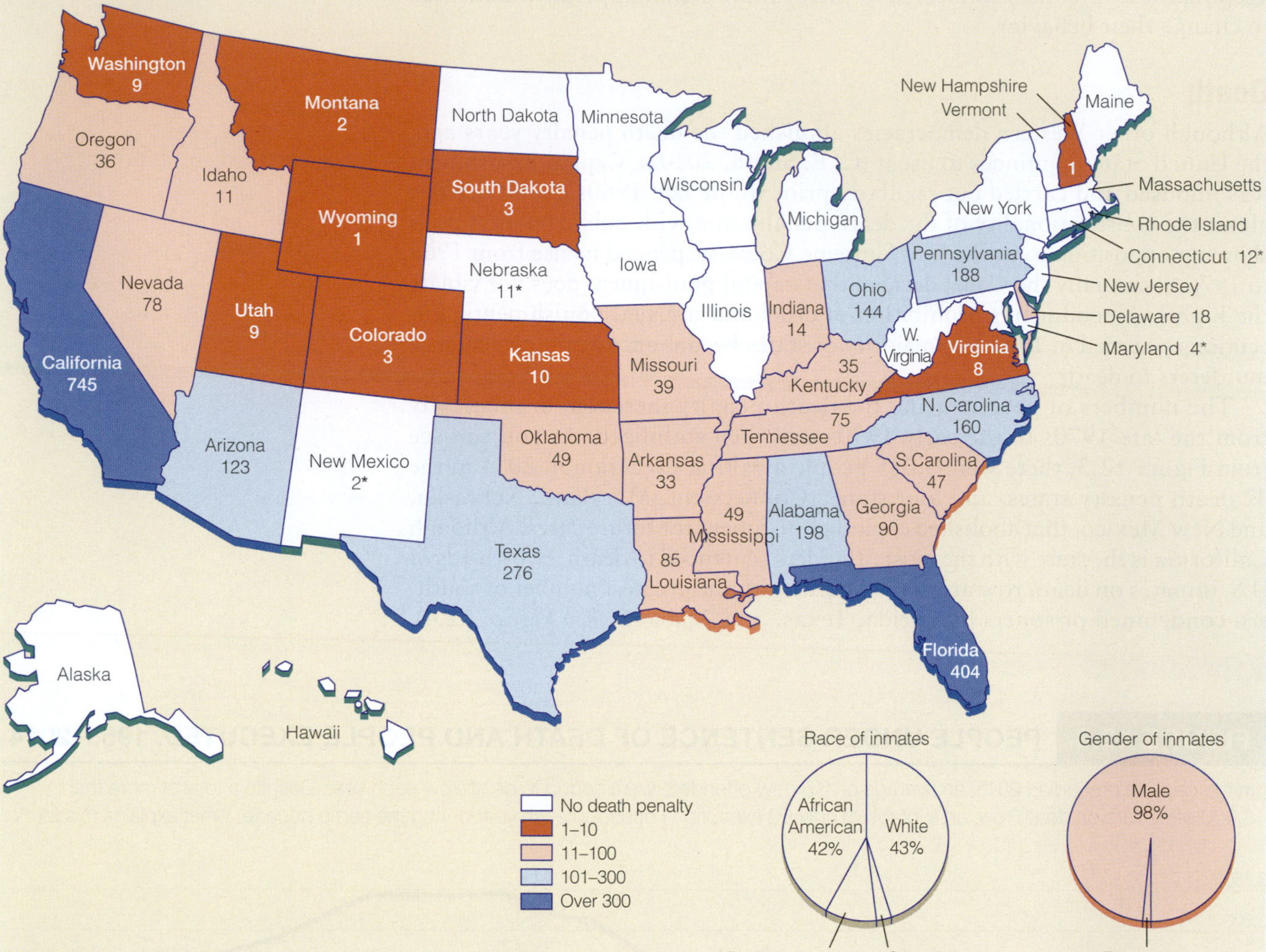

*Connecticut, Maryland, Nebraska, and New Mexico abolished capital punishment, but offenders who were previously convicted of murder and sentenced to death remain on death row.

Sources: Adapted from data by Death Penalty Information Center, *Facts about the Death Penalty*, October 1, 2014 (deathpenaltyinfo.org). *Note*: Nebraska abolished its death penalty in May 2015.

In 1998, there were 295 people nationwide who received death sentences. The number of people added to death row subsequently declined over the years, with only 72 sentenced to death in 2014 (Death Penalty Information Center, 2015). Many observers believe that the public has become less supportive of the death penalty and that juries are more reluctant to impose death sentences (Feuer, 2008). Observers further think that this development stems from the publicity each year surrounding the discovery of innocent people on death row by journalists, students, and lawyers reexamining such cases (Sarat, 2005). Seven innocent people were released from death row in 2014, leading to a total of 150 exonerations since 1973 (Death Penalty Information Center, 2015).

Despite the number of people currently on death row and the number sentenced to death each year, since 1977, no more than 98 people have been executed in a single year. That number of executions occurred in 1999. Since that time, the number of executions has dropped dramatically. In 2014, for example, only 35 executions took place nationwide (Death Penalty Information Center, 2015). This decline is usually attributed to a softening of support for capital punishment among the American public—a trend that appears related to recognition of the risks and flaws that lead to the conviction of innocent defendants (J. Unnever and Cullen, 2005).

The Death Penalty and the Constitution

Death differs from other punishments in that it is final and irreversible. The Supreme Court has therefore examined the decision-making process in capital cases to ensure that it fulfills the Constitution's requirements regarding due process, equal protection, and cruel and unusual punishment. The Court finds that punishments violate the Eighth Amendment's cruel and unusual punishments clause when they clash with "the evolving standards of decency that mark the progress of a maturing society" (*Trop v. Dulles*, 1958). Because life is in the balance, capital cases must be conducted according to higher standards of fairness and more-careful procedures than are other kinds of cases. Several important Supreme Court cases illustrate this concern.

Key Supreme Court Decisions

In ***Furman v. Georgia* (1972)**, the Supreme Court ruled that the death penalty, as administered, constituted cruel and unusual punishment. The decision invalidated the death penalty laws of 39 states and the District of Columbia. A majority of justices found that the procedures used to impose death sentences were arbitrary and unfair (Oshinsky, 2010). Over the next several years, 35 states enacted new capital punishment statutes that provided for better procedures.

***Furman v. Georgia* (1972)**
The death penalty, as administered, constitutes cruel and unusual punishment.

The new laws were tested before the Supreme Court in ***Gregg v. Georgia* (1976)**. The Court upheld those laws that required the sentencing judge or jury to take into account specific aggravating and mitigating factors in deciding which convicted murderers should be sentenced to death. Further, the Court decided that, rather than having a single proceeding determine the defendant's guilt and whether the death sentence would be applied, states should use *bifurcated proceedings*. In this two-part process, the defendant has a trial that determines guilt or innocence and then a separate hearing that focuses exclusively on the issue of punishment. It seeks to ensure a thorough deliberation before someone receives the ultimate punishment.

***Gregg v. Georgia* (1976)**
The Supreme Court's decision reactivating the death penalty after states revised their laws to make decision making about punishment in murder cases more careful and deliberate.

Under the *Gregg* decision, the prosecution uses the punishment-phase hearing to focus attention on the existence of aggravating factors, such as excessive cruelty or a defendant's prior record of violent crimes. The defense may focus on mitigating factors, such as the offender's youthfulness, mental condition, or lack of a criminal record (Kremling et al., 2007). These aggravating and mitigating factors must be weighed before the judge or jury can decide to impose a death sentence. The Supreme Court has ruled that the defendant may not be brought into court for this second hearing wearing chains and shackles. Such visible restraints may influence the jury to favor the death penalty in that they might make the individual seem exceptionally dangerous (*Deck v. Missouri*, 2005). Because of the Court's emphasis on fair procedures and individualized decisions, state appellate courts review trial court procedures in virtually every capital case.

McCleskey v. Kemp (1987)
Rejects a challenge to Georgia's death penalty that was made on the grounds of racial discrimination.

In **McCleskey v. Kemp (1987)**, opponents of the death penalty felt that the U.S. Supreme Court dealt a serious blow to their movement. In this case, the Court rejected a challenge to Georgia's death penalty law, made on the grounds of racial discrimination. Warren McCleskey, an African American, was sentenced to death for killing a white police officer. Before the U.S. Supreme Court, McCleskey's attorney cited research that showed a disparity in the imposition of the death penalty in Georgia, based on the race of the victim and, to a lesser extent, the race of the defendant. Researchers had examined more than 2,000 Georgia murder cases and found that defendants charged with killing whites had received the death penalty 11 times more often than had those convicted of killing African Americans. At that time, although 60 percent of homicide victims in Georgia were African American, all 7 people put to death in that state since 1976 had been convicted of killing white people, and 6 of the 7 murderers were African American (Baldus, Woodworth, and Pulaski, 1994).

By a 5-to-4 vote, the justices rejected McCleskey's assertion that Georgia's capital sentencing practices violated the equal protection clause of the Constitution by producing racial discrimination. The slim majority of justices declared that McCleskey would have to prove that the decision makers acted with a discriminatory purpose in deciding his particular case. The Court also concluded that statistical evidence showing discrimination throughout the Georgia courts did not provide adequate proof. McCleskey was executed in 1991. The decision made it very difficult to prove the existence of racial discrimination in capital cases, but it did not alleviate continuing concerns that death penalty cases can be infected with racial bias (R. N. Walker, 2006).

Atkins v. Virginia (2002)
Execution of the developmentally disabled ("mentally retarded") is unconstitutional.

In June 2002, the Supreme Court broke new ground in a way that heartened opponents of the death penalty. In **Atkins v. Virginia (2002)** it ruled that execution of developmentally disabled defendants was unconstitutional. In its opinion, the Court used the older term *mentally retarded* to refer to these defendants instead of the contemporary term *developmentally disabled*. Daryl Atkins, who has an IQ of 59, was sentenced to death for killing Eric Nesbitt in a 7-Eleven store parking lot. Lower courts had upheld Atkins's sentence based on *Penry v. Lynaugh* (1989), in which the Supreme Court had upheld execution of a defendant with similar developmental disabilities. In that decision it noted that only two states prohibited the death penalty in such cases.

Justice John Paul Stevens, writing for the *Atkins* majority, noted that since 1989 there had been a "dramatic shift in the state legislative landscape," and a national consensus had emerged rejecting execution of the developmentally disabled. He pointed out that among death penalty states, the number prohibiting such executions had gone from 2 to 18. The dissenters, Chief Justice William Rehnquist and Justices Antonin Scalia and Clarence Thomas, disputed that there was a real or lasting consensus against executing such defendants. In the absence of an authentic consensus, Justice Scalia said that the majority had merely imposed their own views as constitutional law.

As the majority opinion noted, the characteristics of developmentally disabled offenders, people with IQs of less than 70, "undermine the strength of the procedural protections." This point is in keeping with the argument of mental health experts who say their suggestibility and willingness to please lead such people to confess. At trial they have problems remembering details, locating witnesses, and testifying credibly in their own behalf.

Roper v. Simmons (2005)
Execution of offenders for murders committed before they were 18 years of age is unconstitutional.

Three years later the Supreme Court further limited the application of capital punishment. In **Roper v. Simmons (2005)**, a five-member majority on the Court declared that the execution of individuals who committed murders as juveniles violates the contemporary societal standards of the Eighth Amendment (C. M. Bradley, 2006). Previously, the Supreme Court had said that offenders could only be executed for crimes that they committed at age 16 or older (*Stanford v. Kentucky,* 1989). At the time of the decision, the United States was the lone democracy among the handful of countries that permitted the execution of juvenile offenders (Blecker, 2006). Justice Anthony Kennedy's majority opinion claimed that society had moved away from permitting such executions. He noted that 30 states had forbidden the imposition of the death penalty on anyone under the age of 18 and that during the preceding decade only three states had actually executed anyone for crimes committed as juveniles. In dissent, Justice Scalia, on behalf of Chief Justice Rehnquist and Justice Thomas, again asserted that the Court was imposing its own views on society. Justice Sandra Day O'Connor, in a separate dissent, argued that the death penalty may be appropriate for some 17-year-old killers, depending on the maturity of the offender and the circumstances of the crime.

In **Ring v. Arizona (2002)**, the Supreme Court ruled that juries, rather than judges, must make the crucial factual decisions regarding whether a convicted murderer should receive the death penalty. The *Ring* decision overturned the law in five states—Arizona, Colorado, Idaho, Montana, and Nebraska—where judges alone had decided whether there were aggravating factors that warrant capital punishment. The decision also raised questions about the procedure in four other states—Alabama, Delaware, Florida, and Indiana—where the judge chose between life imprisonment or death after hearing a jury's recommendation. The Court's opinion also says that any aggravating factors must be stated in the indictment, thus also requiring a change in federal death penalty laws.

Ring v. Arizona (2002)
Juries, rather than judges, must make the crucial factual decisions regarding whether a convicted murderer should receive the death penalty.

The decision results from the implications of the Court's decision in *Apprendi v. New Jersey* (2000). The Court said that any factor that led to a higher sentence than the statutory maximum must be charged in the indictment and found beyond a reasonable doubt by the jury. In the 7-to-2 majority opinion in *Ring v. Arizona,* Justice Ruth Bader Ginsburg wrote that in view of the *Apprendi* ruling, the right to a jury trial "would be senselessly diminished if it encompassed the fact-finding necessary to increase a defendant's sentence by two years, but not the fact-finding necessary to put him to death."

By 2009, all capital punishment states had authorized the use of lethal injection as the preferred method of execution. Several states retained other methods, such as electrocution, to be used in the event that courts ever found lethal injection to be unconstitutional. However, lethal injection faced close scrutiny and potential challenges from lawyers for condemned offenders. Botched executions occurred, in which needles have popped out of offenders' arms during executions or technicians have misapplied the drugs. Although lethal injection was intended to kill offenders by peacefully rendering them unconscious as they die, the reality can be quite different. For example, during one execution witnessed and described by a journalist, the condemned man continued to gasp and violently gag until death came, some 11 minutes after the drugs were administered (Radelet, 2004).

In 2008, the U.S. Supreme Court examined a claim that the use of lethal injection produces unconstitutional "cruel and unusual punishment." By a 7-to-2 vote in **Baze v. Rees (2008)**, the justices concluded that the attorneys for the death row inmates had not proven that the use of lethal injection violates the Eighth Amendment. New issues will arise concerning lethal injection, because the drugs used by most states for such executions are difficult to obtain and no longer manufactured in the United States. In 2011, the federal Drug Enforcement Administration seized an execution drug purchased by the state of Georgia from a supplier in Great Britain because Georgia did not hold a proper license to import that drug (Sack, 2011). It remains to be seen if these shortages affect the number of executions or whether states will simply change

Baze v. Rees (2008)
Lethal injection has not been shown to violate the Eighth Amendment prohibition on cruel and unusual punishments and thus this method of execution is permissible.

the combination of drugs used for their executions in order to administer those drugs that are more easily available.

The future of the death penalty's treatment by the Supreme Court will depend on such factors as who is elected to be president of the United States in future elections, which justices leave the Court in the near future, and the views of the most recent appointees, including Sonia Sotomayor (confirmed in 2009), Elena Kagan (confirmed in 2010), and those appointed by future presidents.

Continuing Legal Issues

The case law since *Furman* indicates that capital punishment is legal as long as it is imposed fairly. However, opponents argue that certain classes of death row inmates should not be executed, because they are insane, did not have effective counsel, or were convicted by a death-qualified jury that excludes participation by those strongly opposed to capital punishment. Other issues exist concerning the length of appeals and American compliance with international law.

Execution of the Insane As we have seen, insanity is a recognized defense for commission of a crime. But should people who become mentally disabled after they are sentenced be executed? The Supreme Court responded to this question in 1986 in *Ford v. Wainwright*. In 1974, Alvin Ford was convicted of murder and sentenced to death. Only after he was incarcerated did he begin to exhibit delusional behavior.

Justice Thurgood Marshall, writing for the majority, concluded that the Eighth Amendment prohibited the state from executing the insane—the accused must comprehend both the fact that he had been sentenced to death and the reason for it. Marshall cited the common-law precedent that questioned the retributive and deterrent value of executing a mentally disabled person.

Critics have also raised questions about the morality of treating an offender's mental illness so that he or she can be executed, a policy opposed by the American Medical Association. The Supreme Court has not directly addressed this issue with regard to death row inmates, but many observers predict that it will eventually be addressed by the Court (Winick, 2010).

Execution for Child Rape

Because of the heinous nature of the crime, several states have sought to enact laws permitting use of the death penalty for adults who rape children, even when the children are not murdered. Since the 1970s, capital punishment has been used exclusively for homicide offenses, so the use of the ultimate punishment for a sex crime would represent an expansion of the death penalty. In 2008, by a narrow 5-to-4 vote, the Supreme Court struck down Louisiana's law applying the death penalty to adults who rape children (*Kennedy v. Louisiana*, 2008). The vote in the case was so close that many observers believe that changes in the Court's composition could lead to a reversal on this issue.

Effective Counsel

The effective performance of the defense attorney can be a key factor in determining whether a defendant is sentenced to death (Brewer, 2005). In *Strickland v. Washington* (1984), the Supreme Court ruled that defendants in capital cases had the right to representation that meets an "objective standard of reasonableness." As noted by Justice O'Connor, the appellant must show "that there is a reasonable probability that, but for the counsel's unprofessional errors, the result of the proceeding would be different."

David Washington was charged with three counts of capital murder, robbery, kidnapping, and other felonies, and an experienced criminal lawyer was appointed as counsel. Against his attorney's advice, Washington confessed to two murders, waived a jury trial, pleaded guilty to all charges, and chose to be sentenced by the trial judge. Believing the situation was hopeless, his counsel did not adequately prepare for the sentencing hearing. On being sentenced to death, Washington appealed. The Supreme Court, however, rejected Washington's claim that his attorney was ineffective because he did not call witnesses, seek a presentence investigation report, or cross-examine medical experts on the defendant's behalf. In other words, although his lawyer did not do as good a job as he wanted, Washington nonetheless received a fair trial.

In recent years the public has learned of cases where the defense attorney has seemed incompetent, even to the point of sleeping at trial. In 1999, the *Chicago Tribune* conducted an extensive investigation of capital punishment in Illinois. Reporters found that 33 defendants sentenced to death since 1977 were represented by an attorney who had been, or was later, disbarred or suspended for conduct that was "incompetent, unethical, or even criminal." These attorneys included David Landau, who was disbarred one year after representing a Will County defendant sentenced to death, and Robert McDonnell, a convicted felon and the only lawyer in Illinois to be disbarred twice. McDonnell had represented four men who landed on death row (K. Armstrong and Mills, 1999). These cases may affect the public's view on fairness, as indicated in What Americans Think.

In March 2000, a federal judge overturned the conviction of Calvin Jerold Burdine after 16 years on death row. At his 1984 trial, Burdine's defense attorney slept through long portions of the proceedings. As the judge said, "Sleeping counsel is equivalent to no counsel at all" (Milloy, 2000).

These highly publicized cases may have caught the attention of the Supreme Court. In 2003 the Court issued a decision that seemed designed to remind lawyers and judges about the need for competent defense attorneys in capital cases. In *Wiggins v. Smith* (2003), the Court found that the Sixth Amendment right to counsel was violated when a defense attorney failed to present mitigating evidence concerning the severe physical and sexual abuse suffered by the defendant during childhood. It remains to be seen whether the justices create clearer or stricter standards for defense attorneys.

Death-Qualified Juries Should people who are opposed to the death penalty be excluded from juries in capital cases? In ***Witherspoon v. Illinois* (1968)**, the Supreme Court held that potential jurors who have general objections to the death penalty or whose religious convictions oppose its use cannot be automatically excluded from jury service in capital cases. However, it upheld the practice of removing, during voir dire (preliminary examination), those people whose opposition is so strong as to "prevent or substantially impair the performance of their duties." Such jurors have become known as "Witherspoon excludables." The decision was later reaffirmed in *Lockhart v. McCree* (1986).

Because society is divided on capital punishment, opponents argue that death-qualified juries do not represent a cross section of the community. Researchers have also found that juries are likely to be nudged toward believing the defendant is guilty and toward an imposition of the death sentence by the very process of undergoing death qualification (Luginbuhl and Burkhead, 1994: 107). There are additional jury issues concerning jurors' potential misperceptions about the judge's instructions for making decisions (Otto, Applegate, and Davis, 2007).

Mark Costanzo points to research that indicates that death qualification has several impacts. First, those who are selected for jury duty are more conviction prone and more receptive to aggravating factors presented during the penalty phase. A second, subtler impact is that jurors answering the questions about their willingness to vote for a death sentence often conclude that both defenders and prosecutors anticipate a conviction and a death sentence

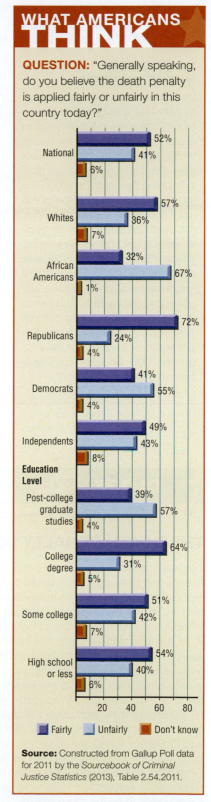

WHAT AMERICANS THINK

QUESTION: "Generally speaking, do you believe the death penalty is applied fairly or unfairly in this country today?"

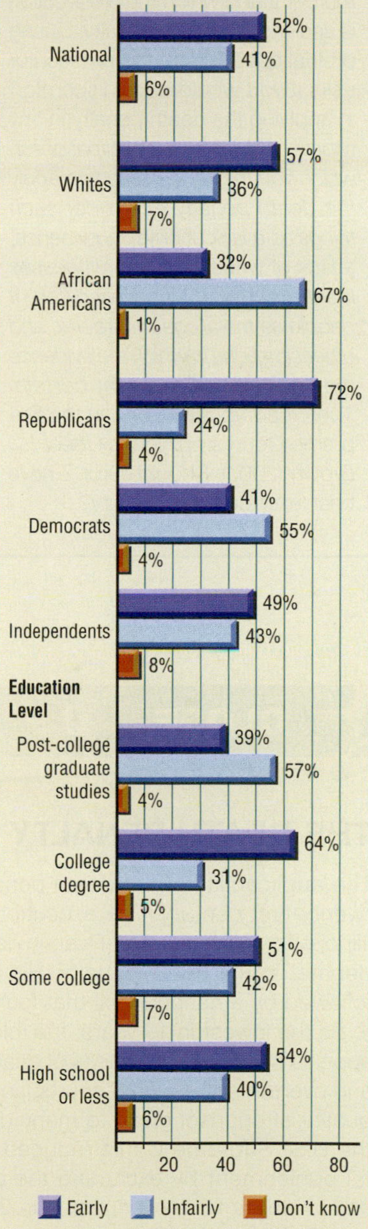

Source: Constructed from Gallup Poll data for 2011 by the *Sourcebook of Criminal Justice Statistics* (2013), Table 2.54.2011.

***Witherspoon v. Illinois* (1968)**
Potential jurors who object to the death penalty cannot be automatically excluded from service; however, during voir dire, those who feel so strongly about capital punishment that they could not give an impartial verdict may be excluded.

CIVIC ENGAGEMENT

YOUR ROLE IN THE SYSTEM

Imagine that you have been called to serve as a potential juror in a murder trial in which the prosecution is seeking the death penalty. During pretrial questioning, the prosecutor asks if you would have discomfort in applying the death penalty in any situations. *Make a list of situations in which you might be hesitant to apply the death penalty—consider such things as a lack of physical evidence, a lack of witnesses, two witnesses identifying two completely different people as the alleged murderer, and other situations in which the evidence may not be 100 percent certain.* Then read about Juror Z in the Supreme Court's opinion in *Uttecht v. Brown* (2007). Should Juror Z have been excluded from the jury?

(Costanzo, 1997). Think about these arguments as you read "Civic Engagement: Your Role in the System."

Appeals The long appeals process for death penalty cases remains a source of ongoing controversy (B. E. Dickson, 2006). The 65 prisoners executed in 2003 were under sentence of death an average of 10 years and 11 months (Bonczar and Snell, 2004). During this waiting period, the state courts review the sentences, as do the federal courts, through the writ of habeas corpus.

The late Chief Justice William Rehnquist actively sought to reduce the opportunities for capital punishment defendants to have their appeals heard by multiple courts. In 1996, President Bill Clinton signed the Antiterrorism and Effective Death Penalty Act, which requires death row inmates to file habeas appeals within one year and requires federal judges to issue their decisions within strict time limits.

Appellate review is a time-consuming and expensive process, but it also makes an impact. From 1977 through 2003, there were 7,061 people who entered prison under sentence of death. During those 26 years, 885 people were executed, 282 died of natural causes, and 2,542 were removed from death row as a result of appellate court decisions and reviews or commutations by governors. (Bonczar and Snell, 2004).

Michael Radelet and his colleagues have examined the cases of 68 death row inmates later released because of doubts about their guilt (Radelet, Lofquist, and Bedau, 1996). This number is equivalent to one-fifth of the inmates executed during the period 1970–1996. Correction of the miscarriage of justice for about one-third of the defendants took four or fewer years, but it took nine years or longer for another one-third of the defendants. Had the expedited appeals process and limitations on habeas corpus been in effect at that time, would these erroneous death sentences have been overturned?

CLOSE UP

THE DEATH PENALTY DEBATE

The applicability of the death penalty has diminished in the twenty-first century. The execution moratorium imposed by Illinois Governor George Ryan in January 2000 reinvigorated debate on the death penalty. His announcement was soon followed by a national poll that found support for the penalty to be the lowest in 19 years; the release of a national study of appeals that found two-thirds of death penalty cases are flawed and overturned by higher courts; and research questioning the quality of counsel given to many defendants. Subsequently, the U.S. Supreme Court reduced the applicability of capital punishment by excluding the developmentally disabled and juveniles from executions. In 2011, the Illinois legislature and Governor Pat Quinn approved legislation to end capital punishment in that state, just as New Jersey had done in 2007. Connecticut and Maryland followed suit in 2012 and 2013, respectively. Nebraska's legislature overrode objections from the governor to do the same in 2015.

Opponents of capital punishment continue the fight to abolish it. They argue that poor people and minorities receive a disproportionate number of death sentences. They also believe that executing people who are teenage, insane, or developmentally disabled is barbaric.

Even the proponents of capital punishment remain dissatisfied with how it is applied. They point to the fact that although more than 3,000 convicted murderers wait on death row, the number of executions since 1976 has never exceeded 98 per year and has declined through the first years of the twenty-first century. The appeals process is a major factor affecting this pace, given that it can delay executions for years.

FOR THE DEATH PENALTY

Supporters argue that society should apply swift, severe punishments to killers to address the continuing problems of crime and violence. Execution should occur quite soon after conviction so that the greatest deterrent value will result. They say that justice requires that a person who murders another must be executed. To do less is to denigrate the value of human life.

The arguments for the death penalty include the following:

- The death penalty deters criminals from committing violent acts.
- The death penalty achieves justice by paying killers back for their horrible crimes.

The Death Penalty: A Continuing Controversy Various developments in the twenty-first century appear to indicate a weakening of support for capital punishment in the United States. In May 2000, the New Hampshire legislature became the first in more than two decades to vote to repeal the death penalty; however, the governor vetoed the bill. New York's capital punishment law was declared unconstitutional by its own state courts in 2004. The New Jersey state legislature and governor eliminated the death penalty in that state in 2007. In March 2011, the governor of Illinois signed a law that eliminated capital punishment. He also commuted the sentences of the 15 offenders on death row so that they are now serving sentences of life without parole (Schwartz and Fitzsimmons, 2011). Illinois had not executed an offender since 2000, when it was discovered that a number of innocent people had been sentenced to death due to flaws in the justice system, including the use of dishonest jailhouse informants and incompetent defense attorneys. Connecticut's legislature and governor approved legislation abolishing the death penalty in 2012, and Maryland's governor and legislative leaders did the same in 2013 (Ariosto, 2012; Witte, 2013). In 2015, the Nebraska legislature overrode the governor's veto to abolish capital punishment when Democratic and Republican senators joined together to change the state's sentencing law (Bosman, 2015).

The extent to which additional states move to abolish capital punishment may depend on the political party with the most influence within the state. Capital punishment is an issue that sparks a strong divide between Democrats and Republicans. When asked in 1993 about the best punishment for murderers, 55 percent of Democrats said the death penalty. By 2014, a poll found 60 percent of Democrats said they favored life imprisonment for murderers. In contrast, 68 percent of Republicans preferred the death penalty for murderers in 1993, and the identical percentage of Republicans still held that view in 2014 (Jones, 2014a).

- The death penalty prevents criminals from doing further harm while on parole.
- The death penalty is less expensive than holding murderers in prison for life.

AGAINST THE DEATH PENALTY

Opponents believe that the death penalty lingers as a barbaric practice from a less civilized age. They point out that most other developed democracies in the world have ceased to execute criminals. Opponents challenge the claim that the death penalty effectively reduces crime. They also raise concerns about whether the punishment can be applied without errors and discrimination.

The arguments against the death penalty include these:

- No hard evidence proves that the death penalty is a deterrent.
- It is wrong for a government to participate in the intentional killing of citizens.
- The death penalty is applied in a discriminatory fashion.
- Innocent people have been sentenced to death.
- Some methods of execution are inhumane, causing painful, lingering deaths.

WHAT SHOULD U.S. POLICY BE?

With more and more people now being sentenced to death row but fewer than 70 executions every year since 2003 and only 35 in 2014, death penalty policy faces a significant crossroads. Will the United States increase the pace of executions, allow the number of capital offenders in prison to keep growing, or increasingly emphasize sentences of life imprisonment without parole for convicted murderers?

DEBATE THE ISSUE

Can the United States create a system to eliminate the problem of innocent people being sentenced to death? List two improvements to the death penalty process that could reduce erroneous convictions. If these improvements work, will it eliminate the risk of erroneous convictions? Should we be willing to take the risk of convicting a few innocent people in order to make sure that many guilty murderers are executed? List two arguments for each side of this final question. Which side is more persuasive?

Bobby O'Lee Phillips is escorted by deputies outside the Covington County Courthouse in Alabama after being sentenced to death for committing a murder after he had escaped from jail. Why might a judge or jury believe that capital punishment is appropriate in this case?

AP Images/Andrew Garner

WHAT AMERICANS THINK

QUESTION: "If you could choose between the following two approaches, which do you think is the better penalty for murder—the death penalty or life imprisonment with absolutely no possibility of parole?"

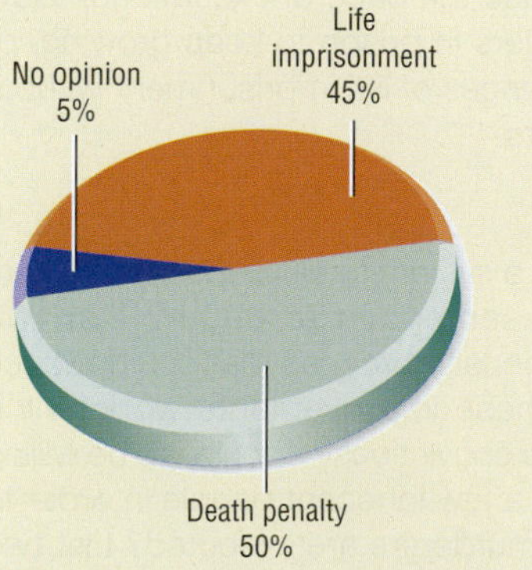

Source: Jeffrey M. Jones, "Americans' Support for Death Penalty Stable," Gallup Poll , October 23, 2014. Reprinted by permission of Gallup Organization.

Concerns about the conviction of innocent people may lead some other states to reconsider the use of capital punishment. Simultaneously, the extraordinary costs of capital trials and appeals are likely to deter many states from seeking to use the punishment widely in murder cases. Because the costs of trials are typically placed on county government, small counties frequently cannot afford to seek the death penalty in murder cases as these trials can last for weeks and require the services of expensive scientific testing and expert witnesses. On the other hand, a future terrorist attack on the United States may intensify public support for capital punishment and spur efforts to expand the penalty. Thus it remains to be seen whether the nation will continue to see diminishing use of the death penalty.

Although public opinion polls show that many Americans support the death penalty, only 72 new death sentences were imposed in 2014, a number that was down from the 126 new death sentences imposed as recently as 2007. In addition, the number of executions remains low, declining from 52 in 2009 to 35 in 2014 (Death Penalty Information Center, 2015). As indicated in "What Americans Think," recent surveys show the public is divided when respondents are asked to choose between life imprisonment (without parole) and death. In addition, as shown in the survey presented earlier in "What Americans Think," one source of division is conflicting views about whether capital punishment is applied fairly (Saad, 2007). Debate on this important public policy issue has gone on for more than 200 years, yet there is still no consensus (J. D. Unnever, Cullen, and Bartkowski, 2006). Read the Close Up feature to examine the two sides to the debate.

The criminal sanction takes many forms, and offenders are punished in various ways to serve various purposes. Table 12.3 summarizes how these sanctions operate and how they reflect the underlying philosophies of punishment.

TABLE 12.3 THE PUNISHMENT OF OFFENDERS

The goals of the criminal sanction are carried out in a variety of ways, depending upon the provisions of the law, the characteristics of the offender, and the discretion of the judge. Judges may impose sentences that combine several forms to achieve punishment objectives.

FORM OF SANCTION	DESCRIPTION	PURPOSES
Incarceration	Imprisonment	
Indeterminate sentence	Specifies a maximum and minimum length of time to be served	Incapacitation, deterrence, rehabilitation
Determinate sentence	Specifies a certain length of time to be served	Retribution, deterrence, incapacitation
Mandatory sentence	Specifies a minimum amount of time that must be served for given crimes	Incapacitation, deterrence.
Good time	Subtracts days from an inmate's sentence because of good behavior or participation in prison programs	Rewards behavior, relieves prison crowding, helps maintain prison discipline
Intermediate Sanctions	Punishment for those requiring sanctions more restrictive than probation but less restrictive than prison	Retribution, deterrence
Administered by the judiciary		
Fine	Money paid to state by offender	Retribution, deterrence
Restitution	Money paid to victim by offender	Retribution, deterrence
Forfeiture	Seizure by the state of property illegally obtained or acquired with resources illegally obtained	Retribution, deterrence
Administered in the community		
Community service	Requires offender to perform work for the community	Retribution, deterrence
Home confinement	Requires offender to stay in home during certain times	Retribution, deterrence, incapacitation
Intensive probation supervision	Requires strict and frequent reporting to probation officer	Retribution, deterrence, incapacitation
Administered institutionally		
Boot camp/shock incarceration	Short-term institutional sentence emphasizing physical development and discipline, followed by probation	Retribution, deterrence, rehabilitation
Probation	Allows offender to serve a sentence in the community under supervision	Retribution, incapacitation, rehabilitation
Death	Execution	Incapacitation, deterrence, retribution

✔POINT

3. What are the three types of sentences used in the United States?

4. What are thought to be the advantages of intermediate sanctions?

5. What requirements specified in *Gregg v. Georgia* must exist before a death sentence can be imposed?

STOP AND ANALYZE: Take the fundamental purposes of punishment and apply them to the types of punishments used in the United States—intermediate sanctions, incarceration, and death. List one or two primary purposes of punishment that are fulfilled by each type of punishment. Are there any purposes that do not appear to be fulfilled by any of the types of punishments?

The Sentencing Process

Regardless of how and where the decision has been made—misdemeanor court or felony court, plea bargain or adversarial context, bench or jury trial—judges carry the responsibility for imposing sentences.

Often difficult, sentencing usually involves more than applying clear-cut principles to individual cases. In one case, a judge may decide to sentence a forger to prison as an example to others, even though the offender represents no threat to community safety and probably does not need rehabilitative treatment. In another case, the judge may impose a light sentence on a youthful offender who has committed a serious crime but may be a good risk for rehabilitation if moved quickly back into society. Sentencing requires balancing the scales of justice between a violated society and the fallible human being who committed a crime.

Legislatures establish the penal codes that set forth the sentences judges can impose. These laws generally give judges discretion in sentencing. However, there may be specific requirements that can tie the hands of judges for specific crimes or offenders. As mentioned previously concerning mandatory minimums, legislatures may specify required sentences for certain crimes. In particular, some legislatures, including Congress, have mandated specific added time periods in prison for crimes committed with firearms. In effect, these sentencing laws appear to have both deterrent and incapacitative objectives with respect to the use of guns for criminal purposes.

In many states, judges have significant discretion in determining sentences for convicted offenders. Judges may combine various forms of punishment in order to tailor the sanction to the offender. The judge may specify, for example, that the prison terms for two charges are to run either concurrently (at the same time) or consecutively (one after the other), or that all or part of the period of imprisonment may be suspended. In other situations, the offender may be given a combination of a suspended prison term, probation, and a fine. The judge may also suspend a sentence as long as the offender stays out of trouble, makes restitution, or seeks medical treatment. Finally, the judge may delay imposing any sentence but retain the power to set penalties at a later date if the offender misbehaves. Read the New Directions in Criminal Justice Policy feature to see how evidence-based practices can be applied to sentencing.

NEW DIRECTIONS IN CRIMINAL JUSTICE POLICY

EVIDENCE-BASED SENTENCING

The Center for Sentencing Initiatives of the National Center for State Courts advocates that states consider implementing evidence-based sentencing practices. The purpose of evidence-based sentencing (EBS) is to reduce recidivism. When criminal punishments are designed with consideration for the goal of reducing reoffending, states may benefit from both a reduction in crime and a potential reduction in the costs associated with sending convicted offenders to prison. The use of EBS is not intended to determine the appropriate severity of punishments for specific offenses. Instead, it is an approach designed to provide useful information to judges so that they can evaluate potential supervision and treatment conditions that may help to reduce the risk that the offender will commit future crimes.

As described by the Center for Sentencing Initiatives, evidence-based sentencing relies on the Risk-Need-Responsivity (RNR) model for the identification of important principles to reduce recidivism. The first principle, *Risk*, posits that treatment and supervision should be tailored to the risk posed by the offenders, with higher-risk offenders requiring more significant supervision and services. The second principle, *Need*, holds that treatments should be designed to address the specific factors that may contribute to the risk that a specific individual will reoffend. The third principle, *Responsivity*, concerns the recognition that individuals will have differing characteristics, education levels, and abilities, thereby requiring consideration of the specific teaching, learning, and treatment approaches that will be effective for each individual.

The risk element is evaluated through assessment tools, including interview questions and evaluation of documents, which gather information about each offender concerning "static factors" that cannot be changed through treatment, such as criminal history and age at first offense. In addition, information is compiled about "dynamic risk factors," such as antisocial attitudes, that can potentially be changed through appropriate treatment and services. Judges can incorporate this information when considering punishment decisions. If a sentencing goal is to reduce the risk of offender recidivism, assessment tools can determine viable intermediate sanctions and services for those

Within the discretion allowed by the code, various elements influence the decisions of judges (B. D. Johnson, 2006). Social scientists believe that several factors influence the sentencing process: (1) the administrative context of the courts, (2) the attitudes and values of judges, (3) the presentence report, and (4) sentencing guidelines.

The Administrative Context of the Courts

Judges are strongly influenced by the administrative context within which they impose sentences (B. D. Johnson, 2005). As a result, differences appear, for example, between the assembly-line style of justice in the misdemeanor courts and the more formal proceedings found in felony courts.

Misdemeanor Courts: Assembly-Line Justice

Misdemeanor or lower courts have limited jurisdiction, because they normally can only impose jail sentences of less than one year. These courts hear about 90 percent of criminal cases. Whereas felony cases are processed in lower courts only for arraignments and preliminary hearings, misdemeanor cases are processed completely in the lower courts. Only a minority of cases adjudicated in lower courts end in jail sentences. Most cases result in fines, probation, community service, restitution, or a combination of these punishments.

Because most lower courts are overloaded, they allot minimal time to each case. Judicial decisions are mass-produced, because actors in the system share three assumptions. First, any person appearing before the court is guilty, because doubtful cases have presumably been filtered out by the police and prosecution. Second, the vast majority of defendants will plead guilty. Third, those charged with minor offenses will be processed in volume, with dozens of cases being decided in rapid succession within a single hour. The citation will be

offenders who do not require incarceration based on severity of offense or threat to public safety.

Advocates of EBS note that additional elements and practices must be in place in order to use risk-related information at sentencing to attempt to reduce reoffending. For example, judges, probation officers, prosecutors, and defense attorneys need training in order to cooperate and coordinate their focus on the prospects for the offender to change his or her behavior. In addition, EBS needs to integrate services and sanctions with a recognition that supervision alone, without treatment and services, will have limited prospects for successfully altering behavior beyond the period of the sanction. Judges also need to be role models who use court hearings to encourage offenders to develop personal motivation to change. When judges are perceived by offenders to be caring, polite, and encouraging, the sentencing and supervision process can reduce the risks of resistance and hostile attitudes that may be produced when judges threaten, lecture, and shame offenders.

Sources: *Arming the Courts with Research: 10 Evidence-Based Sentencing Initiatives to Control Crime and Reduce Costs,* Public Safety Policy Brief No. 8, May 2009, Pew Center on the States; Pamela M. Casey, Roger K. Warren, and Jennifer K. Elek, *Using Offender Risk and Needs Assessment Information at Sentencing: Guidance for Courts from a National Working Group,* National Center for State Courts, 2011; Center for Sentencing Initiatives, *NCSC Fact Sheet: Evidence-Based Sentencing,* National Center for State Courts, August 2014; Roger K. Warren, "Evidence-Based Sentencing: The Application of Principles of Evidence-Based Practice to State Sentencing Practice and Policy," *University of San Francisco Law Review* 43 (2009): 585–634.

DEBATE THE ISSUE

Evidence-based sentencing reflects an effort to incorporate a rehabilitative focus into the design of criminal sanctions. Is this an appropriate job for judges? Do judges know enough about the causes of criminal behavior to accurately apply information from the EBS process to their attempts to tailor an appropriate sanction that will simultaneously punish and reduce the risk of reoffending? If you were the governor of a state, would you recommend that new laws require judges to use EBS? Give three reasons for the decision you would make as a governor.

read by the clerk, a guilty plea entered, and the sentence pronounced by the judge for one defendant after another.

Defendants whose cases are processed through the lower court's assembly line may appear to receive little or no punishment. However, people who get caught in the criminal justice system experience other punishments, whether or not they are ultimately convicted. A person who is arrested, but then released at some point in the process, still incurs various tangible and intangible costs. Time spent in jail awaiting trial, the cost of a bail bond, and days of work lost create an immediate and concrete impact. Poor people may lose their jobs or be evicted from their homes if lost wages keep them from paying rent and other bills. For most people, simply being arrested is a devastating experience. Measuring the psychological and social price of being stigmatized, separated from family, and deprived of freedom is impossible.

The sentencing practices of misdemeanor courts drew national attention when the U.S. Department of Justice issued a report in 2015 on practices in Ferguson, Missouri, that reflected racial bias and favoritism. Read the Inside Today's Controversies feature to evaluate the problems illuminated by the Justice Department report.

INSIDE TODAY'S CONTROVERSIES

THE U.S. DEPARTMENT OF JUSTICE'S INVESTIGATION OF THE FERGUSON, MISSOURI, MUNICIPAL COURT

The public anger and protests in Ferguson, Missouri, after the fatal shooting of unarmed teenager Michael Brown by Officer Darren Wilson in 2014 did not merely reflect objections to the incident and the failure to charge Wilson with a crime. The protests also flowed from long-standing complaints about unfair treatment of African Americans in Ferguson by police officers and the municipal court. In response to the national attention of the resultant civil disorder in Ferguson, the U.S. Department of Justice launched two investigations. One investigation found that federal prosecutors lacked a basis to charge Wilson with a federal crime for any provable racial motive or clear denial of Brown's rights. The other investigation looked more broadly at police and court practices in Ferguson. The second investigation resulted in a scathing report that documented frequently used police practices that violated citizens' rights with unjustified stops, searches, arrests, and applications of force. This second investigation also found that the municipal court worked with the police department to intentionally use municipal code citations, fines, and jailing as mechanisms to improperly produce revenue to fund city government. While Americans typically expect judges and courts to be guardians of the law in order to advance equal justice, the Justice Department report painted a picture of a court operation that appeared to disregard principles of law in order to advance the interests of city officials.

- Statistics showed that Ferguson police officers primarily targeted African American residents for traffic and other citations, often with the intent of writing as many tickets as possible in a single traffic stop. African Americans comprise 67 percent of the population, but received 90 percent of the citations and were subject to 93 percent of the arrests. As a result, court officials could impose burdensome fines that multiplied and increased as poor people, in particular, had difficulty paying on time. For example, one woman "received two parking tickets for a single violation in 2007 that totaled $151 plus fees. Over seven years later, she still owed Ferguson $541—after already paying $550 in fines and fees, having multiple arrest warrants issued against her, and being arrested and jailed on several occasions" (U.S. Department of Justice, 2015).
- City officials specifically communicated to the police department their desire to increase city revenue through issuing more citations.
- While the municipal court lacked the legal authority to impose a fine over $1,000 for any offense, it was not common for individuals who were unable to pay their fines on time to end up paying for more than $1,000 to the city in additional court fees, further citations for failure to appear in court, and forfeited bail payments.
- The federal report found that the municipal court failed to give individuals adequate notice of allegations against them and an opportunity to be heard. When citizens and their attorneys attempted to present arguments in court against the basis for their treatment by the police and the citations issued, they reportedly faced retaliation from the judge and the prosecutor. In one example, an attorney was repeatedly interrupted by the judge during trial and was threatened with being jailed for contempt of court for daring to object to the judge's interruptions, thus stopping the attorney from thoroughly questioning a police officer who had been found to be untruthful in a prior case.
- There were reportedly needlessly complicated court processes that provided opportunities for court officials to increase the number of fines imposed on individuals: "We

AP Images/Dan Joling

In misdemeanor cases, judges' sentencing decisions may be influenced by many factors, including the defendant's remorse, the availability of space in the county jail, and the defendant's prior record. Many offenders are sentenced to probation, fines, and community service. Is it important for judges to impose comparable sentences on offenders who committed similar crimes?

have heard repeated reports, and found evidence in court records, of people appearing in court many times—in some instances on more than ten occasions—to try to resolve a case but being unable to do so and subsequently having additional fines, fees, and arrest warrants issued against them" (U.S. Department of Justice, 2015). Moreover, police officers frequently gave people incorrect dates and times for their court appearances, thus leading to the risk of additional fines even when the citizens followed the officers' instructions.

- Ferguson imposed exceptionally high fines for offenses as compared to the fines imposed for the same offenses in nearby St. Louis suburbs. For example, Ferguson fined people $375 for failing to show proof of auto insurance while the median fine for this offense in nearby communities was $175.
- The Ferguson court issued an extraordinary number of arrest warrants as a means to secure payment for fines rather than to protect public safety: over 9,000 warrants issued in fiscal year 2013 in a community with a population of 21,000 people. In addition, bail amounts set for people to gain release from jail were haphazard and inconsistent with the city's own policies. People arrested for failure to pay minor municipal fines were routinely held in jail for three days and could be rearrested and held again when they were unable to pay.
- A city council member complained that a part-time municipal judge "does not listen to testimony, does not review the reports or the criminal history of defendants, and doesn't let all the pertinent witnesses testify before rendering a verdict." However, the city manager retained the judge by emphasizing his role in collecting money for the city. According to the city manager, "the city cannot afford to lose any efficiency in our courts, nor experience any decrease in fines and forfeitures" (Yokley and Eligon, 2015).
- As the courts were imposing unfair hardships on poor African Americans in order to fund city government, court officials fixed tickets for city officials so that they would not have to pay the fines being imposed on other members of the community. In addition, a newspaper investigation found that the part-time judge deeply involved in fining and jailing the defendants, who were overwhelmingly African Americans, for their failure to pay increasingly accumulating fines for municipal offenses, was himself behind in paying his federal income taxes. He owed the federal government a reported $170,000—but unlike his treatment of poor people who owed a few hundred dollars to Ferguson, he was not subject to the same arrests and jailing that he helped to impose on others.

Sources: Harry Bruinius, "Does Ferguson Run 'Debtor's Prison'? Lawsuit Targets a Source of Unrest," *Christian Science Monitor,* February 9, 2014 (www.csmonitor.com); John Eligon, "Ferguson City Manager Cited in Justice Department Report Resigns," *New York Times*, March 10, 2015 (www.nytimes.com); Campbell Robertson, "A City Where Policing, Discrimination and Raising Revenue Went Hand in Hand," *New York Times,* March 4, 2015 (www.nytimes.com); Jon Swaine, "Ferguson Judge behind Aggressive Fines Policy Resigns as City's Court System Seized," *Guardian,* March 9, 2015 (www.theguardian.com); U.S. Department of Justice, *Investigation of Ferguson Police Department*, Civil Rights Division, U.S. Department of Justice, March 4, 2015; Eli Yokley and John Eligon, "Missouri Court Assigns a State Judge to Handle Ferguson Cases," *New York Times,* March 9, 2015 (www.nytimes.com).

CRITICAL THINKING AND ANALYSIS

Critics argued that Ferguson, Missouri, created a "debtors' prison" environment that punished poor people for their inability to pay and constantly increased their financial burdens for minor offenses solely to generate money for city government. Write a memo that describes specific steps you would recommend to achieve fairness and equal justice by reforming the approach to policing and punishment taken by Ferguson, Missouri, police, prosecutors, and court officials.

Felony Courts

Felony cases are processed and offenders are sentenced in courts of general jurisdiction. Because of the seriousness of the crimes, the atmosphere is more formal and generally lacks the chaotic, assembly-line environment of misdemeanor courts. Caseload burdens can affect how much time individual cases receive. Exchange relationships among courtroom actors can facilitate plea bargains and shape the content of prosecutors' sentencing recommendations. Sentencing decisions are ultimately shaped, in part, by the relationships, negotiations, and agreements among the prosecutor, defense attorney, and judge (Haynes, Ruback, and Cusick, 2010). Table 12.4 shows the types of felony sentences imposed for different kinds of offenses.

Attitudes and Values of Judges

All lawyers recognize that judges differ from one another in their sentencing decisions. Administrative pressures, the influence of community values, and the conflicting goals of criminal justice partly explain these differences. Sentencing decisions also depend on judges' attitudes concerning the offender's blameworthiness, the protection of the community, and the practical implications of the sentence (Steffensmeier and Demuth, 2001). See the "Question of Ethics" feature at the end of the chapter to ask yourself how you might formulate a sentence in a controversial case.

Blameworthiness concerns such factors as offense severity (such as violent crime or property crime), the offender's criminal history (such as recidivist or first timer), and role in commission of the crime (such as leader or follower) (Bushway and Piehl, 2007). For example, a judge might impose a harsh sentence on a repeat offender who organized others to commit a serious crime.

TABLE 12.4 TYPES OF FELONY SENTENCES IMPOSED BY STATE COURTS

Although a felony conviction is often equated with a prison sentence, almost a third of felony offenders receive probation.

MOST-SERIOUS CONVICTION OFFENSE	PERCENTAGE OF FELONS SENTENCED TO		
	PRISON	JAIL	PROBATION
All offenses	41	28	27
Murder	93	2	2
Rape	72	15	10
Robbery	71	14	13
Burglary	49	24	24
Larceny	34	34	28
Drug possession	33	31	30
Drug trafficking	41	26	29
Weapons offenses	45	28	25

Note: For persons receiving a combination of sanctions, the sentence designation came from the most severe penalty imposed—prison being the most severe, followed by jail, and then probation. Rows do not add up to 100 percent because a small percentage of offenders for each crime were sentenced to other nonincarceration sanctions.

Source: Sean Rosenmerkel, Matthew R. Durose, and Donald Farole Jr., "Felony Sentences in State Courts, 2006: Statistical Tables," Bureau of Justice Statistics *Statistical Tables,* December 2009, p. 4.

Similar factors, such as dangerousness, recidivism, and offense severity, influence protection of the community. However, protection focuses mostly on the need to incapacitate the offender or deter would-be offenders.

Finally, the practical implications of a sentence can affect judges' decisions. For example, judges may take into account the offender's ability to "do time," as in the case of an elderly person. They may also consider the impact on the offender's family; a mother with children may receive a different sentence than a single woman would. Finally, costs to the corrections system may play a role in sentencing, as judges consider the number of probation officers or prison crowding (Steffensmeier, Kramer, and Streifel, 1993).

Presentence Report

Even though sentencing is the judge's responsibility, the **presentence report** has become an important ingredient in the judicial mix. Usually a probation officer investigates the convicted person's background, criminal record, job status, and mental condition to suggest a sentence that is in the interests of both the offender and society. Although the presentence report serves primarily to help the judge select the sentence, it also assists in the classification of probationers, prisoners, and parolees for treatment planning and risk assessment. In the report, the probation officer makes judgments about what information to include and what conclusions to draw from that information. In some states, however, probation officers present only factual material to the judge and make no sentencing recommendation. Because the probation officers do not necessarily follow evidentiary rules, they may include hearsay statements as well as firsthand information.

presentence report
A report, prepared by a probation officer, that presents a convicted offender's background and is used by the judge in selecting an appropriate sentence.

Although presentence reports are represented as diagnostic evaluations, critics point out that they are not scientific and often reflect stereotypes. John Rosencrance has argued that in actual practice the presentence report primarily serves to maintain the myth of individualized justice. He found that the present offense and the prior criminal record determine the probation officer's final sentencing recommendation (Rosencrance, 1988). He learned that officers begin by reviewing the case and typing the defendant as one who should fit into a particular sentencing category. They then conduct their investigations in ways that help them gather information to reinforce their early decision.

In the federal court system, the presentence report is supplemented by an additional written report by a *pretrial services officer* (*PSO*). This report focuses on the defendant's behavior and compliance with conditions while out on bail—prior to trial or plea or between the date of conviction and the date of sentencing.

The presentence report is one means by which judges ease the strain of decision making. The report lets judges shift partial responsibility to the probation department. Because they can choose from a substantial number of sentencing alternatives, judges often rely on the report for guidance.

Sentencing Guidelines

Since the 1980s, **sentencing guidelines** have been established in the federal courts and in nearly two dozen state court systems. Such guidelines indicate to judges the expected sanction for particular types of offenses. They are intended to limit the sentencing discretion of judges and to reduce disparity among sentences given for similar offenses (T. Griffin and Wooldredge, 2006). Although statutes provide a variety of sentencing options for particular crimes, guidelines attempt to direct the judge to more-specific actions that should be

sentencing guidelines
A mechanism to indicate to judges the expected sanction for certain offenses, in order to reduce disparities in sentencing.

TABLE 12.5 MINNESOTA SENTENCING GUIDELINES GRID (PRESUMPTIVE SENTENCE LENGTH IN MONTHS)

The italicized numbers in the grid are the range within which a judge may sentence without the sentence being considered a departure. The criminal history score is computed by adding one point for each prior felony conviction, one-half point for each prior gross-misdemeanor conviction, and one-quarter point for each prior misdemeanor conviction.

LESS SERIOUS ⟵⟶ MORE SERIOUS

SEVERITY OF OFFENSE (ILLUSTRATIVE OFFENSES)		CRIMINAL HISTORY SCORE 0	1	2	3	4	5	6 or more
Murder, second degree (intentional murder, drive-by shootings)	XI	306 *261–367*	326 *278–391*	346 *295–415*	366 *312–439*	386 *329–463*	406 *346–480*	426 *363–480*
Murder, third degree *Murder, second degree (unintentional murder)*	X	150 *128–180*	165 *141–198*	180 *153–216*	195 *166–234*	210 *179–252*	225 *192–270*	240 *204–288*
Assault, first degree *Controlled substance crime, first degree*	IX	86 *74–103*	98 *84–117*	110 *94–132*	122 *104–146*	134 *114–160*	146 *125–175*	158 *135–189*
Aggravated robbery, first degree *Controlled substance crime, second degree*	VIII	48 *41–57*	58 *50–69*	68 *58–81*	78 *67–93*	88 *75–105*	98 *84–117*	108 *92–129*
Felony DWI	VII	36	42	48	54 *46–64*	60 *51–72*	66 *57–79*	72 *62–84*
Controlled substance crime, third degree	VI	21	27	33	39 *34–46*	45 *39–54*	51 *44–61*	57 *49–68*
Residential burglary *Simple robbery*	V	18	23	28	33 *29–39*	38 *33–45*	43 *37–51*	48 *41–57*
Nonresidential burglary	IV	12	15	18	21	24 *21–28*	27 *23–32*	30 *26–36*
Theft crimes (over $5,000)	III	12	13	15	17	19 *17–22*	21 *18–25*	23 *20–27*
Theft crimes ($5,000 or less) *Check forgery ($251–$2,500)*	II	12	12	13	15	17	19	21 *18–25*
Sale of simulated controlled substance	I	12	12	12	13	15	17	19 *17–22*

▭ At the discretion of the judge, up to a year in jail and/or other nonjail sanctions can be imposed instead of prison sentences as conditions of probation for most of these offenses. If prison is imposed, the presumptive sentence is the number of months shown.

▭ Presumptive commitment to state prison for all offenses.

Note: First-degree murder has a mandatory life sentence and is excluded from the guidelines by law.

Source: Minnesota Sentencing Guidelines Commission, *Minnesota Sentencing Guidelines and Commentary,* effective August 1, 2014.

taken. The range of sentencing options provided for most offenses is based on the seriousness of the crime and on the criminal history of the offender.

Legislatures—and, in some states and the federal government, commissions—construct sentencing guidelines as a grid of two scores (Tonry, 1993). As shown in Table 12.5, one dimension relates to the seriousness of the offense, and the other to the likelihood of offender recidivism. The offender score is obtained by totaling the points allocated to such factors as the number of juvenile, adult misdemeanor, and adult felony convictions; the number of times incarcerated; the status of the accused at the time of the last offense, whether on probation or parole or escaped from confinement; and employment status or educational achievement. Judges look at the grid to see what sentence a particular offender who has committed a specific offense should receive. Judges may go outside of the guidelines if aggravating or mitigating circumstances exist; however, they must provide a written explanation of their reasons for doing so (Fischman and Schanzenbach, 2011).

Sentencing guidelines are to be reviewed and modified periodically in order to include recent decisions. Given that guidelines are constructed on the basis of past sentences, some critics argue that because the guidelines reflect only what has happened, they do not reform sentencing. Others question the choice of characteristics included in the offender scale and charge that some are used to mask racial criteria. However, Lisa Stolzenberg and Stewart J. D'Alessio (1994) studied the Minnesota guidelines and found, compared with pre-guideline decisions, an 18 percent reduction in disparity for the prison/no-prison outcome and a 60 percent reduction in disparity of length of prison sentences.

One impact of guidelines is that sentencing discretion has shifted from the judge to the prosecutor. Prosecutors can choose the charge and plea bargain; therefore, defendants realize that to avoid the harsh sentences specified for some crimes (such as crack cocaine possession or operating a continuing criminal enterprise), they must plead guilty and cooperate. In fact, federal drug laws give prosecutors discretion to ask judges to give sentence reductions for offenders who have "provided substantial assistance in the investigation or prosecution of another person."

Although guidelines make sentences more uniform, many judges object to having their discretion limited in this manner (Zimmerman, 2011). However, Peter Rossi and Richard Berk (1997) found a fair amount of agreement between the sentences prescribed in the federal guidelines and those desired by the general public.

In 2004, the U.S. Supreme Court decided that aspects of Washington State's sentencing guidelines violated the Sixth Amendment right to trial by jury by giving judges too much authority to enhance sentences based on unproven factual determinations (*Blakely v. Washington*). One year later, the Supreme Court applied the *Blakely* precedent to the federal sentencing guidelines and found a similar violation of the Sixth Amendment when judges enhance sentences based on their own determinations (*United States v. Booker,* 2005). In effect, federal judges are expected to consult the guidelines, but the parameters are not mandatory, and federal judges can make reasonable deviations. Research has found some differences in sentencing under the guidelines when comparing specific district courts (Wu and Spohn, 2010). Yet most sentences in federal courts remain in conformity with the guidelines (U.S. Sentencing Commission, 2006). Observers anticipate that the U.S. Supreme Court will revisit this issue in order to provide direction as to how sentencing guidelines can properly affect—or not—judges' decisions. For example, in 2011 the Court determined that federal judges can consider evidence of an offender's rehabilitation in imposing a sentence that is below those specified in sentencing guidelines (*Pepper v. United States,* 2011).

✔POINT 6. What are the four factors thought to influence the sentencing behavior of judges?

STOP AND ANALYZE: Would it be desirable to have uniform mandatory sentences for each specific crime in order to reduce the influence of discretionary judgments—and potential biases—by individual decision makers in the process? List two arguments in favor of rigid mandatory sentences and two opposing arguments. Which side is most persuasive? What would be the impact of such mandatory sentences on the criminal justice system?

Who Gets the Harshest Punishment?

Harsh, unjust punishments can occur because of sentencing disparities and wrongful convictions. The prison population in most states contains a higher proportion of African American and Hispanic men than appears in the general population. Are these disparities caused by racial prejudices and discrimination, or are other factors at work? Wrongful conviction occurs when people who are in fact innocent are nonetheless found guilty by plea or verdict. Inaccurate results also occur when the conviction of a truly guilty person is overturned on appeal because of due process errors.

Racial Disparities

Research on racial disparities in sentencing is inconclusive. Studies of sentencing in Pennsylvania, for example, found that there was a "high cost of being black, young (21–29 years), and male." Sentences given these offenders resulted in a higher proportion going to prison and for longer terms (Steffensmeier, Ulmer, and Kramer, 1998: 789). Although supporting the Pennsylvania results, research in Chicago; Kansas City, Missouri; and Miami found variation among the jurisdictions as to sentence-length disparities (Spohn and Holleran, 2000). Other research shows disproportionate effects on African American men being sent to prison through mandatory punishments and sentence enhancements (Schlesinger, 2011).

Do these disparities stem from the prejudicial attitudes of judges, police officers, and prosecutors? Are African Americans and Hispanics viewed as a "racial threat" when they commit crimes of violence and drug selling—activities which are thought to be spreading from the urban ghetto to the "previously safe places of the suburbs" (Crawford, Chiricos, and Kleck, 1998: 484)? Are enforcement resources distributed so that certain groups are more closely scrutinized than others?

Scholars have pointed out that the relationship between race and sentencing is complex and that judges must consider many defendant and case characteristics. According to this view, judges assess not only the legally relevant factors of blameworthiness, dangerousness, and recidivism risk, but also race, gender, and age characteristics (Steen, Engen, and Gainey, 2005). The interconnectedness of these variables, not judges' negative attitudes, is what culminates in the disproportionately severe sentences given young black men.

Federal sentencing guidelines were adjusted in 2007 and 2008 to address a highly criticized source of racial disparities in prison sentences for offenders convicted of cocaine-related offenses. The federal sentencing guidelines for crack cocaine offenses—which disproportionately affected African American defendants—were adjusted to be more closely aligned with shorter sentences for possessing and selling similar amounts of powder cocaine, crimes more commonly associated with white offenders. The U.S. Sentencing Commission voted to apply these new guidelines retroactively, meaning that offenders currently serving long sentences for crack cocaine offenses were eligible to be resentenced to shorter terms in prisons, which in many cases began to lead to the release of offenders in 2008 who had already served for longer periods than those required under the new sentencing guidelines (Gezari, 2008; Third Branch, 2008b). In 2010, President Obama signed into law a new statute that reduced, but did not eliminate, the disparities in mandatory sentences for crack and powder cocaine offenders (Eckholm, 2010).

Wrongful Convictions

A serious dilemma for the criminal justice system concerns people who are falsely convicted and sentenced. Although the public expresses much concern over those who "beat the system" and go free, they pay comparatively little attention to those who are innocent, yet convicted. Such cases can be corrected by decisions of the courts or through pardon and clemency decisions by governors (state cases) or the president (federal cases) (Sarat, 2008). Professionals in the justice system are aware of the problem of erroneous convictions, but it can be difficult to prevent it or remedy it (Ramsey and Frank, 2007).

The development of DNA technology has increased the number of people convicted by juries and later exonerated by science. Ronald Huff notes that "because the great majority of cases do not produce biological material to be tested, one can only speculate about the error rate in those cases [without DNA evidence available]" (C. R. Huff, 2002: 2). As of May 2013, there were 306 innocent people who had been released from prison after DNA testing excluded them as perpetrators of the rapes and murders for which they had been convicted and imprisoned. Many of these cases are investigated by the Innocence Project at Cardozo Law School in New York City.

Many other exonerations were not based on DNA evidence but rather on the discovery that police and prosecutors had ignored or hidden evidence, or that the conviction was based on testimony from an untruthful informant. New cases continue to arise that raise questions about the actions of police and prosecutors in seeking to gain convictions without adequate concern for ensuring that the actually guilty individual is the one convicted. For example, in May 2013 the prosecutor in Brooklyn, New York, ordered a review of 50 murder cases investigated by a specific detective. As described in newspaper accounts of the probe, there were

> disturbing patterns, including the detective's reliance on the same eyewitness, a crack-addicted prostitute, for multiple murder prosecutions and his delivery of confessions from suspects who later said they had told him nothing (Robles and Kleinfield, 2013).

The investigation began when a man was freed from prison after serving 23 years for murder based on flawed police work by this particular detective (Robles and Kleinfield, 2013). Unlike the Brooklyn example, however, many prosecutors resist efforts to reexamine cases when questions have been raised concerning the quality of evidence used to obtain a conviction. In those cases,

AP Images/Jonathan Drew

The development of DNA evidence has contributed to the reinvestigation of cases and the release of innocent people who were wrongly confined in prisons for many years. In North Carolina, Joseph Sledge gained release in 2015 after serving 37 years for two murders he did not commit. DNA testing of preserved evidence helped to establish his innocence. How could we improve the justice processes to reduce the risks of erroneous convictions?

it often takes dogged determination by defense attorneys and scrutiny from the news media to create enough pressure to lead to new investigations.

Why do wrongful convictions occur? Eyewitness error, unethical conduct by police and prosecutors, community pressure, false accusations, inadequacy of counsel, and plea-bargaining pressures may all contribute to wrongful convictions (C. R. Huff, 2002). Ronald Huff has proposed a variety of reforms to reduce the likelihood of erroneous convictions. Some of these reforms, such as a state commission to investigate innocence claims, have been enacted by a few states.

Huff's (2002) policy recommendations include the following:

1. States should enact laws to compensate fairly those who are wrongly convicted.
2. When biological evidence is available for testing, defendants should be able to request and receive such tests. The results should be preserved.
3. When eyewitness identification is involved, the testimony of qualified experts and witnesses should be allowed and judges should give cautionary instructions to juries informing them of the possibility of misidentification.
4. No identification procedure (such as lineups) should be conducted without the presence of counsel for the suspect/accused.
5. Police interrogations of suspects should be recorded in full.
6. Criminal justice officials who engage in unethical or illegal conduct contributing to wrongful conviction should be removed from their position and subjected to appropriate sanctions.
7. Criminal case review commissions should be established to review postappellate claims of wrongful conviction and, when appropriate, refer those cases to the proper courts.

The first policy recommendation, compensation for wrongly convicted people, has only been enacted by 26 states, and their statutes vary about the amount of compensation. Florida, for example, pays $50,000 for each year of wrongful imprisonment up to a maximum of $2 million, whereas New Hampshire, by contrast, authorizes only a maximum of $20,000, no matter how long someone was wrongfully imprisoned (CNN, 2012b). There is no constitutional right to compensation. Indeed, in nearly half the states, there is no entitlement of any kind to compensation. In some cases, there may be a possibility of recovering money in a lawsuit, if it can be proven that the police violated an individual's rights. But such cases are not necessarily easy to prove. Moreover, wrongful convictions can be produced by errors instead of rights violations, thereby reducing any possibility for lawsuits.

Whether from racial discrimination or wrongful convictions, unjust punishments do not serve the ideals of justice. They raise fundamental questions about the criminal justice system and its links to the society it serves. Beyond the fact that the real criminal presumably remains free in such cases, the standards of our society are damaged when an innocent person has been convicted.

CHECKPOINT 7. What factors contribute to erroneous convictions?

STOP AND ANALYZE: If your son were arrested for a crime and you believed his claim that he was innocent, are there any steps you could take to reduce the likelihood that he would be subject to an erroneous conviction? Make a list of what you might do to help your son.

A QUESTION OF ETHICS

In February 2014, a national controversy arose when Judge Jean Boyd, a state court judge in Texas, imposed a sentence of ten years of probation on teenager Eric Couch who, as a 16-year-old, killed four people and seriously injured two others when driving while drunk. Couch pleaded guilty to charges of intoxication manslaughter. Prosecutors said Couch drove 70 miles-per-hour in a zone with a speed limit of 40. His blood alcohol level was three times the state limit of 0.08 when he lost control of his speeding truck and hit people changing a flat tire on a vehicle on the side of the road. One passenger in Couch's truck suffered severe brain injuries and can longer move or talk. In addition to the long probation sentence, Couch's family committed to paying for him to go to an in-patient facility for treatment and counseling. National news reporters focused on the case because a psychologist for the defense supported the case for a lenient sentence by saying that Couch suffered from "affluenza," a shorthand term for someone who is so wealthy and spoiled that he does not connect his actions with the likelihood of bad consequences. The victims' families were outraged that the sentence was, in their view, too light by not requiring the youth to serve time in prison.

By contrast, two years earlier Judge Boyd imposed a ten-year sentence on a 14-year-old boy who killed another youth with one punch when the victim fell and hit his head on the pavement. In that case, the defendant could be paroled after five years or be sent to an adult prison at age 19 to serve the final five years. Critics expressed concern that Boyd had imposed a more severe sentence on the 14-year-old, an African American youth who killed one person, than she did on a wealthy white teen who killed four people and seriously injured others.

Does this provide evidence of racial discrimination? Some observers noted that Boyd had sought to emphasize rehabilitation for both boys, but no treatment program would accept the boy who threw the punch. Thus he ended up in juvenile prison. By contrast, Couch's parents were so wealthy that they could afford to send him to a treatment facility in California that cost $450,000 per year per patient.

Wealth discrimination? Racial discrimination? Excessive leniency? Excessive emphasis on rehabilitation without proper concern for other objectives of punishment? These cases raise challenging questions about a judge's responsibilities in sentencing.

Sources: Molly Hennessey-Fiske, "Judge in 'Affluenza' Case Rules Out Jail Time for Teen Driver," *Los Angeles Times,* February 5, 2014 (www.latimes.com); Clare Kim, "Families of 'Affluenza' Teen's Victims Reach Settlements," MSNBC online, March 18, 2014 (www.msnbc.com); Christina Sterbenz, "Judge in 'Affluenza' Case Sentenced Black Teen to 10 Years for Killing a Guy with a Single Punch," *Business Insider,* December 20, 2013 (www.businessinsider.com); Gary Strauss, "No Jail for 'Affluenza' Teen in Fatal Crash Draws Outrage," *USA Today,* February 6, 2014 (www.usatoday.com).

CRITICAL THINKING AND ANALYSIS

Imagine that you were the judge in these two cases. Write a memo describing the sentence that you would impose in each case and the punishment objectives that you would pursue with these sentences. To what extent did your sentences reflect a concern or prediction about the teenagers' future lives after they complete their periods of confinement or probation?

Summary

1 Describe the goals of punishment

- In the United States, the four main goals of the criminal sanction are retribution, deterrence, incapacitation, and rehabilitation.
- Restoration, a new approach to punishment, has not become widespread yet.
- The goals of the criminal sanction are carried out through incarceration, intermediate sanctions, probation, and death.

2 Identify the types of sentences that judges can impose

- Penal codes vary as to whether the permitted sentences are indeterminate, determinate, or mandatory. Each type of sentence makes certain assumptions about the goals of the criminal sanction.
- Good time allows correctional administrators to reduce the sentence of prisoners who live according to the rules. Earned time may be awarded to those who participate in various vocational, educational, and treatment programs.
- The U.S. Supreme Court allows capital punishment only when the judge and jury are allowed to take into account mitigating and aggravating circumstances.
- Judges often have considerable discretion in fashioning sentences to take into account factors such as the seriousness of the crime, the offender's prior record, and mitigating and aggravating circumstances.

3 Discuss what really happens in sentencing

- The sentencing process is influenced by the administrative context of the courts, the attitudes and values of the judges, the presentence report, and sentencing guidelines.

4 Analyze whether the system treats wrongdoers equally

- Many states have formulated sentencing guidelines as a way of reducing disparity among the sentences given offenders in similar situations.
- Harsh, unjust punishments may result from racial discrimination or wrongful convictions.

Questions for Review

1. What are the major differences between retribution, deterrence, incapacitation, and rehabilitation?
2. What is the main purpose of restoration?
3. What are the forms of the criminal sanction?
4. What purposes do intermediate sanctions serve?
5. What has been the Supreme Court's position on the constitutionality of the death penalty?
6. Is there a link between sentences and social class? Between sentences and race?

Key Terms and Cases

determinate sentence (p. 489)
earned time (p. 493)
general deterrence (p. 482)
good time (p. 493)
incapacitation (p. 483)
indeterminate sentence (p. 489)
intermediate sanctions (p. 495)
justice reinvestment (p. 496)
mandatory sentence (p. 491)
presentence report (p. 513)
presumptive sentence (p. 491)
probation (p. 496)
rehabilitation (p. 484)
restoration (p. 485)
retribution (p. 481)
selective incapacitation (p. 484)
sentencing guidelines (p. 513)
shock probation (p. 496)
specific deterrence (p. 482)
Atkins v. Virginia (2002) (p. 500)
Baze v. Rees (2008) (p. 501)
Furman v. Georgia (1972) (p. 499)
Gregg v. Georgia (1976) (p. 499)
McCleskey v. Kemp (1987) (p. 500)
Ring v. Arizona (2002) (p. 501)
Roper v. Simmons (2005) (p. 500)
Witherspoon v. Illinois (1968) (p. 503)

Checkpoint Answers

1 What are the four primary goals of the criminal sanction?

✓ Retribution, deterrence, incapacitation, rehabilitation.

2 What are the difficulties in showing that a punishment acts as a deterrent?

✓ It is impossible to show who has been deterred from committing crimes; punishment isn't always certain; people act impulsively rather than rationally; people commit crimes while on drugs.

3 What are the three types of sentences used in the united States?

✓ Indeterminate, determinate, and mandatory sentences.

4 What are thought to be the advantages of intermediate sanctions?

✓ Intermediate sanctions give judges a greater range of sentencing alternatives, reduce prison populations, cost less than prison, and increase community security.

5 What requirements specified in ***Gregg v. Georgia*** must exist before a death sentence can be imposed?

✓ Judge and jury must be able to consider mitigating and aggravating circumstances, proceedings must be divided into a trial phase and a punishment phase, and there must be opportunities for appeal.

6 What are the four factors thought to influence the sentencing behavior of judges?

✓ The administrative context of the courts, the attitudes and values of judges, the presentence report, and sentencing guidelines

7 What factors contribute to erroneous convictions?

✓ Eyewitness error, unethical conduct by police and prosecutors, inadequate performance by defense attorneys, false accusations, plea bargaining pressures.

PART 4

CORRECTIONS

Throughout history the debate has continued about the most appropriate and effective ways to punish lawbreakers. Over time the corrections system has risen to peaks of excited reform, only to drop to valleys of despairing failure. In Part 4, we examine how the American system of criminal justice currently deals with offenders. The process of corrections is intended to penalize the individual found guilty, to impress upon others that violators of the law will be punished, to protect the community, and to rehabilitate and reintegrate the offender into law-abiding society.

Chapters 13 through 16 will discuss how various influences have structured the U.S. corrections system and how offenders are punished.

As these chapters unfold, recall the processes that have occurred before the sentence was imposed and how they are linked to the ways offenders are punished in the correctional portion of the criminal justice system.

CHAPTER FEATURES

- **New Directions in Criminal Justice Policy** Evidence-Based Practices, Jails, and Mental Illness
- **Close Up** Free Exercise of Religion Inside Prisons
- **Technology and Criminal Justice** Cell Phones in Prisons
- **Close Up** Behind Bars in North America and Europe

CHAPTER 13 Corrections

CHAPTER LEARNING OBJECTIVES

1. Describe how the American system of corrections has developed
2. Analyze the roles federal, state, and local governments play in corrections
3. Discuss the law of corrections and how it is applied to offenders and correctional personnel
4. Describe the direction of community corrections
5. Explain why the prison population has more than quadrupled over the last three decades

CHAPTER OUTLINE

Development of Corrections
- Invention of the Penitentiary
- Reform in the United States
- Reformatory Movement
- Improving Prison Conditions for Women
- Rehabilitation Model
- Community Model
- Crime Control Model

Organization of Corrections in the United States
- Federal Correctional System
- State Correctional Systems
- Private Prisons
- Incarcerated Immigrants

Jails: Detention and Short-Term Incarceration
- Origins and Evolution
- The Contemporary Jail
- Who Is in Jail?
- Managing Jails

The Law of Corrections
- Constitutional Rights of Prisoners
- Law and Community Corrections
- Law and Correctional Personnel

Correctional Policy Trends
- Community Corrections
- Incarceration

Brendan Mcdermid/Reuters/Landov

Throughout 2014 and 2015, horrifying stories appeared in newspapers about abusive practices at Rikers Island, New York City's massive jail for holding pretrial detainees and offenders serving short sentences. In January 2015, for example, six corrections officers were fired because, three years earlier, they hogtied and savagely beat an inmate being held in a cellblock for offenders with mental illness. Critics complained about a culture of silence among corrections officers as officers looked the other way when their colleagues committed acts of misconduct (Winerip, 2015). Prior to 2015, Rikers Island officers proven to have used excessive force seldom received any punishment worse than a brief suspension. However, by 2015, Rikers Island was under intense scrutiny because the U.S. Department of Justice issued a report in August 2014 documenting what it called "a culture of violence" in which teenage inmates, as well as adult offenders, were beaten by staff members. The report documented officers using radios, batons, broomsticks, and pepper spray, and slamming teens' heads into walls, resulting in skull fractures and other injuries. A *New York Times* investigation documented 129 cases of detainees and convicted offenders at Rikers Island suffering serious injuries at the hands of staff members (Weiser and Schwirtz, 2014; Winerip and Schwirtz, 2015).

In the New York state prison system, an extraordinary case also emerged in 2015, as three corrections officers at Attica prison were reportedly the first officers ever to face criminal charges for a nonsexual assault on a prisoner. As reported in news stories, they apparently mistook the prisoner for someone who had yelled an obscenity at officers. Witnesses reportedly described the prisoner as drenched in blood after absorbing fifty kicks and a dozen blows from a baton as prisoners two floors away could hear him scream and beg for his life (Robbins, 2015). Ultimately, as their trial was about to begin, the officers were permitted to resign from their jobs and plead guilty to a single misdemeanor count, thereby avoiding the risk of prison sentences if they were convicted at trial (Robbins and D'Avolio, 2015).

These examples from New York are not representative of the actions of corrections officers throughout the country. Large numbers of corrections officers do difficult jobs with a high degree of professionalism and a strong commitment to following proper rules and procedures. Moreover, shocking stories emerging from jails and prisons that hold the most difficult offenders obscure the fact that most convicted offenders are punished outside of these institutions through probation and intermediate sanctions in the community. However, by bringing these alarming examples to the forefront of public attention, these cases highlight important aspects of corrections. First and foremost, corrections is, in many respects, a world usually hidden away from public scrutiny and attention. Prisons and jails are typically closed institutions whose operations are not visible to outsiders. As a result, there are risks that improper actions can occur in corrections programs and facilities, especially when those actions remain hidden in closed institutions that employ officers and administrators who lack a complete commitment to professionalism. Thus, even in the second decade of the twenty-first century, examples appear with disappointing regularity of improper actions that many people associate with the first decades of the twentieth century and earlier, when people held in prisons and jails were unprotected by law and constitutional rights.

Second, these cases help to remind us that corrections can be a difficult environment for offenders and employees alike. Depending on the correctional context, officials have only limited resources and overcrowded facilities for securely holding or supervising a wide array of defendants and offenders in a safe and appropriate manner. The challenges in corrections are compounded by the need to deal with people suffering from mental illness and drug abuse as well as those who can be angry and violent in reaction to close supervision and confinement under difficult conditions. There are risks that both offenders and corrections officers may "snap" and produce ugly confrontations as they try to live or work in tense or overcrowded conditions.

The foregoing issues present perpetual challenges for corrections. Yet, certain aspects of corrections are changing. A report issued in March 2013 revealed an important development in American corrections: The prison population declined for two years in a row (Pew Center on the States, 2013). This was extraordinary news because prison populations had increased steadily in a dramatic fashion for the preceding 30 years. This new development was especially significant because the size and expense of corrections systems had reached levels few people had imagined possible. Just a few years earlier, a report released by the Pew Center on the States in February 2008 showed that for the first time in history, 1 in 100 American adults were behind bars in prisons (1,596,127) and jails (723,000). The "one in 100" report brought home the fact of the country's tremendously large and then-expanding prison population (Warren, 2008: 3). The United States incarcerates a higher proportion of its population than any other country. China, a country with four times as many people as the United States, is the only country with a comparable number of people in prison (Walmsley, 2014). The United States has less than 5 percent of the world's population, but almost a quarter of the world's prisoners. Even with the recent decrease in prison population, the United States has approximately 35 times more prisoners than Canada while having only 10 times the population of its northern neighbor.

The foregoing developments raise important questions. In particular, why does this gap exist between American justice and that of the rest of the world? What factors led the United States to have large prison populations? Over the past 30 years the U.S. incarceration rate has quadrupled, even though nationwide, crime declined dramatically in the past two decades. While prison populations remain high, the violent crime rate in 2013 was less than half of what it had been in 1991 (BJS, 2015a). The prison populations increased due to the imposition of longer sentences on offenders, including nonviolent drug offenders who were imprisoned in large numbers. The United States uses imprisonment more frequently as a punishment and imposes longer sentences than those seen in other countries' justice systems. The increase in prison populations had significant financial consequences. The larger number of offenders incarcerated in prisons and jails increased the need for new prisons, resulting in a construction boom and increased employment of correctional officers. Correctional budgets climbed an average of 10 percent annually, and many states diverted money from education, welfare, and health programs to meet the soaring needs of corrections.

Today, we appear to be on the verge of a new historic moment as many states and the federal government take specific actions to change sentencing practices in ways that would send fewer people to prison (Hulse, 2015; A. Johnson, 2011; "Indiana's Answer," 2011). A significant factor in states' recent reconsideration of the use of lengthy prison sentences for drug offenders and other non-homicide offenses is the high financial cost of imprisonment at a moment when states face serious budget crises. Thus states are increasingly investing their corrections funds in programs that provide alternatives to incarceration, such as community programs, as well as programs to help offenders succeed in society after they are released from prison (Pew Center on the States, 2013).

Corrections refers to the great number of programs, services, facilities, and organizations responsible for the management of people accused or convicted of criminal offenses. In addition to prisons and jails, corrections includes probation, halfway houses, education and work release programs, parole supervision, counseling, and community service. Correctional programs operate in Salvation Army hostels, forest camps, medical clinics, and urban storefronts.

corrections
The variety of programs, services, facilities, and organizations responsible for the management of people who have been accused or convicted of criminal offenses.

Corrections is authorized by all levels of government, is administered by both public and private organizations, and costs the states $50 billion a year (Pew Center on the States, 2013). A total of nearly 7 million adults and juveniles receive correctional supervision by 750,000 administrators, psychologists, officers, counselors, social workers, and other professionals (L. E. Glaze and Kaeble, 2014). For those held in prisons and jails, the incarceration numbers are not spread evenly across American society. For some groups, the impact is startling. For example, while the incarceration rate per 100,000 for men ages 30 to 34 is 1,187, the rate for African American males in that age group is 6,746. Gender adds another dimension to the picture. Men are 10 times more likely to be in prison or jail, but the incarcerated female population is increasing at a brisker pace. For African American women in that age group, the incarceration rate is 277, while the rate for white women in those ages is 156. Growing older reduces criminal behavior. Although the incarceration rate for males ages 25 to 29 is 1,937 per 100,000, that rate drops to 679 for the 55 to 59 age group (E. Carson, 2014). As we will see later in Chapter 15, the demographic composition of incarcerated populations affects the nature of prisoner behavior, programmatic needs, and challenges facing corrections officials.

In introducing corrections systems, this chapter will examine (1) the history of corrections, (2) the organization of prisons and jails, (3) the context of jails, (4) the law of corrections, and (5) the policy trends in community corrections and incarceration.

Development of Corrections

How did corrections get where it is today? Why are offenders now placed on probation or incarcerated instead of whipped or burned, as in colonial times? Over the past 200 years, ideas about punishment have moved like a pendulum from far in one direction to far in another (Table 13.1). As we review the development of present-day policies, think about how future changes in society may lead to new forms of corrections.

Invention of the Penitentiary

Enlightenment
A movement, during the eighteenth century in England and France, in which concepts of liberalism, rationalism, equality, and individualism dominated social and political thinking.

The late eighteenth century stands out as a remarkable period. At that time, scholars and social reformers in Europe and America were rethinking the nature of society and the place of the individual in it. During the **Enlightenment**, as this period was known, philosophers and reformers challenged tradition with new ideas about the individual, about limitations on government, and about rationalism. As the main intellectual force behind the American Revolution, such thinking laid the foundation of American values. The Enlightenment also affected the new nation's views on law and criminal justice. Reformers began to raise questions about the nature of criminal behavior and the methods of punishment.

Prior to 1800, Americans copied Europeans in using physical punishment as the main criminal sanction. Flogging, branding, and maiming served as the primary methods of controlling deviance and maintaining public safety. For more-serious crimes, offenders were hanged on the gallows.

TABLE 13.1 HISTORY OF CORRECTIONS IN AMERICA

Note the extent to which correctional policies have shifted from one era to the next and are influenced by societal factors.

CORRECTIONAL MODEL						
COLONIAL (1600s–1790s)	PENITENTIARY (1790s–1860s)	REFORMATORY (1870s–1890s)	PROGRESSIVE (1890s–1930s)	MEDICAL (1930s–1960s)	COMMUNITY (1960s–1970s)	CRIME CONTROL (1970s–2000s)
Features						
Anglican Code	Separate confinement	Indeterminate sentences	Individual case approach	Rehabilitation as primary focus of incarceration	Reintegration into community	Determinate sentences
Capital and corporal punishment, fines	Reform of individual	Parole	Administrative discretion	Psychological testing and classification	Avoidance of incarceration	Mandatory sentences
	Power of isolation and labor	Classification by degree of individual reform	Broader probation and parole	Various types of treatment programs and institutions	Vocational and educational programs	Sentencing guidelines
	Penance	Rehabilitative programs	Juvenile courts			Risk management
	Disciplined routine	Separate treatment for juveniles				
	Punishment according to severity of crime					
Philosophical Basis						
Religious law	Enlightenment	National Prison Association	The Age of Reform	Biomedical science	Civil rights movement	Crime control
Doctrine of predestination	Declaration of Independence	Declaration of Principles	Positivist school	Psychiatry and psychology	Critique of prisons	Rising crime rates
	Human perfectibility and powers of reason	Crime as moral disease	Punishment according to needs of offender	Social work practice	Small is better	Political shift to the right
	Religious penitence	Criminals as "victims of social disorder"	Focus on the offender	Crime as signal of personal "distress" or "failure"		New punitive agenda
	Power of reformation		Crime as an urban, immigrant ghetto problem			
	Focus on the act					
	Healing power of suffering					

For example, in the state of New York about 20 percent of all crimes on the books were capital offenses. Criminals were regularly sentenced to death for picking pockets, burglary, robbery, and horse stealing (Rothman, 1971). Jails existed throughout the country, but they served only to hold people awaiting trial or to punish people unable to pay their debts. As in England, the American colonies maintained houses of correction, where offenders were sentenced to terms of "hard labor" as a means of turning them from crime (Hirsch, 1992).

With the spread of Enlightenment ideas during the late eighteenth century, such practices began to wane (Foucault, 1977). Before the French Revolution of 1789, European governments tried to control crime by making public spectacles out of punishments such as torture and hanging. They often branded criminals, literally marking their offense for all to see. They also put the dismembered bodies of capital offenders on public display. In the early nineteenth century, such practices were gradually replaced by "modern" penal systems that emphasized fitting the punishment to the individual offender. The new goal was not to inflict pain on the offender's body but to change the individual and set him or her on the right path.

Clearly, this constituted a major shift in policy. The change from physical (corporal) punishment to correction of the offender reflected new ideas about the causes of crime and the possibility of reforming behavior.

Many people promoted the reform of corrections, but John Howard (1726–1790), sheriff of Bedfordshire, England, was especially influential. His book, *The State of Prisons in England and Wales*, published in 1777, described his observations of the prisons he visited (Howard, 1777/1929). Among generally horrible conditions, the lack of discipline particularly concerned him.

Public response to the book resulted in Parliament's passing the Penitentiary Act of 1779, which called for the creation of a house of hard labor where offenders would be imprisoned for up to two years. The institution would be based on four principles:

1. A secure and sanitary building
2. Inspection to ensure that offenders followed the rules
3. Abolition of the fees charged offenders for their food
4. A reformatory regime

At night, prisoners were to be confined to individual cells. During the day, they were to work silently in common rooms. Prison life was to be strict and ordered. Influenced by his Quaker friends, Howard believed that the new institution should be a place of industry. More important, it should be a place that offered criminals opportunities for penitence (sorrow and shame for their wrongs) and repentance (willingness to change their ways). In short, the **penitentiary** served to punish and to reform.

penitentiary
An institution intended to punish criminals by isolating them from society and from one another so they can reflect on their past misdeeds, repent, and reform.

Howard's idea of the penitentiary was not implemented in England until 1842, which was 50 years after his death. Although England was slow to act, the United States applied Howard's ideas much more quickly.

✓POINT
1. What was the Enlightenment and how did it influence corrections?
2. What were the main goals of the penitentiary?

STOP AND ANALYZE: Why did American society shift from physical punishments to imprisonment? List two beliefs and values that could affect how we approach criminal punishment in the future.

(Answers are at the end of the chapter.)

Reform in the United States

From 1776 to around 1830, a new revolution occurred in the American idea of criminal punishment. Although based on the work of English reformers, the new correctional philosophy reflected many ideas expressed in the Declaration of Independence, including an optimistic view of human nature and of

Time Life Pictures/Mansell/The LIFE Images Collection/Getty Images

Until the early 1800s, Americans followed the European practice of relying on punishment that was physically painful, such as death, flogging, and branding. Would such punishments be appropriate today?

individual perfectibility. Emphasis shifted from the assumption that deviance was part of human nature to a belief that crime resulted from environmental forces. The new nation's humane and optimistic ideas focused on reforming the criminal.

In the first decades of the nineteenth century, the creation of penitentiaries in Pennsylvania and New York attracted the attention of legislators in other states, as well as investigators from Europe. Even travelers from abroad with no special interest in corrections made it a point to include a penitentiary on their itinerary, much as they planned visits to a southern plantation, a textile mill, or a frontier town. By the mid-1800s, the U.S. penitentiary had become world famous.

AP Images/Rick Bowmer/Pool

Traditionally, women's prisons lacked the education and technical job training programs offered inside men's prisons. Instead, women were trained for sewing, typing, cooking, and other skills reflecting a limited view of women's roles in society. Should prisons for men and women today be identical, or are there reasons to have differences in facilities and programs?

The Pennsylvania System

Several groups in the United States dedicated themselves to reforming the institutions and practices of criminal punishment. One of these groups was the Philadelphia Society for Alleviating the Miseries of Public Prisons, formed in 1787. This group, which included many Quakers, was inspired by Howard's ideas. They argued that criminals could best be reformed if they were placed in penitentiaries—isolated from one another and from society to consider their crimes, repent, and reform.

In 1790, the Pennsylvania legislature authorized the construction of two penitentiaries for the solitary confinement of "hardened and atrocious offenders." The first, created out of an existing three-story stone structure in Philadelphia, was the Walnut Street Jail. This 25-by-40-foot building had eight dark cells, each measuring 6 by 8 by 9 feet, on each floor. An outside yard was attached to the building.

Only one inmate occupied each cell, and no communications of any kind were allowed. From a small, grated window high on the outside wall, prisoners "could perceive neither heaven nor earth."

separate confinement
A penitentiary system, developed in Pennsylvania, in which each inmate was held in isolation from other inmates. All activities, including craft work, took place in the cells.

From this limited beginning, the Pennsylvania system of **separate confinement** evolved. It was based on five principles:

1. Prisoners would not be treated vengefully but should be convinced that through hard and selective forms of suffering they could change their lives.
2. Solitary confinement would prevent further corruption inside prison.
3. In isolation, offenders would reflect on their transgressions and repent.
4. Solitary confinement would be punishment because humans are by nature social animals.
5. Solitary confinement would be economical, because prisoners would not need long periods of time to repent, and so fewer keepers would be needed and the costs of clothing would be lower.

The opening of the Eastern Penitentiary near Philadelphia in 1829 culminated 42 years of reform activity by the Philadelphia Society. On

October 25, 1829, the first prisoner, Charles Williams, arrived. He was an 18-year-old African American and had been sentenced to two years for larceny. He was assigned to a cell 12 by 8 by 10 feet with an individual exercise yard 18 feet long. In the cell was a fold-up steel bed, a simple toilet, a wooden stool, a workbench, and eating utensils. Light came from an 8-inch window in the ceiling. Solitary labor, Bible reading, and reflection were the keys to the moral rehabilitation that was supposed to occur within the penitentiary. Although the cell was larger than most in use today, it was the only world the prisoner would see throughout the entire sentence. The only other human voice heard would be that of a clergyman who would visit on Sundays. Nothing was to distract the penitent prisoner from the path toward reform.

In the years between Walnut Street and Eastern, other states had adopted aspects of the Pennsylvania system. Separate confinement was introduced by Maryland in 1809, by Massachusetts in 1811, by New Jersey in 1820, and by Maine in 1823.

Within five years of its opening, Eastern endured the first of several outside investigations. The reports detailed the extent to which the goal of separate confinement was not fully observed, physical punishments were used to maintain discipline, and prisoners suffered mental breakdowns from isolation. Separate confinement had declined at Eastern by the 1860s, when crowding required doubling up in each cell, yet it was not abolished in Pennsylvania until 1913 (Teeters and Shearer, 1957).

The New York System

In 1819, New York opened a penitentiary in Auburn that evolved as a rival to Pennsylvania's concept of separate confinement. Under New York's **congregate system**, prisoners were held in isolation at night but worked with other prisoners in shops during the day. They worked under a rule of silence and were even forbidden to exchange glances while on the job or at meals.

congregate system
A penitentiary system, developed in Auburn, New York, in which each inmate was held in isolation during the night but worked and ate with other prisoners during the day under a rule of silence.

Auburn's warden, Elam Lynds, was convinced that convicts were incorrigible and that industrial efficiency should be the overriding purpose of the prison. He instituted a regime of discipline and obedience that included the lockstep and the wearing of prison stripes. He also started a **contract labor system**. By the 1840s, Auburn was producing footwear, barrels, carpets, harnesses, furniture, and clothing.

contract labor system
A system under which inmates' labor was sold on a contractual basis to private employers who provided the machinery and raw materials with which inmates made saleable products in the institution.

Seeing the New York approach as a great advance, American reformers copied it throughout the Northeast (see Figure 13.1). Advocates said that the inmate production of goods for sale would cover the operating costs. At an 1826 meeting of prison reformers in Boston, the New York system was described in glowing terms:

> At Auburn, we have a more beautiful example still, of what may be done by proper discipline, in a prison well constructed. . . . The unremitted industry, the entire subordination, and subdued feeling among the convicts have probably no parallel among any equal number of convicts. In their solitary cells, they spend the night with no other book than the Bible, and at sunrise they proceed in military order, under the eye of the turnkey in solid columns, with the lock march to the workshops. (Goldfarb and Singer, 1973: 30)

During this period, advocates of the Pennsylvania and New York plans debated on public platforms and in the nation's periodicals. Advocates of both systems agreed that the prisoner must be isolated from society and placed on a disciplined routine. They believed that criminality was a result of corruption pervading the community and that the family and the church did not sufficiently counterbalance. Only when offenders were removed from the

FIGURE 13.1 EARLY PRISONS IN THE UNITED STATES

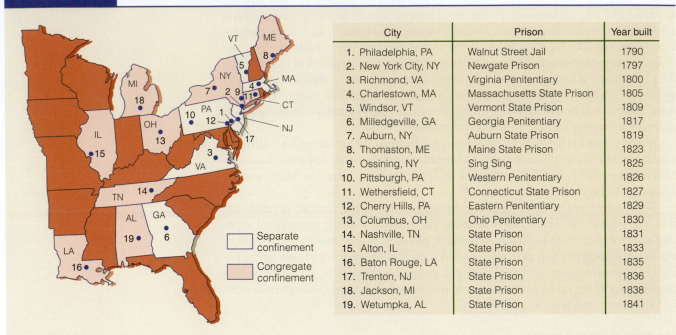

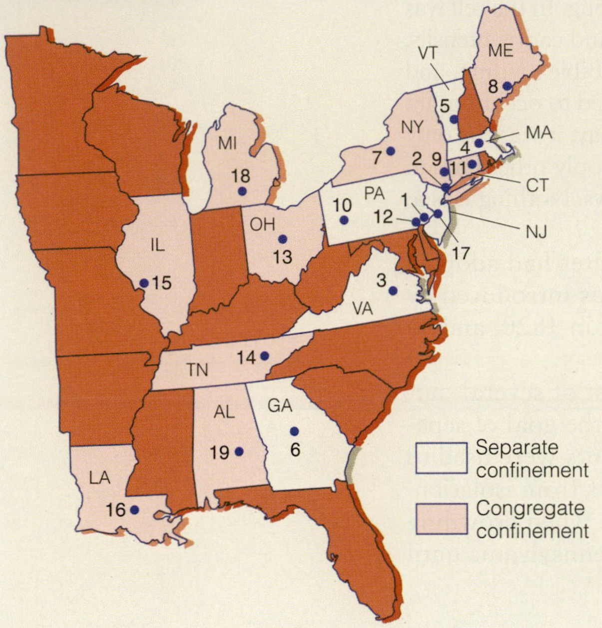

City	Prison	Year built
1. Philadelphia, PA	Walnut Street Jail	1790
2. New York City, NY	Newgate Prison	1797
3. Richmond, VA	Virginia Penitentiary	1800
4. Charlestown, MA	Massachusetts State Prison	1805
5. Windsor, VT	Vermont State Prison	1809
6. Milledgeville, GA	Georgia Penitentiary	1817
7. Auburn, NY	Auburn State Prison	1819
8. Thomaston, ME	Maine State Prison	1823
9. Ossining, NY	Sing Sing	1825
10. Pittsburgh, PA	Western Penitentiary	1826
11. Wethersfield, CT	Connecticut State Prison	1827
12. Cherry Hills, PA	Eastern Penitentiary	1829
13. Columbus, OH	Ohio Penitentiary	1830
14. Nashville, TN	State Prison	1831
15. Alton, IL	State Prison	1833
16. Baton Rouge, LA	State Prison	1835
17. Trenton, NJ	State Prison	1836
18. Jackson, MI	State Prison	1838
19. Wetumpka, AL	State Prison	1841

Source: Adapted from data by Norman Johnston, *Forms of Constraint: A History of Prison Architecture* (Urbana: University of Illinois, 2000).

temptations and influences of society and kept in a silent, disciplined environment could they reflect on their sins and offenses and become useful citizens. The convicts were not inherently depraved; rather, they were victims of a society that had not protected them from vice. While offenders were being punished, they would become penitent and motivated to place themselves on the right path. See Table 13.2 for a comparison of the Pennsylvania and New York systems.

Prisons in the South and West

Scholars tend to emphasize the nineteenth-century reforms in the populous Northeast, neglecting penal developments in the South and the West. Prisons, some following the penitentiary model, were built in four southern states—Georgia, Kentucky, Maryland, and Virginia—before 1817. Later prisons, such as the ones in Jackson, Mississippi (1842), and Huntsville, Texas (1848), were built on the Auburn model. But further expansion ended with the Civil War. With the exception of San Quentin (1852), the sparse population of the West

TABLE 13.2 COMPARISON OF PENNSYLVANIA AND NEW YORK (AUBURN) PENITENTIARY SYSTEMS

	GOAL	IMPLEMENTATION	METHOD	ACTIVITY
Pennsylvania (separate system)	Redemption of the offender through the well-ordered routine of the prison	Isolation, penance, contemplation, labor, silence	Inmates kept in their cells for eating, sleeping, and working	Bible reading, work on crafts in cell
New York (Auburn) (congregate system)	Redemption of the offender through the well-ordered routine of the prison	Strict discipline, obedience, labor, silence	Inmates sleep in their cells but come together to eat and work	Work together in shops making goods to be sold by the state

did not lend itself to the construction of many prisons until the latter part of the nineteenth century.

After the Civil War, southerners began the task of rebuilding their communities and that region's primarily agricultural economy. They lacked funds to build prisons but faced an increasing population of offenders. This approach to corrections was used as a tool of oppression by falsely convicting innocent African Americans in order to maintain the supply of convict laborers (Friedman, 1993). To address their governments' need for revenue, southern states developed the **lease system**. Businesses in need of workers negotiated with the state for the labor (logging, agriculture, mining, railroad construction) and care of prisoners. Because these entrepreneurs had no ownership interest in the prisoners, they subjected the prisoners to worse abuses than they inflicted on slaves prior to the Civil War (Rotman, 1995). As described in Douglas Blackmon's Pulitzer Prize-winning book, *Slavery by Another Name: The Re-Enslavement of Black Americans from the Civil War to World War II* (2008), the corrections system was used, in effect, to perpetuate the enslavement of many African Americans for nearly 80 years after slavery was technically prohibited by the Constitution's Thirteenth Amendment in 1865. Aspects of this slavery were arguably worse, as evidenced by the horrific death rates for these convict-laborers, who died more frequently than slaves did prior to the Civil War. Before 1865, slave owners would lose their investments if their slaves died. By contrast, under this corrections system, they did not care how many of these African Americans prisoners were worked to death under the most dangerous and inhuman conditions. They could always rely on criminal justice officials to provide more slaves by convicting innocent African Americans of imaginary crimes. The prisoner death rate soared. For example, among the 285 prisoners sent to work on the Greenwood and Augusta Railroad between 1877 and 1880, 45 percent lost their lives under the brutal working conditions (Friedman, 1993). As described by historian Lawrence Friedman, "these were young black men in the prime of their lives. You can imagine what it would take, what cruelty, what conditions of work, to kill off almost half of them" (Friedman, 1993: 95).

lease system
A system under which inmates were leased to contractors who provided prisoners with food and clothing in exchange for their labor. In southern states the prisoners were used as agricultural, mining, logging, and construction laborers.

Settlement in the West was slow until the California gold rush of 1849. Except in California, the prison ideologies of the East did not greatly influence penology in the West. Prior to statehood, western prisoners were held in territorial facilities or federal military posts and prisons. Until Congress passed the Anticontract Law of 1887, restricting the employment of federal prisoners, leasing programs existed in California, Montana, Oregon, and Wyoming. In 1852 a lessee chose Point San Quentin and, using convict labor, built two prison buildings. In 1858, after reports of deaths, escapes, and brutal discipline, the state of California took over the facility. The Oregon territory had erected a log prison in the 1850s, but it was soon leased to a private company. On joining the Union in 1859, however, the state discontinued the lease system. In 1877 a state prison modeled on the Auburn plan was built, but with labor difficulties and an economic depression in the 1890s, it was turned over to a lessee in 1895 (McKelvey, 1977: 228).

Reformatory Movement

By the middle of the nineteenth century, reformers had become disillusioned with the penitentiary. Neither the Pennsylvania nor the New York systems or any of their imitators had achieved rehabilitation or deterrence. Most saw this failure as the result of poor administration rather than as a flawed idea. Within 40 years of being built, penitentiaries had become overcrowded, understaffed, and minimally financed. Discipline was lax, brutality was common, and administrators were viewed as corrupt. At Sing Sing Penitentiary in Ossining,

New York, for example, investigators in 1870 discovered "that dealers were publicly supplying prisoners with almost anything they could pay for" and that convicts were "playing all sorts of games, reading, scheming, trafficking" (Rothman, 1980: 18).

Cincinnati, 1870

The National Prison Association (the predecessor of today's American Correctional Association) and its 1870 meeting in Cincinnati embodied a new spirit of reform. In its famous Declaration of Principles, the association advocated a new design for penology: that prisons should operate according to a philosophy of inmate change, with reformation rewarded by release. Sentences of indeterminate length would replace fixed sentences, and proof of reformation—rather than mere lapse of time—would be required for a prisoner's release. Classification of prisoners on the basis of character and improvement would encourage the reformation program. Penitentiary practices that had evolved during the first half of the nineteenth century—fixed sentences, the lockstep, rules of silence, and isolation—were now seen as debasing and humiliating and as destroying inmates' initiative.

Elmira Reformatory

reformatory
An institution for young offenders, emphasizing training, a mark system of classification, indeterminate sentences, and parole.

The first **reformatory** took shape in 1876 at Elmira, New York, when Zebulon Brockway was appointed superintendent. Brockway believed that diagnosis and treatment were the keys to reform and rehabilitation. He questioned each new inmate in order to explore the social, biological, psychological, and "root cause(s)" of the offender's deviance. An individualized treatment program of work and education was then prescribed. Inmates adhered to a rigid schedule of work during the day, followed by courses in academic, vocational, and moral subjects during the evening. Inmates who did well achieved early release.

mark system
A system in which offenders receive a certain number of points at the time of sentencing, based on the severity of their crime. Prisoners can reduce their term and gain release by earning marks to reduce these points through labor, good behavior, and educational achievement.

Designed for first-time felons aged 16–30, the approach at Elmira incorporated a **mark system** of classification, indeterminate sentences, and parole. Each offender entered the institution at grade 2, and if he earned nine marks a month for six months by working hard, completing school assignments, and causing no problems, he could be moved up to grade 1—necessary for release. If he failed to cooperate and violated the rules, he would be demoted to grade 3. Only after three months of satisfactory behavior could he resume on the path toward eventual release. In sum, this system placed "the prisoner's fate, as far as possible, in his own hands" (Pisciotta, 1994: 20).

By 1900 the reformatory movement had spread throughout the nation. However, by the outbreak of World War I in 1914, it was already in decline. In most institutions the architecture, the attitudes of the guards, and the emphasis on discipline differed little from those of the past. Too often, the educational and rehabilitative efforts took a back seat to the traditional emphasis on punishment. Nonetheless, the reformatory movement contributed the indeterminate sentence, rehabilitative programs, and parole. The Cincinnati Declaration of Principles and the reformatory movement set goals that inspired prison activists well into the twentieth century.

✔POINT

3. How did the Pennsylvania and New York systems differ?
4. What was the significance of the Cincinnati Declaration of Principles?

STOP AND ANALYZE: What were the differences between the Pennsylvania, New York, and southern systems and the later Elmira approach? In light of your understanding of human nature, the causes of crime, and the purposes of punishment, which one took the most appropriate approach to imprisonment? Give two reasons for your answer.

Improving Prison Conditions for Women

Until the beginning of the nineteenth century, female offenders in Europe and North America were treated no differently than men and were not separated from them when they were incarcerated. Only with John Howard's 1777 exposé of prison conditions in England and the development of the penitentiary in Philadelphia did attention begin to focus on the plight of the female offender. Among the English reformers, Elizabeth Gurney Fry, a middle-class Quaker, was the first person to press for changes. When she and other Quakers visited London's Newgate Prison in 1813, they were shocked by the conditions in which the female prisoners and their children were living (Zedner, 1995: 333).

News of Fry's efforts spread to the United States. The Women's Prison Association was formed in New York in 1844 with the goal of improving the treatment of female prisoners and separating them from men. Elizabeth Farnham, head matron of the women's wing at Sing Sing from 1844 to 1848, implemented Fry's ideas until male overseers and legislators thwarted her and she was forced to resign.

The Cincinnati Declaration of Principles did not address the problems of female offenders. It only endorsed the creation of separate treatment-oriented prisons for women. Although the House of Shelter, a reformatory for women, was created in Detroit following the Civil War, not until 1873 did the first independent female-run prison open in Indiana. Within the next 50 years, 13 other states had followed this lead.

Three principles guided female-prison reform during this period: (1) the separation of female prisoners from men, (2) the provision of care in keeping with the needs of women, and (3) the management of women's prisons by female staff. "Operated by and for women, female reformatories were decidedly 'feminine' institutions" (Rafter, 1983: 147).

As time passed, the original ideas of the reformers faltered. In 1927 the first federal prison for women opened in Alderson, West Virginia, with Mary Belle Harris as warden. Yet, by 1935 the women's reformatory movement had "run its course, having largely achieved its objective (establishment of separate prisons run by women)" (Rafter, 1983: 165).

✔POINT 5. What principles guided the reform of corrections for women in the nineteenth century?

STOP AND ANALYZE: Should the approach to corrections for women offenders differ from the approach to corrections for men, or should they be treated in identical fashion? Give two arguments in favor of each side of this debate. Which side's arguments are most persuasive?

Rehabilitation Model

In the first two decades of the twentieth century, reformers known as the Progressives attacked the excesses of big business and urban society and advocated government actions against the problems of slums, vice, and crime. The Progressives urged that knowledge from the social and behavioral sciences should replace religious and traditional moral wisdom as the guiding ideas of criminal rehabilitation. They pursued two main strategies: (1) improving conditions in social environments that seemed to be the breeding grounds of crime and (2) rehabilitating individual offenders. By the 1920s, probation, indeterminate sentences, presentence reports, parole, and treatment programs were being promoted as a more scientific approach to criminality.

rehabilitation model
A model of corrections that emphasizes the need to restore a convicted offender to a constructive place in society through some form of vocational or educational training or therapy.

medical model
A model of corrections based on the assumption that criminal behavior is caused by biological or psychological conditions that require treatment.

community corrections
A model of corrections based on the goal of reintegrating the offender into the community.

Although the Progressives were instrumental in advancing the new penal ideas, not until the 1930s did reformers attempt to implement fully what became known as the **rehabilitation model** of corrections. Taking advantage of the new prestige of the social sciences, penologists helped shift the emphasis of corrections. The new approach saw the social, intellectual, or biological deficiencies of criminals as the causes of their crimes. Because most states had in place the essential elements of parole, probation, and the indeterminate sentence, incorporating the rehabilitation model meant adding classification systems to diagnose offenders and treatment programs to rehabilitate them.

Because penologists likened the new correctional methods to those used by physicians in hospitals, this approach was often referred to as the **medical model**. Correctional institutions were to be staffed with people who could diagnose the causes of an individual's criminal behavior, prescribe a treatment program, and determine when the offender was cured and could be safely released to the community.

Following World War II, rehabilitation won new followers. Group therapy, behavior modification, counseling, and several other approaches became part of the "new penology." Yet even during the 1950s, when the medical model was at its height, only a small proportion of state correctional budgets went toward rehabilitation. What frustrated many reformers was that, even while states adopted the rhetoric of the rehabilitation model, custody remained the overriding goal of most institutions in their actual practices.

Because the rehabilitation model failed to achieve its goals, it became discredited in the 1970s. According to critics of rehabilitation, its reportedly high recidivism rates prove its ineffectiveness. Probably the most thorough analysis of research data from treatment programs was undertaken by Robert Martinson. Using rigorous standards, he surveyed 231 studies of rehabilitation programs, including counseling, group therapy, medical treatment, and educational and vocational training. Martinson summarized his findings by saying, "With few and isolated exceptions, the rehabilitative efforts that have been reported so far have had no appreciable effect on recidivism" (Martinson, 1974: 25). The report had an immediate impact on legislators and policy makers, who took up the cry that "Nothing Works!" As a result of dissatisfaction with the rehabilitation model, new reforms emerged.

Community Model

The social and political values of particular periods have long influenced correctional goals. During the 1960s and early 1970s, U.S. society experienced the civil rights movement, the war on poverty, and resistance to the war in Vietnam. People challenged the conventional ways of government. In 1967, the President's Commission on Law Enforcement and the Administration of Justice (1967: 4) argued that the purpose of corrections should be to reintegrate the offender into the community.

Under this model of **community corrections**, the goal of corrections was to reintegrate the offender into the community. Proponents viewed prisons as artificial institutions that hindered offenders from finding a crime-free lifestyle. They argued that corrections should focus on increasing opportunities for offenders to be successful citizens and on providing psychological treatment. Programs were supposed to help offenders find jobs and remain connected to their families and the community. Imprisonment was to be avoided, if possible, in favor of probation, so that offenders could seek education and vocational training that would help their adjustment. The small proportion of offenders who had to be incarcerated would spend a minimal amount of time in prison before release on parole. To promote reintegration, correctional workers were to serve as advocates for offenders in dealing with government agencies providing employment counseling, medical treatment, and financial assistance.

The community model dominated until the late 1970s. It gave way to a new punitiveness in criminal justice, in conjunction with the rebirth of the determinate sentence. Advocates of reintegration claim, as did advocates of previous reforms, that the idea was never adequately tested. Nevertheless, community corrections remains one of the significant ideas and practices in the recent history of corrections.

Crime Control Model

As the political climate changed in the 1970s and 1980s, and with the crime rate at historic levels, legislators, judges, and officials responded with an emphasis on crime control through incarceration and risk containment. The critique of rehabilitation led to changes in the sentencing structures in more than half the states and the abolition of parole release in many.

Compared with the community model, this **crime control model of corrections** is more punitive and makes greater use of incarceration (especially for violent offenders and career criminals), longer sentences, mandatory sentences, and strict supervision of probationers and parolees.

crime control model of corrections
A model of corrections based on the assumption that criminal behavior can be controlled by more use of incarceration and other forms of strict supervision.

The effect of these get-tough policies is demonstrated by the record number of people incarcerated, the greater amount of time being served, the great number of parolees returned to prison, and the huge size of the probation population. Some advocates point to the crime control policies as the reason for the fall of the crime rate. Others ask whether the crime control policies have really made a difference, considering the smaller number of men in the crime-prone age group and other changes in U.S. society that may have actually reduced the crime rate.

The history of corrections in America reflects a series of swings from one model to another. During this early part of the twenty-first century, the time may be ripe for another look at correctional policy. The language now used in criminal justice journals differs markedly from that found in their pages 30 years ago. The optimism that once suffused corrections has waned. The financial and human costs of the retributive crime control policies of the 1990s are now being scrutinized. Are the costs of incarceration and surveillance justified? Has crime been reduced? Is society safer today than it was, say, 25 years ago? Many researchers think not. Looking to the future, will there be a new direction for corrections? If so, what will be its focus?

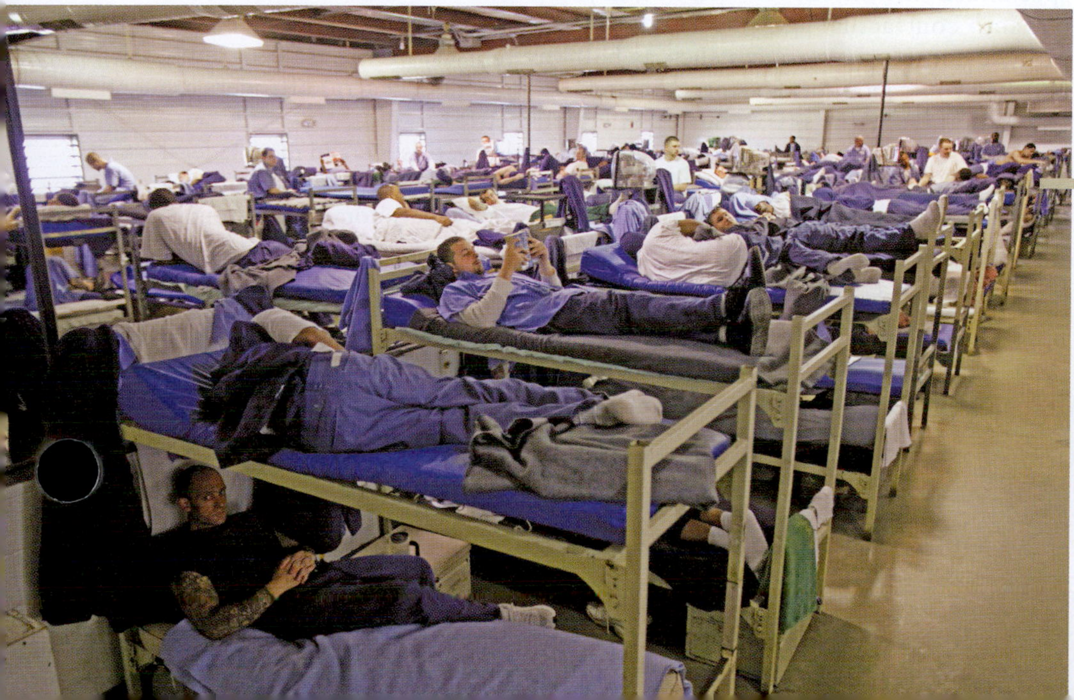

AP Images/Kiichiro Sato

In 2011, the U.S. Supreme Court endorsed a lower court's order that mandated a reduction in California's prison population. Offenders in other states' prisons live under similarly crowded conditions. These conditions cause problems for security, order, and the provision of medical services. How should society address the issue of prison overcrowding?

POINT 6. What are the underlying assumptions of the rehabilitation, community, and crime control models of corrections?

STOP AND ANALYZE: Do you foresee the current state-budget crises affecting the states' future approach to corrections? Which of these three approaches is most likely to be emphasized in the future? Give two reasons for your answer.

Organization of Corrections in the United States

The organization of corrections in the United States is fragmented. Each level of government has some responsibility for corrections. The federal government, the 50 states, over 3,047 counties, and uncounted municipalities and public and private organizations administer corrections at an annual cost in excess of $50 billion (Pew Center on the States, 2013). State and local governments pay about 90 percent of the cost of all correctional activities in the nation.

Federal Correctional System

The correctional responsibilities of the federal government are divided between the Department of Justice, which operates prisons through the Federal Bureau of Prisons, and the Administrative Office of the United States Courts, which covers probation and parole supervision.

Federal Bureau of Prisons

The Federal Bureau of Prisons, created by Congress in 1930, now operates a system of prisons located throughout the nation and is responsible for supervision of over 209,000 inmates, supervised by a staff of more than 38,000. Approximately 82 percent of federal offenders are in facilities run by the Bureau of Prisons, but the others are in privately run or community-based facilities (U.S. Bureau of Prisons, 2015). Facilities and inmates are classified by security level, ranging from Level 1 (the least secure, camp-type settings, such as the Federal Prison Camp at Tyndall, Florida) through Level 5 (the most secure, such as the "supermax" penitentiary at Florence, Colorado). Between these extremes are Levels 2 through 4 federal correctional institutions—other U.S. penitentiaries, administrative institutions, medical facilities, and specialized institutions for women and juveniles. The Bureau of Prisons enters into contractual agreements with states, cities, and private agencies to provide community services such as halfway houses, prerelease programs, and electronic monitoring. Approximately 18 percent of federal offenders are placed in these settings (U.S. Bureau of Prisons, 2015).

Because of the jurisdiction of federal criminal law, prisoners in most federal facilities differ from those in state institutions. Federal prisoners are often a more sophisticated type of criminal, from a higher socioeconomic background, who have committed crimes of extortion, mail fraud, bank robbery, and arson. But since the beginning of the war on drugs in the 1980s, the number of drug offenders has increased and now makes up about 49 percent of the federal inmate population. There is a lower percentage of violent offenders in federal prisons than in most state institutions. Interestingly, about 24 percent of federal prisoners are citizens of other countries (U.S. Bureau of Prisons, 2015).

Federal Probation and Parole Supervision

The Federal Probation and Pretrial Services System, a branch of the Administrative Office of the U.S. Courts, provides probation and parole supervision for federal offenders. The federal judiciary appoints probation officers, who serve the court. The first full-time federal probation officer was appointed in 1927; today nearly 4,000 are assigned to the judicial districts across the country. They assist with presentence investigations but are primarily involved in supervising those on probation and offenders released either on parole or mandatory release. Their average caseload is 70 people.

The Pretrial Services Act of 1982 required pretrial services to be established in each federal judicial district. These services are performed either by probation officers or independently in a separate office of pretrial services. The responsibilities of pretrial services officers are to "collect, verify, and report to the judicial officer information pertaining to the pretrial release of each person charged with an offense" (Administrative Office of the U.S. Courts, 1993).

State Correctional Systems

Although states vary considerably in how they organize corrections, in all states the administration of prisons falls under the executive branch of state government. This point is important, because probation is often part of the judiciary; parole may be separate from corrections; and in most states, jails are run by county governments. The differences can be seen in the proportion of correctional employees who work for the state. In Connecticut, Rhode Island, and Vermont, for example, 100 percent are state employees, compared with 47 percent in California. The remaining 53 percent in California work for county or municipal governments.

Community Corrections

Probation, intermediate sanctions, and parole are the three major ways that offenders are punished in the community. States vary in how they carry out these punishments. In many states, probation and intermediate sanctions are administered by the judiciary, often by county and municipal governments. By contrast, parole is a function of state government. The decision to release an offender from prison is made by the state parole board in those states with discretionary release. Parole boards are a part of either the department of corrections or an independent agency. In states with a mandatory system, the department of corrections makes the release. In all states, a state agency supervises the parolees.

Central to the community corrections approach is a belief in the "least restrictive alternative," the idea that the criminal sanction should be applied only to the minimum extent necessary to meet the community's need for protection, the seriousness of the offense, and society's need for offenders to get their deserved punishment. To this end, probation and parole services are geared to assist and reintegrate the offender into the community.

State Prison Systems

A wide range of state correctional institutions and programs exists for adult felons, including prisons, reformatories, prison farms, forestry camps, and halfway houses. This variety does not exist for women because of the smaller female prisoner population.

States vary considerably in the number, size, type, and location of correctional facilities they have. Louisiana's state prison at Angola, for example, can hold 5,100, whereas specialized institutions house fewer than 100 inmates. Some states (such as New Hampshire) have centralized incarceration in a few institutions, and other states (such as California, New York, and Texas) have a wide mix of sizes and styles—secure institutions, diagnostic units, work camps, forestry centers, and prerelease centers. For example, Oklahoma has

17 correctional facilities, including 1 that is maximum security and 2 others with maximum-security wings. The state also runs 6 community corrections centers. There are also 15 community work centers and 4 private prisons (Oklahoma Department of Corrections, 2015).

State correctional institutions for men are usually classified by level of security: maximum, medium, and minimum. For example, the website of the Minnesota Department of Corrections (2015) characterizes its prisons' security levels as "Level 2-Minimum," "Level 3-Medium," "Level 4-Close," and "Level 5-Maximum." Only one Minnesota prison is classified as Level 5. Each of the other security levels has three institutions. Among the institutions in Minnesota, three have facilities designed to hold prisoners assigned to more than one security level. For example, the Minnesota prisons at Faribault and Lino Lakes have both Level 2 and Level 3 sections, while Stillwater has Level 2 and Level 4 facilities.

Forty states have created prisons that exceed maximum security. About 20,000 inmates are currently held in these supermax prisons. These institutions are designed to hold the most-disruptive, violent, and incorrigible offenders. California's Pelican Bay institution and Connecticut's Northern Correctional Facility are examples of prisons designed to hold the "toughest of the tough." In such institutions, inmates spend up to 23 hours a day in their cells. They are shackled whenever they are out of their cells—during recreation, showers, and telephone calls. All of these measures are designed to send a message to other inmates (Reiter, 2012).

The maximum-security prison (holding about 21 percent of state inmates) is built like a fortress, usually surrounded by stone walls with guard towers, and designed to prevent escape. New facilities are surrounded by double rows of chain-link fences with rolls of razor wire in between and along the tops of the fences. Inmates live in cells, each with its own sanitary facilities. The barred doors may be operated electronically so that an officer can confine all prisoners to their cells with the flick of a switch. The purpose of the maximum-security facility is custody and discipline. It maintains a military-style approach to order, with prisoners following a strict routine. Some of the most famous prisons, such as Attica (New York), Folsom (California), Stateville (Illinois), and Yuma (Arizona) are maximum-security facilities.

The medium-security prison (holding 40 percent of state inmates) externally resembles the maximum-security prison, but it is organized somewhat differently and its atmosphere is less rigid. Prisoners have more privileges and contact with the outside world through visitors, mail, and access to radio and television. The medium-security prison usually places greater emphasis on work and rehabilitative programs. Although the inmates may have committed serious crimes, they are not perceived as hardened criminals.

The minimum-security prison (with 33 percent of state inmates) houses the least-violent offenders, long-term felons with clean disciplinary records, and inmates who have nearly completed their term. The minimum-security prison lacks the guard towers and stone walls associated with correctional institutions. Often, chain-link fencing surrounds the buildings. Prisoners usually live in dormitories or even in small private rooms rather than in barred cells. There is more personal freedom: Inmates may have television sets, choose their own clothes, and move about casually within the buildings. These prisons rely on rehabilitation programs and offer opportunities for education and work release. They also offer reintegration programs and support to inmates preparing for release.

In addition to the three types of institutions just described, a small percentage of state inmates are held in other settings, such as work camps and county jails. Sentenced offenders may remain in local jails while they await transfer to a state prison or when there are agreements between state correctional officials and county sheriffs in response to overcrowding in state prisons. For example, beginning in October 2011, newly sentenced California offenders serving for nonviolent, nonserious, nonsexual crimes were sentenced to three years or less in county jails; this is a change from the previous practice of sending all offenders serving more than one year to state prison (M. Santos, 2013; "California's Prison Realignment," 2011).

State Institutions for Women

Because only 7 percent of the prison population are women, there are relatively few women's facilities (L. E. Glaze and Kaeble, 2014). Although the ratio of arrests is approximately 6 men to 1 woman, the ratio of admissions to state correctional institutions is 18 men to 1 woman. A higher proportion of female defendants is sentenced to probation and intermediate punishments, partly as a result of male offenders' tendency to commit most of the violent crimes. However, the growth rate in number of incarcerated women has exceeded that for men in recent decades. From 2000 to 2013, the male population in state and federal prisons increased 12 percent, whereas that of women increased by 19 percent. (L. E. Glaze and Kaeble, 2014). This growth has been particularly acute in the federal system, which, because of the war on drugs, has had to absorb 6,000 female inmates over the past 20 years. The growth also varies by state—as, for example, Oklahoma incarcerates 10 times as many women per capita as Massachusetts and Rhode Island, largely due to punitive sentencing policies in drug cases (B. Palmer, 2011). The increased number of women in prison has significantly affected the delivery of programs, housing conditions, medical care, staffing, and security.

Female offenders are incarcerated in 98 institutions for women and 93 coed facilities (J. Stephan and Karberg, 2003). Conditions in correctional facilities for women can be more pleasant than those of similar institutions for men. Usually the buildings have no gun towers and barbed wire. Because of the small population, however, most states have only one facility, which is often located in a rural setting far removed from urban centers. Thus women prisoners may be more isolated than men from their families and communities. Pressure from women's organizations and the apparent rise in the incidence of crime committed by women may bring about a greater equality in corrections for men and women.

In the United States, the extensive corrections system affects many offenders and imposes significant financial costs on taxpayers.

As you think about the various kinds of correctional institutions, consider whether average citizens can make a contribution to advancing the goals of corrections. Is there a role for citizens in contributing to rehabilitation efforts or in preparing offenders for release? Read "Civic Engagement: Your Role in the System" as you think about this issue.

CIVIC ENGAGEMENT

YOUR ROLE IN THE SYSTEM

Imagine that you are a member of a fraternity, sorority, church group, or community service organization. You are approached by officials from your state's department of corrections about volunteering your time to work on a public service project in the corrections system. *Make a list of the kinds of contributions that volunteers may be able to make in the corrections system.* Then look at the programs for volunteers in the New Mexico Department of Corrections.

✓POINT

7. What agencies of the U.S. government are responsible for prisons and probation?
8. What agencies of state government are responsible for incarceration, probation, intermediate sanctions, and parole?

STOP AND ANALYZE: Corrections in the United States is extremely fragmented, with many different state systems in addition to the federal system. In light of the budget problems experienced by many states, should the country create a single, unified prison system in order to increase efficiency and save money? Give three reasons for your answer to that question.

Private Prisons

Corrections is a multibillion-dollar government-funded enterprise that purchases supplies and services from the private sector. Many jurisdictions have long contracted with private vendors to provide specific institutional services and to operate facilities and programs for offenders who are released from prison or who are sentenced to community based programs. Businesses furnish food and medical services, educational and vocational training, maintenance, security, and industrial programs. All of this has been referred to as "the corrections–commercial complex," which we discuss later in this chapter.

One response to prison and jail crowding and rising staff costs has come from private entrepreneurs who argue that they can build and run prisons at least as effectively, safely, and humanely as any level of government can, at a profit and at a lower cost to taxpayers. The management of entire institutions for adult felons under private contract was launched in the 1980s (Harding, 2001). Such privately run entities pose serious challenges for supervision and accountability as the government seeks to make sure that they are being run properly (Fathi, 2010).

By the end of 2013, there were 26 states and the federal system contracted to have offenders confined in private prisons. A total of 133,044 prisoners nationwide were housed in private institutions. This reflected a slight decline in the total number of prisoners in private facilities from the prior year (E. Carson, 2014). State budget cuts reduced opportunities for private prisons to make money by filling their cells with prisoners paid for by the government. Thus the Corrections Corporation of America, for example, had 11,600 unoccupied beds in its facilities (N. Cook, 2010).

In 2013, private facilities held 7 percent of all state prisoners and 21 percent of all federal prisoners. Among the states, Texas, with 14,538 inmates housed in private facilities, plus Florida, with 11,801, reported the largest number. Seven states had nearly 20 percent or more of their prison population housed in private prisons, led by New Mexico (43.6 percent), Montana (40.1 percent), Idaho (36.4 percent), Oklahoma (25.6 percent), Hawaii (25.2 percent), Vermont (24 percent), and Mississippi (20 percent). Other than Vermont, the only states

Private prisons are a source of controversy. There are questions about whether they actually save the taxpayers any money. They are opposed by corrections officers' unions because they often provide lower wages and fewer benefits for corrections workers. There is also a philosophical question at the heart of the issue: Should private companies be responsible for carrying out the government's detention and punishment functions?

AP Images/Seth Wenig

outside of the South and West that used private facilities for more than 6 percent of their prisoners were New Jersey (12.2 percent), Indiana (14.8 percent), and Ohio (10.6 percent) (E. Carson, 2014). In light of the American experience, interest in the private prison business has spread overseas to Australia, Great Britain, Brazil, and Denmark ("Private Jails: Locking in the Best Price," 2007).

In addition to inmates held for criminal offenses, 17 percent of the estimated 30,000 individuals detained by the Immigration and Customs Enforcement agency of the U.S. Department of Homeland Security are held in private facilities. The increased pressure to enforce immigration laws has been a financial boon to the private prison industry (Berestein, 2008).

The $1 billion per year private prison business is dominated by two companies—Corrections Corporation of America (CCA) and the GEO Group (formerly known as the Wackenhut Corrections Corporation). CCA now operates the fifth-largest correctional system in the United States. It manages 72,000 beds in 65 facilities in 19 states and the District of Columbia. This makes up half of all beds under contract. Today, because prison population reductions have left many states with excess capacity in their own prisons, the growth of the private prison industry has leveled off. However, the federal government will continue to rely on private facilities to detain people who entered the country in violation of immigration laws and are awaiting hearings and deportation.

Advocates of privately operated prisons claim that they provide the same level of care as the states but do so more cheaply and flexibly. Research on private prisons points to the difficulties of measuring the costs and quality of these institutions (R. A. Oppel, 2011; S. D. Camp and Gaes, 2002). One issue is that many of the "true costs" (fringe benefits, contracting supervision, federal grants) are not taken into consideration. A study of 48 juvenile correctional facilities found little difference between private and public facilities in terms of environmental quality (G. S. Armstrong and MacKenzie, 2003). The Bureau of Justice Statistics found that compared to private prisons, a greater proportion of state facilities provide access to work programs, education programs, and counseling programs; but the percentage of private correctional facilities providing education programs increased after the mid-1990s (J. Stephan and Karberg, 2003).

Supporters of privatization claim that they can run prisons more cheaply than the state. In 1996, the U.S. General Accounting Office issued a report comparing the costs of public and private prisons. After reviewing five separate studies, it could not determine whether privatization saved money (Xiong, 1997). Travis Pratt and Jeff Maahs reanalyzed the results of 24 studies and concluded that private prisons were no more cost-effective than public prisons (Pratt and Maahs, 1999). When savings can be shown, it appears that they are modest and result primarily from personnel-related costs (J. Austin and Coventry, 2001). In 2011, Arizona studied closely the costs of the private prisons that it utilized and found they saved only three cents per prisoner per day in minimum-security facilities, although the savings were more substantial in medium security. One of the ways that Arizona's private prisons saved money was by refusing to accept prisoners that needed expensive medical care—thus the state did not save any money on those prisoners. As one state legislator complained, "It's cherry picking. . . . They leave the most expensive prisoners with the taxpayers and take the easy prisoners" (R. A. Oppel, 2011). More-recent studies continue to raise questions about whether private prisons actually provide the benefits that supporters claim (Kish and Lipton, 2013; Genter, Hooks, and Mosher, 2013).

Political, fiscal, ethical, and administrative issues must be examined before corrections can become too heavily committed to the private ownership and operation of prisons. The political issues, including ethical questions concerning the delegation of social-control functions to people other than state employees, may be the most difficult to overcome (Sigler, 2010). Some people believe that the administration of justice is a basic function of government that should not be delegated. They fear that correctional policy would be skewed because contractors would use their political influence to continue programs not in the public interest. For example, in 2013 a newspaper's analysis of campaign contributions in Oklahoma found that private prison interests had contributed a total of nearly $200,000 in campaign dollars and gifts to 79 of the 149 members of the state legislature (Killman and Hoberock, 2013). Further, some observers fear that the private corporations will press to maintain high occupancy and will "skim off" the best inmates, leaving the most troublesome ones to the public corrections system.

Labor unions have opposed private prisons, pointing out that the salaries, benefits, and pensions of workers at these facilities are lower than those of their public counterparts. Finally, questions have arisen about quality of services, accountability of service providers to corrections officials, and problems related to contract supervision (Egan, 2014; Friess, 2014). Opponents cite the many instances in which privately contracted services in group homes, day-care centers, hospitals, and schools have been terminated because of reports of corruption, brutality, or substandard services. Research has shown that staff turnover as well as escapes and drug use by prisoners are problems in private prisons (S. D. Camp and Gaes, 2002). A number of state legislatures have enacted or are considering new laws to ensure that the private prison industry lives up to its contractual obligations. The idea of privately run correctional facilities has stimulated much interest among the general public and within the criminal justice community, but the future of this approach is quite uncertain. Ironically, despite the questions about the true costs and consequences of private prisons, budget-cutting governors who have a strong belief in the benefits of privatization continue to push for private prisons even without clear evidence of savings (R. A. Oppel, 2011). Read "A Question of Ethics" to consider problems raised by private prisons.

CHECKPOINT 9. What are the arguments in favor of or against privately run prisons?

STOP AND ANALYZE: Does a philosophical problem arise when convicted offenders are sent to privately run prisons? In criminal law, the government imposes punishment on people for breaking the laws made by government. Does this mean that only the government should administer the punishment? List two arguments either supporting or opposing the idea that all criminal punishment should be administered by government.

Incarcerated Immigrants

undocumented immigrants
Foreign-born noncitizens present in the United States without proper papers or approval for either entering the country or remaining beyond a specified date.

There has been an upsurge in the number of noncitizen immigrants in the United States during the past 20 years. The population of **undocumented immigrants** has been estimated at more than 12 million, whereas, since 2000, about 1 million immigrants per year have legally become residents. According to the U.S. Bureau of the Census 6.9 percent of the total U.S. population are noncitizens (Leonhardt, 2007).

Incarcerated immigrants present a complex jurisdictional and operational situation for corrections. Incarcerated immigrants may be classified into three categories.

1. *Undocumented immigrants.* Some noncitizens are detained by the U.S. Immigration and Customs Enforcement (ICE) branch of the Department

of Homeland Security because they have violated immigration laws and are subject to **deportation**. In 2012, a total of 429,000 noncitizens were held while awaiting immigration hearings or deportation. On any given day, approximately 34,000 noncitizens are in ICE custody at ICE facilities, private facilities, or local jails that are paid to detain undocumented immigrants. It costs the government $166 per day to hold each detainee (Childress, 2013; Koulish and Noferi, 2013).

deportation
Formal removal by the federal government of an undocumented immigrant or other noncitizen from the United States for violation of immigration and other laws.

2. *Sentenced undocumented immigrants*. Some undocumented immigrants have been sentenced to prisons and jails for criminal offenses. They must usually serve these sentences before they are handed over to ICE for deportation processing.
3. *Sentenced legal immigrants*. These are noncitizens who are legally in the United States and serving time for a criminal conviction. These people may also be subject to deportation upon completion of the sentence if the offense is serious, such as murder, rape, and drug trafficking, and makes the immigrant ineligible for citizenship.

Noncitizens sentenced for criminal offenses comprise notable portions of the corrections population for the federal prisons and the corrections systems of some states. An estimated 24 percent of sentenced offenders in the custody of the Federal Bureau of Prisons were noncitizens (U.S. Bureau of Prisons, 2015). At the state level, in Arizona for example, 12 percent of sentenced criminal offenders were noncitizens in April 2013 (Arizona Department of Corrections, 2013). However, the data reported by these corrections systems do not specify how many of these noncitizens were legal immigrants and how many were undocumented immigrants. Nationwide, there were more than 72,000 noncitizens serving sentences for crimes in state prisons (BJS, 2013a).

Immigrants in the custody of ICE are not convicted prisoners but are detainees held pursuant to civil immigration laws awaiting disposition of their cases by an administrative judge. According to the U.S. Court of Appeals of the Ninth Circuit (*Jones v. Blanas*, 2004) immigration detainees must be confined under conditions that are less restrictive than those under which criminal pretrial detainees or convicted prisoners are held. In November 2000, the formerly named Immigration and Naturalization Service released the *Detention Operations Manual*, which stipulates detention standards for all facilities holding detainees for more than 72 hours. It is anticipated that the federal government will seek to detain and deport increasing numbers of undocumented immigrants and, amid budget problems, will attempt to detain them as cheaply as possible (Kalhan, 2010). As a result, critics are very concerned that there will be inadequate provision of health care and other services (Hing, 2010), especially for those detainees whose cases are processed slowly and therefore end up with long-term confinement in facilities designed for short-term detentions (Heeren, 2010). Other problems have emerged with ICE detentions, including holding detainees in extended solitary confinement for violating rules, even though such confinement may be especially harmful to people affected by mental illness, and the mistaken detention of more than 800 U.S. citizens whom officials initially suspected might be noncitizens (Carcamo, 2013; Urbina and Rentz, 2013).

Immigrant prisoners present problems for correctional officials. In addition to language and cultural barriers, their deportation status may cause confusion. Questions arise as to the conditions under which detainees must be held when they are assigned to a non-ICE prison or jail. Second, it is generally assumed that undocumented-immigrant offenders must complete their criminal sentence before they enter the deportation process, but questions arise concerning their status as they appeal deportation. ICE has a Criminal Alien Program designed to ensure that criminal noncitizens incarcerated within federal, state, and local facilities are not released into the community before a final order of removal is obtained. (The government's program still uses the older term *alien* to refer to noncitizens within the United States.)

There is also a federal program in which participating jurisdictions can deputize local law enforcement officers to receive training and assist ICE in processing undocumented immigrants. The local officers investigate suspects, both on the street and those held in correctional facilities, whom they think are undocumented immigrants. These officers work with ICE to increase arrests and expedite the deportation process.

But cracks in this program have developed in Virginia's Prince William County. ICE agents are supposed to pick up suspected undocumented immigrants from the jail within 72 hours of their release from county custody. Instead, Prince William jail board chairman Patrick Hurd has said that some inmates are waiting as long as four weeks to be transferred, and the already crowded jail is spending $3 million a year in additional transportation and processing costs. Another factor driving up jail costs is that inmates facing county charges, who in the past might have been released on bail, must now be held for ICE. The county picks up the bill (Miroff, 2008). As a result, a number of counties have announced that they will no longer bear the expense; they will release detained criminal suspects who are eligible for bail, despite the insistence by ICE that counties keep undocumented immigrants in custody (Chanen, 2014).

ICE Rapid Repatriation programs in Arizona and New York provide early release of nonviolent, undocumented-immigrant inmates from state prisons, and then hand them to ICE for deportation. An Arizona corrections review found that 40 percent of incarcerated undocumented immigrants were convicted of violent assaults and were ineligible for early release. Among those who could be released early, 37 percent were convicted of drug or alcohol charges and 18 percent for property crimes (Holstege, 2008).

In the past decade, there has been a sharp escalation in the federal crackdown on undocumented workers. This is best illustrated by the prosecution and sentencing of 297 Guatemalans arrested in a May 12, 2008, raid on a meat-processing plant in Waterloo, Iowa. Ten days later, in unusually swift proceedings, the workers admitted taking jobs using fraudulent social security cards and immigration documents. Two hundred seventy workers were sentenced to five months in prison to be followed by immediate deportation (Preston, 2008). The Iowa raid affected an exceptionally large number of people. Many raids of factories and businesses lead to the arrests of smaller numbers of undocumented workers. More recently, ICE has focused on apprehending noncitizen gang members and others with criminal records. In a five-day operation called "Operation Cross Check" in 2015, ICE arrested 2,000 noncitizens with criminal records in locations throughout the country (Bruer, 2015).

With immigration a "hot" political issue, ICE is under pressure to expedite deportations. Immigration officials are scouring prisons, jails, and courts to identify deportable noncitizens. In the 12-month period ending September 30, 2007, ICE reported that 164,000 criminals had been placed in deportation status, two and one-half times as many as in the prior year. (Londono, 2008). By 2014, that number had risen to more than 178,000. Incarcerated immigrants contribute to prison and jail crowding, access medical services, and cause instability in the general population of some institutions.

Jails: Detention and Short-Term Incarceration

Most Americans do not distinguish between jails and prisons. **Prisons** are federal and state correctional institutions that hold offenders who are sentenced to terms of more than one year. **Jails** are local facilities for the detention of people awaiting trial and sentenced misdemeanants. Jails are also a holding facility for social misfits—drug abusers, prostitutes, those with mental disorders, and disturbers of public order.

prison
An institution for the incarceration of people convicted of serious crimes, usually felonies.

jail
An institution authorized to hold pretrial detainees and sentenced misdemeanants for periods longer than 48 hours. Most jails are administered by county governments; in six jurisdictions, they are administered by state governments.

Origins and Evolution

Jails in the United States descend from feudal practices in twelfth-century England. At that time, an officer of the crown, the reeve, was appointed in each shire (what we call a county) to collect taxes, keep the peace, and run the gaol (jail). Among other duties, the "shire reeve" (from which the word *sheriff* evolved) caught and held in custody, until a court hearing determined guilt or innocence, people accused of breaking the law. With the development of the workhouse in the sixteenth century, the sheriff took on added responsibilities for vagrants and the unemployed who were sent there. The sheriff made a living by collecting fees from inmates and by hiring out their labor.

English settlers brought these institutions to the American colonies. After the Revolution, the local community elected law enforcement officials—sheriffs and constables—to run the jail. As in England, the early American jails were used to detain accused people awaiting trial as well as to shelter misfits.

In the 1800s, the jail began to change in response to the penitentiary movement. In addition to shouldering traditional responsibilities, jails now held offenders serving short terms. The development of probation removed some offenders, as did adult reformatories. However, even with these innovations, the overwhelming majority of accused and convicted misdemeanants were held in jail. This pattern continued to modern times.

The Contemporary Jail

Of the 3,376 jails in the United States, 2,700 have a county-level jurisdiction, and most are administered by an elected sheriff. An additional 600 or so municipal jails are in operation. Only in six states—Alaska, Connecticut, Delaware, Hawaii, Rhode Island, and Vermont—does the state administer jails for adults. There are also an estimated 13,500 police lockups (or "drunk tanks") and similar holding facilities authorized to detain people for up to 48 hours. The Federal Bureau of Prisons operates 12 jails for detained prisoners only, holding a total of 14,000 inmates. There are 47 privately operated jails, under contract to state or local governments, and they house 2.4 percent of the total jail population. On any given day there are 730,000 people housed in jails (T. Minton and Golinelli, 2014)).

As we have seen, the primary function of jails is to hold people awaiting trial and people who have been sentenced for misdemeanors to terms of less than one year. On a national basis, about 62 percent of jail inmates are unconvicted pretrial detainees (T. Minton and Golinelli, 2014). In some states, convicted felons may serve more than one year in jail instead of in prison. For 87 percent of the sentenced population, however, stays in jail are less than one month.

Jails and police lockups shoulder responsibility for housing not only criminal defendants and offenders but also those viewed as problems by society. The criminal justice system is thus linked to other government agencies. People with substance abuse problems or mental illness have become a part of the jail population. They are often reported to the police for their deviant acts, which, although not necessarily illegal, are upsetting to the citizenry (urinating in public, appearing disoriented, shouting obscenities, and so on). Temporary confinement in a lockup or jail may be utilized if no appropriate social service facilities are available. This situation has been likened to a revolving door that shifts these "street people" from the police station to the jail. After an appearance in court, they are often released to the streets to start their cycle through the system all over again.

Ten percent of the national jail population consists of sentenced felons for whom state prisons have no room. They also house people awaiting transportation to prison, such as those convicted of parole or probation violations. This backup of inmates has caused difficulties in some states for judges and jail administrators, who must often put misdemeanants on probation because no jail space is available.

The capacity of jails varies greatly. The 50 largest jurisdictions hold about 30 percent of the nation's jailed inmates. The two jurisdictions with the most inmates, Los Angeles County and New York City, together hold approximately 31,000 inmates in multiple jails, or 4.1 percent of the national total. The Los Angeles County Men's Central Jail alone holds more than 6,000 people, but most jails are much smaller, with two-thirds holding fewer than 50 people (T. D. Minton, 2011).

Who Is in Jail?

With an estimated 13 million jail admissions and releases per year, more people directly experience jails than experience prisons, mental hospitals, and halfway houses combined. Even if we consider that some people of this total are admitted more than once, probably at least 6 to 7 million people are detained at some time during the year. Nationally, 731,000 people, both the convicted and the unconvicted, sit in jail on any one day (T. Minton and Golinelli, 2014). However, the number of people held at any one time in jail does not tell the complete story. Many are held for less than 24 hours; others may reside in jail as sentenced inmates for up to one year; a few may await their trial for more than a year.

Jeff Schrier/MLIVE.COM/Landov

Jails hold presumptively innocent detainees as well as people who have been convicted of crimes. The changing mix of inmates, including people with mental problems, poses a significant challenge for officials who must maintain safety and security within the limited facilities of a jail. If you were a county sheriff, how would you decide which people inside the jail could be safely housed together?

FIGURE 13.2 CHARACTERISTICS OF JAIL INMATES IN U.S. JAILS

Compared with the American population as a whole, jails are disproportionately inhabited by men, minorities, the poorly educated, and those with low income.

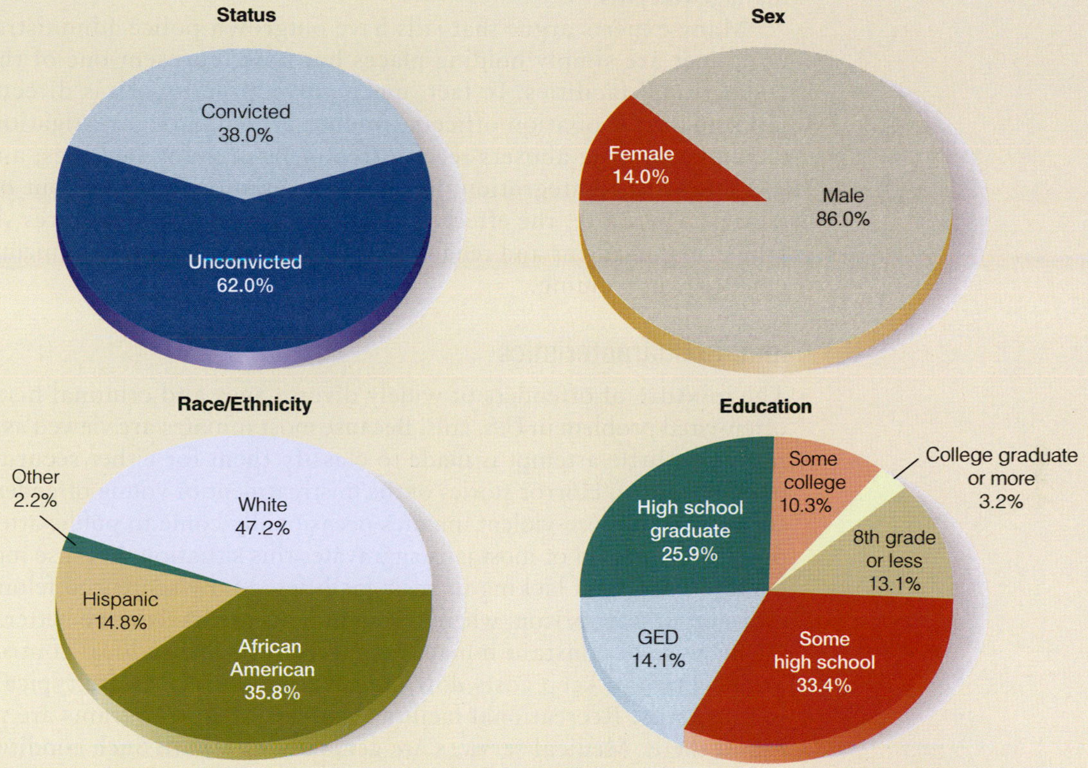

Sources: Todd D. Minton and Daniela Golinelli, *Jail Inmates at Midyear 2013: Statistical Tables*, NCJ 245350 (Washington, DC: U.S. Bureau of Justice Statistics), May 2014; C. W. Harlow, "Education and Correctional Populations," *Bureau of Justice Statistics Bulletin Special Report*, January 2003.

The most recent Annual Survey of Jails shows that about 86 percent of inmates are men and 47 percent are white (T. Minton and Golinelli, 2014). Typically, most jail inmates are under 30 years old and have very little education and income. A significant percentage of jail inmates have mental health problems (Petteruti and Walsh, 2008). During the last decade, as the country has become more anxious about immigrants, local jails' detention of people for immigration violations grew by 100 percent (T. D. Minton, 2011). The demographic characteristics of the jail population differ greatly from those of the national population (Figure 13.2).

Managing Jails

Jail administrators face several problems that good management practices cannot always overcome. These problems include (1) the perceived role of the jail in the local criminal justice system, (2) the inmate population, and (3) fiscal problems.

Role of the Jail

As facilities to detain accused people awaiting trial, jails customarily have been run by law enforcement agencies. We might reasonably expect that the agency that arrests and transports defendants to court should also administer the facility that holds them. Typically, however, neither sheriffs nor deputies have much interest in corrections. They often think of themselves as police officers and of the jail as merely an extension of their law enforcement activities. In some major cities, municipal departments of correction, rather than the police, manage the jails.

Many experts argue that jails have outgrown police administration. Jails no longer are simply holding places but now represent one of the primary correctional facilities. In fact, much correctional work is directed toward jail inmates. Probation officers conduct presentence investigations in jails; alcohol and drug abusers receive treatment in many facilities; and inmates work toward reintegration or perform community service out of some facilities. Therefore, the effective administration of jails requires skills in offender management and rehabilitation that are not generally included in law enforcement training.

Inmate Characteristics

The mixture of offenders of widely diverse ages and criminal histories is an often-cited problem in U.S. jails. Because most inmates are viewed as temporary residents, little attempt is made to classify them for either security or treatment purposes. Horror stories of the mistreatment of young offenders by older, stronger, and more-violent inmates occasionally come to public attention. The physical condition of most jails aggravates this situation, because most are old, overcrowded, and lacking in basic facilities. Many sentenced felons prefer to move on to state prison, where the conditions are likely to be better.

Because of constant inmate turnover and because local control provides an incentive to keep costs down, correctional services are typically lacking in most jails. Recreational facilities and treatment programs are not usually found there. Medical services are generally minimal. Such conditions add to

NEW DIRECTIONS IN CRIMINAL JUSTICE POLICY

EVIDENCE-BASED PRACTICES, JAILS, AND MENTAL ILLNESS

A report in 2014 by the Treatment Advocacy Center, a nonprofit organization focused on expanding the availability of treatment for mental illnesses, reported the striking statistic that there are 10 times as many people with severe mental illnesses in jails and prisons as are confined to psychiatric hospitals. There were an estimated 356,000 prisoners and detainees with severe mental illnesses in prisons and jails and only 35,000 patients in state psychiatric hospitals. Because of the deinstitutionalization movement of the past 40 years, which reduced the populations of mental hospitals in favor of the goal of less-expensive treatment within the community, jails have found themselves on the frontlines of mental illness issues. People with mental illnesses often end up in jails for behaving in unusual ways that upset their fellow citizens, even if their behavior does not clearly constitute a crime.

In light of the challenges facing jails with respect to this issue, many mental health professionals have worked with criminal justice officials to try to develop evidence-based practices that will benefit people needing treatment and also protect safety and security in society. These efforts have produced a number of important recommendations:

- Criminal justice officials, including police, jail officials, and other corrections officials, must collaborate and coordinate with mental health professionals and local health service providers.
- Efforts must be made to evaluate and classify people who enter the jail in order to determine who needs mental health services and the nature of their needs. They should be assigned to safe housing settings that minimize opportunities for suicide or conflict with others and that provide adequate supervision if there is a need for crisis intervention.
- Efforts must be made to develop jail diversion programs that can place eligible people with mental illnesses into alternative living and treatment settings that do not contain the relatively harsh conditions of jail and do not mix them with the diverse populations within jails. Diversion efforts may include the use

the idleness and tensions of the inmates. Suicides and high levels of violence are hallmarks of many jails. In any one year, almost half the people who die while in jail have committed suicide. People with mental illness are among those with the greatest risk of suicide while in jail. They present significant challenges for jail officials who run institutions designed for custody but typically not well-prepared to provide treatment. Read the New Directions in Criminal Justice Policy feature to consider the role of evidence-based practices for addressing the needs of detainees struggling with mental illness.

Fiscal Problems

Jails help to control crime but also drain local resources. The tension between these two public interests often surfaces in debates over expenditures for jail construction and operation. Because resources are often insufficient, many jails are overcrowded, lack programs, and do not have enough officers for effective supervision. In some states, multicounty jails have been created to serve an entire region as a means of operating facilities in a cost-effective way.

As criminal justice policy has become more punitive, jails, like prisons, have become crowded. Even with new construction and with alternatives such as release on recognizance programs, diversion, intensive probation supervision, and house arrest with electronic monitoring, the jail population continues to rise.

✔POINT

10. What are the functions of jails?

11. What are three of the problems affecting jails?

STOP AND ANALYZE: Because jails hold more unconvicted detainees who are presumptively innocent than they hold convicted offenders, should jail conditions and services be more comfortable and generous than those in prisons? Give two arguments for and two arguments against the proposition that jail conditions should be less harsh than those in prisons.

of Crisis Intervention Teams, in which police officers and social workers respond together when there are calls about the behavior of people exhibiting signs of mental illness.

- Alternative programs, such as mental health courts, can often provide treatment and supervision more effectively than treatment that is provided within confinement in jail.
- Jails need to work with service providers to bring mental health professionals into jails to train jail staff and provide treatment programs for detainees and offenders who are confined within these institutions. Larger jails may be able to establish separate housing units for those who are receiving mental health treatment.
- Jails must develop procedures within applicable federal and state guidelines for providing needed medications, including the possibility of involuntarily medicating individuals when medically necessary and permitted by law.
- Jails and other correctional institutions must have special planning for the transition of detainees and offenders with mental disorders from confinement to society, including access to housing assistance and other social services, as well as mental health aftercare plans.

Sources: California Corrections Standards Authority, *Jails and the Mentally Ill: Issues and Analysis* (2014); (http://www.cdcr.ca.gov/COMIO/docs/MENTALLY_ILL_IN_JAILS_PAPER.pdf); Treatment Advocacy Center, *The Treatment of Persons with Mental Illness in Prisons and Jails: A State Survey* (abridged), April 8, 2014 (http://www.tacreports.org/treatment-behind-bars).

DEBATE THE ISSUE

If you were a sheriff who had just received a substantial grant from a private foundation for the purpose of adopting evidence-based practices, what would be your priorities? What agencies and organizations would you contact in order to create well-planned procedures that should be followed when people with mental disorders are brought to your jail by the police?

The Law of Corrections

hands-off policy
Judges should not interfere with the administration of correctional institutions.

Prior to the 1960s, most courts maintained a **hands-off policy** with respect to corrections. Only a few state courts had recognized rights for offenders. Most judges felt that prisoners and probationers did not have protected rights and that courts should not interfere in the operational agencies dealing with probation, prisons, and parole.

Since the 1960s, however, offenders have gained access to the courts to contest correctional officers' decisions and aspects of their punishment that they believe violate basic rights. Judicial decisions have defined and recognized the constitutional rights of probationers, prisoners, and parolees, as well as the need for policies and procedures that respect those rights. As you read "Civic Engagement: Your Role in the System," think about what rights might be protected inside a prison.

CIVIC ENGAGEMENT

YOUR ROLE IN THE SYSTEM

Imagine that in prison your cellmate assaults you and causes painful injuries. *Make a list of any rights that you believe were violated in this situation and what you would do about it.* Then go online and read about what happened to an Illinois prison inmate who raised this complaint.

Chapter 4 presented an overview of the law in relation to the criminal justice system as a whole. In that discussion, we touched on prisoners' rights. Here, we further explore court decisions in relation to the many aspects of corrections.

Bear in mind that corrections law does not just apply to people who have been convicted of committing crimes. It also applies to people being held in jail while they await the processing of their cases. Many of these people will have charges against them dropped. Others will eventually be found not guilty and released. Also remember that anyone in the United States can be arrested. For example, former President George W. Bush and former Vice President Dick Cheney were both arrested for drinking and driving before they achieved high positions in government. You do not need to commit a crime to be arrested. You merely need to be subject to a police officer's discretionary decision to make an arrest. This can happen through being misidentified by a witness or from a variety of everyday acts committed by Americans from all segments of society, such as driving after drinking alcohol or forgetting to carry your driver's license.

Constitutional Rights of Prisoners

***Cooper v. Pate* (1964)**
Prisoners are entitled to the protection of the Civil Rights Act of 1871 and may challenge in federal courts the conditions of their confinement.

The U.S. Supreme Court decision in ***Cooper v. Pate* (1964)** signaled the end of the hands-off policy. The court said that through the Civil Rights Act of 1871 (referred to here as Section 1983), state prisoners were *persons* whose rights are protected by the Constitution. The act imposes *civil liability* on any state or local official who deprives someone of constitutional rights. It allows suits against state officials to be heard in the federal courts. Because of *Cooper v. Pate*, the federal courts now recognize that prisoners may sue state and local officials over such things as brutality by guards, inadequate nutrition and medical care, theft of personal property, and the denial of basic rights.

The first successful prisoners' rights cases involved the most excessive of prison abuses: brutality and inhumane physical conditions. Gradually, however, prison litigation has focused more directly on the daily activities of the institution, especially on those pertaining to the administrative rules that regulate inmates' conduct. The result has been a series of court decisions concerning the First, Fourth, Eighth, and Fourteenth Amendments to the Constitution. (See Appendix A for the full text of these amendments.)

✔POINT
12. What was the hands-off policy?
13. Why is the case of *Cooper v. Pate* important to the expansion of prisoners' rights?

STOP AND ANALYZE: Critics claim that judges interfere with the administration of prisons when they make decisions protecting the rights of convicted offenders. If someone said to you, "People who commit crimes should forfeit all of their rights," can you think of two counterarguments to use in response to this statement?

First Amendment

The First Amendment guarantees freedom of speech, press, assembly, petition, and religion. Many of the restrictions of prison life—access to reading materials, censorship of mail, and rules affecting some religious practices—have been successfully challenged by prisoners in the courts.

Since 1970, courts have extended limited rights of freedom of speech and expression to prisoners. They have required correctional administrators to show why restrictions on these rights must be imposed (Table 13.3). For example, in 1974 the Supreme Court ruled that censorship of mail was permissible only when officials could demonstrate a compelling government interest in maintaining security (*Procunier v. Martinez*). The result has increased the communication between inmates and the outside world. However, in *Turner v. Safley* (1987), the Court upheld a Missouri ban on correspondence between inmates in different institutions as a means of combating gang violence and the communication of escape plans.

The First Amendment prevents Congress from making laws with regard to the establishment of religion or prohibiting its free exercise. Cases concerning the free exercise of religion have caused the judiciary some problems, especially when the religious practice may interfere with prison routine and the maintenance of order.

The growth of the Black Muslim religion in prisons set the stage for lawsuits demanding that this group be granted the same privileges as other faiths (special diets, access to clergy and religious publications, opportunities for group worship). Attorneys for the Black Muslims succeeded in winning several important cases that helped to establish for prisoners the First Amendment right to free exercise of religion. These decisions also helped Native Americans, Orthodox Jews, and other prisoners to practice their religions. Court decisions in some cases have upheld prisoners' rights to be served meals consistent with

TABLE 13.3 SELECTED INTERPRETATIONS OF THE FIRST AMENDMENT AS APPLIED TO PRISONERS

The Supreme Court and other federal courts have made numerous decisions affecting prisoners' rights to freedom of speech and expression and freedom of religion.

CASE	DECISION
Procunier v. Martinez (1974)	Censorship of mail is permitted only to the extent necessary to maintain prison security.
Turner v. Safley (1987)	Inmates do not have a right to receive mail from one another, and rights can be limited by rules "reasonably related to legitimate penological interests."
Beard v. Banks (2006)	In an effort to promote security and rule compliance, policies that deny magazines, newspapers, and photographs to the most incorrigible inmates are constitutional.
Theriault v. Carlson (1977)	The First Amendment does not protect so-called religions that are obvious shams, that tend to mock established institutions, and whose members lack religious sincerity.
Gittlemacker v. Prasse (1970)	The state must give inmates the opportunity to practice their religion but is not required to provide a member of the clergy.
O'Lone v. Estate of Shabazz (1987)	The rights of Muslim prisoners are not violated when a work assignment makes it impossible for them to attend religious services.
Kahane v. Carlson (1975)	An orthodox Jewish inmate has the right to a diet consistent with his religious beliefs unless the government can show cause why it cannot be provided.
Holt v. Hobbs (2015)	Prison may not prohibit Muslim prisoner from growing a short beard as required by his religion.
Cruz v. Beto (1972)	Prisoners who adhere to other than conventional beliefs may not be denied the opportunity to practice their religion.

CLOSE UP

FREE EXERCISE OF RELIGION INSIDE PRISONS

Congress enacted the Religious Land Use and Institutionalized Persons Act (RLUIPA) in 2000, in part, to require corrections officials to demonstrate a compelling justification before carrying out policies and practices that hinder or prevent a prisoner's free exercise of religion under the First Amendment. John Walker Lindh, a prisoner serving a lengthy sentence in a federal prison in Terre Haute, Indiana, filed a lawsuit asserting that corrections officials violated the RLUIPA and First Amendment by barring him from engaging in group prayer with his fellow Muslim prisoners as required by his religion. Prison officials claimed that the inmates would threaten order and security in the institution if they were permitted to gather together regularly for group prayer. Moreover, the officials said the prisoners could fulfill the requirements of their religion by praying individually in their own cells.

The case highlighted an interesting issue about exactly who should be entitled to the protection of constitutional rights. In 2001, Lindh was widely known as "the American Taliban" and arguably regarded at that time as the most hated person in the United States. As he was growing up in a middle-class, suburban white family in California, he had converted to Islam as a teenager and moved to the Middle East to study his religion at a time in life when other Americans would be attending college. When American military and intelligence officers entered Afghanistan in the aftermath of the September 11, 2001, attacks on the World Trade Center in New York City and the Pentagon in Washington, D.C., Lindh was captured among fighters helping the Taliban government that the United States was seeking to defeat. During a prison uprising after Lindh's capture, an American CIA officer

religious dietary laws, to correspond with religious leaders, to possess religious literature, to wear a beard if their belief requires it, and to assemble for services. For example, in 2015 the U.S. Supreme Court ruled that Arkansas could not prevent a Muslim prisoner from growing a half-inch beard as part of his religious practices (*Holt v. Hobbs*). Thus members of religious minorities have broken new legal ground on First Amendment issues. In other cases, however, judges have decided that prison officials have compelling reasons to prevent some of these religious practices. Read the Close Up feature concerning a prisoner's free exercise of religion case in 2013, and think about how you would decide the case if you were a judge.

Fourth Amendment

Hudson v. Palmer (1984)
Prison officials have the authority to search cells and confiscate any materials found.

The Fourth Amendment prohibits unreasonable searches and seizures, but courts have not been active in extending these protections to prisoners. Thus regulations viewed as reasonable to maintain security and order in an institution may be justified. For example, the 1984 decision in ***Hudson v. Palmer*** upheld the authority of officials to search cells and confiscate any materials found.

Table 13.4 outlines some of the Supreme Court's Fourth Amendment opinions. They reveal the fine balance between institutional need and the right to privacy. Body searches have been harder for administrators to justify than cell searches, for example. But body searches have been upheld when they are part of a policy clearly related to an identifiable and legitimate institutional need and when they are not intended to humiliate or degrade. For example, strip searches are justified when prisoners have had contact visits in the visiting room—as opposed to talking to visitors on a phone while seeing each other through a window. In the jail context, the Supreme Court ruled in *Florence v. Board of Chosen Freeholders of County of Burlington* (2012) that all arrestees, even those brought to the jail for minor offenses, can be strip searched before being placed in the jail population, even if there is no reason to suspect that the arrestees are hiding drugs or weapons on their bodies.

was killed. Many Americans wanted Lindh held responsible for the CIA officer's death, since he was present at the prison and widely regarded as a traitor to his country, although there is no evidence that he was actively involved in the death of the American official. Lindh was charged with numerous crimes. He ultimately avoided a life sentence by pleading guilty to two charges, aiding the Taliban and carrying an explosive, in exchange for a 20-year sentence. Given his notoriety and the widely held view that he fought against his own country, should he be entitled to the benefits of rights under the U.S. Constitution?

Lindh filed his lawsuit himself as he worked his way through the initial grievance processes in his prison and the federal Bureau of Prisons. Later, a civil liberties interest group provided a lawyer to carry his case forward in court. Ultimately, Lindh prevailed in 2013, because a federal judge concluded after a trial that the prison officials did not meet the burden required under the RLUIPA that there be a compelling justification for their prohibition on group prayers.

DEBATE THE ISSUE

Should an offender convicted of aiding his country's enemies be entitled to the protection of rights? Should the judge defer to corrections officials when those officials claim that group gatherings within a prison can produce dangerous situations? Who knows best about prisons—judges or wardens? Is freedom of religion so important as a constitutional right that it should be a priority above other considerations? Write a memo giving your assessment of this case and judicial decision.

With the increased employment of both male and female correctional officers, courts have ruled that staff members of one sex should not strip search inmates of the opposite sex except by necessity when a search is needed and no other officers are available. Because of many lawsuits in which male corrections officers groped or sexually abused female prisoners, similar concerns can arise in the supervision of other personal locations, such as showers and bathrooms.

Eighth Amendment

The Constitution's prohibition of cruel and unusual punishments has been tied to prisoners' need for decent treatment and minimum health standards. The identification of Eighth Amendment violations depends on judges' assessment of the specific conditions in a particular prison. Whereas the Supreme Court

TABLE 13.4 SELECTED INTERPRETATIONS OF THE FOURTH AMENDMENT AS APPLIED TO PRISONERS

The Supreme Court and other federal courts have established very limited protections against warrantless searches and seizures.

CASE	DECISION
Lanza v. New York (1962)	Conversations recorded in a jail visitor's room are not protected by the Fourth Amendment.
Bell v. Wolfish (1979)	Strip searches, including searches of body cavities after contact visits, may be carried out when need for such searches outweighs the personal rights invaded.
United States v. Hitchcock (1972)	A warrantless search of a cell is not unreasonable, and documentary evidence found there is not subject to suppression in court. It is not reasonable to expect a prison cell to be accorded the same level of privacy as a home or automobile.
Lee v. Downs (1981)	Staff members of one sex may not normally supervise inmates of the opposite sex during bathing, toilet use, or strip searches.
Hudson v. Palmer (1984)	Officials may search cells without a warrant and seize materials found there.
Florence v. Board of Chosen Freeholders (2012)	All arrestees may be strip searched in jail prior to being placed in the general population, even those arrested for very minor offenses who have raised no suspicions about carrying contraband.

has looked for the unnecessary infliction of pain, in conditions of confinement cases it also requires judges to ask whether corrections officials were deliberately indifferent to inhumane conditions. For example, under the Eighth Amendment, prisoners possess only a limited right to medical care. It is not a right to the best, most-comprehensive diagnosis and treatment. The right is violated only if corrections officials are deliberately indifferent to serious medical needs (*Estelle v. Gamble*, 1976). Thus conditions alone may not be judged as "cruel and unusual" unless accompanied by improper intentions on the part of corrections officials. In the use of force during disturbances within prisons, the Supreme Court gives officials broad authority and finds rights violations only when officials use force maliciously for the purpose of causing injury and pain.

Federal courts have issued rulings based on a combination of various factors—the *totality of conditions*—to determine that living conditions in the institution constitute cruel and unusual punishment. Since the Supreme Court's decision in *Wilson v. Seiter* (1991), prisoners have faced the extra hurdle of proving that corrections officials knew about and were deliberately indifferent to improper conditions and practices. When courts have found brutality, unsanitary facilities, overcrowding, and inadequate food, judges have used the Eighth Amendment to order sweeping changes and even, in some cases, to take over administration of entire prisons or corrections systems. In these cases judges have ordered wardens to follow specific internal procedures and to spend money on certain improvements (Table 13.5).

In 2011, a closely divided Supreme Court upheld lower court decisions ordering California to reduce its prison population, because overcrowded conditions had overwhelmed the prison system's ability to provide proper health care and mental health treatment for prisoners (*Brown v. Plata*, 2011). The competing opinions issued in the case illustrated continuing divisions among the justices about forcing prisons to uphold certain standards for living conditions. The four dissenting justices advocated permitting states to handle their own issues and avoid the risk that public safety would be threatened by early releases (C. E. Smith, 2013).

TABLE 13.5 SELECTED INTERPRETATIONS OF THE EIGHTH AMENDMENT AS APPLIED TO PRISONERS

The Supreme Court and other courts are called on to determine whether correctional actions constitute cruel and unusual punishment.

CASE	DECISION
Ruiz v. Estelle (1975)	Conditions of confinement in the Texas prison system are unconstitutional and remedies must be implemented.
Estelle v. Gamble (1976)	Deliberate indifference to serious medical needs of prisoners constitutes the unnecessary and wanton infliction of pain, and thus violates the Eighth Amendment.
Rhodes v. Chapman (1981)	Double-celling and crowding do not necessarily constitute cruel and unusual punishment. It must be shown that the conditions involve "wanton and unnecessary infliction of pain" and are "grossly disproportionate" to the severity of the crime warranting imprisonment.
Whitley v. Albers (1986)	An innocent prisoner mistakenly shot in the leg during a disturbance does not suffer cruel and unusual punishment if the action was taken in good faith to maintain discipline rather than for the malicious purpose of causing harm.
Wilson v. Seiter (1991)	Prisoners must not only prove that prison conditions are objectively cruel and unusual but also show that they exist because of the deliberate indifference of officials.
Overton v. Bazetta (2003)	Regulations suspending visiting privileges for two years for those prisoners who have "flunked" two drug tests do not violate the cruel and unusual punishments clause. The regulations bear a rational relation to legitimate penological objectives.

POINT 14. What protections do prisoners receive from the First, Fourth, and Eighth Amendments?

STOP AND ANALYZE: Imagine that you are a judge, and prisoners file a lawsuit alleging a violation of the Eighth Amendment prohibition on cruel and unusual punishments because the heating and hot water systems at a prison in snowy Vermont have been broken and unrepaired for weeks during January and February. Should this be considered a violation of the Eighth Amendment that requires the judge to order officials to fix the problem? Give two reasons to support your decision in the case.

Fourteenth Amendment

One word and two clauses of the Fourteenth Amendment are relevant to the question of prisoners' rights. The relevant word is *state*, which is found in several clauses of the Fourteen Amendment. The rights covered by the Amendment protect individuals against actions by states. Through decisions by the Supreme Court in the twentieth century, most of the rights in the Bill of Rights also were considered to be protected against actions by states.

As we saw in Chapter 4, the first important clause concerns procedural due process, which requires that government officials treat all people fairly and justly and that official decisions be made according to procedures prescribed by law. The second important clause is the equal protection clause. Assertions that prisoners have been denied equal protection of the law are based on claims of racial, gender, or religious discrimination.

Due Process in Prison Discipline In ***Wolff v. McDonnell* (1974)**, the Supreme Court ruled that basic procedural rights must be present when decisions are made about the disciplining of inmates for serious rule violations. Specifically, prisoners have a right to receive notice of the complaint, to have a fair hearing, to confront witnesses, to get help in preparing for the hearing, and to be given a written statement of the decision. However, the Court further stated that prisoners do not have a right to cross-examine witnesses and that the evidence presented by the offender shall not be unduly hazardous to institutional safety or correctional goals. The context of corrections and procedures used in prisons is not the same as those in a formal trial at a courthouse.

***Wolff v. McDonnell* (1974)** Basic elements of procedural due process must be present when decisions are made about the disciplining of an inmate.

As a result of these Supreme Court decisions, some of which are outlined in Table 13.6, prison officials have established rules that provide elements of due process in disciplinary and other proceedings. In many institutions, a disciplinary committee receives the charges, conducts hearings, and decides guilt and punishment. Even with these protections, prisoners are still powerless and may risk further punishment if they challenge the warden's decisions too vigorously.

Equal Protection In 1968 the Supreme Court firmly established that racial discrimination may not be official policy within prison walls (*Lee v. Washington*). Segregation can be justified only as a temporary measure during periods when violence between races is demonstrably imminent. In *Johnson v. California* (2005), the Supreme Court refused to defer to the judgment of California administrators that led to racial segregation in prison cells during the first two months of imprisonment as officials sought to evaluate which new prisoners might be gang members. The Court required that officials provide compelling proof of the need to engage in a form of racial segregation that no other state thought necessary to use.

In recent decades, some cases have concerned equal protection issues affecting female offenders. Judges in state courts and lower federal courts have addressed these issues. For example, in a series of decisions spanning nearly two decades, female inmates in Michigan successfully argued that their equal protection rights were violated because programs and services were not as good as

TABLE 13.6 SELECTED INTERPRETATIONS OF THE FOURTEENTH AMENDMENT AS APPLIED TO PRISONERS

The Supreme Court has issued rulings concerning procedural due process and equal protection.

CASE	DECISION
Wolff v. McDonnell (1974)	The basic elements of procedural due process must be present when decisions are made concerning the disciplining of an inmate.
*Baxter v. Palmigiano (*1976)	Although due process must be accorded, an inmate has no right to counsel in a disciplinary hearing.
Vitek v. Jones (1980)	The involuntary transfer of a prisoner to a mental hospital requires a hearing and other minimal elements of due process such as notice and the availability of counsel.
Sandin v. Conner (1995)	Prison regulations do not give rise to protected due process liberty interests unless they place atypical and significant hardships on a prisoner.

those provided to male inmates (*Glover v. Johnson*, 1991). Critics who believe that prisons neglect the needs of women prisoners argue that judges have generally permitted too many differences in facilities and programs for women without providing sufficient attention to issues of equality (Carroll-Ferrary, 2006).

✔POINT 15. Which two clauses of the Fourteenth Amendment have been interpreted by the Supreme Court to apply to prisoners' rights?

STOP AND ANALYZE: Can judges accurately anticipate the consequences of their decisions that shape policies and practices in prisons? Do judges really understand what goes on inside prisons and the problems that corrections officials face in running these institutions? List two possible undesirable consequences that could emerge in the aftermath of decisions by judges that instruct administrators on how to run their institutions in order to respect prisoners' constitutional rights.

A Change in Judicial Direction?

During the past 35 years, the Supreme Court has been less supportive of expanding prisoners' rights, and a few decisions reflect a retreat. In *Bell v. Wolfish* (1979), the justices took pains to say that prison administrators should be given wide-ranging deference in the adoption and execution of policies. In *Daniels v. Williams* (1986) the concept of deliberate indifference surfaced. Here the Court said that prisoners could sue for damages only if officials had violated rights through deliberate actions. This reasoning was extended in *Wilson v. Seiter* (1991), where the Court ruled that a prisoner's conditions of confinement are not unconstitutional unless it can be shown that prison administrators had acted with "deliberate indifference" to basic human needs (Call, 1995; C. E. Smith, 1993).

Many scholars believe that the deliberate-indifference requirement indicates a shift from the use of objective criteria (proof that the inmate suffered conditions protected by the Eighth Amendment) to subjective criteria (the state of mind of correctional officials, namely, deliberate indifference) in determining whether prison conditions are unconstitutional. The retirement of Justice John Paul Stevens from the U.S. Supreme Court in 2010 removed the foremost advocate of prisoners' rights from the nation's highest court (C. E. Smith, 2007). In his judicial opinions, Stevens had advocated a relatively broad conception of prisoners' rights, and from 1976 onward, argued against applying the deliberate-indifference requirement to Eighth Amendment claims. It remains to be seen whether President Obama's two appointees to the Supreme Court, Justices Sonia Sotomayor and Elena Kagan, will demonstrate such outspokenness in protecting against the Supreme Court's current deference to the preferences of corrections officials (C. E. Smith, 2013; C. E. Smith, 2011).

In 1996, Congress passed the Prison Litigation Reform Act, making it more difficult for prisoners to file civil rights lawsuits and for judges to make decisions affecting prison operations. For example, the Act:

- Requires that inmates exhaust the prison's grievance procedure before filing a lawsuit
- Requires judges to dismiss all frivolous lawsuits and makes it more difficult for prisoners with limited funds to file lawsuits without paying at least partial filing fees
- Specifies that judges' orders affecting prisons must automatically expire after two years unless new hearings are held demonstrating that rights violations continue to exist
- Limits prisoners' ability to file additional civil rights lawsuits without full filing fees if they previously had three lawsuits dismissed as frivolous.

Since the Prison Litigation Reform Act became law, the number of Section 1983 lawsuits filed in federal courts has dropped dramatically, even though the number of state prisoners rose after the law was enacted (BJS, 2005).

Impact of the Prisoners' Rights Movement

Although the Supreme Court in recent years reduced its support for the expansion of prisoners' rights, some general changes in American corrections have occurred since the late 1970s. The most obvious are improvements in institutional living conditions and administrative practices. Law libraries or legal assistance is now generally available, communication with the outside is easier, religious practices are protected, inmate complaint procedures have been developed, and due process requirements are emphasized. Prisoners in solitary confinement undoubtedly suffer less neglect than they did before. Although overcrowding is still a major problem, many conditions are much improved and the most brutalizing elements of prison life have diminished. These changes were not entirely the result of court orders, however. They also coincide with the growing influence of college-educated corrections professionals who have sought on their own to improve prisons (C. E. Smith, 2000).

Law and Community Corrections

Although most correctional law concerns prisons and jails, two-thirds of adults under supervision live in the community on probation and parole. However, as with prisoners, offenders in the community are not without rights, and courts have addressed issues concerning due process and searches and seizures.

Conditions of Probation and Parole

Probationers and parolees must live according to conditions specified at the time of their sentencing or parole release. These conditions may substantially diminish their constitutional rights. The conditions typically limit the right of free association by restricting offenders from contact with their crime partners or victims. However, courts have struck down conditions preventing parolees from exercising their First Amendment rights by giving public speeches and receiving publications.

The case of *Samson v. California* (2006) is a good example of the tension between the Fourth Amendment and the goal of making offenders feel able to reintegrate into the community. A police officer saw Donald Samson walking down the sidewalk with a woman and child. The officer knew that Samson was on parole, so he approached and asked Samson if there were any outstanding warrants for his arrest. Samson said "no," and the officer's radio check with the police dispatcher confirmed that Samson had not violated any conditions of parole. Based solely on the fact that Samson was a parolee, the officer decided to search Samson, and he found a small quantity of methamphetamine. Such a search would not be permitted on a regular citizen unless the officer could articulate specific evidence to support reasonable suspicion that the citizen was armed and potentially engaged in criminal activity. Samson's lawyer claimed that the search was improper because there was no reasonable suspicion of wrongdoing. However, by a 6-to-3 vote, the U.S. Supreme Court ruled that officers can conduct such suspicionless searches of parolees simply because the individual is on parole. In fact, Justice Clarence Thomas's majority opinion claimed that "California's ability to conduct suspicionless searches of parolees serves its interest in reducing recidivism, in a manner that aids, rather than hinders, the reintegration of parolees into productive society." By contrast, the dissenting opinion of Justice John Paul Stevens complained that parolees have greater reasonable expectations of privacy than prisoners and that the "requirement of individualized suspicion, in all its iterations, is the shield the Framers selected to guard against the evils of arbitrary action, caprice, and harassment." Such debates illuminate general disagreements about the extent to which parolees and probationers should enjoy the protections of constitutional rights in order to enable them to return successfully to society.

Revocation of Probation and Parole

When probationers or parolees do not obey their conditions of release, they may be sent to prison. If the offender commits another crime, probation or

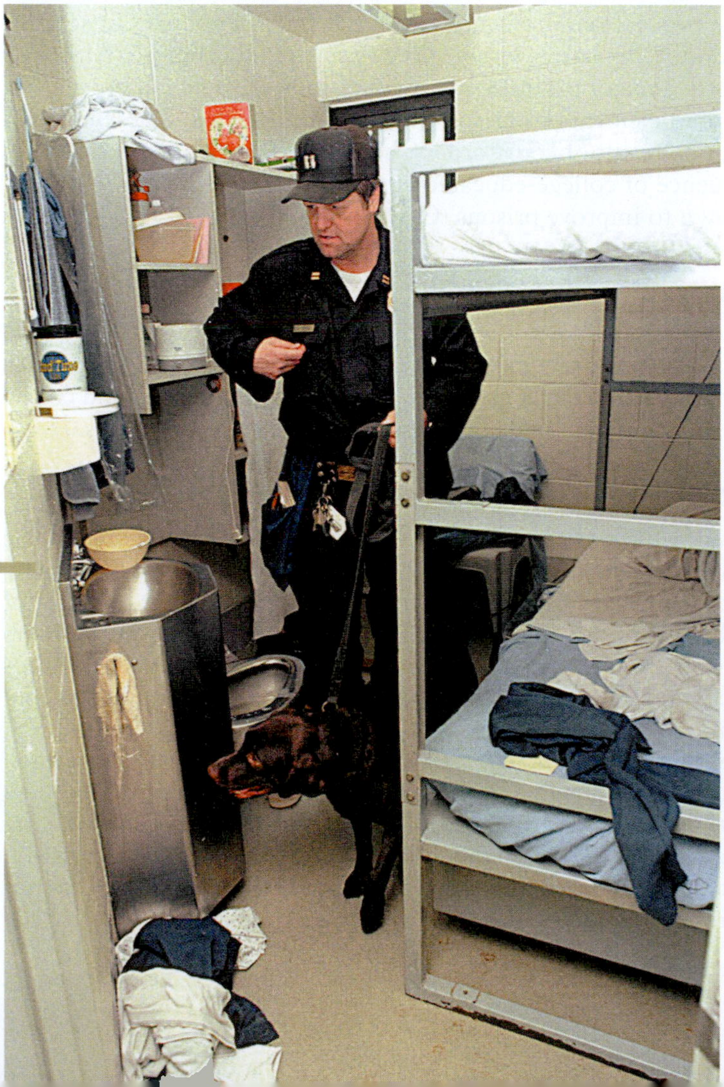

A correctional officer leads a "sniffer" dog through a cell at Big Muddy Correctional Center in Ina, Illinois. A 150-member tactical team conducted this search without giving the prisoners any prior warning. Is there anything that officers might do during such a search that would violate a prisoner's Fourth Amendment right against unreasonable searches and seizures?

AP Images/Southern Illinoisan, Joe Jines

parole will likely be revoked. For minor violations of the conditions (such as missing an Alcoholics Anonymous meeting), the supervising officer has discretion as to whether to seek revocation.

The Supreme Court has addressed the question of due process when revocation is being considered. In ***Mempa v. Rhay* (1967)** the justices determined that a probationer had the right to counsel in revocation and sentencing hearings before a deferred prison sentence could be imposed. Similarly, in ***Morrissey v. Brewer* (1972)**, the court ruled that parolees facing revocation must be given a two-step hearing process. In the first stage, a hearing officer determines whether there is probable cause that a violation has occurred. Parolees have the right to be notified of the charges against them, to know the evidence against them, to be allowed to speak on their own behalf, to present witnesses, and to confront the witnesses against them. In the second stage, the revocation hearing, the parolee must receive a notice of both the charges and the evidence that allegedly supports the charges. The parolee may question any witnesses. The hearing body determines if the violation is sufficiently severe to warrant revocation. It must give the parolee a written statement outlining the evidence with reasons for the decision.

***Mempa v. Rhay* (1967)**
Probationers have the right to counsel at a combined revocation-sentencing hearing.

***Morrissey v. Brewer* (1972)**
Due process rights require a prompt, informal two-part inquiry before an impartial hearing officer prior to parole revocation. The parolee may present relevant information and confront witnesses.

In the following year, the Supreme Court applied the *Morrissey* procedures to probation revocation proceedings in *Gagnon v. Scarpelli* (1973). But in *Gagnon*, the Court also looked at the question of the right to counsel. It ruled that there was no absolute requirement; however, probationers and parolees might be given attorneys on a case-by-case basis, depending on the complexity of the issues, the competence of the offender, and other circumstances.

Law and Correctional Personnel

Just as law governs relationships among inmates, probationers, and parolees, laws and regulations also define the relationships between correctional administrators and their staff. With the exception of those working for corporate or nonprofit entities, correctional personnel are public employees. Here we consider two important aspects of correctional work. First, as public employees, all correctional employees are governed by civil service rules and regulations. Second, correctional clients may sue state employees using Section 1983 (Title 42) of the United States Code. We will examine the liability of correctional personnel with regard to these lawsuits while bearing in mind that employees of corporate-owned private prisons are not subject to the same kinds of lawsuits.

Civil Service Laws

Civil service laws set the procedures for hiring, promoting, assigning, disciplining, and firing public employees. These laws protect public employees from arbitrary actions by their supervisors. Where correctional personnel can join unions, the collective bargaining process develops rules concerning assignments, working conditions, and grievance procedures. These agreements carry the force of law.

Like their counterparts in the private sector, government employees are protected from discrimination. With the Civil Rights Act of 1964, Congress prohibited employment discrimination based on race, gender, national origin, and religion. Subsequent federal legislation prohibits some forms of age discrimination (Age Discrimination in Employment Act) and discrimination against people with disabilities (Americans with Disability Act). States have their own antidiscrimination laws. All these laws have increased the number of minorities and women who work in corrections.

Unlike many public employees, those who work in corrections are in a difficult position. They must assert authority over persons who have shown that they lack self-control or have little regard for society's rules. Whether in prison, in a probationer's home, or on the street, this responsibility creates pressures and difficult—and sometimes dangerous—situations.

Liability of Correctional Personnel

As noted, in *Cooper v. Pate* (1964) the Supreme Court said that Section 1983—the federal civil rights statute—provides a means for prisoners as well as probationers and parolees to bring lawsuits against correctional officials. The meaning of Section 1983 was clarified in *Monell v. Department of Social Services for the City of New York* (1978). The court said that individual public employees and their local agency may be sued when a person's civil rights are violated by the agency's "customs and usages." Specifically, if an individual can show that harm was caused by employees whose wrongful acts were the result of these "customs, practices, and policies, including poor training and supervision," then the employees as well as their local agencies may be sued. Criminal justice officials may avoid liability through the legal concept of "qualified immunity," which arises when they would not have known that their actions violated constitutional rights. However, courts look closely at whether officials should have known the implications of their actions. In *Hope v. Pelzer* (2002), for example, the court denied immunity from lawsuit to Alabama correctional officials who had handcuffed an inmate to a post in the prison yard and denied him adequate water and bathroom breaks for several hours. The decision emphasized that a reasonable officer would have known that this was a violation of the Eighth Amendment prohibition on cruel and unusual punishment.

Although huge financial settlements make headlines, and the numbers of Section 1983 filings are large, few cases come to trial, and very few correctional employees must personally pay financial awards to plaintiffs. However, no correctional employee wants to be involved in such legal situations.

Employees of private prisons are not subject to precisely the same kinds of lawsuits. For example, in *Minneci v. Pollard* (2012), the Supreme Court ruled that a prison inmate could not file a lawsuit in federal court alleging Eighth Amendment rights violations for the denial of medical care by officials at a private prison. Instead, the Court said the prisoner must seek compensation from these private business employees by filing a regular personal injury lawsuit in state court, rather than pursue a case for a constitutional rights violation as they would against government employees.

Correctional Policy Trends

The United States has a huge and expanding population under correctional supervision. Since the middle of the 1970s, the United States has fought a war on crime mainly by increasing the severity of sanctions against offenders. This led to a 500 percent increase in correctional budgets, nearly 4 million people on probation, more than 2 million incarcerated in prisons and jails, and 850,000 under parole supervision (E. Carson, 2014; L. E. Glaze and Kaeble, 2014; T. Minton and Golinelli, 2014). Some states now spend more on prisons than on higher education. These are staggering figures, especially considering the fact that crime has been decreasing for the past decade. These large numbers also pose significant issues for correctional administrators who must plan how to run institutions and control prisoners' behavior. Read the Technology and Criminal Justice feature to see a contemporary problem of growing significance. Figure 13.3 shows the tremendous growth in the

FIGURE 13.3 CORRECTIONAL POPULATIONS IN THE UNITED STATES, 1988–2013

Although the increase in prison populations receives the most publicity, a greater proportion of correctional growth has occurred in probation and parole.

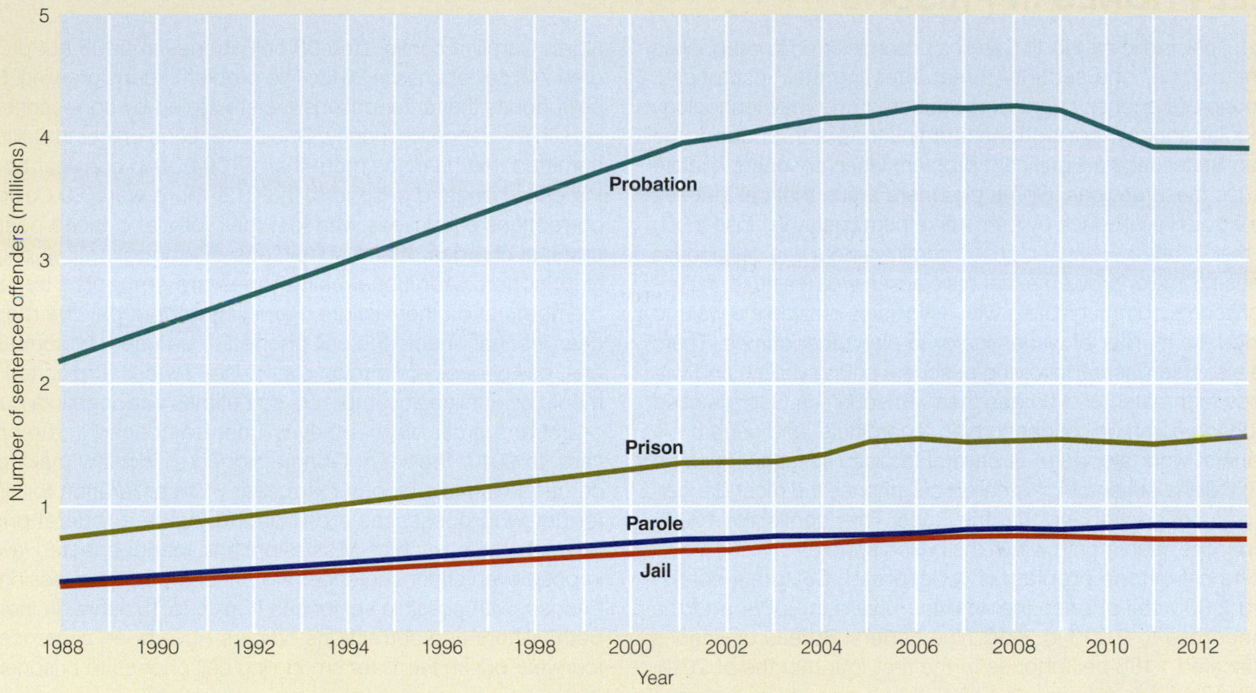

Sources: E. Ann Carson. "Prisoners in 2013," *Bureau of Justice Statistics Bulletin,* September 2014, NCJ 247282; Lauren E. Glaze and Danielle Kaeble, "Correctional Populations in the United States, 2013," *Bureau of Justice Statistics Bulletin,* December 2014, NCJ 248479; Todd Minton and Daniela Golinelli. *Jail Inmates at Midyear 2013: Statistical Tables,* NCJ 245350 (Washington, DC: U.S. Bureau of Justice Statistics), May 2014.

correctional population since the 1980s with the beginning of a decline for probation, jail, and prison in the most recent two-year period. The number on parole, by contrast, has continued to rise as more offenders are released from prison.

Some observers believe that the nation's drop in crime is a result of the harsher arrest and sentencing policies of the past quarter century. Critics say that the "lock 'em up" policies have had little impact on crime and that the fiscal and human costs of current policies severely damage families and communities. Some believe that there now exists a "prison-commercial complex," composed of construction companies, private prison companies, corrections officers' unions, and others who encourage increased spending on imprisonment regardless of need. Let's examine community corrections and incarceration policies so as to better understand current practices and future trends.

Community Corrections

Escalating prison growth has captured the public's attention, yet the numbers of those on probation and parole have actually risen at a faster rate than has the rate of the incarcerated population. Many factors may explain this growth, including more arrests and successful prosecutions, the lower costs

TECHNOLOGY & CRIMINAL JUSTICE

CELL PHONES IN PRISONS

In 2015, officials in the North Carolina prison referred to cell phones as the number one security threat affecting their institutions. Although cell phones might be considered everyday technology in regular society, correctional administrators throughout the United States face a significant problem when prisoners acquire and use these devices. Some prisoners argue that cell phones have a positive influence by permitting them to stay in close touch with their families. However, prison administrators ban cell phones because of major problems that have arisen with their use, including prisoners communicating with associates outside the walls to arrange the murder of witnesses or to plan other crimes. There have also been issues involving prisoners calling victims and witnesses to threaten and harass them. Prisoners in Georgia used cell-phone communications to plan, coordinate, and carry out a prisoners' work stoppage at several facilities simultaneously. In 2013, Indiana prison officials called cell phones the most dangerous piece of contraband that they face: They confiscate 100 to 200 phones each month within the prison system.

The cell-phone problem is widespread. California confiscated 2,800 cell phones inside prison walls in 2008, and the number rose to 9,000 in 2010. The Federal Bureau of Prisons confiscated 1,188 cell phones in the first four months of 2010. North Carolina confiscated 33 cell phones in 2005 but discovered 747 cell phones in 2013. The problem keeps growing. Most cell phones that enter prisons are smuggled by corrections officers in exchange for money. One corrections officer in California admitted that he made more than $100,000 in one year by selling cell phones to prisoners. In 2012, there were 20 California corrections employees who lost their jobs and faced possible criminal charges due to suspicions of smuggling cell phones to prisoners. Additional cell phones are smuggled by family members and other visitors. Family members pay the monthly charges that enable the cell phones to be used. In some prisons, cell phones are thrown over prison fences at planned moments by outside accomplices, sometimes wrapped in a bundle of dirt and grass so that they will not be noticed in the prison yard. In 2010, President Obama signed a new law making it a crime punishable by one extra year of incarceration for an offender who possesses a cell phone inside a federal prison. Several states, such as Mississippi and Idaho, enacted laws to impose even stiffer sentences on prisoners for possessing cell phones, with possible sentences from 5 to 15 years. In Indiana, both visitors and corrections officers have been sentenced to four-year prison terms for smuggling cell phones to prisoners.

of probation compared with incarceration, concerns regarding prison and jail crowding, and the large numbers of felons now being released from prison.

Probation

People on probation under community supervision now make up 57 percent of the correctional population, yet budgets and staffing have not risen accordingly. In many urban areas, probation caseloads are growing well beyond reasonable management levels: 200- and even 300-person caseloads are no longer unusual. Budget and staffing issues have adversely affected parole supervision, too. This has led to a deterioration in the quality of supervision. For example, news reports in 2013 indicated that Alabama's 350 probation and parole officers were so overwhelmed by their responsibility for supervising the state's 67,410 probationers and parolees that they typically saw each offender for only ten minutes each month (Edgemon, 2013). Yet the importance of probation for public safety has never been greater, because some probationers will commit additional crimes. As a result, a renewed emphasis on public safety has arisen. Many agencies have seen a resurgence of intensive and structured supervision for selected offenders.

In many respects, then, probation finds itself at a crossroads. Its workload is growing dramatically and, in light of budget cuts and crowding in prison and jails, will probably continue to do so. Under the strain of this workload and on-again, off-again public support, probation faces a serious challenge. Can its methods of supervision and service be adapted successfully to high-risk offenders?

Officials are developing new techniques to find cell phones, in addition to old-fashioned physical searches of prisoners' personal possessions and bunk areas. In some states, dogs are being trained to sniff for cell-phone batteries during searches. Many corrections officials would like to use jamming technology to prevent cell phones from being used in prisons, but jamming violates federal law and could affect the phones of people living near prisons. Mississippi implemented a system that detects calls and texts going into and out of prisons. With the cooperation of cell-phone companies, a message is sent to the phone announcing that the device will be shut off and made unusable. Mississippi's use of managed cell-phone towers that can control all calls originating in the institution led other states to follow suit, despite the major expense of up to $800,000 for the installation of such towers at a prison.

California officials believe that course of action could significantly reduce the cell-phone problem, with thorough searches of corrections officers as they enter the prison for each shift. However, employee searches would cost millions of dollars in additional wages for corrections officers, because thousands of officers would have to be paid for several additional minutes each day as they remove their shoes and equipment in order to be searched.

Sources: Jack Dolan, "California Prison Guards Union Is Called Main Obstacle to Keeping Cellphones Away from Inmates," *Los Angeles Times*, February 4, 2011 (www.latimes.com); Jack Dolan, "Phone Smuggling Case Costs 20 California Prison Workers Their Jobs," *Los Angeles Times*, October 14, 2012 (www.latimes.com); Troy Kehoe, "Cell Phones Create Ind. Prison Danger," WISH-TV.com, January 31, 2013 (www.wishtv.com); Troy Kehoe, "I Team 8: Hanging Up Prison Cells," WISH-TV.com, January 31, 2013 (www.wishtv.com); Tom McNichol, "Prison Cell-Phone Use a Growing Problem," *Time*, May 26, 2009 (www.time.com); Kim Severson and Robbie Brown, "Outlawed, Cellphones Are Thriving in Prisons," *New York Times*, January 2, 2011 (www.nytimes.com); John Wagner, "As Baltimore Jail Corruption Case Unfolds, Cellphone-Penalty Legislation Returns to Spotlight," *Washington Post*, May 5, 2013 (www.washingtonpost.com); Jonathan Rodriguez, "Cellphones Top Threat in NC Prisons, DOC Says," WNCN News online, January 29, 2015 (www.wncn.com); Sarah Phinney, "Indiana Jails and Prisons Using Phone Sniffing Dogs to Fight Contraband," WDRB News online, March 1, 2015 (www.wdrb.com).

DEBATE THE ISSUE

In times of budget cuts, how will corrections officials be able to keep up with smuggled technology in prisons? Even if Mississippi's system proves to be effective, can other states afford to purchase new technology in order to help them combat cell phones? List three things you would do if you were in charge of solving the cell-phone problem.

Parole

With the incarcerated population more than quadrupling during the past 30 years, it is not surprising that the number of parolees has also grown. Currently over 620,000 felons are released from prison each year, and most of them enter the community under correctional supervision. In 2011, more than 850,000 offenders were under parole supervision, a nearly fourfold increase since 1980 (L. E. Glaze and Kaeble, 2014). After the massive incarceration binge of recent decades, the number on parole could reach 1 million in the next five years, primarily because several states gave renewed emphasis to increasing parole releases as a way to cut expensive prison budgets (Lambert, 2011).

Compared with parolees in 1990, today's parolees are older, have served longer sentences, and have higher levels of substance abuse and mental illness; further, more were sentenced for drug violations. These characteristics increase reentry problems concerning the renewal of family ties, obtaining a job, and living according to parole rules. Most parolees cannot obtain the assistance necessary to reenter the community successfully.

Further, increased numbers of offenders are being returned to prison as parole violators. In 2013, an estimated 164,000 parole violators were returned to prison, constituting more than 25 percent of offenders entering prison that year (E. Carson, 2014). Thus a significant portion of admissions to state prisons each year can be attributed to the return of parolees for committing new crimes or violating conditions of release. Many states are devoting new efforts to more effectively transitioning parolees for reentry into society and then supervising and assisting them more intensively in order to reduce readmissions into the expensive sanction of incarceration. We discuss this trend in Chapter 16.

Incarceration

From 1940 until 1973, the number of people incarcerated in the United States remained fairly stable, with an incarceration rate of about 110 per 100,000 population. However, since 1973, when the overall crime rate started to fall, the incarceration rate has quadrupled, standing at 478 per 100,000 at the end of 2013 (E. Carson, 2014). As we saw in the chapter opener, the United States now has the highest incarceration rate in the developed world (Lambert, 2011).

Every June and December, a census of the U.S. prison population is taken for the Bureau of Justice Statistics. As shown in Figure 13.4, from a low of 98 per 100,000 population in 1972, the incarceration rate steadily rose to a high of 509 in June 2007, with a modest drop at the end of 2013. This corresponds to more than 1.5 million men and women in state and federal prisons. An additional 731,000 were in local jails (T. Minton and Golinelli, 2014). The Close Up feature examines incarceration rates in North America and Europe.

FIGURE 13.4 **INCARCERATION IN FEDERAL AND STATE PRISONS PER 100,000, POPULATION 1940–2013**

Between 1940 and 1973, the incarceration rate held steady. Since that time there has been a continuing increase. The rate today has more than quadrupled since 1970.

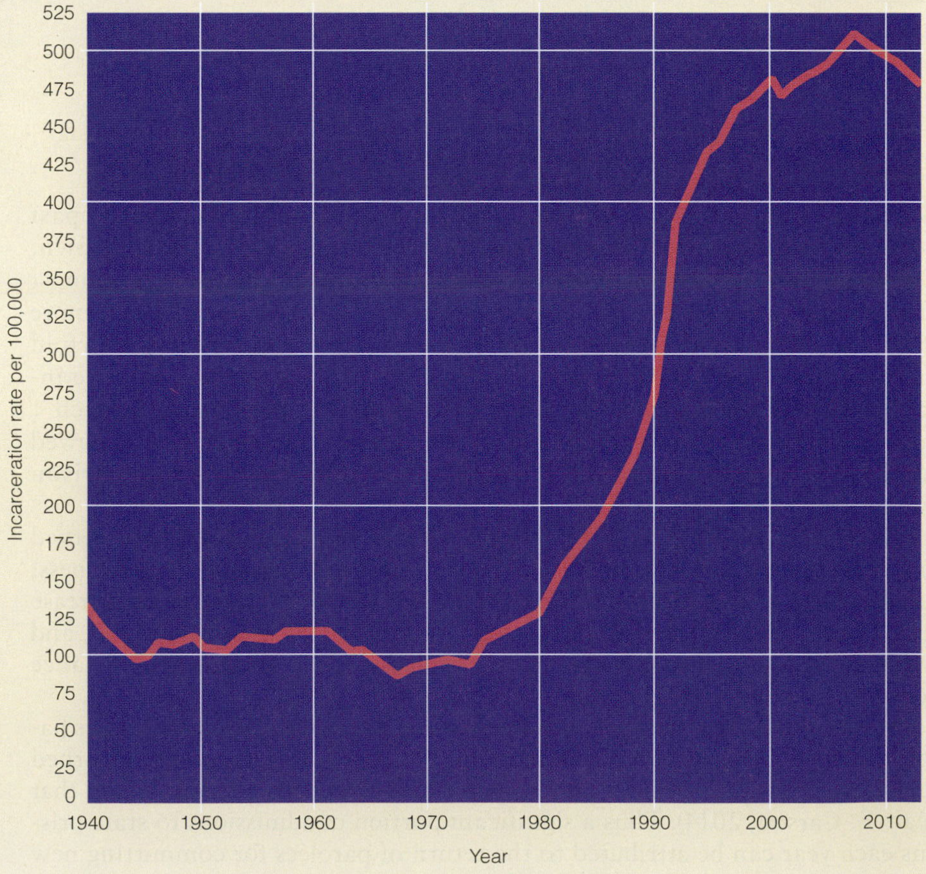

Sources: Bureau of Justice Statistics *Bulletin*, November 2004; *Bulletin*, December 2007; H. West, "Prison Inmates at Midyear 2009: Statistical Tables," *Bureau of Justice Statistics Tables*, June 2010, p. 4; E. Ann Carson and William J. Sabol,. "Prisoners in 2011," Bureau of Justice Statistics *Bulletin*, December 2012; E. Ann Carson, "Prisoners in 2013." Bureau of Justice Statistics *Bulletin*, September 2014, NCJ 247282.

CLOSE UP

BEHIND BARS IN NORTH AMERICA AND EUROPE

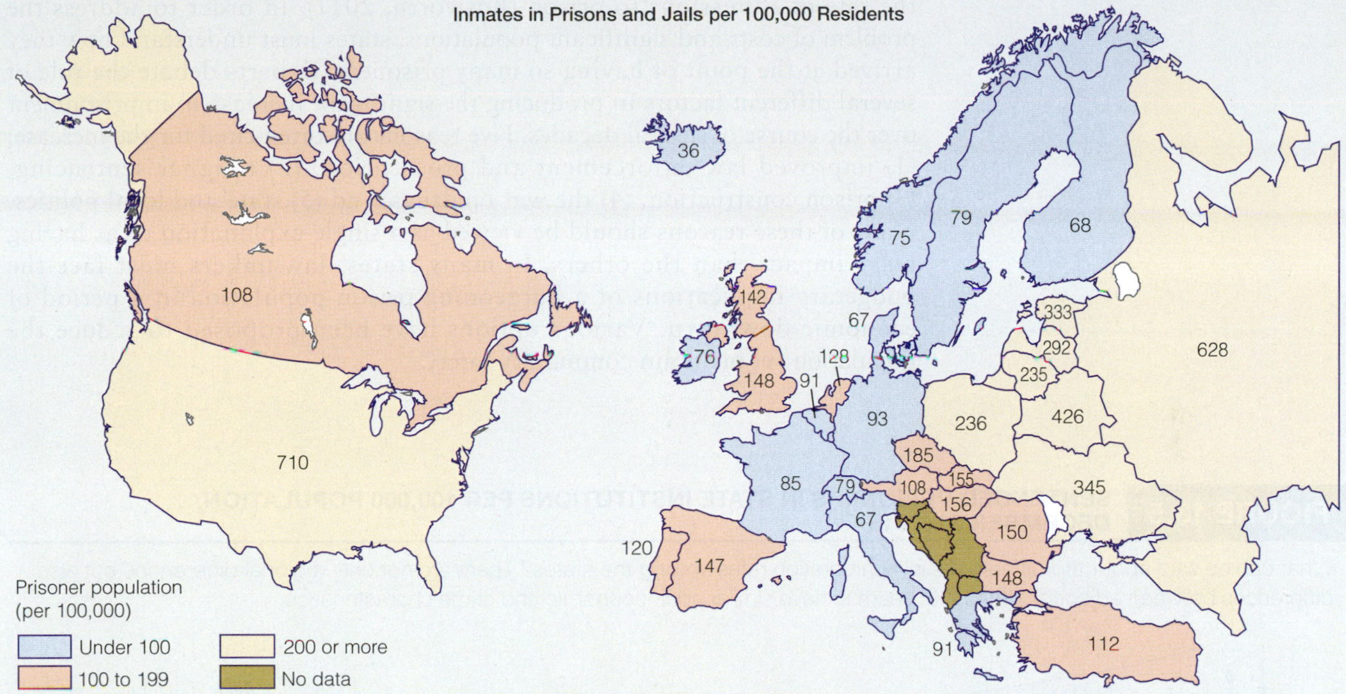

Most western countries have put more people behind bars in recent years, but in none has the incarceration rate risen higher than in the United States. The cause of the extraordinary American figure is not higher levels of crime, for the crime rate in the United States is about the same as in western Europe (except for the rate of homicide, which is 2 to 8 times greater in the United States, mostly because of the ready availability of guns).

The high U.S. rate—which rivals those of former Soviet nations—can be traced primarily to a shift in public attitudes toward crime that began about 30 years ago as apprehension about violence and drugs escalated. Politicians were soon exploiting the new attitudes with promises to get criminals off the streets. Congress and state legislatures, often at the prodding of presidents and governors, promoted "tough on crime" measures, including mandatory sentencing, three-strikes laws, longer sentences, and increased budgets for prison construction.

As a result, the length of sentences, already severe by western European standards, became even more punitive. Consequently, the number of those locked up rose more than fivefold between 1972 and 2008 to more than 2 million. Most of those sentenced in recent years are perpetrators of nonviolent crimes, such as drug possession, that would not ordinarily be punished by long prison terms in other western countries.

Sources: Adapted from Roger Doyle, "By the Numbers," *Scientific American*, August 1999, p. 25; *One in 100: Behind Bars in America, 2008* (Washington, DC: Pew Center on the States, 2008) p. 35; *World Prison Brief: 2008* (London: King's College); map adapted from data by Bureau of Justice Statistics, *Sourcebook of Criminal Justice Statistics* (2013), Table 6.1.2011; E. Ann Carson, "Prisoners in 2013," Bureau of Justice Statistics *Bulletin*, September 2014, NCJ 247282.

DEBATE THE ISSUE

Do these incarceration rates reflect differences in the nature of crime problems, differences in philosophies about punishment, or other factors? Do higher incarceration rates indicate that a country's citizens are safer than those in other countries? List three reasons why you believe the United States has such a relatively high incarceration rate compared to other countries. Can any of these reasons to be changed in order to lower the extent and expense of imprisonment in the United States?

Keep in mind that the size and growth of the prison population is not evenly distributed across the country. As Figure 13.5 shows, the states with the highest incarceration rates are in the South, along with Arizona in the West and Missouri in the Midwest.

At the close of the twenty-first century's first decade, financial problems led many states to initiate efforts to reduce their prison populations or slow the rate of admissions to prison (Bosworth, 2011). In order to address the problem of costs and significant populations, states must understand how they arrived at the point of having so many prisoners. Experts debate the role of several different factors in producing the significant increase in imprisonment over the course of several decades. Five reasons are often cited for the increase: (1) improved law enforcement and prosecution, (2) tougher sentencing, (3) prison construction, (4) the war on drugs, and (5) state and local politics. None of these reasons should be viewed as a single explanation or as having more impact than the others. In many states, lawmakers must face the budgetary implications of a burgeoning prison population in a period of economic downturn. Various options have been proposed to reduce the population yet maintain community safety.

FIGURE 13.5 SENTENCED PRISONERS IN STATE INSTITUTIONS PER 100,000 POPULATION, DECEMBER 31, 2013

What can be said about the differences in incarceration rates among the states? There are not only regional differences but also differences between adjacent states that seem to have similar socioeconomic and crime characteristics.

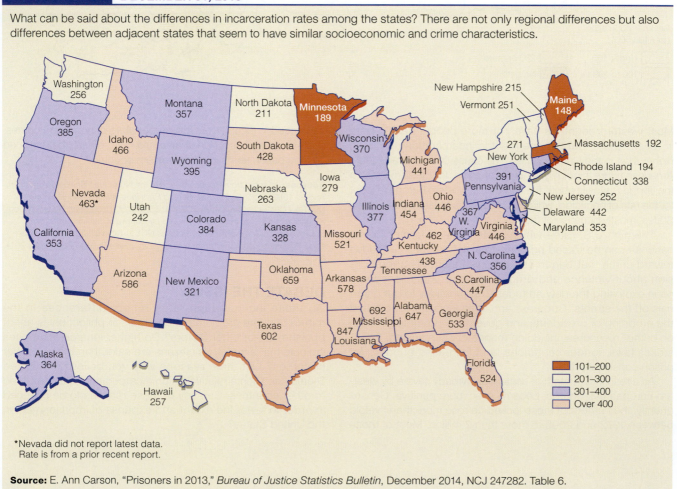

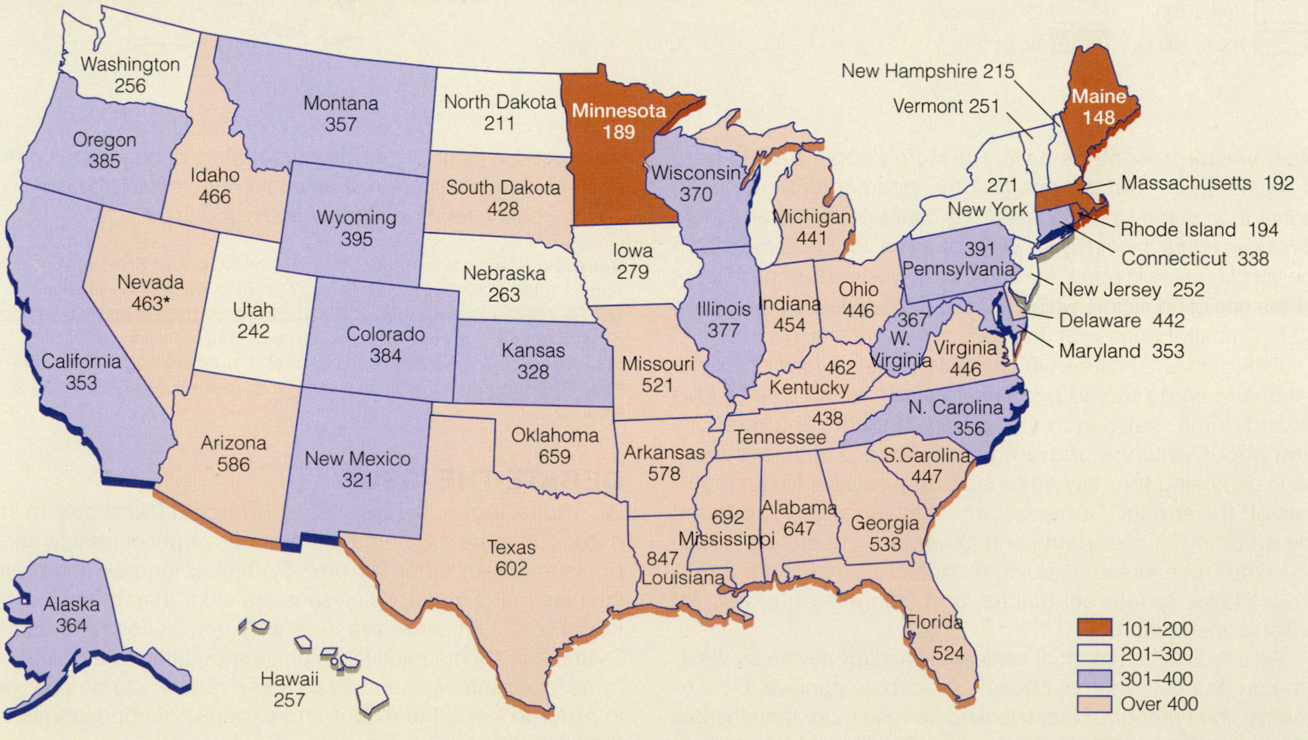

*Nevada did not report latest data. Rate is from a prior recent report.

Source: E. Ann Carson, "Prisoners in 2013," *Bureau of Justice Statistics Bulletin*, December 2014, NCJ 247282. Table 6.

Increased Arrests and More-Likely Incarceration

Some analysts have argued that the billions of dollars spent on the crime problem may be paying off. Not only have arrest rates increased, particularly for some offenses such as drug violations, aggravated assaults, and sexual assaults, but the probability of being sent to prison also has dramatically increased. In 2009, the U.S. Sentencing Guidelines Commission reported that the percentage of federal offenders sent to prison increased over the preceding ten years from 75.4 percent to 85.3 percent (Coyle, 2009).

In addition, the number of offenders returned to prison for parole violations (see Chapter 16) has also increased. Those sent back to prison include parolees convicted of new felonies while in the community and those experiencing parole revocation for technical violations, such as failing to meet with their parole officer or failing a drug test. However, among those sent back for technical violations, an unknown number went back based on being arrested for a new crime. Some of these offenders would have been convicted of new felonies if the prosecutors and parole authorities had wished to pursue these charges rather than just send the offenders straight back to prison to complete the earlier sentence. Much of the growth in total admissions to state prisons can be attributed to parole and probation violators being sent to prison and does not reflect the commission of new crimes or the incarceration of new offenders. In Texas, for example, 77,000 offenders were admitted to prison in 2004, and 46 percent of them were parole or probation violators. Among these violators, nearly 40 percent went to prison for technical infractions rather than for new crimes (Elliott and Murphy, 2005).

Studies have also shown that the increase in drug arrests have led to disproportionate rates of incarceration for African Americans. The research points to police tactics of targeting poor, urban, minority areas for enforcement of drug laws, even though blacks and whites use illegal drugs at roughly the same rate (Heath, 2014; Eckholm, 2008a).

Tougher Sentencing Practices

Some observers think that a hardening of public attitudes toward criminals was reflected in longer sentences, in a smaller proportion of those convicted getting probation, and in fewer being released at the time of the first parole hearing.

In the past three decades, the states and the federal government have passed laws that increase sentences for most crimes. However, the tougher sentences do not seem to be the main factor keeping offenders in prison for longer periods. Between 1990 and 1998 the mean sentence of new court commitments has actually dropped. Rather, it is the 13 percent increase in the amount of time served that affects the total number of inmates. This increase in time served has resulted from the adoption by states of truth-in-sentencing laws that require offenders to serve most of their sentences in prison, and mandatory minimum laws that limit the discretion of judges (JFA Institute, 2007). Keeping people in prison longer seems to account for some of the growth of the incarcerated population. However, recent budget-driven developments may diminish the prior effects of tougher sentencing and contribute to further declines in prison growth.

Prison Construction

The increased rate of incarceration may be related to the creation of additional space in the nation's prisons. Between 1975 and 2000, over 400 prisons were built across the country, at least doubling the number of facilities in each state. Even with the decline in crime rates and tougher economic times in many states, new prison construction continues.

According to organization theorists, available public resources such as hospitals and schools are used to capacity. Prisons are no exception. When prison space is limited, judges reserve incarceration for violent offenders only. However, additional prisons may present a variation of the "Field of Dreams" scenario—build them and they will come. As Joseph Davey has noted, "The presence of empty state-of-the-art prison facilities can encourage a criminal court judge to incarcerate a defendant who may otherwise get probation" (1998: 84).

Prison construction during the 1990s was a growth industry, building 351 adult facilities that added more than 528,000 beds during the decade (A. Beck and Harrison, 2001). The new facilities increased the capacity of state prisons by 81 percent.

For health and security reasons, crowded conditions in existing facilities cannot be tolerated. Many states attempted to build their way out of this dilemma, because the public seemed to favor harsher sentencing policies, which would require more prison space. With many states holding large budget surpluses during the booming economy of the 1990s, legislatures were willing to advance the huge sums required for prison expansion. Pressures from contractors, building-material providers, and correctional-officer unions spurred expansion in a number of states. Yet many states that tried to build their way out of their crowded facilities found that as soon as a new prison came on line, it was quickly filled.

The War on Drugs

Crusades against the use of drugs have recurred in American politics since the late 1800s. The latest manifestation began in 1982, when President Ronald Reagan declared another "war on drugs" and asked Congress to set aside more money for drug enforcement personnel and for prison space. This came at a time when the country faced the frightening advent of crack cocaine, which ravaged many communities and increased the murder rate. In 1987, Congress imposed stiff mandatory minimum sentences for federal drug law violations, and many states copied these sentencing laws. Only in the second decade of the twenty-first century, when concerns about the budgetary costs of large prison populations began to enter legislators' thinking, did drug sentencing practices begin to change and become less severe.

The war on drugs has succeeded on one front by packing the nation's prisons with drug law offenders, but many scholars believe that is about all it has achieved. With additional resources and pressures for enforcement, the number of people sentenced to prison for drug offenses has increased steadily. In 1980, only 19,000, or about 6 percent of state prisoners, had been convicted of drug offenses; by 2003 the number had risen to 250,000. More than 16 percent of state prisoners were incarcerated for drug offenses in 2013, and the percentage in federal prisons was even higher, at 49 percent (E. Carson, 2014; U.S. Bureau of Prisons, 2015). Furthermore, the likelihood of imprisonment and length of sentences increased for drug offenders from the 1980s into the 1990s, and then continued at this level of punishment through the first decade of the twenty-first century (Langan and R. Cohen, 1996; BJS, 2013a).

State and Local Politics

Incarceration rates vary among the regions and states, but why do states with similar characteristics differ in their use of prisons? Can it be that local political factors influence correctional policies?

One might think that each state would show a certain association between crime rates and incarceration rates—the more crime, the more prisoners. Even when states have similar socioeconomic and demographic characteristics—poverty, unemployment, racial composition, drug arrests—unaccountable variations among their incarceration rates exist. For example, North Dakota and South Dakota have similar social characteristics and crime rates, yet the incarceration rate in South Dakota is significantly higher. South Dakota's rate rose from 88 to 428 per 100,000 population from 1980 to 2013. By contrast, North Dakota's rate rose only to 211 per 100,000 population by 2013 (E. Carson, 2014). One can even find similar and contiguous states—such as Connecticut and Massachusetts, Arizona and New Mexico, or Minnesota and Wisconsin—where the state that sometimes has the higher crime rate also has the lower incarceration rate.

Scholars' studies have shown that community leaders often promote the siting of prisons in their towns as a means of economic development. However, some studies show that the touted gains are often not realized (R. S. King, Mauer, and Huling, 2004). A good example of the impact of locating prisons in communities can be found in the state of New York, which in the 1970s passed tough drug-sentencing laws. Over the next 20 years, the state's prison population increased dramatically. Most of the prisoners ended up in new prisons located in the northern, rural, economically impoverished region of the state. The influx of prisoners brought some jobs to the region. Legislative districts whose economy was tied to prison payrolls soon found that their politics was dominated by the union that represents correctional officers (F. Santos, 2008b). Across the nation, 21 counties were found in which at least 21 percent of the residents were inmates. In Concho County, Texas, with a population of 4,000, a full 33 percent of the people counted as residents were offenders housed in the prison (Butterfield, 2004b).

David Greenberg and Valerie West analyzed variations in the levels of incarceration among the 50 states between 1971 and 1991. They found that the volume of crime in a state accounted for only part of the incarceration rate. Here are the major findings of this research.

- States with high violent crime rates have higher levels of incarceration.
- States with higher revenues have higher prison populations.
- States with higher unemployment and where there is a higher percentage of African Americans have higher prison populations.
- States with more-generous welfare benefits have lower prison populations.
- States with more conservatives have not only higher incarceration rates, but their rates grew more rapidly than did the rates of states with fewer conservatives.
- Political incentives for an expansive prison policy transcended Democratic and Republican affiliations. (D. F. Greenberg and West, 2001)

It is at the state level that critics point to the operation of a corrections–commercial complex. They argue that the "punishment industry" influences high incarceration rates during a period of falling levels of crime. Specifically, they point to links among corporations doing business with corrections, government agencies seeking to expand their domain, and legislators promoting tough crime policies that benefit their districts.

Critics of the corrections–commercial complex concept say that the growth of the prison population helped to lower crime rates, that felons deserve to be punished severely, and that the political influences just cited do not drive corrections policy.

Clearly, doubling of the incarceration rate during a single decade seems to stem from several factors, not just one. Given public attitudes toward crime and punishment, fear of crime, and the expansion of prison space, incarceration rates will likely remain high. However, because the costs of this form of punishment more deeply invade the pockets of taxpayers than do other forms of punishment, there are indications that greater emphasis is being placed on alternatives to incarceration. This is reflected in the efforts of specific states to reduce their prison populations so that some of their expensive prisons can be closed. It is also reflected in the dip in imprisonment rates for several states, especially Michigan and California, from 2008 onward.

Community Safety versus Incarceration

Faced with ever-increasing costs of incarceration, many state legislatures are considering budget-cutting proposals that would result in the release of thousands of inmates to parole, halfway houses, or rehabilitation facilities. For example,

- Mississippi's governor has signed a law to allow offenders to go free after serving 25 percent of their sentence.
- Rhode Island lawmakers have approved an expansion of good time, thus setting the stage for substantial savings through shorter prison sentences.
- Kentucky has decided to allow nonviolent, non–sex offenders to serve up to 180 days of their sentences at home.
- Kansas and Michigan enhanced services in the community for ex-offenders in order to facilitate more releases, whereas other states gave more attention to drug treatment programs that are less expensive than incarceration. (Mauer, 2011).

Legislators are faced with the hard task of reducing prison costs while ensuring community safety. A report by the Pew Center on the States addressed the issue of reducing incarceration costs while maintaining public safety. The report argues that "states are paying a high cost for corrections—one that may not be buying them as much in public safety as it should" (Riordan, 2008: 1). According to the Pew Center, some states are attempting to protect public safety and reap corrections savings by holding lower-risk offenders accountable in less costly settings and using intermediate sanctions for parolees and probationers who violate conditions of their release. These include a mix of community based programs such as day reporting centers, treatment facilities, electronic monitoring, and community services. These tactics have been adopted in a number of states including Kansas and Texas (Riordan, 2008). It will be interesting to follow this policy trend to see if legislators are willing to risk the political consequences of being labeled as "soft on crime."

✔POINT

16. What are five explanations for the great increase in the incarcerated population?

17. Why might additional prison construction only aggravate the problem?

STOP AND ANALYZE: Because the size of a state's prison population is affected by a variety of factors, including policies for granting and revoking parole, there is not a single factor that is solely responsible for the nation's significant incarceration rate. In light of what you have read about the factors that led to the increase in the American incarceration rate since the 1980s, what would you recommend if a governor hired you as a consultant on reducing the cost of a state's prison system? List three recommendations that you would make, and state your reasons for each recommendation.

A QUESTION OF ETHICS

Michigan's corrections system decided that it could save money by laying off 370 prison food service workers and, instead, signing a contract with a private company, Aramark, to handle prison food service with its own lower-paid, nonunion employees. By late 2014, within one year of privatizing prison food service, more than 100 Aramark employees had been barred from entering the prisons for various misdeeds, including smuggling cell phones and drugs to prisoners, having sexual contact with prisoners, and even reportedly asking one prisoner to kill another prisoner. In addition, the private company had difficulties fulfilling the required food service standards; problems included running out food and inspection violations, such as the presence of maggots in insufficiently clean food preparation and service areas. Prisoners protested against the inadequacy of the new privatized food service, events that in at least one case led corrections officers to use tear gas to restore order. Similar problems arose when Ohio prisons contracted with Aramark to handle prison food service. Legislators and newspaper editorials in Michigan demanded that the state end the contract, but the governor was reportedly reluctant to terminate the contract for inadequate performance because it had saved the state $12 million in the first year.

Sources: Paul Egan, "Aramark on Notice over Prison Contract," *Lansing State Journal,* June 25, 2014 (www.lansingstatejournal.com); Paul Egan, "Aramark's Record in Other Prison Systems," *Detroit Free Press*, July 13, 2014 (www.freep.com); Paul Egan, "Maggots Found in Second Michigan Prison," *Detroit Free Press,* July 2, 2014 (www.freep.com); Steve Friess, "Aramark Workers Run Amok in Michigan Prisons," *Bloomberg News,* October 2, 2014 (www.bloomberg.com).

CRITICAL THINKING AND ANALYSIS

Should corrections officials and legislators make saving money their highest priority? What if privatization of food service leads to illnesses among the prison population—which can potentially then lead to increased costs for medical care? What if privatization of food service leads to disorder in prisons that puts the safety of corrections officers at risk? Given the food service problems associated with privatization in Michigan, make a list of what you see as the highest priorities that should motivate corrections officials. In addition, what three recommendations would you make to either improve the private company's performance or move in a different direction?

Summary

1 Describe how the American system of corrections has developed

- From colonial days to the present, the methods of criminal sanctions that are considered appropriate have varied.
- The development of the penitentiary brought a shift away from corporal punishment.
- The Pennsylvania and New York systems were competing approaches to implementing the ideas of the penitentiary.
- The Declaration of Principles of 1870 contained the key elements for the reformatory and rehabilitation models of corrections.
- Three principles guided female-prison reform during the nineteenth century: (1) separation from male prisoners, (2) care specialized to women's needs, and (3) management by female staff.
- Although based on the social sciences, the rehabilitative model failed to reduce recidivism.
- The community model of corrections tried to provide psychological treatment and increase opportunities for offenders to be successful citizens.
- The crime control model emphasized incarceration, long and mandatory sentencing, and strict supervision.

2 Analyze the roles federal, state, and local governments play in corrections

- The administration of corrections in the United States is fragmented, in that various levels of government are involved.
- The correctional responsibilities of the federal government are divided between the Federal Bureau of Prisons (of the U.S. Department of Justice) and the Administrative Office of the U.S. Courts.
- In all states, the administration of prisons falls under the executive branch of state government.
- Private prisons may or may not become accepted as a way to address overcrowding.
- Efforts to apprehend undocumented immigrants place additional burdens and costs on jails that must hold these detainees as they are processed for possible deportation.
- Jails, which are administered by local government, hold people awaiting trial and hold sentenced offenders.

- Jail administrators face several problems: (1) the perceived role of the jail in the local criminal justice system, (2) the inmate population, and (3) fiscal problems.

3 Discuss the law of corrections and how it is applied to offenders and correctional personnel

- Until the 1960s the courts held a "hands-off" policy with respect to corrections.
- The rights of offenders are found in the First, Fourth, Eighth, and Fourteenth Amendments to the U.S. Constitution.
- The prisoners' rights movement, through lawsuits in the federal courts, has brought many changes to the administration and conditions of U.S. prisons.
- Decisions of the Supreme Court have affected community corrections through rules governing probation and parole revocation.

4 Describe the direction of community corrections

- The growth of prisons has attracted public attention, but the numbers of offenders on probation and parole have risen at a faster rate.
- Probation is faced with the challenge of supervising high-risk offenders.
- Increasing numbers of offenders are being returned to prison as parole violators.

5 Explain why the prison population has more than quadrupled over the last three decades

- Prison populations rose quite substantially as a result of longer prison sentences, more frequent incarceration of drug offenders, and requirements for serving longer portions of sentences prior to parole.
- The factors affecting prison populations are affected by political choices and policy decisions.

Questions for Review

1. What were the major differences between the New York and Pennsylvania systems in the nineteenth century?
2. What are some of the pressures that administrators of local jails face?
3. What types of correctional programs does your state support? What government agencies run them?
4. Why do some state legislators consider private prisons an attractive option for corrections?
5. What Supreme Court decisions are the most significant for corrections today? What effects has each had on correctional institutions? On probation and parole?
6. What explanations might be given for the increased use of incarceration during the past two decades?

Key Terms and Cases

community corrections (p. 536)
congregate system (p. 531)
contract labor system (p. 531)
corrections (p. 525)
crime control model of corrections (p. 537)
deportation (p. 545)
Enlightenment (p. 526)
hands-off policy (p. 552)
jail (p. 547)
lease system (p. 533)
mark system (p. 534)
medical model (p. 536)
penitentiary (p. 528)
prison (p. 547)
reformatory (p. 534)
rehabilitation model (p. 536)
separate confinement (p. 530)
undocumented immigrants (p. 544)
Cooper v. Pate (1964) (p. 552)
Hudson v. Palmer (1984) (p. 554)
Mempa v. Rhay (1967) (p. 561)
Morrissey v. Brewer (1972) (p. 561)
Wolff v. McDonnell (1974) (p. 557)

Checkpoint Answers

1 What was the Enlightenment and how did it influence corrections?

✓ A period in the late eighteenth century when philosophers rethought the nature of society and the place of the individual in the world. New ideas about society and government arose from the Enlightenment.

2 What were the main goals of the penitentiary?

✓ (1) secure and sanitary building, (2) systematic inspection, (3) abolition of fees, and (4) a reformatory regime.

3 How did the Pennsylvania and New York systems differ?

✓ The Pennsylvania system of separate confinement held inmates in isolation from one another. The New York congregate system kept inmates in their cells at night, but they worked together in shops during the day.

4 What was the significance of the Cincinnati Declaration of Principles?

✓ It advocated indeterminate sentences, rehabilitation programs, classifications based on improvements in character, and release on parole.

5 What principles guided the reform of corrections for women in the nineteenth century?

✓ Separation of women prisoners from men, care in keeping with women's needs, women's prisons staffed by women.

6 What are the underlying assumptions of the rehabilitation, community, and crime control models of corrections?

✓ *Rehabilitation model:* Criminal behavior is the result of a biological, psychological, or social deficiency; clinicians should diagnose the problem and prescribe treatment; when cured, the offender may be released. *Community model:* The goal of corrections is to reintegrate the offender into the community, so rehabilitation should be carried out in the community rather than in prison, if possible; correctional workers should serve as advocates for offenders in their dealings with government agencies. *Crime control model:* Criminal behavior can be controlled by greater use of incarceration and other forms of strict supervision.

7 What agencies of the U.S. government are responsible for prisons and probation?

✓ The Federal Bureau of Prisons of the Department of Justice, and the Administrative Office of the U.S. Courts, which handles probation.

8 What agencies of state government are responsible for incarceration, probation, intermediate sanctions, and parole?

✓ *Incarceration (prisons)*: department of corrections. *Probation:* judiciary or executive branch department. *Intermediate sanctions*: judiciary, probation department, department of corrections. *Parole*: executive agency.

9 What are the arguments in favor of and against privately run prisons?

✓ *In favor*: Claims that costs are lower, yet conditions are the same or better than prisons run by the government. *Opposed*: Incarceration should be a function of government, not an enterprise for private profit. Private interests can skew public policy and do not necessarily save money.

10 What are the functions of jails?

✓ Holding of alleged offenders before trial and incarceration of offenders sentenced to short terms.

11 What are three of the problems affecting jails?

✓ High population turnover, lack of services, scarce resources.

12 What was the hands-off policy?

✓ Judges' belief that prisoners do not have protected rights and that the courts should not become involved in the administration of prisons.

13 Why is the case of *Cooper v. Pate* important to the expansion of prisoners' rights?

✓ *Cooper v. Pate* allowed state prisoners to sue in federal courts in order to challenge conditions of confinement and other rights issues in prisons.

14 What protections do prisoners receive from the First, Fourth, and Eighth Amendments?

✓ First Amendment protects limited rights for religious practices and access to publications; Fourth Amendment provides limited protection for bodily searches; Eighth Amendment protects against inhumane prison conditions.

15 Which two clauses of the Fourteenth Amendment have been interpreted by the Supreme Court to apply to prisoners' rights?

✓ The due process and equal protection clauses.

16 What are five explanations for the great increase in the incarcerated population?

✓ Increased arrests and more-likely incarceration, tougher sentencing, prison construction, the war on drugs, state and local politics.

17 Why might additional prison construction only aggravate the problem?

✓ New prison beds will quickly become filled, since judges will be less hesitant to sentence people to prison and because the correctional bureaucracy needs the space to be used.

CHAPTER FEATURES

- **Technology and Criminal Justice** Technology and Probation
- **Doing Your Part** Probation Volunteer
- **Close Up** Controversies over Forfeiture of Cash and Property
- **New Directions in Criminal Justice Policy** Evidence-Based Practices in Community Corrections

CHAPTER 14 COMMUNITY CORRECTIONS: PROBATION AND INTERMEDIATE SANCTIONS

CHAPTER LEARNING OBJECTIVES

1. Analyze the philosophical assumptions that underlie community corrections
2. Discuss how probation evolved and how probation sentences are implemented today
3. Describe the types of intermediate sanctions and how they are administered
4. Analyze the key issues facing community corrections at the beginning of the twenty-first century

CHAPTER OUTLINE

Community Corrections: Assumptions

Probation: Corrections without Incarceration
- Origins and Evolution of Probation
- Organization of Probation
- Probation Services
- Reliance on Volunteers
- Revocation and Termination of Probation
- Assessing Probation

Intermediate Sanctions in the Community
- Intermediate Sanctions Administered Primarily by the Judiciary
- Intermediate Sanctions Administered in the Community
- Intermediate Sanctions Administered in Institutions and the Community
- Implementing Intermediate Sanctions

The Future of Community Corrections

Joe Raedle/Getty Images

Pop star Justin Bieber was arrested twice in January 2014—first in Florida for careless driving, and then later in California for throwing eggs at his neighbor's house. After his arrest in Florida, Bieber pled guilty to careless driving and resisting arrest and agreed to donate $50,000 to a local charity rather than serve probation.

As punishment for his egg-throwing vandalism in California, he was ordered to serve two years of probation, five days of community service, complete an anger-management program, and pay his neighbor $80,900 in restitution (Reuters, 2014a). However, Bieber has not been able to complete his required community service—his attorney explained that due to an ankle injury, time spent in the recording studio, and the taping of several television programs, he would need extra time to complete the terms of his probation. The judge agreed (F. Brown, 2015).

Does the fact that Bieber is a celebrity affect the type of punishment he has received? Did he receive probation rather than jail due to his fame? Does his celebrity also allow him to extend the deadline for completing his requirements? Would the average person receive such leniency from a judge if he or she had work conflicts or minor injuries? Most people cannot afford to make $50,000 donations to avoid punishment. Does this mean that Bieber was able to buy his freedom? These are serious and important questions. Moreover, Bieber's case stands in stark contrast with the U.S. Department of Justice's report on the local court system, discussed in Chapter 12, where poor people faced jailing and additional fines for failing to pay *parking tickets* in a timely manner. Community corrections is an important aspect of criminal punishment, but we must be concerned about whether they are applied appropriately and fairly.

Since the early nineteenth century, supervision in the community has been recognized as an appropriate punishment for some offenders. Probation was developed in the 1840s and parole followed in the 1870s. By the 1930s every state and the federal government used these forms of community corrections to either punish offenders without incarceration (probation) or to supervise offenders in the community after leaving prison (parole). Intermediate sanctions were developed in the 1980s when people saw the need for punishments that were less restrictive than prison but more restrictive than probation.

Community corrections can be expected to play an increasing role in the criminal justice system. As shown in Figure 14.1, two-thirds of offenders are already under correctional supervision in the community. In an era of state budget cuts, this proportion is likely to increase as states seek alternatives to the high costs of incarceration. Probation and intermediate sanctions are less expensive and, in the view of many criminal justice experts, just as effective as imprisonment for certain categories of offenders.

FIGURE 14.1 PERCENTAGE OF PEOPLE IN EACH CATEGORY OF CORRECTIONAL SUPERVISION

Although most people think of corrections as prisons and jails, in fact, more than three-quarters of offenders are supervised within the community.

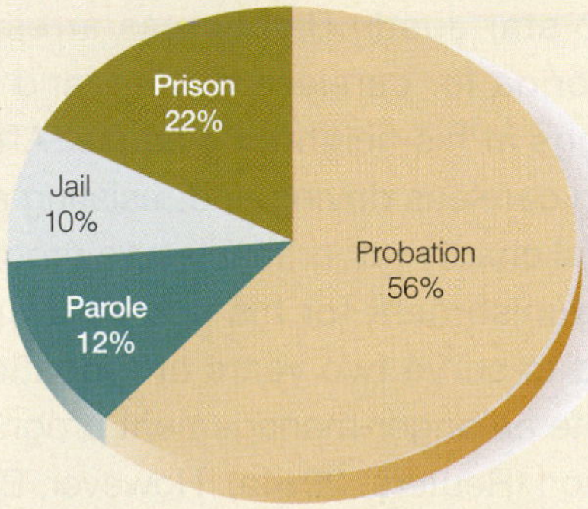

Source: Lauren E. Glaze and Danielle Kaeble, "Correctional Populations in the United States, 2013," Bureau of Justice Statistics *Bulletin,* December 2014, NCJ 248479.

Community Corrections: Assumptions

Community corrections seeks to keep offenders in the community by building ties to family, employment, and other normal sources of stability and success. This model of corrections assumes that the offender must change, but it also recognizes that factors within the community that might encourage criminal behavior (unemployment, for example) must also change.

Four factors are usually cited in support of community corrections:

1. Many offenders' criminal records and current offenses are not serious enough to warrant incarceration.
2. Community supervision is cheaper than incarceration.
3. Rates of **recidivism**, or returning to crime, for those under community supervision are no higher than for those who go to prison.

recidivism
A return to criminal behavior.

4. Ex-inmates require both support and supervision as they try to remake their lives in the community.

Community corrections is based on the goal of finding the "least restrictive alternative"—punishing the offender only as severely as needed to protect the community and to satisfy the public. Advocates call for programs to assist offenders in the community so they will have opportunities to succeed in law-abiding activities and to reduce their contact with the criminal world. Surveys have found there is support for community-based punishments for some types of offenders (see "What Americans Think").

✔POINT 1. What are the four main assumptions underlying community corrections?

STOP AND ANALYZE: Consider the four factors in support of community corrections. Now think of four counterarguments that oppose widespread use of community sanctions. Which set of factors or arguments is most persuasive to you?

(Answers are at the end of the chapter.)

Probation: Corrections without Incarceration

As we have seen, probation is the conditional release of the offender into the community, under the supervision of correctional officials. Although probationers live at home and work at regular jobs, they must report regularly to their probation officers. They must also abide by specific conditions, such as submitting to drug tests, obeying curfews, and staying away from certain people or parts of town.

Probation is significantly less expensive than imprisonment, a fact that has become increasingly important as state budget cuts force justice system officials to consider how to employ expanded use of lower-cost punishments for criminal offenders. The United States court system calculates that the cost of incarcerating a federal prisoner in a Bureau of Prisons facility is $28,948 per year, while the cost of supervising that individual in the community is $3,347 per year—a savings of $25,601 per prisoner per year (U.S. Courts, 2013). When one multiplies the amount saved by the hundreds or thousands of offenders placed on probation rather than sent to prison, that represents a significant reduction in the corrections system's burden on the federal budget. Thus there is consideration for using probation for a larger number of offenders, including those who have committed crimes that led to imprisonment in the past. As indicated in Figure 14.2, although probation is used mainly for lesser offenses, states also use probation for more-serious felonies.

Probation can be combined with other sanctions, such as fines, restitution, and community service. Fulfillment of these other sanctions may, in effect, become a condition for successful completion of probation. The sentencing court retains authority over the probationer, and if he or she violates the conditions or commits another crime, the judge can order the entire sentence to be served in prison.

The number of probationers now under supervision is at a record high and is still rising. Much has been written about overcrowded prisons, but the adult probation population increased steadily from 2000 to 2008, but then dropped slightly each year from 2009 through 2011 (L. E. Glaze and Parks, 2012). Today, nearly 4 million offenders are on probation, yet probation budgets in many states have been cut and probation officers' caseloads have increased as resources are diverted to other priorities (Leu and Cristobal, 2011).

WHAT AMERICANS THINK

QUESTION: "What percent of the people currently in prison in the United States do you think could be released from prison who would not pose a threat to overall public safety?"

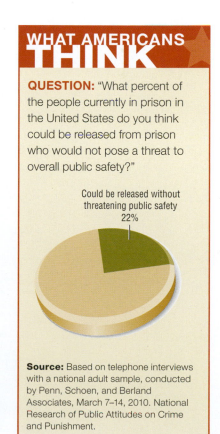

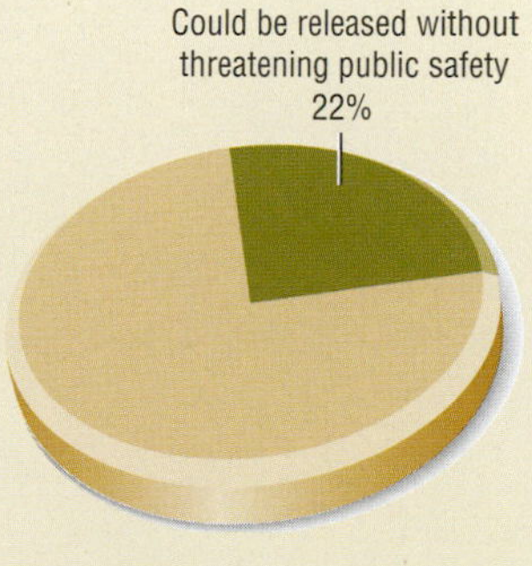

Source: Based on telephone interviews with a national adult sample, conducted by Penn, Schoen, and Berland Associates, March 7–14, 2010. National Research of Public Attitudes on Crime and Punishment.

FIGURE 14.2 MOST-SERIOUS OFFENSES COMMITTED BY OFFENDERS SENTENCED TO PROBATION

Most probationers are serving their sentence because they committed property or drug offenses, but almost 20 percent of probationers have been convicted of violent offenses. Sex offenders comprise the smallest category of people sentenced to probation.

*Totals are affected by rounding

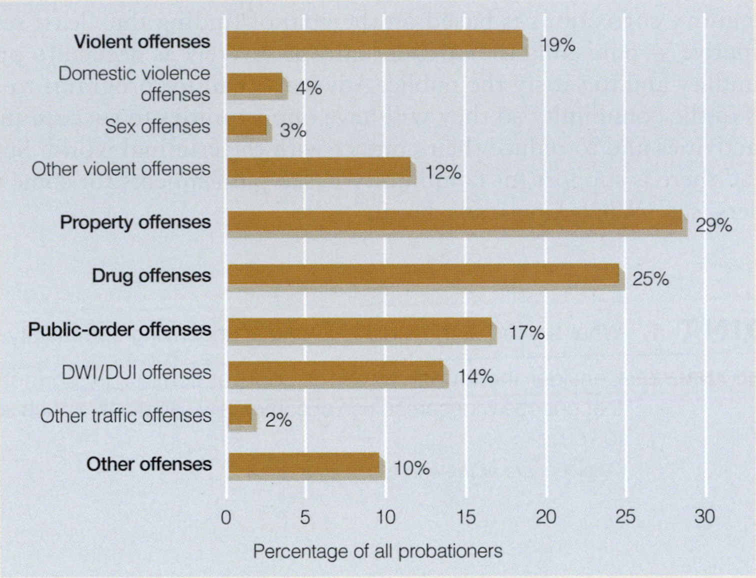

Source: Erinn J. Herberman and Thomas P. Bonczar, "Probation and Parole in the United States, 2013," Bureau of Justice Statistics *Bulletin,* October 2014, NCJ 284029.

Although probation offers many benefits that cause it to be chosen over incarceration, the public often sees it as merely a "slap on the wrist" for offenders. When caseloads in some urban areas are as high as 300 offenders per officer, probation officers cannot provide the level of supervision necessary to ensure compliance and proper behavior by probationers (Edgemon, 2013).

Origins and Evolution of Probation

The historical roots of probation lie in the procedures for reprieves and pardons of early English courts. Probation first developed in the United States when John Augustus, a Boston boot maker, persuaded a judge in the Boston Police Court in 1841 to give him custody of a convicted offender for a brief period and then helped the man to appear to be rehabilitated by the time of sentencing.

Massachusetts developed the first statewide probation system in 1880, and 21 other states had followed suit by 1920. The federal courts were authorized to hire probation officers in 1925. By the beginning of World War II, probation systems were in place in 44 states.

Probation began as a humanitarian effort to allow first-time and minor offenders a second chance. Early probationers were expected not only to obey the law but also to behave in a morally acceptable fashion. Officers sought to provide moral leadership to help shape probationers' attitudes and behavior with respect to family, religion, employment, and free time.

By the 1940s, the development of psychology led probation officers to shift their emphasis from moral leadership to therapeutic counseling. This shift brought three important changes. First, the officer no longer primarily acted as a community supervisor charged with enforcing a particular morality. Second, the officer became more of a clinical social worker whose goal was to help the offender solve psychological and social problems. Third, the offender was expected to become actively involved in the treatment. The pursuit of rehabilitation as the primary goal of probation gave the officer extensive discretion in defining and treating the offender's problems. Officers used their judgment to evaluate each offender in an effort to develop a treatment approach to the personal problems that presumably had led to crime.

During the 1960s, a new shift occurred in probation. Rather than counseling offenders, probation officers provided them with concrete social services such as assistance with employment, housing, finances, and education. This emphasis on reintegrating offenders and remedying the social problems they faced was consistent with federal efforts to wage a "war on poverty." Instead of being a counselor or therapist, the probation officer served as an advocate, dealing with private and public institutions on the offender's behalf.

In the late 1970s, the orientation of probation changed again as the goals of rehabilitation and reintegration gave way to "risk management." This approach, still dominant today, seeks to minimize the probability that an offender will commit a new offense (Cadigan, Johnson, and Lowenkamp, 2012). Risk management reflects two basic goals. First, in accord with the deserved-punishment ideal, the punishment should fit the offense, and correctional intervention should neither raise nor lower the level of punishment.

Second, according to the community protection criterion, the amount and type of supervision are determined according to the risk that the probationer will return to crime. This is measured using "risk assessment instruments," which use characteristics of the offender to determine the risk of rearrest for that person. For example, the Post-Conviction Risk Assessment Tool (PCRA) includes such items as a history of violent offending, alcohol problems, educational attainment, and mental health issues to calculate the probability that an offender will be rearrested during their term of probation (Lowenkamp et al., 2012).

Today there is a growing interest in probation's role as part of **community justice**, a philosophy that emphasizes restorative justice (see Chapter 12), reparation to the victim and the community, problem-solving strategies instead of adversarial procedures, and increased citizen involvement in crime prevention. By breaking away from traditional bureaucratic practices, community justice advocates hope to develop a more flexible and responsive form of local justice initiatives—and many see probation leading the way (Hudson, 2012).

community justice
A model of justice that emphasizes reparation to the victim and the community, approaching crime from a problem-solving perspective, and citizen involvement in crime prevention.

✔POINT

2. Who was John Augustus and what did he do?

3. What is the main goal of probation today?

STOP AND ANALYZE: How is contemporary probation different from—and similar to—the first probation effort by John Augustus?

Organization of Probation

As a form of corrections, probation falls under the executive branch, and people usually see it as a concern of state government. However, in about 25 percent of the states, probation falls to county and local governments. Further, in many states it is administered locally by the judiciary. The state sets the standards and provides financial support and training courses, but about two-thirds of all people under probation supervision are handled by locally administered programs.

In many jurisdictions, although the state is formally responsible for all probation services, the locally elected county judges are in charge. This seemingly odd arrangement produces benefits as well as problems. On the positive side, having probationers under the supervision of the court permits judges to keep closer tabs on them and to order incarceration if the conditions of probation are violated. On the negative side, some judges know little about the goals and methods of corrections, and the probation responsibility adds to the administrative duties of already overworked courts.

Judicially enforced probation seems to work best when the judge and the supervising officer have a close relationship. Proponents of this system say that judges need to work with probation officers whom they can trust, whose presentence reports they can accurately evaluate, and on whom they can rely to report on the success or failure of individual cases.

For the sake of their clients and the goals of the system, probation officers need direct access to corrections and other human services agencies. However, these agencies are located within the executive branch of government. Several states have combined probation and parole services in the same agency to coordinate resources and services better. Others point out, however, that probationers differ from parolees. Parolees already have served prison terms, frequently have been involved in more-serious crimes, and often have been disconnected from mainstream society. By contrast, most probationers have not developed criminal lifestyles to the same degree and do not have the same problems of reintegration into the community.

Probation Services

Probation officers play roles similar to both the police and social workers. In both roles, probation officers must act ethically and professionally to be effective and uphold the purposes of their offices' mission. Read "A Question of

TECHNOLOGY & CRIMINAL JUSTICE

TECHNOLOGY AND PROBATION

Various technological tools are increasingly used by probation officers to enhance their efficiency and effectiveness. At the front end of the probation officers' responsibilities are tasks concerning the evaluation of offenders' backgrounds, criminal records, and level of risk. Initially, as we saw in Chapter 12, this analysis focused on the presentence report prepared by the probation office for use by the judge in determining the sentence. If the judge sentences the offender to probation, then further risk and needs analyses are undertaken to determine appropriate conditions for probation, level of supervision, and need for drug treatment, job training, and other services. For the foregoing tasks, it is important to use complete and accurate information. Thus accurate databases of prior offenses and sentences are essential for determining matters related to sentencing and risk. Justice system agencies have continually improved the detailed content of databases on arrestees and offenders, the ease of drawing specific information from those databases, and the ability to share information across jurisdictions through databases that are accessible nationwide. Many jurisdictions now also use videoconferencing for the development of presentence reports so that probation officers can interview an offender without the offender being moved from the jail or the probation officer being required to travel to a jail. In addition, there are software programs that can quickly help to calculate levels of risk and needed supervision according to developed models of risk assessment. These technological tools present the possibility of making assessments more consistent, accurate, and complete.

Technology also provides tools for supervising probationers and monitoring their compliance with required conditions of probation. Electronic monitoring devices such as ankle "bracelets" or "tethers" can inform probation officers when an offender has left the immediate vicinity of the home telephone when home confinement for specific hours during the day is a component of the probation sentence. Another form of electronic monitoring, GPS devices, can track the locations of probationers and warn probation officers when an offender has traveled to a forbidden location. These devices are especially useful for tracking sex offenders and monitoring their compliance with rules against going near schools and parks. They can also be used with other offenders to keep them away from victims' homes or from parts of town where drug activity occurs. Some critics have pointed out, however, that offenders are not often monitored with regard to their interaction with others who may also be on a tether. For example, two offenders who committed a crime together may be required to limit their interaction, but unless corrections officers are monitoring their locations in tandem, the offenders may violate their terms of probation or parole without notice of the corrections officer.

For probationers who do not require intensive supervision, some jurisdictions have created technology check-in stations that are often called supervision kiosks. Probationers' fingerprints or palm prints are kept in computer databases. At specific times and days, probationers report to the probation office,

Ethics" at the end of the chapter to see examples of ethical problems that have arisen for probation officers.

In their law enforcement role, probation officers supervise clients to keep them out of trouble and enforce the conditions of the sentence. This law enforcement role involves discretionary decisions about whether to report violations of probation conditions. Probation officers are also expected to play a social-worker role by helping clients obtain the housing, employment, and treatment services they need (Bourgon, Gutierrez, and Ashton, 2012). The potential conflict between the roles is great. Not surprisingly, individual officers sometimes emphasize one role over the other. Advocates of evidence-based practices argue that probation officers must find "balanced roles" in which they are "neither indulgent of anti-social attitudes and noncompliance nor authoritative and heavy-handed" (Whetzel et al., 2011: 11). In all of their roles, technology has become increasingly important for enhancing the duties of the probation officer and sponsoring agency. Read the Technology and Criminal Justice feature to consider the many ways that technology can be used in the context of probation.

During the past decade, probation officials have developed methods of classifying clients according to their service needs, the element of risk they pose to the community, and the chance that they will commit another offense (Cadigan et al., 2012). Risk classification fits the deserved-punishment model

identify themselves on a computer through their fingerprints or palm prints, and then answer questions on that computer to verify that they are reporting periodically on schedule, as required by the probation sentence. This method of reporting by computer helps to save the probation officer's scarce time for those higher-risk probationers who need personal supervision from the official through in-person visits and personal counseling. In 2013, the state of Maryland used a supervision kiosk system developed in New York City for the supervision of 7,000 low-risk probationers.

Facial recognition software is being used more frequently in community corrections, with many jurisdictions using these tools to identify probationers who might have absconded or violated the terms of their sentence. Used by the FBI, this software compares faces captured on interstate highway cameras to a database of known offenders. This kind of software is referred to as "biometric," because it uses technology to measure biological patterns.

A major manufacturer of monitoring technology has developed an iPhone app to help track offenders on supervision. The app, called *House Arrest,* uses facial recognition and fingerprint technology so that offenders can virtually "check in" at specific times of day, and officers are also able to reach them by phone if needed. Ideally, this app replaces the need for a monitoring bracelet, but offenders must remember to keep their phone on them at all times, lest they violate the conditions of their supervision.

As in other aspects of criminal justice operations, technology has become increasingly useful and important for probation purposes. However, budget cuts throughout the United States present the likelihood that technology will not be fully used or evenly distributed unless there is a greater emphasis on devoting resources for these purposes.

Sources: "Patent Owner Hopes 'House Arrest' iPhone App Replaces Ankle Bracelets," *City Wire*, March 12, 2015 (thecitywire.com); Keegan Kyle, "After Orange County Lapse, GPS Tracking Gets More Scrutiny," *Orange County Register*, July 8, 2014 (ocregister.com); State of Maryland, Department of Public Safety and Services, "Technology," 2013 (www.dpscs.state.md.us/initiatives/kcs/index_KCS_tech -new.shtml); Jeff Stone, "FBI Adds Facial Recognition to Biometric ID Toolkit," *International Business Times*, September 16, 2014 (ibtimes.com); Emily Sweeney, "Probation 2.0: How Technology Is Changing Probation Work," *Boston Globe,* November 28, 2102 (www.boston.com).

DEBATE THE ISSUE

Are there any issues concerning privacy or misuse of technology that can arise in probation contexts? Are other individuals' privacy interests affected by their living with or interacting with probationers who are being monitored electronically? Are there risks that probation will become too dependent on technology through such methods as supervision kiosks, for example, and thereby fail to devote sufficient human resources for supervision and services? Are there risks that technical failures, such as erroneously believing that an electronic device is working properly, will lead to problems that increased human supervision might have prevented? In your view, what should be the two most significant concerns about reliance on technology in probation?

CIVIC ENGAGEMENT

YOUR ROLE IN THE SYSTEM

Imagine that the voters of your state are presented with a ballot issue seeking approval of a new law that would mandate probation and drug treatment for nonviolent drug offenders instead of sending such individuals to prison or jail. *Make a list of the results and consequences likely to be produced by such a law. Would you vote to favor the ballot issue?* Then look to see the results of California's ballot issue in 2000 on this very subject.

of the criminal sanction in that the most serious cases receive the greatest restrictions and supervision. If probationers live according to the conditions of their sentence, the level of supervision is gradually reduced.

A continuing issue for probation officers is the size of their caseloads. How many clients can one officer effectively handle? In the 1930s the National Probation Association recommended a 50-unit caseload, and in 1967 the President's Commission on Law Enforcement and Administration of Justice reduced it to 35. However, today the national average for adult supervision is about 150, but some urban caseloads exceed 300. The oversized caseload is usually cited as one of the main obstacles to successful probation. In Sacramento, California, $12 million in budget cuts over five years left over 90 percent of the county's 22,000 probationers without any supervision, drug testing, or services, because probation officers simply cannot handle the average caseload of 124 that resulted from staff reductions (Branan, 2013). In such cases, it is hard to see how any goal of the sanctions—deserved punishment, rehabilitation, deterrence, or incapacitation—is being realized. If none of these objectives is being met, the offender is "getting off." As you look at "Civic Engagement: Your Role in the System," consider whether you believe probation serves the interests of society.

Reliance on Volunteers

State budget cuts can increase the use of probation in two ways. First, judges can sentence to probation those offenders who previously would have gone to jail or prison. In a probation sentence in which offenders live in their own homes, these individuals are responsible for their own living expenses and medical care—a significant savings for the state and county when compared to the costs of jail or prison incarceration. Second, state officials can release more offenders early from prison as a means to save money and as a possible avenue to close expensive corrections facilities. For example, in light of overcrowding and the Supreme Court's decision in *Brown v. Plata* (2012) [discussed in Chapter 13], California shifted prisoners from state corrections facilities to county-run jails and community supervision programs run by county probation departments (Mills, 2011). This policy caused county officials to worry that the state would not provide adequate funds for the community supervision of additional offenders, many of whom could have committed more-serious offenses than typical probationers and parolees in the past.

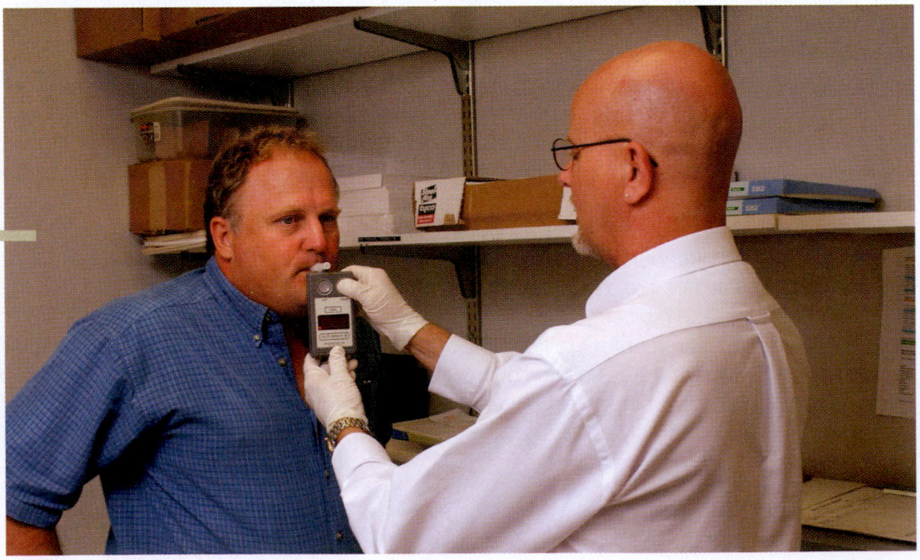

An offender blows into a Breathalyzer device at a probation office in Travis County, Texas. Frequent alcohol and drug testing is a condition of probation for many offenders. Administering these tests has become part of the officer's supervisory role. How difficult is it to monitor the behavior of offenders in the community?

Bob Daemmrich/The Image Works

As criminal justice agencies cope with budget cuts, observers anticipate that there may be greater reliance on volunteers to handle many of the duties previously managed by professionals. For example, when the Los Angeles Police Department faced a $10 million budget cut in 2011, news reporters examined the city's reliance on 700 unpaid trained volunteer officers in the police department's Reserve Corps who serve on a part-time basis for duties that would otherwise be handled by professional officers (Hillard, 2011). Because many cities and counties have well-established programs for using volunteers for probation functions, there is the possibility that volunteers may take a larger role in providing community supervision.

In 1960, Judge Keith Leenhouts in the Detroit suburb of Royal Oak, Michigan, began a Volunteers in Probation (VIP) program. According to the city's website, he utilized hundreds of community volunteers, called "sponsors," who met one-on-one with probationers for 12 hours each month to provide guidance and to serve as willing listeners. After a five-year period, the city found that its recidivism rate was less than 15 percent, whereas the national average was close to 50 percent. Other cities and counties began their own programs, and after he retired as a judge, Leenhouts became the national director of the Volunteers in Probation program that helped localities throughout the country start their own programs (City of Royal Oak website, 2011). The programs continue today in many locations, using the time and talents of thousands of volunteers.

These programs operate according to at least two different models. In one model, the volunteers actually function as unpaid probation officers. After receiving training, they carry out the duties of professionals in order to permit their cities and counties to administer probation programs less expensively. For example, the website of the City of Westminster, Colorado, insists that "volunteers do not do 'social' type activities with the clients" and describes the responsibilities carried out by volunteers: enforce court orders, provide mentoring, monitor compliance with probation terms, write monthly reports on each offender, attend probation court hearings, and attend monthly training sessions (City of Westminster website, 2011). In the second model, volunteers conduct a wider array of activities in support of the probation office. For example, in San Diego County, the Volunteers in Probation program carries out fund-raising activities and clothing drives in order to provide clothing, eye exams, scholarships, emergency funds, and bus passes for probationers who are fulfilling the conditions of probation (www.volunteersinprobation.org, 2015). Read the Doing Your Part feature to see an example of a citizen who donated her time and energy to help offenders succeed.

DOING YOUR PART

PROBATION VOLUNTEER: MARSHA STEINFIELD

In March 2011, Orange County, California, resident Marsha Steinfield received the Outstanding Probation Volunteer award. As a volunteer, she is assigned to the Youth Guidance Center, a facility for juvenile offenders where she tutors students and arranges guest speakers and educational field trips. The Youth Guidance Center includes its own high school and attempts to involve the juveniles in various volunteer activities within the community, including planting trees, reading to small children, cleaning up public parks and beaches, and providing food for the homeless. Volunteers such as Marsha Steinfield can help to create important connections between the community and youthful offenders. By providing mentoring and guidance, volunteers can potentially make a difference in the lives of troubled youths.

✔POINT 4. What are the major tasks of probation officers?

STOP AND ANALYZE: In light of state and county budget cuts, could probation functions be handled by volunteers and churches? Give two arguments in favor of this position and two in opposition. Which perspective is most persuasive?

Revocation and Termination of Probation

Probation ends in one of two ways: (1) the person successfully completes the period of probation, or (2) the probationary status is revoked because of misbehavior. Revocation of probation can occur for either a **technical violation** or the probation officer's discovery that the probationer has committed a new crime, a discovery that typically occurs when the probationer is arrested by the police. Once the officer calls a violation to the attention of the court, the probationer may be arrested (if not already in jail), or summoned for a revocation hearing.

technical violation
The probationer's failure to abide by the rules and conditions of probation (specified by the judge), resulting in revocation of probation.

Technical violations occur when a probationer fails to meet the conditions of a sentence by, for instance, violating curfew, failing a drug test, or using alcohol. Officers have discretion as to whether or not they bring this fact to the attention of the judge. Table 14.1 presents one study of reasons submitted to the court for revocation of probation and the results of revocation in New York State.

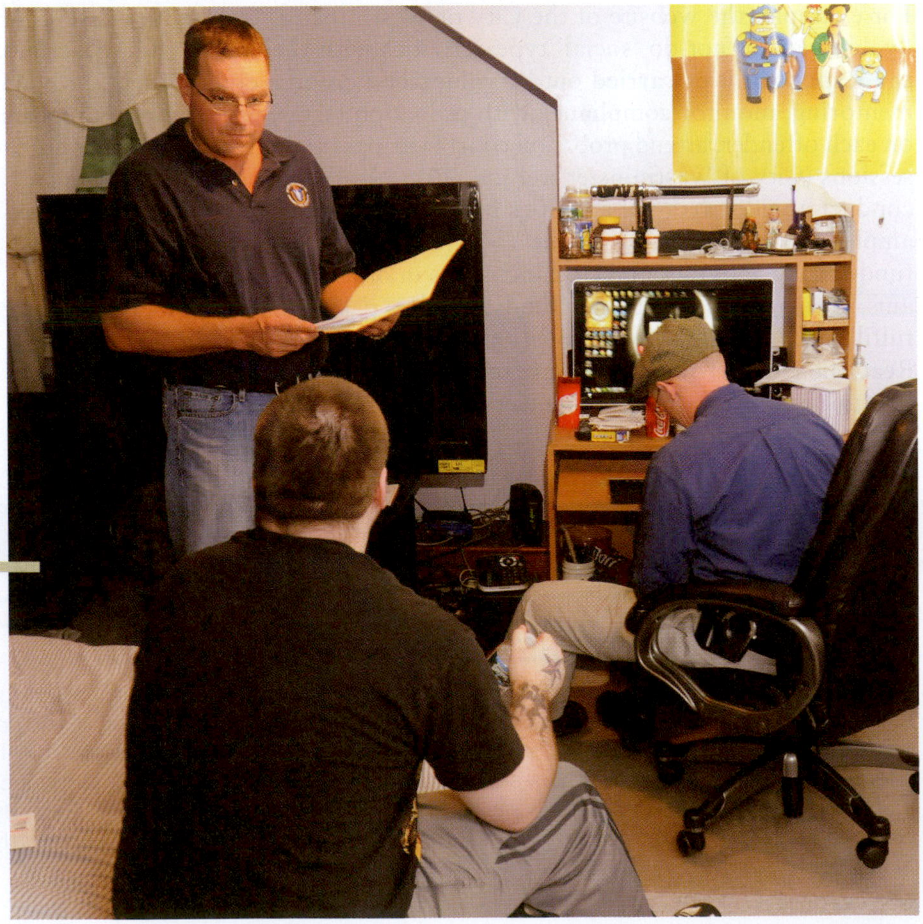
Dave Roback/The Republican/Landov

Probation officers are supposed to help offenders stay out of trouble at the same time that they monitor offenders' behavior. Officers make important discretionary decisions about when to treat rule violations as serious enough to seek revocation of probation and recommend jail for the offender. What qualifications should someone have in order to become a probation officer?

TABLE 14.1 PROBATION REVOCATION HEARINGS: JUSTIFICATIONS AND OUTCOMES

This is a snapshot of the reasons for outstate New York probation officers' recommendation for revocation and the outcomes when probationers were resentenced as a result of revocation.*

VIOLATION REASONS	
Technical violations	54%
Arrest	23
New conviction	13
Abscond (go missing)	11
RESENTENCE AFTER PROBATION REVOCATION†	
Local jail	74%
State prison	15
Probation	4
Intermittent imprisonment	4
Unconditional discharge	2
Fine	1
Total	100%

*The data present reasons and outcomes for the 57 counties outside of New York City. New York City's probation population is much more heavily composed of convicted felons. The outstate counties' mix of misdemeanants and felons on probation may be more similar to the probation populations throughout the country.

†Two additional offenders were sent to juvenile detention facilities.

Source: *New York State Probation Population: 2007 Profile* (Albany: New York State Division of Criminal Justice Services, June 2008).

Probation officers and judges have widely varying notions of what constitutes grounds for revoking probation. When encountering technical violations, probation officers may first try to impose stricter rules, sternly lecture the probationer, and increase the frequency of contacts with the probationer. Yet the probation officer may face special challenges if the probationer does not take seriously the likelihood of consequences for technical violations. Indeed, a study in Wisconsin found that 68 percent of probationers failed on at least one occasion to report as required to the probation officer, in contrast to only 42 percent of parolees committing the same technical violation (Van Stelle and Goodrich, 2009). Unlike parolees who, as we will see in Chapter 16, have already been to prison and therefore may be more likely to fear being sent back, many probationers are young and less experienced with the system. This failure to fulfill probation conditions may demonstrate their greater immaturity as well as their failure to recognize that technical violations could actually lead to incarceration if their probation officer seeks revocation.

The Legislative Analyst's Office for the state of California calculates that it costs the taxpayers an extra $50,000, on average, each time an offender is sent to prison for a probation revocation. That amount includes not only the marginal annual cost of sending an offender to prison, but also the average length of the probationer's prison sentence (17 months), the subsequent cost of parole supervision, and the likelihood that some percentage of these offenders will be sent to prison again for parole violations (M. Taylor, 2009).

Not surprisingly, in these times of shrinking government budgets, the contemporary emphasis is on avoiding incarceration except for flagrant and continual violation of the conditions of probation. Thus most revocations today occur because of a new arrest or conviction. For example, in contrast to the New York State data presented in Table 14.1, a study in Wisconsin of both probation and parole revocations found that the commission of new crimes provided the reason for revocation in a larger percentage of cases (Van Stelle and Goodrich, 2009).

Differences in probation revocation rates among different jurisdictions may reflect a number of different factors. The mix of misdemeanants and felons may differ. Probation officers in different cities and states may be following different guidelines in determining when noncompliance should trigger a revocation recommendation. Attitudes about revocation may differ among judges in different locations. Overcrowding in the local jail may limit the probation officers' and judges' options for imposing revocation sanctions. These varying circumstances can produce differences in probation revocation rates even among counties within the same state. In California, for example, for the years 2005 through 2007, probation revocation rates ranged from 1 percent in Contra Costa County, a large suburban county in the Oakland–San Francisco area, to 28 percent in Imperial County, a sparsely populated desert county that borders Mexico and Arizona. Further, San Diego County had a revocation rate of 7 percent, and the rate for Los Angeles was nearly 11 percent (M. Taylor, 2009). By contrast, for 2007 in the 57 counties outside New York City, there were 77,022 offenders on probation, and 6,775 of those probationers (8.7 percent) were sent to revocation hearings (New York State Division of Criminal Justice Services, 2008). Nationally, in recent years among those probationers who exited probation, 16 percent exited by being sent to prison or jail (L. M. Maruschak and Parks, 2012).

As discussed in Chapter 13, in two cases, *Mempa v. Rhay* (1967) and *Gagnon v. Scarpelli* (1973), the U.S. Supreme Court extended the right to due process by requiring that, before probation can be revoked, the offender is entitled to a preliminary and a final hearing and a right to counsel in some cases. When a probationer is taken into custody for violating the conditions of probation, a preliminary hearing must be held to determine whether probable cause exists to believe that the incident occurred. If there is a finding of probable cause, a final hearing, where the revocation decision is made, is mandatory. At these hearings, the probationer has the right to cross-examine witnesses and to be given notice of the alleged violations and a written report of the proceedings. The Court ruled, though, that the probationer does not have an automatic right to counsel. This decision is to be made on a case-by-case basis. At the final hearing, the judge decides whether to continue probation or to impose tougher restrictions, such as incarceration.

For those who successfully complete probation, the sentence ends. Ordinarily the probationer is then a free citizen again, without obligation to the court or to the probation department.

✔POINT

5. What are the grounds for probation revocation?
6. What rights does a probationer have while revocation is being considered?

STOP AND ANALYZE: Why would a probation officer decline to seek revocation for every technical violation? Does the criminal justice system benefit from such decisions? Give two arguments for each side of this question.

Assessing Probation

Some critics see probation as nothing more than a slap on the wrist, an absence of punishment. Yet the importance of probation for public safety has never been greater: At the end of 2009, data showed that 55 percent of probationers were serving their punishments for committing felony offenses—an increase from 52 percent in 2000 (Herberman and Bonczar, 2014). These offenders have been convicted of serious crimes, yet caseload burdens and limited resources lead many probation officers to meet with individual offenders little more than once per month. In Colorado, the placement of felons on probation caused controversy when ten of them were charged with murder or attempted murder while on probation in a single year (Cardona, 2011). As budget cuts aimed at the expense of imprisonment reduce the number of probation officers and increase the number of offenders assigned to community sanctions, contact between officers and probationers may be further reduced in many jurisdictions. Although probation suffers from poor credibility in the public's eyes, its workload is growing dramatically and, in view of the budget cuts in corrections, will probably continue to do so.

The 2009 report of the Pew Center on the States presents research-based recommendations designed to strengthen community corrections systems, thereby saving money and reducing crime (Pew Center on the States, 2009). These recommendations include the following:

- Sort offenders by risk to public safety to determine appropriate levels of supervision
- Base intervention programs on sound research about what works to reduce recidivism
- Harness advances in supervision technology such as electronic monitoring and rapid-result alcohol and drug tests
- Impose swift and certain sanctions for offenders who break the rules of their release but do not commit new crimes
- Create incentives for offenders and supervision agencies to succeed, and monitor their performance

Although the recidivism rate for probationers is lower than the rate for those who have been incarcerated, researchers question whether this is a direct result of supervision or an indirect result of the maturing of the offenders. Most offenders placed on probation do not become career criminals, their criminal activity is short-lived, and they become stable citizens as they obtain jobs and get married. Most of those who are arrested a second time do not repeat their mistake again.

What rallies support for probation is its relatively low cost: Keeping an offender on probation instead of behind bars costs roughly $1,500 a year (a savings of more than $20,000 a year). However, these savings might not satisfy community members who hear of probationers committing serious violent crimes (Cardona, 2011). Because of budget cuts and many states' efforts to reduce prison populations, it is likely that more people convicted of felonies will be placed on probation in the future. This development presents new challenges for probation, because officers can no longer assume that their clients pose little threat to society and that they have the skills to lead productive lives in the community.

To offer a viable alternative to incarceration, probation services need the resources to supervise and assist their clients appropriately. The new demands on probation have brought calls for increased electronic monitoring and for risk-management systems that provide different levels of supervision for different kinds of offenders.

Intermediate Sanctions in the Community

Dissatisfaction with the traditional means of probation supervision, coupled with the crowding and high cost of prisons, has resulted in a call for intermediate sanctions. These are sanctions that restrict the offender more than does simple probation and that constitute actual punishment for more-serious offenders. The development of new technology, such as electronic monitoring devices that enable the imposition of home confinement, also provides an increasing range of options for intermediate sanctions.

Many experts have supported the case for intermediate sanctions. For example, as Norval Morris and Michael Tonry asserted prior to the recent expansion of community corrections, "Prison is used excessively; probation is used even more excessively; between the two is a near vacuum of purposive and enforced punishments" (Morris and Tonry, 1990: 3). In recent years, 69 percent of convicted felons were incarcerated, the severest sentence, whereas 27 percent received probation, the least severe. Hence nearly all convicted felons received either the severest or the most lenient of possible penalties (Rosenmerkel, Durose, and Farole, 2009). Morris and Tonry urged that punishments be created that are more restrictive than probation yet match the severity of the offense and the characteristics of the offender, and that can be carried out while still protecting the community.

We can view intermediate sanctions as a continuum—a range of punishments that vary in levels of intrusiveness and control, as shown in Figure 14.3. A sentence to probation is often tied to additional intermediate sanctions such as community service, restitution, and alcohol or drug treatment, as seen in Table 14.2.

Probation plus a fine or community service may be appropriate for minor offenses, while at the same time, six weeks of boot camp followed by intensive probation supervision might be right for serious crimes. But some question whether offenders will be able to fulfill the conditions added to probation. Moreover, if prisons are overcrowded, is incarceration a believable threat if offenders fail to comply?

Across the country, state corrections agencies employ many types of intermediate sanctions. They can be divided into (1) those administered primarily by the judiciary (fines, restitution, and forfeiture); (2) those primarily

FIGURE 14.3 CONTINUUM OF INTERMEDIATE SANCTIONS

Judges may use a range of intermediate sanctions, from those imposing a low level of control to those imposing a high level.

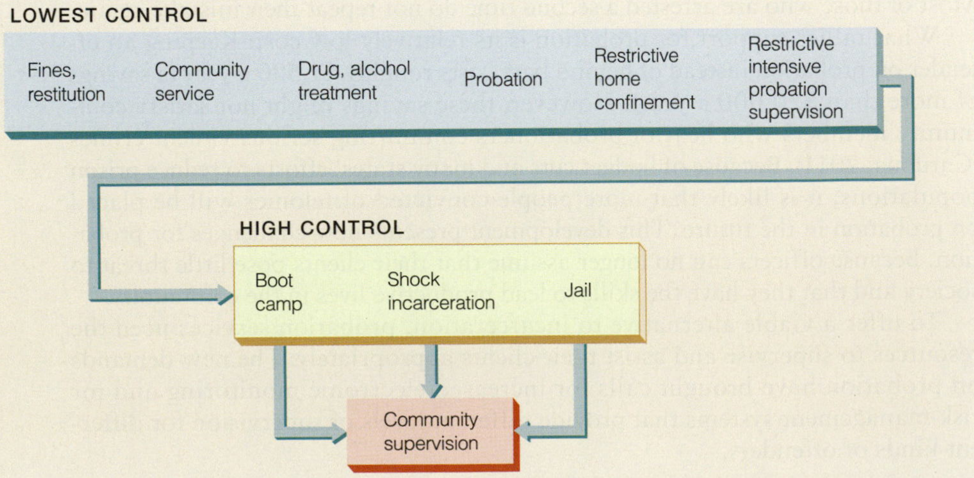

TABLE 14.2 CONDITIONS OF PROBATION SENTENCE RECEIVED MOST OFTEN BY OFFENDERS IN THE 75 LARGEST URBAN COUNTIES

Percentage whose sentence to probation includes:

	COMMUNITY SERVICE	RESTITUTION	TREATMENT	FINE
All Felonies	22%	21%	29%	28%
Violent offenses	27	22	29	26
Property offenses	23	37	18	19
Drug offenses	21	7	45	36
Public order offenses	22	26	16	27
Misdemeanors	26	14	13	27

Source: Brian A. Reeves, "Felony Defendants in Large Urban Counties, 2009: Statistical Tables," Bureau of Justice Statistics, December 2013, p. 32.

administered in the community with a supervision component (home confinement, community service, day reporting centers, and intensive probation supervision); and (3) those that are administered inside institutions and followed by community supervision (boot camp). Furthermore, sanctions may be imposed in combination—for example, a fine and probation, or boot camp with community service and probation.

✔POINT

7. What is the main argument for intermediate sanctions?
8. What is meant by a continuum of sanctions?

STOP AND ANALYZE: Look at the sanctions labeled as "lowest control" in Figure 14.3. In thinking about people who have been convicted of committing crimes, do you see all of these sanctions as actually constituting "punishment" for society's lawbreakers? Give two arguments either in favor of or opposed to viewing these lowest control sanctions as actually constituting punishment for criminal offenders.

Intermediate Sanctions Administered Primarily by the Judiciary

The judiciary administers many kinds of intermediate sanctions. Here we discuss three of them—fines, restitution, and forfeiture. Because all three involve the transfer of money or property from the offender to the government or crime victim, the judiciary is considered the proper body not only to impose the sanction but also to collect what is due.

Fines

Fines are routinely imposed for offenses ranging from traffic violations to felonies. Studies have shown that the fine is used widely as a criminal sanction and that nationally well over $1 billion in fines have been collected annually. Yet, judges in the United States make little use of fines as the *sole* punishment for crimes more serious than motor vehicle violations. Instead, fines typically are used in conjunction with other sanctions, such as probation and incarceration—for example, two years of probation and a $500 fine. A survey of offenders on electronic monitoring (home confinement with electronic device to confirm presence in the home) reported that their sentences included an average of 27 days on monitoring, 493 days

fine
A sum of money to be paid to the state by a convicted person as punishment for an offense.

on probation or parole, and 34 days in jail or prison. In addition, these offenders completed an average of 17 hours of community service and paid approximately $3,600 in fines (J. S. Martin, Hanrahan, and Bowers, 2009).

Many judges cite the difficulty of collecting fines as the reason that they do not make greater use of this punishment. They note that offenders tend to be poor, and many judges fear that fines will be paid from the proceeds of additional illegal acts. Other judges are concerned that relying on fines as an alternative to incarceration will let affluent offenders "buy" their way out of jail while forcing the poor to serve time.

In contrast, fines are used extensively in Europe, are enforced, and are normally the sole sanction for a wide range of crimes. In Germany and Sweden, a majority of all sentenced criminal offenders must pay a fine as their punishment, even in cases involving some serious offenses. To deal with the concern that fines exact a heavier toll on the poor than on the wealthy, Sweden and Germany have developed the day fine, which bases the penalty on the offender's income.

The day fine has been tested in Arizona, Connecticut, Iowa, New York, and Washington (Zedlewski, 2010). For example, if sentenced to a 30-day day fine, an individual who earns $200,000 annually would pay a total of $16,438, whereas an individual who earns only $45,000 per year would pay $3,699 for the same offense. In relative terms, these fines would hit each individual with equivalent force, yet critics question whether for a similar offense a wealthy person should automatically be required to pay a larger fine than a less affluent person. In 2015, Finland imposed a fine of $58,000 on a multimillionaire for a speeding ticket when he drove 64 mph in a 50 mph zone (Thornhill, 2015). These significant fines raise questions in the minds of some observers about the fairness of day fines when applied for minor offenses.

Restitution

restitution
Repayment—in the form of money or service—by an offender to a victim who has suffered some loss from the offense.

Restitution is repayment by an offender to a victim who has suffered some form of financial loss from the crime. It is *reparative* in that it seeks to repair the harm done. In the Middle Ages, restitution was a common way to settle a criminal case. The offender was ordered to pay the victim or do the victim's work. The growth of the modern state saw the decline of such punishments based on "private" arrangements between offender and victim. Instead, the state prosecuted offenders, and punishments focused on the wrong the offender had done to society.

Victim restitution has remained a part of the U.S. criminal justice system, though it is largely unpublicized. In many instances, restitution derives from informal agreements between the police and offenders at the station, during plea bargaining, or in the prosecutor's sentence recommendation. Only since the late 1970s has restitution been institutionalized, usually as one of the conditions of probation.

As with fines, convicted offenders differ in their ability to pay restitution, and the conditions inevitably fall more harshly on less affluent offenders who cannot easily pay. Someone who has the "good fortune" to be victimized by an affluent criminal might receive full compensation, whereas someone victimized by a poor offender might never receive a penny. In Colorado, a corps of investigators work with probation officers monitoring cases, collecting restitution, and working out payment plans if necessary. As a result, collections in Colorado counties have increased by 25 to 50 percent since the late 1980s. However, even in a well-organized system, it can be difficult to collect from many offenders. In 2009, offenders in Colorado still owed an uncollected $563 million in restitution and $215 million in court fines and costs. Pennsylvania, which was less active and organized in collecting from offenders, was owed $1.55 billion by criminal offenders (Crummy, 2009).

Restitution is more easily imposed when the "damage" inflicted can be easily measured—value of property stolen or cost of medical care after a criminal assault, for instance. But what should be the restitution for the terror of an attempted rape?

Forfeiture

With passage of two laws in 1970—the Racketeer Influenced and Corrupt Organizations Act (RICO) and the Continuing Criminal Enterprise Act (CCE)—Congress resurrected forfeiture, a criminal sanction that had lain dormant since the American Revolution. Through amendments in 1984 and 1986, Congress improved ways to implement the law. Similar laws are now found in most states, particularly to deal with trafficking in controlled substances and with organized crime.

Forfeiture is government seizure of property and other assets derived from or used in criminal activity. Assets seized by federal and state agencies through forfeiture can be quite considerable, and have increased significantly in the past 30 years. For example, in 1989, U.S. attorneys recovered $285 million in assets—by 2013, that amount had increased to $2.2 billion (Offices of the U.S. Attorneys, n.d.).

forfeiture
Government seizure of property and other assets derived from or used in criminal activity.

Forfeiture is controversial. Critics argue that confiscating property without a court hearing violates citizens' constitutional rights. Concerns have also been raised about the excessive use of this sanction, because forfeited assets often go into the budget of the law enforcement agency taking the action.

In a 1993 opinion, the Supreme Court ruled that the Eighth Amendment's ban on excessive fines requires that the seriousness of the offense be related to the property that is taken (*Austin v. United States*). The ruling places limits on the government's ability to seize property and invites the judiciary to monitor the government's forfeiture activities when convicted offenders challenge them.

Critics argue that ownership of the seized property is often unclear. For example, in Hartford, Connecticut, a woman's home was seized because her grandson, unbeknownst to her, was using it as a base for selling drugs. Under the Civil Asset Forfeiture Reform Act passed by Congress in 2000, property cannot be seized if owners demonstrate their innocence by a preponderance of evidence. Read more about forfeiture in the Close Up box in this chapter.

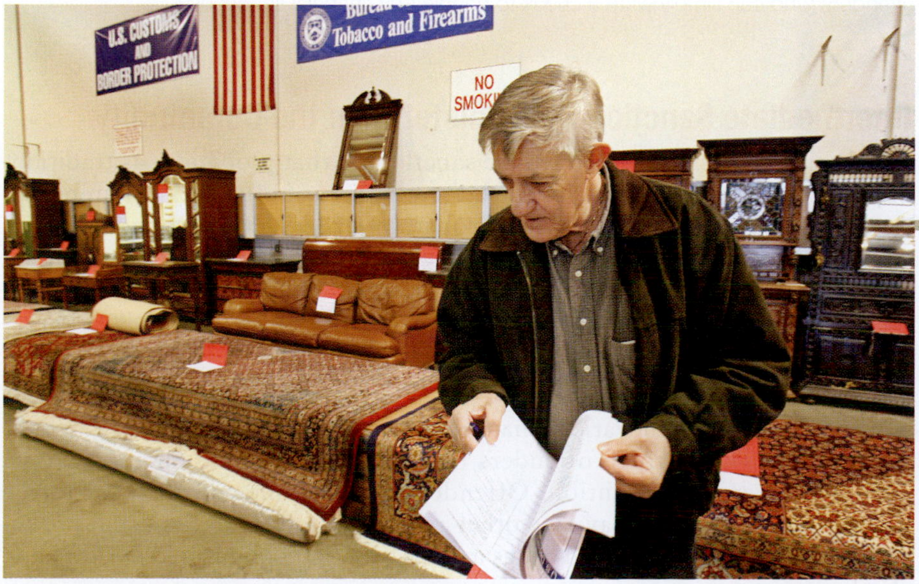

AP Images/Ric Francis

A potential buyer examines property seized by federal officials from Congressman Randy "Duke" Cunningham after his conviction for taking bribes. The property items were presumably obtained through illegal funds and therefore were subject to forfeiture. Should law enforcement officials be permitted to sell the property that they seize from criminal offenders?

CLOSE UP

CONTROVERSIES OVER FORFEITURE OF CASH AND PROPERTY

There has been growing concern over the power of police agencies to seize property, including cash, from people, even when they have not been convicted of a crime. Civil forfeiture laws allow police to seize property from individuals suspected of committing a crime, and then require the property owner to prove that their possessions were acquired legally. Newspaper reports provide numerous accounts of people carrying cash as they head to a casino for a recreational weekend having their money seized by police when stopped for traffic violations. Similarly, small business owners, such as immigrants who may be less familiar or less trusting of the American banking system, have had money seized during traffic stops when they were carrying thousands of dollars on their way to pay for new restaurant equipment or other legitimate business transactions.

Civil forfeiture laws are controversial because police officers, in practice, typically make discretionary decisions about seizures based on their own suspicions and justifications. Contrary to the American justice system's claims that people are presumptively innocent until proven guilty of a crime according the standard of "beyond a reasonable doubt," people subjected to asset forfeitures often face long, expensive legal battles to seek the return of money and property. In effect, they may be required to prove their innocence rather than having police and prosecutors prove that they were engaged in wrongdoing.

Originally developed to target high-level drug distributors, forefeitures have been expanded by some police departments to include smaller amounts of money and property from those accused of committing minor infractions. Police often assume that anyone driving with large amounts of cash is involved in drug trafficking. An investigative study by the *Washington Post* found that since the events of 9-11, police agencies have made over 61,000 seizures of cash without search warrants, totaling more than $2.5 million.

Local police agencies used civil forfeiture laws to seize property under the U.S. Department of Justice's "Equitable Sharing" program, which permitted local police departments to keep a portion of proceeds seized for potential federal law violations after giving a portion to the federal government. However, in light of news media attention to seizures of cash from innocent people, former Attorney General Eric Holder ended aspects of that program in January 2015 and subsequently limited the authority of local police to seize property under federal law. Police officers may still enjoy broad authority to make such seizures under their own states' laws. A significant

CHECKPOINT

9. How do fines, restitution, and forfeiture differ?

10. What are some of the problems of implementing these sanctions?

STOP AND ANALYZE: Financial penalties can be useful as an alternative sanction, but some have argued they are only useful when an offender has the means to pay. If fines were used more extensively in the United States, what solution would you recommend for those too poor to pay fines or restitution? Suggest three alternatives or consequences for those who are too poor to pay. Are these alternatives and consequences fair when compared to those offenders who can simply write a check to handle any financial sanctions?

Intermediate Sanctions Administered in the Community

One basic argument for intermediate sanctions is that probation, as traditionally practiced, is inadequate for the large numbers of offenders whom probation officers must supervise today. Probation leaders have responded to this criticism by developing new intermediate sanction programs and expanding old ones. Four of these are: home confinement, community service, day reporting centers, and intensive supervision probation.

Home Confinement

home confinement
A sentence requiring the offender to remain inside his or her home during specified periods.

With technological innovations that provide for electronic monitoring, **home confinement**, in which offenders must remain at home during specific periods, has gained attention. Offenders under home confinement (often called "house arrest") may face other restrictions such as the usual probation rules against alcohol and drugs as well as strictly monitored curfews and check-in times.

problem with these practices concerns the apparent self-interest of police departments that use seized assets to enhance their own annual budgets, making it very difficult for innocent people to regain possession of improperly seized cash, cars, and other property. As a result, many members of Congress, both Republicans and Democrats, are concerned that the law enforcement authority to seize assets from unconvicted people has gone too far.

Proponents of civil forfeiture laws claim that many high-level drug distribution networks have been disrupted due to these statutes. Advocates of the forfeiture process also argue that victims of economic crime can also benefit from civil forfeiture laws. High-profile offenders like Bernie Madoff and his associates (who defrauded over $20 billion from investment clients) were subject to civil forfeiture laws in order to pay back their victims. Their money, homes, cars, and other assets were seized and sold to reimburse victims for their losses. There are both advantages and disadvantages of forfeiture systems—but does the good outweigh the bad? Consider the situation presented in "Debate the Issue" and enumerate the costs and benefits of forfeiture.

Sources: Leon Neyfakh, "Helicopters Don't Pay for Themselves," *Slate Magazine*, January 16, 2015 (http://www.slate.com); Robert O'Harrow Jr. and Stephen Rich, "Justice Clarifies New Limits on Asset Forfeiture Involving Local, State Police." *Washington Post*, February 11, 2015 (http://washingtonpost.com); Michael Sallah, Robert O'Hallow Jr., and Steven Rich, "Stop and Seize," Washington Post, September 6, 2014 (http://washingtonpost.com); Sarah Stillman, "Taken," New Yorker, August 12, 2013 (http://newyorker.com).

DEBATE THE ISSUE

Many believe that forfeiture laws create an unreasonable intrusion of the government into citizens' lives. Others claim that these laws serve to cripple drug-trafficking organizations, provide restitution to victims, and help police departments financially. Imagine you are a defense attorney who is counseling a client whose home was seized by police after her son was arrested for dealing drugs out of the house without her knowledge. After his arrest, police confiscated the house and planned to sell it at auction. As her attorney, what three points would you make to the judge to argue that the seizure was inappropriate? Next, imagine you are the district attorney handling the same case. What three points would you make to the judge to justify the seizure of the home?

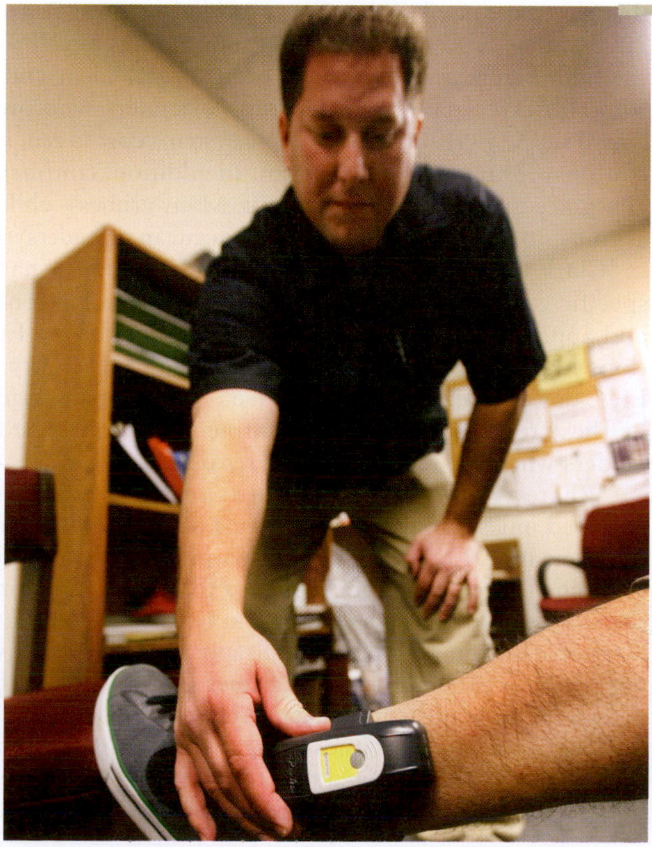

Paul Chinn/San Francisco Chronicle/San Francisco ChronicleCorbis News/Corbis

Electronic monitoring devices are used when offenders are sentenced to home confinement as part of intermediate sanctions in the community. If an offender is sitting at home watching TV and sleeping in his own bedroom, is he really being punished?

Some offenders are allowed to go to a place of employment, education, or treatment during the day but must return to their homes by a specified hour. Those supervising home confinement may telephone offenders' homes at various times of the day or night to speak personally with offenders to make sure they are complying.

Home confinement offers a great deal of flexibility. It can be used as a sole sanction or in combination with other penalties. It can be imposed at almost any point in the criminal justice process: during the pretrial period, after a short term in jail or prison, or as a condition of probation or parole. In addition, home confinement relieves the government of the responsibility to provide the offender with food, clothing, and housing, as it must do in prisons. For these reasons, home confinement programs have grown and proliferated.

The development of electronic monitoring equipment has made home confinement an enforceable sentencing option. The number of offenders currently being monitored is difficult to estimate, because the equipment manufacturers consider this privileged information.

Two basic types of electronic monitoring devices exist. Passive monitors respond only to inquiries; most commonly, the offender receives an automated telephone call from the probation office and is told to place the device on a receiver attached to the phone. Active devices send continuous signals that a receiver picks up; a computer notes any break in the signal.

Despite favorable publicity, certain legal, technical, and correctional issues must be addressed before home confinement with electronic monitoring can become a standard punishment. First, some criminal justice scholars question its constitutionality. Monitoring may violate the Fourth Amendment's protection against unreasonable searches and seizures. The issue is a clash between the constitutionally protected reasonable expectation of privacy and the invasion of one's home by surveillance devices. Second, technical problems with the monitoring devices are still extensive, often giving erroneous reports that the offender is home. Third, offender failure rates may prove to be high. There is little evidence that electronic monitoring reduces recidivism rates (Renzema and Mayo-Wilson, 2005). Some observers believe that four months of full-time monitoring is about the limit before a violation will occur (T. R. Clear and Braga, 1995). Finally, some observers point out that only offenders who own telephones and can afford the $25–$100 per week these systems cost to rent are eligible for the home confinement monitoring program. In addition, confinement to the home is no guarantee that crimes will not occur. Many crimes—child abuse, drug sales, and assaults, to name a few—commonly occur in offenders' residences.

Clark County, Washington, informs offenders that they must meet three specific conditions in order to be eligible for home confinement: "[1] A stable and approved residence; [2] A dedicated line for the EHC equipment (no options like call-waiting or call forwarding); [3] Ability to pay the $15.00 per EHC day plus a $40.00 hookup fee" (www.clark.wa.gov, 2010). As indicated by these requirements, home confinement seems best suited for low-risk offenders who have relatively stable residences.

Whatever the potential benefits of home confinement, they cannot be achieved unless monitoring programs operate appropriately. Newspaper investigations in 2013 found that Florida judges were ordering home confinement for some people who were supposed to be ineligible for such sanctions due to the violent crimes for which they had been convicted. In one county, more than 50 people on home confinement disappeared. Nearly all were eventually caught, but not before some committed crimes and used drugs. In the worst instance, a defendant on home confinement—as part of conditions of bail prior to trial—murdered one of the witnesses against him in his upcoming home invasion trial. County officials noted that the escapees represented only 6 percent of the 900 people assigned to home confinement in Orange County, Florida. However, that small percentage still represented a large number of people who caused harm in the community and raised questions about the effectiveness of the entire home confinement program (Weiner, 2013a; Weiner, 2013b). These problems highlight the need for judges to be careful about which individuals are assigned to home confinement; for equipment to work properly; and for officials to respond quickly and effectively when people violate their assignment to home confinement.

Community Service

A **community service** sentence requires the offender to perform a certain amount of unpaid labor in the community. Community service can take a variety of forms, including assisting in social service agencies, cleaning parks and roadsides, and helping the poor. The sentence specifies the number of hours to be worked and usually requires supervision by a probation officer. Judges can tailor community service to the skills and abilities of offenders. For example, less educated offenders might pick up litter along the highway, and those with schooling might teach reading in evening literacy classes. Many judges order community service when an offender cannot pay a fine. The offender's effort to make reparation to the community harmed by the crime also serves a symbolic function. When singer Chris Brown was convicted of assaulting his girlfriend, the singer Rihanna, newspaper photos showed him shoveling at a police horse stable and working along local roads to fulfill his community service. Such public exposure may also have a "shaming" function of embarrassing people who can be seen publicly by their friends and neighbors as they fulfill the visible requirements of a criminal sentence.

Remember that community service programs require contact between citizens in the community and the offenders fulfilling their sentences. Do the members of the public want offenders providing services to their community organizations? Do they want to be involved in supervising offenders in various contexts? As you read "Civic Engagement: Your Role in the System," think about your own willingness to interact with offenders in the community.

community service
A sentence requiring the offender to perform a certain amount of unpaid labor in the community.

CIVIC ENGAGEMENT

YOUR ROLE IN THE SYSTEM

If you were asked to contribute your time to help make a correctional community service program succeed, what could you do to contribute? *Make a list of things that you could do to help such a program succeed.* Then look at the description of a volunteer opportunity related to the correctional community service program in Washington County, Minnesota.

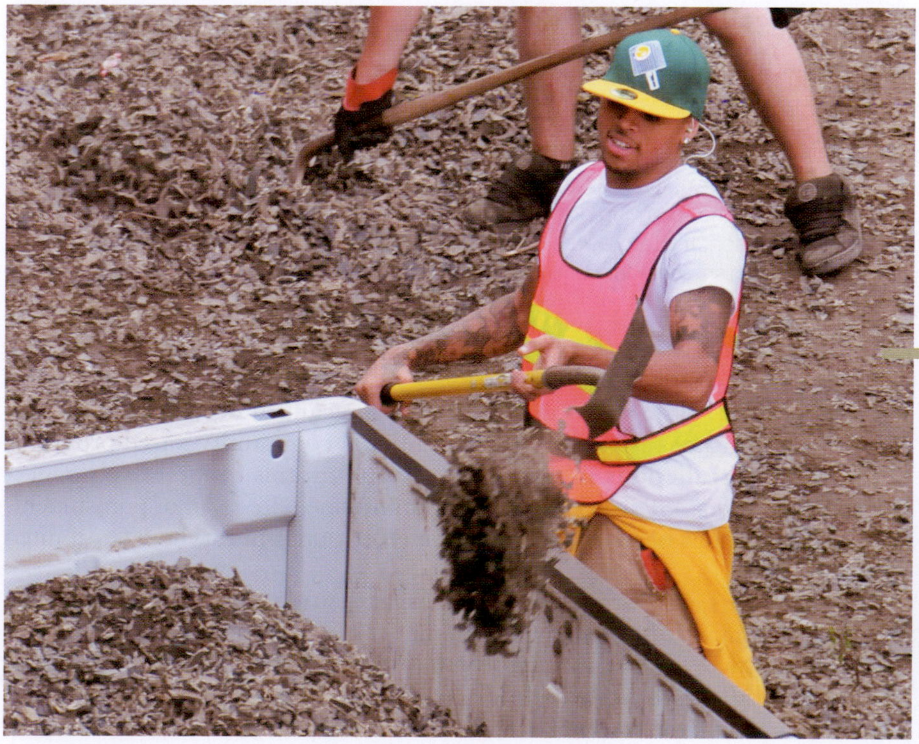

Brandon Todd/Splash News/Newscom

Singer Chris Brown did physical labor outdoors at a police horse stable and elsewhere along roads in fulfillment of his community service sentence. Such sanctions can provide benefits to the community. There may also be a "shaming" effect if offenders are embarrassed to be seen in public fulfilling a criminal punishment. Can you think of creative and effective ways to expand the use of community services sanctions?

Although community service has many supporters, some labor unions and workers criticize it for possibly taking jobs away from law-abiding citizens. In addition, some experts believe that if community service is the only sanction, it may be too mild a punishment, especially for upper-class and white-collar criminals.

Day Reporting Centers

day reporting center
A community correctional center where an offender reports each day to comply with elements of a sentence.

Another intermediate sanction option is the **day reporting center**—a community correctional center to which the offender must report each day to carry out elements of the sentence. Designed to ensure that probationers follow the employment and treatment stipulations attached to their sentence, day reporting centers also increase the likelihood that offenders and the general public will consider probation supervision to be credible.

Most day reporting centers incorporate multiple correctional methods. For example, in some centers offenders must be in the facility for eight hours or report for drug urine checks before going to work. Centers that have a rehabilitation component carry out drug and alcohol treatment, literacy programs, and job searches. Others provide contact levels equal to or greater than intensive supervision programs, in effect, creating a community equivalent to confinement.

So far, there are few evaluations of these programs. One problem common to a newly established program is that strict eligibility requirements result in small numbers of cases entering the program, but the evidence of their effectiveness is mixed. Some have found that these programs can reduce recidivism rates (Ostermann, 2009), but others indicate that offenders who complete these programs may fare worse than those on "regular" parole (Boyle et al., 2013). Evaluation of jail-run day reporting centers find that program participants have lower levels of drug use and absconding. However, because participants were carefully screened for acceptance, applicability may be limited to low-risk cases (Porter, Lee, and Lutz, 2002).

✔POINT
11. What are some of the problems of home confinement?
12. What goes on at a day reporting center?

STOP AND ANALYZE: Think back to the goals of punishment discussed in Chapter 12: retribution, deterrence, incapacitation, rehabilitation, and restorative justice. Which, if any, of these purposes are advanced by intermediate sanctions in the community? For each of the following, list the purposes of punishment that are advanced: home confinement, fines, and restitution. If intermediate sanctions do not advance many (or any) of these purposes, should they be used as punishments for criminal offenders?

Intensive Supervision Probation (ISP)

intensive supervision probation (ISP)
Probation granted under conditions of strict reporting to a probation officer with a limited caseload.

Intensive supervision probation (ISP) is a means of dealing with offenders who need greater restrictions than traditional community-based programs can provide. Jurisdictions in every state have programs to intensively supervise such offenders. ISP uses probation as an intermediate form of punishment, imposing conditions of strict reporting to a probation officer who has a limited caseload.

ISP programs are of two general types: probation diversion and institutional diversion. *Probation diversion* puts those offenders under intensive surveillance who are thought to be too risky for routine supervision. *Institutional diversion* selects low-risk offenders sentenced to prison and provides supervision for them in the community. Daily contact between the probationer and the probation officer may cut rearrest rates. Such contact also gives the probationer greater access to the resources the officer can provide, such as treatment services in the community. Offenders have incentives to obey rules, knowing that they must meet with their probation officers daily and in some cases must speak with them even more frequently. Additional restrictions—electronic monitoring, alcohol and drug testing, community service, and restitution—often are imposed on offenders as well.

ISP programs have been called "old-style" probation, because each officer has only 20 clients and requires frequent face-to-face contact (Jalbert and Rhodes, 2012). Nonetheless, some people question how much of a difference constant surveillance can make to probationers with numerous problems. Such offenders frequently need help to get a job, counseling to deal with emotional and family situations, and a variety of supports to avoid drug or alcohol problems that may have contributed to their criminality. Yet ISP may be a way of getting the large number of drug-addicted felons into treatment.

Because it presents a "tough" image of community supervision and addresses the problem of prison crowding, ISP has become popular among probation administrators, judges, and prosecutors. Most ISP programs require a specific number of monthly contacts with officers, performance of community service, curfews, drug and alcohol testing, and referral to appropriate job-training, education, or treatment programs.

Observers have warned that ISP is not a "cure" for the rising costs and other problems facing corrections systems. Ironically, ISP can also increase the number of probationers sent to prison. All evaluations of ISP find that, probably because of the closer contact with clients, probation officers uncover more violations of rules than they do in regular probation. Therefore, ISP programs often have higher failure rates than do regular probation programs, even though their clients produce fewer arrests (Tonry and Lynch, 1996). Recent analyses of recidivism post-ISP indicates that clients in these programs are not arrested any more frequently than those on "regular" probation, but are more likely to abscond due to higher surveillance (Hyatt and Barnes, 2014).

Another surprising finding is that when given the option of serving prison terms or participating in ISP, many offenders have chosen prison. In New Jersey, 15 percent of offenders withdrew their applications for ISP once they learned the conditions and requirements. Similarly, when offenders in Marion County, Oregon, were asked if they would participate in ISP, one-third chose prison instead (Petersilia, 1990). Apparently some offenders would rather spend a short time in prison, where conditions differ little from their accustomed life, than a longer period under demanding conditions in the community. To these offenders, ISP does not represent freedom, because it is so intrusive and the risk of revocation seems high. There is evidence that offenders' race plays a part in their attitude toward alternative sanctions. As shown in Table 14.3, black and white offenders differ significantly in the reasons why they would choose prison over an alternative sanction.

Despite problems and continuing questions about its effectiveness, ISP has raised confidence about the possibilities for effective probation. Some of the most effective offender supervision has been carried out by these programs. As with regular probation, the size of a probation officer's caseload, within reasonable limits, is often less important for preventing recidivism than is the quality of supervision and assistance provided to probationers. If ISP is properly implemented, it may improve the quality of supervision and services that foster success for more kinds of offenders.

TABLE 14.3 REASONS WHY RESPONDENTS WOULD AVOID AN ALTERNATIVE SANCTION

According to this table, African American offenders are more likely to say that alternatives have too many rules, and that program officers are too hard on the offenders they are monitoring. Can you think of reasons that might explain why African American offenders have more negative views about the intent of criminal justice authorities?

PERCENTAGE INDICATING REASON IS "VERY IMPORTANT" OR "PRETTY IMPORTANT"	WHITE	AFRICAN AMERICAN
Programs like these are too hard to complete.	38.9	40.0
Program rules are too hard to follow.	33.4	52.7
Officers are too hard on the program participants.	33.4	54.5
Serving prison time is easier than alternatives.	46.3	49.1
Failure to complete will result in prison.	68.5	74.1
Living in prison is easier than living outside.	24.5	37.0
Inmates are abused by parole and probation officers.	35.9	53.7
Serving time in prison is less of a hassle: The programs have too many responsibilities.	39.6	55.6

Source: Peter B. Wood and David C. May, "Racial Differences in Perceptions of the Severity of Sanctions: A Comparison of Prison with Alternatives," *Justice Quarterly* 20 (2003): 605–31.

✔POINT 13. How does intensive supervision probation differ from traditional probation?

STOP AND ANALYZE: Remember that California officials calculated that, due to the increased costs of imprisonment, it cost the state an average of $50,000 for every probationer who fails and is subsequently sent to prison. Would it be worthwhile for states, even in difficult budget situations, to invest more money in ISP? Provide two arguments for each side of this question.

Intermediate Sanctions Administered in Institutions and the Community

boot camp
A short-term institutional sentence, usually followed by probation, that puts the offender through a physical regimen designed to develop discipline and respect for authority. Also referred to as shock incarceration.

Among the most publicized intermediate sanctions are the **boot camps**. Often referred to as *shock incarceration,* these programs vary, but all are based on the belief that young offenders (usually 14- to 21-year-olds) can be "shocked" out of their criminal ways.

Boot camps put offenders through a 30- to 90-day physical regimen designed to develop discipline and respect for authority. Like the Marine Corps, most programs emphasize a spit-and-polish environment and keep the offenders in a disciplined and demanding routine that seeks ultimately to build self-esteem. Most camps also include education, job-training programs, and other rehabilitation services. On successful completion of the program, offenders are released to the community. At this point probation officers take over, and the conditions of the sentence are imposed.

Boot camps proliferated in the late 1980s, and by 1995 states and the Federal Bureau of Prisons operated 93 camps for adults and 30 for juveniles. At their peak, boot camps had more than 7,000 offenders. By 2000, about one-third of the camps had closed, and the decline in boot camp operations has continued. In January 2005, the Federal Bureau of Prisons announced that its remaining boot camps would be phased out over six months. Further, the public uproar following the death of teenager Martin Anderson caused Florida to scrap its system of juvenile boot camps. Anderson died after being pummeled by a group of guards at a Panama City boot camp. He had been sent to the camp for joyriding in his grandmother's automobile (C. Miller, Klas, and Fineout, 2006).

Joel Sartenheim/CORBIS

Military-type drills and physical workouts are part of the regimen at most boot camps, such as this one in Massachusetts. Evaluations of boot camps have reduced the initial optimism about this approach. Boot camps have been closed in many states. What are the potential shortcomings of boot camps as punishment?

Evaluations of boot camp programs have reduced the initial optimism about such approaches. Critics suggest that the emphasis on physical training ignores young offenders' real problems. Some point out that, like the military, boot camp builds esprit de corps and solidarity, characteristics that can improve the leadership qualities of the young offender and therefore enhance a criminal career. In fact, follow-up studies of boot camp graduates indicate there is evidence of changes in attitudes (Kurlycheck, 2010), but not necessarily changed behavior in avoiding subsequent criminal acts (Meade and Steiner, 2010). Research has also been found that, like intensive supervision probation, boot camps do not automatically reduce prison crowding. A National Institute of Justice (NIJ) summary of the boot camp experiment noted that they failed to reduce recidivism or prison populations (Parent, 2003).

Defenders of boot camps argue that the camps are accomplishing their goals; the failure lies in the lack of educational and employment opportunities in the participants' inner-city communities. A national study found that few boot camp graduates received any aftercare assistance on returning to their communities (Bourque, Han, and Hill, 1996), but aftercare has been shown to be essential to reducing recidivism rates (Kurlychek and Kempinen, 2006).

Researchers in the United Kingdom recently studied a group of former boot camp attendees for ten years after their release. In this program, young offenders attended a High Intensity Training program (HIT) that contained a strong rehabilitation component post-release. Their findings indicate that some boot camp programs can reduce recidivism in the short term, resulting in a cost savings of $3,600 per boot camp graduate. These costs represent savings due to reduced security expenditures and insurance, less damaged/stolen property, health-related costs of victimization, and reduced costs of responding to crime (Jolliffe, Farrington, and Howard, 2013).

Because boot camps have been popular with the public, which imagines that strict discipline and harsh conditions will instill positive attitudes in young offenders, some camps are likely to continue operating whether or not they are more effective than probation or prison. Some criminal justice experts believe the entire boot camp experiment has been a cynical political maneuver. As Franklin Zimring pointed out more than twenty years ago, "Boot camps are rapidly becoming yesterday's enthusiasm" ("Bust in Boot Camps," 1994: 26).

POINT 14. What are some typical activities at a boot camp?

STOP AND ANALYZE: Boot camps continue to operate even though some research indicates they are not effective at reducing crimes. Should we experiment with approaches that have not been proven effective through social science research? Give two arguments favoring the use of unproven programs and two arguments in opposition.

Implementing Intermediate Sanctions

Although the use of intermediate sanctions has spread rapidly, three major questions have emerged about their implementation: (1) Which agencies should implement the sanctions? (2) Which offenders should be admitted to these programs? (3) Will the "community corrections net" widen as a result of these policies so that more people will come under correctional supervision?

As in any public service organization, administrative politics is an ongoing factor in corrections. In many states, agencies compete for the additional funding needed to run the programs. The traditional agencies of community corrections, such as probation offices, could receive the funding, or the new programs could be contracted out to nonprofit organizations. Probation organizations argue that they know the field, have the experienced staff, and—given the additional resources—could do an excellent job. They correctly point out that a great many offenders sentenced to intermediate sanctions are also on

NEW DIRECTIONS IN CRIMINAL JUSTICE POLICY

EVIDENCE-BASED PRACTICES IN COMMUNITY CORRECTIONS

Significant efforts are being undertaken to identify and verify the effectiveness of programs and then publicize and provide training about effective programs. It is sometimes the case that programs that seem to be a good idea in theory can actually have no impact, or sometimes even do more harm than good. For example, the Scared Straight program, which takes juvenile offenders into adult prisons in an attempt to keep them from committing future crimes, actually increases the chance that juvenile offenders will recidivate. It is for these reasons that programs must be built on a solid foundation of knowing "what works" with regard to community corrections.

One important approach for advancing the use of evidence-based practices is the EPICS program—Effective Practices in Community Supervision. Developed by researchers at the University of Cincinnati, this program is designed to train community corrections officers on how to manage successful interactions with their probationers and parolees using techniques proven effective from research. Specifically, researchers have discovered that there are several important components to effective supervision: (1) the offender's risk of recidivism must be assessed to provide the appropriate level of supervision (high-risk probationers require greater levels of supervision); (2) the corrections officer must understand the factors that cause the probationer to commit a crime, so that the goals of supervision can be determined; and (3) supervision must include a cognitive-behavioral component in order to change dysfunctional thought patterns of clients. For example, an offender who was convicted of theft from a convenience store may have difficulty accepting blame for his actions if he reasons that his crime was "victimless." Restructuring his thought patterns to accept blame by recognizing that the store owner was harmed financially may help reduce his theft in the future.

The EPICS program is designed specifically for high-risk offenders, and corrections officers use a cognitive-behavioral approach when meeting with their clients. There are four components to each meeting:

1. Check-in: The officer determines any immediate needs of the client and discusses how well he or she has been complying with the terms of supervision. This step allows the officer to build a relationship (rapport) with the client, which can reduce future crime.
2. Review: The officer asks how skills learned in prior sessions were applied since the last meeting.
3. Intervention: The officer identifies the most urgent continued needs of the client, teaches news skills, and identifies problematic thinking.
4. Homework and rehearsal: The officer works with the client to set goals for the next meeting, review skills, and work on recurring problems.

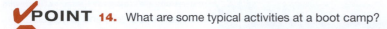

probation. Critics of giving this role to probation services argue that the established agencies are not receptive to innovation. They say that probation agencies place a high priority on the traditional supervision function and would not actively help to solve the offenders' problems.

The different types of offenders who are given intermediate sanctions prompt a second issue in the implementation debate. One school of thought focuses on the seriousness of the offense and the other on the problems of the offender. If offenders are categorized by the seriousness of their offense, they may be given such close supervision that they will not be able to abide by the sentence. Sanctions for serious offenders may accumulate to include, for example, probation, drug testing, addiction treatment, and home confinement. As the number of sentencing conditions increases, even the most willing probationers find fulfilling every one of them difficult.

Some agencies want to accept into their intermediate sanctions program only those offenders who will succeed. These agencies are concerned about their success ratio, especially because of threats to future funding if the program does not reduce recidivism. Critics point out that this strategy leads to "creaming," taking the most promising offenders and leaving those with worse problems to traditional sanctions.

The third issue concerns **net widening**, a process in which the new sanction increases instead of reduces the control over offenders' lives (Phelps, 2013).

net widening
Process in which new sentencing options increase instead of reduce control over offenders' lives.

Officers can adapt portions of this framework to meet the individual needs of their clients. For example, a client with alcohol dependency issues may require a greater focus on eliminating negative thoughts about himself and his prospects for the future. Evaluations of the EPICS program indicate that it is effective in reducing recidivism among graduates, with only 25 percent of EPICS clients being reconvicted for a new crime, as compared to 40 percent of clients on probation.

The literature on evidence-based practices in community corrections makes clear that important challenges extend beyond identifying effective practices and providing training to justice system officials who have face-to-face contact and supervisory responsibility with offenders. There is also an issue of convincing individual officers and agencies to actually incorporate evidence-based practices into their standard routines. When people have been doing their jobs and operating their offices in a certain way over a long period of time, it can be difficult to get them to change their customary practices, even when there is evidence that new approaches will be more effective. In addition, budget cuts can complicate the implementation of new practices because there may be insufficient time or personnel to carry out evidence-based practices in the manner that is most effective.

Sources: James Bonta, Tanya Rugge, Terri-Lynne Scott, Guy Bourgon, and Annie K. Yessine, "Exploring the Black Box of Community Supervision," *Journal of Offender Rehabilitation* 47 (2008): 248–70; Chris Hansen, "Cognitive-Behavioral Interventions: Where They Come from and What They Do," *Federal Probation* 72 (2008): 43–49; Edward J. Latessa, Shelley J. Listwan, and Deborah Koetzle, "What Works (and Doesn't) in Reducing Recidivism (Waltham, MA: Anderson, 2014); Anthony Petrosino, Carolyn Turpin-Petrosino, and James O. Finckenauer, "Well-Meaning Programs Can Have Harmful Effects! Lessons from Experiments of Programs Such as Scared Straight," *Crime & Delinquency* 46 (2000): 354–79; Faye S. Taxman and Steven Belenko, *Implementing Evidence-Based Practices in Community Corrections and Addiction Treatment* (New York: Springer, 2013).

DEBATE THE ISSUE

Are you optimistic that probation officers and other community corrections officials can be trained to effectively help offenders become less likely to commit new crimes? Given the number of people on probation and in other community corrections programs, and the limited number of officials who must supervise these offenders, the available time and resources may make the actual implementation of evidence-based practices an impossible dream. If you are optimistic about the possibility of progress, describe what you see as the two biggest priorities for those seeking to implement evidence-based practices. If you are not optimistic, would you steer time, attention, and resources to other aspects of probation and community corrections? Briefly describe what you would do if you were the head of a local probation office.

This can occur when a judge imposes a more intrusive sentence than usual. For example, rather than merely giving an offender probation, the judge might also require that the offender perform community service. Critics of intermediate sanctions argue that they have created the following:

- *Wider nets.* Reforms increase the proportion of individuals in society whose behavior is regulated or controlled by the state.
- *Stronger nets.* By intensifying the state's intervention powers, reforms augment the state's capacity to control individuals.
- *Different nets.* Reforms transfer jurisdictional authority from one agency or control system to another.

The creation of intermediate sanctions has been advocated as a less costly alternative to incarceration and a more effective alternative to probation. With incarceration rates still at record highs and probation caseloads increasing, intermediate sanctions will probably play a major role in corrections through the first decades of this century. However, correctional reform has always had its limitations, and intermediate sanctions may not achieve the goals of their advocates. Read the New Directions in Criminal Justice Policy feature to consider some of the practices being taught to community corrections officials and used throughout the country.

CHECKPOINT 15. What are three problems in the implementation of intermediate sanctions?

STOP AND ANALYZE: Will the contemporary government budget crisis force states and counties to make a genuine commitment to intermediate sanctions as a means to reduce expensive prison populations? If this happens, what are three likely consequences for society?

The Future of Community Corrections

In 1995 there were 3.7 million Americans under community supervision; by the beginning of 2012 this figure had grown to 4.8 million, so that 1 in 50 American adults was under correctional supervision in the community (L. M. Maruschak and Parks, 2012). Despite this tremendous growth, community corrections still lacks public support. Community corrections can suffer from an image of being "soft on crime." Moreover, news stories about probationers and offenders on home confinement committing murders and other serious crimes can reduce public support, as community corrections appears to threaten public safety (Weiner, 2013a).

Community corrections also faces the challenge that offenders today require closer supervision. The crimes, criminal records, and drug problems of these offenders are often worse than those of lawbreakers of earlier eras. Half of the offenders on probation in 2010 had been convicted of felonies, and 19 percent were guilty of violent felonies (L. Glaze and Bonczar, 2011). These people are supervised by probation officers whose caseloads number in the hundreds. Such officers, and their counterparts in parole, cannot provide effective supervision and services to all their clients.

Community corrections also faces even greater caseload pressures than in the past. With responsibility for about two-thirds of all offenders under correctional supervision, community corrections needs an infusion of additional resources. To succeed, public support for community corrections is essential, but it will come only if citizens believe that offenders are being given appropriate punishments. Opinion polls have shown that the public will support community sanctions only if offenders are strictly supervised. Allowing offenders to "roam free on the streets" with minimal supervision undermines community corrections and raises the question as to why these offenders are not incarcerated (M. G. Turner et al., 1997: 6–26).

Citizens must realize that policies designed to punish offenders in the community yield not mere "slaps on the wrists" but meaningful sanctions, even while these policies allow offenders to retain and rebuild their ties to their families and society. Joan Petersilia argues that too many crime control policies focus solely on the short term. She believes that long-term investments in community corrections will pay off for both the offender and the community (Petersilia, 1996). Consistent with her view, greater efforts have been made in recent years to apply evidence-based practices in probation and other community corrections contexts.

A QUESTION OF ETHICS

Like other officials in the criminal justice system, probation officers work independently on a wide range of tasks. They use their discretion to make decisions, including those with significant impact on others' lives, such as whether to recommend revocation of parole. Thus probation officers, like police officers and corrections officers, need to be professional, ethical, and educated as they make decisions and perform important tasks without anyone directly supervising each moment of their day. Obviously, probation officers need to act properly in treating probationers fairly, avoiding any improper discrimination when making decisions.

Probation officers also must avoid temptations to abuse their power or to enrich themselves using their position of authority. Unfortunately, cases arise occasionally that reveal probation officers falling short of proper behavior. In March 2015, a probation officer in Illinois was arrested for child pornography and official misconduct after persuading juvenile offenders under his supervision to pose for explicit photos. In Florida, a probation officer pled guilty in January 2015 for stealing over $250,000 from the county in which she worked, by falsifying community service documents and taking money directly from parolees. A probation officer in Oregon pled guilty in June 2013 for an inappropriate sexual relationship with a probationer under her supervision. A Michigan probation officer was arraigned in October 2014 for stealing prescription drugs from a client while meeting with her in the courthouse.

CRITICAL THINKING AND ANALYSIS

Even if we cannot prevent unlawful behavior by all probation officers, what can be done to reduce the problems illustrated by the foregoing cases? Selection of better candidates for probation officer positions? Better training? Better supervision? Develop four recommendations to help guard against unethical behavior by probation officers.

Summary

1 Analyze the philosophical assumptions that underlie community corrections

- Community corrections is based on four assumptions: (1) many offenders' records and offenses do not warrant incarceration, (2) community supervision is cheaper than incarceration, (3) recidivism of those under community supervision is no higher than those who go to prison, (4) ex-inmates require support and supervision to remake their lives in the community.
- Community supervision through probation, intermediate sanctions, and parole is a growing part of the criminal justice system.

2 Discuss how probation evolved and how probation sentences are implemented today

- Probation began as a humanitarian effort to allow first-time and minor offenders a second chance.
- Probation is imposed on more than half of offenders. People with this sentence live in the community according to conditions set by the judge and under the supervision of a probation officer.

3 Describe the types of intermediate sanctions and how they are administered

- Intermediate sanctions are designed as punishments that are more restrictive than probation and less restrictive than prison.
- The range of intermediate sanctions allows judges to design sentences that incorporate one or more of these punishments.
- Some intermediate sanctions are implemented by courts (fines, restitution, forfeiture); others in the community (home confinement, community service, day reporting centers, intensive supervision probation); and others in institutions and the community (boot camps).

4 Analyze the key issues facing community corrections at the beginning of the twenty-first century

- Despite tremendous growth, community sanctions lack public support.
- Some offenders require closer supervision with attendant higher costs.
- Caseload pressures often limit supervision effectiveness.
- The use of community sanctions is expected to grow during the next decade, in spite of the problems that occur when implementing these sanctions.

Questions for Review

1. What is the aim of community corrections?
2. What is the nature of probation, and how is it organized?
3. What is the purpose of intermediate sanctions?
4. What are the primary forms of intermediate sanctions?
5. What problems confront parolees upon their release?

Key Terms

boot camp (p. 600)
community justice (p. 581)
community service (p. 597)
day reporting center (p. 598)
fine (p. 591)
forfeiture (p. 593)
home confinement (p. 594)
intensive supervision probation (ISP) (p. 598)
net widening (p. 603)
recidivism (p. 578)
restitution (p. 592)
technical violation (p. 586)

Checkpoint Answers

1 What are the four main assumptions underlying community corrections?

✓ Many offenders' crimes and records do not warrant incarceration; community supervision is cheaper; recidivism rates for those supervised in the community are no higher than for those who serve prison time; ex-inmates require support and supervision as they try to remake their lives in the community.

2 Who was John Augustus and what did he do?

✓ A Boston boot maker who became the first probation officer by taking responsibility for a convicted offender before sentencing; called the father of probation.

3 What is the main goal of probation today?

✓ Risk management.

4 What are the major tasks of probation officers?

✓ To assist judges by preparing presentence reports and to provide assistance and supervision to offenders in the community.

5 What are the grounds for probation revocation?

✓ An arrest for a new offense or a technical violation of the conditions of probation that were set by the judge.

6 What rights does a probationer have while revocation is being considered?

✓ Right to a preliminary and final hearing, right to cross-examine witnesses, right to notice of the alleged violations, and right to a written report of the proceedings. Right to counsel is determined on a case-by-case basis.

7 What is the main argument for intermediate sanctions?

✓ Judges need a range of sentencing options that are less restrictive than prison and more restrictive than simple probation.

8 What is meant by a continuum of sanctions?

✓ A range of punishments reflecting different degrees of intrusiveness and control over the offender.

9 How do fines, restitution, and forfeiture differ?

✓ A fine is a sum of money paid to the government by the offender. Restitution is a sum of money paid to the victim by the offender. Forfeiture is the government seizure of assets derived from or used in criminal activity.

10 What are some of the problems of implementing these sanctions?

✓ Most offenders are poor and cannot pay, and the courts do not always allocate resources for collection and enforcement.

11 What are some of the problems of home confinement?

✓ Home confinement may violate the Fourth Amendment's protections against unreasonable searches, monitoring devices have technical problems, and failure rates are high because offenders cannot tolerate home confinement for very long.

12 What goes on at a day reporting center?

✓ Drug and alcohol treatment, job searches, educational programs, and sometimes just offenders reporting in.

13 How does intensive supervision probation differ from traditional probation?

✓ In ISP the offender is required to make stricter and more-frequent reporting to an officer with a much smaller caseload.

14 What are some typical activities at a boot camp?

✓ Boot camps maintain a spit-and-polish environment and strict discipline; involve offenders in physical activity; and provide educational, vocational, and rehabilitative services.

15 What are three problems in the implementation of intermediate sanctions?

✓ Deciding which agencies should implement the sanctions, deciding which offenders should be admitted to these programs, and the possible widening of the community corrections net.

CHAPTER FEATURES

- **Close Up** One Man's Walk through Atlanta's Jungle: Michael G. Santos
- **Close Up** Survival Tips for Beginners: TJ Granack
- **New Directions in Criminal Justice Policy** Evidence-Based Prison Practices to Reduce Recidivism
- **Doing Your Part** Inside-Out Prison Exchange Program
- **Technology and Criminal Justice** Body Armor Technology for Corrections Officers
- **Inside Today's Controversies** Arming Corrections Officers: Risks and Benefits

CHAPTER 15 INCARCERATION AND PRISON SOCIETY

CHAPTER LEARNING OBJECTIVES

1. Describe the three models of incarceration that have predominated since the 1940s
2. Discuss how a prison is organized
3. Analyze how a prison is governed
4. Describe the role of correctional officers in a prison
5. Discuss what it is like to be in prison
6. Analyze the special needs and problems of incarcerated women
7. Describe the programs and services that are available to prisoners
8. Discuss the nature of prison violence

CHAPTER OUTLINE

The Modern Prison: Legacy of the Past

Goals of Incarceration

Prison Organization

Governing a Society of Captives
- The Defects of Total Power
- Rewards and Punishments
- Gaining Cooperation: Exchange Relationships
- Inmate Leadership
- The Challenge of Governing Prisons

Correctional Officers: At the Forefront of Facing Complex Challenges
- The Officer's Role
- Recruitment of Officers
- Use of Force

Who Is in Prison?
- Elderly Prisoners
- Prisoners with HIV/AIDS
- Prisoners with Mental Illness
- Long-Term Prisoners

The Convict World
- Adaptive Roles
- The Prison Economy

Women in Prison
- The Subculture of Women's Prisons
- Male versus Female Subcultures
- Issues in the Incarceration of Women

Prison Programs
- Classification of Prisoners
- Educational Programs
- Vocational Education
- Prison Industries
- Rehabilitative Programs
- Medical Services

Violence in Prison
- Assaultive Behavior and Inmate Characteristics
- Prisoner–Prisoner Violence
- Prisoner–Officer Violence
- Officer–Prisoner Violence
- Decreasing Prison Violence

Nicole Hill/The Christian Science Monitor/Getty Images

It's 6:30 A.M. The morning whistle blows, and inmates awaken and clean their cells. At 7:00 A.M., another whistle tells inmates that it is time for breakfast. They are escorted to the mess hall to eat, where they have 25 minutes to finish their meals before reporting to work duty. Some inmates work in the laundry; others work in the kitchen or library; others take on janitorial duties to keep the prison clean. After eating lunch at noon, inmates continue working through the afternoon with recreation time at 4:10 P.M. and dinner served at 4:40 P.M. Prisoners spend the evening in their cells, perhaps reading or playing cards. "Lights out" occurs at 9:30 P.M., with the prisoners to be awakened the next morning at 6:30 A.M. to start the daily process again.

In the prison's "Rules and Regulations" handbook, inmates are told that they are entitled to "food, clothing, shelter, and medical attention. Anything else that you get is a privilege." Recreational activities include baseball, handball, and table games. Movies are shown two times per month.

This description is pretty typical of most prisons in the United States. Inmates arise, eat breakfast, work, eat lunch, work or study, eat dinner, and then go to sleep. The day described above, however, is an account of the daily activities at Alcatraz prison, circa 1956. In some ways, prison life has not changed much in the past 60 years. Compare this historical example with the very similar daily schedule in a contemporary high-security state prison (North Carolina Department of Public Safety, 2014):

6 A.M. Wake up

7 A.M. Breakfast

8 A.M. Work at prison job

Noon Lunch (30 minutes)

Lunch to 3 P.M. Work at prison job

3 P.M. Recreation/prison-yard time

4 P.M. Return to cell

5 P.M. Supper (30 minutes)

Supper to 8 P.M. Evening programs—religious services, anger management, addiction, group counseling, etc.

8 P.M. In cell

11 P.M. Lights out

The continuous similarities in daily routines do not mean that prisons have remained unchanged. The mix of offenders serving in prisons has changed, especially with the greater numbers of drug offenders being incarcerated in recent decades. In addition, as American society and culture evolve, those changes can be reflected in the knowledge and expectations of prisoners. For example, the civil rights movement for racial equality was just gathering momentum in 1956, and racial segregation was accepted in certain states' prisons. Today, however, expectations about constitutional rights and freedom from racial discrimination are widely shared among prison officials and prisoners. In addition, technological advancements; social science research on behavior; and formalization of training, policies, and procedures have all changed aspects of contemporary prisons.

What is it like to be incarcerated? What does it mean to the inmates, the guards, and the administrators? Are the officers in charge or do the prisoners "rule the joint"? This chapter explores the lives of the incarcerated, both in prison and as they face release into the community.

As we examine the social and personal dimensions of prison life, imagine visiting a foreign land and trying to learn about its culture and daily activities. The prison may be located in the United States, but the traditions, language, and relationships are unlike anything you have experienced. In the Close Up feature, One Man's Walk through Atlanta's Jungle, Michael Santos, a former long-term prisoner, describes his entry to the U.S. Federal Penitentiary in Atlanta.

The Modern Prison: Legacy of the Past

American correctional institutions have always been more varied than movies or novels portray them to be. Fictional depictions of prison life are typically set in a fortress, the "big house"—the maximum-security prisons where the inmates are tough and the guards are just as tough or tougher. Although big houses predominated in much of the country during the first half of the twentieth century, many prisons were built on another model. In the South, for instance, prisoners worked outside at farm labor, and the massive walled structures were not so common.

The typical big house of the 1940s and 1950s was a walled prison with large, tiered cellblocks, a yard, shops, and industrial workshops. The prisoners, in an average population of about 2,500 per institution, came from both urban and rural areas; they were usually poor, and outside the South, were predominantly white. The prison society was essentially isolated; access to visitors, mail, and other communication was restricted. Prisoners' days were strictly structured, with rules enforced by the guards. A basic division stood between inmates and staff; rank was observed and discipline maintained. In the big house, few treatment programs existed; custody was the primary goal.

During the 1960s and early 1970s, when the rehabilitation model prevailed, many states built new prisons and converted others into "correctional institutions." Treatment programs administered by counselors and teachers became a major part of prison life, although the institutions continued to give priority to the custody goals of security, discipline, and order.

The civil rights movement of the early 1960s profoundly affected prisoners, especially minority inmates. Prisoners demanded their constitutional rights as citizens and greater sensitivity to their needs. As discussed in Chapter 13, the courts began to take notice of the legal rights of prisoners. As inmates gained more legal services, the traditional judicial hands-off policy evaporated. Suddenly, administrators had to respond to the directives of the judiciary and run the institutions according to constitutional mandates.

During the past 30 years, as the population of the United States has changed, so has the prison population. The number of African American and Hispanic inmates has greatly increased. More inmates come from urban areas, and more have been convicted of drug-related and violent offenses. Incarcerated members of street gangs, which are often organized along racial lines, frequently regroup inside prison and contribute to elevated levels of violence. Another major change has been the rising number of correctional officers joining public employee unions, along with the use of collective bargaining to improve working conditions, safety procedures, and training.

Now the focus of corrections has shifted to crime control, which emphasizes the importance of incarceration. As a result, the number of people in prison greatly increased. Some politicians argue that offenders have "cushy" lives and that prisoners should return to the strict regimes found in the early twentieth century. Many states have removed educational and recreational amenities from institutions.

Although today's correctional administrators seek to provide humane incarceration, they must struggle with limited resources and shortages of cell space. Thus, the modern prison faces many of the difficult problems that confront other parts of the criminal justice system: racial conflicts, legal issues, limited resources, and growing populations. Despite these challenges, can prisons still achieve their objectives? The answer to this question depends, in part, on how we define the goals of incarceration.

✔POINT **1.** How does today's prison differ from the "big house" of the past?

STOP AND ANALYZE: As indicated by the preceding section, prisons are not static institutions that remain the same for centuries. They change as society changes. What are two changes in prisons that reflect shifts in American society within the past half-century? What are two possible future changes in prisons that may reflect forthcoming developments in American society?

(Answers are at the end of the chapter.)

Goals of Incarceration

Citing the nature of inmates and the need to protect staff and the community, most people consider security the dominant purpose of a prison. High walls, razor wire, searches, checkpoints, and regular counts of inmates serve the security function: Few inmates escape. More importantly, such features set the tone for the daily operations. Prisons are expected to be impersonal, quasi-military organizations where strict discipline, minimal amenities, and restrictions on freedom constitute the punishment of criminals.

CLOSE UP

ONE MAN'S WALK THROUGH ATLANTA'S JUNGLE: MICHAEL G. SANTOS

I was not expecting to receive the southern hospitality for which Atlanta is famous when the bus turned into the penitentiary's large, circular drive, but neither did I expect to see a dozen uniformed prison guards—all carrying machine guns—surround the bus when it stopped. A month in transit already had passed by the time we made it to the U.S. Penitentiary (USP) in Atlanta, the institution that would hold me (along with over two thousand other felons) until we were transferred to other prisons, we were released, or we were dead.

I left the jail in Tacoma, Washington, on the first of August, but I didn't see the huge gray walls that surround USP Atlanta until the first of September. That month was spent in a bus operated by the U.S. Marshal Service as it moved across the country, picking up federal prisoners in local jails and dropping them off at various Bureau of Prison facilities.

As I crossed the country, I listened to tales from numerous prisoners who sat beside me on the bus. There wasn't much to discuss except what was to come. Each of us was chained at the hands and feet. There were neither magazines to read nor music playing. Mostly people spoke about a riot that had taken place behind USP Atlanta's walls a few months earlier. A lot of the men had been to prison before, and Atlanta would be nothing new. Those prisoners only talked about reuniting with old friends, explaining prison routine, or sat like stone-cold statues waiting for what was to come. I'd never been confined before, so it was hard to tune out the stories that others were telling. While I was listening, though, I remember telling myself that I would survive this sentence. No matter what it took, I would survive.

I was in my early twenties, younger than perhaps every other prisoner on the bus. Pimples spotted my face as I began my term, but I was certain my black hair would be white by the time I finished. I had been sentenced to 45 years by a U.S. district court judge in Tacoma on charges related to cocaine trafficking. I was expected to serve close to 30 years before release. It was hard then—just as it is hard now—to believe the sentence was real. The best thing I could do, I reasoned, was to stay to myself. I'd heard the same rumors that every suburban kid hears about prison. I was anxious about what was to come, but I was determined to make it out alive and with my mind intact. Now it was all to begin!

After the bus stopped, the guards began calling us off by last name and prison number. It is not easy to walk with a 12-inch chain connected to each ankle, and wrists bound to a chain that runs around the waist, but when my name was called, I managed to wobble through the bus's aisle, hop down the steps, and then begin the long march up the stairs leading to the fortress. As I was moving to the prison's doors, I remember glancing over my shoulder, knowing it would be the last time I'd see the world from the outside of prison walls for a long time.

Once inside the institution, the guards began unlocking my chains. About 50 other prisoners arrived with me that day, so the guards had plenty of chains to unlock, but their work didn't stop there. They also had to squeeze us through the dehumanizing admissions machine. The machine begins with photographs, fingerprints, and interrogations. Then comes the worst part, the strip search, where each prisoner stands before a prison official, naked, and responds to the scream: "Lift up your arms in the air! Let me see the back of your hands! Run your fingers through your hair! Open your mouth! Stick your tongue out! Lift your balls! Turn around! Bend over! Spread your ass! Wider! Lift the bottom of your feet! Move on!" The strip search, I later learned, is a ritual Atlanta's officers inflict on prisoners every time they have contact with anyone from outside the walls, and sometimes randomly as prisoners walk down the corridor.

Three models of incarceration have predominated since the early 1940s: the custodial, rehabilitation, and reintegration models. Each is associated with one style of institutional organization.

1. The **custodial model** assumes that prisoners have been incarcerated for the purpose of incapacitation, deterrence, or retribution. It emphasizes security, discipline, and order as they subordinate the prisoner to the authority of the warden. Discipline is strict, and most aspects of behavior are regulated. Having prevailed in corrections before World War II, this model still dominates most maximum-security institutions.
2. The *rehabilitation model*, which reached its height during the 1950s (see Chapter 13) emphasizes treatment programs designed to reform the offender. According to this model, security and housekeeping activities are viewed primarily as preconditions for rehabilitative efforts. Because all aspects of the organization should be directed toward rehabilitation, professional

custodial model
A model of incarceration that emphasizes security, discipline, and order.

There was a lot of hatred behind those walls. Walking through the prison must be something like walking through a jungle, I imagined, not knowing whether others perceive you as predator or prey, knowing that you must remain always alert, watching every step, knowing that the wrong step may be the one that sucks you into the quicksand. The tension is ever present; I felt it wrapped all over, under and around me. I remember it bothering me that I didn't have enough hatred, because not hating in the jungle is a weakness. As the serpents slither, they spot that lack of hatred and salivate over a potential target.

Every prisoner despises confinement, but each must decide how he or she is going to do the time. Most of the men run in packs. They want the other prisoners either to run with them or run away from them. I wasn't interested in doing either. Instead of scheming on how I could become king of the jungle, I thought about ways that I could advance my release date. Earning academic credentials, keeping a clean record, and initiating projects that would benefit the communities both inside and outside of prison walls seemed the most promising goals for me to achieve. Yet working toward such goals was more dangerous than running with the pack; it didn't take me long to learn that prisoners running in herds will put forth more energy to cause others to lose than they will to win themselves. Prison is a twisted world, a menagerie.

I found that a highly structured schedule would not only move me closer to my goals but also would limit potential conflicts inside the prison. There is a pecking order in every prison, and prisoners vying for attention don't want to see others who are cutting their own path. I saw that bullies generally look for weaker targets, so I began an exercise routine that would keep me physically strong. If I were strong, I figured, others would be more reluctant to try me. Through discipline, I found, I could develop physical strength. Yet I've never figured out how to develop the look of a killer, or the hatred off which that look feeds.

I don't know whether the strategies I have developed for doing time are right for everyone. But they are working for me. Still, I know that I may spend many more years in prison. The only fear I have—and as I'm working on my eighth year, it's still here—is that someone will try me and drag me into an altercation that may jeopardize my spotless disciplinary record. I've been successful in avoiding the ever-present quicksand on my walk through the jungle so far, but I know that on any given day, something may throw me off balance, or I may take a wrong step. And one wrong step in this jungle can drown me in quicksand, sucking me into the abysmal world of prison forever. That wrong step also could mean the loss of life, mine or someone else's.

In prison, more than anywhere else I know, understanding that some things are beyond an individual's sphere of control is vital. No matter how much preparation is made, the steel and concrete jungle is a dangerous place in which to live.

Source: Written for this book in 1995 by Michael G. Santos. In August 2012, he was released from federal prison after serving 25 years of a 45-year sentence for drug trafficking. He then spent six months living in a halfway house followed by home confinement prior to his release from Bureau of Prisons' supervision in August 2013.

DEBATE THE ISSUE

Have prison officials failed to do enough to control the environment of prisons if these institutions are, as described here, such dangerous and scary places? Should Americans care at all if prisoners harm each other inside those walls? List two reasons for your perspective on each of these questions. Then list one counterargument that an opponent could present against your position on each question.

treatment specialists have a higher status than do other employees. Since the rethinking of the rehabilitation goal in the 1970s, treatment programs still exist in most institutions, but few prisons conform to this model today.

3. The **reintegration model** is linked to the structures and goals of community corrections. Recognizing that prisoners will be returning to society, this model emphasizes maintaining the offenders' ties to family and community as a method of reform. Prisons following this model gradually give inmates greater freedom and responsibility during their confinement, moving them to halfway houses or work release programs before giving them community supervision.

Although one can find correctional institutions that conform to each of these models, most prisons are mainly custodial. Nevertheless, treatment programs do exist, and because almost all inmates return to society at some point, even the most custodial institutions must prepare them for their reintegration.

reintegration model
A model of a correctional institution that emphasizes maintaining the offender's ties to family and community as a method of reform, recognizing that the offender will be returning to society.

See "What Americans Think" for a look at how the public views the goals of incarceration. However, even as Americans express support for rehabilitation and release programs for nonviolent offenders, there is still a question about whether taxpayers are truly willing to pay for such programs, especially during an era in which state governments are cutting funds for education and other services needed by the general public.

Much is asked of prisons. As Charles Logan notes, "We ask them to correct the incorrigible, rehabilitate the wretched, deter the determined, restrain the dangerous, and punish the wicked" (Logan, 1993: 19). Because prisons are expected to pursue many different and often incompatible goals, they are almost doomed to fail as institutions. Logan believes the mission of prisons is confinement. He argues that the basic purpose of imprisonment is to punish offenders fairly and justly through lengths of confinement proportionate to the seriousness of their crimes. He summarizes the mission of prison as follows: "to keep prisoners—to keep them in, keep them safe, keep them in line, keep them healthy, and keep them busy—and to do it with fairness, without undue suffering, and as efficiently as possible" (Logan, 1993: 21). If the purpose of prisons is punishment through confinement under fair and just conditions, what are the implications of this purpose for correctional managers?

✔POINT 2. What three models of prison have predominated since the 1940s?

STOP AND ANALYZE: If you were asked to choose one—and only one—of the three models as the basis for designing a prison, which would you choose and why?

Prison Organization

The prison's physical features and function set it apart from almost every other institution and organization in modern society. It is a place where a group of employees manage a group of captives. Prisoners must live according to the rules of their keepers, and their movements are sharply restricted. Unlike managers of other government agencies, prison managers:

- Cannot select their clients
- Have little or no control over the release of their clients
- Must deal with clients who are there against their will
- Must rely on clients to do most of the work in the daily operation of the institution—work these clients are forced to do and for which they receive little, if any, compensation
- Must depend on the maintenance of satisfactory relationships between clients and staff

Given these unique characteristics, how should a prison be run? What rules should guide administrators? As the description just given indicates, wardens and other key personnel are asked to perform a difficult job, one that requires skilled and dedicated managers (Vickovic and Griffin, 2014).

Most prisons are expected to fulfill goals related to keeping (custody), using (work), and serving (treatment) inmates. Because individual staff members are not equipped to perform all functions, separate lines of command organize the groups of employees that carry out these different tasks. One group is charged with maintaining custody over the prisoners, another group supervises them in their work activities, and a third group attempts to treat them.

The custodial employees are the most numerous. They are typically organized along military lines, from warden to captain to officer, with accompanying pay differentials down the chain of command. The professional personnel

WHAT AMERICANS THINK

QUESTION: "State prison systems could offer the following four alternative prison policies for people who have committed nonviolent crime. What would you prefer the state to implement?"

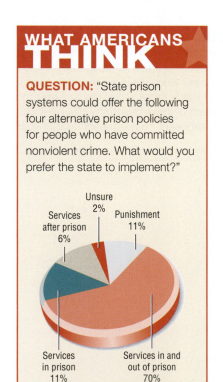

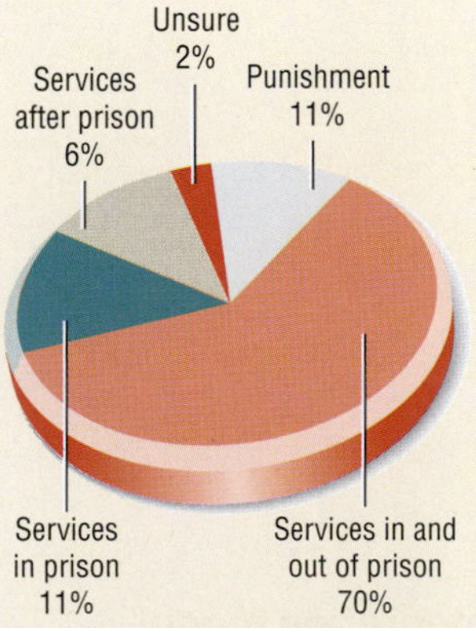

Source: Barry Krisberg and Susan Marchionna, "Attitudes of U.S. Voters toward Prisoner Rehabilitation and Reentry Policies," *Focus* (National Council on Crime and Delinquency), April 2006, p. 3.

FIGURE 15.1 FORMAL ORGANIZATION OF PRISON FOR ADULT FELONS

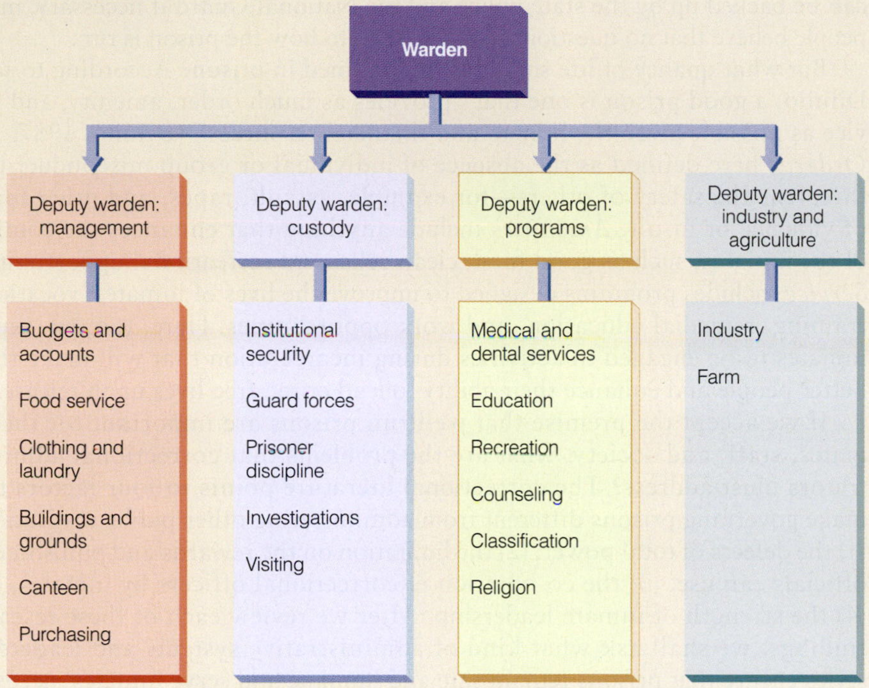

Prison staff are divided into various sections consistent with the goals of the organization. Custodial employees are the most numerous.

associated with the using and serving functions, such as industry supervisors, clinicians, and teachers, are not part of the custodial structure and have little in common with its staff. All employees are responsible to the warden, but the treatment personnel and the civilian supervisors of the workshops have their own salary scales and titles. Figure 15.1 presents the formal organization of staff responsibilities in a typical prison.

The multiple goals and separate lines of command often cause ambiguity and conflict in the administration of prisons. For example, the goals imposed on prisons are often contradictory and unclear. Conflicts between different groups of staff (custodial versus treatment, for instance), as well as between staff and inmates, present significant challenges for administrators.

How, then, do prisons function? How do prisoners and staff try to meet their own goals? Although the U.S. prison may not conform to the ideal goals of corrections and the formal organization may bear little resemblance to the ongoing reality of the informal relations, order is kept and a routine is followed.

✔POINT
3. How do prisons differ from other organizations in society?
4. What are the multiple goals pursued in today's prisons with respect to prisoners?
5. What problems do these goals present to administrators?

STOP AND ANALYZE: How might the multiple goals of prisons collide with each other? Select two of the goals and describe how the pursuit of one goal may make the effective attainment of the other goal more difficult.

Governing a Society of Captives

Much of the public believes that prisons are operated in an authoritarian manner. In such a society, correctional officers give orders and inmates follow those commands. Strictly enforced rules specify what the captives may and may not do. Staff members have the right to grant rewards and to inflict punishment. In theory, any inmate who does not follow the rules could be placed in solitary confinement. Because the officers have a monopoly on the legal means of enforcing rules and can be backed up by the state police and the National Guard if necessary, many people believe that no question should arise as to how the prison is run.

But what quality of life should be maintained in prison? According to John DiIulio, a good prison is one that "provides as much order, amenity, and service as possible given the human and financial resources" (DiIulio, 1987: 12). *Order* is here defined as the absence of individual or group misconduct that threatens the safety of others—for example, assault, rapes, and other forms of violence or insult. *Amenities* include anything that enhances the comfort of the inmates, such as good food, clean cells, and recreational opportunities. *Service* includes programs designed to improve the lives of inmates: vocational training, remedial education, and work opportunities. Here, too, we expect inmates to be engaged in activities during incarceration that will make them better people and enhance their ability to lead crime-free lives upon release.

If we accept the premise that well-run prisons are important for the inmates, staff, and society, what are the problems that correctional administrators must address? The correctional literature points to four factors that make governing prisons different from administering other public institutions: (1) the defects of total power, (2) the limitation on the rewards and punishments officials can use, (3) the co-optation of correctional officers by inmates, and (4) the strength of inmate leadership. After we review each of these research findings, we shall ask what kind of administrative systems and leadership styles ensure that prisons remain safe and humane and serve inmates' needs.

The Defects of Total Power

Imagine a prison society that comprises hostile and uncooperative inmates ruled by force. Prisoners can be legally isolated from one another, put under continuous surveillance, and physically abused until they cooperate. Although all of these things are possible, such practices would probably not be countenanced for long because the public expects correctional institutions to be run humanely.

In reality, the power of officers is limited, because many prisoners have little to lose by misbehaving, and unarmed officers have only limited ability to force compliance with rules. Perhaps more important is the fact that forcing people to follow commands is an inefficient way to make them carry out complex tasks; efficiency is further diminished by the ratio of inmates to officers (typically 9 to 1 in federal prisons and 4.5 to 1 in state prisons) and by the potential danger.

Rewards and Punishments

Correctional officers often rely on rewards and punishments to gain cooperation. To maintain security and order among a large population in a confined space, they impose extensive rules of conduct. Instead of using force to ensure obedience, however, they reward compliance and punish rule violators by granting or denying privileges.

To promote control, officers may follow any of several policies. One is to offer cooperative prisoners rewards such as choice job assignments, residence in the honor unit, and favorable parole reports. Inmates who do not break rules are given good time. Informers may also be rewarded, and administrators may ignore conflict among inmates on the assumption that it keeps prisoners from uniting against authorities.

The system of rewards and punishments has some deficiencies. One is that the punishments for rule breaking do not represent a great departure from the prisoners' usual circumstances. Because inmates are already deprived of many freedoms and valued goods—heterosexual relations, money, choice of clothing, and so on—not being allowed to attend, say, a recreational period does not carry much weight. Further, inmates receive authorized privileges at the start of the sentence that are taken away only if rules are broken, but they receive few rewards for progress or exceptional behavior. However, as an inmate approaches release, opportunities for furloughs, work release, or transfer to a halfway house can serve as incentives to obey rules.

Gaining Cooperation: Exchange Relationships

One way that correctional officers obtain inmate cooperation is by tolerating minor rule infractions in exchange for compliance with major aspects of the custodial regime. The correctional officer plays the key role in these exchange relationships. Officers and prisoners remain in close association both day and night—in the cellblock, workshop, dining hall, recreation area, and so on. Although the formal rules require a social distance between officers and inmates, the physical closeness makes them aware that each relies on the other. The officers need the cooperation of the prisoners so that they will look good to their superiors, and the inmates count on the officers to relax the rules or occasionally look the other way. For example, officers in a Midwestern prison told researcher Stan Stojkovic that flexibility in rule enforcement was especially important as it related to the ability of prisoners to cope with their environment. As one officer said, "Phone calls are really important to guys in this place. . . . You cut off their calls and they get pissed. So what I do is give them a little extra and they are good to me." Yet the officers also told Stojkovic that they would be crazy to intervene to stop illicit sex or drug use (Stojkovic, 1990: 214).

Correctional officers must be careful not to pay too high a price for the cooperation of their charges. Under pressure to work effectively with prisoners, officers may be blackmailed into doing illegitimate favors in return for cooperation. Officers who establish *sub-rosa,* or secret, relationships can be manipulated by prisoners into smuggling contraband or committing other illegal acts. Corrections officers are caught each year smuggling drugs and cell phones to prisoners. In addition, bans on cigarettes inside some prisons have created a

Marjorie Kamys Cotera/Bob Daemmrich Photography/Alamy

Corrections officers face significant challenges in maintaining order and safety while outnumbered by prisoners, especially when many prisons are understaffed. What qualities and skills do corrections officers need in order to be effective?

lucrative and tempting market for corrections officers to smuggle tobacco into institutions and receive payments from the prisoners' relatives. Because scarce tobacco can be worth hundreds of dollars per bag, unethical officers can significantly enhance their incomes through such smuggling—at the same time that they risk being arrested and sent to prison themselves for such illegal activity (Goldschmidt and Shoichet, 2013; Ingold, 2011). News stories every year describe corrections employees being convicted and incarcerated for attempting to smuggle items to prisoners. In March 2015, for example, an officer employed by a private prison company in Washington, D.C., was sentenced to 27 months in prison for accepting $750 to smuggle a cell phone and cigarettes into a correctional facility ("Former Corrections Officer Sentenced," 2015).

Inmate Leadership

In the traditional prison of the big-house era, administrators enlisted the inmate leaders to help maintain order. Inmate leaders had been "tested" over time so that they were neither pushed around by other inmates nor distrusted as stool pigeons. Because the staff could rely on them, they served as the essential communications link between staff and inmates. Their ability to acquire inside information and gain access to higher officials brought inmate leaders the respect of other prisoners and special privileges from officials. In turn, they distributed these benefits to other prisoners, thus bolstering their own influence within the prison society.

Prisons seem to function more effectively now than they did in the recent past. Although prisons are more crowded, riots and reports of violence have declined. In many prisons, the inmate social system may have reorganized, so that correctional officers again can work through prisoners respected by fellow inmates. Yet, some observers contend that when wardens maintain order in this way, they enhance the positions of some prisoners at the expense of others. The leaders profit by receiving illicit privileges and favors, and they increase their influence by distributing benefits.

Further, descriptions of the contemporary maximum-security prison raise questions about administrators' ability to run prisons in this way. In most of today's institutions, prisoners are divided by race, ethnicity, age, and gang affiliation, so that no single leadership structure exists.

The Challenge of Governing Prisons

The factors of total power, rewards and punishments, exchange relationships, and inmate leadership exist in every prison and must be managed. How they are managed greatly influences the quality of prison life. John DiIulio's classic study (1987) challenged the common assumption of many correctional administrators that "the cons run the joint." Instead, successful wardens have made their prisons function well by applying management principles within the context of their own style of leadership. Prisons can be governed, violence can be minimized, and services can be provided to the inmates if correctional executives and wardens exhibit leadership. Governing prisons is an extraordinary challenge, but it can be and has been effectively accomplished.

Consider the example of Warden Dennis Luther, who led a medium-security federal correctional institution in Pennsylvania in the 1990s without any escapes, murders, or suicides, and with only three serious assaults on staff and six serious assaults among prisoners (R. Worth, 1995). Luther emphasized prisoners' involvement through "town hall" meetings, communication and interaction between staff and prisoners on a daily basis throughout the institution, education programs, and, especially, treating everyone within the institution—prisoners and staff—with respect (Peters, 1992; R. Worth, 1995).

Staff members were expected to adhere to a set of principles that included the following:

1. Inmates are sent to prison as punishment and not for punishment.
2. Correctional workers have a responsibility to ensure that inmates are returned to the community no more angry or hostile than when they were committed.
3. Inmates are entitled to a safe and humane environment while in prison.
4. You must believe in man's capacity to change his behavior.
5. Be responsive to inmate requests for action or information. Respond in a timely manner and respond the first time an inmate makes a request. . . .
6. It is important for staff to model the kind of behavior they expect to see duplicated by inmates. . . .
7. There is an inherent value in self-improvement programs such as education, whether or not these programs are related to recidivism. . . .
8. Staff cannot, because of their own insecurities, lack of self-esteem, or concerns about their masculinity, condescend or degrade inmates. . . .
9. Inmate discipline must be consistent and fair.

These rules present high aspirations that are not easily fulfilled, and that are even more difficult to implement in higher-security institutions with more-troubled populations of offenders. The first rule in particular has implications for all of the others. Staff members in prison must avoid the temptation to inflict hassles and punishments on prisoners as a means of asserting their authority or as a way of lashing back against insults and uncooperative behavior. The deprivation of liberty and the constraints of a controlled environment are supposed to be the bases for criminal punishment in prisons. Punishment should not include additional hassles and burdens inflicted by corrections officers through harassing searches, degrading treatment, and arbitrary denial of services (T. R. Clear, 1994). Such actions by corrections officers can contribute to an environment of tension and intensify the prisoners' hostility toward each other and staff.

✔POINT 6. What four factors make the governing of prisons different from administering other public institutions?

STOP AND ANALYZE: If staff members' emotional self-control and respect for prisoners can make positive contributions to effective management of prisons, how can a warden encourage these qualities in staff members who may face insults, spitting, assaults, and angry displays of disobedience by uncooperative offenders? Give three suggestions for how a warden might encourage these qualities in staff members.

Correctional Officers: At the Forefront of Facing Complex Challenges

A prison is simultaneously supposed to keep, use, and serve its inmates. The achievement of these goals depends heavily on the performance of its correctional officers. Their job is not easy. Not only do they work long and difficult hours with a hostile client population, but their superiors also expect them to do so with few resources or punishments at their disposal. Most of what they are expected to do must be accomplished by gaining and keeping the cooperation of the prisoners.

The Officer's Role

Over the past 30 years, the correctional officer's role has changed greatly. No longer responsible merely for "guarding," the correctional officer is now considered a crucial professional who has the closest contact with the prisoners and performs a variety of tasks. Officers are expected to counsel, supervise, protect, and process the inmates under their care. But the officer also works as a member of a complex bureaucratic organization and is expected to deal with clients impersonally and to follow formal procedures. Fulfilling these contradictory role expectations is difficult in itself, and the physical closeness of the officer and inmate over long periods exacerbates this difficulty.

Recruitment of Officers

Employment as a correctional officer is neither glamorous nor popular. The work is thought to be boring, the pay is low, and career advancement is minimal. Studies have shown that one of the primary incentives for becoming involved in correctional work is the security that civil service status provides. In addition, because most correctional facilities are located in rural areas, prison work often is better than other available employment. Because correctional officers are recruited locally, many of them are rural and white, in contrast to the majority of prisoners who come from urban areas and are often either African American or Hispanic (Figure 15.2). Yet some correctional officers see their work as a way of helping people, often the people most in need in U.S. society.

Today, because they need well-qualified, effective correctional officers, states seek to recruit quality personnel. Salaries have been raised so that the average annual pay nationally is $39,000, although states vary in their pay rates for corrections personnel. Thus the lowest-paid 10 percent of corrections officers nationally have salaries below $27,000, while the highest-paid 10 percent earn more than $69,000 (Bureau of Labor Statistics, 2014a). For example, the starting salary for corrections officers in Texas is $29,000; with step increases over time, Texas officers reach a top salary of $39,000 after seven years of service (Texas Department of Criminal Justice, 2014). By contrast, after graduating from the state training academy, corrections officers in California begin their careers making $45,000 with the prospect of earning nearly $74,000 when they reach the top pay grade (California Department of Corrections and Rehabilitation, 2014). Because of attractive pay and retirement benefits, California can receive as many as 120,000 applications for 900 places in a training academy class (Finley, 2011). In other states, however, it is likely

FIGURE 15.2 **RACIAL/ETHNIC COMPOSITION OF CORRECTIONAL OFFICERS AND INMATES, ADULT SYSTEMS, NATIONWIDE**

Although the racial/ethnic composition of correctional officers does not equal the racial/ethnic composition of the inmate population, great strides have been made during the past quarter century.

Sources: Garey Bies, *Corrections Report* (Madison: Wisconsin Association for Correctional Law Enforcement, 2013), p. 15; E. Ann Carson, "Prisoners in 2013," Bureau of Justice Statistics *Bulletin*, September 2014, NCJ 247282, p. 1.

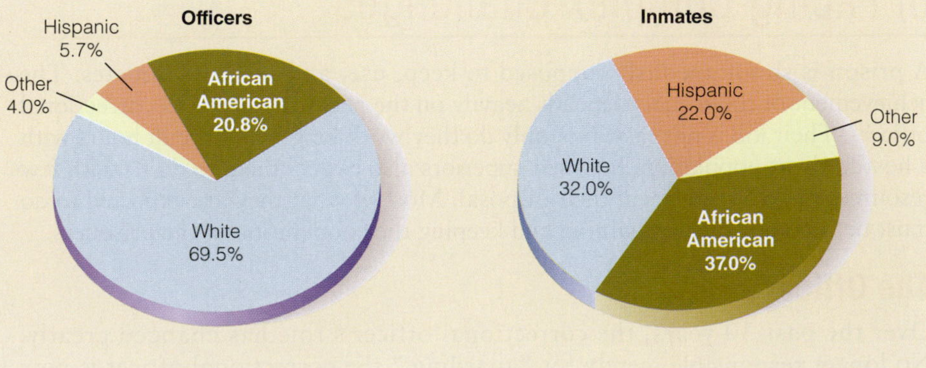

that factors such as low salaries, crowded prisons, and a more violent class of prisoners have contributed to a shortage of correctional officers when other job opportunities are available in the local area.

Special efforts have been made to recruit women and minorities. Approximately 30 percent of correctional officers are members of minority groups and 23 percent are women. The diversification of the corrections workforce can create issues for corrections administrators who must be concerned about performance, effectiveness, and job satisfaction among corrections officers. For example, female officers can have greater perceptions of the risk of victimization on the job than do their male counterparts (J. A. Gordon, Proulx, and Grant, 2013). Research on job satisfaction and job stress has found that "female correctional officers with low levels of job satisfaction will report greater job stress" than other corrections officers (Cheeseman and Downey, 2012: 38). There are also issues about corrections officers' attitudes toward prisoners and whether prisoners' attitudes and behavior with respect to officers vary according to the demographic composition of the workforce.

Most states now have training programs for correctional officers. Ted Conover compares his experience as a "newjack" (recruit) at the Corrections Academy of the State of New York to that of the military's basic training (Conover, 2000: 12–56). During the typical six-week programs, recruits receive at least a rudimentary knowledge of job requirements and correctional rules. The classroom work, however, often bears little resemblance to problems confronted in the cellblock or in the yard. Therefore, on completing the course, the new officer is placed under the supervision of an experienced officer. On the job, the new officer experiences real-life situations and learns the necessary techniques and procedures. Through encounters with inmates and officers, the recruit becomes socialized to life behind the walls and gradually becomes part of that subculture (Crouch and Marquart, 1994: 301).

For most correctional workers, being a custodial officer is a job with limited opportunities for advancement, except for the chance to supervise other custodial officers. Although officers who perform well may be promoted to a higher rank, such as correctional counselor, few ever move into administrative positions. However, in some states and in the Federal Bureau of Prisons, people with college degrees can move up the career ladder to management positions.

AP Images/Elaine Thompson

Much of the work of corrections officers involves searching cells and counting prisoners. Such officers have a saying, "We're all doing time together, except officers are doing it in eight-hour shifts." What are the professional rewards—if any—of working as a corrections officer?

Use of Force

When and how can force be used? Although corporal punishment and the excessive use of force are not permitted, correctional officers use force in many situations. They often confront inmates who challenge their authority or are attacking other inmates. Though unarmed and outnumbered, officers must maintain order and uphold institutional rules. Under these conditions they feel justified in using force.

When and how much force may be used? All correctional agencies now have formal policies and procedures with regard to the legitimate use of force. In general these policies allow only levels of force necessary to achieve legitimate goals. Officers violating these policies may face an inmate lawsuit and dismissal from their job. There are five situations in which the use of force is legally acceptable:

1. *Self-defense:* If officers are threatened with physical attack, they may use a level of force that is reasonable to protect themselves from harm.
2. *Defense of third persons:* As in self-defense, an officer may use force to protect an inmate or another officer. Again, only reasonably necessary force may be used.
3. *Upholding prison rules:* If inmates refuse to obey prison rules, officers may need to use force to maintain safety and security. For example, if an inmate refuses to return to his or her cell, it may be necessary to use handcuffs and forcefully transfer the prisoner.
4. *Prevention of a crime:* Force may be used to stop a crime, such as theft or destruction of property, from being committed.
5. *Prevention of escapes:* Officers may use force to prevent escapes, because escapes threaten the well-being of society as well as order within correctional institutions. Although escape from a prison is a felony, officials may not shoot the fleeing inmate at will, as could be done in the past. Today, agencies differ as to their policies toward escapees. Some limit the use of deadly force to prisoners thought to be dangerous, whereas others require warning shots. However, officers in certain states may face disciplinary action if they fail to use deadly force in certain situations. Although the U.S. Supreme Court has limited the ability of police officers to shoot fleeing felons, the rule has not been applied to correctional officers dealing with escapes.

Correctional departments have detailed sets of policies on the use of force. However, correctional officers face daily challenges that test their self-control and professional decision-making skills. Inmates often "push" officers in subtle ways, such as moving slowly, or they use verbal abuse to provoke officers. Correctional officers are expected to run a "tight ship" and maintain order, often in situations where they are outnumbered and dealing with troubled people. In confrontational situations they must defuse hostility yet uphold the rules—a difficult task at best.

✔POINT
7. What complex challenges face correctional officers?
8. Name three of the five legally acceptable reasons for the use of force.

STOP AND ANALYZE: What should happen when a corrections officer uses force in an inappropriate situation or uses too much force in an approved situation? If you were a warden, what procedures would you put in place to hear excessive-force complaints from prisoners? What would you do if you were persuaded excessive force had been used?

Who Is in Prison?

The age, education, and criminal history of the inmate population influence how correctional institutions function. What are the characteristics of inmates in our nation's prisons? Do most offenders have long records of serious offenses, or are many of them first-time offenders who have committed minor crimes? Do some inmates have special needs that dictate their place in prison? These questions are crucial to an understanding of the work of wardens and correctional officers.

Data on the characteristics of prisoners are limited. The Bureau of Justice Statistics reports that a majority of prisoners are men, aged 25 to 44, and members of minority groups (E. Carson, 2014). Approximately 40 percent of state prisoners have not completed their high school education (Figure 15.3).

Recidivists and those convicted of violent crimes make up a significant portion of the prison population. Previous research showed that 44 percent of prisoners are rearrested within the first year after release and approximately

FIGURE 15.3 **SOCIODEMOGRAPHIC AND OFFENSE CHARACTERISTICS OF STATE PRISON INMATES**

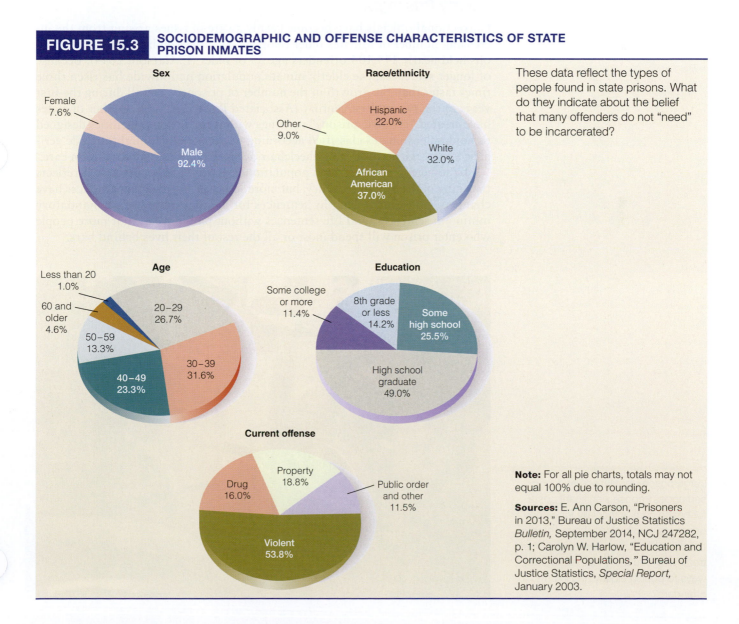

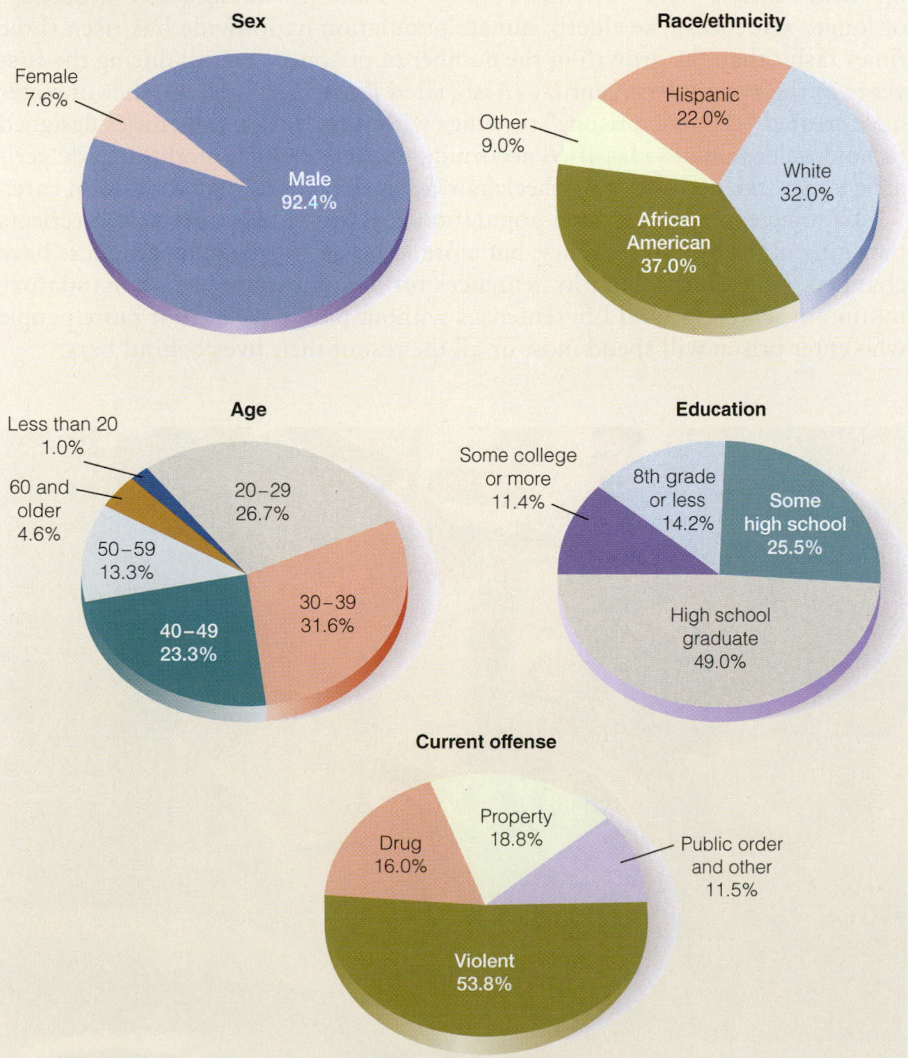

These data reflect the types of people found in state prisons. What do they indicate about the belief that many offenders do not "need" to be incarcerated?

Note: For all pie charts, totals may not equal 100% due to rounding.

Sources: E. Ann Carson, "Prisoners in 2013," Bureau of Justice Statistics *Bulletin,* September 2014, NCJ 247282, p. 1; Carolyn W. Harlow, "Education and Correctional Populations," Bureau of Justice Statistics, *Special Report,* January 2003.

25 percent of all released inmates will return to prison within three years (Langan and Levin, 2002). Most of today's prisoners have a history of persistent criminality. As we will see in Chapter 16, however, there is a significant emphasis by legislators and corrections officials today on facilitating the successful reentry into society by former prison inmates. States are seeking to reduce prison populations and make greater use of less expensive community corrections options. Yet it remains true that parole violators account for a significant portion of admissions to prison each year. In 2013, for example, out of 631,168 prison admissions nationwide, 164,065 or 26 percent were parole violators being returned to prison for committing new crimes or violating conditions of their parole while living under supervision in the community (E. Carson, 2014).

Correctional operations also face challenges from four specific categories of prisoners: the increased number of elderly prisoners, the many prisoners with HIV/AIDS, the thousands of prisoners with mental disorders, and the increase in long-term prisoners.

Elderly Prisoners

Correctional officials have become keenly aware of issues arising from the increasing number of inmates older than age 55. In December 2013, state prisons held nearly 144,104 offenders age 55 or older (E. Carson, 2014). Because of longer sentences, the elderly inmate population nationwide has risen three times faster than the growth in the number of prisoners overall during the first years of the twenty-first century (Associated Press, 2007). A number of states have created "geriatric prisons" or wings within correctional facilities designed to hold older inmates classified according to needs, which might include geriatric issues, the necessity for wheelchair-accessible ramps, and long-term care.

To some extent, the prison population is growing older because it reflects the aging of the overall citizenry, but more so because sentencing practices have changed. Consecutive lengthy sentences for heinous crimes, long mandatory minimum sentences, and life sentences without parole mean that more people who enter prison will spend most or all the rest of their lives behind bars.

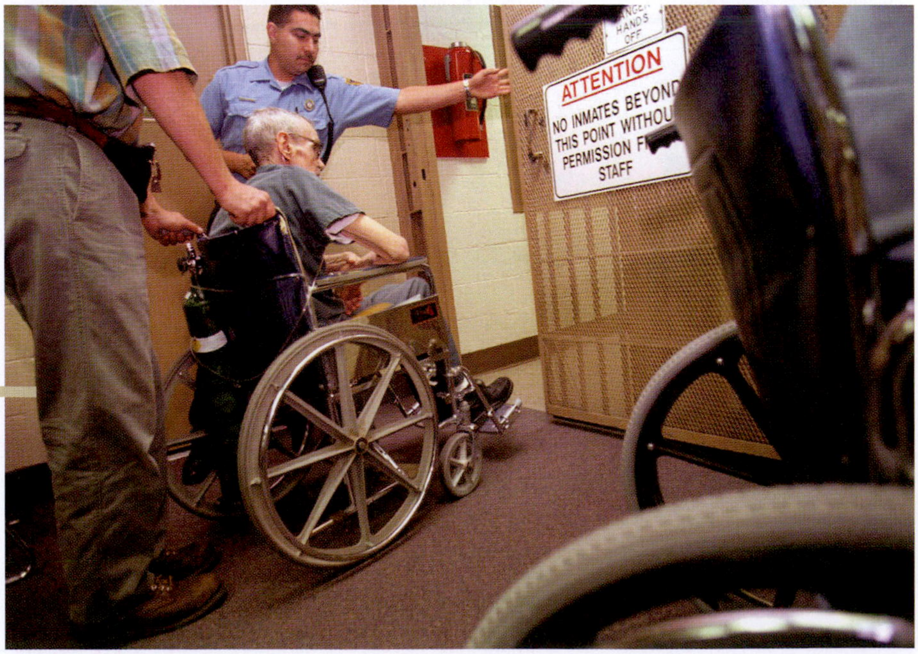

Large prison populations and long sentences impose significant costs for health care, especially for elderly prisoners who typically have chronic conditions that require medication or treatment. Are there less expensive ways to punish elderly and infirm offenders?

Sean Cayton/The Image Works

Elderly prisoners have security and medical needs that differ from those of the average inmate (Habes, 2011). For example, they can't climb into top bunks. In many states, special sections of the institution have been designated for this older population so they will not have to mix with the younger, tougher inmates. New York has opened a dementia unit within the state prison in Fishkill (Hill, 2007). Elderly prisoners are more likely to develop chronic illnesses such as heart disease, stroke, and cancer. The cost for maintaining an elderly inmate averages about $69,000 per year, triple the average cost for other prisoners (Curtin, 2007).

Ironically, while in prison the offender will benefit from much better medical care and live a longer life than if he or she were discharged. As one Georgia inmate has said, "You have to wonder why they haven't . . . let them go home? What can an 80-year-old man in a wheelchair do? Run?" (Associated Press, 2007).

Prisoners with HIV/AIDS

Prison officials face significant challenges in identifying and treating prisoners with HIV and AIDS as well as preventing the spread of the virus. In 2008, there were 21,987 HIV-positive inmates (1.5 percent of the prison population) including 5,174 offenders with AIDS. The rate of confirmed AIDS cases in state and federal prisons is two times higher than the rate in the total U.S. population. In 2006, there were 155 AIDS-related inmate deaths recorded in state and federal prisons (Maruschak, 2009). Although AIDS is the next-leading cause of death in the total prison population behind "natural causes" and suicide, the actual number of deaths has substantially decreased since 1995 (BJS, 2008). Because many inmates who are HIV-infected are undiagnosed, these numbers underestimate the scope of the problem.

The high incidence of HIV/AIDS among prisoners can be traced to increased incarceration of drug offenders. Many of these inmates engaged in intravenous drug use, shared needles, and/or traded sex for drugs or money. Male homosexual activity is also a primary way that HIV is transmitted. But rates of HIV/AIDS are higher among female prisoners (1.9 percent) than male prisoners (1.5 percent) (Maruschak, 2009). Some argue that the government has a compelling interest to educate prisoners about the risk of unprotected sex or drug use in prison and even beyond the walls (Merianos, Marquart, and Damphousse, 1997). In many correctional facilities HIV/AIDS prevention programs are in place.

To deal with offenders who have AIDS symptoms or who test positive for the virus, prison officials can develop policies on methods to prevent transmission of the disease, housing of those infected, and medical care for inmates with the full range of symptoms. Institution administrators are confronting a host of legal, political, medical, budgetary, and attitudinal factors as they decide what actions to take.

Prisoners with Mental Illness

Mass closings of public hospitals for individuals with mental disorders began in the 1960s. At the time, new psychotropic drugs made treating patients in the community seem a more humane alternative to long-term hospitalization. It also promised to be less expensive. Soon, however, people saw that community treatment works only if patients take their medication. Widespread homelessness was the most public sign that the community treatment approach had its shortcomings. With the expansion of prisons and the greater police emphasis on public order offenses, many individuals with psychiatric disorders are now arrested and incarcerated. These inmates tend to catch a revolving door from homelessness to incarceration and then back to the streets. As with other aspects of contemporary corrections, state budget cuts are reducing the already-limited services and programs for those with mental illness within the criminal justice system (Weston, 2011).

As an example, in Miami, the same 97 individuals with mental disorders were arrested a total of 2,200 times and spent a combined 27,000 days in jail over a five-year period, costing taxpayers $13 million (National Public Radio, 2011). Although that striking example concerns a local jail, it gives some sense about the fact that people dealing with mental illness end up in the corrections system, including prisons, when convicted of serious offenses, yet the justice system is ill-equipped to address their problems. A study by the Bureau of Justice Statistics in 2006 found staggering rates of mental illness symptoms among the nation's incarcerated population. The study found that 56 percent of state prisoners, 45 percent of federal prisoners, and 64 percent of jail inmates had either current symptoms or a recent history of mental illness (D. J. James and Glaze, 2006). Many of these individuals may function well in some situations, but others may have great difficulty with comprehending orders, self-control, and appropriate behavior (Fellner, 2006).

Correctional workers are usually unprepared to deal with prisoners with mental illness. Cellblock officers, for instance, often do not know how to respond to disturbed inmates. Although most corrections systems have mental health units that segregate the ill, many inmates with psychiatric disorders live among other prisoners in the general population, where they are teased and otherwise exploited.

The availability and type of mental health treatment programs vary from prison to prison. The two most common types involve therapy/counseling or dispensing medications. One in 7 inmates in state prisons receives psychotropic medications and many of those inmates, plus others with mental health issues, receive counseling (D. J. James and Glaze, 2006). Although some inmates benefit from the regular medication and therapy they receive, others suffer as the stress of confinement deepens their depression, intensifies delusions, or leads to mental breakdown. Some commit suicide. Issues of mental health care and other aspects of medical care for prisoners served as the focal point for a controversial U.S. Supreme Court decision in 2011 that ordered the state of California to reduce its prison population (*Brown v. Plata,* 2011).

Long-Term Prisoners

More prisoners in the United States serve longer sentences than do prisoners in other Western nations. One survey found that nearly 310,000 prisoners are currently serving at least 20-year sentences. Of these inmates, about 10 percent are serving "natural life," which means there is no possibility of parole (C. G. Camp, 2003). The number of inmates serving natural life has nearly tripled since 1992 and they now make up 10 percent of all prisoners (Liptak, 2005; S. Moore, 2009). These long-term prisoners are often the same people who will become elderly offenders, with all the attendant problems. Each life sentence costs taxpayers an estimated $1 million.

Studies show substantial differences in the way the long-termer responds to incarceration. Some, but not others, experience severe stress, depression, and other health problems (Mauer, 2001). Such emotional stress tends to take place earlier rather than later in the sentence as these inmates lose contact with their families.

Long-term prisoners are generally not seen as control problems. They are charged with disciplinary infractions about half as often as are short-term inmates. They do, nonetheless, present challenges for administrators who must find ways of making long terms livable. Experts suggest that administrators follow three main principles: (1) maximize opportunities for the inmate to exercise choice in living circumstances, (2) create opportunities for meaningful living, and (3) help the inmate maintain contact with the outside world (Flanagan, 1995).

Many long-term inmates will eventually be released after spending their prime years incarcerated. Will offenders be able to support themselves when they return to the community at age 50, 60, or 70?

The contemporary inmate population presents several challenges to correctional workers. Resources may not be available to provide rehabilitative programs for most inmates. Even if the resources exist, the goal of maintaining a safe and healthy environment may tax the staff's abilities. These difficulties are multiplied still further by AIDS and the increasing numbers of elderly and long-term prisoners. The contemporary corrections system must also deal with a different type of inmate, one who is more prone to violence, and with a prison society where racial tensions are great. How well it meets this correctional challenge will greatly affect American society.

CHECKPOINT 9. What are the major characteristics of today's prisoners?

STOP AND ANALYZE: Draft a solution to alleviate one of the four problems just discussed: elderly prisoners, prisoners with HIV/AIDS, mental illness in prisons, or prisoners serving long sentences. In light of the budget difficulties faced by states, are there any solutions that can save money?

The Convict World

Inmates of a maximum-security prison do not serve their time in isolation. Rather, prisoners form a society with traditions, norms, networks of relationships and interactions, and a leadership structure (Kreager et al., 2015). Some choose to associate with only a few close friends; others form cliques along racial or "professional" lines. Still others serve as the politicians of the convict society; they attempt to represent convict interests and distribute valued goods in return for support. Just as there is a social culture in the free world, there is a prisoner subculture on the "inside." Membership in a group provides mutual protection from theft and physical assault, the basis of wheeling-and-dealing activities, and a source of cultural identity (Irwin, 1980).

As in any society, the convict world has certain norms and values. Often described as the **inmate code**, these norms and values develop within the prison social system and help to define the inmate's image of the model prisoner. As Robert Johnson notes, "The public culture of the prison has norms that dictate behavior 'on the yard' and in other public areas of the prison such as mess halls, gyms, and the larger program and work sites" (R. Johnson, 2002: 100). Prison is an ultramasculine world. The culture breathes masculine toughness and insensitivity, impugning softness, and emphasizes the use of hostility and manipulation in one's relations with fellow inmates and staff. It makes caring and friendly behavior, especially with respect to the staff, look servile and silly (Sabo, Kupers, and London, 2001). This is a core element of the inmate code, even when differences in other aspects of the code exist in different prisons.

inmate code
The values and norms of the prison social system that define the inmates' idea of the model prisoner.

Former inmate Chuck Terry, who later became a college professor, says that male prisoners must project an image of "fearlessness in the way they walk, talk and socially interact" (Terry, 1997: 26). Because showing emotion is seen as a weakness, inmates must suppress expressions of their true feelings.

The code also emphasizes the solidarity of all inmates against the staff. For example, inmates should never inform on one another, pry into one another's affairs, "run off at the mouth," or put another inmate on the spot. They must be tough and not trust the officers or the principles for which the guards stand. Further, guards are wrong and the prisoners are right.

Famous sociologists who first examined prisons concluded that the code emerges within the institution as a way to lessen the pain of imprisonment (Sykes, 1958); others concluded that it is part of the criminal subculture that prisoners bring with them (Irwin and Cressey, 1962). The inmate who follows the code can be expected to enjoy a certain amount of admiration from other inmates as a "right guy" or a "real man." Those who break the code are labeled "rat" or "punk" and will probably spend their prison life at the bottom of the convict social structure, alienated from the rest of the population and targeted for abuse (Sykes, 1958: 84).

A single, overriding inmate code probably does not exist in today's prisons. Instead, convict society has divided itself along racial lines (Irwin, 1980). The level of adherence to the inmate code also differs among institutions, with greater modifications to local situations found in maximum-security prisons. Still, the core commandments described by Sykes 50 years ago remain. For a somewhat different perspective, see the Close Up box, "Survival Tips for Beginners."

In a changing society that has no single code of behavior accepted by the entire population, administrators' tasks become much more difficult. Those in authority must be aware of the different groups, recognize the norms and rules that members hold, and deal with the leaders of many cliques rather than with a few inmates who have risen to top positions in the inmate society.

✔POINT

10. What are the key elements of the inmate code?

11. Why is it unlikely that a single, overriding inmate code exists in today's prisons?

STOP AND ANALYZE: Imagine if, through a horrible series of events and errors, you were convicted of a crime and sent to prison. How would you find out about what to expect in prison? How would you learn how to behave in prison society? List three things that you would do to avoid making major mistakes while serving your sentence.

Marjorie Kamys Cotera/Bob Daemmrich Photography/Alamy

There is no longer a common inmate code and solidarity among prisoners. Prisoners often divide themselves into racial and ethnic groups. In addition, race-based gangs use threats and violence to gain power and material benefits inside prison society. As a corrections officer, how would you deal with a white supremacist gang or other gangs based on racial and ethnic divisions and conflicts?

CLOSE UP

SURVIVAL TIPS FOR BEGINNERS: TJ GRANACK

Okay, so you just lost your case. Maybe you took a plea bargain. Whatever. The point is you've been sentenced. You've turned yourself over to the authorities and you're in the county jail waiting to catch the next chain to the R Units (receiving) where you'll be stripped and shaved and photographed and processed and sent to one of the various prisons in your state.

So what's a felon to do? Here are some survival tips that may make your stay less hellish:

1. *Commit an Honorable Crime.* Commit a crime that's considered, among convicts, to be worthy of respect. I was lucky. I went down for first-degree attempted murder, so my crime fell in the "honorable" category. Oh, goodie. So I just had to endure the everyday sort of danger and abuse that comes with prison life.
2. *Don't Gamble.* Not cards, not chess, not the Super Bowl. And if you do, don't bet too much. If you lose too much, and pay up (don't even think of doing otherwise), then you'll be known as rich guy who'll be very popular with the vultures.
3. *Never Loan Anyone Anything.* Because if you do, you'll be expected to collect one way or another. If you don't collect, you will be known as a mark, as someone without enough heart to take back his own. . . .
4. *Make No Eye Contact.* Don't look anyone in the eye. Ever. Locking eyes with another man, be he a convict or a guard, is considered a challenge, a threat, and should therefore be avoided.
5. *Pick Your Friends Carefully.* When you choose a friend, you've got to be prepared to deal with anything that person may have done. Their reputation is yours, and the consequences can be enormous.
6. *Fight and Fight Dirty.* You have to fight, and not according to Marquis of Queensbury rules, either. If you do it right, you'll only have to do it once or twice. If you don't, expect regular whoopings and loss of possessions. . . .
7. *Mind Your Own Business.* Never get in the middle of anyone else's discussion/argument/confrontation/fight. Never offer unsolicited knowledge or advice.
8. *Keep a Good Porn Collection.* If you don't have one, the boys will think you're funny. . . .
9. *Don't Talk to Staff, Especially Guards.* Any prolonged discussions or associations with staff makes you susceptible to rumor and suspicion of being a snitch.
10. *Never Snitch.* Or even appear to snitch. And above all, avoid the real thing. And if you do, you'd better not get caught.

Source: From TJ Granack, "Welcome to the Steel Hotel: Survival Tips for Beginners," in *The Funhouse Mirror* (pp. 6–10), edited by Robert Gordon Ellis. Copyright © 2000 by Washington State University Press. Reprinted by permission of Washington State University Press.

Adaptive Roles

John Irwin, who served time in prison as a young man and later became a prominent scholar in criminal justice, produced the classic description of prisoners' roles. On entering prison, a newcomer ("fish") is confronted by the question, "How am I going to do my time?" Some decide to withdraw and isolate themselves. Others decide to become full participants in the convict social system. The choice, influenced by prisoners' values and experiences, helps determine strategies for survival and success.

Most male inmates use one of four basic role orientations to adapt to prison: "doing time," "gleaning," "jailing," and functioning as a "disorganized criminal" (Irwin, 1970: 67).

Doing Time

Men "doing time" view their prison term as a brief, inevitable break in their criminal careers, a cost of doing business. They try to serve their terms with the least amount of suffering and the greatest amount of comfort. They avoid trouble by living by the inmate code, finding activities to fill their days, forming friendships with a few other convicts, and generally doing what they think is necessary to survive and to get out as soon as possible.

Gleaning

Inmates who are "gleaning" try to take advantage of prison programs to better themselves and improve their prospects for success after release. They use the resources at hand: libraries, correspondence courses, vocational training, schools. Some make a radical conversion away from a life of crime.

Jailing

"Jailing" is the choice of those who cut themselves off from the outside and try to construct a life within the prison. These are often "state-raised" youths who have spent much of their lives in institutional settings and who identify little with the values of free society. These are the inmates who seek power and influence in the prison society, often becoming key figures in the politics and economy of prison life.

Disorganized Criminal

A fourth role orientation—the "disorganized criminal"—describes inmates who cannot develop any of the other three orientations. They may be of low intelligence or afflicted with psychological or physical disabilities, and they find functioning in prison society difficult. They are "human putty" to be manipulated by others. These are also the inmates who cannot adjust to prison life and who develop emotional disorders, attempt suicide, and violate prison rules (K. Adams, 1992).

As these roles suggest, prisoners are not members of an undifferentiated mass. Individual convicts choose to play specific roles in prison society. The roles they choose reflect the physical and social environment they have experienced and also influence their relationships and interactions in prison. How do most prisoners serve their time? Although the media generally portray prisons as violent, chaotic places, research shows that most inmates want to get through their sentence without trouble. As journalist Pete Earley found in his study of Leavenworth, roughly 80 percent of inmates try to avoid trouble and do their time as easily as possible (Earley, 1992). Indeed, recent research indicates that the longer prisoners are incarcerated, the more effective they become in coping with stress and challenges by planning for avoiding confrontations and other problems (Leban et al., 2015).

✔POINT 12. What are the four role orientations found in adult male prisons?

STOP AND ANALYZE: If you were a corrections officer, how could you encourage prisoners to become "gleaners," as a way of keeping themselves busy and helping them prepare for life after prison? List two things you might try to say or do.

The Prison Economy

In prison, as outside, individuals want goods and services. Although the state feeds, clothes, and houses all prisoners, amenities are scarce. Prisoners are deprived of everything but bare necessities. Their diet and routine are monotonous and their recreational opportunities scarce. They experience a loss of identity (due to uniformity of treatment) and a lack of responsibility. In short, the prison is relatively unique in having been deliberately designed as "an island of poverty in the midst of a society of relative abundance" (V. Williams and Fish, 1974: 40).

The number of items that a prisoner can purchase or receive through legitimate channels differs from state to state and from facility to facility. For example, inmates in some prisons may have televisions, civilian clothing, and hot plates. Not all prisoners enjoy these luxuries, nor do the few items they are allowed satisfy lingering desires for a variety of other goods. Some state legislatures have decreed that amenities will be prohibited and that prisoners should return to Spartan living conditions.

Recognizing that prisoners do have some needs that are not met, prisons have a commissary or "store" from which inmates may periodically purchase a limited number of items—toilet articles, tobacco, snacks, and other items—in exchange for credits drawn on their "bank accounts." The size of a bank account depends on the amount of money deposited on the inmate's entrance, gifts sent by relatives, and amounts earned in the low-paying prison industries.

However, the peanut butter, soap, and cigarettes of the typical prison store in no way satisfy the consumer needs and desires of most prisoners. Consequently, an informal, underground economy is a major element in prison society. Many items taken for granted on the outside are highly valued on the inside. For example, talcum powder and deodorant become more important because of the limited bathing facilities. Goods and services unique to prison can take on exaggerated importance inside prison. For example, unable to get alcohol, offenders may seek a similar effect by sniffing glue. Or to distinguish themselves from others, offenders may pay laundry workers to iron a shirt in a particular way, a modest version of conspicuous consumption.

Beginning in the 1980s, many studies demonstrated the pervasiveness of this economy. When David Kalinich (1980) studied the State Prison of Southern Michigan in Jackson, he learned that a market economy provides the goods (contraband) and services not available or not allowed by prison authorities. Mark Fleisher (1989) found an inmate running a "store" in almost every cellblock in the U.S. Penitentiary at Lompoc, California. Food stolen (from the kitchen) for late-night snacks, homemade wine, and drugs (marijuana) were available in these "stores." As a principal feature of prison culture, this informal economy reinforces the norms and roles of the social system and influences the nature of interpersonal relationships. The extent of the underground economy and its ability to produce desired goods and services—food, drugs, alcohol, sex, preferred living conditions—vary according to the scope of official surveillance, the demands of the consumers, and the opportunities for entrepreneurship. Inmates' success as "hustlers" determines the luxuries and power they can enjoy.

Because real money is prohibited and a barter system is somewhat restrictive, traditionally the standard currency of the prison economy was cigarettes. Half of the states now ban tobacco in prisons in order to reduce health risks for prisoners and staff (Seaman, 2010). Where still permitted, cigarettes are easily transferable, have a stable and well-known standard of value, and come in "denominations" of singles, packs, and cartons. Furthermore, they are in demand by smokers. Even those who do not smoke keep cigarettes for prison currency. As more prisons become nonsmoking, cans of tuna fish and bars of soap have emerged as new forms of currency.

Certain positions in the prison society enhance opportunities for entrepreneurs. For example, inmates assigned to work in the kitchen, warehouse, and administrative office steal food, clothing, building materials, and even information to sell or trade to other prisoners. The goods may then become part of other market transactions. Thus, the exchange of a dozen eggs for two packs of cigarettes may result in the reselling of the eggs in the form of egg sandwiches made on a hot plate for five cigarettes each. Meanwhile, the kitchen worker who stole the eggs may use the income to get a laundry worker to starch his shirts, to get drugs from a hospital orderly, or to pay another prisoner for sexual favors.

Participation in the prison economy can put inmates at greater risk for victimization while incarcerated (Copes et al., 2010). Economic transactions can lead to violence when goods are stolen, debts are not paid, or agreements are violated. Disruptions of the economy can occur when officials conduct periodic "lockdowns" and inspections. Confiscation of contraband can result in temporary shortages and price readjustments, but gradually business returns. The prison economy, like that of the outside world, allocates goods and services, rewards and sanctions, and it is closely linked to the society it serves.

✔POINT **13.** Why does an underground economy exist in prison?

14. Why are prison administrators wary of the prison economy?

STOP AND ANALYZE: Is it possible to stop the underground economy in prisons? If you were a warden, identify two steps you would take to reduce the problems associated with the underground economy (whether you believe you can completely stop it or not).

Women in Prison

Most studies of prisons have been based on institutions for men. How do prisons for women differ, and what are the special problems of female inmates? Women constitute less than 8 percent (111,287) of the entire U.S. prison population (E. Carson, 2014). However, the growth rate in the number of incarcerated women has exceeded that of men since 1981. In fact, from 2003 to 2013, the population of men in state and federal prisons increased 7 percent, whereas that of women increased by 11 percent (E. Carson, 2014). The war on drugs had a decided impact on the prison population, with the increasing proportion of drug offenders making up the largest category in women's prisons (Kruttschnitt and Gartner, 2003). This growth is particularly acute in the federal system, which has had to absorb thousands of additional female drug offenders during the past 20 years. The increased number of women in prison has significantly affected the delivery of programs, housing conditions, medical care, staffing, and security. As you read "Civic Engagement: Your Role in the System," think about how society should treat women prisoners, particularly in light of the fact that nearly all of them will eventually gain release.

Life in the nation's 98 confinement facilities for women and 93 coed facilities both resembles and differs from that in institutions for men (J. Stephan and Karberg, 2003). Women's prisons are smaller, with looser security and less structured relationships; the underground economy is not as well developed; and female prisoners seem less committed to the inmate code. Women also serve shorter sentences than do men, so their prison society is more fluid as new members join and others leave.

Many women's prisons have the outward appearance of a college campus, often seen as a group of "cottages" around a central administration/dining/program building. Generally these facilities lack the high walls, guard towers, and cyclone fences found at most prisons for men. In recent years, however, the trend has been to upgrade security for women's prisons by adding barbed wire, higher fences, and other devices to prevent escapes.

These characteristics of correctional facilities for women are offset by geographic remoteness and inmate heterogeneity. Few states operate more than one institution for women, so inmates are generally far from children, families, friends, and attorneys. In many institutions, the small numbers of inmates limit the extent to which the needs of individual offenders can be recognized and treated. Housing classifications are often so broad that inmates who are

CIVIC ENGAGEMENT

YOUR ROLE IN THE SYSTEM

Imagine that your fraternity, sorority, church group, or other social-service organization has been asked to participate in programs to help women prisoners prepare for successful reentry into society. *Make a list of needs that women prisoners are likely to have and what measures volunteer groups could take to provide assistance with reentry and success in society.* Then compare your responses with the activities of the Women's Prison Association.

FIGURE 15.4 CHARACTERISTICS OF FEMALE INMATES IN STATE PRISONS

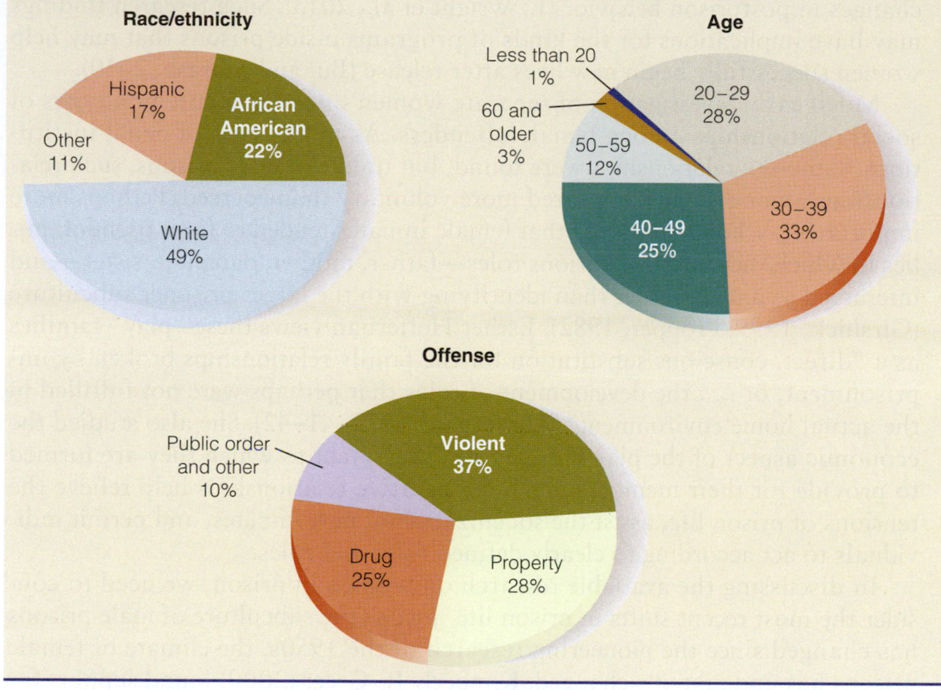

Like their male counterparts, women inmates in state prisons are typically young, have little education, are incarcerated for a serious offense, and include overrepresentation by members of minority groups.

Note: Each pie chart total does not equal 100% due to rounding.

Source: E. Ann Carson. 2014. "Prisoners in 2013," Bureau of Justice Statistics *Bulletin,* September, NCJ 247282.

dangerous or have mental disorders are mixed with women who have committed minor offenses and have no psychological problems. Similarly, available rehabilitative programs are often not used to their full extent, because correctional departments fail to recognize women's problems and needs.

In most respects, we can see incarcerated women, like male prisoners, as disadvantaged losers in this complex and competitive society. However the two groups differ with regard to types of offenses, length of sentences, patterns of drug use, and correctional history. A Bureau of Justice Statistics survey found that 37 percent of female prisoners were sentenced for violent offenses (compared with more than 50 percent of male prisoners), and 25 percent for drug-related offenses (versus 15 percent of men) (E. Carson, 2014). In light of the differences in patterns of offenses, women receive shorter average maximum sentences than do men. Figure 15.4 summarizes some characteristics of female prisoners.

CHECKPOINT 15. What accounts for the neglect of facilities and programs in women's prisons?

STOP AND ANALYZE: Should women's prisons be identical to men's prisons? List two arguments supporting reasons for there to be differences between them and two arguments supporting identical institutions.

The Subculture of Women's Prisons

Studies of the subculture of women's prisons have been less extensive than those of male convict society. Although there have been few ethnographic studies of prisons during the past two decades, recently scholars have given greater attention to interactions, social structure, and social networks in both men's and women's prisons using interview methods (Leban et al., 2015). In women's prisons, particular attention has been paid to the effects of offenders' relationships with family and outside friends, as well as other prisoners, on their success in moving away from criminal behavior after release. It appears that the development and maintenance of positive relationships are associated with changes in postprison behavior (E. Wright et al., 2013). Such research findings may have implications for the kinds of programs inside prisons that may help women successfully begin new lives after release (Bui and Morash, 2010).

Much early investigation of separate women's prisons focused on types of social relationships among female offenders. As in all types of penal institutions, same-sex relationships were found, but unlike in male prisons, such relationships among women appeared more voluntary than coerced. Perhaps more importantly, scholars reported that female inmates tended to form pseudofamilies in which they adopted various roles—father, mother, daughter, sister—and interacted as a unit, rather than identifying with the larger prisoner subculture (Girshick, 1999; Propper, 1982). Esther Heffernan views these "play" families as a "direct, conscious substitution for the family relationships broken by imprisonment, or . . . the development of roles that perhaps were not fulfilled in the actual home environment" (Heffernan, 1972: 41–42). She also studied the economic aspect of the play families and the extent to which they are formed to provide for their members. Such cooperative relationships help relieve the tensions of prison life, assist the socialization of new inmates, and permit individuals to act according to clearly defined roles and rules.

In discussing the available research on women in prison, we need to consider the most recent shifts in prison life. Just as the subculture of male prisons has changed since the pioneering research of the 1950s, the climate of female prisons has undoubtedly changed. Kimberly R. Greer (2000) found support for the idea that prisons for women are less violent, involve less gang activity, and do not have the racial tensions existing in men's prisons; however, the respondents indicated that their interpersonal relationships may be less stable and less familial than in the past. They reported higher levels of mistrust among women and greater economic manipulation.

In another study of prison culture, Barbara Owen (1998) found that the inmates at the Central California Women's Facility, holding over 4,500 women, developed various styles of doing time. Based on the in-prison experience, these styles correspond to the day-to-day business of developing a program of activities and settling into a routine. She observed that the vast majority wanted to avoid "the mix"—"behavior that can bring trouble and conflict with staff and other prisoners." A primary feature of "the mix" is anything for which one can lose good time or can result in being sent to administrative segregation. Being in "the mix" was related to "'homo-secting,' involvement in drugs, fights, of 'being messy,' that is, being involved in conflict and trouble." Owen found that most women want to do their time and go home, but some "are more at home in prison and do not seem to care if they 'lost time'" (Owen, 1998: 179).

Male versus Female Subcultures

Comparisons of male and female prisons are complicated by the nature of the research: Most studies have been conducted in single-sex institutions, and most follow theories and concepts first developed in male prisons. However, the following facts may explain the differences in subculture:

- More than half of male inmates but little more than a third of female inmates are serving time for violent offenses.
- There is less violence in prisons for women than in prisons for men.
- Women show greater responsiveness to prison programs than do men.
- Men's prison populations are divided by security level, but most women serve time in facilities where the entire population is mixed.

- Men tend to segregate themselves by race; this is less true with women.
- Men rarely become intimate with their keepers, but many women share their lives with officers.

A major difference between the two types of prisons relates to interpersonal relationships. Male prisoners act for themselves and are evaluated by others according to how they adhere to subcultural norms. As James Fox (1982) noted in his comparative study of one women's prison and four men's prisons, men believe they must demonstrate physical strength and consciously avoid any mannerisms that might imply homosexuality. To gain recognition and status within the convict community, the male prisoner must strictly adhere to these values. Men form cliques, but not the family networks found in prisons for women. Male norms stress autonomy, self-sufficiency, and the ability to cope with one's own problems, and men are expected to "do their own time." Fox found little sharing in the men's prisons (Fox, 1982).

Women place less emphasis on achieving status or recognition within the prisoner community. Fox writes that women are also less likely "to impose severe restrictions on the sexual (or emotional) conduct of other members" (1982: 100). As noted previously, in prisons for women, close ties seem to exist among small groups akin to extended families. These family groups provide emotional support and share resources.

Some have ascribed the differences between male and female prisoner subcultures to the nurturing, maternal qualities of women. Critics charge that such an analysis stereotypes female behavior and imputes a biological basis to personality where none exists. Of importance as well is the issue of inmate–inmate violence in male and female institutions. The few data that exist indicate that women are less likely to engage in violent acts against other inmates than are men (Kruttschnitt and Krmpotich, 1990). In addition, the violence that occurs is shaped by differences in prison culture within women's institutions (Owen et al., 2008). It will be interesting to see whether such gender-specific differences continue to be found among prisoners as society increasingly views women and men as equals.

✔POINT 16. How do the social relationships among female prisoners differ from those of their male counterparts?

STOP AND ANALYZE: What might be reasons that account for differences in men's and women's behavior, values, and relationships in prison society? List three factors that potentially contribute to the differences.

Issues in the Incarceration of Women

Under pressures for equal opportunity, states seem to believe that they should run women's prisons as they do prisons for men, with the same policies and procedures. However, advocates for female prisoners have urged governments to keep in mind that women inmates have different needs than men do (Bartels and Gaffney, 2011). Understanding the pathways by which women end up incarcerated can also help prison and jail administrators manage their facilities. Many incarcerated women have been victims of physical and sexual abuse, and that history can affect their behavior during incarceration (McCampbell, 2005).

Although departments of corrections have been playing "catch up" to meet the unique needs of women offenders, sexual misconduct by officers persists, along with women prisoners' demands for education and training, medical services, and methods for dealing with the problems of mothers and their children. We next examine each of these issues and the policy implications they pose for the future.

Sexual Misconduct

As the number of female prisoners has increased, cases of sexual misconduct by male correctional officers have escalated. As a result of an investigation of sexual misconduct by officers in the women's prisons of five states—California, Georgia, Illinois, Michigan, and New York—Human Rights Watch reported that male officers had raped, sexually assaulted, and abused female inmates (Culley, 2012). Guards had also "used their near total authority to provide or deny goods and privileges to female prisoners to compel them to have sex or, in other cases, to reward them for having done so" (S. A. Holmes, 1996). A national survey of prisoners estimated that 60,000 prisoners—female and male—experienced sexual victimization, and a majority of the reported victimizations involved corrections officers (A. J. Beck and Harrison, 2007). One reason for the prevalence of misconduct by corrections officers is that even consensual sexual contact between a prisoner and a corrections officer is defined as victimization because of rules against such conduct as well as the status and role differences between the two individuals that create a context for exploitation.

Monetary civil judgments awarded to women for mistreatment while in prison have grown. Officials in California, Georgia, and the District of Columbia have reached out-of-court settlements in class-action suits brought on behalf of women who said they were sexually harassed or assaulted by guards while incarcerated.

To deal with the problem of sexual abuse in prison, states have enacted statutes aimed at sexual misconduct with correctional clients. Although some of these laws are directed toward correctional officers, several states are revising their statutes to include anyone who supervises offenders. Beyond the new laws, corrections faces a great need for the implementation of effective sexual harassment policies, the training of officers, and tougher screening of recruits.

In 2003, Congress and President George W. Bush created a bipartisan National Prison Rape Elimination Commission. The commission studied the issue of sexual assault in correctional settings, focusing on the victimization of women and men that takes place through the actions of both corrections officers and other prisoners. The commission held hearings around the country to study the issue and heard depressing testimony from many victims. The commission gave its report and recommendations to the U.S. attorney general in 2009. The attorney general, in turn, was required to develop proposed regulations to address underlying problems. When Attorney General Eric Holder issued the proposed regulations in 2011, critics complained that the Justice Department's regulations did not do enough to embrace the commission's complete recommendations (A. Clark, 2011). There are concerns that the proposed regulations do not cover probation and parole officers or immigration detention facilities and that there are excessively short deadlines for prisoners to quickly report sexual abuse. In addition, contrary to the commission's recommendations, the proposed regulations still would permit opposite-sex officers to conduct pat-down searches and to view prisoners using a shower or toilet during a cell check—two contexts that were regarded as contributing to sexual humiliation and abuse (Kaiser and Stannow, 2011). It remains to be seen whether the laudable purposes of the commission will ultimately lead to greater protection against sexual abuse of women—and men—prisoners.

Educational and Vocational Training Programs

A major criticism of women's prisons is that they lack the variety of vocational and educational programs available in male institutions. Critics also charge that existing programs tend to conform to sexual stereotypes of "female" occupations—cosmetology, food service, housekeeping, sewing. Such training does not correspond to the wider employment opportunities available to women in today's world. Both men's and women's facilities usually offer educational programs so inmates can become literate and earn general equivalency diplomas (GEDs). There are questions about whether the work assignments available for incarcerated women actually teach the prisoners any marketable job skills and assist in avoiding a return to criminal activity (Richmond, 2014).

Research conducted in the 1970s by Ruth Glick and Virginia Neto (1977) documented and confirmed that fewer programs were offered in women's than in men's institutions and that the existing programs lacked variety. Merry Morash and her colleagues noted changes during the 1980s, but they too found that gender stereotypes shaped vocational programs (Morash, Haarr, and Rucker, 1994). The American Correctional Association reported that the few work assignments available for incarcerated women do not teach marketable job skills (American Correctional Association, 1990). Contemporary scholars advocate gender-responsive programs that take into account how women's pathways into crime and reentry challenges may differ from men's with respect to prior employment experience, domestic violence victimization, parenthood, and drug abuse. However, tailoring programs to address needs of specific women offenders should not be based on traditional sex stereotypes that make assumptions about limited roles for women in employment and society (Holtfreter and Wattanaporn, 2013).

To get a good job, workers must have the education necessary to meet the needs of a complex workplace. However, the educational level of most female offenders limits their access to these occupations. In some institutions, less than half of the inmates have completed high school. Some corrections systems assign these women to classes so they can earn a GED, and other inmates can do college work through correspondence study or courses offered in the institution.

Medical Services

Women's prisons frequently lack proper medical services (R. Roth, 2010). Because of their socioeconomic status and limited access to preventive medical care, women typically have more serious health problems than do men. Compared with men, they have a higher incidence of asthma, drug abuse, diabetes, and heart disorders, and many women also have gynecological problems (BJS, 2008). Although a higher percentage of women than men report receiving medical services in prison, women's institutions are less likely than men's to have a full-time medical staff or hospital facilities.

HIV, tuberculosis, drug addiction, and mental illness affect female prisoners more than they do male inmates. A national survey revealed that a higher percentage of female than male state prison inmates (1.9 percent versus 1.4 percent) tested positive for HIV. In addition, 48 percent of women in state prisons have a recent history of mental health problems, and three-quarters of those prisoners met criteria for substance abuse or dependence prior to imprisonment (Maruschak, 2015; D. J. James and Glaze, 2006; Maruschak, 2009).

Pregnant women also need special medical and nutritional resources. It is estimated that up to 10 percent of incarcerated women are pregnant on admission and similar numbers may have given birth during the previous year. Yet studies have raised questions about the adequacy of prenatal care, nutrition, counseling, and treatment for sexual transmitted diseases in prisons (Clarke et al., 2006). Pregnancies raise numerous issues for correctional policy, including abortion rights, access to delivery rooms and medical personnel, and length of time that newborns can remain with incarcerated mothers. Many pregnant inmates have characteristics (older than 35, history of drug abuse, prior multiple abortions, and sexually transmitted diseases) that indicate the potential for a high-risk pregnancy requiring special medical care (Hotelling, 2008). Several prison systems are attempting to address this problem by allowing nursing infants to stay with their mothers, creating in-prison nurseries, instituting counseling programs, and improving standards of medical care (Campbell and Carlson, 2012).

One controversy that receives regular media attention is the practice of shackling pregnant women while transporting them to the hospital and even chaining them to the bed during delivery (E. Alexander, 2010). Critics note that the use of handcuffs and chains can increase the risk that the pregnant woman will lose her balance and fall during transport, interfere with her ability to move and push during delivery, and impede a doctor's ability to quickly implement cesarean delivery or other surgical procedures. In 2011, for example, the Rhode Island legislature debated whether they would join 11 other states in banning the use of restraints on pregnant prisoners at time of delivery (Klepper, 2011).

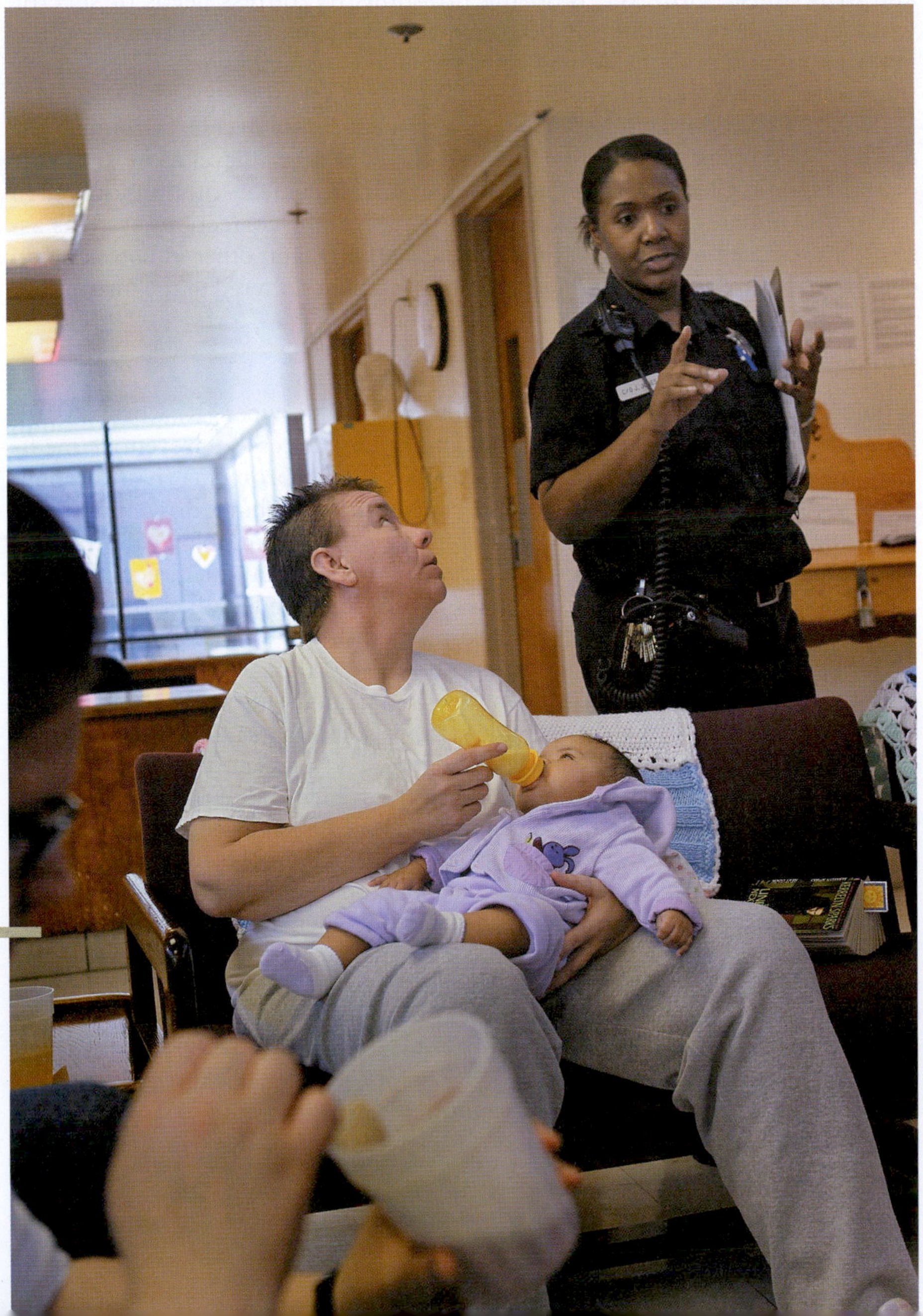

Some institutions have programs to permit mothers in prison to spend time with their children. Should society be more concerned about the impact on children when they have little contact with their incarcerated mothers?

Scott Olson/Getty Images

Mothers and Their Children

Of greatest concern to incarcerated women is the fate of their children. Over 61 percent of women inmates in state prisons are mothers, as are nearly 56 percent of women in federal prisons. Nearly 40 percent have two or more minor children. Thus on any given day, 147,400 children—three-fourths of whom are under 15 years old—have mothers who are in prison. Roughly half of these children do not see their mothers the entire time that the prison sentence is being served (L. Glaze and Maruschak, 2008).

Because about 52 percent of incarcerated mothers were the primary financial providers before they entered prison, they do not have partners to take care of the children. More than 80 percent of these children are cared for by relatives, while 8 percent are with friends of the mother and 11 percent are in state-funded foster care (L. Glaze and Maruschak, 2008).

Imprisoned mothers have difficulty maintaining contact with their children. Because most states have only one or two prisons for women, mothers may be incarcerated 150 miles or more away. Transportation is thus difficult, visits are short and infrequent, and phone calls uncertain and irregular. When the children do visit the prison, the surroundings are strange and intimidating. In some institutions, children must conform to the rules governing adult visitations: strict time limits and no physical contact.

Other correctional facilities, however, seek ways to help mothers maintain links to their children. For example, at Logan Correctional Center, the prison to which all women prisoners in Illinois were moved in 2013, there are a variety of programs (Fak, 2013). The "Mom and Me Camp" brings children ages 7 through 12 together with their imprisoned mothers for three days of activities in the summer. Through the "Family Connections Visitation" program, an outside social service agency transports 30 children and their caregivers, usually their grandmothers, to visit imprisoned mothers each month. The assistance of the outside agency with transportation and arrangements creates visitation opportunities that would otherwise not occur. In the prison's "Operation Storybook" program, incarcerated mothers and grandmothers have the opportunity to read children's books aloud that are recorded and copied on CDs to be sent to their children and grandchildren. The Illinois prison also cooperates with the national Angel Tree program, through which volunteers provide Christmas gifts, summer camp experiences, and mentors for the children of incarcerated mothers. In some states, children can meet with their mothers at almost any time, for extended periods, and in playrooms or nurseries that allow contact. Some states transport children to visit their mothers; some institutions even let children stay overnight with their mothers. A few prisons have family visitation programs that let the inmate, her legal husband, and her children stay together in a mobile home or apartment on prison grounds for up to 72 hours (D'Alessio, Flexon, and Stolzenberg, 2013).

✔POINT

17. What are some of the problems encountered by female prisoners in maintaining contact with their children?

18. How are children cared for while their mothers are incarcerated?

STOP AND ANALYZE: To what extent should society worry about, pay attention to, and spend money on programs for children whose parents are in prison? Give two arguments supporting each side of this debate.

Prison Programs

Modern correctional institutions differ from those of the past in the number and variety of programs provided for inmates. Early penitentiaries included prison industries; educational, vocational, and treatment programs were added when rehabilitation goals became prevalent. For most of the last 35 years, as the public has called for harsher punishment of criminals, legislators have gutted prison educational and treatment programs as "frills" that only "coddled" inmates. There is a debate about whether the government should spend money on education and job-training programs for people who have harmed society. In addition, the great increase in the number of prisoners has limited access to those programs that are still available. Many experts believe that an increase in the availability of prison programs may enable corrections institutions to have beneficial impacts for larger numbers of prisoners. Only in the past few years have legislators given increased resources to programs that seek to prepare soon-to-be-released offenders for successful reentry into society, but these programs do not necessarily include job training or education. They frequently focus on counseling offenders about the challenges that they will face in society.

Administrators argue that job training, education, and other programs help them deal with the problem of time on the prisoners' hands. They know that the more programs prisons offer, the less likely that inmate idleness will turn into hostility—less cell time means fewer tensions. Evidence suggests that inmate education and jobs may positively affect the running of prisons, as well as reduce recidivism. However, in an era of government budget cuts, prison vocational training and education programs are often targeted for reduction because they are less essential than preserving resources for safety and security. In 2010 California cut its prisoner vocational training programs in half and reduced the number of instructional hours for literacy classes and other education programs ("California to Redesign Prison Education," 2011). In other examples, Indiana cut millions of dollars from a program that permitted prisoners to earn college credits, and advocates in North Carolina worried that its prison and training programs would also be targeted for reductions (Slabaugh, 2011; Freskos, 2011).

Classification of Prisoners

classification
The process of assigning an inmate to a category specifying his or her needs for security, treatment, education, work assignment, and readiness for release.

Determining the appropriate program for an individual prisoner usually involves a process called **classification**. A committee—often comprising the heads of the security, treatment, education, and industry departments—evaluates the

NEW DIRECTIONS IN CRIMINAL JUSTICE POLICY

EVIDENCE-BASED PRISON PRACTICES TO REDUCE RECIDIVISM

The National Institute of Corrections promotes evidence-based practices in prisons by holding training sessions and distributing research-based materials on effective practices, procedures, and programs. A central element of evidence-based programming to reduce recidivism is the assessment and classification of prisoners to identify their individual problems and needs. Effective classification requires the use of an assessment instrument that asks appropriate and necessary questions to determine prisoners' needs. One prominent assessment tool is the Level of Service Inventory–Revised instrument that is used in structured interviews with individual prisoners to gather information about 54 items, including criminal history, educational background, family relationships, substance abuse problems, emotional and personal issues, and social attitudes. According to the evidence-practice approach, programs and treatments cannot be provided with effective results unless the needs and problems of prisoners have been accurately assessed.

Other principles of evidence-based practices in prisons include focusing resources on prisoners with the greatest needs and ensuring that programs and treatments are of sufficient duration and appropriate timing to help with successful reentry and avoidance of recidivism. Thus studies indicate that high-risk offenders should spend 40 to 70 percent of their time in highly structured activities and programs in the months preceding their release from prison into community supervision. In addition, there should be extended continuity of treatment during inmate's security level, treatment needs, work assignment, and, eventually, readiness for release.

Classification decisions are often based on the institution's needs rather than those of the inmates. For example, inmates from the city may be assigned to farm work because that is where they are needed. Further, certain popular programs may remain limited, even though the demand for them is great. Thus inmates may find that the few places in, for example, a computer course are filled and that there is a long waiting list. Prisoners are often angered and frustrated by the classification process and the limited availability of programs. Release on parole can depend on a good record of participation in these programs, yet entrance for some inmates is blocked. Read the New Directions in Criminal Justice Policy feature to see how classification is a critical element in evidence-based practices designed to reduce recidivism.

✔POINT

19. Why are prison programs important from the standpoint of prison administrators?

20. How are inmates assigned to programs?

STOP AND ANALYZE: If budget cuts led to the elimination of all vocational training and education programs in prisons, how would that impact daily life for prisoners and corrections officers? List three possible effects from the elimination of these types of programs.

Educational Programs

Surveys have shown that programs offering academic courses are the most popular in corrections systems. Offenders constitute one of the most under-educated groups in the U.S. population. In many systems, all inmates who have not completed eighth grade are assigned full-time to prison school. Many programs provide remedial help in reading, English, and math. They also permit prisoners to earn their GED. As you read "Civic Engagement: Your Role in the System," think about the resources required for presenting successful education programs.

community supervision for those with specific, difficult problems, such as drug addicts and sex offenders. As one state's description of evidence-based practices described the approach and goal, "treatment should be delivered as a life-long plan for changing entrenched negative lifestyle behaviors."

Evidence-based practices also rely on positive reinforcement approaches to help offenders change their attitudes and behavior and learn new ways to think about values, choice of friends, intoxicating substances, and interactions with others. Obviously, the use of effective evidence-based practices does not merely require devoting time and resources to teaching and counseling offenders, but also relies on extensive training for staff members who are responsible for such efforts.

Source: "Evidence Based Correctional Practices," report prepared by the Colorado Division of Criminal Justice based on materials from the National Institute of Corrections, August 2007.

DEBATE THE ISSUE

How much time, money, and staff should be devoted to programs for offenders in prison? In an era of budget cuts, can states afford to present extensive programs when they must reduce prison populations and staffing in order to save money? If you were governor, what would you regard as the greatest benefit to society: cut prisons' budgets to save taxpayers' money or increase spending on corrections programs in order to reduce recidivism? Give two arguments in support of your position.

CIVIC ENGAGEMENT

YOUR ROLE IN THE SYSTEM

Imagine that your instructor assigns a class project: You must start a program to send books to prisoners to help them advance their education and increase their chances of being productive citizens after release. *Write a memo on what books the prisoners would want and need as well as what problems and challenges might hinder the program.* Then compare your ideas with the experience of the Prison Book Program in Massachusetts.

In 1995, there were an estimated 350 college-degree programs in prisons across the nation. However, since that time, funding for such programs has come under attack. The Comprehensive Crime Control Act of 1994 bans federal funding to prisoners for postsecondary education (Buruma, 2005). Many state legislatures have passed similar laws, under pressure from people who argue that tax dollars should not be spent on tuition for prisoners. Among the educational programs that continue, many exist because of voluntary efforts by college and universities. For example, faculty and graduate students, aided by undergraduate teaching assistants, offer courses at two New York prisons through an arrangement that permits prisoners to earn college credits toward an associate degree from Cayuga Community College. The program is funded by a grant from a private foundation as well as contributions from Cornell University (Skorton and Altschuler, 2013). Despite this New York example as a demonstration of how programs can continue without government funding, many colleges and universities around the country are struggling with their own budget cuts and therefore may not be well positioned to voluntarily contribute personnel and resources for prisoner education.

As governors and legislators become increasingly aware of the need to prepare convicted offenders for reentry into society, they may become more willing to devote resources to vocational and educational programs. Recently, there has been some movement toward initiatives to use public money for advanced education in prisons. In 2014, for example, New York Governor Andrew Cuomo proposed spending state money to provide college classes for incarcerated offenders, a practice that had ended 20 years earlier. Many people oppose providing free programs for criminal offenders that law-abiding citizens must struggle to pay for on their own. Ultimately, Cuomo dropped his first effort to add such programs to the state budget (Kaplan, 2014). However, in raising the idea, he may have set the stage for future education initiatives in light of research showing an association between educational opportunities and post-release success in avoiding future criminal behavior (L. Davis et al., 2013; Skorton and Altschuler, 2013). See the Doing Your Part feature for more on prisoner education.

Vocational Education

Vocational education programs attempt to teach offenders a marketable job skill. Unfortunately, too many programs train inmates for trades that already have an adequate labor supply or in which new methods have made the skills taught obsolete.

Offenders often lack the attitudes necessary to obtain and keep a job—punctuality, accountability, deference to supervisors, cordiality to coworkers. Therefore most prisoners not only need to learn a skill but also how to act in the work world. For example, Minnesota's "Affordable Homes Program" teaches prisoners construction skills as they build or remodel homes for low-income families. An evaluation of this program determined that prisoners who participated were more likely to be hired in construction jobs after release, and the state saved over $13 million by using inmate labor. However, graduates of the program did not have reduced rates of criminal behavior after release (Bohmert and Duwe, 2012).

According to Marvin Greenleaf, a 51-year-old prisoner in Illinois who had been sent to prison eleven times since the age of 22, he gained patience, a work ethic, and sense of pride from working in the prison's meat-processing plant. Although he admitted that he had not "applied himself" toward gaining education or skills in his early years as a prisoner, Greenleaf's prison work experience had taught him to believe that "I know I can go there and make something

DOING YOUR PART

INSIDE-OUT PRISON EXCHANGE PROGRAM

Lori Pompa, a criminal justice instructor at Temple University in Philadelphia, developed the Inside-Out Exchange Program in which college courses are taught inside prisons, with each class composed of half college students and half prisoners. The courses are not necessarily about criminal justice. They could be focused on nearly any college-level subject, such as philosophy or English, depending on which college professors are interested in conducting one of their courses inside the prison with a mixed group of students. Special rules are imposed to prevent any risk of improper interactions that might distract from the educational purpose of the course. Thus students and prisoners only know each other's first names, and they must promise not to have any outside contact with each other through correspondence or visits.

Prisoners benefit by participating in an actual college course and interacting with students from outside the prison. Presumably, such experiences help them to gain knowledge as well as confidence about their ability to analyze and discuss intellectual matters with those from other walks of life. In addition, this experience may assist in eventual reentry by making prisoners accustomed to participating in a structured setting with fellow citizens from free society, including reacquainting themselves with social matters of expected language and behavior in the outside world.

Traditional college students presumably benefit from exposure to a wider set of perceptions and experiences when discussing literature, politics, and other subjects with classmates who may be from completely different segments of society, and with whom they would not typically share a classroom. In addition, college students will inevitably learn about the realities of prisoners and prisons. Sharing a class with someone who has such a drastically different life experience can humanize criminal offenders in the eyes of their fellow students. Such interaction helps to personalize the realities of incarceration, something that might, for many, be an abstract concept. It can help broaden traditional students' perspective and encourage them to become more interested and knowledgeable when they vote, discuss, and educate others about the realities of the criminal justice system.

The Inside-Out Exchange Program has spread across the United States and Canada as more universities begin to conduct courses within the program.

Sources: Alex Hilborn, "Sociology Class Sends Students to Prison," *Daily Barometer* [Oregon State University], March 4, 2012 (www.dailybarometer.com); Judy Weightman, "Prison Exchange Program Lets Students, Prisoners Learn as Peers," *Metro Philadelphia,* June 18, 2012 (www.metro.us); "Women See the Other Side," *Toronto Star*, December 27, 2011 (www.thestar.com).

happen on the legitimate side. . . . I can go out and cut somebody's grass. I can go and . . . paint somebody's porch" (Freeman, 2013b). Prison vocational programs have also been reduced through budget cuts, so opportunities in many states have diminished. However, because of the renewed interest in the past few years in reducing populations and helping prisoners reenter society successfully, the vocational programs and their importance have become a focus of increased discussion and planning in several states.

Ty Wright/Bloomberg/Getty Images

Some companies have discovered that prison labor can be more efficient than outsourcing to low-wage countries elsewhere in the world. Are these prisoners doing jobs that otherwise would provide wages to law-abiding citizens?

Prison Industries

Prison industries, which trace their roots to the early workshops of New York's Auburn Penitentiary, are intended to teach work habits and skills that will assist prisoners' reentry into the outside workforce. In practice, institutions rely on prison labor to provide basic food, maintenance, clerical, and other services. In addition, many prisons contain manufacturing facilities that produce goods, such as office furniture and clothing, to be used in correctional and other state institutions.

The prison industries system has had a checkered career. During the nineteenth century, factories were established in many prisons, and inmates manufactured items that were sold on the open market. With the rise of the labor movement, however, state legislatures and Congress passed laws restricting the sale of prison-made goods so that they would not compete with those made by free workers. In 1979, Congress lifted restrictions on the interstate sale of prison-made products and urged correctional administrators to explore with the private sector possible improvements for prison industry programs. Industrial programs would relieve idleness, allow inmates to earn wages that they could save until release, and reduce the costs of incarceration.

The Federal Bureau of Prisons and some states have developed industries, but generally their products are not sold on the free market and the percentage of prisoners employed varies greatly. In the federal prison system, for example, the number of prisoners employed in production jobs shrank from 23,152 in 2008 to 16,115 in 2010 as budget cuts affected these operations. This was a participation reduction from 11.5 percent of federal prisoners to 7.6 percent (K. Johnson, 2010c). Overall, only a limited percentage of prisoners in any prison system tend to enjoy these opportunities to learn skills and produce a small hourly wage for themselves. In the federal prisons, these workers earn $1.15 per hour as government minimum wage laws do not apply to prisoners (K. Johnson, 2010c).

Although there are reductions in prison industries in some corrections systems, there is a controversial increase in work by prisoners in another area, albeit without any plan to necessarily use this work as vocational training. Prisoners are playing an even greater role in the maintenance and upkeep of prisons. They have always had a part in cleaning and cooking, but now states are seeking to save money by using prisoners for broader aspects of repairs and maintenance. Even more controversial is the use of prisoners for tasks outside of prisons: cleaning state park campsites, removing roadkill from highways, painting courthouses, and other types of low-skill labor. Having prisoners perform these tasks can save states money in labor costs, but this approach leads to criticism in an era when many law-abiding citizens who are unemployed are thereby denied a possible opportunity for employment (R. Brown and Severson, 2011).

Although the idea of employing inmates sounds attractive, the inefficiencies of prison work may offset its economic value. Turnover is great because many inmates are transferred among several institutions or released over a two-year period. Many prisoners have little education and lack steady work habits, making it difficult for them to perform many of the tasks of modern production. An additional cost to efficiency is the need to stop production periodically to count heads and to check that tools and materials have not been stolen. In addition, participation in prison industry programs may not reduce recidivism post-release for many inmates (K. M. Richmond, 2012).

Rehabilitative Programs

Rehabilitative programs seek to treat the personal defects thought to have brought about the inmate's criminality. Most people agree that rehabilitating offenders is a desirable goal, but there is much disagreement on the amount of emphasis that these programs should receive. Counseling and special programs are offered in 97 percent of public prisons but only 74 percent of private correctional institutions (J. J. Stephan, 2008).

Reports in the 1970s cast doubt on the ability of treatment programs to stem recidivism. Questions were also raised about the ethics of requiring inmates to participate in rehabilitative programs in exchange for the promise of parole (Martinson, 1974). Supporters of treatment programs argue that certain programs, if properly run, work for certain offenders (Andrews et al., 1990; T. Palmer, 1992).

Most corrections systems still offer a range of psychological, behavioral, and social services programs. How much they are used seems to vary according to the goals of the institution and the attitudes of the administrators. Nationally, relatively little money is spent on treatment services, and these programs reach only a portion of the inmate population. Therefore, although rehabilitative programs remain a part of correctional institutions, their emphasis has diminished. Incarceration's current goal of humane custody implies no effort to change inmates.

Medical Services

Most prisons offer medical services through a full-time staff of nurses augmented by part-time physicians under contract to the corrections system. Nurses take care of routine health care and dispense medicines from a secure in-prison pharmacy; regularly scheduled visits to the prison by doctors can enable prisoners to obtain checkups and diagnoses. For cases needing a specialist, surgery, or emergency medical assistance, prisoners must be transported to local hospitals under close supervision by correctional staff. The aim is for the prison system to be able to provide a range of medical assistance to meet the various needs of the population as a whole. In 2008, most states spent about $5,000 annually per inmate for health care, but some spent up to $12,000 (California) and a few spent under $3,000 (Louisiana, South Carolina, Illinois) (Pew Charitable Trusts, 2013). Costs are also dependent on inmate age—health care costs in Oregon prisons range from $299 per inmate for those under age 30, up to $6, 527 per inmate for those older than 70 (Zaitz, 2011).

Medical services in some states have not kept up with the increase in the incarcerated population. In 1976, the U.S. Supreme Court ruled that prisoners have a constitutional right to health care. In 2011, the Supreme Court's decision in *Brown v. Plata* ordered California to reduce its incarcerated population significantly to reduce overcrowding and create a healthier prison environment. The decision supported earlier findings by lower court judges that the state's failure to provide medical and mental health care was needlessly causing the death of at least one inmate every month and was subjecting prisoners to cruel and unusual punishment, which is prohibited by the Constitution (Liptak, 2011b).

Issues of health care quality and costs can be further complicated in those prison systems that privatize such services. When states pay outside companies to provide doctors and nurses, those companies may have an incentive to increase their profits and reduce their costs by denying needed medical care to prisoners. The profit motive risks creating a collision with ethical and legal obligations to provide adequate health care (K. Leonard, 2012).

While inmates' needs for health care echo those of the general population, prisoners pose two special needs, one due to poverty and the other to aging. Because prisoners as a group are very poor, they often bring to the prison years of neglect of their general health. Other consequences of being poor, such as an inadequate diet and poor hygiene, also affect the general health of the prison population. As we have seen, by far the most extraordinary health problem in contemporary corrections is the burgeoning number of elderly prisoners. Elderly inmates have more complicated and more numerous health problems overall, and they eventually reach an age where they cannot productively participate in prison assignments. Some prison systems have formed nursing and hospice facilities where younger inmates can care for the elderly as they spend their last days on earth behind bars.

POINT

21. Why have legislatures and the general public been so critical of educational and rehabilitative programs in prisons?

22. What problems are encountered in vocational training programs?

23. Why have legislatures restricted prison industries?

STOP AND ANALYZE: Prison programs generate debates between those who believe that lawbreakers are the least-deserving people in society to benefit from education and training and those who believe we must prepare prisoners to reenter society in order to prevent future crime and harm to others. Where do you stand in this debate? Give three reasons for your answer.

Violence in Prison

Prisons provide a perfect recipe for violence. They confine, in cramped quarters, a thousand men, some with histories of violent behavior. While incarcerated, these men are not allowed contact with women and they live under highly restrictive conditions. Sometimes these conditions spark collective violence, as in the riots at Attica, New York (1971), Santa Fe, New Mexico (1980), Atlanta, Georgia (1987), Lucasville, Ohio (1993), and Florence, Colorado (2008).

Although prison riots are widely reported in the news, few people know the level of everyday interpersonal violence in U.S. prisons. When asked specific questions in surveys about forms of assaultive behavior, nearly 20 percent of prisoners reported being threatened or assaulted by other prisoners during a six-month period (Wolff, Shi, and Bachman, 2008). In 2011, the homicide rate was 5 per 100,000 inmates, which is substantially lower than it was in 1980 (54 homicides per 100,000). Similarly, the suicide rate among state prisoners was 14 per 100,000 inmates in 2011, which is also lower than the rate reported in 1980 (34 suicides per 100,000 inmates) (Noonan, 2013; Mumola, 2005).

Although the reductions over three decades demonstrate progress, there are still great numbers of prisoners who live in a state of constant uneasiness, always on the lookout for people who might demand sex, steal their few possessions, or otherwise harm them. In any case, some researchers suggest that the level of violence varies by offender age, institutional security designation, and administrative effectiveness (Maitland and Sluder, 1998). Others point out that prisoners' own behavior affects their likelihood of victimization, with those who have violent prior offenses and those who participate in the prison economy more likely to be victimized in prison (Copes et al., 2010; Kerley, Hochstetler, and Copes, 2009).

Assaultive Behavior and Inmate Characteristics

For the person entering prison for the first time, the anxiety level and fear of violence are especially high. One fish asked, "Will I end up fighting for my life?" Gary, an inmate at Leavenworth, told Pete Earley, "Every convict has three choices, but only three. He can fight (kill someone), he can hit the fence (escape), or he can fuck (submit)" (Earley, 1992: 55). Inmates who are victimized are significantly more likely than others to be depressed and experience symptoms associated with posttraumatic stress, such as nightmares. Even if a prisoner is not assaulted, the potential for violence permeates the environment of many prisons, adding to the stress and pains of incarceration.

Violence in correctional institutions raises serious questions for administrators, criminal justice specialists, and the general public. What causes prison violence? What can be done about it? We consider these questions by examining three main categories of prison violence: prisoner–prisoner, prisoner–officer, and officer–prisoner. First, we discuss three characteristics of prisoners that affect violence: age, race, and mental illness.

Age

Young men aged 16 to 24, both inside and outside prison, are more prone to violence than are their elders. Not surprisingly, 93 percent of adult prisoners are men, with an average age at the time of admission of 27. There is also evidence that younger inmates are more likely to be victimized than are older inmates.

Besides greater physical strength, young men also lack the commitments to career and family that can restrict antisocial behavior. In addition, many have difficulty defining their position in society. Thus they interpret many things as challenges to their status.

"Machismo," the concept of male honor and the sacredness of one's reputation as a man, requires physical retaliation against those who insult one's honor. Some inmates adopt a preventive strategy of trying to impress others with their bravado, which may result in counterchallenges and violence. The potential for violence among such prisoners is clear.

Race

Race has become a major divisive factor in today's prisons (P. Goodman, 2014). Racist attitudes, common in the larger society, have become part of the "convict code," or implicit rules of life. Forced association—having to live with people one would not likely associate with on the outside—exaggerates and amplifies racial conflict. Violence against members of another race may be how some inmates deal with the frustrations of their lives. The shouting of racial slurs against black inmates by a group of white supremacists celebrating Adolf Hitler's birthday is cited as the basis of a riot at the U.S. Penitentiary,

Mikael Karlsson/Alamy

When officers must remove an uncooperative or violent prisoner from a cell, trained cell-extraction teams must overwhelm the prisoner through the use of force while also limiting the risk of injury to themselves. Such events are often filmed to prevent false claims by prisoners that officers used excessive force. Are there additional precautions that these officers should take in order to avoid injuries to themselves or the prisoner?

Florence, Colorado, in 2008 that resulted in the death of two inmates and a brawl involving up to 200 (Burnett and Hartman, 2008).

Mental Illness

Inmates with diagnosed mental illnesses are significantly more likely to be victims of violence in prison than are those with no psychological disorders (Blitz, Wolff, and Shi, 2008), and are more likely to be sexually abused during incarceration (Cristani and Frueh, 2011). Prison is a traumatic experience and can cause mental illness to develop in individuals who were not suffering from it when they arrived. Incarceration can also exacerbate preexisting mental conditions, leaving more inmates in need psychological treatment (J. Rich, Wakeman, and Dickman, 2011). If these prisoners are victimized, their mental condition can worsen, causing even greater problems for them during their incarceration (Listwan et al., 2010).

Prisoner–Prisoner Violence

Although prison folklore may attribute violence to brutal guards, most prison violence occurs between inmates. In its most recent report on the subject, the U.S. Bureau of Justice Statistics said that the rate of prisoner–prisoner assault is 26 attacks per 1,000 inmates (J. Stephan and Karberg, 2003). But official statistics likely do not reflect the true amount of prisoner–prisoner violence, because many inmates who are assaulted do not make their victimization known to prison officials. Instead many spend years in fear of harm. Some inmates request segregation, others lock themselves in, and some are hermits by choice.

Prison Gangs

Racial or ethnic gangs (also referred to as "security threat groups") are now linked to acts of violence in most prison systems. Gangs make it difficult for wardens to maintain control. By continuing their street wars inside prison, gangs make some prisons more dangerous than any American neighborhood. Gangs are organized primarily to control an institution's drug, gambling, loan-sharking, prostitution, extortion, and debt-collection rackets. In addition, gangs protect their members from other gangs and instill a sense of macho camaraderie.

Contributing to prison violence is the "blood-in, blood-out" basis for gang membership: A would-be member must stab a gang's enemy to be admitted and, once in, cannot drop out without endangering his own life. Given the racial and ethnic foundation of gangs, violence between them can easily spill into the general prison population. Some institutions have programs that offer members "a way out" of the gang. Often referred to as "deganging," these programs educate members and eventually encourage them to renounce their gang membership. Critics say that for many this supposed change is only a "way of getting out of lock-down status; proponents counter with 'so what? Their behavior within the prison setting has been modified'" (Carlson, 2001: 13).

Prison gangs exist in the institutions of most states and the federal system. A survey of prisons in the United States found that wardens reported between 2 percent and 50 percent of their inmates were gang members, with an average of 19 percent (Winterdyk and Ruddell, 2010). Although prison gangs are small, they are tightly organized and have even arranged the killing of opposition gang leaders housed in other institutions. Administrators say that prison gangs, like organized crime groups, tend to pursue their "business" interests, yet they are also a major source of inmate–inmate violence as they discipline members, enforce orders, and retaliate against other gangs.

The racial and ethnic basis of gang membership has been documented in several states. Beginning in the late 1960s, a Chicano gang—the Mexican Mafia—whose membership had known each other in Los Angeles—took over the rackets in San Quentin. In reaction, other gangs were formed, including a rival Mexican gang, La Nuestra Familia; CRIPS (Common Revolution in Progress); the Texas Syndicate; the Black Guerrilla Family; and the Aryan Brotherhood (see Table 15.1). Gang conflict in California prisons became so serious in the 1970s that attempts were made to break up the gangs by dividing members among several institutions. As of 2002, however, California had the largest number of prison gang members (5,342), followed by Texas (5,262). Data from 41 different jurisdictions shows that nearly 5 percent of inmates are validated gang members (C. G. Camp, 2003).

TABLE 15.1 CHARACTERISTICS OF MAJOR PRISON GANGS

These gangs were founded in the California prison system during the late 1960s and 1970s. They have now spread across the nation and are viewed as major security threat groups in most corrections systems.

	NAME	MAKEUP	ORIGIN	CHARACTERISTICS	ENEMIES
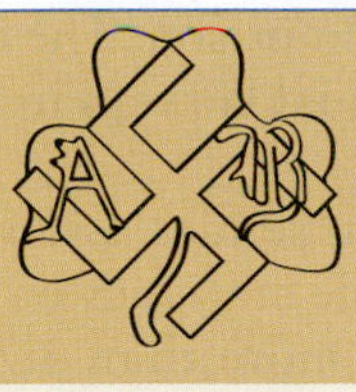	Aryan Brotherhood	White	San Quentin, 1967	Apolitical. Most in custody for crimes such as robbery.	CRIPS, Bloods, BGF
	Black Guerrilla Family (BGF)	African American	San Quentin, 1966	Most politically oriented. Antigovernment.	Aryan Brotherhood, EME
	Mexican Mafia (EME)	Mexican American/ Hispanic	Duel Vocational Center, Los Angeles, late 1950s	Ethnic solidarity, control of drug trafficking.	BGF, NF
	La Nuestra Familia (NF)	Mexican American/ Hispanic	Soledad, 1965	Protect young, rural Mexican Americans.	EME
	Texas Syndicate	Mexican American/ Hispanic	Folsom, early 1970s	Protect Texan inmates in California.	Aryan Brotherhood, EME, NF

Source: Florida Department of Corrections, "Major Prison Gangs" (www.dc.state.fl.us/pub/gangs/prison.html).

Many facilities segregate rival gangs by housing them in separate units of the prison or moving members to other facilities (Winterdyk and Ruddell, 2010). Administrators have also set up intelligence units to gather information on gangs, particularly about illegal acts both in and outside of prison. In some prisons, however, these policies created a power vacuum within the convict society that newer groups with new codes of behavior soon filled.

Prison Rape

Prison rape is a crime hidden by a curtain of silence. Inmate–inmate and inmate–staff sexual contact is prohibited in all prisons; however it exists, and much of it is hidden from authorities. Sexual violence ranges from unwanted touching to nonconsensual sex. When incidents are reported, correctional officers say that it is difficult to distinguish between consensual sexual acts and rapes. Most officers have not caught inmates in the act, and only a few said they ignored violations when they discovered them (Eigenberg, 2000).

The Prison Rape Elimination Act (PREA) enacted by Congress in 2004 establishes a zero-tolerance standard for the incidence of rape in prison. The law requires the U.S. Bureau of Justice Statistics to conduct annual surveys in the nation's prisons and jails to measure the incidence of rape.

Until recently there has been no reliable data on prison sexual assaults. In 2011, the Bureau of Justice Statistics released nationwide statistics based on reports by *prison administrators*. The research found more than 3,700 allegations of inmate-on-inmate sexual assaults among state prison inmates, a rate of 3.2 attacks per 1,000 inmates. Perpetrators of substantiated incidents tended to be male (82 percent), black (45 percent) or white (42 percent). Victims were more likely to be male (77 percent), under the age of 25 (37 percent), and white (73 percent). The report also showed that sexual violence usually involves a single victim (96 percent) and one assailant (88 percent) (Guerino and Beck, 2011).

Another survey published in 2010 based on reports by *inmates* found many times more inmate-on-inmate nonconsensual acts in state and federal prisons. An estimated 30,086 prisoners could have been victims of unwanted sexual contacts based on calculations from the survey sample. Inmates' reports of unwilling sexual contacts with staff members indicated that there could be 41,000 victims in state and federal prisons. Many inmates nationwide reported being injured by the sexual victimization. Injuries included anal or vaginal tearing, knife or stab punctures, broken bones, bruises, black eyes, and other less serious injuries (A. Beck, Harrison, Berzofsky, et al., 2010).

How are we to interpret the results of these two surveys? It is difficult to gauge their accuracy. Prisoners may be fearful of reporting sexual assaults in order to protect their own images or to avoid retaliation by the perpetrators among other prisoners or staff. There may also be false reports by some prisoners to researchers that affect the accuracy of these limited surveys.

For victims of prisoner–prisoner violence, there are few options. According to the "inmate code" one should "stand and fight" one's own battles. For many victims this is not feasible. Alternatively, some may seek the protection of a gang or stronger inmate to whom the victim is beholden. Others may try to fade into the shadows. Still others may seek protective custody. Each option has it pluses and minuses, but none provides victims the ability to serve their time without constantly looking over their shoulders.

Protective Custody

For many victims of prison violence, protective custody offers the only way to escape further abuse. About 5,000 state prisoners are in protective custody.

Life is not pleasant for these inmates (Browne, Cambier, and Agha, 2011). Often they are let out of their cells only briefly to exercise and shower. Inmates who ask to "lock up" have little chance of returning to the general prison population without being viewed as a weakling—a snitch or a punk—to be preyed on. Even when they are transferred to another institution, their reputations follow them through the grapevine.

✔POINT **24.** Which inmate characteristics are thought to be factors in prison violence?

25. Why are gangs such a threat to prison order?

STOP AND ANALYZE: How can prison officials combat the formation, influence, and behavior of prison gangs? Imagine that you are a warden confronted with this problem. List three steps you would take to counteract the problem of gangs and their role in prison violence.

Prisoner–Officer Violence

The mass media have focused on riots in which guards are taken hostage, injured, and killed. However, violence against officers typically occurs in specific situations and against certain individuals. Yearly, inmates assault more than 18,000 staff members (J. Stephan and Karberg, 2003). Correctional officers typically do not carry weapons within the institution, because a prisoner might seize them. However, a few prisons have begun to experiment with equipping officers with conducted energy devices to defend themselves and control offenders (Marley, 2013). Prisoners manage to obtain lethal weapons, such as homemade knives or stolen tools, and can use the element of surprise to injure an officer. In the course of a workday, an officer may encounter situations that require the use of physical force against an inmate—for instance, breaking up a fight or moving a prisoner to segregation. Because such situations are especially dangerous, officers may enlist others to help them minimize the risk of violence. Read A Question of Ethics at the end of the chapter to consider the problem wardens face if corrections officers seek revenge against prisoners who have assaulted an officer.

The officer's greatest fear is unexpected attacks, such as a missile thrown from an upper tier or an officer's "accidental" fall down a flight of stairs. The need to constantly watch against personal attacks adds stress and keeps many officers at a distance from the inmates. Read the Technology and Criminal Justice feature to see how advances in technology may help to reduce injuries for officers.

Officer–Prisoner Violence

A fact of life in many institutions is unauthorized physical violence by officers against inmates. Stories abound of guards giving individual prisoners "the treatment" when supervisors are not looking. Some corrections officers view physical force as an everyday, legitimate tool for asserting authority and maintaining control. In some institutions, authorized "crisis teams" composed of physically powerful officers use their muscle to maintain order.

Correctional officers are expected to follow departmental rules in their dealings with prisoners, yet supervisors generally cannot observe staff–prisoner confrontations directly. Further, prisoner complaints about officer brutality are often not believed until the officer involved gains a reputation for harshness. Even in this case, wardens may feel they must stand behind the officer in order to retain all their officers' support. Read the Inside Today's Controversy feature to consider critics' concerns that the recent trend toward arming corrections officers with conducted energy devices and

TECHNOLOGY & CRIMINAL JUSTICE

BODY ARMOR TECHNOLOGY FOR CORRECTIONS OFFICERS

In prisons throughout the country, inmates are adept at making weapons to defend themselves—or to attack other prisoners and corrections officers. Familiar forms of weapons include razor blades imbedded into toothbrushes, toothbrush handles sharpened into potentially deadly stabbing implements, and metal weapons fashioned from items stolen in the prison kitchen and workshop. One of the most serious potential threats to a corrections officer's life is the possibility of being stabbed. Thus corrections officials have worked to develop and encourage the use of protective clothing.

Early body armor was very stiff and thick, and thereby made it difficult for corrections officers to move freely, such as when they needed to run down a corridor to stop a fight. Modern materials are thinner and bendable; thus contemporary body armor makes it easier for officers to be protected while retaining their full range of movement.

One of the challenges for corrections officers is the fact that not every state will purchase and supply body armor for its officers. With contemporary budget cuts, it is even more difficult for many prisons to afford these expensive items. A parallel issue is the challenge for correctional supervisors to make sure that officers who have such body armor will actually wear it. Many officers do not like to carry the extra weight of protective garb or to endure its extra warmth all day. They may also feel that the body armor diminishes their mobility. Or some officers may believe that they are capable of fighting any prisoner successfully without grave risk of injury.

Sources: Barry Evert, "'Running Naked': Why You Should Wear a Stab-Resistant Vest," *CorrectionsOne*, April 28, 2009 (www.correctionsone.com); U.S. Government Accountability Office, *Bureau of Prisons: Evaluating the Impact of Protective Equipment Could Help Enhance Officer Safety,* GAO-11-410, April 2011.

DEBATE THE ISSUE

In 2011, after a female corrections officer was murdered by a male prisoner in the prison chapel, the Washington State legislature authorized additional money for the purchase of body armor and better communications equipment for individual officers. If you were a member of the legislature, how would you prioritize the purchase of body armor for corrections officers? List three items in the state government's budget that you would be willing to reduce in order to buy body armor.

INSIDE TODAY'S CONTROVERSIES

ARMING CORRECTIONS OFFICERS: RISKS AND BENEFITS

Typically, corrections officers who work among the prisoners inside the walls of a prison must be unarmed. There are often officers armed with rifles on the walls or in towers overlooking the prison yard. There are also firearms, tear gas, and other weapons in locked areas beyond the bars and outside the reach of prisoners. These weapons are available for use if there is a violent disturbance in the prison or if officers must rescue a fellow officer who is being attacked somewhere inside the prison. However, officers who work inside the bars are significantly outnumbered by the prisoners all around them in the cellblocks, dining halls, and recreation yards. If these officers were to be armed, there are grave risks that they would be overpowered by the more numerous prisoners and their weapons would be taken. Thus officers must typically maintain order through their communication skills and their reputation for toughness and fairness as the means to gain respect and cooperation from prisoners.

Many jails have permitted officers to carry conducted energy devices, such as Tasers and other forms of electrical "stun guns." Such devices are useful for jail officers who may need to frequently transport detainees to court for hearings. In addition, the devices can be used for security and control purposes. In Seattle, Washington, for example, jail supervisors were issued conducted energy devices after officers had difficulty stopping a large-scale disturbance by relying on pepper spray and physical force alone. Similarly, jail officers in Marathon County, Wisconsin, were issued conducted energy weapons after an officer armed with only pepper spray suffered a serious head injury when attacked by an inmate. By contrast, there is greater reluctance to have such weapons inside the walls of prisons because prisons hold larger numbers of offenders convicted of serious, violent offenses.

In 2011, Michigan began issuing to corrections officers in its prisons a chemical spray canister containing a substance more powerful than standard pepper spray. They also began issuing conducted energy devices to supervisory officers. The purpose of the weapons was to deter prisoners from assaulting officers and to enable officers to break up fights between prisoners without risking injuries to themselves. Wisconsin followed Michigan's lead in late 2013 by issuing pepper spray to prison officers and conducted energy devices to supervising officers. In both states, corrections officials claimed that prisoners were reluctant to risk being sprayed with a chemical agent or receiving a painful, disabling electrical shock. Thus officers believed that the weapons were increasing safety and security inside the prisons. Indeed, Michigan reported that assaults against corrections employees dropped by one-third, from 688 in 2010 to 458 in 2013, as the state prison population remained at the same level during that chemical sprays will lead to excessive use of force against those held in prisons and jails.

Decreasing Prison Violence

In considering how to reduce violence, corrections administrators must identify and address the factors that contribute to violence. Among these are several factors that can potentially be diminished through administrative actions and planning if sufficient resources are available: (1) inadequate supervision by staff members, (2) architectural design that promotes rather than inhibits victimization, (3) the easy availability of deadly weapons, (4) the housing of violence-prone prisoners near relatively defenseless people, and (5) a general high level of tension produced by close quarters. The physical size and condition of the prison and the relations between inmates and staff also affect violence.

The Effect of Architecture and Size

The fortress-like prison certainly does not create an atmosphere for normal interpersonal relationships, and the size of the larger institutions can create management problems. The massive scale of the mega-prison, which may hold up to 3,000 inmates, provides opportunities for aggressive prisoners to hide weapons, dispense private "justice," and engage more or less freely in other illicit activities.

The size of the population in a large prison may also result in some inmates' "falling through the cracks"—being misclassified and forced to live among more-violent offenders.

Much of the emphasis on the "new generation prisons"—small housing units, clear sight lines, security corridors linking housing units—is designed to limit these opportunities and thus prevent violence.

time period. Because the decline in assaults was not attributable to a decline in prison population, officials credited the deterrent effect of conducted energy devices and the new more-powerful chemical spray carried by officers. Moreover, even though Michigan spent more than $1 million to acquire less-lethal weapons for corrections officers at prisons, the state claimed to save $1.8 million in workers' compensation claims because fewer corrections officers were injured on the job from prisoners' assaults.

Civil liberties advocates and prisoners claimed that officers were too quick to use the weapons in situations that did not require the use of such force and that the weapons were not always used properly. According to one report, a Michigan prisoner lost his vision when struck near the eye with a jolt from a conducted energy device. The fears about the potential overuse of the new weapons are enhanced by reports about the misuse of these devices in jails around the country. For example, a jail officer in South Carolina faced criminal charges after using a conducted energy device in anger on a jail inmate who temporarily closed a cell door to the keep the officer out. A jail officer in Florida was fired after hitting a jail inmate with a jolt from a conducted energy device simply because the inmate expressed curiosity about how the electroshock would feel.

Sources: "Corrections Officer Accused of Unlawfully Using a Taser on an Inmate," WISTV.com, April 3, 2009 (www.wistv.com); Steve Crawford, "Sheriff's Officials Credit Fewer Injuries at Jail to Taser Use," *Augusta Chronicle,* September 3, 2012 (http://chronicle.augusta.com); Paul Egan, "Fewer Assaults on Prison Staff Since TASERs Introduced," *Detroit Free Press,* July 6, 2014 (www.freep.com); Paul Egan, "Tasers in Michigan Prisons Praised," *Detroit Free Press,* February 23, 2012 (www.freep.com); Patrick Marley, "Prison Guards Equipped with Pepper Spray in Response to Inmate Assaults," *Milwaukee Journal Sentinel,* December 21, 2013 (www.jsonline.com); Rachel Myers, "Lee Prison Guard Fired in Taser Row," *Ft. Myers* (FL) *News-Press,* April 10, 2008 (http://archive.news-press.com); Claire Sarafin, "Jailers Carry Tasers Following Attack," WKOW News, April 3, 2013 (www.wkow.com); Jennifer Sullivan, "King County Jail Officers to Carry Tasers," *Seattle Times,* April 19, 2011 (www.seattletimes.com).

CRITICAL THINKING AND ANALYSIS

The introduction of less-lethal weapons that are carried by officers inside the walls of prisons represents a big change from traditional practice. Will views about the benefits of the practice change if prisoners overpower an officer, seize pepper spray and a conducted energy device, and use those weapons against prison employees? How great are the risks that officers will be too quick to use these weapons rather than defuse situations with their communication skills? Similarly, how great are the risks that these weapons may be used improperly, such as for an expression of officers' annoyance and anger rather than out of necessity? Write a memo describing the recommendation you would make about the distribution and use of these less-lethal weapons if you were the director of a state department of corrections.

The Role of Management

The degree to which inmate leaders are allowed to take matters into their own hands can affect the level of violence among inmates. When administrators run a tight ship, security measures prevent sexual attacks in dark corners, the making of "shivs" and "shanks" (knives) in the metal shop, and open conflict among inmate groups. A prison must afford each inmate defensible space, and administrators should ensure that every inmate is secure from physical attack.

Effective prison management can decrease the level of assaultive behavior by limiting opportunities for attacks. Wardens and correctional officers must therefore recognize the types of people with whom they are dealing, the role of prison gangs, and the structure of institutions. John DiIulio argues that no group of inmates is "unmanageable [and] no combination of political, social, budgetary, architectural, or other factors makes good management impossible" (DiIulio, 1991: 12). He points to such varied institutions as the California Men's Colony, the Federal Bureau of Prisons, and the Texas Department of Corrections under the leadership of George Beto. At these institutions, DiIulio claimed that good management practices have resulted in prisons and jails where inmates can "do time" without fearing for their personal safety. Wardens who exert leadership can manage their prisons effectively, so that problems do not fester and erupt into violent confrontations.

In sum, prisons must be made safe places. Because the state puts offenders there, it has a responsibility to prevent violence and maintain order. To exclude violence from prisons, officials may have to limit movement within institutions, contacts with the outside, and the right of inmates to choose their associates. Yet these measures may run counter to the goal of producing men and women who will be accountable when they return to society.

CHECKPOINT 26. What factors are thought to contribute to prison violence?

STOP AND ANALYZE: Think about the role of architectural design in facilitating or preventing prison violence. Draw a design of a prison that would reduce the opportunities for violence. List three aspects of your design that are intended to reduce opportunities for violence.

A QUESTION OF ETHICS

In April 2014, U.S. District Judge James Bredar sentenced former corrections officer Tyson Hinckle to serve two and one-half years in prison for conspiring to severely beat a prisoner at the Roxbury Correctional Institution near Hagerstown, Maryland. Hinckle was one of fifteen corrections officers facing prison terms for beating inmate Kenneth Davis and then erasing security camera footage to destroy evidence of the violence. A total of 22 officers were fired because of the incident. Because Davis had punched a corrections officer, other officers followed the practice of punishing Davis by having officers beat him on three consecutive work shifts. Some officers held Davis down as other officers kicked and beat him. Davis suffered a broken nose, back, and ribs from the beating.

During an earlier sentencing hearing for other convicted officers, an outraged Judge Bredar said, "How in God's name did this culture evolve to the point where officers on three different shifts, including supervisors, came to the conclusion. . . . that the appropriate solution was raw, crude violence? . . . Where was the leadership of this institution and of this state department?"

Sources: "Maryland Correctional Officers Get 2.5 Years Prison for Beating an Inmate—and 13 More Will Be Sentenced," *Daily Mail,* March 10, 2014(www.dailymail.co.uk); "Maryland Correctional Officer Sentenced to Prison for Beating Inmate," WJLA News, April 8, 2014 (www.wjla.com).

CRITICAL THINKING AND ANALYSIS

If you were the warden of a prison, what steps would you take to prevent such illegal and unethical activity by corrections officers? In light of behaviors by prisoners that make officers angry, how can officers be taught to keep calm and how can they be supervised to make sure that they do? Create a list of actions that you would take and explain why you would do each one.

Summary

1 Describe the three models of incarceration that have predominated since the 1940s

- The custodial model emphasizes the maintenance of security, (2) the rehabilitation model views security and housekeeping activities as mainly a framework for treatment efforts, and (3) the reintegration model recognizes that prisoners must be prepared for their return to society.

2 Discuss how a prison is organized

- Most prisons are expected to fulfill goals related to keeping (custody), using (work), and serving (treatment) inmates. The formal organization of prisons is designed to achieve these goals.

3 Analyze how a prison is governed

- The public's belief that the warden and officers have total power over the inmates is outdated.
- Good management through effective leadership can maintain the quality of prison life as measured by levels of order, amenities, and services.
- Four factors make managing prisons different from administering other public institutions: defects of total power, limited use of rewards and punishments, exchange relationships, and strength of inmate leadership.

4 Describe the role of correctional officers in a prison

- Correctional officers, because they are constantly in close contact with the prisoners, are the real linchpins in the prison system. The effectiveness of the institution lies heavily on their shoulders.
- Prison administrators must deal with the special needs of some groups, including elderly prisoners, prisoners with HIV/AIDS, prisoners with mental illness, and long-term prisoners.

5 Discuss what it is like to be in prison

- Inmates do not serve their time in isolation but are members of a subculture with its own traditions, norms, and leadership structure. Such norms are often called the inmate code.
- Today's prisons, unlike those of the past, do not have a uniform inmate code but several, in part because of the influence of gangs.
- Inmates deal with the pain of incarceration by assuming an adaptive role and lifestyle.
- To meet their needs for goods and services not provided by the state, prisoners run an underground economy.

6 Analyze the special needs and problems of incarcerated women

- Women make up only a small portion of the inmate population. This is cited as the reason for the limited programs and services available to female prisoners.
- Social relationships among female inmates differ from those of their male counterparts. Women tend to form pseudofamilies in prison. Many women experience the added stress of being responsible for their children on the outside.

7 Describe the programs and services that are available to prisoners

- Educational, vocational, industrial, and treatment programs are available in prisons. Administrators believe that these programs are important for maintaining order, but they may be among the first items eliminated when a prison must impose budget cuts.

8 Discuss the nature of prison violence

- Violence in prison depends on such things as administrative effectiveness; the architecture and size of prisons; and inmate characteristics such as age, attitudes, and race.
- Violence occurs between prisoners, often through gangs, and between prisoners and guards.

Questions for Review

1. How do modern prisons differ from those in the past?
2. What are the characteristics of prisons that make them different from other institutions?
3. What must a prison administrator do to ensure successful management?
4. What is meant by an adaptive role? Which roles are found in male prison society? In female prison society?
5. How does the convict society in institutions for women differ from that in institutions for men?
6. What are the main forms of prison programs, and what purposes do they serve?
7. What are the forms and causes of prison violence?

Key Terms

classification (p. 640)
custodial model (p. 612)
inmate code (p. 627)
reintegration model (p. 613)

Checkpoint Answers

1 How does today's prison differ from the "big house" of the past?

✓ The characteristics of the inmate population have changed. More inmates are from urban areas and have been convicted for drug-related or violent offenses; the inmate population is fragmented along racial and ethnic lines, prisoners are less isolated from the outside world, and correctional officers have used collective bargaining to improve their working conditions.

2 What three models of prison have predominated since the 1940s?

✓ The custodial, rehabilitation, and reintegration models.

3 How do prisons differ from other organizations in society?

✓ It is a place where a group of workers manages a group of captives.

4 What are the multiple goals pursued in today's prisons with respect to prisoners?

✓ Keeping (custody), using (work), serving (treatment).

5 What problems do these goals present to administrators?

✓ The goals often mean the administration of prisons is marked by ambiguity and conflict.

6 What four factors make the governing of prisons different from administering other public institutions?

✓ The defects of total power, a limited system of rewards and punishments, exchange relations between correctional officers and inmates, and the strength of inmate leadership.

7 What complex challenges face correctional officers?

✓ They are in daily contact with the inmates and therefore must handle the moment-to-moment aspects of discipline and control as they carry out the institutions' detailed policies and procedures.

8 Name three of the five legally acceptable reasons for the use of force.

✓ Self-defense, defense of third person, upholding prison rules, prevention of crime, prevention of escapes.

9 What are the major characteristics of today's prisoners?

✓ Today's prisoners are largely men in their late 20s to early 30s with less than a high school education. They are disproportionately members of minority groups.

10 What are the key elements of the inmate code?

✓ The values and norms of prison society that emphasize inmate solidarity.

11 Why is it unlikely that a single, overriding inmate code exists in today's prisons?

✓ The prison society is fragmented by racial and ethnic divisions.

12 What are the four role orientations found in adult male prisons?

✓ Doing time, gleaning, jailing, and functioning as a disorganized criminal.

13 Why does an underground economy exist in prison?

✓ To provide goods and services not available through regular channels.

14 Why are prison administrators wary of the prison economy?

✓ The prison economy is responsible for the exploitation of prisoners by other prisoners and has the potential for conflict and violence.

15 What accounts for the neglect of facilities and programs in women's prisons?

✓ Because there are relatively few women in prison and they are often confined in a single institution within a state, departments of corrections typically devote their program planning and resources to the larger number of prisons that contain male prisoners.

16 **How do the social relationships among female prisoners differ from those of their male counterparts?**

✓ Men are more individualistic and their norms stress autonomy, self-sufficiency, and the ability to cope with one's own problems. Women share more with one another.

17 **What are some of the problems encountered by female prisoners in maintaining contact with their children?**

✓ The distance of prisons from homes, intermittent telephone privileges, and unnatural visiting environment.

18 **How are children cared for while their mothers are incarcerated?**

✓ Children are either with relatives or in foster care.

19 **Why are prison programs important from the standpoint of prison administrators?**

✓ Programs keep prisoners busy and reduce security problems.

20 **How are inmates assigned to programs?**

✓ Classification by a committee according to the needs of the inmate or of the institution.

21 **Why have legislatures and the general public been so critical of educational and rehabilitative programs in prisons?**

✓ These programs are thought to "coddle" prisoners and give them resources not available to law-abiding citizens.

22 **What problems are encountered in vocational training programs?**

✓ Too many programs train inmates for trades for which there is already an adequate labor supply or in which the skills are outdated. They are inefficient because of the low education level and poor work habits of the prisoners. Production has to be stopped for periodic head counts and checks on tools and materials.

23 **Why have legislatures restricted prison industries?**

✓ Pressures from labor unions whose members make competing products at higher wages.

24 **Which inmate characteristics are thought to be factors in prison violence?**

✓ Age, attitudes, and race.

25 **Why are gangs such a threat to prison order?**

✓ Gang wars continue on the inside.

26 **What factors are thought to contribute to prison violence?**

✓ Inadequate supervision, architectural design, availability of weapons, housing of violence-prone inmates with the defenseless, the high level of tension of people living in close quarters, the physical size and condition of the prison, and the role of management.

CHAPTER FEATURES

- **New Directions in Criminal Justice Policy** Evidence-Based Reentry Practices
- **Close Up** A Personal Encounter with the Parole Process in Michigan
- **Technology and Criminal Justice** Using GPS to Track Parolees
- **Inside Today's Controversies:** The REDEEM Act

CHAPTER 16 REENTRY INTO THE COMMUNITY

CHAPTER LEARNING OBJECTIVES

1 Describe the nature of the "reentry problem"

2 Discuss the origins of parole and the way it operates today

3 Analyze the mechanisms for the release of felons to the community

4 Describe the problems parolees face during their reentry

5 Discuss how ex-prisoners are supervised in the community

6 Analyze how civil disabilities block successful reentry

CHAPTER OUTLINE

Prisoner Reentry
- Contemporary Budget Cuts and Prisoner Release
- Institutional Reentry Preparation Programs

Release and Supervision
- The Origins of Parole
- The Development of Parole in the United States

Release Mechanisms
- Discretionary Release
- Mandatory Release
- Probation Release
- Other Conditional Release
- Expiration Release
- The Parole Board Process
- Impact of Release Mechanisms

Parole Supervision in the Community
- Community Programs following Release
- Work and Educational Release
- Parole Officer: Cop or Social Worker?
- The Parole Bureaucracy
- Adjustments to Life outside Prison
- Revocation of Parole

The Future of Prisoner Reentry

Civil Disabilities of Ex-Felons

Pardon

AP Images/Klas Stolpe/Juneau Empire

The excited looks on the men's faces highlighted the special quality of the occasion. As a group, with their tattoos, scars, and lined faces, they did not call to mind the image of a graduating class. However, with hugs from family members and congratulatory handshakes from corrections officials, they had reason to bask in a moment of accomplishment and optimism—despite the harsh and uncertain reality of the difficulties they would face in finding jobs and reentering society. Through an initiative at the Orleans Parish Prison in New Orleans, these offenders had completed a ten-week course on job skills, self-development, and behavior intended to help them succeed as they neared release from incarceration. Fifty-two-year-old J. C. Alford, who had been in and out of prison since 1977, noted that it was the first time that anyone cared about whether or not he would succeed in society after being released (Chang, 2012).

The New Orleans program is just one example of the rapidly expanding effort to address the fact that many offenders released from prison will simply end up back in the criminal justice system if they do not receive any preparation and support toward their efforts to reenter society successfully. Reentry initiatives do not only involve prerelease education programs; they can also include community corrections centers where released offenders can go to obtain assistance in finding jobs and housing, receive access to counseling, and access a range of additional services, as at the Partners Reentry Center in Anchorage, Alaska. The Anchorage center is a joint project of several nonprofit organizations that receive government grants and private contributions (Boots, 2013).

Newspaper headlines regularly remind us about the risks posed by offenders who are released from prison: "Parolee Arrested Again on Drug Trafficking Charges" ("Parolee Arrested Again," 2015); "Police: Parolee

Arrested after 1 Adult, 2 Kids Stabbed" (Greenwood and Fournier, 2015); "Parolee Arrested for Attempted Murder of Acquaintance Made While in Prison" ("Parolee Arrested for Attempted Murder," 2015). With more than 600,000 people released from state and federal prisons each year, such events can make the public understandably fearful about the return of convicted offenders to their communities. Yet society as a whole must become ready for the return of these offenders and, more importantly, there must be developed programs to prepare these offenders for successful reentry into the general population. Only a small percentage of imprisoned offenders are serving life sentences, as illustrated by a description of the Montana Women's Prison: "Only one inmate . . . is currently serving a life sentence. That means at some point roughly 265 offenders will be released back into society" (Wooley, 2011). Reentry issues are important as an inevitable component of the corrections process, and they have become even more significant as budget crises push states to move offenders back into society more quickly in the effort to reduce prison populations.

Offenders who leave prison, either under parole supervision or after the completion of their sentences, face serious difficulties. Many of them were never successful in mainstream society prior to incarceration, so they are in greater need than other Americans for education, job training, and a reorientation about societal values and proper behavior. Moreover, many offenders will be returning to a community environment where their problems with drugs and alcohol may be renewed. These newly released individuals will seek jobs in a slowly recovering economy that makes finding jobs difficult even for those who do not have criminal records. Even if the criminal record does not stop employers from considering them as likely employees, many of those leaving prison are also encumbered by their limited education and lack of legitimate work experience, and thus have a difficult time competing with other job applicants.

Many offenders stumble when they initially reenter society by failing to obey their conditions of parole, returning to drug use, or quitting education and job-training programs. Some of these offenders will overcome these missteps, perhaps after a stint in jail awakens them to the looming prospect of a return to prison. Although numerous offenders will fail and be returned to prison for parole violations or the commission of new crimes, given the expense of incarceration—$32,000 per year for each imprisoned offender in Pennsylvania, for example—it is in society's interest to find ways to reduce the number returned to prison. Yet, reentry programs are not available for all offenders as they near their release dates.

In this chapter, we examine the mechanisms by which prisoners are released from incarceration; we also look at their supervision in the community. Finally, we discuss the many problems facing parolees as they reenter society.

Prisoner Reentry

Prisoner reentry has become an important public issue. Reentry has been described as a "transient state between liberty and recommitment" (Blumstein and Beck, 2005: 50). It is a limited period of supervision whereby an offender coming out of prison either moves to full liberty in the community or returns to prison for committing a new crime or violating the terms of parole. As indicated by "What Americans Think," many Americans believe that there are too many people in prison.

In response to the increasing recognition of the importance of this issue, in 2013 U.S. Attorney General Eric Holder established the Federal Interagency Reentry Council in 2011 to bring together the leaders of 20 federal agencies to examine the full range of issues and problems related to prisoner reentry. The council was then tasked to create a comprehensive plan toward improving ex-offenders' successful return to society. In the words of former U.S. Attorney General Eric Holder,

> After all, we know reentry is not just a matter of public safety—it's also an issue of housing and health care policy; a question of education and employment; and a fatherhood and family challenge that affects millions across the country every year. (2013)

Holder described the work of the Federal Interagency Reentry Council by saying, "We're calling attention to successful programs, striving to dispel myths about reentry, strengthening our policies, and engaging with an expanding group of allies to advance this comprehensive work" (Holder, 2013). As indicated by the attorney general's statements, there are now increased efforts to address a wide range of issues that may affect successful reentry and to coordinate efforts among agencies at different levels of government.

The sudden flood of offenders leaving prison and the fact that about half will return to prison, either because of a new crime or a parole violation, raise serious questions as to how the criminal justice system deals with the reentry of ex-felons (Durose, Cooper, and Snyder, 2014). Moreover, the ones who avoid a return to prison need significant initial help with respect to housing, employment, and other factors that affect their ability to support themselves and live successfully in free society. What is the crux of this problem?

Jeremy Travis and Joan Petersilia point to several factors that seem to have contributed to the reentry problem (Travis and Petersilia, 2001). They argue that beginning in the 1970s, the power of parole boards to decide whether a prisoner was "ready" to be released was abolished in mandatory release states and severely restricted in discretionary release states. This means that more inmates are automatically leaving prison, ready or not, when they meet the requirements of their sentence. It also means that there has been little or no prerelease planning so that the new parolee has a job, housing, and a supportive family when he or she hits the streets.

A second factor contributing to the reentry problem is the defunding of prison education, job training, and other rehabilitation programs designed to prepare inmates for their return to the community (Gunnison and Helfgott, 2013). States' budget cuts since 2008 affected many government programs, including those focused on reentry and other operations in the corrections system.

Travis and Petersilia also note that the profile of returning prisoners has changed in ways that pose new challenges to successful reentry. In particular, the conviction offense and time served is different than it was 30 years ago. Now, about 30 percent of prisoners released to parole were incarcerated for a drug offense—up from 12 percent in 1985. Although the average time served has also increased by almost a half year since 1990, some drug and violent offenders are exiting prison after very long terms, perhaps 20 or more years. The longer time in prison means a longer period the prisoner has been absent from family and friends.

WHAT AMERICANS THINK

QUESTION: "Do you believe there are too many people in prison in the United States, not enough people in prison, or is the number of people in prison about right?"

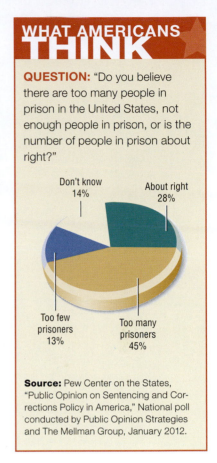

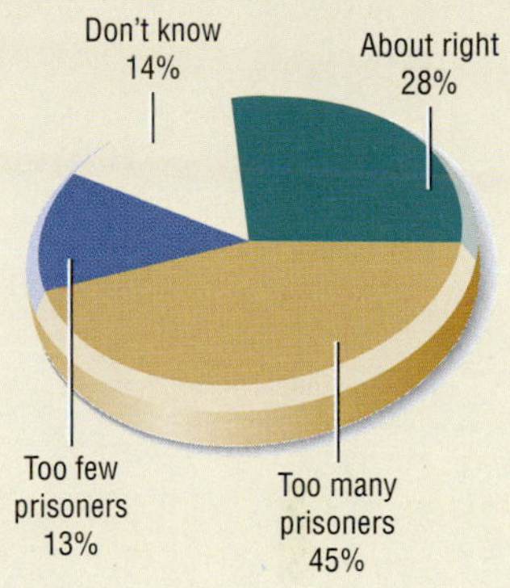

Source: Pew Center on the States, "Public Opinion on Sentencing and Corrections Policy in America," National poll conducted by Public Opinion Strategies and The Mellman Group, January 2012.

How prepared, then, are prisoners to live as law-abiding citizens? Successful prisoner reentry requires that parole and reentry support services focus on linking offenders with community institutions—churches, families, self-help groups, and assistance programs. Research indicates that the prisoners most likely to succeed in the job market are those who had work experience prior to prison, connected to employers prior to release, and had conventional family relationships (Visher, Debus-Sherrill, and Yahner, 2011). Many prisoners do not have these assets as they exit prison. Thus efforts must be made to improve their chances for success in free society. According to Joan Petersilia (2009), because public safety and neighborhood stability depend on successful reentry, communities must share with corrections officials the responsibility for transitioning offenders to the community.

The reentry problem has stimulated action by Congress and the states to provide assistance to parolees and to reduce the staggering amount of recidivism among them. The Second Chance Act of 2007, signed into law by President Bush on April 9, 2008, was designed to ensure the safe and successful return of prisoners to the community. The act provides federal grants to states and communities to support reentry initiatives focused on employment, housing, substance abuse and mental health treatment, and children and family services. See the New Directions in Criminal Justice Policy feature for a look at evidence-based reentry practices.

Contemporary Budget Cuts and Prisoner Release

The economic recession of 2008 and its lingering aftermath produced a drop in employment rates and difficulties for many American businesses and families. When the incomes of families drop and businesses are less profitable, the government receives less tax revenue to fund needed programs, including corrections. Because incarceration is such an expensive form of punishment, with states and

NEW DIRECTIONS IN CRIMINAL JUSTICE POLICY

EVIDENCE-BASED REENTRY PRACTICES

Researchers have studied prisoner reentry programs for decades. Some of this research has provided evidence of specific practices that facilitate reentry and reduce future recidivism. Although many approaches may seem effective on the surface (see Chapter 14), it is only rigorous research and evaluation that can determine what really "works" to reduce recidivism.

Programs focused exclusively on employment training have generally been found to be ineffective; however, recent analyses have indicated that there are some elements of job-skills programs that can benefit inmates leaving prison. In Minnesota, the "EMPLOY" program has been demonstrated to effectively reduce the likelihood of revocation of parole, new arrests, reconviction, and also reincarceration. The unique aspect of EMPLOY is that it is delivered in two parts: First, inmates begin technical training and learn job/employment readiness skills while *still* incarcerated. After release, they receive assistance in community-based programs for one year, continuing the vocational work that was started in prison. Studies show that ex-inmates who successfully complete EMPLOY have found jobs more easily, work more hours, and earn more money. A cost analysis of this program indicates that it saves the State of Minnesota approximately $2.84 million per year due to program participants not reentering the criminal justice system—the costs of arrest, court time, and reincarceration.

Some inmates awaiting release from prison have substance abuse issues that may harm their chances of remaining crime free. Research on "what works" with regard to substance abuse treatment has indicated that the programs with the greatest success are those that focus on the offenders who have the greatest risk of using drugs and include a significant aftercare program (that is, the participant continues to be monitored after the program officially ends).

The Sheridan Correctional Center National Model Drug Prison and Reentry Program in Illinois was created in partnership with researchers and corrections experts based on best practices in the field. Sheridan is a medium-security prison that was remodeled in 2004 to serve only inmates with substance abuse issues. It is considered a therapeutic community, in counties paying as much as $33,000 or more annually to cover the costs of holding each prisoner in a secure facility, government officials began to rethink sentencing policies that had caused prison populations to skyrocket since the 1980s. In particular, they gave consideration to greater utilization of probation and community corrections for nonviolent and drug offenders. In addition, many states sought ways to reduce their prison populations by accelerating the release into the community of nondangerous offenders and those nearing the completion of their sentences. For example, Michigan, a state with budget problems stemming from one of the nation's highest unemployment rates, reduced its prison population from a peak of 51,554 in March 2007 to 43,704 in December 2013 (Sayre, 2014). The reductions enabled the state to save money by closing several prisons. According to the website of the Michigan Department of Corrections, it costs the state an average of $33,822 per year for each offender held in prison, but only $2,379 for each offender under community supervision. Thus the state's reduction of the prison population created substantial financial savings for corrections expenditures. These developments were facilitated, in part, by Michigan's effort to develop reentry programs that would help prisoners become prepared to move back into the community (Pew Center on the States, 2011).

Such efforts to reduce prison populations can be affected by continuing budget difficulties that lead to cuts in reentry programs and thereby diminish the state's ability to prepare offenders to effectively reintegrate into the community. Parole officers in California have higher caseloads than in the past, after the governor took action to release more "lifer" inmates from prison to parole (St. John, 2014). Significant budget cuts (and possible financial mismanagement) in Florida have resulted in understaffed probation and parole departments, with officers having to purchase their own weapons (Pransky, 2015). In 2013, Michigan significantly cut the budget of the Michigan Prisoner Reentry Initiative, which some argue has saved the state significant funds by diverting offenders from parole (Graham, 2013). The governor of Vermont is considering making significant cuts

which every inmate participates in group therapy, counseling, and 12-step programming to deter substance abuse. As inmates progress through the program, they obtain higher levels of responsibility and serve as peer educators for inmates entering the program. A key feature of Sheridan's program is aftercare—inmates must attend up to 90 days of substance abuse treatment in their community *after* release. As indicated by research, aftercare support significantly reduces future recidivism.

Evidence indicates that some programs are more successful than others at keeping former inmates crime free as they transition back into the community. Researchers generally agree that successful strategies begin with assessing the needs of those inmates in the system who are close to release. Because there are many kinds of reentry programming, it is vital that inmates are matched with the approach that best fits their needs and that will give them the tools to help them succeed.

Sources: Grant Duwe, "The Benefits of Keeping Idle Hands Busy: An Outcome Evaluation of a Prisoner Reentry Employment Program," *Crime & Delinquency*, 2011; Grant Duwe, *What Works with Minnesota Prisoners: A Summary of the Effects of Correctional Programming on Recidivism, Employment, and Cost Avoidance*, July 2013 (St. Paul, MN: Minnesota Department of Corrections); Edward J. Latessa and Brian Lovins, "The Role of Offender Risk Assessment: A Policy Maker Guide," *Victims & Offenders* 5(3): 203–19, 2010; Jessica Reichert and Dawn Ruzich, *Community Reentry after Prison Drug Treatment: Learning from Sheridan* Therapeutic *Community Program Participants*, January 2012 (Chicago: Illinois Criminal Justice Information Authority).

DEBATE THE ISSUE

As discussed earlier in the chapter, budget cuts made to correctional programming can reduce the number of programs available to inmates leaving prisons; however, some programs have been shown to be very effective in reducing crime and keeping former inmates from returning to prison. In Kansas, for example, only about 10 percent of releasees who needed substance abuse treatment were able to get it. Imagine you are advising the governor of your state on making cuts to the correctional budget. What are the pros and cons of cutting post-release programs? How might cuts to correctional programs actually end up increasing state costs over time?

to an education program that allows released inmates to complete high school degrees (A. A. Nixon, 2015). At the federal level, according to former U.S. Attorney General Eric Holder, by 2013 the Second Chance Act had provided the basis for the Justice Department to award more than $250 million in grants to 400 reentry programs around the country (Holder, 2013). However, when across-the-board budget cuts took effect in mid-2013 as Congress and President Obama could not reach agreement on issues of federal spending and taxation policies, the federal government's support for reentry was affected. In the second decade of the twenty-first century, state and county governments are facing the problematic results of tough policy choices: They are accelerating the release of prisoners in order to decrease corrections budgets by reducing prison populations. At the same time, many legislatures are cutting or reducing programs and services that help to prepare those prisoners for successful reentry into society.

Institutional Reentry Preparation Programs

Most of this chapter discusses post-release community corrections, especially issues involving parole. In addition to community programs, states are increasingly developing programs within prisons as the first step to begin offenders' preparation for reentry. A few states have created separate institutions dedicated to preparing offenders for reentering society. This enables them to spend the last portion of their sentences in a special facility among other prisoners who are also focused on taking classes to prepare for release. Some correctional officials argue that preparation for reentry should begin at an even earlier point in the prison sentence. As one prison warden said, "[W]e're trying to start the day they come in. . . . [W]hat do you need to do here to prepare yourself [for release?]. . . . We try to get that into their minds immediately (Wooley, 2011).

In 2011, the Pew Center on the States issued a report, entitled *State of Recidivism: The Revolving Door of America's Prisons,* which noted that nationwide, a consistent percentage of offenders—40 percent—was reimprisoned within three years of release. This percentage remained steady throughout the study period of 1999–2007 (Pew Center on the States, 2011). The Pew Center report pointed out that the recidivism rate actually varied by state and that some individual states had seen declines in recidivism even as the national rate hovered at the same level. After examining approaches taken by different states, one of the Pew Center report's recommendations was "begin preparation for release at time of prison admission" (Pew Center on the States, 2011). Contrary to the traditional practice of using prisons for custody, and worrying—if at all—about reentry at the time of release, the report highlighted the need to see the period of imprisonment as a time in which efforts can be made to address offenders' problems and needs. The perspective presented in the report is not advocating treating offenders as "victims of society" who deserve attention and care. Instead, it is merely the practical recognition that society benefits from thinking in advance about the reality that most offenders will eventually be released back into the community. Critics of the prison system have raised this question: If we treat offenders as "monsters" while they are in prison, shouldn't we expect that they will inevitably affect society by acting as "monsters" when they again live among us?

South Carolina, Florida, Indiana, and other states developed reentry preparation programs within prisons to assist offenders with the transition back to society. These programs are often in special facilities and involve spending a specific period of months in the programs just prior to release. Indiana developed an innovation by creating the nation's first prison dedicated to preparation for reentry. The Duvall Residential Center is relatively small—only 350 prisoners nearing their release date—and focuses on providing a range of programs that cover job readiness, business ownership, fatherhood, conflict resolution, financial knowledge, substance abuse treatment, and other concrete subjects (City of Indianapolis, 2015). These programs recognize that successful reentry depends not merely on gaining employment, but also on having sufficient knowledge about finances and asset management to use money wisely for expenses and family responsibilities (L. Martin, 2011).

At Michigan's Detroit Reentry Center, many prerelease offenders spend time preparing for parole at a low-security facility only a few minutes from downtown Detroit. In a building once used by Daimler Chrysler to store automobiles, they attend sessions that include reading skills and training for jobs in food service and as porters. About 200 volunteers assist by providing faith-based programming to inmates, and men at this facility have access to health care through a local hospital (Michigan Department of Corrections, 2015).

The idea of prerelease facilities and programs has gained popular support from the public, including legislators, who recognize that society benefits in many ways, including financially, from helping offenders avoid a return to the expensive environment of prison. Some states are trying to save funds by using closed prisons as reentry centers and homeless shelters (Couch, 2015). Others are cutting funding to reentry to help balance steep corrections budgets. For example, in 2012, the Florida Department of Corrections announced that it would close two reentry facilities as part of an effort to solve a $79 million budget deficit. Closing the centers would result in moving 300 prisoners out of job-training and life-skills courses and back into the general inmate population at other institutions. State legislators and newspaper editorial writers complained that it was shortsighted to target reentry programs for cuts, especially because closing the two centers would only save $1 million, which would barely affect the overall corrections budget deficit. Ultimately, the political pressure and public outcry led Florida's corrections officials to decide keep the reentry facilities in operation (Bousquet, 2012a, 2012b). In other states, however, budget pressures have led to a reduction in reentry programs.

CHECKPOINT **1.** What problems interfere with offenders' reentry into society after imprisonment?

STOP AND ANALYZE: Petersilia suggests that the community assist with the rehabilitation of offenders. List two things community members can do to help parolees stay away from criminal influence.

(Answers are at the end of the chapter).

Release and Supervision

Except for the 7 percent of offenders who die in prison, all inmates will eventually be released to live in the community. Currently about 77 percent of felons will be released on parole and will remain under correctional supervision for a specific period of time. About 19 percent are released at the expiration of their sentence, having "maxed out," and are free to live in the community without supervision.

parole
The conditional release of an inmate from incarceration under supervision after a part of the prison sentence has been served.

Parole is the conditional release of an offender from incarceration but not from the legal custody of the state. Thus offenders who comply with parole conditions and do not violate the law receive an absolute discharge from supervision at the end of their sentences. If a parolee breaks a rule, parole can be revoked and the person returned to a correctional facility. Parole rests on three concepts:

1. *Grace:* The prisoner could be kept incarcerated, but the government extends the privilege of release.
2. *Contract:* The government enters into an agreement with the prisoner whereby the prisoner promises to abide by certain conditions in exchange for being released.

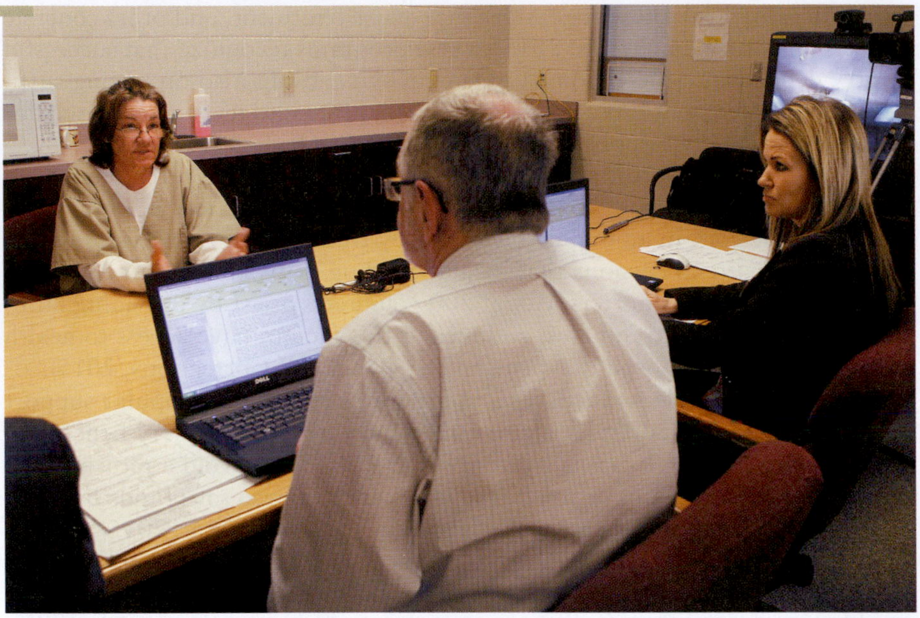

In discretionary release, parole board members make decisions about when a prisoner will be released under parole supervision. Because of the number of cases that they must consider, they cannot spend a great deal of time interviewing specific prisoners. In addition, they cannot know with certainty who will commit crimes in the future. What factors should carry the greatest weight in these parole decisions?

AP Images/The Lexington Herald-Leader, Charles Bertram

3. *Custody:* Even though the offender is released from prison, he or she is still under supervision by the government. Parole is an extension of correctional programs into the community.

Only felons are released on parole; adult misdemeanants are usually released immediately after they have finished serving their sentences. Today over 800,000 people are under parole supervision, a threefold increase since 1985 (Glaze and Kaeble, 2014; Hester, 1987).

The Origins of Parole

Parole in the United States evolved during the nineteenth century from the English, Australian, and Irish practices of conditional pardon, apprenticeship by indenture, transportation of criminals from one country to another, and the issuance of **tickets of leave**. These were all methods of moving criminals out of prison as a response to overcrowding, labor shortages, and the cost of incarceration.

ticket of leave
A system of conditional release from prison, devised by Captain Alexander Maconochie and first developed in Ireland by Sir Walter Crofton.

A key figure in developing the concept of parole in the nineteenth century was Captain Alexander Maconochie, an administrator of British penal colonies in Tasmania and elsewhere in the South Pacific. A critic of definite prison terms, Maconochie devised a system of rewards for good conduct, labor, and study. Under his classification procedure, prisoners could pass through stages of increasing responsibility and freedom: (1) strict imprisonment, (2) labor on government chain gangs, (3) freedom within a limited area, (4) a ticket of leave or parole resulting in a conditional pardon, and (5) full restoration of liberty. Like modern correctional practices, this procedure assumed that prisoners should be prepared gradually for release. The roots of the American system of parole can be seen in the transition from imprisonment to conditional release to full freedom.

Maconochie's idea of requiring prisoners to earn their early release caught on first in Ireland. There, Sir Walter Crofton built on Maconochie's idea that an offender's progress in prison and a ticket of leave were linked. Prisoners who graduated through Crofton's three successive levels of treatment were released on parole under a series of conditions. Most significant was the requirement that parolees submit monthly reports to the police. In Dublin, a special civilian inspector helped releasees find jobs, visited them periodically, and supervised their activities.

POINT
2. In what countries did the concept of parole first develop?
3. What were the contributions of Alexander Maconochie and Sir Walter Crofton?

STOP AND ANALYZE: Think about the concept of parole. One can see how it benefits the offender. How does it benefit society? List three arguable benefits for society from parole.

The Development of Parole in the United States

In the United States, parole developed during the prison reform movement of the latter half of the nineteenth century. Relying on the ideas of Maconochie and Crofton, American reformers such as Zebulon Brockway of the Elmira State Reformatory in New York began to experiment with the concept of parole. After New York adopted indeterminate sentences in 1876, Brockway started to release prisoners on parole. Under the new sentencing law, prisoners could be released when their conduct showed they were ready to return to society.

As originally implemented, the parole system in New York did not require supervision by the police. Instead, volunteers from citizens' reform groups assisted with the parolee's reintegration into society. As parole became more common and applied to larger numbers of offenders, states replaced the volunteer supervisors with correctional employees.

Many individuals and groups in the United States opposed the release of convicts before they had completed the entire sentence that they had earned by their crimes. However, the use of parole continued to spread. By 1900, parole systems were implemented in 20 states; 44 states and the federal government had them by 1932 (Friedman, 1993). Today every state has some procedure for the release of offenders before the end of their sentences. A recent study indicates that around 70 percent of offenders are released from prison conditionally, before the end of their formal sentence (M. S. Bradley and Engen, 2014).

Although it has been used in the United States for more than a century, parole remains controversial. To many people, parole allows convicted offenders to avoid serving the full sentence they deserve. Public pressure in the late 1970s to be tougher on criminals has led half the states and the federal government to restructure their sentencing laws and release mechanisms (Petersilia, 2009).

Release Mechanisms

From 1920 to 1973 there was a nationwide sentencing and release policy. During this period, all states and the federal government used indeterminate sentencing, authorized discretionary release by parole boards, and supervised prisoners after release. They did this all in the interest of the rehabilitation of offenders.

The critique of rehabilitation in the 1970s led to determinate sentencing as the public came to view the system as "soft" on criminals. By 2002, discretionary release by parole boards had been abolished in 16 states. Another 5 states had abolished discretionary release for certain offenses (Petersilia, 2009).

Further, in some states that kept discretionary release, parole boards were reluctant to grant it. In Texas, for example, 57 percent of all cases considered for parole release in 1988 were approved; by 1998 that figure had dropped to just 20 percent (Fabelo, 1999). However, since 2001 the rate of release votes had increased from 25 percent to 31 percent, while simultaneously the number of revocations decreased (Battson, 2012). This could indicate that, at least in Texas, the parole board had improved their ability to accurately assess risk of recidivism for offenders. These trends could also be attributed to the desire to cut budgets by reducing prison populations and using less expensive options for nonviolent offenders.

There are now five basic mechanisms for people to be released from prison: (1) discretionary release, (2) mandatory release, (3) probation release, (4) other

FIGURE 16.1 METHODS OF RELEASE FROM STATE PRISON

Felons are released from prison to the community, usually under parole supervision, through various means depending on the law.

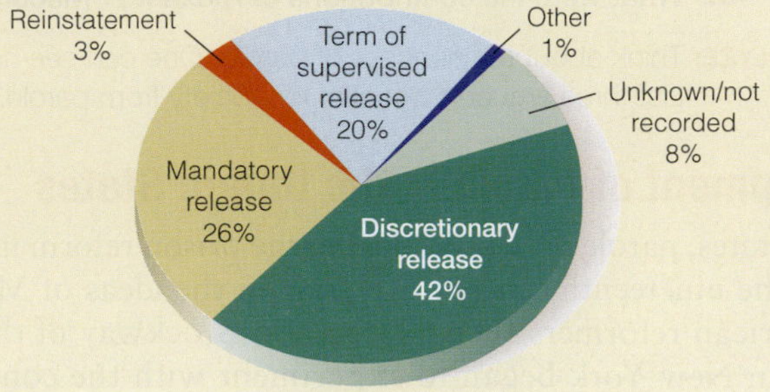

Source: Erinn J. Herberman and Thomas P. Bonczar, "Probation and Parole in the United States, 2013." Bureau of Justice Statistics *Bulletin,* October 2014.

conditional release, and (5) expiration release. Figure 16.1 shows the percentage of felons released by the various mechanisms.

Discretionary Release

discretionary release
The release of an inmate from prison to conditional supervision at the discretion of the parole board, within the boundaries set by the sentence and the penal law.

States retaining indeterminate sentences allow **discretionary release** by the parole board within the boundaries set by the sentence and the penal law. As a conditional release to parole supervision, this approach lets the parole board assess the prisoner's readiness for release within the minimum and maximum terms of the sentence. In reviewing the prisoner's file and asking questions, the parole board focuses on the nature of the offense, the inmate's behavior, and his or her participation in rehabilitation programs. This process places great faith in the ability of parole board members to predict the future behavior of offenders.

Currently, some states are looking to increase discretionary releases as a means to cut budgets by reducing prison populations. The website of the Michigan Department of Corrections, for example, shows that parole approval rates for parole-eligible violent offenders (excluding sex offenders) ranged from 34 percent to 39 percent during the period of 2002 to 2007. The approval rate jumped to 43 percent in 2008 and then above 56 percent for 2009 and 2010 and above 65 percent in 2011, 2012, and 2013, a period when the state was hammered by unemployment and a loss of tax revenue as it suffered some of the nation's worst consequences from the financial crisis of the recession. Did the offenders themselves become much better behaved and rehabilitated so quickly? No. The state made a policy decision that its use of long sentences and a high incarceration rate were excessively expensive and it needed to save money by reducing the prison population and closing some prisons. Increased use of discretionary release on parole was one method to advance this goal.

Mandatory Release

mandatory release
The required release of an inmate from incarceration to community supervision upon the expiration of a certain period, as specified by a determinate-sentencing law or parole guidelines.

Mandatory release occurs after an inmate has served time equal to the total sentence minus good time, if any, or to a certain percentage of the total sentence as specified by law. Mandatory release is found in federal jurisdictions and states with determinate sentences and good-time provisions (see Chapter 12). Without a parole board to make discretionary decisions, mandatory release is a matter of bookkeeping to check the correct amount of good time and other credits and to make sure the sentence has been accurately interpreted. The prisoner is conditionally released to parole supervision for the rest of the sentence. Prior to recent court orders mandating a reduction in the population of its prisons, in California, only prisoners serving life sentences with parole eligibility went through the discretionary release process of parole. All other prisoners—except those on death row or serving life without parole—received mandatory release to parole after serving their determinate sentences.

Probation Release

Probation release occurs when a sentencing judge requires a period of postcustody supervision in the community. Probation release is often tied to shock incarceration, a practice in which first-time offenders are sentenced to a short period in jail ("the shock") and then allowed to reenter the community under supervision. Since 2000, releases to probation have increased from 6 percent to 10 percent.

probation release
The release of an inmate from incarceration to probation supervision, as required by the sentencing judge.

Other Conditional Release

Because of the growth of prison populations, many states have devised ways to get around the rigidity of mandatory release. They place inmates in the community through furloughs, home supervision, halfway houses, emergency release, and other programs (Travis and Lawrence, 2002; Griset, 1995: 307). These types of **other conditional release** also avoid the appearance of the politically sensitive label "discretionary parole."

other conditional release
A term used in some states to avoid the rigidity of mandatory release by placing convicts under supervision in various community settings.

Circumstances may also arise in which prison officials use their discretion to release offenders early instead of going through the usual parole process. In order to close a budget deficit in 2002, Montana corrections officials released nonviolent offenders early from prison and placed them under the supervision of community corrections authorities. An important study of the results of that release showed that those offenders who received this conditional release from prison, instead of going through the usual parole decision process, had higher levels of recidivism (K. Wright and Rosky, 2011). As in other states, a significant portion of admissions to prison can be composed of offenders returning to prison for violating conditions of release or for committing new crimes while under the supervision of community corrections. According to Wright and Rosky, "Montana, in particular, experienced a significant increase in the annual 3-year recidivism rate as a result of the early release program" (901). Thus, when undertaking conditional releases, states need to be aware of preparing prisoners for release and the supervision capabilities of community corrections officials. Otherwise they may end up returning offenders to the expensive environment of imprisonment and thereby undercut the intended financial benefits of reducing prison populations through this mechanism.

The situation faced by Montana illustrates the larger debates about the choices facing states, just as it reflected specific debates within the state of Montana itself. As the authors of the study observed, "Not surprisingly, a public battle among the [Montana Department of Corrections] and legislators, judges, and prosecutors ensued over the appropriateness of the early release program in Montana" (K. Wright and Rosky, 2011: 887). Although there has been a growing consensus among liberal and conservative politicians about rethinking the costs of using incarceration to punish nonviolent offenders (Viguerie, 2013; C. Savage, 2011c), there are debates about the wisdom of releasing prisoners as opposed to a more gradual approach of simply changing sentencing policies as they affect certain offenders ("Our View," 2011; Mauer, 2011).

Litigation can also create pressure to reduce prison populations through releases outside the usual parole process if overcrowding causes constitutional violations. In the provisions of the Prison Litigation Reform Act of 1996, Congress had attempted to limit the ability of judges to order the release of prisoners by mandating that any such decisions be made by three-judge panels rather than by a single judge. However, as the Supreme Court decided with respect to overcrowding and the lack of medical services in California's prisons in *Brown v. Plata* (2011), circumstances can arise in which states may be forced to quickly and creatively find ways reduce prison populations. Because most states are presently seeking ways to save money by reducing the numbers in prison, the prospect for more litigation affecting releases seems unlikely during the current era.

Many states have programs that permit offenders to participate in work release. They work at jobs in the community while living in a lower-security correctional setting, such as a halfway house. These programs ease reentry into the community. Should the government assist offenders in finding jobs?

AP Images/Journal Times, Mark Hertzberg

expiration release
The release of an inmate from incarceration, without any further correctional supervision; the inmate cannot be returned to prison for any remaining portion of the sentence for the current offense.

Expiration Release

An increasing percentage of prisoners receive an **expiration release**. These inmates are released from any further correctional supervision and cannot be returned to prison for their current offense. Such offenders have served the maximum court sentence, minus good time—they have "maxed out."

✓POINT 4. How do discretionary release, mandatory release, other conditional release, and expiration release differ?

STOP AND ANALYZE: What are the advantages and disadvantages of mandatory release at the completion of a sentence rather than a discretionary parole-board decision? List two benefits and two arguable risks or disadvantages of that policy.

The Parole Board Process

State parole boards are typically composed of citizens who are appointed by the governor for fixed terms. For example, the Vermont Parole Board consists of five regular members and two alternates who are appointed for three-year terms by the governor. The Texas Board of Pardons and Paroles consists of seven members appointed by the governor for renewable six-year terms. The people on the Texas board include a former city attorney, a former county attorney, a former juvenile probation officer, a former county sheriff, an individual with experience in business and government, a former military officer, and an individual with experience in education and criminal justice—who is also the spouse of a former top official in the Texas corrections system (Texas Board of Pardons and Paroles, 2014 [www.tdcj.state.tx.us/bpp/brd_members/brd_members.html]; Jennings, 2007). Obviously, the members bring with them values, perspectives, and experiences that inform their judgments about whether offenders should be released on parole. It is possible that the appointment of board members with prior experiences as law enforcement officers, prosecutors, and other connections to the criminal justice system may be intended to include in parole decision making varied perspectives that contain caution and skepticism toward prisoners' claims about having changed themselves. The Texas structure also includes 11 commissioners, all of whom are experienced criminal justice professionals, who join with the parole board members in making decisions about parole.

Parole boards are often described as if the governor's appointees sit together as they question and listen to the parole-eligible prisoner and hear arguments from the prisoner's attorney. In fact, there are differences among the parole processes in various states. For example, parole-eligible prisoners in California, all of whom are serving life sentences, have attorneys at parole hearings, either one whom they hire or one who is appointed for them. In other states, the parole board members interview the prisoner. Elsewhere, the parole board may simply review the written file on the prisoner's progress in prison. There is no single model for what "the parole board process" looks like.

As indicated by the great increase in prison populations in the last few decades, large numbers of prisoners become parole eligible each year—too many to have hearings in front of a state's full parole board. Thus parole processes involve hearings or interviews conducted by only a portion of a parole board, often with other members of the board making decisions based on the report written by their colleague. In some circumstances, if a panel of a board is divided on a decision, the full board may examine the records in the case and make a decision.

In California, for example, each parole hearing is conducted by a 2-member panel. At least 1 of the 2 members is a "commissioner," the title used in that state for the 12 parole board members appointed by the governor. The other member is either a second commissioner or a "deputy commissioner," a state employee who works in the parole process. Immediately after the hearing, the two decision makers leave the hearing room and make a determination. If they disagree about whether to recommend parole, then there will be a second hearing in front of the full 12-member California Board of Parole Hearings. After a unanimous decision by the two-member panel or a vote by the full board, the decision goes to the staff of the board to make sure that there were no errors of law or fact in the process. The decision is then submitted to the governor who can approve the parole, add a condition to the parole release, refer a panel decision to the full board, or in cases of convicted murderers, reverse the decision to grant parole (California Department of Corrections and Rehabilitation, 2014 [www.cdcr.ca.gov/BOPH/lifer_parole_process.html]).

By using only a portion of the parole board for interviews and hearings, states can conduct many interviews and hearings simultaneously. This is the only way that they can handle a large volume of cases. Texas uses a different procedure to handle its 77,619 prisoners who were considered for parole in 2013. The Texas Board of Pardons and Paroles operates out of six different offices around the state, each with three-member panels composed of one board member and two "commissioners." For each parole-eligible prisoner, one member of the panel interviews the prisoner and writes a report while the other two members review that report and the prisoner's written file. If two of the three members approve, then the prisoner gains release under parole supervision (Texas Board of Pardons and Paroles, 2014).

Even small states divide their parole boards for hearings. In Wyoming, the least populous state in the country, a seven-member board sits in three-member hearing panels and conducts some hearings by telephone and video conference (Wyoming Board of Parole, 2013). In Vermont, another of the least populous states, hearings and interviews are conducted by at least three of the parole board's five members and two alternates (Vermont Parole Board, 2015 [http://doc.vermont.gov/about/parole-board]).

Parole board hearings and interviews are much less formal than court proceedings. Board members want the opportunity to ask prisoners about their crimes, their remorse, their attitudes, their disciplinary records and programs in prison, and their concrete plans for where they will live and work if they are granted parole. Prisoners are typically nervous because they do not know exactly what will be asked. They may quickly discover that the board members seem very skeptical about what they say. They may also find that board members lecture them about what they have done wrong in life and issue stern warnings to them about what will happen if they are released and then violate conditions of parole. Because back-to-back interviews or hearings must be scheduled with numerous parole-eligible prisoners on any given day, each individual prisoner may leave the brief encounter feeling very dissatisfied and disappointed, as if he or she did not have a full opportunity to explain how much change has occurred in attitude and behavior since entering prison. When a prisoner feels as if there was not a complete opportunity to make a good, persuasive presentation about being reformed, there is likely to be great anxiety about whether the long-awaited opportunity to speak to a parole board member or panel will actually lead to release.

Crime victims have become much more important participants in the parole decision process in recent decades. Many states have victims' rights laws that require officials to keep victims informed of offenders' upcoming parole consideration and to invite victims to provide input in the process. In California,

CLOSE UP

A PERSONAL ENCOUNTER WITH THE PAROLE PROCESS IN MICHIGAN

[Note: *Dr. Christopher Smith, one of the coauthors of this book, served as the "representative" for Christopher Jones (whose story of arrest and imprisonment appears in Chapter 3) at the parole board interview that ultimately led to Jones's release on parole. This is a first-person account of that process.*]

I agreed to serve as the "representative" for Christopher Jones at his parole interview because I had known him and his family since he was a teenager. As an outside observer, I had seen his self-destruction through drugs and theft crimes, as well as his gradual self-rehabilitation, as I corresponded with him and occasionally visited him during his ten years behind bars. Moreover, I was grateful for his eagerness to present his story in this book so that college students could learn about the justice process through his mistakes and experiences. In Michigan, a parole interview representative is typically a family member or someone else who can vouch for the prisoner's progress and good qualities. In speaking with a former parole board member prior to the interview, I knew that prisoners often had their mothers appear as their representatives. However, this was often counterproductive, because mothers too often made excuses for their children or displayed emotion instead of providing information useful in the parole decision. Although I am trained as a lawyer, Michigan prisoners are not represented by lawyers to argue on their behalf (unlike in California parole hearings); here, the parole candidate is allowed only one representative present to provide personal endorsement and information.

After spending nearly an hour in the prison's visitor waiting room, I was searched and led through several sets of locked doors to a small office. Outside the office, I came upon a dozen or more prisoners fidgeting nervously in a long line of chairs as they waited to be called one-by-one into the interview room. Mr. Jones was in the first chair. He rose to greet me and we were immediately ushered into the office together.

I had driven nearly 250 miles from Lansing, located in the middle of Michigan's Lower Peninsula, to a low-security prison in the Upper Peninsula to be present for the interview. Ironically, the interview was conducted via video conference by one of the ten members of the Michigan's parole board who was physically back in Lansing—the very place I had left the day before and to which I would return later that day. We saw him live on a television screen via a video feed from the prison up north, while he saw us on a screen in his office in Lansing. Video technology permits Michigan to save a substantial amount of money, which previously would have been spent for the parole board members to travel to prisons throughout the state to conduct interviews.

After Mr. Jones introduced me as his representative, the parole board member introduced himself and informed me that he had many questions for Mr. Jones and that I should refrain from speaking until questions were directed to me. The parole board member noted that Mr. Jones had participated in many prison programs and that the file contained an impressive number of letters of support from family members and a minister. The board member asked Mr. Jones about his plan to live with his parents and work for his father's home inspection business. Mr. Jones was asked about how he had changed from when he committed his crimes. The board member pressed Mr. Jones about how he would respond to the availability of drugs and alcohol if he was on parole back in his hometown. Predictably, Mr. Jones, who crime victims and their families are invited to parole hearings where they are permitted to speak, or they can bring a representative to speak for them about the impact of the crime and their concerns about the offender being granted parole. Alternatively, they can submit written statements or audio or video statements for consideration by the board members. At the hearing, the victim is accompanied by a Victim Services Representative from the state's Office of Victim and Survivor Rights and Services. A prosecutor also attends the hearing and may speak about the offender who is being considered for parole. In addition, news reporters may be permitted to attend California parole hearings (California Department of Corrections and Rehabilitation, 2010).

In Wyoming, crime victims are invited to meet with the parole board separately from the prisoner's hearing. Similarly, in Vermont the victim can testify prior to the scheduled appearance of the prisoner before the board. In both of these states, the interviews or hearings are held in private, and the policies about victims' participation are designed to prevent the victim from having a face-to-face encounter with the offender. By contrast, Connecticut is more like California in that the victim is invited to speak at hearings that, though not open to the public, are more available to the public in the sense that they can be recorded and broadcast on public television, just as hearings in California may be covered by the news media in some cases. In all of these states, victims have the option of submitting written statements to be added to the file that is reviewed by the board members. Read the Close Up feature for a personal account of the parole process in Michigan.

had spent years looking forward to the chance to have a parole interview, provided reassuring responses and pledged to stay away from the people, places, and substances that had been his downfall in the past. The board member spoke sternly to him about the consequences of violating the conditions of parole or committing new crimes. During this lecture, Mr. Jones nodded his head and repeatedly said, "Yes, sir, yes, sir."

Throughout the interview with Mr. Jones, I restrained myself from speaking even as I thought of many helpful things that I could say. I kept quiet, however, and then the board member turned to me to ask what I had to add as information for the board's consideration. I gave a brief endorsement of the changes that I had observed over the years Mr. Jones had been in prison and described his participation in education and substance abuse recovery programs. And then the interview was over. It was obvious that the board member had many other interviews that he needed to conduct, so he could not spend more than 15 minutes or so on any individual interview.

I came away from the brief experience without any strong sense about what the decision would be. The interview seemed to go as well as it could have, but it was so short that there was not much information exchanged. Moreover, I wondered whether a parole board member could really trust reassurances from a parole-eligible prisoner, especially a former drug user, when the board member obviously knew that a notable percentage of such offenders return to drugs, violate parole conditions, or commit new crimes once they are back in the community. Obviously, the most significant information for the decision came from the reports and prison disciplinary records in the file. The quick interview gave the board member an opportunity to gain a brief impression of the prisoner's attitude and demeanor. Moreover, it was an opportunity to issue stern warnings to the prisoner about returning to prison for any failure to behave properly on parole. The release decision hinged on this board member's subsequent report and recommendation, which would be significant factors in determining whether at least two of the three board members (including himself) assigned to the case would vote to grant parole.

Ultimately, the parole decision is shaped by impressions and judgments, not just those of the board members, but also those of the prison counselors who write evaluative reports for the file and thereby shape the impressions of the board members. No one can make an absolutely certain prediction about whether a specific prisoner will commit future violations or crimes on parole—not even the prisoner himself. The prisoner may feel determined to succeed, but he does not yet know the practical challenges of parole that await, such as being offered drugs, feeling frustrated by unemployment, or having conflicts with friends and family who have become, in some sense, strangers after years of separation.

DEBATE THE ISSUE

Does this parole interview process, as described, provide enough information to make a decision about whether or not to grant parole? Should the process be changed in any way? Provide three arguments either supporting the interview process as adequate, or supporting specific changes in the process.

CIVIC ENGAGEMENT

YOUR ROLE IN THE SYSTEM

Imagine that the governor has appointed you to serve for a four-year term on your state's parole board. *Make a list of factors that you would consider about an offender in deciding whether to recommend release on parole.* Then look at the website of the Montana Board of Pardons and Parole, a body composed of citizens appointed by the governor, and see the factors that they are supposed to consider.

Impact of Release Mechanisms

Parole release mechanisms do more than simply determine the date at which a particular prisoner will be sent back into the community. Parole release also has an enormous impact on other parts of the system, including sentencing, plea bargaining, and the size of prison populations.

One important effect of discretionary release is that an administrative body—the parole board—can shorten a sentence imposed by a judge. Even in states that have mandatory release, various potential reductions built into the sentence mean that the full sentence is rarely served. Good time, for example, can reduce punishment even if there is no parole eligibility. Consider the role of citizens from the community who serve on parole boards in many states as you read "Civic Engagement: Your Role in the System."

To understand the impact of release mechanisms on criminal punishment, we must compare the amount of time actually served in prison with the sentence specified by the judge. In some jurisdictions, up to 60 percent of felons sentenced to prison are released to the community after their first appearance before a parole board. Eligibility for discretionary release is ordinarily determined by the minimum term of the sentence minus good time and jail time.

Although the statistics vary considerably from state to state, on a national basis felony inmates serve an average of two years and three months before release. Some offenders who receive long sentences actually serve a smaller proportion of such sentences than do offenders given shorter sentences. For example, the average robbery offender is given a term of 91 months and serves 58 percent of the term before being released after 53 months. By contrast, the average aggravated assault offender is given a term of 54 months but serves 66 percent of the term, 36 months. Figure 16.2 shows the average time served and the percentage of the sentence for selected offenses.

Supporters of discretion for the paroling authority argue that parole benefits the overall system. Discretionary release mitigates the harshness of the penal code. If the legislature must establish exceptionally strict punishments as a means of conveying a "tough on crime" image to frustrated and angry voters, parole can effectively permit sentence adjustments that make the punishment fit the crime. Everyone convicted of larceny may not have done equivalent harm, yet some legislatively mandated sentencing rules may impose equally strict sentences. Early release on parole can be granted to an offender who is less deserving of strict punishment, such as someone who voluntarily makes restitution, cooperates with the police, or shows genuine regret. Discretionary release is also an important tool for reducing prison populations in states with overcrowded prisons and budget deficits.

A major criticism of discretionary release is that it shifts responsibility for many primary criminal justice decisions from a judge, who holds legal procedures uppermost, to an administrative board, where discretion rules. Judges know a great deal about constitutional rights and basic legal protections, but parole board members may not have such knowledge. In most states with discretionary release, parole hearings are secret, with only board members, the inmate, and correctional officers present. Often no published criteria guide decisions, and prisoners are given no reason for denial or granting of parole.

Should society place such power in the hands of parole boards? Because there is so little oversight regarding their decision making and so few constraints on their decisions, some parole board members will make arbitrary or discriminatory decisions that are inconsistent with the values underlying our constitutional system and civil rights. Generally, the U.S. legal system seeks to avoid determining people's fate through such methods.

FIGURE 16.2 ESTIMATED TIME TO BE SERVED BY ADULTS CONVICTED OF SELECTED CRIMES

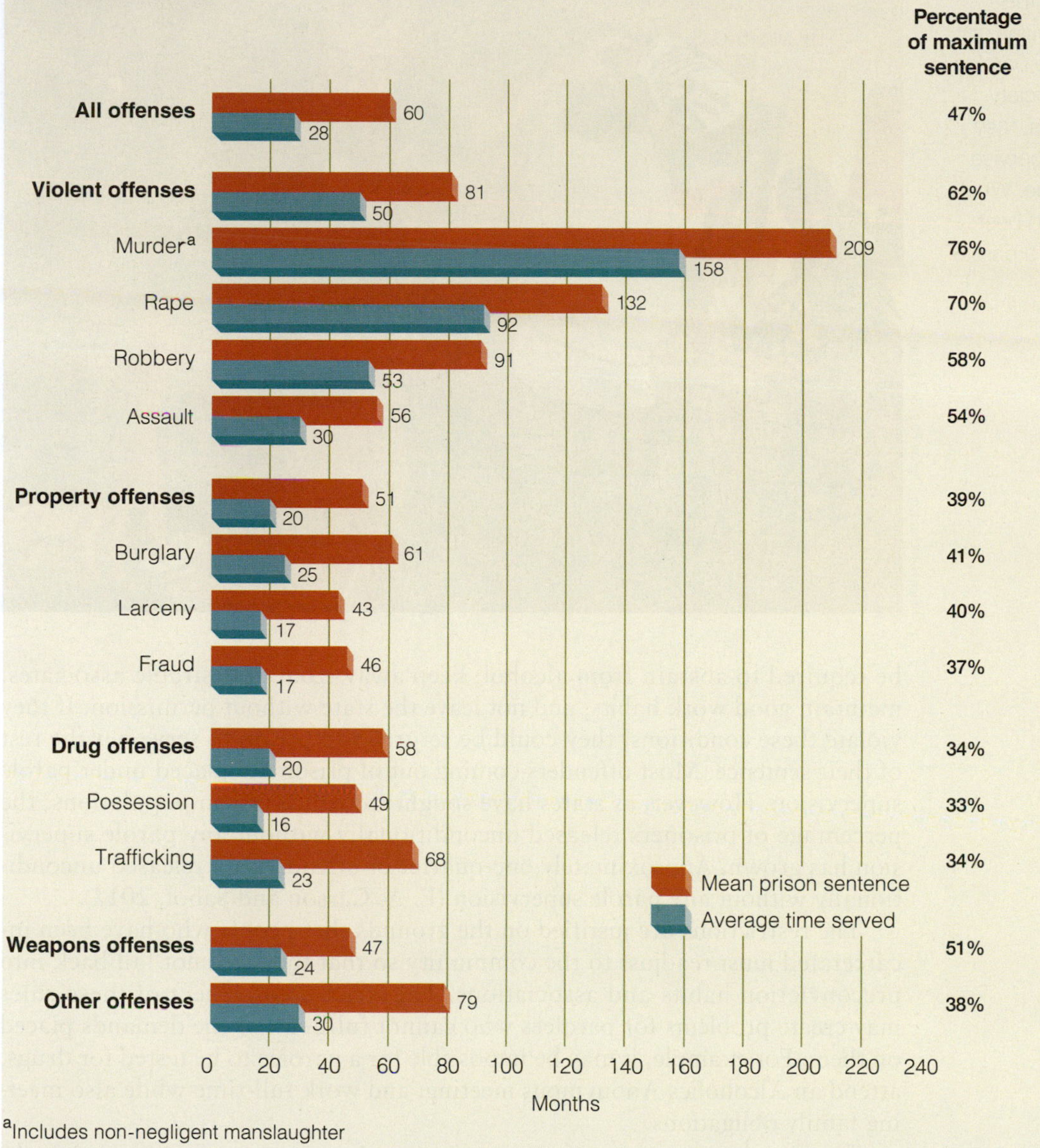

The data indicate that the average felony offender going to prison for the first time spends about two years in prison. How would you expect the public to react to that fact?

Source: Thomas P. Bonczar, *National Corrections Reporting Program: Statistical Tables,* May 5, 2011, Table 9 (www.bjs.gov/index.cfm?ty=pbdetail&iid=2174).

✔POINT
5. Who participates in the parole hearing process?
6. How does parole release influence the rest of the criminal justice system?

STOP AND ANALYZE: In light of the differences in parole and hearing processes used in various states, how do you see the importance (or lack thereof) of involvement by defense attorneys and crime victims? Do they provide helpful information about whether an offender is reformed enough for release? Provide two advantages and two risks that may arise from permitting attorneys to represent prisoners at parole hearings. Provide two advantages and two risks from permitting victims to provide input.

Parole Supervision in the Community

Parolees are released from prison on condition that they abide by laws and follow rules, known as **conditions of release**, designed to aid their readjustment to society and control their movement. As in probation, the parolee may

conditions of release
Conduct restrictions that parolees must follow as a legally binding requirement of being released.

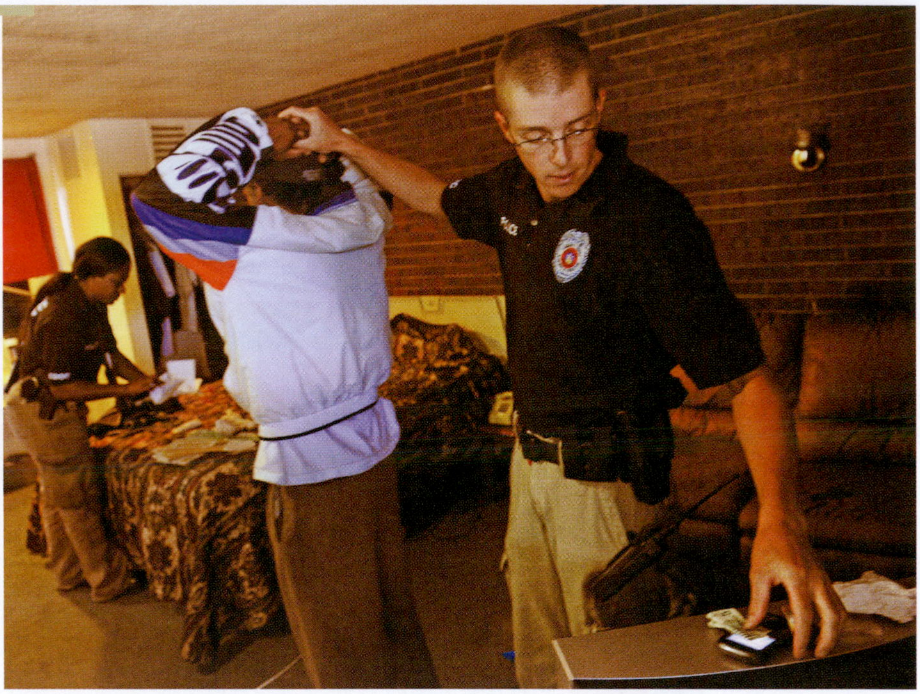

Helen H. Richardson/Denver Post/Getty Images

Parole officers have dual responsibilities for protecting the public from lawbreaking activities of parolees and also helping the parolee transition successfully into society. Depending on their caseloads, they may have limited ability to supervise or help each individual parolee. What training and experience would best prepare a person to become a parole officer?

be required to abstain from alcohol, keep away from undesirable associates, maintain good work habits, and not leave the state without permission. If they violate these conditions, they could be returned to prison to serve out the rest of their sentence. Most offenders coming out of prison are placed under parole supervision. However, as states have sought to reduce prison populations, the percentage of prisoners released unconditionally without any parole supervision has grown. Approximately one-quarter of offenders are released unconditionally without any parole supervision (E. A. Carson and Sabol, 2012).

The restrictions are justified on the grounds that people who have been incarcerated must readjust to the community so that they will not fall back into preconviction habits and associations. The strict enforcement of these rules may create problems for parolees who cannot fulfill all of the demands placed on them. For example, it may be impossible for a parolee to be tested for drugs, attend an Alcoholics Anonymous meeting, and work full-time while also meeting family obligations.

The day they come out of prison, parolees face a staggering array of problems. In most states, they are given only clothes, a token amount of money, a list of rules governing their conditional release, and the name and address of the parole officer to whom they must report within 24 hours. Although a promised job is often a condition for release, an actual job may be another matter. Most former convicts are unskilled or semiskilled, and the conditions of release may prevent them from moving to areas where they could find work. If the parolee is African American, male, and younger than 30, he belongs to the largest category of unemployed workers in the country. Figure 16.3 shows the characteristics of parolees.

Parolees have the added handicap of former convict status. In most states, laws prevent former prisoners from working in certain types of establishments—where alcohol is sold, for example—thus ruling out many jobs. In some states, the fact of having served time is seen as evidence of "a lack of good moral character and trustworthiness" required to obtain a license to be employed as a barber, for example. In many trades, workers must belong to a union, and unions often have restrictions on the admission of new members. Finally, many

FIGURE 16.3 PERSONAL CHARACTERISTICS OF PAROLEES

Prison releasees tend to be men in their thirties who have an inadequate education and were incarcerated for a nonviolent offense.

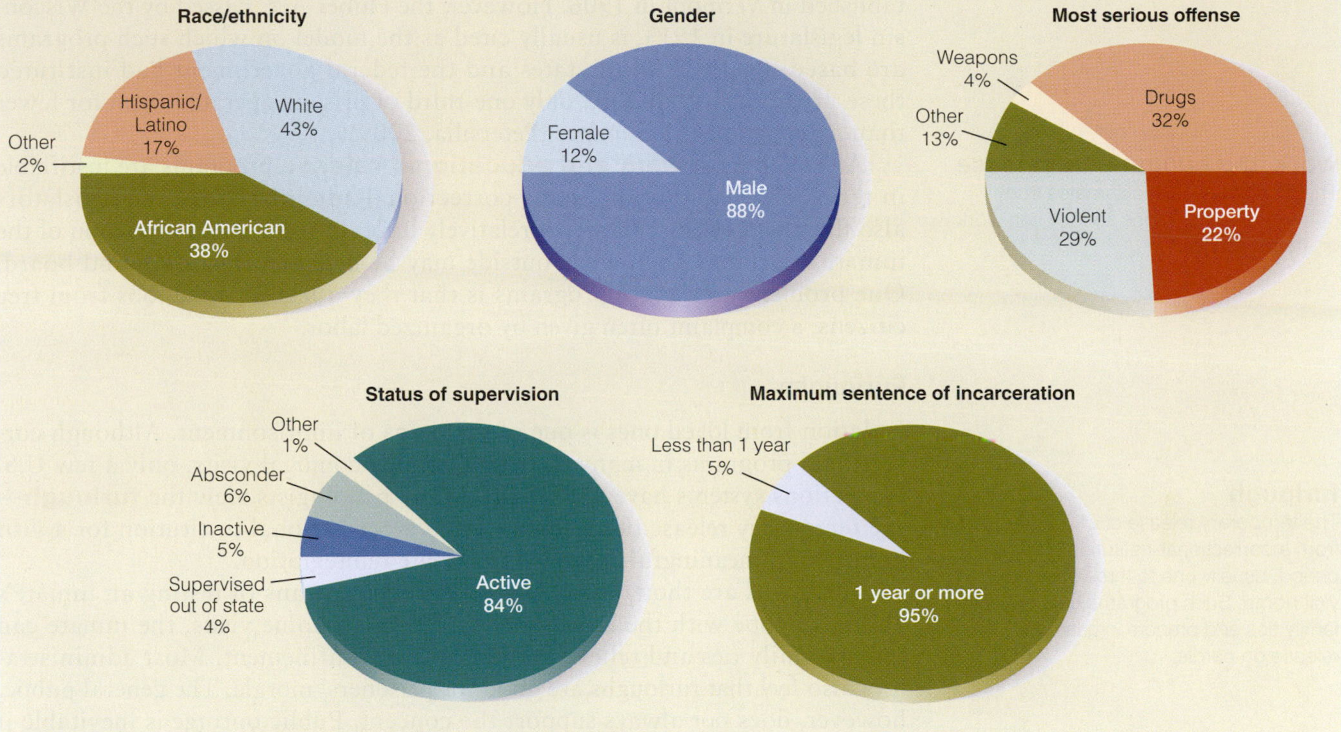

Note: Amounts may not add to 100% due to rounding.

Source: Erinn J. Herberman and Thomas P. Bonczar, "Probation and Parole in the United States, 2013," Bureau of Justice Statistics *Bulletin*, October 2014, NCJ 248029.

parolees, as well as other ex-convicts, face a significant dilemma. If they are truthful about their backgrounds, many employers will not hire them. If they are not truthful, they can be fired for lying if the employer ever learns about their conviction.

Other reentry problems plague parolees. For many, the transition from the highly structured life in prison to open society is too difficult to manage. Many just do not have the social, psychological, and material resources to cope with the temptations and complications of modern life. For these parolees, freedom may be short-lived as they fall back into forbidden activities such as drinking, using drugs, and stealing.

Community Programs Following Release

There are various programs to assist parolees. Some help prepare offenders for release while they are still in prison; others provide employment and housing assistance after release. Together, the programs are intended to help the offender progress steadily toward reintegration into the community. Experts agree that there should be pre- and post-release programs to assist reentry.

Among the many programs developed to help offenders return to the community, three are especially important: work and educational release, furloughs, and residential programs. Although similar in many ways, each offers a specific approach to helping formerly incarcerated individuals reenter the community.

Work and Educational Release

Programs of work and educational release, in which inmates are released from correctional institutions during the day to work or attend school, were first established in Vermont in 1906. However, the Huber Act, passed by the Wisconsin legislature in 1913, is usually cited as the model on which such programs are based. By 1972, most states and the federal government had instituted these programs, yet in 2002 only one-third of prisons operated them for fewer than 3 percent of U.S. inmates (Petersilia, 2009).

work and educational release
The daytime release of inmates from correctional institutions so they can work or attend school.

Although most **work and educational release** programs are justifiable in terms of rehabilitation, many correctional administrators and legislators also like them because they cost relatively little. In some states a portion of the inmate's earnings from work outside may be deducted for room and board. One problem with these programs is that they allegedly take jobs from free citizens, a complaint often given by organized labor.

Furloughs

Isolation from loved ones is one of the pains of imprisonment. Although correctional programs in many countries include conjugal visits, only a few U.S. corrections systems have used them. Many penologists view the **furlough**—the temporary release of an inmate from a correctional institution for a visit home—as a meaningful approach to inmate reintegration.

furlough
The temporary release of an inmate from a correctional institution for a brief period, usually one to three days, for a visit home. Such programs help maintain family ties and prepare inmates for release on parole.

Furloughs are thought to offer an excellent means of testing an inmate's ability to cope with the larger society. Through home visits, the inmate can renew family ties and relieve the tensions of confinement. Most administrators also feel that furloughs are good for prisoners' morale. The general public, however, does not always support the concept. Public outrage is inevitable if an offender on furlough commits another crime or fails to return. Correctional authorities are often nervous about using furloughs, because they fear being blamed for such incidents.

Halfway Houses

As its name implies, the **halfway house** is a transitional facility for soon-to-be-released inmates that connects them to community services, resources, and support. Usually, felons work in the community but reside in the halfway house during nonworking hours. Halfway houses range from secure institutions in the community, with programs designed to assist inmates who are preparing for release on parole, to group homes where parolees, probationers, or others diverted from the system live with minimal supervision and direction. Some halfway houses deliver special treatment services, such as programs designed to deal with alcohol, drug, or mental problems.

halfway house
A correctional facility housing convicted felons who spend a portion of their day at work in the community but reside in the halfway house during nonworking hours.

Residential programs have problems. Few neighborhoods want to host halfway houses or treatment centers for convicts. Community resistance has significantly impeded the development of community-based correctional facilities and even has forced some successful facilities to close. Many communities, often wealthier ones, have blocked placement of halfway houses or treatment centers within their boundaries. One result of the NIMBY ("not in my backyard") attitude is that many centers are established in deteriorating neighborhoods inhabited by poor people, who lack the political power and resources to block unpopular programs. Think about this problem as you read "Civic Engagement: Your Role in the System" and "A Question of Ethics" at the end of the chapter.

A survey found a striking increase in the number of community-based residential corrections facilities. Such facilities were defined as those in which 50 percent or more of residents regularly leave unaccompanied for work or study in the community, thus including halfway houses and similar programs

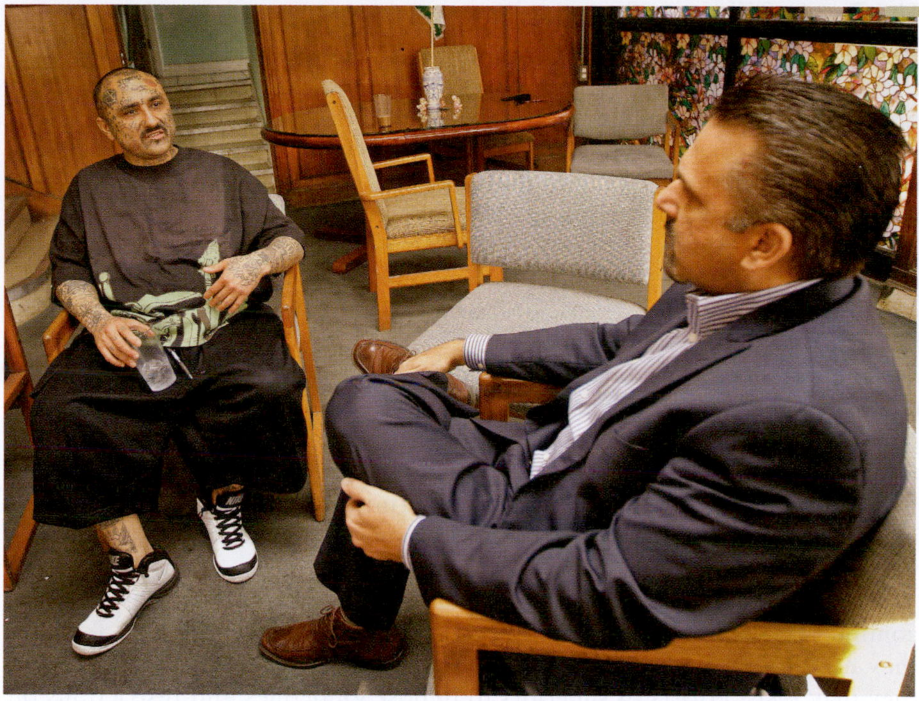

Tony Avelar/The Christian Science Monitor/Getty Images

Community-based corrections facilities, such as halfway houses, provide opportunities for offenders to gradually transition back into the community. How would you react if someone proposed placing a halfway house in your neighborhood? If you would oppose such a facility near your home, where do think such facilities should be located?

that provide substance abuse treatment. What was most notable about the survey was the decrease in the number of public facilities from 297 to 221 between 2000 and 2005 at the same time that private facilities increased from 163 to 308 (J. J. Stephan, 2008). These private facilities undoubtedly rely on contracts from state governments to provide services that the state believes are less expensive in the private sector. The interesting question for contemporary times is whether, in an atmosphere of budget cuts, state governments will find money for the use of such facilities to assist in the reentry of prisoners. Budget reductions may eliminate the availability of funds for outside contracts but, alternatively, depending on the calculations of key decision makers in government, such cuts may instead lead to reliance on private facilities if their use is viewed as a means of saving money (S. Davis, 2012).

CIVIC ENGAGEMENT

YOUR ROLE IN THE SYSTEM

Imagine that the state proposes to purchase a house in your neighborhood to use as a halfway house for sex offenders on parole as they reenter the community. *Make a list of arguments that you would make either for or against the creation of this halfway house.* Then look at one Connecticut community's experience with this issue.

CHECKPOINT **7.** What are three programs designed to ease the reentry of offenders into the community?

STOP AND ANALYZE: Work release programs are not used very often in the United States. Imagine that it is your job to find the job placements for a work release program for prisoners who are preparing to leave prison. How would you explain the benefits of the program to potential employers? List three points that you would make.

Parole Officer: Cop or Social Worker?

After release, a parolee's principal contact with the criminal justice system is through the parole officer, who has the dual responsibility of providing surveillance and assistance. Thus, parole officers are asked to play two different, some might say incompatible, roles: cop and social worker. Whereas parole was originally designed to help offenders make the transition from prison to the community, supervision has shifted ever more toward surveillance, drug testing, monitoring curfews, and collecting restitution. Community safety and security have become major issues in parole services.

The Parole Officer as Cop

In their role as cop, parole officers have the power to restrict many aspects of the parolee's life, to enforce the conditions of release, and to initiate revocation proceedings if parole conditions are violated. Like other officials in the criminal justice system, the parole officer has extensive discretion in low-visibility situations. In many states, parole officers have the authority to search the parolee's house without warning, to arrest him or her without the possibility of bail for suspected violations, and to suspend parole pending a hearing before the board. This authoritarian component of the parole officer's role can give the ex-offender a sense of insecurity and hamper the development of mutual trust.

The parole officer is responsible for seeing that the parolee follows the conditions imposed by the parole board. Typically the conditions require the parolee to: follow the parole officer's instructions; permit the officer to visit the home and place of employment; maintain employment; not leave the state without permission; not marry without permission; not own a firearm; not possess, use, or traffic in narcotics; not consume alcohol to excess; and comply with all laws and be a good citizen.

Parole officers are granted law enforcement powers so as to protect the community from offenders who are coming out of prison. Officers feel that they need discretionary authority to take actions to protect the public, and they may resist efforts of superiors to impose guidelines and restrictions on their discretion (Steiner, Travis, and Markarios, 2011). However, because these powers diminish the possibility for the officer to develop a close relationship with the client, they can weaken the officer's other role of assisting the parolee's readjustment to the community. News stories and lawsuits periodically highlight cases in which parole officers forcefully invade homes, point guns at family members, and damage property as they investigate possible parole violations. The issue of officers potentially going too far in exercising their powers looms large because of impacts on the rights of family members with whom the parolee is residing.

The Parole Officer as Social Worker

Parole officers must act as social workers by helping the parolee find a job and restore family ties. Officers channel parolees to social agencies, such as psychiatric, drug, and alcohol clinics, where they can obtain support services. As caseworkers, officers work to develop a relationship that allows parolees to confide their frustrations and concerns.

Because parolees are not likely to do this if they are constantly aware of the parole officer's ability to send them back to prison, some researchers have suggested that parole officers' conflicting responsibilities of cop and social worker should be separated. Parole officers could maintain the supervisory aspects of the position, and other personnel—perhaps a separate parole counselor—could perform the casework functions. Another option would be for parole officers to be charged solely with social work duties, and local police could check for parole violations.

The Parole Bureaucracy

Although parole officers have smaller caseloads than do probation officers, parolees require more-extensive services. One reason is that parolees, by the very fact of their incarceration, have generally committed much more serious crimes. Another reason is that parolees must make a difficult transition from the highly structured prison environment to a society in which they have previously failed to live as law-abiding citizens. It is exceptionally difficult for a parole officer to monitor, control, and assist clients who may have little knowledge of or experience with living successfully within society's rules.

The parole officer works within a bureaucratic environment. Like most other human services organizations, parole agencies are short on resources and expertise. Because the difficulties faced by many parolees are so complex, the officer's job is almost impossible. As a result, parole officers frequently must classify parolees and give priority to those most in need. For example, most parole officers spend extra time with the newly released. As the officer gains greater confidence in the parolee, the level of supervision can be adjusted to "active" or "reduced" surveillance. Depending on how the parolee has functioned in the community, he or she may eventually be allowed to check in with the officer periodically instead of submitting to regular home visits, searches, and other intrusive monitoring. Technology can help parole officers track offenders—read the Technology and Criminal Justice feature to learn about the pros and cons of GPS technology in monitoring recent prison releasees.

✔POINT **8.** What are some of the rules most parolees must follow while under supervision in the community?
9. What are the major tasks of parole officers?

STOP AND ANALYZE: The dual roles of "cop" and "social worker" can sometimes counter each other. Provide two reasons why parole officers should probably *not* take on one or the other of these roles.

Adjustments to Life Outside Prison

General Adjustments

With little preparation, the ex-offender moves from the highly structured, authoritarian life of the institution into a world that is filled with temptations and complicated problems. Suddenly, ex-convicts who are unaccustomed to undertaking even simple tasks such as going to the store for groceries are expected to assume pressing, complex responsibilities. Finding a job and a place to live are not the only problems the newly released person faces (Arditti and Parkman, 2011). Parolees no longer receive medical care from the government (Sung, Mahoney, and Mellow, 2011). They must handle their own transportation needs for seeking employment, going to work, and meeting with parole officers. The parolee must also make significant social and psychological role adjustments. A male ex-convict, for example, is suddenly required to become not only a parolee but also an employee, a neighbor, a father, a husband, and a son. Women on parole face parallel issues and, as the primary parent prior to incarceration in many situations, they may face extra challenges in reestablishing relationships with children and the capacity to resume parenting. The expectations, norms, and social relations in the free world are very different from those learned in prison. The relatively predictable inmate code is replaced by society's often unclear rules of behavior—rules that the offender had failed to cope with during his or her previous life in free society.

Today's parolees face even greater obstacles in living a crime-free life than did parolees released prior to 1990. Since that time, Congress and many state legislatures have imposed new restrictions on ex-felons. These include denial of many social supports for those convicted of even minor drug crimes: welfare benefits such as food stamps, access to public housing, receipt of student

TECHNOLOGY & CRIMINAL JUSTICE

USING GPS TO TRACK PAROLEES

A number of different technologies have been used to track parolees, most frequently systems using GPS (global positioning systems). With this technology, parole officers can follow the geographic location of parolees, and ensure they avoid areas where they are forbidden to be. This technology can also be used to determine that the parolees are indeed at work, at school, at home, or wherever they are supposed to be.

Although useful, this technology is not perfect. Offenders have been able to remove their GPS "bracelets" and evade tracking. In one high-profile case, a California sex offender under surveillance kidnapped a teenager in 1991. Philip Garrido held the victim hostage in his home for 18 years, even fathering two children with her during her captivity. Even though Garrido had a history of prior sexual violence, he was classified in the "lower risk" monitoring system and frequently traveled farther than his parole allowed, with no follow-up from corrections officials. His "passive" GPS system did not automatically report his location to officials, unlike the "active" systems used for higher-risk parolees. Parole officers were also accused of ignoring over 276 reports of signal loss from his device (Farrell, 2009). His victim later sued the United States government for failing to monitor his whereabouts during her captivity (Berg, 2011).

In 2013, California ordered one company's devices to be removed from all of its nearly 8,000 high-risk parolees, primarily sex offenders and gang members. Those devices were replaced with another manufacturer's GPS device. A study had found that

> Batteries died early, cases cracked, reported locations were off by as much as three miles. Officials also found that tampering alerts failed and offenders were able to disappear by covering the devices with foil, deploying illegal GPS jammers, or ducking into cars or buildings. (St. John, 2013)

Such problems with technology threaten public safety, especially in cases when officials have no idea that a device has been removed or stopped working. The California example demonstrates the need for officials to continually test devices and consider whether alternative hardware would be more reliable or effective.

loans, and, in some states, voting rights. Studies have found that returning inmates often face so many restrictions after long periods of incarceration that the conditions amount to more years of "invisible punishment" (Mauer and Chesney-Lind, 2002: 1). As emphasized by Jeremy Travis (2002), the effects of these policies impact not only the individual parolee, but also their families and communities.

✔POINT 10. What are some of the major problems faced by parolees?

STOP AND ANALYZE: Imagine that you were in prison for several years and then gained release on parole. What kind of job would you seek? Where would you live? Make a list of specific obstacles that you would face—in light of your education and family situation. Make a list of specific assets or advantages, if any, that you would have—also taking into account your own education, family situation, and network of friends. Would you be better off, worse off, or no differently situated than most of today's parolees coming out of prison?

Public Opinion

News accounts of brutal crimes committed by ex-offenders on parole fuel a public perception that parolees are a threat to the community. The murder of 12-year-old Polly Klaas by a parolee in California and the rape and murder of 7-year-old Megan Kanka by a paroled sex offender in New Jersey spurred legislators in more than 35 states and the federal government to enact "sexual offender notification" laws. These laws require that the public be notified of the whereabouts of "potentially dangerous" sex offenders. In some states, paroled sex offenders must register with the police, whereas in others, the immediate neighbors must be informed. Many states now have publicly accessible

However, some states have determined that the use of GPS systems for high-risk sex offenders can both (1) reduce the recidivism of these offenders, and (2) help protect the public by allowing corrections officials to intercept offenders who violate conditions of parole. The state of New Jersey, for example, has determined that the recidivism rates for sex offenders in their GPS monitoring program is lower than the national rate of recidivism. In other cases, parolees wearing GPS devices have been placed at the scene of a crime. Based on data from a GPS monitoring system, police were able to charge Saquan Evans of Syracuse, New York, with homicide in the shooting death of a 20-month-old infant.

North Carolina mandates that certain sex offenders must wear GPS technology for life, which is currently under review by the North Carolina Supreme Court and may go to the Supreme Court of the United States. Torrey Grady has two convictions for sexual offenses, but has argued that wearing a GPS monitor for life is in violation of the Fourth Amendment's ban on unreasonable searches and seizures. The Courts will decide what the limits are on wearing this type of technology.

Sources: P. J. Barnes, *Report on New Jersey's GPS Monitoring of Sex Offenders,* New Jersey State Parole Board, December 5, 2007 (www.state.nj.us/parole/docs/reports/gps.pdf); Emmett Berg, "Jaycee Dugard Sues U.S. over Monitoring of Her Captor," Reuters, September 22, 2011 (www.reuters.com); P. Bulman, "Sex Offenders Monitored by GPS Found to Commit Fewer Crimes," *National Institute of Justice Journal* 271, NCJ 240700 (nij.gov/journals); M. B. Farrell, "Report: GPS Parole Monitoring of Phillip Garrido Failed," *Christian Science Monitor,* November 6, 2009 (www.csmonitor.com); L. Hurley, "U.S. Supreme Court Revives Sex Offender's Ankle Bracelet Case," Reuters, March 30, 2015 (reuters.com); J. O'Hara, "Accused Killer Linked to Child's Death by Eyewitness and Parole GPS," *Syracuse Post-Standard,* March 25, 2011 (www.syracuse.com); Paige St. John, "Tests Found Major Flaws in Parolee GPS Monitoring Devices," *Los Angeles Times,* March 30, 2013 (www.latimes.com).

DEBATE THE ISSUE

It is possible that officials will be tempted to release higher-risk offenders on parole based on a belief that GPS technology will permit close monitoring of these individuals. Do the costs saved by using GPS technology instead of imprisonment outweigh the risks of placing serious offenders in the community? Give two arguments on each side of this issue.

sex offender websites listing the names and addresses of those registered. Additional restrictions have been created by many states to limit where registered sex offenders can live, typically with limits on how close they may reside to schools and playgrounds. Some jurisdictions have become even more restrictive by banning registered sex offenders from beaches, playgrounds, and parks (Lovett, 2012).

These laws have had several consequences, some of them unintended. In some communities, there are so many schools, parks, and playgrounds spread around the town that there can be almost nowhere that a registered sex offender can legally live without violating laws concerning keeping a distance from forbidden locations. Thus some communities have dealt with issues of dozens of registered sex offenders sleeping under bridges or highway overpasses or concentrated together in the same rundown motels just outside of town. As a result, it becomes nearly impossible for these offenders to reintegrate successfully into society. In addition, many critics point to the fact that sex offender registration laws are often written broadly and thus apply to underage teenagers who had consensual sex or even people convicted of indecent exposure for public urination during one night of excessive drinking. The harsh restrictions on these offenders who fall under laws that many people envision as actually designed for violent predators have led to calls for more careful crafting of restrictions and requirements (Lancaster, 2011).

The most serious unintended consequences of these laws occur in incidents when parolees have been "hounded" from communities, their homes have been burned, and neighbors have threatened and assaulted parolees whom they erroneously thought were sex offenders. A worst-case scenario occurred in 2006 when two parolees in Maine were killed by a man intent on murdering registered sex offenders. One of those killed was on the list because at age 19 he had been convicted of having consensual sex with his underage girlfriend. His murder heightened debates about whether online registries create unnecessary risks of violence and include people convicted of behaviors that did not warrant lifetime registration and public notification (G. Adams, 2006).

Revocation of Parole

Always hanging over the ex-inmate's head is the potential revocation of parole for committing a new crime or violating the conditions of release. The public tends to view the high number of revocations as a failure of parole. Corrections officials point to the great number of parolees who are required to be drug-free, employed, and pay restitution—conditions that are difficult for many to fulfill.

Morrissey v. Brewer (1972)
Due process rights require a prompt, informal two-part inquiry before an impartial hearing officer prior to parole revocation. The parolee may present relevant information and confront witnesses.

As discussed in Chapter 13, the Supreme Court ruled in ***Morrissey v. Brewer* (1972)**, that if the parole officer alleges that a technical violation occurred, a two-step revocation proceeding is required. In the first stage a hearing determines whether there is probable cause to believe the conditions have been violated. The parolee has the right to be notified of the charges, to be informed of the evidence, to be heard, to present witnesses, and to confront the witnesses. In the second stage, the parole authority decides if the violation is severe enough to warrant return to prison.

A significant percentage of admissions to prison are parole violators returned to prison because of an arrest or violations of parole conditions. However, the percentage of violators returned to prison varies by state, accounting for a substantial percentage of prison admissions in Vermont (67 percent), Washington (55 percent), and Missouri (48 percent), but only small percentages in such states as Florida (0.3 percent), Virginia (1.2 percent), and North Carolina (4.4 percent). Clearly, states can take very different approaches to dealing with issues of parole violations (Carson and Sabol, 2012). In Michigan, for example, a special "Intensive Detention Reentry Program" rents space for 250 parole violators in two neighboring county jails where offenders are placed for periods of up to 120 days in response to parole violations or arrests for misdemeanors and non-assaultive felonies. The state department of corrections runs programs on behavior change and employment preparation for these offenders with the hope of avoiding the expense of sending them back to prison.

Officials, however, are considering policy alternatives that can deal with the reentry crisis, in which so many ex-prisoners are returned to prison because of new offenses or technical violations. One suggestion for dealing with this problem is the creation of "reentry courts," patterned after drug courts. States around the country have experimented with these courts for the past decade. Judges maintain active oversight of parolees whom they had originally sentenced. Parolees appear before the court on a regular basis so that the judge, together with the parole officer, can assess the ex-inmates' progress in following the parole conditions and adjusting to life in society. Other core elements of the reentry court include (1) the involvement of the judge and correctional officials in evaluating the needs of a prisoner prior to release and in building linkages to family, social services, housing, and work opportunities that would support reintegration; (2) the provision of supportive services such as substance abuse treatment, job training, and family assistance; and (3) a system of sanctions and rewards to encourage positive behavior. A recent evaluation of a reentry court in New York City showed that the program had positive effects for reducing rates of rearrests and reconvictions.

✔POINT

11. What are "sexual offender notification laws"?
12. What two conditions can result in the revocation of parole?
13. What does the U.S. Supreme Court require during the revocation process?

STOP AND ANALYZE: Should criminal justice officials be able to revoke parole without a hearing? Alternatively, should parolees be entitled to a full trial and representation by counsel before parole is revoked, because the revocation decision has such a huge impact on their personal liberty? Give three reasons for your responses to these two questions.

The Future of Prisoner Reentry

For most of the past four decades, parole has been under attack as a symbol of leniency whereby criminals are "let out" early. Public outrage is heightened when the media report the gruesome details of violent crimes committed by parolees. Such crimes in the past have led to calls by legislators for the abolition of parole. Many people argue that without parole, criminals would serve longer terms and there would be greater honesty in sentencing. As indicated in "What Americans Think," however, many Americans recognize that serving a prison sentence can be associated with subsequent lawbreaking when offenders leave prison and cannot fully rejoin society. It can also be in society's interest to think seriously about the issues of reentry and not just focus on the use of extended imprisonment to increase the severity of punishment. Thus there is an increasing recognition today of the value of programs and assistance to help offenders reenter society effectively. Moreover, budgetary problems have led states to recognize the desirability of reducing their expensive prison populations and seek to make more effective use of parole and other community sanctions.

Correctional experts argue that parole plays an important role in the criminal justice system, given that early release from prison must be earned. Discretionary release enables parole boards to individualize punishment, place offenders in treatment programs, and provide incentives for early release. Neither mandatory nor expiration release provides strong incentives for felons to prepare themselves to reenter the community, because the parole date is based solely on the sentence minus good time. Thus corrections officials must seek ways to create and operate reentry preparation programs for those whose release date is not based on good behavior in prison, and for future parolees who earn their early release through improved behavior.

The public typically believes that all offenders should serve their full sentences. The public does not always recognize the amount of money and number of facilities required to incarcerate all offenders for the complete terms of their sentences. Although many offenders are not successfully integrated into the community, most will end up back in free society whether or not they serve their full sentences. Parole and community programs represent an effort to address the inevitability of their return. Even if such programs do not prevent all offenders from leaving the life of crime, they do help some to turn their lives around. The ideas underlying the debates about parole may be reaching the public as many Americans recognize the need for reentry preparation as part of the corrections process. In fact, as shown in "What Americans Think," a large percentage of respondents in the survey believe that reentry planning should be a component of imprisonment from the very beginning of the sentence.

WHAT AMERICANS THINK

QUESTION: "Generally speaking, do you think that people who have served their time in prison for nonviolent offenses and are released back into society today are more likely, less likely, or about the same than they were before their imprisonment to commit future crimes?"

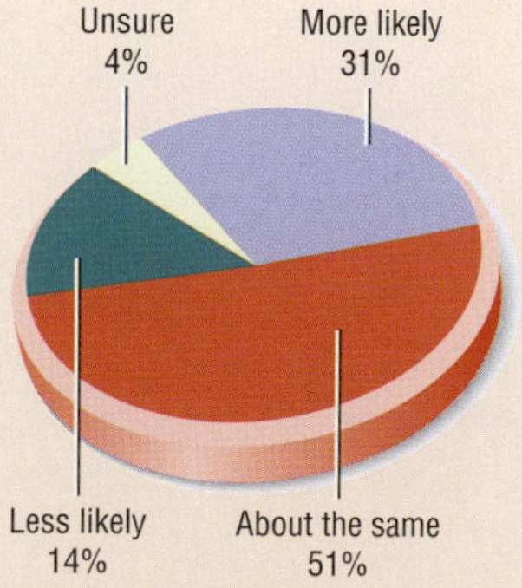

Source: Barry Krisberg and Susan Marchionna, "Attitudes of U.S. Voters toward Prisoners Rehabilitation and Reentry Policies." National Council on Crime and Delinquency, April 2006 (www.nccd-crc.org).

WHAT AMERICANS THINK

QUESTION: "When do you think planning for an incarcerated person's reentry into society should begin?"

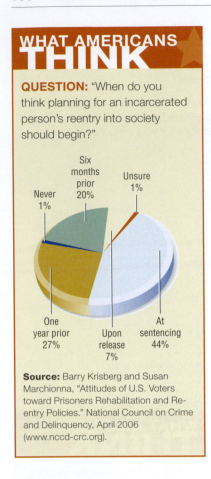

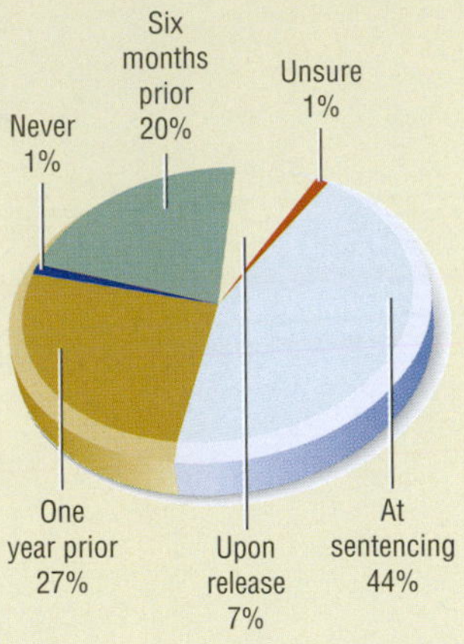

Source: Barry Krisberg and Susan Marchionna, "Attitudes of U.S. Voters toward Prisoners Rehabilitation and Reentry Policies." National Council on Crime and Delinquency, April 2006 (www.nccd-crc.org).

civil disabilities
Legal restrictions that prevent released felons from voting, serving on juries, and holding public office.

Civil Disabilities of Ex-Felons

Once a person has been released from prison, paid a fine, or completed parole or probation, the debt to society—in theory—has been paid and the punishment has ended. For many offenders, however, a criminal conviction is a lifetime burden. In most states, certain civil rights are forfeited forever, some fields of employment are closed, and some insurance or pension benefits may be denied. Depending on the state in which the offender lives, these "invisible punishments" affect parolees regardless of whether an ex-convict successfully obtains steady employment, raises a family, and contributes time to community organizations.

The **civil disabilities** of ex-felons can include loss of the right to vote and to hold public office. In Maine and Vermont, offenders can vote while in prison, but other states remove voting rights during imprisonment. About a dozen states, including Massachusetts, Michigan, and Ohio, automatically restore voting rights after release from prison. Most states, however, continue to bar voting for offenders under community supervision. Thus in states such as North Carolina, Texas, and Wisconsin, voting rights are not restored until offenders complete their criminal punishment, whether it be probation, imprisonment, or parole. A half dozen states permit a restoration of voting rights for those who have committed certain offenses, but not the most serious offenses. Those ex-offenders are permanently barred from voting unless they are successful in filing a petition to have their voting rights restored. Iowa, Kentucky, and Florida bar voting permanently for all ex-felons unless the offender applies for official restoration of voting rights from the governor. Because this last category of most-restrictive states includes the populous state of Florida, there is a significant impact on opportunities for ex-offenders to become completely restored as active members of society (Quandt, 2015). Many ex-offenders in these states will not vote again because the petitioning process is neither easy nor automatic.

Nationally, an estimated 5.9 million Americans are barred from voting, either as incarcerated offenders or as ex-felons in restrictive voting states. This includes 2.2 million African American men and women—1 out of every 13 black men and women are prohibited from voting in the United States (Quandt, 2015). Without the right to vote, those ex-offenders, who may become completely reformed and energetic leaders within their neighborhoods, still cannot be formally involved as leaders in local government or public schools because of an act that they may have committed many years earlier. Researchers have shown that Al Gore would have won the presidency in 2000 if ex-felons had been allowed to vote because of lower-income individuals' tendency to be more supportive of Democratic candidates than Republican candidates (Manza and Uggen, 2006). In the past decade, several states have moved to either lift restrictions on voting for ex-felons or to create new processes that could eventually permit them to regain voting rights. For example, in 2014 Virginia law changed to remove drug offenders from the "serious offenders" category that restricts voting rights. Instead, drug offenses have been grouped in the "less serious" category along with embezzlement, theft, and similar offenses, for which voting rights are not limited (Laris, 2014). Not all states have taken action. For example, in 2011 Florida and Iowa made it more difficult for ex-felons to regain voting rights. Florida requires a waiting period of either five or seven years, depending on the crime, before an individual application can be submitted for restoration of voting rights. Iowa's new Republican governor rescinded the practice of his Democratic predecessor who believed in automatic restoration of voting rights.

Thus Iowa requires an individual application for the governor's approval. Critics who oppose such restrictions believe that there should be one clear national rule: When you have completed your sentence, you can vote again.

Voting may be the most notable civil disability of ex-prisoners, but other legal barriers directly affect those trying to make it after a term in prison. For example, in many states, felons are not allowed to serve on juries, maintain parental rights, or have access to public employment. In many states, ex-felons are prohibited from obtaining a license to practice a trade or profession. Cities often have rules that forbid ex-felons from gaining needed licenses to become taxicab drivers, for example. In another example, Marc LaCloche was taught barbering during the 11 years he served in New York prisons. Upon release his application for a state barbering license was rejected on the grounds that his "criminal history indicates a lack of good moral character and trustworthiness required for licensure" (Haberman, 2005).

Critics of civil disability laws point out that, upon fulfilling the penalty imposed for a crime, the former offender should be assisted to full reintegration into society. They argue that it is counterproductive for the government to promote rehabilitation with the goal of reintegration while at the same time preventing offenders from fully achieving that goal. Supporters of these laws respond that they are justified by the possibility of recidivism and the community's need for protection. Between these two extremes is the belief that not all people convicted of felonies should be treated equally. In other words, to be protected, society needs to place restrictions only on certain individuals.

One way that offenders avoid the consequences of civil disabilities is through **expungement**, a process through which an individual's criminal records are erased from public records. Each state defines whether and how criminal records can be expunged. In some states, such opportunities are limited to youthful offenders who enter guilty pleas and then successfully complete their criminal punishments without causing any problems. However, the impediments to employment and civil disabilities that face ex-offenders on reentry have led some legislatures to consider broadening opportunities for expungement, such as permitting applications from older, nonviolent offenders after a five-year waiting period following the completion of the sentence (K. Gray, 2013).

expungement
Process defined by individual states' laws through which offenders can have their criminal records erased from public records. This process is often focused on youthful offenders who commit nonviolent offenses in their teens or early twenties.

AP Images/Justin Steyer

Prisoners attend a class as part of the Reintegration and Progression Program at the state prison in Monroe, Washington. As a component of learning about healthy living and aggression control, the prisoners participate in classes on meditation. Is meditation a useful subject in these classes? What other subjects do prisoners need to study in order to prepare for release from prison?

Pardon

pardon
An action of the executive branch of state or federal government excluding the offense and absolving the offender from the consequences of the crime.

References to **pardon** are found in ancient Hebrew law. In medieval Europe, the church and monarchies exercised the power of clemency. Pardon later became known as the "royal prerogative of mercy" in England.

Pardons and expungements are not identical. The pardon power rests in the hands of the governor or president to make individual decisions, often based on advice from a pardon commission or an agency within the attorney general's office, which may occur either before a case is prosecuted or after a guilty verdict. Depending on the relevant jurisdiction's laws, a postconviction pardon may not enable a person to treat a criminal conviction as if it never occurred when responding to a question about his or her criminal history in a job interview. Expungements are more frequently a judicial decision and they only occur after there has been a criminal conviction. Usually an expungement will permit the individual to treat the conviction as if it never occurred, although the record may remain available to police officials.

Throughout the United States, the president and state governors may grant clemency in individual cases. The president's power operates with respect to violations of federal criminal law, not criminal convictions under state law. In each state, the governor typically receives recommendations from the state's board of pardons (often combined with the board of parole) concerning individuals who are thought to be deserving of the act. Pardons serve three main purposes: (1) to remedy a miscarriage of justice, (2) to remove the stigma of a conviction, and (3) to mitigate a penalty. Although full pardons for miscarriages of justice are rare, from time to time society hears the story of some individual who has been released from prison after the discovery that he or she was incarcerated by mistake.

INSIDE TODAY'S CONTROVERSIES

THE REDEEM ACT

In July 2014, U.S. Senators Rand Paul (R), Kirsten Gillibrand (D) and Corey Booker (D) introduced the REDEEM Act to Congress. (REDEEM is an acronym for Record Expungement Designed to Enhance Employment.) The act is designed to facilitate employment for parolees and offenders released from prison. Its key proposals include

- Creating a method to seal or expunge nonviolent federal crimes from criminal records
- Improving the accuracy of FBI background checks, which are frequently inaccurate or out-of-date
- Removing the lifetime ban on receiving federal public assistance (such as welfare) for those convicted of felony drug offenses
- Encouraging states to increase the age of criminal responsibility to 18, which can help keep juveniles out of the adult criminal justice system.

The REDEEM Act is supported by politicians from both major political parties as well as by U.S. corporations and antipoverty organizations. Supporters of the REDEEM Act maintain that a federal conviction is a "life sentence to poverty"—a federal conviction makes it difficult, if not impossible, for releasees to find gainful employment and to earn a living wage. In addition, proponents claim that African American men with prior convictions are less likely than their white counterparts to receive callbacks on job interviews. Supporters of the REDEEM Act assert that the legislation would greatly help reduce race disparity in employment.

Some are opposed to the REDEEM Act due to the very notion of sealing or expunging criminal records, which may encourage ex-offenders to forget or fail to own up to their past crimes. Others are concerned about raising the "age of responsibility" for juvenile offenders to 18, believing that the courts should be allowed to charge juveniles as adults for serious crimes (read more about the issue of "waiver" in Chapter 17).

Frequently, governors or presidents issue sentence commutations, a form of pardon that shortens prison sentences or moves a condemned murderer from death row to a life sentence in prison. In March 2015, for example, President Obama commuted the sentences of 22 federal prisoners imprisoned for drug crimes. Several were serving sentences that were longer than the sentences that currently would have been applied for the same drug possession offenses. This set of commutations brought his total commutations and pardons to 43 during his first six years as president, a relatively low number compared to other presidents (Korte, 2015).

The more-typical activity of pardons boards is to erase the criminal records of first-time offenders—often young people—so they may enter those professions whose licensing procedures ban former felons, or so they may obtain certain types of employment— and in general, so they will not have to bear the stigma of a single mistake. In this sense, the actual exercise of pardon power in these cases is very similar to the underlying purposes of state expungement laws that focus on preventing youthful offenders from being scarred for life by the commission of a minor, nonviolent act at a young age.

Since 2009, laws have been changed in 41 states to ease restrictions on ex-inmates. In addition to expanding expungement, some states have issued "certificates of recovery," which provide ex-inmates with a certificate for completing certain rehabilitative programs. These can be shown to employers as evidence that the ex-inmate has willingness to improve. Other states, such as Minnesota, New Mexico, and Indiana, have enacted laws to remove questions about prior criminal record and convictions from job applications. Finally, Louisiana, Rhode Island, and several other states have created pre-adjudication programs, in which an offender is found guilty but can avoid a formal conviction by participating in conditional programming, such as job training, educational programs, or drug treatment (Subramanian, Moreno, and Gebreselassie, 2014). Read more about proposed changes in the federal law that may reduce civil disabilities in the Inside Today's Controversies feature.

Others challenge the proposal's lifting of the current lifetime ban for some federal welfare programs for those who have been convicted of nonviolent drug offenses. They raise the argument that instead of using public assistance for living expenses, it is likely that former drug offenders would use the funds to purchase illegal drugs. State laws on public assistance for ex-offenders vary considerably. Ten states mandate a complete lifetime ban from social welfare benefits for those convicted of drug crimes. However, other legislatures take a softer approach and allow food stamps and public assistance for those drug offenders who comply with drug testing, attend drug treatment programs, or otherwise follow the conditions of their release from prison. The REDEEM Act would invalidate any state law banning public assistance for these offenders.

So far, political support for the REDEEM Act seems stronger than countervailing opposition. In addition to the bipartisan support in Congress, business leaders, civil liberties groups, and others have rallied support for the REDEEM Act since its introduction in Congress.

Sources: Freddie Allen, "Bipartisan Support for Broader Hiring Practices for Ex-Offenders," *North Dallas Gazette* (northdallasgazette.com), April 1, 2015; Chandra Bozelko, "'REDEEM' Act Belies Redemption," *Baltimore Sun*, October 17, 2014 (baltimoresun.com); Legal Action Center, Opting Out of Federal Ban on Food Stamps and TANF, December 2011 (lac.org); Amanda Turkel, "Corey Booker and Rand Paul Team Up on Criminal Justice Reform," Huffington Post (www.huffingtonpost.com), July 8, 2014; Rebecca Vallas, "Why Congress Should Pass the REDEEM Act," March 12, 2015, *Common Dreams* (commondreams.org).

CRITICAL THINKING AND ANALYSIS

The civil disabilities that follow former inmates can create circumstances that lead them back to crime. The REDEEM Act aims to remove specific civil disabilities for ex-inmates, allowing them to more easily procure employment. However, the sealing and expungement of criminal records are controversial. Should people convicted of crimes be allowed a "clean slate" after they have served their time? Should prospective employers have the right to know if employees have been convicted of a crime, even after records are expunged? Write a memo that takes a stand on each of these questions, and provide two points to support your opinions for each question.

✔POINT **14.** What is a civil disability? Give three examples.

15. What purposes does pardoning serve?

STOP AND ANALYZE: In theory, the punishment for the crime is the loss of liberty during the period of incarceration or some other sanction specified in the sentence. What then justifies a continuing loss of equal rights and opportunities after the sentence has been served? Give two arguments favoring some forms of civil disability for ex-felons. Then list the restrictions that are most appropriate for ex-felons. Provide the strongest arguments against the specific items on your list. After working through this exercise, where do you fundamentally stand on this issue?

A QUESTION OF ETHICS

NEIGHBORHOOD RESISTANCE TO PLACEMENT OF COMMUNITY CORRECTIONS PROGRAMS AND FACILITIES

Community corrections programs and aftercare are vital components of a releasee's transition out of prison; however, there is considerable public debate over the best location for these centers. Given that many parolees have limited access to personal transportation, it can be difficult for them to travel long distances to visit their parole officer or attend important rehabilitative programs. Placing community corrections programs in neighborhoods would give parolees easy access to these centers, but many neighborhood residents have a "Not In My Backyard" (NIMBY) attitude toward allowing these offices in their area. Expressing concerns over safety and increased crime, these residents fear that increased parolee foot traffic will make their neighborhoods more dangerous.

For example, in Amelia Island, Florida, a halfway house where 12 men live has faced opposition by residents. As part of the American Recovery Program, these men are working to become sober, gain employment,and reconnect with their families. Neighborhood residents, however, are fearful. One (anonymous) resident says, "I believe that everybody should have a second chance. We should help those people with whatever, but not in my neighborhood" (McKee, 2015).

CRITICAL THINKING AND ANALYSIS

Is there any way to meet the competing demands of (1) providing parolees easy access to valuable services, but also (2) keeping neighborhoods safe and crime free? If you were the spokesperson for the Florida Department of Corrections, how would you respond to the statement by the Amelia Island resident?

Source: K. McKee, "Neighbors Say 'Not In My Neighborhood' to Amelia Island Halfway House," *Action News Jacksonville.* March 18. 2015 (www.actionnewsjax.com).

Summary

1 Describe the nature of the "reentry problem"

- The successful reentry of ex-prisoners to the community has become a pressing problem.
- About 600,000 felons are released to the community each year.
- Preventing recidivism by assisting parolees to become law-abiding citizens requires government effort.

2 Discuss the origins of parole and the way it operates today

- Parole in the United States evolved during the nineteenth century from the English, Australian, and Irish practices of conditional pardon, apprenticeship by indenture, transportation, and the issuance of tickets of leave.
- The ideas of Captain Alexander Maconochie, Sir Walter Crofton, and Zebulon Brockway played a major role in the development of parole.

3 Analyze the mechanisms for the release of felons to the community

- Conditional release from prison on parole is the primary method by which inmates return to society. While on parole, they remain under correctional supervision.

- There are five types of release: discretionary release, mandatory release, probation release, other conditional release, and expiration release.
- Parole boards exercise the discretion to consider various factors in making the decision to release.
- Parolees are released from prison on the condition that they do not again violate the law and that they live according to rules designed both to help them adjust to society and to control their movements.
- Parole officers are assigned to assist ex-inmates in making the transition to society and to ensure that they follow the conditions of their release.

4 Describe the problems parolees face during their reentry

- Upon release, offenders face a number of problems, such as finding housing and employment and renewing relationships with family and friends.
- Community corrections assumes that reentry should be a gradual process through which parolees should be assisted. Work and educational release, halfway houses, and furloughs are geared to ease the transition.

5 Discuss how ex-prisoners are supervised in the community

- Each releasee is assigned a parole officer whose role is part cop and part social worker.
- The parole officer's work combines supervision and assistance.
- Parole may be revoked for commission of a crime or for violating the rules governing the parolee's supervision.

6 Analyze how civil disabilities block successful reentry

- Society places restrictions on many ex-felons. State and federal laws prevent offenders from entering certain professions and occupations.
- Voting rights and the right to hold public office are sometimes denied to ex-felons.
- A small number of offenders obtain pardons for their crimes and have their civil rights reinstated, usually after successfully completing their time on parole.

Questions for Review

1. What are the basic assumptions of parole?
2. How do discretionary release, mandatory release, probation release, other conditional release, and expiration release differ?
3. What are the roles of the parole officer?
4. What problems confront parolees upon their release?

Key Terms and Cases

civil disabilities (p. 686)
conditions of release (p. 675)
discretionary release (p. 668)
expiration release (p. 670)
expungement (p. 687)
furlough (p. 678)
halfway house (p. 678)
mandatory release (p. 668)
other conditional release (p. 669)
pardon (p. 688)
parole (p. 665)
probation release (p. 669)
ticket of leave (p. 666)
work and educational release (p. 678)
Morrissey v. Brewer (1972) (p. 684)

Checkpoint Answers

1 What problems interfere with offenders' reentry into society after imprisonment?

✓ Ex-offenders often have significant personal problems, such as substance abuse, as well as a lack of job skills, job experience, and the necessary knowledge and habits to succeed in the workplace and function in a free society. Their criminal records will also create barriers to being hired in many jobs. In addition, budget cuts have reduced programs designed to help facilitate reentry.

2 In what countries did the concept of parole first develop?

✓ England, Australia, Ireland.

3 What were the contributions of Alexander Maconochie and Sir Walter Crofton?

✓ Captain Alexander Maconochie developed a classification procedure through which prisoners could get increasing responsibility and freedom. Sir Walter Crofton linked Maconochie's idea of an offender's progress in prison to the ticket of leave and supervision in the community.

4 How do discretionary release, mandatory release, other conditional release, and expiration release differ?

✓ *Discretionary release* is the release of an inmate from incarceration to conditional supervision at the discretion of the parole board within the boundaries set by the sentence and the penal law. *Mandatory release* is the required release of an inmate from incarceration to community supervision upon the expiration of a certain period as specified by a determinate sentencing law. *Other conditional release* is the release of an inmate who has received a mandatory sentence from incarceration to a furlough, halfway house, or home supervision by correctional authorities attempting to deal with a crowding problem. *Expiration release* is the release of an inmate from incarceration without any further correctional supervision; the inmate cannot be returned to prison for any remaining portion of the sentence for the current offense.

5 Who participates in the parole hearing process?

✓ States use different processes for parole considerations, sometimes hearings with two or three board members, possibly including a civil servant professional (deputy commissioner) and sometimes just an interview by one board member. The prisoner participates, and there can be input in some form from victims who want to express themselves. There may be family members or other representatives of the prisoner who offer their opinions. In some states, the prisoners may be represented by attorneys, and prosecutors may also participate.

6 How does parole release influence the rest of the criminal justice system?

✓ Parole release affects sentencing, plea bargaining, and the size of prison populations.

7 What are three programs designed to ease the reentry of offenders into the community?

✓ Work and educational release programs, furlough programs, and halfway houses.

8 What are some of the rules most parolees must follow while under supervision in the community?

✓ Make required reports to parole officer, do not leave the state without permission, do not use alcohol or drugs, maintain employment, attend required treatment programs.

9 What are the major tasks of parole officers?

✓ Surveillance and assistance.

10 What are some of the major problems faced by parolees?

✓ Finding housing and employment, having a shortage of money, and reestablishing relationships with family and friends.

11 What are "sexual offender notification laws"?

✓ Laws requiring that the public be notified of the whereabouts of potentially dangerous sex offenders.

12 What two conditions can result in the revocation of parole?

✓ (1) Arrest for a new crime; (2) technical violation of one or more of the conditions of parole.

13 What does the U.S. Supreme Court require during the revocation process?

✓ A two-step hearing process. The first stage determines if there is probable cause to believe the conditions of parole have been violated. In the second stage, a decision is made as to whether the violation is severe enough to warrant a return to prison.

14 What is a civil disability? Give three examples.

✓ Ex-felons may be required forfeit certain civil rights such as the right to vote, to serve on juries, and to hold public office. Ex-felons are restricted from certain types of employment as well.

15 What purposes does pardoning serve?

✓ To remedy a miscarriage of justice, to remove the stigma of a conviction, to mitigate a penalty.

PART 5

Alexander Raths/Shutterstock.com

THE JUVENILE JUSTICE SYSTEM

Crimes committed by juveniles are a serious national problem. The Uniform Crime Reports (UCR) reveal that nearly 9 percent of all arrests in 2013 were suspects younger than 18 years of age. Children who are charged with crimes, who have been neglected by their parents, or whose behavior is otherwise judged to require official action, enter the juvenile justice system, an independent process that is interrelated with the adult system.

Many of the procedures used in handling juvenile problems are similar to those used with adults, but the overriding philosophy of juvenile justice is somewhat different, and the state may intrude into the lives of children to a much greater extent. In recent years, political and legal moves have been made to reduce the differences in the procedures of the two systems.

CHAPTER FEATURES

- **Close Up** Youth Violence Reduction Programs
- **New Directions in Criminal Justice Policy** Evidence-Based Diversion Programs
- **Doing Your Part** Teen Court
- **Inside Today's Controversies:** Solitary Confinement for Juveniles
- **Technology and Criminal Justice** Cyberbullying and "Sexting"

CHAPTER 17 JUVENILE JUSTICE

CHAPTER LEARNING OBJECTIVES

1. Describe the extent of youth crime in the United States
2. Discuss how the juvenile justice system developed and the assumptions on which it was based
3. Analyze what determines the jurisdiction of the juvenile justice system
4. Describe how the juvenile justice system operates
5. Analyze some of the problems facing the American system of juvenile justice

CHAPTER OUTLINE

Youth Crime in the United States

The Development of Juvenile Justice
- The Puritan Period (1646–1824)
- The Refuge Period (1824–1899)
- The Juvenile Court Period (1899–1960)
- The Juvenile Rights Period (1960–1980)
- The Crime Control Period (1980–2005)
- The "Kids Are Different" Period (2005–present)

The Juvenile Justice System
- Age of Clients
- Categories of Cases under Juvenile Court Jurisdiction

The Juvenile Justice Process
- Police Interface
- Intake Screening at the Court
- Pretrial Procedures
- Transfer (Waiver) to Adult Court
- Adjudication
- Disposition
- Corrections

Problems and Perspectives

Michael Sears/Milwaukee Journal Sentinel/MCT) Milwaukee Journal Sentinel/ MCT/Landov

In December 2014, two 12-year-old girls in the quiet town of Waukesha, Wisconsin, lured a classmate into the woods near their home after inviting her for a sleepover. They stabbed the victim 19 times, but she survived the assault. The assailants, A. W. and M. G., whose names were protected by several news media organizations because of their youthful ages, claimed they commited the assault to please Slender Man, a fictional online character (Reuters, 2014b). They reportedly believed that by killing the victim, they would be welcomed as minions to Slender Man's home in the Wisconsin woods and that their families would be safe from him (Hathaway, 2015).

Because of their adamant belief that Slender Man is real, the girls' attorneys argued that they were both incompetent to stand trial as adults and should be tried in the juvenile court system on lower charges of second-degree attempted murder. After psychological evaluation, both girls were found competent to stand trial and a judicial ruling indicated they would be charged with attempted first-degree murder in adult court (Fieldstadt, 2015).

There are serious implications for the decision to try the girls as adults. If tried in the Wisconsin juvenile court, they can only be incarcerated until they turn 25 years of age; however, if tried as adults, they could face up to 65 years in an adult prison (K. Richmond, 2015). *Waiver*, the process of transferring juvenile offenders to the adult court, is governed by each state's law. Thus, the procedure varies significantly from state to state. In every state, waiver of juveniles to adult court can generate controversy. Critics complain that juveniles should not be held to the same standards and face the same punishments as adults. Should the courts assume that juveniles truly understand the consequences of their actions? Are the more-severe penalties typically reserved for adult offenders appropriate for juvenile offenders? Is it safe for juvenile offenders to serve sentences in adult facilities? There are continuing disagreements and debates about each of these questions.

Although the juvenile justice system is separate from the adult criminal justice system, the key values of freedom, fairness, and justice undergird both structures. The formal processes of each differ mainly in emphasis, not in values. Although different, the systems are interrelated. One cannot separate the activities and concerns of policing, courts, and corrections from the criminal problems of youth. With juveniles committing a notable portion of criminal offenses, officials in the adult system must pay serious attention to the juvenile system as well.

Youth Crime in the United States

In Brooklyn, New York, a 16-year-old girl is arrested for beating a 15-year-old girl to unconsciousness; her prior arrests include charges of stabbing a family member and beating her own grandmother. Three boys in Kansas City, Missouri, are charged with vandalism after leaping back-first onto cars in a prank that goes viral on social media. A teenager in Indiana is charged with arson after setting a rental home on fire. In Atlanta, a male high school student is accused of lying in wait for a female student to pass by, then raping her in the school. Such dramatic criminal acts make headlines. Are these only isolated incidents, or is the United States facing a major increase in youth crime?

The juvenile crime incidents just described are unusual. In a nation with 74 million people younger than age 18, about 875,000 arrests of juveniles occur each year, only 43,000 of which (about 5 percent) are for violent crimes (FBI, 2014a: Table 41). After rising from 1988 through 1994, the number of index crimes (those considered "serious" by the FBI) committed by juveniles dropped to an all-time low in 2012 (Puzzanchera, 2014). Public opinion reflects the reality of declining crime rates in the United States, with Americans less concerned about crime than in many past years. As shown in "What Americans Think," the public is most concerned about issues related to the economy and government.

WHAT AMERICANS THINK

QUESTION: "What do you think is the most important problem facing this country today?"

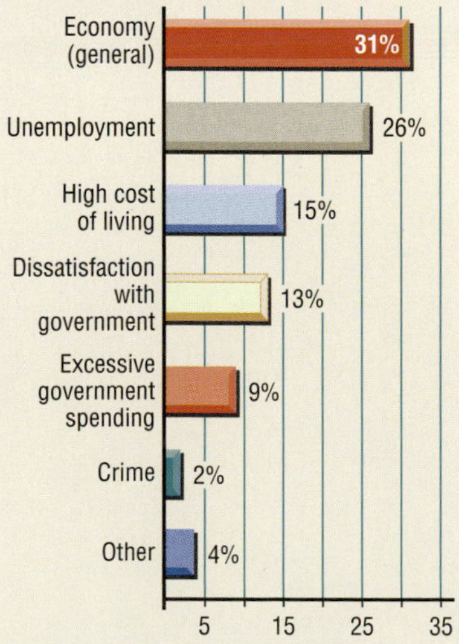

Source: Bureau of Justice Statistics, *Sourcebook of Criminal Justice Statistics* (2015), Table 2.1.2012.

Youth crimes range from UCR Index Crimes (for example murder, rape, robbery, assault) to less serious crimes such as liquor-law violations, gambling, and disorderly conduct (see Figure 17.1). Consistent with the trends just discussed, and although about 1.5 million delinquency cases were handled in the juvenile court in 2009, the decline in caseloads since the mid-1990s is the largest since 1960. Most juvenile crimes are committed by young men, but young women make up an increasing percentage of juveniles appearing in court. In the 1980s, young men were arrested 8 times more than young women for violent crimes; but by 2012 the arrest rate for young men was only 4 times more than for young women (Puzzanchera, 2014). This trend has occurred primarily because the number of arrests for boys has decreased at a faster rate than the number of arrests for girls (Puzzanchera, 2014).

Criminologists have tried to explain the "epidemic" of violent youth crime that erupted in the mid-1980s, which reached its peak in 1993. Among the explanations, two are heard frequently. One explanation uses a "cohort" approach, arguing that during the 1980s the increase in violence was due to an increase in the prevalence of exceptionally violent individuals—so-called "super predators." Critics of this approach say that the birth cohort that peaked during the early 1990s was not at all exceptional with respect to involvement in violence in their younger years (P. J. Cook and Laub, 2002: 2). In addition, there

FIGURE 17.1 PERCENTAGE OF ARRESTS OF PEOPLE YOUNGER THAN 18 YEARS OLD (ROUNDED)

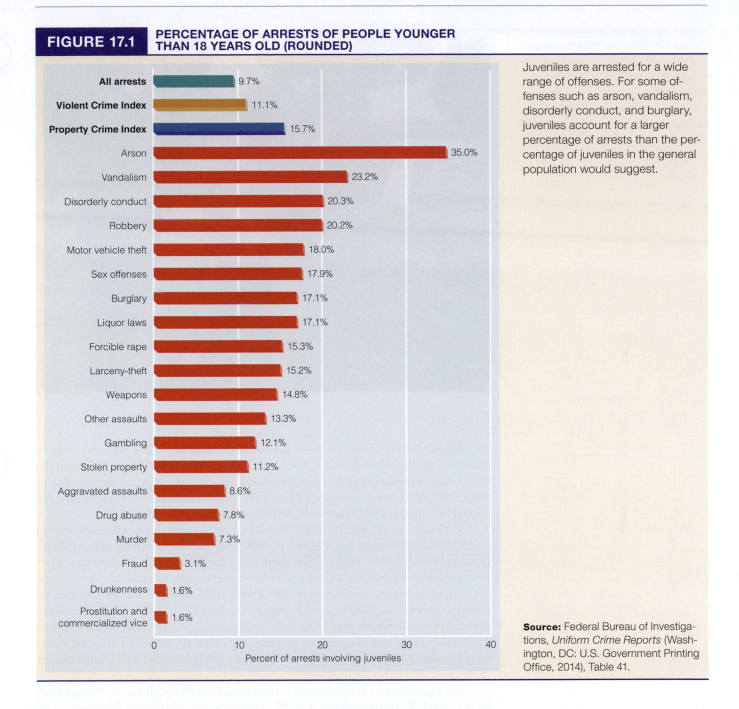

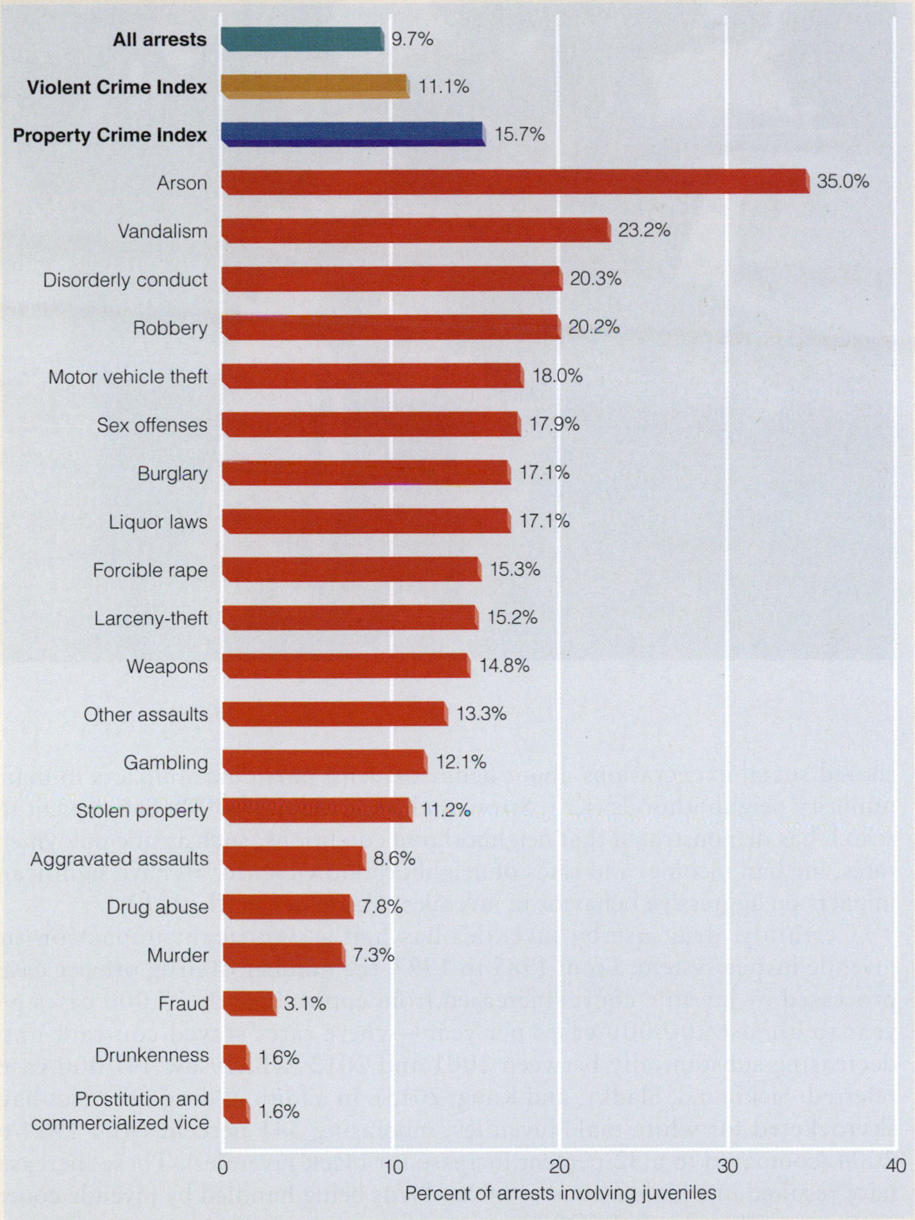

Juveniles are arrested for a wide range of offenses. For some offenses such as arson, vandalism, disorderly conduct, and burglary, juveniles account for a larger percentage of arrests than the percentage of juveniles in the general population would suggest.

Source: Federal Bureau of Investigations, *Uniform Crime Reports* (Washington, DC: U.S. Government Printing Office, 2014), Table 41.

was little evidence that "super predators" even existed, and much of the attention given to this explanation was blamed on media hype (Haberman, 2014).

A second explanation focuses on environmental factors during the epidemic period that influenced the rise in violent youth crime. Scholars holding this position point to the impact of the drug trade, especially crack cocaine and the related increase in the number of youths carrying and using guns. Alfred Blumstein (2002) suggests that as more juveniles, particularly inner-city minority males, were recruited into the drug trade, they armed themselves with guns and used those firearms in battles over market turf.

Other factors may have also played a role—violent crime by youth was most prevalent in neighborhoods with deteriorating social and economic conditions. These changes led to increases in family instability and reductions in

Gangs can draw youths into serious criminal activities. What kinds of programs might lure young people away from the attractions of the image of toughness, solidarity, respect, and power that youths may believe to be offered by gang membership?

Robert Nickelsberg/Getty Images News/Getty Images

shared social expectations about behavior, with particular impacts in many minority neighborhoods (K. J. Strom and MacDonald, 2007). Subsequent research has demonstrated that neighborhood conditions, such as unemployment rates, median income, and rates of neighborhood violence, all have significant impacts on aggressive behavior in juveniles (Vanfossen et al., 2010).

Certainly, drug use by juveniles has had a significant impact on the juvenile justice system. From 1985 to 1997, the number of drug offense cases processed by juvenile courts increased from approximately 77,000 cases per year to almost 200,000 cases per year—where rates stayed constant until decreasing substantially between 2001 and 2012 (which saw 147,000 cases referred: Sickmund, Sladky, and Kang, 2015). In addition, drug use cases have skyrocketed for white male juveniles, increasing 341 percent from 1984 to 2004 (compared to a 32 percent increase for black juveniles). These increases have resulted in a higher number of caseloads being handled by juvenile courts in the past 20 years (Stahl, 2008).

Youth gangs are another factor influencing violent youth crime. Gangs such as the Black P. Stone Nation, CRIPS (Common Revolution in Progress), and Bloods first came to police attention in the 1970s. The National Youth Gang Survey estimates that there are now more than 29,400 gangs with 756,000 members in the United States, and that highly populated areas accounted for the largest number of gang-related homicides (Egley and Howell, 2012). Gangs are a primary source of fear and peril in many neighborhoods. Especially where gang members are armed, the presence of the gang can destabilize neighborhood life. Youth gangs are not restricted to large cities—crackdowns on violence in cities can sometimes force gang behavior into suburban areas (Sanchez and Giordano, 2008). Fear of being a crime victim can lead youths to seek protection through gang membership without realizing that gang members are actually more likely than other juveniles to be victims of violence and property crimes (Melde, Esbensen, and Taylor, 2009).

Although juvenile delinquency, neglect, and dependency have been concerns since the nation's early decades, a separate system to deal with these problems did not evolve until the early twentieth century. The contemporary juvenile justice system has gone through a major shift of emphasis as well. The remainder of the chapter explores the history of juvenile justice, the process it follows today, and some of the problems associated with it.

✓POINT 1. What might explain the "epidemic" of violent crime committed by juveniles that peaked in the 1990s?

STOP AND ANALYZE: There appears to be a strong link between drug use and delinquency rates. What might you recommend to lawmakers to help reduce juvenile drug use so that delinquency rates can be decreased?

(Answers are at the end of the chapter.)

The Development of Juvenile Justice

The system and philosophy of juvenile justice that began in the United States during the social reform period of the late nineteenth century was based on the idea that the state should act as a parent in advancing the interest of the child. This view remained unchallenged until the 1960s, when the Supreme Court ushered in the juvenile rights period. With the rise in juvenile crime in the 1980s, the juvenile justice system shifted again, to one focusing on the problem of controlling youth crime. Today people are again reexamining the philosophy and processes of the juvenile justice system.

The idea that children should be treated differently from adults originated in the common law and in the chancery courts of England. The common law had long prescribed that children younger than seven years of age were incapable of felonious intent and were therefore not criminally responsible. Children aged 7 to 14 could be held accountable only if it could be shown that they understood the consequences of their actions.

The English chancery courts, established during the Middle Ages, heard only civil cases, mainly concerning property. However, under the doctrine of ***parens patriae***, which held the king to be the father of the realm, the chancery courts exercised protective jurisdiction over all children, particularly those involved in questions of dependency, neglect, and property. At this time the criminal courts, not a separate juvenile court, dealt with juvenile offenders. In legitimizing the actions of the state on behalf of the child, however, the concept of *parens patriae* laid the groundwork for the development of juvenile justice.

parens patriae The state as parent; the state as guardian and protector of all citizens (such as juveniles) who cannot protect themselves.

Table 17.1 outlines the shifts in how the United States has dealt with the problems of youth. These shifts fall into six periods of American juvenile justice history. Each was characterized by changes in juvenile justice that reflected the social, intellectual, and political currents of the time. During the past 200 years, population shifts from rural to urban areas, immigration, developments in the social sciences, political reform movements, and the continuing problem of youth crime have all influenced how Americans have treated juveniles.

The Puritan Period (1646–1824)

English legal rules and procedures were maintained in the American colonies and continued into the early years of American independence in the nineteenth century. The earliest attempt by a colony to deal with problem children was passage of the Massachusetts Stubborn Child Law in 1646. With this law, the Puritans of the Massachusetts Bay Colony imposed the view that the child was evil, and they emphasized the need for the family to discipline and raise youths. Those who would not obey their parents were dealt with by the law.

TABLE 17.1 JUVENILE JUSTICE DEVELOPMENTS IN THE UNITED STATES

PERIOD	MAJOR DEVELOPMENTS	CAUSES AND INFLUENCES	JUVENILE JUSTICE SYSTEM
Puritan 1646–1824	Massachusetts Stubborn Child Law (1646)	A. Puritan view of child as evil B. Economically marginal agrarian society	Law provides: A. Symbolic standard of maturity B. Support for family as economic unit
Refuge 1824–1899	Institutionalization of deviants; House of Refuge in New York established (1825) for delinquent and dependent children	A. Enlightenment B. Immigration and industrialization	Child seen as helpless, in need of state intervention
Juvenile Court 1899–1960	Establishment of separate legal system for juveniles; Illinois Juvenile Court Act (1899)	A. Reformism and rehabilitative ideology B. Increased immigration, urbanization, large-scale industrialization	Juvenile court institutionalized legal responsibility of child
Juvenile Rights 1960–1980	Increased "legalization" of juvenile law; *Gault* decision (1967); Juvenile Justice and Delinquency Prevention Act (1974) calls for deinstitutionalization of status offenders	A. Criticism of juvenile justice system on humane grounds B. Civil rights movement by minority groups	Movement to define and protect rights as well as to provide services to children
Crime Control 1980–2005	Concern for victims, punishment for serious offenders, transfer to adult court of serious offenders, protection of children from physical and sexual abuse	A. More-conservative public attitudes and policies B. Focus on serious crimes by repeat offenders	System more formal, restrictive, punitive; increased percentage of police referrals to court; incarcerated youths stay longer periods
"Kids Are Different" 2005–present	Elimination of death penalty for juveniles, focus on rehabilitation, states increasing age of transfer to adult court	A. *Roper v. Simmons* (2005) B. Scientific evidence on youth's biological, emotional, and psychological development	Recognition that juveniles are less culpable than adults

Sources: Portions adapted from Barry Krisberg, Ira M. Schwartz, Paul Litsky, and James Austin, "The Watershed of Juvenile Justice Reform," *Crime and Delinquency* 32 (January 1985): 5–38; U.S. Department of Justice, *A Preliminary National Assessment of the Status Offender and the Juvenile Justice System* (Washington, DC: U.S. Government Printing Office, 1980), 29.

✔POINT
2. Until what age were children exempt from criminal responsibility under common law?
3. What was the jurisdiction of the English chancery court?
4. What is meant by the doctrine of *parens patriae*?

STOP AND ANALYZE: In what sense can a court or the government act as a "parent" to a child? Parents provide not only discipline, but also love and care to their children. Can a court (or judge) really take on this role?

The Refuge Period (1824–1899)

As the population of American cities began to grow during the early 1800s, the problem of youth crime and neglect became a concern for reformers. Just as the Quakers of Philadelphia had been instrumental during the same period in reforming correctional practices, other groups supported changes toward the education and protection of youths. These reformers focused their efforts primarily on the urban immigrant poor, seeking to have parents declared "unfit" if their children roamed the streets and were apparently "out of control." Not all such children were engaged in criminal acts, but the reformers believed that children would end up in prison if their parents did not discipline them and train them to abide by the rules of society. The state would use its power to prevent delinquency. The solution was to create "houses of

During the nineteenth century, reformers were alarmed by the living conditions of inner-city youths. Reformers in Chicago ushered in the juvenile justice system. Would it have been better to permit youthful offenders to receive the same punishments as adults offenders? Would that approach actually better fulfill the nation's goal of "equal justice under law"?

refuge" where these children could learn good work and study habits, live in a disciplined and healthy environment, and develop "character."

The first of these institutions was the New York House of Refuge, which opened in 1825. This half-prison, half-school housed destitute and orphaned children as well as those convicted of crime (Friedman, 1993: 164). Similar facilities followed in Boston, Philadelphia, and Baltimore. Children were placed in these homes by court order, usually because of neglect or vagrancy. They often stayed until they were old enough to be legally regarded as adults. The houses were run according to a strict program of work, study, and discipline.

Some states created "reform schools" to provide the discipline and education needed by wayward youth in a "homelike" atmosphere, usually in rural areas. The first, the Lyman School for Boys, opened in Westborough, Massachusetts, in 1848. A similar Massachusetts reform school for girls opened in 1855 for "the instruction . . . and reformation, of exposed, helpless, evil disposed and vicious girls" (Friedman, 1993: 164). Institutional programs began in New York in 1849, Ohio in 1850, and Maine, Rhode Island, and Michigan in 1906.

Despite these reforms, children could still be arrested, detained, tried, and imprisoned. Even in states that had institutions for juveniles, the criminal justice process for children was the same as that for adults.

The Juvenile Court Period (1899–1960)

With most states providing services to neglected youth by the end of the nineteenth century, the problem of juvenile criminality became the focus of attention. Progressive reformers pushed for the state to provide individualized care and treatment to deviants of all kinds—adult criminals, the mentally ill, juvenile delinquents. They urged adoption of probation, treatment, indeterminate sentences, and parole for adult offenders and succeeded in establishing similar programs for juveniles.

Referred to as the "child savers," these upper-middle-class reformers sought to use the power of the state to "save" children from a life of crime (Platt, 1977). They shared a concern about the role of environmental factors on behavior and a belief that benevolent state action could solve social problems. They also believed the claim of the new social scientists that they could treat the problems underlying deviance.

Reformers wanted a separate juvenile court system that could address the problems of individual youths by using flexible procedures that, as one reformer said, "banish entirely all thought of crime and punishment" (Rothman, 1980: 213). They put their idea into action with the creation of the juvenile court.

Passage of the Juvenile Court Act by Illinois in 1899 established the first comprehensive system of juvenile justice. The act placed under one jurisdiction cases of dependency, neglect, and delinquency ("incorrigibles and children threatened by immoral associations as well as criminal lawbreakers") for children younger than 16. The act had four major elements:

1. A separate court for delinquent, dependent, and neglected children.
2. Special legal procedures that were less adversarial than those in the adult system.
3. Keeping child offenders separate from adult offenders in all portions of the justice system.
4. Programs of probation to assist the courts in deciding what the best interest of the state and the child entails.

Activists such as Jane Addams, Lucy Flower, and Julia Lathrop, of the settlement house movement; Henry Thurston, a social work educator; and the National Congress of Mothers successfully promoted the juvenile court concept. By 1904, ten states had implemented procedures similar to those of Illinois. By 1917, all but three states provided for a juvenile court.

The philosophy of the juvenile court derived from the idea that the state should deal with a child who broke the law much as a wise parent would deal with a wayward child. The doctrine of *parens patriae* again helped legitimize the system. Procedures would be informal and private, records would be confidential, children would be detained apart from adults, and probation and social workers would be appointed. Even the vocabulary and physical setting of the juvenile system were changed to emphasize diagnosis and treatment instead of findings of guilt. The term *criminal behavior* was replaced by *delinquent behavior* when referring to the acts of children. The terminology reflected the underlying belief that these children could be "cured" and returned to society as law-abiding citizens.

Because procedures were not to be adversarial, lawyers were unnecessary. The main professionals attached to the system were psychologists and social workers, who could determine the juvenile's underlying behavioral problem. These reforms, however, took place in a system in which children lacked the due process rights held by adults.

Although the creation of the juvenile court was a positive development for juveniles in general, some contemporary researchers criticize the tendency for these reformers to hold different standards for girls and boys. For example, girls found guilty of the status offense of "promiscuity" were frequently incarcerated until adulthood (age 18) for their own protection. Boys were rarely charged with this type of offense.

The Juvenile Rights Period (1960–1980)

Until the early 1960s, few questioned the sweeping powers of juvenile justice officials. When the U.S. Supreme Court expanded the rights of adult defendants, however, lawyers and scholars began to criticize the extensive discretion given to juvenile justice officials. In a series of decisions (Figure 17.2), the U.S. Supreme Court expanded the rights of juveniles.

FIGURE 17.2 **MAJOR DECISIONS BY THE U.S. SUPREME COURT REGARDING THE RIGHTS OF JUVENILES**

Since the mid-1960s, the Supreme Court has gradually expanded the rights of juveniles but has continued to recognize that the logic of the separate system for juvenile offenders justifies differences from some adult rights.

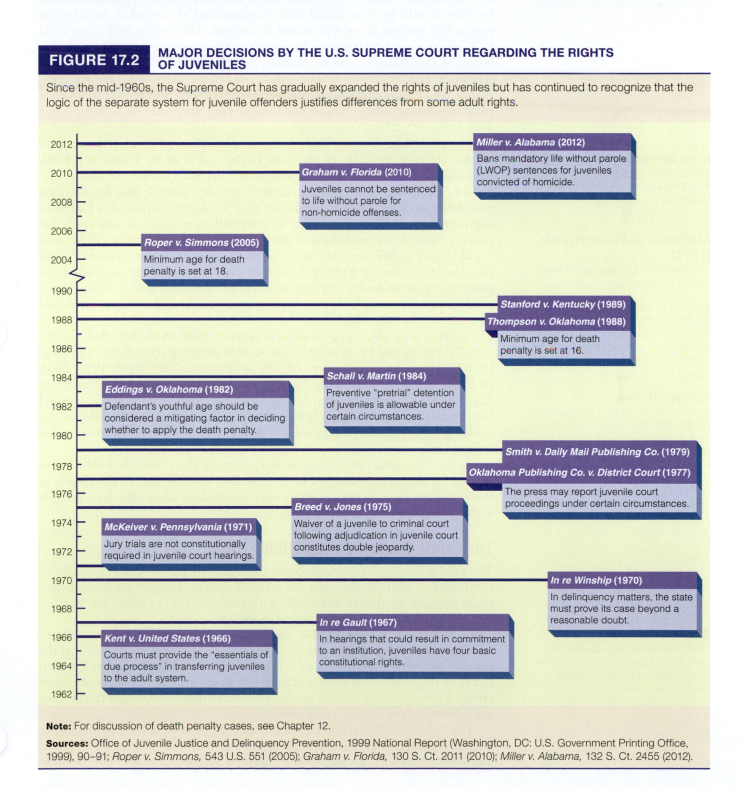

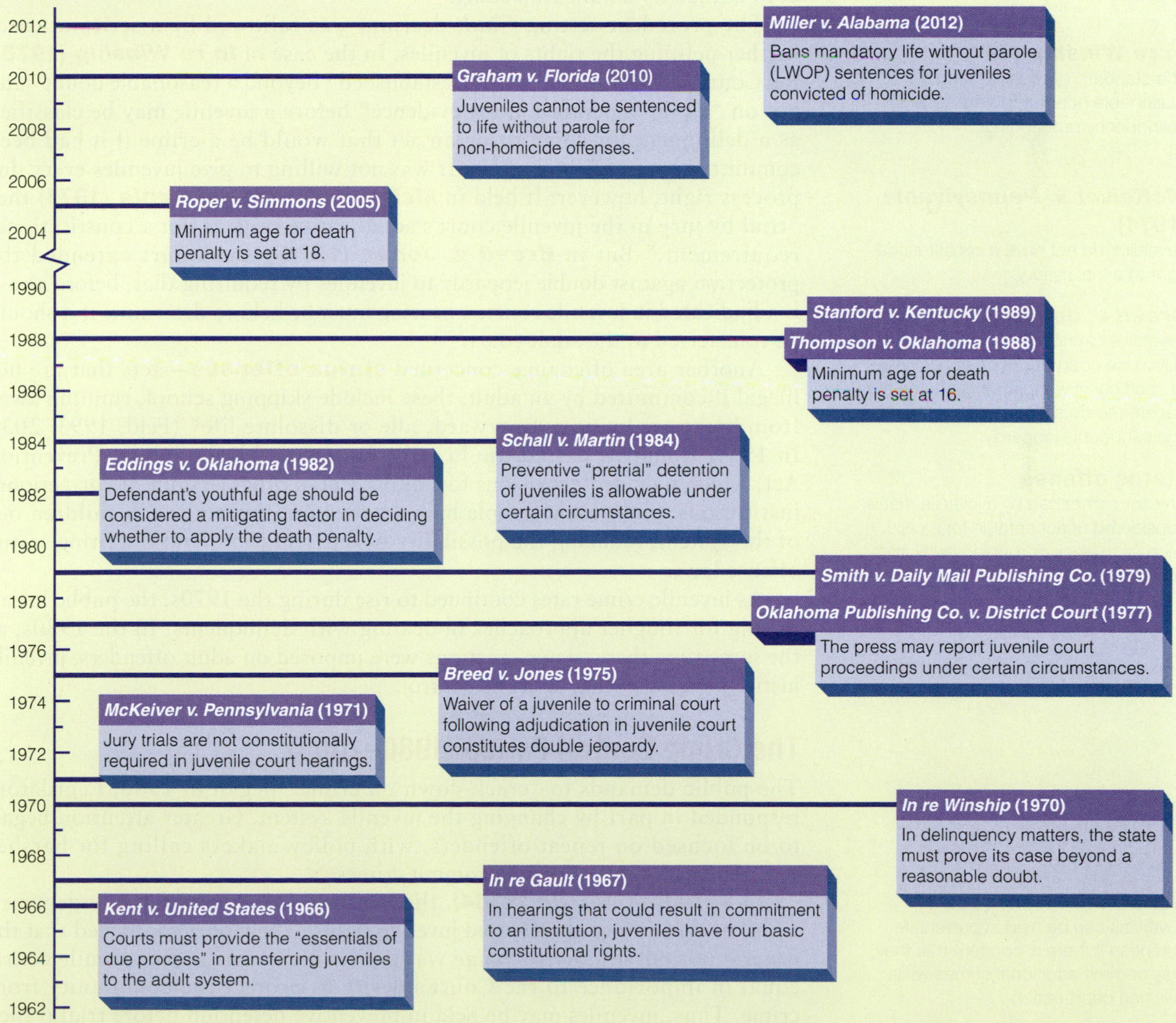

Note: For discussion of death penalty cases, see Chapter 12.

Sources: Office of Juvenile Justice and Delinquency Prevention, 1999 National Report (Washington, DC: U.S. Government Printing Office, 1999), 90–91; *Roper v. Simmons,* 543 U.S. 551 (2005); *Graham v. Florida,* 130 S. Ct. 2011 (2010); *Miller v. Alabama,* 132 S. Ct. 2455 (2012).

In the first of these cases, *Kent v. United States* (1966), the Supreme Court ruled that juveniles had the right to counsel at a hearing at which a juvenile judge may waive jurisdiction and pass the case to the adult court.

In re Gault (1967)
Juveniles have the right to counsel, to confront and examine accusers, and to have adequate notice of charges when confinement is a possible punishment.

In re Gault (1967) extended due process rights to juveniles. Fifteen-year-old Gerald Gault had been sentenced to six years in a state training school for making a prank phone call. Had he been an adult, the maximum punishment for making such a call would have been a fine of $5 to $50 or imprisonment for two months at most. Gault was convicted and sentenced in an informal proceeding without being represented by counsel. The justices held that a child in a delinquency hearing must be given certain procedural rights, including notice of the charges, right to counsel, right to confront and cross-examine witnesses, and protection against self-incrimination. Writing for the majority, Justice Abe Fortas emphasized that due process rights and procedures have a place in juvenile justice: "Under our Constitution the condition of being a boy does not justify a kangaroo court."

In re Winship (1970)
The standard of proof beyond a reasonable doubt applies to juvenile delinquency proceedings.

McKeiver v. Pennsylvania (1971)
Juveniles do not have a constitutional right to a trial by jury.

Breed v. Jones (1975)
Juveniles cannot be found delinquent in juvenile court and then transferred to adult court without a hearing on the transfer; to do so violates the protection against double jeopardy.

status offense
Any act committed by a juvenile that is considered unacceptable for a child, such as truancy or running away from home, but that would not be a crime if it were committed by an adult.

The precedent-setting *Gault* decision was followed by a series of cases further defining the rights of juveniles. In the case of **In re Winship (1970)**, the Court held that proof must be established "beyond a reasonable doubt" and not on "a preponderance of the evidence" before a juvenile may be classified as a delinquent for committing an act that would be a crime if it had been committed by an adult. The Court was not willing to give juveniles every due process right, however: It held in **McKeiver v. Pennsylvania (1971)** that "trial by jury in the juvenile court's adjudicative stage is not a constitutional requirement." But in **Breed v. Jones (1975),** the Court extended the protection against double jeopardy to juveniles by requiring that, before a case is adjudicated in juvenile court, a hearing must be held to determine if it should be transferred to the adult court.

Another area of change concerned **status offenses**—acts that are not illegal if committed by an adult; these include skipping school, running away from home, or living a "wayward, idle or dissolute life" (Feld, 1993: 203). In 1974, Congress passed the Juvenile Justice and Delinquency Prevention Act, which included provisions for taking status offenders out of correctional institutions. Since then, people have worked on diverting such children out of the system, reducing the possibility of incarceration, and rewriting status offense laws.

As juvenile crime rates continued to rise during the 1970s, the public began calling for tougher approaches in dealing with delinquents. In the 1980s, at the same time that stricter sanctions were imposed on adult offenders, juvenile justice policies shifted to crime control.

The Crime Control Period (1980–2005)

The public demands to "crack down on crime" began in 1980. Legislators responded in part by changing the juvenile system. Greater attention began to be focused on repeat offenders, with policy makers calling for harsher punishment for juveniles who commit crimes.

Schall v. Martin (1984)
Juveniles can be held in preventive detention if there is concern that they may commit additional crimes while awaiting court action.

In **Schall v. Martin (1984)**, the Supreme Court significantly departed from the trend toward increased juvenile rights. The Court confirmed that the general notion of *parens patriae* was a primary basis for the juvenile court, equal in importance to the Court's desire to protect the community from crime. Thus, juveniles may be held in preventive detention before trial if they are deemed a "risk" to the community.

The *Schall* decision reflects the ambivalence permeating the juvenile justice system. On one side are the liberal reformers, who call for increased procedural and substantive legal protections for juveniles accused of crime. On the other side are conservatives devoted to crime control policies and alarmed by the rise in juvenile crime.

Crime control policies brought many more juveniles to be tried in adult courts. As noted by Alex Kotlowitz, "the crackdown on children has gone well beyond those accused of violent crimes" (1994: 40). Data from the National Juvenile Court Data Archive show that delinquency cases waived to the adult criminal courts increased dramatically from 1987 to 1994, but have since decreased and remained steady since 2001 (B. Adams and Addie, 2010: 186). In addition, some claim that increased penalties on juvenile offenders disproportionately affect minority youth more than white youth (Feld, 1999, 2004).

The "Kids Are Different" Period (2005–Present)

Some observers believe that a new period in juvenile justice may be developing. In ***Roper v. Simmons* (2005)**, the case discussed in Chapter 12, the United States Supreme Court ruled that executions were unconstitutional for crimes committed by those younger than 18 years of age. Similarly, in ***Graham v. Florida* (2010)**, the Court decided that life imprisonment without possibility of parole (LWOP) for juvenile offenders was unconstitutional in non-homicide cases. Two years later, in ***Miller v. Alabama* (2012)** the Court also deemed mandatory LWOP unconstitutional for juvenile homicide offenders. A majority of the Supreme Court's justices ruled that these harsh punishments for juveniles, when mandated by the state legislature without leaving any discretion for the judge or jury, were out of step with the contemporary values of society and therefore they violated the Eighth Amendment prohibition on cruel and unusual punishments.

***Roper v. Simmons* (2005)**
No death penalty for offenders who commit a murder while younger than age 18.

***Graham v. Florida* (2010)**
Juvenile offenders cannot be sentenced to life imprisonment without possibility of parole (LWOP) for non-homicide crimes.

***Miller v. Alabama* (2012)**
Juvenile homicide offenders cannot be sentenced to mandatory life without possibility of parole (LWOP) imprisonment.

These important rulings arguably signaled a new era of juvenile justice. In *Roper, Graham*, and *Miller*, the Court focused on the issue of culpability, and decided that juveniles were less culpable than adults due to a number of different factors related to physical and emotional development involving the growth and maturation process of the human brain (MacArthur Foundation, 2007b). In another case in 2011, the Supreme Court relied on developmental factors in redefining the law concerning *Miranda* warnings. Additional research into the development of juveniles indicates that intellectual maturity occurs at age 16, but other factors (such as avoiding impulsiveness) are not fully developed until early adulthood (ages 24–26). In addition, studies indicate that the large majority of juvenile offenders grow out of antisocial behavior as they become adults, and most juvenile delinquency is limited to adolescence (Steinberg, Cauffman, and Monahan, 2015). Scientific research has spurred a growing recognition of the brain development differences between teens and adults. These findings provide a basis for new programs and proposed laws designed to reemphasize treating juveniles differently than adults for purposes of rehabilitation and punishment. This is not to say that juveniles accused of crimes cannot be held responsible for their actions. Researchers studying this issue argue that juvenile brain development does not imply that juvenile offenders should avoid punishment, but that the punishment should be more lenient than an adult convicted of the same crime.

Current program trends aimed at helping juvenile offenders are rooted in the principles of rehabilitation and the prevention of delinquency. Such programs are not yet widespread nor fully developed. For example, there are few low-cost substance abuse programs for juveniles outside of correctional institutions—therefore, a poor juvenile must be incarcerated to receive such assistance without significant personal financial expense. Reducing drug use before it accelerates delinquency would seem to be the key to keeping juveniles crime free, and thus there is increasing interest in developing more programs that are accessible to youths in the community. Research is also focusing on the relationship between parents and children, and how parenting programs may help to keep kids out of the juvenile courts (MacArthur Foundation, 2007a). Read more about several successful prevention programs in the Close Up feature.

waiver
Procedure by which the juvenile court waives its jurisdiction and transfers a juvenile case to the adult criminal court.

As indicated by the 2014 example of the Slender Man stabbing case described in the chapter opener, judicial **waiver** is used to waive or relinquish juvenile court jurisdiction and move juveniles into adult court for prosecution and punishment. The use of waiver declined dramatically from 1996 to 2010, reaching the lowest number of cases waived since 1988. This decrease in waiver mirrors the decrease in violent juvenile crime during that period (Puzzanchera and Addie, 2014). Recent changes in a few states indicate that waiver is becoming less popular. Several states are considering the abolition of juvenile waiver by increasing their minimum age for adult trial to 18. The REDEEM Act (discussed in Chapter 16) recommends the expungement of juvenile offenses committed before the age of 15, and provides incentives for states to raise the age of criminal responsibility to 18 (Booker, 2015). Research on public attitudes also indicates that U.S. citizens are becoming less supportive of waiver, and believe it should be used "sparingly and selectively" and only when the adult justice system is able to provide a rehabilitative component to punishment for juveniles (Applegate, Davis, and Cullen, 2009).

The current movement for more-lenient treatment of juveniles is still in its infancy. It is unknown how states will react to changes reflected in *Roper v. Simmons*, *Graham v. Florida*, and *Miller v. Alabama*, and there is still considerable support for the "get tough" stance toward older juveniles. The Supreme Court has allowed California's "three strikes" law, for example, to count juvenile convictions as "strikes," thereby mandating long sentences for repeat offenders (*Nguyen v. California*, 2009). Opponents point out that this violates the spirit of the *parens patriae* philosophy (Juvenile Law Center, 2008). In many places, the juvenile court, where the use of discretion and the desire to rehabilitate were previously uppermost goals, employs a system of rules and procedures similar to those in adult courts.

In spite of the increasingly tough policies directed at juvenile offenders in the late twentieth century, changes that occurred during the juvenile rights

CLOSE UP

YOUTH VIOLENCE REDUCTION PROGRAMS

Several cities have initiated programs to reduce and prevent juvenile violence. The Philadelphia Youth Violence Reduction Partnership (YVRP) was created to reduce Philadelphia's homicide rate and keep high-risk teenagers from killing or being killed themselves. Participants in this program have been convicted of at least one violent or drug-related offense in the past. The program utilizes increased supervision of offenders combined with opportunities for employment, mentoring, health care, and drug treatment programs. They specifically identify risk factors for delinquency focused on characteristics describing the individual (social ties, drug use, victimization history), the family (delinquent siblings, family poverty and violence), the school (poor school, frequent truancy), the community (availability of drugs and firearms, crime rate), and peers (gang membership, drug use). To determine if this program had a significant effect on crime rates, researchers collected homicide data from police departments; tracked participants; and interviewed probation officers, police, and street workers to obtain their input as well. Analysis of these data indicated that the police districts that implemented this program had lower homicide rates than other districts in Philadelphia.

"Operation Peacekeeper" in Stockton, California aims to reduce gun-related violence among gang members. The period continue to affect the system profoundly. Lawyers are now routinely present at court hearings and other stages of the process, adding a note of formality that was not present 30 years ago. Status offenders seldom end up in secure punitive environments, such as training schools. The juvenile justice system looks more like the adult justice system than it did, but it remains less formal. Its stated intention is also less harsh: to keep juveniles in the community whenever possible.

✔POINT

5. What was the function of a "house of refuge"?
6. What were the major elements of the Illinois Juvenile Court Act of 1899?
7. What was the main point of the *In re Gault* decision?
8. How did the decline in juvenile crime in the 1990s affect juvenile justice policy?
9. What reasons has the Supreme Court given for disallowing the use of the death penalty and other harsh sentences for juveniles?

STOP AND ANALYZE: The Supreme Court was deeply divided over the issue of whether sentences of death for murder and life without parole for non-homicide offenses are out of step with the values of contemporary society. Do you think society's contemporary values would reject those sentences for juveniles? If you were a lawyer, what evidence could you present to a court that reflects society's current values concerning the punishment of juveniles today?

The Juvenile Justice System

Juvenile justice operates through a variety of procedures in different states; even different counties within the same states vary in their processes. Because the offenses committed by juveniles are mostly violations of state laws, there is little federal involvement in the juvenile justice system. Despite internal differences, the juvenile justice system is characterized by two key factors: (1) the age of clients and (2) the categories of cases under juvenile court jurisdiction.

program uses youth outreach workers, who are "streetwise young men and women" with special training in working with these youths. They work in neighborhood settings to assist youth and also act as positive role models, and work with gang-involved youth to educate them on the consequences of gang membership and a violent lifestyle. Research has indicated that gun violence dropped dramatically in Stockton during the evaluation period.

Sources: Adapted from the Office of Juvenile Justice and Delinquency Prevention "Model Programs Guide" (www.ojjdp.gov/mpg), and the National Gang Center "Philadelphia Youth Violence Reduction Partnership" (www.nationalgangcenter.gov).

DEBATE THE ISSUE

Operation Peacekeeper is designed to prevent youth from engaging in violent activities related to gang membership; however, some argue that funds spent on programs such as these are better spent on the "back end" of the system—strengthening the police response to crime and the juvenile court response. Others argue that using funds on the "front end" will save significant costs, because successful prevention programs will reduce associated expenditures for the police, juvenile courts, and corrections down the road. What is the most effective use of public funds with regard to delinquency?

Age of Clients

Age normally determines whether a person is processed through the juvenile or the adult justice system. The upper age limit for original juvenile court jurisdiction varies from 16 to 18. In 39 states and the District of Columbia, it is the 18th birthday; in 10 states, the 17th; and in the remaining 2 states, the 16th birthday. In 45 states, judges have the discretion to transfer juveniles to adult courts through a waiver hearing. Figure 17.3 shows the age at which juveniles can be transferred to adult court.

Categories of Cases under Juvenile Court Jurisdiction

Four types of cases fall under the jurisdiction of the juvenile justice system: delinquency, status offenses, neglect, and dependency. Mixing together young criminals with children who suffer from their parents' inadequacies dates from the earliest years of juvenile justice.

delinquent
A child who has committed an act that if committed by an adult would be a criminal act.

Delinquent children have committed acts that if committed by an adult would be criminal—for example, auto theft, robbery, or assault. Juvenile courts handle about 1.2 million delinquency cases each year, 72 percent involving male delinquents, and 33 percent involving African Americans. Among the criminal charges brought before the juvenile court, 26 percent are for crimes against persons, 36 percent for property offenses, 12 percent for drug law violations, and 26 percent for public order offenses (Hockenberry and Puzzanchera, 2014a). Table 17.2 shows the distribution of delinquency cases that are referred to juvenile court.

FIGURE 17.3 THE YOUNGEST AGE AT WHICH JUVENILES MAY BE TRANSFERRED TO ADULT CRIMINAL COURT BY WAIVER OF JUVENILE JURISDICTION

The waiver provisions of states vary greatly, and no clear regional or other factor explains the differences.

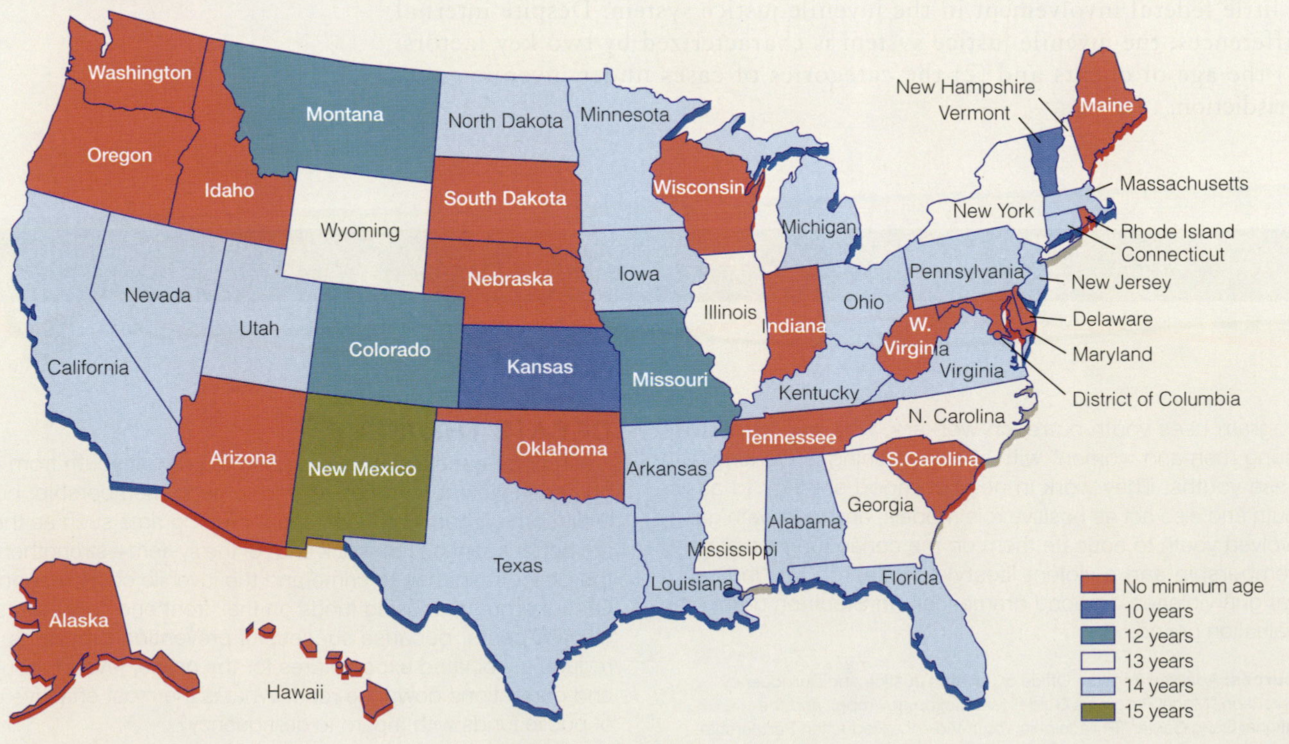

Source: Adapted from data by Office of Juvenile Justice and Delinquency Prevention, *OJJDP Statistical Briefing Book* (www.ojjdp.gov/ojstatbb/structure_process/qa04110.asp?qaDate=2011). Released on December 17, 2012.

TABLE 17.2 DISTRIBUTION OF DELINQUENCY CASES REFERRED TO JUVENILE COURT

Juvenile courts in the United States handled about 1.2 million criminal cases in 2011. This was a decline of 34% from the number handled in 1997.

PERCENTAGE OF TOTAL CASES DISPOSED, 2011

26%	**Crimes against persons**	**Percentages**
	Homicide	Less than 1
	Forcible rape	Less than 1
	Robbery	2
	Other personal offenses	2
	Aggravated assault	3
	Simple assault	18
	Other violent sex offenses	1
36%	**Property crimes**	
	Burglary	6
	Larceny/theft	18
	Motor vehicle theft	1
	Arson	Less than 1
	Vandalism	6
	Trespassing	3
	Stolen property offenses	1
	Other property offenses	1
12%	**Drug violations**	
26%	**Public order offenses**	
	Weapons offenses	2
	Obstruction of justice	12
	Disorderly conduct	7
	Liquor law violations	1
	Nonviolent sex offenses	1
	Other public order offenses	2

Source: Sarah Hockenberry and Charles Puzzanchera, *Delinquency Cases in Juvenile Courts, 2011* (Washington, DC: U.S. Government Printing Office, December 2014).

Recall that status offenses are acts that are illegal only if they are committed by juveniles. Status offenders have not violated a penal code; instead they are charged with being ungovernable or incorrigible: as runaways, truants, or **PINS** (persons in need of supervision). Status offenders make up about 9 percent of the juvenile court caseload. Although female offenders account for only 28 percent of delinquency cases, they make up 41 percent of the status offense cases (Hockenberry and Puzzanchera, 2014b).

PINS
Acronym for "person(s) in need of supervision," a term that designates juveniles who are either status offenders or thought to be on the verge of trouble.

Some states do not distinguish between delinquent offenders and status offenders; they label both as juvenile delinquents. Those judged to be ungovernable and those judged to be robbers may be sent to the same correctional institution.

Beginning in the early 1960s, many state legislatures attempted to distinguish status offenders and to exempt them from a criminal record. In states that have decriminalized status offenses, juveniles who participate in these activities may now be classified as dependent children and placed in the care of child-protective agencies.

Juvenile justice also deals with problems of neglect and dependency—situations in which children are viewed as being hurt through no fault of their own because their parents have failed to provide a proper environment for them. People see the state's role as acting as a parent to a child whose own parents are unable or unwilling to provide proper care. Illinois, for example, defines a **neglected child** as one who is receiving inadequate care because of some action or inaction of his or her parents. This may include not being sent to school, not receiving medical care, being abandoned, living in an injurious environment, or not receiving some other care necessary for the child's well-being. A **dependent child** either has no parent or guardian or is receiving inadequate care because of the physical or mental disability of the parent. The law governing neglected and dependent children is broad and includes situations in which the child is viewed as a victim of adult behavior.

neglected child
A child who is receiving inadequate care because of some action or inaction of his or her parents.

dependent child
A child who has no parent or guardian or whose parents cannot give proper care.

Nationally about 75 percent of the cases referred to the juvenile courts are delinquency cases, 20 percent of which are status offenses. Twenty percent are dependency and neglect cases, and about 5 percent involve special proceedings, such as adoption. The system, then, deals with both criminal and noncriminal cases. Often juveniles who have done nothing wrong are categorized, either officially or in the public mind, as delinquents. In some states little effort is made in detention facilities or in social service agencies to separate the classes of juveniles prior to their judicial hearings.

✔POINT 10. What are the jurisdictional criteria for the juvenile court?

STOP AND ANALYZE: Why do most state laws use 18 as the age of majority? Is there something special that occurs at age 18 that indicates a shift from "juvenile" to "adult"? Would you use a specific age, or design some other basis for deciding whether to try an older teen as a juvenile or adult? Why?

The Juvenile Justice Process

Underlying the juvenile justice system is the philosophy that police, judges, and correctional officials should focus primarily on the interests of the child. Prevention of delinquency is the system's justification for intervening in the lives of juveniles who are involved in either status or criminal offenses.

In theory at least, juvenile proceedings are to be conducted in a nonadversarial environment. The juvenile court is to be a place where the judge, social workers, clinicians, and probation officers work together to diagnose the child's situation and select a treatment program to attack that problem.

Juvenile justice is a bureaucracy based on an ideology of social work. It is staffed primarily by people who think of themselves as members of the helping professions. Not even the recent emphasis on crime control and punishment has removed the treatment philosophy from most juvenile justice arenas. However, political pressures and limits on resources may stymie the implementation of this philosophy by focusing on the punishment of offenders rather than the prevention of delinquency, even though the public is more willing to pay for prevention programs and rehabilitation than incarceration (T. Baker et al., 2013).

Like the adult system, juvenile justice functions within a context of exchange relationships between officials of various government and private agencies that influence decisions. The juvenile court must deal not only with children and their parents, but also with patrol officers, probation officers, welfare officials, social workers, psychologists, and the heads of treatment institutions—all of whom have their own goals, perceptions of delinquency, and concepts of treatment.

FIGURE 17.4 THE JUVENILE JUSTICE SYSTEM

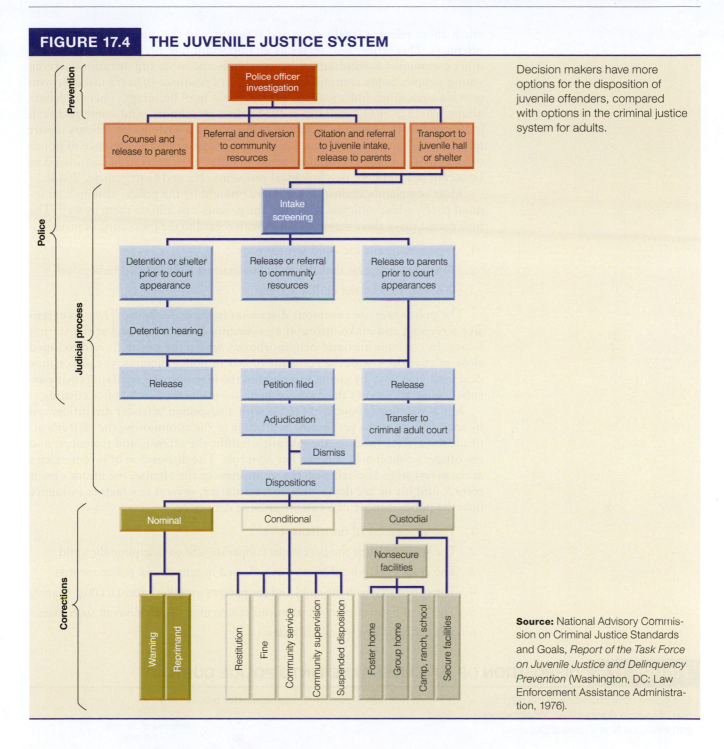

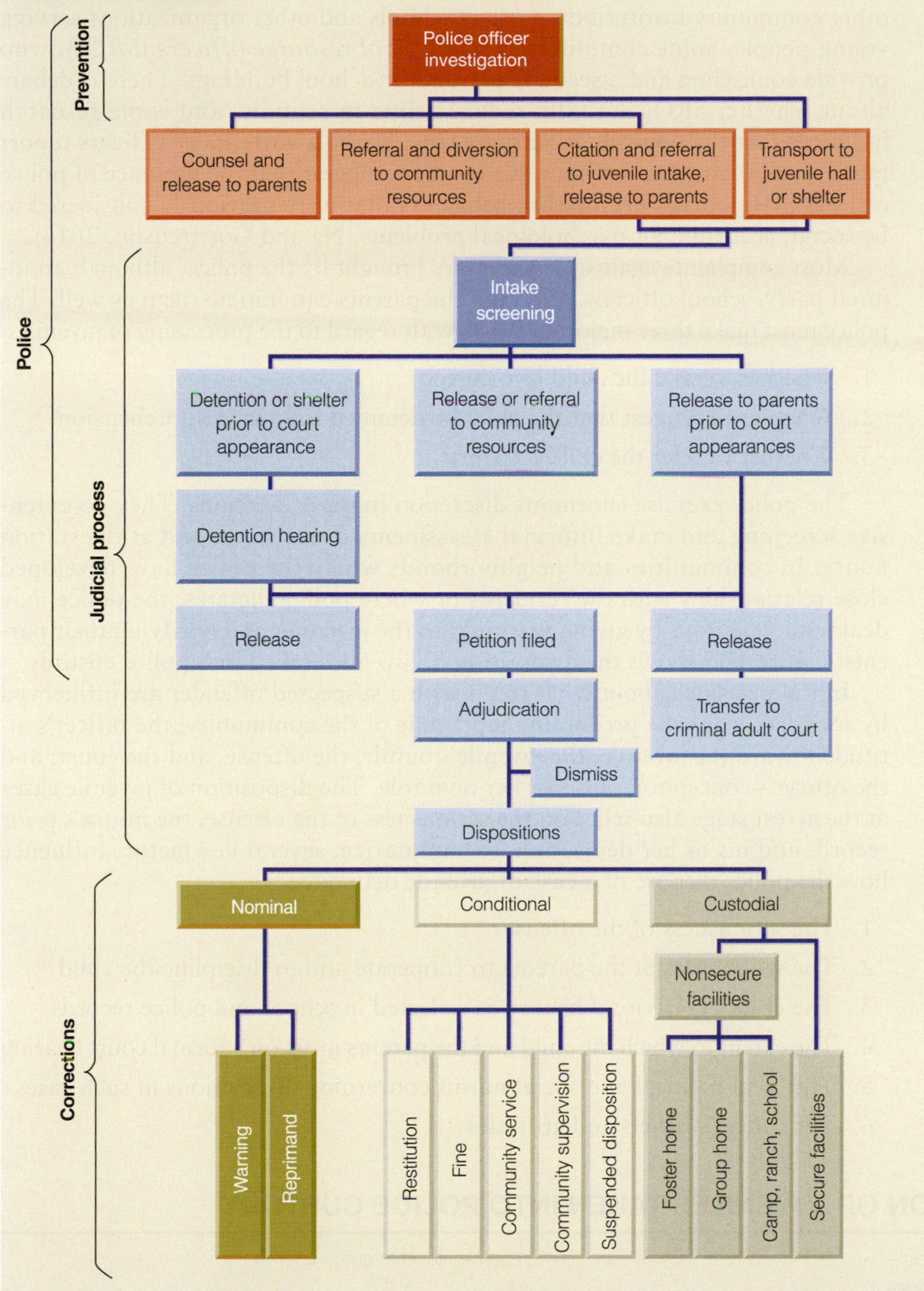

Decision makers have more options for the disposition of juvenile offenders, compared with options in the criminal justice system for adults.

Source: National Advisory Commission on Criminal Justice Standards and Goals, *Report of the Task Force on Juvenile Justice and Delinquency Prevention* (Washington, DC: Law Enforcement Assistance Administration, 1976).

Figure 17.4 outlines the sequence of steps that are taken from the point of police investigation through to correctional disposition, which have not changed drastically in many years. As you examine this figure, compare the procedures with those of the criminal justice system for adults. Note the various options available to decision makers and the extensive discretion that they may exercise.

Police Interface

Many police departments, especially those in cities, have special juvenile units. The juvenile officer is often selected and trained to relate to youths, knows much about relevant legal issues, and is sensitive to the special needs of young offenders. This officer also serves as an important link between the police and other community institutions, such as schools and other organizations serving young people. Some communities hire *school resource officers* (*SROs*), who provide counseling and a security presence in school buildings. There is debate about whether SROs actually reduce crime in schools, and some research indicates that the opposite is actually true. Schools with police officers report more crime than those without. Researchers suggest that the presence of police officers may actually criminalize behaviors that were previously considered to be social, academic, or psychological problems (Na and Gottfredson, 2013).

Most complaints against juveniles are brought by the police, although an injured party, school officials, and even the parents can initiate them as well. The police must make three major decisions with regard to the processing of juveniles:

1. Whether to take the child into custody
2. Whether to request that the child be detained following apprehension
3. Whether to refer the child to court

The police exercise enormous discretion in these decisions. They do extensive screening and make informal assessments in the street and at the station house. In communities and neighborhoods where the police have developed close relationships with the residents or where policy dictates, the police may deal with violations by giving warnings to the juveniles and notifying their parents. Figure 17.5 shows the disposition of juveniles taken into police custody.

Initial decisions about what to do with a suspected offender are influenced by such factors as the predominant attitude of the community; the officer's attitude toward the juvenile, the juvenile's family, the offense, and the court; and the officer's conception of his or her own role. The disposition of juvenile cases at the arrest stage also relies on the seriousness of the offense, the minor's prior record, and his or her demeanor. To summarize, several key factors influence how the police dispose of a case of juvenile delinquency:

1. The seriousness of the offense
2. The willingness of the parents to cooperate and to discipline the child
3. The child's behavioral history as reflected in school and police records
4. The extent to which the child and the parents insist on a formal court hearing
5. The local political and social norms concerning dispositions in such cases
6. The officer's beliefs and attitudes

FIGURE 17.5 DISPOSITION OF JUVENILES TAKEN INTO POLICE CUSTODY

The police have discretion in the disposition of juvenile arrest cases. What factors can influence how a case is disposed?

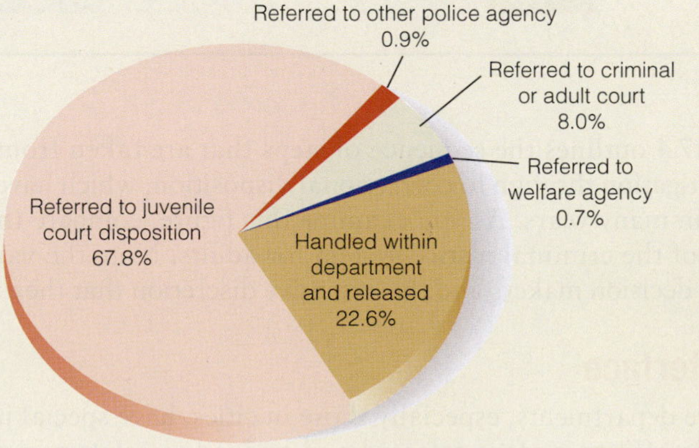

Source: Federal Bureau of Investigation, *Uniform Crime Reports 2013* (Washington DC: U.S. Government Printing Office, 2014), Table 68.

In dealing with juveniles, police often confront issues concerning the *Miranda* warnings and the *Mapp* unreasonable search and seizure rulings. Although the language of these decisions is not explicit, most jurisdictions now provide the *Miranda* protections. But questions remain as to the ability of juveniles to waive these rights. In 1979, the Supreme Court ruled in **Fare v. Michael C. (1979)** that a child may waive his or her rights to an attorney and to protections against self-incrimination. But the Court said that juvenile court judges must evaluate the totality of circumstances under which the minor made these decisions, to ensure that they were voluntary. The Court later specified that police must take the offender's age into account when deciding whether a minor is officially in the custody of the police, stating that "children will often feel bound to submit to police questioning when an adult in the same circumstances would feel free to leave" (*J. D. B. v. North Carolina*, 2011).

Fare v. Michael C. (1979)
By examining the totality of circumstances, trial court judges must evaluate the voluntariness of juveniles' waiving their rights to an attorney and to protections against self-incrimination.

On the issue of unreasonable searches and seizures prohibited by the Fourth Amendment, the Court has not been as forthcoming. State courts interpreted *Gault* to extend these provisions, but in 1985 the Supreme Court ruled in **New Jersey v. T. L. O. (1985)** that school officials can search students and their lockers. The justices recognized that children do have Fourth Amendment rights, yet a search could be viewed as reasonable if (1) it is based on a suspicion of lawbreaking and (2) it is required to maintain order, safety, and discipline in the school.

New Jersey v. T. L. O. (1985)
School officials may search a student if they have a reasonable suspicion that the search will produce evidence that a school rule or a criminal law has been violated.

Faced with problems of drug use and students carrying weapons in the public schools, administrators have taken steps to enforce rules so as to increase security. This has led to conflicts concerning the right to privacy versus school safety. In 1995, the Supreme Court said certain students, such as athletes, could be subject to random drug testing. The case, **Vernonia School District v. Acton (1995)**, concerned a seventh grader's parents who refused to sign a urinalysis consent form. As a result their son, James Acton, was kept off of the football team. The court ruled that the testing was constitutional in the interest of ensuring a safe learning environment even though the student had not exhibited suspicious behavior. The Supreme Court later expanded school officials' authority to impose drug testing by permitting schools to require students to submit to random drug testing in order to participate in non-sports extracurricular activities, such as band and choir (*Board of Education v. Earls*, 2002). The Supreme Court has not approved mandatory drug testing of all students in a public school. It has simply permitted schools to develop and apply testing policies to students as a condition of participation in extracurricular activities. In addition, the Court has also recognized limits on school officials' authority to conduct searches. In *Safford Unified School District v. Redding* (2009), the Court ruled that public school officials cannot conduct a strip search of a student to look for drugs. In this case, the search was based on inaccurate information reported to school authorities by another student.

Vernonia School District v. Acton (1995)
To ensure a safe learning environment, school officials may require random drug testing of students involved in extracurricular school sports teams.

Although young people commit many serious crimes, the juvenile function of police work is concerned largely with order maintenance. In most incidents of this sort, the law is ambiguous, and blame cannot easily be assigned. Many offenses committed by juveniles that involve physical or monetary damage are minor infractions: breaking windows, hanging around the business district, disturbing the peace, public sexual behavior, and shoplifting. Here the function of the investigating officer is not so much to solve crimes as to handle the often legally uncertain complaints involving juveniles. The officer seeks both to satisfy the complainant and to keep the youth from future trouble. Given this emphasis on settling cases within the community—instead of strictly enforcing the law—the police power to arrest is a weapon that can be used to deter juveniles from criminal activity and to encourage them to conform to the law.

Intake Screening at the Court

The juvenile court processing of delinquency cases begins with a referral in the form of a petition, not with an arrest warrant as in the adult system. When a petition is filed, an intake hearing is held, over which a hearing officer presides. During this stage, the officer determines whether the alleged facts are sufficient for the juvenile court to take jurisdiction or whether some other action would be in the child's best interest.

diversion
The process of screening children out of the juvenile justice system without a decision by the court.

Nationally, 46 percent of all referrals are disposed of at this stage, without formal processing by a judge. **Diversion** is the process of screening children out of the system without a decision by the court, thereby limiting their involvement in the formal juvenile justice system. In approximately 41 percent of these cases, the charges are dismissed; another 22 percent are diverted to an informal probation, and the remaining 37 percent are placed in a mental health facility, other treatment facility, or are assigned to serve some agreed-on alternative sanction in the community (Hockenberry and Puzzanchera, 2014a). You can read about evidence-based diversion programs in the New Directions in Criminal Justice Policy Feature.

Pretrial Procedures

When a decision is made to refer the case to the court (54 percent of cases), the court holds an initial hearing. Here, the juveniles are informed of their rights and told that if a plea is given it must be voluntary.

detention hearing
A hearing by the juvenile court to determine if a juvenile is to be detained or released prior to adjudication.

If the juvenile is to be detained pending trial, most states require a **detention hearing**, which determines if the youth is to be released to a parent or guardian or to be held in a detention facility until adjudication. Some children are detained to keep them from committing other crimes while

NEW DIRECTIONS IN CRIMINAL JUSTICE POLICY

EVIDENCE-BASED DIVERSION PROGRAMS

The juvenile justice system is increasingly reliant on evidence-based programs that have been tested by rigorous scientific research. Many of these programs are designed to divert juveniles from the justice system to avoid the stigma and impact of being processed in the formal court system.

In Michigan, the Adolescent Diversion Project (ADP) was created by Michigan State University using the tenets of three theories of juvenile delinquency: social control, social learning, and labeling theories (see Chapter 2). Student volunteers at MSU are trained to work with juvenile offenders to determine their specific needs and then help to strengthen their skills in areas in which they might be lacking. For example, some juveniles may benefit from strengthening their family relationships, while others may need help structuring their free-time activities. Evaluations of this program have indicated that youth who complete the program have a lower recidivism rate than those who are processed in the juvenile courts.

New York has implemented a similar program with the same name, in which 16- and 17-year-old offenders are diverted from adult court processing (in New York, offenders in these age groups are automatically tried as adults). This ADP program aims to divert juvenile offenders from the adult system in order to avoid the civil disabilities experienced by many adult offenders (see Chapter 16). Judges who have received specific training related to adolescent brain development, substance abuse, and other issues relevant to adolescent offenders can make a determination of the offender's suitability for the ADP. Evaluations of this program indicate that the juvenile offenders who experience ADP have similar recidivism rates to those offenders who are processed in the adult system—indicating that diversion awaiting trial. Others are held to protect them from the possibility of harm from gang members or parents. Still others are held because if released they will likely not appear in court as required. Nationally, about 21 percent of all delinquency cases involve detention between referral to the juvenile court and disposition of the case (Hockenberry and Puzzanchera, 2014a).

The conditions in many detention facilities are poor; abuse is often reported. In some rural areas, juveniles continue to be detained in adult jails even though the federal government has pressed states to hold youths in separate facilities. In 2003, the city of Baltimore, Maryland, unveiled a new juvenile detention facility, meant to expedite juvenile cases and centralize services to delinquent youth. The new facility was later termed a "monstrosity," with poor lines of sight (meaning officers cannot easily observe and supervise the juvenile detainees), overcrowding, and increasing rates of violence within its walls (Bykowicz, 2008). A 2010 evaluation determined that the high rates of violence in the facility had begun to decrease (Dedel, 2010), with greater reductions in violence from 2010 to 2012 (Moroney, 2014). Baltimore currently holds juveniles charged as adults in the same facility as adult offenders, which has been a source of controversy as well. In 2013, officials determined that this facility was controlled by gang members, and that guards had been sneaking in contraband (Toobin, 2014). While some recommended that a separate jail be constructed for juveniles being tried as adults, the State of Maryland decided that the low numbers of these juveniles did not warrant new construction, and will build a facility for juvenile offenders as part of the Baltimore City Detention Center reconstruction (Duncan, 2013). Most recently, the U.S. Department of Justice has faulted the center for mistreatment of juvenile detainees, several of whom were kept in solitary confinement for up to 143 days (Fenton, 2015).

Based on the belief that detaining youth accelerates their delinquent behaviors, some jurisdictions have attempted to stem the tide of rising numbers of juveniles in detention. In Durham, North Carolina, a new program is being implemented to keep 16- and 17-year-olds who commit minor crimes out of the juvenile justice system. Their "Misdemeanor Diversion Program" allows juvenile

---

does not increase their risk of recidivism. It also avoids the civil disabilities that often result from formal charges.

The State of Texas has implemented the Front-End Diversion Initiative (FEDI), a diversion program specifically for juvenile offenders with mental health needs. Intake officers with special training determine whether an offender should be evaluated for mental health issues. If the offender qualifies, then prosecution of the juvenile is deferred for six months. During this time, the individual works with a probation officer who is specially trained to help the juvenile set goals and to create a plan to meet those goals. The educational, mental health, family, and community needs of the juvenile are all assessed and worked on during the program. Evaluations of the program indicate that FEDI significantly reduced the rate of juveniles adjudicated—they were able to successfully avoid prosecution by meeting the goals set by their probation officer.

Sources: Adapted from the U.S. Department of Justice, Office of Juvenile Justice and Delinquency Prevention online "Model Programs Guide" (www.ojjdp.gov/mpg/) and "Crime Solutions" websites (crimesolutions.gov).

DEBATE THE ISSUE

Each of these programs was created based on a foundation of criminological theory and assessed using valid research methodologies. Diversion of juveniles from formal processing may help reduce their recidivism rates as well as the stigma (and civil disabilities) faced by those with criminal convictions. Supporters of these programs point out they are less expensive than incarceration, and more effective. With limited budgets, should the juvenile justice system be spending funds on diversion, or focusing their efforts on policing and incarceration? Which strategy might best reduce crime rates?

offenders to complete community service requirements and avoid being charged as adults, which would otherwise occur under state law (Oleniacz, 2014).

Transfer (Waiver) to Adult Court

In 1997, an 11-year-old boy named Nathaniel Abraham shot and killed a man outside a convenience store in Pontiac, Michigan. At the time, Michigan law specified no minimum age for transfer of a juvenile to adult court. Nathaniel's case was waived to adult court and he stood trial for the homicide. The jury, however, refused to convict him of the crime of homicide in the first degree, which would have necessitated incarceration in an adult prison. Instead, they found him guilty of second-degree homicide, allowing the judge to use his discretion to place Nathaniel in a juvenile facility. Nathaniel's case attracted national attention, because it highlighted the difficulty of deciding what to do with children and teens who commit offenses as serious as those committed by the most violent adult offenders. As you read "Civic Engagement: Your Role in the System," consider how you might react if you were a juror in regular criminal court considering the case of a youthful defendant.

CIVIC ENGAGEMENT

YOUR ROLE IN THE SYSTEM

Imagine that you were a juror in the case of 11-year-old Nathaniel Abraham who shot and killed a man—someone that he did not know—who was walking into a convenience store. Apparently, he had come into possession of a gun and was simply interested in trying it out. *Make a list of arguments favoring and opposing convicting him as an adult defendant. How do you think you would vote during the jury's deliberations?* Then read about a study that indicates jurors may become biased in favor of conviction when they learn that a youthful defendant in adult court has been sent there by the juvenile court.

One of the first decisions to be made after a juvenile is referred is whether a case should be transferred to the criminal (adult) justice system. In 45 states, juvenile court judges may waive their jurisdiction. This means that after considering the seriousness of the charge, the age of the juvenile, and the prospects of rehabilitation, the judge can transfer the case to adult court. In 29 states, certain violent crimes such as murder, rape, and armed robbery are excluded by law from the jurisdiction of the juvenile courts. In 1970, only 3 states allowed prosecutors the authority to decide whether to file in adult or juvenile court. Today, 15 states give prosecutors the authority to do so (P. Griffin, 2011). Critics question whether prosecutors will "make better informed and more appropriate 'criminal adulthood' decisions than would judges in an adversarial waiver hearing" (Feld, 2004: 599). See "What Americans Think" for a look at public attitudes about transferring juveniles to the adult court.

A "tougher" approach to juvenile crime took hold in the 1970s, which led to an increase in the number of cases transferred to adult court. Several states expanded their ability to transfer juveniles by excluding certain crimes from juvenile court jurisdiction, or lowering their minimum age for transfer to adult court. Several states specify no minimum age for certain offenses (note the number of states in Figure 17.3 that can waive a juvenile regardless of his or her age).

Although the laws regarding waiver have not changed much in recent years, there is evidence that it is being used less frequently and for more-serious offenses. Waived cases represent less than 1 percent (about 6,000) of delinquency cases, and the likelihood of waiver varies by offense, offender age, and offender race. In all, violent offenders make up the majority of those transferred to adult court (50 percent), followed by property offenders (30 percent), drug offenders (12 percent), and public order offenders (8 percent). In addition, African American youths are more likely to be waived than are white youths, although this is partially due to differences in offending patterns and the gap between African American and white youth is growing smaller (Puzzanchera and Addie, 2014). A study of 40 large urban counties found that nearly two-thirds of juvenile felony defendants in adult court were charged with violent crime, compared with one-quarter of adult defendants (Rainville and Smith, 2003).

One result of the decreased use of waiver is that fewer juveniles are being sent to adult state prisons. In 1995, almost 6,500 juvenile offenders were sent to adult prison; by 2009, that number had dropped to just under 3,000—a decrease of 57 percent (Sickmund and Puzzanchera, 2014). Supporters of waiving juveniles to adult court argue that serious crime deserves a serious punishment. Critics of the policies claim that waiver subverts the intent of the juvenile justice system, and exposes juvenile offenders to harsh conditions in adult prisons—where they are vulnerable to physical and sexual victimization (DeJong and Merrill, 2000). In addition, those juveniles tried in adult courts are more likely to reoffend after release (MacArthur Foundation, 2007c; Redding 2010).

Adjudication

Juvenile courts deal with almost 1.2 million delinquency cases each year (Hockenberry and Puzzanchera, 2014a). *Adjudication* is the trial stage of the juvenile justice process. If the child has not admitted to the charges and the case has not been transferred to the adult court, an adjudication hearing is held to determine the facts in the case and, if appropriate, label the juvenile as "delinquent."

The Supreme Court's decision in *Gault* and other due process rulings mandated changes that have altered the philosophy and actions of the juvenile court. Contemporary juvenile proceedings are more formal than those of the past, although still more informal than adult courts. The parents and child must receive copies of petitions with specific charges; counsel may be present, and free counsel can be appointed if the juvenile cannot pay; witnesses can be cross-examined; and a transcript of the proceedings must be kept.

As with other Supreme Court decisions, local practice may differ sharply from the procedures spelled out in the high court's rulings. Juveniles and their

WHAT AMERICANS THINK

QUESTION: "Which statement do you agree with more?

1. Putting convicted youth under the age of 18 in adult jails and prisons makes them MORE likely to commit future crimes than if they were placed in a youth facility.

Agree 57%

2. Putting youth under the age of 18, who are charged with or convicted of crimes, in adult jails and prisons makes them LESS likely to commit future crimes than if they were placed in a youth facility.

Agree 27%

Source: GBA Strategies, "Campaign for Youth Justice: Youth Justice System Survey" (October 11, 2011). Retrieved from gbastrategies.com.

AP Images/Phil Coale

Alex King, age 13, is escorted into a Florida courtroom where he and his 14-year-old brother Derek were convicted of beating their father to death with a baseball bat as he slept. They were sentenced to, respectively, 7- and 8-year sentences of imprisonment. Should youthful offenders who commit such serious crimes always be tried as adults and given the same punishments as adults?

parents often waive their rights in response to suggestions from the judge or probation officer. The lower social status of the offender's parents, the intimidating atmosphere of the court, and judicial hints that the outcome will be more favorable if a lawyer is not present are reasons the procedures outlined in *Gault* might not be followed. The litany of "getting treatment," "doing what's right for the child," and "working out a just solution" may sound enticing, especially to people who are unfamiliar with the intricacies of formal legal procedures. In practice, then, juveniles still lack many of the protections given to adult offenders. Some of the differences between the juvenile and adult criminal justice systems are listed in Table 17.3.

The increased concern about crime has given prosecuting attorneys a more prominent part in the system. In keeping with the traditional child-saver philosophy, prosecuting attorneys rarely appeared in juvenile court prior to the *Gault* decision. Now that a defense attorney is present, the state often uses legal counsel as well. In many jurisdictions, prosecutors are assigned to deal specifically with juvenile cases. Their functions are to advise the intake officer, administer diversion programs, negotiate pleas, and act as an advocate during judicial proceedings.

TABLE 17.3 THE ADULT AND JUVENILE CRIMINAL JUSTICE SYSTEMS

Compare the basic elements of the adult and juvenile systems. To what extent does a juvenile have the same rights as an adult? Are the different decision-making processes necessary because a juvenile is involved?

	ADULT SYSTEM	JUVENILE SYSTEM
Philosophical assumptions	Decisions made as result of adversarial system in context of due process rights	Decisions made as result of inquiry into needs of juvenile within context of some due process elements
Jurisdiction	Violations of criminal law	Violations of criminal law, status offenses, neglect, dependency
Primary sanctioning goals	Retribution, deterrence, rehabilitation	Retribution, rehabilitation
Official discretion	Widespread	Widespread
Entrance	Official action of arrest, summons, or citation	Official action, plus referral by school, parents, other sources
Role of prosecuting and defense attorneys	Required and formalized	Sometimes required; less structured; poor role definition
Adjudication	Procedural rules of evidence in public jury trial required	Less formal structure to rules of evidence and conduct of trial; no right to public trial or jury in most states
Treatment programs	Run primarily by public agencies	Broad use of private and public agencies
Terminology	Arrest	Referral
	Preliminary hearing	Intake
	Prosecution	Adjudication
	Sentencing	Disposition
	Parole	Aftercare
APPLICATION OF BILL OF RIGHTS AMENDMENTS		
Fourth: Unreasonable searches and seizures	Applicable	Applicable
Fifth: Double jeopardy	Applicable	Applicable (re: waiver to adult court)
Self-incrimination	Applicable (*Miranda* warnings)	Applicable
Sixth: Right to counsel	Applicable	Applicable
Public trial	Applicable	Applicable in less than half of states
Trial by jury	Applicable	Applicable in less than half of states
Fourteenth: Right to treatment	Not applicable	Applicable

Ann Hermes/The Christian Science Monitor via Getty Images

The concept of restorative justice is applied to juveniles in some settings. Teen courts, for example, deal with less serious offenses, often before formal charges have been brought. Teens are judged by their peers, and typically the sentences include restitution, ranging from community service to letters of apology. Is this an effective way to deal with youthful offenders?

Juvenile proceedings and court records have traditionally remained closed to the public to protect the child's privacy and potential for rehabilitation. Thus, judges in the adult courts usually do not have access to juvenile records. This means that people who have already served time on juvenile probation or in juvenile institutions may be erroneously perceived to be first-time offenders when they are processed for crimes as adults. Some people argue that adult courts should have access to juvenile records and that young criminals should be treated more severely than adults to deter them from future illegal activity.

Disposition

If the court makes a finding of delinquency, the judge will schedule a dispositional hearing to decide what action should be taken. Typically, before passing sentence the judge receives a predispositional report prepared by a probation officer. Similar to a presentence report, it serves to assist the judge in deciding on a disposition that is in the best interests of the child and is consistent with the treatment plan developed by the probation officer.

The court finds most juveniles to be delinquent at trial, because the intake and pretrial processes normally filter out cases in which a law violation cannot be proved. Besides dismissal, four other choices are available: (1) probation, (2) intermediate sanctions, (3) custodial care, and (4) community treatment.

Juvenile court advocates have traditionally believed that rehabilitation is the only goal of the sanction imposed on young people. For most of the twentieth century, judges sentenced juveniles to indeterminate sentences so that correctional administrators could decide when release was appropriate. As in the adult criminal justice system, indeterminate sentences and unbridled discretion in juvenile justice have faced attack during the last three decades. Several states have tightened the sentencing discretion of judges, especially with regard to serious offenses. Washington State, for example, has adopted a determinate sentencing law for juveniles. In other states, a youth can be transferred more readily than before to the adult court for adjudication and sentencing. Jurisdictions such as the District of Columbia, Colorado, Florida, and Virginia have passed laws requiring mandatory sentences for certain offenses committed by juveniles.

Corrections

Many aspects of juvenile corrections resemble those of adult corrections. Both systems, for example, mix rehabilitative and retributive sanctions. However, juvenile corrections differs in many respects from the adult system. Some of the differences flow from the *parens patriae* concept and the youthful, seemingly innocent people with whom the system deals. At times, the differences show up in formal operational policies, such as contracting for residential treatment. At other times, the differences appear only in the style and culture of an operation, as they do in juvenile probation.

One predominant aim of juvenile corrections is to avoid unnecessary incarceration. When children are removed from their homes, they are inevitably damaged emotionally, even when the home life is harsh and abusive, because they are forced to abandon the only environment they know. Further, placing children in institutions has labeling effects; the children may perceive themselves as bad because they have received punitive treatment, and children who see themselves as "bad" may behave that way. Finally, treatment is believed to be more effective when the child is living in a normal, supportive home environment. For these reasons, noninstitutional forms of corrections are seen as highly desirable in juvenile justice and have proliferated in recent years. See "Doing Your Part" for a novel program emphasizing restorative justice for minor violations.

DOING YOUR PART

TEEN COURT

A 15-year-old boy was caught with marijuana on school property. Rather than be referred to juvenile court, his case is heard by a jury of his peers—a group of teens—who decide on the appropriate outcome of the case. During questioning, the defendant indicated an interest in studying culinary arts, so one jury member suggested he spend time volunteering somewhere that involved cooking. The final disposition involved writing a code of ethics, apologizing to his school, and paying court fees.

In Ingham County, Michigan, the Lansing Teen Court Program has provided diversion services to over 200 juvenile offenders since its creation in 2000. Rather than face an adult judge, Lansing Teen Court uses teenagers from around the county to serve as a jury of peers for juveniles referred for low-level offenses. The teen jury works together to decide how the offender can repair the harm done by his/her delinquency, and decide on the most appropriate social services to assist the offender to maintain a delinquency-free lifestyle. Since the creation of the Lansing Teen Court, over 4,500 youths have been recruited and trained to serve as peer jurors, bailiffs, and clerks.

The defendants must be first offenders who agree to plead guilty, who are referred to the Teen Court where a jury of teenage volunteers, who have been trained in the Teen Court's processes and goals, will determine their punishments. Punishments often emphasize restorative justice by requiring community service and restitution.

Defendants may also be required to write letters of apology to victims and write honor codes that will force them to think about and learn from their experiences. A faculty member from Cooley Law School in Lansing serves as the "judge" who ensures that the proceedings remain serious and that fair procedures are followed.

In many Teen Courts, teenagers who have gained experience as jurors later serve as "attorneys" in these cases, either arguing for specific punishments as "prosecutors" or serving as "defense attorneys" who support the defendant's explanation for why the offenses occurred. The jury carefully questions the defendant and then reaches a unanimous decision about punishment. These courts are relatively informal in the sense that they do not follow formal trial rules, but they are serious affairs in which the defendant and other participants are expected to be well-dressed and respectful of the process.

Sources: Drawn from Larry O'Connor, "Lansing Teen Court," *Capital Gains*, May 11, 2011 (www.capitalgainsmedia.com); Thomas M. Cooley Law School, "Teen Court Celebrates 10th Anniversary at Cooley Law School," October 22, 2010 (www.cooley.edu); Ingham Teen Court, 2013. (www.childandfamily.org/teen-court).

Probation

In 64 percent of adjudicated cases, the juvenile delinquent is placed on probation and released to the custody of a parent or guardian (Hockenberry and Puzzanchera, 2014a). Often the judge orders that the delinquent undergo some form of education or counseling. The delinquent can also be required to pay a fine or make restitution while on probation.

Juvenile probation operates in much the same way that adult probation does, and sometimes the same agency carries it out. In two respects, however, juvenile probation can differ markedly from adult probation. First, juvenile probation officers have smaller caseloads. Second, the juvenile probation officer is often infused with the sense that the offender is worthwhile and can change and that the job is valuable and enjoyable. Such attitudes make for greater creativity than adult probation officers usually exhibit. For example, a young offender can be paired with a "big brother" or "big sister" from the community.

Intermediate Sanctions

Although probation and commitment to an institution are the system's two main dispositional options, intermediate sanctions served in the community account for 12 percent of adjudicated juvenile cases (Hockenberry and Puzzanchera, 2014a). Judges have wide discretion to warn, to fine, to arrange for restitution, to order community service, to refer a juvenile for treatment at either a public or a private community agency, or to withhold judgment.

Judges sometimes suspend judgment—that is, continue a case without a finding—when they wish to put a youth under supervision but are reluctant to apply the label "delinquent." The judge holds off on giving a definitive judgment but can give one, should a youth misbehave while under the informal supervision of a probation officer or parents.

Custodial Care

Of those juveniles declared delinquent, 24 percent are placed in public or private facilities. The placement rate of juveniles over time has decreased from about 1 in 3 adjudicated juveniles in 1985, to about 1 in 4 juveniles in 2012 (Sickmund, Sladky, and Kang, 2015). The national incarceration rate per 100,000 juveniles aged 10 to 18 is 196—this includes juveniles held both prior to trial and as a

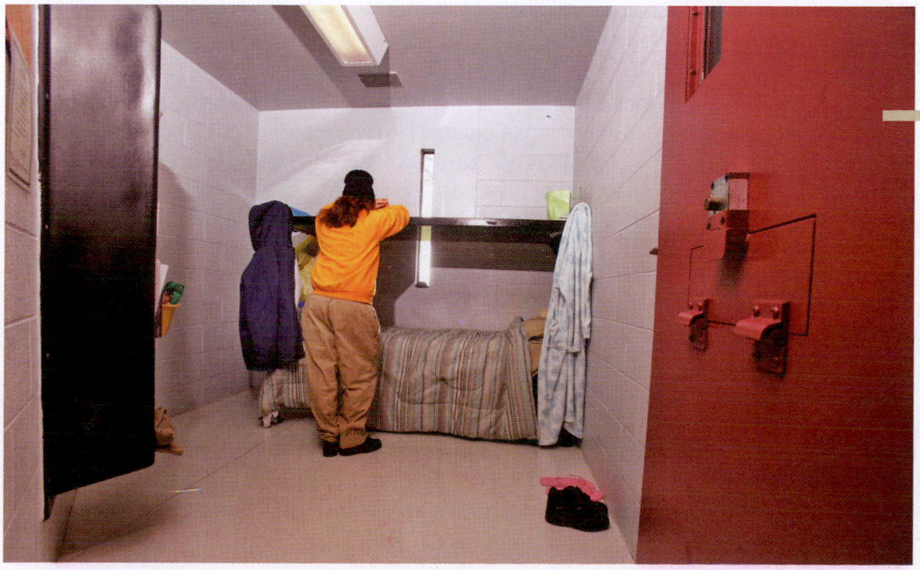

AP Images/The Columbus Dispatch, Tom Dodge

Detention inside a juvenile facility can be an intimidating experience for many youths. They may be threatened, bullied, or assaulted by older or larger teens. The physical condition of the facilities and the limited nature of programs may contribute to the difficult experience of living there. Are taxpayers willing to pay for the personnel and facilities necessary to provide a good environment for implementing effective treatment programs for juvenile offenders?

WHAT AMERICANS THINK

QUESTION: Respondents' views on the best punishment for juveniles adjudicated guilty of "homicide" and "assisted homicide."

Homicide: Which of the following punishments should an adolescent convicted of committing a homicide receive?

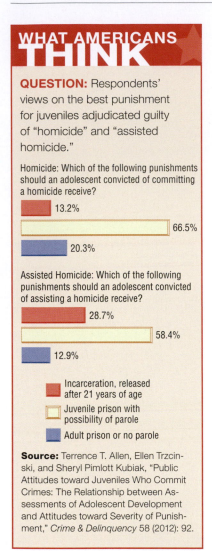

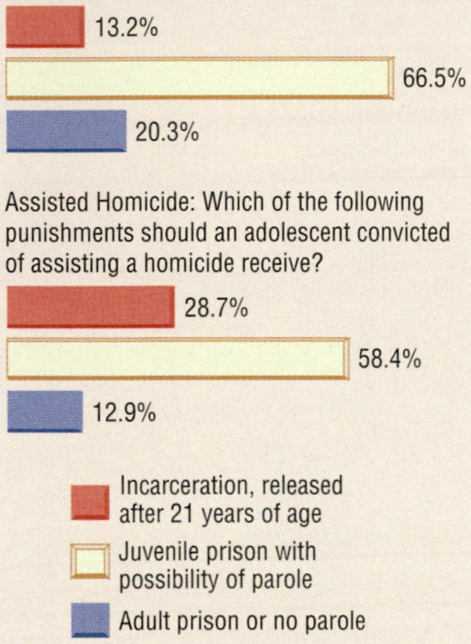

Source: Terrence T. Allen, Ellen Trzcinski, and Sheryl Pimlott Kubiak, "Public Attitudes toward Juveniles Who Commit Crimes: The Relationship between Assessments of Adolescent Development and Attitudes toward Severity of Punishment," *Crime & Delinquency* 58 (2012): 92.

sentence of incarceration. Like the adult incarceration rate, these rates vary widely among the states, with the highest rate in the District of Columbia (618) and the lowest in Vermont (59). The number of juveniles incarcerated in public and private facilities decreased steadily from 1997 through 2011, with only a few states exhibiting increased rates of incarceration of juvenile delinquents during that period (District of Columbia, Idaho, Nebraska, North Dakota, West Virginia; Hockenberry, 2014). See "What Americans Think" for a picture of public attitudes toward prisons for juveniles.

Policy makers are concerned that a larger percentage of African American juveniles are incarcerated compared to white juveniles. For example, a 2003 study estimated that about 33 percent of black males born in 2001 would spend time incarcerated eventually, compared to 6 percent of white males (Bonczar, 2003). Another study (Figure 17.6) found that the disproportionate confinement of minority juveniles stems from discretionary decisions at early stages of the process. Thus, if more African American juveniles are detained than others, more of them will likely be adjudicated in juvenile court, and more placed in residential facilities. Some research suggests that juvenile court actors have biased perceptions of minority juveniles, and thus they receive more-severe treatment at all levels of the juvenile justice system (Leiber and Mack, 2003). Others have indicated the importance of examining both race and gender when analyzing court outcomes, as girls are generally treated more leniently than boys in the justice system (Guevara, Herz, and Spohn, 2006). There is some evidence, however, that recent changes in criminal justice policies have helped to reduce the disparities in sentencing related to race (J. Davis and Sorenson, 2013).

Institutions for juvenile offenders are classified as either nonsecure or secure. *Nonsecure* placements (foster homes, group homes, camps, ranches, or schools) include a significant number of non-offenders—youths referred for abuse, neglect, or emotional disturbance. *Secure* facilities, such as reform schools and training schools, deal with juveniles who have committed serious violations of the law and have significant personal problems. Most secure juvenile facilities are small, designed to hold 40 or fewer residents. However, many states have at least one facility holding 200 or more hard-core delinquents who are allowed limited freedom.

INSIDE TODAY'S CONTROVERSIES

SOLITARY CONFINEMENT FOR JUVENILES

In the state of New York, juvenile offenders who are 16 or 17 years old are automatically tried as adults. If convicted and incarcerated, they are sent to adult facilities as punishment. Offenders convicted in New York City who receive a jail sentence are sent to Riker's Island, one of the largest jails in the world. Prior to 2015, if these teens misbehaved or otherwise broke the rules, they faced time in solitary confinement—23 hours per day in a 6-by-8-foot concrete cell with no human companionship. New York City officially ended the use of solitary confinement for juvenile offenders on January 1, 2015, but they will continue to use Riker's Island (an adult facility) to hold juvenile offenders. The June 2015 suicide of Kalief Browder has once again drawn attention to this issue. Mr. Browder was 16 years old when he was arrested on suspicion of burglary in 2010 and held at Riker's for over three years without trial, much of it in solitary confinement. He attempted suicide several times during his incarceration, but had been trying to complete his education after the charges against him were dropped (Gonnerman, 2015).

Psychiatrists have spoken out about the use of solitary confinement for juveniles, indicating that it can result in depression, anxiety, and psychosis; and that juvenile offenders are at higher risk for these illnesses than adults due to their stage of emotional development. In addition, more suicides take place in juvenile facilities when the individual is in solitary confinement.

The American Civil Liberties Union has called for the end of solitary confinement for juvenile offenders nationwide, given the risk of psychological harm and suicide. Pointing to the research indicating that juveniles do not have the same emotional and psychological development as adults, they indicate this punishment will cause great physical, emotional, and developmental harm to juveniles—especially those with prior trauma or a disability.

FIGURE 17.6 REPRESENTATION OF AFRICAN AMERICAN JUVENILES IN THE JUVENILE JUSTICE SYSTEM COMPARED WITH THEIR PROPORTION OF THE POPULATION

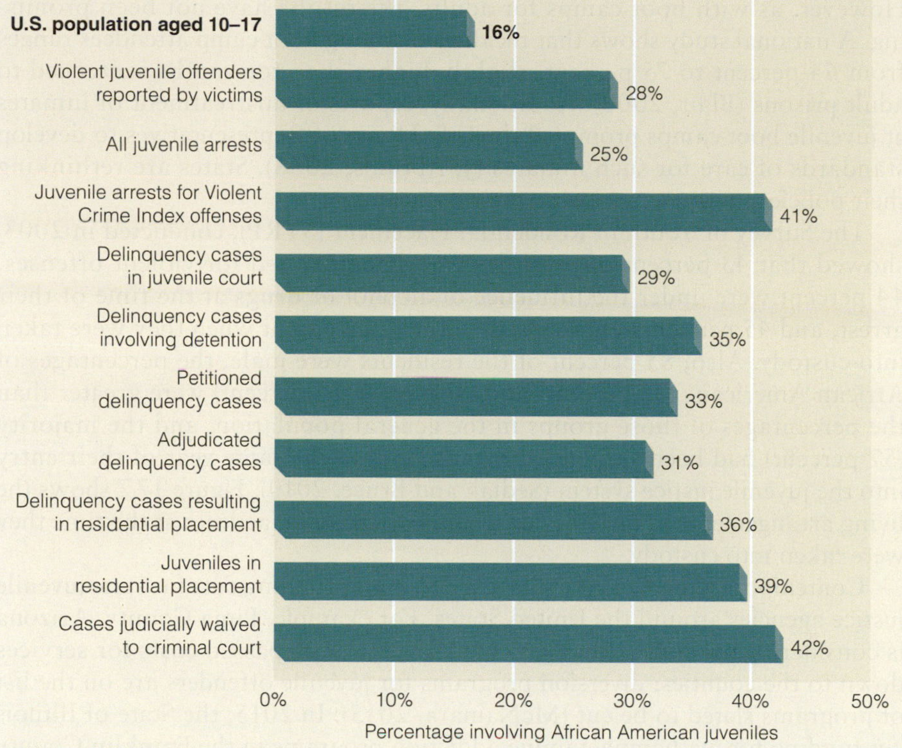

Source: Melissa Sickmund, "Juveniles in Corrections," in *National Report Series Bulletin* (Washington, DC: Office of Juvenile Justice and Delinquency Prevention, June 2004), 12.

Because the residents are younger and somewhat more volatile than adults, behavioral control is often an everyday issue, and fights and aggression are common. Poor management practices can lead to difficult situations. Severe punishments, such as the use of solitary confinement for juveniles, have recently come under fire. Read more about this in the Inside Today's Controversies feature.

Several lawsuits have been filed by juvenile offenders in an attempt to end this practice and gain remuneration for poor treatment. In 2014, the state of Ohio agreed to phase out the use of solitary confinement for juvenile offenders (*S. H. v. Reed*, 2008). Also in 2014, the state of Illinois agreed to improve conditions at juvenile facilities, including eliminating solitary confinement for disciplinary reasons, after the ACLU filed a court case on behalf of a juvenile detainee (*R. J. vs. Jones*, 2012). A lawsuit brought by two juveniles against the State of New Jersey resulted in a $400,000 settlement payment after these individuals were placed in solitary confinement for extended periods of time (*T. D. and O. S. v. Mickens et al.*, 2010).

Sources: American Academy of Child and Adolescent Psychiatry, *Solitary Confinement of Juvenile Offenders*, April 2012 (aacap.org); American Civil Liberties Union, *Alone and Afraid: Children Held in Solitary Confinement and Isolation in Juvenile Detention and Correctional Facilities*, June 2014 (aclu.org); Trey Bundy and Daffodil J. Altan, "For Teens at Riker's Island, Solitary Confinement Pushes Mental Limits," *Center for Investigative Reporting*, March 4,2014 (cironline.org); Lauren Kirchner, "Why Solitary Confinement Hurts Juveniles More than Adults," *Pacific Standard Magazine*, October 9, 2014 (psmag.com).

CRITICAL THINKING AND ANALYSIS

If solitary confinement has been demonstrated to be harmful, especially to juveniles, why is it still used in juvenile and adult facilities on juvenile offenders? If it is outlawed, how can correctional administrators maintain order and punish juvenile offenders who are disruptive and threaten order and safety? Should solitary confinement be used to protect juvenile detainees from other inmates looking to cause them harm? Which is the greater harm faced by detainees—solitary confinement or victimization at the hands of older inmates?

Boot camps for juvenile offenders saw a growth spurt in the early 1990s, with an increased focus by politicians to "get tough on crime." By 1997, more than 27,000 teenagers were passing through 54 camps in 34 states annually. However, as with boot camps for adults, the results have not been promising. A national study shows that recidivism among boot camp attendees ranges from 64 percent to 75 percent, slightly higher than for youths sentenced to adult prisons (Blair, 2000). Additionally, reports of mistreatment of inmates at juvenile boot camps prompted the U.S. House of Representatives to develop standards of care for such inmates (J. Abrams, 2008). States are rethinking their policies, with many closing their programs.

The Survey of Youth in Residential Placement (SYRP), conducted in 2003, showed that 43 percent of juveniles were incarcerated for violent offenses, 44 percent were under the influence of alcohol or drugs at the time of their arrest, and 45 percent were living with only one parent when they were taken into custody. Also, 85 percent of the residents were male, the percentages of African Americans (32 percent) and Hispanics (24 percent) were greater than the percentages of those groups in the general population, and the majority (57 percent) had been suspended from school in the same year of their entry into the juvenile justice system (Sedlak and Bruce, 2010). Figure 17.7 shows the living arrangements of juveniles in secure correctional facilities at the time they were taken into custody.

Contemporary budget crises have led to major funding cuts for state juvenile justice agencies around the United States. For example, Pima County, Arizona is considering substantial budget cuts after the state passed costs for services down to the counties; diversion programs for juvenile offenders are on the list of programs slated to be cut (McNamara, 2015). In 2015, the State of Illinois cut funding for methamphetamine addiction programs in the Franklin County Juvenile Detention Center (Long, 2015). In Utah, the Wasatch Youth Center, which houses up to 46 juvenile sex offenders, faces closure due to state budget cuts (Boyd, 2015). It is unclear how these cuts will impact the rate of juvenile delinquency in these areas, but the lack of treatment options for juveniles does not bode well for their ability to avoid criminal behavior as adults.

Institutional Programs

Because of the emphasis on rehabilitation that has dominated juvenile justice for much of the past 50 years, a wide variety of treatment programs has been used. Counseling, education, vocational training, and an assortment of psychotherapy methods have been incorporated into the juvenile correctional programs of most states. Unfortunately, research has raised many questions about the effectiveness of rehabilitation programs in juvenile corrections. For example, incarceration in a juvenile training institution primarily seems to

FIGURE 17.7 FAMILY BACKGROUND OF YOUTH IN CUSTODY, AT TIME OF ARREST

Most youths in custody lived with only one parent at the time of their referral to juvenile court.

Source: Andrea J. Sedlak and Carol Bruce, "Youth's Characteristics and Backgrounds," *Juvenile Justice Bulletin* (Washington, DC: Office of Juvenile Justice and Delinquency Prevention, December 2010) (www.ncjrs.gov/pdffiles1/ojjdp/227730.pdf).

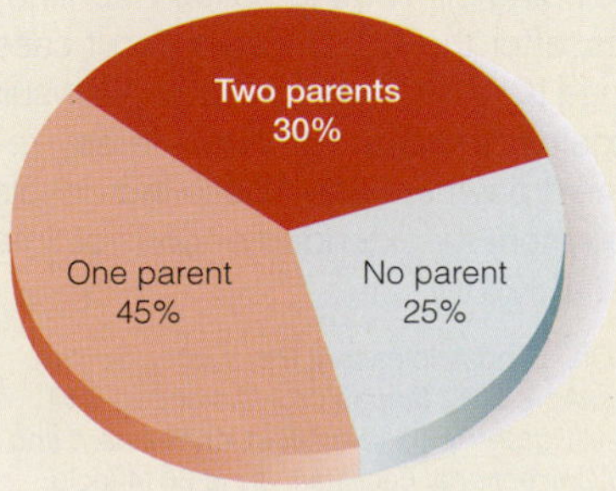

prepare many offenders for entry into adult corrections. John Irwin's (1970) concept of the state-raised youth is a useful way of looking at children who come in contact with institutional life at an early age, lack family relationships and structure, become accustomed to living in a correctional facility, and cannot function in other environments. Current recommendations focus on the importance of prevention and keeping first-time juvenile offenders out of placement and in their homes, with family (Ryan, Abrams, and Huang, 2014).

Aftercare

The juvenile equivalent of parole is known as **aftercare**. Upon release, the offender is placed under the supervision of a juvenile parole officer who assists with educational, counseling, and treatment services. Well-implemented and individualized aftercare programs have lowered recidivism rates for juvenile offenders (C. James et al., 2013). In fact, some scholars identify lack of aftercare as a primary reason why boot camps failed (Kurlychek and Kempinen, 2006). As with the adult system, juveniles may be returned to custodial care should they violate the conditions of their parole. As you read "Civic Engagement: Your Role in the System," consider how people in the community may be able to contribute to the success of aftercare.

CIVIC ENGAGEMENT

YOUR ROLE IN THE SYSTEM

Imagine that you have been asked to serve as a mentor to a youth who has been released from a juvenile detention facility. *Make a list of the things that you would say and do to attempt to be a positive influence for a delinquent youth. Write a brief statement describing what you think you might be able accomplish.* Then read about the mentoring programs available in the state of Louisiana.

aftercare
Juvenile justice equivalent of parole, in which a delinquent is released from a custodial sentence and supervised in the community.

Community Treatment

In the past decade, treatment in community-based facilities has become much more common. Today many private, nonprofit agencies contract with states to provide services for troubled youths. Community-based options include foster homes, in which juvenile offenders live with families, usually for a short period, and group homes, often privately run facilities for groups of 12 to 20 juvenile offenders. Each group home has several staff personnel who work as counselors or houseparents during 8- or 24-hour shifts. Group home placements provide individual and group counseling, allow juveniles to attend local schools, and offer a more structured life than most of the residents have received in their own homes. However, critics suggest that group homes often are mismanaged and may do little more than "warehouse" youths.

Reforms developed to increase the use of community treatment can also have unintended effects elsewhere in the system. For example, a 2012 report on the Texas juvenile corrections system found that as more offenders were diverted to community programs, the secure institutional settings were left with higher concentrations of the most difficult offenders. In the wake of these changes, youth-on-youth assaults increased from 17 assaults per 100 detained youths in 2007 to 54 assaults per 100 youths in 2011. The institutions also experienced a similar rise in assaults against staff by youths (Grissom, 2012).

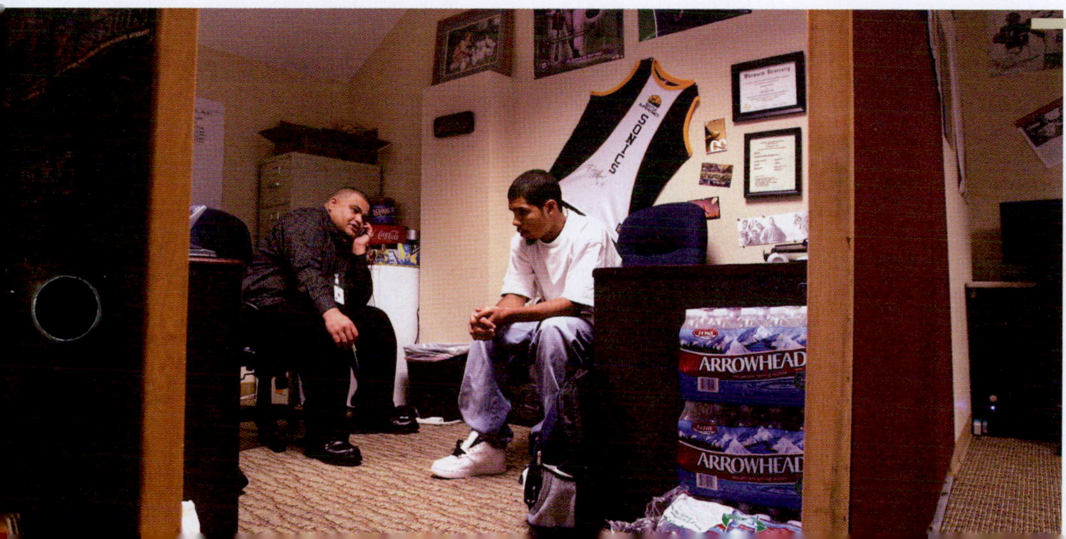

AP Images/Elaine Thompson

Staff member Vincent Vaielua (left) talks to a youth at an evening reporting center run by the Pierce County Juvenile Court in Tacoma, Washington. Many courts develop community programs in an effort to avoid confining youthful offenders in juvenile corrections institutions. What are the potential advantages and benefits of emphasizing community-based programs?

Criminal justice planners think very carefully about the impacts of new policies, yet it can be very difficult to anticipate what issues may arise. Read "A Question of Ethics" at the end of the chapter to consider how less-lethal weapons are used in juvenile facilities to manage behavior.

✔POINT

11. What three discretionary decisions do the police make with regard to processing juveniles?

12. What are the costs and benefits of trying juveniles in adult court?

13. What is the purpose of diversion?

14. What are five sentencing dispositions available to the judge?

STOP AND ANALYZE: Juvenile records are sealed and generally cannot be used against adult offenders. Why would such a policy exist? Would it make more sense to allow juvenile records to be used routinely in adult criminal proceedings? State your view and give two reasons to support your position.

Problems and Perspectives

Much of the criticism of juvenile justice has emphasized the disparity between the treatment ideal and the institutionalized practices of an ongoing bureaucratic system. Commentators have focused on how the language of social reformers has disguised the day-to-day operations that lack the elements of due process and in which custodial incarceration is all too frequent. Other criticisms claim that the juvenile justice system does not control juvenile crime.

The juvenile court, in both theory and practice, is a remarkably complex institution that must perform a wide variety of functions. The juvenile justice system must play such a range of roles that goals and values will inevitably collide.

In many states, the same judges, probation officers, and social workers are asked to deal with both neglected children and young criminals. Although departments of social services usually deal primarily with cases of neglect, the distinction between the criminal and the neglected child is often not maintained.

TECHNOLOGY & CRIMINAL JUSTICE

CYBERBULLYING AND "SEXTING"

In recent years there are more and more incidents of juveniles using technology to engage in harmful acts. In addition to cyberbullying, teens are increasingly "sexting," in which they engage in sexually explicit conversations and share explicit images via text messaging and cell phones. This behavior falls under the criminal law in most states, due to the illegality of child pornography. In a Michigan City (Indiana) high school, investigators are looking into widespread sexting among students, reminding them that this constitutes child pornography—even if done by juveniles. Four Illinois teens may be charged for taking and disseminating nude photos—two of the four were girls who took nude "selfies" (aged 15 and 17). The others were boys at the high school who sent the pictures to classmates. In early 2015, four girls middle school girls, ages 12 and 13, sent nude photos of themselves to a group of their male classmates. Experts warn that sexting is on the rise, especially among middle school students; and unfortunately, legislation on this issue is not being created fast enough to keep up with technology.

There is considerable confusion among school administrators about how to handle sexting when they find it. A middle school in Massachusetts discovered that one of its 14-year-old students had sent nude pictures of herself to a few classmates, who had circulated the pictures to others. Rather than contact the police, the school confiscated as many phones as possible to search for evidence. In some communities, the police and prosecutor may prefer to see school officials confiscate phones, delete images, and impose suspensions and other school discipline rather than use the scarce resources of the

In addition to recognizing that the juvenile system has organizational problems, society must acknowledge that little is known about the causes of delinquency and its prevention or treatment. Over the years, people have advanced various social and behavioral theories to explain delinquency. One generation looked to slum conditions as the cause of juvenile crime, and another pointed to the affluence of the suburbs. Psychologists sometimes point to masculine insecurity in a matriarchal family structure, and some sociologists note the peer-group pressures of the gang. This array of theories has led to an array of proposed—and often contradictory—treatments. In such confusion, those interested in the problems of youth may despair. What is clear is that we need additional research on the causes of delinquency and the treatment of juvenile offenders.

Youth gangs pose unique problems to those making decisions in the juvenile justice system. Gangs are responsible for a significant amount of delinquency in communities, and these gangs also thrive in correctional institutions (particularly adult institutions). How does the presence and behavior of youth gangs affect juvenile justice policy? Recent research has indicated gang members are more likely than non-gang members to carry guns, thereby also increasing the likelihood of severe or lethal violence among these groups. Gang members are also more likely to receive longer sentences, given that gang membership and weapon ownership can increase the severity of punishment for juveniles (Melde, Esbensen, and Taylor, 2009).

In recent years, juveniles have been engaging in delinquent behavior online. The phenomenon of "cyberbullying" involves the use of computers, cell phones, and other electronic devices by youth to mistreat and harm their peers. Approximately 24 percent of adolescents have been bullied online, while approximately 16 percent of youth admit to cyberbullying others (Cyberbullying Research Center, 2014). Although additional inquiry is necessary, cyberbullying has been correlated with traditional bullying and various forms of school violence (Hinduja and Patchin, 2007). Read the Technology and Criminal Justice feature to gain insight about the interaction between delinquency and technology.

What trends may foretell the future of juvenile justice? The conservative crime control policies that hit the adult criminal justice system—with their

criminal justice system to pursue this form of teen misbehavior. The varying attitudes of police and prosecutors, as well as the limits of their budgets, may lead to different outcomes for youths who are caught sexting, depending on the community in which they live. The fates of individual juveniles, especially if they are entered into the justice system instead of merely experiencing school discipline, may also depend on the extent to which victims' parents complain and insist on action by criminal justice officials. Rapid changes in technology and behavior have made it difficult for the criminal justice system to keep up with the range of consequences resulting from this phenomenon.

Sources: WGN Web Desk, "High School Sexting Investigation in Michigan City". *WGN News*, March 19, 2015 (wgntv.com); Natalie Hayes, "Ridgewood High School Students Face Charges over Nude Photos," *Chicago Tribune*, March 16, 2015 (chicagotribune.com); Elizabeth Janney, "Kids Sexting Happens 'on a Daily Basis': Harford County Detective," *Bel Air Patch*, April 1, 2015 (patch.com); Victoria Warren, "Everett Police Investigating Middle School Sexting," *WHDH News*, March 9, 2015t (wdhd.com).

DEBATE THE ISSUE

Should juveniles who send sexually explicit pictures of themselves via cell phone be charged with a crime? Should other students who forward such pictures to others be charged with the crime of child pornography? Consider the purposes of laws against child pornography—are they designed to prosecute these types of behaviors? List two arguments that express your position on this issue.

WHAT AMERICANS THINK

QUESTION: When asked to select the punishment that youths should receive if found guilty of killing another person (under a variety of circumstances), respondents answered:

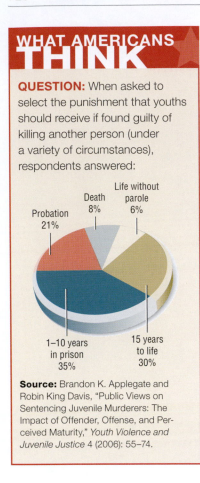

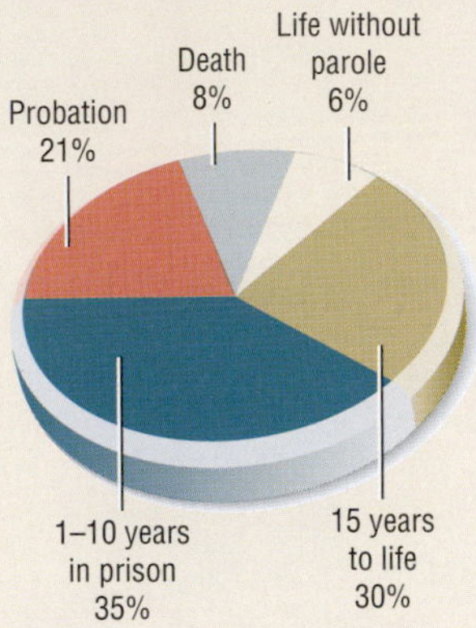

Source: Brandon K. Applegate and Robin King Davis, "Public Views on Sentencing Juvenile Murderers: The Impact of Offender, Offense, and Perceived Maturity," *Youth Violence and Juvenile Justice* 4 (2006): 55–74.

emphasis on deterrence, retribution, and getting tough—have also influenced juvenile justice in the past 20 years. One can point to growing levels of overcrowding in juvenile institutions, increased litigation challenging the abuse of children in training schools and detention centers, and higher rates of minority youth incarceration. All of these problems have emerged during a period of declining youth populations and fewer arrests of juveniles. With a renewed focus on juvenile crime under the philosophy that "kids are different," the juvenile justice system may be embarking on a less severe path to dealing with juvenile offenders.

On the other hand, future developments and events might ultimately lead to a continuation of the crime control orientation in many states. We must wait to see if we are truly moving into a new era that recognizes and focuses on the vast developmental differences between juveniles and adults. For example, the Supreme Court's ban on the execution of offenders for crimes committed prior to the age of 18 is not necessarily permanent. *Roper v. Simmons* was decided on a 5-to-4 vote of the Supreme Court's justices. Thus a change in the Court's composition may lead to the reinstatement of the death penalty for juveniles in some states if a newly appointed future justice replaces a supporter of the *Roper* majority and votes to reverse the decision when the issue arises in a new case.

Such a change may seem primarily symbolic, because only a small number of offenders who committed crimes as juveniles were actually executed in the decades prior to *Roper*. Between 1973 and 2000, there were 17 juvenile offenders executed, mostly in the state of Texas. All but one of these offenders were age 17 at the time of their offense (Sickmund, 2004). In addition, there does not appear to be strong public opinion supporting the death penalty for juvenile offenders (Applegate and Davis, 2006) (see "What Americans Think" regarding attitudes toward punishment).

Yet, even if a reversal of the *Roper* decision does not lead to many executions of youthful murderers, a new Supreme Court decision would weaken the "kids are different" message that the Court announced in *Roper*. As a result, a future increase in youth crime or highly publicized gang violence could lead policy makers to turn back toward crime control priorities or otherwise slow the current trend toward reemphasizing treatment and rehabilitation for youthful offenders. In recent decades, the United States has not shown a consistent, firm commitment to the original rehabilitative goals of the juvenile justice system. Thus it remains to be seen which priorities will shape the system's approach to punishing youthful offenders in the future.

A QUESTION OF ETHICS

In 2015, the U.S. Department of Justice ended a six-year study of the juvenile probation camps in Los Angeles County, California. The investigation of these probation camps began in 2006, after reports of abuses by guards against juveniles. The accusations included complaints of excessive use of force (including overuse of pepper spray) and misconduct by officers such as drinking on the job. Officers argue that the responsible use of less-lethal weapons, such as pepper spray, can be useful for controlling rowdy populations found in juvenile facilities.

Sources: Michael Barba, "SF Juvenile Hall Counselors Call for Safety Reforms, Mace, *San Francisco Examiner*, March 18, 2015 (sfexaminer.com); Abby Sewell, "Federal Monitoring of L.A. County Juvenile Probation Camps Ending," *Los Angeles Times*, April 3, 2015 (latimes.com).

CRITICAL THINKING AND ANALYSIS

What ethical considerations arise when staff members of a juvenile corrections facility choose to pepper spray rather than to physically restrain a violent or out-of-control teenager? Are there risks that staff will use such weapons too quickly without attempting to understand the nature and source of the problem? Does the use of such weapons communicate to the juvenile offenders that it is legitimate to use weapons and violence to solve conflicts? Might such weapons be used inconsistently or in discriminatory ways when deciding which juveniles to spray rather than restrain? Describe the policies and training that you would develop for instructing staff members on when to use pepper spray—if at all—and when to use physical restraint.

Summary

1 Describe the extent of youth crime in the United States

- Crimes committed by juveniles have increased since 1980, even though crimes of violence in general have decreased.

2 Discuss how the juvenile justice system developed and the assumptions on which it was based

- The history of juvenile justice comprises six periods: Puritan, Refuge, Juvenile Court, Juvenile Rights, Crime Control, and "Kids Are Different."
- Creation of the juvenile court in 1899 established a separate juvenile justice system.
- The *In re Gault* decision by the U.S. Supreme Court in 1967 brought due process to the juvenile justice system.

3 Analyze what determines the jurisdiction of the juvenile justice system

- The juvenile system handles cases based on the ages of youths who are affected by status offenses, delinquency, dependency, and neglect.

4 Describe how the juvenile justice system operates

- Decisions by police officers and juvenile intake officers dispose of a large portion of the many cases that are never referred to the court.
- In juvenile court, most cases are settled through a plea agreement.
- After conviction or plea, a disposition hearing is held. Before passing sentence, the judge reviews the offense and the juvenile's social history.
- Possible dispositions of a juvenile case include suspended judgment, probation, community treatment, or institutional care.
- Juvenile court jurisdiction may be waived so that youths can be tried in the adult criminal justice system, but this appears to be decreasing in recent years.
- Options for juvenile corrections include probation, intermediate sanctions, custodial care, institutional programs, aftercare, and community treatment.

5 Analyze some of the problems facing the American system of juvenile justice

- Juvenile justice faces issues of racial disparities in punishment; criminal activity by gangs; and new behavioral problems, such as cyberbullying, which involve computers, tablets, and cell phones.
- It remains to be seen whether the current move toward increased rehabilitation will continue or whether crime control policies will be a primary priority.

Questions for Review

1. What are the major historical periods of juvenile justice in the United States?
2. What is the jurisdiction of the juvenile court system?
3. What are the major processes in the juvenile justice system?
4. What are the sentencing and institutional alternatives for juveniles who are judged delinquent?
5. What due process rights do juveniles have?

Key Terms and Cases

aftercare (p. 725)
delinquent (p. 708)
dependent child (p. 710)
detention hearing (p. 714)
diversion (p. 714)
neglected child (p. 710)
parens patriae (p. 699)
PINS (p. 709)
status offense (p. 704)
waiver (p. 706)
Breed v. Jones (1975) (p. 704)
Fare v. Michael C. (1979) (p. 713)
Graham v. Florida (2010) (p. 705)
In re Gault (1967) (p. 704)
In re Winship (1970) (p. 704)
McKeiver v. Pennsylvania (1971) (p. 704)
Miller v. Alabama (2012) (p. 705)
New Jersey v. T. L. O. (1985) (p. 713)
Roper v. Simmons (2005) (p. 705)
Schall v. Martin (1984) (p. 704)
Vernonia School District v. Acton (1995) (p. 713)

Checkpoint Answers

1 **What might explain the "epidemic" of violent crime committed by juveniles that peaked in the 1990s?**

✓ Two theories: (1) the presence of a large number of violent super predators in the age cohort; (2) environmental factors, such as the inner-city drug trade and increased use of guns by juveniles.

2 **Until what age were children exempt from criminal responsibility under common law?**

✓ Age seven.

3 **What was the jurisdiction of the English chancery court?**

✓ Chancery courts had protective jurisdiction over children, especially those involved in cases concerning dependency, neglect, and property.

4 **What is meant by the doctrine of *parens patriae*?**

✓ The state acting as parent and guardian.

5 **What was the function of a "house of refuge"?**

✓ To provide an environment where neglected children could learn good work and study habits, live in a disciplined and healthy environment, and develop character.

6 **What were the major elements of the Illinois Juvenile Court Act of 1899?**

✓ A separate court for delinquent, dependent, and neglected children; special legal procedures that were less adversarial than those in the adult system; separation of children from adults throughout the system; programs of probation to assist judges in deciding what is in the best interest of the state and the child.

7 **What was the main point of the *In re Gault* decision?**

✓ Procedural rights for juveniles, including notice of charges, right to counsel, right to confront and cross-examine witnesses, and protection against self-incrimination.

8 **How did the decline in juvenile crime in the 1990s affect juvenile justice policy?**

✓ A decrease in the use of judicial waiver to move youthful offenders from juvenile court to adult court.

9 **What reasons has the Supreme Court given for disallowing the use of the death penalty and other harsh sentences for juveniles?**

✓ The Court has argued that juveniles cannot have the same degree of blameworthiness as adults due to their physical and emotional immaturity and impulsiveness.

10 **What are the jurisdictional criteria for the juvenile court?**

✓ The age of the juvenile, usually younger than 16 or 18, and the type of case: delinquency, status offenses, neglect, and dependency.

11 **What three discretionary decisions do the police make with regard to processing juveniles?**

✓ Whether to take the child into custody, whether to request that the child be detained, whether to refer the child to court.

12 **What are the costs and benefits of trying juveniles in adult court?**

✓ *Costs*: youth tried as adults receive longer sentences, are likely to be incarcerated with criminal (and potentially abusive) adults, and are more likely to recidivate post-release than youth not transferred. *Benefit*: sends "get tough" message to juvenile offenders.

13 **What is the purpose of diversion?**

✓ To avoid formal proceedings when the child's best interests can be served by treatment in the community.

14 **What are five sentencing dispositions available to the judge?**

✓ Possible sentencing options include dismissal, probation, commitment to institution, intermediate sanctions (warning, fine, restitution, community service, treatment, withholding judgment), custodial care, institutional programs, aftercare, community treatment.

APPENDIX A

Constitution of the United States: Criminal Justice Amendments

The First Ten Amendments to the Constitution, Known as the Bill of Rights, Became Effective on December 15, 1791.

I. Congress shall make no law respecting an establishment of religion, or prohibiting the free exercise thereof; or abridging the freedom of speech, or of the press, or the right of the people peaceably to assemble, and to petition the Government for a redress of grievances.

IV. The right of the people to be secure in their persons, houses, papers, and effects, against unreasonable searches and seizures, shall not be violated, and no warrants shall issue but upon probable cause, supported by oath or affirmation, and particularly describing the place to be searched, and the persons or things to be seized.

V. No person shall be held to answer for a capital or otherwise infamous crime, unless on a presentment or indictment of a grand jury, except in cases arising in the land or naval forces or in the militia when in actual service in time of war or public danger; nor shall any person be subject for the same offense to be twice put in jeopardy of life or limb; nor shall be compelled in any criminal case to be a witness against himself, nor be deprived of life, liberty, or property, without due process of law; nor shall private property be taken for public use without just compensation.

VI. In all criminal prosecutions the accused shall enjoy the right to a speedy and public trial, by an impartial jury of the State and district wherein the crime shall have been committed, which district shall have been previously ascertained by law, and to be informed of the nature and cause of the accusation; to be confronted with the witnesses against him; to have compulsory process for obtaining witnesses in his favor, and to have the assistance of counsel for his defense.

VIII. Excessive bail shall not be required, nor excessive fines imposed, nor cruel and unusual punishments inflicted.

The Fourteenth Amendment became Effective on July 28, 1868.

XIV. SECTION 1. All persons born or naturalized in the United States, and subject to the jurisdiction thereof, are citizens of the United States and of the State wherein they reside. No State shall make or enforce any law which shall abridge the privileges or immunities of citizens of the United States; nor shall any State deprive any person of life, liberty, or property, without due process of law; nor deny to any person within its jurisdiction the equal protection of the laws.

APPENDIX B

Understanding and Using Criminal Justice Data

When it comes to numbers, criminal justice is somewhat like baseball. Both require a wealth of quantitative data to answer a variety of questions. Casual baseball fans want to know who has the highest batting average in the league or how many runs a certain pitcher gives up per game. More-serious fans might want information that can help them judge whether statistics on various events (home runs, stolen bases, sacrifice bunts) support one or more of the manager's strategies.

Similarly, people interested in criminal justice need quantitative data to describe events as well as to make inferences about trends or about the impact of different policies. They want to know, for example, how much crime there is, whether crime is on the increase and which types of crimes are increasing or decreasing, whether strong gun-control laws are linked to a decrease in violent crime, or what effects correctional policies have on the likelihood that criminals will break the law in the future.

Researchers constantly gather, analyze, and disseminate quantitative information that fosters an understanding of the dimensions of crime and the workings of the criminal justice system. As a student in this course and as an informed citizen, you need to be able to read about these data intelligently and to make valid inferences about them.

In this text, as in most criminal justice books and articles, quantitative data often are reported in graphs and tables that organize the information and highlight certain aspects of it. The way the material is presented reflects the writer's choices about what is important in the raw data that underlie the graphic display. So that you can better interpret and use quantitative information, this appendix provides some pointers on reading graphic presentations and tips for interpreting raw data.

Reading Graphs and Tables

Writers use graphs and tables to organize information so that key factors stand out. Although you may be tempted to try to take in the meaning of such displays in one quick glance, you will need to *analyze* what is being presented so that you do not misinterpret the material.

To begin, read the title and descriptive caption carefully to find out what the data do and do not represent. For example, consider the title of Figure B.1: "Violent Crime Trends Measured by UCR and NCVS." The title tells you that the data presented pertain to *violent* crime (not all crime) and that the *sources* of the information are reports to police (Uniform Crime Reports) and victimization surveys (National Crime Victimization Survey). Knowing where the data come from is important, because different means of data collection have their own strengths and weaknesses. So what this figure presents is not a directly observed picture of crime trends, but a picture that has been filtered through two distinct methods of measuring crime (these measures of crime are described in Chapter 1.) In general, always note the sources of the data before drawing conclusions from a graphic display.

After reading the title and caption, study the figure itself. Note that the graph compares the number of crimes from 1993 to 2013 as reported by the two types of surveys. As indicated in the caption, the data are presented in terms of the *number* of victimizations, not the relative *frequency* of crime (a crime *rate*). For this reason you need to be cautious in making inferences about what the data show about crime trends. In baseball, a graph showing an increase in the number of home runs hit over a certain period would not prove that home runs were becoming more common if, during the same period, new teams were added to the league. More teams and more games being played would naturally lead to an increase in the total number of home runs. Similarly, if the U.S. population were increasing over the 20-year period of the data presented, we may observe an increase in the *number* of crimes due to the greater number of Americans. The fact that the number of crimes has been consistently *decreasing* even as the number of Americans has been increasing has been a topic of much speculation by criminologists.

FIGURE B.1 VIOLENT CRIME TRENDS MEASURED BY UCR AND NCVS

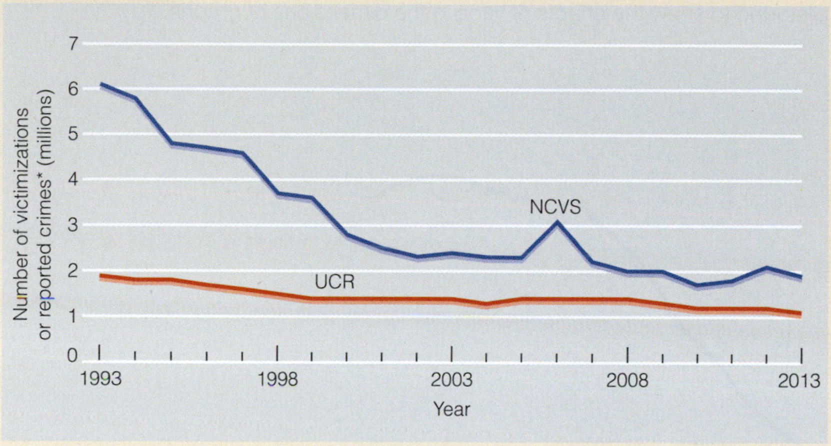

Note that this chart contains the number of violent victimizations reported to police from 1993 to 2013, rather than the rate of victimizations.

*Includes NCVS violent crimes of rape, robbery, aggravated assault, and simple assault, and UCR violent crimes of murder and non-negligent manslaughter, forcible rape, robbery, and aggravated assault.

Sources: Bureau of Justice Statistics, 2015, Table: "Number of Serious Violent Victimizations by Population Size, 1993–2013." Generated using the NCVS Victimization Analysis Tool at www.bjs.gov. May 5, 2015; Federal Bureau of Investigation (2014), Crime in the United States, Table 1 (www.fbi.gov).

Also note that the data show what has happened over two decades. Even though the lines in the graph depict trends during that period, they do *not* in themselves forecast the future. There are statistical procedures that could be used to predict future trends based on certain assumptions, but such projections are not a part of this figure.

A final caution about graphic display in general: The form in which data are presented can affect or even distort your perception of the content. For example, a graph showing incarceration rates in the United States from 1978 to 2013 could be drawn with a shorter or longer time line (see Figure B.2). Figure B.2(a) shows the graph in normal proportions. If the time line is made shorter in relation to the incarceration rate scale, as in Figure B.2(b), the changes in incarceration rates will appear to be more drastic than if the line is longer. By the same token, the height chosen for the vertical axis affects the appearance of the data and can influence the way the data are interpreted—including a greater range of values makes the line appear "flatter" and the increase less severe. How does your impression of the same data change when you compare Figure B.2(b) with B.2(c)?

Although much more could be said about interpreting graphical displays, these brief comments alert you to the need to carefully review data presented in graphic form. In criminal justice, as in baseball, you need to actively question and think about the information you encounter, in order to become a serious student of the game.

Three Types of Graphs

You will find three types of graphs in this book: bar graphs, pie graphs (or pie charts), and line graphs. All three are represented in Figure B.3. Each graph displays information concerning public opinion about crime.

Figure B.3(a) is a pie graph. Pie graphs show the relative sizes of the parts of a single whole. Usually these sizes are reported as percentages. In this case, respondents were asked in 2011 if they were afraid to walk alone in their neighborhoods at night. The whole consists of all the responses taken together, and the portions of the "pie" represent the percentage of respondents who chose each option. The pie graph indicates that a majority (61 percent) of respondents in the survey are not afraid to walk alone in their neighborhoods at night. The same data could have been reported in a bar graph, but it would not have been as clear that a single whole was divided into parts.

Whenever data are presented as percentages of a whole—whether in a pie graph, a table, or another display—the percentages should add up to 100 percent. Often, however, the sum may be slightly over or under 100 because of what is known as *rounding error*. Rounding error can occur when percentages are rounded to the nearest whole number. For instance, you might notice that the two values in Figure B.3(a) only add to 99 percent. This could be due to the rounding down of one or both of the values. Where rounding error occurs, the figure or table will usually have a note indicating this fact.

Figure B.3(b) is a bar graph. Bar graphs compare quantities organized in different categories. Sometimes, these percentages add to 100 percent, as in pie graphs. In this case, each bar represents the percentage of poll respondents who report that they "frequently or occasionally" worry about these types of crimes. Because respondents can indicate that they worry about more than one of these crime types, this chart adds up to more than 100 percent. The lengths of the bars (or their heights, when a bar graph is oriented vertically) allow for a visual comparison of the quantities associated with each category of

FIGURE B.2 **INCARCERATION RATES IN THE UNITED STATES, 1978–2013**

The panels of graphs (b) and (c) are intentionally distorted to show the effects of varying the dimensions of graphs.

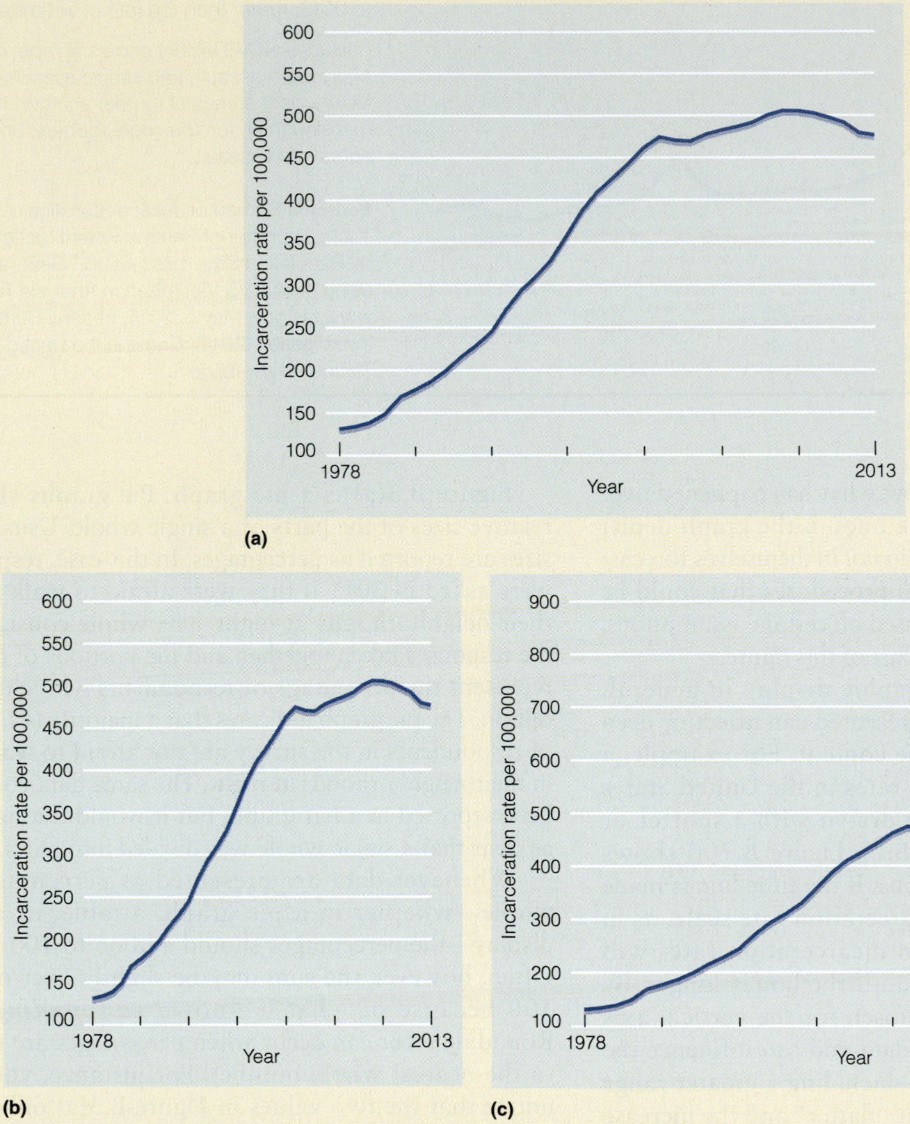

Source: Bureau of Justice Statistics, 2015, Table: "Imprisonment Rate of Sentenced Prisoners under the Jurisdiction of State or Federal Correctional Authorities per 100,000 U.S. Residents, December 31, 1978–2013." Generated using the Corrections Statistical Analysis Tool (www.bjs.gov).

response. In this case, you can readily see that when the data were collected in 2011, about two-thirds of respondents reported they were concerned about being the victim of identity theft. Respondents in this survey reported that they were not as concerned about being killed or harmed at work by a coworker (6 percent). The creator of a graph of this type needs to take care that the sizes of the bars are visually proportionate to the quantities they represent. A bar graph that is drawn unscrupulously or carelessly can make the difference in quantities appear larger or smaller than it really is. Intentionally or not, graphs that appear in the mass media often exaggerate some effect in this way. The lesson here is to go beyond looking at the shape of the graph. Use the scales provided on the axes to directly compare the numbers being depicted and verify your visual impression.

Figure B.3(c) is a line graph. Line graphs show the relationship between two or more variables. The variables in question are indicated by the labels on the vertical axis

FIGURE B.3 CRIME: IN THE NATION, IN OUR NEIGHBORHOOD

Crime remains one of the most important problems facing Americans. Most Americans say that crime has increased in their neighborhood in the past year.

(a) Is there any area where you live—that is, within a mile—where you would be afraid to walk alone at night? (Survey of adults, 2011):

(b) How often do you, yourself, worry frequently or occasionally about the following things? (Percentage responding "yes": survey of Americans, 2011):

(c) Is there more crime in your area than there was a year ago, or less? (Survey of adults, 2003–2011):

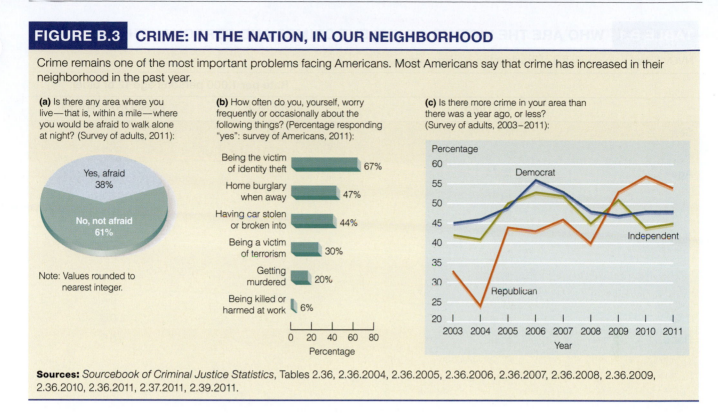

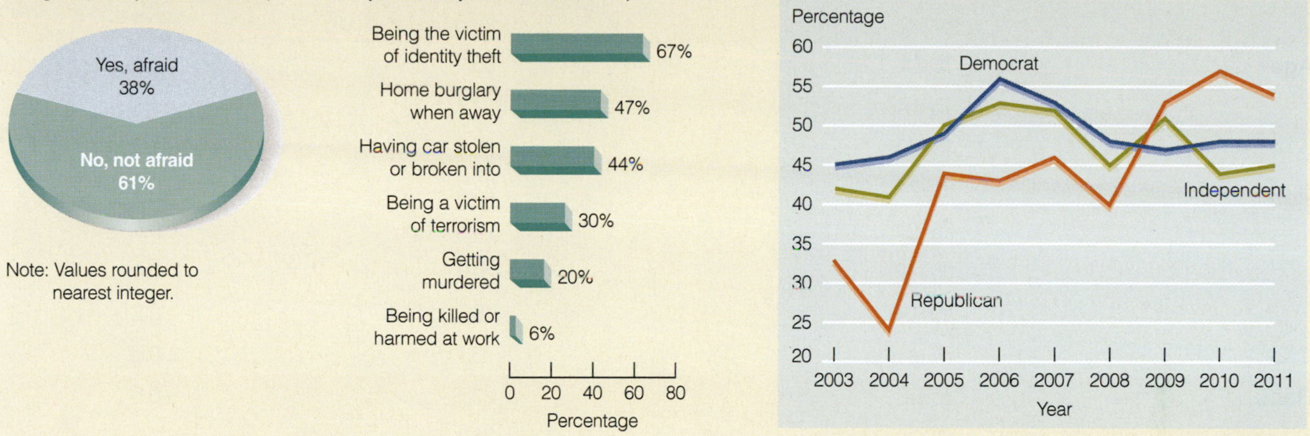

Sources: *Sourcebook of Criminal Justice Statistics*, Tables 2.36, 2.36.2004, 2.36.2005, 2.36.2006, 2.36.2007, 2.36.2008, 2.36.2009, 2.36.2010, 2.36.2011, 2.37.2011, 2.39.2011.

and the longitudinal (horizontal) axis of the graph. In this case, the variable on the vertical axis is the percentage of people, broken out by self-identified political party, who say that there is more crime in their neighborhoods than a year before. The variable on the longitudinal axis is time, reported as years when the survey question was asked. In 2003, for instance, 33 percent of Republicans indicated there was more crime in their neighborhoods than one year before, compared to 42 percent of Independents and 45 percent of Democrats. Drawing a line through the points that show the percentage associated with each response for each year allows for a graphic presentation of how opinions have changed over time within each group. The same data could have been presented in a table, but this would have made it harder to see the direction of change in opinion. Line graphs are especially well suited to showing data about trends. Think about how we might compare the data in this chart to those presented in Figure B.1, which indicated that the number of violent crimes in the United States has been generally decreasing since 2003. It appears that perceptions about crime may not match the reality.

Analyzing Tables

All these points about graphic presentations in general apply also to tables. When you see a table, read the title and descriptive information carefully, note the source of the data, and be aware of how the presentation itself affects your perception of the content.

Tables relate two or more variables by organizing information in vertical columns and horizontal rows. In Table B.1, the columns give data about victimization rates for two categories of crime in 2013: violent crime and personal theft. The rows of the table show categories of victims organized by sex, age, race, Hispanic origin, household income, and so forth. Reading down a column allows you to compare information about personal theft, for example, for different types of victims. By inspecting each column in turn, you can see that the rates for both types of crime victimization are higher for people aged 12–20 than for those in other age groups, for those with lower incomes, and so on. Reading across a row, for example, "Divorced," allows you to compare violent crime with personal theft for people who are divorced.

Like other types of data displays, tables often require close study beyond the particular information being highlighted by the writer. When you come across a table, read down the columns and across the rows to discover for yourself the shape of the information being reported. Be careful, however, to notice how the data are organized and to distinguish between the data themselves and any inferences you draw from them. In this case, for example, you might be struck by the higher victimization rates reported by people who have never married compared with the rates reported by those who are married. Before you speculate about why this is so, note that the data for marital status are not broken out by age. People under

TABLE B.1 WHO ARE THE VICTIMS OF VIOLENT CRIMES AND PERSONAL THEFT?

NVCVS data help clarify the characteristics of crime victims.

		Rate per 1,000 persons age 12 or older	
	VICTIMS	VIOLENCE	PERSONAL THEFT*
Sex	Male	23.7	0.5
	Female	22.7	0.5
Age	12–14	65.1	0.4
	15–17	39.2	1.5
	18–20	35.9	1.3
	21–24	32.2	0.8
	25–34	29.6	0.6
	35–49	20.3	0.4
	50–64	18.7	0.2
	65 or older	3.1	0.5
Race	White	22.7	0.5
	African American	25.2	0.4
	Other race	11.4	1.3
	Two or more races	74.1	0.6
Household Income	Less than $7,000	84.0	1.0
	$7,000–$14,999	62.3	1.7
	$15,000–$24,999	31.8	0.2
	$25,000–$34,999	21.6	0.7
	$35,000–$49,999	22.8	0.3
	$50,000–$74,999	17.8	0.2
	$75,000 or more	14.4	0.3
Marital Status	Never married	36.3	0.8
	Married	10.7	0.3
	Divorced	8.6	0.5
	Widowed	34.4	0.8
	Separated	73.2	1.4
Region	Northeast	27.5	0.9
	Midwest	23.7	0.4
	South	18.0	0.5
	West	27.3	0.4
Residence	Urban	25.9	0.9
	Suburban	23.3	0.4
	Rural	16.9	0.2

*Personal theft includes only purse snatching and pocket picking.

Source: Bureau of Justice Statistics, 2015, Table: "Rate of Violent Victimizations, and Personal Thefts/Larcenies by Sex, Age, Race, Hispanic Origin, Household Income, Marital Status, Region, and Residence, 1993–2013." Generated using the NCVS Victimization Analysis Tool (www.bjs.gov).

age 25 are more likely than those who are older to be victimized (see the data under "age"). Because these younger people are far more likely than older ones to be unmarried, the difference in victimization rates for married and unmarried people may be largely accounted for by age rather than by marital status. The table does not provide enough information to tell to what extent this might be the case.

In summary, data are presented in tables and graphs so they can be more easily grasped. But before you decide that you have truly understood the information, read the item and accompanying commentary attentively and be aware of the ways the writer has chosen to organize and display the data. By working with graphic presentations and posing questions to yourself as you read them, you also make the important information easier to remember.

Understanding Raw Data

Data that you see in graphs and tables have already been sifted and organized. As a student of criminal justice, you also encounter raw (or "whole") data. For example, the *Sourcebook of Criminal Justice Statistics* (Table 3.106.2012) reports that there were 14,827 homicides in the category of "murder and non-negligent manslaughter" in the United States in 2012. These are the killings that result from intentional criminal acts that we typically describe in crime data as "murders." Data often are expressed in terms of the *rate* at which an event occurs for a certain number of people in the population. The murder rate in 2012 was 4.7 murders per 100,000 people in the United States. The formula for determining the rate is:

$$\frac{\text{Number of murders}}{\text{Total U.S. population}} \times 100{,}000 = \text{Rate per } 100{,}000$$

For some purposes, the total figures (the raw data) are needed; for other purposes, percentages are more informative; and for still other purposes, expressing data as a rate is most useful. To illustrate this point, consider the following example of data about incarceration in two different states.

On December 31, 2013, there were 60,200 offenders held in the prisons of Michigan and 50,100 in the prisons of Louisiana. How does incarceration in these states compare? Michigan has a larger prison population than Louisiana, but what if more people live in Michigan? We would expect states with higher populations to incarcerate more people. Knowing the number of prisoners does not allow you to draw many conclusions about incarceration in these states. If, however, the numbers are expressed as a rate, the difference in the sizes of the two state populations would be taken into consideration and a much clearer picture would result.

Although Louisiana has fewer prisoners than Michigan, the incarceration rate in Louisiana (1,420 prisoners per 100,000 population) is considerably higher than in Michigan (790 per 100,000). On a national basis, the number of incarcerated people on December 31, 2013, represents a rate of 910 prisoners for every 100,000 U.S. residents, so the rate in Louisiana was significantly higher than in both Michigan and in the United States as a whole. In fact, Louisiana has the highest incarceration rate in the country (L. E. Glaze and Kaeble, 2014).

Sources of Criminal Justice Data

To a large extent, criminal justice researchers depend on data collected and analyzed by agencies of the government. Many of these sources are cited throughout this book. In particular, the Bureau of Justice Statistics of the U.S. Department of Justice produces the *Sourcebook of Criminal Justice Statistics,* an annual compilation of data on most aspects of crime and justice; the *Bulletin,* which regularly publishes issues focusing on a single topic related to police, courts, and corrections; and the *Special Report,* a publication that presents findings from specific research projects. The National Institute of Justice, also an arm of the U.S. Department of Justice, publishes *Research in Brief,* which offers summary versions of major research studies. *Crime in the United States,* published each August by the Department of Justice, contains data collected through the FBI's Uniform Crime Reports system.

The libraries of most colleges and universities hold these publications in the government documents or reference section. Ask your librarian to help you find them. You can also access most of these publications on the Internet.

GLOSSARY

A

accusatory process The series of events from the arrest of a suspect to the filing of a formal charge with a court (through an indictment or information).

administrative regulations Rules made by government agencies to implement specific public policies in areas such as public health, environmental protection, and workplace safety.

adversarial system Basis of the American legal system in which a passive judge and jury seek to find the truth by listening to opposing attorneys who vigorously advocate on behalf of their respective sides.

affidavit Written statement of fact, supported by oath or affirmation, submitted to judicial officers to fulfill the requirements of probable cause for obtaining a warrant.

aftercare Juvenile justice equivalent of parole, in which a delinquent is released from a custodial sentence and supervised in the community.

aggressive patrol A patrol strategy designed to maximize the number of police interventions and observations in the community.

anomie A breakdown in and disappearance of the rules of social behavior.

appeal A request to a higher court that it review actions taken in a completed lower-court case.

appellate courts Courts that do not try criminal cases but hear appeals of decisions of lower courts.

***Arizona v. Gant* (2009)** An arrest does not justify a vehicle search if the handcuffed driver has already been removed and poses no danger to officers or to the preservation of evidence.

arraignment The court appearance of an accused person in which the charges are read and the accused, advised by a lawyer, pleads guilty or not guilty.

assigned counsel An attorney in private practice assigned by a court to represent an indigent. The attorney's fee is paid by the government with jurisdiction over the case.

***Atkins v. Virginia* (2002)** Execution of the developmentally disabled ("mentally retarded") is unconstitutional.

B

bail An amount of money specified by a judge to be paid as a condition of pretrial release to ensure that the accused will appear in court as required.

***Barron v. Baltimore* (1833)** The protections of the Bill of Rights apply only to actions of the federal government.

***Baze v. Rees* (2008)** Lethal injection has not been shown to violate the Eighth Amendment prohibition on cruel and unusual punishments and thus this method of execution is permissible.

bench trial Trial conducted by a judge who acts as fact finder and determines issues of law. No jury participates.

biological explanations Explanations of crime that emphasize physiological and neurological factors that may predispose a person to commit crimes.

boot camp A short-term institutional sentence, usually followed by probation, that puts the offender through a physical regimen designed to develop discipline and respect for authority. Also referred to as shock incarceration.

***Bordenkircher v. Hayes* (1978)** A defendant's rights were not violated by a prosecutor who warned that failure to agree to a guilty plea would result in a harsher sentence.

***Boykin v. Alabama* (1969)** Defendants must state that they are voluntarily making a plea of guilty.

***Breed v. Jones* (1975)** Juveniles cannot be found delinquent in juvenile court and then transferred to adult court without a hearing on the transfer; to do so violates the protection against double jeopardy.

"broken windows" theory Influential theory about increases in fear and crime within neighborhoods when there is insufficient police attention to seemingly minor public order offenses such as vandalism, loitering, aggressive panhandling, and prostitution.

C

case law Court decisions that have the status of law and serve as precedents for later decisions.

chain of command Organizational structure based on a military model with clear definition of ranks to indicate authority over subordinates and obligations to obey orders from superiors.

challenge for cause Removal of a prospective juror by showing that he or she has some bias or some other legal disability. The number of these challenges permitted to attorneys is potentially unlimited.

***Chimel v. California* (1969)** Supreme Court decision that endorsed warrantless searches for weapons and evidence in the immediate vicinity of people who are lawfully arrested.

circumstantial evidence Evidence, provided by a witness, from which a jury must infer a fact.

citation A written order or summons, issued by a law enforcement officer, often directing an alleged offender to appear in court at a specified time to answer a criminal charge.

civil disabilities Legal restrictions that prevent released felons from voting, serving on juries, and holding public office.

civil forfeiture The confiscation of property by the state because it was used in or acquired through a crime. In recent years the police have used civil forfeiture to seize property that they believe was purchased with drug profits.

civil law Law regulating the relationships between or among individuals, usually involving property, contract, or business disputes.

civilian review board Citizens' committee formed to investigate complaints against the police.

classical criminology A school of criminology that views behavior as stemming from free will, that demands responsibility and accountability of all perpetrators, and that stresses the need for punishments severe enough to deter others.

classification The process of assigning an inmate to a category specifying his or her needs for security, treatment, education, work assignment, and readiness for release.

clearance rate The percentage rate of crimes known to the police that they believe they have solved through an arrest; a statistic used to measure a police department's productivity.

Commission on Accreditation for Law Enforcement Agencies (CALEA) Nonprofit organization formed by major law enforcement executives' associations to develop standards for police practices and policies; on request, will review police agencies and award accreditation upon meeting those standards.

common law The Anglo-American system of uncodified law, in which judges follow precedents set by earlier decisions when they decide new but similar cases. The substantive and procedural criminal law was originally developed in this manner but was later codified—set down in codes—by state legislatures.

community corrections A model of corrections based on the goal of reintegrating the offender into the community.

community justice A model of justice that emphasizes reparation to the victim and the community, approaching crime from a problem-solving perspective, and citizen involvement in crime prevention.

community prosecution An approach to advance effective prosecution and crime prevention by placing prosecutors in close contact with citizens and neighborhood groups in an effort to identify and solve problems while enhancing cooperation between the community and the prosecutor's office.

community service A sentence requiring the offender to perform a certain amount of unpaid labor in the community.

conditions of release Conduct restrictions that parolees must follow as a legally binding requirement of being released.

congregate system A penitentiary system, developed in Auburn, New York, in which each inmate was held in isolation during the night but worked and ate with other prisoners during the day under a rule of silence.

constitution The basic laws of a country or state defining the structure of government and the relationship of citizens to that government.

continuance An adjournment of a scheduled case until a later date.

contract counsel An attorney in private practice who contracts with the government to represent all indigent defendants in a county during a set period of time and for a specified dollar amount.

contract labor system A system under which inmates' labor was sold on a contractual basis to private employers who provided the machinery and raw materials with which inmates made saleable products in the institution.

control theories Theories holding that criminal behavior occurs when the bonds that tie an individual to society are broken or weakened.

***Cooper v. Pate* (1964)** Prisoners are entitled to the protection of the Civil Rights Act of 1871 and may challenge in federal courts the conditions of their confinement.

corrections The variety of programs, services, facilities, and organizations responsible for the management of people who have been accused or convicted of criminal offenses.

counts Each separate offense of which a person is accused in an indictment or an information.

crime A specific act of commission or omission in violation of the law, for which a punishment is prescribed.

crime control model A model of the criminal justice system that assumes freedom is so important that every effort must be made to repress crime; it emphasizes efficiency, speed, finality, and the capacity to apprehend, try, convict, and dispose of a high proportion of offenders.

crime control model of corrections A model of corrections based on the assumption that criminal behavior can be controlled by more use of incarceration and other forms of strict supervision.

criminogenic traits Factors thought to bring about criminal behavior in an individual.

custodial model A model of incarceration that emphasizes security, discipline, and order.

cybercrimes Offenses that involve the use of one or more computers.

D

dark figure of crime A metaphor referring to the significant yet undefined extent of crime that is never reported to the police.

day reporting center A community correctional center where an offender reports each day to comply with elements of a sentence.

defense attorney The lawyer who represents accused or convicted offenders in their dealings with criminal justice officials.

delinquent A child who has committed an act that if committed by an adult would be a criminal act.

demonstrative evidence Evidence that is not based on witness testimony but demonstrates information relevant to the crime, such as maps, X-rays, and photographs; includes real evidence involved in the crime.

dependent child A child who has no parent or guardian or whose parents cannot give proper care.

deportation Formal removal by the federal government of an undocumented immigrant or other noncitizen from the United States for violation of immigration and other laws.

detention hearing A hearing by the juvenile court to determine if a juvenile is to be detained or released prior to adjudication.

determinate sentences A sentence that fixes the term of imprisonment at a specific period.

differential response A patrol strategy that assigns priorities to calls for service and then determines the appropriate response depending on the importance or urgency of the call.

direct evidence Eyewitness accounts.

directed patrol A proactive form of patrolling that directs resources to known high-crime areas.

discovery A prosecutor's pretrial disclosure, to the defense, of facts and evidence to be introduced at trial.

discretionary release The release of an inmate from prison to conditional supervision at the discretion of the parole board within the boundaries set by the sentence and the penal law.

diversion The process of screening children out of the juvenile justice system without a decision by the court.

domestic violence The term commonly used to refer to intimate partner violence or violent victimization between spouses, boyfriends, and girlfriends, or those formerly in intimate relationships. Such actions account for a significant percentage of the violent victimizations experienced by women.

double jeopardy The subjecting of a person to prosecution more than once in the same jurisdiction for the same offense; prohibited by the Fifth Amendment.

drug courts Specialized courts that impose drug testing and counseling requirements on substance abusers and monitor their progress instead of sending them immediately to jail or prison.

due process model A model of the criminal justice system that assumes freedom is so important that every effort must be made to ensure that criminal justice decisions are based on reliable information; it emphasizes the adversarial process, the rights of defendants, and formal decision-making procedures.

E

earned time Reduction in a prisoner's sentence as a reward for participation in educational or other rehabilitation programs, and for work assignments, such as disaster relief and conservation projects.

Enlightenment A movement, during the eighteenth century in England and France, in which concepts of liberalism, rationalism, equality, and individualism dominated social and political thinking.

entrapment The defense that the police induced the individual to commit the criminal act.

***Escobedo v. Illinois* (1964)** Police cannot refuse access to an attorney for arrested suspects who ask to see one.

evidence-based practices Policies developed through guidance from research studies that demonstrate which approaches are most useful and cost-effective for advancing desired goals.

excessive use of force Applications of force against individuals by police officers that violate either departmental policies or constitutional rights by exceeding the level of force permissible and necessary in a given situation.

exclusionary rule The principle that illegally obtained evidence must be excluded from a trial.

exigent circumstances When there is a threat to public safety or the risk that evidence will be destroyed, officers may search, arrest, or question suspects without obtaining a warrant or following other usual rules of criminal procedure.

expiration release The release of an inmate from incarceration, without any further correctional supervision; the inmate cannot be returned to prison for any remaining portion of the sentence for the current offense.

expungement Process defined by individual states' laws through which offenders can have their criminal records erased from public records. This process is often focused on youthful offenders who commit nonviolent offenses in their teens or early twenties.

F

***Fare v. Michael C.* (1979)** By examining the totality of circumstances, trial court judges must evaluate the voluntariness of juveniles' waiving their rights to an attorney and to protections against self-incrimination.

felonies Serious crimes usually carrying a penalty of incarceration for more than one year or the death penalty.

fine A sum of money to be paid to the state by a convicted person as punishment for an offense.

***Florida v. J. L.* (2000)** Police officers may not conduct a stop-and-frisk search based solely on an anonymous tip.

forfeiture Government seizure of property and other assets derived from or used in criminal activity.

frankpledge A system in old English law in which members of a tithing, a group of ten families, pledged to be responsible for keeping order and bringing violators of the law to court.

fundamental fairness A legal doctrine supporting the idea that so long as a state's conduct maintains basic standards of fairness, the Constitution has not been violated.

furlough The temporary release of an inmate from a correctional institution for a brief period, usually one to three days, for a visit home. Such programs help maintain family ties and prepare inmates for release on parole.

***Furman v. Georgia* (1972)** The death penalty, as administered, constitutes cruel and unusual punishment.

fusion centers Centers run by states and large cities that analyze and facilitate sharing of information to assist law enforcement and homeland security agencies in preventing and responding to crime and terrorism threats.

G

general deterrence Punishment of criminals that is intended to provide an example to the general public and to discourage the commission of offenses.

geographic information system (GIS) Computer technology and software that enable law enforcement officials to map problem locations to better understand calls for service and the nature and frequency of crimes and other specific issues within specific neighborhoods.

***Gideon v. Wainwright* (1963)** Indigent defendants have a right to counsel when charged with serious crimes for which they could face six months or more incarceration.

going rate Local court officials' shared view of the appropriate sentence for the offense, based on the defendant's prior record and other case characteristics.

good faith exception When police act in honest reliance on a warrant, the evidence seized is admissible even if the warrant is later proved to be defective.

good time A reduction of an inmate's prison sentence, at the discretion of the prison administrator, for good behavior or participation in vocational, educational, or treatment programs.

***Graham v. Florida* (2010)** Juvenile offenders cannot be sentenced to life imprisonment without possibility of parole (LWOP) for non-homicide crimes.

grand jury A body of citizens that determines whether the prosecutor possesses sufficient evidence to justify the prosecution of a suspect for a serious crime.

***Gregg v. Georgia* (1976)** The Supreme Court's decision reactivating the death penalty after states revised their laws to make decision making about punishment in murder cases more careful and deliberate.

H

habeas corpus A writ or judicial order requesting the release of a person being detained in a jail, prison, or mental hospital. If a judge finds the person is being held improperly, the writ may be granted and the person released or granted a new trial.

halfway house A correctional facility housing convicted felons who spend a portion of their day at work in the community but reside in the halfway house during nonworking hours.

hands-off policy Judges should not interfere with the administration of correctional institutions.

***Herring v. United States* (2009)** When officers act in good faith reliance on computerized records concerning outstanding warrants, evidence found in a search incident to arrest is admissible even if the arrest was based on an erroneous record that wrongly indicated the existence of a warrant.

home confinement A sentence requiring the offender to remain inside his or her home during specified periods.

Hudson v. Palmer (1984) Prison officials have the authority to search cells and confiscate any materials found.

identity theft The theft of social security numbers, credit card numbers, and other information in order to secure loans, withdraw bank funds, and purchase merchandise while posing as someone else. The unsuspecting victim will eventually lose money in these transactions.

Illinois v. Rodriguez (1990) Officers may rely on reasonable beliefs that a person giving consent to a search has authority to do so even if the person actually lacks authority over the apartment, house, or vehicle.

I

In re Gault (1967) Juveniles have the right to counsel, to confront and examine accusers, and to have adequate notice of charges when confinement is a possible punishment.

In re Winship (1970) The standard of proof beyond a reasonable doubt applies to juvenile delinquency proceedings.

incapacitation Depriving an offender of the ability to commit crimes against society, usually by detaining the offender in prison.

inchoate offense Conduct that is criminal even though the harm that the law seeks to prevent has been merely planned or attempted but not done.

incident-driven policing A reactive approach to policing emphasizing a quick response to calls for service.

incorporation The extension of the due process clause of the Fourteenth Amendment to make binding on state governments the rights guaranteed in the first ten amendments to the U.S. Constitution (the Bill of Rights).

indeterminate sentences A period, set by a judge, that specifies a minimum and a maximum time to be served in prison. Sometime after the minimum, the offender may be eligible for parole. Because it is based on the idea that the time necessary for treatment cannot be set, the indeterminate sentence is closely associated with rehabilitation.

indigent defendants People facing prosecution who do not have enough money to pay for their own attorneys and court expenses.

inevitable discovery exception Improperly obtained evidence can be used when it would later have inevitably been discovered without improper actions by the police.

inmate code The values and norms of the prison social system that define the inmates' idea of the model prisoner.

inquisitorial system Basis of legal system in Europe in which the judge takes an active role in investigating the case and asking questions of witnesses in court.

intelligence-led policing An approach to policing, in conjunction with concerns about homeland security, that emphasizes gathering and analyzing information to be shared among agencies in order to develop cooperative efforts to identify, prevent, and solve problems.

intensive supervision probation (ISP) Probation granted under conditions of strict reporting to a probation officer with a limited caseload.

intermediate sanctions A variety of punishments that are more restrictive than traditional probation but less severe and costly than incarceration.

internal affairs unit A branch of a police department that receives and investigates complaints alleging violations of rules and policies on the part of officers.

Interpol The International Criminal Police Organization through which countries cooperate in investigating crimes, especially situations in which lawbreakers have crossed international borders or participated in multicountry criminal activities.

J

jurisdiction The geographic territory or legal boundaries within which control may be exercised; the range of a court's authority.

jury A panel of citizens selected according to law and sworn to determine matters of fact in a criminal case and to deliver a verdict of guilty or not guilty.

justice reinvestment Evidence-based policies intended to reduce spending on imprisonment, with the money saved being reinvested in alternative sanctions and programs that hold offenders accountable, protect public safety, and reduce the risk of reoffending.

K

Kentucky v. King (2011) Police officers can use the exigent circumstances justification to conduct a warrantless search even when their own actions, such as knocking loudly on the wrong door in an apartment building, lead to the sounds inside the dwelling that trigger the belief in the necessity of an immediate search.

Kyllo v. United States (2001) Law enforcement officials cannot examine a home with a thermal-imaging device unless they obtain a warrant.

L

labeling theories Theories emphasizing that the causes of criminal behavior are found not in the individual but in the social process that labels certain acts as deviant or criminal.

latent fingerprints Impressions from the ridges on the fingertips that are left behind on objects due to natural secretions from the skin or contaminating materials, such as ink, blood, or dirt, which were present on the fingertips at the time of their contact with the objects.

law enforcement intelligence Information, collected and analyzed by law enforcement officials, concerning criminal activities and organizations such as gangs, drug traffickers, and organized crime.

law enforcement The police function of controlling crime by intervening in situations in which the law has clearly been violated and the police need to identify and apprehend the guilty person.

learning theories Theories that see criminal behavior as learned, just as legal behavior is learned.

lease system A system under which inmates were leased to contractors who provided prisoners with food and clothing in exchange for their labor. In southern states the prisoners were used as agricultural, mining, logging, and construction laborers.

legal responsibility The accountability of an individual for a crime because of the perpetrator's characteristics and the circumstances of the illegal act.

legal sufficiency The presence of the minimum legal elements necessary for prosecution of a case. When a prosecutor uses legal sufficiency as the customary criterion for prosecuting cases, a great many are accepted for prosecution, but the majority of them are disposed of by plea bargaining or dismissal.

legalistic style Style of policing that emphasizes strict enforcement of laws and reduces officers' authority to handle matters informally.

life course theories Theories that identify factors affecting the start, duration, nature, and end of criminal behavior over the life of an offender.

lifestyle-exposure theory Approach to understanding the unequal distribution of crime and victimization that examines the differential exposure to crime of demographic groups, such as the young or the poor, based on where they live and work and engage in leisure activities.

line functions Police components that directly perform field operations and carry out the basic functions of patrol, investigation, traffic, vice, juvenile, and so on.

local legal culture Norms, shared by members of a court community, which center on how cases should be handled and how a participant should behave in the judicial process.

mala in se Offenses that are wrong by their very nature.

M

mala prohibita Offenses prohibited by law but not wrong in themselves.

mandatory release The required release of an inmate from incarceration to community supervision upon the expiration of a certain period, as specified by a determinate-sentencing law or parole guidelines.

mandatory sentences A sentence determined by statutes and requiring that a certain penalty be imposed and carried out for convicted offenders who meet certain criteria.

***Mapp v. Ohio* (1961)** Evidence obtained through illegal searches by state and local police must be excluded from use at trial.

mark system A system in which offenders receive a certain number of points at the time of sentencing, based on the severity of their crime. Prisoners can reduce their term and gain release by earning marks to reduce these points through labor, good behavior, and educational achievement.

***Maryland v. King* (2013)** U.S. Supreme Court decision that endorsed the legality of collecting DNA samples from individuals arrested but not yet convicted of serious offenses.

***McCleskey v. Kemp* (1987)** Rejects a challenge to Georgia's death penalty that was made on the grounds of racial discrimination.

***McKeiver v. Pennsylvania* (1971)** Juveniles do not have a constitutional right to a trial by jury.

medical model A model of corrections based on the assumption that criminal behavior is caused by biological or psychological conditions that require treatment.

***Mempa v. Rhay* (1967)** Probationers have the right to counsel at a combined revocation-sentencing hearing.

mens rea "Guilty mind" or blameworthy state of mind, necessary for legal responsibility for a criminal offense; criminal intent, as distinguished from innocent intent.

merit selection A reform plan by which judges are nominated by a commission and appointed by the governor for a given period. When the term expires, the voters are asked to approve or disapprove the judge for a succeeding term. If the judge is disapproved, the committee nominates a successor for the governor's appointment.

***Miller v. Alabama* (2012)** Juvenile homicide offenders cannot be sentenced to mandatory life without possibility of parole (LWOP) imprisonment.

***Miranda v. Arizona* (1966)** Before questioning a suspect held in custody, police officers must inform the individual of the right to remain silent and the right to have an attorney present during questioning.

misdemeanors Offenses less serious than felonies and usually punishable by incarceration of no more than one year, probation, or intermediate sanctions.

money laundering Moving the proceeds of criminal activities through a maze of businesses, banks, and brokerage accounts in order to disguise their origin.

***Morrissey v. Brewer* (1972)** Due process rights require a prompt, informal two-part inquiry before an impartial hearing officer prior to parole revocation. The parolee may present relevant information and confront witnesses.

motion An application to a court requesting that an order be issued to bring about a specified action.

N

National Crime Victimization Surveys (NCVS) Interviews of samples of the U.S. population conducted by the Bureau of Justice Statistics to determine the number and types of criminal victimization, and thus, the extent of unreported as well as reported crime.

National Incident-Based Reporting System (NIBRS) A reporting system in which the police describe each offense in a crime incident, together with data describing the offender, victim, and property.

neglected child A child who is receiving inadequate care because of some action or inaction of his or her parents.

net widening Process in which new sentencing options increase instead of reduce control over offenders' lives.

***New Jersey v. T. L. O.* (1985)** School officials may search a student if they have a reasonable suspicion that the search will produce evidence that a school rule or a criminal law has been violated.

***Nix v. Williams* (1984)** Decision in which the Supreme Court created the "inevitable discovery" exception to the exclusionary rule.

nolle prosequi An entry made by a prosecutor on the record of a case and announced in court to indicate that the charges specified will not be prosecuted. In effect, the charges are thereby dismissed.

nonpartisan election An election in which candidates' party affiliations are not listed on the ballot.

***North Carolina v. Alford* (1970)** A plea of guilty may be accepted for the purpose of a lesser sentence from a defendant who maintains his or her innocence.

O

occupational crime A criminal offense committed through opportunities created in a legal business or occupation. Officials' examination of and hunt for evidence in or on a person or place in a manner that intrudes on reasonable expectations of privacy.

open fields doctrine Officers are permitted to search and to seize evidence, without a warrant, on private property beyond the area immediately surrounding the house.

order maintenance The police function of preventing behavior that disturbs or threatens to disturb the public peace or that involves face-to-face conflict among two or more people. In such situations, the police exercise discretion in deciding whether a law has been broken.

organized crime A framework for the perpetration of criminal acts—usually in fields, such as gambling, drugs, and prostitution—providing illegal services that are in great demand.

other conditional release A term used in some states to avoid the rigidity of mandatory release by placing convicts under supervision in various community settings.

P

pardon An action of the executive branch of state or federal government excluding the offense and absolving the offender from the consequences of the crime.

parens patriae The state as parent; the state as guardian and protector of all citizens (such as juveniles) who cannot protect themselves.

parole The conditional release of an inmate from incarceration under supervision after a part of the prison sentence has been served.

partisan election An election in which candidates openly endorsed by political parties are presented to voters for selection.

patrol units The core operational units of local police departments that deploy uniformed officers to handle the full array of police functions for service, order maintenance, and law enforcement.

penitentiary An institution intended to punish criminals by isolating them from society and from one another so they can reflect on their past misdeeds, repent, and reform.

peremptory challenge Removal of a prospective juror without giving any reason. Attorneys are allowed a limited number of such challenges.

PINS Acronym for "person(s) in need of supervision," a term that designates juveniles who are either status offenders or thought to be on the verge of trouble.

plain view doctrine Officers may examine and use as evidence, without a warrant, contraband or evidence that is in open view at a location where they are legally permitted to be. Police officers assigned for duty in schools to assist in order maintenance while also developing positive relationships with students that may assist in delinquency prevention.

political crime An act, usually done for ideological purposes, that constitutes a threat against the state (such as treason, sedition, or espionage) or a criminal act by a state.

positivist criminology A school of criminology that views behavior as stemming from social, biological, and psychological factors. It argues that punishment should be tailored to the individual needs of the offender.

***Powell v. Alabama* (1932)** An attorney must be provided to a poor defendant facing the death penalty.

presentence report A report, prepared by a probation officer, that presents a convicted offender's background and is used by the judge in selecting an appropriate sentence.

presumptive sentence A sentence for which the legislature or a commission sets a minimum and maximum range of months or years. Judges are to fix the length of the sentence within that range, allowing for special circumstances.

preventive detention Holding a defendant for trial, based on a judge's finding that, if the defendant were released on bail, he or she would flee or would endanger another person or the community.

preventive patrol Making the police presence known, in order to deter crime and to make officers available to respond quickly to calls.

prisons An institution for the incarceration of people convicted of serious crimes, usually felonies.

proactive Acting in anticipation, such as an active search for potential offenders that is initiated by the police without waiting for a crime to be reported. Arrests for victimless crimes are usually proactive.

probable cause Reliable information indicating that evidence will likely be found in a specific location or that a specific person is likely to be guilty of a crime.

probation release The release of an inmate from incarceration to probation supervision, as required by the sentencing judge.

probation A sentence that the offender is allowed to serve under supervision in the community.

problem-oriented policing An approach to policing in which officers routinely seek to identify, analyze, and respond to the circumstances underlying the incidents that prompt citizens to call the police.

procedural criminal law Law defining the procedures that criminal justice officials must follow in enforcement, adjudication, and corrections.

procedural due process The constitutional requirement that all people be treated fairly and justly by government officials. An accused person can be arrested, prosecuted, tried, and punished only in accordance with procedures prescribed by law.

property crimes Crimes in which property is damaged or stolen.

prosecuting attorney A legal representative of the state with sole responsibility for bringing criminal charges; in some states referred to as district attorney, state's attorney, or county attorney.

psychological explanations Explanations of crime that emphasize mental processes and behavior.

public defender An attorney employed on a full-time, salaried basis by the government to represent indigents.

public order crimes Acts, such as public drunkenness and disorderly conduct, that threaten society's well-being and make citizens fearful.

public policy Priorities and actions developed by government to use public resources as a means to deal with issues affecting society.

public safety exception When public safety is in jeopardy, police may question a suspect in custody without providing the *Miranda* warnings.

R

reactive Acting in response, such as police activity in response to notification that a crime has been committed.

real evidence Physical evidence such as a weapon, records, fingerprints, stolen property—objects actually involved in the crime.

reasonable doubt The standard used by a juror to decide if the prosecution has provided enough evidence for conviction.

reasonable expectations of privacy Standard developed for determining whether a government intrusion of a person or property constitutes a search because it interferes with individual interests that are normally protected from government intrusion.

reasonable suspicion A police officer's belief, based on articulable facts, that criminal activity is taking place, so that intruding on an individual's reasonable expectation of privacy is necessary.

recidivism A return to criminal behavior.

reformatory An institution for young offenders, emphasizing training, a mark system of classification, indeterminate sentences, and parole.

rehabilitation model A model of corrections that emphasizes the need to restore a convicted offender to a constructive place in society through some form of vocational or educational training or therapy.

rehabilitation The goal of restoring a convicted offender to a constructive place in society through some form of vocational or educational training or therapy.

reintegration model A model of a correctional institution that emphasizes maintaining the offender's ties to family and community as a method of reform, recognizing that the offender will be returning to society.

release on recognizance (ROR) Pretrial release granted on the defendant's promise to appear in court, because the judge believes that the defendant's ties in the community guarantee that he or she will appear.

repetitive victimization The victimization of an individual or household by more than one crime during a relatively short period of time.

restitution Repayment—in the form of money or service—by an offender to a victim who has suffered some loss from the offense.

restoration Punishment designed to repair the damage done to the victim and community by an offender's criminal act.

retribution Punishment inflicted on a person who has infringed on the rights of others and so deserves to be penalized. The severity of the sanction should fit the seriousness of the crime.

revictimization The victimization of an individual more than once over a long period time such as repeat incidents of domestic violence spread out over several years.

***Ricketts v. Adamson* (1987)** Defendants must uphold the plea agreement or risk going to trial and receiving a harsher sentence.

***Ring v. Arizona* (2002)** Juries, rather than judges, must make the crucial factual decisions regarding whether a convicted murderer should receive the death penalty.

***Roper v. Simmons* (2005)** Execution of offenders for murders committed before they were 18 years of age is unconstitutional.

***Roper v. Simmons* (2005)** No death penalty for offenders who commit a murder while younger than age 18.

routine activities theory A variation of the lifestyle approach that sees crime arise in times and places where there is a convergence of specific elements: motivated offenders, suitable victims, and a lack of capable guardians to prevent or deter criminal acts.

S

***Santobello v. New York* (1971)** When a guilty plea rests on a promise of a prosecutor, the promise must be fulfilled.

***Schall v. Martin* (1984)** Juveniles can be held in preventive detention if there is concern that they may commit additional crimes while awaiting court action.

Section 1983 lawsuits Civil lawsuits authorized by a federal statute against state and local officials and local agencies when citizens have evidence that their federal constitutional rights have been violated by these authorities.

seizure Situations in which police officers use their authority to deprive people of their liberty and property.

selective incapacitation Making the best use of expensive and limited prison space by targeting for incarceration those individuals whose detention will do the most to reduce crime in society.

self-incrimination The act of exposing oneself to prosecution by being forced to respond to questions whose answers may reveal that one has committed a crime. The Fifth Amendment protects defendants against compelled self-incrimination. In any criminal proceeding, the prosecution must prove the charges by means of evidence other than the involuntary testimony of the accused.

sentencing guidelines A mechanism to indicate to judges the expected sanction for certain offenses, in order to reduce disparities in sentencing.

separate confinement A penitentiary system, developed in Pennsylvania, in which each inmate was held in isolation from other inmates. All activities, including craft work, took place in the cells.

service style Style of policing in which officers cater to citizens' desire for favorable treatment and sensitivity to individual situations by using discretion to handle minor matters in ways that seek to avoid embarrassment or punishment.

service The police function of providing assistance to the public, usually in matters unrelated to crime.

sheriff Top law enforcement official in county government. The sheriff was an exceptionally important police official during the country's westward expansion and continues to bear primary responsibility for many local jails.

shock probation A sentence in which the offender is released after a short incarceration and resentenced to probation.

slave patrols Distinctively American form of law enforcement in southern states that sought to catch and control slaves through patrol groups that stopped and questioned African Americans on the roads and elsewhere in public places.

social conflict theories Theories that assume criminal law and the criminal justice system are primarily a means of controlling the poor and the have-nots.

social process theories Theories that see criminality as normal behavior. Everyone has the potential to become a criminal, depending on (1) the influences that impel one toward or away from crime and (2) how one is regarded by others.

social structure theories Theories that attribute crime to the existence of a powerless lower class that lives with poverty and deprivation and often turns to crime in response.

socialization The process by which the rules, symbols, and values of a group or subculture are learned by its members.

sociological explanation Explanations of crime that emphasize the social conditions that bear on the individual as causes of criminal behavior.

specific deterrence Punishment inflicted on criminals to discourage them from committing future crimes.

state attorney general A state's chief legal officer, usually responsible for both civil and criminal matters.

status offense Any act committed by a juvenile that is considered unacceptable for a child, such as truancy or running away from home, but that would not be a crime if it were committed by an adult.

statutes Laws passed by legislatures. Statutory definitions of criminal offenses are found in penal codes.

stop Government officials' interference with an individual's freedom of movement for a duration that typically lasts for a limited number of minutes and only rarely exceeds one hour.

stop-and-frisk search Limited search approved by the Supreme Court in *Terry v. Ohio* that permits officers to pat down clothing of people on the streets if there is reasonable suspicion of dangerous criminal activity.

strict liability An obligation or duty that when broken is an offense that can be judged criminal without a showing of *mens rea,* or criminal intent; usually applied to regulatory offenses involving health and safety.

subculture The symbols, beliefs, and values shared by members of a subgroup of the larger society.

substantive criminal law Law defining acts that are subject to punishment and specifying the punishments for such offenses.

sworn officers Police employees who have taken an oath and been given powers by the state to make arrests and use necessary force, in accordance with their duties.

system efficiency Policy of the prosecutor's office that encourages speedy and early disposition of cases in response to caseload pressures. Weak cases are screened out at intake, and other nontrial alternatives are used as a primary means of disposition.

T

technical violation The probationer's failure to abide by the rules and conditions of probation (specified by the judge), resulting in revocation of probation.

***Tennessee v. Garner* (1985)** Deadly force may not be used against an unarmed and fleeing suspect unless necessary to prevent the escape and unless the officer has probable cause to believe that the suspect poses a significant threat of death or serious injury to the officers and others.

***Terry v. Ohio* (1968)** Supreme Court decision endorsing police officers' authority to stop and frisk suspects on the street when there is reasonable suspicion that they are armed and involved in criminal activity.

testimony Oral evidence provided by a legally competent witness.

theory of differential association The theory that people become criminals because they encounter more influences that view criminal behavior as normal and acceptable than influences that are hostile to criminal behavior.

ticket of leave A system of conditional release from prison, devised by Captain Alexander Maconochie and first developed in Ireland by Sir Walter Crofton.

totality of circumstances test Flexible test established by the Supreme Court for identifying whether probable cause exists to justify the issuance of a warrant.

transnational crime Profit-seeking criminal activities that involve planning, execution, or victimization that crosses national borders.

trial courts of general jurisdiction Criminal courts with jurisdiction over all offenses, including felonies. In some states, these courts also hear appeals.

trial courts of limited jurisdiction Criminal courts with trial jurisdiction over misdemeanor cases and preliminary matters in felony cases. Sometimes these courts hold felony trials that may result in penalties below a specified limit.

trial sufficiency The presence of sufficient legal elements to ensure successful prosecution of a case. When a prosecutor uses trial sufficiency as the customary criterion for prosecuting cases, only cases that seem certain to result in conviction at trial are accepted for prosecution. Use of plea bargaining is minimal; good police work, and court capacity to go to trial are required.

U

U.S. marshals Federal law enforcement officials appointed to handle duties in western territories and today bear responsibility for federal court security and apprehending fugitives.

undocumented immigrants Foreign-born noncitizens present in the United States without proper papers or approval for either entering the country or remaining beyond a specified date.

Uniform Crime Reports (UCR) Annually published statistical summary of crimes reported to the police, based on voluntary reports to the FBI by local, state, and federal law enforcement agencies.

United States attorneys Officials responsible for the prosecution of crimes that violate the laws of the United States; appointed by the president and assigned to a U.S. district court jurisdiction.

***United States v. Drayton* (2002)** Police officers are not required to inform people of their right to decline when police ask for consent to search.

***United States v. Jones* (2012)** Law enforcement officials cannot place a GPS device on a vehicle to monitor its movements based on their own discretion without obtaining a warrant or having another proper justification.

***United States v. Salerno and Cafero* (1987)** The preventive detention provisions of the Bail Reform Act of 1984 are upheld as a legitimate use of government power designed to prevent people from committing crimes while on bail.

USA Patriot Act A federal statute passed in the aftermath of the terrorist attacks of September 11, 2001, which broadens government authority to conduct searches and wiretaps and that expands the definitions of crimes involving terrorism.

V

***Vernonia School District v. Acton* (1995)** To ensure a safe learning environment, school officials may require random drug testing of students involved in extracurricular school sports teams.

victim precipitation The role of victims in fostering the context or triggering the action that led to their victimization in a crime.

victimless crimes Offenses involving a willing and private exchange of illegal goods or services that are in strong demand. Participants do not feel they are being harmed, but these crimes are prosecuted on the ground that society as a whole is being harmed.

victimology A field of criminology that examines the role the victim plays in precipitating a criminal incident and the impact of crimes on victims.

violent crimes Crimes against people in which force is employed to rob, produce physical injury, or cause death.

visible crime An offense against persons or property that is committed primarily by members of the lower social classes. Often referred to as "street crime" or "ordinary crime," this type of offense is the one most upsetting to the public.

voir dire A questioning of prospective jurors in order to screen out people the judge or attorneys think might be biased or otherwise incapable of delivering a fair verdict.

W

waiver Procedure by which the juvenile court waives its jurisdiction and transfers a juvenile case to the adult criminal court.

watch system Practice of assigning individuals to night observation duty to warn the public of fires and crime that was first introduced to the American colonies in Boston and that later evolved into a system of paid, uniformed police.

watchman style Style of policing that emphasizes order maintenance and tolerates minor violations of law as officers use discretion to handle small infractions informally but make arrests for major violations.

***Williams v. Florida* (1970)** Juries of fewer than 12 members are permitted by the U.S. Constitution.

***Witherspoon v. Illinois* (1968)** Potential jurors who object to the death penalty cannot be automatically excluded from service; however, during voir dire those who feel so strongly about capital punishment that they could not give an impartial verdict may be excluded.

***Wolff v. McDonnell* (1974)** Basic elements of procedural due process must be present when decisions are made about the disciplining of an inmate.

work and educational release The daytime release of inmates from correctional institutions so they can work or attend school.

workgroups A collection of individuals who interact in the workplace on a continuing basis, share goals, develop norms regarding how activities should be carried out, and eventually establish a network of roles that differentiates the group from others and that facilitates cooperation.

working personality A set of emotional and behavioral characteristics developed by a member of an occupational group in response to the work situation and environmental influences.

REFERENCES

"Aaron Hernandez Trial: Prosecutors Continue to Detail Police Evidence Tying Him to Murder." 2015. ABC News online, February 20. http://abcnews.go.com.

Aaronson, D. and S. Patterson. 2013. "Modernizing Jury Instructions in the Age of Social Media," *Criminal Justice* (American Bar Association) 27:4–10.

Abid, A. 2012. "Restorative Justice in the Gilded Age: Shared Principles Underlying Two Movements in Criminal Justice." *Criminal Law Brief* 8:29–42.

Abrahamson, S. S. 2004. "The State of the State Courts." *Judicature* 87:241–42.

Abrams, J. 2008. "House Sets Standards for Juvenile Boot Camps." Associated Press, June 25. www.ap.org.

Adams, B. 2012. "Utah's Cardall Family Settles Lawsuit over Taser Death." *Salt Lake City Tribune*. December 29. www.sltrib.com.

Adams, B., and S. Addie. 2010. *Delinquency Cases Waived to Criminal Court, 2007*. NCJ230167. Washington, DC: U.S. Office of Juvenile Justice and Delinquency Prevention.

Adams, G. 2006. "Sex Offenders' Killer Studied Lists." *Maine Sun Journal*, April 26. www.sunjournal.com.

Adams, K. 1992. "Adjusting to Prison Life." In *Crime and Justice: A Review of Research*, vol. 16, ed. M. Tonry. Chicago: University of Chicago Press, 275–359.

———. 1999. "What We Know about Police Use of Force." In *Use of Force by Police: Overview of National and Local Data*. Washington, DC: U.S. Government Printing Office.

Aden, H., and C. Koper. 2011. "The Challenges of Hot Spot Policing." *Transnational Criminology* (Summer), 6–7.

Administrative Office of the U.S. Courts. 1993. *Guide to Judiciary Policies and Procedures: Probation Manual*, vol. 10. [mimeograph]

———. 2005. "Need for DNA Testing Taxes Courts." *The Third Branch* 37 (February): 3.

Ahmadi, S. 2011. "The Erosion of Civil Rights: Exploring the Effects of the Patriot Act on Muslims in America." *Rutgers Race and the Law Journal* 12:1–55.

Albanese, J. 2011. *Transnational Crime and the 21st Century*. New York: Oxford University Press.

Alderman, K. 2012. "Honor amongst Thieves: Organized Crime and the Illicit Antiquities Trade." *Indiana Law Review* 45:601–27.

Alexander, E. 2010. "Unshackling Shawanna: The Battle over Chaining Women Prisoners during Labor and Delivery." *University of Arkansas-Little Rock Law Review* 32:435–459.

Alexander, M. 2012. *The New Jim Crow: Mass Incarceration in the Age of Colorblindness*. New York: New Press.

Alley, M. E., E. M. Bonello, and J. A. Schafer. 2002. "Dual Responsibilities: A Model for Immersing Midlevel Managers in Community Policing." In *The Move to Community Policing: Making Change Happen*, eds. M. Morash and J. Ford. Thousand Oaks, CA: Sage, 112–25.

Almasy, S., and H. Yan. 2014. "Protesters Fill Streets across Country as Ferguson Protests Spread Coast to Coast." CNN.com. November 26. www.cnn.com.

Alvarez, L. 2014. "Florida Man's Fiancée Contradicts Parts of His Testimony in Killing of Teenager." *New York Times*, February 11. www.nytimes.com.

Amar, A. R. 1997. *The Constitution and Criminal Procedure: First Principles*. New Haven, CT: Yale University Press.

American Bar Association. 2010. National Database on Judicial Diversity in State Courts. apps.americanbar.org/abanet/jd/display/national.cfm.

American Correctional Association. 1990. *The Female Offender: What Does the Future Hold?* Alexandria, VA: Kirby Lithographic.

Anderson, G., R. Litzenberger, and D. Plecas. 2002. "Physical Evidence of Police Officer Stress." *Policing* 25:399–420.

Andrews, D. A., I. Zinger, R. D. Hoge, J. Bonta, P. Gendreau, and F. T. Cullen. 1990. "Does Correctional Treatment Work? A Clinically Relevant and Psychologically Informed Meta-analysis." *Criminology* 28:369–404.

Anglen, R. 2008. "Judge Rules for Taser in Cause-of-Death Decisions." *Arizona Republic*, May 2. www.azcentral.com.

Antonio, M. E. 2006. "Jurors' Emotional Reactions to Serving on a Capital Jury." *Judicature* 89:282–88.

Applegate, B. K., and R. K. Davis. 2006. "Public Views on Sentencing Juvenile Murderers: The Impact of Offender, Offense, and Perceived Maturity." *Youth Violence and Juvenile Justice* 4:55–74.

Applegate, B. K., R. K. Davis, and F. T. Cullen. 2009. "Reconsidering Child Saving: The Extent and Correlates of Public Support for Excluding Youths from the Juvenile Court." *Crime & Delinquency*, 55(1): 51–77.

Archibold, R. 2007. "Officials See a Spread in Activity of Gangs." *New York Times*, February 8. www.nytimes.com.

Arditti, J. A., and T. Parkman. 2011. "Young Men's Reentry after Incarceration: A Development Paradox." *Family Relations* 60:205–20.

Arena, K., and K. Bohn. 2008. "Rape Victim Pushes for Expanded DNA Database." CNN.com, May 12. www.cnn.com.

Ariosto, D. 2012. "Connecticut Becomes 17th State to Abolish Death Penalty." CNN.com, April 25. www.cnn.com.

Arizona Department of Corrections. 2013. *Corrections at a Glance*. April. www.azcorrections.gov.

Armstrong, G. S., and M. L. Griffin. 2007. "The Effect of Local Life Circumstances on Victimization of Drug-Involved Women." *Justice Quarterly* 24 (1): 80–105.

Armstrong, G. S., and D. L. MacKenzie. 2003. "Private versus Public Juvenile Facilities: Do Differences in Environmental Quality Exist?" *Crime & Delinquency* 49 (October): 542–63.

Armstrong, K. 2015. "In Aaron Hernandez Trial, Judge and Prosecutor Argue over Text Messages." *New York Daily News*, February 20.

Armstrong, K., F. Davila, and J. Mayo. 2004. "Public Defender Profited while His Clients Lost." *Seattle Times*, April 12. www.seattletimes.com.

Armstrong, K., and S. Mills. 1999. "Death Row Justice Derailed." *Chicago Tribune*, November 14, 15, p. 1.

Arnold, N. 2008. "Madison Murder Prompts Look at 911 Procedures." WBAY-TV, May 5. www.wbay.com.

Associated Press. 2005. "Panel Faults County's Public Defender Load." *Seattle Post-Intelligencer*, November 23. seattlepi.nwsource.com.

———. 2007. "Elderly Inmates Clogging Nation's Prisons." *USA Today*, September 30. www.usatoday.com.

———. 2014. "Eyewitnesses recount moment Michael Dunn Shot, Killed Teen over Loud Music." *New York Daily News*, February 7. www.nydailynews.com.

———. 2015. "Officer Describes Faulkner University Student's Fatal Shooting." Tuscaloosa (Alabama) News, January 9. www.tuscaloosanews.com.

"Attorney General Invites Public to Community Meetings to Highlight Statewide Victim Services Reorganization Plan." 2012. Office of Attorney General website. www.state.ia.us/government/ag/latest_news/releases/oct_2012/Victim_Services_Reorg.html.

Austin, J., and G. Coventry. 2001. "Emerging Issues on Privatizing Prisons." *Corrections Forum* 10 (December): 11.

Austin, P. 2011. "Seal Beach Man Sentenced in Corrupt Bail Bond Scheme." *Los Alamitos-Seal Beach Patch*, January 28. losalamitos.patch.com/articles/seal-beach-man-sentenced-in-corrupt-bail-bond-scheme.

Aviram, H., J. Seymour, and R. Leo. 2010. "Moving Targets: Placing the Good Faith Doctrine in the Context of Fragmented Policing." *Fordham Urban Law Journal* 37:709–42.

Aviv, R. 2015. "Your Son Is Deceased." *New Yorker*, February 2, pp. 36–47.

Axtman, K. 2005. "A New Motion to Make Jury Service More Attractive." *Christian Science Monitor*, May 23, pp. 2–3.

Bagley, A. W. 2011. "Don't Be Evil: The Fourth Amendment in the Age of Google, National Security, and Digital Papers and Effects." *Albany Law Journal of Science and Technology* 21:153–91.

Bagnato, C. F. 2010. "Change Is Needed: How Latinos Are Affected by the Process of Jury Selection." *Chicana/o-Latina/o Law Review* 29:59–67.

"Bail Denied to Retired Fla. Officer Charged in Fatally Shooting Man in Movie Theater." *New York Daily News,* February 7, 2014. www.nydailynews.com.

Baker, A. 2008. "Police Data Shows Increase in Street Stops." *New York Times*, May 6. www.nytimes.com.

———. 2010. "New York Minorities More Likely to Be Frisked." *New York Times*, May 12. www.nytimes.com.

———. 2013. "Sex Charges in Connecticut Are Dissected on Internet." *New York Times*, March 20. www.nytimes.com.

Baker, A., and J. Goldstein. 2011. "Police Tactic: Keeping Crime Reports off the Books." *New York Times*, December 30. www.nytimes.com.

Baker, L. A. 2010. "Supreme Court Cases 2009–2010 Term." *FBI Law Enforcement Bulletin* (November). www.fbi.gov/stats-services/publications/law-enforcement-bulletin/Nov%202010/title-1.

Baker, P. 2010. "Obama Signs Law Narrowing Cocaine Sentencing Disparities." *New York Times*, August 3. www.nytimes.com.

Baker, P., and S. Shane. 2010. "Suspect Was Tracked through Phone Numbers." *New York Times,* May 5. www.nytimes.com.

Baker, T., H. M. D. Cleary, J. T. Pickett, and M. G. Gertz. 2013. "Crime Salience and Public Willingness to Pay for Child Saving and Juvenile Punishment." *Crime & Delinquency* 58(1): 78–102.

Baldus, D. C., G. Woodworth, and C. A. Pulaski. 1994. *Equal Justice and the Death Penalty: A Legal and Empirical Analysis*. Boston: Northeastern University Press.

Baldas, T. 2014. "Cancer Doc Admits Scam, Giving Patients Unneeded Chemo." *Detroit Free Press*. September 17. www.freep.com.

Bandy, D. 1991. "$1.2 Million to Be Paid in Stray-Bullet Death." *Akron Beacon Journal,* December 3, p. B6.

Banks, C., and S. Tauber. 2014. "U.S. District Court Decision-Making in USA PATRIOT Act Cases after September 11." *Justice System Journal* 35:39–61.

Barnes, C. W., and R. Kingsnorth. 1996. "Race, Drug, and Criminal Sentencing: Hidden Effects of the Criminal Law." *Journal of Criminal Justice* 24:39–55

Barnes, J. C., K. M. Beaver, and B. B. Boutwell. 2011. "Examining the Genetic Underpinnings of Moffitt's Developmental Taxonomy: A Behavioral Genetic Analysis." *Criminology* 49:923–54.

Barnes, K., D. Sloss, and S. Thaman. 2009. "Place Matters (Most): An Empirical Study of Prosecutorial Decision-Making in Death-Eligible Cases." *Arizona Law Review* 51:305–79.

Barragan, J., and M. Toohey. 2014. "Neighbor Says Shooter Sought Fresh Start in Austin." *Austin American-Statesman*. November 28. www.statesman.com.

Barrett, C., M. Bergman, and R. Thompson. 2014. "Women in Federal Law Enforcement: The Role of Gender Role Orientations and Sexual Orientation in Mentoring." *Sex Roles* 71:21–32.

Barry, D. 2014. "Notes May Recount a Pennsylvania Trooper's Death." *New York Times*, October 8. www.nytimes.com.

Barry, J. M. 2012. "Prosecuting the Exonerated: Actual Innocence and the Double Jeopardy Clause." *Stanford Law Review* 64:535–86.

Bartels, L., and A. Gaffney. 2011. *Good Practices in Women's Prisons: A Literature Review.* Canberra, Australia: Australian Institute of Criminology.

Bast, C. M. 1995. "Publication of the Name of a Sexual Assault Victim: The Collision of Privacy and Freedom of the Press." *Criminal Law Bulletin* 31:379–99.

Battson, H. 2012. "Parole Granted More Often, Revoked Less." News Release from Texas Department of Corrections Board of Pardons and Paroles, August 13. http://www.tdcj.state.tx.us/bpp/parole_increase.pdf.

Baude, W. 2010. "Last Chance on Death Row." *Wilson Quarterly* 34:18–21.

Baxter, S. 2011. "Santa Cruz County Sheriff's Office Hires San Jose Police Officers Poised for Layoffs." *San Jose Mercury News*, May 16. www.mercurynews.com.

Bayley, D. 1994. *Police for the Future*. New York: Oxford University Press.

———. 1998. *What Works in Policing?* New York: Oxford University Press.

Beaver, K. M., J. P. Wright, M. DeLisi, and M. G. Vaughn. 2008. "Genetic Influences on the Stability of Low Self-Control: Results from a Longitudinal Sample of Twins." *Journal of Criminal Justice* 36(6): 478–85.

Beck, A., and P. Harrison. 2001. "Prisoners in 2000." NCJ 188207. Bureau of Justice Statistics *Bulletin,* August.

Beck, A., P. Harrison, M. Berzofsky, S. Caspar, and C. Krebs. 2010. *Sexual Victimization in Prisons and Jails by Inmates, 2008–09*. NCJ 231169. Washington, DC: Bureau of Justice Statistics. August.

Beck, A. J., and P. M. Harrison. 2007. "Sexual Victimization in State and Federal Prisons Reported by Inmates, 2007." NCJ 219414. Bureau of Justice Statistics, *Special Report*, December.

Becker, Howard S. 1963. *Outsiders: Studies in the Sociology of Deviance*. New York: Free Press.

Beichner, D., and C. Spohn. 2012. "Modeling the Effects of Victim Behavior and Moral Character on Prosecutors' Charging Decisions in Sexual Assault Cases." *Violence and Victims* 27:3–24.

Bell, D. 1967. *The End of Ideology*. 2nd. rev. ed. New York: Collier.

Belson, K., and V. Mather. 2015. "Aaron Hernandez Found Guilty of First-Degree Murder." *New York Times*, April 15. www.nytimes.com

Bennett, C. 2011. "Feds Issue Warning for Lone-wolf Terror Attacks in Wake of bin Laden Killing." *NewYork Post*, May 10. www.nypost.com.

Bennion, E. 2011. "Death Is Different No Longer: Abolishing the Insanity Defense Is Cruel and Unusual under *Graham v. Florida*." *DePaul Law Review* 61:1–56.

Berestein, L. 2008. "Detention Dollars." *San Diego Union Tribune*, May 4. www.signonsandiego.com/uniontrib/20080504/news_lz1b4dollars.html.

Bermudez, E. 2008. "Are Crime and Immigration Linked?" *Oregonian*, May 4. www.oregonlive.com.

Bernstein, D., and N. Isackson. 2014. "The Truth about Chicago's Crime Rates." *Chicago Magazine* April. www.chicagomag.com.

Bersin, A. D. 2012. "Lines and Flows: The Beginning and End of Borders." *Brooklyn Journal of International Law* 37:389–406.

Betts, S. 2014. "Court Gives Former Camden Charity President Extension in Embezzlement Lawsuit." *Bangor Daily News*, December 24. Retrieved from http://bangordailynews.com.

Bichler, G., and L. Gaines. 2005. "An Examination of Police Officers' Insights into Problem Identification and Problem Solving." *Crime & Delinquency* 51:53–74.

"Big Changes Ahead for King County Deputies and Seattle Police Officers." 2011. KCPQ-TV, April 25. www.q13fox.com.

Bindas, M., S. Cooper, D. K. DeWolf, and M. J. Reitz. 2010. "The Washington Supreme Court and the State Constitution: A 2010 Assessment." *Gonzaga Law Review* 46:1–56.

Bisbee, J. 2010. "Oklahoma Indigent Defense System Struggles to Survive Cuts." *Oklahoman*, April 14. newsok.com.

BJS (Bureau of Justice Statistics). 1988. *Report to the Nation on Crime and Justice*. 2nd ed. Washington, DC: U.S. Government Printing Office.

———. 2005. "Law Enforcement Statistics—2000." www.ojp.usdoj.gov/bjs/lawenf.htm.

———. 2008. *Employment and Earnings Bulletin*, vol. 55 (January). www.bls.gov.

———. 2013a. *Sourcebook of Criminal Justice Statistics*. Washington, DC: U.S. Department of Justice.

———. 2013b. "Tribal Law Enforcement." BJS.gov website. bjs.gov/index.cfm?ty=tp&tid=75.

———. 2015a. *Sourcebook of Criminal Justice Statistics*. http://www.albany.edu/sourcebook/about.html.

———. 2015b. Table: Number of Violent Victimizations by Sex and Victim-Offender Relationship. Generated using the NCVS Victimization Analysis Tool at www.bjs.gov.

Blackmon, D. 2008. *Slavery by Another Name: The Re-Enslavement of Black Americans from the Civil War to World War II*. New York: Random House.

Blair, J. 2000. "Ideas and Trends; Boot Camps: An Idea Whose Time Came and Went." *New York Times*, January 2. nytimes.com.

Blankenship, G. 2013. "Board Adopts Hotly Debated Plea Bargain Ethics Opinion." *Florida Bar News*, January 1. www.floridabar.org.

Blecker, R. 2006. "'A Poster Child for Us'." *Judicature* 89 (5): 297–301.

Blitz, C. L., N. Wolff, and J. Shi. 2008. "Physical Victimization in Prison: The Role of Mental Illness." *International Journal of Law and Psychiatry* 31:385–93.

Bluestein, G. 2011. "State Budget Cuts Clog Criminal Justice System." *Seattle Post Intelligencer*, October 26. www.seattlepi.com.

Blumberg, A. 1967. "The Practice of Law as a Confidence Game." *Law and Society Review* 1:11–39.

Blumstein, A. 2002. "Youth, Guns, and Violent Crime". *The Future of Children*, 12(2):38–53.

Blumstein, A., and A. Beck. 2005. "Reentry as a Transient State between Liberty and Recommitment" (with Allen J. Beck). In *Prisoner Reentry and Crime in America*, eds. Jeremy Travis and Christy Visher. New York: Cambridge University Press 50–79.

Bogdanich, W. 2008. "Heparin Find May Point to Chinese Counterfeiting." *New York Times*, March 20. www.nytimes.com.

Bohmert, M. B., and G. Duwe. 2012. "Minnesota's Affordable Homes Program: Evaluating the Effects of a Prison Work Program on

Recidivism, Employment, and Cost Avoidance." *Criminal Justice Policy Review* 23:327–51.

Boland, B., E. Brady, H. Tyson, and J. Bassler. 1983. *The Prosecution of Felony Arrests*. Washington, DC: Bureau of Justice Statistics.

Bonczar, T .P. 2003. *Prevalence of Imprisonment in the U.S. Population*. NCJ 197976. Washington, DC: Office of Juvenile Justice and Delinquency Prevention.

Bonczar, T. P., and T. L. Snell. 2004. "Capital Punishment, 2003." Bureau of Justice Statistics *Bulletin*, November.

Bonneau, C. W. 2004. "Patterns of Campaign Spending and Electoral Competition in State Supreme Court Elections." *Justice System Journal* 25 (1): 21–38.

Bontrager, S., W. Bales, and T. Chiricos. 2005. "Race, Ethnicity, Threat and the Labeling of Convicted Felons." *Criminology* 43 (3): 589–622.

Booker, C. 2015. "The REDEEM Act." Retrieved from www.booker.senate.gov.

Boots, M.T. 2013. "New Prisoner Re-entry Center Takes Aim at Criminal Recidivism." *Anchorage Daily News*, October 2. www.adn.com.

Bornstein, B. H., and E. Greene. 2011. "Jury Decision Making: Implications for and from Psychology." *Current Directions in Psychological Science* 20:63–7.

Bosman, J. 2015. "Nebraska Bans Death Penalty, Defying a Veto," *New York Times*, May 27. www.nytimes.com.

Bosworth, M. 2011. "Penal Moderation in the United States? Yes We Can." *Criminology & Public Policy* 10:335–43.

Bourgon, G., L. Gutierrez, and J. Ashton. 2012. "The Evolution of Community Supervision Practice: The Transformation from Case Manager to Change Agent." *Federal Probation* (September): 27–35.

Bourque, B. B., M. Han, and S. M. Hill. 1996. "A National Survey of Aftercare Provisions for Boot Camp Graduates." In *Research in Brief*. Washington, DC: National Institute of Justice.

Bousequet, S. 2012a. "Plan to Close Prison Re-entry Centers Angers Lawmakers." *Tampa Bay Times*, March 2. www.tampabay.com.

———. 2012b. "Prison System Will Keep Re-entry Centers Open." *Tampa Bay Times*, March 7. www.tampabay.com.

Bowen, D. M. 2009. "Calling Your Bluff: How Prosecutors and Defense Attorneys Adapt Plea Bargaining Strategies to Increased Formalization." *Justice Quarterly* 26:2–29.

Bowers, J. 2010. "Legal Guilt, Normative Innocence, and the Equitable Decision Not to Prosecute." *Columbia Law Review* 110:1655–726.

Boyd, R. 2015. "Budget Cuts in Utah Could Mean Closure of Center that Houses Juvenile Sex Offenders." Fox 13 News, January 28. fox13now.com.

Boyle, D. J., L. M. Ragusa-Salerno, J. L. Lanterman, and A. F. Marcus. 2013. "An Evaluation of Day Reporting Centers for Parolees." *Criminology & Public Policy* 12(1):117–43.

Bradley, C. 1992. "Reforming the Criminal Trial." *Indiana Law Journal* 68:659–64.

Bradley, C. M. 2006. "The Right Decision on the Juvenile Death Penalty." *Judicature* 89 (5): 302–5.

Bradley, M. S., and R. L. Engen. 2014. "Leaving Prison: A Multilevel Investigation of Racial, Ethnic, and Gender Disproportionality in Correctional Release." *Crime & Delinquency* (online before print). doi: 10.1177/0011128714557023.

Braga, A., C. Winship, T. R. Tyler, J. Fagan, and T. L. Meares. 2014. "The Salience of Social Contextual Factors in Appraisals of Police Interactions with Citizens: A Radomized Factorial Experiment." *Journal of Quantitative Criminology* 30:599–627.

Braga, A. A. 1999. "Problem-Oriented Policing in Violent Crime Places: A Randomized Controlled Experiment." *Criminology* 37:541–80.

Braga, A. A., A. V. Papachristos, and D. M. Hureau. 2010. "The Concentration and Stability of Gun Violence at Micro Places in Boston, 1980–2008." *Journal of Quantitative Criminology* 26:33–53.

Braithwaite, J. 2007. "Encourage Restorative Justice." *Criminology & Public Policy* 6:689–96.

Branan, B. 2013. "Sacramento County Probation Officers Have Highest Caseload in the State." *Sacramento Bee*, April 10. www.sacbee.com.

Brandenburg, B., and M. Berg. 2012. "The New Storm of Money and Politics around Judicial Retention Elections." *Drake Law Review* 60:703–13.

Brandl, S. 1993. "The Impact of Case Characteristics of Detectives' Decision Making." *Justice Quarterly* 10 (September): 395–415.

Brandl, S., and Frank, J. 1994. "The Relationship between Evidence, Detective Effort, and the Disposition of Burglary and Robbery Investigations." *American Journal of Police* 13:149–68.

Brandon, K. 1999. "Legal Abortions Tied to Decline in Crime." *Hartford Courant*, August 8, p. A5.

Bray, K. 1992. "Reaching the Final Chapter in the Story of Peremptory Challenges." *UCLA Law Review* 40:517–55.

Brennan, P. A., S. A. Mednick, and J. Volavka. 1995. "Biomedical Factors in Crime." In *Crime*, eds. J. Q. Wilson and J. Petersilia. San Francisco: ICS Press.

Brennan, P. K. 2006. "Sentencing Female Misdemeanants: An Examination of the Direct and Indirect Effects of Race/Ethnicity." *Justice Quarterly* 23 (1):60–95.

Brennan, S. 2012, "Police-Reported Crime Statistics in Canada, 2011," Statistics Canada website www.statcan.gc.ca.

Breslin, D. M. 2010. "Judicial Merit-Retention Elections in Pennsylvania." *Duquesne Law Review* 48:891–907.

Brewer, T. W. 2005. "The Attorney–Client Relationship in Capital Cases and Its Impact on Juror Receptivity to Mitigation Evidence." *Justice Quarterly* 22 (3): 340–63.

Brezosky, L. 2012. "Bail Bondsman Sentenced in Corrupt Judge Case." MySanAntonio.Com, February 14. www.mysanantonio.com/news/article/Bail-bondsman-sentenced-in-corrupt-judge-case-3323702.php.

Bridges, K. L. 2004. "The Forgotten Constitutional Right to Present a Defense and Its Impact on the Acceptance of Responsibility-Entrapment Debate." *Michigan Law Review* 103:367–96.

Bright, S. B. 1994. "Counsel for the Poor: The Death Sentence Not for the Worst Crime but for the Worst Lawyer." *Yale Law Journal* 103:1835.

Brink, B. 2014. "Paul Lee, Seattle Pacific University Shooting Victim, Was a 'Brother to Everybody,' Family Says." *Oregon Live*, June 12, http://www.oregonlive.com.

Britt, C. 2000. "Social Context and Racial Disparities in Punishment Decisions." *Justice Quarterly* 17:707–32.

Broeder, D. W. 1959. "The University of Chicago Jury Project." *Nebraska Law Review* 38:774–803.

Bronsteen, J. 2010. "Retribution's Role." *Indiana Law Journal* 84:1129–56.

Brown, F. 2015. "Lawyer Says Justin Bieber Is Making Progress on Probation Terms." CBS News, February 10. www.cbsnews.com.

Brown, R., and K. Severson. 2011. "Enlisting Prison Labor to Close Budget Gaps." *New York Times*, February 24. www.nytimes.com.

Brown, R. A., and J. Frank. 2006. "Race and Officer Decision Making: Examining Differences in Arrest Outcomes between Black and White Officers." *Justice Quarterly* 23:96–126.

Browne, A., A. Cambier, and S. Agha. 2011. "Prisons within Prisons: The Use of Segregation in the United States." *Federal Sentencing Reporter* 24:46–49.

Bruce, M. 2003. "Contextual Complexity and Violent Delinquency among Black and White Males." *Journal of Black Studies* 35:65–98.

Bruer, W. 2015. "ICE Arrests More Than 2,000 Fugitive Immigrants." CNN.com, March 9. www.cnn.com

Bruni, F. 2013. "Colorado's Marijuana Muddle." *New York Times*, January 14. www.nytimes.com.

Brunson, R. K. 2007. "'Police Don't Like Black People': African American Young Men's Accumulated Police Experiences." *Criminology & Public Policy* 6:71–102.

Bueermann, J. 2012. "Being Smart on Crime with Evidence-Based Policing." *National Institute of Justice Journal* 269 (March):12–15.

Buettner, R. 2013. "Appeal Denied, Ex-consultant Is Off to Jail." *New York Times*, March 20. www.nytimes.com.

Bui, H. and M. Morash. 2010. "The Impact of Network Relationships, Prison Experiences, and Internal Transformation on Women's Success after Prison Release." *Journal of Offender Rehabilitation* 49:1–22.

Buie, L. 2014. "Curtis Reeves, Suspect in Movie Theater Shooting, Released on Bail." *Tampa Bay Times*, July 11, 2014. www.tampabay.com.

Bulman, P. 2010. "Police Use of Force: The Impact of Less-Lethal Weapons and Tactics." *National Institute of Justice Journal* 267:4–10.

Bunch. J., J. Clay-Warner, and M. Lei. 2012. "Demographic Characteristics and Victimization Risk: Testing the Mediating Effects of Routine Activities." *Crime & Delinquency*, published online December 6. cad.sagepub.com.

Bureau of Justice Assistance (BJA). 1998. *1996 National Survey of State Sentencing Structures*. Washington, DC: U.S. Government Printing Office.

Bureau of Labor Statistics. 2014a. "Correctional Officers" in *Occupational Outlook Handbook* online. www.bls.gov/ooh/protective-service/correctional-officers.htm.

Bureau of Labor Statistics. 2014b. "Employment Situation Summary." *Economic News Release*. December 5. www.bls.gov.

Burke, A. 2012. "Prosecutors and Peremptories." *Iowa Law Review* 97:1467–88.

Burnett, S., and T. Hartman. 2008. "Guards Fired Warning Shots in Deadly Riot at Florence Prison, Officials Say." *Rocky Mountain News*, April 22. m.rockymountainnews.com/news/2008/Apr/22/2-florence-inmates-killed-by-guards/.

Burns, J. L. 2010. "The Future of Problem-Solving Courts: Inside the Courts and Beyond." *University of Maryland Journal of Race, Religion, Gender and Class* 10:73–87.

Burns, J. M. 2009. *Packing the Court: The Rise of Judicial Power and the Coming Crisis of the Supreme Court.* New York: Penguin Press.

Buruma, I. 2005. "What Teaching a College-Level Class at a Maximum Security Correctional Facility Did for the Inmates—and for Me." *New York Times Magazine,* February 20, pp. 36–41.

Bushway, S., A. Redlich, and R. Norris. 2014. "An Explicit Test of Plea Bargaining in the 'Shadow of the Trial.'" *Criminology* 52:723–54.

Bushway, S. D., and A. M. Piehl. 2001. "Judging Judicial Discretion: Legal Factors and Racial Discrimination in Sentencing." *Law and Society Review* 35:733–64.

"The Bust in Boot Camps." *Newsweek,* February 20, 1994. www.thedailybeast.com/newsweek/1994/02/20/the-bust-in-boot-camps.html.

Butler, P. 2010. "One Hundred Years of Race and Crime." *Journal of Criminal Law and Criminology* 100:1043–60.

Butterfield, F. 2004a. "Repaving the Long Road Out of Prison." *New York Times,* May 4. www.nytimes.com.

———. 2004b "Study Tracks Boom in Prisons and Notes Impact on Counties." *New York Times,* April 30, p. A15.

Buzawa, E. and A. Buzawa. 2013. "Evidence-Based Prosecution: Is It Worth the Cost?" *Criminology and Public Policy* 12:491–506.

Bykowicz, J. 2008. "Juvenile Center Home to Despair." *Baltimore Sun,* May 25. baltimoresun.com.

Bynum, T., and S. Varano. 2002. "The Anti-ang Initiative in Detroit: An Aggressive Enforcement Approach to Gangs." In *Policing Gangs and Youth Violence,* ed. Scott H. Decker. Belmont, CA: Wadsworth, 214–38.

Cade, N. W. 2012. "An Adaptive Approach for an Evolving Crime: The Case for an International Cyber Court and Penal Code." *Brooklyn Journal of International Law* 37:1139–75.

Cadigan, T. P. 2007. "Pretrial Services in the Federal System: Impact of the Pretrial Services Act of 1982." *Federal Probation* 71 (2): 10–15.

Cadigan, T. P., J. L. Johnson, and C. T. Lowenkamp. 2012. "The Re-validation of the Federal Pretrial Services Risk Assessment (PTRA)." *Federal Probation* (September): 3–9.

Caldwell, H. M. 2011. "Coercive Plea Bargaining: The Unrecognized Scourge of the Justice System." *Catholic University Law Review* 61:63–96.

Calhoun, F. 1990. *The Lawmen.* Washington, DC: Smithsonian Institution.

California Department of Corrections and Rehabilitation. 2010. *Parole Suitability Hearing Handbook: Information for Victims and Their Families.* www.cdcr.ca.gov/Victim_Services/docs/BPHHandbook.pdf.

———. 2014. "Career Opportunities." California Department of Corrections and Rehabilitation website. www.cdcr.ca.gov_opportunities/por/documents.html.

"California to Redesign Prison Education Programs." 2011. *Correctional News,* March 16. www.correctionalnews.com.

"California's Prison Realignment Has Perils, Potential." 2011. *Modesto Bee,* November 19. www.modesto.com.

Call, J. E. 1995. "Prison Overcrowding Cases in the Aftermath of *Wilson v. Seiter.*" *Prison Journal* 75 (September): 390–405.

Callahan, D. G. 2013. "Oxford Settles Taser Lawsuit." *Dayton Daily News,* March 7. www.daytondailynews.com.

Callahan, L. A., M. A. McGreevy, C. Cirincione, and H. J. Steadman. 1992. "Measuring the Effects of the Guilty but Mentally Ill (GBMI) Verdict." *Law and Human Behavior* 16:447–62.

Callahan, R. 2002. "Scientists: Liars Are Betrayed by Their Faces." Associated Press Wire Service, January 2.

Cammack, M. E. 2010. "The Exclusionary Rule: The Rise and Fall of the Constitutional Exclusion Rule in the United States." *American Journal of Comparative Law* 58:631–58.

Camp, C. G. 2003. *Corrections Yearbook, 2002.* Middletown, CT: Criminal Justice Institute.

Camp, S. D., and G. G. Gaes. 2002. "Growth and Quality of US Private Prisons: Evidence from a National Survey." *Criminology & Public Policy* 1:427–50.

Campbell, J., and J. R. Carlson. 2012. "Correctional Administrators' Perceptions of Prison Nurseries." *Criminal Justice & Behavior* 39:1063–74.

Cancino, J. M., and R. Enriquez. 2004. "A Qualitative Analysis of Officer Peer Retaliation: Preserving the Police Culture." *Policing: International Journal of Police Strategies and Management* 27:320–40.

Candiotti, S. 2015. "Aaron Hernandez's Fiancee Granted Immunity in Murder Trial." CNN.com, February 10. www.cnn.com

Canes-Wrone, B., T. Clark, and J. Park. 2012. "Judicial Independence and Retention Elections." *Journal of Law, Economics, and Organization* 28:211–34.

Carcamo, C. 2013. "Report: Some Citizens Detained at Immigration Officials' Request." *Los Angeles Times,* February 20. www.latimes.com.

Cardona, F. 2011. "Colorado Probation under the Gun after Rash of Felonies." *Denver Post,* March 27. www.denverpost.com.

Carlson, P. M. 2001. "Prison Interventions: Evolving Strategies to Control Security Threat Groups." *Corrections Management Quarterly* 5 (Winter): 10–22.

Carr, J. G. 1993. "Bail Bondsmen and the Federal Courts." *Federal Probation* 57 (March): 9–14.

Carr, P. J., L. Napolitano, and J. Keating. 2007. "We Never Call the Cops and Here Is Why: A Qualitative Examination of Legal Cynicism in Three Philadelphia Neighborhoods." *Criminology* 45:445–80.

Carroll-Ferrary, N. L. 2006. "Incarcerated Men and Women, the Equal Protection Clause, and the Requirement of 'Similarly Situated.'" *New York Law School Law Review* 51:594–617.

Carson, D. 2009. "Detecting, Developing, and Disseminating Detectives' 'Creative' Skills." *Policing and Society* 19:216–25.

Carson, E. 2014. "Prisoners in 2013." NCJ 247282. Bureau of Justice Statistics *Bulletin,* September.

Carson, E. A., and W. J. Sabol. 2012. "Prisoners in 2011." NCJ 239808. Bureau of Justice Statistics *Bulletin,* December.

Carter, D. A. 2009. "To Catch the Lion, Tether the Goat: Entrapment, Conspiracy, and Sentencing Manipulation." *Akron Law Review* 42:135–84.

Carter, J. G., S. W. Phillips, and S. M. Gayadeen. 2014. "Implementing Intelligence-Led Policing: An Application of Loose-Coupling Theory." *Journal of Criminal Justice* 42:433–42.

Carter, J. G., and M. Rip. 2013. "Homeland Security and Public Health: A Critical Integration." *Criminal Justice Policy Review* 24:573–600.

Caspi, A., J. McClay, T. E. Moffitt, J. Mill, J. Martin, I. W. Craig, A. Taylor, and R. Poulton. 2002. "Role of Genotype in the Cycle of Violence in Maltreated Children." *Science* 297:851–54.

Cassell, P., and R. Fowles. 1998. "Handcuffing the Cops? A Thirty-Year Perspective on *Miranda's* Harmful Effects on Law Enforcement." *Stanford Law Review* 50:1055–145.

Catalano, S. M. 2007. *Intimate Partner Violence in the United States.* Washington, DC: U.S. Bureau of Justice Statistics.

Cauffman, E., L. Steinberg, and A. R. Piquero. 2005. "Psychological, Neuropsychological, and Physiological Correlates of Serious Antisocial Behavior in Adolescence: The Role of Self-Control." *Criminology* 43:133–76.

CBS News. 2004. "John Hinckley Wants More Freedom," November 8. www.cbsnews.com.

Centers for Disease Control and Prevention. 2013. "Youth Violence: National Statistics," http://www.cdc.gov.

Chacon, J. M. 2010. "Border Exceptionalism in the Era of Moving Borders." *Fordham Urban Law Journal* 38:129–52.

Champagne, A., and K. Cheek. 1996. "PACs and Judicial Politics in Texas." *Judicature* 80:26–29.

Champion, D. J. 1989. "Private Counsels and Public Defenders: A Look at Weak Cases, Prior Records, and Leniency in Plea Bargaining." *Journal of Criminal Justice* 17:253–63.

Chanen, D. 2014. "Hennepin County No Longer Will Honor 'ICE Hold' Requests," *Minneapolis Star Tribune,* June 12. www.startribune.com.

Chang, C. 2012. "Behind, but Few Have Access to the Classes." *New Orleans Times-Picayune,* May 29. www.nola.com.

Chapman, S. G. 1970. *Police Patrol Readings.* 2nd ed. Springfield, IL: Thomas.

Chappell, A. T., and L. Lanza-Kaduce. 2010. "Police Academy Socialization: Understanding the Lessons Learned in a Paramilitary-Bureaucratic Organization." *Journal of Contemporary Ethnography* 39:187–214.

Chapper, J. A., and R. A. Hanson. 1989. *Understanding Reversible Error in Criminal Appeals.* Williamsburg, VA: National Center for State Courts.

"Charging Common Criminals under Terrorism Laws Doesn't Fit in America's Justice Values." 2003. *Asheville Citizen-Times,* July 23. www.citizentimes.com.

Chavez, P. 2005. "Shooting Raises Racial Tension in L.A." *Sacramento Union,* February 21. www.sacunion.com.

Cheeseman, K. A., and R. A. Downey. 2012. "Talking 'Bout My Generation': The Effect of 'Generation' on Correctional Employee Perceptions of Work Stress and Job Satisfaction." *Prison Journal* 92:24–44.

Chen, C., and D. Wilbur. 2014. "Heroin Resurgence in U.S. Sparked by Cheap Cost, Access." *Business Week,* February 4. www.businessweek.com.

Cheng, E. K. 2006. "Should Judges Do Independent Research on Scientific Issues?" *Judicature* 90:58–61.

Chermak, S., and E. McGarrell. 2004. "Problem-Solving Approaches to Homicide: An Evaluation of Indianapolis Violence Reduction Partnership." *Criminal Justice Policy Review* 15:161–92.

Chertoff, M., and D. Robinson. 2012. "Check One and the Accountability Is Done: The Harmful Impact of Straight-Ticket Voting on Judicial Elections." *Albany Law Review* 75:1773–97.

Chiang, E. 2010. "Indigent Defense Invigorated: A Uniform Standard for Adjudicating Preconviction Sixth Amendment Claims." *Temple Political & Civil Rights Law Review* 19:443–75.

Childress, S. 2013. "Why ICE Released Those 2,000 Immigrant Detainees." PBS *Frontline*, March 19. www.pbs.org.

Chiricos, T., K. Padgett, and M. Gertz. 2000. "Fear, TV News, and the Reality of Crime." *Criminology* 38:755–85.

Christensen, P. H. 2008. "Crime Prevention Takes Teamwork." *Spokesman Review*, April 17. www.spokesmanreview.com.

Church, T. W. 1985. "Examining Local Legal Culture." *American Bar Foundation Research Journal* 1985 (Summer): 449.

Cieply, M. 2011. "Mel Gibson to Plead Guilty in Abuse of Former Girlfriend." *New York Times*, March 10. www.nytimes.com.

City of Indianapolis. 2015. "Duvall Residential Center." www.indy.gov.

City of Seattle. 2015. "Seattle Police Department Jobs." http://www.seattle.gov/policejobs/benefits-and-salary/salary.

Clancy, T. K. 2010. "The Irrelevancy of the Fourth Amendment in the Roberts Court." *Chicago-Kent Law Review* 85:191–208.

Clark, A. 2011. "A Muted Effort to Reduce Prison Rape." *American Prospect*, April 11. prospect.org.

Clark, M. 2013. "Sequester Cuts at Justice Department Threaten Local Drug Investigations." *Stateline* (Daily News Service of the Pew Charitable Trusts), April 2. www.pewstates.org.

Clarke, J. G., M. R. Hebert, C. Rosengard, J. S. Rose, K. M. DaSilva, and M. D. Stein. 2006. Reproductive Health Care and Family Planning Needs among Incarcerated Women." *American Journal of Public Health* 96:834–39.

Clear, T., G. Cole, and M. Reisig. 2012. *American Corrections*, 10th ed. Belmont, CA: Cengage Wadsworth.

Clear, T., and D. Karp. 1999. *Community Justice: Preventing Crime and Achieving Justice*. New York: Westview Press.

Clear, T. R. 1994. *Harm in American Penology*. Albany: State University of New York Press.

Clear, T. R., and A. A. Braga. 1995. "Community Corrections." In *Crime*, eds. J. Q. Wilson and J. Petersilia. San Francisco: ICS Press, 421–44.

Cleary, H. 2014. "Police Interviewing and Interrogation of Juvenile Suspects: A Descriptive Examination of Actual Cases." *Law and Human Behavior* 38:271–82.

Cliff, G., and C. Desilets. 2014. "White Collar Crime: What It Is and Where It's Going." *Notre Dame Journal of Law, Ethics & Public Policy* 28:481–523.

Clisura, A. 2010. "None of Their Business: The Need for Another Alternative to New York's Bail Bond Business." *Journal of Law and Policy* 19:307–51.

CNN. 2004a. "Boston Police Accept 'Full Responsibility' in Death of Red Sox Fan." October 22. www.cnn.com.

———. 2004b. "Police Review Policy after Tasers Used on Kids." November 14. www.cnn.com.

———. 2005 "Pregnant Woman: 'Maternal Instinct' Helped Kill Attacker." February 14. www.cnn.com.

———. 2012. "Wrongful Conviction Compensation Statutes." CNN.com. Accessed May 14, 2013. www.cnn.com.

Cochran, J. C., and P. Y. Warren. 2012. "Racial, Ethnic, and Gender Differences in Perceptions of the Police: The Salience of Officer Race within the Context of Racial Profiling." *Journal of Contemporary Criminal Justice* 28(2): 206–27.

Cohen, A. 2012. "How Andrea Yates Lives, and Lives with Herself, a Decade Later." *Atlantic*, March 12. www.theatlantic.com

Cohen, T. H., and T. Kyckelhahn. 2010. "Felony Defendants in Large Urban Counties, 2006." NCJ 228944. Bureau of Justice Statistics *Bulletin*, May.

Coker, D. 2014. "'Stand Your Ground' in Context: Race, Gender, and Politics." *University of Miami Law Review* 68:943–59.

Collins, J. 2005. *Preventing Identity Theft in Your Business: How to Protect Your Business, Customers, and Employees*. New York: Wiley.

Comey, J. B. 2013. "Statement before the Senate Committee on Homeland Security and Government Affairs." Washington, D.C., November 14. www.fbi.gov

Commission on Accreditation for Law Enforcement Agencies. 2006. *Standards for Law Enforcement Accreditation*. 5th ed. Fairfax, VA: Commission on Accreditation for Law Enforcement Agencies.

"Concern Mounts over Anti-terrorism Law." 2005. *Michigan Daily*, April 7. www.michigandaily.com.

Conover, T. 2000. *Newjack: Guarding Sing Sing*. New York: Random House.

Conti, N. 2011. "Weak Links and Warrior Hearts: A Framework for Judging Self and Others in Police Training." *Police Practice and Research: An International Journal* 12:410–23.

Cook, N. 2010. "How the Recession Hurts Private Prisons." *Newsweek*, June 29. www.thedailybeast.com/newsweek/2010/06/30/how-the-recession-hurts-private-prisons.html.

Cook, P. J., and J. H. Laub. 2002. "After the Epidemic: Recent Trends in Youth Violence in the United States." In *Crime and Justice: A Review of Research*, vol. 29, ed. Michael Tonry. Chicago: University of Chicago Press.

Cooney, M. 1994. "Evidence as Partisanship." *Law and Society Review* 28:833–58.

Cooper, F. R. 2010. "Masculinities, Post-racialism and the Gates Controversy: The False Equivalence between Officer and Civilian." *Nevada Law Journal* 11:1–43.

Cooprider, K. 2014. "A Descriptive Analysis of Pretrial Services at the Single-Jurisdictional Level." *Federal Probation* (December) 78:9–15.

Copeland, L. 2011. "Sales Double of DUI Checkpoint App, CEO Says." *Lansing State Journal*, May 18. www.lsj.com.

Copes, H., G. E. Higgins, R. Tewksbury, and D. Dabney. 2010. "Participation in the Prison Economy and Likelihood of Physical Victimization." *Victims and Offenders* 6:1–18.

Cornwell, E., and V. Hans. 2011. "Representation through Participation: A Multilevel Analysis of Jury Deliberations." *Law & Society Review* 45:667–98.

Costinett, A. H. 2011. "'In a Puff of Smoke': Drug Crime and the Perils of Subjective Entrapment." *American Criminal Law Review* 48:1757–87.

Costanzo, M. 1997. *Just Revenge*. New York: St. Martin's Press.

Couch, R. 2015. "Some States Are Closing Prisons and Turning Them into Homeless Shelters, Reentry Centers." *Huffington Post*, February 5. www.huffingtonpost.com.

Coutts, L., and F. Schneider. 2004. "Police Officer Performance Appraisal Systems: How Good Are They?" *Policing: International Journal of Police Strategies and Management* 27:67–81.

Covey, R. D. 2009. "Signaling and Plea Bargaining's Innocence Problem." *Washington and Lee Law Review* 66:73–131.

———. 2011. "Longitudinal Guilt: Repeat Offenders, Plea Bargaining, and the Variable Standard of Proof." *Florida Law Review* 63:431–55.

Cowell, A. J., N. Broner, and R. DuPont. 2004. "The Cost-Effectiveness of Criminal Justice Diversion Programs for People with Serious Mental Illness Co-occurring with Substance Abuse." *Journal of Contemporary Criminal Justice* 20:292–315.

Coyle, M. 2009. "New Report Shows Sharp Rise in Prison Time for Federal Offenders." *National Law Journal*, February 12. www.law.com.

Crandall, S. 2013. Teacher Who Had Sex with Students Sentenced to 20 Years." Fox4 News online, November 13. www.fox4news.com.

Crawford, C. 2000. "Gender, Race, and Habitual Offender Sentencing in Florida." *Criminology* 38 (February): 263–80.

Crawford, C., T. Chiricos, and G. Kleck. 1998. "Race, Racial Threat, and Sentencing of Habitual Offenders." *Criminology* 36 (August): 481–512.

Cristani, A. S., and B. C. Frueh. 2011. "Risk of Trauma Exposure among Persons with Mental Illness in Jails and Prisons: What Do We Really Know?" *Current Opinion in Psychiatry* 24:431–35.

Crooke, C. 2013. "Women in Law Enforcement." *Community Policing Dispatch*, vol. 6, July (U.S. Department of Justice e-newsletter). http://cops.usdoj.gov/html/dispatch/07-2013/women_in_law_enforcement.asp.

Crouch, B. M., and J. M. Marquart. 1994. "On Becoming a Prison Guard." In *The Administration and Management of Criminal Justice Organizations*, 2nd ed., ed. S. Stojokovic, J. Klofas, and D. Kalinich. Prospect Heights, IL: Waveland Press.

Crowe, K. 2014. "Police, Fire Layoffs Planned." *Albany Times Union*, November 22. www.timesunion.com.

Crummy, K. 2009. "Colorado Criminals Owe State's Victims Nearly $778 Million." *Denver Post*, September 24. www.denverpost.com.

Cruz, C. 2014. "Ybarra Chose SPU for Shootings Because He Was Unfamiliar with It, Journal Says." *Seattle Times*, July 22.

Cruz, C., and M. Baker. 2014. "SPU Shooting Suspect Raised in Home of Tumult." *Seattle Times*, July 19.

Cullen, F. T., T. Leming, B. Link, and J. Wozniak. 1985. "The Impact of Social Supports in Police Stress." *Criminology* 23:503–22.

Culley, R. 2012. " 'The Judge Didn't Sentence Me to be Raped': *Tracy Neal v. Michigan Department of Corrections*: A 15-Year Battle against the Sexual Abuse of Women Inmates in Michigan." *Women and Criminal Justice* 22:206–25.

Cunningham, L. 2010. "New York's Post-verdict Scheme for the Treatment of Insanity Acquittees: Balancing Public Safety with Rights of the Mentally Ill." *Journal of Civil Rights and Economic Development* 25:81–98.

Cunningham, W. C., J. J. Strauchs, and C. W. Van Meter. 1990. *Private Security Trends, 1970 to the Year 2000*. Boston: Butterworth-Heinemann.

Curtin, 2007. "The Continuing Problem of America's Aging Prison Population and the Search for a Cost-Effective and Socially Acceptable Means of Addressing It." *Elder Law Journal* 15:473–502.

Cyberbullying Research Center. 2014. "Cyberbullying Facts." http://cyberbullying.us/research/facts/.

Dabney, D. 2009. "Observations egarding Key Operational Realities in a Compstat Model of Policing." *Justice Quarterly* 27:28–51.

Dabney, D., H. Copes, R. Tewksbury, and S. Hawk-Tourtelot. 2013. "A Qualitative Assessment of Stress Perceptions among Members of a Homicide Unit." *Justice Quarterly* 30:811–36.

Daftary-Kapur, T., R. Dumas, and S. D. Penrod. 2010. "Jury Decision-Making Biases and Methods to Counter Them." *Legal and Criminological Psychology* 15:133–54.

Daigle, L. E., and B. S. Fisher. 2013. "The Recurrence of Victimization." In *Victims of Crimes*, 4th ed., eds. R. C. Davis, A. J. Lurigio, and S. Herman. Los Angeles: Sage. 371–400.

Daleiden, C. 2012. "Identity Theft and Consumer Protection under the Fair Credit Reporting Act." *Hawaii Bar Journal* 16 (June): 4–10.

D'Alessio, S., J. Flexon, and L. Stolzenberg. 2013. "The Effect of Conjugal Visitation on Sexual Violence in Prison." *American Journal of Criminal Justice* 38:13–26.

Damron, G., E. Anderson, and J. Wisely. 2013. "Wayne County Prosecutor Kym Worthy Cuts Start to Affect Suburbs." *Detroit Free Press*, April 1. www.freep.com.

Dansky, Kara. 2008. "Understanding California Sentencing." *University of San Francisco Law Review* 43:45–86.

Dantzker, M. L. 2011. "Psychological Preemployment Screening for Police Candidates: Seeking Consistency if Not Standardization." *Professional Psychology: Research and Practice* 42:276–83.

Davey, J. D. 1998. *The Politics of Prison Expansion: Winning Elections by Waging War on Crime*. Westport, CT: Praeger.

Davey, M. 2010. "Abortion Foe Found Guilty in Doctor's Killing." *New York Times*, January 30. www.nytimes.com.

———. 2015. "Governor of Michigan Vetoes Bill on Guns." *New York Times,* January 15. www.nytimes.com.

Davey, M., and J. Bosman. 2014. "Protests Flare After Ferguson Police Officer Is Not Indicted." *New York Times,* November 24. www.nytimes.com.

Davey, M. M., Wines, E. Eckholm, and R. Oppel. 2014. "Raised Hands and the Doubts of a Grand Jury." *New York Times*, November 29. www.nytimes.com.

Davies, T. Y. 1983. "A Hard Look at What We Know (and Still Need to Learn) about the 'Costs' of the Exclusionary Rule: The NIJ Study and Other Studies of 'Lost' Arrests." *American Bar Foundation Research Journal* 1983:611–90.

Davis, E., and L. Robinson. 2014. "Modeling Successful Researcher–Practitioner Partnerships: The International Association of Chiefs of Police Research Advisory Committee." *Translational Criminology* (Fall):4–5, 8.

Davis, J., and J. R. Sorenson. 2013. "Disproportionate Minority Confinement of Juveniles: A National Examination of Black–White Disparity in Placements, 1997–2006." *Crime & Delinquency* 59:115–39.

Davis, L., R. Bosick, J. Steele, J. Saunders, and J. Miles. 2013. *Evaluating the Effectiveness of Correctional Education*. Santa Monica, CA: Rand Corporation.

Davis, S. 2012. "Ionia Site Targeted in Budget Proposal." *Lansing State Journal*, April 7. www.lsj.com.

Dean, B. 2011. "Police Chief Laments Criminals' Access to Military-Style Guns." *Oklahoman*, January 16. newsok.com.

Death Penalty Information Center. 2008 "Cases of Innocence: 1973–Present." www.deathpenaltyinfo.org.

———. 2015. *Facts about the Death Penalty.* http://www.deathpenaltyinfo.org/documents/FactSheet.pdf.

Decker, J. F., and P. G. Baroni. 2011. "'No' Still Means 'Yes': The Failure of the 'Non-consent' Reform Movement in American Rape and Sexual Assault Law." *Journal of Criminal Law and Criminology* 101:1081–169.

Dedel, K. 2010. "Fifth Monitor's Report for the Baltimore City Juvenile Justice Center (BCJJC) for the Period of July 1, 2009 through December 31, 2009." One in 37 Research. www.djs.state.md.us.

DeJong, C., and E. S. Merrill. 2000. "Getting 'Tough on Crime': Juvenile Waiver and the Criminal Court." *Ohio Northern University Law Review* 27:175–96.

DeJong, C., S. Mastrofski, and R. Parks. 2001. "Patrol Officers and Problem Solving: An Application of Expectancy Theory." *Justice Quarterly* 18:31–61.

Demleitner, N. V. 2009. "Good Conduct Time: How Much and for Whom? The Unprincipled Approach of the Model Penal Code." *Florida Law Review* 61:777–95.

Dervan, L., and V. Edkins. 2013. "The Innocent Defendant's Dilemma: An Innovative Empirical Study of Plea Bargaining's Innocence Problem." *Journal of Criminal Law and Criminology* 103:1–48.

Desmarais, S., R. Van Dorn, R. Telford, J. Petrila, and T. Coffey. 2012. "Characteristics of START Assessments Completed in Mental Health Jail Diversion Programs." *Behavioral Sciences and the Law* 30:448–69.

Devers, L. 2011. *Plea and Charge Bargaining: Research Summary.* Washington, DC: U.S. Bureau of Justice Assistance.

Dewan, S. 2007. "An SOS for 911 Systems in Age of High-Tech." *New York Times*, April 6. www.nytimes.com.

———. 2009. "Prosecutors Block Access to DNA Testing for Inmates." *New York Times*, May 18. www.nytimes.com.

Diamond, S. S., D. Peery, F. Dolan, and E. Dolan. 2009. "Achieving Diversity on the Jury: Jury Size and the Peremptory Challenge." *Journal of Empirical Legal Studies* 6:425–49.

Dickerson, B. 2008. "Hard Lemonade, Hard Price." *Detroit Free Press*, April 28. www.freep.com.

Dickson, B. E. 2006. "Effects of Capital Punishment on the Justice System: Reflections of a State Supreme Court Justice." *Judicature* 89 (5): 278–81.

Diedrich, J., and G. Barton. 2013. "New Milwaukee Police Procedures Address Racial Profiling, Crime Data." *Milwaukee Journal Sentinel,* February 7. www.jsonline.com.

DiIulio, J. J., Jr. 1987. *Governing Prisons*. New York: Free Press.

———. 1991. *No Escape: The Future of American Corrections.* New York: Basic Books.

———. 1993. "Rethinking the Criminal Justice System: Toward a New Paradigm." In *Performance Measures for the Criminal Justice System*. Washington, DC: Bureau of Justice Statistics, 1–18.

Dillehay, R. C., and M. R. Sandys. 1996. "Life under *Wainwright v. Witt:* Juror Dispositions and Death Qualification." *Law and Human Behavior* 20:147–65.

Dixon, J. 2008. "Policy Essay: Mandatory Domestic Violence Arrest and Prosecution Policies: Recidivism and Social Governance." *Criminology & Public Policy* 7:663–70.

Dodge, J., and M. Pogrebin. 2001. "African-American Policewomen: An Exploration of Professional Relationships." *Policing* 24:550–52.

Doerner, J. K., and S. Demuth. 2010. "The Independent and Joint Effects of Race/Ethnicity, Gender, and Age on Sentencing Outcomes in US Federal Courts." *Justice Quarterly* 27:1–27.

Donziger, S. R., ed. 1996. *The Real War on Crime: The Report of the National Criminal Justice Commission*. New York: HarperCollins.

Dority, B. 2005. "The USA Patriot Act Has Decimated Many Civil Liberties." In *Homeland Security: Current Controversies,* ed. Andrea Nakaya. Detroit: Thomson/Gale, 130–6.

Dow, S. B. 2010. "'Step Outside, Please': Warrantless Doorway Arrests and the Problem of Constructive Entry." *New England Law Review* 45:7–38.

Drash, W. 2009. "911 Caller in Gates Arrest Never Referred to 'Black Suspects.'" CNN.com. www.cnn.com.

Drimmer, J. 1997. "America' s Least Wanted: We Need New Rules to Stop Abuses." *Washington Post,* September 21, p. C6.

Dubail, J. 2009. "Cuyahoga County Jury Pay Cut to Save Money," May 14. www.cleveland.com.

Dugan, A. 2014. "In U.S., 37% Do Not Feel Safe Walking at Night Near Home." Gallup Poll website. November 24. www.gallup.com.

Dugan, L. 1999. "The Effect of Criminal Victimization on a Household's Moving Decision." *Criminology* 37:903–30.

Dugdale, R. 1910. *The Jukes: Crime, Pauperism, Disease, and Heredity*. 4th ed. New York: Putnam.

Duncan, I. 2013. "Lawmakers Call for Replacement of Baltimore Jail." *Baltimore Sun*, December 11. http://baltimoresun.com.

Durose, M. R., A. D. Cooper, and H. N. Snyder. 2014. "Recidivism of Prisoners Released in 30 States in 2005: Patterns from 2005 to 2010." NCJ244205. Bureau of Justice Statistics, *Special Report.*

Durose, M. R., and P. A. Langan. 2007. "Felony Sentences in State Courts, 2004." NCJ 215646. Bureau of Justice Statistics *Bulletin*, July.

Durose, M. R., E. L. Schmitt, and P. Langan. 2005. *Contacts between Police and the Public: Findings from the 2002 National Survey*. Washington, DC: Bureau of Justice Statistics, April.

Dzur, A. 2011. "Restorative Justice and Democracy: Fostering Public Accountability for Criminal Justice." *Contemporary Justice Review* 14:367–81.

Earley, P. 1992. *The Hot House: Life nside Leavenworth Prison.* New York: Bantam Books.

Eastman, S. C. 2012. "Jordan Davis Shooting: Charges Upgraded to First Degree Murder in Slaying of Unarmed Teen." *Huffington Post*, December 13. www.huffingtonpost.com

Eaton, L., and L. Kaufman. 2005. "In Problem-Solving Court, Judges Turn Therapist." *New York Times,* April 26. www.nytimes.com.

Eckholm, E. 2008a. "Reports Find Racial Gap in Drug Arrests." *New York Times*, May 6, p. A21.

———. 2008b. "US Shifting Prison Focus to Reentry into Society." *New York Times,* April 8. www.nytimes.com.

———. 2010. "Congress Moves to Narrow Cocaine Sentencing Disparities." *New York Times*, July 28. www.nytimes.com.

———. 2013. "With Police in Schools, More Children in Court." *New York Times,* April 12. www.nytimes.com.

Edelman, M. W. 2010. "Strength to Love: A Challenge to the Privatized Prison Industry." *Child Watch Column* (Children's Defense Fund), December 10. www.childrensdefense.org.

Edgemon, E. 2013. "10 Minutes per Month: Alabama Probation, Parole Officers Get Little

Time with 67,410 They Oversee." *Birmingham News,* May 20. blog.al.com.

Editorial Board. 2014. "When New York City Police Walk Off the Job." *New York Times*, December 30. www.nytimes.com.

Edkins, V. 2011. "Defense Attorney Plea Recommendations and Client Race: Does Zealous Representation Apply Equally to All?" *Law and Human Behavior* 35:413–25.

Edwards, C. 2014. "Ending Identity Theft and Cyber Crime." *Biometric Technology Today* 2:9–11.

Effron, L., and M. Keneally. 2015. "'American Sniper' Trial: Eddie Routh Attorney Says Jurors Who Saw Movie Didn't Hurt Case." ABC News online, February 25. www.abcnews.go.com

Egan, P. 2014. "Aramark on Notice over Prison Contract," *Lansing State Journal,* June 25. www.lansingstatejournal.com.

Egelko, B. 2014. "2 San Francisco Police Officers Convicted of Corruption." SFGATE.com, December 5. www.sfgate.com

Egley, A., and J. C. Howell. 2012. *Highlights of the 2010 National Youth Gang Survey*. NCJ 237542. Washington, DC: Office of Juvenile Justice and Delinquency Prevention.

Ehrhard, S. 2008. "Plea Bargaining and the Death Penalty: An Exploratory Study." *Justice System Journal* 29:313–27.

Eichenwald, K. 2006. "On the Web, Pedophiles Extend Their Reach." *New York Times*, August 21. www.nytimes.com.

Eigeman, A. 2013. "San Diego Coalition Aims to Stem Gang Violence Despite Police Cuts." *Nonprofit Quarterly*, March 18. www.nonprofit.org.

Eigenberg, H. 2000. "Correctional Officers, and Their Perceptions of Homosexuality, Rape, and Prosecution in Male Prisons." *Prison Journal* 80 (December): 415–33.

Eisenberg, T., P. Hannaford-Agor, V. P. Hans, N. L. Mott, G. T. Munsterman, S. J. Schwab, and M. T. Wells. 2005. "Judge–Jury Agreement in Criminal Cases: A Partial Replication of Kalven and Zeisel's *The American Jury*. *Journal of Empirical Legal Studies* 2:171–206.

Eisenstein, J., R. B. Flemming, and P. F. Nardulli. 1988. *The Contours of Justice: Communities and Their Courts*. Boston: Little, Brown.

Eisenstein, J., and H. Jacob. 1977. *Felony Justice: An Organizational Analysis of Criminal Courts*. Boston: Little, Brown.

Eith, C., and M. R. Durose. 2011. "Contacts between Police and the Public, 2008." NCJ234599. Bureau of Justice Statistics, *Special Report*, October.

Eitle, D., and S. Monahan. 2009. "Revisiting the Racial Threat Thesis: The Role of Police Organizational Characteristics in Predicting Race-Specific Drug Arrest Rates." *Justice Quarterly* 26:528–61.

Eligon, J., and T. Kaplan. 2012. "New York State Set to Add All Convict DNA to Its Database." *New York Times*, March 13. www.nytimes.com.

Elliott, J., and B. Murphy. 2005. "Parole, Probation Violators Add to Crowding." *Houston Chronicle,* January 20. www.chron.com/disp/story.mpl/special/05/legislature/3000503.html.

Ellis, H. 2014. "Effects of a Crisis Intervention Team (CIT) Training Program upon Police Officers before and after Crisis Intervention Team Training." *Archives of Psychiatric Nursing* 28 (February): 10–16.

Emmelman, D. S. 1996. "Trial by Plea Bargain: Case Settlement as a Product of Recursive Decisionmaking." *Law and Society Review* 30:335–60.

Engber, D. 2005. "Does the FBI Have Your Fingerprints?" *Slate,* April 22. slate.msn.com/id/2117226.

Engel, R. S., and J. Calnon. 2004. "Examining the Influence of Drivers' Characteristics during Traffic Stops with Police: Results from a National Survey." *Justice Quarterly* 21:49–90.

Engel, R. S., J. M. Calnon, and T. J. Bernard. 2002. "Theory and Racial Profiling: Shortcomings and Future Directions in Research." *Justice Quarterly* 19:249–73.

Enion, M.R. 2009. "Constitutional Limits on Private Policing and the State's Allocation of Force." *Duke Law Journal* 59:519–51.

Epp, C. R. 2009. *Making Rights Real: Activists, Bureaucrats, and the Creation of the Legalistic State*. Chicago: University of Chicago Press.

Epp, C. R., S. Maynard-Moody, and D. Haider-Markel. 2014. *Pulled Over: How Police Stops Define Race and Citizenship*. Chicago: University of Chicago Press.

Epstein, L., and J. Segal. 2007. *Advice and Consent: The Politics of Judicial Appointments*. New York: Oxford University Press.

Erez, E., and J. Roberts. 2013. "Victim Participation in the Criminal Justice System." In *Victims of Crimes*, 4th ed., eds. R. C. Davis, A. J. Lurigio, and S. Herman. Los Angeles: Sage, pp. 251–70.

Esposito, R. 2010. "FBI and ATF Turf War Creates 'Confusion' at Bomb Scenes." abcnews.go.com/Blotter/fbi-atf-turf-war-creates-confusion-bomb-scenes/story?id=11410254.

European Institute for Crime Prevention and Control. 2014. *European Sourcebook of Crime and Criminal Justice Statistics—2014*. http://europeansourcebook.org/.

Fabelo, T. 1999. *Biennial Report to the 76th Texas Legislature*. Austin, TX: Criminal Justice Policy Council.

Faddis, C. S. 2010. "Nuclear Plants Need Real Security." CNN.com, March 15. www.cnn.com/2010/OPINION/03/15/faddis.nuclear.plant.security/index.html.

Fak, M. 2013. "Musical Chairs Complete with Dwight Women Transferred to Logan County Correctional Center." *Logan County Herald*, March 30. www.logancountyherald.com.

Farole, D. J., and L. Langton. 2010. "County-Based and Local Public Defender Offices, 2007." NCJ 231175. Bureau of Justice Statistics, *Special Report*, September.

Farrell, G. 1995. "Preventing Repeat Victimization." *Crime and Justice* 19:469–534.

Farrington, David. 2010. "Life-Course and Developmental Theories in Criminology." In *The Sage Handbook of Criminological Theory,* ed. E. McLaughlin and Tim Newburn. Thousand Oaks, CA: Sage

Fathi, D. C. 2010. "The Challenge of Prison Oversight." *American Criminal Law Review* 47:1453–62.

FBI (Federal Bureau of Investigation). 2008. "Cyber Solidarity: Five Nations, One Mission." March 18. www.fbi.gov.

———. 2013a. "Quick Facts." FBI Website. www.fbi.gov.

———. 2013b. *Today's FBI: Facts and Figures, 2013–2014*. Washington, DC: U.S. Department of Justice.

———. 2014a. *Crime in the United States, 2013* (Uniform Crime Reports-UCR). FBI website. www.fbi.gov.

———. 2014b. *Law Enforcement Officers Killed and Assaulted, 2013*. FBI website. www.fbi.gov.

———. 2014c. *Today's FBI: Facts and Figures, 2013–2014*. FBI website. www.fbi.gov.

FBI Press Release. 2012. "Portsmouth Bail Bondsman Sentenced to 30 Months in Prison for Bribing Public Officials." November 2. www.fbi.gov.

Feehan, J. 2014. "Teacher Sentenced to 17 Months for Sexual Relations with Student." *Toledo Blade,* August 5. www.toledoblade.com.

Feeney, F. 1998. *German and American Prosecution: An Approach to Statistical Comparison*. Washington, DC: Bureau of Justice Statistics.

Feinberg, M. E., M. T. Greenwood, and D. W. Osgood. 2004. "Readiness, Functions, and Perceived Effectiveness in Community Prevention Coalitions: A Study of Communities That Care." *American Journal of Community Psychology* 33:163–77.

Feingold, D. A. 2005. "Human Trafficking." *Foreign Policy* 150:26–30.

Feld, B. C. 1993. "Criminalizing the American Juvenile Court." In *Crime and Justice: A Review of Research,* vol. 17, ed. M. Tonry. Chicago: University of Chicago Press, 197–280.

———. 1999. *Bad Kids: Race and the Transformation of the Juvenile Court*. New York: Oxford.1999.

———. 2004. "Editorial Introduction: Juvenile Transfers." *Criminology & Public Policy* 3 (November): 599–603.

Felice, J. D., and J. C. Kilwein. 1992. "Strike One, Strike Two. . . : The History and Prospect for Judicial Reform in Ohio." *Judicature* 75:193–200.

Fellner, J. 2006. "A Corrections Quandary: Mental Illness and Prison Rules." *Harvard Civil Rights–Civil Liberties Law Review* 41:391–412.

Felson, M., and R. Boba. 2010. *Crime and Everyday Life*, 4th ed. Los Angeles: Sage.

Fenton, J. 2015. "Baltimore Jail Faulted for Harsh Treatment of Youth Detainees," Baltimore Sun, April 8. baltimoresun.com.

Ferguson, J. 2009. "Professional Discretion and the Use of Restorative Justice Programs in Appropriate Domestic Violence Cases: An Effective Innovation. *Criminal Law Brief* 4:3–17.

Fernandez, M. 2014. "Despite Chaos, Police in Ferguson React with Restraint Not Shown after August Killing." *New York Times*, November 25. www.nytimes.com

Fernandez, M., and K. Jones. 2013. "Suspect in Texas Veteran's Killing Was Hospitalized." *New York Times,* February 7. www.nytimes.com

Ferrise, A. 2014. "Cleveland Police Never Reviewed Independence Personnel File before Hiring Officer Who Shot Tamir Rice." Cleveland.com website. December 3. www.cleveland.com

Feuer, A. 2006. "For ex-FBI Agent Accused in Murders, a Case of What Might Have Been." *New York Times*, April 15. www.nytimes.com.

———. 2008. "An Aversion to the Death Penalty, but No Shortage of Cases." *New York Times*, March 10. www.nytimes.com.

Fields, G. 2008. "Murder Spike Poses Quandary." *Wall Street Journal*, May 6. online.wsj.com.

Fields, G., and J. R. Emshwiller. 2012. "Federal Guilty Pleas Soar as Bargains Trump Trials." *Wall Street Journal,* September 23. online.wsj.com.

Fieldstadt, E. 2015. "Judge Rules 'Slender Man' Stabbing Suspects Will Be Tried as Adults." NBC News, March 13. nbcnews.com.

Finley, A. 2011. "California Prison Academy: Better Than a Harvard Degree." *Wall Street Journal*, April 30. www.wsj.com.

Finn, B., M. Shively, J. McDevitt, W. Lassiter, and T. Rich. 2005. *Comparison of Activities and Lessons Learned among 19 School Resource Officer (SRO) Programs*. Boston: Abt Associates.

Finn, M. 2013. "Evidence-Based and Victim-Centered Prosecutorial Policies: Examination of Deterrent and Therapeutic Jurisprudence Effects on Domestic Violence." *Criminology and Public Policy* 12:443–72.

Firozi, P. 2014a. "5 Things to Know about Ferguson Police Department," *USA Today*, August, 19, 2014, www.usatoday.com

Firozi, P. 2014b. "Police Ticket Quotas Get Warning." *USA Today*, June 20, p. 4B.

Fischman, J., and M. Schanzenbach. 2011. "Do Standards of Review Matter? The Case of Federal Criminal Sentencing." *Journal of Legal Studies* 40:405–37.

Fishbein, D. H. 1990. "Biological Perspectives in Criminology." *Criminology* 28:27–72.

Fitzpatrick, B. T. 2010. "Questioning Reform: On the Merits of Merit Selection." *Advocate* (State Bar of Texas), 53:67–70.

Flanagan, T. J., ed. 1995. *Long-Term Imprisonment*. Thousand Oaks, CA: Sage.

Flango, V. E. 1994. *Habeas Corpus in State and Federal Courts*. Williamsburg, VA: National Center for State Courts.

Fleisher, M. 1989. *Warehousing Violence*. Newbury Park, CA: Sage.

Fliegelman, O. 2015. "Made in China: Face IDs." *New York Times*, February 6 www.nytimes.com.

Flores, Aileen. 2014a. "Council of Judges Says Commissioners Court Misled Public on Indigent Defense Pay Issue." *El Paso Times*, April 9. www.elpasotimes.com.

———. 2014b. "Indigent Defense System Debated: Other Texas Counties Take Judges Out of Process." *El Paso Times*, April 20. www.elpasotimes.com.

Florida Office of Program Policy Analysis and Government Accountability. 2010. *Intermediate Sanctions for Non-violent Offenders Could Produce Savings*, Report No. 10–27 (March).

———. 2014. "Expansion Drug Courts Can Produce Positive Outcomes through Prison Diversion and Reduced Recidivism,". Report No. 14-02, January.

Flowers, R. 2010. "The Role of the Defense Attorney: Not Just an Advocate." *Ohio State Journal of Criminal Law* 7:647–52.

Foley, S. 2013. "The Newly Murky World of Searches Incident to Lawful Arrest: Why the Gant Restrictions Should Apply to All Searches Incident to Arrest." *University of Kansas Law Review* 61:753–83.

Forman, J., Jr. 2004. "Community Policing and Youth as Assets." *Journal of Criminal Law and Criminology* 95:1–49.

Forman, S. J. 2015. "The #Ferguson Effect: Opening the Pandora's Box of Implicit Racial Bias in Jury Selection." *Northwestern University Law Review Online* 109:171–79.

"Former Corrections Officer Sentenced to 27 Months in Prison For Taking Cash to Smuggle Contraband into Facility." Press Release, U.S. Attorney for the District of Columbia, March 26, 2015. http://www.justice.gov/usao-dc/pr/former-corrections-officer-sentenced-27-months-prison-taking-cash-smuggle-contraband-0.

Foucault, M. 1977. *Discipline and Punish*. Trans. A. Sheridan. New York: Pantheon.

Fox, J. G. 1982. *Organizational and Racial Conflict in Maximum Security Prisons*. Lexington, MA: Lexington Books.

———. 2013. "Vandalia Prison Continues Educational Programs, Despite State's Budget Cuts." *Decatur Herald Review*, January 19. www.herald-review.com.

Freskos, B. 2011. "Education in N.C. Prisons Is Top of the Class." *Wilmington Star News*, May 20. www.starnewsonline.com.

Freud, S. (1923). *The Ego and the Id*. London: Hogarth Press.

Fridell, L. 1990. "Decision Making of the District Attorney: Diverting or Prosecuting Intrafamilial Child Sexual Abuse Offenders." *Criminal Justice Policy Review* 4:249–67.

Friedersdorf, C. 2014. "California Can't Police Its Own Cops Stealing Nude Photos of Women." *Atlantic*, October 29. www.thatlantic.com.

Friedman, L. M. 1993. *Crime and Punishment in American History*. New York: Basic Books.

Friedrichs, D. O. 2010. *Trusted Criminals: White Collar Crime in Contemporary Society*. 4th ed. Belmont, CA: Cengage.

Friess, S. 2014. "Aramark Workers Run Amok in Michigan Prisons," *Bloomberg News*, October 2. www.bloomberg.com.

Gannon, M. 2006. "Crime Statistics in Canada, 2005." *Juristat* 26 (4): 1–23 [Canadian Centre for Justice Statistics Catalogue 85-002].

Garcia, M. 2005. "N.Y. Using Terrorism Law to Prosecute Street Gang." *Washington Post*, February 1, p. A3.

Garner, J. H., C. D. Maxwell, and C. G. Heraux. 2002. "Characteristics Associated with the Prevalence and Severity of Force Used by the Police." *Justice Quarterly* 19:705–46.

Gartner, R., A. N. Doob, and F. E. Zimring. 2011. "The Past as Prologue? Decarceration in California Then and Now." *Criminology & Public Policy* 10:291–325.

Garvey, C. 2002. "Risk Assessment: Looking for Chinks in the Armor." In *Readings in Security Management*, ed. Robert McCrie. New York: ASIS International, 99–104.

Gau, J., N. Corsaro, and R. K. Brunson. 2014. "Revisiting Broken Windows Theory: A Test of the Mediation Impact of Social Mechanisms on the Disorder–Fear Relationship." *Journal of Criminal Justice* 42:579–88.

Gebo, E., N. Stracuzzi, and V. Hurst. 2006. "Juvenile Justice Reform and the Courtroom Workgroup: Issues of Perception and Workload." *Journal of Criminal Justice* 34:425–33.

Gelman, A., J. Fagan, and A. Kiss. 2007. "An Analysis of the New York City Police Department's 'Stop-and-Frisk' Policy in the Context of Claims of Racial Bias," *Journal of the American Statistical Association* 102:813–23.

Genter, S., G. Hooks, and C. Mosher. 2013. "Prisons, Jobs, and Privatization: The Impact of Prisons on Employment Growth in Rural US Counties, 1997–2004." *Social Science Research* 42:596–610.

German, M., and J. Stanley. 2007. *What's Wrong with Fusion Centers?* New York: American Civil Liberties Union.

Gershman, B. L. 1993. "Themes of Injustice: Wrongful Convictions, Racial Prejudice, and Lawyer Incompetence." *Criminal Law Bulletin* 29:502–15.

Gerstein, C. 2013. "Plea Bargaining and the Right to Counsel at Bail Hearings." *Michigan Law Review* 111:1513–34.

Gertner, N. 2010. "Juries and Originalism: Giving 'Intelligible Content' to the Right to a Jury Trial." *Ohio State Law Journal* 71:935–58.

Gesch, C. B., S. M. Hammond, S. H. Hampson, A. Eves, and M. J. Crowder. 2002. "Influence of Supplementary Vitamins, Minerals, and Essential Fatty Acids on the Antisocial Behavior of Young Adult Prisoners." *British Journal of Psychiatry* 181:22–28.

Gest, T. 2001. *Crime and Politics: Big Government's Erratic Campaign for Law and Order.* New York: Oxford University Press.

Gezari, V. M. 2008. "Cracking Open." *Washington Post*, June 1. www.washingtonpost.com.

Giacomazzi, A. L., S. Riley, and R. Merz. 2004. "Internal and External Challenges to Implementing Community Policing: Examining Comprehensive Assessment Reports from Multiple Sites." *Criminal Justice Studies* 17:223–37.

Gill, M., and C. Howell. 2014. "Policing Organisations: The Role of Corporate Security Function and the Implications for Suppliers." *Police Science & Management* 16:65–75.

Ginther, M., F. Shen, R, Bonnie, M. Hoffman, O. Jones, R. Marois, and K. Simons. 2014. "The Language of Mens Rea." *Vanderbilt Law Review* 67:1327–72.

Giordano, P. C., M. A. Longmore, R. D. Schroeder, and P. M. Seffrin. 2008. "A Life-Course Perspective on Spirituality and Desistance from Crime." *Criminology* 46 (1): 99–131.

Girshick, L. B. 1999. *No Safe Haven: Stories of Women in Prison*. Boston: Northeastern University Press.

Glaberson, W. 2002. "On Eve of Trial, Ex-officer Agrees to Perjury Term in Louima Case." *New York Times*, September 22, p. 1.

Glanz, J., and D. Rohde. 2006. "Panel Faults US-Trained Afghan Police." *New York Times*, December 4. www.nytimes.com.

Glasheen, C., S. Hedden, L. Kroutil, M. Pemberton, and I. Goldstrom. 2012. "Past Year Arrest among Adults in the United States: Characteristics of and Association with Mental Illness and Substance Abuse." *CBQHSQ Data Review* (Center for Behavioral Health Statistics and Quality). November. www.samhsa.gov/data/2k12/DataReview/DR008/CBHSQ-datareview-008-arrests-2012.pdf.

Glaze, L. 2011. "Correctional Population in the United States, 2010." NCJ236319. Bureau of Justice Statistics *Bulletin*, December.

Glaze, L., and T. P. Bonczar. 2011. "Probation and Parole in the United States, 2010." NCJ 236019. Bureau of Justice Statistics *Bulletin*, November.

Glaze, L., and L. Maruschak. 2008. "Parents in Prison and Their Minor Children." NCJ 222984. Bureau of Justice Statistics, *Special Report*, August.

Glaze, L. E., and D. Kaeble. 2014. "Correctional Populations in the United States, 2013." NCJ 248479. Bureau of Justice Statistics *Bulletin*, December.

Glaze, L. E., and E. Parks. 2012. "Correctional Populations in the United States, 2011." NCJ 239972. Bureau of Justice Statistics *Bulletin*, November.

Glick, R. M., and V. V. Neto. 1977. *National Study of Women's Correctional Programs*. Washington, DC: U.S. Government Printing Office.

Glueck, S., and E. Glueck. 1950 *Unraveling Juvenile Delinquency*. New York: Commonwealth Fund.

Goddard, H. H. 1902. *The Kallikak Family*. New York: Macmillan.

Goheen, W. 2013. "One Dead after Officer Involved Shooting in Flint." WNEM-TV5, June 5. www.wnem.com.

Goldberg, C. 2010. "In Theory, in Practice: Judging State Jurisdiction in Indian Country." *University of Colorado Law Review* 81:1027–65.

Goldfarb, R. L. 1965. *Ransom: A Critique of the American Bail System*. New York: Harper & Row.

Goldfarb, R. L., and L. R. Singer. 1973. *After Conviction*. New York: Simon & Schuster.

Goldkamp, J., C. Irons-Guynn, and D. Weiland. 2002. "Community Prosecution Strategies:

Measuring Impact." *Bureau of Justice Assistance Bulletin*. November.

Goldkamp, J. S. 1985. "Danger and Detention: A Second Generation of Bail Reform." *Journal of Criminal Law and Criminology* 76:1–75.

Goldman, S., and E. Slotnick. 1999. "Clinton's Second Term Judiciary: Picking Judges under Fire." *Judicature* 82:264–85.

Goldschmidt, D., and C. E. Shoichet. 2013. "Former Guards Accused of Smuggling Cell Phones into Texas Prison." CNN.com, February 28. www.cnn.com.

Goldstein, H. 1977. *Policing a Free Society*. Cambridge, MA: Ballinger.

———. 1979. "Improving Policing: A Problem-Oriented Approach." *Crime & Delinquency* 25:236–57.

———. 1990. *Problem-Oriented Policing*. New York: McGraw-Hill.

Goldstein, J. 2013. "Judge Tells Ex-Chief of Police Not to Turn Testimony into a Speech." *New York Times*, April 9. www.nytimes.com.

Gonnerman, J. 2015. "Kalief Browder, 1993–2015." *New Yorker*, June 7. Newyorker.com.

Gooch, A. D. 2010. "Admitting Guilt by Professing Innocence: When Sentence Enhancements Based on Alford Pleas Are Unconstitutional." *Vanderbilt Law Review* 63:1755–93.

Goode, E. 2002. "Jobs Rank Low as Risk Factors for Suicide." *New York Times*, November 12. www.nytimes.com.

Goodman, J. 1994. *Stories of Scottsboro*. New York: Random House.

Goodman, P. 2014. "Race in California's Prison Fire Camps for Men: Prison Politics, Space, and the Racialization of Everyday Life." *American Journal of Sociology* 120:352–94.

Goodnough, A. 2011. "Pharmacies Besieged by Addicted Thieves." *New York Times*, February 6. www.nytimes.com.

Gordon, J. 2005. "In Patriots' Cradle, the Patriot Act Faces Scrutiny." New York Times, April 24. www.nytimes.com.

Gordon, J. A., B. Proulx, and P. H. Grant. 2013. "Trepidation among the "Keepers": Gendered Perceptions of Fear and Risk of Victimization among Corrections Officers." *American Journal of Criminal Justice* 38:245–65.

Gordon, S. 2013. "Through the Eyes of Jurors: The Use of Schemas in the Application of 'Plain-Language' Jury Instructions," *Hastings Law Journal* 64:643–77.

Gorenstein, N. 2011. "Family Wins $1.2 Million Settlement in Police Shooting." *Philadelphia Inquirer*, April 7. articles.philly.com.

Gottfredson, M., and T. Hirschi. 1990. *A General Theory of Crime*. Stanford, CA: Stanford University Press.

Governor's Office on Drug Control Policy. 2006. *Iowa's Drug Control Strategy, 2006*. http://www.iowa.gov/odcp/images/pdf/Strategy_06.pdf.

Graber, C. 2013. "Invention Could Scope Out Counterfeit Drugs." *Scientific American*, November 11. www.scientificamerican.com.

Grady, D. 2003. "FDA. Outlines Plan to Counter Growing Trade in Counterfeit Pharmaceuticals." *New York Times*, October 3. www.nytimes.com.

Graham, L. 2013. "Snyder Administration to Cut Program That Has Saved Hundreds of Millions in Prison Costs." *Michigan Radio*, September 9. www.michiganradio.org.

Gray, C. 2004. "The Good News in Republican Party of *Minnesota v. White*." *Judicature* 87:271–72.

Gray, K. 2013. "Some Felons Could Get Records Erased under Bill Heading to Michigan House." *Detroit Free Press*, May 17. www.freep.com.

Green, G. S. 1997. *Occupational Crime*. 2nd ed. Belmont, CA: Wadsworth.

Greenberg, A. 2010. "Full-Body Scan Technology Deployed in Street-Roving Vans." *Forbes*, August 24. www.forbes.com.

Greenberg, D. F., and V. West. 2001. "State Prison Populations and Their Growth, 1971–1991." *Criminology* 39 (August): 615–54.

Greenberg, J., and E. Brotman. 2014. "Strict Vicarious Criminal Liability for Corporations and Corporate Executives: Stretching the Boundaries of Criminalization." *American Criminal Law Review* 51:79–98.

Greene, J. A. 1999. "Zero Tolerance: A Case Study of Police Policies and Practices in New York City." *Crime & Delinquency* 45 (April): 171–87.

Greenhouse, L. 2008. "Justices Accept Question of Prosecutors as Lawyers or Managers." *New York Times*, April 15. www.nytimes.com.

———. 2015. "It's All Right with Sam." *New York Times*, January 7. www.nytimes.com.

Greenwood, P., J. M. Chaiken, and J. Petersilia. 1977. *Criminal Investigation Process*. Lexington, MA: Lexington Books.

Greenwood, T., and H. Fournier. 2015. "Police: Parolee Arrested after 1 Adult, 2 Kids Stabbed." *Detroit News*, March 11. www.detroitnews.com.

Greer, K. R. 2000. "The Changing Nature of Interpersonal Relationships in a Women's Prison." *Prison Journal* 80 (December): 442–68.

Griffin, A. 2012. "Judges to Decide Fate of Wesleyan Killer's Fate." *Hartford Courant*. February 28. articles.courant.com.

Griffin, K. 2009. "Criminal Lying, Prosecutorial Power, and Social Meaning." *California Law Review* 97:1515–68.

Griffin, P. 2011. "National Overviews." State Juvenile Justice Profiles. Pittsburgh: National Center for Juvenile Justice. www.ncjj.org/stateprofiles.

Griffin, T., and J. Wooldredge. 2006. "Sex-Based Disparities in Felony Dispositions before versus after Sentencing Reform in Ohio." *Criminology* 44(4): 893–923.

Griset, P. L. 1994. "Determinate Sentencing and the High Cost of Overblown Rhetoric: The New York Experience." *Crime & Delinquency* 40 (4): 532–48.

———. 1995. "The Politics and Economics of Increased Correctional Discretion over Time Served: A New York Case Study." *Justice Quarterly* 12 (June): 307–23.

Grissom, B. 2011. "Proposals Could Make It Harder to Leave Prison." *New York Times*, March 12. www.nytimes.com.

Grissom, B. 2012. "More Young Inmates Attack One Another." *New York Times*, March 12. www.nytimes.com.

Gross, J. P. 2013. "Rationing Justice: The Underfunding of Assigned Counsel Systems," Part I of *Gideon at 50: A Three-Part Examination of Indigent Defense in America*. Washington, DC: National Association of Criminal Defense Lawyers.

Gross-Shader, C. 2011. "Partnerships in Evidence-Based Policing." *Translational Criminology* (Summer): 8–9.

Grovum, J. 2014. "Voting Rights for Felons in the Table in Several States." February 21. www.usatoday.com.

Grubb, A., and E. Turner. 2012. "Attribution of Blame in Rape Cases: A Review of the Impact of Rape Myth Acceptance, Gender Role Conformity and Substance Use on Victim Blaming." *Aggression and Violent Behavior* 17:443–52.

Gruber, A. 2012. "A 'Neo-feminist' Assessment of Rape and Domestic Violence Law Reform." *Journal of Gender, Race & Justice* 15:583–615.

Guerino, P., P. M. Harrison, and W. J. Sabol. 2011. "Prisoners in 2010." NCJ 236096. Bureau of Justice Statistics *Bulletin*. December.

Guevara, L., D. Herz, and C. Spohn. 2006. "Gender and Juvenile Justice Decision Making: What Role Does Race Play?" Feminist Criminology 1:258–82.

Guiora, A. N. 2012. "Due Process and Counterterrorism." *Emory International Law Review* 26:163–88.

Gunnell, J. J., and S. J. Ceci. 2010. "When Emotionality Trumps Reason: A Study of Individual Processing Style and Juror Bias." *Behavioral Sciences and the Law* 28:850–77.

Gunnison, E. and J. B. Helfgott. 2013. *Offender Reentry: Beyond Crime and Punishment*. Lynne Rienner Publishers.

Haarr, R. N., and M. Morash. 1999. "Gender, Race, and Strategies of Coping with Occupational Stress in Policing." *Justice Quarterly* 16:303–36.

Haberman, C. 2005. "He Did Time, So He's Unfit to Do Hair." *New York Times*, March 4. www.query.nytimes.com/mem/tnt.html?tntget=2005/03/04/nyregion.html.

Haberman, C. 2014. "When Youth Violence Spurred 'Superpredator' Fear." *New York Times*, April 6. www.nyt.com.

Habes, H. 2011. "Paying for the Graying: How California Can More Effectively Manage Its Growing Elderly Inmate Population." *Southern California Interdisciplinary Law Journal* 20:395–424.

Hackett, D. P., and J. M. Violanti, eds. 2003. *Police Suicide: Tactics for Prevention*. Springfield, IL: Thomas.

Hagan, F. E. 1997. *Political Crime: Ideology and Criminality*. Needham Heights, MA: Allyn & Bacon.

Hall, J. 1947. *General Principles of Criminal Law*. 2nd ed. Indianapolis: Bobbs-Merrill.

Hall, M., and C. Bonneau. 2013. "Attack Advertising, the *White* Decision, and Voter Participation in State Supreme Court Elections." *Political Research Quarterly* 66:115–26.

Hall, M. G. 1995. "Justices as Representatives: Elections and Judicial Politics in the United States." *American Politics Quarterly* 23:485–503.

Hall, W. K., and L. T. Aspin. 1987. "What Twenty Years of Judicial Retention Elections Have Told Us." *Judicature* 70:340–47.

Hambling, D. 2005. "Police Toy with 'Less Lethal' Weapons." April 30. www.newscientist.com.

Handy, R. 2012. "Parolee Arrested in Drug Bust." *Colorado Springs Gazette*, March 9. www.gazette.com.

Hanlon, M. 2007. "Run Away the Ray-Gun is Coming: We Test US Army's New Secret Weapon." *Daily Mail*, September 18. www.dailymail.co.uk.

Hannaford-Agor, P. 2011. "Systematic Negligence in Jury Operations: Why the Definition of Systematic Exclusion in Fair Cross Section Claims Must Be Expanded." *Drake Law Review* 59:762–98.

Hans, V. P., D. H. Kaye, B. M. Dann, E. J. Farley, and S. Albertson. 2011. "Science in the Jury Box: Jurors' Comprehension of Mitochondrial DNA Evidence." *Law and Human Behavior* 35:60–71.

Hans, V. P., and N. Vidmar. 2008. "The Verdict on Juries." *Judicature* 91:226–30.

Hanson, R. A., and J. Chapper. 1991. *Indigent Defense Systems*. Williamsburg, VA: National Center for State Courts.

Hanson, R. A., and H. W. K. Daley. 1995. *Challenging the Conditions of Prisons and Jails: A Report on Section 1983 Litigation*. Washington, DC: Bureau of Justice Statistics.

Harcourt, B. and J. Ludwig. 2006. "Broken Windows: New Evidence from New York City and a Five-City Social Experiment." *University of Chicago Law Review* 73:271–320.

Harding. R. 2001. "Private Prisons." In *Crime and Justice: A Review of Research*, vol. 27, ed. M. Tonry. Chicago: University of Chicago Press, 265–346.

Hargreaves, S. 2012. "Counterfeit Goods Becoming More Dangerous." CNN Money.com, September 27. money.cnn.com.

Harlow, C. W. 2000. "Defense Counsel in Criminal Cases." NCJ 179023. Bureau of Justice Statistics, *Special Report*, November.

Harrell, E., and L. Langton. 2013. "Victims of Identity Theft, 2012." Bureau of Justice Statistics *Bulletin*, NCJ 243779. December.

Harrell, E., L. Langton, M. Berzofsky, L. Couzens, and H. Smiley-McDonald. 2014. *Household Poverty and Nonfatal Violent Victimization, 2008–2012*. NCJ248384.

Harrendorf, S., M. Heiskanen, and S. Malby, eds. 2010. *International Statistics on Crime and Justice*. Helsinki: European Institute for Crime Prevention and Control (HEUNI).

Harrington, E. 2010. "Police 'Outgunned' by Criminals; Add Assault Rifles to Shifts." WBOC-TV, March 11. www.wboc.com.

Harris, J., and P. Jesilow. 2000. "It's Not the Old Ball Game: Three Strikes and the Courtroom Workgroup." *Justice Quarterly* 17:185–204.

Harrison, C. 2011. "Ten Rules for Great Jury Selection: With Some Lessons from Texas Case Law." *Defense Counsel Journal* 78:29–54.

Hartley, R., S. Madden, and C. Spohn. 2007. "Prosecutorial Discretion: An Examination of Substantial Assistance Departures in Federal Crack-Cocaine and Powder-Cocaine Cases." *Justice Quarterly* 24 (3): 382–407.

Hartley, R. E., and K. Bates. 2006. "Meeting the Challenge of Educating Court Managers." *Judicature* 90 (2): 81–88.

Hastie, R., S. Penrod, and N. Pennington. 1983. *Inside the Jury*. Cambridge, MA: Harvard University Press.

Hathaway, J. 2015. "Slender Man Stab Tweens to Be Tried as Adults for Attempted Homicide." Gawker, March 13. gawker.com.

Hauser, C. 2008. "A Precinct's Hard Road Back." *New York Times*, February 24. www.nytimes.com.

Hawaii Department of Public Safety. 2013. "Law Enforcement Division." Hawaii Department of Public Safety website. dps.hawaii.gov/about/divisions/law-enforcement-division/.

Hayes, L. 2012. "National Study of Jail Suicide: 20 Years Later." *Journal of Correctional Health Care* 18:233–45.

Haynes, S. H., B. Ruback, and G. R. Cusick. 2010. "Courtroom Workgroups and Sentencing: The Effects of Similarity, Proximity, and Stability." *Crime & Delinquency* 56:126–61.

Healy, J. 2013. "Colorado Reels after Killing of Top Official over Prisons." *New York Times*, March 20. www.nytimes.com.

Heath, B. 2014. "Investigation: ATF Drug Stings Targeted Minorities." *USA Today*, July 20. www.usatoday.com.

Heeren, G. 2010. "Pulling Teeth: The State of Mandatory Immigration Detention." *Harvard Civil Rights–Civil Liberties Law Review* 45:601–34.

Heffernan, E. 1972. *Making It in Prison*. New York: Wiley.

Hegsted, M. 2005. "Sniper's Conviction Upheld." *Potomac News*, April 23. www.potomacnews.com.

Heil, E. 2014. "Sen. Mark Udall's Son Charged with Trespassing, Heroin Possession." *Washington Post*, January 30. www.washingtonpost.com.

Heise, M. 2009. "Federal Criminal Appeals: A Brief Empirical Perspective." *Marquette Law Review* 93:825–43.

Henning, K. 2013. "Criminalizing Normal Adolescent Behavior in Communities of Color: The Role of Prosecutors in Juvenile Justice Reform." *Cornell Law Review* 98:383–461.

Hensley, T. R., J. A. Baugh, and C. E. Smith. 2007. "The First-Term Performance of Chief Justice John Roberts." *Idaho Law Review* 43:625–42.

Herberman, E. J., and T. P. Bonczar. 2014. "Probation and Parole in the United States, 2013." NCJ 248029. Bureau of Justice Statistics *Bulletin*, October.

Herbert, S. 1996. "Morality in Law Enforcement: Chasing "Bad Guys" with the Los Angeles Police Department." *Law and Society Review* 30:799–818.

Hermann, P. 2014. "Air Force Major Charged in Child Pornography Case." *Washington Post*, January 31. www.washingtonpost.com.

"Hernandez Jurors See Police Video." 2015. ESPN News online, February 17. http://espn.go.com.

Hester, T. 1987 *Correctional Populations in the United States, 1985*. NCJ 103957. Washington, DC: U.S. Department of Justice.

Heumann, M. 1978. *Plea Bargaining*. Chicago: University of Chicago Press.

Heyman, M. 2014. "Lost in Translation: Criminal Jury Trials in the United States." *British Journal of American Legal Studies* 3:1–35.

Hickey, T. J. 1993. "Expanding the Use of Prior Act Evidence in Rape and Sexual Assault." *Criminal Law Bulletin* 29:195–218.

Hickman, M., and B. Reaves. 2006. *Local Police Departments, 2003*. NCJ210118. Washington, DC: U.S. Department of Justice, Bureau of Justice Statistics.

Hill, M. 2007. "New York Prison Creates Dementia Unit." *Washington Post*, May 29. www.washingtonpost.com.

Hillard, G. 2011. "In Tight Times, LA Relies on Volunteer Police." National Public Radio website, May 19. www.npr.org.

Hinduja, S. 2004. "Perceptions of Local and State Law Enforcement Concerning the Role of Computer Crime Investigative Teams." *Policing: International Journal of Police Strategies and Management* 27:341–57.

———. 2007. "Neutralization Theory and Online Software Piracy: An Empirical Analysis." *Ethics and Information Technology* 9(3): 187–204.

Hinduja, S., and J. Patchin. 2007. "Offline Consequences of Online Victimization: School Violence and Delinquency." *Journal of School Violence* 6(3): 89–112.

———. 2013. "Social Influences on Cyberbullying Behaviors Among Middle and High School Students." *Journal of Youth and Adolescence* 42:711–22.

Hing, B. O. 2010. "Systemic Failure: Mental Illness, Detention, and Deportation." *University of California Davis Journal of International Law and Policy* 16:341–82.

Hipp, J. R., and D. K. Yates. 2011. "Ghettos, Thresholds, and Crime: Does Concentrated Poverty Really Have an Accelerating Increasing Effect on Crime?" *Criminology* 49:955–90.

Hirsch, A. J. 1992. *The Rise of the Penitentiary*. New Haven, CT: Yale University Press.

Hirschi, T. 1969. *Causes of Delinquency*. Berkeley: University of California Press.

Hirten, M. 2014. "Free Speech and Terrorism." *Lansing City Pulse*, November 10. http://www.lansingcitypulse.com/lansing/article-10872-free-speech-and-terrorism.html.

Ho, T. 1998. "Retardation, Criminality, and Competency to Stand Trial among Mentally Retarded Criminal Defendants: Violent versus Non-violent Defendants." *Journal of Crime and Justice* 21:57–70.

Hockenberry, S. 2014. Juveniles in Residential Placement. Juvenile Offenders and Victims Bulletin. NCJ 246826. Washington, DC: Office of Juvenile Justice and Delinquency Prevention.

Hockenberry, S., and C. Puzzanchera. 2014a. Delinquency Cases in Juvenile Court, 2011. Juvenile Offenders and Victims Fact Sheet. NCJ 248409. Washington, DC: Office of Juvenile Justice and Delinquency Prevention.

———. 2014b. Juvenile Court Statistics, 2011. Pittsburgh: National Center for Juvenile Justice.

Hoffman, M. 1999. "Abolish Peremptory Challenges." *Judicature* 82:202–4.

Hoffmann, H. L. 2006. "Rehnquist and Federal Habeas Corpus." In *The Rehnquist Legacy*, ed. C. Bradley. New York: Cambridge University Press.

Holder, E. 2013. Speech at National Association of Counties Legislative Conference, March 4, 2013, Washington, DC. www.justice.gov.

Hollander-Blumoff, R. 2012. "Crime, Punishment, and the Psychology of Self-Control." *Emory Law Journal* 61:501–53.

Holmes, O. W., Jr. 1881. *The Common Law*. Boston: Little, Brown.

Holmes, S. A. 1996. "With More Women in Prison, Sexual Abuse by Guards Becomes Greater Concern." *New York Times*, December 27, p. A18.

Holstege, S. 2008. "Ariz. Deportation Policy a Model, Feds Say," *Arizona Republic*, April 15. www.azcentral.com/arizonarepublic/news/articles/0415deport0414.html?&wired.

Holt, T., and A. Bossler. 2012. "Predictors of Patrol Officer Interest in Cybercrime Training and Investigation in Selected United States Police Departments." *Cyberpsychology, Behavior, and Social Networking*. 15:464–72.

Holt, T. J., and A. M. Bossler. 2009. "Examining the Applicability of Lifestyle-Routine Activities Theory for Cybercrime Victimization." *Deviant Behavior* 30(1): 1–25.

———. 2014. "An Assessment of the Current State of Cybercrime Scholarship." *Deviant Behavior* 35:20–40.

Holtfreter, K., and K. A. Wattanaporn. 2013. "The Transition from Prison to Community Initiative: An Evaluation of Gender Responsiveness for Female Offender Reentry." *Criminal Justice and Behavior* 41:41–57.

Homan, C. 2010. "Michigan Lawmakers to Debate Bringing Good Time Back for Prisoners," *Holland Sentinel*, February 15. www.hollandsentinel.com.

Horne, P. 2006. "Policewomen: Their First Century and the New Era." *The Police Chief*, 73 (9), September. policechiefmagazine.org.

Horwitz, S. 2013. "New FBI Director James B. Comey Stunned by Impact of Sequestration on Agents in the Field." *Washington Post*, September 27. www.washingtonpost.com.

Hotelling, B. A. 2008. "Perinatal Needs of Pregnant, Incarcerated Women." *Journal of Perinatal Education* 17:37–44.

Howard, J. 1929. *The State of Prisons in England and Wales*. London: J. M. Dent. Originally published in 1777.

Howley, S., and C. F. Dorris. 2013. "Legal Rights for Crime Victims in the Criminal Justice System." In *Victims of Crimes*, 4th ed., R. C. Davis, A. J. Lurigio, and S. Herman, eds. Los Angeles: Sage, 271–92.

Hu, W., and N. Schweber. 2012. "Bus Driver Found Not Guilty of Manslaughter in I-95 Crash." *New York Times*, December 7. www.nytimes.com.

Hubert, C. 2010. "Placerville Shooting Fuels Debate about Use of Deadly Force against Mentally Ill." *Sacramento Bee*, April 4. www.sacbee.com.

Hudson, J. 2012. "Contemporary Origins of Restorative Justice Programming: The Minnesota Restitution Center." *Federal Probation* (September): 49–55.

Huebner, B. M. 2005. "The Effect of Incarceration on Marriage and Work over the Life Course." *Justice Quarterly* 22 (3): 281–301.

Huetteman, E. 2015. "Senate Panel Approves Loretta Lynch to be Attorney General." *New York Times,* February 26, 2015. www.nytimes.com.

Huey, L. 2010. "'I've Seen This on CSI': Criminal Investigations' Perceptions about the Management of Public Expectations in the Field." *Crime, Media, and Culture* 6:49–68.

Huff, C. R. 2002. "Wrongful Conviction and Public Policy: The American Society of Criminology 2001 Presidential Address." *Criminology* 40: 1–18.

Huff, J. M. 2010. "Warrantless Entries and Searches under Exigent Circumstances: Why Are They Justified and What Types of Circumstances Are Considered Exigent?" *University of Detroit/Mercy Law Review* 87:373–414.

Hulse, C. 2015. "Unlikely Cause Unites the Left and the Right: Justice Reform." *New York Times*, February 18. www.nytimes.com.

Hult, J. 2011. "Pay, Retention Central to Prison Talks about Prison." *Sioux Falls Argus Leader*, May 15. www.argusleader.com.

Humes, K. R., N. A. Jones, and R. R. Ramirez. 2011. "Overview of Race and Hispanic Origin: 2010." *2010 Census Briefs* (March). Washington, DC: U.S. Census Bureau.

Hundley, K., S. T. Martin, and C. Humburg. 2012. "Florida 'Stand Your Ground' Law Yields Some Shocking Outcomes Depending on How Law Is Applied." *Tampa Bay Times*, June 1. www.tampabay.com.

Hunnicutt, T. 2010. "Budget Cuts Have Left Abuse Victims to Rely on Volunteers." *Los Angeles Daily News*, August 22. www.dailynews.com.

Hunter, G. 2014. "Cops: Detroit Shooting Suspect on Bond Shoots Again." *Detroit News,* September 6. www.detroitnews.com.

Hyatt, J. M., and G. C. Barnes. 2014. "An Experimental Evaluation of the Impact of Intensive Supervision on the Recidivism of High-Risk Probationers." *Crime & Delinquency* (online publication prior to print publication). http://www.sagepub.com/journals/Journal200959.

"Indiana's Answer to Prison Costs." 2011. *New York Times*, January 17. www.nytimes.com.

"Indigent Defense." 2011. U.S. Office of Justice Programs *Fact Sheet*, December. http://ojp.gov/newsroom/factsheets/ojpfs_indigentdefense.html.

Ingold, J. 2011. "Prison Black Market a Steal: Correctional Officers Get Drawn into Contraband Smuggling." *Denver Post*, December 18. www.denverpost.com.

Internet Crime Complaint Center. 2011. *2010 Internet Crime Report*. Washington, DC: U.S. Department of Justice.

———. 2012. *2011 Internet Crime Report*. Glen Allen, VA: National White Collar Crime Center.

———. 2014. *2013 IC3 Annual Report*. Washington, DC: Federal Bureau of Investigation.

Ioannou, S., V. Gallese, and A. Merla. 2014. "Thermal Infrared Imaging in Psychophysiology: Potentialities and Limits." *Psychophysiology* 51:951–63.

Iribarren, C. J., J. H. Markovitz, D. R. Jacobs, P. J. Schreiner, M. Daviglus, and J. R. Hibbeln. 2004. "Dietary Intake of n-3, n-6 Fatty Acids and Fish: Relationship with Hostility in Young Adults—the CARDIA Study." *European Journal of Clinical Nutrition* 58:24–31.

Irwin, J. 1970. *The Felon*. Englewood Cliffs, NJ: Prentice-Hall.

———. 1980. *Prisons in Turmoil*. Boston: Little, Brown.

———. 2013. "Prisoner Re-entry an Investment in Public Safety." *Detroit Free Press*, May 24. www.freep.com.

Irwin, J., and D. Cressey. 1962. "Thieves, Convicts, and the Inmate Culture." *Social Problems* 10:142–55.

Ith, I. 2001. "Taser Fails to Halt Man with Knife; Seattle Officer Kills 23-Year-Old." *Seattle Times,* November 28, p. A1.

Itzkoff, D. 2010. "Wesley Snipes Surrenders to Begin Sentence on Tax Convictions." *New York Times*, December 9. www.nytimes.com.

Izadi, E. 2015. "'American Sniper' Trial: Why Prosecutors Often Don't Seek the Death Penalty." *Washington Post*, March 6. www.washingtonpost.com.

Jacobs, E. T. 2012. "Online Sexual Solicitation of Minors: An Analysis of the Average Predator, His Victims, What Is Being Done and Can Be Done to Decrease the Occurrences of Victimization." *Cardozo Public Law, Policy & Ethics Journal* 10:505–37.

Jacobs, J. B., and C. Panarella. 1998. "Organized Crime." In *The Handbook of Crime and Punishment,* ed. M. Tonry. New York: Oxford University Press, 159–77.

Jacobs, J. B., C. Panarella, and J. Worthington. 1994. *Busting the Mob: United States v. Cosa Nostra*. New York: New York University Press.

Jacobs, T. 2015. "Unconscious Racial Bias Taints the Legal System." *Pacific Standard*. January 15. www.psmag.com.

Jacoby, J. 1979. "The Charging Policies of Prosecutors." In *The Prosecutor,* ed. W. F. McDonald. Beverly Hills, CA: Sage.

———. 1995. "Pushing the Envelope: Leadership in Prosecution." *Justice System Journal* 17:291–307.

Jain, N. 2011. "Engendering Fairness in Domestic Violence Arrests: Improving Police Accountability through the Equal Protection Clause." *Emory Law Journal* 60:1011–48.

Jaksic, V. 2007. "Public Defenders, Prosecutors Face a Crisis in Funding." *National Law Journal*, March 27. www.law.com.

Jalbert, S. K., and W. Rhodes. 2012. "Reduced Caseloads Improve Probation Outcomes." *Journal of Crime and Justice* 35:221–38.

James, C., G. J. Stams, J. J. Asscher, A. K. DeRoo, and P. H. van der Lann. 2013. "Aftercare Programs for Reducing Recidivism among Juvenile and Young Adult Offenders: A Meta-analytic Review." *Clinical Psychology Review*, 33:263–74.

James, D. J., and L. E. Glaze. 2006. "Mental Health Problems of Prison and Jail Inmates." NCJ 213600. Bureau of Justice Statistics, *Special Report*, September.

Jenks, C. 2015. "Civil Liberties and Indefinite Detention of U.S. Citizens." *Harvard Journal of Law and Public Policy* (forthcoming 2015).

Jennings, D. 2007. "Man Named in Fix TYC Failures Is Hailed." Texas Cable News, March 11. www.txcn.com.

Jervis, R. 2015. "'American Sniper' Killer Found Guilty in Murders." *USA Today,* February 25. www.usatoday.com.

JFA Institute. 2007. *Unlocking America: Why and How to Reduce America's Prison Population.* Washington, DC: JFA Institute.

Johnson, A. 2011. "Sentencing Overhaul Would Save State $78 Million." *Columbus Dispatch*, May 5. www.dispatchpolitics.com.

Johnson, B., and S. Betsinger. 2009. "Punishing the 'Model Minority': Asian-American Criminal Sentencing Outcomes in Federal District Courts." *Criminology* 47:1045–89.

Johnson, B. D. 2005. "Contextual Disparities in Guidelines Departures: Courtroom Social Contexts, Guidelines Compliance, and Extralegal Disparities in Criminal Sentencing." *Criminology* 43 (3): 761–96.

———. 2006. "The Multilevel Context of Criminal Sentencing: Integrating Judge- and County-Level Influences." *Criminology* 44(2): 259–98.

Johnson, C. 2013. "Some Public Defenders Warn: 'We Have Nothing Left to Cut.'" National Public Radio, April 10. www.npr.org.

Johnson, D. T. 1998. "The Organization of Prosecution and the Possibility of Order." *Law and Society Review* 32:247–308.

Johnson, K. 2010a. "How Racial Profiling in America Became the Law of the Land." *Georgetown Law Journal* 98:1005–77.

———. 2010b. "Police Training Halts as Agencies Face Budget Cuts." *USA Today*, October 4. www.usatoday.com.

———. 2010c. "Prison Workforce Feels Pinch." *USA Today*, July19. www.usatoday.com.

Johnson, K., O. Dorell, and E. Weise. 2014. "Official: North Korea behind Sony Hack." *USA Today*, December 18. www.usatoday.com.

Johnson, M., and L. Johnson. 2012. "Bail: Reforming Policies to Address Overcrowded Jails, the Impact of Race on Detention, and Community Revival in Harris County, Texas." *Northwestern Journal of Law and Social Policy* 7:42–87.

Johnson, M. P. 2008. *Typologies of Domestic Violence*. Boston: Northeastern University Press.

Johnson, R. 2002. *Hard Time: Understanding and Reforming the Prison*. 3rd ed. Belmont, CA: Wadsworth.

———. 2011. "Suspect Mental Disorder and Police Use of Force." *Criminal Justice and Behavior* 38:127–45.

Johnson, S. 2008. "The Judicial Behavior of Justice Souter in Criminal Cases and the Denial of a Conservative Counterrevolution." *Pierce Law Review* 7:1–37.

Jolliffe, D., D. P. Farrington, and P. Howard. 2013. "How Long Did It Last? A 10-year Reconviction Follow-Up Study of High Intensity Training for Young Offenders." *Journal of Experimental Criminology*, 9:515–31.

Jones, J. M. 2014a. "Americans' Support for Death Penalty Stable." Gallup Poll. October 23. www.gallup.com.

———. 2014b. "Drop among Nonwhites Drives Police Honesty Ratings Down." Gallup Poll. December 18. www.gallup.com.

Jonsson, P. 2014. "Authorities Look at 'Anti-government' Motive in Austin Shooting." *Christian Science Monitor.* November 28. www.csmonitor.com.

———. 2015. "How Police Can Get It Right." *Christian Science Monitor,* February 8, 2015. www.csmonitor.com.

Jordan, J. 2002. "Will Any Woman Do? Police, Gender and Rape Victims." *Policing* 25:319–44.

Joy, P. 2015. "Race Matters in Jury Selection." *Northwestern University Law Review Online* 109:180–86.

Juvenile Law Center. 2008. *People v. Nguyen.* www.jlc.org/litigation/People_v._Nguyen_/.

Kaiser, D., and L. Stannow. 2011. "Prison Rape and the Government." *New York Review of Books*, March 24, pp. 26–28.

Kalhan, A. 2010. "Rethinking Immigration Detention." *Columbia Law Review Sidebar* 110:42–58.

Kalinich, D. B. 1980. *Power, Stability, and Contraband.* Prospect Heights, IL: Waveland Press.

Kamisar, Y. 2012. "The Rise, Decline, and Fall (?) of *Miranda.*" *Washington Law Review* 87:965–1039.

Kampeas, R. 2001. "Terror Attacks Bring Profound Changes in FBI Focus, Challenges for New Director." Associated Press News Service, October 27.

Kane, R. J. 2005. "Compromised Police Legitimacy as a Predictor of Violent Crime in Structurally Disadvantaged Communities." *Criminology* 43:469–98.

Kane, R. J., and M. D. White. 2009. "Bad Cops: A Study of Career-Ending Misconduct among New York City Police Officers." *Criminology & Public Policy* 8:737–69.

Kang, C., C. Timberg, and E. Nakashima. 2014. "Sony's Hacked Emails Expose Spats, Director Calling Angelina Jolie a 'Brat'." *Washington Post* December 11. www.washingtonpost.com.

Kang, M. and K. Stokes. 2014. "After 2 Deadly Shootings in a Week, Seattle Major Says, 'We Must Find a Solution.'" *KPLU News*, 88.5. Retrieved from http://kplu.org.

"Kansas City Police Officer Convicted of Corruption." 2014. KSDK News, April 5. www.ksdk.com.

Kaplan, T. 2014. "Cuomo Drops Plan to Use State Money to Pay for College Classes for Inmates." *New York Times,* April 2. www.nytimes.com.

Karmen, A. 2001. *Crime Victims.* 4th ed. Belmont, CA: Wadsworth.

Karnowski, S. 2008. "City's I-35W Bridge Response Generally Praised." Associated Press, April 22. www.twin cities.com.

KATC-TV. 2010. "New Prison 'Good Time' Law Frees 463." KATC.com, October 27. www.katc.com.

Kaye, D. 2014. "Why So Contrived? Fourth Amendment Balancing, Per Se Rules, and DNA Databases after *Maryland v. King*. *Journal of Criminal Law and Criminology* 104:535–95.

Kazemian, L., C. McCoy, and M. Sacks. 2013. "Does Law Matter? An Old Bail Law Confronts the New Penology. *Punishment and Society*, 15:43–70.

Kelling, G. L. 1985. "Order Maintenance, the Quality of Urban Life, and Police: A Line of Argument." In *Police Leadership in America,* ed. W. A. Geller. New York: Praeger.

———. 1992. "Measuring What Matters: A New Way of Thinking about Crime and Public Order." *City Journal* 2 (Spring): 21–31.

Kelling, G. L., and C. M. Coles. 1996. *Fixing Broken Windows: Restoring and Reducing Crime in Our Communities.* New York: Free Press.

Kelling, G. L., and M. Moore. 1988. "The Evolving Strategy of Policing." In *Perspectives on Policing,* no. 13. Washington, DC: National Institute of Justice.

Kelling, G. L., T. Pate, D. Dieckman, and C. E. Brown. 1974. *The Kansas City Preventive Patrol Experiments: A Summary Report.* Washington, DC: Police Foundation.

Kelly, H. 2012. "Police Embracing Tech that Predicts Crime." CNN.com, July 9. www.cnn.com/2012/07/09/tech/innovation/police-tech.

Kennedy, K. 2013. "Gunshot Wounds Drive Up Government Health Care Costs." *USA Today,* March 4. www.usatoday.com.

Kenney, D. J., and J. O. Finckenauer. 1995. *Organized Crime in America.* Belmont, CA: Wadsworth.

Kenny, J. 2012. "Criminal Foreplay: The Process from Target Selection to Victimization." *Journal of Applied Security Research* 7:439–51.

Kenny, K. 2009. "When Cultural Tradition and Criminal Law Collide: Prosecutorial Discretion in Cross-Cultural Cases." *Judicature* 92:216–19.

Kerley, K. R., A. Hochstetler, and H. Copes. 2009. "Self-Control, Prison Victimization, and Prison Infractions." *Criminal Justice Review* 34:553–68.

Kerlikowske, R. G. 2004. "The End of Community Policing: Remembering the Lessons Learned," *FBI Law Enforcement Bulletin* 73 (April): 6–11.

KGO-TV. 2013. "FBI: Layoffs Take Toll on California Police Departments." KGO-TV Online, March 14. abclocal.go.com/kgo/story?section=news/state&id=9028245

Kidder, D. L. 2005. "Is It 'Who I Am', 'What I Can I Get Away With,' or 'What You've Done to Me'? A Multi-theory Examination of Employee Misconduct." *Journal of Business Ethics* 57:389–98.

Kilgannon, C., and N. Cohen. 2009. "Cadets Trade the Trenches for Firewalls." *New York Times*, May 11. www.nytimes.com.

Killman, C., and B. Hoberock. 2013. "Lawmakers Benefit from Private Prison Donations." *Tulsa World.* May 19. www.tulsaworld.com.

Kim, J. 2009. "Secrecy and Fairness in Plea Bargaining with Multiple Defendants." *Journal of Economics* 96:263–76.

Kim, K., and M. Denver. 2011. *A Case Study on the Practices of Pretrial Services and Risk Assessment in Three Cities.* Washington, D.C.: District of Columbia Policy Institute.

Kimberly, J. 2003. "House Passes Crime Lab Bill." *Houston Chronicle,* May 2. www.houstonchronicle.com.

King, N. J., F. Cheesman, and B. Ostrom. 2007. *Habeas Litigation in the US District Courts.* Williamsburg, VA: National Center for State Courts.

King, N. J., and J. L. Hoffmann. 2010. *Habeas Corpus for the Twenty-First Century.* Chicago: University of Chicago Press.

King, R. S., M. Mauer, and T. Huling. 2004. "An Analysis of the Economics of Prison Siting in Rural Communities." *Criminology & Public Policy* 3 (July): 453–80.

Kingsnorth, R., R. MacIntosh, and S. Sutherland. 2002. "Criminal Charge or Probation Violation? Prosecutorial Discretion and Implications for Research in Criminal Court Processing." *Criminology* 40:553–77.

Kirby, S., A. Quinn, and S. Keay. 2010. "Intelligence-Led and Traditional Policing Approaches to Open Drug Markets—A Comparison of Offenders," *Drugs and Alcohol Today* 10:13–19.

Kirk, D. S. 2012. "Residential Change as a Turning Point in the Life Course of Crime: Desistance or Temporary Cessation?" *Criminology* 50:329–57.

Kirkpatrick, D. D. 2005a. "Alito Memos Supported Expanding Police Powers." *New York Times*, November 29. www.nytimes.com.

———. 2005b. "In Secretly Taped Conversations, Glimpses of the Future President." *New York Times,* February 20. www.nytimes.com.

Kish, R. J., and A. F. Lipton. 2013. "Do Private Prisons Really Offer Savings Compared with Their Public Counterparts?" *Economic Affairs* 33:93–107.

Klahm, C., and R. Tillyer. 2010. "Understanding Police Use of Force: A Review of the Evidence." *Southwest Journal of Criminal Justice* 7:214–39.

Klain, E. 2012. "President Obama Signed the National Defense Authorization Act—Now What?" *Forbes*, January 2. www.forbes.com.

Klaus, P. 2007. "Crime and the Nation's Households, 2005." NCJ 217198. Bureau of Justice Statistics *Data Brief*, April.

Kleck, G., B. Sever, S. Li, and M. Gertz. 2005. "The Missing Link in General Deterrence Research." *Criminology* 43 (3): 623–59.

Klein, D. 1973. "The Etiology of Female Crime: A Review of the Literature." *Issues in Criminology* 8(2): 3–30.

Klein, D. W. 2010. "Rehabilitating Mental Disorder Evidence after *Clark v. Arizona*: Of Burdens, Presumptions, and the Right to Raise Reasonable Doubt." *Case Western Law Review* 60:645–86.

Klepper, D. 2011. "RI House Passes Pregnant Inmate Handcuff Rules." *Boston Globe*, May 25. www.boston.com.

Klinger, D. 2012a. "On the Problems and Promise of Research on Lethal Police Violence: A Research Note." *Homicide Studies* 16:78–96.

———. 2012b. "Police Training as an Instrument of Accountability." *St. Louis University Law Review* 32:111–21.

Klockars, C. B. 1985. "Order Maintenance, the Quality of Urban Life, and Police: A Different Line of Argument." In *Police Leadership in America,* ed. W. A. Geller. New York: Praeger.

Knake, R. N. 2010. "The Supreme Court's Increased Attention to the Law of Lawyering: Mere Coincidence or Something More?" *American University Law Review* 59:1499–572.

Kocieniewski, D. 2007. "So Many Crimes, and Reasons Not to Cooperate." *New York Times*, December 30. www.nytimes.com.

Konczal, M. 2013. "Does Dodd–Frank Really End 'Too Big to Fail'?" *Washington Post*, March 2. www.washingtonpost.com.

Koper, C. 1995. "Just Enough Police Presence: Reducing Crime and Disorderly Behavior by Optimizing Patrol Time in Crime Hot Spots." *Justice Quarterly* 12 (December): 649–72.

Koper, C. S., and E. Mayo-Wilson. 2006. "Police Crackdowns on Illegal Gun Carrying: A Systematic Review of Their Impact on Gun Crime." *Journal of Experimental Criminology* 2:227–61.

Korte, G. 2015. "Obama Gives Drug Offenders a Break." *Lansing State Journal*, April 1, p. 3B.

Kotlowitz, A. 1994. "Their Crimes Don't Make Them Adults." *New York Times Magazine,* February 13, p. 40.

Koulish, R., and M. Noferi. 2013. "Unlocking Immigrant Detention Reform." *Baltimore Sun*, February 20. articles.baltimoresun.com.

Krauss, C. 1994. "No Crystal Ball Needed on Crime." *New York Times,* November 13, sec. 4, p. 4.

Kreager, D., D. Schaefer, M. Bouchard, D. Haynie, S. Wakefield, J. Young, and G. Zajac. 2015. "Toward a Criminology of Inmate Networks." *Justice Quarterly* (online first publication before print version). http://www.acjs.org/pubs/167_669_2916.cfm.

Kremling, J., M. D. Smith, J. K. Cochran, B. Bjerregaard, and S. J. Fogel. 2007. "The Role of Mitigating Facts in Capital Sentencing before and after *McKoy v. North Carolina*." *Justice Quarterly* 24(3): 357–81.

Krischke, S. 2010. "Absent Accountability: How Prosecutorial Impunity Hinders the Fair Administration of Justice in America." *Journal of Law and Policy* 19:395–434.

Kruttschnitt, C., and K. Carbone-Lopez. 2006. "Moving beyond the Stereotypes: Women's Subjective Accounts of Their Violent Crime. *Criminology* 44 (2): 321–51.

Kruttschnitt, C., and R. Gartner, 2003. "Women's Imprisonment," *Crime and Justice: A Review of Research* 30:55–135.

Kruttschnitt, C., and S. Krmpotich. 1990. "Aggressive Behavior among Female Inmates: An Exploratory Study." *Justice Quarterly* 7 (June): 371–89.

KTKA News. 2011. "Shawnee Co. Looks to Cost Cuts with Early Retirement, Jury Pay Cuts." KTKA.com, February 10. www.ktka.com.

Kubrin, C. E., S. F. Messner, G. Deane, K. McGeever, and T. D. Stuckey. 2010. "Proactive Policing and Robbery Rates across US Cities." *Criminology* 48:57–97.

Kurlychek, M. 2010. "Transforming Attitudinal Change into Behavioral Change: The Missing Link." *Criminology and Public Policy* 9:119–26.

Kurlychek, M., and C. Kempinen. 2006. "Beyond Boot Camp: The Impact of Aftercare on Offender Re-entry." *Criminology & Public Policy,* 5:363–88.

Kurtz, H. 1997. "The Crime Spree on Network News." *Washington Post,* August 12, p. 1.

Kurz, D. 2012. "Roll Call and the Second Shift: The Influences of Gender and Family on Police Stress." *Police Practice and Research: An International Journal* 13:71–86.

Kutnjak Ivkovic, S. 2009. "Rotten Apples, Rotten Branches, and Rotten Orchards: A Cautionary Tale of Police Misconduct." *Criminology & Public Policy* 8:777–85.

Kyckelhahn, T. 2014. *Justice Expenditures and Employment Extracts, 2010*, NCJ 247019. http://www.bjs.gov.

Kyckelhahn, T., and T. Martin. 2013. *Justice Expenditure and Employment Extracts, 2010—Preliminary.* NCJ 242544. Washington, D.C.: Bureau of Justice Statistics, July 1.

Lambert, L. 2011. "States Seek to Escape Rising Prison Costs." Reuters News Service, May 20. www.reuters.com.

Lancaster, R. N. 2011. "Sex Offenders: The Last Pariahs." *New York Times*, August 20. www.nytimes.com

Langan, P., and R. Cohen. 1996. *State Court Sentencing of Convicted Felons, 1992.* NCJ 152696. Washington, DC: Bureau of Justice Statistics, May.

Langan, P., and D. Levin. 2002. "Recidivism of Prisoners Released in 1994." NCJ 193427. Bureau of Justice Statistics, *Special Report*, June.

Langton, L., and D. Farole. 2010. "State Public Defender Programs, 2007." NCJ 228229. Bureau of Justice Statistics, *Special Report*, September.

Laris, M. 2014. "Voting-Rights Quest in Va. Will Become Easier for Ex-Prisoners Held on Serious Drug Charges." *Washington Post*, April 18. www.washingtonpost.com.

Laski, L. 2012. "Compelled Acquittal by Reason of Mental Disease or Defect in Arkansas." *Arkansas Law Review* 65:899–928.

Lasley, J. R., J. Larson, C. Kelso, and G. C. Brown. 2011. "Assessing the Long-Term Effects of Officer Race on Police Attitudes toward the Community: A Case for Representative Bureaucracy Theory." *Police Practice and Research: An International Journal* 12:474–91.

Laub, J. H., and R. J. Sampson. 2003. *Shared Beginnings, Divergent Lives: Delinquent Boys to Age 70.* Cambridge, MA: Harvard University Press.

Lauritsen, J., and N. White. 2001. "Putting Violence in Its Place: The Influence of Race, Ethnicity, Gender, and Place on the Risk for Violence." *Criminology & Public Policy* 1:37–59.

Lavandera, E. 2008. "Cleared by DNA, Man Tries to Reclaim His Life." CNN.com, May 16. www.cnn.com.

Lave, T. R. 1998. "Equal before the Law." *Newsweek*, July 13, p. 14.

Lawrence, A. 2009. *Cutting Corrections Costs: Earned Time Policies for State Prisoners.* Denver, CO: National Conference of State Legislatures.

Lawrence, A., and D. Lyons. 2013. "Justice Reinvestment." *Crime Brief* (National Conference of State Legislatures), July. http://www.ncsl.org/Documents/CJ/July2013CrimeBrief.pdf.

Lawson, B. 2011. "Bribery Conviction of Army Major and His Wife in Decatur Brings Corruption Probe Tally to 16." *Huntsville Times*, March 2. www.al.com.

Le, V., P. Bell, and M. Lauchs. 2013. "Elements of Best Practices in Policing Transnational Organized Crime: Critical Success Factors for International Cooperation." *International Journal of Management and Administrative Sciences* 2:24–34.

Leban, L., S. Cardwell, H. Copes, and T. Brezina. 2015. "Adapting to Prison Life: A Qualitative Examination of the Coping Process among Incarcerated Offenders." *Justice Quarterly* (online publication first before print version). http://www.acjs.org/pubs/167_669_2916.cfm.

———. 2011. "Riding along with the Cops in Murdertown, USA." *New York Times*, April 15. www.nytimes.com.

Lee, V. 2013. "New San Francisco Court Program Helps Military Veterans." KGO-TV website, April 4. abclocal.go.com/kgo/story?section=news/local/san_francisco&id=9053406.

Lehti, M., and Aromaa, K. 2006. "Trafficking for Sexual Exploitation." *Crime and Justice* 34:133–227.

Leiber, M. J., and K. Y. Mack. 2003. "The Individual and Joint Effects of Race, Gender, and Family Status on Juvenile Justice Decision-Making." *Journal of Research in Crime & Delinquency* 40:34–70.

Leland, J. 2014. "Drug-Selling Charges Dropped Against Man Arrested in Hoffman Case." *New York Times,* August 28. www.nytimes.com.

Leo, R. 2008. *Police Interrogation and American Justice*. Cambridge, MA: Harvard University Press.

Leo, R. A. 1996a. "The Impact of *Miranda* Revisited." *Journal of Criminal Law and Criminology* 86:621–92.

———. 1996b. " *Miranda*'s Revenge: Police Interrogation as a Confidence Game." *Law and Society Review* 30:259–88.

Leonard, J. 2002. "Dropping 'Nonlethal' Beanbags as Too Dangerous." *Los Angeles Times*, June 3, p. 1.

Leonard, K.. 2012. "Privatized Prison Health Care Scrutinized." *Washington Post,* July 21. www.washingtonpost.com.

Leonhardt, D. 2007. "Immigrants and Prison," *New York Times*, May 30. www.nytimes.com.

Lersch, K. M. 2002. "Are Citizen Complaints Just Another Measure of Officer Productivity? An Analysis of Citizen Complaints and Officer Activity Measures." *Police Practices and Research* 3:135–47.

Lersch, K. M., and L. Kunzman. 2001. "Misconduct Allegations and Higher Education in a Southern Sheriff's Department." *American Journal of Criminal Justice* 25:161–72.

Lett, C., and R. Ellis. 2015. "'American Sniper' Trial: Deputy Says Defendant Explained Killings." CNN.com, February 25. www.cnn.com.

Leu, M., and M. J. Cristobal. 2011. "Probation Officers Hit By Statewide Budget Cuts." *Illinois Statehouse News*, March 18. illinois.statehousenewsonline.com.

Levin, B. 2013. "American Gangsters: RICO, Criminal Syndicates, and Conspiracy Law as Market Control." *Harvard Civil Rights-Civil Liberties Law Review* 48:105–64.

Levine, J. P. 1992. Juries and Politics. Belmont, CA: Wadsworth.

Lewis, E. 2007. *Realizing Justice: Defender Caseload Report 2007.* Frankfort: Kentucky Department of Public Advocacy.

Lewis, N. 1999. "Prosecutors Urged to Allow Appeals on DNA." *New York Times*, September 28, p. 14.

Lichtblau, E. 2012. "Police Are Using Tracking as Routine Tool." *New York Times*, March 31. www.nyt.com.

Lightfoot, E., and M. Umbreit. 2004. "An Analysis of State Statutory Provisions for Victim–Offender Mediation." *Criminal Justice Policy Review* 15:418–36.

Lineberger, K. 2011. "The United States–El Salvador Extradition Treaty: A Dated Obstacle in the Transnational War against Mara Salvatrucha (MS-13)." *Vanderbilt Journal of Transnational Law* 44:187–216.

Lippke, R. L. 2010. "Rewarding Cooperation: The Moral Complexities of Procuring Accomplice Testimony." *New Criminal Law Review* 13:90–118.

Liptak, A. 2005. "To More Inmates, Life Term Means Dying behind Bars." *New York Times,* October 2. www.nytimes.com.

———. 2008. "Illegal Globally, Bail for Profit Remains in US." *New York Times*, January 29. www.nytimes.com.

———. 2011a. "$14 Million Jury Award to Ex-inmate Is Dismissed." *New York Times,* March 29. www.nytimes.com.

———. 2011b. "Justices, 5–4, Tell California to Cut Prisoner Population." New York Times, May 23. www.nytimes.com.

———. 2012. "In Supreme Court Term, Striking Unity on Major Cases." *New York Times,* June 30. www.nytimes.com.

———. 2013a. "Budget Cuts Imperil Federal Court System, Roberts Says." *New York Times,* December 31, 2013. www.nytimes.com.

———. 2013b. "Supreme Court Rejects Challenge to Surveillance Law." *New York Times,* February 26. www.nytimes.com.

Liska, A. E., and S. F. Messner. 1999. *Perspectives on Crime and Deviance*. 3rd ed. Upper Saddle River, NJ: Prentice-Hall.

Listwan, S. J., C. J. Sullivan, R. Agnew, F. T. Cullen, and M Colvin. 2013. "The Pains of Imprisonment Revisited: The Impact of Strain on Inmate Recidivism." *Justice Quarterly* 30:144–68.

Listwan, S. J., M. Colvin, D. Hanley, and D. Flanner. 2010. "Victimization, Social Support, and Psychological Well-Being: A Study of Recently Released Prisoners." *Criminal Justice and Behavior* 37:1140–59.

Lithwick, D., and J. Turner. 2003. "A Guide to the Patriot Act, Part 4." *Slate,* September 11. slate.msn.com.

Loeffler, C. E. 2013. "Does Imprisonment Alter the Life Course? Evidence on Crime and Employment from a Natural Experiment." *Criminology* 51:137–66.

Loewen, B. 2013. "Jordan Johnson Acquitted of Rape." *Montana Kaimin*, March 1. www.montanakaimin.com.

Logan, C. 1993. "Criminal Justice Performance Measures in Prisons." In *Performance Measures for the Criminal Justice System*. Washington, DC: Bureau of Justice Statistics, 19–60.

Logan, C., and J. J. DiIulio Jr. 1993. "Ten Deadly Myths about Crime and Punishment in the United States." In *Criminal Justice: Law and Politics,* ed. G. F. Cole. Belmont, CA: Wadsworth, 486–502.

Lombroso, C. 1968 [1912]. *Crime: Its Causes and Remedies*. Montclair, NJ: Patterson Smith.

Londono, E. 2008. "US Steps Up Deportation of Immigrant Criminals," *Washington Post,* February 27, p. A01.

Long, J. 2014. "No Change of Venue Decision in Michael Dunn Retrial." *First Coast News*, September 8. www.firstcoastnews.com.

———. 2015. "Illinois Budget Cuts Jeopardize Juvenile Meth Treatment Program." KFVS News, March 19. kfvs12.com.

Lopez, C. 2010. "Disorderly (mis)Conduct: The Problem with 'Contempt of Cop' Arrests," *American Constitution Society Issue Brief,* June. Washington, DC: American Constitution Society.

Lord, R., and A. Anderson. 2014. "Pittsburgh Leads Way in Fighting Cybercrime." *Pittsburgh Post-Gazette* June 16. www.post-gazette.com.

Lord, V. B., and M. Sloop. 2010. "Suicide by Cop: Police Shooting as a Method of Self-Harming." *Journal of Criminal Justice* 38:889–95.

Lovett, I. 2012. "Public-Place Laws Tighten Rein on Sex Offenders." *New York Times*, May 29. www.nytimes.com.

Loviglio, J. 2002. "Judge Reverses Himself, Will Allow Fingerprint-Analysis Testimony." Associated Press Wire Service, March 13. Lexis-Nexis.

Lowenkamp, C. T., J. L. Johnson, A. M. Holsinger, S. W. VanBenschoten, and C. R. Robinson. 2012. "The Federal Post Conviction Risk Assessment (PCRA): A Construction and Validation Study." *Psychological Services*. http://www.apadivisions.org/division-18/publications/journals/index.aspx.

Luginbuhl, J., and M. Burkhead. 1994. "Sources of Bias and Arbitrariness in the Capital Trial." *Journal of Social Issues* 7:103–12.

Lum, C., C. Koper, and C. Telep. 2011. "The Evidence-Based Policing Matrix." *Journal of Experimental Criminology* 7:3–26.

Lum, C., C. W. Telep, C. S. Koper, and J. Grieco. 2012. "Receptivity to Research in Policing," *Justice Research and Policy* 14:61.

Lundman, R., and R. Kaufman. 2003. "Driving While Black: Effects of Race, Ethnicity, and Gender on Citizen Self-Reports of Traffic Stops and Police Actions." *Criminology* 41:195–220.

Lunney, L. A. 2009. "Has the Fourth Amendment Gone to the Dogs?: Unreasonable Expansion of Canine Sniff Doctrine to Include Sniffs of the Home." *Oregon Law Review* 88:829–903.

Luthern, A. 2014. "Police, Prosecutors Use New Tools to Help Domestic Violence Victims." *Milwaukee Journal Sentinel,* December 25. www.jsonline.com.

Lynch, D. 1999. "Perceived Judicial Hostility to Criminal Trials: Effects on Public Defenders in General and on Their Relationships with Clients and Prosecutors in Particular." *Criminal Justice and Behavior* 26:217–34.

Lynch, J. 1995. "Crime in International Perspective." In *Crime,* eds. J. Q. Wilson and J. Petersilia. San Francisco: ICS Press, 11–38.

Lynem, J. N. 2002. "Guards Call for Higher Wages, More Training: Industry Faces Annual Staff Turnover Rate of up to 300%." *San Francisco Chronicle,* August 22, p. B3.

MacArthur Foundation. 2007a. "Creating Turning Points for Serious Adolescent Offenders: Research on Pathways to Desistance" (Issue Brief 2, MacArthur Foundation Research Network on Adolescent Development and Juvenile Justice). Philadelphia: MacArthur Foundation.

———. 2007b. "Less Guilty by Reason of Adolescence" (Issue Brief 3, MacArthur Foundation Research Network on Adolescent Development and Juvenile Justice). Philadelphia: MacArthur Foundation.

———. 2007c. "The Changing Borders of Juvenile Justice: Transfer of Adolescents to Adult Criminal Court" (Issue Brief 5, MacArthur Foundation Research Network on Adolescent Development and Juvenile Justice). Philadelphia: MacArthur Foundation

MacCoun, R. J., A. Saiger, J. P. Kahan, and P. Reuter. 1993. "Drug Policies and Problems: The Promises and Pitfalls of Cross-National Comparisons." In *Psychoactive Drugs and Human Harm Reduction: From Faith to Science,* eds. N. Heather, E. Nadelman, and P. O'Hare. London: Whurr.

Mackey, R. 2010. "Somali Pirates Convicted in Virginia." *New York Times*, November 24. www.nytimes.com.

MacLean, C., and S. Wilks. 2012. "Keeping Arrows in the Quiver: Mapping the Contours of Prosecutorial Discretion." *Washburn Law Journal* 52:59–85.

Maddox, J. 2012. "Florida Teen Dead after Row That Began with Loud-Music Complaint, Suspect Jailed." CNN.com, November 26. www.cnn.com.

Maggi, L. 2005. "Courts Look at Indigent Defense." *New Orleans Times-Picayune,* April 14. www.nola.com.

Main, F., and N. Korecki. 2011. "Former SOS Cops Charged with Federal Civil Rights Violations," *Chicago Sun Times*, April 7. www.suntimes.com.

Maitland, A. S., and R. D. Sluder. 1998. "Victimization and Youthful Prison Inmates: An Empirical Analysis." *Prison Journal* 78:55–73.

Mallory, S. 2012. *Understanding Organized Crime.* 2nd ed. Sudbury, MA: Jones and Bartlett.

"Man Gets 1 Year for Making Fake Prescription Drugs." 2014. WMTV News, August 5. www.nbc15.com.

"Man Found Not Guilty in Father's Death." 2014. *Des Moines Register*, August 7. www.desmoinesresgister.com.

Mann, C. R. 1993. *Unequal Justice: A Question of Color*. Bloomington: Indiana University Press.

Mann, J. 2012. "St. Louis Jury Rejects Liability Suit against Taser." *St. Louis Post Dispatch*, December 13. www.stltoday.com.

———.2014. "Webster Groves Ballet Teacher Sentenced to 10 Years for Sex with Student." *St. Louis Post Dispatch*, July 7. www.stltoday.com.

Mannheimer, M. 2011. "Not the Crime but the Cover-Up: A Deterrence-Based Rationale for the Premeditation-Deliberation Formula." *Indiana Law Journal* 86:879–937.

Manning, A. 2012. "Local Officials Look to State to Pay Indigent-Defense Bills." *Columbus Dispatch,* February 26. www.dispatch.com.

Manning, P. K. 1977. *Police Work*. Cambridge, MA: MIT Press.

Mansker, N., and N. Devins. 2011. "Do Judicial Elections Facilitate Popular Constitutionalism? Can They? *Columbia Law Review Sidebar* 111:27–37.

Manza, J. and C. Uggen. 2006. *Locked Out: Felony Disenfranchisement and American Democracy*. New York: Oxford.

March, A. P. 2010. "Insanity in Alaska." *Georgetown Law Journal* 98:1481–514.

Margasak, L. 2006. "Guards Say Homeland Security HQ Insecure." Associated Press, March 6. www.sfgate.com.

———. 2007. "Ill-Trained, Underpaid Guard Terror Targets." Associated Press, May 29. news.aol.com.

Marimow, A. E. 2013. "John Hinckley Case Attorneys Debate Plans for Unsupervised Visits." *Washington Post*, January 24. www.washingtonpost.com.

Markoff, J. 2009. "Old Trick Threatens the Newest Weapons." *New York Times*, October 27. www.nytimes.com.

Markon, J. 2008. "FBI, ATF Battle for Control of Cases." *Washington Post*, May 10. www.washingtonpost.com.

Marley, P. 2013. "Prison Guards Equipped with Pepper Spray in Response to Inmate Assaults: Some State Corrections Supervisors Getting Tasers." *Milwaukee Journal Sentinel,* December 21. www.jsonline.com.

Marsh, J. R. 2001. "Reducing Unnecessary Detention: A Goal or Result of Pretrial Services?" *Federal Probation,* December, pp. 16–19.

"Martial Arts Teacher Sentenced for Sex with Teen." 2014. CBS Baltimore News online, August 13. http://baltimore.cbslocal.com.

Martin, J. S., K. Hanrahan, and J. H. Bowers. 2009. "Offenders' Perceptions of House Arrest and Electronic Monitoring." *Journal of Offender Rehabilitation* 48:547–70.

Martin, K. 2008. "The New Domestic Surveillance Regime: Ineffective Counterterrorism That Threatens Civil Liberties and Constitutional Separation of Powers." *Advance: The Journal of the American Constitution Society Issue Groups*. 2 (2): 51–61.

Martin, L. 2011. "Debt to Society: Asset Poverty and Prisoner Reentry." *Review of Black Political Economy* 38:131–143.

Martin, S. E. 2005. "Women Officers on the Move." In *Critical Issues in Policing,* 5th ed., eds. Roger G Dunham and Geoffrey P. Alpert. Long Grove, IL: Waveland Press.

Martinson, R. 1974. "What Works? Questions and Answers about Prison Reform." *Public Interest,* Spring, p. 25.

Maruschak, L. 2009. "HIV in Prisons, 2007–2008." NCJ 228307. Bureau of Justice Statistics *Bulletin,* December.

———. 2015. "HIV in Prisons, 2001–2010," Bureau of Justice Statistics *Bulletin* NCJ238877 (revised March 24, 2015).

Maruschak, L. M., and E. Parks. 2012. "Probation and Parole in the United States, 2011." NCJ 239686. Bureau of Justice Statistics *Bulletin*, November.

Mascaro, L. 2011. "Patriot Act Provisions Extended Just in Time." *Los Angeles Times*, May 27. www.latimes.com.

Maschke, K. J. 1995. "Prosecutors as Crime Creators: The Case of Prenatal Drug Use." *Criminal Justice Review* 20:21–33.

Mashhood, F., and C. O'Rourke. 2013. "State Funds for Crime Victim Services Organizations at Risk." *Austin American-Statesman*, January 2. www.statesman.com.

Maske, M. 2009. "Vick Heads Home for Confinement." *Washington Post*, May 21. www.washingtonpost.com.

Massey, B. 2011. "Chief Justice Appeals for New Mexico Court Budgets." Bloomberg News Service, January 25. www.bloomberg.com.

Mastrofski, S. D., M. D. Reisig, and J. D. McCluskey. 2002. "Police Disrespect toward the Public: An Encounter-Based Analysis." *Criminology* 40:519–52.

Mastrofski, S. D., and J. J. Willis. 2010. "Police Organization Continuity and Change: Into the Twenty-First Century." *Crime and Justice* 39:55–144.

Mastrofski, S. D., J. J. Willis, and J. B. Snipes. 2002. "Styles of Patrol in a Community Policing Context." In *The Move to Community Policing: Making Change Happen*, eds. M. Morash and J. Ford. Thousand Oaks, CA: Sage, 81–111.

Matthews, C. 2014. "The 10 Most Corrupt States in the U.S." *Fortune*. June 10. www.fortune.com.

Matthews, S. K. 2011. "Self-Complexity and Crime: Extending General Strain Theory." *Justice Quarterly* 28:863–902.

Maudsley, H. 1974. *Responsibility in Mental Disease*. London: Macmillan.

Mauer, M. 2011. "Opposing View: Reduce Prison Populations." *USA Today*, May 24. www.usatoday.com.

Mauer, M., and M. Chesney-Lind, eds. 2002. *Invisible Punishment: The Collateral Consequences of Mass Imprisonment*. New York: New Press.

Mawby, R., K. Boakye, and C. Jones. 2014. "Policing Tourism: The Emergence of Specialist Units." *Policing and Society*. Initial publication online at www.tandonline.com.

Maxwell, S. R. 1999. "Examining the Congruence between Predictors of ROR and Failures to Appear." *Journal of Criminal Justice* 27:127–41.

Maxwell, S. R., and C. Maxwell. 2000. "Examining the 'Criminal Careers' of Prostitutes within the Nexus of Drug Use, Drug Selling, and Other Illicit Activities." *Criminology* 38:787–809.

Mayhew, P., and J. J. M. van Dijk. 1997. *Criminal Victimisation in Eleven Industrial Countries*. The Hague, Netherlands: Dutch Ministry of Justice.

"Mayor Disagrees with Verdict in PPB Use-of-Force Suit." 2014. KGW.com, September 30. www.kgw.com.

McAuliff, B .D., and T. D. Duckworth. 2010. "I Spy with My Little Eye: Jurors' Detection of Internal Validity Threats in Expert Evidence." *Law and Human Behavior* 34:489–500.

McCannon, B. 2013. "Prosecutor Elections, Mistakes, and Appeals." *Journal of Empirical Legal Studies* 10:696–714.

McCampbell, S. W. 2005. *Gender Responsive Strategies for Women Offenders*. Washington, DC: National Institute of Corrections.

McCarthy, B. 2011. "Biggest Earners in New Orleans Police Details Are Often High-Ranking Officers Overseeing the Jobs." *New Orleans Times-Picayune*, May 15. www.nola.com.

McCarthy, J. 2014. "Most Americans Still See Crime Up over Last Year." Gallup Poll website. November 21. www.gallup.com.

McCartney, A. 2011. "Mel Gibson Pleads Guilty to Battery Charge of Ex-girlfriend." *Chicago Sun Times*, March 12. www.suntimes.com.

McConville, M. 2000. "Plea Bargaining: Ethics and Politics." In *The Judicial Role in Criminal Proceedings*, ed. Sean Doran and John Jackson. Oxford, England: Hart, 67–91.

McCormack, S. 2015. "Demographics of North Charleston Police Department Tell a Familiar Story." *Huffington Post*, April 8. www.huffingtonpost.com.

McCoy, C. 1993. *Politics and Plea Bargaining: Victims' Rights in California*. Philadelphia: University of Pennsylvania Press.

———. 1995. "Is the Trial Penalty Inevitable?" Paper presented at the annual meeting of the Law and Society Association, Phoenix, Arizona, June.

McCullagh, D. 2010. "Feds Admit Storing Checkpoint Body Scan Images." CNET News, August 4. news.cnet.com.

McGarrell, E., S. Chermak, A. Weiss, and J. Wilson. 2001. "Reducing Firearms Violence through Directed Police Patrol." *Criminology & Public Policy* 1:119–48.

McGraw, S. and T. Gabriel. 2014. "Answers Still Elusive after Arrest of Eric Frein in Killing of State Trooper." *New York Times*, October 31. www.nytimes.com.

McKee, K. 2015. "Neighbors Say 'Not In My Neighborhood' to Amelia Island Halfway House," *Action News Jacksonville*. March 18. www.actionnewsjax.com.

McKelvey, B. 1977. *American Prisons*. Montclair, NJ: Patterson Smith.

McKendrick, J. 2013. "10 Most Stressful and 10 Least Stressful Jobs of 2013." Smart Planet website, February 19. www.smartplanet.com/blog/bulletin/10-most-stressful-and-10-least-stressful-jobs-of-2013/13177.

McKinley, J. 2014. "Study Finds Racial Disparity in Criminal Prosecutions." *New York Times*, July 8. www.nytimes.com.

McLamb, S. 2011. "State Bill Proposes Sales Ban on Bullet Proof Vests to Citizens." WBTV-TV, March 30. www.wbtv.com.

McLaughlin, M. 2014. "Seattle Pacific University Shooting Leaves at Least 1 Dead." *Huffington Post*, June 5. http://huffingtonpost.com.

McMahon, P. 2002. "311 Lightens Load for Swamped 911 Centers." *USA Today*, March 5. www.usatoday.com.

McNamara, P. 2015. "Budget Cuts Threaten Pima County Court Programs." Tuscon.com, March 30.

McNulty, T. L., and P. E. Bellair. 2003. "Explaining Racial and Ethnic Differences in Adolescent Violence: Structural Disadvantage, Family Well-Being, and Social Capital." *Justice Quarterly* 20:1–31.

McVicker, S. 2005. "Officer Downloads Driver's Nude Photos off Phone." *Houston Chronicle*, March 25. www.chron.com.

Meade, B., and B. Steiner. 2010. "The Total Effects of Boot Camps that House Juveniles: A Systematic Review of the Evidence." *Journal of Criminal Justice* 38:841–53.

Meese, E., and P. J. Larkin. 2012. "Reconsidering the Mistake of Law Defense." *Journal of Criminal Law and Criminology* 102:725–84.

Meier, R. F., and T. D. Miethe. 1993. "Understanding Theories of Criminal Victimization." In *Crime and Justice: A Review of Research*, ed. M. Tonry. Chicago: University of Chicago Press.

Melde, C., M. T. Berg, and F. Esbensen. 2014. "Fear, Social Interactions, and Violence Migration." *Justice Quarterly* (ahead-of-print), 1–29.

Melde, C., F. Esbensen, and T. J. Taylor. 2009. "'May Piece Be with You': A Typological Examination of the Fear and Victimization Hypothesis of Adolescent Weapon Carrying." *Justice Quarterly* 26:348–76.

Melendez, L. 2011. "BART's Citizen Review Board Questions SFPD Investigation." KGO-TV website, September 19. abclocal.go.com/kgo.

———. 2014. "SF Celebrates First Year of Vet Court." KGO-TV website, March 5. http://abclocal.go.com/kgo/story?section=news/local/san_francisco&id=9456255

Mentzer, A. 1996. "Policing in Indian Country: Understanding State Jurisdiction and Authority." *Law and Order* (June): 24–9.

Merianos, D. E., J. W. Marquart, and K. Damphousse. 1997. "From the Outside In: Using Public Health Data to Make Inferences about Older Inmates." *Crime & Delinquency* 43 (July): 298–314.

Messerschmidt, J. W. 1993. *Masculinities and Crime: Critique and Reconceptualization of Theory*. Lanham, MD: Rowman & Littlefield.

Messner, S. F., and R. Rosenfeld. 2006. *Crime and the American Dream*. 4th ed. Belmont, CA: Wadsworth.

Messner, S. F., S. Galea, K. J. Tardiff, M. Tracy, A. Bucciarelli, T. M. Piper, V. Frye, and D. Vlahov. 2007. "Policing, Drugs, and the Homicide Decline in New York City in the 1990s." *Criminology* 45:385–413.

Meyer, J. 2008. "LAPD Leads the Way in Local Counter-Terrorism." *Los Angeles Times*, April 14. www.latimes.com.

Michigan Department of Corrections. 2015. "Detroit Reentry Center (DRC)." www.michigan.gov/corrections.

Miethe, T. D. 1985. "The Myth and Reality of Victim Involvement in Crime: A Review and Comment on Victim-Precipitation Research." *Sociological Focus* 18:209–20.

———. 1995. "Fear and Withdrawal from Urban Life." *Annals of the American Academy of Political and Social Science* 539 (May): 14–27.

Mihm, S. 2006. "No Ordinary Counterfeit." *New York Times*, July 23. www.nytimes.com.

Miller, C., M. Klas, and G. Fineout. 2006. "Violent End Revealed," *Miami Herald*, February 18. www.miamiherald.com.

Miller, J. L., and J. J. Sloan. 1994. "A Study of Criminal Justice Discretion." *Journal of Criminal Justice* 22:107–23.

Miller, M., and M. Guggenheim. 1990. "Pretrial Detention and Punishment." *Minnesota Law Review* 75:335–426.

Miller, M. K., D. M. Flores, and A. N. Dolezilek. 2007. "Addressing the Problem of Courtroom Stress." *Judicature* 91:60–9.

Miller, S. 2013. "Michigan Budget Cuts Lead to Police Lay Offs, Less Training." *Central Michigan Life*, January 7. www.cm-life.com.

Miller, S. L, K. Zielaskowski, and E. A. Plant. 2012. "The Basis of Shooter Biases: Beyond Cultural Stereotypes." *Personality and Social Psychology Bulletin* 38:1358–66.

Milloy. 2000. "Judge Frees Texas Inmate Whose Lawyer Slept at Trial," *New York Times*, March 2, p. A19.

Mills, D. 2011. "Governor's Budget Would Impact Prison, Probation Systems." *Livermore Patch*, January 12. livermore.patch.com.

Minnesota Department of Corrections. 2015. "Adult Facilities." Department of Corrections website. www.doc.state.mn.us.

Minton, T., and D. Golinelli. 2014. *Jail Inmates at Midyear 2013: Statistical Tables*. NCJ 245350. Washington, D.C.: U.S. Bureau of Justice Statistics.

Minton, T. D. 2011. *Jail Inmates at Midyear 2010: Statistical Tables*. Washington, DC: U.S. Bureau of Justice Statistics.

Miroff, N. 2008."Detainee Program Strains Va. Jail," *Washington Post*, April 8, p. A01.

Misjak, L. 2013. "Police Interview Tossed in Child Death Case." *Lansing State Journal,* March 1, p. 3A.

Moffitt, T. 1993. "Adolescence-Limited and Life-Course-Persistent Antisocial Behavior: A Developmental Taxonomy." *Psychology Review*, 100(4): 674–701.

Mongrain, S., and J. Roberts. 2009. "Plea Bargaining with Budgetary Constraints." *International Review of Law and Economics* 29:8–12.

Monkkonen, E. H. 1981. *Police in Urban America, 1869–1920*. Cambridge, England: Cambridge University Press.

———. 1992. "History of the Urban Police." In *Modern Policing,* eds. M. Tonry and N. Morris. Chicago: University of Chicago Press, 547–80.

Moore, M. 1992. "Problem-Solving and Community Policing." In *Modern Policing,* ed. M. Tonry and N. Morris. Chicago: University of Chicago Press, 99–158.

Moore, M., and G. L. Kelling. 1983. "To Serve and to Protect: Learning from Police History." *Public Interest,* Winter, p. 55.

Moore, S. 2009. "Number of Life Terms Hits Record." *New York Times*, July 22. www.nytimes.com.

Moore, T. 2011. "'East Coast Rapist' Caught, Officials Say after Man's DNA Linked to Spree of Sex Assaults." *New York Daily News*, March 5. www.dailynews.com.

Moran, D. 2014. "On DNA, Prosecutors Can't Handle the Truth." *Detroit News,* October 13. www.detroitnews.com.

Morash, M., and J. K. Ford, eds. 2002. *The Move to Community Policing: Making Change Happen*. Thousand Oaks, CA: Sage.

Morash, M., J. K. Ford, J. P. White, and J. G. Boles. 2002. "Directing the Future of Community-Policing Initiatives." In *The Move to Community Policing: Making Change Happen,* ed. M. Morash and J. Ford. Thousand Oaks, CA: Sage, 277–88.

Morash, M., and R. N. Haarr. 2012. "Doing, Redoing, and Undoing Gender: Variation in Gender Identities of Women Working as Police Officers." *Feminist Criminology* 7:3–23.

Morash, M., R. N. Haarr, and L. Rucker. 1994. "A Comparison of Programming for Women and Men in the US Prisons in the 1980s." *Crime & Delinquency* 40 (April): 197–221.

Morgan, D. 2013. "Impressed by Fairfield Police Crisis Intervention Team." *Connecticut Post,* February 20. www.ctpost.com/opinion/article/Impressed-by-Fairfield-Police-Crisis-Intervention-4294457.php.

Moroney, N. 2014. "Juvenile Justice Monitoring Unit, 2013 Annual Report." Baltimore, MD: Office of the Attorney General.

Morris, N., and M. Tonry. 1990. *Between Prison and Probation: Intermediate Punishments in a Rational Sentencing System*. New York: Oxford University Press.

Mosher, C., T. Miethe, and D. Phillips. 2002. *The Mismeasure of Crime*. Thousand Oaks, CA: Sage.

Mueller, R .S. 2008. "Statement of FBI Director before the House Judiciary Committee," (April 23). www.fbi.gov.

———. 2011. "FBI Director Statement before the Senate Committee on Appropriations, Subcommittee on Commerce, Justice, Science, and Related Agencies," April 7. www.fbi.gov.

Muftic, L. R., and D. E. Hunt. 2012. "Victim Precipitation: Further Understanding the Linkage between Victimization and Offending in Homicide." *Homicide Studies,* October 11. hsx.sagepub.com/content/early/2012/10/09/1088767912461785.abstract.

Mumola, C. J. 2005. "Suicide and Homicide in State Prisons and Local Jails." NCJ 210036. Bureau of Justice Statistics, *Special Report,* August.

Murphy, C. 2014. "Police Chief Discusses Millions in Budget Cuts to Department." Fox10 TV, March 17. Fox10tv.com.

Murphy, P. V. 1992. "Organizing for Community Policing." In *Issues in Policing: New Perspectives,* ed. J. W. Bizzack. Lexington, KY: Autumn Press, 113–28.

———. 2013. "John Hinckley, Who Shot Reagan, Seeks More Time at Mom's House." *Los Angeles Times*, February 25. www.latimes.com.

Na, C., and D. Gottfredson. 2013. "Police Officers in Schools: Effects on School Crime and the Processing of Offending Behaviors." *Justice Quarterly* 30 (4):619–50.

Nakamura, D. 2011. "Obama Signs Defense Bill, Pledges to Maintain Legal Rights of US Citizens." *Washington Post*, December 31. www.washingtonpost.com.

Nakashima, E., and A. Peterson. 2014. "Report: Cybercrime and Espionage Costs $445 Billion Annually." *Washington Post*, June 9. www.washingtonpost.com.

Nalla, M. 2002. "Common Practices and Functions of Corporate Security: A Comparison of Chemical, Financial, Manufacturing, Service, and Utility Industries." *Journal of Security Administration* 25:33–46.

Nardulli, P. F. 1986. "Insider Justice: Defense Attorneys and the Handling of Felony Cases." *Journal of Criminal Law and Criminology* 79:379–417.

National Association of Women Judges. 2014. "2013 Representation of United States State Court Women Judges." http://www.nawj.org/us_state_court_statistics_2013.asp.

National Public Radio. 2011. "Nation's Jails Struggle with Mentally Ill Prisoners." *All Things Considered* website, September 4. www.npr.org.

Nelson, A. J. 2014. "Judge Commits Teen to Psych Unit." *Omaha World-Herald*, December 9. www.omaha.com.

"New Cyberbullying Law Generates First Juvenile Sentence in Union County." *Suburban News*. July 29. http://www.nj.com/suburbannews/index.ssf/2014/07/new_cyberbullying_law_generate.html.

"New NYCLU Report Finds NYPD Stop-and-Frisk Practices Ineffective, Reveals Depth of Racial Disparities." 2012. New York Civil Liberties Union website. www.nyclu.org.

New York Division of Criminal Justice Services. 2013. "Police Employment Police Basic Court FAQ." New York Division of Criminal Justice Services website. www.criminaljustice.ny.gov/ops/training/bcpo/bcpo05.htm#furthertraining.

New York State Division of Criminal Justice Services. 2008. *New York State Probation Population: 2007 Profile*. Albany, NY: New York State Division of Criminal Justice Services, June.

Newman, J. 2012. "Drunk Security Contractors in Afghanistan? Again?" *Huffington Post,* October 19. www.huffingtonpost.com/joe-newman/afghanistan-drunk-contractors_b_1989290.html.

Newport, F. 2013. "Americans Unsure if Best Times for US Are Past or to Come." Gallup Poll, January 2. www.gallup.com.

Nicholas, S. C. Kershaw, and A. Walker. 2007. "Crime in England and Wales, 2006/7." *Home Office Statistical Bulletin*. London: UK Home Office. www.homeoffice.gov.uk.

Nixon, A. A. 2015. "Governor Proposes Cuts in Prison Education Program." *VTDigger.org*, January 28. www.vtdigger.org.

Nixon, R. 2012. "New Law Clears the Way for Airports to Drop TSA Screeners." *New York Times*, March 15. www.nytimes.com.

Noble, R. K. 2006. "All Terrorism Is Local, Too." *New York Times*, August 13. www.nytimes.com.

Noblet, A., J. Rodwell, and A. Allisey. 2009. "Job Stress in the Law Enforcement Sector: Comparing the Linear, Non-linear, and Interaction Effects of Working Conditions." *Stress and Health* 25:111–20.

Nolan, J. 2003. "Redefining Criminal Courts: Problem-Solving and the Meaning of Justice." *American Criminal Law Review* 40:1541–66.

Nolan, J. L. 2010. "Drug Treatment and Problem-Solving Courts in Comparative Perspective." *Journal of Health Care Law and Policy* 13:31–47.

Noonan, M. 2013. "Mortality in Local Jails and State Prisons, 2000-2011." *Bureau of Justice Statistics Statistical Tables,* NCJ 242186.

Norris, F. 2011. "After Years of Red Flags, a Conviction." *New York Times*, April 21. www.nytimes.com.

North Carolina Department of Public Safety. 2014. "24 Hours in Prison." North Carolina Department of Public Safety Website. http://www.doc.state.nc.us/DOP/HOURS24.htm.

Nowlin, J. W. 2012. "The Warren Court's House Built on Sand: From Security in Persons, Houses, Papers, and Effects to Mere Reasonableness in Fourth Amendment Doctrine." *Mississippi Law Journal* 81:1017–82.

"Obama's Speech on N.S.A. Phone Surveillance." 2014. *New York Times*, January 17. www.nytimes.com.

Oberfield, Z. W. 2012. "Socialization and Self-Selection: How Police Develop Their Views about Using Force." *Administration and Society* 44:702–30.

O'Brien, A., and K, Thom. 2014. "Police Use of TASER Devices in Mental Health Emergencies: A Review." *International Journal of Law and Psychiatry* 37:420–26.

O'Brien, B. 2009. "A Recipe for Bias: An Empirical Look at the Interplay between Institutional Incentives and Bounded Reality in Prosecutorial Decision Making." *Missouri Law Review* 74:999–1048.

Odegard, Kyle. 2015. "New Chief, New Programs for Albany Police." *Albany* (OR) *Democrat-Herald*, February 1. http://democratherald.com.

Office on Drug Control Policy. 2006. *Iowa's Drug Control Strategy, 2006*. http://www.iowa.gov/odcp/images/pdf/Strategy_06.pdf.

Offices of the United States Attorneys. n.d. "Annual Statistical Reports." http://justice.gov.

Ofgang, K. 2013. "Governor Brown's 'Crippling' Budget Cuts to Force Court to Go Ahead head with Shutdown Plans." *Metropolitan News Enterprise*, January 14. www.metnews.com/articles/2013/cour011413.htm.

Ogletree, C. J., Jr., M. Prosser, A. Smith, and W. Talley Jr. 1995. *Beyond the Rodney King Story: An Investigation of Police Misconduct in Minority*

Communities. Boston: Northeastern University Press.

O'Harrow, R. 2008. "Centers Tap into Personal Databases." *Washington Post*, April 2. www.washingtonpost.com.

O'Harrow, R., S. Horwitz, and S. Rich. 2015. "Holder Limits Seized-Asset Sharing Process that Split Billions with Local, State Police." *Washington Post*, January 16. www.washingtonpost.com.

O'Harrow, R., and S. Rich. 2014. "Asset Seizures Fuel Police Spending." *Washington Post*, October 11. www.washingtonpost.com.

O'Hear, M. M. 2006. "The End of *Bordenkircher*: Extending the Logic of *Apprendi* to Plea Bargaining." *Washington University Law Review* 84:835–49.

———. 2007. "Plea Bargaining and Victims: From Consultation to Guidelines." *Marquette Law Review* 91:323–47.

———. 2008. "Plea Bargaining and Procedural Justice." *Georgia Law Review* 42:407–15.

Okada, Y. 2006. "Lay Participation in Japanese Criminal Trials and Citizens' Attitudes toward the Legal Profession." Paper presented at the annual meeting of the American Society of Criminology. Los Angeles, CA.

O'Keefe, K. 2010. "Two Wrongs Make a Wrong: A Challenge to Plea Bargaining and Collateral Consequence Statutes through Their Integration." *Journal of Criminal Law and Criminology* 100:243–77.

Oklahoma Department of Corrections. 2011. "Facts at a Glance," March 31. www.doc.state.ok.us.

Oklahoma Department of Corrections. 2015. Oklahoma Department of Corrections website. http://www.ok.gov/doc/Facilities.html.

Oleniacz, L. 2014. "Durham Minor Misdemeanor Diversion Program Launches for 16, 17-year-olds." *Herald Sun*, April 4. Heraldsun.com.

Oleson, J. C., M. Van Nostrand, C. T. Lowenkamp, T. Cardigan, and J.Woodredge. 2014. "Pretrial Detention Choices and Federal Sentencing." *Federal Probation* (June issue), 78:12–18.

Olivares, K., V. Burton, and F. Cullen. 1996. "The Collateral Consequences of a Felony Conviction: A National Study of State Legal Codes Ten Years Later." *Federal Probation* 60:10–8.

Oliver, W. M. 2002."9-11, Federal Crime Control Policy, and Unintended Consequences." *ACJS Today* 22 (September–October): 1–6.

Oppel, R. A. 2011. "Private Prisons Found to Offer Little in Savings." *New York Times*, May 18. www.nytimes.com.

Oppel, R. 2011. "Sentencing Shift Gives New Leverage to Prosecutors." *New York Times*, September 25. www.nytimes.com.

Ordonez, F. 2011. "Charlotte Expanding Officer Recruiting." *Charlotte Observer*, May 15. www.charlotteobserver.com.

Orlov, Rick. 2014. "Los Angeles Raids on Illegal Prescription Drugs to be Stepped Up." *Los Angeles Daily News*, October 2. www.dailynews.com.

Oshinsky, D. 2010. *Capital Punishment on Trial:* Furman v. Georgia *and the Death Penalty in Modern America*. Lawrence: University Press of Kansas.

Osowski, C. 2014. "Accused Movie Theater Shooter, Curtis Reeves, Heads Back to Pasco Court." News Channel 8 online, November 19, 2014. www.wfla.com.

Ostermann, M. 2009. "An Analysis of New Jersey's Day Reporting Center and Halfway Back Program: Embracing the Rehabilitative Ideal through Evidence-Based Practices," *Journal of Offender Rehabilitation* 48:139–53.

Otto, C. W., B. K. Applegate, and R. K. Davis. 2007. "Improving Comprehension of Capital Sentencing Instructions: Debunking Juror Misconceptions." *Crime & Delinquency* 53:502–17.

"Our View: Don't Just Cut Prisoners Loose" 2011. [Editorial]. *USA Today*, May 24. www.usatoday.com.

Owen, B. 1998. *"In the Mix": Struggle and Survival in a Woman's Prison*. Albany: State University of New York Press.

Owen, B., J. Wells, J. Pollock, B. Muscat, and S. Torres. 2008. *Gendered Violence and Safety: A Contextual Approach to Improving Security in Women's Facilities*. Report prepared for the U.S. Department of Justice. http://www.prearesourcecenter.org/sites/default/files/library/105-genderedviolenceandsafetyfinalreportnovember2008.pdf.

Owens, E. 2009. "More Time, Less Crime? Estimating the Incapacitative Effects of Sentence Enhancements." *Journal of Law and Economics* 52:551–73.

Oxley, J. C. 2014. "Explosive Detection: How We Got Here and Where Are We Going?" *International Journal of Energetic Materials and Chemical Propulsion* 13:373–81.

Packer, H. L. 1968. *The Limits of the Criminal Sanction*. Stanford, CA: Stanford University Press.

Palmer, B. 2011. "Oklahoma's Female Inmate Population Skyrockets." *Oklahoman*, January 30. newsok.com.

Palmer, T. 1992. *The Re-emergence of Correctional Intervention*. Newbury Park, CA: Sage.

Paoline, E., and W. Terrill. 2007. "Police Education, Experience, and the Use of Force." *Criminal Justice and Behavior* 34:179–96.

Parent, D. 2003 *Correctional Boot Camps: Lessons from a Decade of Research*. Washington, DC: National Institute of Justice.

"Parolee Arrested Again on Drug Trafficking Charges." 2015. *Central Kentucky News*, March 25. www.centralkynews.com.

"Parolee Arrested for Attempted Murder of Acquaintance Made While in Prison." 2013. *Salt Lake Tribune*, March 13. www.sltrib.com.

Patterson, D. 2011. "The Impact of Detectives' Manner of Questioning on Rape Victims' Disclosure." *Violence against Women* 17:1349–73.

Peart, N. 2011. "Why Is the NYPD after Me?" *New York Times*, December 17. www.nytimes.com.

"Perdue OKs Bill to Expand Use." 2008. *Augusta (GA) Chronicle*, May 8. chronicle.augusta.com.

Perrine, J., V. Speirs, and J. Horwitz. 2010. "Fusion Centers and the Fourth Amendment." *Capital University Law Review* 38:721–87.

Peters, T. 1992. *Liberation Management*. New York: Knopf.

Petersilia, J. 1990. "When Probation Becomes More Dreaded than Prison." *Federal Probation*, March, p. 24.

———. 1996. "A Crime Control Rationale for Reinvesting in Community Corrections." *Perspectives* 20 (Spring): 21–29.

———. 2009. *When Prisoners Come Home: Parole and Prisoner Reentry*. New York: Oxford University Press.

Peterson, A., E. Yahr, and J. Warrick. 2014. "Leaks of Nude Celebrity Photos Raise Concerns about Security of the Cloud." *Washington Post*, September 1. www.washingtonpost.com

Peterson, M. 2005. *Intelligence-Led Policing: The New Intelligence Architecture*. Washington, DC: U.S. Bureau of Justice Assistance.

Peterson, R. 2012. "The Central Place of Race in Crime and Justice." *Criminology* 50:303–27.

Petteruti, A., and N. Walsh. 2008. *Jailing Communities: The Impact of Jail Expansion and Effective Public Safety Strategies*. Washington, DC: Justice Policy Institute.

Pew Center on the States. 2009. *One in 31: The Long Reach of American Corrections*. Washington, DC: Pew Charitable Trusts.

———. 2011. *State of Recidivism: The Revolving Door of America's Prisons*. Washington, DC: Pew Charitable Trusts.

———. 2013. "More Than Half of States Cut Imprisonment Rates from 2006 to 2011." Press Release, March 8. www.pewstates.org

Pew Charitable Trusts. 2012. *Public Opinion on Sentencing and Corrections Policy in America*, March. www.pewstates.org/research/analysis/public-opinion-on-sentencing-and-corrections-policy-in-america-85899380361.

———. 2013. *Managing Prison Health Care Spending*. Washington, D.C.: The Pew Charitable Trusts. www.pewstates.org.

Phelps, M. S. 2013. "The Paradox of Probation: Community Supervision in the Age of Mass Incarceration." *Law and Policy* 35:51–80.

Phillips, S. 1977. *No Heroes, No Villains*. New York: Random House.

Pickett, J. T., T. Chiricos, K. M. Golden, and M. Gertz. 2012. "Reconsidering the Relationship between Perceived Neighborhood Racial Composition and Whites' Perceptions of Victimization Risk: Do Racial Stereotypes Matter?" *Criminology* 50:145–86.

Pickett, J. T., D. Tope, and R. Bellandi. 2014. "Taking Back Our Country': Tea Party Membership and Support for Punitive Crime Control Policies." *Sociological Inquiry* 84:167–90.

Pinguelo, F. M., W. Lee, and B. W. Muller. 2012. "Virtual Crimes, Real Damages Part II: What Businesses Can Do Today to Protect Themselves from Cybercrime, and What Public–Private Partnerships Are Attempting to Achieve for the Nation Tomorrow." *Virginia Journal of Law and Technology* 17:75–88.

Pinkerton, J. 2011. "Shootings by Officers Down in '10." *Houston Chronicle*, January 17. www.chron.com.

Pisciotta, A. W. 1994. *Benevolent Repression: Social Control and the American Reformatory-Prison Movement*. New York: New York University Press.

Pizzi, W. T., and M. B. Hoffman. 2001. "Jury Selection Errors on Appeal." *American Criminal Law Review* 38:1391–442.

Place, T. 2013. "Closing Direct Appeal to Ineffectiveness Claims: The Supreme Court of Pennsylvania's Denial of State Constitutional Rights." *Widener Law Journal* 22:687–719.

Platt, A. 1977. *The Child Savers*. 2nd ed. Chicago: University of Chicago Press.

Podgor, E. 2010. "The Tainted Federal Prosecutor in an Overcriminalized Justice System." *Washington and Lee Law Review* 67:1569–85.

"Police: Drug-Laden Drone Crashes Near U.S.-Mexico Border." CBS-Los Angeles website, January 21. http://losangeles.cbslocal.com/2015/01/21/police-drug-laden-drone-crashes-near-u-s-mexico-border/.

"Police: Man Fired 100-Plus Rounds Downtown." 2014. *Victoria* (TX) *Advocate*. November 28. www.victoriaadvocate.com.

"Police Officer Acquitted in 95-Year-Old's Beanbag Gun Death." 2015. My FOX Chicago News. February 4. www.myfoxchicago.com.

"Police Silence Fuels Distrust." 2015. *Daytona Beach* (FL) *News Journal*, January 28. www.news-journalonline.com.

Ponulo, J. D., J. Dempsey, E. Maeder, and L. Allen. 2010. "The Effects of Victim Gender, Defendant Gender, and Defendant Age on

Juror Decision Making." *Criminal Justice and Behavior* 37:47–63.
Porter, R, S. Lee, and M. Lutz. 2002. *Balancing Punishment and Treatment: Alternatives to Incarceration in New York City.* New York: Vera Institute of Justice.
Poston, B. 2012. "Crimes Underreported by Police Include Robbery, Rape." *Milwaukee Journal Sentinel,* August 25. www.jsonline.com.
Pransky, N. 2015. "Officers Say Corrections Cuts Keep Them Off the Road." *Florida Today,* March 23. www.floridatoday.com.
Pratt, T. C., and J. Maahs. 1999. "Are Private Prisons More Cost Effective Than Public Prisons? A Meta-analysis of Evaluation Research Studies." *Crime & Delinquency* 45 (July): 358–71.
Preller, A. E. 2012. "Jury Duty Is a Poll Tax: The Case for Severing the Link between Voter Registration and Jury Service." *Columbia Journal of Law and Social Problems* 46:1–42.
President's Commission on Law Enforcement and the Administration of Justice. 1967. *The Challenge of Crime in a Free Society*. Washington, DC: U.S. Government Printing Office.
Press, E. 2006. "Do Immigrants Make Us Safer?" *New York Times Magazine*, December 3, pp. 20–4.
Preston, J. 2005. "Rape Victims' Eyes Were Covered, but a Key Clue Survived." *New York Times,* April 28. www.nytimes.com.
———. 2008. "270 Illegal Immigrants Sent to Prison in Federal Push," *New York Times*, May 24, p. A1.
Price, M. 2009. "Performing Discretion or Performing Discrimination: Race, Ritual, and Peremptory Challenges in Capital Jury Selection." *Michigan Journal of Race and Law* 15:57–107.
Primus, E. B. 2010. "A Structural Vision of Habeas Corpus." *California Law Review* 98:1–57.
"Private Jails: Locking in the Best Price." 2007. *Economist*, January 25. www.economist.com /node/8599146.
Propper, A. 1982. "Make-Believe Families and Homosexuality among Imprisoned Girls." *Criminology* 20:127–39.
Provine, D. M. 1996. "Courts in the Political Process in France." In *Courts, Law, and Politics in Comparative Perspective,* eds. H. Jacob, E. Blankenburg, H. Kritzer, D. M. Provine, and J. Sanders. New Haven, CT: Yale University Press, 177–248.
Prussel, D., and K. Lonsway. 2001. "Recruiting Women Police Officers." *Law and Order* 49 (July): 91–6.
Puzzanchera, C. 2014. *Juvenile Arrests 2012*. Washington, DC: Office of Juvenile Justice and Delinquency Prevention.
Puzzanchera, C., and S. Addie. 2014. "Delinquency Cases Waived to Adult Court, 2010." Juvenile Offenders and Victims Fact Sheet. NCJ 243042. Washington, DC: Office of Juvenile Justice and Delinquency Prevention.
Quandt, K. 2015. "1 in 13 African-American Adults Prohibited from Voting in the United States." Moyers & Company, March 24. www .billmoyers.com.
Quesada, M.. 2014. Questions Linger after Michael Dunn First Degree Murder Mistrial." *First Coast News*, February 16, 2014. www.firstcoastnews .com.
Radelet, M. L. 2004. "Post-*Furman* Botched Executions." www.deathpenaltyinfor.org /article.php?scid=8&did =478.
Radelet, M. L., H. A. Bedeau, and C. E. Putnam. 1992. *In Spite of Innocence*. Boston: Northeastern University Press.
Radelet, M. L., W. S. Lofquist, and H. A. Bedau. 1996. "Prisoners Released from Death Rows since 1970 Because of Doubts about Their Guilt." *Thomas M. Cooley Law Review* 13:907–66.
Radford, D. 2010. "County Budget Cuts Threaten Services for Victims of Domestic Violence, Sexual Assault." *Renton Reporter*, September 23. www.pnwlocalnews.com.
Raeder, M. 2009. "Post-conviction Claims of Innocence." *Criminal Justice* 24:14–26.
Rafter, N. H. 1983. "Prisons for Women, 1790–1980." In *Crime and Justice,* 5th ed., eds. M. Tonry and N. Morris. Chicago: University of Chicago Press.
Rainville, G., and S. Smith. 2003. "Juvenile Felony Defendants in Criminal Courts." NCJ 197961. Bureau of Justice Statistics, *Special Report*, May.
Ramos, N. (2014). "Maine Philanthropist Accused of Embezzling $3.8M." *Boston Globe*, November 16. www.bostonglobe.com.
Ramsey, R. J., and J. Frank. 2007. "Perceptions of Criminal Justice Professionals Regarding the Frequency of Wrongful Conviction and the Extent of System Errors." *Crime & Delinquency* 53:436–70.
Rand, M. R., and J. E. Robinson. 2011. *Criminal Victimization in the United States, 2008—Statistical Tables*, May. NCJ 231137.
Randolph, E. D. 2001. "Inland Police Like New Weaponry." *Riverside* (CA) *Press-Enterprise,* November 24, p. B4.
Ratcliffe, J., T. Taniguchi, E. Groff, and J. Wood. 2011. "The Philadelphia Foot Patrol Experiment: A Randomized Controlled Trial of Police Patrol Effectiveness in Violent Crime Hotspots." *Criminology* 49:795–831.
Ratcliffe, J. H., T. Taniguchi, and R. B. Taylor. 2009. "The Crime Reduction Effects of Public CCTV Cameras: A Multi-method Approach." *Justice Quarterly* 26:746–70.
Reaves, B. 2006. "Violent Felons in Large Urban Counties." NCJ 205289. Bureau of Justice Statistics, *Special Report*, July.
———.2011. "Census of State and Local Law Enforcement Agencies, 2008." NCJ233982. Bureau of Justice Statistics *Bulletin,* July.
———. 2012. "Federal Law Enforcement Officers, 2008." NCJ238250. Bureau of Justice Statistics *Bulletin,* June.
———. 2013. "Felony Defendants in Large Urban Counties, 2009: Statistical Tables." NCJ 243777. Bureau of Justice Statistics *Bulletin*, December.
Reaves, B. A. 2010. *Local Police Departments, 2007.* Washington, DC: U.S. Bureau of Justice Statistics.
Reaves, T. 2012. "Cabarrus County Settles $1 Million Taser Lawsuit." *Kannapolis* (NC) *Independent Tribune*, December 28. www.hickoryrecord.com.
Redding, R. E. 2010. Juvenile Transfer Laws: An Effective Deterrent to Delinquency?" *Juvenile Justice Bulletin,* June. Washington, DC: Office of Juvenile Justice and Delinquency Programs.
Redlich, A., S. Liu, H. Steadman, L. Callahan, and P. Robbins. 2012. "Is Diversion Swift? Comparing Mental Health Court and Traditional Criminal Justice Processing." *Criminal Justice and Behavior* 39:420–33.
Redlich, A. D., A Summers, and S. Hoover. 2010. "Self-Reported False Confessions and False Guilty Pleas among Offenders with Mental Illness." *Law and Human Behavior* 34:79–90.
Regan, P., and T. Monahan. 2014. "Fusion Accountability and Intergovernmental Information Sharing." *Publius: The Journal of Federalism* 44:475–98.
Regoli, R. M., J. P. Crank, and R.G. Culbertson. 1987. "Rejoinder—Police Cynicism: Theory Development and Reconstruction." *Justice Quarterly* 4:281–86.
Regoli, R. M., and J. D. Hewitt. 1994. *Criminal Justice*. Englewood Cliffs, NJ: Prentice- Hall.
Reichers, L. M., and R. R. Roberg. 1990. "Community Policing: A Critical Review of Underlying Assumptions." *Journal of Police Science and Administration* 17:105–14.
Reid, T. V. 1996. "PAC Participation in North Carolina Supreme Court Elections." *Judicature* 80:21–5.
———. 2000. "The Politicization of Judicial Retention Elections: The Defeat of Justices Lamphier and White." In *Research on Judicial Selection 1999*. Chicago: American Judicature Society, 45–72.
———. 2004. "Assessing the Impact of a Candidate's Sex in Judicial Campaigns and Elections in North Carolina." *Justice System Journal* 25 (2): 183–207.
Reiman, J. 1996. . . . *And the Poor Get Prison: Economic Bias in American Criminal Justice*. Boston: Allyn & Bacon.
Reinert, A. 2012. "Revisiting 'Special Needs' Theory via Airport Searches." *Northwestern University Law Review Colloquy* 106:207–29.
Reisig, M. D. 2002. "Citizen Input and Police Service: Moving beyond the "Feel Good" Community Survey." In *The Move to Community Policing: Making Change Happen,* eds. M. Morash and J. Ford. Thousand Oaks, CA: Sage, 43–60.
———. 2010. "Community and Problem-Oriented Policing," *Crime and Justice* 39:2–53.
Reisig, M. D., W. Bales, C. Hay, and X. Wang. 2007. "The Effect of Racial Inequality on Black Male Recidivism." *Justice Quarterly* 24 (3): 408–34.
Reisig, M. D., K. Holtfreter, and M. Morash. 2006. "Assessing Recidivism Risk across Female Pathways to Crime." *Justice Quarterly* 23 (3): 384–405.
Reisig, M. D., J. D. McCluskey, S. D. Mastrofski, and W. Terrill. 2004. "Suspect Disrespect toward the Police." *Justice Quarterly* 21:241–68.
Reiss, A. J., Jr. 1988. *Private Employment of Public Police*. Washington, DC: National Institute of Justice.
———. 1992. "Police Organization in the Twentieth Century." In *Crime and Justice: A Review of Research,* vol. 15, eds. M. Tonry and N. Morris. Chicago: University of Chicago Press, 51–97.
Reiter, K. A. 2012. "Parole, Snitch, or Die: California's Supermax Prisons and Prisoners, 1997–2007." *Punishment and Society* 14:530–63.
Rembert, D., and H. Henderson. 2014. "Correctional Officer Excessive Use of Force: Civil Liability under Section 1983." *Prison Journal* 94:198–219.
Renzema, M., and E. Mayo-Wilson. 2005. "Can Electronic Monitoring Reduce Crime for Moderate to High-Risk Offenders?" *Journal of Experimental Criminology* 1:215–37.
Reuters. 2014a. "Justin Bieber Gets Two Years Probation for Egging Incident." *Huffington Post Entertainment*, July 9. www.huffingtonpost.com.
———. 2014b. "Wisconsin Girls in Slenderman Case Ruled Competent to Stand Trial," Chicago Tribune, December 18. chicagotribune.com.
Rhodes, K., M. Dichter, C. Kothari, S. Marcus, and C. Cerulli. 2011. "The Impact of Children in Legal Actions Taken by Women Victims of Intimate Partner Violence." *Journal of Family Violence* 26:355–64.
Riccardi, N. 2009. "Cash-Strapped States Revise Laws to Get Inmates out." *Los Angeles Times*, September 5. www.latimes.com.
Riccucci, N., G. Van Ryzin, and C. Lavena. 2014. "Representative Bureaucracy in Policing: Does

It Increase Perceived Legitimacy?" *Journal of Public Administration Research and Theory* 24:537–51.

Rich, J., S. E. Wakeman, and S. L. Dickman. 2011. "Medicine and the Epidemic of Incarceration in the United States." *New England Journal of Medicine* 364:2081–83.

Richey, W. 2006. "US Creates Terrorist Fingerprint Database." *Christian Science Monitor*, December 27, pp. 1, 4.

Richinick, M. 2014. "Michael Dunn Sentenced to Life in 'Loud Music' Trial." MSNBC.com, October 17. www.msnbc.com.

Richmond, K. M. 2012. "The Impact of Federal Prison Industries Employment on the Recidivism Outcomes of Female Inmates." *Justice Quarterly* 31:719–45. doi: 10.1080/07418825.2012.668924.

Richmond, T. 2015. "Judge Rules Slender Man Stabbing Suspects Will Be Tried as Adults," News Radio 620 WTMJ, March 13. 620wtmj.com.

Riddell, K. 2014. "Hoffman's Death Highlights U.S. Spike in Heroin Use." *Washington Times*, February 3. www.washingtontimes.com.

Ring, W. 2005. "Backlogs in Labs Undercut DNA's Crime-Solving Value." *Lansing* (MI) *State Journal*, April 28, p. A3.

Ringhand, L. A., and C. M. Collins. 2011. "May It Please the Senate: An Empirical Analysis of the Senate Judiciary Committee Hearings of Supreme Court Nominees, 1939–2009." *American University Law Review* 60:589–639.

Riordan, J. 2008. "Pew Report Finds More than 1 in 100 Adults Are behind Bars," Press Release, Pew Center on the States, February 28. www.pewcenteronthestates.org/news_room_detail.aspx?id=35912.

Ripoll-Nunez, K. J., and R. P. Rohner. 2006. "Corporal Punishment in Cross-Cultural Perspective: Directions for a Research Agenda." *Cross-Cultural Research* 40 (2): 220–49.

Ritter, N. 2010. "Solving the Problem of Untested Evidence in Sexual Assaults." *National Institute of Justice Journal* 267 (Winter): 18–20.

Roane, K. R., and D. Morrison. 2005. "The CSI Effect." *US News and World Report,* April 25. www.usnews.com.

Robbins, L. 2011. "A Fateful Stop for Candy for a Helper to So Many." *New York Times*, November 1. www.nytimes.com.

Robbins, T. 2015. "A Brutal Beating Wakes Attica's Ghosts." *New York Times,* February 28. www.nytimes.com.

Robbins, T., and L. D'Avolio. 2015. "3 Attica Guards Resign in Deal to Avoid Jail." *New York Times,* March 2. www.nytimes.com.

Roberg, R., and S. Bonn. 2004. "Higher Education and Policing: Where Are We Now?" *Policing: International Journal of Police Strategies and Management* 27:469–86.

Roberts, J. 2013. "Effective Plea Bargaining Counsel." *Yale Law Journal* 122:2650–74.

Robertson, C. 2014. "In a Mississippi Jail, Convictions and Counsel Appear Optional." *New York Times,* September 24. www.nytimes.com.

Robinson, Wesley. 2014. "Chief: York City Budget Cuts Would Reduce Police Force to Patrol Unit and Detective Division." PennLive.com, November 20. www.pennlive.com.

Robles, F., and N. R. Kleinfield. 2013. "Review Ordered of 50 Brooklyn Murder Cases." *New York Times,* May 12. www.nytimes.com.

Rodriguez, N. 2005. "Restorative Justice, Communities, and Delinquency: Whom Do We Reintegrate?" *Criminology & Public Policy* 4:103–30.

———. 2007. "Restorative Justice at Work: Examining the Impact of Restorative Justice Resolutions on Juvenile Recidivism." *Crime & Delinquency* 53:355–79.

Roettger, M. E., and R. R. Swisher. 2011. "Associations of Fathers' History of Incarceration with Sons' Delinquency and Arrest among Black, White, and Hispanic Males in the United States." *Criminology* 49:1109–147.

Rogers, B. 2014. "Reports: Sentence Doubled for Teacher in Sex Case." *Houston Chronicle,* January 14. www.chron.com.

Rogers, M. 2010. "Cops Trained in Crisis Intervention Less Likely to Use Force on Mentally Ill." *Salt Lake City Tribune*, April 18. www.sltrib.com.

———. 2011. "Cardell's Taser Death Inspires Utah Police Training." *Salt Lake City Tribune*, May 12. www.sltrib.com.

Rojek, J., G. Alpert, and H. Smith. 2012. "The Utilization of Research by Police." *Police Practice and Research: An International Journal* 13:329–41.

Rojek, J., R. Rosenfeld, and S. Decker. 2012. "Policing Race: The Racial Stratification of Searches in Police Traffic Stops." *Criminology* 50:993–1024.

Romney, L. 2012. "Task Force Seeks to Change California's Mental Health Commitment Law." *Los Angeles Times*, April 8. articles.latimes.com/2012/apr/08/local/la-me-mental-health-task-force-20120409.

Rose, M., and J. Abramson. 2011. "Data, Race, and the Courts: Some Lessons on Empiricism from Jury Representation Cases." *Michigan State University Law Review* 2011:911–63.

Rosen, L. 1995. "The Creation of the Uniform Crime Report: The Role of Social Science." *Social Science History* 19 (Summer): 215–38.

Rosenbaum, J. L. 1989. "Family Dysfunction and Female Delinquency." *Crime & Delinquency* 35:31–44.

Rosencrance, J. 1988. "Maintaining the Myth of Individualized Justice: Probation Presentence Reports." *Justice Quarterly* 5:235.

Rosenfeld, R., and R. Fornango. 2014. "The Impact of Police Stops on Precinct Robbery and Burglary Rates in New York City, 2003–2010." *Justice Quarterly* 31:96–122.

Rosenfeld, R., R. Fornango, and A. F. Rengifo. 2007. "The Impact of Order-Maintenance Policing on New York City Homicide and Robbery Rates, 1988–2001." *Criminology* 45:355–83.

Rosenmerkel, S., M. Durose, and D. Farole. 2009. "Felony Sentences in State Courts, 2006—Statistical Tables," *Bureau of Justice Statistics Statistical Tables,* December. bjs.ojp.usdoj.gov/

Rossi, P. H., and R. A. Berk. 1997. *Just Punishments: Federal Guidelines and Public Views Compared*. New York: Aldine DeGruyter.

Roth, A. 2010. "Database-Driven Investigations: The Promise—and Peril—of Using Forensics to Solve 'No-Suspect' Cases." *Criminology & Public Policy* 9:421–28.

Roth, J. 2014. "The Anomaly of Entrapment." *Washington University Law Review* 91:979–1034.

Roth, R. 2010. "Obstructing Justice: Prisons as Barriers to Medical Care for Pregnant Women." *UCLA Women's Law Journal* 18:79–105.

Rothman, D. J. 1971. *The Discovery of the Asylum: Social Order and Disorder in the New Republic.* Boston: Little, Brown.

———. 1980. *Conscience and Convenience.* Boston: Little, Brown.

Rotman, E. 1995. "The Failure of Reform." In *Oxford History of the Prison*, ed. N. Morris and D. J. Rothman. New York: Oxford University Press.

Rousey, D. C. 1984. "Cops and Guns: Police Use of Deadly Force in Nineteenth-Century New Orleans." *American Journal of Legal History* 28:41–66.

"RTD Finds Credit Card Skimmers at Light Rail Stations." 2014. Fox31 News. November 5. http://kdvr.com.

Ruderman, W. 2013. "New Tool for Police Officers: Records at Their Fingertips." *New York Times*, April 11. www.nytimes.com.

Rushford, M. 2009. "The False Promise and Lethal Consequences of Releasing Inmates." *CJLF Report* (Criminal Justice Legal Foundation), August. www.cjlf.org.

Ryan, J. P., L. S. Abrams, and H. Huang. 2014. "First-Time Violent Juvenile Offenders: Probation, Placement, and Recidivism." Social Work Research 38:7–18.

Rydberg, J., and W. Terrill. 2010. "The Effect of Higher Education on Police Behavior." *Police Quarterly* 13:92–120.

Saad, L. 2007. "Racial Disagreement over Death Penalty Has Varied Historically." *Gallup Poll Report*, July 30. www.gallup.com.

Sabo, D., T. A. Kupers, and W. London. 2001. "Gender and the Politics of Punishment." In *Prison Masculinities,* eds. D. Sabo, T. A. Kupers, and W. London. Philadelphia: Temple University Press, 3–18.

Sack, K. 2011. "Executions in Doubt in Fallout over Drug." *New York Times*, March 16. www.nytimes.com.

Saletan, W. 2012. "Killers in Kevlar." Slate.com, August. 14. www.slate.com.

Salter, M. 2014. "Toys for the Boys? Drones, Pleasure and Popular Culture in the Militarisation of Policing." *Critical Criminology* 22:163–77.

Sampson, R. J., and J. H. Laub. 1993. *Crime in the Making: Pathways and Turning Points through Life*. Cambridge, MA: Harvard University Press.

Sampson, R. J., J. D. Morenoff, and S. Raudenbush. 2005. "Social Anatomy of Racial and Ethnic Disparities in Violence." *American Journal of Public Health* 95:224–32.

Samuelson, R. J. 1999. "Do We Care about Truth?" *Newsweek,* September 6, p. 76.

Sanchez, C. E., and M. Giordano. 2008. "Gang Activity in Suburbs Acknowledged." *Nashville Tennessean,* April 28. tennessean.com.

———. 2008."Plan to Close Prisons Stirs Anxiety in Rural Towns." *New York Times*, January 27. www.nytimes.com.

Santos, M. 2013. "California's Realignment: Real Prison Reform or Shell Game?" *Huffington Post,* March 11. www.huffingtonpost.com.

Sarat, A. 2005. "Innocence, Error and the 'New Abolitionism': A Commentary." *Criminology & Public Policy* 4:45–54.

———. 2008. "Memorializing Miscarriages of Justice: Clemency Petitions in the Killing State." *Law and Society Review* 42 (1): 183–224.

Saufley, L. I. 2010. "Funding Justice: The Budget of the Maine Judicial Branch." *Maine Law Review* 62:671–87.

Savage, C. 2011a. "Developments Rekindle Debate over Best Approach for Terrorism Suspects." *New York Times,* October 13. www.nytimes.com.

———. 2011b. "In a Reversal, Military Trials for 9/11 Cases." *New York Times*, April 4. www.nytimes.com.

———. 2011c. "Trend to Lighten Harsh Sentence Catches on in Conservative States." *New York Times*, August 12. www.nytimes.com.

Savage, D. G. 2008. "Supreme Court to Hear Challenge to DC Gun Law." March 17. www.latimes.com.

Sayre, M. 2014. "Efforts to Reduce Michigan's Prison Population through Sentencing and Parole Reform." *Michigan Policy Network*, July 29. michiganpolicy.com.

Scalia, J. 2002. "Prisoners Petitions Filed in US District Courts, 2000, with Trends 1980–2000." Bureau of Justice Statistics, *Special Report*, January.

Scarborough, B. K., T. Z. Like-Haislip, K .J. Novak, W. L. Lucas, and L. F. Alarid. 2010. "Assessing the Relationship between Individual Characteristics, Neighborhood Context, and Fear of Crime." *Journal of Criminal Justice* 38 (4): 819–26.

Schafer, J. A. 2002. "The Challenge of Effective Organizational Change: Lessons Learned in Community-Policing Implementation." In *The Move to Community Policing: Making Change Happen*, ed. M. Morash and J. Ford. Thousand Oaks, CA: Sage, 243–63.

Schaible, L., and V. Gecas. 2010. "The Impact of Emotional Labor and Value Dissonance on Burnout among Police Officers." *Police Quarterly* 13:316–41.

Schaldenbrand, A. M. 2010. "The Constitutional and Jurisdictional Limitations of In Rem Jurisdiction in Forfeiture Actions: A Response to International Forfeiture and the Constitution—The Limits of Forfeiture Jurisdiction over Foreign Assets under 28 U.S.C. 1355(B)(2)." *Syracuse Journal of International Law and Commerce* 38:55–90.

Schlesinger, T. 2011. "The Failure of Race Neutral Policies: How Mandatory Terms and Sentencing Enhancements Contribute to Mass Incarceration." *Crime & Delinquency* 57:56–81.

———. 2013. "Racial Disparities in Pretrial Diversion: An Analysis of Outcomes among Men Charged with Felonies and Processed in State Courts." *Race and Justice* 3 (3): 210–238.

Schmidt, M. 2014. "In Policy Change, Justice Dept. to Require Recording of Interrogations." *New York Times,* May 22. www.nytimes.com.

Schmitt, E., and D. Rohde. 2007. "Reports Assail State Department on Iraq Security." *New York Times*, October 23. www.nytimes.com.

Schmitt, R. B. 2008. "FBI Is Called Slow to Join the Terrorism Fight." *Los Angeles Times*, May 9. www.latimes.com.

Schultz, J. S. 2011. "More on Spotting ATM Skimmers." *New York Times*, February 1. www.nytimes.com.

Schwartz, A. 2013. "Chicago's Video Surveillance Cameras: A Pervasive and Poorly Regulated Threat to Our Privacy." *Northwestern Journal of Technology and Intellectual Property* 11:47–60.

Schwartz, J. 2009. "Effort Begun to End Voting for Judges." *New York Times*, December 23. www.nytimes.com.

Schwartz, J., and E. G. Fitzsimmons. 2011. "Illinois Governor Signs Capital Punishment Ban." *New York Times*, March 9. www.nytimes.com.

Schwirtz, M. 2013. "In 2 Trailers, the Neighbors Nobody Wants." *New York Times*, February 4. www.nytimes.com.

Seaman, A. M. 2010. "States with Tobacco-Free Prisons." *USA Today*, March 25. www.usatoday.com.

Secret, M. 2010. "NYC Misdemeanor Defendants Lack Bail Money." *New York Times*, December 2. www.nytimes.com.

Sedlak, A. J., and C. Bruce. 2010. "Youth's Characteristics and Backgrounds." NCJ 227730. *Juvenile Justice Bulletin*. Washington, DC: Office of Juvenile Justice and Delinquency Prevention.

Seelye, K. Q., W. K. Rashbaum, and M. Cooper. 2013. "Boston Bomb Suspect Is Captured after Standoff." *New York Times*, April 19. www.nytimes.com.

Segal, L., B. Ngugi, and J. Mana. 2011. "Credit Card Fraud: A New Perspective on Tackling an Intransigent Problem." *Fordham Journal of Corporate and Financial Law* 16:743–81.

Sen, M. 2014. "Minority Judicial Candidates Have Changed." *Judicature* 98:46–53.

Senzarino, P. 2014. "Barlas Found Not Guilty by Reason of Insanity in Father's Death." *Mason City* (Iowa) *Globe Gazette*, December 31. Globegazette.com.

———. 2013a. "Closing Arguments Presented in Crooks Trial." *Mason City* (Iowa) *Globe Gazette*, May 10. Globegazette.com.

———. 2013b. "Noah Crooks Convicted of Second-Degree Murder in Mom's Slaying." *Mason City* (Iowa) *Globe Gazette*, May 13. Globegazette.com.

Seron, C., J. Pereira, and J. Kovath. 2006. "How Citizens Assess Just Punishment for Police Misconduct." *Criminology* 44:925–60.

Serwer, A. 2009. "Reversing Rockefeller." *American Prospect*, April 1. www.prospect.org

Sever, M. 2010. "No More Pay for Portage Jurors: Annual $28,000 Earmarked for Fees at Issue; Cost of Murder Trials Cited." *Kent Record Courier*, January 29. www.recordpub.com.

Shamir, H. 2012. "A Labor Paradigm for Human Trafficking." *UCLA Law Review* 76–136.

Shane, S., and R. Nixon. 2007. "In Washington, Contractors Take On Biggest Role Ever." *New York Times*, February 4. www.nytimes.com.

Shapiro, B. 1997. "Sleeping Lawyer Syndrome." *Nation,* April 7, pp. 27–29.

Sharp, E., and P. Johnson. 2009. "Accounting for Variation in Distrust of Local Police." *Justice Quarterly* 26:157–182.

Shay, G. 2009. "What We Can Learn about Appeals from Mr. Tillman's Case: More Lessons from Another DNA Exoneration." *University of Cincinnati Law Review* 77:1499–553.

Sheeran, T. J. 2010. "Amid Cuts, Ohio Judge Tells Citizens to Carry Guns." *Ohio Free Press*, April 9. www.ohiofreepress.com.

"Shells near Ex-NFL Star's Alleged Victim, in Car, from Same Gun: Witness." 2015. *New York Times*, February 25. www.nytimes.com.

Shelton, D. E. 2008. "The 'CSI Effect': Does It Really Exist?" *National Institute of Justice Journal*, 259 (March): 1–6.

Shen, F. X. 2011. "How We Still Fail Rape Victims: Reflecting on Responsibility and Legal Reform." *Columbia Journal of Gender and Law* 22:1–79.

Sheridan, M., and S. S. Hsu. 2006. "Localities Operate Intelligence Centers to Pool Terror Data." *Washington Post*, December 31. www.washingtonpost.com.

Sherman, L. W. 1983. "Patrol Strategies for Police." In *Crime and Public Policy,* ed. J. Q. Wilson. San Francisco: ICS Press, 149–54.

Sherman, L. W. 1995. "The Police." In *Crime,* eds. J. Q. Wilson and J. Petersilia. San Francisco: ICS Press, 327–48.

Sherman, L. W., P. R. Gartin, and M. E. Buerger. 1989. "Hot Spots of Predatory Crime: Routine Activities and the Criminology of Place." *Criminology* 27:27–55.

Sherman, L. W., and D. A. Weisburd. 1995. "General Deterrent Effects of Police Patrol in Crime 'Hot Spots': A Randomized Controlled Trial." *Justice Quarterly* 12 (December): 625–48.

Shermer, L. O., and B. D. Johnson. 2010. "Criminal Prosecutions: Examining Prosecutorial Discretion and Charge Reductions in US Federal District Courts." *Justice Quarterly* 27:394–430.

Shigihara, A. M. 2013. "It's Only Stealing a Little a Lot: Techniques of Neutralization for Theft among Restaurant Workers." *Deviant Behavior* 34:494–512.

Shover, N. 1998. "White-Collar Crime." In *The Handbook of Crime and Punishment,* ed. M. Tonry. New York: Oxford University Press, 133–58.

Sickmund, M. 2004. "Juveniles in Corrections." In *National Report Series Bulletin*. Washington, DC: Office of Juvenile Justice and Delinquency Prevention, June.

Sickmund, M., and C. Puzzanchera. 2014. Juvenile Offenders and Victims: 2014 National Report." Pittsburg: National Center for Juvenile Justice.

Sickmund, M., A. Sladky, and W. Kang. 2015. "Easy Access to Juvenile Court Statistics: 1985–2012." Pittsburgh: National Center for Juvenile Justice. http://www.ojjdp.gov/ojstatbb/ezajcs/.

Sidel, R. 2014. "Home Depot's 56 Million Credit Card Breach Bigger Than Target's." *Wall Street Journal* September 18. www.wsj.com.

Sigler, M. 2010. "Private Prisons, Public Functions, and the Meaning of Punishment." *Florida State University Law Review* 38:149–78.

Silverman, E. 1999. *NYPD Battles Crime*. Boston: Northeastern University Press.

Simmons, A., and B. Rankin. 2010. "Gwinnett Cuts Pay Rate for Defending Indigent." *Atlanta Journal Constitution*, February 1. www.ajc.com.

Simmons, R. 2012. "The New Reality of Search Analysis: Four Trends Created by New Surveillance Technologies." *Mississippi Law Journal* 81:991–1014.

Simons, M. 2010. "Prosecutorial Discretion in the Shadow of Advisory Guidelines and Mandatory Minimums." *Temple Political & Civil Rights Law Review* 19:377–87.

Simpson, S. S. 2013. "White-Collar Crime: A Review of Recent Developments and Promising Directions for Future Research." *Annual Review of Sociology* 39:309–31.

Skipp, C. 2010. "A Law for Sex Offenders under a Miami Bridge." *Time*, February 1. www.time.com.

Skogan, W. G. 1990. *Disorder and Decline: Crime and the Spiral of Decay in America*. New York: Free Press.

———. 1995. "Crime and Racial Fears of White Americans." *Annals of the American Academy of Political and Social Science* 539 (May): 59–71.

Skogan, W. G., and M. G. Maxfield. 1981. *Coping with Crime*. Newbury Park, CA: Sage.

Skolnick, J. H. 1966. *Justice without Trial: Law Enforcement in a Democratic Society*. New York: Wiley.

Skolnick, J. H., and D. H. Bayley. 1986. *The New Blue Line*. New York: Free Press.

Skolnick, J. H., and J. J. Fyfe. 1993. *Above the Law: Police and Excessive Use of Force*. New York: Free Press.

Skorton, D., and G. Altschuler. 2013. "College behind Bars: How Educating Prisoners Pays Off." *Forbes*, March 25. www.forbes.com.

Skutch, J. 2015. "Former Savannah-Chatham Police Chief Willie Lovett Sentenced to 7.5 Years in Prison." *Savannah Morning News*, February 6. http://savannahnow.com.

Slabaugh, S. 2011. "Inmate Education Programs Facing Major Budget Cuts." *Muncie Star Press*, May 21. www.thestarpress.com.

Slobodzian, J. A. 2008. "TV Footage Shows Police Beating Suspects." *Philadelphia Inquirer*, May 7. www.philly.com.

Slocum, L., A. F. Rengifo, T. Choi, and C. R. Herrmann. 2013. "The Elusive Relationship between Community Organizations and Crime: An Assessment across Disadvantaged Areas of the South Bronx." *Criminology* 51:167–216.

Slocum, L., S. S. Simpson, and D. A. Smith. 2005. "Strained Lives and Crime: Examining Intra-individual Variation in Strain and Offending in a Sample of Incarcerated Women." 43 (4): 1067–110.

Smith, C. E. 1990. United States Magistrates in the Federal Courts: Subordinate Judges. New York: Praeger.

———. 1993. "Justice Antonin Scalia and Criminal Justice Cases." *Kentucky Law Journal* 81:187–212.

———. 1994. "Imagery, Politics, and Jury Reform." *Akron Law Review* 28:77–95.

———. 1995a. "The Constitution and Criminal Punishment: The Emerging Visions of Justices Scalia and Thomas." *Drake Law Review* 43:593–613.

———. 1995b. "Federal Habeas Corpus Reform: The State's Perspective." *Justice System Journal* 18:1–11.

———. 1995c. "Judicial Policy Making and Habeas Corpus Reform." *Criminal Justice Policy Review* 7:91–114.

———. 1997. *The Rehnquist Court and Criminal Punishment*. New York: Garland.

———. 1999a. "Criminal Justice and the 1997–98 US Supreme Court Term." *Southern Illinois University Law Review* 23:443–67.

———. 1999b. *Law and Contemporary Corrections*. Belmont, CA: Wadsworth.

———. 2000. "The Governance of Corrections: Implications of the Changing Interface of Courts and Corrections." In *Boundary Changes in Criminal Justice Organizations*, vol. 2, *Criminal Justice 2000*. Washington, DC: National Institute of Justice, U.S. Department of Justice, 113–66.

———. 2004a. "The Bill of Rights after September 11th: Principles or Pragmatism?" *Duquesne Law Review* 42:259–91.

———. 2004b. *Constitutional Rights: Myths and Realities*. Belmont, CA: Wadsworth.

———. 2007. "Justice John Paul Stevens and Prisoners' Rights." *Temple Political & Civil Rights Law Review* 17:83–107.

———. 2010a. "Justice John Paul Stevens and Capital Punishment." *Berkeley Journal of Criminal Law* 15:205–60.

———. 2010b. "Justice John Paul Stevens: Staunch Defender of *Miranda* Rights." *DePaul Law Review* 60:99–140.

———. 2011. "The Changing Supreme Court and Prisoners' Rights." *Indiana Law Review* 44:853–88.

———. 2013. "*Brown v. Plata,* the Roberts Court, and the Future of Conservative Perspectives on Rights behind Bars." *Akron Law Review* 46:519–50.

———. 2014. "What I Learned about Stop-and-Frisk from Watching My Black Son." Atlantic online. April 1. http://www.theatlantic.com/national/archive/2014/04/what-i-learned-about-stop-and-frisk-from-watching-my-black-son/359962/

Smith, C. E., C. DeJong, and J. D. Burrow. 2002. *The Supreme Court, Crime, and the Ideal of Equal Justice*. New York: Peter Lange.

Smith, C. E., and H. Feldman. 2001. "Burdens of the Bench: State Supreme Courts' Non-judicial Tasks." *Judicature* 84:304–9.

Smith, C. E., and J. Hurst. 1996. "Law and Police Agencies' Policies: Perceptions of the Relative Impact of Constitutional Law Decisions and Civil Liabilities Decisions." Paper given at the annual meeting of the American Society of Criminology (November), Chicago.

Smith, C. E., and A. Sanford. 2013. "The Roberts Court and Wrongful Convictions." *St. Louis Public Law Review* 32:307–28.

Smith, M. 2015. "Regulation Law Enforcement's Use of Drones: The Need for State Legislation." *Harvard Journal on Legislation* (forthcoming 2015).

Snedker, K. A. (2010). "Neighborhood Conditions and Fear of Crime: A Reconsideration of Sex Differences." *Crime & Delinquency* (December 3), published online before print. doi: 10.1177/0011128710389587.

Socia, K. M. 2014. "Residence Restrictions Are Ineffective, Inefficient, and Inadequate: So Now What?" *Criminology and Public Policy* 13:179–88.

Solomon, A. L., J. W. L. Osborne, S. F. LoBuglio, J. Mellow, and D. A. Mukamal. 2008. *Life after Lockup: Improving Reentry from Jail to the Community*. Washington, DC: Urban Institute.

Sommers, S., and S. Marotta. 2014. "Racial Disparities in Legal Outcomes: On Policing, Charging Decisions, and Criminal Trial Proceedings." *Policy Insights from the Behavioral and Brain Sciences* 1:103–11.

Sommers, S. 2009. "On the Obstacles to Jury Diversity." *Jury Expert* 21:1–10.

Soree, N. B. 2013. "Show and Tell, Seek and Find: A Balanced Approach to Defining a Fourth Amendment Search and the Lessons of Rape Reform." *Seton Hall Law Review* 43:127–227.

Souryal, S. S., D. W. Potts, and A. I. Alobied. 1994. "The Penalty of Hand Amputation for Theft in Islamic Justice." *Journal of Criminal Justice* 22:249–65.

Southall, A. 2014. "Eric Frein, Suspect in Pennsylvania Trooper's Death, Is Captured after 7-Week Manhunt." *New York Times*, October 30. www.nytimes.com.

Spangenberg Group. 2007. "Rates of Compensation Paid to Court-Appointed Counsel in Non-capital Felony Cases at Trial: A State-by-State Overview." American Bar Association Bar Information Program, June 2007.

Spangenberg, R. L., and M. L. Beeman. 1995. "Indigent Defense Systems in the United States." *Law and Contemporary Problems* 58:31–49.

Sparrow, M. K., M. H. Moore, and D. M. Kennedy. 1990. *Beyond 911: A New Era for Policing*. New York: Basic Books.

Spears, J. W., and C. C. Spohn. 1997. "The Effect of Evidence Factors and Victim Characteristics on Prosecutors' Charging Decisions in Sexual Assault Cases." *Justice Quarterly* 14:501–24.

Spelman, W. G., and D. K. Brown. 1984. *Calling the Police: Citizen Reporting of Serious Crime*. Washington, DC: Police Executive Research Forum.

Spencer, C. 2000. "Nonlethal Weapons Aid Lawmen: Police Turn to Beanbag Guns, Pepper Spray to Save Lives of Defiant Suspects." *Arkansas Democrat-Gazette,* November 6, p. B1.

Spitzer, S. 1975. "Toward a Marxian Theory of Deviance." *Social Problems* 22:638–51.

Spohn, C. 2011. "Unwarranted Disparity in the Wake of the *Booker/Fanfan* Decision: Implications for Research and Policy." *Criminology & Public Policy* 10:1119–27.

Spohn, C., and D. Holleran. 2000. "The Imprisonment Penalty Paid by Young, Unemployed Black and Hispanic Male Offenders." *Criminology* 38:281–306.

———. 2001. "Prosecuting Sexual Assault: A Comparison of Charging Decisions in Sexual Assault Cases Involving Strangers, Acquaintances, and Intimate Partners." *Justice Quarterly* 18:651–85.

Sridharan, S., L. Greenfield, and B. Blakley. 2004. "A Study of Prosecutorial Certification Practice in Virginia." *Criminology & Public Policy* 3:605–32.

Srubas, P. 2011. "Marinette County: DA to State on Cuts—Tell Us What Crimes Not to Prosecute." *Green Bay Press Gazette*, May 5. www.greenbaypressgazette.com.

Staba, D. 2007. "Killer of 3 Women in Buffalo Area Is Given a Life Term." *New York Times*, August 15. www.nytimes.com.

Stafford, M. C., and M. Warr. 1993. "A Reconceptualization of General and Specific Deterrence." *Journal of Research in Crime & Delinquency* 30 (May): 123–35.

Stahl, M. B. 1992. "Asset Forfeiture, Burden of Proof, and the War on Drugs." *Journal of Criminal Law and Criminology* 83:274–337.

Stahlkopf, C., M. Males, and D. Macallair. 2010. "Testing Incapacitation Theory: Youth Crime and Incarceration in California." *Crime & Delinquency* 56:253–68.

Stanko, E. 1988. "The Impact of Victim Assessment on Prosecutors' Screening Decisions: The Case of the New York District Attorney's Office." In *Criminal Justice: Law and Politics,* 5th ed., ed. G. F. Cole. Pacific Grove, CA: Brooks/Cole.

Staples, B. 2012. "California Horror Stories and the 3-Strikes Law." *New York Times*, November 24. www.nytimes.com.

Starkey, B. S. 2012. "A Failure of the Fourth Amendment and Equal Protection's Promise: How the Equal Protection Clause Can Change Discriminatory Stop and Frisk Policies." *Michigan Journal of Race and Law* 18:131–87.

St. Clair, S., and J. Gorner. 2013. "City Plans $4.1 Million Settlement in Fatal Police Shooting." *Chicago Tribune,* February 8. articles.tribune.com.

Steen, S., R. L. Engen, and R. R. Gainey. 2005. "Images of Danger and Culpability: Racial Stereotyping, Case Processing, and Criminal Sentencing." *Criminology* 43 (2): 435–68.

Steffensmeier, D., and S. Demuth. 2001. "Ethnicity and Judges' Sentencing Decisions: Hispanic-Black-White Comparisons." *Criminology* 39:145–78.

Steffensmeier, D., B. Feldmeyer, C. T. Harris, and J. T. Ulmer. 2011. "Reassessing Trends in Black Violent Crime 1980–2008: Sorting out the 'Hispanic Effect' in Uniform Crime Reports Arrests, National Crime Victimization Survey Offender Estimates, and US Prisoner Counts. *Criminology* 49:197–252.

Steffensmeier, D., J. Kramer, and C. Streifel. 1993. "Gender and Imprisonment Decisions." *Criminology* 31:411–46.

Steffensmeier, D., J. Schwartz, H. Zhong, and J. Ackerman. 2005. "An Assessment of Recent Trends in Girls' Violence Using Diverse Longitudinal Sources: Is the Gender Gap Closing?" *Criminology* 43 (2): 355–406.

Steffensmeier, D., J. Ulmer, and J. Kramer. 1998. "The Interaction of Race, Gender, and Age in Criminal Sentencing: The Punishment Cost of Being Young, Black, and Male." *Criminology* 36:763–97.

Steinberg, J. 1999. "The Coming Crime Wave Is Washed Up." *New York Times,* January 3, p. 4-WK.

Steinberg, L., E. Cauffman, and K. C. Monahan. 2015. "Psychosocial Maturity and Desistance from Crime in a Sample of Serious Juvenile Offenders." *Juvenile Justice Bulletin* (NCJ 248391). Washington, DC: Office of Juvenile Justice and Delinquency Prevention.

Steiner, B., L. Travis, and M. Markarios. 2011. "Understanding Parole Officers' Responses to Sanctioning Reform." *Crime & Delinquency* 57:222–46.

Stephan, J., and J. Karberg. 2003, August. *Census of State and Federal Correctional Facilities, 2000.* Washington, DC: Bureau of Justice Statistics.

Stephan, J. J. 2008. "Census of State and Federal Correctional Facilities, 2005." NCJ 222182. Bureau of Justice Statistics *Bulletin,* October.

Steward, D., and M. Totman. 2005. *Racial Profiling: Don't Mind If I Take a Look, Do Ya? An Examination of Consent Searches and Contraband Hit Rates at Texas Traffic Stops.* Austin: Texas Justice Coalition.

St. John, P. 2014. "As More Inmates Are Released from Prison, More Parolees Return." *LA Times,* December 27. www.latimes.com.

Stoddard, E. R. 1968. "The Informal 'Code' of Police Deviancy: A Group Approach to Blue-Coat Crime." *Journal of Criminal Law, Criminology, and Police Science* 59:204–11.

Stojkovic, S. 1990. "Accounts of Prison Work: Corrections Officers' Portrayals of Their Work Worlds." *Perspectives on Social Problems* 2:211–30.

Stolzenberg, L., and S. J. D'Alessio. 1994. "Sentencing and Unwarranted Disparity: An Empirical Assessment of the Long-Term Impact of Sentencing Guidelines in Minnesota." *Criminology* 32:301–10.

Streb, M. J., B. Frederick, and C. LaFrance. 2007. "Contestation, Competition, and the Potential for Accountability in Intermediate Appellate Court Elections." *Judicature* 91 (2): 70–78.

Streib, V. 2010. "Innocence: Intentional Wrongful Conviction of Children." *Chicago-Kent Law Review* 85:163–77.

Streitfeld, D. 2008. "R. Kelly Is Acquitted in Child Pornography Case." *New York Times,* June 14. www.nytimes.com.

Strickland, C. 2011. "Regulation without Agency: A Practical Response to Private Policing in *United States v. Day.*" *North Carolina Law Review* 89:1338–62.

Strodtbeck, F., R. James, and G. Hawkins. 1957. "Social Status in Jury Deliberations." *American Sociological Review* 22:713–19.

Strom, K., M. Berzofsky, B. Shook-Sa, K. Barrick, C. Daye, N. Horstmann, and S. Kinsey. 2010. *The Private Security Industry: A Review of the Definitions, Available Data Sources, and Paths Moving Forward,* report prepared for US Bureau of Justice Statistics (December). www.njrs.gov/pdffiles1/bjs/grants/232781.pdf.

Strom, K. J., and M. J. Hickman. 2010. "Unanalyzed Evidence in Law-Enforcement Agencies: A National Examination of Forensic-Processing in Police Departments." *Criminology & Public Policy* 9:381–404.

Strom, K. J., and J. M. MacDonald. 2007. "The Influence of Social and Economic Disadvantage on Racial Patterns in Youth Homicide over Time." *Homicide Studies* 11:50–69.

Stroshine, M. S. 2005. "Information Technology Innovations in Policing." In *Critical Issues in Policing,* 5th ed., ed. R. G. Dunham and G. P. Alpert. Long Grove, IL: Waveland Press, 172–83.

Subramanian, R., R. Moreno, and S. Gebreselassie. 2014. *Relief in Sight? States Rethink the Collateral Consequences of Criminal Conviction, 2009–2014.* New York: Vera Institute of Justice.

Sullivan, C. M. (2012, October). *Domestic Violence Shelter Services: A Review of the Empirical Evidence,* Harrisburg, PA: National Resource Center on Domestic Violence. http://www.dvevidenceproject.org.

Sullivan, E. 2013. "Local Police Grapple with Response to Cybervrimes." *Lexington Herald Leader.*" April 13. www.kentucky.com.

Sullivan, K. M. 2003. "Under a Watchful Eye: Incursions on Personal Privacy." In *The War on Our Freedoms: Civil Liberties in an Age of Terrorism,*" ed. R. C. Leone and G. Anrig Jr. New York: Public Affairs, 128–46.

Sundby, S. E. 2010. "War and Peace in the Jury Room: How Capital Juries Reach Unanimity." *Hastings Law Journal* 62:103–53.

Sung, H., A. M. Mahoney, and J. Mellow. 2011. "Substance Abuse Treatment Gap among Adult Parolees: Prevalence, Correlates, and Barriers." *Criminal Justice Review* 36:40–77.

Sutherland, E. H. 1947. *Criminology.* 4th ed. Philadelphia: Lippincott.

———. 1949. *White-Collar Crime.* New York: Holt, Rinehart, and Winston.

———. 1950. "The Sexual Psychopath Laws." *Journal of Criminal Law and Criminology* 40 (January–February): 543–54.

Swirko, C. 2012. "Budget Cuts Force Tough Decisions on Prosecutors." *Gainesville Sun,* December 17. www.gainesville.com.

Sykes, G. M. 1958. *The Society of Captives.* Princeton, NJ: Princeton University Press.

Sylvester, R. 2011. "Dallas DA Established Unit to Look into Old Cases." *Wichita Eagle,* February 13. www.kansas.com/2011/02/13/1718594/dallas-da-established-unit-to.html.

Tark, J., and G. Kleck. 2004. "Resisting Crime: The Effects of Victim Action on the Outcomes of Crimes." *Criminology* 42:861–909.

Tavernise, S. 2011. "Ohio County Losing Its Young to Painkillers' Grip." *New York Times,* April 19. www.nytimes.com.

Taxman, F. S., and S. Belenko, 2013. *Implementing Evidence-Based Practices in Community Corrections and Addiction Treatment.* New York: Springer.

Taylor, B., C. Koper, and D. J. Woods. 2010. "A Randomized Controlled Trial of Different Policing Strategies at Hot Spots of Violent Crime." *Journal of Experimental Criminology* 7:149–81.

Taylor, M. 2009. *Achieving Better Outcomes for Adult Probation.* Sacramento: Legislative Analyst's Office, May.

Teeters, N. K., and J. D. Shearer. 1957. *The Prison at Philadelphia, Cherry Hill: The Separate System of Penal Discipline, 1829–1913.* New York: Columbia University Press.

Telep, C., and D. Weisburd. 2012. "What Is Known about the Effectiveness of Police Practices in Reducing Crime and Disorder?" *Police Quarterly* 15:331–57.

Telep, C., R. Mitchell, and D. Weisburd. 2014. "How Much Time Should the Police Spend at Crime Hot Spots? Answers from a Police Agency Directed Randomized Field Trial in Sacramento, California." Justice Quarterly 31:905–33.

Tepfer, D. 2013. "Towns to Pay $3.5M in Deadly Raid." *Connecticut Post,* February 20. www.ctpost.com.

Terrill, W., E. A. Paoline III, and P. K. Manning. 2003. "Police Culture and Coercion." *Criminology* 41:1003–34.

Terry, C. 1997. "The Function of Humor for Prison Inmates." *Journal of Contemporary Criminal Justice* 13:23–40.

Texas Board of Pardons and Paroles. 2011. *Parole Handbook.* www.tdcj.state.tx.us/documents/parole/PIT_English.pdf.

Texas Board of Pardons and Paroles. 2014. *Annual Statistical Report: Fiscal Year 2013.* Austin, TX: Texas Board of Pardons and Paroles.

Texas Department of Criminal Justice. 2014. "Correctional Officer Salary." Texas Department of Criminal Justice website. www.tdcj.state.tx.us.

Thaman, S. C. 2000. "The Separation of Questions of Law and Fact in the New Russian and Spanish Jury Verdicts." In *The Judicial Role in Criminal Proceedings,* eds. Sean Doran and John Jackson. Oxford, England: Hart, 51–63.

The Third Branch. 2008a. "Economics of CJA Regulations Costly to Attorneys." Administrative Office of the U.S. Courts. Vol. 40 (4), April. www.uscourts.gov.

———. 2008b. "National Summits Help Federal Courts Prepare for Sentence Reduction Requests." Administrative Office of the U.S. Courts. Vol. 40 (2), February, pp. 1–3, 6. www.uscourts.gov.

Thomas, P. 2011. "Mississippi Should Consider Jury Reforms Similar to Those Adopted in Michigan," *MS Litigation Review and Commentary,* July 21. www.mslitigationreview.com.

Thompson, R. A. 2001. "Police Use of Force against Drug Suspects: Understanding the Legal Need for Policy Development." *American Journal of Criminal Justice* 25:173–97.

Thornhill, T. 2015. "Finnish Man Given £40,000 Speeding Ticket for Going 14mph over Limit." *Daily Mail,* March 15. http://dailymail.co.uk.

"Thumb on the Scale." 2013. *Economist,* January 26. www.economist.com.

Thurman, Q., J. Zhao, and A. Giacomazzi. 2001. *Community Policing in a Community Era.* Los Angeles: Roxbury.

Tonry, M. 1993. "Sentencing Commissions and Their Guidelines." In *Crime and Justice,* vol. 17, ed. M. Tonry. Chicago: University of Chicago Press.

Tonry, M. 1995. *Malign Neglect: Race, Crime, and Punishment in America.* New York: Oxford University Press.

———. 1998. Introduction to *Handbook of Crime and Punishment,* ed. M. Tonry. New York: Oxford University Press, 22–3.

Tonry, M., and M. Lynch. 1996. "Intermediate Sanctions." In *Crime and Justice,* vol. 20, ed. M. Tonry. Chicago: University of Chicago Press, 99–144.

Toobin, J. 2014. "'This Is My Jail': Where Gang Members and Female Guards Set the Rules." *New Yorker,* April 14. http://www.newyorker.com/magazine/2014/04/14/this-is-my-jail.

Travis, J. 2002. "Invisible Punishment: An Instrument of Social Exclusion." In *Invisible Punishment: The Collective Consequences of Mass Imprisonment,* eds. M. Mauer and M. Chesney-Lind. New York: New Press, 15–36.

Travis, J., and S. Lawrence. 2002. *Beyond the Prison Gates: The State of Parole in America.* Washington, DC: Urban Institute.

Travis, J., and J. Petersilia. 2001. "Reentry Reconsidered: A New Look at an Old Question." *Crime & Delinquency,* July, 291–313.

Truman, J. L., and L. Langton. 2014. "Criminal Victimization, 2013." NCJ247648. Bureau of Justice Statistics *Bulletin.*

Truman, J., L. Langton, and M. Planty. 2013. "Criminal Victimization, 2012." NCJ 243389. Bureau of Justice Statistics *Bulletin.* October.

Truman, J. L., and M. Planty. 2012. "Criminal Victimization, 2011." NCJ 239437. Bureau of Justice Statistics *Bulletin*, October.

Truman, J. L., and M. R. Rand. 2010. "Criminal Victimization, 2009." NCJ 231327. Bureau of Justice Statistics *Bulletin,* October.

Tse, D., D Chen, Q. Liu, F. Wang, Z. Wei. 2014. "Emerging Issues in Cloud Storage Security: Encryption, Key Management, Data Redundancy, Trust Mechanism." *Multidisciplinary Social Networks Research* 473:297–310.

Turner K. B., and J. B. Johnson. 2006. "The Effect of Gender on the Judicial Pretrial Decision of Bail Amount Set." *Federal Probation* 70 (1): 56–62.

Turner, M. G., F. T. Cullen, J. L. Sundt, and B. K. Applegate. 1997. "Public Tolerance for Community-Based Sanctions." *Prison Journal* 77 (March): 6–26.

Tyler, T. R., and C. J. Wakslak. 2004. "Profiling and Police Legitimacy: Procedural Justice, Attributions of Motive, and Acceptance of Police Authority." *Criminology* 42:253–81.

Twyman, A. S. 2005. "Police Policy on Mentally Ill Questioned." *Philadelphia Inquirer,* April 18. www.philly.com.

Uchida, C. 2005. "The Development of the American Police: An Historical Overview." In *Critical Issues in Policing,* ed. R. G. Dunham and G. P. Alpert. Long Grove, IL: Waveland Press, 20–40.

Uchida, C., and T. Bynum. 1991. "Search Warrants, Motions to Suppress and 'Lost Cases': The Effects of the Exclusionary Rule in Seven Jurisdictions." *Journal of Criminal Law and Criminology* 81:1034–66.

Ulmer, J. T., J. Eisenstein, and B. Johnson. 2010. "Trial Penalties in Federal Sentencing: Extra Guidelines Factors and District Variation." *Justice Quarterly* 27:560–92.

Ulmer, J. T., M.T. Light, and J. H. Kramer. 2011. Racial Disparity in the Wake of the *Booker /Fanfan* Decision." *Criminology & Public Policy* 10:1077–118.

Unah, I. 2010. "Choosing Who Will Die: The Effect of Race, Gender, and Law in Prosecutorial Decisions to Seek the Death Penalty in Durham County, North Carolina." *Michigan Journal of Race and Law* 15:135–79.

United Nations Office on Drugs and Crime (UNODC). 2011. *Research Report: Estimating Illicit Financial Flows Resulting from Drug Trafficking and Other Transnational Organized Crimes,* October. Vienna: UNODC.

University of Pittsburgh Medical Center. 2005. "Lead in Environment Causes Violent Crime, Reports University of Pittsburgh Researcher at AAAS." *UPMC News Release,* February 18. www.sciencedaily.com/releases /2005/02/050223145108.htm.

Unnever, J., and F. T. Cullen. 2005. "Executing the Innocent and Support for Capital Punishment: The Implications for Public Policy." *Criminology & Public Policy* 4:3–38.

Unnever, J. D., F. T. Cullen, and J. P. Bartkowski. 2006. "Images of God and Public Support for Capital Punishment: Does a Close Relationship with a Loving God Matter?" *Criminology* 44 (4): 835–66.

Uphoff, R. J. 1992. "The Criminal Defense Lawyer: Zealous Advocate, Double Agent, or Beleaguered Dealer?" *Criminal Law Bulletin* 28:419–56.

Urbina, I., and C. Rentz. 2013. "Immigrants Held in Solitary Cells, Often for Weeks." *New York Times*, March 23. www.nytimes.com.

U.S. Bureau of Prisons. 2013. "About the Bureau of Prisons." Federal Bureau of Prisons website. www.bop.gov.

———. 2015. "About Our Facilities." Federal Bureau of Prisons website. www.bop.gov.

United States Courts. 2013. "Supervision Costs Significantly Less than Incarceration in Federal System." July 18. http://uscourts.gov.

U.S. Department of Health and Human Services. 2007. "Illicit Drug Use, by Race/Ethnicity, in Metropolitan and Non-metropolitan Counties: 2004 and 2005." *NSDUH Report* (National Survey on Drug Use and Health), June 21.

———. 2012. "Information on Poverty and Income Statistics: A Summary of 2012 Current Population Survey Data." *ASPE Issue Brief*, September 12. aspe.hhs.gov/hsp/12 /povertyandincomeest/ib.shtml.

U.S. Department of Justice. 1997. *Principles of Prosecution*. Washington, DC: U.S. Government Printing Office.

———. 2011. "Hacker Pleads Guilty to Identity Theft and Credit Card Fraud Resulting in Losses of More Than $36 Million." Press release, April 21. www.justice.gov.

———. 2014. "Former Hell's Angel Member Pleads Guilty to Methamphetamine Trafficking." FBI Press Release. August 20. www.fbi.gov

———. 2013. "Facts and Figures 2013." U.S. Marshals Service website. January 10. www.usmarshals.gov.

U.S. Marshals Services. 2014. *Fact Sheet: Facts and Figures 2014*. www.usmarshals.gov.

U.S. President's Commission on Law Enforcement and Administration of Justice. 1967. *The Challenge of Crime in a Free Society*. Washington, DC: U.S. Government Printing Office.

U.S. Sentencing Commission. 2006. *Final Report on the Impact of* United States v. Booker *on Federal Sentencing*. Washington, DC: U.S. Sentencing Commission.

Utz, P. 1978. *Settling the Facts*. Lexington, MA: Lexington Books.

van de Brunt, H., and W. Huisman. 2007. "Organizational Crime in the Netherlands." *Crime and Justice* 35:217–60.

Van Natta, D. 2011. "Race Issues Confront the Miami Police in the Killings of Seven Black Men." *New York Times*, March 23. www .nytimes.com.

Van Stelle, K., and J. Goodrich. 2009. *The 2008/2009 Study of Probation and Parole Revocation*. Madison: University of Wisconsin Population Health Institute, June.

Vanfossen, B., C. H. Brown, S. Kellam, N. Sokoloff, and S. Doering. 2010. "Neighborhood Context and the Development of Aggression in Boys and Girls." *Journal of Community Psychology*, 38:329–49.

VanNostrand, M. 2010. "Alternatives to Pretrial Detention: Southern District of Iowa, A Case Study." *Federal Probation* (December): 11–15.

Varano, S. P., J. D. McCluskey, J. W. Patchin, and T. S. Bynum. 2004. "Exploring the Drug–Homicide Connection." *Journal of Contemporary Criminal Justice* 20:369–92.

Vaughn, M. S. 2001. "Assessing the Legal Liabilities in Law Enforcement: Chiefs' Views." *Crime & Delinquency* 47:3–27.

Velez, M. B., C. J. Lyons, and B. Boursaw. 2012. "Neighborhood Housing Investments and Violent Crime in Seattle, 1981–2007." *Criminology* 50:1025–56.

Vermont Parole Board. 2010. *The Vermont Parole Board Manual*. www.doc.state.vt.us/about /parole-board/pb-manual.

Vickovic, S., and M. Griffin. 2014. "A Comparison of Line and Supervisory Officers and the Impact of Support on Commitment to the Prison Organization." *Criminal Justice Policy Review* 25:719–42.

Viguerie, R. A. 2013. "A Conservative Case for Prison Reform." *New York Times*, June 9. www.nytimes.com.

Vila, B., and D. J. Kenney. 2002. "Tired Cops: The Prevalence and Potential Consequences of Police Fatigue." *National Institute of Justice Journal* 248:16–21.

Villiers, de, M. 2011. "Enabling Technologies of Cyber Crime: Why Lawyers Need to Understand It." *Pittsburgh Journal of Technology, Law and Policy* 11:1–25.

Virtanen, M. 2014. "Report Details NY Indigent Defense Caseloads." *Wall Street Journal,* September 24. www.wsj.com

Visher, C., Debus-Sherrill, and J. Yahner, 2011. "Employment after Prison: A Longitudinal Study of Former Prisoners." *Justice Quarterly* 28:698–718.

Vogel, M. 1999. "The Social Origins of Plea Bargaining: Conflict and the Law in the Process of State Formation, 1830–1860." *Law and Society Review* 33:161–246.

Vogel, M., and S. F. Messner. 2012. "Social Correlates of Delinquency for Youth in Need of Mental Health Services: Examining the Scope Conditions of Criminological Theories." *Justice Quarterly* 29:546–72.

von Hirsch, A. 1976. *Doing Justice*. New York: Hill and Wang.

Vorenberg, A. 2012. "Indecent Exposure: Do Warrantless Searches of a Student's Cell Phone Violate the Fourth Amendment?" *Berkeley Journal of Criminal Law* 17:62–96.

Wade, N. 2006. "Wider Use of DNA Lists Is Urged in Fighting Crime." *New York Times*, May 12. www.nytimes.com.

Walker, L., and L. A. Hayashi. 2007. "Pono Kaulike: A Hawaii Criminal Court Provides Restorative Justice Practices for Healing Relationships." *Federal Probation* 71 (3): 18–24.

Walker, P. 1998. "Felony and Misdemeanor Defendants Filed in the US District Courts during Fiscal Years 1990–95: An Analysis of the Filings of Each Offense Level." *Journal of Criminal Justice* 26:503–11.

Walker, R. N. 2006. "How the Malfunctioning Death Penalty Challenges the Criminal Justice System." *Judicature* 89 (5): 265–9.

Walker, S. 1984. "'Broken Windows' and Fractured History: The Use and Misuse of History in Recent Police Patrol Analysis." *Justice Quarterly* 1 (March): 79–82.

———. 1993. *Taming the System: The Control of Discretion in Criminal Justice 1950–1990.* New York: Oxford University Press.

———. 1999. *The Police in America.* 3rd ed. New York: McGraw-Hill.

———. 2001. *Sense and Nonsense about Crime and Drugs: A Policy Guide.* 5th ed. Belmont, CA: Wadsworth

Walker, S., C. Spohn, and M. DeLeone. 2012. *The Color of Justice: Race, Ethnicity, and Crime in America,* 5th ed. Belmont, CA: Cengage Wadsworth.

Walker, S., and K. B. Turner. 1992. "A Decade of Modest Progress: Employment of Black and Hispanic Police Officers, 1983–1992." Omaha: Department of Criminal Justice, University of Nebraska at Omaha.

Walker, S., and B. Wright. 1995. "Citizen Review of the Police, 1994: A National Survey." In *Fresh Perspectives*. Washington, DC: Police Executive Research Forum.

Walmsley, R. 2014. World Prison Population List, 10th ed. International Centre for Prison Studies. http://www.prisonstudies.org/sites/prisonstudies.org/files/resources/downloads/wppl_10.pdf.

Walpin, G. 2003. "America's Adversarial and Jury Systems: More Likely to Do Justice." *Harvard Journal of Law and Public Policy* 25:175–86.

Walsh, D. 2013. "The Dangers of Eyewitness Identification: A Call for Greater State Involvement to Ensure Fundamental Fairness." *Boston College International and Comparative Law Review* 36:1415–53.

Walsh, J. A., and B. T. Muscat. 2013. "Reaching Underserved Victim Populations." In *Victims of Crimes*, 4th ed. R. C. Davis, A. J. Lurigio, and S. Herman. Los Angeles: Sage, 293–324.

Walsh, W. F., and G. F. Vito. 2004. "The Meaning of Compstat." *Journal of Contemporary Criminal Justice* 20:51–69.

Walton, F. V. 2014. "Missouri AG Confirms that Michael Brown Grand Jury Misled by St. Louis DA." *Daily Kos,* December 4. www.dailykos.com.

Warr, M. 1993. "Fear of Victimization." *Public Perspective,* November–December, pp. 25–28.

———. 2008. *One in 100: Behind Bars in America 2008*. Washington, DC: Pew Center on the States.

Warren, P., D. Tomaskovic-Devey, W. Smith, M. Zingraff, and M. Mason. 2006. "Driving While Black: Bias Processes and Racial Disparity in Police Stops." *Criminology* 44 (3): 709–38.

Warren, R. 2007. "Evidence-Based Practices and State Sentencing Policy: Ten Policy Initiatives to Reduce Recidivism." *Indiana Law Journal* 82:1307–17.

Wasserman, D. T. 1990. *A Sword for the Convicted: Representing Indigent Defendants on Appeal*. New York: Greenwood Press.

Watson, R. A., and R. G. Downing. 1969. *The Politics of the Bench and Bar: Judicial Selection under the Missouri Nonpartisan Court Plan*. New York: Wiley.

Weinberg, S. 2003. "Unbecoming Conduct." *Legal Affairs,* November–December, pp. 28–33.

Weiner, J. 2013a. "Monitoring Programs Have History of Trouble." *Orlando Sentinel*, May 25. www.orlandosentinel.com.

———. 2013b. "Review of Home Confinement Program Finds Lost Defendants, New Crime." *Orlando Sentinel*, March 23. www.orlandosentinel.com.

Weisburd, D. 2011. "The Evidence for Place-Based Policing." *Translational Criminology* (Summer), pp. 10–11, 16.

Weisburd, D., S. D. Mastrofski, A. M. McNally, R. Greenspan, and J. J. Willis. 2003. "Reforming to Preserve: Compstat and Strategic Problem Solving in American Policing." *Criminology & Public Policy* 2:421–56.

Weisburd, D., C. W. Telep, J. C. Hinkle, and J. E. Eck. 2010. "Is Problem-Oriented Policing Effective in Reducing Crime and Disorder?" *Criminology & Public Policy*. 9:139–72.

Weiser, B. 2011. "Defendant in 3 Killings Seeks to Give Guilty Plea." *New York*, March 11. www.nytimes.com.

Weiser, B., and M. Schwirtz. 2014. "U.S. Inquiry Finds a 'Culture of Violence' against Teenage Inmates at Rikers Island." *New York Times,* August 4. www.nytimes.com.

Weiss, D. C. 2009. "Fear of Financial Ruin Has More Potential Jurors Claiming Hardship." *American Bar Association Journal,* September 2. www.abajournal.com.

Weitzer, R. 2002. "Incidents of Police Misconduct and Public Opinion." *Journal of Criminal Justice* 30:397–408.

Welch, M. 1994. "Jail Overcrowding: Social Sanitation and the Warehousing of the Urban Underclass." In *Critical Issues in Crime and Justice,* ed. A. Roberts. Thousand Oaks, CA: Sage, 249–74.

Welch, W. M. 2010. "States Seek Savings in the Courtroom." *USA Today*, April 1. www.usatoday.com

Welsh, B. C., and D. P. Farrington. 2009. "Public Area CCTV and Crime Prevention: An Updated Systematic Review and Meta-analysis." *Justice Quarterly* 26:716–45.

Welsh, D. 2011. "Procedural Justice Post-9/11: The Effects of Procedurally Unfair Treatment of Detainees on Perceptions of Global Legitimacy." *University of New Hampshire Law Review* 9:261–96.

Weston, A. 2011. "Budget Cuts Force Jail Time for Mentally Ill." *Columbia Missourian*, March 12. www.columbianmissourian.com.

WFTS Webteam. 2015. "Accused Theater Shooter Curtis Reeves Has Pre-Trial Hearing, Trial Date Set." ABC Action News online, January 29. www.abcactionnews.com.

Wheater, E. 2014. "Insanity Verdict Doesn't Mean Metzker-Madsen Walks Free." WHOTV.com. November 7. WHOTV.com.

Whetzel, J., M. Paparozzi, M. Alexander, and C. T. Lowenkamp. 2011. "Goodbye to a Worn-Out Dichotomy: Law Enforcement, Social Work, and a Balanced Approach (A Survey of Federal Probation Officer Attitudes)." *Federal Probation* 75:7–12.

White, J. 2004. *Defending the Homeland*. Belmont, CA: Thomson/Wadsworth.

White, M. D., J. A. Cooper, J. Saunders, and A. J. Raganella. 2010. "Motivations for Becoming a Police Officer: Re-assessing Officer Attitudes and Job Satisfaction after Six Years on the Street." *Journal of Criminal Justice* 38:520–30.

White, M. D., and J. Ready. 2009. "Examining Fatal and Nonfatal Incidents Involving the Taser: Identifying Predictors of Suspect Death Reported in the Media." *Criminology and Public Policy* 8:865–91.

White, M. S. 1995. "The Nonverbal Behaviors in Jury Selection." *Criminal Law Bulletin* 31:414–45.

White, T., and E. Baik. 2010. "Venire Reform: Assessing the State and Federal Efforts to Attain Fair, Cross-Sectional Representation in Jury Pools." *Journal of Social Sciences* 6:113–18.

Whitebread, C. H., and C. Slobogin. 2000. *Criminal Procedure: An Analysis of Cases and Concepts*. 4th ed. Westbury, NY: Foundation Press.

Widom, C. S. 1995. *Victims of Childhood Sexual Abuse: Later Criminal Consequences*. Washington, DC: U.S. Dept. of Justice, Office of Justice Programs, National Institute of Justice.

Wilbanks, W. 1987. *The Myth of a Racist Criminal Justice System*. Pacific Grove, CA: Brooks/Cole.

Williams, C. J. 2010. "Weighed Down by Recession Woes, Jurors Are Becoming Disgruntled." *Los Angeles Times*, February 15. www.latimes.com.

Williams, H., and P. V. Murphy. 1990. "The Evolving Strategy of Police: A Minority View." In *Perspectives on Policing,* 13. Washington, DC: National Institute of Justice.

Williams, M. S. 2006. "The Process of Becoming a Judge for Women and Men." *Judicature* 90 (3): 104–13.

Williams, T. 2012. "Brutal Crimes Grip an Indian Reservation." *New York Times*, February 2. www.nytimes.com.

Williams, V., and M. Fish. 1974. *Convicts, Codes, and Contraband*. Cambridge, MA: Ballinger.

Willis, J. J., S. D. Mastrofski, and D. Weisburd. 2004. "Compstat and Bureaucracy: A Case Study of Challenges and Opportunities for Change." *Justice Quarterly* 21:463–96.

Wilson, J. M. 2008. *Community Policing and Crime: The Process and Impact of Problem-Solving in Oakland*. Santa Monica, CA: Rand.

———. 2010. *Police Recruitment and Retention for the New Millennium: The State of Knowledge*. Santa Monica, CA: Rand.

Wilson, J. Q. 1968. *Varieties of Police Behavior*. Cambridge, MA: Harvard University Press.

Wilson, J. Q., and B. Boland. 1979. *The Effect of the Police on Crime*. Washington, DC: U.S. Government Printing Office.

Wilson, J. Q., and R. Herrnstein. 1985. *Crime and Human Nature*. New York: Simon & Schuster.

Wilson, J. Q., and G. L. Kelling. 1982. "Broken Windows: The Police and Neighborhood Safety." *Atlantic Monthly,* March, pp. 29–38.

Wilson, M. D. 2010. "An Exclusionary Rule for Police Lies." *American Criminal Law Review* 47:1–55.

Winerip, M. 2015. "Rikers Officer Who Hogtied and Beat an Inmate in 2012 Are Fired." *New York Times,* January 21. www.nytimes.com.

Winerip, M., and M. Schwirtz. 2015. "Even as Many Eyes Watch, Brutality at Rikers Island Persists." *New York Times,* February 21. www.nytimes.com.

Wines, M. 2014. "Are Police Bigoted?" *New York Times,* August 30. www.nytimes.com.

Winick, B. J. 1995. "Reforming Incompetency to Stand Trial and Plead Guilty." *Journal of Criminal Law and Criminology* 85:571–624.

———. 2010. "The Supreme Court's Evolving Death Penalty Jurisprudence: Severe Mental Illness as the Next Frontier." *Boston College Law Review* 50:785–858.

Winkeljohn, M. 2002. "A Random Act of Hate: Duckett's Attack Linked to Racism." *Atlanta Journal and Constitution,* August 4, p. E1.

Winter, C. 2013. "Edible Bar Codes Aim to Swallow the Counterfeit Drug Market." *Bloomberg Business Week*, September 4. www.bloomberg.com.

Winter, M. 2015. "North Miami Police Use Faces of Black Men as Targets." *USA Today,* January 15. www.usatoday.com.

Winterdyk, J., and R. Ruddell. 2010. "Managing Prison Gangs: Results from a Survey of US Prison Systems." *Journal of Criminal Justice* 38:730–36.

Winton, R., and C. Saillant. 2011. "Lindsay Lohan Has Mixed Day in Court." *Los Angeles Times,* April 23. www.latimes.com.

Withrow, B., and J. Dailey. 2012. "Racial Profiling Litigation: Current Status and Emerging Controversies." *Journal of Contemporary Criminal Justice* 28:122–45.

Witte, B. 2013. "Maryland Death Penalty Repeal Signed into Law by Martin O'Malley." *Huffington Post*, May 2. www.huffingtonpost.com.

Wolcott, R. J. 2015. "Former Northern Michigan Teacher Sentenced to up to 10 Years behind

Bars in Student Sex Case." MLIVE.com, January 21. www.mlive.com.
Wolf, R. 2014. "Outside Groups Seeking to Sway Judicial Elections." *USA Today,* October 30. www.usatoday.com.
Wolff, N., J. Shi, and R. Bachman. 2008. "Measuring Victimization inside Prisons." *Journal of Interpersonal Violence* 23:1343–62.
Wood, S. 2014. "Camden Escapes Most-Dangerous Status—on Technicality." Philly.Com. December 4. www.philly.com.
Wool, J. 2005. "Beyond *Blakely*: Implications of the *Booker* Decision for State Sentencing Systems." *Policy and Practice Review* (Vera Institute of Justice), February, pp. 1–7.
Wooldredge, J. 2012. "Distinguishing Race Effects on Pre-trial Release and Sentencing Decisions." *Justice Quarterly* 29:41–75.
Wooldredge, J. D., and K. Masters. 1993. "Confronting Problems Faced by Pregnant Inmates in State Prisons." *Crime & Delinquency* 39 (April): 195–203.
Wooley, B. 2011. "Inside the Montana Women's Prison: Preparing for Reentry." KAJ18 News, November 4. www.kaj18.com.
Worden, A. P. 1993. "The Attitudes of Women and Men in Policing: Testing Conventional and Contemporary Wisdom." *Criminology* 31 (May): 203–24.
———. 1995. "The Judge's Role in Plea Bargaining: An Analysis of Judges' Agreement with Prosecutors' Sentencing Recommendations." *Justice Quarterly* 12:257–78.
Worrall, J. L., and T. V. Kovandzic. 2007. "COPS Grants and Crime Revisited." *Criminology* 45:159–90.
Worth, R. 1995. "A Model Prison." *Atlantic Monthly* (November), pp. 38–44.
Worth, R. F. 2001. "73 Tied to Genovese Family Are Indicted, Officials Say." *New York Times,* December 6, p. A27.
Wright, E., D. DeHart, B. Koons-Witt, and C. Crittenden. 2013. "'Buffers' against Crime? Exploring the Roles and Limitations of Positive Relationships among Women in Prison." *Punishment and Society* 15:71–95.
Wright, K., and J. Rosky. 2011. "Too Early Is Too Soon: Lessons from the Montana Department of Corrections Early Release Program." *Criminology and Public Policy* 10:881–908.
Wu, J., and C. Spohn. 2010. "Interdistrict Disparity in Sentencing in Three US District Courts." *Crime & Delinquency* 56:290–322.
Wu, Y. 2014. "Race/Ethnicity and Perceptions of Police: A Comparison of White, Black, Asian, and Hispanic Americans." *Policing and Society* 24:135–57.
Wyoming Board of Parole. 2014. *Policy and Procedure Manual*. Cheyenne, WY: State of Wyoming.
Xie, M., K. Heimer, and J. L. Lauritsen. 2012. "Violence against Women in US Metropolitan Areas: Change in Women's Status and Risk, 1980–2004." *Criminology* 50:105–43.
Xie, M., J. L. Lauritsen, and K. Heimer. 2012. "Intimate Partner Violence in US Metropolitan Areas: The Contextual Influences of Police and Social Services." *Criminology* 50:961–92.
Xiong, N. 1997. "Private Prisons: A Question of Savings," *New York Times*, July 13, D5.
Yaniv, O. 2011. "Ex-Giants Great Lawrence Taylor Declared Sex Offender, Sentenced to 6 Years Probation in Hooker Case." *New York Daily News*, March 22. www.nydailynews.com.
Yardley, W. 2006. "DNA Samples Link 4 Murders in Connecticut." *New York Times*, June 8. www.nytimes.com.
Zaitz, L. 2011. "Oregon Taxpayers Pay Spiraling Cost of Prison Health Care with No Solution in Sight." Oregon Live online news, June 18. www.oregonlive.com.
Zak, D. 2012. "Newtown School Shooting's First Responders Deal with Searing Memories." *Washington Post*, December 30. www.washingtonpost.com.
Zalman, M., and B. Smith. 2007. "The Attitudes of Police Executives toward *Miranda* and Interrogation Policies." *Journal of Criminal Law and Criminology* 97:873–942.
Zedlewski, E. 2010. "Alternatives to Custodial Supervision: The Day Fine." NCJ 230401. National Institute of Justice Discussion Paper, April. www.ncjrs.gov.
Zedner, L. 1995. "Wayward Sisters." In *The Oxford History of Prisons,* ed. N. Morris and D. J. Rothman. New York: Oxford University Press, 329–61.
Zernike, K. 2007. "Violent Crime in Cities Shows Sharp Surge," *New York Times*, March 9. www.nytimes.com.
Zhang, Y., L. Hoover, J. Zhao. 2014. "Geographic Information Effects on Police Efficacy: An Evaluation of Empirical Assessments." *International Journal of Applied Geospatial Research* 5:30–43.
Zhang, Y., L. Zhang, and M. S. Vaughn. 2011. "Indeterminate and Determinate Sentencing Models: A State-Specific Analysis of Their Effects on Recidivism." *Crime & Delinquency.* doi: 10.1177/0011128709354047.
Zhao, J. S., N. He, and N. Loverich. 2003. "Community Policing: Did It Change the Basic Functions of Policing in the 1990s? A National Follow-Up Study." *Justice Quarterly* 20:697–724.
Zhao, J. S., N. P. He, N. Loverich, and J. Cancino. 2003. "Marital Status and Police Occupational Stress." *Journal of Crime and Justice* 26:23–46.
Zimmerman, E. 2011. "The Federal Sentencing Guidelines: A Misplaced Trust." *University of Michigan Journal of Law Reform* 43:841–70.
Zimring, F. 2007. "Protect Individual Punishment Decisions from Mandatory Penalties." *Criminology & Public Policy* 6:881–86.
Zinser, L. 2008. "Vick Pleads Guilty to Dogfighting Charge." *New York Times*, November 26. www.nytimes.com.
Zinser, L., and N. Schweber. 2010. "Lawrence Taylor Charged with Rape." *New York Times*, May 6. www.nytimes.com.
Zweig, J., and J. Yahner. 2013. "Providing Services to Victims of Crime." In *Victims of Crimes*, 4th ed., ed. R. C. Davis, A. J. Lurigio, and S. Herman. Los Angeles: Sage, 325–348.

NAME INDEX

F

G

H

SUBJECT INDEX

A

B

C

D

E

F

G

K

L

M

Q

R

T

U

V

W

Y

Z